2012-2013

U.S. Notary Reference Manual

A Guide to Notarization Requirements
for All U.S. States and Jurisdictions

Charles N. Faerber
NATIONAL NOTARY ASSOCIATION

Published by:

National Notary Association
9350 De Soto Ave.
Chatsworth, CA 91311-4926
Telephone: (818) 739-4000
Fax: (818) 700-0920

Website: NationalNotary.org
Email: nna@NationalNotary.org

Copyright © 2011 National Notary Association
ALL RIGHTS RESERVED.
Eleventh Edition

Library of Congress Cataloging-In-Publication Data is available for this publication.

ISSN No. 1527-3512
ISBN 978-1-59767-096-8

Previously published as the
Notary Seal & Certificate Verification Manual

No part of this book may be reproduced, stored in a retrieval system, or transmitted in whole or part, in any form or by any means, electronic, mechanical, photographic, audial, digital or otherwise, without prior written permission from the publisher.

The *U.S. Notary Reference Manual* is designed to provide accurate and authoritative information on notarial practices. It is provided with the understanding that the publisher is not engaged in rendering legal, accounting or other professional services. If legal advice or other expert, professional assistance is required, the services of a competent professional should be sought.

The contact information in this *U.S. Notary Reference Manual* is correct and current at the time of its publication. Web addresses and phone numbers of commissioning agencies are subject to change.

The *U.S. Notary Reference Manual* is revised and published every two years.

Table of Contents

Author's Foreword. . . . .*iv*

Publisher's Preface. . . . .*v*

Introduction . . . .*vi*
    Purposes of This *Manual*. . . . .*vi*
    What This *Manual* Contains . . . .*vi*
    Who Will Find This *Manual* Useful . . . . . .*vi*
    Important Information . . . .*vii*

Notary Seals, Powers, Certificates and Procedures for U.S. States and Jurisdictions:

Alabama 1
Alaska. 9
American Samoa 21
Arizona. 33
Arkansas. 49
California 59
Colorado. 77
Connecticut. 91
Delaware 105
District of Columbia. 117
Florida 125
Georgia. 143
Guam 159
Hawaii 169
Idaho 185
Illinois. 197
Indiana 211
Iowa 219
Kansas 227
Kentucky. 237
Louisiana. 245
Maine 257
Maryland. 269
Massachusetts 279
Michigan. 293
Minnesota 303
Mississippi. 315
Missouri 329
Montana 341
Nebraska. 353
Nevada 363
New Hampshire 379
New Jersey 389
New Mexico 399
New York 411

North Carolina. 423
North Dakota 445
Northern Marianas 461
Ohio. 469
Oklahoma 481
Oregon 491
Pennsylvania 507
Puerto Rico 521
Rhode Island. 533
South Carolina. 549
South Dakota 561
Tennessee 571
Texas 583
Utah 599
Vermont 609
Virginia. 617
Virgin Islands, U.S. 635
Washington. 643
West Virginia. 653
Wisconsin 665
Wyoming 675

Appendices:

Appendix 1: Table of Enactment of Model
    and Uniform Laws (2011) 687

Appendix 1A: Model Notary Act (2010) 689

Appendix 1B: Revised Uniform Law on
    Notarial Acts (2010). 743

Appendix 2: Uniform Law on Notarial Acts
    (1982). 765

Appendix 3: Uniform Recognition of
    Acknowledgments Act (1968) 773

Appendix 4: Uniform Acknowledgment Act
    (1939, Amended 1960) 779

Appendix 5: Uniform Foreign
    Acknowledgments Act (1914) 783

Appendix 6: Uniform Acknowledgments
    Act (1892) 785

Appendix 7: Hague Convention on
    Authentication (1961) 787

About the NNA 791
To Order More Copies 793

Author's Foreword

If Notary laws were uniform across the United States, there would be no need for this *U.S. Notary Reference Manual*. Unfortunately, they are not.

Because each state sets its own notarial rules, the seals, certificates, duties and procedures of Notaries differ markedly across the nation. Yet, daily, thousands of legal documents are sent from state to state — already notarized or to be notarized and returned — and under our federal Constitution a notarization lawfully performed in one state must be accepted as valid in any other.

Facilitates Cross-Border Document Exchange

How can it be known if a paper received from another state has been lawfully notarized and is therefore acceptable for recording or evidentiary use? And, in preparing a document for notarization in another state, how can the proper notarial format and authentication procedures in that second state be learned?

This *Manual* provides that vital information. And, in this edition, again, data is given not only for the 50 states and District of Columbia but also for the five other major jurisdictions in the U.S. political family: American Samoa, Guam, Northern Marianas, Puerto Rico and U.S. Virgin Islands.

The *Manual* contains a wealth of information for persons drafting, preparing, analyzing, validating, investigating or relying on legal documents that have been or will be notarized.

For example, this volume will be valuable for county recorders scrutinizing out-of-state Notary seals; for attorneys drafting documents that will be notarized in another jurisdiction; for public investigators tracking down a Notary's official records; for foreign consular officials seeking information on state authentication procedures; and for many other professionals concerned about the correctness of legal documents.

Useful to Interstate Employers of Notaries

It can also be useful to Notaries themselves and to interstate organizations employing Notaries in different jurisdictions. Each of the 56 separate state and territorial chapters is a distillation of available information on Notary duties — based on statutes, administrative rules, gubernatorial executive orders, court rulings, attorney general opinions, official directives form Notary-regulating officials, and official recommendations in state Notary handbooks and websites. Thus, this reference book may additionally serve as a guide for Notaries in any included jurisdiction as to their obligations under law, with the understanding that it should be supplemented by the Notary's further study of the lengthier key texts it may reference.

Appendices Hold Model and Uniform Laws

In addition, the Appendices of this *Manual* helpfully reprint the full, annotated text of the National Notary Association's *Model Notary Act* of 2010, along with the six pertinent uniform laws affecting notarial acts that have been promulgated since 1892 by the National Conference of Commissioners on Uniform State Laws (Uniform Law Commission). Most states have enacted one or several of these important models, *in toto* or in amended form. A "Table of Enactment of Model and Uniform Laws (2011)" at the beginning of the Appendices indicates which states have enacted which prototype laws.

Also included, at the end of the Appendices, is the text of the influential Hague Convention on authentication, along with a list of the countries that currently adhere to this important treaty. This Convention, repeatedly referred to in state Notary laws, considerably simplifies the exchange of notarized documents between the subscribing nations.

CHARLES N. FAERBER
Vice President of Notary Affairs
National Notary Association

Publisher's Preface

No one is better prepared to author this *2012–2013 U.S. Notary Reference Manual* than Charles N. Faerber, who has both tracked and influenced important developments impacting the American Notary Public office as an executive of the National Notary Association since 1978.

Mr. Faerber is widely recognized as one of the nation's foremost experts on Notary regulations, customs and practices. Currently, he serves as the NNA's Editor-at-Large and its Vice President of Notary Affairs.

Representing the Association, Mr. Faerber frequently lectures at seminars and conferences. He has appeared as an expert witness on notarization in court and testified before state legislative committees considering new laws affecting Notaries or the performance of notarial acts. As an expert on eNotarization issues, he has also been heavily involved in a variety of groundbreaking collaborations with industry and government to implement electronic notarization.

Served on Uniform and Model Law Panels

He served as an adviser on the panel of the National Conference of Commissioners on Uniform State Laws that drafted the *Uniform Law on Notarial Acts* (1982). On three occasions he has been the drafting coordinator for the NNA-recruited national panels of governmental officials, attorneys, business executives and technical experts who produced the *Model Notary Acts* of 1984, 2002 and 2010. Over the years, the different versions of the *Model Notary Act* have been enacted or adopted by over 40 U.S. states and territorial jurisdictions.

A graduate of Dartmouth College in Hanover, New Hampshire, Mr. Faerber earned a master's degree in mass communications/journalism from San Diego State University. Before joining the NNA in 1978, he worked for several years as a newspaper reporter and editor.

His role as author/compiler of the *2012–2013 U.S. Notary Reference Manual* and of the previous 10 editions of the biennially published *Manual* is enabled by his careful regular tracking of legislation in all states affecting Notaries and notarial acts. The accuracy of the *Manual's* information has been verified by each state and jurisdiction whose laws and regulations are covered.

Editor-at-Large of NNA Publications

As Editor-at-Large, he also regularly contributes to *The National Notary* magazine, the *Notary Bulletin* eNewsletter and all other NNA publications and periodicals. He supervised the compilation and drafting of the NNA's popular state *Notary Law Primers* and of the *Notary Home Study Course,* and has been involved in the development of a variety of other educational programs for the Association.

Over the years, Mr. Faerber has become a highly respected and much-consulted source of information for state officials, lawmakers and attorneys across the nation on matters related to or affecting Notaries. He has also represented the National Notary Association in both national and international forums, including the founding meeting of a global organization for common law Notaries (World Organization of Notaries) at Henley-on-Thames, England, in 2009.

His *U.S. Notary Reference Manual* has emerged over two decades as the definitive and internationally recognized compendium of information about the American Notary Public office, useful as a guide to those who set or rely on the rules governing notarization, including Notaries themselves.

MILT VALERA
President and Publisher
National Notary Association

Introduction

PURPOSES OF THIS MANUAL

The *U.S. Notary Reference Manual* is a first-of-its-kind and one-of-a-kind reference source with three specific purposes:

First, to assist anyone trying to verify the genuineness and correctness of legal forms completed by Notaries anywhere in the United States or its jurisdictions.

Second, to assist anyone in any state or nation in preparing a legal document that will be notarized in the United States.

Third, to provide definitive, complete and up-to-date information on notarial procedures throughout the country.

WHAT THIS MANUAL CONTAINS

Among the information included in this *Manual* for all U.S. jurisdictions:

- Notary seal specifications and samples.
- Notary certificate wording and requirements.
- Officials with notarial powers other than Notaries.
- Authorized and unauthorized acts by Notaries, particularly in regard to taking proof of execution in lieu of acknowledgment and certifying copies.
- Authentication procedures for notarial acts.
- Wording for oaths and affirmations administered by Notaries.
- Notary procedures, fees, disqualifications, recordkeeping requirements and other pertinent data.
- Information that will help in finding a particular Notary and in obtaining that Notary's official records.
- State offices that can answer questions about Notaries and notarial procedures.
- County offices that can provide assistance in locating a Notary, obtaining a Notary's records or in authenticating a notarial act.
- Citations of pertinent state laws, regulations, court cases and official directives.
- Statutory provisions regarding digital or electronic signatures/documents that affect notarization.

WHO WILL FIND THIS MANUAL USEFUL

Any person in an industry relying on the authenticity and correctness of real estate papers, powers of attorney, affidavits and other legal documents will find this *Manual* invaluable. It is particularly useful for:

- Attorneys
- Consuls
- County recorders
- Document examiners
- Document fraud investigators
- Escrow officers
- Immigration authorities
- Import/export businesspersons
- Legal educators
- Legal publishers
- Legislative staffs
- Municipal and county officials
- Paralegals
- Seal manufacturers
- State and federal officials
- Title investigators

In addition, Notaries themselves will find this *Manual* extremely useful, especially in the states where official guidelines are so scant that they must devise their own certificate wording and recordkeeping procedures.

In short, any individual, agency or firm — U.S. or foreign — engaged in intrastate, interstate, or international law or commerce and depending on the validity of witnessed documents will find this *Manual* to be a unique, definitive and immensely helpful reference source and practical guide.

IMPORTANT INFORMATION

The preceding pages have defined what the *U.S. Notary Reference Manual* can do. This section defines its limitations.

Notary Powers

Beyond the scope of this *Manual* are detailed procedures for Notaries who, in their official capacity, are authorized to:

1. Open safe deposit boxes;
2. Issue subpoenas and summonses;
3. Take depositions;
4. Execute protests;
5. Perform marriages;
6. Prepare documents other than basic acknowledgment and jurat forms in the state of Louisiana and the commonwealth of Puerto Rico, both of whose notarial regulations derive from a Latin Civil Law heritage, and in certain Common Law states, namely Florida and Alabama, where attorneys may now qualify to become Civil Law Notaries for international transactions;
7. Perform specialized notarial duties in certain states that may require further qualifications of the Notary, such as the vehicle-conveyancing-related duties in Pennsylvania that are performed only by specially qualified Notaries.

Other Notarial Officers

This *Manual* only lists the particular officers who, under state law, have power to take acknowledgments and proofs of execution in lieu of acknowledgment — not the vast range of local, state and federal officers who may be authorized to administer oaths and affirmations.

Notary Certificates

All notarial certificates in this book are reprinted verbatim from state law except that:

1. "He" is usually replaced by "he/she" or "he/she/they."
2. Blank spaces are added when missing in the statutory form to accentuate insertions to be written in by the Notary: e.g., "… of (name of corporation) …" becomes "… of _____ (name of corporation) …."
3. To heighten clarity, "officer" may be replaced by "notarizing officer."
4. Venue ("State of _____, County of _____") is added if it does not appear in the statutory form.
5. The need to affix the Notary's signature, seal, title and commission expiration date is indicated when statute requires these items, whether or not the statutory form itself so indicates.
6. Commas may be added on rare occasions to enhance understanding: e.g., "… before me _____ (name of Notary) personally appeared …" becomes "… before me, _____ (name of Notary), personally appeared …."
7. Even more rarely, self-evident errors in the statutory form may be corrected: e.g., "… title of acknowledging officer …" becomes "… title of officer taking acknowledgment …."

All certificates of uniform laws appearing in the Appendices, however, are reprinted verbatim.

Time Sensitivity

Most Notary regulations are legislatively enacted and, thus, subject to change at any time. Though this *Manual* is revised and updated every two years, and its printing timed to encompass the vast majority of pertinent legislative changes made during a given year of publication, there will inevitably be changes in the intervening year that cannot be included.

All users of this *Manual* should be aware of its time-sensitivity and rely only on its latest edition.

Important Note

Extraordinary efforts have been made to corroborate through official sources the accuracy, completeness, and timeliness of information in the *U.S. Notary Reference Manual*. In every state, territory or commonwealth, the official Notary-regulating office was consulted to verify critical information. However, users of the *Manual* are encouraged to contact these officials on their own (telephone numbers, addresses and websites are listed under "Notary Administration" on the first page of each chapter) to obtain the latest available information on any critical point. ■

Alabama

NOTARY SEAL

"For the authentication of his or her official acts, each notary shall provide a seal of office, which shall present, by its impression or stamp, the name, office, and the state for which he or she was appointed" (COA 36-20-72).

Acknowledgements No Longer Exempted

As a result of a law (Act No. 2011-295) that took effect January 1, 2012, Alabama Notaries must now affix a seal of office for every notarial act involving a document. According to the office of the Secretary of State, the act of acknowledgement is no longer exempted from the seal requirement, as it had been pursuant to an Alabama Attorney General Opinion (95-00289) of August 16, 1995.

Kind

Embosser: According to the office of the Secretary of State, the embosser remains as the only permitted official Notary seal, though an inked stamp may be used in addition to the embosser (COA 36-20-72). Indeed, in authenticating

Example

The above typical, actual-size example of an embossing Notary seal is allowed by Alabama law. Formats other than this may also be permitted.

NOTARY ADMINISTRATION

While Alabama's county probate judges appoint and commission the state's Notaries, these judges must report to the Alabama Secretary of State the name, county, date of issuance and date of expiration of each Notary commission (COA36-20-70[a]).

NOTE: Effective January 1, 2012, all Alabama Notaries are commissioned with statewide ("state at large") jurisdiction under Act No. 2011-295 (i.e., Senate Bill 54). Notary commissions with countywide powers existing on that date remain in effect only until commission expiration (COA 36-20-70[b]).

Office of Secretary of State
Administrative Services
Notaries Public   1-334-242-7205
State Capitol, Rm. S-105
P.O. Box 5616
Montgomery, AL 36103-5616

Websites: Secretary of State: www.sos.
state.al.us/AdminServices/
NotaryPublic.aspx
County Probate Judges:
www.sos.state.al.us/vb/
officials/index.aspx

NOTARY RULES

COA — CODE OF ALABAMA
MNP — MANUAL FOR NOTARIES PUBLIC IN THE STATE OF ALABAMA

Most Notary rules are in the Code of Alabama:

a. Title 36, Chapter 20, "Notaries Public";

b. Title 35, Chapter 4, "Conveyances and Creation of Estates."

Other still helpful guidelines for Notaries are in "A Manual For Notaries Public in the State of Alabama," formerly issued (1989) by the Alabama State Bar's Young Lawyers' Section.

notarized documents to be sent abroad, the office insists on an embosser.

Shape/Size
Not specified by statute.

Components
1. Name of Notary;
2. Notary's office ("Notary Public");
3. Name of state ("Alabama" or "State of Alabama").

NOTE: Notaries holding commissions on the effective date, January 1, 2012, of Act No. 2011-295 may continue to use existing seals indicating "State-at-Large" or county jurisdiction until their commissions expire (COA 36-20-70[b]). After December 31, 2015, no such seals should be in use.

Seal of Civil Law Notary
"The Alabama Civil-law Notary's original handwritten signature and an original rubber stamp or embossed impression of the civil-law notary's seal shall be affixed by the civil-law notary to all documents executed by the civil-law notary while acting as an Alabama Civil-law Notary under Act No. 99-449. The civil-law notary shall not allow any other person to sign or seal a document using the civil-law notary's official signature or seal" (Ala. Admin. Code 820-6-3-.01[2]). The signature and seal must be registered with the Secretary of State. Under "Other Notarial Officers" below, see also "Civil Law Notaries."

Format of Seal: "The civil-law notary's seal may be an embossing seal or a rubber stamp and may be circular or square in shape and shall not be more than two inches nor less than one inch in diameter if circular, or more than two inches on each side nor less than one inch on each side if square" (Ala. Admin. Code 820-6-3-.01[3]).

NOTARY POWERS

Alabama Notaries are authorized to perform the following notarial acts (COA 36-20-73):
1. Take acknowledgments and proofs*;
2. Administer oaths**;
3. Execute protests;
4. "Exercise such other powers as, according to commercial usage or the laws of this state, may belong to notaries public."

* Proof by Two Subscribing Witnesses: If not acknowledged, conveyances must be proved by two subscribing witnesses (COA 35-4-68).

** Oath Wording and Ceremony: "Everyone is familiar with the question, 'Do you swear (or affirm) to tell the truth, the whole truth, and nothing but the truth, so help you God?' The affiant need not hold his hand on the Bible, but he should raise his right hand at the time the question is asked and he answers in the affirmative" (MNP).

Signature by Mark
"(I)f he is not able to sign his name, then his name must be written for him, with the words 'his mark' written against the same, or over it; the execution of such conveyance must be attested by one witness or, where the party cannot write, by two witnesses who are able to write and who

Examples
The above are typical, actual-size examples of Alabama Civil Law Notary seals, which may be square or circular and affixed by an inking rubber stamp or an embosser. Other formats may also be permitted.

must write their names as witnesses; or, if he can write his name but does not do so and his name is written for him by another, then the execution must be attested by two witnesses who can and do write their names" (COA 35-4-20).

NOTARY DON'TS

Disqualifying Interests

Notarizing for Close Relatives Discouraged: "(R)esearch does not reveal any law that prohibits a notary public from notarizing a relative's or spouse's signature. However, the better practice would be for a notary public to refrain from notarization of the signature of his or her spouse or immediate family member so the impartiality of the notary public would not be an issue should the authentication of the document be questioned" (Ala. Atty. Gen. Opinion 95-00289 of August 16, 1995).

Notarization by Stockholder: A Notary who is a stockholder in a corporation, national banking association, building and loan association or savings and loan association may notarize deeds, mortgages, or other conveyances for the organization, as long as the Notary holds no more than 1 percent of the total issued and outstanding capital stock and holds no office in the organization (COA 35-4-25).

NOTARY SIGNING AGENTS

Currently, there are no statutes, regulations or rules expressly governing, prohibiting or restricting the operation of Notary Signing Agents within the state of Alabama.

Court Allows Closings but No Advice

A 1983 ruling by the Alabama Supreme Court allows real estate closings to be conducted by appropriately skilled non-attorneys as long as unauthorized legal advice or assistance is not provided to the involved parties at the closings — *Coffee County Abstract and Title Co. v. State ex rel. Norwood*, 445 So.2d852 (Ala. 1983).

In *Coffee County*, agents of a title company were accused of providing unauthorized legal advice during a real estate closing in which two single persons were purchasing a townhouse. When one of the purchasers asked the title agent about what would happen to the property's title in the event of the death of either purchaser, the agent provided erroneous information — resulting in a later lawsuit.

The Alabama Supreme Court ruled in the case that it was the unauthorized practice of law for Coffee County Abstract and Title to be "conducting real estate closings in Alabama at which officers or employees of (the title company) give legal advice or express opinions as to the effect of legal documents, whether or not the closing is incidental to issuance of title insurance."

The Court pointed out, "If the parties to the transaction raise a legal question at the closing, the title company should stop the proceeding and instruct them to consult their attorneys."

NOTARY FEES

The maximum fees that an Alabama Notary may charge for a notarial act are (COA 36-20-74):
1. Taking an acknowledgment or proof: $5;
2. Administering an oath: $5;
3. Executing a protest: $5;
4. Giving any other certificate and affixing seal of office: $5.

NOTARY CERTIFICATES

Acknowledgment certificates for "conveyances and instruments of every description admitted to record" must be substantially in the forms prescribed by COA 35-4-29, which have been slightly modified as follows in "A Manual for Notaries Public in the State of Alabama":

Acknowledgment for Individual (COA 35-4-29 and MNP):

State of _____)
County of _____)

I, _____ (name of officer), a Notary Public in and for said County in said State (or for said State at Large), hereby certify that _____, whose name is signed to the foregoing _____, and who is known to me, acknowledged before me on this day that, being informed of the contents of the above and foregoing _____, he/she executed the same voluntarily on the day the same bears date.

    Given under my hand (and official seal of office) this _____ day of _____, 20__.

_____
Notary Public   *(Seal)*
My commission expires: _____

Acknowledgment for Corporation (COA 35-4-29 and MNP):

State of _____)
County of _____)

    I, _____ (name of officer), a Notary Public in and for said County in said State (or for said State at Large), hereby certify that _____, whose name as _____ (title) of the _____, a corporation, is signed to the foregoing _____, and who is known to me, acknowledged before me on this day that, being informed of the contents of the above and foregoing _____, he/she, as such officer and with full authority, executed the same voluntarily for and as the act of said corporation on the day the same bears date.

    Given under my hand (and official seal of office) this _____ day of _____, 20__.

_____
Notary Public   *(Seal)*
My commission expires: _____

Acknowledgment for Corporation as Representative (COA 35-4-29 and MNP):

State of _____)
County of _____)

    I, _____ (name of officer), a Notary Public in and for said County in said State (or for said State at Large), hereby certify that _____, whose name as _____ (title) of _____, a corporation, as _____ (representative capacity) of the estate of _____ (or as the case might be), is signed to the above and foregoing _____, and who is known to me, acknowledged before me on this day, that being informed of the contents of said _____,

he/she, as such officer, and with full authority, executed the same voluntarily for and as the act of said corporation, acting in its capacity as _____ as aforesaid.

    Given under my hand (and official seal of office) this _____ day of _____, 20__.

_____
Notary Public   *(Seal)*
My commission expires: _____

Acknowledgment for Official or Other Person in Representative Capacity (COA 35-4-29 and MNP):

State of _____)
County of _____)

    I, _____ (name of officer), a Notary Public in and for said County in said State (or for said State at Large), hereby certify that _____, whose name as _____ (here state representative capacity) is signed to the foregoing _____, and who is known to me, acknowledged before me on this day that, being informed of the contents of the above and foregoing _____, he/she, in his/her capacity as such _____, executed the same voluntarily on the day the same bears date.

    Given under my hand (and official seal of office) this _____ day of _____, 20__.

_____
Notary Public   *(Seal)*
My commission expires: _____

Form of Probate of Conveyance with Two Subscribing Witnesses (COA 35-4-30):

State of _____)
County of _____)

    I, _____ (name and title of officer), hereby certify that _____, a subscribing witness to the foregoing conveyance, known to me, appeared before me on this day and being sworn, stated that _____, the grantor, voluntarily executed the same in his/her presence, and in the presence of the other subscribing witness, on the day the same bears date; that he/she attested the same in the presence of the grantor and of the other witness, and that such other

witness subscribed his/her name as a witness in his/her presence.
    Given under my hand and official seal of office this _____ day of _____, 20__.

_____
Notary Public   Seal
My commission expires: _____

Improper Acknowledgments Cured

"When a validly executed instrument, not properly acknowledged and recorded, has for 10 years been of record in the office of the judge of probate, the original or a duly certified transcript thereof shall have the same force and effect as evidence as such original or transcript would have had had such instrument been duly acknowledged and recorded" (COA 35-4-72).

ELECTRONIC NOTARIZATIONS

The state of Alabama has not yet adopted statutes or regulations expressly establishing rules, definitions and procedures for electronic notarization.

UETA Recognizes Notary's eSignature

Alabama has adopted the Uniform Electronic Transactions Act (House Bill 170 of 2001, effective January 1, 2002) and its provision on "Notarization and acknowledgment," thereby recognizing the legal validity of electronic signatures used by Notaries:

"If a law requires a signature or record to be notarized, acknowledged, verified, or made under oath, the requirement is satisfied if the electronic signature of the person authorized to perform those acts, together with all other information required to be included by other applicable law, is attached to or logically associated with the signature or record" (COA 8-1A-11).

URPERA Does Not Require Seal Image

Alabama has adopted the Uniform Real Property Electronic Recording Act (COA 35-4-120 through 35-4-127), including the following provision:

"A requirement that a document or a signature associated with a document be notarized, acknowledged, verified, witnessed, or made under oath is satisfied if the electronic signature of the person authorized to perform that act, and all other information required to be included, is attached to or logically associated with the document or signature. A physical or electronic image of a stamp, impression, or seal need not accompany an electronic signature" (COA 35-4-122).

NOTARY RECORDS

With legislative enactment of Act No. 2011-295 (Section 2), the requirement was repealed that each Alabama Notary "keep a fair register of all his official acts" (formerly COA 36-20-7), effective January 1, 2012. Also repealed were requirements in COA 36-20-8 through 10 related to delivery of these records to the county probate judges upon the Notary's death, resignation, removal or commission expiration.

Notaries May Still Keep Records

Even with enactment of Act No. 2011-295, nothing prevents an Alabama Notary from continuing or beginning to keep a record of all official acts. Indeed, the benefits to the public and Notary of such a record have been extolled by officials in the office of the Alabama Secretary of State.

AUTHENTICATION OF NOTARIAL ACTS

County Probate Judges

Except in the case of apostilles, an authenticating certificate for an Alabama Notary must first be obtained from the county probate judge who has commissioned the Notary before a "certification" may be attached to a notarized document by the office of the Secretary of State. (In Jefferson County, the circuit court clerk issues authenticating certificates for Notaries.)

Secretary of State

Apostilles and certifications for Notaries are issued by the Secretary of State's office. Notarized documents to be sent to countries that have not signed the Hague Convention on authentication must be accompanied by an authenticating certificate from the appropriate probate judge (website, "Authentications").

Fee: $5 (check or money order) per document for an apostille or authentication of a probate judge's certificate. Payable to "Secretary of State."

Address:
Secretary of State
Document Authentication
100 N. Union Street, Ste. 770
Montgomery, Alabama 36130

Telephone: 1-334-242-5325

Procedure: Mail or present in person the original notarized document(s) and the appropriate fee(s). When mailed, an "Authentication Submittal Form" (available on the website) should accompany the notarized document(s). County authentication of the Notary's commission is first necessary if the document will be sent to a non-Hague country. A stamped, self-addressed envelope or air bill should be included. Allow five business days for processing. "Your document must have an original signature and embossed (raised) seal of a currently commissioned Alabama public official" such as a Notary, probate judge or circuit clerk (website, "Authentications").

Certifying Acts of Civil Law Notaries

"If certification of a civil law notary's authority is necessary for a particular document or transaction, it must be obtained from the Secretary of State. Upon receipt of a written request from a civil law notary and the fee prescribed by the Secretary of State, the Secretary of State shall issue a certification of the civil law notary's authority, in a form prescribed by the Secretary of State, which shall include a statement explaining the legal qualifications and authority of a civil law notary in this state. The fee prescribed for the issuance of the certification under this section or an apostille shall not exceed twenty dollars ($20) per document. The Secretary of State may adopt rules to implement this section" (COA 36-20-55).

COMMISSIONING AND ADMINISTRATION

In Alabama, county probate judges appoint and commission Notaries, and all Notaries appointed on or after January 1, 2012, hold statewide Notary powers. Formerly, Notaries were appointed with either countywide or statewide ("state-at-large") powers. "All existing notaries public functioning on (January 1, 2012) shall continue to function pursuant to their existing authority for the remainder of their existing commission" (COA 36-20-70[b]).

The probate courts keep the Notary's application paperwork, including a record of the sureties for the Notary's bond. The probate judges report to the Alabama Secretary of State the name, county, date of issuance, and date of expiration of each Notary commission (COA 36-20-70[a]. "(T)he records filed with (the Secretary's) office regarding the appointment and commissioning of notaries are a matter of public record and are available for review by the general public" (website, "Notaries Public").

Applying for Commission

Qualifications: While county probate judges do have discretion to appoint Notaries, according to a spokesperson for the Secretary of State's office, judges must follow certain guidelines: "I am not aware of any authority that would allow the qualifications to vary from county to county. In Atty. Gen Op. No. 1995-0289… the AG opined that in order to be an Alabama notary, the resident must possess all legal requirements' to be an officer in this state. Moreover, in Atty. Gen. Op. No. 1995-0274, the AG opined that one who has been or is convicted of a felony cannot serve as a notary public. However, if a convicted felon, who has not served in office, receives a pardon, which specifically restores to him his civil and political rights, such pardon removes the disabilities accompanying a felony conviction, including the ineligibility to hold office. I am also unaware of any provision in state law that would allow a probate judge to require a notary applicant to pass a qualifying course or test."

The qualification of being a registered voter of the state may not be imposed. The Alabama Supreme Court in *Babcooke v. Duncan*, 866 So.2d 431 (Ala. 1986), ruled that requiring applicants for a Notary appointment to be qualified electors was a denial of equal protection under the law.

Course or Test: Whether an applicant for a Notary appointment must pass a qualifying course or test is at the discretion of the appointing county probate judge.

Application: The probate judges of each Alabama county set application rules and procedures for the commissioning of Notaries. By law, the probate judge may collect a fee of $10 for issuance of a Notary commission. (COA 36-20-70[a]). In all counties, Notaries must provide a $25,000 bond, with the surety(ies) approved by the probate judge (COA 36-20-71[a]). Notaries carrying a $10,000 bond on January 1, 2012, need not obtain a $25,000 bond until commission expiration (COA 36-20-71[b]). "An individual desiring to become a notary public has to show evidence of a bond for the term of appointment before appointment" (Ala. Atty. Gen. Opinion 95-00289 of August 16, 1996).

Non-Residents Do Not Qualify: "An individual must apply in the county of his residency to become a notary public .... A person who resides in another state, but who works in Alabama, cannot be appointed and commissioned as a notary public in this state" (Ala. Atty. Gen. Opinion 95-00289 of August 16, 1995).

Online Search: Alabama's Notaries, both regular and Civil Law, are listed on the Secretary of State's website ("Government Records Inquiry System"). The list of Notaries may be searched by name or bonding company.

Changes of Status

If Notary Changes Name: "There is no statutory authority by which a probate judge may amend or reissue a notary's record of appointment to authorize the notary to use a newly acquired name. However, if the notary so desires, she may reapply for a new notary commission in her newly acquired or married name" (Ala. Atty. Gen. Opinion 95-00220 of May 17, 1995).

If Notary Moves from County: State-at-large Notaries do not vacate their offices upon moving from their counties, however, a spokesperson for the Secretary of State's office advised that "it may be that a better practice for a notary for the state at large would be to get a new commission in his/her county of residence if the notary moves from the county where the commission was initially obtained."

COUNTY PROBATE JUDGES

To contact an Alabama county probate judge to obtain an authenticating certificate for a Notary, or to obtain the register of a former Notary, telephone 1-XXX-555-1212, using the following area codes, and ask for the number of the "county judge of probate."

County	City/Town	Area Code
Autauga	Prattville	(334)
Baldwin	Bay Minette	(251)
Barbour	Clayton/Eufaula	(334)
Bibb	Centreville	(205)
Blount	Oneonta	(205)
Bullock	Union Springs	(334)
Butler	Greenville	(334)
Calhoun	Anniston	(256)
Chambers	Lafayette	(334)
Cherokee	Centre	(256)
Chilton	Clanton	(205)
Choctaw	Butler	(205)
Clarke	Grove Hill	(251)
Clay	Ashland	(256)
Cleburne	Heflin	(256)
Coffee	Enterprise/New Brockton	(334)
Colbert	Tuscumbia	(256)
Conecuh	Evergreen	(251)
Coosa	Rockford	(256)
Covington	Andalusia	(334)
Crenshaw	Luverne	(334)
Cullman	Cullman	(256)
Dale	Ozark	(334)
Dallas	Selma	(334)
DeKalb	Fort Payne	(256)
Elmore	Wetumpka	(334)
Escambia	Brewton	(251)
Etowah	Gadsden	(256)
Fayette	Fayette	(205)
Franklin	Russellville	(256)
Geneva	Geneva	(334)
Greene	Eutaw	(205)
Hale	Greensboro	(334)
Henry	Abbeville	(334)
Houston	Dothan	(334)
Jackson	Scottsboro	(256)
Jefferson*	Birmingham	(205)
Lamar	Vernon	(205)
Lauderdale	Florence	(256)
Lawrence	Moulton	(256)
Lee	Opelika	(334)
Limestone	Athens	(256)
Lowndes	Hayneville	(334)
Macon	Tuskegee	(334)
Madison	Huntsville	(256)

County	City/Town	Area Code
Marengo	Linden	(334)
Marion	Hamilton	(205)
Marshall	Guntersville	(256)
Mobile	Mobile	(251)
Monroe	Monroeville	(251)
Montgomery	Montgomery	(334)
Morgan	Decatur	(256)
Perry	Marion	(334)
Pickens	Carrollton	(205)
Pike	Troy	(334)
Randolph	Wedowee	(256)
Russell	Phenix City	(334)
St. Clair	Ashville	(205)
Shelby	Columbiana	(205)
Sumter	Livingston	(205)
Talladega	Talladega	(256)
Tallapoosa	Dadeville	(256)
Tuscaloosa	Tuscaloosa	(205)
Walker	Jasper	(205)
Washington	Chatom	(251)
Wilcox	Camden	(334)
Winston	Double Springs	(205)

* In Jefferson County, the circuit clerk issues authenticating certificates for Notaries.

OTHER NOTARIAL OFFICERS

Besides Notaries Public, the following officers have power to take acknowledgments and proofs of conveyances within the state (COA 35-4-24):

1. Judges of the supreme court, court of civil appeals, court of criminal appeals, circuit court and district court;
2. Clerks of the above courts;
3. Registers of the circuit court;
4. Judges of the court of probate.

Civil Law Notaries

The Alabama Secretary of State may appoint as a "Civil Law Notary" any member of the Alabama Bar admitted to the practice of law for at least five years. Such Notaries may execute "authentic acts," including notarial deeds and "minutes," as well as "brevets," a private document in which the Civil Law Notary attests to the authenticity of a signature, fact or contract; brevets may also be used to "prescribe oaths, certify a translation or a copy of a document that is not part of the civil law notaries protocol, or certify the identity of any object or thing." Civil Law Notaries keep copies of the originals of their acts in a "protocol." They may also execute all other acts of a regular Alabama Notary. See COA 36-20-50 through 36-20-55, as amended on September 26, 2001; see also Alabama Administrative Code, Chapters 820-6-1 through 820-6-4 and the Secretary of State's website ("Civil Law Notaries").

QUICK FACTS

Notary Jurisdiction
Effective January 1, 2012, all Alabama Notaries are commissioned with statewide jurisdiction under Act No. 2011-295 (i.e., Senate Bill 54). Notary commissions with countywide powers existing on that date remain in effect only until commission expiration (COA 36-20-70[b]).

Notary Term Length
Four years (COA 36-20-70[a]), expiring at midnight on the commission expiration date. Willfully notarizing with an expired commission is a Class C misdemeanor (COA 36-20-75).

Notary Bond
$25,000 for all Notaries commissioned on or after January 1, 2012 (COA 36-20-71[a]).
Notaries carrying a $10,000 bond on January 1, 2012, need not obtain a $25,000 bond until commission expiration (COA 36-20-71[b]).

Alaska

NOTARY SEAL

An Alaska Notary must authenticate all official acts with a seal of office (AS 44.50.064[a]), and the seal's format must be as follows:

Kind

Inked Stamp or Photocopiable Embosser: "With regard to each paper document being notarized, a sharp, legible, photographically reproducible impression or depiction of a notary public's official seal shall be affixed ... on the notarial certificate near the notary public's official signature" (AS 44.50.065[a]).

"If using an embossing seal, take care to shade over the raised portion of the seal so that it complies with the requirement that it be 'photographically reproducible'" (website, "Frequently Asked Questions").

NOTARY ADMINISTRATION

Office of Lieutenant Governor
Notary Public Office 1-907-465-3509
240 Main St. 1-877-764-1234
Suite 301 (mail)
(State Capitol Bldg., Room 315 [walk-in])
Juneau, AK 99801

Website: http://ltgov.alaska.gov/treadwell/notaries.html

NOTARY RULES

AS — *Alaska Statutes*

Most Notary rules are in the Alaska Statutes:

a. Title 44, Chapter 50, "Notaries Public";

b. Title 9, Chapter 63, Sections 09.63.050 through 09.63.100 of which are cited as the "Uniform Recognition of Acknowledgments Acts."*

* This is the *Uniform Recognition of Acknowledgments Act* of 1968, adopted with minor revisions.

Notary Public
JANE Q. DOE
State of Alaska
My Commission Expires Jan. 30, 2015

RICHARD A. ROE
NOTARY
PUBLIC
STATE OF ALASKA

Examples

The above typical, actual-size examples of circular and rectangular seals are allowed by Alaska law. Formats other than these may also be permitted.

Embosser May Supplement Stamp: "An embossed seal impression that is not photographically reproducible may be used in addition to, but not in place of, the seal impression or depiction required by (a) of this section" (AS 44.50.065[c]).

Shape/Size

Circular or Rectangular: Circular, not over 2 inches in diameter; or rectangular, not over 1 inch wide and $2^{1}/_{2}$ inches long; or in electronic form as authorized by the Lieutenant Governor (AS 44.50.064[b][2]).

Components

An Alaska Notary Public's official seal must contain (AS 44.50.064[b][1]):
1. Name of Notary exactly as on commission;
2. "Notary Public";
3. "State of Alaska".

OPTIONAL: Commission expiration date and/or commission number (website, "Frequently Asked Questions").

Expiration Date Must Appear

The Notary's commission expiration date must be affixed on the document along with the Notary's seal and signature (AS 09.63.100[b][1]).

"If you are not prompted for the expiration date of your commission as part of the notarial certificate it must be included anyway, either as part of your notary seal or by indicating 'My commission expires (date)' near your signature on your notarial certificate" (website, "Frequently Asked Questions").

"When performing notarizations as a limited governmental notary you will indicate that your commission expires 'with office'" (website, "Applications for Limited Governmental Commissions").

Affix Seal at Time of Notarization

Whether on a paper document or an electronic one, the Notary's seal must be affixed "only at the time the notarial act is performed" (AS 44.50.065[a][2] and 44.50.065[d]).

Illegible Seal Impression

"For a notarized paper document, illegible information within a seal impression or depiction may be typed or printed legibly by the notary public adjacent to, but not within, the impression or depiction" (AS 44.50.065[b]).

"If any elements of the seal are illegible, print the missing information so that it is legible" (website, "Frequently Asked Questions").

Postmaster's Stamp

U.S. postmasters in Alaska may act as Notaries. When they do so, they must affix the post office cancellation stamp in lieu of the Notary seal (AS 44.50.180[b]).

Seal Placement

"Place the seal in a blank space as near as possible to your signature. Never place the seal over any signatures or document wording" (website, "Frequently Asked Questions").

Recorded Document: "If the document bearing the notarized signature will be submitted for recording please avoid placing your seal within two inches of the top margin of the page and within one inch of the remaining margins of the document. The recorder's office charges a $50.00 non-standard document fee for any documents submitted for recording that do not meet their margin requirements" (website, "Frequently Asked Questions").

If No Room for Seal

"What should I do if there is not enough room for an embosser seal or rubber stamp information on a document? – In most instances, a separate notary certificate may be affixed to the document. This is called a loose certificate, and the notary should place the seal half on the loose portion of the certificate and half on the original document. However, the loose certificate is not always accepted and the person requesting the notarization is responsible for making sure with the receiving agency of the document that a separate notary certificate attached to the document is acceptable" (website, "Frequently Asked Questions").

Security of Seal

The Notary must "ensure that another person does not possess or use the official seal" because it is "the exclusive property of the notary public" (AS 44.50.064[a]).

"When not in use, a notary public's official seal shall be kept secure and under the exclusive control of the notary public" (AS 44.50.064[c]).

Lost or Stolen Seal

"Within 10 days after a notary public's official seal is stolen or lost, or the security of the notary public's official electronic seal is compromised, the notary public shall provide the lieutenant governor with written notification of the theft, loss, or compromised security. After the notary public has provided the lieutenant governor with the notification, the notary public shall provide the lieutenant governor with any additional information that the lieutenant governor requests about the compromise of the seal" (AS 44.50.064[d]).

Seal To Be Destroyed, Defaced

"In order to avoid misuse, a notary public's official seal shall be destroyed or defaced

"(1) upon the notary public's resignation or death;

"(2) upon the revocation or termination by the lieutenant governor of the notary public's commission; or

"(3) when the notary public's term of commission ends if the notary public has not received a new commission ..." (AS 44.50.064[e]).

Notary's Signature Requirements

"When performing a notarization, a notary public shall

"(1) sign in the notary public's own handwriting, on the notarial certificate, exactly and only the name indicated on the notary public's commission certificate, or sign an electronic document by electronic means as authorized by regulations adopted by the lieutenant governor; and

"(2) affix the official signature only at the time the notarial act is performed" (AS 44.50.063[a]).

NOTARY POWERS

Alaska Notaries are authorized to perform the following notarial acts (44.50.060 and 09.63.120):
1. Take acknowledgments*;
2. Administer oaths** and affirmations**, especially in executing jurats***;
3. Attest documents;
4. Execute protests**** (AS 45.03.505[b]).

* Acknowledgments: An acknowledger must appear before the Notary and indicate to the Notary that the acknowledger voluntarily affixed his or her signature on the document for the purposes stated in the document (AS 44.50.062[5][A]).

"Acknowledged before me" means that "the person taking the acknowledgment either knew or had satisfactory evidence that the person acknowledging is the person named in the instrument or certificate" (AS 09.63.090[2]).

"An acknowledgment is a declaration by a person before a notarial officer that he or she has signed a record for the purposes stated in the record and, if the record is signed in a representative capacity, that the individual signed the record with proper authority and signed it as the act of the individual or entity identified in the record. When a document contains an acknowledgment, it does not have to be signed in a notary's presence, but the document signer must still appear before the notary to acknowledge that he or she signed the document and agrees to the contents" (website, "Frequently Asked Questions").

** Oath, Affirmation Wording: The Lieutenant Governor's website ("Frequently Asked Questions") recommends the following wording for oaths and affirmations associated with documents (see "Jurats," below):

Oath. "I do solemnly swear that the statements in this document are true, so help me God."

Affirmation. "I do solemnly affirm that the statements in this document are true."

*** Jurats: "A jurat is part of an affidavit in which the notary states that the affidavit was signed and sworn to before the notary. When a document contains a jurat, it must be signed in a notary's presence, and the document signer must swear to the truthfulness of the statement in the document" (website, "Frequently Asked Questions").

"A notary public may not ... affix the notary public's official seal to a document unless the person who is to sign the document ... gives an oath or affirmation if required under law or if the notarial certificate states that the document was signed under oath or affirmation ..." (AS 44.50.062[5][B]).

**** Protests: While the changes to Alaska's Notary law that took effect in 2005 through enactment of House Bill 97 (Chapter 60) repealed the authority of Alaska Notaries to execute protests, another section of Alaska law (AS 45.03.505) still empowers Notaries to perform them. However, the Lieutenant Governor's website ("Notary Law Comparison") discourages the practice: "(T)he Notarial Protest appears to be a very technical process that would now be beyond the scope of duties (and technical prowess) of the contemporary Alaska notary. We caution our notaries not to become involved in a protest without first consulting our office."

Authority to Take Depositions Removed

The changes to Alaska's Notary law that took effect in 2005 through enactment of House Bill 97 (Chapter 60) only removed from the Notary statutes the Notary's general authority to "take" (in the sense of transcribing) spoken testimony for depositions and affidavits. "Signatures on depositions and affidavits may require notarization — and under the current law any notary is still allowed to perform notarizations of signatures related to these documents — but the preparation of the document itself is not the proper venue of the notary. The changes here are intended to clarify that point, not ... to prevent any notary from performing a notarization related to an affidavit or deposition" (website, "Notary Law Comparison").

These changes thus do not affect the Notary's continuing authority to administer oaths and affirmations and execute jurats for depositions and affidavits. The 2005 law changes also did not remove from the Alaska Rules of Civil Procedure (Rule 28) the authorization for Notaries as oath-administering officials to take depositions when so duly authorized.

No Authority to Certify Copies

Based on a 1992 Alaska Attorney General's opinion, Notaries do not have authority to certify copies of documents, according to the Notary Public Office.

"Alaska's notaries do not have the authority to certify documents or photocopies of documents. When it is necessary to authenticate a photocopy of a document ... it may be possible to use a process called Copy Certification by Document Custodian. Anybody except an individual functioning in the capacity of Notary Public can certify a document (as custodian) using this process. The person (custodian) that is certifying the document signs a statement and their signature on that statement is notarized" (website, "Authentications and Apostilles"). See the "Copy Certification by Document Custodian" form below, under "Notary Certificates."

However, the Notary Public Office points out that copy certifications by document custodians are not universally accepted and that the document custodian therefore should first check with the intended recipient to ensure that such a form will suffice. Further, "(i)t is against the law to make photocopies of ... Alaska Vital Statistics documents (AS 18.50.320[5]). The Lieutenant Governor will not be able to authenticate photocopies of Vital Statistic documents even if they have been properly notarized via the Copy Certification by Document Custodian process" (website, "Authentications and Apostilles").

Personal Appearance Required

"A notary public may not ... affix the notary public's official seal to a document unless the person who is to sign the document ... appears ... before the notary public" (AS 44.50.062[5][A]).

"The personal appearance of the signer before the Notary during the act of notarization is required by law" (website, "Frequently Asked Questions").

Identifying Signers

"Unless the signer is personally known to the Notary, Alaska Statute requires persons appearing before a notary to produce government-issued identification containing the photograph and signature of the person signing or government-issued ID containing the signature of the person signing without a photograph and another valid identification containing the photograph and signature of the person signing (AS 44.50.062[5][C])" (website, "Frequently Asked Questions").

Documentary Identification Requirements: "A Notary public may not ... affix the notary public's official seal to a document unless the person who is to sign the document ... is personally known to the notary public, produces government-issued identification containing the photograph and signature of the person signing, or produces

"(i) government-issued identification containing the signature of the person signing, but without a photograph; and

"(ii) another valid identification containing the photograph and signature of the person signing" (AS 44.50.062[5][C]).

Determining Willingness and Competence

"What three things should a notary screen for? — a. Identity. b. Willingness. c. Competency" (website, "Frequently Asked Questions").

Willingness: "If you suspect a person is being forced to sign a document, you should refuse to notarize the document. If you fear violence, you might notarize and then contact the police" (website, "Frequently Asked Questions").

Indeed, Alaska law states that no notarization may be performed unless the person who is to sign the document "appears and signs the document before the notary public or, for an acknowledgment, appears and indicates to the notary public that the person voluntarily affixed the person's signature on the document for the purposes stated within the document" (AS 44.50.062[5][A]).

Competence: "While you scan the document for any printed title or other document identification, ask the signer to describe the document to you as well (use both sources of information to describe the document in your journal). If the signer is unable to describe what the document is, or is having a difficult time conveying that information, it may be an indication that they are not competent to sign....

"The constituent should be able to communicate with you in some fashion and have the ability to indicate a basic understanding of the contents of the document. If there is doubt about competency, you may consult an available expert, such as the constituent's doctor or attorney. However, your common sense should prevail. If the constituent cannot communicate intelligibly, the notarization should not be performed" (website, "Frequently Asked Questions").

Signature by Mark

"When a physical handicap or illiteracy prevents a signer from writing his or her signature in the normal fashion, a mark (usually an 'X') may be used. This type of signature requires two witnesses in addition to the notary" (website, "Frequently Asked Questions").

Foreign-Language Documents

"What should a notary do if asked to notarize a document written in a foreign language? — First, the notary and the signer must be able to communicate directly without the assistance of a translator. If the notary and signer can't communicate directly the notary must decline the notarization and the signer should find a notary fluent in the language.

"If direct communication with the signer is possible but the notary can't read the body of the document, notaries have the discretion to either continue with the notarization or they may decline the notarization for reasons discussed below. Either way, every document bearing a notarized signature must also contain a notarial certificate and the notarial certificate must be in a language that the notary understands.

"If you decide that you are unable to perform the notarization please try to assist the signer in finding a notary that can work with them or direct them to contact the (state) notary office for assistance.

"In some cases, foreign language documents may be drafted such that the notary's name is embedded in the body of the document. Alaska law specifically prohibits notaries from performing notarizations if they are named in the body of the document.

"The safest course of action for a the notary is to defer the notarization to a notary fluent in the language the document is constructed in.

We have a resources Web page where we list Alaska notaries who are available to perform foreign language notarizations" (website, "Frequently Asked Questions").

Signing on Penalty of Perjury

"A matter required or authorized to be supported, evidenced, established, or proven by the sworn statement, declaration, verification, certificate, oath, or affidavit, in writing of the person making it (other than a deposition, an acknowledgment, an oath of office, or an oath required to be taken before a specified official other than a notary public) may be supported, evidenced, established, or proven by the person certifying in writing 'under penalty of perjury' that the matter is true. The certification shall state the date and place of execution, the fact that a notary public or other official empowered to administer oaths is unavailable, and the following: 'I certify under penalty of perjury that the foregoing is true'" (AS 09.63.020[a]).

NOTARY DON'TS

Alaska Notaries may:
1. NOT "make representations to have powers, qualifications, rights, or privileges that the office of notary public does not have" (AS 44.50.061[c]);
2. NOT "influence a person to enter into or avoid a transaction involving a notarial act by the notary public" (AS 44.50.062[2]).

Certificate Selection Unauthorized

"A notary public who is not an attorney may complete but may not select notarial certificates, and may not assist another person in drafting, completing, selecting, or understanding a document or transaction requiring a notarial act" (AS 44.50.061[a]).

"A notarization is incomplete without notarial wording. It is not the notary's role or obligation to decide what type of notarial act is needed for a given document. This is a legal decision. The signer should be asked to find out what kind of certificate is appropriate. This information may be acquired through an attorney or from the issuing or receiving agencies of the document. If the constituent provides the appropriate wording, the notary may affix the notarial certificate as a courtesy" (website, "Frequently Asked Questions").

Blank or Incomplete Certificates

"A notary public may not ... affix the notary public's signature or seal on a notarial certificate that is incomplete" (AS 44.50.062[3]).

Disqualifying Interests

"A notary public may not ... perform a notarial act if the notary public

"(A) is a signer of or named in the document that is to be notarized; or

"(B) will receive directly from a transaction connected with the notarial act a commission, fee, advantage, right, title, interest, cash, property, or other consideration exceeding in value the normal fee charged by the notary for the notarial act" (AS 44.50.062[6]).

Family Members: "Alaska Statutes do not specifically forbid notarizing the signatures of relatives....

"If there is any reason to believe that a document may be contested, or if the actions related to the document may prove controversial, it would be best in those situations to avoid performing notarizations for relatives.

"If you are unsure about the wisdom or propriety of involving yourself in a notarization for a relative it would be best to refuse to participate in the notarization" (website, "Frequently Asked Questions").

NOTARY SIGNING AGENTS

Currently, there are no statutes, regulations or rules expressly recognizing, governing, prohibiting or restricting the operation of Notary Signing Agents within the state of Alaska.

NOTARY FEES

Fees for Notaries Public are not currently addressed in the Alaska Statutes. Setting and charging fees is left entirely up to the Notary's discretion.

Must Provide Fee Schedule

"A notary public may not ... charge a fee for a notarial act unless a fee schedule has been provided to the signer before the performance of the notarial act" (AS 44.50.062[4]).

Fees Prohibited

Limited Governmental Notaries: Limited governmental Notaries "may not charge or receive a fee or other consideration for notarial services" (AS 44.50.039[3]).

Postmasters: U.S. postal regulations do not allow postmasters to charge fees for notarizations.

NOTARY CERTIFICATES

Alaska has adopted the *Uniform Recognition of Acknowledgments Act* with minor revisions, including the short-form certificates (AS 09.63.100[a]) for:

1. Acknowledgment by individual;
2. Acknowledgment by corporation;
3. Acknowledgment by limited liability company;
4. Acknowledgment by partnership;
5. Acknowledgment by attorney in fact;
6. Acknowledgment by public officer, trustee, or personal representative.

In order to conform with Alaska law, the Notary's seal and commission expiration date must be added to the above certificates, and the judicial district should be noted in the venue rather than the county. The six certificates appear below as forms 09.63.100(a)(1) through (6).

Judicial District Preferred: Alaska is divided into "boroughs" rather than counties, and, on a larger scale, into four judicial districts. The venue of each notarial certificate should state the judicial district in which the notarization was performed (First, Second, Third or Fourth — see "Venue Districts," below). An official in the Lieutenant Governor's office emphasized the importance of including the pertinent city or municipality in the venue, because judicial districts may be "cryptic."

Acknowledgment by Individual (AS 09.63.100[a][1]):

State of Alaska,
_____ Judicial District
(or County or Municipality of _____)

The foregoing instrument was acknowledged before me this _____ (date) by _____ (name of person who acknowledged).

_____ *(Signature of person taking acknowledgment)*
_____ *Title or Rank*
_____ *Serial Number, if any* (SEAL)

(NOTARY'S COMMISSION EXPIRATION DATE [if not included in seal])

Acknowledgment by Corporation (AS 09.63.100[a][2]):

State of Alaska,
_____ *Judicial District*
(or County or Municipality of ____)

The foregoing instrument was acknowledged before me this _____ (date) by _____ (name of corporate officer or agent), _____ (title of corporate officer or agent), of _____ (name of corporation acknowledging), a _____ (state or place of incorporation) corporation, on behalf of the corporation.

_____ *(Signature of person taking acknowledgment)*
_____ *Title or Rank*
_____ *Serial Number, if any* (SEAL)

(NOTARY'S COMMISSION EXPIRATION DATE [if not included in seal])

Acknowledgment by Limited Liability Company (AS 09.63.100[a][3]):

State of Alaska,
_____ *Judicial District*
(or County or Municipality of ____)

The foregoing instrument was acknowledged before me this _____ (date) by _____ (name of member or manager), member (or manager) of _____ (name of limited liability company acknowledging), a _____ (state or place of the company's organization) limited liability company, on behalf of the limited liability company.

_____ *(Signature of person taking acknowledgment)*
_____ *Title or Rank*
_____ *Serial Number, if any* (SEAL)

(NOTARY'S COMMISSION EXPIRATION DATE [if not included in seal])

Acknowledgment by Partnership (AS 09.63.100[a][4]):

State of Alaska,
_____ *Judicial District*
(or County or Municipality of ____)

The foregoing instrument was acknowledged before me this _____ (date) by _____ (name of acknowledging partner or agent), partner (or agent) on behalf of _____ (name of partnership), a partnership (or limited partnership or limited liability partnership).

_____ *(Signature of person taking acknowledgment)*
_____ *Title or Rank*
_____ *Serial Number, if any* (SEAL)

(NOTARY'S COMMISSION EXPIRATION DATE [if not included in seal])

Acknowledgment by Attorney in Fact (AS 09.63.100[a][5]):

State of Alaska,
_____ *Judicial District*
(or County or Municipality of ____)

The foregoing instrument was acknowledged before me this _____ (date) by _____ (name of attorney in fact) as attorney in fact on behalf of _____ (name of principal).

_____ *(Signature of person taking acknowledgment)*
_____ *Title or Rank*
_____ *Serial Number, if any* (SEAL)

(NOTARY'S COMMISSION EXPIRATION DATE [if not included in seal])

Acknowledgment by Public Officer, Trustee, or Personal Representative (AS 09.63.100[a][6]):

State of Alaska,
_____ *Judicial District*
(or County or Municipality of ____)

The foregoing instrument was acknowledged before me this _____ (date) by _____ *(name of acknowledging public officer, trustee or personal representative), _____ (title of position).*

_____ *(Signature of person taking acknowledgment)*
_____ *Title or Rank*
_____ *Serial Number, if any*   (SEAL)

(NOTARY'S COMMISSION EXPIRATION DATE [if not included in seal])

In addition, the following certificates are prescribed elsewhere in statute and on the Lieutenant Governor's website:

Jurat Certificate (AS 09.63.030[b]):

State of Alaska,
_____ *Judicial District*
(or County or Municipality of ____)

Subscribed and sworn to or affirmed before me at _____ on _____ (date).

_____ *(Signature of officer)*   (SEAL)
_____ *(Title of officer)*

(NOTARY'S COMMISSION EXPIRATION DATE [if not included in seal])

Verification with Jurat (AS 09.63.040[c]):

State of Alaska,
_____ *Judicial District*
(or County or Municipality of ____)

I, _____, say on oath or affirm that I have read the foregoing (or attached) document and believe all statements made in the document are true.

_____ *(Signature)*

Subscribed and sworn to or affirmed before me at _____ on _____ (date).

_____ *(Signature of officer)*   (SEAL)
_____ *(Title of officer)*

(NOTARY'S COMMISSION EXPIRATION DATE [if not included in seal])

Copy Certification by Document Custodian (website, "Authentications and Apostilles"):

State of Alaska,
_____ *Judicial District*
(or County or Municipality of ____)

I, _____ (name of document custodian), hereby affirm that the attached reproduction of _____ (document description) is a true, correct and complete photocopy of a document in my possession.

_____ *(Signature of custodian)*
_____ *(Address of custodian)*

Subscribed and sworn to before me this ___ day of _____, 20___.

_____ *(Signature of Notary)*   (SEAL)

(NOTARY'S COMMISSION EXPIRATION DATE [if not included in seal])

Form of Acknowledgment Certificate

"The form of a certificate of acknowledgment … shall be accepted in the state if

"(1) the certificate is in a form prescribed by the laws or regulations of the state;

"(2) the certificate is in a form prescribed by the laws or regulations applicable in the place in which the acknowledgment is taken; or

"(3) the certificate contains the words 'acknowledged before me' or their substantial equivalent" (AS 09.63.080).

Attaching Certificates

"Is it proper for the notarial certificate to be an attachment to the document? – Yes. However, the notarial certificate should be identified in some way as belonging to that document. You might, for example, write in the margin, 'This certificate is attached to a _____ (name of document) dated _____, and signed by _____'" (website, "Frequently Asked Questions").

Postmaster Certificates

When performing notarial acts, U.S. postmasters must: sign each notarial certificate; include their title ("Postmaster"), the name of the post office and the date of notarization; affix the post office cancellation stamp in lieu of the Notary seal; and complete all other required elements of the notarial certificate (AS 44.50.180[b]).

ELECTRONIC NOTARIZATIONS

Official Signature May Be Electronic

When performing a notarization, a Notary may "sign an electronic document by electronic means as authorized by regulations adopted by the lieutenant governor" and must "affix the official signature only at the time the notarial act is performed" (AS 44.50.063[a]).

If a Notary wishes to notarize using an electronic signature, the Notary "shall comply in a timely manner with a request by the lieutenant governor to supply … information regarding the notary public's electronic signature" (AS 44.50.063[b]).

Reporting Security Compromise: "Within 10 days after the security of a notary public's electronic signature has been compromised, the notary public shall provide the lieutenant governor with written notification that the signature has been compromised. After the notary public has provided the lieutenant governor with the notification, the notary public shall provide the lieutenant governor with any additional information that the lieutenant governor requests about the compromise of the signature" (AS 44.50.063[c]).

Electronic Seal

"A notary public may use a seal in electronic form on electronic documents notarized by the notary public as authorized by regulations adopted by the lieutenant governor. The seal shall be affixed only at the time the notarial act is performed" (AS 44.50.065[d]).

NOTARY RECORDS

While Alaska law does not require Notaries to keep a record of their official acts, the practice of record-keeping by Notaries has long been encouraged by the Lieutenant Governor's office. Indeed, the Lieutenant Governor's website ("Frequently Asked Questions") states:

"You are not required by law to keep permanent record of your notarizations, however, this office cannot emphasize enough the importance of recording every notarization you perform in a proper notary journal. Journal entries should be sequentially numbered and any journal or recording system where the pages are not physically bound together (or logically bound in the case of electronic notary journals) in a manner that prevents them from being inserted or removed from the journal by the notary should be avoided. If a notarized document is lost or altered, or if certain facts about the transaction are later challenged, the journal becomes valuable evidence. It can protect the rights of citizens and help notaries defend themselves against false accusations."

Principal Should Sign Journal

"Record information about the act in your Notary journal and have the signer sign your journal. Pay attention to how the signer signs your journal. It should be an easy fluid movement. Any awkwardness related to the making of the signature may be an indication of attempted forgery….

"Carefully compare the signature on the document against the signatures on the ID card and your journal" (website, "Frequently Asked Questions").

Must Scan Document to Make Entry

The "Alaska Notary Handbook," formerly published by the Lieutenant Governor (final edition 2004), stated: "You do not have an unrestricted right or duty to read a document. However, you have the right and duty to scan the document in order to perform your record keeping duties.

"You should refuse to notarize a document when the person requesting the notarization will not permit you to examine the document sufficiently to be able to perform the duty imposed on you by law or rules of practice."

AUTHENTICATION OF NOTARIAL ACTS

Authenticating certificates for Alaska Notaries, including apostilles, are issued by the state Lieutenant Governor's office.

Fee: $5 per authenticating certificate, for an apostille or "certificate of authority" (AS 44.19.024). Payable to "State of Alaska."

Address:
Office of Lieutenant Governor
Authentications Department
240 Main St., Suite 301
Juneau, AK 99801

Telephone: 1-907-465-3509

Procedure: Mail or present in person the original notarized document(s) and the appropriate fee. Indicate the nation to which the document will be sent, and include a contact telephone number and a return mailing address. An improperly notarized document will be rejected for authentication. "Unless other arrangements have been clearly requested and provided for, your order will be processed and returned at no extra cost to you by regular U.S. mail to any domestic location that you indicate" (website, "Authentications and Apostilles").

Pre-Screening Encouraged: "Faxing the notarized pages of your notarized documents prior to sending your order allows us to verify that your documents have been properly notarized by an actively commissioned Alaska notary (or that we will be able to authenticate the signatures of other State officials) and that they meet all of the requirements for authentication. This screening process also allows us to accomplish some of the necessary preparation work before we actually receive your original documents. Having this work done by the time we physically receive your order can mean the difference between being able to return your documents on the same day we receive them or having to wait until the following business day.

"To take advantage of this service, fax only the notarized pages (or those that have been signed and sealed by a State official) of your documents to (907) 465-5400. Please include a cover sheet with your name, contact numbers and the name of the country that will be receiving your authenticated documents. We will review the notarizations and contact you with the results. If your notarizations include embossed (a raised seal made with a crimping device) notary seals, please be sure to darken the raised portion of the seal with a pencil or ink before you send your fax. If steps are not taken to darken the seal it will not show up on the fax and will appear as an incomplete notarization" (website, "Authentications and Apostilles").

Document Custodian Certifications: The Lieutenant Governor's website ("Authentications and Apostilles") points out that the Copy Certification by Document Custodian process may be a method to get a Notary involved and thereby enable documents, particularly school transcripts, to be authenticated by the state: "After you have determined that a Copy Certification by Document Custodian will be acceptable to the recipient country, create your photocopy, add the Copy Certification by Document Custodian notarial certificate to your document and obtain the services of a commissioned Notary Public to administer the oath and notarize your signature. It is most desirable to add the wording directly to the photocopy (front or back), but you can add a loose certificate (separate piece of paper containing the notarial wording) if necessary." See the "Copy Certification by Document Custodian" form above, under "Notary Certificates."

This method is not lawful for certifying vital statistics documents (e.g., birth certificates), which may only be certified by their designated official custodians.

COMMISSIONING AND ADMINISTRATION

The office of Alaska's Lieutenant Governor appoints, commissions, regulates and maintains records on the state's Notaries (AS 44.50.010[a] and 45.50.072).

A Notary may provide the Lieutenant Governor with an address, telephone number and email address that is to be kept confidential. However, a nonconfidential address and telephone number must also be provided (AS 44.50.071[a]).

Applying for Commission

Qualifications: An applicant for a commission as an Alaska Notary Public must: (a) be at least 18 years old, (b) be a resident of Alaska and physically present in the state for a minimum of 30 days with the intent to remain indefinitely, (c) be legally residing in the United States, (d) not have been convicted or incarcerated for a felony in the 10 years before the commission takes effect and (e) not have had a Notary commission revoked for failure to obey the law or maintain residency or for incompetence or malfeasance in the past 10 years (AS 01.10.055, 44.50.020, 44.50.036 and 44.50.068[a]).

Two types of commission are available: a commission for Notaries "without limitation" and one for "limited governmental" Notaries. The latter commission type is only for use by federal, state and municipal employees on official business and has an open-ended term for the duration of government employment. One person may hold both types of commission concurrently (AS 44.50.010 and 44.50.039).

No Course or Test: No course of instruction is required of applicants for a Notary commission in Alaska.

"However, we do highly recommend all Notaries Public to go through a training course. This will better equip any Notary Public (to deal) with the various situations that will arise in their duties as an Alaska Notary Public" (website, "Alaska Notary Training").

Application: For a Notary commission without limitation, the completed application form must be submitted with a $40 application fee payable to "State of Alaska" and a $1,000 surety bond. If the surety is personal rather than commercial, the signature of the surety on the bond form must be notarized.

For a limited governmental Notary commission, there is no bond requirement. For applicants who are employed by the State of Alaska, there is no application fee (federal and municipal government employees are not exempt from the fee). A completed application for a limited governmental commission requires a signed statement from the applicant's employer that the commission is needed to conduct official government business.

For both types of commission, the applicant's signature on the oath of office on the application form must be notarized prior to submission (AS 44.50.032 through 44.50.035 and website, "Commission Applications").

"There is no special application process for people who have previously been notaries or who have current commissions that are nearing expiration" (website, "Notary Commission Renewals").

Postmasters: Postmasters who perform notarial acts are not required to hold a Notary commission or to be bonded (AS 44.50.180[d]).

Non-Residents: Non-residents of Alaska may not qualify for a Notary commission in the state.

Online Search: Anyone may search the Alaska Notary Data Files "to keep track of recently issued commissions or to locate any current Alaska notary. An Excel spreadsheet containing the same data is also available" (website, "Alaska Notary Data Files").

Changes of Status

"Within 30 days after change of a notary public's name, mailing address, or physical address, the notary public shall, on a form provided by the lieutenant governor, submit written notification of the change, signed by the notary public" (AS 44.50.066[a]). The relevant form may be downloaded from the Lieutenant Governor's website. The Notary's signature on the form must be notarized before submission (website, "Name and Address Change Form").

If Notary's Name Changes: When a Notary is reporting a name change, he or she must include a $5 fee for a replacement certificate of commission (AS 44.19.024 and 44.50.066[c]). The Notary must continue to use the former name when notarizing until written notification has been provided to the surety for the Notary's bond, a replacement certificate of commission has been received from the Lieutenant Governor and a new seal has been obtained to reflect the name change (AS 44.50.066[d]).

If Notary Resigns: To resign a commission, a Notary must notify the Lieutenant Governor in writing of the effective date. A Notary who no longer meets the requirements of Chapter 44.50 must immediately resign (AS 44.50.067).

VENUE DISTRICTS

Alaska's major cities are in the judicial districts indicated below. An official in the Office of the Lieutenant Governor suggests that the municipality (city or town) be inserted in the venue by the Notary rather than – or in addition to – the judicial district: "The law allows either to be used but the judicial districts are very large areas that are not very meaningful in this context. The municipality is the more precise piece of information and most of the notaries have a better grasp of what city they are in (which is not necessarily the case when it comes to judicial districts)."

To contact a district superior court clerk, telephone long distance information — 1-907-555-1212 — and ask for the phone number of the clerk for the appropriate district.

First District:	Juneau
	Sitka
	Ketchikan
	Wrangell
	Petersburg
Second District:	Nome
	Kotzebue
	Barrow
Third District:	Anchorage
	Kenai
	Kodiak
	Palmer
	Valdez
Fourth District:	Fairbanks
	Bethel

OTHER NOTARIAL OFFICERS

Besides Notaries Public, the following officers have ex officio power to take acknowledgments and administer oaths and affirmations in the state (AS 09.63.010):

1. A justice, judge or magistrate of a court of the State of Alaska or of the United States;
2. A clerk or deputy clerk of a court of the State of Alaska or of the United States;
3. A United States postmaster (AS 44.50.180[a]);
4. A U.S. military officer (AS 09.63.050[4]);
5. A municipal clerk when carrying out official duties (AS 29.20.380);
6. The Alaska Lieutenant Governor when carrying out official duties (AS 24.05.160);
7. The presiding officer of each legislative house of Alaska when carrying out official duties (AS 24.05.170).

Limited Governmental Notaries

"Limited governmental notaries public" — either state, municipal or federal employees — may be commissioned and authorized to notarize for official governmental business only. The term of each such governmental Notary coincides with the term of employment. Such Notaries may not charge or receive a fee for their notarial services (AS 44.50.010 and 44.50.039).

However, "(a) person who is a state, municipal, or federal employee commissioned as a limited governmental notary public may also be commissioned as a notary public without limitation" (AS 44.50.010[c]).

U.S. Postmasters

Under Alaska statute (AS 44.50.180), U.S. postmasters in Alaska may act as Notaries. See "Postmaster Certificates," above, under "Notary Certificates" for further information.

QUICK FACTS

Notary Jurisdiction
Statewide (AS 44.50.010).

Notary Term Length
Four years (AS 44.50.010[b]), expiring at midnight on the commission expiration date.

Limited Governmental Notaries: "The term of a limited governmental notary public coincides with the term of government employment" (AS 44.50.010[b]).

Notary Bond
$1,000 (AS 44.50.034[a]). The Notary's surety may be a commercial bonding company or a business organization or private individual, but not the Notary (website, "Frequently Asked Questions").

American Samoa

NOTARY SEAL

An American Samoa Notary must affix an image of an official seal on every paper document notarized (ASCA 31.0339[b]) and the seal's format must be as follows:

Kind

Inked Stamp or Adhesive Label: "Near the notary's official signature on the notarial certificate of a paper document, the notary shall affix a sharp, legible, permanent, and photographically reproducible image of the official seal …" (ASCA 31.0340[a]).

Embosser Not Used by Itself: "An embossed seal impression that is not photographically reproducible may be used in addition to but not in lieu of the seal described in subsection (a)" (ASCA 31.0340[c]).

Shape/Size

Rectangular: The official seal must have "a border in a rectangular shape no larger than 1 inch by 2 inches, surrounding the required words" (ASCA 31.0340[a][5]).

Components

The official seal of an American Samoa Notary must include (ASCA 31.0340[a]):
1. Name of Notary exactly as indicated on commission;
2. Serial number of Notary's commission;
3. Words "Notary Public" and "Territory of American Samoa" and "My commission expires (commission expiration date)";
4. Notary's business address.

Adhesive Label: "Any seal image affixed by an adhesive label shall bear a preprinted sequential number which shall be recorded in the journal of notarial acts for its respective notarization" (ASCA 311.0339[e]).

Illegible Information: "Illegible information within a seal impression may be typed or printed legibly by the notary adjacent to but not within the impression" (ASCA 31.0340[b]).

Richard A. Roe
NOTARY PUBLIC No. 9876
Territory of American Samoa
1234 Main St., Pago Pago, A.S. 96799
My commission expires Jan. 30, 2014

Example

The above typical, actual-size example of a Notary seal is allowed by the law of American Samoa. Rectangular formats other than this may also be permitted.

NOTARY ADMINISTRATION

American Samoa Government
Secretary of American Samoa
Office of the Governor   1-684-633-4116
A.P. Lutali Executive Office Bldg., Utulei
Pago Pago, American Samoa 96799

Website: http://americansamoa.gov/

NOTARY RULES

ASCA — AMERICAN SAMOA CODE ANNOTATED
CPR — NOTARY PUBLIC CODE OF PROFESSIONAL
     RESPONSIBILITY

Statutory rules for Notaries are in the American Samoa Code Annotated, Title 31 ("Professions"), Sections 31.0301 through 31.0366, which is the Notary Act of 2007 (Public Law 30-18 as amended by Public Law 30-21), effective October 29, 2008. These laws are in the "American Samoa Notary Public Handbook," available from the Secretary's office.

For the mandatory course, Notary commission applicants are additionally required to study and keep as a guide the National Notary Association's "Notary Public Code of Professional Responsibility," available from the Secretary and from the NNA.

Seal Affixed at Time of Act

"An image of the seal shall be affixed only at the time the notarial act is performed" (ASCA 31.0339[c]).

Authorization to Sell or Make Seal

A seal vendor or manufacturer must apply for a permit from the Secretary of American Samoa, who charges $50 for the permit and maintains a controlled-access telephone number or Internet site to allow vendors and manufacturers to confirm the business mailing address of Notaries (ASCA 31.0341[a]).

Each seal purchaser must present to the vendor or manufacturer a photocopy of his or her Notary commission and a Certificate of Authorization to Purchase a Notary Seal from the Secretary. The purchaser must appear in person and be identified as the individual named in the commission and Certificate of Authorization, either through personal knowledge or satisfactory evidence of identity (ASCA 31.0341[b] and [c]).

"For each Certificate of Authorization to Purchase a Notary Seal, a vendor or manufacturer shall make or sell one and only one seal, plus, if requested by the person presenting the Certificate, one and only one embossing seal" (ASCA 31.0341[d]).

The vendor must affix an image of all seals on the Certificate of Authorization and send it to the Secretary, retaining a copy of the Certificate and related Notary commission for two years (ASCA 31.0341[e]).

A vendor who fails to comply with ASCA 31.0341 is guilty of a class B misdemeanor, punishable upon conviction by imprisonment of not more than six months and/or a fine of not more than $500, with additional civil liability not precluded (ASCA 31.0341[g]).

<u>Name or Business Address Change</u>: To obtain a new seal after a name or business address change, the Notary must present to the vendor or manufacturer a copy of the Confirmation of Notary's Name or Address Change from the Secretary in accordance with Sections 31.0351 and 31.0352 (ASCA 31.0341[f]).

Seal Is Notary's Exclusive Property

"A notary shall keep an official seal that is the exclusive property of the notary. The seal shall not be possessed or used by any other person, nor surrendered to an employer upon termination of employment" (ASCA 31.0339[a]).

"When not in use, the seal shall be kept secure and accessible only to the notary" (ASCA 31.0339[d]).

Lost or Stolen Seal

"Within 10 days after the seal of a notary is stolen, lost, damaged, or otherwise rendered incapable of affixing a tangible image, the notary, after informing the appropriate law enforcement agency in the case of theft or vandalism, shall notify the Secretary by any means providing a tangible receipt or acknowledgment, including certified mail and electronic transmission, and also provide a copy or number of any pertinent police report. Upon receipt of such notice the Secretary shall issue to the notary a new Certificate of Authorization to Purchase a Notary Seal, which shall be presented to a seal vendor in accordance with section 31.0341" (ASCA 31.0339[f]).

Disposition of Seal

"As soon as reasonably practicable after resignation, revocation, or expiration of a notary commission, or death of the notary, the seal shall be destroyed or defaced so that it may not be misused" (ASCA 31.0339[g]; 31.0354[a]; and 31.0355).

Official Signature

When notarizing a paper document, a Notary must (ASCA 31.0338): (a) sign by hand on the notarial certificate exactly and only the name indicated on the Notary's commission, (b) not sign using a facsimile stamp or an electronic or other printing method, and (c) affix the signature only at the time the notarization is performed.

NOTARY POWERS

Every Notary of American Samoa who is a "United States National" (i.e., born in the Territory of American Samoa, or a citizen of the United States, and owing allegiance to the United States [ASCA 31.0307(u)]) is empowered to perform the following notarial acts (ASCA 31.0320):

1. Take acknowledgments*;
2. Administer oaths** and affirmations***;
3. Execute jurats****;
4. Witness signatures*****;
5. Certify copies******.

NOTE: A Notary of American Samoa who is not a United States National is empowered only to perform acknowledgments, signature witnessings and copy certifications — and not to perform any notarial acts entailing administration of oaths or affirmations.

* Acknowledgments: "'Acknowledgment' means a notarial act in which an individual at a single time and place:
"1. appears in person before the notary and presents a document;
"2. is personally known to the notary or identified by the notary through satisfactory evidence; and
"3. indicates to the notary that the signature on the document was voluntarily affixed by the individual for purposes stated within the document and, if applicable, that the individual had due authority to sign in a particular representative capacity" (ASCA 31.0307[a]).

** Oaths: "'Oath' means a notarial act, or part thereof, which is legally equivalent to an affirmation and in which an individual at a single time and place:
"1. appears in person before the notary;
"2. is personally known to the notary or identified by the notary through satisfactory evidence; and
"3. makes a vow of truthfulness or fidelity on penalty of perjury while invoking a deity or using any form of the word 'swear'" (ASCA 31.0307[k]).

*** Affirmations: "'Affirmation' means a notarial act, or part thereof, which is legally equivalent to an oath and in which an individual at a single time and place:
"1. appears in person before the notary;
"2. is personally known to the notary or identified by the notary through satisfactory evidence; and
"3. makes a vow of truthfulness or fidelity on penalty of perjury, based on personal honor and without invoking a deity or using any form of the word 'swear'" (ASCA 31.0307[b]).

**** Jurats: "'Jurat' means a notarial act in which an individual at a single time and place:
"1. appears in person before the notary and presents a document;
"2. is personally known to the notary or identified by the notary through satisfactory evidence;

"3. signs the document in the presence of the notary; and
"4. takes an oath or affirmation from the notary vouching for the truthfulness or accuracy of the signed document" (ASCA 31.0307[g]).

***** Signature Witnessings: "'Signature witnessing' means a notarial act in which an individual at a single time and place:
"1. appears in person before the notary and presents a document;
"2. is personally known to the notary or identified by the notary through satisfactory evidence; and
"3. signs the document in the presence of the notary" (ASCA 31.0307[t]).

****** Copy Certifications: "'Copy certification' means a notarial act in which a notary:
"1. is presented with a document that is neither a vital record, a public record, nor publicly recordable;
"2. copies or supervises the copying of the document using a photographic or electronic copying process;
"3. compares the document to the copy; and
"4. determines the copy is accurate and complete" (ASCA 31.0307[d]).

Identifying Signers

"'Satisfactory evidence of identity' means identification of an individual based on:
"1. at least one current document issued by a federal, state, territorial, or tribal government agency bearing the photographic image of the individual's face and signature and a physical description of the individual, though a properly stamped passport without a physical description is acceptable; or
"2. the oath or affirmation of one credible witness unaffected by the document or transaction who is personally known to the notary and who personally knows the individual, or of 2 credible witnesses unaffected by the document or transaction who each personally knows the individual and shows to the notary documentary identification as described in subparagraph (a) of this subsection" (ASCA 31.0307[q]).

Personal Knowledge of Identity: "'Personal knowledge of identity' and 'personally knows' mean familiarity with an individual resulting from interactions with that individual over a period of time sufficient to dispel any reasonable uncertainty that the individual has the identity claimed" (ASCA 31.0307[n]).

Credible Witness: "'Credible witness' (means) an honest, reliable, and impartial person who personally knows an individual appearing before a notary and takes an oath or affirmation from the notary to vouch for that individual's identity" (ASCA 31.0307[e]).

Notarization of Signature by Mark

"A notary may certify the affixation of a signature by mark on a document presented for notarization if:

"1. the mark is affixed in the presence of the notary and of 2 witnesses unaffected by the document;

"2. both witnesses sign their own names beside the mark;

"3. the notary writes below the mark: 'Mark affixed by (name of signer of mark) in presence of (names and addresses of witnesses) and undersigned notary under section 31.0320(d) of the Notarial Act of 2007': and

"4. the notary notarizes the signature by mark through an acknowledgment, jurat, or signature witnessing" (ASCA 31.0320[d] and 31.0345[1]).

Notary May Sign for Another Person

"A notary may sign the name of a person physically unable to sign or make a mark on a document presented for notarization if:

"1. the person directs the notary to do so in the presence of 2 witnesses unaffected by the document;

"2. the notary signs the person's name in the presence of the person and the witnesses;

"3. both witnesses sign their own names beside the signature;

"4. the notary writes below the signature: 'Signature affixed by notary in the presence of (names and addresses of person and 2 witnesses) under section 31.0320(e) of the Notarial Act of 2007': and

"5. the notary notarizes the signature through an acknowledgment, jurat, or signature witnessing" (ASCA 31.0320[e] and 31.0345[2]).

Notarizing outside Workplace

"A notary may but is not required to perform a notarial act outside the notary's regular workplace or business hours" (ASCA 31.0322[c]).

NOTARY DON'TS

Prohibitions

"A notary shall not perform a notarial act if the principal:

"1. is not in the notary's presence at the time of notarization;

"2. is not personally known to the notary or identified by the notary through satisfactory evidence;

"3. shows a demeanor which causes the notary to have a compelling doubt about whether the principal knows the consequences of the transaction requiring a notarial act; or

"4. in the notary's judgment, is not acting of his or her own free will" (ASCA 31.0320[c]).

Disqualifications

"A notary is disqualified from performing a notarial act if the notary:

"1. is a party to or named in the document that is to be notarized;

"2. will receive as a direct or indirect result any commission, fee, advantage, right, title, interest, cash, property, or other consideration exceeding in value the fees specified in section 31.0330(a);

"3. is a spouse, domestic partner, ancestor, descendant, or sibling of the principal, including in-law, step, or half relatives; or

"4. is an attorney who has prepared, explained, or recommended to the principal the document that is to be notarized" (ASCA 31.0321[a]).

Signing Agent May Collect Fee: "Notwithstanding subsection (a)(2), a notary may collect a fee for an assignment as a signing agent if payment of that fee is not contingent upon the signing of any document" (ASCA 31.0321[b]).

Improper Cause for Refusal

"A notary shall not refuse to perform a notarial act based on the principal's race, advanced age, gender, sexual orientation, religion, national origin, health or disability, or status as a non-client or non-customer of the notary or the notary's employer" (ASCA 31.0322[a]).

Proper Cause for Refusal: "A notary shall perform any notarial act ... for any person requesting such an act who tenders the appropriate fee specified in section 31.0330(a), unless:

"1. the notary knows or has good reason to believe that the notarial act or the associated transaction is unlawful;

"2. the act is prohibited under section 31.0320(c) (see "Prohibitions" above);

"3. the number of notarial acts requested practicably precludes completion of all acts at once, in which case the notary shall arrange for later completion of the remaining acts…" (ASCA 31.0322[b]).

Improper Influence

"A notary shall not influence a person either to enter into or avoid a transaction involving a notarial act by the notary, except that the notary may advise against a transaction if section 31.0322(b)(1) applies" (ASCA 31.0323[a]). The cited Section 31.0322(b)(1) refers to when the Notary "knows or has good reason to believe that the notarial act or the associated transaction is unlawful."

Notary Does Not Investigate: "A notary has neither the duty nor the authority to investigate, ascertain, or attest the lawfulness, propriety, accuracy, or truthfulness of a document or transaction involving a notarial act" (ASCA 31.0323[b]).

Improper Notarial Certificates

An American Samoa Notary shall (ASCA 31.0324):

1. NOT execute a notarial certificate containing information known or believed by the Notary to be false;
2. NOT affix an official signature or seal on a notarial certificate that is incomplete;
3. NOT provide or send a signed or sealed notarial certificate to another person with the understanding that it will be completed or attached to a document outside the notary's presence.

Improper Documents

An American Samoa Notary shall (ASCA 31.0325):

1. NOT notarize a signature on a blank or incomplete document;
2. NOT notarize a signature on a document without notarial certificate wording;
3. NOT certify or authenticate a photograph.

Intent to Deceive or Defraud

"A notary shall not peform any official action with the intent to deceive or defraud" (ASCA 31.0326).

Testimonials

"A notary shall not use the official notary title or seal to endorse, promote, denounce, or oppose any product, service, contest, candidate, or other offering" (ASCA 31.0327).

Unauthorized Practice of Law

A non-attorney American Samoa Notary shall (ASCA 31.0328):

1. NOT determine the type of notarial act or certificate to be used, if certificate wording is not provided or indicated for a document;
2. NOT assist another person in drafting, completing, selecting or understanding a document or transaction requiring a notarial act;
3. NOT claim to have powers, qualifications, rights or privileges that the office of Notary does not confer, including the power to counsel on immigration matters.

Duly Qualified, Trained May Decide: "This section does not preclude a notary who is duly qualified, trained or experienced in a particular industry or professional field from selecting, drafting, completing, or advising on a document or certificate related to a matter within that industry or field" (ASCA 31.0328[c]).

Non-English Advertising

"A non-attorney notary who advertises notarial services in a language other than English shall include in the advertisement, letterhead, or sign the following, prominently displayed in the same language:

"1. the statement: 'I am not an attorney and have no authority to give advice on immigration or other legal matters'; and

"2. the fees for notarial acts specified in section 31.0330(a)" (ASCA 31.0328[e]).

'Notario' Prohibited: "A notary may not use the term 'notario publico' or any equivalent non-English term in any business card, advertisement, notice, or sign" (ASCA 31.0328[f]).

Criminal Sanctions

Felony: "In performing a notarial act, a notary is guilty of a class D felony, punishable upon conviction by a fine not exceeding $5,000 or imprisonment of up to five years, or both, for knowingly:

"1. failing to require the presence of a principal at the time of the notarial act;

"2. failing to identify a principal through personal knowledge or satisfactory evidence; or

"3. executing a false notarial certificate under Section 31.0324" (ASCA 31.0361[a]).

Misdemeanor: "A notary who knowingly perform or fails to perform any other act prohibited or mandated respectively by this Act may be guilty of a class A misdemeanor, punishable upon conviction by a fine not exceeding $1,000 or imprisonment of up to one year, or both" (ASCA 31.0361[b]).

NOTARY SIGNING AGENTS

Notary Signing Agents may operate within the Territory of American Samoa, but with the following restriction: "Notwithstanding (Section 31.0321[a][2], a notary may collect a fee for an assignment as a signing agent if payment of that fee is not contingent upon the signing of any document" (ASCA 31.0321[b]). The cited Subsection (a)(2) refers to the Notary's disqualification if receiving any commission fee, advantage, right, title, interest, cash, property or other consideration exceeding in value the fees allowed by statute for performing a notarial act.

NOTARY FEES

The maximum fees that may be charged by an American Samoa Notary for notarial acts are (ASCA 31.0330[a]):

1. Taking an acknowledgment: $10 per signature;
2. Executing a jurat: $10 per signature;
3. Administering an oath or affirmation without a signature: $20 per person;
4. Witnessing a signature: $10 per signature;
5. Certifying a copy: $5 per page, with a minimum total charge of $10.

Fee May Be Waived

"For performing a notarial act, a notary may charge the maximum fee specified in section 31.0330, charge less than the maximum fee, or waive the fee" (ASCA 31.0329[a]).

No Discrimination in Charging Fees

"A notary shall not discriminatorily condition the fee for a notarial act on the attributes of the principal as delineated in section 31.0322(a), though a notary may waive or reduce fees for humanitarian or charitable reasons" (ASCA 31.0329[b]).

Travel Fees

"A notary may charge a travel fee when traveling to perform a notarial act if:

"1. the notary and the person requesting the notarial act agree upon the travel fee in advance of the travel; and

"2. the notary explains to the person requesting the notarial act that the travel fee is both separate from the notarial fee…and neither specified nor mandated by law" (ASCA 31.0330[b]).

Payment Prior to Act

Prior to the performance of a notarial act, a Notary may require payment of the lawful fees for the requested act and for any travel to perform the act (ASCA 31.0331[a]).

Any fees paid to a Notary prior to the performance of a notarization are non-refundable if (a) the act was completed or (b) in the case of travel fees, the act was not completed for reasons stated in Section 31.0322(b)(1) or (2) after the Notary had traveled to meet the principal (ASCA 31.0331[b]).

Fees of Employee Notary

"An employer may prohibit an employee who is a notary from charging for notarial acts performed on the employer's time, but shall not condition imposition of a fee on attributes of the principal as described in section 31.0322(a)" (ASCA 31.0332[a]). These attributes include status as a non-client or non-customer of the Notary's employer.

Private Employer: "A private employer shall not require an employee who is a notary to surrender or share fees charged for any notarial acts" (ASCA 31.0332[b]).

Governmental Employer: "A governmental employer who has absorbed an employee's costs in becoming or operating as a notary shall require any fees collected for notarial acts performed on the employer's time either to be waived or surrendered to the employer to support public programs" (ASCA 31.0332[c]).

Notice of Fees

"Notaries who charge for their notarial services shall conspicuously display in their places of business, or present to each principal outside their places of business, an English-language or Samoan-language schedule of fees for notarial acts, as specified in section 31.0330(a). No part of any notarial fee schedule shall be printed in smaller than 10-point type" (ASCA 31.0333).

NOTARY CERTIFICATES

The following notarial certificates are prescribed by American Samoa's Notary Act of 2007:

General Acknowledgment (ASCA 31.0342):

A Notary must use a certificate in substantially the following form in notarizing the signature or mark of persons acknowledgment for themselves or as partners, corporate officers, attorneys in fact, or in other representative capacities.

Territory of American Samoa
County of _____

On this _____ *day of* _____, *20*____, *before me, the undersigned Notary, personally appeared* _____ *(name of document signer), (personally known to me) (proved to me through identification documents allowed by law, which were* _____,*) (proved to me on the oath or affirmation of* _____, *who is personally known to me and stated to me that he/she personally knows the document signer and is unaffected by the document,) (proved to me on the oath or affirmation of* _____ *and* _____, *whose identities have been proven to me through documents allowed by law and who have stated to me that they personally know the document signer and are unaffected by the document,) to be the person whose name is signed on the preceding or attached document, and acknowledged to me that he/she signed it voluntarily for its stated purpose(.)*

(as partner for _____, *a partnership.)*

(as _____ *for* _____, *a corporation.)*

(as attorney in fact for _____, *the principal.)*

(as _____ *for* _____, *(a) (the)* _____.*)*

_____
(Official signature and seal of Notary)

Jurat (ASCA 31.0343):

A Notary must use a jurat certificate in substantially the following form in notarizing a signature or mark on an affidavit or other sworn or affirmed written declaration.

Territory of American Samoa
County of _____

On this _____ *day of* _____, *20*____, *before me, the undersigned Notary, personally appeared* _____ *(name of document signer), (personally known to me) (proved to me through identification documents allowed by law, which were* _____,*) (proved to me on the oath or affirmation of* _____, *who is personally known to me and stated to me that he/she personally knows the document signer and is unaffected by the document,) (proved to me on the oath or affirmation of* _____ *and* _____, *whose identities have been proven to me through documents allowed by law and who have stated to me that they personally know the document signer and are unaffected by the document,) to be the person who signed the preceding or attached document in my presence and who swore or affirmed to me that the contents of the document are truthful and accurate to the best of his/her knowledge and belief.*

_____
(Official signature and seal of Notary)

Signature Witnessing (ASCA 31.0344):

A Notary must use a certificate in substantially the following form when notarizing a signature or mark to confirm that it was affixed in the Notary's presence without administration of an oath or affirmation.

Territory of American Samoa
County of _____

On this _____ day of _____, 20____, before me, the undersigned Notary, personally appeared _____ (name of document signer), (personally known to me) (proved to me through identification documents allowed by law, which were _____,) (proved to me on the oath or affirmation of _____, who is personally known to me and stated to me that he/she personally knows the document signer and is unaffected by the document,) (proved to me on the oath or affirmation of _____ and _____, whose identities have been proven to me through documents allowed by law and who have stated to me that they personally know the document signer and are unaffected by the document,) to be the person who signed the preceding or attached document in my presence.

_____
(Official signature and seal of Notary)

Certified Copy (ASCA 31.0346):

A Notary must use a certificate in substantially the following form in notarizing a certified copy.

Territory of American Samoa
County of _____

On this _____ day of _____, 20____, I certify that the (preceding) (following) (attached) document is a true, exact, complete, and unaltered copy made by me of _____ (description of document), (presented to me by the document's custodian, _____,) (held in my custody as a notarial record,) and that, to the best of my knowledge, the copied document is neither a vital record, a public record nor a publicly recordable document, certified copies of which may be available from an official source other than a Notary.

_____
(Official signature and seal of Notary)

ELECTRONIC NOTARIZATIONS

The Territory of American Samoa has not yet adopted statutes or regulations expressly establishing rules, definitions and procedures for electronic notarization.

NOTARY RECORDS

"A notary shall keep, maintain, protect, and provide for lawful inspection a chronological official journal of notarial acts that is a permanently bound book with numbered pages" (ASCA 31.0334[a]). "A notary shall safeguard the journal and all other notarial records and surrender or destroy them only by rule of law, by court order, or at the direction of the Secretary" (ASCA 31.0337[e]).

No More Than One Active Journal

"A notary shall keep no more than one active journal at the same time" (ASCA 31.0334[b]).

Entries

"For every notarial act, the notary shall record in the journal at the time of notarization at least the following:

"1. the date and time of day of the notarial act;

"2. the type of notarial act;

"3. the type, title, or a description of the document or proceeding;

"4. the signature, printed name, and address of each principal;

"5. the evidence of identity of each principal, in the form of either: a statement that the person is 'personally known' to the notary; a notation of the type of identification document, its issuing agency, its serial or identification number, and its date of issuance or expiration; or the signature, printed name and address of each credible witness swearing or affirming to the person's identity, and, for credible witnesses who are not personally known to the notary, a description of identification documents relied on by the notary;

"6. the fee, if any, charged for the notarial act" (ASCA 31.0335[a]).

Signature Required: At the time of notarization, the Notary's journal must be signed by (a) each principal signer, (b) each credible witness swearing or affirming to the identity of a principal, and (c) each witness to a signature by mark or to a signing by the notary on behalf of a person physically unable to sign (ASCA 31.0336).

No Social Security or Credit Card Number: "A notary shall not record a social security or credit card number in the journal, unless such number is used as a serial or identification number for an identification document relied upon by the notary for identification purposes" (ASCA 31.0335[b]).

Record Circumstances of Incompletion: The Notary must record in the journal the circumstances for not completing a notarization (ASCA 31.0335[c]).

Record Request to Inspect or Copy: "As required in section 31.0337(a) (see below), a notary shall record in the journal the circumstances of any request to inspect or copy an entry in the journal, including the requester's name, address, signature, and evidence of identity. The reason for refusal to allow inspection or copying of a journal entry shall also be recorded" (ASCA 31.0335[d]).

Inspection and Copying of Journal

"In the notary's presence, any person may inspect an entry in the official journal of notarial acts during regular business hours, but only if:

"1. the person's identity is personally known to the notary or proven through satisfactory evidence;

"2. the person affixes a signature in the journal in a separate, dated entry;

"3. the person specifies the month, year, type of document, and name of the principal for the notarial act or acts sought; and

"4. the person is shown only the entry or entries specified" (ASCA 31.0337[a]).

Providing a Copy: "Upon complying with a request under subsection (a), the notary shall provide a copy of a specified entry or entries in the journal at a cost of not more than $2.00 per copy; other entries on the same page shall be masked. If a certified copy of an entry in a bound book is requested, the additional cost is as specified in section 31.0330" (ASCA 31.0337[d]).

Cause for Denying Access: "If the notary has a reasonable and explainable belief that a person bears a criminal or harmful intent in requesting information from the notary's journal, the notary may deny access to any entry or entries" (ASCA 31.0337[b]).

Official Access to Journal: "The journal may be examined without restriction by a law enforcement officer in the course of an official investigation, subpoenaed by court order, or surrendered at the direction of the Secretary" (ASCA 31.0337[c]).

Security of Journal

"When not in use, the journal shall be kept in a secure area under the exclusive control of the notary, and shall not be used by any other notary nor surrendered to an employer upon termination of employment" (ASCA 31.0337[f]).

Lost, Stolen or Damaged Journal

"Within 10 days after the journal is stolen, lost, destroyed, damaged, or otherwise rendered unusable or unreadable as a record of notarial acts, the notary, after informing the appropriate law enforcement agency in the case of theft or vandalism, shall notify the Secretary by any means providing a tangible receipt or acknowledgment, including certified mail and electronic transmission, and also provide a copy or number of any pertinent police report" (ASCA 31.0337[g]).

Resignation, Revocation or Expiration

"Upon resignation, revocation, or expiration of a notary commission, or death of the notary, the journal and notarial records shall be delivered to the Office of the Secretary of American Samoa in accordance with sections 31.0351 to 31.0355" (ASCA 31.0337[h]).

Delivery within 30 Days: "(a) Except as provided in subsection (b), when a notary commission expires or is resigned or revoked, the notary shall…within 30 days after the effective date of resignation, revocation, or expiration, send to the Office of the Secretary of American Samoa by any means providing a tangible receipt or acknowledgment, including certified mail and electronic transmission, the notarial journal and records, in accordance with the requirements of the same office.

"(b) A former notary who intends to apply for a new commission and whose previous commission or application was not revoked or denied by this Territory, need not deliver the journal and records within 30 days after commission expiration, but must do so within 3 months after expiration unless recommissioned within that period" (ASCA 31.0354).

Death of Notary: If a Notary dies during the commission term or before fulfilling the requirements of ASCA 31.0354, the Notary's personal representative must notify the Secretary in writing and, within 30 days after the death, "send to the Office of the Secretary of American Samoa, care of the Office of the Governor by any means providing a tangible receipt or acknowledgment, including certified mail and electronic transmission, the notary's journal of notarial acts and any other notarial records, in accordance with requirements of the same office" (ASCA 31.0355).

AUTHENTICATION OF NOTARIAL ACTS

Secretary of American Samoa

Certificates of authority and apostilles authenticating a Notary's commission are issued by the Secretary of American Samoa (ASCA 31.0350).

Fees: For issuing a certificate of authority or an apostille, the Secretary may charge $25.

COMMISSIONING AND ADMINISTRATION

The Secretary of American Samoa, located within the Office of the Governor, commissions, regulates and maintains records on the islands' Notaries (ASCA 31.0309[a]).

Applying for Commission

Qualifications: An applicant for a commission as an American Samoa Notary must (ASCA 31.0309[b]): (a) be at least 18 years of age, (b) have a regular place of work or business in the Territory of American Samoa, as defined in ASCA 31.0307(p), (c) reside legally in American Samoa, (d) read and write English and (e) submit fingerprints to allow a criminal background check.

Course and Test Required: An applicant for a first-time or renewal commission must pass a course of instruction requiring a written examination (ASCA 31.0309[b][5]). The course must be at least three hours, approved by the Secretary and taken within the three months preceding application (ASCA 31.0316[a]). The content of the course and the basis for the written examination are notarial laws, procedures and ethics (ASCA 31.0316[b]). An approved course is offered by the Secretary at American Samoa Community College.

Application: An application must be made on paper forms determined by the Secretary (ASCA 31.0314) and the application package must include: (a) a certificate evidencing successful completion of a course of instruction, (b) a declaration of the applicant notarized by an American Samoa Notary (ASCA 31.0317), (c) a full set of fingerprints of the applicant on a Department of Public Safety fingerprint card, along with a copy of the applicant's traffic record from High Court, both attached to the application, and (d) a non-refundable application fee of $100 (ASCA 31.0318[a]).

"Successful applicants will be notified by letter from the Secretary of American Samoa and will then be required to pay a $500 security bond with the Revenue Office of the Department of Treasury. A receipt of payment of said bond shall be provided to the Secretary before a commission is issued. An applicant who is denied a commission will also be informed by letter and allowed to retake the exam on a date to be announced by the Secretary, but no later than 20 days from the date of the issuance of said letter" (formerly posted on the American Samoa Government's official website).

Changes of Status

Change of Address: "Within 10 days after the change of a notary's residence, business, or mailing address, the notary shall send to the Secretary by any means providing a tangible receipt or acknowledgment, including certified mail and electronic transmission, a signed notice of the change, giving both old and new addresses" (ASCA 31.0351[a]).

If the business address changes, the Notary must not notarize until (ASCA 31.0351[b]): (a) the notice described above has been delivered or transmitted, (b) a "Confirmation of Notary's Name or Address Change" has been received from the Secretary, and (c) a new seal bearing the new business address has been obtained.

Change of Name: "Within 10 days after the change of notary's name by court order or marriage, the notary shall send to the Secretary by any means providing a tangible receipt or acknowledgment, including certified mail and electronic transmission, a signed notice of the change, giving both former and new names, with a copy of any official authorization for such change" (ASCA 31.0352[a]).

A Notary with a new name must continue to use the former name when notarizing until (ASCA 31.0352[b]): (a) the notice described above has been delivered or transmitted, (b) a "Confirmation of Notary's Name or Address Change" has been received from the Secretary, and (c) a new seal bearing the new name exactly as in the Confirmation has been obtained.

Resignation: "A notary who resigns his or her commission shall send to the Secretary by any means providing a tangible receipt or acknowledgment, including certified mail and electronic transmission, a signed notice indicating the effective date of resignation" (ASCA 31.0353[a]).

If a Notary no longer resides in or maintains a regular place of work or business in American Samoa, or becomes permanently unable to perform notarial duties, that Notary must resign his or her commission (ASCA 31.0353[b]).

OTHER NOTARIAL OFFICERS

Oaths, Acknowledgments for Any Purpose

Besides Notaries, the following officials of American Samoa have notarial powers — ex officio — including the authority to administer oaths and affirmations and to take acknowledgments for any purpose (ASCA 43.0110[a]):
1. Governor;
2. Secretary of American Samoa;
3. Attorney General;
4. Chief Justice, Associate Justice or Clerk of the High Court;
5. Such other persons as may be appointed by the Secretary of American Samoa.

Oaths, Acknowledgments for Use in Samoa

The following officials have authority to administer oaths and affirmations and to take acknowledgments to be used within the limits of American Samoa (ASCA 43.0110[a]):
1. Associate Judges of the High Court in all cases within the Court's jurisdiction;
2. Associate Judges of the High Court and clerks of the District Court in all cases within the District Court's jurisdiction;
3. Members of the Legislature in accordance with provisions of ASCA 2.1001;
4. Those individuals appointed by the Secretary of American Samoa; and
5. Boards of Investigation appointed by the Governor pursuant to ASCA 4.0302 may administer oaths.

QUICK FACTS

Notary Jurisdiction
The three islands of Manu'a and the island of Tutuila, including Aunu'u and Swains Islands.

Notary Term Length
Two years (ASCA 31.0310).

Notary Bond
$500 (ASCA 31.0311[a]), deposited with the Office of the Secretary and payable to any person, conditioned on the Notary's misconduct as defined in ASCA 31.0307(l).

Exhaustion of Bond: "If a notary bond has been exhausted by claims paid out, the Secretary shall suspend the notary's commission until: (1) a new bond is obtained by the notary; and (2) the notary's fitness to serve the remainder of the commission term is determined by the Secretary" (ASCA 31.0311[b]).

A–C

Arizona

NOTARY ADMINISTRATION

Office of Secretary of State
Business Services Division
Notary Section   1-602-542-4758
1700 West Washington Street, 7th Floor
Phoenix, AZ 85007-2888

Southern Arizona Satellite Office:
Arizona State Complex Building
400 West Congress
Second Floor, Room 252   1-520-628-6583
Tucson, AZ 85701

Website: www.azsos.gov/business_
services/notary/

NOTARY RULES

ARS — Arizona Revised Statutes
AAC — Arizona Administrative Code
RM — Notary Public Reference Manual

Most Notary rules are in the Arizona Revised Statutes:

a. Title 41, Chapter 2, Article 2 ("Notaries Public");

b. Title 41, Chapter 2, Article 3 ("Electronic Notarization");

c. Title 33, Chapter 4, Article 5 ("Uniform Recognition of Acknowledgments Act"*);

d. Title 33, Chapter 4, Article 6 ("Acknowledgments").

* This is the *Uniform Recognition of Acknowledgments Act* of 1968, adopted virtually intact as ARS 33-501 through 33-508.

Other guidelines are in the "Notary Public Reference Manual" (Revised July 2011) issued by the Secretary of State and available on the website.

NOTARY SEAL

An Arizona Notary must authenticate all official acts with a seal of office, and the seal's format must be as follows (ARS 41-313[E][2], [3] and 41-321[B]):

Kind

Inked Rubber Stamp: The Arizona Notary's seal must be a rubber stamp that prints in dark ink, including the colors "dark blue, dark purple, dark green or dark brown. Red ink or ink not viewable on all copy or fax machines is unacceptable" (RM).

Embosser Not Official Seal: "A notary public may possess only one official seal but may also possess and use an embossing seal that may be used only in conjunction with the notary public's official seal. An embossing seal is not an official seal of a notary public" (ARS 41-321[B]).

Seal Image Not Needed on e-Document: Under the Uniform Real Property Electronic Recording Act (URPERA), "(a) physical or electronic image of a stamp, impression or seal need not accompany an electronic signature" (ARS 11-487.02[C]).

Shape/Size

Any Shape but Size Limited: "A notary public's official seal may be any shape and shall produce a stamped seal that is no more than one and one-half inches high and two and one-half inches wide" (ARS 41-321[B]).

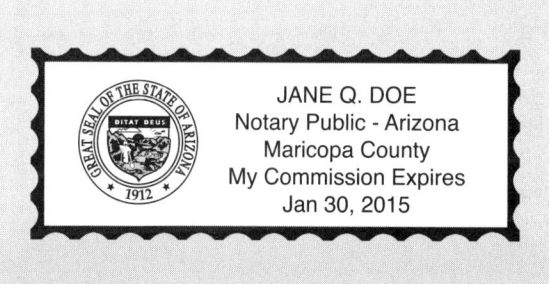

Examples
The above typical, actual-size example of a Notary seal is allowed by Arizona law. Formats other than this may also be permitted.

Arizona

Components

The Notary's official stamp seal must imprint the following (ARS 41-313[E][2]):
1. Name of Notary exactly as it appears on the commission application;
2. "Notary Public";
3. Name of county in which commissioned;
4. Great Seal of the State of Arizona;
5. Expiration date of commission*.

* "Upon reappointment as a notary, the notary must obtain a new seal that contains the notary's new commission expiration date before he or she performs any notarizations" (RM).

Placement of Seal

"It is recommended that the notary seal be placed just below the notarial certificate and to the left, if possible. The notary should not stamp over signatures or other writing if possible. However if there is insufficient space on a document to affix the notary seal, it is better to stamp over pre-printed language than to stamp over signatures" (RM).

Seal Vendor Keeps Commission Copy

"A vendor of notary seals may not provide an official seal to a person unless the person presents a photocopy of the person's notarial commission. The vendor shall retain the photocopy for four years" (ARS 41-321[A]).

"If a bonding agent uses an out-of-state vendor to obtain a notary seal, that vendor is still required to obtain a copy of the commission certificate before making a notary seal. By making Arizona notary seals, the vendor is bound by Arizona law and needs to receive, and keep on file for four years, a copy of the commission certificate (ARS 41-321)" (RM).

Seal Belongs to Notary, Not Employer

"A notary public is a public officer commissioned by this state and the following apply without regard to whether the notary public's employer or any other person has paid the fees and costs for the commissioning of the notary public, including costs for the official seal and journals: … A notary public's official seal and commission and any journal that contains only public record entries remain the property of the notary public" (ARS 41-312[C][1]).

Seal Loss or Theft

"Within ten days after the loss or theft of an official journal or seal, the notary shall deliver to the secretary of state, by certified mail or other means providing a receipt, a signed notice of the loss or theft. The notary also shall inform the appropriate law enforcement agency in the case of theft" (ARS 41-323[B]). For any Notary's failure to comply, the Secretary of State may impose a civil penalty of $25 (ARS 41-323[C]). A "Notice of Loss or Theft — Journal and/or Seal" may be downloaded from the Secretary of State's website.

"The shape and ink color of the replacement seal should be different than the original seal….Once the new seal is received, the notary public should describe the replacement seal to the law enforcement agency to which the theft of the original seal was reported. The notary should also contact the Secretary of State in writing with a description of the new seal. The notary public should also document in his or her journal when he or she started to use the replacement seal" (RM).

Seal Delivered to Secretary of State

"On the resignation or revocation of a notarial commission or the death of a notary, the notary seal, notarial journal and records, except those records of notarial acts that are not public record, shall be delivered by certified mail or other means providing a receipt to the secretary of state. If a notary does not apply for reappointment, on expiration of the notarial commission the notary seal, journal and records shall be delivered to the secretary of state as required for resignation under this subsection. A notary who neglects for three months thereafter to deposit such records, seal and papers, or the personal representative of a deceased notary who neglects for three months after his appointment to deposit such records, seal and papers, shall forfeit to the state not less than fifty nor more than five hundred dollars" (ARS 41-317[A]).

Signature of Notary

"SIGN the document near the title of 'Notary Public.' The notary must use his or her OFFICIAL, wet SIGNATURE, not a facsimile (stamp or other means) of a signature on the document. The official name on the notary seal and the notary's official signature must be used exactly as the commissioned name on file with the Secretary of State's Office" (RM).

NOTARY POWERS

Arizona Notaries are authorized to perform the following notarial acts (ARS 41-313 and 33-501):
1. Take acknowledgments*;
2. Administer oaths and affirmations**;
3. Execute jurats***;
4. Certify copies****.

* Identifying Acknowledgers: "The person taking an acknowledgment shall certify that: 1) The person acknowledging appeared before him and acknowledged he executed the instrument, and 2) The person acknowledging was known to the person taking the acknowledgment or that the person taking the acknowledgment had satisfactory evidence that the person acknowledging was the person described in and who executed the instrument" (ARS 33-503).

"'Acknowledgment' means a notarial act in which a notary certifies that a signer, whose identity is proven by satisfactory evidence, appeared before the notary and acknowledged that the signer signed the document" (ARS 41-311[1]).

** Oath/Affirmation Wording: "'Oath' or 'affirmation' means a notarial act or part of a notarial act in which a person make a vow in the presence of the notary under penalty of perjury, with reference made to a supreme being in the case of an oath" (ARS 41-311[9]).

"A notary should ask the signer or credible person to: Raise his or her right hand. If for any reason a right hand cannot be raised, then the signer shall raise their left hand … the oath or affirmation should be given as follows: Ask the signer or credible person to either: 1) Repeat the oath statement…; or 2) Answer the question…" (RM).

The "Arizona Notary Public Reference Manual" suggests the following sample wording for oaths/affirmations:

"OATH SAMPLE #1 — JURAT. Choose one: Please repeat the oath statement, by either swearing or affirming: *'I, [insert signer's name], swear or affirm that the contents of this document are true and correct.'* (OR) Please answer the oath question with 'I do swear' or 'I do affirm': *'Do you swear or affirm that the contents of this document are true and correct?'*

"OATH SAMPLE #2 — CREDIBLE PERSON. Choose one: Please repeat the oath statement, by either swearing or affirming: *'I, [insert credible person's name], [swear or affirm] that the person appearing before you and who signed this document in your presence is the person that he or she claims to be.'* (OR) Please answer the oath question with 'I do swear' or 'I do affirm': *'Do you swear or affirm that that the person appearing before me and who signed this document in my presence is the person he or she claims to be?'*"

*** Jurats: "'Jurat' means a notarial act in which the notary certifies that a signer, whose identity is proven by satisfactory evidence, has made in the notary's presence a voluntary signature and has taken an oath or affirmation vouching for the truthfulness of the signed document" (ARS 41-311[5]).

**** Certified Copies: "'Copy certification' means a notarial act in which the notary certifies that the notary made a photocopy of an original document that is neither a public record nor publicly recordable" (ARS 41-311[3]). "If the notary does not have access to a copy machine the notary must not perform the copy certification. If the notary has access to a copy machine, they must verify the document presented is an original document. A copy certification cannot be performed on copies of a document or a certified copy. If the document presented is not an original, the notary must refuse the copy certification" (RM).

According to the "Arizona Notary Public Reference Manual," examples of documents that are publicly recordable are marriage licenses, birth and death certificates, divorce papers, court records and real estate deeds.

"The notary writes or types, on the face of each copy, the notarial language…" (RM).

'Personal Knowledge' Defined

"'Personal knowledge' means familiarity with an individual resulting from interactions with that person over a sufficient time to eliminate reasonable doubt that the individual has the identity claimed" (ARS 41-311[10]).

'Satisfactory Evidence' Defined

"'Satisfactory evidence of identity' means:
"(a) Proof of identity is evidenced by one of the following:
"(i) An unexpired driver license that is issued by a state or territory of the United States.
"(ii) An unexpired passport that is issued by the United States department of state.

"(iii) An unexpired identification card that is issued by any branch of the United States armed forces.

"(iv) Any other unexpired identification card that is issued by the United States government or a state or tribal government, that contains the individual's photograph, signature and physical description and that contains the individual's height, weight, color of hair and color of eyes.

"(v) The oath or affirmation of a credible person who is personally known to the notary and who personally knows the individual.

"(vi) The oath or affirmation of a credible person who personally knows the individual and who provides satisfactory evidence of identity pursuant to item (i), (ii), (iii) or (iv) of this subdivision.

"(vii) Personal knowledge of the individual by the notary.

"(b) In addition to subdivision (a), for the purposes of a real estate conveyance or financing, proof of identity may be evidenced by one of the following:

"(i) A valid unexpired passport that is issued by the United States government.

"(ii) A valid unexpired passport that is issued by a national government other than the United States government and that is accompanied by a valid unexpired visa or other documentation that is issued by the United States government and that is necessary to establish an individual's legal presence in the United States.

"(iii) Any other valid unexpired identification that is deemed acceptable by the United States department of homeland security to establish an individual's legal presence in the United States and that is accompanied with supporting documents as required by the United States department of homeland security" (ARS 41-311[11]).

Screening for Comprehension and Willingness

The "Notary Public Reference Manual" states that a Notary "has the right to refuse the notarization" if he or she senses that the signer does not comprehend the transaction or is not proceeding willingly, or both (RM).

Requirements for Every Notarial Act

"B. Notaries Public shall perform the notarial acts prescribed (in ARS 41-313[A]) only if:

"1. The signer is in the presence of the notary at the time of notarization.

"2. The signer signs in a language that the notary understands.

"3. Subject to subsection D, the signer communicates directly with the notary in a language they both understand or indirectly through a translator who is physically present with the signer and notary at the time of the notarization and communicates directly with the signer and the notary in languages the translator understands.

"4. The notarial certificate is worded and completed using only letters, characters and a language that are read, written and understood by the notary public.

"C. If a notary attaches a notarial certificate to a document using a separate sheet of paper, the attachment must contain a description of the document that includes at a minimum the title or type of document, the document date, the number of pages of the document and any additional signers other than those named in the notarial certificate.

"D. A notary may perform a notarial act on a document that is a translation of a document that is in a language that the notary does not understand only if the person performing the translation signs an affidavit containing an oath or affirmation that the translation is accurate and complete. The notarized translation and affidavit shall be attached to the document and shall contain all of the elements described in subsection C" (ARS 41-313).

Foreign-Language Requirements

Notaries may perform a notarial act only if the signer signs in a language that the notary understands, and "the notarial certificate is worded and completed using only letters, characters and a language that is read, written and understood by the notary public" (ARS 313[B][2] and [4]).

Notarizing Foreign-Language Documents: "If a document is written in a foreign language, the notary public must be able to read enough of that language to describe the document in his or her journal to ensure he or she is not attesting to information outside the scope of his or her authority. . . If the document is written in a foreign language and the notary does not have a general understanding of the language, the notary must refuse the notarization" (RM).

Notarizing Written Translations: "A Notary may perform a notarial act on a document that is a translation of a document that is in a language that the Notary does not understand only if the person performing the translation signs an affidavit containing an oath or affirmation that the translation is accurate and complete. The notarized translation and affidavit shall be attached to the document and shall contain" a description of the document that includes the title or type of document, the document date, the number of pages of the document and any additional signers other than those named in the notarial certificate (ARS 41-313[D] and [C]).

Oral Translations: A signer must be able to communicate "directly with the notary in a language they both understand or indirectly through a translator who is physically present with the signer and notary at the time of the notarization and communicates directly with the signer and the notary in languages the translator understands" (ARS 41-313[B][3]).

Signature by Mark

"A notary can notarize a thumb print or an 'X' mark as a 'signature' or 'subscription.'

"These include any kind of mark when a person cannot write, provided that the person's name is written near the mark and the mark is witnessed by a person who writes his or her own name as witness.

"If a person who cannot write is either known to the notary or can provide sufficient evidence of his identity to the notary, the notary can then write the person's name near his or her mark" (RM and ARS 1-215[37]).

Non-English Advertising

Any non-attorney Notary who advertises notarial services in a language other than English, with the exception of a single desk plaque, must post or include with the ad a notice of conspicuous size in English and the other language stating: "I am not an attorney and cannot give legal advice about immigration or any other legal matters." Violation is a class 6 felony and the offender's Notary's commission must be permanently revoked (ARS 41-329).

In addition, "use of false or misleading advertising in which the notary public has represented (holding) duties, rights or privileges that the notary public does not possess by law" is cause for commission revocation or suspension (ARS 41-330[A][5]).

NOTARY DON'TS

An Arizona Notary Public may:
1. NOT notarize the Notary's own signature (ARS 41-328[B]);
2. NOT notarize the signature of any person who is related to the Notary "by marriage or adoption" (ARS 41-328[B]);
3. NOT notarize a document "if the notary is an officer of any named party, if the notary is a party to the document or if the notary will receive any direct material benefit from the transaction that is evidenced by the notarized document that exceeds in value the fees prescribed pursuant to section 41-316" (ARS 41-328[C]).
4. NOT execute a jurat on a document that is incomplete, meaning "a document that has not been signed where a signature line is provided or where other obvious blanks appear in the document or that lacks a notarial certificate" (ARS 41-311[4] and 41-328[A]);
5. NOT execute a certificate containing a statement known by the Notary to be false (ARS 41-330[A][10]);
6. NOT complete a certificate at a different time than when the Notary's signature and seal are affixed (ARS 41-330[A][8]);
7. NOT notarize for a signer who is not present, because the signer must be "in the presence of the notary at the time of notarization" (ARS 41-313[B][1]);
8. NOT use false or misleading advertising representing that the Notary has duties, rights or privileges that the law does not confer (ARS 41-329);
9. NOT perform any act involving dishonesty, fraud or deceit with the intent to substantially benefit the notary or another person or to substantially injure another person (ARS 41-330[A][7]).

Blank Spaces or Incomplete Documents

"A jurat cannot be performed on a document that contains blank spaces or that is incomplete. There is no such limitation when performing acknowledgments, although the Secretary of State's office recommends that a notary public not notarize a document containing obvious blank spaces… " (RM).

Notarizing for Blood Relatives

"Arizona law states notaries cannot notarize for anyone related to the notary by marriage or adoption…. (This) does allow notaries to notarize for a brother or sister but not a brother-in-law or sister-in-law.

"Many courts have found that a sibling relationship implies some type of financial or beneficial interest in transactions involving other family members thereby negating an argument for impartiality.

"Just because the law allows a notary public to notarize for blood relatives, it is not a recommended action" (RM).

Not a Disqualification

Corporations: Stockholders, directors, officers or employees of a corporation may notarize a document affecting the corporation, unless the Notary is, individually or as a corporate representative, a party to the document (ARS 41-320).

"Subject to section 41-320, a notary public shall not perform a notarization on a document if the notary is an officer of any named party, if the notary is a party to the document or if the notary will receive any direct material benefit from the transaction that is evidenced by the notarized document that exceeds in value the fees prescribed pursuant to section 41-316 (ARS 41-328[C]).

Cooperatives: Officers, directors and members of cooperatives may take acknowledgment of documents involving the cooperative (ARS 10-2082).

Notary Employer Don'ts

An employer of an Arizona Notary Public may:
1. NOT keep the Notary seal, commission or journal containing only public record entries of any employee, whether the employer paid for the seal, commission or journal (ARS 41-312[C][1]);
2. NOT prohibit an employee from notarizing while "off duty" nor demand the notarial fees received for such acts (ARS 41-312[C][2]);
3. NOT "limit the notary public's services to customers or other persons designated by the employer" (ARS 41-312[C][3]);
4. NOT cancel the Notary bond or commission of any employee who terminates employment (ARS 41-312[D]).

Valid Reasons for Refusing to Notarize

"If a reasonable request is made, a notary public shall notarize a document under the guidelines in this ("Notary Public Reference Manual"). A notary public cannot refuse a notarization of a document if a reasonable request is made. A notary can however, refuse a notarization if the document or the signer does not meet other requirements listed in this manual..." (RM).

The "Notary Public Reference Manual" gives the following circumstances in which a Notary must or should refuse to notarize:

"The signer must be in the notary's presence and present the document to the notary. If not, the notary must refuse the notarization....

"A notary should refuse a notarization if he or she has no personal knowledge of the individual, there is no credible person, and the signer does not have an appropriate form of identification that meets the standards of ARS § 41-311....

"If a notary feels for any reason that the form of identification presented by the requestor is fraudulent, the notary may refuse the notarization. However, the notary should document the refusal in his or her journal....

"If the signatures look different and the notary is unsure if the same person made the signatures, the notary may request that the signer sign the document again, or may refuse the notarization....

"If a notary doubts the authenticity of the POA (power of attorney) produced or otherwise is uncomfortable performing the notarization, he or she should refuse the notarization and document the reason for the refusal in his or her notary journal...."

Do Not Provide Commission Copy

"To prevent fraud, a notary should not provide a copy of the certificate to anyone other than the vendor who creates the notary's seal" (RM and ARS 41-321)....

"While a notary may show another his or her commission certificate, in an effort to prevent fraud, a notary should not provide a copy of the commission certificate to anyone. If a customer needs proof of a notary's authority, he or she may contact the Secretary of State's Office" (RM).

"Certificates do not have to be posted, but must be kept in a safe place and, if requested, be presented as proof of a notary public's commission" (RM and ARS 41-311[2]).

NOTARY SIGNING AGENTS

Notary Signing Agents may operate within the state of Arizona and in doing so they must observe the fee, mileage and per diem guidelines outlined immediately below. "Companies and employers may not ask notaries public to charge more than the $2 fee. This request violates Arizona rules" (RM).

NOTARY FEES

The maximum fees that Arizona Notaries may receive or advertise are as follows (ARS 41-316[A] and Arizona Administrative Code [AAC], Rule 2-12-1102):
1. Taking an acknowledgment: $2 per signature;
2. Administering an oath or affirmation without a signature: $2 per person;
3. Executing a jurat: $2 per signature;
4. Certifying a copy: $2 per page certified.

Mileage and Per Diem Allowed

When traveling to perform a notarial act, "(n)otaries public may be paid an amount up to the amount authorized for mileage expenses and per diem subsistence for state employees as prescribed by title 38, chapter 4, article 2" (ARS 41-316[B]). The Arizona General Accounting Office currently authorizes 44.5 cents-per-mile reimbursement for use of private vehicles.

To confirm the current fees Arizona Notaries may charge for mileage and per diem, contact the office of the Secretary of State.

Fees Collected outside Workplace

"A notary public may perform notarizations outside the workplace of the notary's employer except during those times normally designated as the notary public's hours of duty for that employer. All fees received by a notary public for notarial services provided while not on duty remain the property of the notary public" (ARS 41-312[C][2]).

No Fee for Pension Papers

Notaries may not charge for taking an acknowledgment in connection with a claim for a federal "pension, allotment, allowance, compensation, insurance or other benefits ..." (ARS 39-122).

No Fee for Military Oaths

An oath-administering officer may not charge for administering an oath or affirmation required in the military service (ARS 26-160).

Fees Conspicuously Posted

Notaries must keep posted at all times in a conspicuous place in their offices a complete list of the fees they are allowed to charge (ARS 38-412).

Overcharging

A Notary may not "advertise or charge or receive a fee for performing a notarial act except as specifically authorized by rule" (ARS 41-316). For charging more than the fee allowed by AAC R2-12-1102, the Notary is liable to the aggrieved party for an amount four times the fee unlawfully asked and received, and is guilty of a Class 5 felony (ARS 38-413).

Same Fees for All Is Best Policy

A Notary Public may charge up to $2 per signature, less than $2 per signature or charge no fee. However, according to the "Notary Public Reference Manual," "fees shall be set and be consistent. That is, the same fee should be charged for each notarization."

Fees for Electronic Notaries

An Electronic Notary may not charge more than $25 for performing a notarial act (AAC R2-12-1207). See "Electronic Notarizations," below.

NOTARY CERTIFICATES

Arizona has adopted the *Uniform Recognition of Acknowledgments Act* virtually intact, including the short-form certificates (ARS 33-506) for:
1. Acknowledgment by individual;
2. Acknowledgment by corporation;
3. Acknowledgment by partnership;
4. Acknowledgment by attorney in fact;
5. Acknowledgment by public officer, trustee or personal representative.

The Notary's seal must be added to these certificates.

For the text of the certificates, see ARS 33-505 and 33-506 or the "Uniform Recognition of Acknowledgments Act (1968)," Section 6, in Appendix 3.

The "Arizona Notary Public Reference Manual" also prescribes the following sample certificates for Notaries:

Acknowledgment by Individual Sample (RM):

State of Arizona   )
)
County of _____)

On this _____ day of _____, 20___, before me personally appeared _____(name of signer), whose identity was proven to me on the basis of satisfactory evidence to be the person who he or she claims to be, and acknowledged that he or she signed the above/attached document.

(Seal) _____ (Notary's Signature)
Notary Public

Jurat Sample (RM):

State of Arizona   )
)
County of _____)

Subscribed and sworn (or affirmed) before me this _____ day of _____, 20___, by _____ (name of signer).

(Seal) _____ (Notary's Signature)
Notary Public

Copy Certification Sample (RM):

State of Arizona   )
)
County of _____)

I, _____ (name of Notary), a Notary Public, do certify that, on the _____ day of _____, 20___, I personally made the above/attached copy of _____ (document title) from the original, and it is a true, exact, complete, and unaltered copy.

(Seal) _____ (Notary's Signature)
Notary Public

Format for Acknowledgment Certificate

"The form of a certificate of acknowledgment used by a person whose authority is recognized under (Uniform Recognition of Acknowledgments Act, Section 1) shall be accepted in this state if:
"1. The certificate is in a form prescribed by the laws or regulations of this state, or
"2. The certificate is in a form prescribed by the laws or regulations applicable in the place in which the acknowledgment is taken, or
"3. The certificate contains the words 'acknowledged before me,' or their substantial equivalent" (ARS 33-504).

Document Must Have Certificate: "The secretary of state may refuse to appoint any person as a notary public or may revoke or suspend the commission of any notary public for… (n)otarizing a document that contains no notarial certificate" (ARS 41-330[A][12]).

Notary May Not Determine Certificate

"If a document does not contain a notarial certificate but the individual wants his or her signature notarized, the notary public must ask the requestor which type of notarization he or she wants. The individual requesting the notarization determines the type of notarial certificate.
"Once this is determined the notary public can type, stamp, or neatly handwrite this information on the document or attach a certificate…" (RM).

Correcting Certificates

"When an acknowledgment is properly made, but defectively certified, any party interested may bring an action in the superior court to obtain a judgment correcting the certificate" (ARS 33-513).
"If any part of the notarial certificate is incorrect, the notary public should either cross out and initial the incorrect words with ink or cross out the entire wording and type or write in the correct wording. Do not attempt to erase or use correction fluid or tape" (RM).

Attaching a Certificate

"A notary may use an additional sheet of paper to attach the notarial certificate to a document if there is no room left on the document. If the notary attaches a certificate, the notary should title the page with the words 'Notarial Acknowledgment', 'Notarial Jurat', or 'Copy Certification'.
"The notary must also describe the attached document on the page containing the notarial certificate in as great of detail as possible, in order to prevent someone from attaching the attach certificate it to a different document.
"The description must include at a minimum:
- Type/Title of Document
- Document Date

- Number of pages attached
- Any additional signers other than those listed in the notarial certificate.

"The office also recommends that document pages be numbered, such as '1 of 1' or '1 of 2,' etc.

"Caution: While a notary might be inclined to affix his or her seal to all pages in a packet, the seal should only be affixed on the page with the notarial certificate. If the notary wants, he or she may use an embossing seal on the additional pages or simply initial the attached pages in order to indicate that those pages were part of the packet presented to them, but they should not affix their notary seal to the pages without a notarial certificate" (RM).

False Certificate Penalty

"A public officer authorized by law to make or give any certificate or other writing, who makes and delivers as true such a certificate or writing containing a statement which he knows is false, is guilty of a class 6 felony" (ARS 38-423).

"A person who acknowledges, certifies, notarizes, procures or offers to be filed, registered or recorded in a public office in this state an instrument he knows to be false or forged, which, if genuine, could be filed, registered or recorded under any law of this state or the United States, or in compliance with established procedure is guilty of a class 6 felony" (ARS 39-161).

Recording Requirements

Effective January 1, 1991, Arizona county recorders will not accept documents for recording, including notarial certificates, which do not comply with the following (ARS 11-480):

1. Printing must be 10-point type (pica) or larger.

2. Margins of at least $1/2$ inch at the top, bottom and sides must be bare of all print, writing, seals or other markings. At least 2 inches should be left at the top of the first page.

3. No document may be larger than $8 1/2$ inches in width and 14 inches in length.

ELECTRONIC NOTARIZATIONS

Effective July 18, 2000, the state adopted the Arizona Electronic Transactions Act (ARS 44-7001 through 44-7016), recognizing the legal validity of electronic signatures used by Notaries and establishing a basis for other statutes and regulations that empower Arizona Notaries to perform electronic notarizations.

Notary's Use of Electronic Signature

"Notwithstanding Title 41, Chapter 2, Article 2, if the law requires a signature or record to be notarized, acknowledged, verified or made under oath, that requirement is satisfied if a notary completes a notarial act on the electronic message or document. That notarial act on the electronic message or document is complete without the imprint of the notary's seal if all of the following apply:

"1. The electronic message or document is signed pursuant to this chapter or section 41-132 in the presence of a notary. (NOTE: Section 41-132 requires use of public key technology.)

"2. The notary confirms that the electronic signature on the electronic message or document is verifiably the electronic signature issued to the signer pursuant to this chapter or section 41-132.

"3. The notary electronically signs with an electronic signature that is consistent with this chapter, any electronic notary law or any other applicable law.

"4. The following information appears electronically within the message electronically signed by the notary:

"(a) The notary's full name and commission number exactly as it appears on the notary's commission.

"(b) The words 'electronic notary public', 'state of Arizona' and 'my commission expires on (date)'.

"(c) The address of the notary's principal place of contact exactly as it appears on the notary's commission.

"(d) The notary's e-mail or other electronic address exactly as it appears on the notary's commission" (ARS 44-7011).

<u>Time Stamp Token Required</u>: "If a law requires a signature or record to be notarized, acknowledged, verified or made under oath, that requirement is satisfied if all of the following are true:

"1. A secure electronic signature of the individual who is authorized to perform those acts and all other information that is required to be included pursuant to any other applicable law are applied to a secure electronic record.

"2. The secure electronic record has a time stamp token that is both:

"(a) Created by a party recognized by the secretary of state.

"(b) In a form that is accepted by the secretary of state to do all of the following:
(i) Reasonably verify the validity of the signing party's secure electronic signature.
(ii) Reasonably establish the time of signing.
"3. The secure electronic record cannot be altered without invalidating the time stamp token" (ARS 44-7034).

Electronic Notaries

The Arizona Revised Statutes contains unusually ample and detailed rules governing the regulation of Electronic Notaries and the performance of electronic notarial acts (Title 41, Chapter 2, Article 3, Sections 41-351 through 41-370).

The Arizona Administrative Code also sets rules for Electronic Notaries in Title 2 ("Administration"), Chapter 12 ("Office of the Secretary of State"), Article 12 ("Electronic Notary").

Electronic Notary Application: The basic qualifications for becoming an Arizona Electronic Notary (ARS 41-353[F]) are essentially the same as for becoming a regular Notary in the state (ARS 41-312[E]), and similarly the Secretary of State may impose a training course requirement (ARS 41-353[I]).

To become an Electronic Notary, the applicant must fill out a form provided by the Arizona Secretary of State and submit it to the Secretary (AAC R2-12-1201). Within 90 days of submitting the application, the applicant must register with the Secretary "possession of an approved electronic notary token" (AAC R2-12-1201). The application must include a $25,000 surety bond (AAC R2-12-1202).

Electronic Notary Journal: The Electronic Notary must "keep a journal of all electronic acts in bound paper form with the same form as required in ARS § 41-319 ..." (AAC R2-12-1203). If the Electronic Notary also holds a regular Notary commission under ARS 41-312 and the commission dates are identical for the two commissions, then the Electronic Notary may also use the regular journal as the required Electronic Notary paper journal (AAC R2-12-1203). "If the dates are not identical, then the electronic notary shall maintain two separate journals."

For failure to deposit the electronic journal and records with the Secretary of State, a civil penalty may be imposed of not more than $500 (AAC R2-12-1209).

Electronic Notary Token: To obtain an Electronic Notary Token, evidence of an Electronic Notary commission must first be presented to the provider (AAC R2-12-1204); only one Token may be provided to a given Electronic Notary.

An Electronic Notary Token must contain: (a) the commission number of the Electronic Notary; (b) the full name of the Electronic Notary; (c) the commission expiration date; (d) a link to the commission record of the Electronic Notary on the Secretary of State's official website; and (e) any applicable information relative to ARS 41-132 (AAC R2-12-1204).

Fees for Electronic Notarial Acts: An Electronic Notary may not charge more than $25 for any of the following electronic acts: acknowledgment, oath or affirmation, jurat or any other notarial act (AAC R2-12-1207).

Penalties: For failure to provide signed notice to the Secretary of State of loss, theft or compromise of the Electronic Notary's journal, a penalty fee may be imposed of $10 per use of the Electronic Notary Token up to a maximum of $500 (R2-12-1208). "When audit trail is not recoverable, the maximum of $500 shall be imposed upon the electronic notary for each failure to provide proper notice of a loss, theft, or compromise of the electronic notary's journal" (AAC R2-12-1208).

For failure to provide signed notice of each loss, theft or compromise of any of the materials or processes used in creating an Electronic Notary Token a civil penalty of $10 per day may be assessed up to a maximum of $500 for each such failure (AAC R2-12-1209).

Electronic Notary Powers

When requested, electronic Notaries may perform the following notarial acts (ARS 41-355[A]):
1. Take electronic acknowledgments*.
2. Administer oaths and affirmations relating to electronic documents and electronic notarial acts.
3. Perform jurats** relating to electronic documents and electronic notarial acts.

* Electronic Acknowledgment: "'Electronic acknowledgment' means a notarial act in which an electronic notary electronically certifies that the signer, whose identity is proven by satisfactory evidence, either: (a) Appeared before the electronic notary and acknowledged that the signer executed the instrument. (b) Provided secure electronic acknowledgment that the signer executed the electronic instrument presented to the electronic notary" (ARS 41-351[3]).

** Electronic Jurat: "'Electronic jurat' means an electronic notarial act in which the electronic notary certifies that a signer, whose identity is proven by satisfactory evidence, has made in the electronic notary's presence a voluntary electronic signature or mark and has taken an oath or affirmation vouching for the truthfulness of the signed electronic document" (ARS 41-351[6]).

eNotarization Requirements

Electronic Notaries Public may perform the notarial acts above only if:

"1. The signer is in the presence of the notary at the time of notarization.

"2. The signer signs in a language that the notary understands.

"3. Subject to subsection D (below), the signer communicates directly with the notary in a language they both understand or indirectly through a translator who is physically present with the signer and notary at the time of the notarization and communicates directly with the signer and the notary in languages the translator understands.

"4. The notarial certificate is worded and completed using only letters, characters and a language that are read, written and understood by the notary public" (ARS 41-355[B].

Components of eDocuments: "A notarized electronic document that is completed in the presence of an electronic notary consists of the following:

"1. A complete electronic document.

"2. A signature or mark that is affixed to the document by the signer.

"3. A time and date statement that is contained within the electronic notary token.

"4. An electronic notary token that is affixed by the electronic notary to the document" (ARS 41-355[E].

"On completion of the notarized electronic document, any change to any of the elements prescribed in subsection E of this section invalidates the notarized electronic document (ARS 41-355[F]).

Additional Duties of eNotary: An Arizona Electronic Notary shall also:

"1. Keep, maintain and protect as a public record a journal of all official acts performed by the notary as prescribed in Section 41-361 and in the form prescribed by the secretary of state.

"2. Provide and keep the materials and processes to create an electronic notary token as approved by the secretary of state.

"3. Authenticate with the electronic notary token all official acts and affix the date of the expiration of the notary's commission as an electronic notary on every document that the electronic notary electronically signs.

"4. Respond to any requests for information and comply with any investigations that are initiated by the secretary of state or the office of the attorney general" (ARS 41-355[G]).

URPERA

Arizona has adopted the Uniform Real Property Electronic Recording Act (URPERA), effective January 1, 2006, including the following requirement on electronic notarization:

"A requirement that a document or a signature associated with a document be notarized, acknowledged, verified, witnessed or made under oath is satisfied if the electronic signature of the person authorized to perform that act, and all other information required to be included, is attached to or logically associated with the document or signature. A physical or electronic image of a stamp, impression or seal need not accompany an electronic signature" (ARS 11-487.02[C]).

NOTARY RECORDS

Every Notary must "keep, maintain and protect as a public record a journal of all official acts performed by the notary" (ARS 41-313[E]).

Bound and Chronological Journal

"The notary shall keep a paper journal and, except as prescribed by subsection E, shall keep only one journal at a time. The notary shall record all notarial acts in chronological order" (ARS 41-319[A]). "Additionally, although not required by law, use of a permanently bound journal is recommended for the notary's protection. Permanently bound pages are more difficult to remove or lose, than loose-leaf pages" (RM).

Public and Non-Public Records

Except for entries whose disclosure would violate the attorney-client privilege or which are confidential under federal or state law, "the notary's journal is a public record that may be viewed by or copied for any member of the public, but only upon presentation to the notary of a written request that details the month and year of the notarial act, the name of the person whose signature was notarized and the type of document or transaction" (ARS 41-319[F]).

If one or more entries in a notary public's journal are not public records, the notary public may keep one journal that contains entries that are not public records and one journal that contains entries that are public records (ARS 41-319[E]).

"The notary shall furnish, when requested, a certified copy of any public record in the notary's journal. Records of notarial acts that violate the attorney-client privilege or that are confidential pursuant to federal or state law are not a public record" (ARS 41-319[A]).

"A notary shall not let the requestor view all journal entries. The notary shall only copy the transaction requested and cover the entries above and below before making a copy of the records" (RM).

Abortion Record Not Public: "Notwithstanding section 41-319, the notarized statement of parental consent (to an abortion) and the description on the document or notarial act recorded in the notary journal are confidential and are not public records" (ARS 36-2152[A]).

Required Entries

Each journal entry must include at least the following entries (ARS 41-319[A]):

1. The date of the notarial act;
2. A description of the document or type of notarial act ("Even though the law says a description of the document OR type of notarial act, the Secretary of State recommends the notary public fill in both fields if offered in the journal" [RM].);
3. The printed full name, signature and address of each person for whom a notarial act is performed;
4. The type of satisfactory evidence of identity for each person for whom the notarial act is performed, if other than the Notary's personal knowledge, including a description of the identification document, its serial or ID number, and its date of issuance or expiration;
5. The fee, if any, charged for the notarial act.

However, if a Notary has personal knowledge of the identity of a signer, items 1 through 4 above "may be satisfied by the notary retaining a paper or electronic copy of the notarized documents for each notarial act" (ARS 41-319[B]).

Further, "(i)f a notary does more than one notarization for an individual within a six month period, the notary shall have the individual provide satisfactory evidence of identity the first time the notary performs the notarization for the individual but may not require satisfactory evidence of identity or the individual to sign the journal for subsequent notarizations performed for the individual during the six month period" (ARS 41-319[C]).

"If a notary performs more than one notarization of the same type for a signer either on like documents or within the same document and at the same time, the notary may group documents together and make one journal entry for the transaction" (ARS 41-319[D]).

Refusals Should Be Noted: "If a notary refuses a notarization for any reason, the notary should always make a notation in his or her journal about the refusal and the grounds for doing so in case legal action ensues over the refusal" (RM).

Credible Witness Must Sign Journal: The "Notary Public Reference Manual" directs each credible witness to sign the Notary's journal, along with the principal signer.

Records Kept Five Years

"While a notary public is commissioned, a notary public shall keep all records and journals of the notary's acts for at least five years after the date the notarial act was performed. On receipt of the records and journals from a notary public who no longer is commissioned, the secretary of state shall keep all records and journals of notaries public deposited in the secretary of state's office for five years and shall give certified copies thereof when required, and for the copy certifications the secretary of state shall receive the same fees as are by law allowed to notaries public. The copy certifications shall be as valid and effectual as if given by a notary public" (ARS 41-317[B]).

Surrendering Notarial Records

Except for notarial records that would violate the attorney-client privilege or that are confidential under federal or state law, the official journal and records of Notaries who vacate their office through resignation, revocation, death or commission expiration without reappointment must be deposited with the secretary of state, who must keep these records for five years and who may issue certified copies for the same fees as a Notary (ARS 41-317[A]). A Notary or, in the case of the Notary's death, a personal representative has three months to deposit these records with the county recorder, upon penalty of a $50-$500 forfeiture.

Records of a Notary that are not regarded as "public records" (i.e., their disclosure would violate the attorney-client privilege or they are confidential under federal or state law) may be kept by the Notary's employer (ARS 41-319[E]).

Employer Keeps Non-Public Journal

"A notary public's journal that contains entries that are not public records is the property of the employer of that notary public and shall be retained by that employer if the notary public leaves that employment. A notary public's journal that contains only public records is the property of the notary public without regard to whether the notary public's employer purchased the journal or provided the fees for the commissioning of the notary public" (ARS 41-319[E]).

"The notary public shall not relinquish the journal to the employer if the journal contains public records (ARS 41-312[C]). A journal that contains only nonpublic records is property of the employer when the notary leaves that employment" (RM).

Prima Facie Evidence

Certified copies of a Notary's records and official papers are prima facie evidence of the facts therein stated (Rules of Civil Procedure 44).

Journal Loss or Theft

"Within ten days after the loss or theft of an official journal or seal, the notary shall deliver to the secretary of state, by certified mail or other means providing a receipt, a signed notice of the loss or theft. The notary also shall inform the appropriate law enforcement agency in the case of theft" (ARS 41-323[B]). A "Notice of Loss or Theft — Journal and/or Seal" may be downloaded from the Secretary of State's website.

Willful Destruction of Records

"Any person who knowingly destroys, defaces or conceals any journal entry or records belonging to the office of a notary public shall forfeit to the state an amount not exceeding five hundred dollars and shall be liable for damages to any party injured thereby" (ARS 41-318).

Court Reporter's Records

Under ARS 41-324, court reporters are exempt from notating in their Notary journals oaths and affirmations administered in judicial proceedings. However, they must fulfill the journal requirement for all other notarizations they perform (RM).

Record of Electronic Acts

An Electronic Notary must keep a journal of all electronic acts in a bound paper form, just as is kept for paper-based notarizations (AAC R2-12-1203). If the Notary's regular and electronic commissions have identical term dates, only one journal is needed; if the dates are not identical, then two journals are needed. For further information on the Electronic Notary's journal, see "Electronic Notarizations" earlier in this chapter.

AUTHENTICATION OF NOTARIAL ACTS

Secretary of State

Authenticating certificates for Notaries, including apostilles, are issued by the Arizona Secretary of State's office (ARS 41-325 and 41-326).

Fee: $3 per document for a certificate authenticating a Notary, including an apostille. (Note: While a fee of $3 is cited on the website by the Notary Department, ARS 41-126[A][12] states that the fee for "issuing a certificate as to official capacity of a notary public and affixing a seal to the certificate" is $18.) Payable to the Secretary of State.

Mailing Address:
Arizona Secretary of State
Attention: Business Services, Notary Section
1700 West Washington, 7th Floor
Phoenix, AZ 85007-2888

Telephone: 1-602-542-6187 or 800-458-5842
(within Arizona)

Walk-in for Same-Day Service: Phoenix Customer Service Center
State Capitol Executive Tower
1700 West Washington Street
First Floor, Room 103
1-602-542-4285

Walk-in for Same-Day Service: Tucson
Arizona State Complex Building
400 W. Congress
Second Floor, Room 252
1-520-628-6583

Procedure: Mail or present in person the original notarized document(s) with the appropriate fee. For return mail, a stamped, addressed envelope is required. Indicate the nation to which the document will be sent. The average turnaround time for mailed documents is five business days. "You are urged to include your name and daytime telephone number so that we may contact you should any question arise when processing your document(s)" (website, "Frequently Asked Questions"). An "Apostille/ Certificate of Authentication Request Form" is available on the Secretary of State's website.

COMMISSIONING AND ADMINISTRATION

Arizona's Secretary of State appoints, regulates and maintains records on the state's Notaries (ARS 41-312).

"Except for the (Notary's) name and business address, all information on the application is confidential and may not be disclosed to any person other than the applicant, the applicant's personal representative or an employee or officer of the federal, state or local government who is acting in an official capacity" (ARS 41-312[F]).

Applying for Commission

Qualifications: An applicant for a commission as an Arizona Notary Public must (ARS 41-312[E]): (a) be at least 18 years old, (b) be an Arizona resident for tax purposes (i.e., claim an Arizona residence as a primary residence on state and federal tax forms), (c) be a citizen or legal permanent resident of the United States, (d) not have been convicted of a felony unless civil rights have been restored, (e) not have had an Arizona Notary commission revoked, in which case the Secretary may deny an appointment for an indefinite period, and (f) be able to read and write English.

No Course or Test: Currently, no course of instruction or test is required of applicants for a Notary commission in Arizona, although "the secretary of state may require that applicants and suspended notaries present proof of attendance at a notary training course before receiving their commissions or before reinstatement of a suspended commission. Any applicant who is required to attend a notary training course must complete the training within ninety days before renewing their commissions. The secretary of state may assess a fee ... for administering notary training courses..." (ARS 41-312[H]).

Free workshops are regularly presented by the Secretary of State's office for interested Notaries and applicants.

Every Notary must keep "as a reference a manual that is approved by the secretary of state and that describes the duties, authority and ethical responsibilities of notaries public" (ARS 41-312[E][5]). Accordingly, the "Notary Public Reference Manual" may be downloaded from the Secretary of State's website.

Application: Effective April 29, 2008, Notary bonds must be submitted to the Secretary of State along with the commission application rather than to a superior court clerk, as before. A check or money order for $43 — consisting of a $25 application fee (ARS 41-126[A]) and an $18 bond filing fee — must be included. An expedited application costs an additional $25. The oath of office appears on the Notary bond, which must be notarized. The $5,000 bond must be obtained in duplicate form, with one form sent to the Secretary of State and the other retained by the Notary. Bonds may not be issued more than 60 days before or 30 days after the commissioning date (ARS 41-315[B]).

Renewal Process: "Notaries public may submit a renewal application, new bond and filing fees to the Secretary of State's Office up to 60 days prior to the expiration of a commission. Notaries public may continue to notarize until midnight of the expiration date of a current commission" (RM). "If you failed to notify us about a change in your mailing address or about a lost or stolen journal or seal within the time limits specified in ARS 41-323, you must also pay the $25 civil penalty per offense before we will renew your commission ..." (website, "Frequently Asked Questions").

Non-Residents: Persons who do not have a primary residence in Arizona may not qualify for a Notary commission in the state.

Online Search: Through the Arizona Secretary of State's website ("Search for a Notary"), the state's roster of Notaries may be searched by commission number, first and last name, business name, business zip code, county and commission date range.

Changes of Status

If Notary Moves: "Within thirty days after the change of a notary's mailing, business or residential address, the notary shall deliver to the secretary of state, by certified mail or other means providing a receipt, a signed notice of the change that provides both the old and new addresses" (ARS 41-323[A]). There is a $25 civil penalty for failure to make such a notification. A "Notary Public Address/Name Change Form" should be used; it may be downloaded from the Secretary of State's website.

If Notary Changes Name: "A notary public who has a change of surname may continue to use the official seal and commission in the notary public's prior name until that commission expires. The notary shall sign the changed surname on the line that is designated for the notary public's signature on the notarial certificate. Immediately below that signature, the notary public shall sign the name under which the notary was commissioned. The notary public shall notify the secretary of state's office within thirty days of the notary's change of surname. Failure to notify the secretary of state of this change of surname is evidence of the notary's failure to fully and faithfully discharge the duties of a notary" (ARS 41-327). A "Notary Public Address/Name Change Form" should be used; it may be downloaded from the Secretary of State's website.

If Notary Resigns: Notaries who resign their office must submit a written resignation to the Governor of Arizona (ARS 38-294[2]). A form letter ("Notary Public Resignation Letter") may be downloaded from the Secretary of State's website. This letter should be delivered by certified mail. If the Notary's records and seal are not delivered to the Secretary of State's office within three months of resignation, a fine of $50 to $500 may be imposed (ARS 41-317).

COUNTY OFFICES

Effective April 29, 2008, Arizona Senate Bill 1174 removed from the state's counties all former functions related to the authenticating of notarial acts, the filing of Notary bonds and oaths, and the depositing of Notary journals and records, and centralized those functions in the office of the Secretary of State. However, some Notary-related records from previous years may still be retained by the counties. To contact an Arizona county official to inquire about such records, telephone long-distance information — 1-XXX-555-1212 — and ask for the number of the superior court clerk or the recorder for the appropriate county:

County	City/Town	Area Code
Apache	St. Johns	(928)
Cochise	Bisbee	(520)
Coconino	Flagstaff	(928)
Gila	Globe	(928)
Graham	Safford	(928)
Greenlee	Clifton	(928)
La Paz	Parker	(928)
Maricopa	Phoenix	(602)
Mohave	Kingman	(928)
Navajo	Holbrook	(928)
Pima	Tucson	(520)
Pinal	Florence	(520)
Santa Cruz	Nogales	(520)
Yavapai	Prescott	(928)
Yuma	Yuma	(928)

OTHER NOTARIAL OFFICERS

Besides Notaries Public, the following officers have power to take acknowledgments within the state (ARS 33-511):
1. A judge of a court of record;
2. A clerk or deputy clerk of a court having a seal;
3. A recorder of deeds;
4. A justice of the peace;
5. A county recorder.

Court Reporters

"A. Court reporters who administer oaths and affirmations in judicial proceedings are exempt from the provisions of this chapter other than section 41-315 (Notary bond requirement). Court reporters who are commissioned as notaries and who perform notarial acts outside of judicial proceedings are subject to all provisions of this chapter and of other laws of this state that regulate notaries public.

"B. A court reporter who prepares a transcript of a judicial proceeding shall attach a certificate page to the transcript. On the certificate page, the court reporter shall attest to the fact that the reporter administered an oath or affirmation to each witness whose testimony appears in the transcript.

"C. An affidavit of nonappearance that is prepared by a court reporter does not need to be witnessed by a notary" (ARS 41-324).

QUICK FACTS

Notary Jurisdiction
Statewide (ARS 41-312[A]).

Notary Term Length
Four years (ARS 41-312[A]), expiring at midnight on the commission expiration date, which is exactly four years less one day from the commission starting date.

Notary Bond
$5,000, with surety approved by the Secretary of State (ARS 41-315 and AAC R2-12-1103). A licensed surety must execute the bond.

Arkansas

NOTARY SEAL

An Arkansas Notary must affix a seal of office "(u)nder or near (the) notary public's official signature on every notary certificate" and the seal's format must be as follows (AC 21-14-107[b]):

Kind

Inked Rubber Stamp or Embosser: "The seal shall be clear and legible and capable of photographic reproduction" (AC 21-14-107[b]).

The "Arkansas Notary Public Handbook" states, "When using an embosser, it is advisable to use an ink pad or carbon over the seal so that it can be photocopied."

Shape/Size

Not specified by law.

Components

1. Name of Notary (exactly as in official signature);
2. Name of county where Notary's bond is filed;
3. "Notary Public";
4. "Arkansas";
5. Commission expiration date;
6. Commission number issued by Secretary of State, if any. Such numbers were issued starting January 1, 2006 (AC 21-14-101[g]).

Examples

The above typical, actual-size examples of Notary seals are allowed by Arkansas law. Formats other than these may also be permitted.

State Seal or Outline Prohibited

"A notary seal shall not include the Seal of the State of Arkansas or an outline of the state" (AC 21-14-107[c]).

NOTARY ADMINISTRATION

Office of Secretary of State
Business & Commercial
 Services Division   1-501-682-3409
1401 W. Capitol Ave., Ste. 250
Little Rock, AR
72201-1094   1-888-233-0325

Website: www.sos.arkansas.gov/BCS/
 Pages/notaryPublic.aspx

NOTARY RULES

AC — Arkansas Code
NPH — Arkansas Notary Public Handbook

Most Notary rules are in the Arkansas Code:

a. Title 21, Chapter 14, "Notaries Public";

b. Title 16, Chapter 47, "Acknowledgment and Proof of Instruments," Subchapter 2 of which is the "Uniform Acknowledgment Act."*

* This is the Uniform Acknowledgment Act of 1939, adopted virtually intact.

Other guidelines for Notaries are in the "Arkansas Notary Public Handbook" published by the Secretary of State and available on the website.

Commission Expiration Date Must Appear

"Every notary public shall attach to any certificate of acknowledgment or jurat to an affidavit that he or she may make a statement of the date on which his or her commission will expire ...

"No acknowledgment or other act of a notary public shall be held invalid on account of the failure to comply with this section" (AC 21-14-108).

Title of Officer Taking Acknowledgment

"The certificate of the acknowledging officer shall be completed by his signature, his official seal if he has one, the title of his office, and if he is a notary public, the date his commission expires" (AC 16-47-208).

Signature of Notary

"At the time of notarization, the notary public shall sign his or her official signature on every notary certificate ...

"The official signature shall be the signature on file with the Secretary of State at the time of signing" (AC 21-14-107[a]).

Facsimile Signature and Seal Use by Notary

"Any notary public may affix a notary certificate bearing the notary's facsimile signature and facsimile seal in lieu of the notary's public's manual signature and rubber or embossed seal on a commercial document, after filing with the Secretary of State:

"1. The notary public's manual signature certified by the notary public under oath;

"2. A general description of the types of commercial documents to be notarized by facsimile signature and seal;

"3. The name and manual signature of any other person or persons signing the commercial document by manual or facsimile signature; and

"4. The written consent of any other person or persons signing the commercial documents to the use of the notary public's facsimile signature and facsimile seal on the commercial documents" (AC 21-14-202).

For filing with the state, a "Registration of Facsimile Signature and Seal of Notary Public" is downloadable from the Arkansas Secretary of State's website.

Facsimile Signature and Seal Defined: "'Facsimile signature' means the reproduction by engraving, imprinting, stamping or other means of a manual signature of a notary public...'Facsimile seal' means the reproduction by engraving, imprinting, stamping, or other means of the seal of office of a notary public, containing the information described in 21-14-107(b)(2)…" (AC 21-14-201).

'Commercial Document' Defined: A commercial document is defined as "any instrument, certificate, report, billing, affidavit, or other document which is required to bear a notary certificate by the terms of a purchase order, contract, bid specification, construction standard, testing standard, or other commercial standard, specification, or practice" (AC 21-14-201[3][A]).

Commercial document does "not include any deed or other instrument in writing for the conveyance of any real estate or by which any real estate may be affected in law or equity" (AC 21-14-201[3][B]).

Duties and Effect Unchanged: "A notary public shall have the same duties when affixing a notary certificate with the notary public's facsimile signature and facsimile seal on a commercial document as when signing a notary certificate with the notary public's manual signature and rubber or embossed seal, and nothing in this subchapter shall remove any duty or responsibility imposed on a notary public by law, except as specifically provided in this subchapter" (AC 21-14-204).

"Notary certificates which are signed by facsimile signature and sealed by facsimile seal under the provisions of this subchapter shall have the same force and effect as notary certificates signed by manual signature and bearing a rubber or embossed seal for all purposes" (AC 21-14-205).

Seal Must Not Be Surrendered

"The seal and certificate of the notary public commission are the exclusive property of the notary public and must be kept in the exclusive control of the notary public ...

"The seal and certificate of the notary public commission shall not be surrendered to an employer upon termination of employment, regardless of whether or not the employer paid for the seal or for the commission" (AC 21-14-107[d] and [e]).

Seal of Resigned Notary to Be Destroyed

"The resigning notary public shall destroy his or her official seal immediately upon resignation" (AC 21-14-203[b]).

NOTARY POWERS

Arkansas Notaries are authorized to perform the following notarial acts (AC 21-14-104 through 21-14-106):
1. Take acknowledgments* and proofs**;
2. Administer oaths*** and affirmations;
3. Take affidavits (AC 16-45-102) and depositions****;
4. Certify copies*****;
5. Make declarations and protests (AC 16-46-211).

* Taking Acknowledgments: "The officer taking the acknowledgment shall know or have satisfactory evidence that the person making the acknowledgment is the person described in and who executed the instrument" (AC 16-47-205).

** Proof by Subscribing Witness: Deeds may be recorded if proved by one or more subscribing witnesses (AC 18-12-206[b]).

*** Oath: "An oath is a formal statement by which a person appearing before a notary swears (or affirms): 1) That the statement or group of statements is the truth; or 2) That the testimony he/she will give will be the truth; or 3) That he/she will faithfully perform the duties of a public office" (NPH).

The following is recommended as an oath of office for public officials: "I, _____, do solemnly swear (or affirm) that I will support the Constitution of the United States and the Constitution of the State of Arkansas, and that I will faithfully discharge the duties of the office of _____, upon which I am now about to enter."

The following is recommended as an oath for corporate officials: "I, _____, hereby enter into the position of _____ on behalf of _____ corporation. I affirm that I will fulfill these duties to the best of my ability and perform in accordance with the law and in the best interest of the corporation."

**** Depositions: "A notary has two functions in connection with depositions. First, the notary may be asked to take the witness' oath to tell the truth. Second, after the deposition has been transcribed, the notary may be asked to certify that the written transcript is a complete and accurate record of what was said at the deposition" (NPH).

"However, Arkansas court rules now require all depositions to be attested by a certified court reporter. If this is not done, the deposition will not be accepted by Arkansas courts" (NPH).

***** Certified Copies: "A notary public may supervise the making of a photocopy of an original document and attest that the document is a copy if the document is not: (1) A vital record in this state, another state, a territory of the United States, or another country; or (2) A public record, if a copy can be made by the custodian of the public record" (AC 21-14-106[b]).

"The notary may supervise the photocopy being made, or may make the copy himself/herself. The notary may keep a copy for his/her records to later ascertain that the certified document has not been altered" (NPH).

Identifying Document Signers

"The notary's greatest responsibility is to be certain of the identity of each person whose signature he/she will notarize. A good guide is to require some form of proper identification unless the notary personally recognizes the person whose signature is to be notarized" (NPH).

Legislation effective March 3, 1989, makes it unlawful for a Notary to witness any signature on any document unless the Notary either: "(1) Witnesses the signing of the instrument and personally knows the signer or is presented proof of the identity of the signer; or (2) Recognizes the signature of the signer by virtue of familiarity with the signature" (AC 21-14-111[a]).

"For purposes of this section, 'personally knows' means having an acquaintance, derived from association with the individual, which establishes the individual's identity with at least a reasonable certainty" (AC 21-14-111[c]).

Any Notary violating the rules of the above rules may be guilty of a Class A misdemeanor (AC 21-14-111[b]).

NOTARY DON'TS

Misleading Advertising

"The Secretary of State may deny the application of any person for appointment or reappointment or revoke the commission of any notary public during such notary public's term of appointment if the notary public ... (k)nowingly uses false or misleading advertising in which the notary public represents that the notary public has powers, duties, rights, or privileges that the notary public does not possess by law" (AC 21-14-112[a][3]).

Advertising Immigration Services: "a. Any notary public who chooses to use the term 'notario', 'notario publico', or any similar term in any advertisement shall include in the advertisement the following notice:

"'I AM NOT A LICENSED ATTORNEY AND CANNOT ENGAGE IN THE PRACTICE OF LAW. I AM NOT A REPRESENTATIVE OF ANY GOVERNMENTAL AGENCY WITH AUTHORITY OVER IMMIGRATION OR CITIZENSHIP AND I CANNOT OFFER LEGAL ADVICE OR OTHER ASSISTANCE REGARDING IMMIGRATION.'

"b. The notice shall be provided in both English and Spanish" (AC 4-109-103).

In the Spanish language, the notice would read:

"YO NO SOY UN ABOGADO MATRICULADO Y NO PUEDO EJERCER EN LA PRÁCTICA DE LEYES. YO NO SOY UN REPRESENTANTE DE NINGUNA AGENCIA GUBERNAMENTAL CON AUTORIDAD SOBRE INMIGRACIÓN O CIUDADANÍA NORTEAMERICANA Y NO PUEDO PROVEER CONSEJOS LEGALES U OTRA ASISTENCIA CON RESPECTO A INMIGRACIÓN."

The above does not apply to an attorney licensed in the state of Arkansas (AC 4-109-104).

Notary's Disqualifying Interest

"By law, a notary who is a party to an instrument, either individually or as a representative of a corporation which is a party to the instrument, may NOT perform any notarial act concerning that instrument. However, a corporate employee may notarize documents to which the corporate employer is a party, as long as the notary is not involved, either individually or as a representative of the corporate party" (NPH).

"A notary public cannot notarize his/her own signature, or a document to which the notary is party, or from which the notary would gain direct or indirect financial benefit" (NPH).

Corporate Employees: Notaries who are employees, stockholders, directors or officers of a bank or other corporation may notarize for that bank or corporation, unless the Notary is a party to the transaction, either individually or as a representative (AC 21-14-109).

Class A Misdemeanor for Witnessing Violation

"A notary public violating Arkansas law in respect to witnessing signatures shall be guilty of a Class A misdemeanor, punishable by a fine of up to $1,000 or up to one year in jail. In addition, his/her commission shall be revoked and he/she cannot be recommissioned for ten (10) years. A notary who violates Arkansas law as to fees charged shall also be guilty of a misdemeanor.

"The Secretary of Stte has been given the power to investigate complaints by the general public against notaries" (NPH).

NOTARY SIGNING AGENTS

Currently, there are no statutes, regulations or rules expressly governing, prohibiting or restricting the operation of Notary Signing Agents within the state of Arkansas.

NOTARY FEES

Arkansas Notaries may receive the following fees (AC 21-6-309):
1. For each certificate and seal: $5;
2. For each protest and record of same: $5;
3. For each notice of protest: $5.

Overcharging Is a Misdemeanor

Overcharging by a Notary is a misdemeanor punishable by a fine of not less than $100 (AC 21-6-309).

NOTARY CERTIFICATES

Arkansas has adopted the *Uniform Acknowledgment Act*, including the certificates (AC 16-47-207) for:
1. Acknowledgment by individual;
2. Acknowledgment by corporation;
3. Acknowledgment by attorney in fact;
4. Acknowledgment by any public officer or deputy thereof, or by any trustee, administrator, guardian or executor.

The Notary's seal and commission expiration

date must be added to each of these certificates, as required by Arkansas law.

For the text of the certificates, see "Uniform Acknowledgment Act (1939, amended 1960)," Section 7, in Appendix 4.

Acknowledgment by Corporation of Real Estate Document (AC 18-12-207 and 16-47-107):

For all documents executed by a corporation that affect title to real estate located in Arkansas, the following certificate should be used:

State of _____
County of _____

On this ____ day of _____, 20__, before me, _____, a Notary Public (or before any officer within this State or without the State now qualified under existing law to take acknowledgments), duly commissioned, qualified and acting, within and for said County and State, appeared in person the within named _____ and _____ (being the person or persons authorized by said corporation to execute such instrument, stating their respective capacities in that behalf), to me personally well known, who stated that they were the _____ and _____ of the _____, a corporation, and were duly authorized in their respective capacities to execute the foregoing instruments for and in the name and behalf of said corporation, and further stated and acknowledged that they had so signed, executed and delivered said foregoing instrument for the consideration, uses and purposes therein mentioned and set forth.

IN TESTIMONY WHEREOF, I have hereunto set my hand and official seal this ____ day of _____, 20__.

_____ (SEAL)
(Signature of Notary Public)
My commission expires: _____.

In addition, the following notarial certificates are permitted by the Secretary of State in the "Arkansas Notary Public Handbook":

Acknowledgment by Individual (NPH):

State of Arkansas
County of _____

On this the _____ day of _____, 20____, before me, _____ (name of Notary), the undersigned Notary, personally appeared _____ (name[s] of signer[s]), known to me (or satisfactorily proven) to be the person whose name(s) is/are subscribed to the within instrument and acknowledged that he/she/they executed the same for the purposes therein contained.

In witness whereof I have hereunto set my hand and official seal.

_____ (SEAL)
Notary Public
My commission expires: _____.

Copy Certification (NPH):

State of Arkansas
County of _____

I, _____ (name of Notary), certify this is a true and perfect copy of the original document presented to me on this ____ day of _____, 20___.

_____ (SEAL)
Notary Public
My commission expires: _____.

Affidavit (NPH):

I, _____ (name of affiant), being duly sworn, depose and say as follows:

(STATEMENTS)

_____
(Signature of Affiant)

State of Arkansas
County of _____

Subscribed and sworn before me this ____ day of _____, 20___.

_____ (SEAL)
Notary Public
My commission expires: _____.

Deposition (NPH):

I, _____ (name of witness), do hereby certify that the foregoing contains a full, complete and accurate transcript of the testimony given at my deposition taken the _____ day of _____, 20__.

_____
(Signature of Witness)

State of Arkansas
County of _____

Subscribed and sworn before me this _____ day of _____, 20__.

_____ (SEAL)
Notary Public
My commission expires: _____.

Acknowledgment by Person Serving in or with U.S. Armed Forces:

If a commissioned officer on active service with the U.S. armed forces uses the following certificate, no venue or authentication is required (AC 16-47-213):

On this _____ day of _____, 20__, before me, _____, the undersigned officer, personally appeared _____ (Serial No. _____), known to me or satisfactorily proven to be serving in or with the armed forces of the United States (a dependent of _____ [Serial No. _____], a person serving in or with the armed forces of the United States) and to be the person whose name is subscribed to the within instrument and acknowledged that he/she executed the same for the purposes therein contained. And the undersigned does further certify that he/she is at the date of this certificate a commissioned officer of the rank stated below and is in the active service of the armed forces of the United States.

_____ *(Signature of the Officer)*

_____
Rank and Serial No. of Officer and Unit

Certificate Size

To be acceptable for recording, all documents and notarial certificates (except plats, surveys and instruments executed before January 1, 2004) must be on $8^1/_2$-by-11-inch paper and have a $2^1/_2$-inch margin at the top right of the first page and across the bottom of the last page, and a $^1/_2$-inch margin on the sides and bottom of all pages (AC 14-15-402).

ELECTRONIC NOTARIZATIONS

The state of Arkansas has not yet adopted statutes or regulations expressly establishing rules, definitions and procedures for electronic notarization.

UETA Recognizes Notary's E-Signature

Arkansas has adopted the Uniform Electronic Transactions Act (Act 905 of 2001) and its provision on notarization, thereby recognizing the legal validity of electronic signatures used by Notaries:

"If a law requires a signature or record to be notarized, acknowledged, verified, or made under oath, the requirement is satisfied if the electronic signature of the person authorized to perform those acts, together with all other information required to be included by other applicable law, is attached to or logically associated with the signature or record" (AC 25-32-111).

Electronic Records and Signatures Act: The state earlier had adopted the Arkansas Electronic Records and Signatures Act (Act 718 of 1999), with the following provision pertinent to electronic notarization (AC 25-31-104):

"(a) Any person may, but shall not be required to, accept or agree to be bound by an electronic record which is:

"(1) Executed or adopted with an electronic signature; and

"(2) Witnessed or notarized using an electronic signature, when that acceptance or agreement is otherwise required to be witnessed or notarized.

"(b) When a person or other entity accepts or agrees to be bound by an electronic record as provided in this section, then any rule of law which requires:

"(1) A record of that type to be in writing shall be deemed satisfied;

"(2) A signature shall be deemed satisfied; and

"(3) A witness or notary shall be deemed satisfied by the electronic signature of the witness or notary."

URPERA Does Not Require Seal Image

In 2007 Arkansas adopted the Uniform Real Property Electronic Recording Act (Act 734), including the following provision (AC 14-2-303[c]):

"A requirement that a document or a signature associated with a document be notarized, acknowledged, verified, witnessed, or made under oath is satisfied if the electronic signature of the person authorized to perform that act, and all other information required to be included, is attached to or logically associated with the document or signature. A physical or electronic image of a stamp, impression, or seal need not accompany an electronic signature."

Notarization Scanned for Court eFiling

The Supreme Court of Arkansas on June 17, 2010, published a court rule permitting the state's courts to adopt e-filing. The rule does not require courts to transition to e-filing, but creates a one-year transition period for the courts that choose to do so. While Arkansas has enacted the Uniform Electronic Transactions Act, Sections 24-32-117 and -118 stipulate that each state agency must decide whether to accept electronic records for filing. Thus, this court rule was necessary for the courts in Arkansas to move forward in utilizing electronic records and signatures.

Section 8 of the rule permits electronic signatures on electronic documents filed with a court. An electronic signature may be a typed name, facsimile, typographical or digital signature. Section 8(b) states that all documents that are required to be notarized must be signed and notarized conventionally (i.e., on paper). After the documents are executed, they then may be submitted electronically to the court. That is, they can be scanned and then submitted.

NOTARY RECORDS

"The law does not require a notary to keep any record of his/her official acts, but it is recommended to do so.

"A register or journal will offer an excellent way of recalling past notarial acts. If a notary is called upon to testify in court, a register or journal may help establish what actually took place. The notary's records and official papers are admissible as evidence in all Arkansas courts" (NPH).

Recommended Entries

The "Arkansas Notary Public Handbook" further suggests that, for each notarial act performed, the Notary should record the following information in the register:

1. Date of notarial act;
2. Type of act performed;
3. Type of document involved;
4. Name and address of each person whose signature was notarized;
5. Signature of each person whose signature was notarized;
6. A "Notes" section of personal annotations.

Certified Copies of Records Are Evidence

"All declarations and protests made and acknowledgments taken by a notary public and certified copies of the notary public's records and official papers shall be received as evidence of the facts therein stated in all the courts of this state" (AC 21-14-110).

Journal of Revokee

"After a notary public receives notice from the Secretary of State that such notary's commission has been revoked, unless such revocation has been enjoined such notary shall immediately send or have delivered to the Secretary of State such notary's journal of notarial acts, all other papers and copies relating to such notary's notarial acts, and such notary's official seal" (AC 21-14-112[c]).

AUTHENTICATION OF NOTARIAL ACTS

Secretary of State

Authenticating certificates for Notaries, both "certifications" and apostilles, are issued only by the Arkansas Secretary of State's office.

Fee: $10 per document for an apostille, but only $5 per document if the document will be sent to a nation not subscribing to the Hague treaty. Checks should be made payable to the "Secretary of State." No credit cards are accepted.

Mailing Address:
Office of Secretary of State
Business & Commercial Services
Attention: Notary
State Capitol
Little Rock, AR 72201-1094

Physical Address:
1401 West Capitol Ave.
Victory Bldg., Suite 250
Little Rock, AR 72201

Telephone: 1-501-682-3409
1-888-233-0325

Procedure: Mail or present in person the original notarized document, along with the fee. If mailed, no stamped, return envelope is required, unless priority or express return is requested; otherwise, it will be returned by regular mail. The turnaround time on most requests is 24 to 48 hours (website, "Apostille/Certification").

COMMISSIONING AND ADMINISTRATION

The Arkansas Secretary of State appoints, commissions, regulates and maintains records on the state's Notaries (AC 21-14-101).

Applying for Commission

Qualifications: An applicant for appointment as an Arkansas Notary must (AC 21-14-101[b]):

(a) be a U.S. citizen or a permanent resident alien, (b) be a legal resident of Arkansas or a legal resident of an adjoining state who is employed in Arkansas, (c) be at least 18 years old, (d) be able to read and write English and (e) not have had his or her Notary commission revoked in the past 10 years.

No Course or Test: Neither education nor testing is mandated for Notary commission applicants, though a 30-question "Notary Public Quiz," with answers provided, is made available to applicants. In addition, the Secretary of State offers a free 90-minute "Notary Public Seminar" on the second Wednesday of each month at the Business & Commercial Services offices in Little Rock; space is limited and registration is required beforehand. This same free class periodically tours the state (website, "Upcoming Notary Seminars").

Application: The application form must be notarized and then submitted to the Secretary of State's office, along with the $20 application fee (AC 21-14-101[c]), a copy of the executed $7,500 surety bond or contract and, in the case of an applicant who is a permanent resident alien, a notarized declaration of domicile, which has been recorded with the circuit clerk.

After the application has been received and processed by the Secretary of State's office, the applicant will be sent three oath-of-office forms and a commission identification number. Within 30 days from the commission starting date, the applicant must complete and file one of these oath forms at the office of the circuit court clerk in the county of residence or employment, along with the original surety bond or contract (AC 21-14-101[d] and [e]). The applicant will retain a second oath form after the clerk signs it. The third oath form, depending on county rules, must be returned to the Secretary of State either by the applicant or the clerk, also within 30 days from the commission starting date. After receiving the oath-of-office form, the Secretary's office will issue an identifying wallet card to the new Notary.

To renew the commission, a new application and $20 fee must be submitted to the Secretary of State no more than 30 calendar days prior to commission expiration (AC 21-14-108[c]).

Non-Residents: Legal residents of adjoining states who are employed in Arkansas may become Notaries (AC 21-14-101[b]).

Online Search: The state's roster of Notaries may be searched at www.sos.arkansas.gov/corps/notary/index.php by a Notary's last name, city, county or filing number. Information provided includes the Notary's address, standing, commission starting and expiration dates and bonding information.

Changes of Status

Within 30 days, Notaries are required to notify the Secretary of State and the local circuit court clerk of any change in their status which would alter the information on file with the Secretary and the court clerk, providing to both a certified copy of any pertinent marriage certificate (AC 21-14-103). A "Change of Personal Information" form is downloadable from the website. If a court order is involved, as with a name change, the Secretary must be provided with a certified copy of the order within 30 calendar days of its filing with the court clerk.

<u>If Notary Moves to New County</u>: Notaries who move their residences to a new county, or out-of-state residents who move their place of employment to a new county, must notify the Secretary of State in writing and file the original bond in the new county (AC 21-14-102). The bonding company must also be notified.

<u>When and How Notary Must Resign</u>: The Notary Public must send a signed letter of resignation to the Arkansas Secretary of State and return the commission if the Notary: (a) wishes no longer to be a Notary, (b) does not maintain legal residence or employment within Arkansas during the term of appointment or (c) is required to resign pursuant to a court order of Arkansas or any other state (AC 21-14-203[b]). "The resigning notary public shall destroy his or her official seal immediately upon resignation."

CIRCUIT CLERKS

To contact an Arkansas county circuit clerk for assistance in locating a Notary whose bond and oath have been filed in that county, telephone long-distance information — 1-XXX-555-1212 — using the following area codes:

County	City/Town	Area Code
Arkansas	DeWitt/Stuttgart	(870)
Ashley	Hamburg	(870)
Baxter	Mountain Home	(870)
Benton	Bentonville	(479)
Boone	Harrison	(870)
Bradley	Warren	(870)
Calhoun	Hampton	(870)
Carroll	Berryville	(870)
Chicot	Lake Village	(870)
Clark	Arkadelphia	(870)
Clay	Piggott/Corning	(870)
Cleburne	Heber Springs	(501)
Cleveland	Rison	(870)
Columbia	Magnolia	(870)
Conway	Morrilton	(501)
Craighead	Jonesboro	(870)
Crawford	Van Buren	(479)
Crittenden	Marion	(870)

County	City/Town	Area Code
Cross	Wynne	(870)
Dallas	Fordyce	(870)
Desha	Arkansas City	(870)
Drew	Monticello	(870)
Faulkner	Conway	(501)
Franklin	Ozark	(479)
Fulton	Salem	(870)
Garland	Hot Springs	(501)
Grant	Sheridan	(870)
Greene	Paragould	(870)
Hempstead	Hope	(870)
Hot Spring	Malvern	(501)
Howard	Nashville	(870)
Independence	Batesville	(870)
Izard	Melbourne	(870)
Jackson	Newport	(870)
Jefferson	Pine Bluff	(870)
Johnson	Clarksville	(479)
Lafayette	Lewisville	(870)
Lawrence	Walnut Ridge	(870)
Lee	Marianna	(870)
Lincoln	Star City	(870)
Little River	Ashdown	(870)
Logan	Paris/Booneville	(479)
Lonoke	Lonoke	(501)
Madison	Huntsville	(479)
Marion	Yellville	(870)
Miller	Texarkana	(870)
Mississippi	Blytheville	(870)
Monroe	Clarendon	(870)
Montgomery	Mount Ida	(870)
Nevada	Prescott	(870)
Newton	Jasper	(870)
Ouachita	Camden	(870)
Perry	Perryville	(501)
Phillips	Helena	(870)
Pike	Murfreesboro	(870)
Poinsett	Harrisburg	(870)
Polk	Mena	(479)
Pope	Russellville	(479)
Prairie	Des Arc	(870)
Pulaski	Little Rock	(501)
Randolph	Pocahontas	(870)
Saint Francis	Forrest City	(870)
Saline	Benton	(501)
Scott	Waldron	(479)
Searcy	Marshall	(870)
Sebastian	Fort Smith	(479)
Sevier	De Queen	(870)
Sharp	Ash Flat	(870)
Stone	Mountain View	(870)

County	City/Town	Area Code
Union	El Dorado	(870)
Van Buren	Clinton	(501)
Washington	Fayetteville	(479)
White	Searcy	(501)
Woodruff	Augusta	(870)
Yell	Danville	(479)

OTHER NOTARIAL OFFICERS

Besides Notaries, the following officers are authorized to take acknowledgments in Arkansas (AC 16-47-202):
1. Judge of a court of record, or any former judge of a court of record who served at least four years;
2. Clerk of a court of record;
3. Commissioner or registrar or recorder of deeds;
4. Justice of the peace;
5. Master in chancery or registrar in chancery.

QUICK FACTS

Notary Jurisdiction
Statewide (AC 21-14-101[a][2] and 21-14-104).

Notary Term Length
Ten years (AC 21-14-101).

Notary Bond
$7,500, through either (a) "a surety insurer authorized to do business in Arkansas ... to be approved by the Secretary of State," or (b) a surety contract issued by a general business corporation registered with the state insurance commissioner (AC 21-14-101[d] and 21-14-108[d]).

California

NOTARY SEAL

A California Notary Public must authenticate all official acts with a seal of office (GC 8207). The seal's format must be as follows:

Kind

Inked Stamp or Embosser:
"The seal of every notary public shall be affixed by a seal press or stamp that will print or emboss a seal which legibly reproduces under photographic methods the required elements of the seal" (GC 8207). Because of the inconvenience of "smudging" an embossment to make it photographable, virtually all California Notaries use inked stamps as their official seal. Some, however, use embossers in addition to their stamps.

Shape/Size

Rectangular, not more than 1 inch wide by 2½ inches long; or circular, not more than 2 inches in diameter (GC 8207). Rectangular inking seals are nearly universal in the state.

Border

"A serrated or milled edged border" must surround all of the components below (GC 8207).

Components

A California Notary Public's official seal must contain (GC 8207):
1. Name of Notary;
2. California state seal;
3. "Notary Public";
4. Name of county where Notary's oath and bond are filed;
5. Commission expiration date;
6. Notary commission number;
7. Seal manufacturer identification number.

Examples

The above typical, actual-size examples of Notary seals are allowed by California law. Formats other than these may also be permitted.

NOTARY ADMINISTRATION

Office of Secretary of State
Business Programs Division
Notary Public Section   1-916-653-3595
P.O. Box 942877
(1500 11th St., 2nd Floor)
Sacramento, CA 94277-0001

Website: www.ss.ca.gov/business/notary/

NOTARY RULES

GC — *California Government Code*
CC — *California Civil Code*
NPH — *Notary Public Handbook*
NN — *Notary News newsletter*

Most Notary rules are in:

a. California Government Code, Title 2, Division 1, Chapter 3, "Notaries Public";

b. California Civil Code, Sections 1181 through 1197.

Other guidelines for Notaries are in the "Notary Public Handbook" and the "Notary News" newsletters, both issued by the California Secretary of State and available on the website.

Subdivision Maps

A Notary need not affix a seal on an acknowledgment certificate on a subdivision map as long as the Notary's name, county of principal place of business, and commission expiration date are typed or printed below the Notary's signature (GC 66436[c]).

If Seal Not Photographable

"A notary acknowledgment shall be deemed complete for recording purposes without a photographically reproducible official seal of the notary public if the seal, as described in Section 8207, is present and legible, and the name of the notary, the county of the notary's principal place of business, the notary's telephone number, the notary's registration number, and the notary's commission expiration date are typed or printed in a manner that is photographically reproducible below, or immediately adjacent to, the notary's signature in the acknowledgment" (GC 27201.5[a]).

Seal Substitute on Electronic Document

Under California's Electronic Recording Delivery Act of 2004, "(w)hen a signature is required to be accompanied by a notary's seal or stamp, that requirement is satisfied if the electronic signature of the notary contains all of the following:

"1. The name of the notary.

"2. The words 'Notary Public.'

"3. The name of the county where the bond and oath of office of the notary are filed.

"4. The sequential identification number assigned to the notary, if any.

"5. The sequential identification number assigned to the manufacturer or vendor of the notary's physical or electronic seal, if any" (GC 27391[e]).

Attributes of Notary Seal

According to the Secretary of State's website, a Notary seal must be all of the following: (a) unique to the person using it, (b) capable of verification, (e) under the sole control of the person using it and (d) accepted in the same format and appearance as transmitted (website, "Procedures and Guidelines for the Issuance of Notary Public Seals").

Authorization for Seal Purchase

Notaries purchasing an official seal must present to the manufacturer a "certificate of authorization" from the Secretary of State. Manufacturers must keep a record of seals sold. Each certificate of authorization is returned to the Secretary of State bearing an impression of the new seal and stating the manufacturer's ID number (GC 8207.3[a] through [d]). Manufacturers of Notary seals must have been issued a permit to sell such seals by the Secretary of State (GC 8207.2[a] and website, "Seal Manufacturer Permits").

Seal Kept in Locked, Secured Area

"The seal shall be kept in a locked and secured area, under the direct and exclusive control of the notary. Failure to secure the seal shall be cause for the Secretary of State to take administrative action against the commission held by the notary public pursuant to Section 8214.1" (GC 8207).

"Any notary public ... who willfully fails to keep the seal of the notary public under the direct and exclusive control of the notary public, or who surrenders the seal of the notary public to any person not otherwise authorized by law to possess the seal of the notary, shall be guilty of a misdemeanor" (GC 8228.1[a]). See also GC 8214.1(o).

Seal Not Surrendered to Employer

"The official seal of a notary public is the exclusive property of that notary public, and shall not be surrendered to an employer upon the termination of employment, whether or not the employer paid for the seal, or to any other person" (GC 8207).

Seal Only for Official Use

"A notary public shall not use the official notarial seal except for the purpose of carrying out the duties and responsibilities as set forth in this chapter" (GC 8207).

Lost, Destroyed, Damaged Seals

"Any notary whose official seal is lost, misplaced, destroyed, broken, damaged, or is rendered otherwise unworkable shall immediately mail or deliver written notice of that fact to the Secretary of State. The Secretary of State, within five working days after receipt of the notice, if requested by a notary, shall issue a certificate of authorization which a notary may use to obtain a replacement seal" (GC 8207.3[e]). There is no fee for the certificate of authorization. For a stolen seal, a police report should be included, if possible (NPH).

County Change May Be Reflected in Seal

A Notary who transfers a principal place of business from one California county to another may choose to file a new bond, or a duplicate of the original bond, and a new oath in the new county. If this is done, the Notary must within 30 days obtain a new official seal bearing the name of the new county (GC 8213[b]).

Name Change Reflected in Seal

After a name change by the Notary and the resulting issuance by the Secretary of State of an amended commission reflecting the new name, and within 30 days after filing a new oath and amended bond with the county clerk, the Notary must obtain a seal bearing the new name (GC 8213[c]).

When Seal Must Be Surrendered to Court

"Upon conviction of any offense in this chapter, or of Section 6203, or of any felony, of a person commissioned as a notary public, in addition to any other penalty, the court shall revoke the commission of the notary public and shall require the notary public to surrender to the court the seal of the notary public. The court shall forward the seal, together with a certified copy of the judgment of conviction, to the Secretary of State" (GC 8214.8).

Seal Must Be Destroyed or Defaced

"The notary, or his or her representative, shall destroy or deface the seal upon termination, resignation, or revocation of the notary's commission" (GC 8207).

Notary Signature Must Be Original

All acknowledgments, depositions, affidavits, oaths, affirmations and copy certifications "shall be signed by the notary public in the notary public's own handwriting" (GC 8205[a][2] through [4]).

NOTARY POWERS

California Notaries are authorized to perform the following notarial acts:

1. Take acknowledgments and proofs* (GC 8205[a][2] and CC 1195[a][2]);
2. Administer oaths** and affirmations** (GC 8205[a][3]) ;
3. Take depositions and affidavits*** (GC 8205[a][3]);
4. Certify copies of powers of attorney (GC 8205[a][4] and Probate Code 4307[b][2]) or copies of entries in the Notary's own journal if ordered by the Secretary of State (GC 8205[b][1]) or by a court (GC 8206[e]);
5. Authorize confidential marriages, but only after screening and approval of the Notary by a local county clerk**** (Family Code 530[a]);
6. Demand acceptance and payment of foreign and inland bills of exchange, or promissory notes, and protest them for nonacceptance and nonpayment, "and, with regard only to the nonacceptance or nonpayment of bills and notes, to exercise any other powers and duties that by the law of nations and according to commercial usages, or by the laws of any other state, government, or country, may be performed by notaries"***** (GC 8205[a][1]).

* <u>Proofs of Execution by Subscribing Witness</u>: Just as proofs of execution by a subscribing witness have long been prohibited by law on grant deeds, mortgages, deeds of trust, quitclaim deeds, and security agreements, effective January 1, 2012, proofs of execution also become prohibited on powers of attorney and any instrument that requires the Notary to obtain a journal thumbprint from the signer of the document. Proofs are still allowed on trustee's deeds resulting from foreclosure and on deeds of reconveyance (GC 27287 and CC 1195[b]).

The subscribing witness must say under oath that he or she personally knows the principal; that he or she either saw the principal sign the document or took the principal's acknowledgment; and that he or she signed the document as a witness at the request of the principal. The subscribing witness must have been requested by the principal to get the document notarized (CC 1197, Code of Civil Proc. [CCP] 1935 and NPH).

The subscribing witness's identity must be proved to the Notary on the sworn or affirmed word of a credible witness. The credible witness must personally know the subscribing witness, must be personally known by the Notary and must present an acceptable identification document to the Notary (CC 1196 and NPH).

<u>Proof Through Handwriting</u>: In the event a subscribing witness and principal are dead, cannot be found, or refuse to appear, there are

procedures for a proof through handwriting (CC 1198-9).

** Wording for Oaths and Affirmations: "There is no prescribed wording for the oath, but an acceptable oath would be 'Do you swear or affirm that the statements in this document are true?' When administering the oath, the signer and notary public traditionally each raise their right hand but this is not a legal requirement" (NPH).

"An oath, affirmation, or declaration in an action or proceeding, may be administered by obtaining an affirmative response to one of the following questions:

"(1) 'Do you solemnly state that the evidence you shall give in this issue (or matter) shall be the truth, the whole truth, and nothing but the truth, so help you God?';

"(2) 'Do you solemnly state, under penalty of perjury, that the evidence that you shall give in this issue (or matter) shall be the truth, the whole truth, and nothing but the truth?'" (CCP 2094[a]).

*** Identifying Affiants: "When executing a jurat, a notary shall administer an oath or affirmation to the affiant and shall determine, from satisfactory evidence as described in Section 1185 of the Civil Code, that the affiant is the person executing the document. The affiant shall sign the document in the presence of the notary" (GC 8202[a]).

For the purposes of preparing for submission forms required by the U.S. Citizenship and Immigration Service, and only for such purposes, a Notary Public may also accept for identification any documents or declarations acceptable to the USCIS (GC 8230).

"If a notary public executes a jurat and the statement sworn or subscribed to is contained in a document purporting to identify the affiant, and includes the birthdate or age of the person and a purported photograph or finger or thumbprint of the person so swearing or subscribing, the notary public shall require, as a condition to executing the jurat, that the person verify the birthdate or age contained in the statement by showing either: (a) A certified copy of the person's birth certificate, or (b) An identification card or driver's license issued by the Department of Motor Vehicles" (GC 8230).

**** Authorizing Confidential Marriages: Citing Family Code, Section 503, the "Notary Public Handbook" says the following:

"A notary public who is interested in obtaining authorization to issue confidential marriage licenses may apply for approval to the county clerk in the county in which the notary public resides. A notary public must not issue a confidential marriage license unless he or she is approved by the county clerk having jurisdiction. The county clerk offers a course of instruction, which a notary public must complete before authorization will be granted. Additionally, in order for a notary public to perform the marriage, he/she must be one of the persons authorized under Family Code sections 400 to 402 (e.g., priest, minister, or rabbi). The county clerk in the county where the notary public resides may or may not approve the authorization to issue confidential marriage licenses. The county clerk should be consulted if the notary public is interested in obtaining approval" (NPH).

The fee for an application for approval to authorize confidential marriages is $300 (Family Code 536[a]). Authorization only applies in the one county.

The form that a Notary completes when notarizing a confidential marriage license is a jurat.

***** Protests: Effective January 1, 2012, only Notaries employed by a financial institution who perform protests in the course of their employment may perform this notarial act (GC 8205[a][1], GC 8208 and Commercial Code 3505[b]).

Identifying Document Signers

IMPORTANT NOTE: Separate pieces of legislation taking effect January 1, 2008, and January 1, 2009, collectively prohibit California Notaries from any longer relying solely on "personal knowledge" to identify document signers, credible witnesses or subscribing witnesses, and remove reference to personal knowledge from the statutory notarial certificates for an acknowledgment (CC 1189[a][1]) and a jurat (GC 8202[b]). Every principal signer may now be identified only through "satisfactory evidence," as defined below.

Further, every credible witness must now identify him- or herself to the Notary through presentation of an identification document prescribed by statute (see below), though only one credible witness is needed if that witness is personally known by the Notary.

Finally, a subscribing witness now may only be identified on the oath or affirmation of a credible witness who personally knows the subscribing witness, is personally known by the Notary, and presents an acceptable identification document to the Notary.

Satisfactory Evidence Defined: "The acknowledgment of an instrument shall not be taken unless the officer taking it has satisfactory evidence that the person making the acknowledgment is the individual who is described in and who executed the instrument" (CC 1185[a]). In executing a jurat, as well, the Notary must determine the identity of the affiant based on satisfactory evidence (GC 8202[a]).

Satisfactory evidence of identity "means the absence of any information, evidence, or other circumstances which would lead a reasonable person to believe that the person … is not the individual he or she claims to be and any one of the following" (CC 1185[b]):

1. The sworn word of one or two credible witnesses, identified through statutorily prescribed ID cards (below), that the signer does not have any of the IDs described below, that the witness personally knows the signer as the individual named in the document, that the witness does not have a financial interest and is not named in the document, and that the witness has a "reasonable belief … that the circumstances of the person ,,, are such that it would be very difficult or impossible for that person to obtain another form of identification" (CC 1185[b][1][A] and [b][2]; or

2. Reasonable reliance on a California driver's license or nondriver's ID or a U.S. passport, as long as they are current or issued within the past five years (CC 1185[b][3]); or

3. Reasonable reliance on any of the following IDs, as long as they contain a photograph, signature, and physical description of the bearer, and an identifying number, and they are current or issued in the past five years:

a. A U.S. state driver's license or official nondriver's ID; or

b. A Canadian or Mexican driver's license issued by an appropriate public agency; or

c. A U.S. military ID; or

d. A foreign passport, if it has been stamped by U.S. immigration authorities; or

e. An employee ID issued by an agency or office of the State of California, or by an agency or office of a city, county, or city and county, in California; or

f. An inmate ID issued by the California Department of Corrections, if the signer is in custody (CC 1185[b][4]).

Failure to Identify Witness: For the Notary's failure to obtain the required documentary evidence of identity of a credible witness, the Secretary of State or any prosecutor may sue to impose a civil penalty of $10,000 (CC 1185[b][1][B]).

Advance Health Care Directives

California's statutory "Advance Health Care Directive" must either be signed or acknowledged in the presence of a Notary or in the presence of two witnesses. If the signer is a patient in a skilled nursing facility, a patient advocate or ombudsman must sign either as one of the two required witnesses or in addition to the notarization (Probate Code 4675 and 4701).

Foreign-Language Documents

"A notary public can notarize a signature on a document in a foreign language with which the notary public is not familiar, since a notary public's function only relates to the signature and not the contents of the document. The notary public should be able to identify the type of document being notarized for entry in the notary public's journal. If unable to identify the type of document, the notary public must make an entry to that effect in the journal (e.g., 'a document in a foreign language'). The notary public should be mindful of the completeness of the document and must not notarize the signature on the document if the document appears to be incomplete. The notary public is responsible for completing the acknowledgment or jurat form" (NPH).

Signature by Mark

Statute prescribes no special notarial certificates for signings by mark, since a mark is considered a signature. However, notarization of a mark requires two witnesses, one of whom must write the principal's name near the mark and both of whom must sign their own names to the document (CCP 17[a] and GC 16).

"A notary public is not required to identify the two persons who witnessed the signing by mark or to have the two witnesses sign the notary's journal. Exception: If the witnesses were acting in the capacity of credible witnesses in establishing the identity of the person signing by mark, then the witnesses' signatures should be entered in the notary's journal" (NPH).

In addition to the Notary's certificate, the "California Recorders' Document Reference Manual" has recommended that the following or substantially similar wording appear on any recorded document that has been signed by mark:

_____ *(name), being unable to write, made his/her mark in our presence and requested the first of the undersigned to write his/her name, which he/she did, and we now subscribe our names as witnesses thereto.*

Witnesses

_____

_____

Homeowners Association Elections

A California Notary Public has been designated as one of the officers, including any volunteer poll worker with a county registrar of voters and any licensee of the California Board of Accountancy, who may act as an "independent third party" (ITP) to inspect an election in a "common interest development" (an incorporated or unincorporated homeowners association) (CC 1363.03[c][2]).

NOTARY DON'TS

According to statute, California's "Notary Public Handbook" and other directives of the Secretary of State, Notaries may:

1. NOT notarize their own signatures (GC 8224.1);
2. NOT use the title "Notary Public," nor the seal, except for lawful notarial duties (GC 8207);
3. NOT use the term Notario Publico or other non-English equivalents, nor advertise in a foreign language without, in both languages, posting the statutory fees and the statement: "I am not an attorney and, therefore, cannot give legal advice about immigration or any other legal matters" (GC 8219.5[a] and [c]);
4. NOT advertise as a Notary while holding him- or herself out as an immigration expert (GC 8223[a]);
5. NOT enter data on immigration forms unless the Notary is an attorney or a qualified and bonded immigration consultant (GC 8223[b] and [c] and Business and Professions Code 22440-22447);
6. NOT refuse to notarize in any lawful transaction upon payment of the fees allowed by law, whether or not the signer is a customer* (GC 6110);
7. NOT use an interpreter to communicate with a signer** (NPH).

* 'Business Purposes Only' Refusals: Notaries may enter into an agreement with an employer who has paid their notarial fees and for their supplies whereby the Notary's services are limited "solely to transactions directly associated with the business purposes of the employer" (GC 8202.8). According to state officials, this only permits the Notary, during business hours, to refuse to notarize signatures on documents in which the employer is not named or acting as an agent. It does not permit the Notary to refuse to notarize for noncustomers.

** Direct Communication Required: "When notarizing a signature on a document, a notary public must be able to communicate with their customer in order for the signer to either swear to or affirm the contents of an affidavit or to acknowledge the execution of the document. An interpreter should not be used, as vital information could be lost in the translation .... [T]he customer should be referred to a notary who speaks the customer's language" (NPH).

Incomplete Documents

"If presented with a document for notarization, which the notary public knows from his or her experience to be incomplete or is without doubt on its face incomplete, the notary public must refuse to notarize the document" (NPH). See also GC 8205(a)(2).

Disqualifying Interests

A Notary who has a direct financial or beneficial interest in a transaction must not notarize in connection with that transaction. A Notary is considered to have a disqualifying interest if that Notary: (a) with respect to a financial transaction, is named individually as a principal; or (b) with respect to a real-property transaction, is named individually as a grantor, grantee, mortgagor, mortgagee, trustor, trustee, beneficiary, vendor, vendee, lessor or lessee (GC 8224).

Exceptions: A Notary who is an agent, employee, insurer, attorney, escrow officer or lender for a person with a financial or beneficial interest may notarize in transactions involving the client or employer (GC 8224).

Relatives: "A notary public is not prohibited from notarizing for relatives or others, unless doing so would provide a direct financial or beneficial interest to the notary public. With California's community property law, care should be exercised if notarizing for a spouse or a domestic partner" (NPH).

False Acknowledgment Form Is Forgery

A law effective January 1, 2006, makes a Notary guilty of the crime of forgery if he or she issues an acknowledgment certificate knowing it to be false. Any person who falsifies the acknowledgment of a Notary is also guilty of forgery (Penal Code 470[d]). Forgery is punishable by imprisonment in the state prison, or by imprisonment in the county jail, for not more than one year (Penal Code 470a).

False certification by a Notary is also a misdemeanor under GC 6203[a].

NOTARY SIGNING AGENTS

Currently, there are no statutes, regulations or rules expressly governing, prohibiting or restricting the operation of Notary Signing Agents within the state of California.

NOTARY FEES

The maximum fees that a California Notary may charge for a notarial act are:
1. Notarizing a signature, either by acknowledgment, proof or jurat: $10 per signature of principal (GC 8211[a] and [b]);
2. Administering an oath or affirmation, apart from a jurat: $10 per person (GC 8211[b]);
3. For all services rendered in connection with taking a deposition: $20, plus $5 for the oath and $5 for the certificate (GC 8211[c]);
4. For certifying a copy of a power of attorney, $10 (GC 8211[e]);
5, For a photocopy of a journal entry: $0.30 (GC 8206[c]).

Protest Fees No Longer Allowed

Effective January 1, 2012, Notaries may no longer charge a fee for any notarial service relating to a protest.

Notary Need Not Charge

"(A) notary public may decide to charge no fee or an amount that is less than the maximum amount prescribed by law. The charging of a fee and the amount of the fee charged is at the discretion of the notary public or the notary public's employer, provided it does not exceed the maximum fees" (NPH).

Travel Fees

"A notary is permitted to charge a fee, aside from the notarization fee, for traveling and other services completed as part of their notarial service, such as duplication of copies, provided that the customer is apprised of these charges in advance" (NN, 2000).

Military, Government Notaries

Notaries appointed for military bases may not charge for notarial services performed on the base (GC 8203.6).

Notaries appointed to act for certain public agencies under GC 8202.5 must charge for notarial services and remit the fee to the employing agency (GC 6100).

Immigration Fees

Nonattorney Notaries may not charge more than $10 for any services related to a set of immigration forms for one person, apart from the above notarial fees (GC 8223[b]).

No Fees for Voting Materials

"No fee may be charged to notarize signatures on vote by mail ballot identification envelopes or other voting materials" (GC 8211[d]).

No Fees for Veteran Claims

"In accordance with Section 6107, no fee may be charged to a United States military veteran for notarization of an application or a claim for a pension, allotment, allowance, compensation, insurance, or any other veteran's benefit" (GC 8211[f]).

No Fee for Circulator's Affidavit

Under Elections Code Section 8080, no fee may be charged by a Notary for verifying any nomination document or circulator's affidavit.

California

A–C

NOTARY CERTIFICATES

Effective January 1, 1993, only the so-called "all-purpose" certificate wording prescribed by California Civil Code Section 1189(a) may be used for any and every acknowledgment taken and filed in the state, regardless of the signer's representative capacity. Effective January 1, 2006, however, the all-purpose certificate wording may no longer be just "in substantially the following form" but must be in exactly the following form and no other, as prescribed by statute:

All-Purpose Acknowledgment (CC 1189[a][1]):

State of California   )

County of _____   )

On _____ (date) before me, _____ (here insert name and title of the notarizing officer), personally appeared _____, who proved to me on the basis of satisfactory evidence to be the person(s) whose name(s) is/are subscribed to the within instrument and acknowledged to me that he/she/they executed the same in his/her/ their authorized capacity(ies)*, and that by his/her/their signature(s) on the instrument the person(s), or the entity upon behalf of which the person(s) acted, executed the instrument.

I certify under PENALTY OF PERJURY under the laws of the State of California that the foregoing paragraph is true and correct.

WITNESS my hand and official seal.

Signature _____   (Notary Seal)

* Authorized Capacity: "The certificate of acknowledgment of an instrument executed on behalf of an incorporated or unincorporated entity by a duly authorized person in the form specified in Section 1189 shall be prima facie evidence that the instrument is the duly authorized act of the entity named in the instrument and shall be conclusive evidence thereof in favor of any good faith purchaser, lessee, or encumbrancer. 'Duly authorized person,' with respect to a domestic or foreign corporation, includes the president, vice president, secretary, and assistant secretary of the corporation" (CC 1190).

False Certificate: $10,000 Penalty

"A notary public who willfully states as true any material fact that he or she knows to be false shall be subject to a civil penalty not exceeding ten thousand dollars ($10,000). An action to impose a civil penalty under this subdivision may be brought by the Secretary of State in an administrative proceeding or any public prosecutor in superior court, and shall be enforced as a civil judgment. A public prosecutor shall inform the Secretary of any civil penalty imposed under this section" (CC 1189[a][2]). See also GC 8214.1(l).

If Document Will Be Filed out of State

"On documents to be filed in another state or jurisdiction of the United States, a California notary public may complete any acknowledgment form as may be required in that other state or jurisdiction on a document, provided the form does not require the notary to determine or certify that the signer holds a particular representative capacity or to make other determinations and certifications not allowed by California law" (CC 1189[c]).

Acknowledgments Taken outside California

"Any certificate of acknowledgment taken in another place shall be sufficient in this state if it is taken in accordance with the laws of the place where the acknowledgment is made" (CC 1189[b]).

Proof by Subscribing Witness (CC 1195[c]):

State of California   )
*   ) ss.*
County of _____   )

On _____ (date), before me, the undersigned, a Notary Public for the state, personally appeared _____ (name of subscribing witness), proved to me to be the person whose name is subscribed to the within instrument, as a witness thereto, on the oath of _____ (name of credible witness), a credible witness who is known to me and provided a satisfactory identifying document. _____ (name of subscribing witness), being by me duly sworn, said that he/she was present and saw/heard _____ (name[s] of principal[s]), the same person(s) described in and whose name(s) is/are subscribed to the within or attached instrument in his/her/their authorized capacity(ies) as (a) party(ies) thereto, execute or acknowledge executing the same, and that said affiant subscribed his/her name to the within or attached instrument as a witness at the request of _____ (name[s] of principal[s]).

WITNESS my hand and official seal.

Signature _____ (Notary Seal)

Acknowledgment before Commissioned Military Officer by Person Serving with U.S. Armed Forces (CC 1183.5):

On this the ____ day of _____, 20 ___, before me, _____, the undersigned officer, personally appeared _____, known to me (or satisfactorily proven) to be (a) serving in the armed forces of the United States, (b) a spouse of a person serving in the armed forces of the United States, or (c) a person serving with, employed by, or accompanying the armed forces of the United States and outside the Canal Zone, Puerto Rico, Guam and the Virgin Islands, and to be the person whose name is subscribed to the within instrument and acknowledged that he/she executed the same. And the undersigned does further certify that he/she is at the date of this certificate a commissioned officer of the armed forces of the United States having the general powers of a Notary Public under the provisions of Section 936 or 1044a of Title 10 of the United States Code (Public Law 90-632 and 101-510).

(SIGNATURE OF OFFICER, RANK, BRANCH OF SERVICE AND CAPACITY IN WHICH SIGNED)

Jurat (GC 8202[b]):

State of California   )
*   )**
County of _____   )

Subscribed and sworn to (or affirmed) before me on this ____ day of _____, 20 ___, by _____, proved to me on the basis of satisfactory evidence to be the person(s) who appeared before me.

Signature _____ (Notary Seal)

* Jurats performed by Notaries serving on military bases must include the name of the base as well as the state and county in which the act was performed (GC 8203.5).

Jurat Alternative

When California law requires a sworn statement (except for a deposition, an oath of office, or an oath required to be taken before an official other than a Notary), it may be signed on penalty of perjury in lieu of a Notary's jurat (CCP 2015.5). The format is as follows:

Within California (CCP 2015.5[a]):

I certify (or declare) under penalty of perjury that the foregoing is true and correct.

(SIGNATURE OF PRINCIPAL)

(DATE AND PLACE OF EXECUTION)

Within or without California (CCP 2015.5[b]):

I certify (or declare) under penalty of perjury under the laws of the State of California that the foregoing is true and correct.

(SIGNATURE OF PRINCIPAL)

(DATE OF EXECUTION)

Copy Certification – Power of Attorney (NPH):

State of California   )
*   ) ss.*
County of _____   )

I, _____ (name of notary), Notary Public, certify that on _____ (date), I examined the original power of attorney and the copy of the power of attorney. I further certify that the copy is a true and correct copy of the original power of attorney.

Signature _____ (Notary Seal)

ELECTRONIC NOTARIZATIONS

The state of California has not yet adopted statutes or regulations expressly and comprehensively establishing rules, definitions and procedures for electronic notarization.

Online Notarization Not Legal

The following appears in a "Customer Alert" on the Secretary of State's website:

"Online webcam notarization is invalid and illegal in the State of California.

"A private company claims to have the first online notarization website and has sent misleading information and made false claims to California notaries public concerning a new online notarization service. The web-based platform purports to allow a person to submit copies of identification over the Internet and to use a webcam in lieu of a personal appearance in front of a notary public. Appearance via webcam does not meet the requirements for notarization in California.

"California notaries public are authorized under current law to perform electronic notarizations as long as all the requirements for a traditional paper-based notarial act are met, including the use of a seal for all but two specific documents used in real estate transactions. California law requires a person to appear personally before a notary public to obtain notarial acts like acknowledgments or jurats. This means the party must be physically present before the notary public. A video image or other form of non-physical representation is not a personal appearance in front of a notary public under current state or federal laws. The technology solution offered by this private company does not comply with California law" (website, "Customer Alert – Online Notarization Services Are Not Legal in California").

Recognizes Notary's eSignature

California has adopted its own version of the Uniform Electronic Transactions Act (CC 1633.1 through 1633.17), including the following provision recognizing the legal validity of electronic signatures used by Notaries:

"(a) If law requires that a signature be notarized, the requirement is satisfied with respect to an electronic signature if an electronic record includes, in addition to the electronic signature to be notarized, the electronic signature of a notary public together with all other information required to be included in a notarization by other applicable law.

"(b) In a transaction, if a law requires that a statement be signed under penalty of perjury, the requirement is satisfied with respect to an electronic signature, if an electronic record includes, in addition to the electronic signature, all the information as to which the declaration pertains together with a declaration under penalty of perjury by the person who submits the electronic signature that the information is true and correct" (CC 1633.11).

Seal Substitute on Electronic Document

Under California's Electronic Recording Delivery Act (ERDA) of 2004, "(w)hen a signature is required to be accompanied by a notary's seal or stamp, that requirement is satisfied if the electronic signature of the notary contains all of the following:

"1. The name of the notary.

"2. The words 'Notary Public.'

"3. The name of the county where the bond and oath of office of the notary are filed.

"4. The sequential identification number assigned to the notary, if any.

"5. The sequential identification number assigned to the manufacturer or vendor of the notary's physical or electronic seal, if any" (GC 27391[e]).

<u>Certain Digital Documents Recordable</u>: Under the ERDA, certain digital electronic documents ("records") may be electronically recorded — reconveyances, substitutions of trustee and assignments of deed of trust — and thus these same documents may also be electronically notarized (GC 27397.5[a]).

"'Digital electronic record' means a record containing information that is created, generated, sent, communicated, received, or stored by electronic means, but not created in original paper form" (GC 27390[b][3]).

Electronic Records

"If a law requires that a record be retained, the requirement is satisfied by retaining an electronic record of the information with the record, if the electronic record reflects accurately the information set forth in the record at the time it was first generated in its final form as an electronic record or otherwise, and the electronic record remains accessible for later reference" (CC 1633.12[a]).

Electronic Health Care Directives

An advance health care directive or power of attorney for health care may be in electronic form if its electronic signature is acknowledged before a Notary Public (Probate Code 4673[b]).

If a digital signature is used, either it must meet the requirements of Government Code Section 16.5 and the California Code of Regulations (CCR), Title 2, Division 7, Chapter 10, Sections 22000 to 22005, or it must employ an algorithm approved by the National Institute of Standards and Technology.

To meet these requirements, the digital signature must (a) be unique to the person using it, (b) be capable of verification, (c) be under the sole control of the person using it, (d) be linked to data in such a manner that if the data are changed, the signature is invalidated, (e) exist with the document and not by association in separate files and (f) be bound to a digital certificate (GC 16.5 and 2 CCR 22000 through 22005).

Acceptable Technologies

"Public key cryptography" and "signature dynamics" are designated as acceptable technologies for public entities using electronic signatures (2 CCR 22003).

NOTARY RECORDS

Every California Notary must keep "one active sequential journal at a time, of all official acts performed as a notary public. The journal shall be kept in a locked and secured area, under the direct and exclusive control of the notary" (GC 8206[a][1]).

Required Entries

The entries must include (GC 8206[a]):

1. Date, time and type of each official act;
2. Character (type or title) of every document "sworn to, affirmed, acknowledged or proved before the notary";
3. Signature of each person whose signature is notarized, including the signature of any subscribing witness (NPH);
4. Statement regarding the type of satisfactory evidence* relied on to identify the signer;
5. Fee charged for the notarial act, or, if no fee was charged, "No Fee" or "0" (NPH);
6. If document is a deed, quitclaim deed or deed of trust affecting real property, or a power of attorney document, the right thumbprint** (or any other available print) of the signer.

* Satisfactory Evidence: "If identity was established by satisfactory evidence pursuant to Section 1185 of the Civil Code, the journal shall contain the signature of the credible witness swearing or affirming to the identity of the individual or the type of identifying document, the government agency issuing the document, the serial or identifying number of the document, and the date of issue or expiration of the document.... If the identity of the person ,,, was established by the oaths or affirmations of two credible witnesses whose identities are proven to the notary public by presentation of any (acceptable identifying) document, the notary public shall record in the journal the types of documents identifying the witnesses, the identifying numbers on the documents identifying the witnesses, and the dates of issuance or expiration of the documents identifying the witnesses" (GC 8206[a][2][D] and [E]).

** Thumbprint Requirement: The need for a journal thumbprint for powers of attorney and certain types of deeds became effective January 1, 1996. The requirement does not, however, apply to a deed of reconveyance or a trustee's deed resulting from a decree of foreclosure or a nonjudicial foreclosure pursuant to Civil Code Section 2924 (GC 8206[a][2][G]). From January 1, 1993, to December 31, 1995, this thumbprint requirement only applied to property in Los Angeles County.

For the Notary's failure to obtain a journal thumbprint as required, a civil fine of up to $2,500 may be imposed by the Secretary of State or any public prosecutor (GC 8214.23[a]).

Inspection, Copying of Journal

"Upon written request of any member of the public, which request shall include the name of the parties, the type of document, and the month and year in which notarized, the notary shall supply a photostatic copy of the line item representing the requested transaction at a cost of not more than thirty cents ($0.30) per page" (GC 8206[c]).

"Upon receiving a request for a copy of a transaction pursuant to subdivision (c) of Section 8206, the notary shall respond to the request within 15 business days after receipt of the request and either supply the photostatic copy requested or acknowledge that no such line item exists. In a disciplinary proceeding for noncompliance with subdivision (c) of Section 8206 or this section, a notary may defend his or her delayed action on the basis of unavoidable, exigent business or personal circumstances" (GC 8206.5).

Inspection by Employer: "A notary public who is an employee shall permit inspection and copying of journal transactions by a duly designated auditor or agent of the notary public's employer, provided that the inspection and copying is done in the presence of the notary public and the transactions are directly associated with the business purposes of the employer. The notary public, upon the request of the employer, shall regularly provide copies of all transactions that are directly associated with the business purposes of the employer, but shall not be required to provide copies of any transaction that is unrelated to the employer's business. Confidentiality and safekeeping of any copies of the journal provided to the employer shall be the responsibility of that employer" (GC 8206[d]).

Inspection by Government Order: "The notary public shall provide the journal for examination and copying in the presence of the notary public upon receipt of a subpoena duces tecum or a court order, and shall certify those copies if requested" (GC 8206[e]).

A Notary must furnish certified copies of the Notary's journal upon written request from the Secretary of State (GC 8205[b][1]). A Notary must respond within 30 days to any written request, sent by certified mail from the Secretary of State, for information relating to the Notary's official acts (GC 8205[b][2]).

"The Secretary of State or a peace officer, as defined in Sections 830.1, 830.2, and 830.3 of the Penal Code, possessing reasonable suspicion and acting in his or her official capacity and within his or her authority, may enforce the provisions of this chapter through the examination of a notary public's books, records, letters, contracts, and other pertinent documents relating to the official acts of the notary public" (GC 8228).

Electronic Records

"If a law requires that a record be retained, the requirement is satisfied by retaining an electronic record of the information with the record, if the electronic record reflects accurately the information set forth in the record at the time it was first generated in its final form as an electronic record or otherwise, and the electronic record remains accessible for later reference" (CC 1633.12[a]).

Rules for Surrender of Journal

"The journal of notarial acts of a notary public is the exclusive property of that notary public, and shall not be surrendered to an employer upon termination of employment, whether or not the employer paid for the journal, or at any other time. The notary public shall not surrender the journal to any other person, except the county clerk, pursuant to Section 8209, or immediately, or if the journal is not present then as soon as possible, upon request to a peace officer investigating a criminal offense who has reasonable suspicion to believe the journal contains evidence of a criminal offense, as defined in Sections 830.1, 830.2, and 830.3 of the Penal Code, acting in his or her official capacity and within his or her authority. If the peace officer seizes the notary journal, he or she must have probable cause as required by the laws of this state and the United States. A peace officer or law enforcement agency that seizes the journal shall notify the Secretary of State by facsimile within 24 hours, or as soon as possible thereafter, of the name of the notary public whose journal has been seized. The notary public shall obtain a receipt for the journal, and shall notify the Secretary of State by certified mail within 10 days that the journal was relinquished to a peace officer. The notification shall include the period of the journal entries, the commission number of the notary public, the expiration date of the commission, and a photocopy of the receipt. The notary public shall obtain a new sequential journal. If the journal relinquished to a peace officer is returned to the notary public and a new journal has been obtained, the notary public shall make no new entries in the returned journal" (GC 8206[d]).

Willful failure to provide access to the journal upon request by a peace officer may be grounds for denying, revoking or suspending a Notary commission (GC 8214.1[r]). In addition, for such failure to provide access to the journal a civil fine of up to $2,500 may be imposed by the Secretary of State or any public prosecutor (GC 8214.21).

Lost, Stolen, Damaged Journal

"If a sequential journal of official acts performed by a notary public is stolen, lost, misplaced, destroyed, damaged, or otherwise rendered unusable as a record of notarial acts and information, the notary public shall immediately notify the Secretary of State by certified or registered mail. The notification shall include the period of the journal entries, the notary public commission number, and the expiration date of the commission, and when applicable, a photocopy of any police report that specifies the theft of the sequential journal of official acts" (GC 8206[b]).

Improper Maintenance of Journal

A law taking effect January 1, 2006, clarifies that a person who solicits, coerces or influences a Notary to improperly maintain the Notary's journal is guilty of a misdemeanor (GC 8225[a]).

Another law taking effect that same date states that a "notary public who willfully fails to perform any duty required of a notary public under Section 8206 ... shall be guilty of a misdemeanor" (GC 8228.1[a]). This section of the Government Code covers requirements related to the Notary's journal. The misdemeanor penalty therefore applies if the Notary willfully fails to do any of the following: properly maintain, secure or retain the journal; notify the Secretary of State if the journal is lost, stolen, rendered unusable or surrendered to a peace officer; or permit a lawful inspection or copying of the journal (GC 8206[a] through [e]). See also GC 8214.1(o).

Destroying, Defacing, Concealing Journal: To "knowingly destroy, deface, or conceal" notarial records is a misdemeanor and carries potential civil liability (GC 8221[a]).

Custodian of Notary Journals

If a Notary resigns, is removed from office, or allows his or her commission to expire without recommissioning within 30 days, that individual must surrender all notarial journals to the clerk of the county in which the Notary's oath of office is filed. For failure to deliver these records within 30 days, the Notary is guilty of a misdemeanor and personally liable for any resulting damages (GC 8209[a]).

"In case of the death of a notary public, the personal representative of the deceased shall promptly notify the Secretary of State of the death of the notary public and shall deliver all notarial records and papers of the deceased to the clerk of the county in which the notary public's official oath of office is on file" (GC 8209[b]).

Ten years after deposit of any journal(s), if no request has been made for the records, the clerk may destroy the journal(s) upon court order (GC 8209[c]).

AUTHENTICATION OF NOTARIAL ACTS

County Clerk Offices

Locally, authenticating certificates for Notaries may be obtained at the office of the county clerk where the Notary has filed an oath and bond. This is the county named in the Notary's seal.

Secretary of State

Authenticating certificates for California Notaries and public officials, including apostilles, are issued by the Notary Public Section of the Secretary of State's office (website, "Apostille or Certification").

Fee: $20 per document, for an authenticating certificate for a Notary or county clerk or for an apostille. For walk-in requests, add $6 for each different signature requiring authentication. When submitting by mail, payment may be made by check or money order, payable to "Secretary of State." When submitting in person, credit cards also may be used. Cash is accepted only for walk-in requests at the Sacramento office (website, "Apostille or Certification").

Mailing:
Office of Secretary of State
Notary Public Section
P.O. Box 942877
Sacramento, CA 94277-0001

In Person (Main Office):
Office of Secretary of State
Notary Public Section
1500 11th St., 2nd Floor
Sacramento, CA 95814

Telephone: 1-916-653-3595

In Person (Regional Office):
Office of Secretary of State
Los Angeles Office
300 South Spring St., Room 12513
South Tower, 12th Floor
Los Angeles, CA 90013

Telephone: 1-213-897-3062

Procedure: Requests may be submitted by mail only to the Sacramento office, or in person at either the Sacramento or the Los Angeles office. Mail or present in person the original notarized document(s) or the certified copy from the county clerk and the appropriate fee, indicating the country of destination. When mailing, include an addressed return envelope and allow approximately three to five business days after receipt of the request in the Sacramento office for processing of the request.

NOTE: The Los Angeles office authenticates only signatures of public officials other than Notaries. The signature of a Notary Public must be authenticated by the Notary's local county clerk before submission for authentication at the Los Angeles office (website, "Apostille or Certification").

Online Verification of Apostilles: Apostilles issued by the California Secretary of State on or after October 1, 2006, may be electronically verified on the Secretary's website (website, "Verification of Apostilles").

COMMISSIONING AND ADMINISTRATION

The California Secretary of State appoints, commissions, regulates and maintains records on the state's Notaries (GC 8200). "Information on (the) form filed by an applicant with the Secretary of State, except for his or her name and address, is confidential ..." (GC 8201.5).

Applying for Commission

Qualifications: An applicant for a commission as a California Notary Public: (a) must be at least 18 years old, and (b) must be a legal resident of California, unless he or she is commissioned to notarize on a military base on recommendation of the commanding officer, in which case the applicant must be a U.S. citizen (GC 8201[a][1] and [2], 8203.1 and 8203.2). Applicants also must pass a background check by both the FBI and the California Department of Justice, including submission of fingerprints (GC 8201.1[a] through [d]). "Applicants found to be non-compliant with child or family support orders will be issued temporary term notary public commissions. Notaries public found to be non-compliant after the commission is issued may be subject to commission suspension or revocation" (website, "Qualifications"). See also Family Code 17520.

Course and Exam Required: For all commissions issued on or after July 1, 2005, applicants must take an approved six-hour course of study at least once. Applicants for recommissioning must take a three-hour refresher course (GC 8201[a][3] and [b][2]). To qualify for the three-hour course, renewing Notaries must submit an application before the current commission expires; otherwise the six-hour course must be taken again. Upon completing the required course, applicants will receive a "Proof of Completion" certificate. A list of approved Notary education vendors is available on the Secretary of State's website (website, "Complete Approved Education").

After taking the course, the applicant must pass a proctored written examination, based on the "Notary Public Handbook" (GC 8201[a][4]). The "Handbook" and additional study materials for the exam are available on the Secretary of State's website. Some education vendors offer the exam at the end of their seminar-style courses. A passing score is 70% (website, "Register for the Exam" and "Take the Exam").

The state-contracted proctor for each exam is Cooperative Personnel Services (CPS); registration for the exam with CPS can be made online or by calling (916) 263-3520. Results will be available about 15 business days after the exam date. CPS will email exam results to the applicant, if an email address was provided in the application; otherwise, results will be sent by regular mail. Exam results will not be discussed over the phone (website, "Register for the Exam" and "Take the Exam").

Applicants must bring the following items to the exam site: (a) current photo identification (e.g., driver's license), (b) a completed application form, including a 2-by-2-inch color passport photo of the applicant attached to the back of the form, (c) the "Proof of Completion" certificate for the course, (d) the registration confirmation letter and (e) the $40 testing and application fee (or $20 for persons taking the exam over), payable to the "Secretary of State" (GC 8201[b] and 8201.5; website, "Take the Exam").

Application: Applicants who pass the exam will have their applications sent to the Secretary of State for processing (website, "Take the Exam").

Applicants then will be sent information about providing a full set of fingerprints at an electronic "LiveScan" site. The prints will be submitted to the California Department of Justice (processing cost $32) and to the FBI (cost $19) for a criminal background check on the applicant. Electronic fingerprinting is required of all first-time and renewing applicants. Prints must be taken within one year of the exam, or retesting will be required. The following items must be brought to the LiveScan site: (a) current photo identification, (b) a completed LiveScan form, downloadable on the Secretary of State's website, and (c) the fingerprint processing fees and an additional "rolling fee," which may vary from site to site (GC 8201.1[f]; website, "Qualifications" and "Submit Fingerprints via LiveScan").

Upon commissioning, a packet will be mailed to the Notary that includes: (a) a cover letter and instructions on how to proceed, (b) the commission certificate, (c) two "Notary Public Oath and Certificate Filing" forms, (d) a "Certificate of Authorization to Manufacture Notary Public Seals," and (e) a list of authorized seal manufacturers (website, "Await Commission Packet").

Filing Oath, Bond with County Clerk: The new Notary has 30 days to take an oath of office before, and file the oath and a $15,000 surety bond with, the clerk of the county in which the Notary maintains a principal place of business. Alternatively, the oath may be taken before a Notary in that county, and the oath and bond then are filed with the county clerk within 30 days by certified mail. A copy of the oath is then sent to the Secretary of State, with the original retained by the county clerk for at least one year after commission expiration. The bond is sent to the county recorder for recording, after which it is mailed back to the Notary (GC 8212 and 8213[a] and [e]).

If the applicant fails to file the oath and bond within the prescribed time, the applicant must reapply. New and renewing Notaries who completed an approved six-hour course of study and passed the exam must attach a current "Proof of Completion" certificate and the required photo to a new application and submit them, along with a check for $20, to the Secretary of State. Because the commission has expired, renewing Notaries who completed a three-hour refresher course must re-take the six-hour course and exam. They must submit a new "Proof of Completion" certificate for the six-hour course, a new application, the required photo and the $20 fee. In all cases, the applicant will need to have his or her fingerprints retaken at a LiveScan site (NPH).

Non-Residents: A non-resident of California may not become a Notary in the state.

Online Search: By clicking "Online Notary Public Listing" on the website, anyone can download a list of Notaries who hold active commissions in California. The active-Notary file is updated daily and includes: (a) Notary's full name and suffix, if any; (b) name of the Notary's employer, if any; (c) Notary's mailing address; (d) county in which the Notary's oath and bond are filed; and (e) commission number and expiration date.

Changes of Status

If Notary Moves: Notaries who move their business, residence and/or mailing address must inform the Secretary of State by certified mail within 30 days of the move. "Willful failure to notify the Secretary of State of a change of address shall be punishable as an infraction by a fine of not more than five hundred dollars ($500)" (GC 8213.5). A letter or the Secretary's change of address form, available on the website, may be used (NPH).

Because California Notaries have statewide jurisdiction, Notaries who move from one county to another need not refile their oath and bond in the new county. If they choose to do so, however, within 30 days of the filing they must obtain a new seal bearing the name of the new county (GC 8213[b]).

If Notary Changes Name: If a Notary changes his or her name, a "Notary Public Name Change" form must be filed with the Secretary of State, who will issue an amended commission. Willful failure to do so may result in a fine of $500 (GC 8213.6). Within 30 days after issuance of the amended commission, the Notary must file a new oath of office and a bond amendment with the clerk of the county in which the Notary's principal place of business is located, Within 30 days after the filing, the Notary must obtain a seal with the new name (GC 8213[c]).

If Notary Resigns: "If you want to resign your commission, send a letter of resignation to the Secretary of State's office; within 30 days deliver all of your notarial journals, records and papers to the county clerk in which your current oath of office is on file; and destroy the seal" (NPH).

California

COUNTY CLERKS

To contact a California county clerk to obtain an authenticating certificate for a Notary, or to seek assistance in locating a Notary, telephone long-distance information — 1-XXX-555-1212, and ask for the phone number of the clerk for the appropriate county.

County	City/Town	Area Code
Alameda	Oakland	(510)
Alpine	Markleeville	(530)
Amador	Jackson	(209)
Butte	Oroville	(530)
Calaveras	San Andreas	(209)
Colusa	Colusa	(530)
Contra Costa	Martinez	(925)
Del Norte	Crescent City	(707)
El Dorado	Placerville	(530)
	So. Lake Tahoe	(530)
Fresno	Fresno	(559)
Glenn	Willows	(530)
Humboldt	Eureka	(707)
Imperial	El Centro	(760)
Inyo	Independence	(760)
Kern	Bakersfield	(661)
Kings	Hanford	(559)
Lake	Lakeport	(707)
Lassen	Susanville	(530)
Los Angeles	Los Angeles	(310)
	Lancaster	(661)
	Norwalk	(562)
	Van Nuys	(818)
Madera	Madera	(559)
Marin	San Rafael	(415)
Mariposa	Mariposa	(209)
Mendocino	Ukiah	(707)
Merced	Merced	(209)
Modoc	Alturas	(530)
Mono	Bridgeport	(760)
Monterey	Salinas	(831)
Napa	Napa	(707)
Nevada	Nevada City	(530)
Orange	Santa Ana	(714)
Placer	Auburn	(530)
Plumas	Quincy	(530)
Riverside	Riverside	(951)
Sacramento	Sacramento	(916)
San Benito	Hollister	(831)
San Bernardino	San Bernardino	(909)
San Diego	San Diego	(619)
	Chula Vista	(619)
	El Cajon	(619)
	Kearny Mesa	(858)
	San Marcos	(760)
San Francisco	San Francisco	(415)
San Joaquin	Stockton	(209)
San Luis Obispo	San Luis Obispo	(805)
San Mateo	Redwood City	(650)
Santa Barbara	Santa Barbara	(805)
	Lompoc	(805)
	Santa Maria	(805)
Santa Clara	San Jose	(408)
Santa Cruz	Santa Cruz	(831)
Shasta	Redding	(530)
Sierra	Downieville	(530)
Siskiyou	Yreka	(530)
Solano	Fairfield	(707)
Sonoma	Santa Rosa	(707)
Stanislaus	Modesto	(209)
Sutter	Yuba City	(530)
Tehama	Red Bluff	(530)
Trinity	Weaverville	(530)
Tulare	Visalia	(559)
Tuolumne	Sonora	(209)
Ventura	Ventura	(805)
Yolo	Woodland	(530)
Yuba	Marysville	(530)

OTHER NOTARIAL OFFICERS

Statewide Jurisdiction

Besides Notaries Public, the following officers have statewide power to take acknowledgments and proofs (CC 1180):
1. A judge or retired judge of a superior court;
2. A justice, retired justice or clerk of any court of appeal;
3. A justice, retired justice or clerk of the state Supreme Court;
4. The secretary of the California Senate and the chief clerk of the Assembly.

Certified shorthand reporters who are not Notaries may administer oaths and affirmations for depositions and charge a fee (CCP 2093[b]).

Limited Jurisdiction

Within the jurisdiction for which they are elected or appointed, the following officials may take acknowledgments and proofs (CC 1181):

1. A retired judge of a municipal or justice court;
2. A clerk of a superior court;
3. A county clerk or counsel;
4. A city clerk or attorney;
5. A court commissioner;
6. A district attorney;
7. A clerk of a board of supervisors;
8. The secretary of the California Senate and the chief clerk of the Assembly.

Deputies

When any of the above officials are authorized by law to appoint a deputy, the acknowledgment or proof may be taken by the deputy in the name of the principal (CC 1184).

Seal

Officers taking acknowledgments or proofs must affix their signature and seal (if they are required by law to have one) and state the name of their office (CC 1193). Court officials must use a seal in authenticating their acts (GC 68074), as must county clerks (GC 26807).

QUICK FACTS

Notary Jurisdiction
Statewide (GC 8200). However, federal civil servants commissioned to serve as Notaries on a U.S. military base in California may notarize only on that base (GC 8203.2 and 8203.3).

Notary Term Length
Four years (GC 8204). The commission of a Notary serving on a U.S. military base is terminated if the Notary ceases to be a federal civil-service employee on that base (GC 8203.4).

Notary Bond
$15,000, with a state-licensed surety company (GC 8212).

A–C

Colorado

NOTARY ADMINISTRATION

Office of Secretary of State
Business and Licensing Division
Notary Program   1-303-894-2200
1700 Broadway, Suite 200   Ext. 9500
Denver, CO 80290

Website: http://www.sos.state.co.us/
pubs/notary/notaryHome.html

NOTARY RULES

CRS — *Colorado Revised Statutes*
CCR — *Code of Colorado Regulations*
NH — *Notary Handbook*

Most Notary rules are in the Colorado Revised Statutes, Title 12, Article 55 ("Notaries Public"):

a. Part 1, "General Provisions" also known as the "Notaries Public Act";

b. Part 2, "Uniform Recognition of Acknowledgments Act."*

 * This is the *Uniform Recognition of Acknowledgments Act* of 1968, adopted virtually intact.

Many guidelines for eNotarization are in the Code of Colorado Regulations' "Rules Concerning Electronic Notarization" (8 CCR 1505-11).

Other guidelines for Notaries are in the "Notary Handbook" (Revised Aug. 10, 2011) issued by the Secretary of State and available on the website.

NOTARY SEAL

A Colorado Notary must affix an official seal on every notarial certificate, and the seal's format must be as follows (CRS 12-55-112):

Kind

<u>Inked Rubber Stamp or Embosser</u>: "Under or near such notary's official signature on every notary certificate, a notary public shall rubber stamp or emboss clearly and legibly such notary's official seal .... The indentations made by the seal embosser shall not be applied on the document where the notary certificate appears in a manner that will render illegible or incapable of photographic reproduction any of the printed marks or writing" (CRS 12-55-112).

<u>Electronic Signature Replaces Seal</u>: "In the case of notarization of an electronic record, the application of a notary's electronic signature in lieu of a handwritten signature and rubber stamp seal or seal embosser is sufficient" (CRS 12-55-112[4.5]).

Size/Shape

Not specified. "Colorado law does not have any size, shape, or color of ink restrictions for notary seals ... Also, the law has no preference for one type of seal over the other" (NH, "Notarial Certificate or Notarization").

Examples

Above are actual-size examples of typical Notary seals allowed by Colorado law. Formats other than these may also be permitted.

Components

Only the following components are authorized:
1. Outline or border of seal;
2. Name of Notary, exactly as in official signature;
3. "Notary Public";
4. "State of Colorado".

NOTE: "The notary's commission expiration date, if included on the seal, must be placed outside the outline" (website, "Frequently Asked Questions").

Commission Expiration Date Must Appear

"Under or near such notary's official signature on every notary certificate, a notary public shall write or stamp 'my commission expires (commission expiration date)'" (CRS 12-55-112[3]).

"Your commission expiration date is not required to be on your notary stamp/seal. You may hand-write your commission expiration date in your notarizations or order a separate stamp for the date" (NH, "Colorado Notary Seals, Stamps and Journals").

Illegibility

"The illegibility of any of the information required by this section does not affect the validity of a document or transaction" (CRS 12-55-112[5]).

Avoid Stamping over Signature, Text: "Do not stamp or emboss the seal over signatures and avoid stamping or embossing over text" (website, "Frequently Asked Questions").

Obtaining a Seal

In order to obtain a Notary seal or stamp, or a journal, the Notary's commission certificate must be presented to the office supplier (website, "Notary E-File Instructions").

Lost Seal

"Every notary public shall send or have delivered notice to the secretary of state within thirty days after the notary loses or misplaces such notary's journal of notarial acts, or official seal, or the notary becomes aware that any other person has electronic control of his or her electronic signature" (CRS 12-55-113).

Wrongful Possession

"Any person who unlawfully possesses and uses a notary's journal, an official seal, a notary's electronic signature, or any papers, copies, or electronic records relating to notarial acts is guilty of a class 3 misdemeanor" (CRS 12-55-118).

Death, Resignation, Revocation, Moving

For disposition of the Notary's seal and journal when the Notary dies, resigns, has the commission revoked or moves from the state, see "Death, Resignation, Revocation, Move" under "Changes of Status," near the end of this chapter.

Notary's Signature

"At the time of notarization, a notary public shall sign such notary's official signature on every notary certificate or in the case of an electronic record, a notary public shall affix his or her electronic signature" (CRS 12-55-112[1]).

NOTARY POWERS

Colorado Notaries are authorized to perform the following notarial acts (CRS 12-55-102[1] and 110[1]):
1. Take acknowledgments* and proofs**;
2. Administer oaths and affirmations***;
3. Certify true copies****;
4. Take depositions and affidavits, including circulator's***** affidavits;
5. "Perform any other act permitted by law," including protests and notices of dishonor (CRS 4-3-501 through 506).

* Performing an Acknowledgment: "The person taking an acknowledgment shall certify that: (a) The person acknowledging appeared before him and acknowledged he executed the instrument; and (b) The person acknowledging was known to the person taking the acknowledgment or that the person taking the acknowledgment had satisfactory evidence that the person acknowledging was the person described in and who executed the instrument" (CRS 12-55-205).

"In an acknowledgment, the notary is guaranteeing that, while the signer was in the notary's presence, the notary identified him or her, and that the signer appeared to be willing and able to execute the document. The notary also guarantees that s/he witnessed the 'execution' of the document, which is its completion by signing. Technically, most (documents) don't have to be signed in the notary's presence. However, the best practice would be to have the client sign

... in front of the notary" (website, "Frequently Asked Questions").

** Taking Proof of Execution: "(The Notary) shall examine such subscribing witness upon oath or affirmation, and shall reduce his testimony to writing and require the witness to subscribe the same, endorsed upon or attached to such deed or other writing, and shall thereupon grant a certificate that such witness was personally known or was proved to him by the testimony of at least one witness (who shall be named in such certificate) to be a subscribing witness to the deed or instrument of writing to be proved, that such subscribing witness was lawfully sworn and examined by him, and that the testimony of the said officer was reduced to writing and by said subscribing witness subscribed in his presence" (CRS 38-30-136).

*** Wording for Oaths/Affirmations: Colorado's "Notary Handbook" suggests the following wording for oaths and affirmations:

"Do you affirm (swear) under penalty of perjury that you are _____ (name of individual swearing or affirming) and that what you are about to say is true (so help you God)?"

"Do you affirm (swear) under penalty of perjury that you are _____ (name of individual swearing or affirming) and that you have read and understood _____ (document name) and that to the best of your knowledge and belief it is true (so help you God)?"

"Do you affirm (swear) under penalty of perjury that you are _____ (name of individual swearing or affirming) and that you have executed this _____ (type of document executed) and that it is your free act and deed (so help you God)?"

"A jurat is a signed statement by the notary stating that the signer (1) personally appeared before the notary, (2) signed the document in the presence of the notary, and (3) took an oath or affirmation administered by the notary, e.g. 'Do you swear that the statements in this document are true, so help you God?' or 'Do you affirm that the statements in this document are true?'" (NH, "Definitions").

**** Certified Copy Requested in Writing: "A notary public may certify a facsimile of a document if the original of the document is exhibited to him, together with a signed written request stating that:

"(a) A certified copy or facsimile of the document cannot be obtained from the office of any clerk and recorder of public documents or custodian of documents in this state; and

"(b) The production of a facsimile, preparation of a copy, or certification of a copy of the document does not violate any state or federal law" (CRS 12-55-120[1]).

As a notarial record, the Notary must retain not only the written request, but also one of the two copies made of the original document, per CRS 12-55-120(2) (NH, "Copy Certifications").

"Make sure the copies are 'complete, full, true, and exact facsimiles' of the original. A notary is responsible for the accuracy of the copies. The notary may make a manual comparison...but most notaries ensure accuracy by making the copies themselves" (NH, "Copy Certifications").

"Can a notary certify a birth, death, marriage, or divorce certificate? — No. The Clerk and Recorder of the county in which the documents were originally recorded must certify recorded documents regarding real property, marriages or divorces. In the case of divorce, the Clerk of the Court that issued the Decree of Dissolution of Marriage can provide a certified copy of the Order. The Vital Records section of the Colorado Department of Public Health and Environment is the only place you can get official copies of birth or death certificates" (website, "Notary Public FAQs").

"A Colorado notary public should not notarize documents issued and certified by a Colorado Public Official" (website, "Apostilles and Authentications").

***** Taking Circulator's Affidavits: In order to have an initiative placed on the Colorado ballot, circulators must obtain the necessary number of signatures of qualified electors and then have their own signature notarized in an affidavit that is attached to the petition. Proper notarization of a circulator's affidavit requires that: (a) the circulator appear in person before the Notary; (b) the circulator date and fully and accurately complete the affidavit with all required information; (c) the Notary, in addition to identifying the circulator in conformance with CRS 12-55-110, ensure that the circulator presents an approved form of identification with a residence address in Colorado as specified in CRS 1-1-104(19.5)(b); and (d) on a designated blank line on the affidavit form, the Notary specify the form of identification used to satisfy CRS 1-1-104(19.5)(b).

Acceptable identification under CRS 1-1-104(19.5) includes one of the following IDs, provided that the ID shows the address of the elector in the state of Colorado:

1. Colorado driver's license;
2. Identification card issued by the Colorado Department of Revenue;
3. U.S. passport;
4. Employee identification card with a photograph issued by any branch, department, agency or entity of the U.S. government or of Colorado, or by any county, municipality, board, authority or other political subdivision of Colorado;
5. Pilot's license issued by the Federal Aviation Administration or other authorized U.S. federal agency;
6. U.S. military identification card with photograph;
7. Copy of a current utility bill, bank statement, government check, paycheck or other government document that shows the name and address of the elector;
8. Medicare or Medicaid card issued by the U.S. Health Care Financing Administration;
9. Certified copy of a birth certificate for the elector issued in the United States;
10. Certified documentation of naturalization;
11. Student identification card with a photograph, issued by an institution of higher learning in Colorado.

As with any notarization, the Notary must first positively identify the circulator using personal knowledge or a form of satisfactory evidence — see "Identifying and Screening Signers" section immediately below.

The Notary should record the ID document satisfying CRS 12-55-110 in the journal and, as a best practice, record the document satisfying CRS 1-1-104(19.5)(b) in the additional information column of the journal.

If the notarization of the circulator's affidavit does not comply with the requirements of statute, the affidavit is invalid and must be rejected by the Secretary of State.

Identifying and Screening Signers

"No notary shall sign a certificate or other statements as to a notarial act to the effect that a document or any part thereof was attested by an individual, unless:

"(a) Such individual has attested such document or part thereof while in the physical presence of such notary; and

"(b) Such individual is personally known to such notary as the person named in the certificate, statement, document, or part thereof, or such notary receives satisfactory evidence that such individual is the person so named. For purposes of this paragraph (b), "Satisfactory evidence" includes but is not limited to the sworn statement of a credible witness who personally knows such notary and the individual so named, or a current identification card or document issued by a federal or state governmental entity containing a photograph and signature of the individual who is so named" (CRS 12-55-110[4]).

Personal Knowledge of Identity: "Personal knowledge of the client… is generally the best identification a notary can have for any type of transaction" (NH, "Acknowledgments").

Assessing Competence: "Assess the client's competence and understanding of the document. Again, a wise notary does not do any type of notarization for a client who is obviously not competent. However, a notary has a little more responsibility for this assessment of acknowledgments than on other types of notarization.

"If a client is, for example, obviously drunk or drugged or otherwise disoriented, or too ill to communicate or know what is happening, or too young to understand the transaction at all, a notary should not take the client's acknowledgment. Such a client cannot meaningfully acknowledge a document or execute it as his/her own act and deed.

"This assessment can be made in the course of a brief discussion of the transaction …" (NH, "Acknowledgments").

"A notary should be certain that all parties understand what they are signing and swearing or affirming to" (NH, "Definitions").

No Duress Permitted: "Be satisfied that the client is not under duress or being coerced to make the acknowledgment. Acknowledgments must be voluntary. They must be the 'free acts and deeds' of the client" (NH, "Acknowledgments").

Foreign-Language Documents

"If the country to which the document is going requires a foreign language notarization, the notary is free to do so. However, the notary must also notarize the same document in English" (website, "Common Mistakes to Avoid").

Accommodating Signer's Physical Limits

"(1) A notary public may certify as to the subscription or signature of an individual when it appears that such individual has a physical limitation that restricts such individual's ability to sign by writing or making a mark, pursuant to the following:

"(a) The name of an individual may be signed, or attached electronically in the case of an electronic record, by another individual other than the notary public at the direction and in the presence of the individual whose name is to be signed and in the presence of the notary public.

"(b) The words 'Signature written by' or 'Signature attached by' in the case of an electronic record, '(name of individual directed to sign or directed to attach) at the direction and in the presence of (name as signed) on whose behalf the signature was written' or 'attached electronically' in the case of an electronic record, or words of substantially similar effect shall appear under or near the signature.

"(2) A notary public may use signals or electronic or mechanical means to take an acknowledgment from, administer an oath or affirmation to, or otherwise communicate with any individual in the presence of such notary public when it appears that such individual is unable to communicate verbally or in writing" (CRS 12-55-110.5).

Wills

Effective July 1, 2010, an enacted Colorado law allows Notaries to take the acknowledgment of a signature on a will (CRS 15-11-502[1][c]). It allows a Colorado Notary to notarize the signature of a testator (person making the will) or of witnesses attesting to the proper execution of the will in a procedure that makes the will "self-proving."

NOTARY DON'TS

Disqualifying Interests

Notaries are disqualified from notarizing when they (CRS 12-55-110[2]):

1. Are named, individually, as a party;
2. May receive directly as a result any advantage, right, title, interest, cash or property exceeding in value the fee for notarizing.

A Notary may not notarize his or her own signature (website, "Frequently Asked Questions").

Notarizing for Relatives: "A notary is not specifically prohibited from witnessing and notarizing the signatures of a spouse or relatives, however a notary public who has a disqualifying interest in a transaction may not legally perform any notarial act in connection with such transaction. If the document were to be questioned for any cause, the notarial act may be scrutinized more closely than if the notary were not a spouse or relative. Also, if the witnessed document is one from which you may derive a benefit, your right to receive that benefit may be jeopardized. To avoid later questioning of the notary's impartiality, as well as accusations of undue influence, it is always safest for a signer to find a Notary who is not related…" (website, "Frequently Asked Questions").

False Advertising

A Notary's commission may be revoked or denied if the Notary "knowingly uses false or misleading advertising in which such notary represents that such notary has powers, duties, rights, or privileges that such notary does not possess by law" (CRS 12-55-107[1][d] and [h]).

Foreign-Language Ads: A nonattorney Notary who advertises notarial services in a language other than English must include in the ad or sign the following statement, both in English and the other language (CRS 12-55-110.3[1]): "I am not an attorney licensed to practice law in the state of Colorado and I may not give legal advice or accept fees for legal advice." This statement must be "clearly visible." Oral advertisements or solicitations, including those on radio or television, must contain the same message but need not use the exact language.

In addition, nonattorney Notaries who advertise in a language other than English must post in their places of business "in a highly visible location," in both English and the other language, a list of fees permitted by law for notarial services; the statement cited in the above paragraph must also be included (CRS 12-55-110.3[2]).

In any ad, English or foreign-language, a nonattorney Notary is prohibited from "(u)sing the phrase 'notario' or 'notario publico' to advertise the services of a notary public, whether by sign, pamphlet, stationery, or other written communication or by radio, television, or other nonwritten communication" (CRS 12-55-110.3[3][b][V]).

Immigration Consultants: "A notary public who is not a licensed attorney in the state of

Colorado shall not represent or advertise himself or herself as an immigration consultant or an expert on immigration matters" (CRS 12-55-110.3[3]).

Notary Does Not Select Act

"A notary actually does not decide which notarial act to perform for a particular document. A smart notary asks the client which notarial act is being requested. The client...will know who wanted the document notarized in the first place, or who its intended recipient is. From that person or entity, the client can find out which notarial act is required" (NH, "Oaths and Affirmations vs. Acknowledgments").

Blank Documents

For notarizing any blank document, a Notary's commission may be revoked (CRS 12-55-107[1][g] and 12-55-110[3]).

"A Notary should skim the document for blanks and ask the document signer to fill them in. If they are intended to be left blank, then the signer can line through them or write N/A" (website, "Frequently Asked Questions"). "This provision does not require blanks to be filled in with specific information. A client may put 'Not Applicable,' or 'X,' or a line, scribble, or other material in such spaces. A notary may then notarize the document, as long as no blanks remain in it" (NH, "What Does the Notary Law Prohibit").

Pre-Dating and Post-Dating Prohibited

"A notary may not pre- or post-date any notarial certificate no matter how a client may plead or bully for an exception and no matter what date is on the document itself" (website, "Frequently Asked Questions").

If Document Has No Date: "(I)f there is space for a date (on the document) it should be filled in with the correct date or lined through by the document signer. If the document simply doesn't have a date, it is acceptable to notarize it and record in your journal that the document has no date" (website, "Frequently Asked Questions").

NOTARY SIGNING AGENTS

Currently, there are no statutes, regulations or rules expressly governing, prohibiting or restricting the operation of Notary Signing Agents within the state of Colorado.

NOTARY FEES

"The fees of notaries public may be, but shall not exceed, five dollars ($5) for each document attested by a person before a notary, except as otherwise provided by law. The fee for each such document shall include the following incidental services of such notary: (a) Receiving evidence of such person's identity as enumerated in section 12-55-110(4); (b) Administering an oath or affirmation to such person; and (c) Signing and sealing a certificate or statement of such notary that is included in or attached to such document and evidences that the document was attested before such notary" (CRS 12-55-121).

Fees for Electronic Acts

The maximum fee a Colorado Notary Public may charge for performing an electronic notarization is $10 (website, "Frequently Asked Questions").

NOTARY CERTIFICATES

Colorado has adopted the *Uniform Recognition of Acknowledgments Act*, including the short-form certificates (CRS 12-55-208) for:

1. Acknowledgment by individual;
2. Acknowledgment by corporation;
3. Acknowledgment by partnership;
4. Acknowledgment by attorney in fact;
5. Acknowledgment by public officer, trustee or personal representative.

The Notary's seal and commission expiration date must be added to each short-form certificate prescribed by the *Act*.

For the text of these certificates, see "Uniform Recognition of Acknowledgments Act (1968)," Section 6, in Appendix 3.

Format for Acknowledgment Certificate

"The form of a certificate of acknowledgment ... shall be accepted in this state if: (a) The certificate is in a form prescribed by the laws or regulations of this state; or (b) The certificate is in a form prescribed by the laws or regulations applicable in the place in which the acknowledgment is taken; or (c) The certificate contains the words 'acknowledged before me', or their substantial equivalent" (CRS 12-55-206).

Colorado law additionally prescribes the following certificates:

Written Affirmation/Oath (CRS 12-55-119):

(TEXT OF AFFIRMATION OR OATH)

(SIGNATURE)

Subscribed and affirmed (or sworn to) before me in the county of _____, State of Colorado, this ____ day of _____, 20__, by _____.

(NOTARY'S SIGNATURE, SEAL, COMMISSION EXPIRATION DATE)

Certified Copy (CRS 12-55-120[2]):

*State of Colorado,
County (or City) of _____,*

I, _____ (name of Notary), a Notary Public in and for said state, do certify that on _____ (date), I carefully compared with the original the attached facsimile of _____ (type of document) and the facsimile I now hold in my possession. They are complete, full, true, and exact facsimiles of the document they purport to reproduce.

(NOTARY'S SIGNATURE, SEAL, COMMISSION EXPIRATION DATE)

Correcting Notarial Certificates

"Only the document signer has authority to make any changes on the document; likewise, only the notary can correct the certificate. When you are correcting a notarial certificate simply line through the mistake with ink, write the correction above or beside, initial and date the correction" (website, "Frequently Asked Questions").

ELECTRONIC NOTARIZATIONS

"Colorado is one of the first states to have specific statutory and regulatory provisions on electronic notarization actually in effect (12-55-106.5[1]), not just under consideration or initial or 'pilot program' use. In fact, Colorado has rules in effect that allow e-notarization by simple, secure, and easily available means and, at the same time, preserve the basic transaction safeguards that notarization has historically provided ....

"Most importantly: electronic notarization does not change a notary's basic duties, functions, and responsibilities. The requirements of law ... are not waived or altered when a notary uses an electronic signature. A notary must still be in the client's presence, identify the client, and administer an oath to, or take an acknowledgment from, that client" (NH, "Electronic Notarization").

"Currently, the uses for electronic notarization are limited. An e-notarization involves a document in electronic format that is signed and notarized electronically, then filed or transmitted electronically to its intended destination. They may be used in transactions between private parties who agree to such use, such as contracts requiring notarization that are emailed or otherwise transmitted electronically between the parties. Some counties within Colorado are accepting certain forms of electronic documents for filing, but only from submitters with whom they have contractual arrangements" (website, "Electronic Notary Public").

'Remote Notarization' Unauthorized

"Electronic notarization does not mean remote notarization. As with all notarizations the signer must appear in the physical presence of the notary to affirm, swear, or acknowledge the document to be notarized" (website, "Electronic Notary Public").

UETA Recognizes Notary's eSignature

Recognizing the legal validity of electronic signatures used by Notaries, Colorado has adopted the Uniform Electronic Transactions Act, including the provision on notarization and acknowledgment (CRS 24-71.3-111):

"If a law requires a signature or record to be notarized, acknowledged, verified or made under oath, the requirement is satisfied if the electronic signature of the person authorized to perform those acts, together with all other information required to be included by other applicable law, is attached to or logically associated with the signature or record."

Colorado

Power to Notarize Electronically

"Every notary public is empowered to ... (t)ake acknowledgments and other unsworn statements, proof of execution, and attest documents and electronic records ..." (CRS 12-55-110[1][a]).

"At the time of notarization, a notary public shall sign such notary's official signature on every notary certificate or in the case of an electronic record, a notary public shall affix his or her electronic signature" (CRS 12-55-112[1]).

Electronic Signature Replaces Seal: "In the case of notarization of an electronic record, the application of a notary's electronic signature in lieu of a handwritten signature and rubber stamp seal or seal embosser is sufficient. A notary shall not use an electronic signature unless:

"(a) The notary uses a journal if maintaining such journal is required by section 12-55-111; and

"(b) The notary attaches to the document a document authentication number issued by the Secretary of State" (CRS 12-55-112[4.5]).

Document Authentication Number: "'Document authentication number' means a number issued by the Secretary of State that includes the Secretary of State's accounting system validation number issued to each notary upon commissioning and a randomly generated number that when used together may constitute the notary's electronic signature and identify both the individual notary and the document to which the document authentication number has been affixed" (8 CCR 1505-11, Rule 1[1]).

Notary's Electronic Signature

"1. In every instance, the electronic signature of a notary public shall contain the following elements, all of which shall be immediately perceptible and reproducible in the electronic record to which the notary's electronic signature is attached: The notary's name; the words 'NOTARY PUBLIC' and 'STATE OF COLORADO'; a document authentication number issued by the Secretary of State; and the words "my commission expires" followed by the expiration date of the notary's commission. A notary's electronic signature shall conform to any standards promulgated by the secretary of state.

"2. The secretary of state shall promulgate rules necessary to establish standards, procedures, practices, forms, and records relating to a notary's electronic signature.

"3. To the extent the provisions of this part 1 (of Title 12, Article 55, i.e., 'Notaries Public Act') differ from the requirements of the federal 'Electronic Signatures in Global and National Commerce Act,' 15 U.S.C. sec. 7001 et seq., the provisions of this part 1 are intended to modify, limit, or supersede the requirements of such act, as provided for in section 7002(a) of such act" (CRS 12-55-106.5).

Two Types of Electronic Signature: "There are two types of electronic signatures that Colorado provides for in the statute and in the rules:

"1. The document authentication numbers issued by the Secretary of State and used as the electronic signature,

"2. An electronic signature purchased from private sector vendors such as Verisign… when used in conjunction with the document authentication numbers issued by the Secretary of State" (NH, "Electronic Notarization").

Wrongful Use of Electronic Signature: "Any person who unlawfully possesses and uses a notary's journal, an official seal, a notary's electronic signature, or any papers, copies, or electronic records relating to notarial acts is guilty of a class three misdemeanor" (CRS 12-55-118).

"Every notary public shall send or have delivered notice to the secretary of state within thirty days after the notary loses or misplaces such notary's journal of notarial acts, or official seal, or the notary becomes aware that any other person has electronic control of his or her electronic signature" (CRS 12-55-113).

Electronic Signature Registration

"Commissioned notaries, or notaries applying for a commission, may apply to be an eNotary by submitting a completed 'Notice of Intent to Notarize Electronically' to the office of the Secretary of State" (website, "Electronic Notary Public").

Rule 2 of the "Rules Concerning Electronic Notarization" (8 CCR 1505-11) sets the following registration guidelines:

"1. Before performing any electronic notarization, an applicant or a notary shall file with the Secretary of State a notification of intent to notarize documents electronically. This notification may be submitted at the time of application for a notary commission or at any subsequent time during the notary's term of commission.

"2. A submitted notification shall not be

deemed filed until it has been approved and an approval certificate has been issued by the Secretary of State. A notification submitted at the time of application for a commission shall not be deemed filed unless and until the application is accepted and the notary is commissioned by the Secretary of State and the approval certificate has been issued.

"3. Notification of intent to notarize electronically shall be on forms prescribed by the Secretary of State, and shall include a statement whether the applicant or notary will use only document authentication numbers as his or her electronic signature. If the applicant or notary indicates an intention to use a different electronic signature than document authentication numbers, then the notification of intent shall also be accompanied by an example of the electronic signature that will be used by the applicant or notary, and shall include the following information:

"(a) A description of the technology that will be used for the notary's electronic notarizations, specifically for the creation of the notary's electronic signature;

"(b) The name, address, telephone number, and web or e-mail address of the supplier or vendor of such technology; and

"(c) Such other information as the Secretary of State finds necessary to confirm that the technology complies with the requirements of the Colorado Notaries Public Act, article 55 of title 12 of the Colorado Revised Statutes.

"4 If the notary is certified to notarize electronically:

"(a) The Secretary of State will: (1) Provide an electronic log to the notary that contains a series of document authentication numbers. Such log shall constitute the journal referenced in section 12-55-104[2] CRS. (2) Maintain a record of the series of numbers issued at the offices of the Secretary of State.

"(b) The notary may use the document authentication numbers provided in the electronic log as the notary's electronic signature, provided that the notary's name, the words 'NOTARY PUBLIC' and 'STATE OF COLORADO', and the words 'my commission expires,' followed by the expiration of the notary's commission, accompany each authentication number so used.

"(c) A different document authentication number shall be used for each electronic notarization that the notary performs.

"(d) A notary shall take reasonable measures to secure his or her journal or authentication numbers against access or use by other persons, and shall not, under any circumstances, permit such access or use by another.

"(5) Any form of electronic signature must:

"(a) Be discrete to the individual submitting the electronic signature;

"(b) Be retrievable from the electronic document in perceivable form."

Fee for Electronic Notarization

The maximum fee that a Colorado Notary Public may charge for performing an electronic notarization is $10 (website, "Frequently Asked Questions").

Expiration of Power to Notarize Electronically

"1. The approval to electronically notarize shall expire when:

"(a) The commission for which it was filed expires;

"(b) The commission for which it was filed is revoked;

"(c) Thirty days have elapsed after the notary's name changes, unless the notary sooner submits a change of name pursuant to section 12-55-114 CRS, including with the submission, if the notary uses a different signature than the document authentication numbers issued by the Secretary of State, a description and example of the notary's new electronic signature, in accord with section 3 of Rule 2 of these Rules Concerning Electronic Notarization.

"(d) The notary, during his or her commission term, resigns the commission, is convicted of a felony, ceases to reside in Colorado, or dies;

"(e) The technology described in the notification changes;

"(f) The technology described in the notification expires or is revoked, if applicable; or;

"(g) The supplier or vendor goes out of business or for any other reason no longer supplies the technology described in the notification.

"2. Except as provided in section (3) of this Rule 3, when a notary's approval to notarize electronically expires, the notary or the notary's duly authorized representative shall, within 30 days after such expiration, permanently erase, delete, or destroy the notary's electronic notarization software, if applicable, and, if the notary has elected to use document authentication numbers provided by the Secretary of State as his or her electronic signature, any and all unused authentication numbers.

"3. If a notary's signature notification expires solely on account of the expiration of the notary's commission, the notary need not permanently erase, delete, or destroy the electronic notarization software if the notary is recommissioned and reregisters his or her electronic signature within 30 days after the commission expiration" (8 CCR 1505-11, Rule 3).

Electronic Affirmation

"If an affirmation is to be administered by the notary public in an electronic record, the person taking the affirmation shall attach his or her electronic signature thereto. Within the affirmation, the notary shall add the fact that the document has been subscribed and affirmed, or sworn to before me in the county of _____, state of Colorado, this _____ day of _____, 20___.

"(notary's electronic signature)" (CRS 12-55-119[2]).

Journal Entry for Each Electronic Act

"The journal must be used for every notarial act whenever an electronic signature is used.

"The journal should include all of the information required by the statutes for the use of a journal for acknowledgments affecting real estate and should include the pen and ink signature of the signer who uses an electronic signature. Some notaries actually capture the thumbprint of a signer, however, the Secretary of State does not take a position on this practice" (NH, "Electronic Notarization").

'Pictorial Notaries' Law Repealed

As part of legislation enacted in 2009 (Senate Bill 111), a former statutory provision (CRS 12-55-106.7) allowing Notaries to authenticate and transmit encrypted photographs of individuals electronically — for use by motor vehicle offices, credit card companies and other entities needing authenticated photos — has been repealed.

NOTARY RECORDS

"Colorado law requires notaries public to keep a journal entry for every notarial act. There is an exception, if the notarized document is retained by the notary's firm or employer in the regular course of business. However, if documents are misfiled, lost, destroyed, or are otherwise unrecoverable, the notary may be exposed to considerable liability. Therefore, every notary is strongly encouraged to keep a well-maintained journal" (website, "Frequently Asked Questions"). The requirement to keep a record of every notarial act became effective July 1, 2009. See also "Records of Notary Employee" below.

Bound Book Not Required

"A journal is not necessarily kept in a bound book printed for the specific purpose of recording notarial acts. Those are handy to have, since they feature built-in reminders of the types of information a notary may want to track on his/her notarizations. They are not required by law, however. A notary may keep a journal in a diary, a spiral notebook, a calendar, a file folder, or on a computer, as far as the Notaries Public Act is concerned" (NH, "Notary Journal").

Components of Journal Entry

"A notary journal is a 'day-to-day' chronological record of a notary's official acts" (NH, "Notary Journal").

"For each notarial act, a notary's journal may contain the following information:

"(a) The type and date of the notarial act;

"(b) The title or type of document or proceeding that was notarized and the date of such document or proceeding, if different than the date of the notarization;

"(c) The name of each person whose oath, affirmation, acknowledgment, affidavit, declaration, deposition, protest, verification, or other statement is taken;

"(d) The signature and address of each person whose oath, affirmation, acknowledgment, affidavit, declaration, deposition, protest, verification, or other statement is taken;

"(e) The signature, printed name, and address of each witness to the notarization;

"(f) Any other information the notary considers appropriate to record that concerns the notarial act" (CRS 12-55-111[2]).

For Notarized Electronic Signatures: In the website ("Frequently Asked Questions"), Notaries are directed also to record a "certificate of authentication of each notarized electronic signature by the provider of the electronic signature or each person whose oath, affirmation, acknowledgment, affidavit, declaration, deposition, protest, verification, or other statement is taken."

Certified Copies: Wording of the statutory form for a certification of a facsimile indicates that the Notary should keep an additional copy of the original document as a notarial record ("… I carefully compared with the original attached facsimile of _____ and the facsimile I now hold in my possession …") (CRS 12-55-120). The Notary also keeps the written and signed request required by law.

Multiple Signers: "If two signers appear before the notary at the same time, the names may appear on the same certificate. Because it is two separate notarizations, two entries must be made in the journal" (website, "Frequently Aksed Questions").

Lost Journal

"Every notary public shall send or have delivered notice to the secretary of state within thirty days after the notary loses or misplaces such notary's journal of notarial acts, or official seal, or the notary becomes aware that any other person has electronic control of his or her electronic signature" (CRS 12-55-113).

Records of Notary Employee

In the case of a Notary employee, the statutory mandate to keep a record "shall not apply to any document or electronic record where the original or a copy of such document or electronic record contains the information otherwise required to be entered in the notary's journal and such original or copy or electronic record is retained by the notary's firm or employer in the regular course of business" (CRS 12-55-111[3][a]).

"For purposes of this subsection (3), 'firm' includes but is not limited to an office where the business of a real estate broker, lawyer, title insurance company, title insurance agent, or other licensed professional is regularly carried on and the records of such business are regularly maintained" (CRS 12-55-111[3][c]).

Nonetheless, "no firm, employer, or professionally licensed person shall prohibit an employee who is a notary from maintaining a journal of his or her notarial acts in the regular course of business of such firm, employer, or professionally licensed person" (CRS 12-55-111[3][b]). Indeed, in the "Notary Handbook" and on the website, the Colorado Secretary of State strongly urges Notary employees to keep a record of all their notarial acts.

All Electronic Acts Recorded

Except as law otherwise prescribes, "for each electronic record or document signed by the notary public, the notary public shall record the document authentication number issued by the secretary of state for each document authenticated in the journal pursuant to this section" (CRS 12-55-111[4]).

"The journal must be used for every notarial act whenever an electronic signature has been used.

"The journal should include all of the information required by the statutes for the use of a journal for acknowledgments affecting real estate and should include the pen and ink signature of the signer who uses an electronic signature. Some notaries actually capture the thumbprint of a signer, however, the Secretary of State does not take a position on this practice" (NH, "Electronic Notarization").

Wrongful Possession of Journal

"The journal is maintained by the notary and kept in his/her possession" (NH, "Notary Journal").

"Any person who unlawfully possesses and uses a notary's journal, an official seal, a notary's electronic signature, or any papers or copies, or electronic records relating to notarial acts is guilty of a class 3 misdemeanor" (CRS 12-55-118).

Death, Resignation, Revocation, Move

For disposition of the Notary's journal and seal when the Notary dies, resigns, has a commission revoked, or moves from the state, see "Death, Resignation, Revocation, Move" under "Changes of Status," below.

AUTHENTICATION OF NOTARIAL ACTS

Secretary of State

Authenticating certificates for Notaries, called "certificates of magistracy," as well as apostilles, are issued by the Colorado Secretary of State (CRS 12-55-109[1]).

Fee: $5 per document. For expedited service (in person only): $15 per document. The fee is payable to "Colorado Secretary of State."

Mailing/Walk-In Address:
Colorado Secretary of State
Notary Program
1700 Broadway, Suite 200
Denver, CO 80290

Telephone: 1-303-894-2200, Ext. 9500

Procedure: Mail or present in person the original properly notarized document(s), along with the appropriate fee and a completed "Authentication Request Form," which can be downloaded from the website. All blanks in the document must have been filled in or crossed out by the signer, and all signatures must be original. "For assurance of delivery of your completed documents(s), we recommend utilizing an express or overnight delivery service such as FedEx or UPS. A prepaid waybill or prepaid label must be included if you would like us to return your document(s) using these shipping methods. Walk-in customers can drop off documents to be processed and picked up the following business day after 10:30 a.m., or placed in return mail normally within 5-7 business days of receipt in our office. Expedited service is available for hand-delivered documents only. No appointment is necessary" (website, "Apostilles and Authentications").

"According to Colorado law, documents must be notarized in English in order to receive an apostille or certificate of magistracy. If the country to which the document is going requires a foreign language notarization, the notary is free to do so. However, the notary must also notarize the same document in English" (website, "Common Mistakes to Avoid").

Electronic Verification: Online verification of the authenticity of an apostille or other authentication issued by the Colorado Secretary of State is now available (website, "Apostilles and Authentication").

County and Court Officials

"A notary public may record his certificate of authority (from the secretary of state) in any county of this state and, after such recording, the county clerk and recorder of such county may issue a certificate that such person is a notary public, the date of expiration of his commission, and any other fact concerning such notary public which is required by the laws of this state" (CRS 12-55-109[2]). IMPORTANT NOTE: county recording of Notary certificates is optional and rarely done.

"A notary public may exhibit to the judge or clerk of any court of record his certificate of authority (from the secretary of state), and the said judge or clerk may thereupon issue a certificate that such person is a notary public, the date of expiration of his commission, and any other fact concerning such notary which is required by the laws of this state" (CRS 12-55-109[3]).

COMMISSIONING AND ADMINISTRATION

The Colorado Secretary of State appoints, commissions and maintains records on the state's Notaries (CRS 12-55-103). The data provided on the Notary commission application becomes public information (website, "To become a notary…").

Applying for Commission

Qualifications: An applicant for a Colorado Notary Public commission must: (a) be a resident of Colorado, (b) be at least 18 years old, (c) be able to read and write the English language, (d) be familiar with Colorado's Notary law (e) not have been convicted of a misdemeanor involving dishonesty, as defined in CRS 12-55-102(1.4), during the last five years, (f) never have had a felony conviction and (g) never have had a Notary commission revoked.

Training and Exam Required: To become a first-time Colorado Notary or to renew a Notary commission expired more than 30 days, applicants must first take a training class and pass an exam (website, "How to Become a Colorado Notary"). Colorado law gives the Secretary of State authority to set rules for this class and exam (CRS 12-55-103.5[2]). For the training, applicants have the choice of taking (a) a classroom or online course conducted for a fee by any educational vendor on an approved list (website, "Notary Public Training") or (b) a free class offered by the Secretary's staff (website, "Secretary of State Office Notary Public Training"). The two-hour classes offered by the Secretary, with pre-registration required for the limited space, are held in Denver at 1700 Broadway, 3rd Floor, Aspen Conference Room; smaller classes are offered at other sites within 35 miles of the

Secretary's office. Handouts are not provided and all needed instructional materials may be downloaded from the website beforehand.

The online, open-book exam requires about 25 minutes and must be taken on a PC, not a Mac, using the Internet Explorer browser, with the latest version of Java. Upon successful completion, a certificate to evidence passage of the exam is printed out (website, "Colorado Notary Testing Process").

Application: The filing fee is only $10 if the application is filled out by typing in the responses online, but $50 if it is filled out by hand using pen and ink (website, "Colorado Notary Application Process"). After completion, the online application is printed out by the applicant, signed in front of a Notary, and mailed or delivered to the Secretary's office, along with a copy of: (a) both sides of an acceptable ID (i.e., a Colorado driver's license or non-driver's ID, a U.S. military ID, a Native American tribal ID with photo, or an I-551 resident alien card; and (b) a certificate showing completion of state-approved Notary training; and (c) a certificate showing a passing grade on the required Notary exam. Upon commissioning, an email will be sent informing the applicant of the Notary ID and password, which will enable online access to the state's Notary system and printing out of the Notary commission certificate. This commission certificate must be presented to an office supplier in order to obtain a Notary seal or stamp and a journal (website, "Notary E-File Instructions").

Renewal applications may be submitted no earlier than 90 days before expiration of the Notary's commission (website, "Frequently Asked Questions").

Non-Residents: Non-residents of Colorado may not become Notaries in the state.

Online Search: On the Web site, through "Verify a Colorado Notary Public," the current status of Notary may be confirmed.

Changes of Status

If Notary Changes Name: Within 30 days after changing a name, the Notary must send or have delivered a notice to the Secretary of State, including a sample of the Notary's new handwritten official signature, containing the surname and at least the initial of the first name (CRS 12-55-114[2]). A name change form is available in the "Forms" link on the website. "A copy of an acceptable identification document in (the) new name is required" (website, "Frequently Asked Questions"). No fee is paid. A name change may be filed electronically.

If Notary Moves within State: Within 30 days after changing a business or residence address, or a telephone number, the Notary must send or have delivered a notice of such change to the Secretary of State (CRS 12-55-114[1]). No fee is required. An address change may be filed electronically. In the case of a home address change, a new Notary commission certificate will be sent to the Notary or made available for printing (website, "Frequently Asked Questions"). If the move is out of state, see immediately below.

Death, Resignation, Revocation, Move: If a Notary dies during the term of appointment, the heirs or personal representative, "as soon as reasonably possible" after death, must send or have delivered to the Secretary of State the Notary's official journal, papers and seal, if available (CRS 12-55-115[1]).

Likewise, a Notary who resigns the commission or ceases to have a business or residence address in the state must send or have delivered to the Secretary of State a letter of resignation and the Notary's official journal, papers and seal — whereupon the commission ceases to be in effect (CRS 12-55-115[2]). A "Notary Public Termination Form" is available on the website for this purpose.

A Notary notified that the commission has been revoked must immediately send or have delivered to the Secretary of State the Notary's official journal, papers and seal (CRS 12-55-107[3]).

COUNTY CLERKS

Though Colorado county clerks have statutory authority to issue authenticating certificates for Notaries who have filed a certificate from the Secretary of State (CRS 12-55-109[2]), such filing by the Notary is optional and rarely done. To contact a Colorado county clerk, telephone long-distance information — 1-XXX-555-1212 — and ask for the phone number of the appropriate county clerk for the following jurisdictions.

Colorado

A–C

County	City/Town	Area Code
Adams	Brighton	(303)
Alamosa	Alamosa	(719)
Arapahoe	Littleton	(303)
Archuleta	Pagosa Springs	(970)
Baca	Springfield	(719)
Bent	Las Animas	(719)
Boulder	Boulder	(303)
Broomfield	Broomfield	(303)
Chaffee	Salida	(719)
Cheyenne	Cheyenne Wells	(719)
Clear Creek	Georgetown	(303)
Conejos	Conejos	(719)
Costilla	San Luis	(719)
Crowley	Ordway	(719)
Custer	Westcliffe	(719)
Delta	Delta	(970)
Denver	Denver	(720)
Dolores	Dove Creek	(970)
Douglas	Castle Rock	(303)
Eagle	Eagle	(970)
Elbert	Kiowa	(303)
El Paso	Colorado Springs	(719)
Fremont	Canon City	(719)
Garfield	Glenwood Springs	(970)
Gilpin	Central City	(303)
Grand	Hot Sulphur Springs	(970)
Gunnison	Gunnison	(970)
Hinsdale	Lake City	(970)
Huerfano	Walsenburg	(719)
Jackson	Walden	(970)
Jefferson	Golden	(303)
Kiowa	Eads	(719)
Kit Carson	Burlington	(719)
Lake	Leadville	(719)
La Plata	Durango	(970)
Larimer	Fort Collins	(970)
Las Animas	Trinidad	(719)
Lincoln	Hugo	(719)
Logan	Sterling	(970)
Mesa	Grand Junction	(970)
Mineral	Creede	(719)
Moffat	Craig	(970)
Montezuma	Cortez	(970)
Montrose	Montrose	(970)
Morgan	Fort Morgan	(970)
Otero	La Junta	(719)
Ouray	Ouray	(970)
Park	Fairplay	(719)
Phillips	Holyoke	(970)
Pitkin	Aspen	(970)
Prowers	Lamar	(719)
Pueblo	Pueblo	(719)
Rio Blanco	Meeker	(970)
Rio Grande	Del Norte	(719)
Routt	Steamboat Springs	(970)
Saguache	Saguache	(719)
San Juan	Silverton	(970)
San Miguel	Telluride	(970)
Sedgwick	Julesburg	(970)
Summit	Breckenridge	(970)
Teller	Cripple Creek	(719)
Washington	Akron	(970)
Weld	Greeley	(970)
Yuma	Wray	(970)

QUICK FACTS

Notary Jurisdiction
Statewide.

Notary Term Length
Four years (CRS 12-55-103), expiring at midnight on the commission expiration date.

Notary Bond
Effective July 1, 1993, a Notary bond is no longer required by law. However, "(n)othing… shall be construed to deny a notary public the right to obtain a surety bond and/or insurance on a voluntary basis to provide coverage for liability" (CRS 12-55-116[3]).

Connecticut

NOTARY SEAL

A Connecticut Notary Public may use a seal of office but is not required by law to do so (CGS 47-5a). "Even though the use of a seal is optional, state law does prescribe the format of the seal to be used" (NPM).

Optional but Encouraged

"A notary public, except a state police major, captain, lieutenant or sergeant appointed as a notary public…may keep and use an official notarial seal" (CGS 3-94j).

Historically, officials in the office of Connecticut's Secretary of the State have encouraged use of Notary seals: "A Notary Public is not required by state statute to use a seal. However, this office does recommend that a seal be used and particularly for documents going out of state" — Deputy Secretary of the State Harry Hammer (1975).

If a Notary seal is used, its impression should be affixed near the notary's official signature on the notarial certificate, and its format must be as described below (CGS 3-94k). "When using the seal, the impression should be affixed near but not over, the notary's signature" (NPM).

Kind

Embosser or Inked Stamp: Not specified by law, but an embosser is traditional and perhaps

Examples

The above typical, actual-size example of an optional Notary seal is allowed by Connecticut law. Formats other than this may also be permitted. The embosser is most common.

NOTARY ADMINISTRATION

Office of Secretary of the State
Notary Public STET   1-860-509-6100
P.O. Box 150470
Hartford, CT 06115-0470

Website: http://www.sots.ct.gov/sots/cwp/browse.asp?A=3184#

NOTARY RULES

CGS — CONNECTICUT GENERAL STATUTES
NPM — NOTARY PUBLIC MANUAL

Most Notary rules are in the Connecticut General Statutes:

a. Title 3, Chapter 33, "Notaries Public";

b. Title 1, Chapter 6, "Uniform Acknowledgment Act";*

c. Title 1, Chapter 8, "Uniform Recognition of Acknowledgments Act".**

* This is the *Uniform Acknowledgment Act* of 1939, adopted with amendments.

** This is the *Uniform Recognition of Acknowledgments Act* of 1968, adopted virtually intact.

Other guidelines for Notaries are in the "Notary Public Manual" (Revised January 10, 2011) issued by the Secretary of the State and available online.

suggested by the statute, which refers to "an impression of the notarial seal." State officials have long expressed preference for an embossing Notary seal: e.g., "A rubber stamp seal is not prohibited but an embossed type is preferred" — Deputy Secretary of the State Harry Hammer (1975).

Size/Shape

Not specified by law, though a circular embossment is traditional.

Components
1. Notary's name exactly as it appears on certificate of appointment;
2. "Notary Public";
3. "Connecticut";
4. OPTIONAL IN SEAL: "My commission expires _____ (date)".

Commission Expiration Date Must Appear
If the words, "My commission expires _____ (date)," do not appear in the seal, they may appear in an inked stamp impression (CGS 3-94k).

If a seal is not used or if the seal does not contain an expiration date, an inked stamp such as is printed below may be affixed below the Notary's signature, with the date either printed or written in by hand (NPM):

```
JANE Q. DOE
Notary Public
My Commission Expires on Jan. 31, 2015
```

But, if the Notary does not elect to use either a seal or a stamp, the words "Notary Public" and "My commission expires _____ (date)" must be typed or printed legibly near the Notary's official signature (CGS 3-94k).

Notary's Signature
"In any circumstance when a notary's signature is required, it must always be the original signature of the notary signed exactly as the name appears on the notary's Certificate of Appointment. If a seal and/or stamp is not used, the notary should type, stamp or print legibly his/her name in close proximity to his/her signature. The notary cannot use a signature stamp, and no other person can sign on behalf of the notary" (NPM).

"It is important for the notary to remember that he/she must sign his/her name exactly as it appears on his/her certificate of appointment and notary seal" (NPM).

Police Seal
State police majors, captains, lieutenants and sergeants who are Notaries may take acknowledgments and administer oaths and affirmations in police matters only, using the seal of the state police as a notarial seal (CGS 3-94e).

Seal, Stamp Not Surrendered to Employer
"Such seal shall not be used by any other person or surrendered to any employer upon termination of the notary's employment" (CGS 3-94j).

"All seals and stamps are obtained from private vendors at the notary's own expense and always remain the property of the notary. This is true even if the notary's employer paid for these items. The only person who has the authority to possess and use a notary's seal and/or stamp is the notary whose name appears on the seal" (NPM).

Lost or Stolen Seal
"If a notary seal or stamp is lost or stolen, the notary should notify both the local police and the Office of the Secretary of the State. The notary should also notify the Department of Motor Vehicles, Dealers, Repairers and Emissions Division, in writing, at 60 State Street, Wethersfield, CT 06109. The Secretary's office will note the loss or theft to protect the notary. If the notary chooses to replace the seal, some distinguishing element may be introduced to differentiate the new seal" (NPM).

Seal Must Be Destroyed
"A notary shall immediately destroy the notary's notarial seal upon resigning as a notary or upon the revocation, lapse or expiration of such person's appointment as a notary" (CGS 3-94j).

"As soon as possible after the death of a notary public, the notary's personal representative shall destroy the notary's official notarial seal, if any …" (CGS 3-94q).

NOTARY POWERS

Connecticut Notaries are authorized to perform the following notarial acts (CGS 1-57):
1. Take acknowledgments* and proofs;
2. Execute jurats**;
3. Administer oaths*** and affirmations****;
4. Take depositions and issue subpoenas for depositions in civil actions and probate proceedings***** (CGS 52-148a – e);
5. Execute protests (CGS 42a-3-509).

* <u>Identifying Acknowledgers</u>: "For an acknowledgment to be properly taken, each of the following requirements should be fulfilled. The signer must: (1) personally appear before the notary. (2) acknowledge that he/she signed the instrument in question. (3) state that it is his/her

free act and deed" (NPM).

"The officer taking the acknowledgment shall know or have satisfactory evidence that the person making the acknowledgment is the person described in and who executed the instrument" (CGS 1-32).

Personal knowledge of identity "means familiarity with an individual resulting from interaction with that individual over a period of time sufficient to eliminate any reasonable doubt that the individual has the identity claimed" (CGS 3-94a[8]).

Satisfactory evidence of identity "means identification of an individual based on (A) at least two current documents, one issued by a federal or state government and containing the individual's signature and either a photograph or physical description, and the other by an institution, business entity or state government or the federal government and containing at least the individual's signature or (B) the oath or affirmation of a credible person who is personally known to the notary public and who personally knows the individual" (CGS 3-94a[9]).

"Remember social security cards and birth certificates are not to be used as a form of identification ....

"Like all witnesses the credible-witness should be honest, competent and ideally, without interest in the transaction. The notary must administer an oath or affirmation to the credible witness" (NPM).

** Jurats: A jurat is "a notarial act in which a notary public certifies that a signatory, whose identity is personally known to the notary public or proven on the basis of satisfactory evidence, has made, in the notary public's presence, a voluntary signature and taken an oath or affirmation vouching for the truthfulness of the signed document" (CGS 3-94a[2]).

*** Oath Ceremony and Wording: Notaries are empowered to administer oaths by CGS 1-24. "The ceremony to be used, by persons to whom an oath is administered, shall be the holding up of the right hand; but when any person, by reason of scruples of conscience, objects to such ceremony or when the court or authority by whom the oath is to be administered has reason to believe that any other ceremony will be more binding upon the conscience of the witness, such court or authority may permit or require any other ceremony to be used" (CGS 1-22).

Oath wording for a witness must be as follows (CGS 1-25): "You solemnly swear that the evidence you shall give, concerning the case now in question, shall be the truth, the whole truth and nothing but the truth; so help you God." An oath for an affiant may be as follows (NPM): "Do you solemnly swear that the statements contained herein are true to the best of your knowledge and belief, so help you God?" The person to whom an oath is administered should answer, "I do" (NPM).

Wording for oaths of office for the following offices and positions is dictated by statute (CGS 1-25): members of the General Assembly, executive and judicial officers; Notaries; voters; attorneys; grand jurors empaneled in court; petit and alternate jurors in criminal causes; jurors and alternate jurors in civil causes; voir dire; interpreters in court, in a criminal case or for a deaf or hearing-impaired juror; assessors; plaintiffs; members and judge-advocate of a court-martial; polling officials.

If not otherwise dictated by law, the following oath of office may be used: "Do you solemnly swear that you will faithfully discharge, according to law, your duties as _____ to the best of your ability, so help you God?"

**** Affirmation Wording: "When any person, required to take an oath, from scruples of conscience declines to take it in the usual form or when the court is satisfied that any person called as a witness does not believe in the existence of a Supreme Being, a solemn affirmation may be administered to him in the form of the oath prescribed, except that instead of the word 'swear' the words 'solemnly and sincerely affirm and declare' shall be used and instead of the words 'so help you God' the words 'upon the pains and penalties of perjury for false statement' shall be used" (CGS 1-23).

***** Depositions and Subpoenas: Officials in the office of the Secretary of the State caution that the Notary's statutory authority to take depositions and to issue subpoenas under CGS 52-149a through 52-148e is seldom used and should only be exercised by Notaries who have a technical knowledge of the methods and steps to be employed. "The notary can refer a person seeking this service to the clerk of the court in which the action is being heard or to an attorney. Court clerks have the authority to issue subpoenas on behalf of pro se clients" (NPM).

Certified Copy Alternative

"Under Connecticut law, notaries have no authority to prepare 'certified' or 'true' copies of any documents. It is a very common request and notaries should be prepared to meet such requests in a helpful manner. This office recommends that all notaries use the following procedure:

"The notary should request that the person presenting the document make a photocopy and prepare a written statement, that may be attached to or written on the photocopy itself, stating that it is a true copy of the original. The individual then verifies under oath, administered by the notary, that the statement is true. The requesting party signs the statement in the notary's presence and (a) form of jurat ... is attached and completed by the notary.

"This procedure will work well in the great majority of cases, however it cannot be used in connection with certain types of public records. A 'public record' is one filed with and maintained by a public record keeper, such as a town clerk, or the Secretary of the State, often pursuant to a statutory requirement. Copies of public records are 'certified' when the authority having custody of the records confirms that they are true and accurate copies of the originals.

"Section 7-62a of the Connecticut General Statutes ... entitled 'Illegal issuance of certificates,' specifically prohibits anyone other than a town clerk/registrar of vital statistics or the Commissioner of Public Health from preparing certified copies of certificates of birth, marriage, death or fetal death. This provision acts as a safeguard against the falsification of information in these certificates. These records are viewed as critical or 'vital' records and are maintained by public record keepers to insure the accuracy and integrity of the information they contain. If an individual requires a certified copy of such a document, he/she should be directed to the public record keeper who has custody of those records. A notary should never perform a notarial act in connection with a photocopy of any such document" (NPM).

Ascertaining Competence

"The notary should always be confident that the individual requesting notarial services is competent. Competence simply means that the individual understands the meaning of his/her actions. The notary should refuse to perform any notarial act for a person who is clearly incompetent. If a question of an individual's competence arises, the notary may consult that person's physician or attorney" (NPM).

Notarizing for Minors: "Notaries will occasionally be asked to perform notarial acts for younger persons. Two issues arise in such cases that make these transactions different from the usual notarial act. Frequently, younger persons do not have adequate forms of identification to meet the requirement for satisfactory proof of identification. One means of addressing this obstacle is to recommend that the notarial act be performed by a notary who personally knows the individual.

"Another option would be to obtain identification through the oath or affirmation of a credible witness ... The second issue is that of competence. The notary must be confident that the younger person understands the nature of the document he/she is signing" (NPM).

Deed Witnesses

In addition to acknowledgement before a Notary or other authorized official, two witnesses are required in executing a deed for real property in Connecticut (CGS 47-5).

Wills

"A notary should only perform a notarial act in connection with a will if the instrument specifically provides for such act. (See Section 45a-251 of the Connecticut General Statutes ...)

"If a notary is uncertain as to how to perform a notarial act in connection with a will, the notary should seek the advice of an attorney or refuse to perform the notarial act. A notary public is not trained or authorized to assist persons in the execution of wills. If the testator asks the notary for assistance, the notary should refer that person to an attorney. The notary should be particularly cautious with regard to holographic, or 'handwritten' wills" (NPM).

Foreign-Language Documents

"On occasion, notaries public will be asked to perform notarial acts in connection with documents prepared in a language that they do not understand. The notary should use his/her best judgment when deciding whether or not to perform a notarial act under these circumstances.

"If the notary decides to proceed with the notarial act, he/she should at a minimum, be able to determine the nature of the document(s) and if the notary keeps a journal this notarial act should be noted in his/her journal. When performing a notarial act in connection with documents that he/she cannot understand, he/she should only sign a notarial certificate ... in a language he/she can read and understand" (NPM).

Translations: "(A) notary public has no authority to certify translations. If a notary public has the ability to prepare translations of documents from one language to another he/she cannot notarize the translation. The statement as to the accuracy of the translation can be made under oath. However, the oath and notarial certificate must be completed by another notary or by another person authorized to administer oaths. The notary cannot perform both acts in connection with the same document" (NPM).

Use of Foreign-Language Terms: "Notaries ... should never use a foreign-language term to describe their office. The use of such a term could mislead a person seeking notarial services into believing that the notary had the authority to provide services, which are not allowed under Connecticut's notary law" (NPM).

Certificate Should Be Displayed

"The certificate (of appointment) is evidence of the public office that the notary holds and should be kept in a safe place. We recommend that notaries display their certificates where they perform their notarial duties" (NPM).

NOTARY DON'TS

A Connecticut Notary may:
1. NOT perform any official action with intent to deceive or defraud (CGS 3-94h);
2. NOT use the Notary's title or seal in an endorsement or promotional statement for any product, service, contest or other offering (CGS 3-94h);
3. NOT "unreasonably refuse to perform notarial acts in lawful transactions for any requesting person who tenders payment of the statutory fee" (CGS 3-94f);
4. NOT certify the accuracy of a translation using the Notary title or seal (NPM);
5. NOT certify corporate information, such as the fact that a particular corporation exists or the incumbency of officers (NPM);
6. NOT forfeit impartiality by "advis(ing) or influenc(ing) a person to enter into or refrain from entering into a lawful transaction that involves a notarial act to be performed by the notary" (NPM);
7. NOT notarize a blank document (NPM).

Unreasonably Refusing to Serve

"It is very important that notaries always remember the public nature of the office they hold. It is the duty of all notaries to serve the public and they may not unreasonably refuse to perform a notarial act for any member of the public who tenders the statutory fee and meets all requirements prescribed by statute" (NPM).

Disqualifying Interests

"A notary public is disqualified from performing a notarial act if the notary is a signatory of the document that is to be notarized" (CGS 3-94g).

"It is impossible for a notary to be a witness to his own act. It is strictly prohibited by Connecticut law" (NPM).

"A notary must always remain impartial and cannot advise or influence a person to enter into or refrain from entering into a lawful transaction that involves a notarial act to be performed by the notary" (NPM).

Pursuant to Public Act No. 91-110, effective May 22, 1991, Notaries are no longer disqualified from performing notarial acts in transactions from which they will receive a commission, fee or other consideration that exceeds the value of the statutory Notary fee, or from performing notarial acts for relatives. "It is important for the notary to remember that all notarial acts must be performed with impartiality. The Office of the Secretary of the State strongly recommends that notaries exercise great caution when performing notarial acts in transactions where the notary has some beneficial interest, or which involve family members. In certain instances, the notary may choose to voluntarily disqualify him/herself from performing notarial acts in connection with such transactions" (NPM).

Witness May Notarize: "Persons who only witness the signing of a document are not considered to be signatories and, therefore, may also perform notarial acts in connection with documents they have witnessed" (NPM). In Connecticut, there usually are two witnesses to a real property deed.

Cooperatives: A Notary who is an officer, trustee or member of a cooperative may take acknowledgments of documents in which the cooperative is a party or beneficiary (CGS 33-239).

NOTARY SIGNING AGENTS

Some Notary Signing Agents do operate in the state of Connecticut but not without challenge, particularly from members of the Real Property Section of the Connecticut Bar Association. Connecticut real estate attorneys hold that conducting a closing for the sale or purchase of real property, or for a loan secured by real property, is the practice of law and an activity open only to licensed lawyers. Even so, there are no statutes, regulations or official directives that expressly govern, regulate or restrict the operation of Notary Signing Agents within the state of Connecticut.

NOTARY FEES

The maximum fee that a Connecticut Notary may charge for any notarial act is $5, plus an additional 35 cents for each mile of travel (CGS 3-95).

NOTARY CERTIFICATES

Connecticut has adopted the *Uniform Acknowledgment Act*, including the certificates (CGS 1-34) for:
1. Acknowledgment by individual;
2. Acknowledgment by corporation;
3. Acknowledgment by attorney in fact;
4. Acknowledgment by any public officer or deputy thereof, or by any trustee, administrator, guardian or executor.

For the text of the above certificates, see "Uniform Acknowledgment Act (1939, amended 1960)," Section 7, in Appendix 4.

Connecticut has also adopted the *Uniform Recognition of Acknowledgments Act*, including the short-form certificates (CGS 1-62) for:
1. Acknowledgment by individual;
2. Acknowledgment by corporation;
3. Acknowledgment by partnership;
4. Acknowledgment by attorney in fact;
5. Acknowledgment by any public officer trustee, or personal representative.

For the text of these certificates, see "Uniform Recognition of Acknowledgments Act (1968)," Section 6, in Appendix 3.

The Notary's commission expiration date and the words "Notary Public" must be added to each of the above certificates, as required by law.

Form of Acknowledgment Certificate

"The form of a certificate of acknowledgment used by a person whose authority is recognized under (*Uniform Recognition of Acknowledgments Act*, Section 1) shall be accepted in this state if: 1) The certificate is in a form prescribed by the laws or regulations of this state; 2) the certificate is in a form prescribed by the laws or regulations applicable in the place in which the acknowledgment is taken; or 3) the certificate contains the words 'acknowledged before me,' or their substantial equivalent" (CGS 1-60).

Acknowledgment by Individual (CGS 1-34[1] and NPM):

State of Connecticut
County of _____ ss. (Town/City)

On this the ____ day of _____, 20__, before me _____ (name of Notary), the undersigned officer, personally appeared _____ (name of individual or individuals), known to me (or satisfactorily proven) to be the person(s) whose name(s) is/are subscribed to the within instrument and acknowledged that he/she/they executed the same for the purposes therein contained.

In witness whereof I hereunto set my hand.

_____ (Signature of Notary)
Notary Public
Date Commission Expires: _____

Acknowledgment by Individual Identified by Credible Witness (NPM):

State of Connecticut
County of _____ ss. (Town/City)

On this the ____ day of _____, 20__, before me _____ (name of Notary), the undersigned Notary Public, personally appeared _____ (name of individual or individuals), proved to me on the basis of satisfactory evidence, in the form of the oath/ affirmation of _____ (name of credible witness, personally known to the Notary), to be the person(s) whose name(s) is/are subscribed to the within instrument and acknowledged that he/she/they executed the same for the purposes therein contained.

In witness whereof I hereunto set my hand.

_____ *(Signature of Notary)*
Notary Public
Date Commission Expires: _____

Acknowledgment by Signer by Mark (NPM):

"If a person cannot sign his or her name because of a physical handicap or illiteracy a mark can serve as a signature. A mark, usually an "X," can suffice. Two witnesses in addition to the notary should be present when a person signs by mark. The name of the person who signs by mark should be written near the mark by one of the witnesses. The witnesses should also subscribe their own names to the document as witnesses, and to the notary's journal. The following form is a widely used signature certificate" (NPM).

State of Connecticut
County of _____ ss. (Town/City)

On this the _____ day of _____, 20__, before me, the undersigned Notary Public, personally appeared _____ (name of signer by mark), known to me (or proved to me on the basis of satisfactory evidence) to be the person who made and acknowledged making his/her mark on the within instrument in my presence and in the presence of the two persons indicated below who have signed the within instrument as witnesses, one of whom, _____ (name of witness), also wrote the name of the signer by mark near the mark.

_____ *(Signature of Notary)*
Notary Public
Date Commission Expires: _____

_____
(Witness's Name and Address)

_____
(Witness's Name and Address)

Acknowledgment by Corporation (CGS 1-34[2] and NPM):

State of Connecticut
County of _____ ss. (Town/City)

On this the _____ day of _____, 20__, before me _____ (name of Notary), the undersigned officer, personally appeared _____ (name of officer), who acknowledged himself/herself to be the _____ (title of officer) of _____ (name of corporation), a corporation, and that he/she as such _____ (title of officer), being authorized so to do, executed the foregoing instrument for the purposes therein contained, by signing the name of the corporation by himself/herself as _____ (title of officer).

In witness whereof I hereunto set my hand.

_____ *(Signature of Notary)*
Notary Public
Date Commission Expires: _____

Acknowledgment by Limited Liability Company (CGS 1-34[5]):

State of Connecticut
County of _____ ss. (Town/City)

On this the _____ day of _____, 20__, before me, _____ (name of Notary), the undersigned officer, personally appeared _____ (name of signer), who acknowledged himself/herself to be the _____ (title) of _____ (name of company), a member-managed/manager-managed limited liability company, and that he/she, as such _____ (title), being authorized so to do, executed the foregoing instrument for the purposes therein contained, by signing the name of the limited liability company by himself/herself as _____ (title).

In witness whereof I hereunto set my hand.

_____ *(Signature of Notary)*
Notary Public
Date Commission Expires: _____

(Also, see the shorter acknowledgment certificate for a limited liability company in CGS 1-62[6].)

Connecticut

A–C

Acknowledgment by Registered Limited Liability Partnership (CGS 1-34[6]):

State of Connecticut
County of _____ ss. (Town/City)

On this the _____ day of _____, 20__, before me, _____ (name of Notary), the undersigned officer, personally appeared _____ (name of signer), who acknowledged himself/herself to be the _____ (title) of _____ (name of partnership), a registered limited liability partnership, and that he/she, as such _____ (title), being authorized so to do, executed the foregoing instrument for the purposes therein contained, by signing the name of the registered limited liability partner-ship by himself/herself as _____ (title).

In witness whereof I hereunto set my hand.

_____ (Signature of Notary)
Notary Public
Date Commission Expires: _____

(Also, see the shorter acknowledgment certificate for a registered limited liability partnership in CGS 1-62[7].)

Acknowledgment by Military Officer (CGS 1-38):

U.S. military officers with the rank of second lieutenant or higher may take the acknowledgment of persons serving with the armed forces or their dependents, wherever located. No authentication is necessary, and failure to state a venue will not invalidate the document. The certificate should be substantially in the following form:

On this the _____ day of _____, 20__, before me, _____, the undersigned officer, personally appeared _____ (name and serial number, if any), known to me (or satisfactorily proven) to be serving in or with the armed forces of the United States (or a dependent of _____ [name and serial number, if any], a person serving in or with the armed forces of the United States) and to be the person whose name is subscribed to the within instrument and acknowledged that he/she executed the same for the purposes therein contained.

And the undersigned does further certify that he/she is at the date of this certificate a commissioned officer of the rank stated below and is in the active service of the armed forces of the United States.

(OFFICER'S SIGNATURE, RANK, SERIAL NUMBER AND COMMAND TO WHICH ATTACHED)

Jurat for Affidavit (NPM):

Subscribed and sworn to before me this _____ day of _____, 20__.

_____ (Signature of Notary)
Notary Public
Date Commission Expires: _____

ELECTRONIC NOTARIZATIONS

The state of Connecticut has not yet adopted statutes or regulations expressly establishing rules, definitions and procedures for electronic notarization.

UETA Recognizes Notary's eSignature

Connecticut has adopted the Uniform Electronic Transactions Act (Public Act No. 02-68, effective October 1, 2002), including the following provision on notarization and acknowledgment, thereby recognizing the legal validity of electronic signatures used by Notaries:

"If a law requires a signature or record to be notarized, acknowledged, verified or made under oath, the requirement is satisfied if the electronic signature of the person authorized to perform such acts, together with all other information required to be included by other applicable law, is attached to or logically associated with the signature or record."

No Seal Image for Electronic Recording

Connecticut has adopted the Uniform Real Property Electronic Recording Act (URPERA) through enactment of Public Act 08-56 — effective October 1, 2009 — including the following provision related to the Notary's seal:

"A requirement that a document or a signature associated with a document be notarized, acknowledged, verified, witnessed or made under oath is satisfied if the electronic signature of the person authorized to perform that act, and all other information required to be included, is attached to or logically associated with the document or signature. A physical or electronic image of a stamp, impression or seal need not accompany an electronic signature" (CGS 7-35cc[c]).

Video-Conference 'Notarization' Unauthorized

"Notarization via video-conference is not allowed. The signer is not considered to have 'personally appeared' before the notary, as required by statute. Additionally, a Connecticut notary does not have the authority to notarize within the state when the signer is out of state" (NPM).

NOTARY RECORDS

"Connecticut state law does not require that notaries maintain a journal of their notarial acts. However, it is the very strong recommendation of the Office of the Secretary of the State that they do so. The journal is a record of the notarial acts performed and could be vital in protecting the notary from possible liability. The journal should be a bound book to prevent loss of pages, and the notary should record the following information for each transaction" (NPM):

    1. Date and time of the notarial act;
    2. Nature or type of notarial act performed;
    3. Description of the document or proceeding;
    4. Signature, printed name and address of each person for whom a notarial act is performed;
    5. Method by which a person's identity has been determined;
    6. Fee, if any charged; and
    7. Place where the notarial act was performed.

AUTHENTICATION OF NOTARIAL ACTS

Town Clerk

Locally, authenticating certificates for a Notary may be obtained at the office of the town clerk where the Notary has filed a certificate of appointment and oath of office (CGS 7-33a); authenticating certificates for justices of the peace and superior court commissioners are also available from the town clerk. For a given Notary, an authenticating certificate may be available at more than one town clerk office: if the Notary has a principal place of business in other than the town of residence, the Notary may also file an appointment and oath with the clerk in that other town (CGS 3-94c).

Fee: $2.

Secretary of the State

Authenticating certificates for Connecticut Notaries, including apostilles, are also issued by the Secretary of the State's office.

Fee: $40 per certificate, covering either an authenticating certificate for the Notary, an apostille, or an authenticating certificate for the town clerk. For documents used in connection with foreign adoptions, however, the fee is only $15 per certificate. For expedited (within 24 hours) service, add $50 per certificate to the above fees, but adoptions cannot be expedited. Personal checks are accepted and payable to "Secretary of the State". Visa and Mastercard are also accepted.

    Mail Address:
    Authentications and Apostilles
    Office of Secretary of the State
    P.O. Box 150470
    Hartford, CT 06115–0470

    Courier Only:
    Office of Secretary of the State
    Authentications and Apostilles
    30 Trinity Street
    Hartford, CT 06106

    Telephone: 1-860-509-6002

Procedure: Mail or present in person the original notarized document(s) and the appropriate fee. Customers may complete the "Authentication/Apostille Order Form" — available on the Secretary's website — or provide a cover letter that includes the following information: name; company name (if applicable); street address; city; state; zip code; daytime telephone number; and country in which the document(s) will be used. All orders will be returned by first class mail, unless the customer provides for an alternative prepaid delivery service.

"For other documents, such as diplomas and school transcripts, we recommend the following procedure: The person in possession of the document can make a photocopy and prepare a written statement that may be attached to or written on the photocopy, stating that the copy is a true and correct copy of the original. The individual will then verify the statement under oath before a notary public and the notary will indicate by a jurat that he or she has administered an oath to the testator" (website, "Authentications and Apostilles").

"Orders for Expedited Service submitted by mail must be clearly marked with the words 'Expedited Service' on the outside of the envelope" (Authentication/Apostille Order Form).

COMMISSIONING AND ADMINISTRATION

The Secretary of the State appoints, regulates and maintains records on Connecticut's Notaries (CGS 3-94b and 3-94m).

Applying for Commission

Qualifications: An applicant for a commission as a Connecticut Notary Public must (CGS 3-94b[b]): (a) be at least 18 years old and (b) reside in or have a principal place of business in Connecticut. The Secretary of the State may deny appointment to any person who has been convicted of a felony or other crime involving dishonesty or moral turpitude, who has had a previous Notary commission revoked, or who has engaged in some form of notarial misconduct (NPM).

Written Test Required: Each applicant under oath must pass the written examination incorporated into the application form. All questions must be completed correctly before the applicant may be appointed.

Application: The application (CGS 3-94b[b][4]) must be completed in the applicant's own handwriting, except for the recommendation of an individual who has personally known the applicant for at least one year and is not legally related to the applicant. "Certificate of Character," which must be filled out and signed by a public official or a reputable business or professional person who is unrelated to the applicant and has known the applicant for at least one year. The nonrefundable application fee is $120. The jurat on the form must be completed by a Notary (not the applicant) or other oath-administering official.

For renewals, no later than three months prior to the expiration date of an appointment as Notary, a renewal application will be mailed to the Notary at the last reported residence address. The renewal application fee is $60.

Filing Certificate of Appointment: A "Certificate of Appointment" will be sent to the new Notary. Within 30 days of its receipt, and before performing notarial acts, the Notary must file this Certificate with its oath of office with the clerk of the town in which the Notary resides or, for a non-resident of Connecticut, the clerk of the town in which the Notary's principal place of business is located (CGS 3-94c[c]). While the oath of office on the Certificate may be taken before any oath-administering official (including another Notary), many Notaries find it convenient to take this oath from the town clerk at the same time they record their Certificate. The recording of the oath and appointment will be confirmed by the town clerk on the Certificate. The recording fee is $10 (CGS 7-34a). (Notaries also have the option of recording their Certificate of Appointment in other towns.)

Non-Residents: A resident of another state may become a Notary if the person's principal place of business is in Connecticut (CGS 3-94b).

Changes of Status

If Notary Moves: Within 30 days after a change of residence address (or address of principal place of business, for nonresidents) the Notary must inform the Secretary of the State in writing (CGS 3-94n). Even non-residents must report a change in residence address. A form for reporting an address change may be downloaded from the Web site or photocopied from the "Notary Public Manual." The filing fee is $15.

If the move is to a new town or city, the Notary must then, within 30 days after issuance of a replacement Certificate of Appointment by the Secretary, record this certificate with the town clerk of the new municipality; but failure to do so will not invalidate any notarial act performed by that Notary.

"A notary public who ceases to either reside within the state or have one's principal place of business in the state shall immediately resign as a notary ..." (CGS 3-94p).

If Notary Changes Name: "If a notary who is a Connecticut resident changes his or her name or residence address, the notary is required to report that change to the Secretary of State's Office within thirty days. Nonresident notaries must maintain a principal place of business in Connecticut and must report any change in their business address, as well as changes in residence address. Forms for reporting such charges are available from (the) Web site's forms page. When completed, the forms must be filed with the Secretary's office with the appropriate fees ($15.00 for Change of Name and Change of Address, $5.00 for Duplicate Certificates).

"When the form has been processed, a new certificate (of appointment) will be issued. It is not necessary for the notary to take an oath of office upon receiving a replacement certificate, but if the notary has relocated to a new town of residence or principal place of business, the replacement certificate must be recorded with the town clerk in the new town of residence." (website, "Applying for Appointment...").

"When a notary files a name change with the Office of the Secretary of the State, that change of name becomes effective the date of issuance of a new Certificate of Appointment. A notary, who uses a seal or stamp, will have to obtain a new seal or stamp reflecting the name change" (NPM).

If Notary Resigns: To resign, a signed, written notice of resignation must be filed with the Secretary of the State, indicating an effective date. The seal must also must be defaced or destroyed (NPM).

If Notary's Appointment Is Revoked: Within 30 days after the resignation, revocation or suspension of a Notary's certificate of appointment, the Secretary of the State must notify all town clerks within the state (CGS 3-94m). The town clerk of any municipality in which such Notary's certificate of appointment, or a replacement certificate, has been recorded must note the resignation, revocation or suspension, and the effective date thereof on the appropriate municipal record.

If Notary Dies: "As soon as possible after the death of a notary public, the notary's personal representative shall destroy the notary's official notarial seal, if any, and file a signed, written notice, with the secretary of the state, indicating that the notary public has died and the date of death" (CGS 3-94q).

TOWN CLERKS

To contact a Connecticut town clerk to obtain an authenticating certificate for a Notary, or to seek assistance in locating a Notary, telephone long-distance information — 1-XXX-555-1212 — using the following area codes:

Andover (860)
Ansonia (203)
Ashford (860)
Avon (860)
Barkhamstead (860)
Beacon Falls (203)
Berlin (860)
Bethany (203)
Bethel (860)
Bethlehem (203)
Bloomfield (860)
Bolton (860)
Bozrah (860)
Branford (203)
Bridgeport (203)
Bridgewater (860)
Bristol (860)
Brookfield (203)
Brooklyn (860)
Burlington (860)
Canaan (860)
Canterbury (860)
Canton (860)
Chaplin (860)
Cheshire (203)
Chester (860)
Clinton (860)
Colchester (860)
Colebrook (860)
Columbia (860)
Cornwall (860)
Coventry (860)
Cromwell (860)
Danbury (203)
Darien (203)
Deep River (860)
Derby (203)
Durham (860)
Eastford (860)
East Granby (860)
East Haddam (860)
East Hampton (860)
East Hartford (860)
East Haven (203)
East Lyme (860)
Easton (203)
East Windsor (860)
Ellington (860)
Enfield (860)
Essex (860)
Fairfield (203)
Farmington (860)
Franklin (860)
Glastonbury (860)
Goshen (860)
Granby (860)
Greenwich (203)
Griswold (860)
Groton (860)
Guilford (203)
Haddam (860)
Hamden (203)
Hampton (860)
Hartford (860)
Hartland (860)
Harwinton (860)
Hebron (860)
Kent (860)
Killingly (860)
Killingworth (860)
Lebanon (860)
Ledyard (860)
Lisbon (860)
Litchfield (860)
Lyme (860)
Madison (203)
Manchester (860)
Mansfield (860)
Marlborough (860)
Meriden (203)
Middlebury (203)
Middlefield (860)
Middletown (860)
Milford (203)
Monroe (860)
Montville (860)
Morris (860)
Naugatuck (203)
New Britain (860)
New Canaan (203)

New Fairfield (203)
New Hartford (860)
New Haven (203)
Newington (860)
New London (860)
New Milford (860)
Newtown (203)
Norfolk (860)
North Branford (203)
North Canaan (860)
North Haven (203)
No. Stonington (860)
Norwalk (203)
Norwich (860)
Old Lyme (860)
Old Saybrook (860)
Orange (203)
Oxford (203)
Plainfield (860)
Plainville (860)
Plymouth (860)
Pomfret (860)
Portland (860)
Preston (860)
Prospect (203)
Putnam (860)
Redding (203)
Ridgefield (203)
Rocky Hill (860)
Roxbury (860)
Salem (860)
Salisbury (860)
Scotland (860)
Seymour (203)
Sharon (860)
Shelton (203)
Sherman (860)
Simsbury (860)
Somers (860)
Southbury (203)

Southington (860)
South Windsor (860)
Sprague (860)
Stafford (860)
Stamford (203)
Sterling (860)
Stonington (860)
Stratford (860)
Suffield (860)
Thomaston (860)
Thompson (860)
Tolland (860)
Torrington (860)
Trumbull (203)
Union (860)
Vernon (860)
Voluntown (860)
Wallingford (203)
Warren (860)
Washington (860)
Waterbury (203)
Waterford (860)
Watertown (860)
Westbrook (860)
West Hartford (860)
West Haven (203)
Weston (203)
Westport (203)
Wethersfield (860)
Willington (860)
Wilton (203)
Winchester (860)
Windham (860)
Windsor (860)
Windsor Locks (860)
Wolcott (203)
Woodbridge (203)
Woodbury (203)
Woodstock (860)

Bridgeport, City of (203)
Danbury, City of (203)
Derby, City of (203)
Groton, City of (860)
Waterbury, City of (203)

OTHER NOTARIAL OFFICERS

In addition to Notaries Public, the following officers have power to take acknowledgments within the state (CGS 1-29):

1. A judge of a court of record;
2. A family support magistrate;
3. A clerk or deputy clerk of a court having a seal;
4. A commissioner of deeds;
5. A town clerk or assistant town clerk (CGS 47-5a);
6. A justice of the peace;
7. An attorney admitted to the state bar;
8. A commissioner of the superior court (CGS 47-5a).

Attorney Acting outside State

"An acknowledgment of any instrument pertaining to real property located in this state or a power of attorney may be made outside the state before an attorney admitted to the bar in this state" (CGS 1-30, 1-31 and 1-31a).

Police Notaries

State police majors, captains, lieutenants and sergeants who are Notaries may only notarize for police matters, using the state police seal as the notarial seal and not charging for their acts (CGS 3-94e). They must resign their commissions upon terminating employment with the police.

QUICK FACTS

Notary Jurisdiction
Statewide (CGS 3-94c).

Attorney Acting Outside State: An acknowledgment of any instrument pertaining to real property located in Connecticut, or a power of attorney, may be made outside the state, anywhere in the world, before a non-Notary attorney admitted to the Connecticut bar (CGS 1-30, 1-31 and 1-31a).

Notary Term Length
Five years (CGS 3-94c), expiring at midnight on the last day of the anniversary month of appointment five years later. "A notary public's appointment expires at midnight on the 'commission expiration date' that appears on his/her Certificate of Appointment" (NPM).

Notary Bond
Not required by law.

Liability of Employer: "An employer of a notary shall be liable to any person for any damages proximately caused to that person by the notary's official misconduct related to the employer's business, if the employer directed, encouraged, consented to, ratified or approved the notary's official misconduct, either in the particular transaction or, implicitly, by previous actions in at least one similar transaction" (CGS 3-94l[b]). The employer may also be liable to the Notary in certain circumstances involving coercion by the employer (CGS 3-94l[c]).

A–C

Delaware

NOTARY SEAL

A Delaware Notary must authenticate all official acts with a seal of office (29 DC 4309 and 4310) — effective June 24, 1999, with legislative enactment of Chapter 65, Volume 72. Prior to this date, seals had been optional for Notaries.

Kind

<u>Black-Inked Rubber Stamp or Embosser</u>: "Each notary public shall provide, keep and use a seal that is either an engraved embossed seal or a black-inked rubber stamp seal to be used on the paper document being notarized" (29 DC 4310[a]).

<u>Seal Must Be Sharp, Legible, Permanent</u>: "Near the notary's official signature on the notarial certificate of a paper document, the notary shall affix a sharp, legible, permanent, and photographically reproducible image of the official seal, or, to an electronic document, the notary shall attach an official electronic seal" (29 DC 4327[b][4]).

NOTARY ADMINISTRATION

Office of Secretary of State
Notary Public Section   1-302-739-4111
John G. Townsend Bldg.
401 Federal St., Suite 4
Dover, DE 19901

(P.O. Box 898
Dover, DE 19903)

Website: http://notary.delaware.gov/

NOTARY RULES

DC — DELAWARE CODE

Most Notary rules are in the Delaware Code, Title 29, Chapter 43, "Notaries Public."*

* *The Uniform Law on Notarial Acts of 1982, adopted with numerous changes and additions, is included as Sections 4321 through 4329.*

"For embossed seals, taking a pencil across the seal or using seal impression inkers (available from most notary suppliers) are both good options" (formerly on the Secretary's website).

Shape/Size

Not specified.

Components

1. Name of Notary, exactly as it appears on commission;
2. "Notary Public";
3. "State of Delaware";
4. "My Commission expires on (date)" *.

* For Limited Governmental Notaries, the expiration date is replaced with "My Commission expires upon office".

Non-Conforming Seals

"If the official seal of any notary public is not engraved in conformity with this section, it shall not invalidate an official act, but such act shall be as valid as though the seal had been engraved in conformity with the requirements of this section …

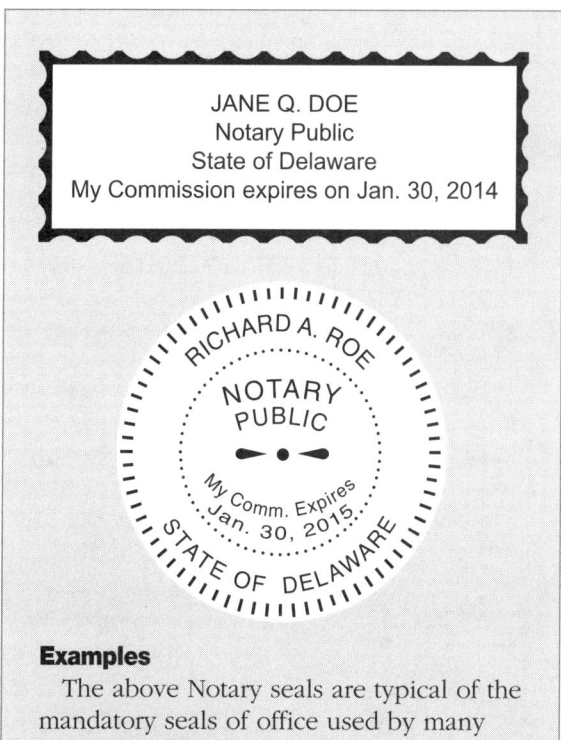

Examples

The above Notary seals are typical of the mandatory seals of office used by many Delaware Notaries.

"Any notary public failing to comply with the requirements of this section may be removed by the Governor for neglect" (29 DC 4310[b] and [h]).

Commission Expiration Date Must Appear

The Notary's commission expiration date must appear on the notarial certificate, "but omission of that information may subsequently be corrected" (29 DC 4327[a]).

Notary's Name, Title Must Be Photocopiable

"(a) Any document presented to the recorder for recording which contains a certificate of a notarial act as defined by §§ 4321(3) and 4327 of Title 29 (existing or as amended), shall, in addition to other matters which may be required by law, identify the name and title of the notarial officer who executed the certificate in a legible manner which is suitable for micrographic or electronic reproduction.

"(b) The use of a typewriter, printer or rubber stamp which when applied to the instrument produces the printed information required by subsection (a) of this section shall also be authorized.

"(c) The recorder may refuse to record any document that contains a certificate of a notarial act which does not comply with subsection (a) of this section unless the person recording the instrument pays a penalty equal to the authorized recording fee for said document.

"(d) The recording of any instrument which does not comply with subsection (a) of this section shall not affect its validity or admissibility as a public record" (9 DC 9611).

Rubber Stamp Use Encouraged: "Notaries must now legibly identify their name and title on all documents to be recorded as public land records. To accomplish this, the use of a typewriter or rubber stamp is encouraged" (spokesperson for office of Secretary of State).

Loss, Theft or Compromise of Seal

The Secretary of State must be notified within 10 days of any loss, theft or compromise of the Notary's official physical or electronic seal (29 DC 4310[g]). Notification by email (notary@delaware.gov) is acceptable, and should include the name on the Notary commission and a brief explanation of the circumstances of the loss or damage. In the case of theft or vandalism, the Notary must also inform the appropriate law enforcement agency (website, "Lost Notary Seal"). In the case of an electronic seal, the Secretary's office will disable use of the missing technology.

Employer Does Not Keep Seal

"Even if your employer pays for the commission and stamp, when you leave employment, your stamp/seal, commission and journal/record book … leave with you" (website, "Frequently Asked Questions").

Seal of Limited Governmental Notary

Under 29 DC 4306(d), the seals of limited governmental Notaries appointed by the Governor must conform with Section 4310(d), except that the commission expiration date must be replaced by "My Commission expires upon office." For a further discussion of limited governmental Notaries, see "Other Notarial Officers," at the end of this chapter.

Notary's Signature

"In acting as a notary public, a notary shall sign the notary's name exactly and only as it appears on the commission …" (29 DC 4310[d]). The name on the commission must include the first, middle and last names — either using all names in full, or using an initial for either the first or middle name, but not for both (website, "Notary Public Application Instructions").

NOTARY POWERS

Delaware Notaries are authorized to perform the following notarial acts (29 DC 4321[13]):
1. Take acknowledgments* (also DC 4309);
2. Administer oaths** and affirmations**;
3. Take verifications upon oath or affirmation;
4. Witness or attest signatures***;
5. Certify or attest copies****;
6. Execute protests***** of negotiable instruments.

* Acknowledgments: "'Acknowledgment' shall mean a statement by a person that the person has executed an instrument for the purposes stated therein. If the instrument is executed in a representative capacity, an acknowledgment certifies that the person who signed the instrument did so with proper authority and executed the instrument as the act of the person or entity stated therein" (29 DC 4321[1]).

** <u>Oaths and Affirmations</u>: For the purpose of executing criminal warrants, oaths and affirmations may be administered by trained court or law enforcement personnel "via videophone, telephone, secure electronic means or in person" (11 DC 222 [21]). A spokesperson for the state Notary Public Section advised that the "average Notary" will never encounter such a situation.

*** <u>Witnessing or Attesting Signatures</u>: "In witnessing or attesting a signature, the notarial officer must determine, either from personal knowledge of identity or from satisfactory evidence of identity, that the signature is that of the person appearing before the officer and named therein" (20 DC 4322[c]).

**** <u>Certifying Copies</u>: "In certifying or attesting a copy of a document the notary public must supervise the making of a photocopy of an original document and shall attest to the authenticity of such copy. Notaries public, however, shall not attest to copies of official or public records, only of documents that cannot be certified by a public official" (29 DC 4322[d]). For example, Notaries may not certify a copy of a recorded deed nor of a birth certificate (website, "Frequently Asked Questions").

In a copy certification, the Notary "[c]opies or supervises the copying of the document using a photographic or electronic copying process," compares the original document to the copy, and determines that the copy is "accurate and complete" (29 DC 4321[3]).

***** <u>Protests</u>: "In making or noting a protest of a negotiable instrument, a notarial officer must determine the matters set forth in Section 3-505 of Title 6" (29 DC 4322[e]).

Identifying Signers

Both a Notary and an Electronic Notary "must ensure, either from personal knowledge of identity or from satisfactory evidence of identity as defined in § 4321 of this title, that the individual whose presence and signature is being certified is in fact the person he or she claims to be" (29 DC 4309[a]).

<u>Personal Knowledge</u>: "'Personal knowledge of identity' or 'personally knows' means familiarity with an individual resulting from interactions with that individual over a period of time sufficient to dispel any reasonable uncertainty that the individual has the identity claimed" (29 DC 4321[16]).

<u>Satisfactory Evidence</u>: "'Satisfactory evidence of identity' means identification of an individual based on:

"i. Examination of 1 or more of the following documents bearing a photographic image of the individual's face and signature: a United States Passport, a certificate of United States citizenship, a certificate of naturalization, an unexpired foreign passport, an alien registration card with photograph, a state-issued driver's license or a state-issued identification card or a United States military card; or

"ii. The oath or affirmation of 1 credible witness unaffected by the document or transaction who is personally known to the notary and who personally knows the individual or of 2 credible witnesses unaffected by the document or transaction who each personally knows the individual and shows to the notary documentary identification as described in subdivision (i)" (29 DC 4321[21]).

"'Credible witness' means an honest, reliable, and impartial person who personally knows an individual appearing before a notary and takes an oath or affirmation from the notary to confirm that individual's identity" (29 DC 4321[4]).

Determining Signer's Competence

"Although this is not specifically addressed in the law, many experts recommend that the notary make a limited inquiry into the person's ability to understand the contents of the document that the person is signing. The notary can make a quick assessment by asking the person if he or she understands the document. As a best practice, a notary should refuse to notarize the signature of a person who appears unable to understand the document or who appears to be under the influence of drugs or alcohol" (website, "Frequently Asked Questions").

Foreign-Language Documents

"Delaware law does not prohibit notarizing documents in a foreign language. As long as the notary can determine if the document contains any blank spaces, the notarization can occur as usual" (website, "Frequently Asked Questions").

NOTARY DON'TS

No Notarization without Physical Presence
"A notary public or electronic notary public shall not notarize a document without the person signing the document being personally present" (29 DC 4309[c]).

Document with Blanks Should Not Be Notarized
"[I]f blanks remain in a document after notarization takes place, the possibility exists that the document can be altered. A notary should do everything possible to ensure the integrity of the document being notarized. Therefore, if you are presented a document that contains blanks, please indicate these to the signer. The signer must fill in the blanks with information or if the blank does not apply, the signer should write in 'N/A' or 'not applicable.' The notarization cannot proceed until all blanks are filled in" (website, "Frequently Asked Questions").

Document Needs Notarial Wording
"[If] presented a document without any notarial wording ... [t]he signer will need to provide that information. The signer may need to check with an attorney, or the issuing or receiving agencies of the document to see what is required" (website, "Frequently Asked Questions").

Disqualifying Interests
"[I]f the document to be notarized contains any financial gain or beneficial interest to the notary, the notary should decline to notarize since he or she would not be an impartial witness" (website, "Frequently Asked Questions").

Notarizing for Relatives: "This is not addressed in Delaware law; however, since a notary public by definition is an impartial witness, the best practice would be not to notarize the signature of a relative" (website, "Frequently Asked Questions").

NOTARY SIGNING AGENTS

As a result of a ruling by the Delaware Supreme Court on May 31, 2000, only an attorney licensed to practice law in Delaware may conduct a closing related to the sale or refinancing of real property in the state — see In Re Mid-Atlantic Settlement Ser., 755 A.2d 389 (Del. Supr. 2000). Thus, Notary Signing Agents and other non-attorneys may not operate at such a closing in the state without a presiding attorney present. The only exception is for home equity loans, but then only a lender acting in a pro se capacity may conduct the closing in lieu of an attorney.

NOTARY FEES

"The maximum fee a notary public can charge for any paper notarial act is $5" (29 DC 4311[a]).

Electronic Acts
"The maximum fee a notary public can charge for any electronic notarial act is $25" (29 DC 4311[b]).

"The Secretary may establish a schedule of fees for each electronic notarial act or service, not to exceed $10 per notarial act or service" (29 DC 4307[c]).

Overcharging
For charging more than the statutory maximum fees, the commission of the offending Notary may be revoked, and reappointment will not be allowed for at least two years (29 DC 4311[c]).

Notary Need Not Charge
"A notary public may choose to waive any fee for any notarial act; provided, however, that a notary public may not waive any fee or fees for an electronic notarial act or service assessed pursuant to § 4307(c) of this title" (29 DC 4311[d]).

Workplace and Non-Workplace Notarizations
"You may perform notarizations outside of your workplace after work hours and collect fees associated with such notarizations. Your employer has the right to collect any fees associated with notarizations performed as part of your employment" (website, "Frequently Asked Questions").

NOTE: This does not apply to Electronic Notaries who are appointed based upon current employment specified under 29 DC 4302(c)(2)-(4), nor to other types of Notary who have limitations specifically set forth within 29 DC Chapter 43.

No Charge for Veterans' Affairs
Notaries appointed to serve veterans' groups, including the American Legion, may not charge for their services (29 DC 4306[a]).

No Notary may charge for notarizing any document required by the Veterans Administration and relating to the claim of a veteran or a veteran's relative (29 DC 4312).

NOTARY CERTIFICATES

Delaware has adopted the *Uniform Law on Notarial Acts*, including the short-form certificates (29 DC 4328) for:
1. Acknowledgment by individual;
2. Acknowledgment by representative;
3. Verification upon oath or affirmation;
4. Witnessing or attesting signature;
5. Attesting copy of document.

For the text of these certificates, see "Uniform Law on Notarial Acts (1982)," Section 8, in Appendix 2. The seal of the Notary is not optional and must be affixed to each of the above certificates.

Requirements for Any Notarial Certificate

"(a). A notarial act must be evidenced by a certificate signed and dated by a notarial officer. The certificate must include identification of the jurisdiction in which the notarial act is performed and the title of the office that the notarial officer holds and may include the official stamp or seal of office, or the electronic notary's electronic seal. If the officer is a notary public, the certificate must also indicate the date of expiration, if any, of the commission of office, but omission of that information may subsequently be corrected. If the officer is a commissioned officer on active duty with the military services of the United States, it must also include the officer's rank.

"(b). A certificate of a notarial act is sufficient if it meets the requirements of subsection (a) of this section and it:

"1. Is in the short form set forth in Section 4328 of this title;

"2. Is in a form otherwise prescribed by the law of this State;

"3. Is in a form prescribed by the laws or regulations applicable in the place in which the notarial act was performed; or

"4. Sets forth the actions of the notarial officer, and those are sufficient to meet the requirements of the designated notarial act" (29 DC 4327).

ELECTRONIC NOTARIZATION

Effective February 1, 2009, statutory rules were put in place for electronic notarization in Delaware through the comprehensive revision of Chapter 43 ("Notaries Public") of Title 29 of the Delaware Code. The state has ambitious plans for establishing a nationwide system for electronic notarization that commissions out-of-state residents as Delaware eNotaries: "When fully deployed, the Delaware eNotary system will provide a complete suite of eNotary Trust products including electronic notarization, electronic archiving of notarized documents, and authentication. The e-notarization service, built on a Microsoft SharePoint platform, will allow qualified Delaware eNotaries to acknowledge digital documents, manage journal records and archive transactional data over a web-enabled network" (See http://governor.delaware.gov/news/2010/). However, "the State of Delaware is not issuing electronic notary commissions at this time" (website, "Frequently Asked Questions").

Becoming an Electronic Notary

Under Chapter 43, the Governor with the assistance of the Secretary of State may appoint and commission "electronic notaries," who must be at least 18 years of age and demonstrate their good character and reputation, as well as a reasonable need for an Electronic Notary commission, and be a legal resident of Delaware or a non-resident who either (29 DC 4302[c]):

1. maintains an office or regular place of employment in the state; or

2. is an attorney-at-law in good standing licensed in any state or jurisdiction of the United States, or is a legal assistant or paralegal working under the direct supervision of such an attorney-at-law who is already a Delaware Electronic Notary and demonstrated a need for such legal assistants and paralegals to become Electronic Notaries; or

3. is a current employee of a banking, trust or insurance company in any state or U.S. jurisdiction, and such company must have previously submitted to the Delaware Secretary of State and had approved an application showing that the company is in good standing and has a reasonable need for permitting one or more of its employees to become an Electronic Notary under Delaware law; or

4. is a current employee of a U.S. federal government agency or unit, and such agency or unit must have previously submitted to the Delaware Secretary of State and had approved an application showing that such agency or unit has a reasonable need for permitting one or more of its employees to become an Electronic Notary under Delaware law, and such employees, once appointed, must perform electronic notarial acts only in the course of their official duties.

<u>Non-Resident Applicants</u>: Non-resident applicants must state their residential and Delaware employment street addresses in their applications, subsequently notifying the Secretary within 30 days of any change (29 DC 4301[c]), and those without a Delaware employment address must designate a registered agent in Delaware for service of process.

<u>Term of Office</u>: The term of office for an Electronic Notary is two years and the non-refundable application fee is $60 (29 DC 4307[b]).

<u>Registration Form</u>: An applicant to become an Electronic Notary must submit a registration form that includes: (a) a description of the technology(ies) that will be used to perform electronic notarizations; (b) information about any licensed authority that will issue the registrant's electronic signature; (c) the electronic signature, "which shall be unique to the notary"; and (d) evidence that the registrant has taken a course of instruction, "whether in the classroom, distance learning or online" (29 DC 4302[d]). Continuing education will be required during the two-year term.

<u>Oath of Office</u>: "The notaries and resident electronic notaries shall severally take and subscribe the oath or affirmation prescribed by Article XIV of the Constitution. The nonresident electronic notaries shall severally take and subscribe the oath or affirmation on a commission issued by the Secretary before a notary public or other officer authorized to administer oaths. Notaries and electronic notaries shall be exempt from the recordation of the oath of office prescribed by Title 9 Section 9605(a). Notaries and electronic notaries shall not be permitted to perform notarial acts until a copy of the fully executed commission is received by the Secretary in an electronic or paper document format deemed acceptable by the Secretary" (29 DC 4308).

Performing Electronic Notarial Acts
"The notary's official electronic seal and signature shall be attached to an electronic document in a manner that is capable of independent verification and prevents any subsequent changes or modifications to the electronic document" (29 DC 4310[e]). "In acting as a notary public, a notary shall ... execute the notary's electronic signature in a manner that attributes such signature to the notary public identified on the commission" (29 DC 4310[d]).

"A notary performing electronic notarial acts shall:

"1. Use an electronic seal and signature that conform to generally accepted standards for secure electronic notarization;

"2. Use the notary's electronic seal and signature only for the purpose of performing electronic notarial acts;

"3. Take reasonable steps to ensure that any registered device used to create an electronic signature is current and has not been revoked or terminated by its issuing or registering authority;

"4. Keep the electronic seal and signature secure under the notary's exclusive control and shall not allow them to be used by any other person; and

"5. Take reasonable steps to ensure the integrity, security and authenticity of electronic notarizations" (29 DC 4310[f]).

"An electronic notarial act performed by a notary public or other person authorized in this title shall constitute a notarial act under the laws of this State, provided that the official signature and seal of an electronic notary:

"1. Shall be attached to or logically associated with the document;

"2. Shall be independently verifiable; and

"3. Will be invalidated if the underlying document is modified" (29 DC 4322[f]).

<u>Electronic Notary Seal</u>: "The electronic seal required by § 4309 of this title shall be used in the transaction of all official electronic notarial acts and shall contain the notary's name exactly as it appears on the commission, the words 'My Commission expires on' and the commission expiration date and the words 'Notary Public' and 'State of Delaware' (29 DC 4310[c]).

"'Electronic notary seal' or 'electronic seal' means information within a notarized electronic document that confirms the notary's name, jurisdiction, and commission expiration date and generally corresponds to data in notary seals used on paper documents" (29 DC 4321[11]).

Loss, Theft of Electronic Seal, Signature: Within 10 days of discovering that the Notary's physical or electronic seal, electronic signature, e-Notary ID card, or electronic journal have been lost, stolen or compromised, the Notary must notify the Secretary of State, "who shall disable use of the missing technology on any electronic system of the Secretary" (29 DC 4310[g]). In the case of theft or vandalism, the Notary must also inform the appropriate law enforcement agency (website, "Lost Notary Seal."). To be reinstated as an Electronic Notary, the individual may submit a new registration form.

Expiration or Resignation of Office: Any Electronic Notary whose commission expires or who wishes to resign must "immediately erase, delete or destroy the coding, disk, certificate, card, software or password that enables the electronic affixation of the notary's official electronic signature or seal and shall so certify to the Secretary" (29 DC 4307[e]). Failure to do so may result in a $500 civil penalty.

Jurisdiction of Electronic Notary: "An electronic notarial act performed by a person appointed by the Governor under this Chapter shall be deemed to have been performed within this State" (29 DC 4323[d]).

Electronic Authentication: "On a notarized electronic document transmitted to another state or country outside of the United States, electronic evidence of the authenticity of the official signature and seal of an electronic notary of the State of Delaware, shall be attached to or logically associated with the document and shall be in the form of an electronic certificate of authority signed by the Secretary that is independently verifiable and will be invalidated if the underlying document is modified" (29 DC 4329[a]).

Electronic Journal of Notarial Acts: Electronic Notaries must "keep, maintain, protect and provide for lawful inspection an electronic journal of notarial acts" that contains a record of every electronic notarization performed (29 DC 4314). For content of the electronic journal and security rules, see "Electronic Journal" below, under "Notary Records."

UETA Recognizes Notary's e-Signature

Delaware has adopted the Uniform Electronic Transactions Act (6 DC 12A-101 through 12A-117), including the following provision on notarization, thereby recognizing the legal validity of electronic signatures used by Notaries:

"If a law requires a signature or record to be notarized, acknowledged, verified or made under oath, the requirement is satisfied if the electronic signature of the person authorized to perform those acts, together with all other information required to be included by other applicable law, is attached to or logically associated with the signature or record" (6 DC 12A-111).

No Seal Image for Electronic Recording

Delaware has adopted the Uniform Real Property Electronic Recording Act (URPERA) — see Title 25, Chapter 1, Subchapter V ("Electronic Recording") of the Delaware Code — including the following provision related to the Notary's seal:

"A requirement that a document or a signature associated with a document be notarized, acknowledged, verified, witnessed, or made under oath is satisfied if the electronic signature of the person authorized to perform that act, and all other information required to be included, is attached to or logically associated with the document or signature. A physical or electronic image of a stamp, impression, or seal is not required to accompany an electronic signature" (25 DC 182[c]).

NOTARY RECORDS

While Notaries need not keep a record of their paper-based notarial acts, Electronic Notaries must "keep, maintain, protect and provide for lawful inspection an electronic journal of notarial acts" that contains a record of every electronic notarization performed (29 DC 4314). "[I]t is not required by law but is highly recommended that a notary keep [a record book or journal] for his or her own records" (website, "Frequently Asked Questions").

Electronic Journal

For each electronic notarial act, the Electronic Notary must record the following in the e-journal at the time of notarization (29 DC 4314[b]):

1. The date and time of day of the notarial act;
2. The type of notarial act;
3. The type, title or a description of the

document or proceeding;

4. The printed name and address of each person whose signature is notarized or who requests a notarial act;

5. The evidence of identity of each principal, in the form of either: a statement that the person is "personally known" to the Notary; a notation of the type of identification document relied on, along with its identifying number; or the printed name and address of the credible witness swearing to or affirming the person's identity;

6. The fee, if any, charged for the notarial act; and,

7. Such other information as the notary may deem to be necessary and appropriate.

A Social Security or credit card number may not be recorded in the journal.

Electronic Journal Security: "A notary shall keep the official journal secure under the notary's exclusive control and shall not allow it to be used by any other person (29 DC 4314[d]).

"A notary shall maintain a backup record of an electronic journal and ensure protection of such backup record from unauthorized use. The Secretary shall establish standards for backup records" (29 DC 4314[e]).

Loss, Theft, Compromise of Journal: The Secretary of State must be notified immediately of the electronic journal's loss, theft or compromise (29 DC 4310[g]).

Employer Does Not Keep Journal: "When you leave employment, your stamp/seal, commission and journal/record book … leave with you" (website, "Frequently Asked Questions").

AUTHENTICATION OF NOTARIAL ACTS

Secretary of State

Authenticating certificates for Notaries, including apostilles, are issued by the Division of Corporations in the Delaware Secretary of State's office. (See "Certifications, Apostilles and Authentication of Documents" at www.corp.delaware.gov.)

Fee: $30 for each document, whether for a certificate of authentication or apostille, payable to "Delaware Secretary of State." For any private citizen seeking certification for personal purposes (adoption, death certificate, school transcript, etc.), see "Discounted Fees" below. Also note "Expedited Service Fees" below.

Address:
Delaware Secretary of State
Division of Corporations
John G. Townsend Building
401 Federal St., Suite 4
Dover, DE 19901

Telephone: 1-302-739-3073

Procedure: Mail or present in person the original notarized document(s), along with appropriate fees. Indicate the nation to which the document will be sent. "Any document that is in a foreign language must have the English translation attached to it. The English version must be notarized" (See "Certifications, Apostilles & Authentication of Documents" at www.corp.delaware.gov.)

Discounted Fees: "The Delaware Division of Corporations can apostille or authenticate documents notarized by a Delaware Notary. … When such services are requested for personal use (such as an adoption) the Division discounts its fees as follows: $30.00 for 1 or more documents that are presented simultaneously. This fee structure enables prospective international adoptive parents to minimize their costs by having all of their apostille and authentication documents processed at one time. As a further convenience, requests received via mail are typically processed on the same business day and hand delivered requests will be completed within 2 hours. To help expedite your request, mailed requests must include a cover memo clearly stating the purpose of the request (e.g., adoption in China). Documents may be either hand delivered, mailed or express mailed …" (See "Frequently Asked Questions" at www.corp.delaware.gov.)

Expedited Service Fees: For expedited service for commercial use, the following fees apply: Priority 1 (1-hour), $1000; Priority 2 (2-hour), $500; same-day, $50; 24-hour, $40. No expedited fees are charged for paperwork required by a private individual for personal purposes (e.g., adoption). (See "Certifications, Apostilles & Authentication of Documents at www.corp.delaware.gov.)

COMMISSIONING AND ADMINISTRATION

While Delaware's Notaries are appointed by the Governor (29 DC 4301), it is the Secretary of State who directly regulates and maintains records on them.

Applying for Commission

Qualifications: An applicant for a commission as a Delaware Notary Public must: (a) be at least 18 years old, (b) maintain a legal residence within Delaware, except for non-residents who maintain a Delaware workplace, (c) have a reasonable need for a Notary commission and (d) have a good character and reputation (29 DC 4301[b]). Individuals convicted of a felony who have not had their rights restored as well as applicants convicted of a crime involving dishonesty or moral turpitude are not eligible for a Delaware Notary commission (website, "Notary Public").

(See "Electronic Notarizations" above for qualifications for an Electronic Notary commission.)

No Course or Test: No course of instruction or test is required of applicants for a Delaware Notary commission. As an aid to Notaries, however, the state website contains a link to Delaware statutes and to frequently asked questions.

Application: "Notary applications and renewals will now be submitted online. As part of this online process, an email address will be required since all correspondence, including commission certificates and renewal notices will be sent electronically by email. During the application process, each notary applicant will establish a notary profile which will be used to track the status of applications, and update information and renew commissions in the future. Existing notaries will receive a letter with instructions to provide an email address and create a profile" (website, "Notary Public").

"Effective October 11, 2010, all notary applications and renewals must be submitted using the online system" (website, "Frequently Asked Questions"). Applicants no longer submit letters of reference. "The notary profile has been designed into the new system to allow the notary to track application status, manage information and renew commissions. For example, if a notary moves or changes employers, the notary will be able to log into the profile and make the change" (website, "Frequently Asked Questions").

Besides "Notary Profiles" for individuals, organizations that anticipate multiple employees or members becoming Notaries may opt to create a "Corporate Profile." A Corporate Profile is mandatory for companies located outside Delaware, but not for Delaware companies. "However, any organization that anticipates a high volume of notary activity may establish a depository account with the Secretary of State to manage this activity" (website, "Corporate Application"). Approved organizations will be issued a Company ID number that individual applicants must enter on their applications. Certain service organizations (e.g., veterans, fire fighting, ambulance and rescue groups) and state and police agencies employing Limited Governmental Notaries are also asked to create a Corporate Profile.

Renewing Notaries will receive an email reminder approximately 30 days before commission expiration, and another 10 days before expiration if a new application has not yet been submitted.

First-time applicants must apply for a two-year term and the non-refundable application fee is $60. Renewing applicants may apply for either a two-year term ($60 fee) or a four-year term ($90 fee), and the application should be submitted no sooner than two months prior to commission expiration. Valid methods of payment are electronic only, including electronic checks from business or personal checking accounts, and Visa, MasterCard, and Discover credit card charges.

Filing Oath of Office: Once the Notary receives the commission certificate by email, he or she should print it out, sign it, take the oath of office before another Notary Public, and then return a copy to the Notary Public Section of the Secretary of State's office (website, "Frequently Asked Questions").

Legislation effective in July of 2009 simplified the former oath-filing process by designating the Secretary of State as a central filing office for the keeping of Notary oaths of office; formerly, the oaths were filed with the local county recorders of deeds. "The notaries and resident electronic notaries shall severally take and subscribe the oath or affirmation prescribed by Article XIV of the Constitution. The nonresident electronic notaries shall severally take and subscribe the oath or affirmation on a commission issued by the Secretary before a notary public or other officer authorized to administer oaths. Notaries and electronic notaries shall be exempt from the recordation of the oath of office prescribed by Title 9 Section 9605(a). Notaries and electronic notaries shall not be permitted to perform notarial acts until a copy of the fully executed commission is received by the Secretary in an electronic or paper document deemed acceptable by the Secretary" (29 DC 4308).

Non-Residents: Out-of-state residents may qualify for a Notary commission if they maintain an office or a regular place of employment in Delaware (29 DC 4301[c]). Their applications must include both a residential and a Delaware employment street address.

Changes of Status

If Notary Changes Name: If the Notary's name has changed during the commission term, the Notary may either (a) perform notarizations by signing both old and new names (e.g., "Jane A. Doe now known as Jane A. Smith") until the commission expires or (b) log into the Notary's online profile and change the name there. Once the Notary Public Section receives notification of the change, the Notary will be sent a name-change certificate by email, so that he or she may obtain a new stamp. There is no charge for this service (website, "Frequently Asked Questions").

If Notary's Address Changes: Non-resident Notaries must notify the Secretary of State of any change of residential or Delaware employment street address within 30 days of such change (29 DC 4301[c]). A Notary may log into his or her Notary profile to update the information. If there is any problem with the information submitted, the Notary Public Section will contact the Notary (website, "Frequently Asked Questions").

If Notary's Email Address Changes: A Delaware Notary is required to have an active email address to receive his or her commissioning certificate and renewal notices and other communications from the state. If the Notary's email address changes, the Notary cannot update it within the notary profile, but "... will need to contact the Notary Public Section at 302-739-4111 or by email at notary@delaware.gov to update [the] email address" (website, "Frequently Asked Questions").

Resignation: Every notary who wishes to resign from office or who no longer meets the qualifications for a commission during their term of office shall immediately mail or deliver the official commission to the Secretary, who shall cancel the same" (29 DC 4307[d]).

COUNTY RECORDERS

As a result of legislation effective July 16, 2009, Delaware Notaries Public no longer file their new commissions and oaths of office in the office of one of the three county recorders of deeds.

OTHER NOTARIAL OFFICERS

Besides Notaries Public, the following officers have power to perform notarial acts within the state (29 DC 4323):

1. A judge, clerk or deputy clerk of any court of the state;

2. An attorney licensed to practice law in the state;

3. Other persons authorized by state law to administer oaths or perform other specific notarial acts.

Justices of Peace and Secretary of Finance

"The Governor shall appoint every person who is appointed to the office of justice of the peace and as Secretary of Finance also as a notary public. The Secretary of Finance shall only act as a notary public in connection with work performed in carrying out the duties of the office. The notary commission of any person appointed a notary public under this section shall terminate at the same time such person's term of office terminates" (29 DC 4303).

Court Reporters of Supreme Court

"The Governor may, upon the request of the Chief Justice of the Supreme Court, appoint any of the official court reporters as a notary public" (29 DC 4305).

Bank Notaries

"The Governor shall appoint 1 notary public for each trust company, bank, banking association or branch or branches thereof in this State, whether state or national, chartered or organized under the laws of this State or of the United States" (29 DC 4304).

Veterans' Organization Notaries

One Notary may be appointed without charge for each veterans' organization for a term of four years, notarizing only for veterans' business, and for that of their families and dependents, and not charging for their notarial services (29 DC 4306[a]).

Fire, Ambulance and Rescue Volunteers

"The Governor may, upon the request of any administrative head of any volunteer fire company or volunteer ambulance and rescue company, appoint 1 notary public for each requesting organization for a term of 4 years, without charge to any appointee, chief or organization. Any such notary, so appointed, shall have no authority to perform any duties with respect to such office or to take affidavits or acknowledgments, except on documents and papers in connection with and for the benefit of any members of the organizations listed herein to include their families or dependents. The notaries public, so appointed, shall make no charge to any service rendered" (29 DC 4306[b]).

Electronic Notaries for Police

"Upon the request of the administrative head of any State, County, municipal, or local governmental agency or unit of this State whose personnel include full-time police officers who are statutorily responsible for the prevention or investigation of crime involving injury to persons or property and who are authorized to execute search warrants and to make arrests (hereinafter called a 'qualified police agency'), the Governor shall appoint a sufficient number of electronic notaries public as may be requested by the administrative head to facilitate the law enforcement responsibilities of the agency or unit. The appointments shall be for a term of 2 years, without charge to the appointee, administrative head, or police agency, except for costs…under Section 4307(b) for special identification cards, hardware, or other related materials and technologies or training (29 DC 4306[c])." Notaries so appointed must use their notarial powers only on police business and may not charge for their electronic acts.

Limited Governmental Notaries

Under 29 DC 4306(d), the Governor may appoint as limited governmental Notaries employees of state governmental agencies or units or of police agencies as defined in 29 DC 4306(c). These appointments expire at the end of the Notary's employment. Such Notaries may perform notarial acts only in the course of their governmental duties, and they may not charge. Their Notary seals must comply with Section 4310(a), except the commission expiration date must be replaced by "My Commission expires upon office."

QUICK FACTS

Notary Jurisdiction
Statewide.

Notary Term Length
Two or four years (29 DC 4307). The first term must be two years, but renewing Notaries may request a two-year or a four-year term. The term of office for a Delaware Electronic Notary is two years.

Notary Bond
Not required by law.

D–H

District of Columbia

NOTARY SEAL

A District of Columbia Notary must authenticate all official acts with a seal of office (CDC 1-1204), and the seal's format must be as follows:

Kind

Inked Embosser: "An embossment inker shall be used in conjunction with the official seal, making the impression legible, permanent, and photographically reproducible" (17 DCMR 2403.6).

"In the case that the document being notarized is made of a non-porous material, such as Mylar or a similar material to which standard ink will not adhere an embossed seal shall be used alone or in conjunction with a non-porous, permanent ink that dries through evaporation, which will adhere without smearing" (17 DCMR 2403.7).

Shape/Size

The seal must have a "border in a circular shape no larger than 1.75 inches surrounding the required words" (17 DCMR 2403.4[e]).

Components

The District of Columbia Notary seal must contain the following components (17 DCMR 2403.4):

Example

The above actual-size example of a typical inked embosser Notary seal is allowed by District of Columbia law. Formats varying from than this may also be permitted.

NOTARY ADMINISTRATION

Office of Secretary of District of Columbia
Office of Notary Commissions
  and Authentications
441 4th St., N.W.
Room 810S   1-202-727-3117
Washington, DC 20001

Website: http://os.dc.gov/os/site/default.asp

NOTARY RULES

CDC — *District of Columbia Official Code*
DCMR — *District of Columbia Municipal Regulations*
NPH — *District of Columbia Notary Public Handbook*

Many Notary rules are in the District of Columbia Official Code:

a. Title 1, Chapter 12, "Notaries Public";

b. Title 42, Chapter 1, "Acknowledgments," including significant portions of the "Uniform Law on Notarial Acts," Sections 42-142 through 42-148*.

  * This is the *Uniform Law on Notarial Acts* of 1982, adopted largely intact but with the Notary seal made mandatory instead of optional and with the Notary's power to certify copies eliminated.

There are additional rules in the District of Columbia Municipal Regulations:

c. Title 17 ("Business, Occupations and Professions"), Chapter 24, "Notaries Public."

Other guidelines for Notaries are in the "District of Columbia Notary Public Handbook" (2008), issued by the Office of Notary Commissions and Authentications.

1. At top, name of Notary, exactly as indicated on commission;
2. In center, "Notary Public";

3. In center, commission expiration date;
4. At bottom, "District of Columbia".

Seals Issued Before Dec. 15, 2010: "Notaries public commissioned prior to December 15, 2010, may use an official seal that does not comply with Section 2403.4 provided that seal is made visible with an embosser inker and coupled with an expiration stamp on all notarizations" (17 DCMR 2403.8). "Notaries public commissioned on or after December 10, 2010, must obtain an embosser that complies with Section 2403.4 upon being newly- or reappointed (IT DCMR 2403.9). Enforcement of the preceding provisions by the Office of Commissions and Authentications began on October 1, 2011 (website, "Special Communication").

Placement of Seal
"Make a seal impression in a blank space, not over signatures and dates. Usually space is provided to the left of the notary's signature for the seal impression. If space is not provided, the seal should be placed near (the Notary's) signature" (NPH).

Seal Affixed at Time of Notarization
"A notary public shall affix his or her official signature and official seal on every document notarized, at the time the notarial act is performed" (17 DCMR 2403.5).

Official Signature and Seal Samples
"Each notary public commissioned in the District shall file his or her official signature and an impression of his or her official seal with the Office of the Secretary of the District of Columbia" (17 DCMR 2403.1).

No Seal Image for Electronic Notarization
"A requirement that a document or a signature associated with a document be notarized, acknowledged, verified, witnessed, or made under oath is satisfied if the electronic signature of the person authorized to perform that act, and all other information required to be included, is attached to or logically associated with the document or signature. A physical or electronic image of a stamp, impression, or seal is not required to accompany an electronic signature" (CDC 42-1232).

Seal Is Exclusive Property of Notary
"A notary shall keep an official seal that is the exclusive property of the notary. When not in use, the seal shall be kept secure and accessible only to the notary" (17 DCMR 2403.2).

Seal Not for Use by Another Person
"The seal shall not be possessed or used by any other person, nor be used for any purpose other than performing lawful notarizations" (17 DCMR 2403.3).

Seal Is Exempt from Execution
"A notary's official seal and his official documents shall be exempt from execution (i.e., subpoena)" (CDC 1-1206).

NOTARY POWERS

District Notaries are authorized to perform the following notarial acts (CDC 1-1210):
1. Take acknowledgments* and proofs;
2. Administer oaths and affirmations**;
3. Execute jurats*** (CDC 42-142), also called "verifications upon oath or affirmation," such as for depositions and for affidavits "to be used before any court, judge, or officer within the District";
4. Witness or attest signatures****;
5. Execute protests***** for foreign and inland bills of exchange (CDC 1-1207, 1-1208);
6. "(P)erform such other acts, for use and effect beyond the jurisdiction of the District, as according to the law of any state or territory of the United States or any foreign government in amity with the United States may be performed by notaries public" (CDC 1-1209).

* Acknowledgments: "In taking an acknowledgment, the notarial officer shall determine from personal knowledge or satisfactory evidence that the person who appears before the officer and makes the acknowledgment is the person whose true signature is on the instrument" (CDC 42-142[a]).

** Oaths and Affirmations: "An oath is a spoken, solemn promise to a Supreme Being that is made before a Notary: 'I solemnly swear that the statements in this document are true, so help me God'" (NPH). "An affirmation is a spoken, solemn promise on one's personal honor, with no reference to a Supreme Being that is made before a Notary: 'I solemnly affirm that the statements in this document are true'" (NPH).

*** Jurats: "In executing a jurat, a notary guarantees that the signer personally appeared before the notary, was given an oath or affirmation by the notary attesting to the truthfulness of the document, and signed the document in the notary's presence" (NPH).

"In taking a verification upon oath or affirmation, the notarial officer shall determine from personal knowledge or satisfactory evidence that the person who appears before the officer and makes the verification is the person whose true signature is on the statement verified" (CDC 42-142[b]).

**** Witness or Attest Signatures: "In witnessing or attesting a signature, the notarial officer shall determine from personal knowledge or satisfactory evidence that the signature is the signature of the person who appears before the officer and is named in the instrument" (CDC 42-142[c]).

***** Protests: "Bank drafts on foreign countries are usually called 'bills of exchange.' To distinguish them from other drafts they are sometimes called foreign bills of exchange, and the others are sometimes called inland bills of exchange. A protest is a formal declaration made by a notary public at the request of the holder on non-acceptance or non-payment of a bill of exchange. These generally apply to notaries who work in banks" (NPH). District Notaries may also "exercise such other powers and duties as by the law of nations and according to commercial usages notaries public may do" (CDC 1-1207).

Protest procedures are covered in CDC 28:3-501 through 28:3-505.

Identifying Document Signers

In taking an acknowledgment or a verification upon oath or affirmation, or in witnessing or attesting a signature, the Notary must identify the document signer through satisfactory evidence of identity.

Satisfactory Evidence of Identity Defined: "A notarial officer shall have satisfactory evidence that a person is the person whose true signature is on a document if the person is:

"1. Personally known to the notarial officer;

"2. Identified upon the oath or affirmation of a credible witness personally known to the notarial officer; or

"3. Identified on the basis of identification documents" (CDC 42-142).

"As a DC Notary Public, you are the one who decides whether or not the person has identified him or herself. Recommended forms of identification are government issued driver's licenses, passports, or employee identification cards; however, you may consider other forms of documentation acceptable. Remember that you are responsible for all official acts you perform, and challenges to your performance could result in losing your commission, fines, and prosecution for perjury" (NPH).

Notary Must Be Available to All

"Remember that Public means you must be available to all during your posted hours" (NPH).

Personal Appearance Always Required

"The person for whom you are notarizing a document must be in your presence in the District of Columbia at the time the document is notarized" (NPH).

Notary Must Exhibit Sign

"One of the first things to do is hang out your sign. Non-Government notaries public are required to display a "NOTARY PUBLIC" sign at your registered location of business (home or office" (NPH).

"Each notary public must exhibit a sign" (17 DCMR 2404.1). "The provisions of this section do not apply to notaries functioning in the government service" (17 DCMR 2404.2).

NOTARY DON'TS

Do Not Read Notarized Documents

"Notaries Public do not read the documents presented for notarization, nor are they required to understand or have knowledge of the document's contents" (NPH).

Do Not Certify Records

"You do not have authority to…certify a public record, a publicly recorded document such as a birth or death certificate, marriage license, a school record or diploma, a professional license, or any other public document or record" (NPH).

May Certify Notarial Record: A Notary, "when required, shall give a certified copy of any record in his office to any person upon payment of the fees therefor" (CDC 1-1211). A Notary may execute a copy of a protest, based on the Notary's records (CDC 1-1212).

Disqualifying Interests

"As a DC Notary Public, you should not carry out an official act for any matter in which you are personally involved, either directly or indirectly" (NPH). According to the "Handbook," this means that Notaries have no authority to take their own oaths, affidavits, acknowledgments or depositions; to serve as a witness for their own personal documents; nor to notarize their own signatures.

<u>Notarizing for Relatives</u>: Notaries should refrain from performing notarial acts for members of their immediate families. "Doing so is not against the law, but it may result in a conflict of interest and gives the matter an air of impropriety" (NPH).

<u>Corporate Notaries</u>: A Notary who is a stockholder, director, officer or employee of a bank, trust company or other corporation may notarize for that corporation unless the Notary is a party to the instrument, either individually or as a representative of the corporation. However, "it shall be unlawful for any notary public to take the oath of an officer or director of any bank or trust company of which he is an officer, or to take an oath of any person verifying a report of such bank or trust company to the Comptroller of the Currency or the Superintendent of Banking and Financial Institutions ..." (CDC 26-110).

<u>Acting before U.S. Government</u>: Notaries may not notarize for matters in which they are employed as counsel, attorney or agent, or in which they are in any way interested, before any agency of the U.S. government (CDC 1-1201).

NOTARY SIGNING AGENTS

Currently, there are no statutes, regulations or rules expressly governing, prohibiting or restricting the operation of Notary Signing Agents within the District of Columbia.

NOTARY FEES

The fees of District Notaries are (CDC 1-1213[c]):

1. Taking an acknowledgment or proof: $2 per signature;
2. Administering an oath or affirmation, including jurat, seal: $2;
3. Taking an affidavit, including jurat, seal: $2;
4. Any other notarial act: $2.

Government Notary Does Not Charge

"Government-only notaries are not permitted to charge a fee for your notarial services, as you are only permitted to notarize government documents" (NPH). "Government employees who have separate commissions may not charge any fee for notarial service performed during hours of active duty as a government employee" (17 DCMR 2401.4).

"If you work in government but you want to also make money as a notary public, you must apply for a 'dual commission'...This means that you must pay the commissioning fee and get a bond for yourself, and you can only do this if you are a DC resident" (NPH). For more information on dual commissions, see "Applying for Commission" under "Commissioning and Administration," below.

Employer May Set Fee Policy

"If you become a Notary Public at the request of your employer, please note that your employer is permitted to set their own policy for fees. Although (the employer) may not charge more than the fee permitted by law, your employer may decide whether to charge a fee and who keeps it (you or the company)" (NPH).

Overcharging

For overcharging, a Notary may be fined $100 and removed from office (CDC 1-1214).

NOTARY CERTIFICATES

The District of Columbia has adopted much of the *Uniform Law on Notarial Acts*, including the short-form certificates (CDC 42-148) for:

1. Acknowledgment by individual;
2. Acknowledgment by representative;
3. Verification upon oath or affirmation;
4. Witnessing or attesting signature.

Under District law, a Notary seal is mandatory on these certificates, not optional as indicated.

For the text of the certificates, see "Uniform Law on Notarial Acts (1982)," Section 8, in Appendix 2.

Format for Notarial Certificate

"a. A notarial act shall be evidenced by a certificate signed and dated by a notarial officer. The certificate shall include identification of the jurisdiction in which the notarial act is performed and the title of the office of the notarial officer and shall include the official stamp or seal of office. If the officer is a notary public, the certificate shall indicate the expiration date, if any, of the commission of office. Omission of the expiration date information may subsequently be corrected. If the officer is a commissioned officer on active duty in the military service of the United States, as provided in 10 U.S.C. sec. 936, the certificate shall include the officer's rank and title of office.

"b. A certificate of a notarial act shall be sufficient if the certificate meets the requirements of subsection (a) of this section and:

"1. Is in the short form set forth in section 42-148;

"2. Is in a form otherwise prescribed by the law of the District;

"3. Is in a form prescribed by a law or regulation applicable in the place where the notarial act was performed; or

"4. Sets forth the actions of the notarial officer and those actions are sufficient to meet the requirements of the designated notarial act" (CDC 42-147).

Jurat Certificate (NPH):

District of Columbia: SS

Subscribed and sworn to before me on this _____ day of _____, 20 _____.

*(Inked Embosser   (Signature
Seal)   of Notary)*

*Notary Public, District of Columbia
My commission expires on _____*

ELECTRONIC NOTARIZATIONS

The District of Columbia has not yet adopted regulations expressly establishing rules, definitions and procedures for electronic notarization.

UETA Recognizes Notary's E-Signature

The District of Columbia has adopted the Uniform Electronic Transactions Act (CDC 28-4001 through 28-4918), including the following provision on notarization, thereby recognizing the legal validity of electronic signatures used by Notaries.

"If a law requires a signature or record to be notarized, acknowledged, verified, or made under oath, the requirement is satisfied if the electronic signature of the person authorized to perform those acts, together with all other information required to be included by other applicable law, is attached to or logically associated with the signature or record" (CDC 29-4910).

URPERA Requires No Seal Image

In 2005, the Council of the District of Columbia enacted the Uniform Real Property Electronic Recording Act (CDC 42-1231 through 1235), including the following provision related to electronic notarization (CDC 42-1232[c]):

"A requirement that a document or a signature associated with a document be notarized, acknowledged, verified, witnessed, or made under oath is satisfied if the electronic signature of the person authorized to perform that act, and all other information required to be included, is attached to or logically associated with the document or signature. A physical or electronic image of a stamp, impression, or seal is not required to accompany an electronic signature."

NOTARY RECORDS

"Each notary public shall keep a fair record of all his official acts, except such as are mentioned in Section 1-1210, and when required, shall give a certified copy of any record in his office to any person upon payment of the fees therefor" (CDC 1-1211). (NOTE: Mentioned in Section 1-1210 are: acknowledgments and proofs, depositions, oaths and affirmations and affidavits to be used before any court, judge or officer within the District.)

Required Entries

The "District of Columbia Notary Public Handbook" specifies the following journal entries for each notarial act:

1. Name and address of each person for whom a document is notarized;

2. Date of person's appearance before the Notary;
3. Method by which each person was identified to the Notary;
4. Type of document notarized;
5. Fee charged;
6. Signature of each person signing the document.

ONCA May Scrutinize Journal

"If your service is ever questioned, ONCA (Office of Notary Commissions and Authentications) may ask you to submit your logbook. If ONCA requests your logbook and finds that you have not been keeping it up-to-date, your commission could be revoked" (NPH).

Three-Month Summary for Reappointment: When applying for reappointment, a Notary who is entitled to charge fees must submit a summary of his or her notarial business for the past three months preceding the date of application for reappointment; this summary must be based on actual records, not estimates (17 DCMR 2406).

At Notary's Death, Resignation, Removal

Upon the death, resignation or removal from office of a Notary, the Notary's records and official papers must be deposited in the office of the Mayor of the District of Columbia or the Mayor's designated agent (CDC 1-1215).

AUTHENTICATION OF NOTARIAL ACTS

Office of Secretary of District of Columbia

An authenticating certificate for a District of Columbia Notary may be obtained at the Office of the Secretary of the District ("Each notary public shall file his signature and deposit an impression of his official seal with the Mayor of the District of Columbia or his designated agent, and the Mayor or his designated agent may certify to the authenticity of the signature and official seal of the notary public" [CDC 1-1205]. "Certificates issued by the Mayor of the District of Columbia may be signed by the Executive Secretary" [CDC 1-1216]).

Fee: A fee of $15 per authenticating certificate, including an apostille (17 DCMR 2407.3). Check or money order payable to "District of Columbia Treasurer." In-person transactions may be paid for by credit card or check. No cash is accepted.

Mail or In-Person:
Office of Secretary of Dist. of Columbia
Notary Commissions and Authentications
441 4th Street, N.W.
Room 810S
Washington, DC 20001

Telephone: 1-202-727-3117

Procedure: Mail or present in person the original notarized document(s), along with the proper fee and a self-addressed, stamped envelope. In a cover letter, indicate the nation to which the document will be sent, as well as the requester's name, address and phone number. "The document must be either notarized by a DC notary public, or signed by an authorized head of a DC government agency" (website, "Document Authentication").

COMMISSIONING AND ADMINISTRATION

The District of Columbia's Notaries are appointed by the Secretary of the District through the Notary Commissions and Authentications Office (17 DCMR 2400.2 and 2410.1; CDC 1-1201).

Applying for Commission

Qualifications: An applicant for a commission as a District of Columbia Notary Public must (17 DCMR 2400.2[c]): (a) be at least 18 years old and (b) live or work in the District.

Four Categories of Notary: There are four categories of Notary and the first step in the application process is for the applicant to decide which type of Notary he or she wants to be:

1. *Resident Notary.* "You can be a resident notary if you live in the District of Columbia. Resident notaries may use their commission anywhere in Washington, DC, whether at work or home" (NPH).

2. *Non-Resident Notary.* "You can apply to be a nonresident notary if you work in the District of Columbia but live elsewhere. As a nonresident notary, you may only notarize documents where you work, such as a bank, post office, or law firm" (NPH).

3. *Government Notary.* "You can become a

government notary if you work for the DC or Federal Government within Washington, DC, regardless of where you live. As a government notary you may only notarize official government documents" (NPH). The commission terminates on leaving government service.

4. *Dual Commission Notary.* "You can receive a Dual Commission if you are a District resident who works for the DC or Federal Government. With a dual commission you can notarize documents at work or home (NPH and 17 DCMR 2401.3).

Application: A complete application includes the following items (NPH and 17 DCMR 2402.1): (a) the names, addresses and phone numbers or email addresses of three individuals willing to be character references (17 DCMR 2402.2); (b) a letter from the applicant's employer stating the need for notarial services or, if the applicant is self-employed, from the applicant on letterhead (17 DCMR 2400.5 through .7 and 2401.1); (c) a completed application form; and (d) a check or money order to "DC Treasurer" for the commissioning fee of $75 (17 DCMR 2409). District and federal government Notaries are exempt from the fee — except for dual commission applicants (CDC 1-1201).

Training and Exam: In order to become a Notary, an applicant must demonstrate a basic knowledge of the rules and regulations governing Notaries, summarized in the "District of Columbia Notary Public Handbook" (17 DCMR 2402.3). This is done through attendance at an oral training/exam session conducted by the Office of Notary Commissions and Authentications. After the application is processed, the applicant will be notified of the date and time of the next such scheduled session, which are offered twice a month, usually on Mondays, at 441 4th Street, N.W. (also known as One Judiciary Square) at the Office of the Secretary of the District.

Seal, Bond and Oath: After passing the training/exam, the applicant must obtain a Notary seal of office and a $2,000 bond. District government Notaries are exempt from bonding. Within 60 days of passing the training/exam, the applicant must make an appointment to come to the Office of Notary Commissions and Authentications to be officially commissioned. Each applicant must bring a District of Columbia Notary seal embosser, Notary surety bond, and personal identification, which must be shown to get into the building to claim the commission; the new Notary must then take the oath of office and submit signature and seal samples, which are retained by the Office to authenticate documents notarized by the Notary (CDC 1-1205; 17 DCMR 2403.1 and 2407.1).

Reappointment: At least 45 days before a Notary's commission expires, the Office of Notary Commissions and Authentications will send reappointment application materials to the Notary. Additional training is not required unless the Notary's commission has been expired for one year or more (NPH). When applying for reappointment, a Notary who is entitled to charge fees must submit a summary of his or her notarial business for the past three months preceding the date of application for reappointment; the summary must be based on actual records, not estimates (17 DCMR 2406).

Online Search: On the Secretary's website, an interactive mapping system provides seekers of notarial services with individualized directions to the offices or residences of District Notaries who are available to serve the public.

Changes of Status

If Notary Moves within District: Notaries must immediately notify the Office of Notary Commissions and Authentications in writing of a new address within the District (17 DCMR 2405.1). The bonding company must also be notified (NPH).

If Notary Changes Name: When the Notary's name changes, the Notary must immediately inform the Mayor's office (17 DCMR 2405.1), specifically the Office of Notary Commissions and Authentications. The Notary's bonding company must also be notified. In addition, a Notary whose name changed due to marriage, divorce or adoption must: (a) complete and submit a new application for a Notary commission; (b) present an official government document showing the official name change; and (c) get a new Notary seal and complete a new signature card with seal impressions reflecting the change (NPH).

If Notary Changes Employer: In writing, the Notary must immediately notify the Mayor's office, specifically the Office of Notary Commissions and Authentications, of any change of business address (17 DCMR 2405.1). "Your commission can be transferred to your new place of employment if your new office is physically located in the District of Columbia, and you tell us about it. To make such a transfer, your new employer must submit a letter explaining why they need a notary public and where and during what hours you will be available (to) perform notarial duties" (NPH).

"The commission of a government employee shall be terminated when the employee leaves government service" (17 DCMR 2401.2).

Any change in office hours by the Notary must also be reported to the Office of Notary Commissions and Authentications (17 DCMR 2405.1).

If Notary Resigns: Notaries must resign their commissions by notifying the Office of Notary Commissions and Authentications in writing, stating the effective date of resignation. Notarial records must also be turned in to the Office (CDC 1-1215). Notaries must resign if they move out of the District or cease to be employed in a business physically located within the District. A government Notary must resign upon leaving his or her governmental post (17 DCMR 2401.2).

OTHER NOTARIAL OFFICERS

In addition to Notaries Public, the following officers have power to perform notarial acts within the District:
1. A judge, clerk, or deputy clerk of any court of the District (CDC 42-143);
2. U.S. federal officers as listed in CDC 42-145, including judges, clerks and deputy clerks of a U.S. court, U.S. military officers and U.S. foreign service and consular officers.

Police Property Clerk

The Property Clerk of the District's Metropolitan Police has all the powers conferred upon District Notaries (CDC 5-119.04).

QUICK FACTS

Notary Jurisdiction
District of Columbia. "District of Columbia commissions can be used only in the District of Columbia. You may not notarize documents in Maryland or Virginia, or any other place that is not DC" (NPH).

Notary Term Length
Five years (CDC 1-1202), expiring at midnight on the commission expiration date.

Government Notary Must Resign: "The government notary must resign his/her commission on leaving government service" (NPH).

Notary Bond
$2,000, with security "to be approved by the Mayor of the District of Columbia or his designated agent" (CDC 1-1203). Notaries for the District government do not need bonds.

Florida

NOTARY SEAL

A Florida Notary must affix a seal of office on all documents notarized, and the seal's format must be as follows (FS 117.05[3][a]):

Kind

Inked Rubber Stamp: "The rubber stamp seal must be affixed to the notarized paper document in photographically reproducible black ink" (FS 117.05[3][a]).

Notaries commissioned prior to January 1, 1992, were allowed to use embossers as their official seals until commission expiration. However, effective January 1, 1996, no Florida Notary may use an embosser as the sole official seal.

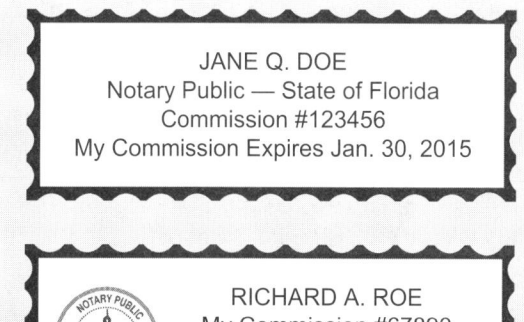

Examples

The above typical, actual-size examples of Notary seals are allowed by Florida law. Formats other than these may also be permitted.

NOTARY ADMINISTRATION

In Florida, two major state officials are involved with the administration of Notaries: the Secretary of State (Department of State), whose office oversees the commissioning process and keeps records on Notaries, and the Governor, whose office educates and assists Notaries in performing their duties.

A. Department of State
   Division of Corporations
   Notary Commissions and
      Certifications Section   1-850-245-6975
   P.O. Box 6327
   Tallahassee, FL 32314

   Website: http://notaries.dos.state.fl.us/index.html

B. Executive Office of the Governor
   Notary Section   1-850-922-6400
   Room 209, The Capitol
   Tallahassee, FL 32399-0001

   Website: www.flgov.com/notary

NOTARY RULES

FS — FLORIDA STATUTES
RMN — GOVERNOR'S REFERENCE MANUAL FOR NOTARIES

Most Notary regulations are in the Florida Statutes:

a. Chapter 117, "Notaries Public";

b. Chapter 695, "Record of Conveyances of Real Estate."

Other guidelines for Notaries are in the "Governor's Reference Manual for Notaries" (Updated Nov. 1, 2001).

Embosser an Addition, Not Substitute: "An impression-type seal may be used in addition to the rubber stamp seal, but the rubber stamp seal shall be the official seal for use on a paper document, and the impression-type seal may not be substituted therefor" (FS 117.05[3][a]).

"If you choose to use an impression seal, your name should be correct and the seal should contain the words 'Notary Public – State of Florida'" (RMN).

Shape/Size

Not specified.

Components

1. Name of Notary;
2. "Notary Public – State of Florida";
3. Commission number;
4. Commission expiration date.

<u>Great Seal Use Prohibited</u>: "The name of the notary's bonding company may be included on the seal but is not required.... Some companies that produce notary seals include a symbol or emblem on the stamp, such as the Capitol dome, a flag, an eagle, etc., but this is optional. No emblem or symbol is required. Additionally, you may NOT use the Great Seal of the State of Florida on your notary seal" (RMN).

Notary's Name Printed, Typed or Stamped

"Every notary public shall print, type, or stamp below his or her signature on a paper document his or her name exactly as commissioned" (FS 117.05[3][a]).

No Seal for Electronic Notarization

According to FS 117.021(3), for an electronic notarization a Notary must affix the information contained in his or her physical seal—but need not affix the image of the physical seal itself. "Neither a rubber stamp nor an impression type seal is required for an electronic notarization" (FS 668.50[11][a]). See also FS 695.27[3] in the Uniform Real Property Electronic Recording Act.

If Seal Prints Imperfectly

"If you get an imperfect imprint of your rubber stamp seal, you should affix the seal again as closely to the first imprint as possible. This may present a problem if the document has limited space. You should never affix your seal over writing, and, if necessary, you may have to resort to the margin area of the document. You may also need to stamp your seal at an angle in order to make it fit the available space" (RMN).

To Prevent Seal Smearing on Mylar

"When affixing my notary seal on a recording plat, my notary seal impression smears. Can you offer a solution?

"(A)n official suggested preserving the ink seal imprint by spraying it immediately with an aerosol acrylic sealer. We experimented using Krylon No. 1303 Crystal Clear Acrylic Spray Coating and found this to be a satisfactory solution...

"The best solution, however, was ... (using a) non-porous, permanent ink that dries through evaporation, like Phillips Industrial Marking Ink #40A, (which) will adhere to mylar without smearing ... The companies also recommended using this ink with a special balsa wood stamp pad, rather than the usual felt or foam rubber stamp pad ..." (RMN).

Lost Seal

"A notary public whose official seal is lost, stolen, or believed to be in the possession of another person shall immediately notify the Department of State or the Governor in writing" (FS 117.05[3][d]). "Additionally, if your seal was stolen, you should file a report with the local law enforcement agency" (RMN).

"Keep your seal in a secure location to avoid its loss or misuse" (RMN).

Unlawful Possession of Seal

"Any person who unlawfully possesses a notary public official seal or any papers or copies relating to notarial acts is guilty of a misdemeanor of the second degree ..." (FS 117.05[3][e]).

"The notary public official seal and the certificate of notary public commission are the exclusive property of the notary public and must be kept under the direct and exclusive control of the notary public. The seal and certificate of commission must not be surrendered to an employer upon termination of employment, regardless of whether the employer paid for the seal or for the commission" (FS 117.05[3][c]).

An employer may not keep an employee's Notary seal, even if the employer paid for it. "If your employer does not comply, you should file a report with the law enforcement agency having jurisdiction. This may protect you in the event that your seal is used and a complaint is filed against you" (RMN).

Resigning Notary Destroys Seal

"(A) resigning notary public shall destroy his or her official notary public seal of office, unless the Governor requests its return" (FS 117.01[5][b]).

Notary's Signature

"A notary public may not use a name or initial in signing certificates other than that by which the notary public is commissioned" (FS 117.107[1]).

Signature Need Not Be in Black Ink: "(Florida law) provides that the official notary seal, the rubber stamp seal, must be affixed with 'photographically reproducible black ink.' However, the Notary law does not specify a color of ink to be used when signing a notarial certificate. Therefore, if you prefer, you may use a color of ink, other than black, in signing your name to distinguish between an original and a photocopy of your notarial certificate" (RMN).

Facsimile Signature Stamp: "A notary public may not sign notarial certificates using a facsimile signature stamp unless the notary public has a physical disability that limits or prohibits his or her ability to make a written signature and unless the notary public has first submitted written notice to the Department of State with an exemplar of the facsimile signature stamp" (FS 117.107[2]).

NOTARY POWERS

Florida Notaries are authorized to perform the following notarial acts (FS 117.03 and 117.04):
1. Take acknowledgments*;
2. Administer oaths** and affirmations, as when executing jurats** for affidavits and depositions;
3. Attest copies (FS 117.05[12])***;
4. Solemnize marriages (FS 117.045);
5. Verify vehicle identification numbers (FS 319.23[3][a]);
6. Certify contents of safe deposit boxes (FS 655.94).

* Acknowledgments: "Acknowledgment — A formal declaration before an authorized official (a notary public) by a person signing an instrument that such execution is his or her free act and deed. The term also refers to the notary's certificate on the document indicating that it was so acknowledged" (RMN).

** Form of Oath: "A notarization requiring an oath begins with the administration of an oath or affirmation. The courts have held that there should be a verbal exchange between the notary and the document signer in which the signer indicates that he or she is taking an oath. An oath similar to one administered in court by a judge or bailiff would be sufficient. Or, you may simply ask, 'Do you swear (or affirm) that the information contained in this document is true?' After receiving an affirmative answer, you must complete a proper notarial certificate indicating that an oath or affirmation was taken" (RMN).

In some cases, a signed declaration may substitute for a notarized oath if it contains the following language: "Under penalties of perjury, I declare that I have read the foregoing (document) and that the facts stated in it are true" (FS 92.525).

Notaries may not "take" (i.e., transcribe) depositions and affidavits by authority of their notarial office, but they may administer oaths and affirmations to deponents and affiants for these documents and execute jurats on them.

*** Certifying (Attesting) Copies: "A notary public may supervise the making of a photocopy of an original document and attest to the trueness of the copy, provided the document is neither a vital record in this state, another state, a territory of the United States, or another country, nor a public record, if a copy can be made by the custodian of the public record" (FS 117.05[12][a]).

"The making of the photocopy must be supervised by the notary public. It is not sufficient for the notary public to compare the photocopy with the original document. The notary public must actually make the photocopy or supervise another person while he or she makes the photocopy" (RMN).

Included among the documents whose copies may NOT be attested by a Notary because they are public records are (RMN): birth certificate, marriage certificate, death certificate, certificate of citizenship or naturalization, documents filed in a court proceeding, documents recorded by the clerk of the court, public records in government offices, student records (transcripts, etc.) kept in public education offices, filed federal or state income tax forms, professional licenses issued by the state and any document for which photocopying is prohibited.

Included among the documents whose copies MAY be attested by a Notary, as long as the original is not officially filed or recorded, are (RMN): Florida driver's license, Florida vehicle title, Social Security card, diploma, medical record, U.S. passport, bill of sale, contact, lease, resident alien card ("green card") and a personal letter.

Identifying Document Signers

"A notary public may not notarize a signature on a document unless he or she personally knows, or has satisfactory evidence, that the person whose signature is to be notarized is the individual who is described in and who is executing the instrument. A notary public shall certify in the certificate of acknowledgment or jurat the type of identification, either based on personal knowledge or other form of identification, upon which the notary public is relying" (FS 117.05[5]):

Personal Knowledge Defined: Personally knows "means having an acquaintance, derived from association with the individual, which establishes the individual's identity with at least a reasonable certainty."

Satisfactory Evidence Defined: Satisfactory evidence "means the absence of any information, evidence, or other circumstances which would lead a reasonable person to believe that the person whose signature is to be notarized is not the person he or she claims to be and any one of the following:

"1. The sworn written statement of one credible witness personally known to the notary public or the sworn written statement of two credible witnesses whose identities are proven to the notary public upon the presentation of satisfactory evidence that each of the following is true:

"a. That the person whose signature is to be notarized is the person named in the document;

"b. That the person whose signature is to be notarized is personally known to the witnesses;

"c. That it is the reasonable belief of the witnesses that the circumstances of the person whose signature is to be notarized are such that it would be very difficult or impossible for that person to obtain another acceptable form of identification;

"d. That it is the reasonable belief of the witnesses that the person whose signature is to be notarized does not possess any of the identification documents specified in subparagraph 2.; and

"e. That the witnesses do not have a financial interest nor are parties to the underlying transaction; or

"2. Reasonable reliance on the presentation to the notary public of any one of the following forms of identification, if the document is current or has been issued within the past 5 years and bears a serial or other identifying number:

"a. A Florida identification card or driver's license issued by the public agency authorized to issue driver's licenses;

"b. A passport issued by the Department of State of the United States;

"c. A passport issued by a foreign government if the document is stamped by the United States Immigration and Naturalization Service (sic);

"d. A driver's license or an identification card issued by a public agency authorized to issue driver's licenses in a state other than Florida, a territory of the United States, or Canada or Mexico;

"e. An identification card issued by any branch of the armed forces of the United States;

"f. An inmate identification card issued on or after January 1, 1991, by the Florida Department of Corrections for an inmate who is in the custody of the department;

"g. An inmate identification card issued by the United States Department of Justice, Bureau of Federal Prisons, for an inmate who is in the custody of the department;

"h. A sworn, written statement from a sworn law enforcement officer that the forms of identification for an inmate in an institution of confinement were confiscated upon confinement and that the person named in the document is the person whose signature is to be notarized; or

"i. An identification card issued by the United States Immigration and Naturalization Service (sic)."

Signature by Mark

"A notary public may notarize the signature of a person who signs with a mark if:

"1. The document signing is witnessed by two disinterested persons;

"2. The notary prints the person's first name at the beginning of the designated signature line and the person's last name at the end of the designated signature line; and

"3. The notary prints the words 'his (or her) mark' below the person's signature mark" (FS 117.05[14][b]).

Notary Must Accommodate Disabled People

"A notary public must make reasonable accommodations to provide notarial services to persons with disabilities" (FS 117.05[14]).

Blind Signers: "A notary public may notarize the signature of a person who is blind after the notary public has read the entire instrument to that person" (FS 117.05[14][a]).

Signing for Disabled: "A notary public may sign the name of a person whose signature is to be notarized when that person is physically unable to sign or make a signature mark on a document if:
"1. The person with a disability directs the notary to sign in his or her presence;
"2. The document signing is witnessed by two disinterested persons;
"3. The notary writes below the signature the following statement: 'Signature affixed by notary, pursuant to s. 117.05[14]), Florida Statutes,' and states the circumstances of the signing in the notarial certificate" (FS 117.05[14][d]).

Serving as Both Witness and Notary

"Generally, a notary public may sign as one of the witnesses and as the notary public on a document. In fact, it is a common practice among Florida notaries, particularly on real estate transactions ... In addition, a Florida court has held that 'there is nothing to prevent a notary from also being a witness.' See *Walker v. City of Jacksonville*, 360 So.2d 52 (1978). However, before signing as a witness, the notary should ensure that the document does not require the notarization of the witnesses' signatures" (RMN).

Must Be 'Mentally Capable of Understanding'

"A notary public may not notarize a signature on a document if it appears that the person is mentally incapable of understanding the nature and effect of the document at the time of notarization" (FS 117.107[5]).

The Notary has discretion to refuse to notarize when "the signer appears to be drunk, sedated, or disoriented" (RMN).

NOTARY DON'TS

Florida Notaries may (FS 117.107):
1. NOT notarize the signature of a person who is not present, subject to a $5,000 fine;
2. NOT notarize their own signatures (FS 117.05[1]);
3. NOT notarize an incomplete or blank document, except "an endorsement or assignment in blank of a negotiable or nonnegotiable note and the assignment in blank of any instrument given as security for such note";
4. NOT notarize a blank document or blank notarial certificate ("A notary public may not affix his signature to a blank form of affidavit or certificate of acknowledgment and deliver that form to another person with the intent that it be used as an affidavit or acknowledgment.");
5. NOT notarize the signature of a person known by the Notary to have been adjudicated mentally incapacitated;
6. NOT as a non-attorney advertise notarial services in a language other than English without conspicuously posting or stating the following notice, in both languages: "I AM NOT AN ATTORNEY LICENSED TO PRACTICE LAW IN THE STATE OF FLORIDA, AND I MAY NOT GIVE LEGAL ADVICE OR ACCEPT FEES FOR LEGAL ADVICE"; nor literally translate "Notary Public" into a language other than English (FS 117.05[10]-[11]);
7. NOT "take the acknowledgment of a person who does not speak or understand the English language, unless the nature and effect of the instrument to be notarized is translated into a language which the person does understand";
8. NOT "take the acknowledgment of a person who is blind until the notary public has read the instrument to such person" (FS 117.05[14][a]);
9. NOT "change anything in a written instrument after it has been signed by anyone" nor amend a notarial certificate after the notarization is complete;
10. NOT certify the identity of a person in a photograph ("Rather, you should certify that the statement concerning the photograph was signed and sworn to in your presence by John Doe" [RMN]);
11. NOT certify a translation ("However, you may notarize the signature of the translator on an affidavit where the translator certifies and swears to the accuracy of his or her translation" [RMN]);
12. NOT provide signature guarantees ("This duty is usually performed by officials in the banking and securities industry" [RMN]);
13. NOT "certify the authenticity of objects, such as art or sports memorabilia" (RMN);

14. NOT certify or judge contest results (RMN);
15. NOT certify a person's residency or citizenship status (RMN);
16. NOT notarize when the Notary "knows or suspects that the transaction is illegal, false, or deceptive" (RMN).

Proof of Execution Not Allowed

According to the "Governor's Reference Manual for Notaries," a proof of execution by a subscribing witness may not be performed by a Florida Notary; the principal signer must always appear before the Notary. "Remember then, if a co-worker, family member, or anyone else asks you to notarize another person's signature based on a sworn statement that he or she saw the person sign the document, JUST SAY NO!!"

However, a procedure is prescribed by FS 695.03(1) whereby a signed real estate document lacking notarization whose signer cannot be located or is deceased may be prepared for recordation by the "proof" of one of the subscribing witnesses. In such a rare instance, the Notary would notarize a "certificate of proof" or an affidavit of proof signed by the witness using a standard jurat (RMN).

Telephone Oaths Forbidden

"Although depositions may be taken over the telephone, the deponent must be in the physical presence of the notary public, or other official authorized to administer oaths, at the time the oath or affirmation is given. There is no exception to the presence requirement, even if the attorneys for both parties stipulate otherwise. (See Attorney General Opinion, No. 92-95, December 23, 1992.) This means that, if you are asked to swear in a person over the phone, you must decline. A notary, or other authorized official, would have to be present with the deponent for the administration of the oath or affirmation" (RMN).

Phone Verification of Signature Prohibited: "Some notaries mistakenly believe that they may call the signer on the telephone to verify the signature and then proceed with the notarization. Florida law prohibits a notary from notarizing any signature if the signer is not present at the time of the notarization" (RMN).

Refusing to Notarize

According to the "Governor's Reference Manual for Notaries," Notaries have discretion to refuse to notarize, even if only because they would be "inconvenienced." However, "(a) notary should never exercise his or her authority in a discriminatory manner," and should refuse in a tactful manner.

The "Manual" cites the following as justifiable reasons for refusing to notarize: a failure or inability to pay the Notary fee; the notarization is requested after regular business hours; the notarization request is on a holiday; the Notary is busy with other work or activities; the Notary would be inconvenienced; the Notary is ill; the Notary is uncomfortable with the request; the signer is a minor; the document is written in a language the Notary cannot read; the Notary is asked to travel.

Notarizing for Customers Only: "(L)imiting bank employees to notarizing only for bank customers is not considered unlawful discrimination. Most notaries are employed in businesses or government agencies which conduct business beyond the provision of notary services. These entities are not required to permit their employees to neglect their duties of employment so as to be available to the general public for notary services" (RMN).

Disqualifying Interests

"(I)t is unlawful for a notary public to notarize his own signature" (FS 117.05[1]).

Employee Does Not Have Financial Interest: "A notary public may not notarize a signature on a document if the notary public has a financial interest in or is a party to the underlying transaction; however, a notary public who is an employee may notarize a signature for his or her employer, and this employment does not constitute a financial interest in the transaction nor make the notary a party to the transaction under this subsection as long as he or she does not receive a benefit other than his or her salary and the fee for services as a notary public authorized by law" (FS 117.107[12]).

Does Owner Have Financial Interest?: "As a business owner, would I have a financial interest in the transactions being notarized for my company's business?

"Section 117.107(12), Florida Statutes, provides that you may not be the notary for a transaction in which you have a financial interest or to which you are a party .... When you are unsure whether you are a party to or have a financial interest in a particular transaction, it is always safer to err on the side of caution and decline to notarize.... Keep in mind that, as a notary, you should be a disinterested third party ..." (RMN)

Attorney Does Not Have Financial Interest: "For purposes of this subsection, a notary public who is an attorney does not have a financial interest in and is not a party to the underlying transaction evidenced by a notarized document if he or she notarizes a signature on that document for a client for whom he or she serves as an attorney of record and he or she has no interest in the document other than the fee paid to him or her for legal services and the fee authorized by law for services as a notary public" (FS 117.107[12]).

Relatives: Notaries may not notarize the signatures of their own spouses, sons, daughters, mothers or fathers (FS 117.107[11]). However, according to state officials, they may perform marriages for relatives:

"Q: May I perform a marriage ceremony for a member of my family, specifically my daughter? A: Yes. You may perform a marriage ceremony for a person who is related by blood or marriage. The prohibition against notarizing the signature of a spouse, son, daughter, mother, or father does not apply because you are not notarizing the signature of the bride and groom. You are only certifying that the couple have been joined in marriage according to the laws of the State of Florida. See Attorney General Opinion, 91-70 (1991) ..." (Governor's website, "Marriage Q & A").

NOTARY SIGNING AGENTS

Currently, there are no statutes, regulations or rules expressly governing, prohibiting or restricting the operation of Notary Signing Agents within the statute of Florida.

NOTARY FEES

"The fee of a notary public may not exceed $10 for any one notarial act, except as provided in section 117.04 (i.e., rite of matrimony fee)" (FS 117.05[2][a]).

Fee for Solemnizing Nuptials

"For solemnizing the rites of matrimony, the fee of a notary public may not exceed those provided by law to the clerks of the circuit court for like services" (FS 117.045). The current such fee charged by clerks is $30 (FS 28.24[24]).

No Fee for Absentee Ballot

A Notary may not charge a fee for witnessing an absentee ballot in an election (FS 117.05[2][b]).

Government Notaries

Notaries employed by a state, county or city government agency, board, commission or department must charge for their notarial services (except for loyalty oaths and government vehicle tags and titles) and these fees must be deposited in the governmental body's general operating fund (FS 116.35 through 116.38). "The chief administrative officer of any such agency, board, commission or department may, upon determining that such service should be performed as a public service, authorize such service to be performed free of charge."

Certain Officers May Not Charge

The following officers are Notaries only in connection with their official duties and may not charge for notarial services: law enforcement officers, correctional officers, including probation officers, traffic accident investigation officers and traffic infraction enforcement officers (FS 117.10).

Itemized List of Charges

"If you charge fees for other services not directly related to your notary services, you should provide your customer with an itemized list of charges beforehand" (RMN).

NOTARY CERTIFICATES

Any jurat or certificate of acknowledgment must contain the following elements (FS 117.05[4]):

1. The venue stating the location of the notarization in the format "State of Florida, County of _____";

2. The type of notarial act performed, whether an oath or acknowledgment, as evidenced by the word "sworn" or "acknowledged";

3. A statement that the signer personally

appeared before the Notary at the time of notarization;

4. The true date of the notarial act;
5. The name of the person whose signature is being notarized ("It is presumed, absent such specific notation by the notary public, that notarization is to all signatures.");
6. The specific type of identification the Notary is relying on in identifying the signer, either based on personal knowledge or satisfactory evidence;
7. The Notary's official signature;
8. The Notary's name — typed, printed or stamped below the signature;
9. The Notary's official seal affixed below or to either side of the Notary's signature.

Florida law prescribes the following certificates of acknowledgment, not precluding the use of other forms:

Short Form Acknowledgment by Individual (FS 695.25[1]):

STATE OF FLORIDA
COUNTY OF _____

The foregoing instrument was acknowledged before me this _____ *(date) by* _____ *(name of person acknowledging), who is personally known to me or who has produced* _____ *(type of identification) as identification.*

_____ *(Signature) (Seal)*

_____ *(Notary's Name printed, typed or stamped)*
_____ *(Title or Rank)*
_____ *(Serial number, if any)*

Acknowledgment by Individual (FS 117.05[13][b]):

STATE OF FLORIDA
COUNTY OF _____

The foregoing instrument was acknowledged before me this _____ *day of* _____, *20*____ *(year), by* _____ *(name of person acknowledging).*

_____ *(Signature) (Seal)*

_____ *(Notary's Name printed, typed or stamped)*

____ *Personally known*
____ *OR Produced identification*
Type of identification produced: _____

Acknowledgment by Individual Signing by Mark (FS 117.05[14][c]):

STATE OF FLORIDA
COUNTY OF _____

The foregoing instrument was acknowledged before me this _____ *day of* _____, *20*____ *(year), by* _____ *(name of person acknowledging), who signed with a mark in the presence of these witnesses:* _____ *(names of two witnesses).*

_____ *(Signature) (Seal)*

_____ *(Notary's Name printed, typed or stamped)*

____ *Personally known*
____ *OR Produced identification*
Type of identification produced: _____

Acknowledgment of Signature Affixed on Behalf of Person Unable to Sign (FS 117.05[14][d]):

STATE OF FLORIDA
COUNTY OF _____

The foregoing instrument was acknowledged before me this _____ *day of* _____, *20*____ *(year), by* _____ *(name of person acknowledging) and subscribed by* _____ *(name of Notary) at the direction of and in the presence of* _____ *(name of person acknowledging), and in the presence of these witnesses:* _____ *(names of two witnesses).*

_____ *(Signature) (Seal)*

_____ *(Notary's Name printed, typed or stamped)*

____ *Personally known*
____ *OR Produced identification*
Type of identification produced: _____

Acknowledgment by Representative (FS 117.05[13][c]):

STATE OF FLORIDA
COUNTY OF _____

The foregoing instrument was acknowledged before me this _____ day of _____, 20____ (year), by _____ (name of person acknowledging) as _____ (type of authority, e.g., officer, trustee, attorney in fact) for _____ (name of party on behalf of whom instrument was executed).

_____ (Signature)   (Seal)

_____ (Notary's Name printed, typed or stamped)

____ Personally known
____ OR Produced identification
Type of identification produced: _____

Short Form Acknowledgment by Corporation (FS 695.25[2]):

STATE OF FLORIDA
COUNTY OF _____

The foregoing instrument was acknowledged before me this _____ (date) by _____ (name of officer or agent, title of officer or agent) of _____ (name of corporation acknowledging), a _____ (state or place of incorporation) corporation, on behalf of the corporation. He/she is personally known to me or has produced _____ (type of identification) as identification.

_____ (Signature)   (Seal)

_____ (Notary's Name printed, typed or stamped)
_____ (Title or Rank)
_____ (Serial number, if any)

Short Form Acknowledgment by Partnership (FS 695.25[3]):

STATE OF FLORIDA
COUNTY OF _____

The foregoing instrument was acknowledged before me this _____ (date) by _____ (name of acknowledging partner or agent), partner (or agent) on behalf of _____ (name of partnership), a partnership. He/she is personally known to me or has produced _____ (type of identification) as identification.

_____ (Signature)   (Seal)

_____ (Notary's Name printed, typed or stamped)
_____ (Title or Rank)
_____ (Serial number, if any)

Short Form Acknowledgment by Attorney in Fact (FS 695.25[4]):

STATE OF FLORIDA
COUNTY OF _____

The foregoing instrument was acknowledged before me this _____ (date) by _____ (name of attorney in fact) as attorney in fact, who is personally known to me or who has produced _____ (type of identification) as identification on behalf of _____ (name of principal).

_____ (Signature)   (Seal)

_____ (Notary's Name printed, typed or stamped)
_____ (Title or Rank)
_____ (Serial number, if any)

Short Form Acknowledgment by Public Officer, Trustee or Personal Representative (FS 695.25[5]):

STATE OF FLORIDA
COUNTY OF _____

The foregoing instrument was acknowledged before me this _____ (date) by _____ (name and title of position), who is personally known to me or who has produced _____ (type of identification) as identification.

_____ (Signature)   (Seal)

_____ (Notary's Name printed, typed or stamped)
_____ (Title or Rank)
_____ (Serial number, if any)

Type of ID Must be Specified in Certificate

"A notary public shall certify in his certificate of acknowledgment or jurat the type of identification, either based on personal knowledge or other form of identification, upon which the notary public is relying" (FS 117.05[5]).

Jurat (FS 117.05[13][a]):

STATE OF FLORIDA
COUNTY OF _____

Sworn to (or affirmed) and subscribed before me this _____ day of _____, 20____ (year), by _____ (name of person making statement).

_____ *(Signature)*   *(Seal)*

_____ *(Notary's Name printed, typed or stamped)*

____ Personally known
____ OR Produced identification
Type of identification produced: _____

Jurat for Signer by Mark (FS 117.05[14][c]):

STATE OF FLORIDA
COUNTY OF _____

Sworn to and subscribed before me this _____ day of _____, 20____ (year), by _____ (name of person making statement), who signed with a mark in the presence of these witnesses: _____ (names of two witnesses).

_____ *(Signature)*   *(Seal)*

_____ *(Notary's Name printed, typed or stamped)*

____ Personally known
____ OR Produced identification
Type of identification produced: _____

Jurat for Signature Affixed on Behalf of Person Unable to Sign (FS 117.05[14][d]):

STATE OF FLORIDA
COUNTY OF _____

Sworn to (or affirmed) before me this _____ day of _____, 20____ (year), by _____ (name of person making statement), and subscribed by _____ (name of Notary) at the direction of and in the presence of _____ (name of person making statement), and in the presence of these witnesses: _____ (names of two witnesses).

_____ *(Signature)*   *(Seal)*

_____ *(Notary's Name printed, typed or stamped)*

____ Personally known
____ OR Produced identification
Type of identification produced: _____

Jurat with Affidavit (RMN):

STATE OF FLORIDA
COUNTY OF _____

Before me this day personally appeared _____ (name of affiant), who, being duly sworn, deposes and says:

(FACTS SWORN TO OR AFFIRMED BY AFFIANT)

Sworn to (or affirmed) and subscribed before me this _____ day of _____, 20____, by _____ (name of affiant).

_____ *(Signature)*   *(Seal)*

_____ *(Notary's Name printed, typed or stamped)*

____ Personally known
____ OR Produced identification
Type of identification produced: _____

Jurat with Deposition (RMN):

STATE OF FLORIDA
COUNTY OF _____

In my capacity as a Notary Public of the State of Florida, I certify that on the _____ day of _____, 20____ (year), at _____ a.m./p.m., _____ (name of deponent) personally appeared before me and took an oath (or affirmation) for the purposes of giving testimony in the matter:

_____

_____ (Signature)   (Seal)

_____ (Notary's Name printed, typed or stamped)

____ Personally known
____ OR Produced identification
Type of identification produced: _____

Attested Copy Certificate (FS 117.05[12][b]):

"This notarial certificate should be typed, stamped or written on the front or back of the photocopy or may be attached as a separate page" (RMN).

STATE OF FLORIDA
COUNTY OF _____

On this ____ day of _____, 20___ (year), I attest that the preceding or attached document is a true, exact, complete, and un-altered photocopy made by me of _____ (description of document) presented to me by the document's custodian, _____, and, to the best of my knowledge, that the photocopied document is neither a vital record nor a public record, certified copies of which are available from an official source other than a notary public.

_____ (Signature)   (Seal)

_____ (Name of Notary printed, typed or stamped)

Written Statement of Credible Witness

In circumstances when signers do not have valid identification, Notaries may identify signers through the "sworn written statement" of one personally known credible witness or of two credible witnesses who are identified through ID cards (FS 117.05[5][b]).

"When using these methods of identification, it is a good practice to have the witnesses also sign the document being notarized. Although not required, if the document has sufficient space, you may want to print or type the witness's statement on the notarized document itself. If it is on a separate page, then you should keep it in your records, rather than attach it to the notarized document" (RMN).

The following credible witness affidavit forms are suggested by the state, not excluding the use of other forms with the same information:

Affidavit for Two Credible Witnesses (RMN):

Under the penalties of perjury, I declare that the person appearing before _____ (name of Notary) is personally known to me as _____ (name of person whose signature is to be notarized) and is the person named in the document requiring notarization; that I believe it would be difficult or impossible for this person to obtain another form of acceptable identification; and that I do not have a financial interest in and am not a party to the underlying transaction.

_____ (Signature of Witness 1)
_____ (Name of Witness 1)
_____ (Date)

_____ (Signature of Witness 2)
_____ (Name of Witness 2)
_____ (Date)

STATE OF FLORIDA
COUNTY OF _____

Sworn to and subscribed before me this ____ day of _____, 20___ (year), by _____ (name of witness), who produced _____ (type of identification) as identification, and by _____ (name of witness) who produced _____ (type of identification) as identification.

_____ (Signature)   (Seal)

_____ (Notary's Name printed, typed or stamped)

Affidavit for One Credible Witness (RMN):

Under the penalties of perjury, I declare that the person appearing before _____ (name of Notary) is personally known to me as _____ (name of person whose signature is to be notarized) and is the person named in the document requiring notarization.

_____ (Signature of Witness)
_____ (Name of Witness)
_____ (Date)

STATE OF FLORIDA
COUNTY OF _____

Sworn to and subscribed before me this ____ day of _____, 20____ (year), by _____ (name of witness), who is personally known to me.

_____ (Signature)   (Seal)

_____ (Notary's Name printed, typed or stamped)

Affidavit for Document Translation (RMN):

The "Governor's Reference Manual for Notaries" prescribes this form for notarizing the signature of a document translator, pointing out that "(c)ertifying a translation is not an authorized duty of a Florida notary public" and that a Notary may not notarize his or her own signature on such a translator's affidavit:

STATE OF FLORIDA
COUNTY OF _____

Before me this day personally appeared _____ (name of translator), who being duly sworn, deposes and says:
I am fluent in both _____ (language 1) and _____ (language 2). I certify that I have accurately translated the attached document, _____ (name or description of document), from _____ (language 1) into _____ (language 2).

_____ (Signature of Translator)
_____ (Address of Translator)

Sworn to and subscribed before me this ____ day of _____, 20____, by _____ (name of translator).

_____ (Signature)   (Seal)

_____ (Typed, printed or stamped name of Notary)

____ Personally known
____ OR Produced identification
Type of identification produced: _____

'Loose' Certificates

"Preprinted notarial certificates designed to be attached to a document should be used only in rare circumstances .... If you do, be sure to state in the notarial certificate the exact document and signature to which the notarization applies" (RMN).

Altering Certificate for Two-Named Signer

"In some instances, individuals may need to sign a document with their former name after making the necessary updates to their identification cards. A classic situation arises when a woman changes her name after marriage and has to sign a document, such as a warranty deed, in her former name. You may notarize her signature if she signs both names, but you may want to indicate that fact in your notarial certificate.

"For an acknowledgment, you could state, 'The foregoing instrument was acknowledged before me this _____ day of _____, 20___, by Mary Smith, who represented to me that she was formerly known as Mary Jones, and who provided a Florida driver license, No. 123 45 678 890 in the name of Mary Smith as identification.' You may also want to include information such as the date of birth, expiration date, or physical description" (RMN).

Abbreviations Inadequate in Certificates

"We have seen notarized documents where the notary simply noted 'PK' or 'DL,' meaning 'personally known' or 'driver's license.' These abbreviations are not clear, and we recommend that you make more specific notations about identification. Although not required, it is a good practice to indicate the identification number and the state or county that issued the card. This will help protect you in case a signer later claims that he or she did not sign the document and did not appear before you for the notarization" (RMN).

ELECTRONIC NOTARIZATIONS

Effective January 1, 2008, the Florida Legislature created FS 117.021 to authorize electronic notarization:

"1. Any document requiring notarization may be notarized electronically. The provisions of ss. 117.01, 117.03, 117.04, 117.05(1) - (11), and (14), 117.105, and 117.107 apply to all notarizations under this section.

"2. In performing an electronic notarial act, a notary public shall use an electronic signature that is:

"a. Unique to the notary public;

"b. Capable of independent verification;

"c. Retained under the notary public's sole control and

"d. Attached to or logically associated with the electronic document in a manner that any subsequent alteration to the electronic document displays evidence of the alteration.

"3. When a signature is required to be accompanied by a notary public seal, the requirement is satisfied when the electronic signature of the notary public contains all of the following seal information:

"a. The full name of the notary public exactly as provided on the notary public's application for commission;

"b. The words 'Notary Public State of Florida';

"c. The date of expiration of the commission of the notary public; and

"d. The notary public's commission number.

"4. Failure of a notary public to comply with any of the requirements of this section may constitute grounds for suspension of the notary public's commission by the Executive Office of the Governor.

"5. The Department of State may adopt rules to ensure the security, reliability, and uniformity of signatures and seals authorized in this section."

Administrative Code's eNotarization Rules

Effective January 26, 2010, rules were put in place in the Florida Administrative Code by the Department of State (FS 117.021[5]) that set basic definitions for electronic notarizations (1N-5.001) and dictate how a Notary's electronic signature and seal information must be affixed on an electronic document (1N-5.002):

Definitions: "1. 'Capable of independent verification' means any interested person may reasonably determine the notary's identity, the notary's relevant authority and that the electronic signature is the act of the particular notary identified by the signature.

"2. 'Electronic document' means information that is created, generated, sent, communicated, received, or stored by electronic means.

"3. 'Electronic notarization' and 'electronic notarial act' means an official act authorized under Section 117.021(1), F.S., using electronic documents and electronic signatures.

"4. 'Electronic Notary System' means a set of applications, programs, hardware, software, or technology designed to enable a notary to perform electronic notarizations.

"5. 'Electronic signature' means an electronic sound, symbol, or process attached to or logically associated with an electronic document and executed or adopted by a person with the intent to sign the electronic document or record.

"6. 'Attached to or logically associated with' means the notary's electronic signature is securely bound to the electronic document in such a manner as to make it impracticable to falsify or alter, without detection, either the signature or the document.

"7. 'Unique to the notary public' means the notary's electronic signature is attributable solely to the notary public to the exclusion of all other persons.

"8. 'Retained under the notary public's sole control' means accessible by and attributable solely to the notary to the exclusion of all other persons and entities, either through being in the direct physical custody of the notary or through being secured with one or more biometric, password, token, or other authentication technologies in an electronic notarization system that meets the performance requirements of Sections 117.021(2) and (3), F.S.

"9. 'Public key certificate' means a computer-based record that:

"a. Identifies the certification authority issuing it;

"b. Names or identifies its subscriber;

"c. Contains the subscriber's public key; and

"d. Is digitally signed by the certification authority issuing it" (FAC 1N-5.001).

Notary's Electronic Signature: "1. In performing an electronic notarial act, a notary shall execute an electronic signature in a manner that attributes such signature to the notary public identified on the official commission.

"2. A notary shall take reasonable steps to ensure the security, reliability and uniformity of electronic notarizations, including, but not limited to, the use of an authentication procedure such as a password, token, card or biometric to protect access to the notary's electronic signature or the means for affixing the signature.

"3. The notary's electronic signature and seal information may be affixed by means of a public key certificate.

"4. The notary's electronic signature and seal information may be affixed by means of an electronic notary system.

"5. Any public key certificate or electronic notary system that is used to affix the Notary's electronic signature and seal information shall be issued at the third or higher level of assurance as defined by the U. S. National Institute of Standards and Technology (NIST) Special Publication 800-63 (NIST800-63), Electronic Authentication Guideline Version 1.0.2., available at NIST's website www.csrc.nist.gov which may be accessed at the following URL: http://csrc.nist.gov/publications/nistpubs/800-63/SP800-63V1_0_2.pdf" (FAC 1N-5.002).

Electronic Recording Authorized by URPERA

Florida has also enacted the Uniform Real Property Electronic Recording Act (URPERA) — FS 695.27 — but with a unique definition of "electronic signature": "'Electronic signature' means an electronic sound, symbol, or process that is executed or adopted by a person with the intent to sign the document and is attached to or logically associated with a document such that, when recorded, it is assigned the same document number or a consecutive page number immediately following such document" (FS 695.27[2]).

URPERA Also Stipulates: "A requirement that a document or a signature associated with a document be notarized, acknowledged, verified, witnessed, or made under oath is satisfied if the electronic signature of the person authorized to perform that act, and all other information required to be included, is attached to or logically associated with the document or signature. A physical or electronic image of a stamp, impression, or seal need not accompany an electronic signature" (FS 695.27[3]).

UETA Recognizes Notary's eSignature

Florida has adopted the Uniform Electronic Transaction (sic) Act (FS 668.50[1] through 668.50[20]), including the provision on notarization, thereby recognizing the legal validity of electronic signatures used by Notaries.

"If a law requires a signature or record to be notarized, acknowledged, verified, or made under oath, the requirement is satisfied if the electronic signature of the person authorized by applicable law to perform those acts, together with all other information required to be included by other applicable law, is attached to or logically associated with the signature or record. Neither a rubber stamp nor an impression type seal is required for an electronic notarization" (FS 668.50[11][a]).

All Notaries Instructed on eNotarization

"A first-time applicant for a notary commission must submit proof that the applicant has, within 1 year prior to the application, completed at least 3 hours of interactive or classroom instruction, including electronic notarization, and covering the duties of the notary public. Courses satisfying this section may be offered by any public or private sector person or entity registered with the Executive Office of the Governor and must include a core curriculum approved by that office" (FS 668.50[11][b]).

NOTARY RECORDS

Florida's Notaries Public are not required by law to keep a record of their official acts. The law does say, however, that "(a)ny person who unlawfully possesses a notary public official seal or any papers or copies relating to notarial acts is guilty of a misdemeanor of the second degree ..." (FS 117.05[9]).

Journal Use Endorsed by Governor

The "Governor's Reference Manual for Notaries" strongly endorses the policy of recording every notarial act in a journal:

"The best way to protect yourself is to document your notarial acts in a journal (record book or log) ...

"Florida law does not require the use of a notary journal; however, ... the Governor's Task Force on Notaries Public in 1989 recommended the mandatory use of journals. Although the Legislature did not follow that recommendation, many notaries in Florida are beginning to voluntarily use a journal ...

"We recommend that your journal be bound (not loose-leaf) and have consecutively numbered pages, so that a page could not be removed without being detected."

Required Components of Entries

The "Governor's Reference Manual for Notaries" specifies that the Notary's journal should include the following information for each official act:

1. the date of the notarial act;
2. the type of notarial act: oath, acknowledgment, attested photocopy, marriage;
3. the title or a brief description of the document;
4. the principal's printed name, exactly as he or she signed the document;
5. the principal's address;
6. the principal's signature;
7. the type of identification relied upon in identifying the principal, including the serial number, expiration date, date of birth, etc.;
8. the fee charged for the notary service; and
9. any additional comments you consider important; for example, the principal is blind and you read the document to him or her.

Record Journal Entry First: "When using a journal to record your notarizations, it is a good idea to complete the journal entry prior to the notarization to ensure that the party does not leave before the necessary information is recorded" (RMN).

Journal Fingerprints Not Prohibited: "Florida law does not require, nor authorize, notaries to take fingerprints from persons whose signatures they notarize. Many notary journals or records books allow space for a thumbprint, but this feature is optional. If there is no objection from the signer, you may record a thumbprint in your journal. However, you should not refuse to provide notary services based solely on the person's refusal to provide a fingerprint in your record book" (RMN).

Important Considerations

The "Governor's Reference Manual for Notaries" also points out important considerations for Notaries in keeping, or deciding whether to keep, a journal of their official acts: (a) journals can be used to refresh the Notary's memory about an event that occurred years earlier, and if kept consistently, may be relied upon for court testimony; (b) journals can prove the Notary's compliance with the law; (c) for a journal to be reliable, the Notary must make sure that every notarial act and any special circumstances related to that act are entered; a journal must not be shared with another notary; (d) the journal must be safeguarded; and (e) a completed journal must be kept for at least five years after the date of its last entry.

AUTHENTICATION OF NOTARIAL ACTS

Secretary of State

Authenticating certificates for Notaries, including apostilles, are issued only by the office of Florida's Secretary of State (FS 15.16). "A notary public is not required to record his or her notary public commission in an office of a clerk of the circuit court. If certification of the notary public's commission is required, it must be obtained from the Secretary of State" (FS 117.103).

Fees: $10 per notarized document for a certificate of notarial authority, including an apostille. Any certified copy of a document obtained from a clerk of the circuit court costs an additional $10 for a total of $20 per document (Dept. of State website, "Procedure for Document Authentication"). Check or money order payable to "Department of State."

Address:
Department of State
Division of Corporations
Apostille Certification
P.O. Box 6800
Tallahassee, FL 32314-6800

Telephone: 1-850-245-6945

In Person or Courier Service:
Department of State
Division of Corporations
Apostille Section
2661 Executive Center Circle (Clifton Bldg.)
Tallahassee, FL 32301

Procedure: "Documents must be submitted with original signatures; copies cannot be certified" (Dept. of State website, "Procedure for Document Authentication"). Mail or present in person the original notarized document(s), along with the appropriate fee. If mailed, enclose a cover letter indicating the country of destination and include an addressed, stamped envelope and a telephone number in case there are questions. Allow five working days for processing. No expedited service is offered. Enclose a prepaid air bill if the document(s) will be returned by courier service.

COMMISSIONING AND ADMINISTRATION

Though Florida's Notaries are appointed by the Governor (FS 117.01[1]), whose office provides instructional literature and information for appointees, it is the Secretary of State's Notary Commissions and Certifications Section that performs the ministerial function of issuing commissions to the state's Notaries and maintaining records on them (FS 117.01[2]). The Governor's Notary Section was established in July 1992 after the Legislature appropriated funds to educate and assist the state's Notaries Public. "The main function of the Notary Section — to educate and assist Notaries — is accomplished in several ways: by publishing and distributing educational materials, particularly the notary laws and the 'Governor's Reference Manual for Notaries'; by answering telephone inquiries from Notaries; by conducting notary seminars; and maintaining the online Notary Education Course. Although the Governor's Notary Section is not authorized to offer legal advice to Notaries, we do make every effort to help Notaries understand their duties" (Governor's website, "Introduction").

The application for a Notary commission is maintained by the Department of State for the full term of a Notary's commission. The application and the information it contains, except for the Social Security number, are a public record and may be disclosed to any person upon request.

Applying for Commission

Qualifications: An applicant for a commission as a Florida Notary Public must: (a) be at least 18 years old, (b) be a legal resident of Florida and (c) if ever convicted of a felony, have had civil rights restored.

Course of Instruction Required: All first-time applicants for a Notary commission, within one year prior to application, must complete a three-hour interactive or classroom course offered by the state or by a provider approved by the Executive Office of the Governor (FS 668.50[11][b]). The course must cover electronic notarization. An online interactive course is offered by the state.

Application: Applications are normally submitted to the Department of State both electronically and in paper format by the state-approved company — the so-called "Notary Processor" — providing the applicant's $7,500 Notary bond. "Most of these companies provide 'one-stop shopping' — they furnish an application, pay the state fees, write your notary bond, and supply your notary seal. You make one payment to the company…Please note that the State does not give out applications or provide notary seals" (Governor's website, "How to Become a Notary"). The application form includes an oath of office and an "Affidavit of Character," which must be signed by a person unrelated to the applicant who has known the applicant for at least one year. For non-citizens of the United States, a recorded "Declaration of Domicile" (available at a county clerk's office) must be included with the application. A signed certificate of completion for the required three-hour Notary course must also be submitted. The total state fees are $39, which includes a $25 application fee, a $10 commission fee and a $4 education surcharge.

"The application process for reappointment is exactly the same as for a first-time appointment… When applying for a renewal commission, treat it as a new application and do not refer…the Notary Commissions and Certifications Section to your previous application for information" (RMN).

Commission Mailed to Bonding Company: "The notary commission is printed by the Department of State and mailed to your bonding agency. Typically, the company will forward it to you, and your notary seal will follow within a few days. The entire process should be completed within 2-3 weeks, unless your application requires special handling" (Governor's website, "How to Become a Notary").

Non-Residents: Persons who do not reside in Florida may not become Notaries in the state.

Online Search: The Florida Department of State's online "Notary Search" allows access to the Notary database by submitting a Notary's last name, first name, commission number or zip code at http://notaries.dos.state.fl.us/not001.html. Included in the data provided for a given Notary are the commission starting and expiration dates, bonding agency and mailing address.

"Daily activity journals reporting updates to the Notaries Public database are available … and may be downloaded as ASCII comma-delimited text files" (Dept. of State website, "Notary Public Access System").

Changes of Status

If Notary Moves: "A notary public shall notify, in writing, the Department of State of any change in his business address, home telephone number, business telephone number, home address, or criminal record within 60 days after such change" (FS 117.01[2]). A Notary "who does not maintain legal residence in this state during the entire term of appointment" must resign his or her commission in a signed letter to the Governor (FS 117.01[5][b]).

If Notary Changes Name: "Any notary public who lawfully changes his name shall, within 60 days after such change, forthwith request an amended commission from the Secretary of State ... (who) shall issue an amended commission to the notary public in the new name. A rider to the notary public's bond must accompany the notice of change form. After submitting the required notice of change form and rider to the Secretary of State, the notary public may continue to perform notarial acts in his former name for 60 days or until receipt of the amended commission, whichever date is earlier" (FS 117.05[9]).

"Any notary public who lawfully changes his name during the term of the commission must request an amended commission from one of the bonding agencies that has been approved by submitting

"1. a completed notice of name change form (DS-DE 77A)

"2. current commission

"3. rider to current notary public bond

"4. $25 check or money order (payable to Department of State)

"A notice of name change form must be sent to the Division via electronic transfer" (Dept. of State website, "About the Notary Commissions and Certifications Section").

If Notary Resigns: A resignation of a Notary Public commission must be submitted to the Florida Governor's Notary Section.

COUNTY CLERKS

In Florida, Notaries do not file oaths, bonds and seal/signature samples at the county level, and, thus, county officials do not normally issue authenticating certificates for Notaries nor keep records on Notaries.

OTHER NOTARIAL OFFICERS

Besides Notaries, the following officers may take acknowledgments and proofs within the state and the seal of the court or officer must be used (FS 695.03):

1. A judge, clerk or deputy clerk of any court;

2. A U.S. commissioner or magistrate.

Law Enforcement, Correctional Officers

Law enforcement officers, correctional officers, correctional probation officers, traffic-accident investigation officers, and traffic infraction enforcement officers, as defined in FS 943.10 and 316.640, have power to administer oaths in the performance of their official duties (FS 117.10). They may not notarize their own signatures.

Florida Civil-Law Notaries

The Florida Secretary of State may appoint attorneys in good standing who have practiced law in the state for at least five years as "Florida civil-law Notaries" with worldwide jurisdiction. Equivalent to the notarial officers of Latin nations (Notarios, Notaires, etc.), these officers are authorized to issue "authentic acts" and must maintain a "protocol," or registry of their acts. Civil-law Notaries may also exercise the powers of regular Florida Notaries, including the power to perform marriages. (See FS 118.10 and 118.12; and Florida Admin. Code 1C-18.001.)

"(T)here is a required exam that is preceded by an optional two day training held (at) various locations throughout the state. The location of the training and exam site is determined by the location of the majority of the pool of applicants" (Dept. of State website, "Civil Law Notary").

The same legislative act (Chapter 97-241, Laws of 1997) that created the office of Florida civil-law Notary to interact with Latin Notaries also repealed the statutes authorizing the Florida Governor to appoint general commissioners of deeds to notarize in jurisdictions outside the state of Florida.

Timeshare Commissioners of Deeds

The Florida Governor may appoint "timeshare commissioners of deeds," with four-year terms, to notarize documents abroad related to purchase of timeshare property in a foreign country (FS 721.97).

QUICK FACTS

Notary Jurisdiction
Statewide (FS 117.01[1]).

Notary Term Length
Four years (FS 117.01[1]), expiring at midnight on the commission expiration date.
"Any notary public who knowingly acts as a notary public after his or her commission has expired is guilty of a misdemeanor of the second degree ..." (FS 117.05[8]).

Notary Bond
$7,500, "approved and filed with the Department of State and executed by a surety company for hire duly authorized to transact business in this state" (FS 117.01[7][a]).

Employer's Liability: "The employer of a notary public shall be liable to the persons involved for all damages proximately caused by the notary's official misconduct, if the notary public was acting in the scope of his or her employment at the time of notary engaged in the official misconduct" (FS 117.05[6]).

Georgia

NOTARY SEAL

A Georgia Notary must authenticate all official acts with a seal of office, and the seal's format — for Notaries commissioned or renewing their commissions on or after July 1, 1985 — must be as follows (OCGA 45-17-6):

Kind

Inked Stamp or Embosser: "The embossment of notarial certificates by the notary's seal shall be authorized but not necessary, and the use of a rubber or other type stamp shall be sufficient for imprinting the notary's seal. A scrawl shall not be a sufficient notary seal. An official act must be documented by the notary's seal" (OCGA 45-17-6[a][1]).

Shape/Size

Not specified by statute.

Examples

The above typical, actual-size examples of Notary seals are allowed by Georgia law. Formats other than these may also be permitted.

NOTARY ADMINISTRATION

While Georgia's superior court clerks appoint and commission the state's Notaries, these clerks must forward each Notary's name, address, signature, age, sex and term of appointment to the Georgia Superior Court Clerks' Cooperative Authority (OCGA 45-17-4), and Notaries are required to report changes in their official status to the Authority. In addition to maintaining a central database on the state's Notaries, the GSCCCA sends out commission renewal notifications, and issues apostilles for notarial acts.

Georgia Superior Court Clerks'
  Cooperative Authority
Notary Division   1-404-327-6023
1875 Century Blvd., Suite 100
Atlanta, GA 30345

Website: www.gsccca.org/Projects/
            aboutnp.asp

NOTARY RULES

OCGA — Official Code of Georgia Annotated
GNH — Georgia Notary Handbook

Most Notary rules are in the Official Code of Georgia Annotated, Title 45, Chapter 17 ("Notaries Public").

Other guidelines for Notaries are in the "Georgia Notary Handbook" (6th Edition, 2009) issued through the Georgia Superior Court Clerks' Cooperative Authority.

Components

1. Name of Notary, as it appears on commission;
2. "Notary Public";
3. "Georgia" or "GA";
4. Name of county of Notary's appointment.

OPTIONAL: "Georgia law does not require the notary's expiration date (on the seal), but we strongly recommend that you include this information on your notary stamp" (GNH).

Commission Expiration Date Required

Georgia county recording officials require that the Notary's commission expiration date appear on deeds and other documents presented for recording in the state. This date need not appear within the Notary's seal.

"A document is generally valid if the expiration date is mistakenly left out. The wise Notary will always include the expiration date. If no stamp is handy, the expiration date may be handwritten" (website, "Frequently-Asked Questions").

Seal Absence Before 1986 Won't Invalidate

"No document executed prior to July 1, 1986, which would otherwise be eligible for recording in the real property records maintained by any clerk of superior court or constitute record notice or actual notice of any matter to any person shall be ineligible for recording or fail to constitute such notice because of noncompliance with the requirement that the document contain a notary seal" (OCGA 45-17-6[a][2]).

Date Not Necessary for Deeds

"(a) Except as otherwise provided in this Code section, in documenting a notarial act, a notary public shall sign on the notarial certificate, by hand in ink, only and exactly the name indicated on the notary's commission and shall record on the notarial certification the exact date of the notarial act.

"(b) The requirement of subsection (a) of this Code section for recording of the date of the notarial act shall not apply to an attestation of deeds or any other instruments pertaining to real property" (OCGA 45-17-8.1).

"In documenting a notarial act, a Notary shall sign the notarial certification in ink exactly as the name appears on the notary commission and shall also record the exact date of the notarial act. However, in connection with attestation of deeds or other instruments pertaining to real property, the date of the notarial act shall not be required" (website, "Georgia State Law").

Obtaining Seal without Authorization

"It shall be unlawful for any person, firm, or corporation to supply a notary public seal to any person unless the person has presented the duplicate original of the certificate commissioning the person as a notary public. It shall be unlawful for any person to order or obtain a notary public seal unless such person is commissioned as a notary public" (OCGA 45-17-6[b]).

Lost or Stolen Seal

"Within ten days of the loss or theft of an official notarial seal, the notary public shall send to the appointing clerk of superior court, with a copy to the Georgia Superior Court Clerks' Cooperative Authority, a written notice of the loss or theft" (OCGA 45-17-14).

"Do not allow others to have access to your notary seal or any other tools or papers related to your official duties. Keep your seal locked in a secure location at all times" (GNH).

Destruction of Notary Seal

"A notary public whose commission expires and who does not apply for renewal of such commission or whose application for renewal of a commission is denied shall destroy the official notary seal" (OCGA 45-17-18). Revocation or resignation of a commission also requires the Notary to destroy the seal (OCGA 45-17-16 and 45-17-17).

Seal Belongs to Notary, Not Employer

"Even though an employer may pay for a notary's commission…(w)hen you leave your place of employment, your commission and supplies go with you. Your employer may not require you to leave your stamp or seal, commission certificate, or recordbook behind….(T)he notary's stamp and other materials may be used only by the notary" (GNH).

Signature by Hand in Ink

A Georgia Notary Public is required to sign on the notarial certificate, by hand in ink, only and exactly the name indicated on the Notary's commission (OCGA 45-17-8.1[a]).

NOTARY POWERS

Georgia Notaries are authorized to perform the following notarial acts (OCGA 45-17-8):
1. Take acknowledgments*;
2. Administer oaths** and affirmations**;
3. Witness affidavits and take verifications upon oath or affirmation (jurats);
4. Witness or attest signatures***;
5. Certify copies****;
6. Perform "such other acts as they are authorized to perform by other laws of this state."

* <u>Acknowledgments</u>: "The acknowledgment is an act in which a document signer personally appears before a notary, is positively identified, and verbally admits to signing a document freely for the purposes therein stated. The notary certifies in a notarial certificate that these actions were completed…

"To take an acknowledgment, the notary must ask the signer a question in substantially the following form: 'Do you acknowledge and declare that this is your signature, that you understand this document, and that you willingly signed the document for the purposes stated herein?'….As with an oath or affirmation, the notarial act is not complete and is not valid if the ceremony is not verbalized. An acknowledgment differs from an oath in that the document does not have to be signed in the notary's presence. The document could have been signed at some point earlier than the date the signer appears before the notary to acknowledge the signing and execution of the document" (GNH).

** Oaths and Affirmations: "When administering an oath, the notary must perform a verbal ceremony; that is, the notary makes a verbal statement that the oath-taker repeats verbatim, or asks a question in which the oath-taker makes an affirmative response. An oath must be given in person. If the oath is for a written document, the person will also sign the document in the notary's presence.

"Notaries may administer any oath required by state law, including an Oath of Office to public officials. If preferred, the notary may ask the signer to raise his/her right hand in a pledging gesture. Such a ceremony impresses upon the signer the solemnity of the oath taken. The best way to administer an oath…is for the notary to simply ask the oath-taker the question: 'Do you solemnly swear under the penalties of perjury that the information contained in this document or statement is the truth, so help you God?'…If the signer is unable to speak, the signer may nod or use some other gesture to indicate agreement or write a response….

"If a person objects to taking an oath, Georgia law allows an affirmation in lieu of an oath. An affirmation is legally equivalent to an oath…. There is no reference to a Supreme Being in an affirmation….To administer an affirmation, the notary simply asks the signer or affirmant: 'Do you solemnly affirm under the penalties of perjury that the information contained in this document or statement is the truth?'" (GNH).

*** Witnessing or Attesting: "'Attesting' and 'attestation' are synonymous and mean the notarial act of witnessing or attesting a signature or execution of a deed or other written instrument, where such notarial act does not involve the taking of an acknowledgment, the administering of an oath or affirmation, the taking of a verification, or the certification of a copy" (OCGA 45-17-1).

In witnessing a signature, the Notary certifies that (a) the signer personally appeared before the Notary at the time of notarization, (b) the signer was positively identified by the Notary and (c) the signer affixed the signature in the presence of the Notary (GNH).

**** Certifying Copies: Georgia Notaries may make certified copies "provided that the document presented for copying is an original document and is neither a public record nor a publicly recorded document certified copies of which are available from an official source other than a notary and provided that the document was photocopied under supervision of the notary" (OCGA 45-17-8[a][6]).

"Documents which can be copied and certified by a Georgia notary public include: business transactions, school diplomas, personal letters, a social security card, insurance policies, accounting statements, contracts, lease agreements, invoices or bills of sale, student permission forms, consent to give medical treatment forms, living wills, and consent to travel forms.

"A Georgia notary public is prohibited from making certified copies of publicly recordable documents which include: deeds, mortgages, and other instruments dealing with real estate, vital records, birth certificates, marriage records, divorce decrees, powers of attorney, probated wills, student records or transcripts from public schools, colleges or universities, military discharges, Uniform Commercial Code documents, court pleadings, documents marked 'filed' or 'recorded,' most documents retained by a government office, Certificates of Naturalization, Certificates of Citizenship, Declarations of Intention to Become a Citizen, foreign passports" (website, "Notary Information").

"A Georgia notary public may make a certified copy of a U.S. Passport using the passport holder's affidavit and certified copy guidelines provided by GSCCCA" (website, "Notary Information"). See "Notary Certificates" later in this chapter for a sample passport affidavit.

"School transcripts must be signed by an issuing official of the school in the presence of a notary public. The notary cannot act as the issuing official and the notary for a transcript document" (website, "Notary Information").

"(N)or is a certification by a notary public that a document is a certified or true copy of an original document evidence to show that such notary public had knowledge of the contents of the document so certified" (OCGA 45-17-8[f]).

Screening for Identity, Volition, Sanity

"In performing any notarial act, a notary public shall confirm the identity of the document signer, oath taker, or affirmant based on personal knowledge or on satisfactory evidence" (OCGA 45-17-8[e]).

Personal Knowledge: "You personally know someone when you have interacted with that person over a substantial period of time. This time period should be long enough for you to feel confident that the person is who he says he is....A friend of long standing, a coworker who you have known for a significant period of time, or a neighbor who has lived near you long enough for you to reasonably know the person are examples of personally knowing. On the other hand, someone you were told about, or someone you met for the first time the day before are examples of people you do not personally know" (GNH).

Documentary Evidence: The "Georgia Notary Handbook" cites the following ID documents as examples of satisfactory evidence: (a) a Georgia driver's license or non-driver's ID; (b) a U.S. passport; (c) a foreign passport duly stamped by the USCIS; (d) a driver's license or non-driver's ID issued by another state, a U.S. territory, Canada or Mexico; (e) an ID card issued by any branch of the U.S. military for active duty personnel, retirees or dependents; (f) a permanent resident or "green card" issued by the USCIS.

Credible Witnesses: "There are some people who have no form of identification....In such cases, there are two forms of credible witness statements that may be used.

"1. The notary personally knows someone who the notary thinks is both disinterested and believable and who personally knows the person who has no identification.

"2. There are two credible witnesses that the notary does not know, but who have satisfactory identification and personally know the person who has no identification" (GNH).

According to the "Handbook," each credible witness must make a written statement swearing that all of the following are true: (a) the credible witness personally knows the signer named in the document; (b) the signer does not possess acceptable documentary identification; (c) the signer has no reasonable way to obtain satisfactory identification; and (d) the witness has no financial interest in the transaction, nor is a party to it.

The "Handbook" states that the Notary must make a journal entry for each witness, in addition to the entry for the notarization.

"The credible witness affidavit must be used only for signers who have no identification. It must not be used as a convenience for someone who has no identification simply because the person has lost the identification card or left it somewhere else. That person will have to obtain a new identification card or retrieve the one he has" (GNH).

Ascertain Sanity, Voluntariness: "A Notary may, and should, refuse to witness a signature whenever any question exists as to the identity of the signer, the sanity of the signer, or the voluntariness of the signature" (website, "Frequently-Asked Questions").

Ads for Notarial Services

"A notary who is not an attorney licensed to practice law in this state who advertises the person's services as a notary public in English or any other language, by radio, television, signs, pamphlets, newspapers, other written communication, or in any other manner, shall post or otherwise include with the advertisement the notice set forth in this subsection in English and in every other language used for the advertisement. The notice shall be of a conspicuous size, if in writing, and shall state: 'I AM NOT AN ATTORNEY LICENSED TO PRACTICE LAW IN THE STATE OF GEORGIA, AND I MAY NOT GIVE LEGAL ADVICE OR ACCEPT FEES FOR LEGAL ADVICE.' If the advertisement is made by radio or television, the statement may be modified but must include substantially the same message" (OCGA 45-17-8.2[b]).

"A notary required to comply with the provisions of subsection (b) (above) of this Code section shall prominently post at the notary public's place of business a schedule of fees established by law which a notary may charge. The fee schedule shall be written in English and in any non-English language in which the notary services were solicited and shall contain the notice required in subsection (b) of this Code section, unless the notice is otherwise prominently posted at the notary public's place of business" (OCGA 45-17-8.2[e]).

Immigration Assistance Rules

Georgia's Registration of Immigration Assistance Act (OCGA 43-20A-1 through 43-20A-21) prescribes special rules for "immigration assistance" (OCGA 43-20A-2[7]) that impact certain activities of Notaries:

1. The Act defines certain immigration-related duties that may only be performed by a licensed "immigration assistance provider" (OCGA 43-20A-2[8]). Among the services an immigration assistance provider licensee may perform is "(n)otarizing signatures on government agency forms, provided that the person performing the service is a notary public commissioned in the State of Georgia and is lawfully present in the United States" (OCGA 43-20A-5[a][5]).

2. Any non-attorney offering immigration assistance – including notarization of immigration documents – "shall post signs at his or her place of business setting forth information in English and in every other language in which the person provides or offers to provide immigration assistance. Each language shall be on a separate sign. Signs shall be posted in a location where the signs will be visible to clients. Each sign shall be at least 12 inches by 17 inches and shall contain the following statement: 'I AM NOT AN ATTORNEY LICENSED TO PRACTICE LAW AND MAY NOT GIVE LEGAL ADVICE OR ACCEPT FEES FOR LEGAL ADVICE'" (OCGA 43-20A-6[b]). In addition, any non-attorney who advertises immigration assistance in a language other than English must include the above statement in a conspicuous position in the ad, both in English and in the language of the ad (OCGA 43-20A-6[c]).

3. The Act prohibits a non-attorney from representing or advertising, "in conjunction with immigration assistance, other titles or credentials, including but not limited to 'notary public' or 'immigration consultant,' that could cause a client to believe that the person possesses special professional skills or is authorized to provide advice on an immigration matter; provided, however, that a certified notary public may use the term 'notary public' if, the use is accompanied by the statement that the person is not an attorney and the term 'notary public' is not translated to another language" (OCGA 43-20A-6[e][2]).

For violations of the Act, the Secretary of State may assess civil penalties of $1,000 to $50,000 (OCGA 43-20A-7).

Notary Not Responsible for Contents

Notarization does not indicate that the Notary had knowledge of the contents of the document notarized or of the copy certified (OCGA 45-17-8[f]).

NOTARY DON'TS

A Georgia Notary may:

1. NOT be obligated to notarize "for a transaction which the Notary knows or suspects is illegal, false, or deceptive" (OCGA 45-17-8[b]);
2. NOT "execute a notarial certificate containing a statement known by the notary to be false nor perform any action with an intent to deceive or defraud" upon penalty of misdemeanor (OCGA 45-17-8[d] and 45-17-20);
3. NOT be obligated to notarize for a person who is being coerced (OCGA 45-17-8[b]);
4. NOT be obligated to notarize for a document signer "whose demeanor causes compelling doubts about whether the person knows the consequences of the transaction requiring the notarial act" (OCGA 45-17-8[b]);
5. NOT be obligated to notarize "in situations which impugn and compromise the notary's impartiality" as specified in OCGA 45-17-8(c)(1) (OCGA 45-17-8[b]);
6. NOT "make claims to have or imply he has powers, qualifications, rights, or privileges that the office of notary does not authorize, including the powers to counsel on immigration matters and to give legal advice" (OCGA 45-17-8.2[a]);
7. NOT, as a nonattorney, represent or advertise that the Notary is a "legal consultant" or an expert on legal matters (OCGA 45-17-8.2[c]);
8. NOT use the term "Notario Publico";
9. NOT issue attachments or garnishments nor approve bonds for that purpose, nor

issue a summons in a dispossessory case, though attesting an affidavit in such cases is allowed (OCGA 45-17-10);
10. NOT notarize nomination and recall petitions, nor petitions for paupers' affidavits, which the notary has circulated and signed as an elector (OCGA 21-2-132, 21-2-170, 21-4-5 and 21-4-8).

No Exceptions to Physical Presence

"(T)he signer MUST be present before the notary, no exceptions" (GNH).

May Not Translate and Notarize

"Documents translated from English to a foreign language must be signed by the translator in the presence of a notary public. The notary cannot act as the translator and the notary for a translated document (OCGA 45-17-8[c][1] & [2])" (website, "Notary Information").

May Not Authenticate Photographs

"A Georgia notary public is not authorized to certify the authenticity of photographs" (website, "Notary Information").

May Not Serve as Notary and Witness

To enable recording, a witness in addition to the Notary is required on documents affecting real property.

"Can I sign as a witness in addition to acting as a notary on a document? — A Notary is disqualified from performing a notarial act when he or she is also a party to the document for which notarization is required" (website, "Frequently-Asked Questions").

No Blanks or Missing Pages

"(T)he signer must present the notary with a complete document, not just the signature page. The notary must be assured there are no blanks in the document that should be filled in at the time of notarization" (GNH).

Disqualifying Interests

A Notary is disqualified from notarizing when (OCGA 45-17-8[c]):
1. The Notary is a signer of the document; or
2. The Notary is a party to the document or transaction for which the notarial act is required.

<u>Bank/Corporate Notary Not Disqualified</u>: A Notary who is a stockholder, director, officer or employee of a bank or other corporation may notarize for bank or corporate transactions, except that such a Notary may not notarize his or her own signature (OCGA 45-17-12).

<u>Notarizing for Relatives</u>: "Notary News," published by the Georgia Superior Court Clerks' Cooperative Authority, stated: "Although the statutes do not forbid notarizing the signature of relatives, it is not a good idea. If the notarized document is ever challenged in court, it might be determined that you were not acting as an impartial witness when the document was notarized."

No Intent to Deceive

"The notary must never execute a notarial certificate that contains a false statement. He or she must never perform an action with the intent to deceive or defraud" (GNH).

Notary Not Vouching for Contents

"The signature of a notary public documenting a notarial act shall not be evidence to show that such notary public had knowledge of the contents of the document so signed, other than those specific contents which constitute the signature, execution, acknowledgment, oath, affirmation, affidavit, verification, or other act which the signature of that notary public documents…" (OCGA 45-17-8[f]).

NOTARY SIGNING AGENTS

In an opinion released November 10, 2003, the Georgia Supreme Court approved UPL Advisory Opinion 2003-2 and thereby dictated that only licensed attorneys — and not laymen such as Notary Signing Agents — may handle closings of home loans and other real estate transactions. "(W)e have consistently held that it is the unauthorized practice of law for someone other than a duly-licensed Georgia attorney to close a real estate transaction or to prepare or facilitate the execution of such deed(s) for the benefit of a seller, borrower, or lender," the opinion stated.

NOTARY FEES

The maximum fees that a Georgia Notary may charge for a notarial act are (OCGA 45-17-11):

1. Taking an acknowledgment: $2;
2. Administering an oath or affirmation: $2;
3. Any other certificate: $2.

Extra Fee for Authenticating Certificate

"The Notary may, upon request of the person asking for notary service, charge an additional $2.00 for providing a certificate from the Clerk of Superior Court of the effectiveness of the notary commission" (website, "Notary Laws …").

"It shall not be lawful for any notary public to charge a greater sum than $4.00 for each service performed. Said sum shall include a fee of $2.00 for performing the notarial act and a fee of $2.00 for an attendance to make proof as a notary public and certifying to same if such certification, which shall be issued by the clerk of superior court of the county in which the notary public was appointed or the Georgia Superior Court Clerks' Cooperative Authority, is required. Registering shall be paid for by the party who has the service performed. The fee for all official acts which the notary may perform shall be the same as those prescribed for other officers who are likewise permitted to perform them" (OCGA 45-17-11[b]).

Announce Fees Before Notarizing

Prior to performing a notarization, the Notary must inform the person requesting the act of the fee (OCGA 45-17-11[d]).

Fees Need Not Be Charged

A Notary is not obligated to charge fees for notarial acts (OCGA 45-17-11[c]).

Travel Fees

"The law does not address travel fees for notarial acts. In the absence of any statutory rule, notaries are allowed to charge a fee for travel as long as the signer is aware that a travel fee is charged and that the travel fee is billed separately from any fee for notary service, and carefully detailed regarding the additional charges" (GNH).

Fees Must Be Posted for Ads

Notaries who advertise their services must "prominently post" in their offices a statutory fee schedule in both English and any other language used in the ads (OCGA 45-17-8.2[e]). The following statement must also appear in every language used in the ads: "I AM NOT AN ATTORNEY LICENSED TO PRACTICE LAW IN THE STATE OF GEORGIA, AND I MAY NOT GIVE LEGAL ADVICE OR ACCEPT FEES FOR LEGAL ADVICE" (OCGA 45-17-8.2[b]).

NOTARY CERTIFICATES

Georgia's Notary statutes do not prescribe language for acknowledgments and other acts. The following format is common on deeds and other documents affecting real property that are recorded:

Signed, sealed and delivered in the presence of

_____   _____
Unofficial Witness   Grantor

_____   _____
Notary Public   Grantor
State of Georgia

(NOTARY'S SEAL AND COMMISSION EXPIRATION DATE)

Because Georgia statute does not prescribe certificates for the various notarial acts, the Georgia Superior Court Clerks' Cooperative Authority recommends the following forms for Notaries:

Acknowledgment by Individual (website):

State of Georgia
County of _____

This instrument was acknowledged before me this ____ *day of* _____, 20___, *by* _____ *(name of signer).*

____ *Personally Known*
____ *Produced Identification*
Type and # of ID _____

_____ *(Notary signature)*

(Seal)

_____ *(Notary name typed, stamped or printed)*

Notary Public, State of Georgia

Jurat (website):

State of Georgia
County of _____

    Sworn to (or affirmed) and subscribed before me this _____ day of _____, 20___, by _____ (name of person making statement).

____ Personally Known
____ Produced Identification
Type and # of ID _____

_____ (Notary signature)

(Seal)

_____ (Notary name typed, stamped or printed)

Notary Public, State of Georgia

Signature Witnessing (website):

State of Georgia
County of _____

    Signed before me this ____ day of _____, 20___, by _____ (name of signer).

____ Personally Known
____ Produced Identification
Type and # of ID _____

_____ (Notary signature)

(Seal)

_____ (Notary name typed, stamped or printed)

Notary Public, State of Georgia

Affidavit Certificate with Jurat (website):

State of Georgia
County of _____

    _____ (printed name of affiant) personally appeared before me and took an oath that the following is true and correct: (Here insert facts to be sworn to or affirmed by affiant)

_____ (Affiant signature)

    Sworn to (or affirmed) and subscribed before me this _____ day of _____, 20___, by _____ (name of person making statement).

____ Personally Known
____ Produced Identification
Type and # of ID _____

_____ (Notary signature)

(Seal)

_____ (Notary name typed, stamped or printed)

Notary Public, State of Georgia

Certified Copy Certificate (website):

State of Georgia
County of _____

    On this _____ day of _____, 20___, I certify that the preceding or attached document is a true, exact, complete, and unaltered photocopy made by me from the original document of _____ _____ (description of document), presented to me by the document's custodian, _____ (name of custodian), and that, to the best of my knowledge, the photocopied document is neither a public record nor a publicly recordable document, certified copies of which are available from an official source other than a notary public.

____ Personally Known
____ Produced Identification
Type and # of ID _____

_____ (Notary signature)

(Seal)

_____ (Notary name typed, stamped or printed)

Notary Public, State of Georgia

Certified Copy by Document Custodian with Jurat (website):

State of Georgia
County of _____

I, _____ (name of document custodian), swear/affirm that the foregoing (or attached) is a true and complete copy of _____ (title or description of document), made by me, and the photocopied document is not a vital record, a public record, or a publicly recordable document, certified copies of which are available from an official source other than a notary public.

_____
(Affiant/custodian signature)

Sworn to (or affirmed) and subscribed before me this _____ day of _____, 20___, by _____ (name of affiant/custodian).

____ *Personally Known*
____ *Produced Identification*
Type and # of ID _____

_____ *(Notary signature)*
(Seal)

_____ *(Notary name typed, stamped or printed)*

Notary Public, State of Georgia

Translator's Certificate with Jurat (website):

State of Georgia
County of _____

I, _____ (name of translator), swear/affirm that I know the English language and the _____ language(s), and can translate from any of them into the other, and that the attached is an accurate and complete translation of _____ (description of document), made by me from _____ into _____.

_____ *(Translator signature)*

_____
(Translator printed name)

Sworn to (or affirmed) and subscribed before me this _____ day of _____, 20___, by _____ (name translator).

____ *Personally Known*
____ *Produced Identification*
Type and # of ID _____

_____ *(Notary signature)*
(Seal)

_____ *(Notary name typed, stamped or printed)*

Notary Public, State of Georgia

Passport Affidavit with Certified Copy Certificate (website):

State of Georgia
County of _____

Before me this _____ day of _____, 20____, personally appeared _____ (name of passport bearer/affiant), who under oath or affirmation makes the following statements:

I am the legal bearer of United States Passport No. _____, issued on _____ and expiring on _____. My date of birth is _____. I hereby authorize a Notary Public to issue a certified copy of my passport from the original.

_____
(Passport bearer/affiant signature)

Sworn to (or affirmed) and subscribed before me this _____ day of _____, 20___, by _____ (name of passport bearer/affiant).

____ *Personally Known*
____ *Produced Identification*
Type and # of ID _____

_____ *(Notary signature)*
(Seal)

_____ *(Notary name typed, stamped or printed)*

Notary Public, State of Georgia

CERTIFICATE OF CERTIFIED COPY

State of Georgia
County of _____

On this ____ day of _____, 20___, I certify that the preceding or attached document is a true, exact, complete, and unaltered photocopy made by me of an original United States Passport in the name of _____, Passport No. _____, issued on _____ and expiring on _____, presented to me by the document's custodian, _____, and that, to the best of my knowledge, this passport is neither a public record nor a publicly recordable document, certified copies of which are available from an official source other than a notary public.

_____ *(Notary signature)*

(Seal)
_____ *(Notary name typed, stamped or printed)*

Notary Public, State of Georgia

Form of Certificate

"In the taking of acknowledgments and the performing of other notarial acts requiring certification, a certificate endorsed upon or attached to the instrument or document, which certificate shows the date of the notarial act and which states, in substance, that the person appearing before the officer acknowledged the instrument as his act or made or signed the instrument or document under oath, shall be sufficient for all intents and purposes. The instrument or document shall not be rendered invalid by the failure to state the place of execution or acknowledgment" (OCGA 45-17-33).

ELECTRONIC NOTARIZATIONS

The state of Georgia has not yet adopted extensive and specific statutes or regulations expressly establishing rules, definitions and procedures for electronic notarization.

Paper-Based Requirements Still Apply

"The fact that notarial acts may be performed electronically does not affect the requirements of the notary law or a notary's responsibilities. The same steps are followed for an electronic notarization as for a standard paper and ink notarization" (GNH).

According to the "Georgia Notary Handbook," Notaries performing electronic notarial acts must still: (a) require the personal physical appearance of the signer at the time of the notarial act, (b) positively identify the signer, (c) ascertain the signer's free will to sign, and (d) determine that the signer appears to understand the import of the transaction. All other elements of the paper-based notarial act — including making a journal entry, completing a notarial certificate and administering any required oath to the signer — must also be performed according to current rules.

UETA Recognizes Notary's eSignature

Georgia has enacted the Uniform Electronic Transaction Act (OCGA 10-12-1 through 10-12-20), including the provision on notarization and acknowledgment:

"If a law requires a signature or record to be notarized, acknowledged, verified, or made under oath, such requirement shall be satisfied if the electronic signature of the person authorized to perform those acts, together with all other information required to be included by other applicable law, is attached to or logically associated with the signature or record" (OCGA 10-12-11).

URPERA Does Not Require Seal Image

Georgia has enacted the Uniform Real Property Electronic Recording Act (OCGA 44-2-35 through 44-2-39.2), including:

"A requirement that a document or a signature associated with a document be notarized, acknowledged, verified, witnessed, or made under oath is satisfied if the electronic signature of the person authorized to perform that act, and all other information required to be included by other applicable law, is attached to or logically associated with the document or signature. A physical or electronic image of a stamp, impression, or seal need not accompany an electronic signature" (OCGA 44-2-37[c]).

NOTARY RECORDS

"Although Georgia does not require use of a recordbook...GSCCCA recommend(s) that every notary use a notary recordbook to minimize liability and to keep track of every notarial service performed. Some notaries prefer to keep copies of all the documents over which they have performed a notarial act. This is not a good idea... because of privacy issues" (GNH).

Recordbook Should Be Bound

"Every time you perform any notarial duty, you should record certain facts about the notarial act in a recordbook. For your protection, your recordbook should be securely bound with numbered pages. The entries should be consecutively numbered as well. All this is designed to prevent someone from tampering with your book or altering it in some way" (GNH).

Entries

According to the "Georgia Notary Handbook," the Notary's journal or recordbook should contain:

1. Information about the signer, such as name, address and phone number. ("The single most important piece of information you will record in the recordbook is the signer's original signature...prov(ing) that the signer personally appeared for the notarization.")
2. Identification information, such as the specific type of ID presented, a partial ID number, and the ID expiration date.
3. A document description, including its title or type and its date.
4. The notarial act's type, date and time of day.
5. The fee for the notarization. ("Also note any fees for additional services or expenses that you pass along to your customers.")
6. Any pertinent additional information, such as comments about special circumstances (e.g., "The signer was blind.") and accommodations, and witness signatures and contact data.
7. A signer thumbprint is optional. ("Since Georgia does not require a signer to provide a thumbprint, you cannot decline to notarize if your signer refuses to provide a thumbprint.")

Journal Is Notary's Exclusive Property

"Do not share recordbooks and keep your recordbook locked up with your notary seal. Do not give access to your notarial records. If you have to go to court to testify about a notarization, you need to be able to put your hands on the recordbook in an instant and be assured that no one has tampered with your book" (GNH).

Journal Does Not Go to Employer: "Even though an employer may pay for a notary's commission...(w)hen you leave your place of employment, your commission and supplies go with you. Your employer may not require you toleave your stamp or seal, commission certificate, or recordbook behind" (GNH).

AUTHENTICATION OF NOTARIAL ACTS

For Non-Hague Convention Nations

An authenticating certificate for a document notarized in Georgia that will be sent abroad to a country not subscribing to the Hague Convention on authentication must be obtained from the clerk of the county superior court that has commissioned the Notary (OCGA 45-17-19) at a fee of $2. (See "Extra Fee for Authenticating Certificate," above, under "Notary's Fees.") Then, another certificate authenticating that of the county clerk and bearing the state's Great Seal must be obtained from the Georgia Secretary of State.

Fees: $10 per document, payable to the "Secretary of State."

Address:
Office of Secretary of State
Elections Division
2 Martin Luther King Jr. Drive, SE
West Tower, Suite 1104
Atlanta, GA 30334-1530

Telephone: 1-404-656-2871

Website: www.sos.state.ga.us/elections/commissions/default.htm

Procedure: The document must be notarized and the Notary's signature must first be certified by the clerk of the superior court in the county where the Notary was commissioned. The signature from the county clerk's office must be an original pen-and-ink signature. The county certification must be attached to each document prior to authentication. Documents may be mailed or presented in person to the Secretary of State's office.

"For university and college transcripts/diplomas; these must be certified by the registrar with an original pen in hand signature or must be notarized in Georgia and certified by the clerk of the superior court in the county where the notary is commissioned" ("Great Seal Certification," Georgia Secretary of State's website).

For Hague Convention Nations

Since May 1, 1998, the Georgia Superior Court Clerks' Cooperative Authority has been authorized to affix apostilles on notarized documents sent to Hague Convention-subscribing nations (OCGA 45-17-19[a][2]) and to affix regular "certificates of authentication" as necessary on notarized documents sent to other U.S. jurisdictions.

Fees: $2 per document for a "domestic certification"; $3 per document for an apostille. Check or money order payable to "GSCCCA."

Address:
Georgia Superior Court Clerks' Cooperative Authority
Notary Division
1875 Century Blvd., Suite 100
Atlanta, GA 30345

Telephone: 1-404-327-6023
1-800-304-5175

Website: www.gsccca.org/Projects/apost.asp

Procedure: The notarized document may be mailed or presented in person, along with the fee. The country of destination should be indicated.
"If mailing your documents, please include a self-addressed, postage-paid envelope of the carrier of your choice ..." (website, "Apostilles").
"Submitted documents must be originals or certified copies with pen-in-hand signatures of notaries public or public officials" (website, "Notary Information").

COMMISSIONING AND ADMINISTRATION

In Georgia, the clerks of the county superior courts appoint and commission Notaries (OCGA 45-17-1.1). "The clerk shall ... keep a record of the names, addresses, signatures, ages, sex, and the terms of all notaries public whom he appoints" (OCGA 45-17-5). Upon appointing a Notary, a superior court clerk sends to the Georgia Superior Court Clerks' Cooperative Authority a copy of the certificate of appointment. The GSCCCA keeps a record of each Notary's name, address, signature, age, sex and term of appointment (OCGA 45-17-4).

Applying for Commission

Qualifications: An applicant for a commission as a Georgia Notary Public must: (a) be at least 18 years old, (b) be a U.S. citizen or a legal resident of the United States, (c) have and provide at the time of application the applicant's operating telephone number, (d) be able to read and write the English language and (e) be a legal resident of the state of Georgia and of the Georgia county in which the application is made or, if an out-of-state resident, be regularly employed or carrying out a business or profession in that county (OCGA 45-17-2). To prove county residency, the applicant must submit one of the following to the superior court (OCGA 45-17-2.1): a valid Georgia driver's license, U.S. passport, voter identification card, or other ID issued by a local or state or the U.S. government.

A Georgia Notary commission may be denied by the clerk of the superior court due to: (a) the applicant's criminal history; (b) revocation, suspension or restriction of any Notary commission or professional license in any state; (c) commission of any of the prohibited acts listed in OCGA 45-17-15(a); or (d) a finding by the Georgia Bar or any court that the applicant engaged in the unauthorized practice of law (GNH).

No Course or Test: No course of instruction or test is required of applicants for a Notary commission in Georgia. An online Notary Public training course that explains Georgia notary law, presents best practices and teaches how to handle difficult or unusual notarial acts is available at http://training.gsccca.org.

Application: The application form for first-time or renewing Notaries is available online for residents of many Georgia counties (at www.gsccca.org/Projects/npapp.asp). If the applicant's county of residence is not listed on the "Notary Online Application," the applicant should obtain an application from the office of the county superior court clerk and submit the completed form in person to the court clerk's office.

The application must be signed by two endorsers, who must be 18 years of age or older, residents of the county, unrelated to the applicant, and these endorsers must have known the applicant at least one month (OCGA 45-17-2.1[b]). A notarized declaration from the applicant is also part of the application. For an online submission, the application must be printed out, signed by the applicant and the two endorsers and presented in person at the clerk's office for processing. The application filing fee payable to the superior court clerk is $37. Information in the application is a matter of public record (OCGA 45-17-2.2).

"At the time the clerk of the superior court issues a certificate of appointment…said officer shall also issue to the appointee a duplicate original of such certificate. The presentation of such duplicate original, either by mail or in person, to the supplier of a notary public seal shall be necessary to authorize such supplier to make up a notary public seal and deliver it to the appointee" (OCGA 45-17-5[b]).

Non-Residents: Residents of bordering states (Alabama, Florida, North Carolina, South Carolina and Tennessee) who regularly work or carry on a business or profession in Georgia may be commissioned as Notaries by the superior court clerk of the county in which they regularly work or conduct business (OCGA 45-17-7).

Online Search: Through the "Notary Index Search" (www.gsccca.org/search/Notary/), the roster of current Notaries may be searched by name, county, city, postal code, range of date of appointment or expiration or e-mail address.

Changes of Status

If Notary Moves: Notaries who change their business or residence address (whichever was used for the purpose of appointment) within the state must notify the appointing superior court clerk in writing within 30 days of the change, with a copy to the Georgia Superior Court Clerks' Cooperative Authority (OCGA 45-17-13[a]). Both old and new addresses must be provided. Any change in the Notary's telephone number also requires notification. Notaries ceasing to reside or work in the state are subject to having their commission revoked by the superior court clerk (OCGA 45-17-15[a]).

"If the notary moves to another county within the State of Georgia…(t)here is no need for the notary to resign his or her commission in the old county of residence. When the notary's commission comes up for renewal, the notary will apply to the new county of residence for the new commission. Nor does the notary have to purchase a new swtamp until his or her commission is renewed in the new county of residence" (GNH).

If Notary Changes Name: Notaries who change their name must notify the appointing superior court clerk in writing, including the new signature and any new address, within 30 days of the change, with a copy to the Georgia Superior Court Clerks' Cooperative Authority (OCGA 45-17-13[b]). Both old and new names must be provided. Upon receiving a confirmation from the clerk and obtaining a new seal, the Notary may again begin notarizing with the new name.

If Notary's Commission Is Revoked: Notaries whose commissions are revoked must destroy their official seal and deliver all appointment papers to the appointing clerk within 10 days of receiving notice of revocation from this clerk (OCGA 45-17-16), a copy of which is sent to the Georgia Superior Court Clerks' Cooperative Authority.

If Notary Resigns: Notaries who resign their commission must send a signed letter of resignation to the appointing superior court clerk (with a copy to the Georgia Superior Court Clerks' Cooperative Authority) along with the appointment papers (OCGA 45-17-17). They must also destroy their official seal.

It would be wise for a Notary to resign the commission before it is revoked by the clerk of the superior court in cases where the Notary (a) moves out of state or, for a non-resident Notary, no longer works in the state, or (b) can no longer, for whatever reason, read or write the English language (GNH).

SUPERIOR COURT CLERKS

To contact a Georgia superior court clerk to obtain an application to become a Notary, an authenticating certificate for a Notary, or to seek assistance in locating a given Notary, search online at http://www.gsccca.org/clerks/ or telephone long-distance information — 1-XXX-555-1212 — using the following area codes:

County	City/Town	Area Code	County	City/Town	Area Code
Appling	Baxley	(912)	Elbert	Elberton	(706)
Atkinson	Pearson	(912)	Emanuel	Swainsboro	(478)
Bacon	Alma	(912)	Evans	Claxton	(912)
Baker	Newton	(229)	Fannin	Blue Ridge	(706)
Baldwin	Milledgeville	(478)	Fayette	Fayetteville	(770)
Banks	Homer	(706)	Floyd	Rome	(706)
Barrow	Winder	(770)	Forsyth	Cumming	(770)
Bartow	Cartersville	(770)	Franklin	Carnesville	(706)
Ben Hill	Fitzgerald	(229)	Fulton	Atlanta	(404)
Berrien	Nashville	(229)	Gilmer	Ellijay	(706)
Bibb	Macon	(478)	Glascock	Gibson	(706)
Bleckley	Cochran	(478)	Glynn	Brunswick	(912)
Brantley	Nahunta	(912)	Gordon	Calhoun	(706)
Brooks	Quitman	(229)	Grady	Cairo	(229)
Bryan	Pembroke	(912)	Greene	Greensboro	(706)
Bulloch	Statesboro	(912)	Gwinnett	Lawrenceville	(770)
Burke	Waynesboro	(706)	Habersham	Clarkesville	(706)
Butts	Jackson	(770)	Hall	Gainesville	(770)
Calhoun	Morgan	(229)	Hancock	Sparta	(706)
Camden	Woodbine	(912)	Haralson	Buchanan	(770)
Candler	Metter	(912)	Harris	Hamilton	(706)
Carroll	Carrollton	(770)	Hart	Hartwell	(706)
Catoosa	Ringgold	(706)	Heard	Franklin	(706)
Charlton	Folkston	(912)	Henry	McDonough	(770)
Chatham	Savannah	(912)	Houston	Perry	(478)
Chattahoochee	Cusseta	(706)	Irwin	Ocilla	(229)
Chattooga	Summerville	(706)	Jackson	Jefferson	(706)
Cherokee	Canton	(678)	Jasper	Monticello	(706)
Clarke	Athens	(706)	Jeff Davis	Hazlehurst	(912)
Clay	Fort Gaines	(229)	Jefferson	Louisville	(478)
Clayton	Jonesboro	(770)	Jenkins	Millen	(478)
Clinch	Homerville	(912)	Johnson	Wrightsville	(478)
Cobb	Marietta	(770)	Jones	Gray	(478)
Coffee	Douglas	(912)	Lamar	Barnesville	(770)
Colquitt	Moultrie	(229)	Lanier	Lakeland	(229)
Columbia	Evans	(706)	Laurens	Dublin	(478)
Cook	Adel	(229)	Lee	Leesburg	(229)
Coweta	Newnan	(770)	Liberty	Hinesville	(912)
Crawford	Knoxville	(478)	Lincoln	Lincolnton	(706)
Crisp	Cordele	(229)	Long	Ludowici	(912)
Dade	Trenton	(706)	Lowndes	Valdosta	(229)
Dawson	Dawsonville	(706)	Lumpkin	Dahlonega	(706)
Decatur	Bainbridge	(229)	Macon	Oglethorpe	(478)
DeKalb	Decatur	(404)	Madison	Danielsville	(706)
Dodge	Eastman	(478)	Marion	Buena Vista	(229)
Dooly	Vienna	(229)	McDuffie	Thomson	(706)
Dougherty	Albany	(229)	McIntosh	Darien	(912)
Douglas	Douglasville	(770)	Meriwether	Greenville	(706)
Early	Blakely	(229)	Miller	Colquitt	(229)
Echols	Statenville	(229)	Mitchell	Camilla	(229)
Effingham	Springfield	(912)	Monroe	Forsyth	(478)

County	City/Town	Area Code	County	City/Town	Area Code
Montgomery	Mt. Vernon	(912)	White	Cleveland	(706)
Morgan	Madison	(706)	Whitfield	Dalton	(706)
Murray	Chatsworth	(706)	Wilcox	Abbeville	(229)
Muscogee	Columbus	(706)	Wilkes	Washington	(706)
Newton	Covington	(770)	Wilkinson	Irwinton	(478)
Oconee	Watkinsville	(706)	Worth	Sylvester	(229)
Oglethorpe	Lexington	(706)			
Paulding	Dallas	(770)			
Peach	Fort Valley	(478)			
Pickens	Jasper	(706)			
Pierce	Blackshear	(912)			
Pike	Zebulon	(770)			
Polk	Cedartown	(770)			
Pulaski	Hawkinsville	(478)			
Putnam	Eatonton	(706)			
Quitman	Georgetown	(229)			
Rabun	Clayton	(706)			
Randolph	Cuthbert	(229)			
Richmond	Augusta	(706)			
Rockdale	Conyers	(770)			
Schley	Ellaville	(229)			
Screven	Sylvania	(912)			
Seminole	Donalsonville	(229)			
Spalding	Griffin	(770)			
Stephens	Toccoa	(706)			
Stewart	Lumpkin	(229)			
Sumter	Americus	(229)			
Talbot	Talbotton	(706)			
Taliaferro	Crawfordville	(706)			
Tattnall	Reidsville	(912)			
Taylor	Butler	(478)			
Telfair	McRae	(229)			
Terrell	Dawson	(229)			
Thomas	Thomasville	(229)			
Tift	Tifton	(229)			
Toombs	Lyons	(912)			
Towns	Hiawassee	(706)			
Treutlen	Soperton	(912)			
Troup	LaGrange	(706)			
Turner	Ashburn	(229)			
Twiggs	Jeffersonville	(478)			
Union	Blairsville	(706)			
Upson	Thomaston	(706)			
Walker	LaFayette	(706)			
Walton	Monroe	(770)			
Ware	Waycross	(912)			
Warren	Warrenton	(706)			
Washington	Sandersville	(478)			
Wayne	Jesup	(912)			
Webster	Preston	(229)			
Wheeler	Alamo	(912)			

OTHER NOTARIAL OFFICERS

Besides Notaries, the following officers have authority to attest the documents enumerated in OCGA 44-2-14, but, except for judges, only in the county in which they hold their offices (OCGA 44-2-15):

1. A judge of a court of record, including a municipal court;
2. A magistrate;
3. A clerk or deputy clerk of a superior court, or of a city court created by special act of the General Assembly.

U.S. Military Officers

"All commissioned officers of all branches of the armed services of the United States of America are constituted ex officio notaries public of this state and as such are authorized, within and outside this state and within and outside the United States of America, to administer oaths, take acknowledgments, and attest instruments conveying or affecting property in Georgia . ... A statement of his rank following the signature of any such officer shall be evidence of the fact of his rank and no seal shall be necessary" (OCGA 45-17-30).

Court Reporters

Certified court reporters who are officially designated to take testimony have authority to administer oaths to deponents (OCGA 9-11-28).

QUICK FACTS

Notary Jurisdiction
Statewide (OCGA 45-17-9).

Notary Term Length
Four years (OCGA 45-17-5[a]), expiring at midnight on the commission expiration date.

Notary Bond
No bond is required by law.

Guam

NOTARY SEAL

A Guam Notary must affix the impressions of TWO seals on each notarial certificate, an inked stamp and an embosser (5 GCA 33412). Their formats must be as follows:

Kind

Black-Inked Stamp: "Near the notary's official signature on a notarial certificate, the notary shall affix in black ink a sharp, legible, and photographically reproducible inked stamp impression of the notarial seal …" (5 GCA 33412[a]).

AND Embosser: "An embossed seal impression that may be photographically reproducible… shall be used in addition to but not in lieu of the seal described in subsection (a)" (5 GCA 33412[c]).

Examples
The above typical, actual-size examples of Notary seals are allowed by Guam law. Formats other than these may also be permitted.

NOTARY ADMINISTRATION

Office of the Attorney General
Administration Division   1-671-475-3324
287 West O'Brien Drive
Hagatna, GU 96910

Website: www.guamattorneygeneral.com

NOTARY RULES

GCA — GUAM CODE ANNOTATED

Most Notary rules are in the Guam Code Annotated, Title 5, Chapter 33 ("Notaries Public"), which may be cited as the "Model Notary Law."

Much other information for Notaries may be found on the Attorney General's website under "Frequently Asked Questions."

Shape/Size

Black-Inked Stamp: Rectangular is mandatory (5 GCA 33412[a][4]).

Embosser: Circular is customary, though not specified by law.

Border

Black-Inked Stamp: "A rectangular border surrounding the required words" (5 GCA 33412[a][4]).

Embosser: Not specified by law.

Components

Black-Inked Stamp: A rectangular inking stamp should have the following information (5 GCA 33412[a]):
1. Notary's name exactly as on commission;
2. "Notary Public in and for Guam, U.S.A."*;
3. "My commission expires (expiration date)"**;
4. Notary's business or residence address.

* For commissions issued on or after October 7, 1997, the term "Territory of Guam" is banned from the Notary seal as a demeaning allusion to a colonial past (1 GCA 420).

** "The commission expiration date must be an integral part of the inked stamp notarial seal and may not be inserted into the impression" (5 GCA 33412[b]).

Embosser: An embossing seal should contain the following information (5 GCA 33412[c]):
1. Notary's name exactly as on commission;
2. "Notary Public in and for Guam, U.S.A."*.

* See note above regarding use of the term "Territory of Guam."

Illegible Information in Seal

"Illegible information within an inked stamp impression of the notarial seal may be typed or printed legibly by the notary adjacent to but not within the impression" (5 GCA 33412[b]).

Seal Not to Be Surrendered

"A notary shall keep an official notarial seal that is the exclusive property of the notary and that may not be used by any other person or surrendered to an employer upon termination of employment" (5 GCA 33411[a]).

Seal to Be Destroyed

"Upon resignation, revocation, or expiration of a notarial commission, or death of the notary, any seal having the expiration date of the commission on it must be destroyed in accordance with Article 7 of this Chapter. A new seal must be obtained, under § 33413 of this Chapter, for any new commission. The notary need not destroy the embossing seal, if any, nor obtain a new embossing seal, if there is no time lapse between the expiration of one commission and the granting of another commission" (5 GCA 33411[b]).

"When a notarial commission is resigned, revoked, or expires, the notary shall … (a)s soon as reasonably practical, destroy the official seal …" (5 GCA 33554[a][1]).

Obtaining a Notary Seal

"A vendor may not provide a notary seal, either inking or embossing, to a person claiming to be a notary, unless the person presents the following documents, which the vendor must retain for a period of three (3) years: A photocopy of the person's notarial commission, attached to a notarized declaration …" (5 GCA 33413[a]).

"A notary applying for a seal as a result of a name change shall present a copy of the Confirmation of Notary's Name Change from the Attorney General in place of the Application for a Notary Seal" (5 GCA 33413[b]).

For failure to comply with these rules, a seal vendor is guilty of a petty misdemeanor (5 GCA 33413[c]).

Lost or Stolen Seal

"Within ten (10) days after the loss or theft of any official journal or seal, the notary shall deliver to the Attorney General, by certified mail or other means providing a receipt, a signed notice of the loss or theft, and inform the appropriate law enforcement agency in the case of theft" (5 GCA 33552).

Wrongful Possession: "Any person who knowingly obtains, conceals, defaces, or destroys the seal, journal, or official records of a notary is guilty of a third degree felony" (5 GCA 33521).

Notary's Signature

"In completing a notarial act, a notary shall sign on the notarial certificate exactly and only the name indicated on the notary's commission" (5 GCA 33410).

NOTARY POWERS

Guam Notaries are authorized to perform the following notarial acts (5 GCA 33301):
1. Take acknowledgments*;
2. Administer oaths and affirmations**;
3. Execute jurats***;
4. Perform copy certifications****.

* Acknowledgments: "Acknowledgment means a notarial act in which a notary certifies that a signer, whose identity is proven on the basis of satisfactory evidence, has admitted, in the notary's presence, having signed a document voluntarily for its stated purpose" (5 GCA 33104[1]).

** Oaths and Affirmations: "Oath and affirmation mean a notarial act or part thereof in which a notary certifies that a person made a vow in the presence of the notary on penalty of perjury, with reference made to a Supreme Being for an oath" (5 GCA 33104[10]).

*** Jurats: "Jurat means a notarial act in which a notary certifies that a signer, whose identity is proven on the basis of satisfactory evidence, has made, in the notary's presence, a voluntary signature and taken an oath or affirmation vouching for the truthfulness of the signed document" (5 GCA 33104[6]).

**** Certifying Copies: "Copy certification means a notarial act in which a notary certifies having made a photocopy of a document that is neither a public record nor publicly recordable" (5 GCA 33104[3]). "College transcripts are considered 'public records' which may only be copy certified by the registrar of the college issuing the transcript" (website, "Frequently Asked Questions").

A Notary must retain as an official notarial record a duplicate photocopy of each certified copy (5 GCA 33402[b]).

Identifying Document Signers

In taking acknowledgments and executing jurats, the Notary must positively identify each signer on the basis of "satisfactory evidence," which means identification of an individual based on: "(i) any current passport or (ii) an official identification issued by a federal or state government with the individual's photograph and signature or (iii) personal knowledge of identity" (5 GCA 33104[13]).

Foreign passports are included in the term "any current passport" (website, "Frequently Asked Questions"). "An expired identification document is legally void, and therefore, insufficient proof of identification, even if it expired only yesterday" (website, "Frequently Asked Questions").

"State includes any state of the United States, any United States territory, possession or commonwealth, and the District of Columbia" (5 GCA 33104[14]).

"Personal knowledge of identity means familiarity with an individual resulting from contact with that individual over a period of time sufficient to eliminate every reasonable doubt that the individual has the identity claimed" (5 GCA 33104[12]).

Ascertaining Competence

"Q. Someone brings his aged mother to me and wants me to (notarize) her signature on a document. His mother appears unable to comprehend what is going on. Should I notarize her signature?

"A. If you have any questions whatsoever of the mental or physical competence of the party signing whose signature you are asked to notarize, you should always obtain legal advice first on how you should act in the situation to avoid becoming involved in a lawsuit. You may also tell the son that he should seek legal advice as to what he is asking you to do concerning the document" (website, "Frequently Asked Questions").

Government Notaries

"The Attorney General may commission any number of (Guam) government employees to act as notaries, but notaries so empowered may perform notarial acts only during their hours of employment with their respective government agencies. Such acts include the notarization for members of the public or for fellow employees, of any forms or statements which any government agency requires before transmittal from or submission to such agency.... No fees may be charged for notarial services performed by a notary empowered under this section" (5 GCA 33220[a] and [e]).

Upon leaving employment with the government of Guam, such "government Notaries" must immediately resign their commissions and dispose of their journals and seals as provided in 5 GCA 33553 and 33554 (5 GCA 33220[f]).

Foreign-Language Documents

"There is no statutory prohibition from you notarizing a foreign language document or notarial certificate. However, you should perform notarial acts only if you can read and understand the language the document is written in. The same is true for a document written in a foreign language, but which has attached a notarial certificate in English. Even if you can read and understand the notarial certificate, unless you also understand the foreign language in which the document is written, it is best if you do not perform the notarial act. The document should be translated fully into English before you notarize the signer's signature so you have no doubt whatsoever in your mind as to exactly what you are doing" (website, "Frequently Asked Questions").

Signers Who Cannot Read or Write

When notarizing for persons who cannot read or write, including blind signers, the Notary should read, but not interpret or explain, the document to the person whose mark will be notarized on that document (website, "Frequently Asked Questions").

NOTARY DON'TS

A Guam Notary may:
1. NOT influence a person to enter into or not enter into a lawful transaction involving a notarial act by that same Notary (5 GCA 33303[a]);
2. NOT refuse to perform a notarial act in a lawful transaction for any requesting person who tenders the appropriate statutory fee (5 GCA 33303[b]);
3. NOT "execute a certificate containing a statement known by the notary to be false or perform any official action with intent to deceive or defraud" (5 GCA 33304);
4. NOT "endorse or promote any product, service, contest, or other offering if the notary's title or seal is used in the endorsement or promotional statement" (5 GCA 33305).

Improper Influence

"Any person who knowingly solicits, coerces, or in any way influences a notary to commit official misconduct is guilty of a third degree felony" (5 GCA 33522).

Signer Must Appear

"A notary who knowingly performs a notarization for a person who does not appear before the notary or at the notary's office is guilty of a third degree felony" (5 GCA 33512).

Telephone Notarizations: "Q. Someone faxed a document to me with his signature on it. He is on the telephone and wants me to (notarize) his signature. May I do so?

"A. No. You may not take an acknowledgment over the telephone even if you personally know the signer" (website, "Frequently Asked Questions").

Unauthorized Practice of Law

"a. A non-attorney notary may complete but may not select notarial certificates, and may not assist another person in drafting, completing, selecting, or understanding a document or transaction requiring a notarial act.

"b. This section does not preclude a notary who is duly qualified in a particular profession from giving advice relating to matters in that professional field.

"c. A notary shall not make representations to have powers, qualifications, rights or privileges that the office of notary does not have, including the providing of legal advice unless the notary is also a licensed attorney.

"d. A non-attorney notary who advertises notarial services in any language shall include in the advertisement, notice, or sign the following statement, prominently displayed in the same language: 'I am not an attorney and have no authority to give advice on any legal matters'" (5 GCA 33306).

Disqualifications

A Notary is disqualified from performing notarial acts if the Notary:
1. Is a signer of or named in the document that is to be notarized;
2. Will receive directly from a transaction connected with the notarial act any commission, fee (except for attorneys), advantage, right, title, interest, cash, property or other consideration exceeding in value the allowed statutory fee for performing a notarial act;
3. Is related to the person whose signature is to be notarized as a spouse, sibling or lineal ascendant or descendant as defined in 15 GCA 809 (5 GCA 33302). Lineal descendants include legally adopted children (website, "Frequently Asked Questions").

Other Relatives Not Disqualified: "Notaries are not disqualified from performing notarial acts for their uncles and aunts, nieces and nephews, and cousins. Notaries are also not disqualified from performing notarial acts for their stepchildren or stepbrother or stepsister, or for any relative of their spouse. However, great caution should be exercised even if the notary is not disqualified based upon the relationship because there may be other reasons for disqualification" (website, "Frequently Asked Questions").

Loan Officers on Commission Disqualified: Whether a bank loan officer may notarize documents for mortgage loans depends on whether the officer will derive a commission fee from the transaction. "For example, let's say that the transaction involves a $200,000 residential mortgage loan. The mortgage officer receives a monthly salary of $2,000. In addition, the bank wants to pay the mortgage loan officer 1% of each transaction closed. The notary may receive his bank salary without violating the Law, because his salary is not directly related to the transaction, but is contingent upon his overall duties with his employer. The proposed 1% commission for closing the loan, however, is directly related to the transaction, and the notary would be benefiting from closing the transaction. Thus, if the mortgage loan officer plans on receiving the commission fee directly resulting from the transaction, then he would be disqualified from performing any notarial acts related to the transaction. He may not then notarize any mortgage documents" (website, "Frequently Asked Questions").

Blank Spaces in Document

"Documents should never be altered after the notarial act is performed. Therefore, all blanks should be filled in prior to the document being signed...(Y)ou should ask the signer to fill in all the blanks or cross the blanks out first. If the client refuses, then you should decline to officiate" (website, "Frequently Asked Questions").

Notarizing for Minors

"Q. May I notarize a document for a minor?
"A. No. The minor should seek a private attorney for legal assistance" (website, "Frequently Asked Questions").

If Signer Does Not Speak English

"Q. If I am asked to (notarize) the signature of a foreign national on a document written in English, and the person appearing before me does not speak English, should I go ahead and notarize his signature?
"A. No. Since the document is written in English, you cannot possibly take the acknowledgment of a person who does not speak or understand the English language" (website, "Frequently Asked Questions").

Impersonation

"Any person not a notary who knowingly acts as or otherwise impersonates a notary is guilty of a third degree felony. Impersonation includes performing notarial acts when the commission of the person performing has expired or been revoked or the person has resigned his or her commission" (5 GCA 33520).

NOTARY SIGNING AGENTS

Currently, there are no statutes, regulations or rules expressly governing, prohibiting or restricting the operation of Notary Signing Agents within Guam.

NOTARY FEES

The maximum fees that a Guam Notary may charge for a notarial act are (5 GCA 33310[a]):
1. Taking an acknowledgment or proof, including the seal and certificate: for the first two signatures, $10 each; for each additional signature, $8;
2. Administering an oath or affirmation: $10 per person;
3. Executing a jurat, including the oath or affirmation: $10 per signature;
4. Certifying a copy: $10 per certificate.

Photocopy of Journal Entry

For providing an uncertified photocopy of an entry in a Notary's journal of notarial acts, the Notary may charge no more than $5 per photocopy (5 GCA 33404[b]). If a certified copy of a journal entry is requested, the Notary may charge the standard $10 for copy certification.

Travel Fees

A Notary may charge a "reasonable" travel fee when traveling to perform a notarial act if: (a) the Notary first explains to the person requesting the notarial act that the travel fee is separate from the statutory fee for notarizing specified above, and is neither specified nor mandated by law; and (b) the Notary and the person requesting the notarial act agree upon the travel fee in advance (5 GCA 33310[b]).

No Charge by Government Notaries

A Notary who is an employee of the government of Guam may not demand or receive any fee or compensation for performing notarial duties for government work during normal business hours (5 GCA 33220[e] and 33310[a]).

Fees of Employee Notary

While a Notary may agree to allow an employer to collect the Notary's fees for notarial acts, the "employer is not entitled to notarial fees and may not keep them if collected." These fees belong to the Notary (website, "Frequently Asked Questions").

A Notary who works for an employer, such as a bank, may charge the employer's customers for the performance of notarial acts. "Your employer may not prevent you from charging its customers for any notarial act if you decide to so charge…. However, you may decide not to charge your employer's customers. Whatever you do, you should set a uniform policy for yourself, or have an agreement with your employer, and follow it" (website, "Frequently Asked Questions").

Fees Must Be Posted

Guam Notaries must display an English-language schedule of the statutory maximum fees for notarial acts. No part of this fee schedule may be printed in smaller than 10-point type (5 GCA 33311).

"If you are a non-attorney notary, you must also display the wording 'I am not an attorney and have no authority to give advice on any legal matters'" (website, "Frequently Asked Questions").

NOTARY CERTIFICATES

Guam statute prescribes the following notarial certificates:

General Acknowledgment (5 GCA 33450):

"A notary shall use a certificate in substantially the following form in notarizing the signature or mark of persons acknowledging for themselves or as partners, corporate officers, attorneys in fact, or in other representative capacities, or may use such other forms of certificates as are otherwise authorized by statute" (5 GCA 33450):

Guam, U.S.A.

On this _____ day of _____, 20___, before me, the undersigned Notary, personally appeared _____, the person(s) whose name(s) is/are signed on the preceding or attached document, and acknowledged to me that he/she/they signed it voluntarily for its stated purpose(.)

(as partner for _____, a partnership.)

(as _____ for _____, a corporation.)
(as attorney in fact for _____, the principal.)
(as _____ for _____, a/the _____.)
(by mark before _____ and _____, subscribing witnesses.)

(OFFICIAL NOTARY SIGNATURE AND SEALS)

Jurat (5 GCA 33452):

"A notary shall use a jurat certificate in substantially the following form in notarizing a signature on an affidavit, deposition, or other sworn or affirmed written declaration" (5 GCA 33452):

Guam, U.S.A.

Subscribed and sworn to before me this _____ day of _____, 20___, by _____.

(OFFICIAL NOTARY SIGNATURE AND SEALS)

Certified Copy Certificate (5 GCA 33453):

Guam, U.S.A.

On this _____ day of _____, 20___, I certify that the preceding or attached document, and the duplicate retained by me as a notarial record, are true, exact, (complete)/(stated portion of _____ [named document]), and unaltered photocopies made by me of _____ (description of the document), (presented to me by the document's custodian, _____,)/(held in my custody as a notarial record,) and that, to the best of my knowledge, are neither public records nor publicly recordable documents, certified copies of which are available from an official source other than a Notary.

(OFFICIAL NOTARY SIGNATURE AND SEALS)

ELECTRONIC NOTARIZATIONS

Guam has not yet adopted statutes or regulations expressly establishing rules, definitions and procedures for electronic notarization.

NOTARY RECORDS

A Guam Notary "shall keep, maintain, protect as a public record, and provide for lawful inspection a chronological, permanently bound, official journal of notarial acts, containing numbered pages" (5 GCA 33401).

Required Journal Entries

"For every notarial act, the notary shall record in the journal before the time of notarization at least the following" (5 GCA 33402[a] and [c]):

1. The date and time of day of the notarial act;
2. The type of notarial act;
3. A description of the document or proceeding;
4. The signature and printed name and address of each person for whom a notarial act is performed;
5. The evidence of identity of each person for whom a notarial act is performed, in the form of a description of the identification document, its issuing agency, its serial or ID number, and its date of issuance (if expired); or a statement that the Notary has "personal knowledge" of the person's identity;
6. The fee, if any, charged for the notarial act;
7. The address where the notarization was performed, if not the Notary's business address;
8. The reason(s) for refusing to perform a notarial act, other than lack of proof of identity.

Duplicate of Each Certified Copy: A notary shall retain as an official record a duplicate photocopy of each certified copy (5 GCA 33402[b]).

Signature in Journal: "At the time of notarization, the notary's journal must be signed, as applicable, by: (1) The person for whom a notarial act is performed; and (2) The two (2) witnesses to a signature by mark of a document that is notarized" (5 GCA 33403).

Record of Request for Journal Photocopy: "Q. I have a client requesting a photocopy of an entry from my journal. Do I have to record this request in my journal and have the client sign?

"A. No. Only if the client wants a certified photocopy of an entry must you record the requested act in your journal and have the client sign your journal" (website, "Frequently Asked Questions").

Journal Must Be Safeguarded

"A notary shall safeguard the journal and other notarial records as valuable public documents and never destroy them, except at the direction of the Attorney General.... The journal must be kept in the exclusive custody of the notary, and may not be used by any other notary or surrendered to an employer upon termination of employment" (5 GCA 33404[c] and [d]).

Defining 'Exclusive Control': "Q. If I leave my notarial journal in the family car, am I violating the Law?

"A. Yes. A notary must be in exclusive control of his notarial journal at all times. For example, you may leave it at your personal work station or desk at your office so long as you have exclusive use of the area. You do not have exclusive control over shared work spaces. Furthermore, if you leave your journal in the family car which others drive, then you have also lost control over your journal and are in violation of the Law" (website, "Frequently Asked Questions").

Inspection of Journal

Except when the journal is delivered to the Attorney General, or disposed of in accordance with 5 GCA, Chapter 10 or any other law, "a journal of notarial acts is an official public record that may be inspected only in the notary's presence by an individual whose identity is personally known to the notary or proven on the basis of satisfactory evidence, who specifies the notarial act sought, and who signs the notary's journal" (5 GCA 33404[a]).

Fee for Photocopy: For providing an uncertified photocopy of an entry in a Notary's journal of notarial acts, the Notary may charge no more than $5 per photocopy (5 GCA 33404[b]). If a certified copy of a journal entry is requested, the Notary may charge the standard $10 for copy certification (5 GCA 33310[a]).

Inspection upon Renewal: According to instructions for renewing Notaries on the Attorney General's website: "The journals of all notaries who are renewing applicants will be inspected for compliance in the notary's presence as provided for by 5 G.C.A. § 33404. Please bring your journal with you when you are submitting your renewal application. If for any reason our office cannot inspect your journal at that time, we will give you an appointment for a later date" (website, "Application Instructions").

Lost or Stolen Journal

"Within ten (10) days after the loss or theft of any official journal or seal, the notary shall deliver to the Attorney General, by certified mail or other means providing a receipt, a signed notice of the loss or theft, and inform the appropriate law enforcement agency in the case of theft" (5 GCA 33552).

Wrongful Possession: "Any person who knowingly obtains, conceals, defaces, or destroys the seal, journal, or official records of a notary is guilty of a third degree felony" (5 GCA 33521).

Disposal of Journal

"Upon the request of the Attorney General or upon resignation, revocation, or expiration of a notarial commission, or death of the notary, whichever comes first, the notarial journal shall be delivered by personal service, certified mail or other means providing a receipt to the Attorney General's office" (5 GCA 33404[e]).

This delivery must be made within 30 days after the effective date of resignation, revocation or expiration (5 GCA 33554[a][2]).

If the Notary dies, the heirs or legal representative must deliver to the Attorney General's office "as soon as reasonably practical ... by certified mail or other means providing a receipt (i) a notice of the date of death and (ii) the notarial journal and records" (5 GCA 33555).

Journal Is Official Public Document: "Q. Is my notary journal an official public document?

"A. Yes. That's why you must turn it in to the Attorney General's office upon the expiration or earlier termination of your commission, and we will hold it in safekeeping as a public record. You must treat your notary journal as a public record at all times" (website, "Frequently Asked Questions").

AUTHENTICATION OF NOTARIAL ACTS

Office of Attorney General

Regular "certificates of authority" for Guam Notaries are issued by the office of the Attorney General (5 GCA 33601[a][1]).

Apostilles for Guam Notaries are issued by the Director or Deputy Director of Guam's Department of Administration; the Lieutenant Governor imprints the Great Seal of Guam on these apostilles. When the Department of Administration issues an apostille, it must verify the authenticity of the Notary's commission and signature with the Attorney General (5 GCA 33601[a][3]).

Fee: $50 for either a certificate of authority or an apostille (5 GCA 33601[b]).

Address:
Office of Attorney General
Administration Division
287 West O'Brien Drive
Hagatna, GU 96910

Telephone: 1-671-475-3324

Procedure: Mail or deliver the original notarized document to the Attorney General's Administration Division. If mailed, indicate the country of destination and include an addressed, stamped envelope. If an apostille is required, the notarized document will be routed, along with the certificate of authority attached by the Attorney General's office, to the Government of Guam's Department of Administration for additional attachment of the apostille, which bears the imprint of the Great Seal of Guam; it will then be forwarded to the indicated address.

COMMISSIONING AND ADMINISTRATION

The Attorney General of Guam commissions, regulates and maintains records on the island jurisdiction's Notaries Public (5 GCA 33201[a]).

Applying for Commission

Qualifications: An applicant for a commission as a Guam Notary Public must: (a) be at least 18 years old, (b) reside on Guam, (c) read and write English and (d) be a citizen of the United States (5 GCA 33201[b][1] through [4]).

Exam Required: Passage of a written 45-minute, closed-book examination is required only for first-time applicants who are neither attorneys licensed in Guam or non-attorneys who are authorized to administer oaths pursuant to another law.

The Attorney General's office reserves the right, however, to require renewing or any other applicants to retake the exam if there is any indication that an applicant does not understand Guam's Notary laws. Also, if there is a gap between commissions of even one day, the applicant must take the exam again. Currently, the exam consists of 25 multiple-choice questions, and a passing score requires four errors or less. Applicants are given two chances to pass the exam. An exam time and place are scheduled after the application is submitted. Normally, exam sessions are scheduled once a month (5 GCA 33201[a][5] and 33212[a] and [c]; website, "Frequently Asked Questions" and "Application Instructions").

Application: The application for a Notary commission includes an applicant "Declaration," which the applicant must complete and sign. The applicant's signature must be notarized by another Notary, and the application must be submitted to the Guam Attorney General with the following documents attached: (a) a clearance from the Guam Police Department issued within 30 days of submission of the application, (b) proof of prior payment of a $100 application fee to the Treasurer of Guam (waived for a government-employed applicant), (c) for government applicants, a written declaration signed by the applicant's department or agency head stating that the commission applied for is in the public interest and (d) for first-time applicants, the "Evidence of Notarial Bond" form (which contains a statement to be completed by the Attorney General that the applicant has passed the exam and that a bond therefore may be issued), or, for renewals, the original bond (5 GCA 33203, 33210, 33213, 33214 and 33220[c]; website, "Application Instructions").

The renewal process is the same as for an initial commission (5 GCA 33204). All renewing applicants must submit the application no earlier than 30 days prior to commission expiration; for a renewal submitted after expiration, the applicant must retake the exam. The journals of all renewing Notaries will be inspected for compliance in the Notary's presence as provided for by 5 GCA 33404 (website, "Application Instructions").

Changes of Status

If Notary Changes Name: Within 30 days, Notaries who change their names must inform the Attorney General, giving both the old and new names and an effective date for the change. Notaries also must provide a certified copy of a document evidencing the name change (e.g., marriage certificate or court order). Upon receipt of the signed notice, the Attorney General will schedule an appointment for the Notary to sign a specimen card. After obtaining new seals, informing the surety and receiving a confirmation of the change from the Attorney General, the Notary may begin notarizing using the new name (5 GCA 33551 and website, "Frequently Asked Questions").

If Notary Moves: Within 30 days after changing a home or work address, the Notary must inform the Attorney General's office by certified mail or other means providing a receipt, indicating both the old and new addresses (5 GCA 33550).

If Notary Resigns: A Notary who resigns must deliver to the Attorney General by certified mail, or other means providing a receipt, a notice indicating the effective date of resignation (5 GCA 33553).

If Notary Dies: If a Notary dies, the heirs or legal representative, as soon as reasonably practical after death, must deliver to the Attorney General by certified mail, or other method providing a receipt, a notice of the death and the notarial journal and records (5 GCA 33555).

OTHER NOTARIAL OFFICERS

Court Reporters and Other Court Officers

"None of the provisions of this Chapter (i.e., 5 GCA Chapter 33, "Notaries Public," also known as the "Model Notary Law") applies to any certification by official court reporters of transcripts of trials or other Court proceedings, or to the authentication of Court documents by other ministerial officers of the Court pursuant to statute or Court rule" (5 GCA 33103.1).

U.S. Military Officers

"Any commissioned officer of the Armed Forces of the United States, while on active duty, who is authorized to administer oaths by the Uniform Code of Military Justice, may administer oaths and affirmations, take depositions, affidavits, and acknowledgments of deeds, grants, transfers and other instruments of writing, and powers of attorney, of any person who for the time being is on active duty with the Armed Forces of the United States, in the same manner as a Notary Public" (5 GCA 33701).

QUICK FACTS

Notary Jurisdiction
Entire island of Guam (5 GCA 33202 and 33220[b]).

Notary Term Length
Four years (5 GCA 33202 and 33220[b]), expiring at midnight on the commission expiration date (website, "Frequently Asked Questions").

Notarizing after Expiration: Knowingly notarizing after commission expiration is a third degree felony (5 GCA 33520).

Notary Bond
$1,000, executed by a licensed surety. "The bond shall not be canceled, revoked or modified without the express written authorization of the Attorney General, which shall be given only in extraordinary circumstances" (5 GCA 33203).

Employer Liability: "An employer of a notary is liable to any person for all damages proximately caused that person by the notary's official misconduct in performing a notarization related to the employer's business, only if the employer directed, encouraged, consented to, or approved the notary's misconduct, either in the particular transaction, or as implied by previous actions in at least one (1) similar transaction" (5 GCA 33501[c]).

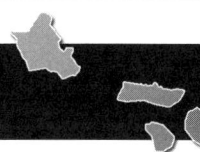

Hawaii

NOTARY SEAL

A Notary Public of Hawaii must authenticate all official acts with a seal of office (HRS 456-3 and HAR 5-11-5[b]), and the seal's format must be as follows:

Kind

Rubber Inked Stamp or Embosser: Each Notary must "constantly keep an engraved seal of office or a rubber stamp facsimile seal …" (HRS 456-3).

As an official seal, the Notary may use either an inked stamp or an embosser but not both (HAR 5-11-5[a]). Only one seal specimen may be filed with the local circuit court.

Shape/Size

Circular: The Notary's seal or stamp must be circular, not over 2 inches in diameter, with "a serrated or milled edge border" (HAR 5-11-5[c]).

Components

Effective May 5, 2008, the following four components are mandatory (HRS 456-3 and HAR 5-11-5[a]):
1. Notary's name;
2. Commission number;

Examples
The above typical, actual-size example of a Notary seal is allowed by Hawaii law. Other circular formats may also be permitted.

NOTARY ADMINISTRATION

Department of Attorney General
Notary Public Program   1-808-586-1216
425 Queen Street   1-808-586-1217
Honolulu, HI 96813

Website: http://hawaii.gov/ag/notary

NOTARY RULES

HRS — HAWAII REVISED STATUTES
HAR — HAWAII ADMINISTRATIVE RULES
NPM — NOTARY PUBLIC MANUAL

Many Notary rules are in the Hawaii Revised Statutes:

a. Chapter 456, "Notaries Public"

b. Chapter 502, "Acknowledgments; Proof of Instruments"

The comprehensive Chapter 5-11 ("Notaries Public") was added to the *Hawaii Administrative Rules* on May 5, 2008, by the Department of the Attorney General "to clarify and implement chapter 456, Hawaii Revised Statutes" (HAR 5-11-1).

Other guidelines for Notaries are in the "Notary Public Manual" (revised September 2010), published by the Attorney General and available on the website.

3. "Notary Public";
4. "State of Hawaii".

(According to the Attorney General's office, the Notary's commission expiration date may not appear in the seal or stamp.)

Failure to Maintain Seal or Stamp: For failure to maintain a seal or stamp as described above, the Attorney General may impose a fine of $20 (HRS 456-9[c][1]).

Name, Expiration Date Must Appear

"The notary public … shall always add to an

official signature the typed or printed name of the notary and a statement showing the date that the notary's commission expires" (HRS 456-3). See also HAR 5-11-6(b).

The name in the Notary seal or stamp does not suffice as the required "typed or printed name"; this name must be affixed apart from the seal or stamp (NPM).

The title of the notarizing officer, whether "Notary Public" or other official, must also appear on the notarial certificate (HRS 502-41).

Seal and Signature Filed with Circuit Court

"Each person appointed and commissioned a notary public under this chapter shall forthwith file a literal or photostatic copy of the person's commission, an impression of the person's seal, and a specimen of the person's official signature with the clerk of the circuit court of the circuit in which the notary public resides. Each person appointed and commissioned a notary public under this chapter may also, at the person's option, file the above-named documents with the clerk of any other circuit court" (HRS 456-4).

Seal or Stamp Must Reflect Name Change

After a Notary has informed the Attorney General's Notary Public Office of a legal name change and has received a new commission certificate bearing the new name, the Notary must relinquish the old seal or stamp to the Office (website, "Name Change Form"). Before notarizing under the new name, the Notary must obtain a new seal or stamp and submit to the circuit court clerk new seal or stamp and signature specimens.

Two Notary Seals or Stamps Needed

It may be necessary for a Notary to affix two pairs of Notary seals and signatures to a document if certain required information does not appear in the wording of an acknowledgment or jurat. See "'Certification Statement' Describes Document," under "Notary Certificates."

Loss, Misplacement, Theft of Seal or Stamp

Within 10 days after a loss, misplacement or theft of a Notary's seal or stamp, the Notary must send a written notice to the Attorney General. In the case of theft, the Notary must also inform the appropriate law enforcement agency and deliver to the Attorney General a copy of the law enforcement agency's report of the theft (HAR 5-11-18). For failure to do so, the Attorney General may impose a fine of $20 (HRS 456-9[c][6]).

Disposing of Seal or Stamp

"Upon resignation, death, expiration of term of office without reappointment, or removal from or abandonment of office, the notary public shall immediately deliver the notary's seal to the attorney general who shall deface or destroy the same. If any notary fails to comply with this section within ninety days of the date of the notary's resignation, expiration of term of office without reappointment, or removal from or abandonment of office or if the notary's personal representative fails to comply with this section within ninety days of the notary's death, then the notary public or the notary's personal representative shall forfeit to the State not more than $200, in the discretion of the court, to be recovered in an action to be brought by the attorney general on behalf of the State" (HRS 456-3). See also HRS 456-9[c][2] and HAR 5-11-5[d] and 5-11-17.

Notary's Signature

"A notary public shall sign on every notarial certificate, at the time of notarization, the notary public's official signature as filed with the clerk of the circuit court in the circuit in which the notary public resides and as the notary public's name appears on the notary public's seal" (HAR 5-11-6[a]).

"A notary must sign the notary's official signature in the same manner as it appears on the notary's seal. For example, if the notary's name is 'John Doe' on the notary's seal, he signs in the same form: i.e., 'John Doe' and not 'J. Doe'" (NPM).

NOTARY POWERS

Hawaii Notaries are authorized to perform the following notarial acts:
1. Take acknowledgments* (HAR 5-11-4 and HRS 502-50[a]);
2. Administer oaths** and affirmations** (HAR 5-11-4 and HRS 456-13);
3. Execute jurats***;
4. Witness the signing of documents (HAR 5-11-4 and NPM);
5. Execute protests (HAR 5-11-4 and HRS 456-10 through 456-12);
6. Certify copies of the Notary's record**** (HRS 456-15).

* <u>Acknowledgments</u>: "For an acknowledgment, the notary certifies that the signer

personally appeared before the notary. The signer is positively identified and acknowledges signing the document as the signer's own free act and deed" (website, "General Notary Questions").

"No acknowledgment of any conveyance or other instrument, except as provided by this chapter, whereby any real estate is conveyed or may be affected, shall be taken, unless the person offering to make the acknowledgment is personally known to the officer taking the acknowledgment to be the person whose name is subscribed to the conveyance or instrument as a party thereto, or is proved to be such by the oath or affirmation of a credible witness known to the officer or by production of a current identification card or document issued by the United States, this State, any other state, or a national government that contains the bearer's photograph and signature" (HRS 502-48).

** Oaths and Affirmations: "An oath is a solemn pledge, made by a person (often referred to as the affiant) with an appeal to God or a Supreme Being to attest to the truth of the person's statement. When an affiant's conscience will not permit the affiant to use the term 'swear,' an affirmation is permissible. Instead, the notary should substitute the term 'affirm' for the term 'swear.' In all cases, whether it is an oath or affirmation, the notary should respect the solemnity of the oath and require the affiant to raise the affiant's hand before administering the oath" (NPM).

The following words may be used to administer an oath or affirmation to a witness in a judicial proceeding: "Do you solemnly swear or affirm that the testimony you are about to give will be the truth, the whole truth and nothing but the truth?" (HRS 621-12).

"The following is an example of an oath that can be administered with an affidavit: 'You do solemnly swear or affirm that the statements made in this affidavit are the truth, the whole truth, and nothing but the truth.' The affiant answers, 'I do'" (NPM).

*** Jurats: Although Hawaii statute does not explicitly authorize Notaries to execute jurats, this notarial act is referenced repeatedly in HRS Chapter 456 and HAR Chapter 5-11. See, for example, HRS 456-6, 456-9(c)(3) and 456-21(a)(4), and HAR 5-11-7 and 5-11-8.

"For a jurat, the notary certifies that the signer personally appeared before the notary. The signer is positively identified and, after signing the document in the notary's presence, takes an oath or affirmation that the statements contained in the document are true" (website, "General Notary Questions").

**** Certifying Copies: Wording in HRS 456-15, which deals with the Notary's record book, suggests that certifying copies of entries in the Notary's record book is a notarial act: "All copies or certificates granted by the notary shall be under the notary's hand and notarial seal and shall be received as evidence of such transactions."

According to the Attorney General's website ("General Notary Questions"), a Notary may not certify a copy of a birth certificate, marriage certificate or passport.

Identifying Document Signers

"No acknowledgment, jurat, or other instrument shall be taken, unless the person offering to make the acknowledgment, jurat, or instrument is personally known to the notary public to be the person whose name is subscribed to the acknowledgment, jurat, or instrument as a party thereto, or is proved to be such by the oath or affirmation of a credible witness known to the notary public, or by production of a current identification card or document issued by the United States, this State, or any other state, or a national government that contains the bearer's photograph and signature" (HAR 5-11-7).

"The ID must be a current ID card or document issued by the United States, this State, or any other state, or a national government that contains the bearer's photograph and signature (e.g., a driver's license, state ID, military ID or a passport)" (website, "General Notary Questions").

'Personally Known' Defined: Personally known "means having an acquaintance, derived from association with the individual, which establishes the individual's identity with at least a reasonable certainty" (HRS 456-1.6).

Failure to Identify: A Notary commits the offense of "failure to verify identity and signature" for knowingly notarizing a document under the following circumstances:

1. If the Notary witnesses the signing of the document and "fails to verify the identity of the signer by personally knowing the signer or by comparing the personal appearance of the signer with satisfactory proof of the signer's identity"; or

2. If the Notary does not witness the signing of the document and "fails to verify the identity of the signer by personally knowing the signer or by comparing the personal appearance of the signer with satisfactory proof of the signer's identity; or fails to verify the signature of the signer by recognizing the signature of the signer by personal familiarity with the signature, or by comparing the signature with satisfactory proof of the signer's signature" (HRS 456-20[a]).

It is a misdemeanor to commit this offense, and conviction results in automatic revocation of the Notary's commission (HRS 456-20[b] and [c]).

Identifying Attorney in Fact: To confirm an attorney in fact's authority to sign a document on behalf of another person, the original power of attorney — not a copy — must be presented to the Notary, who must ensure that it grants such power to sign (website, "General Notary Questions").

Notary Must Initial Changes

"Before notarizing any document, the notary public should inspect the document and ascertain whether there are interlineations, erasures, or other changes. If there are changes, the notary should call them to the attention of the person who is signing the document. If the changes are approved, the notary public places the notary's initials in the margin of the document opposite each interlineation, erasure, or change. (For the protection of the notary, it is also advisable to have the person who is signing the document initial each interlineation, erasure, or change)" (NPM).

Statutory Requirement for Acknowledgment: "Every notary public or the officer authorized to take acknowledgments to instruments, before taking any acknowledgment, shall first carefully inspect any instrument proposed to be acknowledged before the notary public or officer, and ascertain whether there are any interlineations, erasures, or changes in the instrument. If there are any interlineations, erasures, or changes, the notary public or officer shall call the attention thereto of the person offering to acknowledge the instrument. If they are approved, the acknowledging officer (the Notary) shall place the officer's initials in the margin of the instrument opposite each interlineation, erasure, or change. The initialing by the officer taking the acknowledgment is prima facie evidence of the extent of the interlineations, erasures, or changes and of the fact that the same were made prior to acknowledgment of the instrument, but does not preclude proof to the contrary" (HRS 502-61).

A Notary or other officer failing to perform the above duty may be fined not more than $200 (HRS 502-62).

Initialing Necessary for Recording: No document acknowledged in Hawaii may be recorded in the state unless such interlineations, erasures and changes are initialed by the officer taking the acknowledgment. If the document is acknowledged outside Hawaii, the interlineation, erasure or change must be initialed by the party(ies) to the document or by the notarizing officer (HRS 502-63).

Procedures for validating a document with an interlineation, erasure or other change but without an initial are described in HRS 502-50[b].

Notary May Sign for Disabled

"A notary may sign the name of a person physically unable to sign or to make a mark on a document presented for notarization; provided that the notary is satisfied that the person has voluntarily given consent for the notary to sign on the person's behalf, if the notary writes, in the presence of the person: 'Signature affixed by notary pursuant to section 456-19, Hawaii Revised Statutes.' beneath the signature, and if a doctor's written certificate is provided to the notary certifying that the person is unable to physically sign or make a mark because of the disability, and that the person is capable of communicating the person's intention" (HRS 456-19).

Signing by Mark: The "Notary Public Manual" indicates that notarization of a signature by mark must include a notarial certificate drafted to reflect the circumstances of the signing: "If a person is able to make a mark on a document, the notarization forms should reflect that the person is signing by mark. In such instances, an attorney may require the presence of at least two impartial witnesses to witness the signing by mark, and the notarial certificate will be drafted to reflect their presence. Thereafter, the person places the person's mark on the document and the notary indicates that it is the mark of the person in question. Example: X (mark of John Doe)."

NNA Code Must Be Followed

"Every notary public shall perform notary public duties in accordance with chapter 456, HRS, (and) this chapter, and the notary public code of professional responsibility as adopted by the National Notary Association, and as any of these may be amended" (HAR 5-11-3).

"In addition to any other acts or conditions provided by law, the attorney general may refuse to renew, reinstate, or restore, or may revoke, suspend, deny, or condition, a commission of any applicant or notary public who violates any of the provisions of chapter 456, HRS, and this chapter, and to seek fines or to otherwise discipline a notary public for any cause authorized by law, including but not limited to the following: ... Conduct or practice contrary to the notary public code of professional responsibility as adopted by the National Notary Association" (HAR 5-11-39[a][12]).

To view or download *The Notary Public Code of Professional Responsibility*, go to www.nationalnotary.org and click "Notary Resources," then click "Publications."

Available to Public

"A notary public shall provide notarial services to the public during all normal business hours of operation where the notary public is employed" (HAR 5-11-11[b]).

"Although a notary public may be commissioned to perform services in connection with work for his/her employer, the notary is nonetheless a public officer and as such is required to provide notarial service to the general public" (NPM).

This requirement does not apply to Notaries in government service (HAR 5-11-11[c]).

<u>Sign Must Be Displayed</u>: Nongovernmental Notaries must conspicuously display within their places of business a sign no smaller than 3 inches by 5 inches bearing the words "Notary Public" (HAR 5-11-11[a]).

NOTARY DON'TS

According to the "Notary Public Manual," Notaries may:

1. NOT notarize their own signatures;
2. NOT perform telephone notarizations;
3. NOT delegate the performance of a notarial act to another, such as a clerk or deputy;
4. NOT notarize a document for someone unable to speak with the Notary in the same language;
5. NOT notarize a document unless satisfied that the statements in the notarial certificate are true and correct;
6. NOT withhold services from the general public, except for specially commissioned government Notaries who may notarize for government business only.

In addition, "General Notary Questions" on the website indicates that a Notary may:

7. NOT notarize for anyone who appears unable to understand what he or she is signing;
8. NOT notarize a document that the Notary believes contains deceptive or fraudulent information;
9. NOT notarize a document with blank spaces that the signer indicates will be filled in after notarization;
10. NOT notarize if the signer is being pressured or coerced into signing;
11. NOT notarize the signature of an attorney in fact unless an original power of attorney is presented;
12. NOT notarize a document with corrections or erasures without verifying and initialing the changes.

Disqualifying Interests

"(A) notary public cannot certify to, or act in, a matter in which the notary has a personal interest.... One who has a beneficial interest in a document, no matter how small or nominal the interest, cannot act as a notary public relative to that document. Therefore, one partner cannot as a notary public take the oath of his co-partner in a matter in which the partnership has an interest" (NPM).

<u>Corporate Employee or Officer</u>: A Notary who is an officer, employee, shareholder, director or agent of a corporation, trust company, bank or building and loan association may notarize for the corporation, trust company, bank or association — except if the Notary is individually a party to the document (HRS 456-14 and NRM).

<u>Notarizing for Spouse</u>: Hawaii Notaries may notarize for their spouses, provided the Notary

does not have a personal beneficial interest: "Mere relationship to a party does not disqualify a notary. Thus, a wife, who is a notary public, may notarize her husband's documents, provided she does not derive a beneficial interest therefrom" (NPM).

Notarizing While Impaired

A Notary may be disciplined for being "addicted to, dependent on, or a habitual user of a narcotic, barbiturate, amphetamine, hallucinogen, opium, or cocaine, or other drugs or derivatives of a similar nature" (HAR 5-11-39[a][7]). A Notary also may be disciplined for practicing as a Notary Public while the ability to practice is impaired by alcohol, drugs, or mental instability, or substantially impaired by physical disability" (HAR 5-11-39[a][8]).

False or Misleading Representations

A Notary may be disciplined by the Attorney General for allowing "the notary public's name or title to be used deceptively, fraudulently, or in false or misleading advertising, or [for] making untruthful or improbable statements" (HAR 5-11-39[a][6]).

Foreign-Language Documents

"Should I notarize a document in a foreign language? — Only if you have a thorough understanding of the foreign language in which the document is written. Also, you should not notarize a document written in English if the parties to the document who appear before you speak a foreign language unfamiliar to you. You should refer the parties to a notary who speaks the foreign language, or to the foreign consulate, or to an attorney" (website, "General Notary Questions").

NOTARY SIGNING AGENTS

Currently, there are no statutes, regulations or rules prohibiting or restricting the operation of Notary Signing Agents within the state of Hawaii.

Charging of 'Round Sum' Not Permitted

Note below under "Notary Fees" (i.e., "Other Charges") that "the charging of a round sum for notarial and other services together is not permissible" (NPM).

NOTARY FEES

The maximum fees that Hawaii Notaries may charge for notarial acts are (HRS 456-17):
1. Taking an acknowledgment: $5 per signer for one original and one duplicate original; plus $2.50 per signer for every duplicate original beyond the first;
2. Administering an oath, including preparing a certificate: $5 for one original and four duplicate originals, if needed; plus $2.50 for every duplicate original beyond four;
3. Taking a deposition: $5 for each certificate;
4. Preparing any other official certificate: $5;
5. Executing a protest: $5 for noting protest of commercial paper, or any other protest; $5 for each notice and certified copy of the protest.

For administering a loyalty oath to a government employee or official, a Notary may not charge a fee (NPM).

Other Charges

"The notary may make further charges for unofficial services, but the charging of a round sum for notarial and other services together is not permissible. A notary may charge less than the statutory fees for the notary's acts" (NPM).

Income Tax License

"A notary who charges for the notary's official services must secure a State gross income tax license. Fees collected by the notary are subject to the State general excise tax" (NPM).

Government Notaries

Specially appointed government Notaries may not charge in notarizing for government matters (HRS 456-18).

If urgent necessity requires government Notaries to notarize in nongovernmental matters, they must charge the standard fee for the notarial act(s), and these fees will be handed over to the state. Government Notaries may, with prior approval of the Attorney General, pay for their own commission and bond, in which case they may charge for notarizing in nongovernmental matters (HRS 456-18[3]).

NOTARY CERTIFICATES

Contents of Acknowledgment Certificate

"The certificate of acknowledgment shall state in substance that the person who executed the instrument appeared before the officer granting the certificate and acknowledged or stated that the person executed the same, and that such person was personally known to the officer granting such certificate to be the person whose name is subscribed to the instrument as a party thereto, or was proved to be such by the oath or affirmation of a credible witness known to the officer whose name shall be inserted in the certificate. It shall not be ground for the rejection of any such certificate, or for refusing to accept such instrument for record or in evidence, that the certificate fails to state that the person making the acknowledgment stated or acknowledged that the instrument was executed freely or voluntarily by the person or as the person's free act and deed" (HRS 502-42).

For knowingly including any false or misleading statement in a certificate, the notarizing officer may be fined $1,000 and/or imprisoned for one year (HRS 502-54).

Spelling of Signer's Name: "The notary should insert the name carefully, making sure that the name on the document or instrument agrees exactly with the name inserted in the acknowledgment. If the signer's middle name is spelled out in the instrument, the notary should spell it out in the acknowledgment and make sure that the party signs the person's full name exactly as it appears on the document" (NPM).

'Certification Statement' Describes Document

A law that took effect May 5, 2008, discourages fraudulent reattachment of notarial certificates: "Every acknowledgment or jurat shall be evidenced by a certificate signed and dated by a notary public. The certificate shall include the printed name of the notary public, the official stamp or seal of the notary public, identification of the jurisdiction in which the notarial act is performed, identification or description of the document being notarized, which shall be close in proximity to the jurat or acknowledgment, and the number of pages and date of such document" (HAR 5-11-8).

Knowingly failing to include any of the above when notarizing a document — "failure to authenticate with a certification statement" — is a misdemeanor and punishable under HRS Chapter 706. Conviction for this offense results in automatic commission revocation (HRS 456-21). The Attorney General also may impose a $500 fine (HRS 456-9[c][3]).

The following sample "certification statement" is of a type suggested by the Department of the Attorney General. To comply with HAR 5-11-8, it should be stamped in close proximity to acknowledgment or jurat wording:

```
Document Date: _____    No. Pages: ____
Notary Name: _____    _____ Circuit
Doc. Description: _____
_____
_____
_____

_____  _____
Notary Signature  Date
NOTARY CERTIFICATION     (Stamp or Seal)
```

If the format above is used, then the Notary must affix his or her official seal and signature twice on the same document: once with the acknowledgment or jurat wording, and once on the "certification statement."

Only One Seal Required: Alternatively, the data required by HAR 5-11-8 may be incorporated into the acknowledgment or jurat wording. In that case, the Notary may affix his or her seal and signature only once (website, "Important Information Regarding Chapter 5-11, Hawaii Admin Rules" and "Frequently Asked Questions about the New Notary Rules"). For an example of an acknowledgment form in which the data required in the "certification statement" has instead been incorporated into the acknowledgment wording, see the sample certificate printed below at the end of this section ("ONLY ONE NOTARY SEAL REQUIRED — Optional 'All Purpose' Acknowledgment [HRS 501-41(6)]"). Its wording is suggested by the Department of the Attorney General.

If Statement on Separate Page: "It is best to include the description of the document on the same page and in 'close proximity' to or included in the acknowledgment or jurat. If you use a separate certificate, and there is no room for that certificate on the page on which the acknowledgment or jurat is contained, indicate on that page that there is a notary certificate on the next page, such as by typing: 'Notary Certificate on next page'" (website, "Frequently Asked Questions about the New Notary Rules").

If Document Bears No Date: "What should I write on the certificate for the date of a document that is undated? — You should write 'undated at time of notarization'" (website, "Frequently Asked Questions about the New Notary Rules").

Acknowledgment by Individual (HRS 502-41[1]):

State of Hawaii   )
*   ) ss.*
County of _____)

On _____ (date), before me personally appeared _____ (name[s] of signer[s]), to me known to be the person (or persons) described in and who executed the foregoing instrument, and acknowledged that the person (or persons) executed the same as the person's (or persons') free act and deed.

(Notary's Signature)   (Stamp or Seal)

(Printed Name of Notary Public)
My commission expires: _____

Document Date: _____   No. Pages: ____
Notary Name: _____   _____ Circuit
Doc. Description: _____
_____
_____
_____

_____ _____
Notary Signature   Date
NOTARY CERTIFICATION   (Stamp or Seal)

Acknowledgment by Unknown Individual Whose Identity Is Proved by Credible Witness (HRS 502-43):

State of Hawaii   )
*   ) ss.*
County of _____)

On _____ (date), personally appeared before me _____ (name of signer), satisfactorily proved to me to be the person described in and who executed the within instrument, by the oath of _____ (name of credible witness), a credible witness for that purpose, to me known and by me duly sworn, and the person, _____ (name of signer), acknowledged that the person executed the same freely and voluntarily for the uses and purposes therein set forth.
(Notary's Signature) (Stamp or Seal)

(Printed Name of Notary Public)
My commission expires: _____

Document Date: _____   No. Pages: ____
Notary Name: _____   _____ Circuit
Doc. Description: _____
_____
_____
_____

_____ _____
Notary Signature   Date
NOTARY CERTIFICATION   (Stamp or Seal)

Acknowledgment by Corporation (NPM):

State of Hawaii   )
*   ) ss.*
County of _____)

On _____ (date), before me personally appeared _____ and _____, to me personally known, who being by me duly sworn, did say that they are the _____ and _____, respectively, of _____ Corporation, and that the seal affixed to the instrument is the corporate seal* of the corporation, and that the instrument was signed and sealed* on behalf of the corporation by authority of its board of directors and _____ and _____ *acknowledged the instrument to be the free act and deed of the corporation.*

(Notary's Signature) (Stamp or Seal)

(Printed Name of Notary Public)
My commission expires: _____

```
Document Date: _____    No. Pages: ____
Notary Name: _____    _____ Circuit
Doc. Description: _____
_____
_____
_____
_____  ____
Notary Signature   Date
NOTARY CERTIFICATION    (Stamp or Seal)
```

* <u>If No Corporate Seal Exists</u>: "If the corporation has no corporate seal, the notary should line out and initial 'the seal affixed to the instrument is the corporate seal of the corporation' and add 'and the corporation has no corporate seal'" (NPM). The Notary should also line out and initial the ensuing words "and sealed."

Acknowledgment by Corporation or Partnership (HRS 502-41[3]):

State of Hawaii   )
*   ) ss.*
County of _____)

On _____ (date), before me personally appeared _____ (name of signer), to me personally known, who, being by me duly sworn (or affirmed), did say that the person is the president (or other officer, partner, or agent of the corporation, or partnership) of _____ (name of corporation or partnership), and that the instrument was signed in behalf of the corporation (or partnership) by authority of its board of directors (partners or trustees), and _____ (name of signer) acknowledged the instrument to be the free act and deed of the corporation (or partnership).

(Notary's Signature) (Stamp or Seal)

(Printed Name of Notary Public)
My commission expires: _____

```
Document Date: _____    No. Pages: ____
Notary Name: _____    _____ Circuit
Doc. Description: _____
_____
_____
_____
_____  ____
Notary Signature   Date
NOTARY CERTIFICATION    (Stamp or Seal)
```

Acknowledgment by Attorney in Fact (HRS 502-41[2]):

State of Hawaii   )
*   ) ss.*
County of _____)

On _____ (date), before me personally appeared _____ (name of attorney in fact), to me known to be the person who executed the foregoing instrument in behalf of _____ (name of principal) and acknowledged that the person executed the same as the free act and deed of said _____ (name of principal).

(Notary's Signature) (Stamp or Seal)

(Printed Name of Notary Public)
My commission expires: _____

```
Document Date: _____    No. Pages: ____
Notary Name: _____    _____ Circuit
Doc. Description: _____
_____
_____
_____
_____  ____
Notary Signature   Date
NOTARY CERTIFICATION    (Stamp or Seal)
```

<u>Notary Should Verify Authority</u>: "An acknowledgment of an individual acting by power of attorney should never be notarized unless the notary is completely satisfied that the attorney-in-fact does indeed have the authority to sign the instrument for the individual executing the instrument, and that the power of the attorney is in full force and effect" (NPM).

Acknowledgment by Corporation through Attorney in Fact (HRS 502-41[4]):

State of Hawaii   )
*   ) ss.*
County of _____)

On _____ (date), before me personally appeared _____ (name of attorney in fact), to me personally known, who being by me duly sworn (or affirmed) did say that the person is the attorney in fact of _____ (name of corporation), duly appointed under power of attorney dated _____, recorded* in book _____, at page _____/as document no._____; and that the foregoing instrument was executed in the name and behalf of said _____ (name of corporation) by _____ (name of attorney in fact) as its attorney in fact; and _____ (name of attorney in fact) acknowledged the instrument to be the free act and deed of _____ (name of corporation).

(Notary's Signature) (Stamp or Seal)

(Printed Name of Notary Public)
My commission expires: _____

Document Date: _____   No. Pages: ____
Notary Name: _____   _____ Circuit
Doc. Description: _____
_____
_____
_____

_____ _____
Notary Signature   Date
NOTARY CERTIFICATION   (Stamp or Seal)

Acknowledgment by Corporation through Another Corporation as Its Attorney in Fact (HRS 502-41[5]):

State of Hawaii   )
*   ) ss.*
County of _____)

On _____ (date), before me personally appeared _____ (name of corporate officer or agent), to me personally known, who, being by me duly sworn (or affirmed) did say that the person is the _____ (president or other officer or agent of the corporation acting as attorney) of _____ (name of corporation acting as attorney in fact) and that _____ (name of corporation acting as attorney in fact) is the attorney in fact of _____ (name of principal corporation on whose behalf the attorney in fact corporation is acting), duly appointed under power of attorney dated _____, recorded* in book _____, at page _____/as document no. ____; that the foregoing instrument was executed in the name and behalf of _____ (name of principal corporation) by _____ (name of corporation acting as attorney in fact) as its attorney in fact; that the instrument was so executed by _____ (name of corporation acting as attorney in fact) by authority of its board of directors; and _____ (name of corporate officer or agent of corporation acting as attorney in fact) acknowledged the instrument to be the free act and deed of _____ (name of principal corporation).

(Notary's Signature)   (Stamp or Seal)

(Printed Name of Notary Public)
My commission expires: _____

Document Date: _____   No. Pages: ____
Notary Name: _____   _____ Circuit
Doc. Description: _____
_____
_____
_____

_____ _____
Notary Signature   Date
NOTARY CERTIFICATION   (Stamp or Seal)

---

* <u>If Power of Attorney Not Recorded</u>: "In case the enabling power of attorney has not previously been recorded, omit the reference to its place of record and insert in lieu thereof the words 'which power of attorney is now in full force and effect'" (HRS 502-41[4] and [5]).

Optional 'All-Purpose' Acknowledgment (HRS 502-41[6]):

State of Hawaii   )
) ss.
County of _____)

On _____ (date), before me personally appeared _____ (name of signer), to me personally known, who, being by me duly sworn (or affirmed), did say that such person executed the foregoing instrument as the free act and deed of such person, and if applicable in the capacity shown, having been duly authorized to execute such instrument in such capacity.

(Notary's Signature)   (Stamp or Seal)

(Printed Name of Notary Public)
My commission expires: _____

Document Date: _____   No. Pages: ____
Notary Name: _____   _____ Circuit
Doc. Description: _____
_____
_____
_____

_____ _____
Notary Signature   Date
NOTARY CERTIFICATION   (Stamp or Seal)

ONLY ONE SEAL REQUIRED — Optional 'All Purpose' Acknowledgment (HRS 502-41[6] and Dept. of Atty. Gen.):

State of Hawaii   )
) ss.
County of _____)

On this _____ day of _____, 20___, in the _____ Circuit Court, State of Hawaii, before me personally appeared _____, to me personally known or proved to me on the basis of satisfactory evidence to be the person(s) whose name(s) is/are subscribed to this instrument, who, being by me duly sworn or affirmed, did say that he/she executed the foregoing instrument identified or described as _____ as his/her free act and deed, and if applicable, in the capacity shown having been duly authorized to execute such instrument in such capacity. The foregoing instrument is dated _____ and contained _____ pages at the time of this acknowledgment/certification.

_____
Printed Name
NOTARY PUBLIC, STATE OF HAWAII
My commission expires: _____

_____   (Stamp or Seal)
Signature of Notary Public

Venue on Certificates

All notarial certificates must include the venue — that is, the place in which the notarial act occurs (HRS 502-41 and HAR 5-11-8). Hawaii's "Notary Public Manual" interprets this requirement as follows:

"Because a notarial certificate … requires a notary to indicate thereon the venue or location of the notarial act, a notary should be aware that the State is divided into four judicial circuits (HRS § 603-1), for venue purposes, as follows:

"1. The first judicial circuit is the island of Oahu and all other islands belonging to the State not hereinafter mentioned, and the district of Kalawao on the island of Molokai [Designated venue 'City and County of Honolulu'];

"2. The second judicial circuit includes the islands of Maui, Molokai (except the district of Kalawao), Lanai, Kahoolawe, and Molokini [Designated venue 'County of Maui'];

"3. The third judicial circuit is the island of Hawaii [Designated venue 'County of Hawaii']; and

"4. The fifth judicial circuit includes the islands of Kauai and Niihau [Designated venue 'County of Kauai']."*

* There is no fourth judicial circuit.

ELECTRONIC NOTARIZATION

The state of Hawaii has not yet adopted statutes or regulations expressly establishing rules, definitions and procedures for electronic notarization.

UETA Recognizes Notary's eSignature

Hawaii has adopted its own version of the

Uniform Electronic Transactions Act (HRS Chapter 489E), including the provision on notarization, thereby recognizing the legal validity of electronic signatures used by Notaries:

"If a law requires a signature or record to be notarized, certified, acknowledged, verified, or made under oath or seal, the requirement is satisfied if the electronic signature or seal of the person authorized to perform those acts, together with all other information required to be included by other applicable law, is attached to or logically associated with the signature or record" (HRS 489E-11).

URPERA Permits Notary's eSignature

Effective July 1, 2009, Hawaii has enacted its own version of the Real Property Electronic Recording Act (HRS 502-121 through 502-125). The Act enables registrars of the Hawaii Bureau of Conveyances to record land records in electronic format and authorizes Notaries to use electronic signatures in notarizing such electronic land records:

"Any requirement that a document or a signature associated with a document be notarized, acknowledged, verified, witnessed, or made under oath shall be satisfied if the electronic signature of the person authorized to perform that act, and all other information required to be included, is attached to or logically associated with the document or signature. It shall not be necessary to accompany an electronic signature with a physical or electronic image or a stamp, impression, or seal" (HRS 502-122[c]).

NOTARY RECORDS

"Every notary public shall record at length in a book of records all acts, protests, depositions, and other things, by the notary noted or done in the notary's official capacity" (HRS 456-15).

Format of Record

"The record book shall be bound with a soft cover and shall not exceed eleven inches in height and sixteen and one-half inches in width when fully opened" (HAR 5-11-9[b]).

"The pages of the record book shall be consecutively numbered" (HAR 5-11-9[c]).

"The Notary public shall always provide and print legibly on the information page of each record book the notary public's name, business address, commission number, and commission expiration date, the book number, and the beginning and ending dates of the notarial acts recorded in the book" (HAR 5-11-9[d]).

"The notary public shall always print legibly the notary public's name on the top left corner and the notary public's commission number on the top right corner of each set of pages of transactions in each record book" (HAR 5-11-9[e]).

Required Entries

"For each official act, the notary shall enter in the book:

"(1) The type, date, and time of day of the notarial act;

"(2) The title or type and date of the document or proceeding and the nature of the act, transaction, or thing to which the document relates;

"(3) The signature, printed name, and address of each person whose signature is notarized and of each witness;

"(4) Other parties to the instrument; and

"(5) The manner in which the signer was identified" (HRS 456-15).

Failure to Keep Record: For failure to keep such a record as described above, the Attorney General may impose a fine of $200 (HRS 456-9[c][4]).

Open to Inspection

"The (notarial) records, both while in the custody of the acknowledging officer and after ... filing (with the attorney general), shall be open at all reasonable times to the inspection of any responsible person, without fee or reward" (HRS 502-73).

"You may view the notary's notarial record books by first sending to the (Attorney General's office) a written request with any information you have, such as the name of the notary public, the type of transaction, the date, and the signer's name. Depending upon the date of the record book, the record book may be in storage or still in the possession of the notary. Once we have all the information, we will check our records for the particular notary public" (website, "General Notary Questions").

The Attorney General may charge $5 for certification of each notarial transaction in a notary's record book that is in the possession of the Attorney General, with an additional 25 cents charged for each copied page (HAR 5-11-46[a][12] and [13]).

Disposition of Journal

"The records of each notary public shall be deposited with the office of the attorney general upon the resignation, death, expiration of each term of office, or removal from or abandonment of office. If any notary fails to comply with this section within ninety days of the date of the resignation, expiration of any term of office, or removal from or abandonment of office or if the notary's personal representative fails to comply with this section within ninety days of the notary's death, then the notary or the notary's personal representative shall forfeit to the State not less than $50 nor more than $500, in the discretion of the court, in an action brought by the attorney general on behalf of the State" (HRS 456-16). See also HRS 456-9[c][5] and HAR 5-11-9[f] and 5-11-17.

The requirement that notarial records be deposited with the state Attorney General's office took effect on July 1, 2002. Up to that date, each Notary deposited his or her official records of notarial acts with the clerk of the circuit court of the judicial circuit in which the particular Notary resided.

Loss, Misplacement or Theft of Journal

Within 10 days of loss, misplacement or theft of a Notary's journal, the Notary must send a written notice to the Attorney General. In the case of theft, the Notary must also inform the appropriate law enforcement agency and deliver to the Attorney General a copy of the agency's report of the theft (HAR 5-11-18). For failure to do so, the Attorney General may impose a fine of $20 (HRS 456-9[c][6]).

Acknowledgment-Takers to Keep Records

"All judges and other officers authorized by law to take acknowledgments to instruments, besides the certificate of acknowledgment indorsed upon the instrument, shall keep a record of every acknowledgment in a book of records. Each record shall set forth at least the date of acknowledgment, the parties to the instrument, the persons acknowledging, the date, and some memorandum as to the nature of the instrument acknowledged" (HRS 502-71).

AUTHENTICATION OF NOTARIAL ACTS

Circuit Court Clerk

Locally, an authenticating certificate for a Hawaii Notary may be obtained at the office of any clerk of the circuit court where the Notary has filed a copy of his or her commission and specimens of his or her seal and signature. Notaries must file these items with the circuit court of the circuit in which the Notary resides but may also, at their discretion, file them with the clerk of any other circuit court (HRS 456-4). As a result, it may be possible to obtain an authenticating certificate for a given Notary in more than one county.

Fee: Circuit court fees for issuing a certificate of authentication are set by the Hawaii Supreme Court (HRS 456-9[b]). Currently, there is a $3 fee for authenticating each notarized document (Lieutenant Governor's website, "Apostilles and Certifications").

Lieutenant Governor

Authenticating certificates validating the acts of circuit court clerks and apostilles validating the acts of Notaries are issued by the Hawaii Lieutenant Governor.

"When an Apostille is issued, the Lieutenant Governor authenticates the notary public's signature. When a Certification is issued, the Court Clerk must verify the notary public's signature and commission before the Lieutenant Governor can issue a Certification" (Lieutenant Governor's website, "Apostilles and Certifications").

All documents submitted to the Lieutenant Governor for authentication must be notarized by a duly commissioned Hawaii Notary. Birth, death and marriage certificates and divorce decrees may be notarized only by personnel in Hawaii's Department of Health, Vital Records.

Fee: $1 (check or money order) per document for either an apostille or an authenticating certificate.

Address:
Office of Lieutenant Governor
State Capitol, 5th Floor
415 South Beretania St.
Honolulu, HI 96813

Telephone: 1-808-586-0255

Procedure: The first step is to complete and sign the "Application for Apostille or Certification of Documents," which may be downloaded from the Lieutenant Governor's website. Mail or present in person the application and the original notarized document(s), along with the attached circuit court certificate(s) of authentication, when necessary, and the appropriate fee.

COMMISSIONING AND ADMINISTRATION

The Hawaii Attorney General appoints, commissions and maintains records on the state's Notaries (HRS 456-1[a], 456-1.5 and 456-8).

Applying for Commission

Qualifications: An applicant for a Notary commission in the state of Hawaii must: (a) be at least 18 years old, (b) be a resident of Hawaii and (c) be a U.S. citizen, U.S. national or permanent resident alien authorized to work in the United States (HRS 456-2, HAR 5-11-21[b][5] and NPM).

In addition, the Hawaii Administrative Rules allow denial of a Notary commission based on an inability to read, write or speak English with understanding (HAR 5-11-39[a][5]) or on being "addicted to, dependent on, or a habitual user of a narcotic, barbiturate, amphetamine, hallucinogen, opium, or cocaine, or other drugs or derivatives of a similar nature" (HAR 5-11-39[a][7]).

Application: Before taking the mandatory examination (see below), an applicant must submit a completed application to the Notary Public Office of the Hawaii Attorney General. The application must include a nonrefundable $10 application fee; a letter from a state resident (not an employer or relative of the applicant) vouching for the applicant's integrity; and a letter from the applicant's employer or, if the applicant is self-employed, from the applicant, justifying the applicant's need for a commission and acknowledging that a Notary is a public officer (HAR 5-11-21[a] and 5-11-46[a][1]).

If the application is for commission as a government Notary, then the letter of justification must come from the head of the applicant's government department. The letter must justify the applicant's need for a commission and must designate the applicant to perform, at no change, notarial services pertaining to the government department (HRS 456-18 and HAR 5-11-21[c]).

Regardless of the type of commission being applied for, the applicant's signature on the affidavit and oath at the end of the application must be notarized prior to submission (HRS 456-2 and HAR 5-11-21[d]).

Test Required: Upon approval of the application, the applicant will be notified of the examination date, time and place. The exam is given on Oahu at least once a month and on the other islands periodically.

This is a written, closed-book exam, with a minimum passing score of 80%. The exam fee is $10. The exam results and instructions on what to do next will be mailed to the applicant within 30 calendar days (HAR 5-11-32, 5-11-33 and 5-11-46; website, "Application for Notary Public Commission").

Filing Bond, Seal and Signature: Upon being informed of passage of the exam, the applicant must pay a fee of $40 for issuance of the commission (HRS 456-9[a][1] and HAR 5-11-46[a][5]). The commission-issuance fee is waived for government Notaries (HRS 456-18[2][B]).

Before notarizing, the new Notary must obtain a $1,000 surety bond and a seal of office. The bond must be purchased from a surety company authorized to do business in Hawaii, must be approved by a judge of the circuit court and then must be filed with the clerk of the circuit court of the judicial circuit in which the Notary resides (HRS 456-5). Government Notaries need not be bonded (HRS 456-18[2][C]).

In addition to the bond, the Notary also must deposit the following with the clerk of his or her circuit court: (a) a copy of the new commission, (b) an impression of the Notary seal or stamp and (c) a specimen of the Notary's official signature. At the Notary's option, the same items may be filed with any other circuit court clerk(s), thereby enabling authentication of the Notary's acts by the additional clerk(s) (HRS 456-4).

Circuit court fees for filing a copy of a Notary commission are set by the Hawaii Supreme Court (HRS 456-9[b]). Currently, there is a $6 fee for the filing of a commission (Hawaii State Judiciary website, "Circuit Court Filing Fees and Costs"). This filing fee is waived for government Notaries (HRS 456-18[2][A]).

Timely Renewal Essential: A renewal notice is mailed to each Notary approximately two months before commission expiration (website, "General Notary Questions").

"Each notary public shall be responsible for renewing the notary public's commission on a timely basis... . The failure to renew a commission in a timely manner may cause the commission to be forfeited, if the attorney general finds that the failure was done knowingly ..." (HRS 456-1[b]). "A failure to renew shall be deemed knowingly if notice of renewal is sent to the last address on file for the notary public and the notary public fails to complete all the requirements ..." (HAR 5-11-13[a]). A renewal is timely if received by the Attorney General before or on the current commission's expiration date (HAR 5-11-23[a]).

Other than the timing restrictions, the renewal process is the same as for the initial application in regards to requirements and fees (HRS 456-9[a][2] and HAR 5-11-23[b] and 5-11-46[a][2], [6] and [7]).

Non-Residents: Non-residents of Hawaii may not qualify for a commission in the state.

Changes of Status

"Each notary public shall file the notary public's name, employer, residence and business addresses and telephone numbers, and occupation with the attorney general, and shall notify the attorney general of any change, in writing, within thirty days of the change" (HAR 5-11-10[a]). See also HRS-456-1(a).

The Attorney General has authority to revoke a Notary's commission if any change "renders the holding of such commission by the notary no longer necessary for the public good and convenience" (HRS 456-1[a]).

If Notary Changes Name: The notice of name change, sent to the Attorney General by the Notary within 30 days of the change, must state the old and new names and the effective date of the change, and it must include a copy of the legal documentation for the change, as well as the new signature of the a Notary (HAR 5-11-10[b]). The fee for a commission name change is $10 (HAR 5-11-46[a][9]).

A "Name Change Form" may be downloaded from the Attorney General's website. Upon receipt of the new commission certificate bearing the new name, the Notary must relinquish the old seal or stamp to the Notary Public Office (website, "Name Change Form"). Before beginning to notarize under the new name, the Notary must obtain a new seal or stamp and submit to the circuit court clerk new seal and signature specimens and a bond bearing the new name.

If Notary Changes Address or Employer: The notice of residence and/or business address change, sent to the Attorney General by the Notary within 30 days of the change, must state the old and new address(es) and the effective date of the change(s) (HAR 5-11-10[c]). The fee for a change in the Notary's judicial circuit is $10 (HAR 5-11-46[a][10]).

A "Residence Address Change Form" and an "Employment Change Form" may be downloaded from the website. If the Notary changes employers as well as employment address, the new employer must provide a letter justifying continuation of the Notary's commission (website, "Employment Change Form"). If the Notary moves out of state, the commission is terminated (HAR 5-11-39[a][4]).

If Notary Resigns: "A notary public may resign the notary public's commission, and shall ... (s)urrender the notary's public's commission certificate, seal, and notarial record books ..." (HAR 5-11-16[a][1]). Items must be surrendered to the Attorney General's office within 90 days of resignation (HAR 5-11-17[a]).

A "Resignation of Commission" form may be downloaded from the website.

CIRCUIT COURT CLERKS

To contact a clerk of the circuit court to obtain an authenticating certificate for a Notary, or to seek assistance in locating a given Notary, telephone long-distance information — 1-808-555-1212 — and ask for the phone number of the appropriate clerk from the following circuits:

First Judicial Circuit:
    City and County of Honolulu (includes Oahu and other islands not mentioned below)

Second Judicial Circuit:
    County of Maui; county seat at Wailuku (includes Maui, Molokai, Lanai, Molokini and Kahoolawe)

Third Judicial Circuit:
County of Hawaii; county seat at Hilo (includes island of Hawaii)

Fifth Judicial Circuit:*
County of Kauai; county seat at Lihue (includes Kauai and Niihau)

* There is no Fourth Judicial Circuit.

OTHER NOTARIAL OFFICERS

Besides Notaries, the following officials may take acknowledgments (HRS 502-50[a]):
1. A registrar of conveyances or the registrar's deputy;
2. A judge of a court of record.

Only Judge May Take Proof

"If any person having executed an instrument within the State, dies, or departs from the State, without having acknowledged the instrument, or refuses to acknowledge it, or if the person has acknowledged it but such acknowledgment has not been duly certified by the officer before whom made and for any reason neither proper certification nor a new acknowledgment can be secured, the instrument may be entered as of record on proof of its execution by a subscribing witness thereto before the judge of the land court or a judge of a circuit court of the State. If all the subscribing witnesses to the conveyance or other instrument are dead or out of the State, the same may be proved before any court in the State by proving the handwriting of the person executing the same and any subscribing witness. For the purposes of this section a notary public or person who wrongfully undertakes to act as such, may be deemed a subscribing witness" (HRS 502-50[a]).

Limited Access to Government Notaries

"A government notary whose fees and bond are waived is... limited by law to performing notarial services pertaining to the business of the government, except where the occasion is deemed by the head of the department of the government unit to be one of urgent necessity and convenience" (NPM).

QUICK FACTS

Notary Jurisdiction
Statewide (HRS 456-1).

Notary Term Length
Four years (HRS 456-1[a] and HAR 5-11-12).

Notary Bond
A Notary's bond must be $1,000, provided by a surety authorized to do business in Hawaii, as approved by a judge of the circuit court (HRS 456-5). Specially appointed government Notaries need not be bonded (HRS 456-18[2][C]).

Notary's Liability Limited: "In the performance of a notarial act, a notary's liability shall be limited to a failure by the notary to perform properly the actions required for the jurat, acknowledgment, or other notarial act. The notary's liability shall not be based on statements in a notarized document apart from the notarial certificate" (HRS 456-6[a]).

Idaho

NOTARY ADMINISTRATION

Office of Secretary of State
Notary Department   1-208-332-2810
450 N. 4th St.
P.O. Box 83720
Boise, ID 83720-0080

Website: www.sos.idaho.gov/notary/
npindex.htm

NOTARY RULES

IC — IDAHO CODE
NPH — IDAHO NOTARY PUBLIC HANDBOOK

Most Notary rules are in the Idaho Code:

a. Title 51, Chapter 1, "Idaho Notary Public Act";

b. Title 55, Chapter 7, "Acknowledgments."

Guidelines for Notaries also appear in the "Idaho Notary Public Handbook" published by the Secretary of State and available on the website.

NOTARY SEAL

An Idaho Notary must affix an official seal on every notarial certificate "below or near" the Notary's signature, and the format must be as follows (IC 51-106):

Kind

Inked Rubber Stamp. "Each notary public whose current commission became effective on or after July 1, 1998, shall provide and keep an official seal which shall be a rubber stamp with a serrated or milled edge border in a rectangular or circular form, which includes the words 'Notary Public,' the notary public's name, the words 'State of Idaho,' and nothing more" (IC 51-106[2]). Ink color is not specified, but "the color should be one that will fax, copy or scan clearly" (NPH).

Prior to July 1, 2004, embossers had also been allowed as official Notary seals.

Shape/Size

Rectangular or circular, but size not specified.

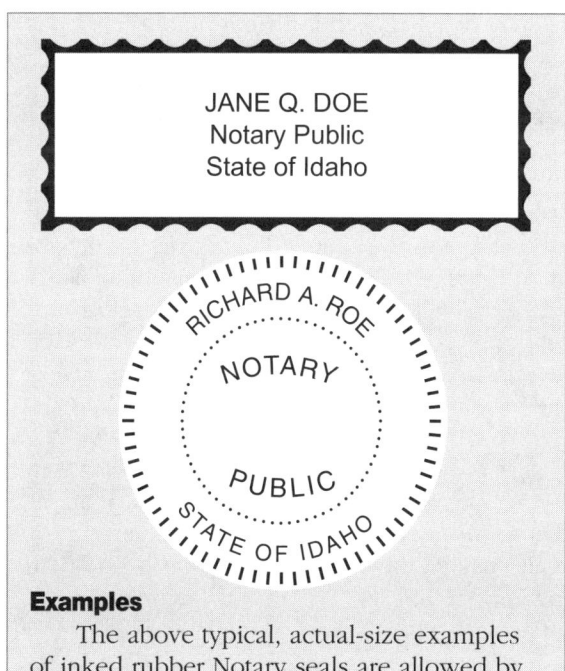

Examples

The above typical, actual-size examples of inked rubber Notary seals are allowed by Idaho law.

Border

A "serrated or milled edge border" is required.

Components

1. Name of Notary;
2. "Notary Public";
3. "State of Idaho".

"There can be no other information or graphics on the seal" (NPH).

Commission Expiration Date Must Appear

"On each notary certificate, the notary public shall immediately following his signature state the date of the expiration of his commission in substantially the following form:

"'My commission expires on _____, 20__'" (IC 51-109[8]).

Wrongful Possession of Notary Seal

"Any person who shall steal or wrongfully

possess a notary public's seal with the intent to use it in the commission of any crime shall be guilty of a felony" (IC 51-119[4]).

New Seal for Name Change

"To effect a change of name for Notary purposes, (the Notary must) purchase a new rubber stamp seal from a Stationery Store, Office Supply or Stamp Company" (website, "Notary Public Change of Name ...").

If Employer Keeps Seal

"If your employer does not allow you to take your stamp with you, you should ask that it be destroyed and you can purchase a new one" (website, "Frequently Asked Questions").

Seal Must be Destroyed

The seal of a resigned, removed or deceased Notary must be destroyed (IC 51-116).

NOTARY POWERS

Idaho Notaries are authorized to perform the following notarial acts (IC 51-107):

1. Take acknowledgments* and proofs**;
2. Administer oaths*** and affirmations;
3. Certify copies****;
4. Certify affidavits or depositions of witnesses including verifications*****;
5. Perform other acts that may be permitted by law (see also IC 55-724).

* Identifying Acknowledgers: "Each notary public shall exercise reasonable care in the performance of his duties generally, and shall exercise a high degree of care in ascertaining the identity of any person whose identity is the subject of a notarial act" (IC 51-111[1]).

"The essence of taking an acknowledgment consists of positively identifying the signer of a document. The signer need not sign in the notary's presence, but must personally appear before the notary and unambiguously state that the signature on the document is his or hers" (NPH). The notarizing officer must personally know the acknowledger or base the identification on "satisfactory evidence from a credible source" (IC 55-707), such as "the sworn identification of the signer by a person known to the notary, or by presentation by the signer of satisfactory identification such as a current photo-bearing driver's license, military identification card, or passport" (NPH).

If the acknowledger is signing in a representative capacity, the notarizing officer must also know or have satisfactory evidence from a credible source that the individual is a corporate or governmental officer, or a partner in a partnership, as applicable (IC 55-707).

"One of the most common situations involving notary fraud is that of a husband conveying community property without his wife's knowledge by using an impostor to sign and acknowledge a deed in place of his wife. A notary should not, therefore, rely on a 'husband's' introduction as a means of identifying a 'wife' when taking the 'wife's' acknowledgment" (NPH).

** Proof by Subscribing Witness: The identity of a subscribing witness must be personally known to the officer taking the proof, or it must be proved by the oath of a credible witness (IC 55-719).

The place of residence of any subscribing witness must appear in the Notary's certificate of proof (IC 55-723).

Officers authorized to take proof of instruments are empowered in such proceedings to employ and swear interpreters, and, as prescribed in the Idaho Code of Civil Procedure, to administer oaths or affirmations, to issue subpoenas and to punish for contempt (IC 55-724).

There are procedures for a proof of execution by handwriting when signers and subscribing witnesses are dead or unavailable (IC 55-721 and 55-722).

*** Oath/Affirmation Wording: "The difference between an oath and an affirmation is that an oath (swearing) impliedly invokes a deity and an affirmation does not. The affirmation is used when the maker of a statement has religious or other objections to the use of an oath. Both forms are effective to invoke the perjury statute against the maker of a false statement" (NPH).

An oath or affirmation administered by a Notary must be in substantially the following form (IC 51-109[3]): "You do solemnly swear (or affirm) that the testimony you shall give in the matter in issue shall be the truth, the whole truth, and nothing but the truth." The person taking the oath or affirmation must then respond affirmatively.

**** Certifying Copies: "If a certified copy of a document cannot be obtained from any recorder or custodian of public documents, and if certification of a copy of the document by a notary public is otherwise permissible, a notary public may certify a copy of the document ..." (IC 51-109[7]).

"This means that a notary cannot certify copies of such things as birth certificates, deeds, marriage licenses, articles of incorporation, college or high school transcripts, military discharge papers, or any other document, a certified copy of which can be obtained from an official custodian. In essence, the documents which a notary can certify include such things as his or her own official records, records of entities such as corporations or associations, and reports of nongovernmental bodies" (NPH).

The original cannot itself be a copy. "The document of which the copy is made must be an original, not a copy; in other words, a notary cannot certify a copy of a copy of any kind. Before certifying the copy, the notary must make a careful page-for-page comparison of it with the original to ensure that it is complete and accurate. If the certification certificate cannot be put on the copy itself, it should be affixed to the copy by some permanent or semipermanent means such as a grommet or staple" (NPH).

***** Jurats and Verifications: In executing a jurat, "the notary certifies: (1) that the maker personally appeared before the notary on the date and in the county indicated; (2) that the maker signed the statement in the notary's presence; and (3) that the notary administered the oath or affirmation to the maker" (NPH).

"A verification is similar to an oath or affirmation, but is made on behalf of an entity other than an individual and includes a recitation of the authority of the signer to make the statement. The format for the verification certificate is set out in subsection (4) of section 51-109, I.C." (NPH).

If Person Is Unable to Sign

Effective July 1, 2007, Idaho law provides procedures for a signing by mark and for notarizing a signature by mark, as well as for a Notary signing the name of a person who cannot sign or make a mark and then notarizing that signature (IC 51-107).

Signing by Mark: A Notary may certify the affixation of a signature by mark on a document presented for notarization if: (a) the signer is unable to handwrite the signer's name, (b) the mark is affixed in the presence and under the direct observation of the Notary, (c) the Notary writes below the mark, "Mark affixed by (printed name of signer by mark)" and (d) the Notary notarizes the mark through a certificate of acknowledgment or verification. (See required forms under "Notary Certificates.")

The website ("Frequently Asked Questions") also directs that "a credible witness familiar with the signer" be present, citing IC 73-114: "Have the credible witness write the marker's name by the mark. The credible witness will also sign as the witness. Have the credible witness sign the notary journal and make a special note if a journal is being used."

If Person Cannot Sign or Make Mark: A Notary may sign the name of a person physically unable to sign or make a mark on a document presented for notarization if: (a) the person directs the Notary to do so in the presence of a witness unaffected by the document, (b) the Notary signs the person's name in the presence of the person and the witness, (c) the witness signs the document beside the signature, (d) the Notary writes below the signature, "Signature affixed by Notary in the presence of (names of person and witness)" and (e) the Notary notarizes the signature through a certificate of acknowledgment or verification. (See required forms under "Notary Certificates," below.)

NOTARY DON'TS

Idaho Notaries may (IC 51-112):
1. NOT engage in any fraudulent or deceptive conduct related to notarial duties;
2. NOT fail to use the requisite care in identifying a person whose identity is an essential element of a notarial act;
3. NOT represent or imply by use of the title "Notary" that they have qualifications, powers, duties, rights or privileges that under law they do not possess;
4. NOT engage in the unauthorized practice of law;
5. NOT endorse or promote any product, service, contest or other offering if the Notary's title is used in the endorsement;
6. NOT refuse to notarize without some justifiable basis (NPH).

Conditions Invalidating Notarial Act

"Without excluding other conditions which may impair the validity of a notarial act, the following conditions invalidate the notarial act:

"(a) Failure of the notary public to require a person whose acknowledgment is taken to personally appear before him;

"(b) Failure of the notary public to administer an oath or affirmation when the notary certificate indicates that he has administered it;

"(c) As to only the notary public who performs the notarial act and any party who shares the same beneficial interest in the transaction, the existence of a disqualifying interest" (IC 51-117).

Disqualifying Interests

A Notary may notarize any signature but his or her own, as long as there is no conflict of interest (NPH).

A Notary may not notarize for a transaction in which the Notary is named as a party or shares the same beneficial interest as a party to the transaction (IC 51-108[3]). This does not apply to judicial proceedings. "Neither the notary public nor any party sharing the same beneficial interest as the notary public in the transaction may raise the issue of disqualifying interest in an attempt to invalidate the transaction. The issue of disqualifying interest may not be raised between parties neither of whom shares the same beneficial interest as the notary public."

One spouse may not notarize a deed affecting community property for the other spouse, nor may a partner notarize for another partner in a matter affecting the partnership (NPH).

"If a notary performs a notarial act despite having a disqualifying interest in the transaction, it does not automatically invalidate the transaction. However, it does make the transaction subject to attack by a party whose interest is adverse to that shared by the notary and the person for whom he or she performed the notarial act" (NPH).

Notary May Not Select Notarial Act

"There is a particular form of certificate for each type of notarial act, and a notary must know and use the proper form for the type of act he or she is requested to perform. It is not, however, the notary's function to determine what type of notarial act is required with regard to a request for 'notarization' of a document" (NPH).

Refusing to Notarize

"The Notary Public law does not address this question specifically, however, since you are a public servant it could be considered discrimination and therefore unconstitutional to refuse notarizing a document without some basis" (NPH).

NOTARY SIGNING AGENTS

Currently, there are no statutes, regulations or rules expressly governing, prohibiting or restricting the operation of Notary Signing Agents within the state of Idaho.

Secretary of State's Guidelines

The following four paragraphs express the Idaho Secretary of State's position on the operation of Notary Signing Agents within the State (website, "Frequently Asked Questions"):

"Notary signing agents are employed by private companies. They are not certified or commissioned by the State of Idaho beyond the normal notary application process. A notary signing agent has no special powers and must adhere to Idaho notary law in all transactions. It is illegal for a notary or a notary signing agent to give legal advice, explain legal documents or aid customers in completing legal or immigration forms. Idaho Code 51-110 states a Notary public may, for any notarial act, charge a fee not to exceed two dollars ($2.00). In addition to the fee, a notary public may be compensated for actual and reasonable expense of travel to a place where a notarial act is be performed.

"The Idaho Secretary of State's office urges notaries to exercise caution in considering signing agent or mobile notary offers. We recommend contacting the Department of Insurance and the Department of Finance before venturing into a business as a 'Mobile Notary' or 'Signing Agent' to ensure that you are not in violation of the Independent Escrow Act or Closing Agent licensing.

"If a bank or mortgage company wants to employ a notary to perform notary services, act as a 'signing agent' or 'mobile notary officer' and wants to pay more than the statutory rate, that is up to them. However, the fee a notary may charge for their services is set forth in state laws as described above. Neither the notary nor a third party charging notary fees as part of the services they provide should exceed the statutory fees in charging for notary services.

"Please be sure to explain the fees assessed to the customer as to what portion of the fee is for the notarial services."

NOTARY FEES

The maximum fee an Idaho Notary may charge for any notarial act is $2 (IC 51-110 and 51-112[e]). Notaries need not charge (NPH).

Travel Expense: "In addition to the fee, a notary public may be compensated for actual and reasonable expense of travel to a place where a notarial act is to be performed" (IC 51-110[2]).

Employer Cannot Take Fees: "An employer shall not require a notary public in his employment to surrender to him a fee, if charged, or any part thereof. An employer may, however, preclude such notary public from charging a fee for a notarial act performed in the scope of his employment" (IC 51-110[3]).

NOTARY CERTIFICATES

Certificates for notarial acts authorized by Idaho law must be substantially in the following forms:

Acknowledgment by Individual (IC 55-710):

State of Idaho, county of _____, ss.

On this _____ day of _____, in the year of 20__, before me _____ (here insert the name and quality of the notarizing officer), personally appeared _____, known or identified to me (or proved to me on the oath of _____), to be the person whose name is subscribed to the within instrument, and acknowledged to me that he/she/they executed the same.

*(NOTARY'S SIGNATURE AND SEAL)
My commission expires on _____, 20__.*

Acknowledgment by Individual Personally Known by Notary (NPH):

*State of Idaho   )
) ss.
County of _____)*

On this _____ day of _____, in the year of 20__, before me, _____, a Notary Public, personally appeared _____, personally known to me to be the person(s) whose name(s) is(are) subscribed to the within instrument, and acknowledged to me that he(she)(they) executed the same.

*(SEAL)   Notary Public
My commission expires on _____, 20__.*

Acknowledgment by Individual with Identity Proven by Credible Witness (NPH):

*State of Idaho   )
) ss.
County of _____)*

On this _____ day of _____, in the year of 20__, before me _____, personally appeared _____, and satisfactorily proved to me to be the signer of the above instrument by the oath of _____, a competent and credible witness for that purpose, by me duly sworn, and acknowledged to me that he (she) executed the same.

*(SEAL)   Notary Public
My commission expires on _____, 20__.*

Acknowledgment by Individual with Identity Proven by Satisfactory Evidence (NPH):

*State of Idaho   )
) ss.
County of _____)*

On this _____ day of _____, in the year of 20__, before me, _____, a Notary Public, personally appeared _____, proved to me on the basis of satisfactory evidence to be the person(s) whose name(s) is (are) subscribed to the within instrument, and acknowledged that he (she)(they) executed the same.

(SEAL)   Notary Public
My commission expires on _____, 20__.

Acknowledgment by Corporation (IC 55-711):

State of Idaho, county of _____, ss.

On this _____ day of _____, in the year of 20__, before me _____ (here insert the name and quality of the notarizing officer), personally appeared _____, known or identified to me (or proved to me on the oath of _____), to be the president, or vice-president, or secretary or assistant secretary, of the corporation that executed the instrument or the person who executed the instrument on behalf of said corporation, and acknowledged to me that such corporation executed the same.

(NOTARY'S SIGNATURE AND SEAL)
My commission expires on _____, 20__.

Acknowledgment by Limited Liability Company (IC 55-711A):

State of Idaho, county of _____, ss.

On this _____ day of _____, in the year of 20__, before me _____ (here insert name and quality of the notarizing officer), personally appeared _____, known or identified to me (or proved to me on the oath of _____), to be the manager or a member of the limited liability company that executed the instrument or the person who executed the instrument on behalf of said limited liability company and acknowledged to me that such limited liability company executed the same.

(NOTARY'S SIGNATURE AND SEAL)
My commission expires on _____, 20__.

Acknowledgment by Attorney in Fact (IC 55-712):

State of Idaho, county of _____, ss.

On this _____ day of _____, in the year of 20__, before me _____ (here insert the name and quality of the notarizing officer), personally appeared _____, known or identified to me (or proved to me on the oath of _____), to be the person whose name is subscribed to the within instrument as the attorney in fact of _____, and acknowledged to me that he/she subscribed the name of _____ thereto as principal, and his/her own name as attorney in fact.

(NOTARY'S SIGNATURE AND SEAL)
My commission expires on _____, 20__.

Acknowledgment by Official or Fiduciary (IC 55-713):

The certificate of acknowledgment for a trustee, executor, administrator, guardian, sheriff, receiver or other official representative must be substantially in the following form:

State of Idaho, county of _____, ss.

On this _____ day of _____, in the year of 20__, before me _____ (here insert the name and quality of the notarizing officer), personally appeared _____, known or identified to me (or proved to me on the oath of _____), to be the person whose name is subscribed to the within instrument as _____ (here insert the official or representative capacity in which the instrument is executed) and acknowledged to me that he/she/they executed the same as such _____ (here insert again the official or representative capacity in which the instrument is executed).

(NOTARY'S SIGNATURE AND SEAL)
My commission expires on _____, 20__.

Acknowledgment by Partnership (IC 55-714):

State of Idaho, county of _____, ss.

On this _____ day of _____, in the year of 20__, before me _____ (here insert the name and quality of the notarizing officer), personally appeared _____, known or identified to me (or proved to me on the oath of _____), to be one of the partners in the partnership of _____ (here insert partnership name signed to instrument), and the partner or one of the partners who subscribed said partnership name to the foregoing instrument, and acknowledged to me that he/she executed the same in said partnership name.

(NOTARY'S SIGNATURE AND SEAL)
My commission expires on _____, 20__.

Acknowledgment by Corporation as Partner in Partnership (IC 55-707A[4]):

State of Idaho   )
*   ) ss.*
County of _____)
   On this ____ day of _____, 20__, before me, _____, a notary public in and for said state, personally appeared _____ (name of signer), known or identified to me (or proved to me on the oath of _____) to be the _____ (signer's title) of _____ (name of corporation), a _____ (state in which incorporated) corporation, one of the partners in the partnership of _____ (name of partnership), a _____ (state in which partnership formed) partnership, and the partner or one of the partners who subscribed said partnership name to the foregoing instrument, and acknowledged to me that he executed the written instrument on behalf of said corporation, and that such corporation executed the same in said partnership name.

   IN WITNESS WHEREOF, I have hereunto set my hand and affixed my official seal the day and year in this certificate just above written.

   (NOTARY'S SIGNATURE AND SEAL)
   My commission expires on _____, 20__.

Acknowledgment by State or Political Subdivision (IC 55-715):

The certificate of acknowledgment for any document executed in the name of the State of Idaho or of any county, political subdivision or municipal, quasi-municipal or public corporation must be substantially in the following form:

State of Idaho, county of _____, ss.

   On this ____ day of _____, in the year of 20__, before me _____ (here insert the name and quality of the notarizing officer), personally appeared _____, known or identified to me (or proved to me on the oath of _____), to be the _____ (here insert the official capacity of the officer making the acknowledgment) of the _____ (here insert the name of state, county, subdivision or corporation executing the instrument) that executed the said instrument, and acknowledged to me that such _____ (here insert name of state, county, political subdivision, municipal or public corporation executing the instrument) executed the same.

   (NOTARY'S SIGNATURE AND SEAL)
   My commission expires on _____, 20__.

Acknowledgment by Signer by Mark (IC 55-712A):

X (Mark)

Mark affixed by _____ (printed or typewritten name of person signing by mark) in the presence of the undersigned Notary.

State of Idaho   )
*   ) ss.*
County of _____)

   On this ____ day of _____, in the year of 20__, before me, _____ (name and title of notarizing officer), personally appeared _____ (name of signer by mark), known or identified to me (or proved to me on the oath of _____) to be the person whose name is subscribed to the within instrument, and acknowledged to me that he/she executed the same by affixing his/her mark thereto.

   (NOTARY'S SIGNATURE AND SEAL)
   My commission expires on _____, 20__.

Acknowledgment by Person Physically Unable to Sign or Make Mark (IC 55-712B):

(SIGNATURE OF PERSON MADE BY NOTARY)

(SIGNATURE OF WITNESS)

Signature affixed by Notary in the presence of _____ (names of person and witness).

State of Idaho   )
*   ) ss.*
County of _____)

   On this ____ day of _____, in the year of 20__, before me, _____ (name and title of notarizing officer), personally appeared _____, known or identified to me (or proved to me on the oath of _____) to be the person whose name is subscribed to the within instrument, and acknowledged to me that he/she executed the same by directing the undersigned Notary to affix his/her signature thereto.

(NOTARY'S SIGNATURE AND SEAL)
My commission expires on _____, 20__.

Certificate to Witness and Verify Signing by Mark (IC 51-109[5]):

X (Mark)

Mark affixed by _____ (name of signer by mark) in the presence of the undersigned Notary, _____ (name of Notary).

State of Idaho   )
*   ) ss.*
County of _____)

I, _____, a Notary Public, do hereby certify that on this ____ day of _____, 20__, personally appeared before me, _____ (name of signer by mark), who, being by me first duly sworn, declared that he made his/her mark on the foregoing instrument, and that the statements therein contained are true.

(NOTARY'S SIGNATURE AND SEAL)
My commission expires on _____, 20__.

Certificate to Witness and Verify Signature Affixed by Notary for Person Physically Unable to Sign or Make Mark (IC 51-109[6]):

(SIGNATURE OF PERSON MADE BY NOTARY)

(SIGNATURE OF WITNESS)

Signature affixed by Notary in the presence of _____ (names of person and witness).

State of Idaho   )
*   ) ss.*
County of _____)

I, _____, a Notary Public, do hereby certify that on this ____ day of _____, 20__, personally appeared before me, _____ (name of person unable to sign or make mark), who, being by me first duly sworn, declared that he/she signed the foregoing instrument by directing the undersigned Notary to sign the instrument for him/her, and that the statements therein contained are true.

(NOTARY'S SIGNATURE AND SEAL)
My commission expires on _____, 20__.

Subscribing Witness Certificate

"An officer taking proof of the execution of any instrument must, in his certificate endorsed thereon or attached thereto, set forth all the matter required by law to be done or known by him, or proved before him on the proceeding, together with the names of all the witnesses examined before him, their places of residence respectively, and the substance of their testimony" (IC 55-723).

Verification by Corporation (IC 51-109[4]):

"A certificate of verification of an instrument shall follow the maker's signature and shall identify the notary public and certify that the maker personally appeared, was sworn, stated his authority for making the instrument, and averred the truth of the statements therein. For example, the verification of a corporate document by an officer of the corporation should be in substantially the following form:"

State of Idaho   )
*   ) ss.*
County of _____)

I, _____, a Notary Public, do hereby certify that on this ____ day of _____, 20__, personally appeared before me _____, who, being by me first duly sworn, declared that he/she is the _____ of _____, that he/she signed the foregoing document as _____ of the corporation, and that the statements therein contained are true.

(NOTARY'S SIGNATURE AND SEAL)
My commission expires on _____, 20__.

Idaho

Basic Jurat (IC 51-109[2]):

State of Idaho   )
*   ) ss.*
County of _____)

Subscribed and sworn (or affirmed) before me this ____ day of _____, 20__.

(NOTARY'S SIGNATURE AND SEAL)
My commission expires on _____, 20__.

Certified Copy (IC 51-109[7]):

State of Idaho   )
*   ) ss.*
County of _____)

I, _____, a Notary Public, do certify that on _____, 20__, I carefully compared the attached copy of _____ (describe document) with the original. It is a complete and true copy of the original document.

(NOTARY'S SIGNATURE AND SEAL)
My commission expires on _____, 20__.

Format of Certificate

"The notary may write or type the necessary certificate on the document. If there is no room at the bottom it can be put on the back of the document. If there is absolutely no room anywhere on the actual document to affix the notary certificate you may attach the certificate on a separate sheet of paper. This should only be done as a last resort" (NPH).

"The seal and signature of the notary without some sort of certificate are meaningless and of no value" (NPH).

ELECTRONIC NOTARIZATIONS

The state of Idaho has not yet adopted statutes or regulations expressly establishing rules, definitions and procedures for electronic notarization.

UETA Recognizes Notary's E-Signature

Effective July 1, 2000, Idaho adopted the Uniform Electronic Transactions Act (IC 28-50-101 through 28-50-120), including the following provision on notarization and acknowledgment, thereby recognizing the legal validity of electronic signatures used by Notaries:

"If a law requires a signature or record to be notarized, acknowledged, verified, or made under oath, the requirement is satisfied if the electronic signature of the person authorized to perform those acts, together with all other information required to be included by other applicable law, is attached to or logically associated with the signature or record" (IC 28-50-111).

URPERA Does Not Require Seal Image

In 2007, Idaho adopted the Uniform Real Property Electronic Recording Act, including the following provision (IC 31-2903[3]): "A requirement that a document or a signature associated with a document be notarized, acknowledged, verified, witnessed, or made under oath is satisfied if the electronic signature of the person authorized to perform that act, and all other information required to be included, is attached to or logically associated with the document or signature. A physical or electronic image of a stamp, impression or seal need not accompany an electronic signature."

NOTARY RECORDS

"One way of establishing evidence of the exercise of the required degree of care is to keep a journal of notarial acts. Although a journal is not required by law, it could be used to relieve a notary from personal liability in a case where his or her negligence is alleged as the cause of a loss" (NPH).

Minimum Recommended Entries

"The journal should include as a minimum the date of the notarial act, the name and signature of the person appearing before the notary and the type of act performed. It may also be useful to note the means of identification of the person who appeared and the type of document to which the notarial act pertained" (NPH).

Journal Is Property of Notary

"If you keep a journal it is the property of the notary" (website, "Frequently Asked Questions").

AUTHENTICATION OF NOTARIAL ACTS

Secretary of State

Authenticating certificates for Notaries, including apostilles, are issued only by the Idaho Secretary of State's office.

Fee: $10, for either a regular "authentication" or an apostille. Payable to "Secretary of State." Payment methods include cash, check, credit card, money order and cashier's check.

Regular Mail Address:
Office of Secretary of State
Notary Department
P.O. Box 83720
Boise, ID 83720-0080

Overnight Mail Address:
Office of Secretary of State
Notary Department
450 N. 4th St. (SE corner of 4th and State)
Boise, ID 83702

Telephone: 1-208-332-2810

Procedure: Mail or present in person the original notarized document(s), along with the appropriate fee. "School documents must be signed by a school official and notarized" (website, "Notaries, Apostilles and Authentication"). Indicate the name of the country to which the document will be sent. An "Apostille/Certificate of Authentication Request Form," downloadable from the website, may be used to transmit all needed information. Requests are processed daily. "While-you-wait" service is not always possible. The document and authentication certificate will be returned or forwarded to any requesting location by first-class mail. "If overnight service is required a pre-addressed, pre-paid airbill must be enclosed with the request" (website, "Notaries, Apostilles and Authentications").

COMMISSIONING AND ADMINISTRATION

The Idaho Secretary of State appoints, regulates and maintains records on the state's Notaries (IC 51-103).

Applying for Commission

Qualifications: An applicant for appointment as an Idaho Notary Public must (IC 51-104): (a) be at least 18 years old, (b) be a resident of or employed in the state of Idaho, (c) be able to read and write the English language and (d) not have been removed from office for misconduct nor convicted of a serious crime within the last 10 years. Lawful resident aliens may be appointed as Notaries (NPH).

No Course or Test: No course of instruction or examination is required to become a Notary Public in Idaho.

"You must read and understand the (Notary Public) Act, not just because the law requires it (which it does), but because you need the knowledge in order to perform your job as a notary" (NPH).

Application: Prior to submitting the application, the applicant must obtain — or already have — a rubber stamp seal, in addition to a $10,000 Notary bond. Employees of the State of Idaho who need a Notary commission to perform their duties must obtain both the application and the bond from the Bureau of Risk Management (IC 51-105[2]). A specimen of the seal must be affixed to the application. The applicant's signature and oath must be notarized on the application (IC 51-105[1]). The application fee is $30, but this fee is waived if the applicant is an officer or employee of a state, county, city or district government within Idaho and the Notary commission will be used in the scope of the applicant's employment.

Commission "renewal" applications may be submitted up to 90 days prior to expiration of the current commission.

Non-Residents: Non-residents of Idaho who are employed or doing business in the state may become Idaho Notaries (IC 51-104).

Online Search: The Idaho Secretary of State's "Notary Public Online Search" allows a search of the state's roster of Notaries by attributes of the Notary including commission number, bonding company, name, city and commission expiration date, at www.sos.idaho.gov/online/notary/notarySearch.jsp. Information provided includes the Notary's address, surety firm, commission expiration date and commission number.

Reports of all new commissions and renewals filed during a given month are also available online. Each report includes the notary's name, mailing address (if given) and commission starting and expiration dates.

Changes of Status

If Notary Changes Name or Residence: "Any notary public whose name or residence changes during his term of office shall within sixty (60) days after such change submit written notice thereof to the secretary of state" (IC 51-111[2]). This requires a $5 filing fee, but a written notice of a change of mailing address requires no fee (NPH). A special form to indicate these changes is available on the website. Name changes will require a new seal with a new name.

"(O)nce you have moved out of state you have 30 days to submit notice of resignation unless still employed in Idaho. 51-113(e) and 51-115(2) I.C." (NPH).

If the Secretary of State receives credible information that a Notary no longer resides in Idaho, a "notice of opportunity to rebut" must be sent to the Notary's last known address by certified return receipt mail; if no rebuttal is made within 45 days, the Notary's commission will be cancelled (IC 51-114[5]).

If Notary Resigns: Notaries may voluntarily resign by mailing or delivering a letter of resignation to the Secretary of State (IC 51-115[1]).

Any Notary who becomes ineligible to hold office must submit a letter of resignation within 30 days thereafter (IC 51-115[2]).

If a Notary becomes incompetent, the conservator or guardian must submit a letter of resignation on the Notary's behalf within 30 days thereafter (IC 51-115[3] and 51-113[d]).

If a Notary dies in office, a personal representative must mail or deliver notice to the Secretary of State within 30 days thereafter (IC 51-115[4]).

Notaries who are state employees and whose bond has been provided by the Bureau of Risk Management must resign their commissions upon termination of employment with the state (IC 51-113[g]).

If Bond Is Cancelled: Cancellation of the Notary's bond by the bonding or surety company or by the Bureau of Risk Management is cause for removal of the Notary from office by the Secretary of State (IC 51-113[f]). The company or Bureau must file a prompt written notice with the Secretary of State of any such cancellation (IC 51-114[6]).

Notaries whose bonds are cancelled by a private employer due to the Notary's departure from the company, thus cancelling the commission, may apply for a new commission (website, "Frequently Asked Questions").

COUNTY CLERKS

In the state of Idaho, county clerks have no involvement in the administration of the Notary Public program nor in the authentication of notarial acts.

OTHER NOTARIAL OFFICERS

Statewide Jurisdiction

Acknowledgments and proofs may be taken anywhere within the state by the following officers, besides Notaries Public (IC 55-701):
1. A justice or clerk of the state Supreme Court;
2. A U.S. commissioner;
3. The Secretary of State.

Limited Jurisdiction

Besides Notaries Public, the following officers may take acknowledgments and proofs within the city, county or district for which they were elected or appointed (IC 55-702):
1. A judge or a clerk of a court of record;
2. A county recorder;
3. A justice of the peace.

When any of the above officers are authorized by law to appoint a deputy, the acknowledgment or proof may be taken by the deputy as well (IC 55-706).

QUICK FACTS

Notary Jurisdiction

Statewide and outside the state for certain documents. "The powers of a notary public ... may be exercised outside the state only in connection with a deed or other writing to be admitted to record in the state of Idaho" (IC 51-107[2]).

Notary Term Length

Six years (IC 51-103[2]), expiring at midnight on the commission expiration date.

Notary Bond

$10,000, issued by a bonding or surety company authorized to do business in the state or, if the Notary is employed by the state and the commission is required for employment, by the state Bureau of Risk Management (IC 51-105[2]).

Employer May Be Jointly Liable: "The employer of a notary public shall be jointly and severally liable with such notary public for all damages proximately caused by the official misconduct of such notary public if: (a) The notary public was acting within the scope of his employment; and (b) The employer had actual knowledge of, or reasonably should have known of, the notary public's official misconduct" (IC 51-118[2]).

Illinois

NOTARY SEAL

An Illinois Notary must authenticate all official acts with a seal of office (5 ILCS 312/3-101[a] and 6-103[a]), and the seal's format must be as follows:

Kind

Black-Inked Rubber Stamp: At the time of each notarial act, "a notary public shall officially sign every notary certificate and affix the rubber stamp seal clearly and legibly using black ink, so that it is capable of photographic reproduction" (5 ILCS 312/3-101[b] and 3-102[l]).

Shape/Size

Rectangular: Not more than 1 inch high by $2^{1}/_{2}$ inches long, surrounding the components (5 ILCS 312/3-101[a][4]).

Border

A "serrated or milled edge border" (5 ILCS 312/3-101[a][4]).

Components

1. "Official Seal";
2. Notary's commissioned name;
3. "Notary Public";
4. "State of Illinois";
5. "My commission expires _____".

"The Illinois Notary Public Act requires that the expiration date be imprinted on the seal. This date may not be handwritten" (NPH).

Illegibility

"The illegibility of any of the information required by this Section does not affect the validity of a transaction" (5 ILCS 312/3-101[b] and 3-102[l]).

Seal May Not Overprint Signature

"Do not imprint your seal over your signature in a notarization. All information must be legible" (NPH).

NOTARY ADMINISTRATION

Office of Secretary of State
Index Department
Notary Public Division   1-217-782-7017
111 East Monroe Street
Springfield, IL 62756

Website: www.cyberdriveillinois.com/
departments/index/notary/
home.html

NOTARY RULES

ILCS — ILLINOIS COMPILED STATUTES
NPH — ILLINOIS NOTARY PUBLIC HANDBOOK

Most Notary rules are in the Illinois Compiled Statutes, including:

a. "The Illinois Notary Public Act," Chapter 5, Sections 312/1-101 through 7-109;

b. "Uniform Recognition of Acknowledgments Act,"* Chapter 765, Sections 30/1 through 10.

* This is the *Uniform Recognition of Acknowledgments Act* of 1968, adopted virtually intact.

Other guidelines for Notaries are in the "Illinois Notary Public Handbook" (December 2010), issued by the Secretary of State and available on the website.

OFFICIAL SEAL
JANE Q. DOE
Notary Public – State of Illinois
My Commission Expires Jan 30, 2015

Example

The above typical, actual-size example of a Notary seal is allowed by law. Formats other than this may also be permitted.

Seal to Be Destroyed or Defaced

When the Notary's commission terminates through revocation, resignation or death, "(t)he Notary, or the Notary's heirs, should destroy or deface the seal so that it may not be misused" (NPH).

Wrongful Possession of Seal

"Any person who unlawfully possesses a notary's official seal is guilty of a misdemeanor and punishable upon conviction by a fine not exceeding $1,000" (5 ILCS 312/7-107).

"Can my employer keep my seal and (commission) certificate if I leave the company? — No. The seal and certificate are considered the property of the notary public. Also, if you lose possession of your seal, it is recommended that you resign your commission" (NPH).

"What should I do if my notary seal is stolen? — Report the theft to the police. If for any reason you lose possession of your seal, it is recommended that you resign your commission" (NPH).

Notary Signature

At the time of each notarial act, "a notary public shall officially sign every notary certificate …" (5 ILCS/3-101[b] and 3-102[l]).

"A notary public shall not use any name or initial in signing certificates other than that by which the notary was commissioned" (5 ILCS 312/6-104[a]).

"Sign your name on notarial certificates exactly as it appears on your commission …" (NPH).

"If a notary is commissioned as JOHN M. DOE …, he must sign his name that way. Signing as J. M. Doe or using any other variation is not acceptable" (NPH).

Facsimile Signatures Forbidden: "Notaries may not use facsimile signature stamps in signing their official certificates. A signature must be written in ink as commissioned. In addition, a facsimile signature may not be notarized" (NPH).

NOTARY POWERS

Illinois Notaries are authorized to perform the following notarial acts (5 ILCS 312/6-101[a] and 6-102[a] through [c] and 765 ILCS 30/2):

1. Take acknowledgments* and proofs;
2. Administer oaths and affirmations;
3. Take verifications upon oath or affirmation**;
4. Witness or attest signatures***.

* Acknowledgments: "'Acknowledgment' means a declaration by a person that the person has executed an instrument for the purposes stated therein and, if the instrument is executed in a representative capacity, that the person signed the instrument with proper authority and executed it as the act of the person or entity represented and identified therein" (5 ILCS 312/6-101[b]).

"The person taking an acknowledgment shall certify that:

"(1) The person acknowledging appeared before him (or her) and acknowledged he (or she) executed the instrument; and

"(2) The person acknowledging was known to the person taking the acknowledgment, or … the person taking the acknowledgment had satisfactory evidence that the person acknowledging was the person described in and who executed the instrument" (765 ILCS 30/4).

"The taking of an acknowledgment consists of positively identifying the signer of a document. The signer need not sign in the notary's presence but must personally appear before the notary and state that the signature on the document is his or hers. Acknowledgments may be taken in an individual capacity or in a representative capacity …" (NPH).

** Verifications upon Oath or Affirmation: "'Verification upon oath or affirmation' means a declaration that a statement is true made by a person under oath or affirmation" (5 ILCS 312/6-101[c]).

"The verification upon oath or affirmation is a declaration that a statement is true and was made by a person upon oath or affirmation. The person requesting this notarial act must personally appear before the notary and sign the document in the presence of the notary. There is no prescribed wording for the oath, but an acceptable oath would be: 'Do you swear (or affirm) that the statements in this document are true.

"Verification upon oath may be taken in an individual capacity or in a representative capacity" (NPH).

*** Witness or Attest Signatures: "(W)hen witnessing a signature on a document … an oath is not necessary or required. The person requesting the notarial act must personally appear before the notary and sign the document in the presence of the notary" (NPH).

Transcribing Affidavits and Depositions

While Illinois Notaries have statutory authority to "take affidavits and depositions" (5 ILCS 255/2), this function of transcribing spoken words into written is most often performed today by certified shorthand reporters. Notaries may, however, execute a verification upon oath or affirmation on an affidavit or deposition that has already been transcribed. For further information, see "Officers for Oaths, Affidavits, Depositions" below, under "Other Notarial Officers."

Identifying Document Signers

The following identification requirements apply to acknowledgments, to verifications upon oath or affirmation and to witnessing or attesting signatures:

"(T)he notary public must determine, either from personal knowledge or from satisfactory evidence," that the person appearing before the Notary is the person whose true signature is on the document (5 ILCS 312/6-102[a] through [c]).

"A notary public has satisfactory evidence that a person is the person whose true signature is on a document if that person: (1) is personally known to the notary; (2) is identified upon the oath or affirmation of a credible witness personally known to the notary; or (3) is identified on the basis of identification documents. Until July 1, 2013, identification documents are documents that are valid at the time of the notarial act, issued by a state agency, federal government agency, or consulate, and bearing the photographic image of the individual's face and signature of the individual" (5 ILCS 312/6-102[d]).

NOTE: On July 1, 2013, unless further action is taken by the Illinois General Assembly, the above provision (describing the required attributes of an acceptable ID document) will terminate, along with other provisions of a four-year pilot program in effect from June 1, 2009, through June 30, 2013 — see "Pilot Program for Cook County Conveyances" below.

'Vancura' Case Reversal by High Court

In the widely publicized case of *Vancura v. Katris*, the Illinois Supreme Court ruled on October 7, 2010, that employers of Notaries do not have a common law duty, going beyond statutory requirements, to train and supervise their Notary employees, thus reversing an Illinois Appellate Court decision of December 2008. The Appellate Court had held the owner of a Chicago photocopy shop liable in part for an employee's notarization of a forged signature.

The Illinois Supreme Court ruled that the "burdens and liabilities on a notary public ... are personal to the notary, rather than shared with his or her employer. Thus ... when a notary public wrongfully or negligently exercises the powers of the office, it is the notary alone who becomes liable.... (T)he employer is liable only if the employer 'consented to' the misconduct of the notary; that is, if the employer committed some malfeasance of its own" (*Vancura v. Katris*, 2010 IL 108652).

Conveyances Must Be Notarized

Effective January 1, 2007, with enactment of Illinois House Bill 4760 (Chapter 94-821), "(w)henever any deed or instrument of conveyance or other instrument to be made a matter of record is executed, the signatures of the parties making the conveyance shall be acknowledged (sic) by a notary public appointed and commissioned by the Secretary of State or by one of the courts or officers designated in Section 20 of this Act. Failure to comply with this provision shall not invalidate the instrument" (765 ILCS 5/35c).

Pilot Program for Cook County Conveyances

A four-year pilot program imposes special duties on Illinois Notaries who notarize "Documents of Conveyance" for "Residential Real Property" in Cook County (5 ILCS 312/3-102). Established in 2008 by Public Act 988, this anti-fraud program is in effect from June 1, 2009, through June 30, 2013.

Document of Conveyance means "a written instrument that transfers or purports to transfer title effecting a change in ownership to Residential Real Property," but it excludes: (a) court-ordered conveyances such as quitclaim deeds executed pursuant to a divorce settlement or transfers in the administration of a probate estate; (b) judicial sale deeds, such as those that foreclose a mortgage or enforce a judgment; (c) deeds transferring ownership to a trust, where the beneficiary is also the grantor; (d) deeds from grantors to themselves to change the nature or type of their tenancy; (e) deeds from a grantor to the grantor and another person in order to establish a joint tenancy; (f) deeds executed to the mortgagee in lieu of foreclosure of a mortgage; and (g) deeds transferring ownership to a grantor trust where the beneficiary includes the grantor (5 ILCS 312/3-102[b][1]).

Residential Real Property is defined as "a building or buildings located in Cook County, Illinois, and containing one to 4 dwelling units or an individual residential condominium unit" (5 ILCS 312/3-102[b][4]).

Notarial Record Created by Notary: A "Notarial Record" must be created by the Notary for each person whose signature is notarized in connection with a Document of Conveyance. This Notarial Record must contain (5 ILCS 312/3-102[c]):
  1. The date of the notarial act;
  2. The type, title or a description of the Document of Conveyance, the Property Index Number (PIN) and the street address of the property;
  3. The signature, printed name and residence street address of each person whose signature is notarized and a certification by each person stating, "The undersigned grantor hereby certifies that the real property identified in this Notarial Record is Residential Real Property as defined in the Illinois Notary Public Act";
  4. A description of the satisfactory evidence of identity relied on by the Notary to identify the signer(s);
  5. The fee charged for the notarization; the Notary's home or business phone number, residence street address and commission expiration date; and the name and street address of the Notary's employer or principal;
  6. The right thumbprint of the signer or agent in a physical or electronic medium, or, if that print is not available, the left thumbprint or the print of any other available finger.

Obtaining a Thumbprint: "The notary public shall require the person signing the Document of Conveyance (including an agent acting on behalf of a principal under a duly executed power of attorney), whose signature is the subject of the notarial act, to place his or her right thumbprint on the Notarial Record. If the right thumbprint is not available, then the notary shall have the party use his or her left thumb, or any available finger, and shall so indicate on the Notarial Record. If the party signing the document is physically unable to provide a thumbprint or fingerprint, the notary shall so indicate on the Notarial Record and shall also provide an explanation of that physical condition. The notary may obtain the thumbprint by any means that reliably captures the image of the finger in a physical or electronic medium" (5 ILCS 312/3-102[c][6]).

Disposition of Notarial Record: "If a notarial act under this Section is performed by a notary who is a principal, employee, or agent of a Title Insurance Company, Title Insurance Agent, Financial Institution, or attorney at law, the notary shall deliver the original Notarial Record to the notary's employer or principal within 14 days after the performance of the notarial act for retention for a period of 7 years as part of the employer's or principal's business records. In the event of a sale or merger of any of the foregoing entities or persons, the successor or assignee of the entity or person shall assume the responsibility to maintain the Notarial Record for the balance of the 7-year business records retention period. Liquidation or other cessation of activities in the ordinary course of business by any of the foregoing entities or persons shall relieve the entity or person from the obligation to maintain Notarial Records after delivery of Notarial Records to the Recorder of Deeds of Cook County, Illinois" (5 ILCS 312/3-102[d]). "Financial Institution" is defined as an Illinois or federally chartered bank, savings and loan association, savings bank, credit union or trust company (5 ILCS 312/3-102[b][2]).

"If a notarial act is performed by a notary who is not a principal, employee, or agent of a Title Insurance Company, Title Insurance Agent, Financial Institution, or attorney at law, the notary shall deliver the original Notarial Record within 14 days after the performance of the notarial act to the Recorder of Deeds of Cook County, Illinois for retention for a period of 7 years, accompanied by a filing fee of $5 (5 ILCS 312/3-102[e]).

"No copies of the original Notarial Record may be made or retained by the Notary. The Notary's employer or principal may retain copies of the Notarial Records as part of its business records, subject to applicable privacy and confidentiality standards" (5 ILCS 312/3-102[g]).

"The Notarial Records or other medium containing the thumbprint or fingerprint required by subsection (c)(6) shall be made available or disclosed only upon receipt of a subpoena duly authorized by a court of competent jurisdiction. Such Notarial Record or other medium shall not be subject to disclosure under the Freedom of Information Act and shall not be made available to any other party, other than a party in succession of interest to the party maintaining the Notarial Record or other medium pursuant to subsection (d) or (e)" (5 ILCS 312/3-102[i]).

Fee of Notary: Until July 1, 2013, an Illinois Notary may charge up to $25 for any notarial act performed pursuant to Section 3-102 (5 ILCS 312/3-104[a]).

Applicability of Pilot Program: "As a notary outside Cook County, am I affected by the new law? — The law affects all notaries in Illinois who notarize a document of conveyance of residential property located in Cook County" (NPH).

"Do I have to participate in the pilot project and notarize conveyances of real property located in Cook County? — No. The law does not require that. You may, however, want to discuss company policy with your employer" (NPH).

Notarial Record Sample Form: At the end of this chapter, see the Notarial Record form (5 ILCS 312/3-102[f]) recommended by the office of the Illinois Secretary of State on its website ("Publications & Forms"). This form is based on the Notarial Record form developed by the National Notary Association with input from the Cook County Recorder of Deeds.

NOTARY DON'TS

Illinois Notaries may:
1. NOT affix a signature to a blank affidavit or acknowledgment certificate and deliver that form for use by another person (5 ILCS 312/6-104[c]) or notarize any blank or incomplete document (NPH);
2. NOT notarize for a person known by the Notary to have been adjudged mentally ill unless the person has been restored to mental health as a matter of record (5 ILCS 312/6-104[d]);
3. NOT take the acknowledgment of a blind person unless the Notary has read the document to the person (5 ILCS 312/6-104[e]);
4. NOT take the acknowledgment of anyone who does not speak or understand English unless the nature and effect of the instrument to be notarized is translated into a language which the person does understand (5 ILCS 312/6-104[f]);
5. NOT change anything in a document after it has been signed (5 ILCS 312/6-104[g]);
6. NOT, as a non-attorney, fill in the blanks on a document, other than the notarial certificate, or assist anyone in preparing a document (5 ILCS 312/6-104[h]);
7. NOT fail to transmit or forward funds taken from a person for whom a notarization is performed for the express purpose of transmitting or forwarding such money, upon penalty of personal liability for any loss sustained because of such failure (5 ILCS 312/6-104[i]);
8. NOT notarize a stamped facsimile signature (NPH);
9. NOT certify copies of documents or signatures (website, "Certifying Official Documents for Foreign Use").

Immigration Restrictions for Notaries

No non-attorney Notary may act or represent him- or herself as an immigration expert unless the Notary is a "designated entity" as defined in the Code of Federal Regulations (8 CFR 245a.1) or is accredited by the Board of Immigration Appeals as an "accredited immigration representative" (5 ILCS 312/3-103[c]). "According to federal law, no person, unless an attorney, shall fill out legalization forms or applications related to the Immigration Reform and Control Act of 1986 unless he or she has been authorized to do so by the (USCIS) or the Board of Immigration Appeals" (NPH).

Any non-attorney Notary who is not an accredited immigration representative and who advertises notarial services in a language other than English must place the following notice in all advertising materials (with the exception of a single desk plaque), in both English and the other language(s): "I AM NOT AN ATTORNEY LICENSED TO PRACTICE LAW IN ILLINOIS AND MAY NOT GIVE LEGAL ADVICE OR ACCEPT FEES FOR LEGAL ADVICE." Additionally, in no ad or other communication or document may the Notary "literally translate from English into another language terms or titles including, but not limited to, notary public, licensed, attorney, lawyer, or any other term that implies the person is an attorney. To illustrate, the word 'notario' is prohibited under this provision" (5 ILCS 312/103[a]). In addition to the notice prescribed above, all non-attorney or unaccredited Notaries who advertise in a language other than English must prominently post in their places of business a schedule of notarial fees in both English and the other language(s) (5 ILCS 312/3-103[b]).

No Notary who is not an attorney or an accredited immigration representative may accept payment for providing legal advice, analysis or interpretation. A violation of this provision may impose a fine of three times the amount collected ($1,001 minimum) and does not prevent further civil remedies or criminal charges (5 ILCS 312/3-103[e] and [f]).

Secretary's Basic Rules of Notarization

In his introductory letter in the "Illinois Notary Public Handbook," Secretary of State Jesse White prescribes the following "basic rules for proper and safe notarization: 1) Keep your notary seal in a safe place; 2) Do not notarize a signature unless the signer is present at the time of notarization; 3) Do not lend your stamp to anyone, including your employer; 4) Do not identify a document signer on the word of a friend or employer who is not willing to take an oath; 5) Sign your name on notarial certificates exactly as it appears on your commission and affix your seal."

Notary Disqualifications

"A notary public shall not acknowledge [sic] any instrument in which the notary's name appears as a party to the transaction" (5 ILCS 312/6-104[b]). "A notary public may not notarize his or her own signature and may not notarize any document in which the notary's name appears as a party to the transaction," even if the Notary is signing on behalf of a corporation (NPH).

Notarizing for Relatives: According to the "Illinois Notary Public Handbook," a Notary may notarize the signature of his or her spouse, children, and other relatives.

Notarizing Powers of Attorney: Effective July 1, 2011, signatures on powers of attorney for property must be both witnessed and notarized. An Illinois Notary who notarizes a signature on a power of attorney for property may not simultaneously serve in the capacity of witness to the signature. Further, a Notary may not notarize a signature on a power of attorney for property if that Notary is:

"(1) the attending physician or mental health service provider of the principal, or a relative of the physician or provider;

"(2) an owner, operator, or relative of an owner or operator of a health care facility in which the principal is a patient or resident;

"(3) a parent, sibling, or descendant, or the spouse of a parent, sibling, or descendant, of either the principal or any agent or successor agent, regardless of whether the relationship is by blood, marriage, or adoption;

"(4) an agent or successor agent for property" (755 ILCS 45/3 3.6).

NOTARY SIGNING AGENTS

With the enactment of Illinois Senate Bill 2718 (215 ILCS 155), effective June 20, 2006, Notary Signing Agents no longer have to operate "under the radar" in the state of Illinois. Their activities — once a matter of debatable legality — became clearly sanctioned by statute.

Formerly, Illinois Notary Signing Agents were limited to performing loan closings for lenders who handled the entire transaction without the assistance of a title company. Otherwise, they were required to become "independent escrowees" and to maintain expensive insurance, bonding and securities in order to act at closings for title companies. With the enactment of SB 2718, Illinois Signing Agents are now considered lawful escrow agents who can perform closings when hired as independent contractors by a title insurance firm or agent.

Independent Contractors May Be at Closings

"'Escrow Agent' means any title insurance company or any title insurance agent, including independent contractors of either, acting on behalf of a title insurance company which receives deposits, in trust, of funds or documents, or both, for the purpose of effecting the sale, transfer, encumbrance or lease of real property to be held by such escrow agent until title to the real property that is the subject of the escrow is in a prescribed condition" (215 ILCS 155/3[8]).

"'Independent Escrowee' means any firm, person, partnership, association, corporation or other legal entity, other than a title insurance company or a title insurance agent, which receives deposits, in trust, of funds or documents, or both, for the purpose of effecting the sale, transfer, encumbrance or lease of real property to be held by such escrowee until title to the real property that is the subject of the escrow is in a prescribed condition.... 'Independent Escrowee' does not include employees or independent contractors of a title insurance company or title insurance agent authorized by a title insurance company to perform closing, escrow, or settlement services" (215 ILCS 155/3[9]).

NOTARY FEES

The maximum fee that may be charged by an Illinois Notary for any notarial act is $1, "and, until July 1, 2013, up to $25 for any notarial act performed pursuant to Section 3-102" (5 ILCS 312/3-104[a]) — see "Pilot Program for Cook County Conveyances" above, under "Notary Powers."

A Notary is not required to charge a fee (NPH).

Immigration Services Fees

Fees for a Notary, agency or any other person who is not an attorney but who is an "accredited representative" filling out immigration forms are limited to the following (5 ILCS 312/3-104[b]):

1. $10 per form completion;
2. $10 per page for the translation of another language into English when such a translation is required for immigration forms;
3. $1 for notarizing;
4. $3 to execute any procedures necessary to obtain a document required to complete immigration forms;
5. A maximum of $75 for any one complete application.

The above fees do not include application fees for submission of immigration forms. Violation of these fees is regarded as a Class A misdemeanor for the first offense and a Class 3 felony for a second or subsequent offense committed within five years (5 ILCS 312/3-104[b]).

Fee Schedule with Non-English Ads: Notaries who are neither attorneys nor accredited immigration representatives who advertise in a language other than English must prominently post in their places of business a schedule of notarial fees in both English and the other language(s) (5 ILCS 312/3-103[b]).

Fees Prohibited for Legal Services: "No notary public who is not an attorney or an accredited representative shall accept payment in exchange for providing legal advice or any other assistance that requires legal analysis, legal judgment, or interpretation of the law" (5 ILCS 312/3-103[e]).

"'Accredited immigration representative' means a not-for-profit organization recognized by the Board of Immigration Appeals under 8 C.F.R. 292.2(a) and employees of those organizations accredited under 8 C.F.R. 292.2(d)" (5 ILCS 312/1-104[c]).

Notary Must Keep Records, Provide Receipts

"All notaries public must provide receipts and keep records for fees accepted for services provided. Failure to provide receipts and keep records that can be presented as evidence of no wrongdoing shall be construed as a presumptive admission of allegations raised in complaints against the notary for violations related to accepting prohibited fees" (5 ILCS 312/3-104[d]).

NOTARY CERTIFICATES

Illinois has adopted the *Uniform Recognition of Acknowledgments Act*, including the short-form certificates for (765 ILCS 30/7):

1. Acknowledgment by individual;
2. Acknowledgment by corporation;
3. Acknowledgment by partnership;
4. Acknowledgment by attorney in fact;
5. Acknowledgment by any public officer, trustee or personal representative.

For the text of the certificates see "Uniform Recognition of Acknowledgments Act (1968)," Section 6, in Appendix 3.

Under Illinois law, the Notary's seal must be affixed to the above certificates (5 ILCS 312/3-101[a] and 6-103[a]).

In addition, the following statutory certificates are also acceptable for notarial acts authorized by Illinois law. The short forms are based substantially on forms in 1982's *Uniform Law on Notarial Acts*:

Short Form Acknowledgment by Individual (5 ILCS 312/6-105[a]):

State of Illinois
County of _____

This instrument was acknowledged before me on _____ *(date) by* _____ *(name/s of person/s).*

(SIGNATURE AND SEAL OF NOTARY)

Short Form Acknowledgment by Representative (5 ILCS 312/6-105[b]):

State of Illinois
County of _____

This instrument was acknowledged before me on _____ (date) by _____ (name/s of person/s) as _____ (type of authority, e.g., officer, trustee, etc.) of _____ (name of party on behalf of whom instrument was executed).

(SIGNATURE AND SEAL OF NOTARY)

Short Form Verification upon Oath or Affirmation by Individual (5 ILCS 312/6-105[c]):

State of Illinois
County of _____

Signed and sworn (or affirmed) to before me on _____ (date) by _____ (name/s of person/s making statement).

(SIGNATURE AND SEAL OF NOTARY)

Short Form for Witnessing or Attesting Signature (5 ILCS 312/6-105[d]):

State of Illinois
County of _____

Signed or attested before me on _____ (date) by _____ (name/s of person/s).

(SIGNATURE AND SEAL OF NOTARY)

Short Form Verification upon Oath or Affirmation by Representative (NPH):

State of Illinois
County of _____

Signed and sworn (or affirmed) to before me on _____ (date) by _____ (name of person) as _____ (type of authority, e.g., officer, trustee, etc.) of _____ (name of party on behalf of whom instrument was executed).

(SIGNATURE AND SEAL OF NOTARY)

Acknowledgment of Signer by Mark (NPH):

"(W)hen an individual requests a notarial act and the individual is prevented by disability or illiteracy from writing a signature ... (t)ake these precautions: positively identify the individual; ensure that there are two persons to witness the signature-by-mark in addition to yourself (the Notary); write in the name of the signer-by-mark near the mark on the document, and complete this form" (NPH):

State of Illinois
County of _____

This instrument was acknowledged before me on _____ (date) by _____ (name of person), who made and acknowledged making his/her mark on the instrument in my presence and in the presence of two persons who have signed below.

(SIGNATURE AND SEAL OF NOTARY)

_____ (signature and address of witness)
_____ (signature and address of witness)

Format of Notarial Certificate

"(a) A notarial act must be evidenced by a certificate signed and dated by the notary public. The certificate must include identification of the jurisdiction in which the notarial act is performed and the official seal of office.

"(b) A certificate of a notarial act is sufficient if it meets the requirements of subsection (a) and it:

"(1) is in the short form set forth in Section 206-105;

"(2) is in a form otherwise prescribed by the law of this State; or

"(3) sets forth the actions of the notary public and those are sufficient to meet the requirements of the designated notarial act" (5 ILCS 312/6-103).

<u>Format of Acknowledgment Certificate</u>: "The form of a certificate of acknowledgment ... shall be accepted in this State if:

"(1) The certificate is in a form prescribed by the laws or regulations of this State;

"(2) The certificate is in a form prescribed by the laws or regulations applicable in the place in which the acknowledgment is taken; or

"(3) The certificate contains the words 'acknowledged before me,' or their substantial equivalent" (765 ILCS 30/5).

ELECTRONIC NOTARIZATIONS

The state of Illinois has not yet adopted statutes or regulations expressly authorizing rules, definitions, and procedures for electronic notarization.

Seal Image Not Required

In 2007, Illinois enacted the Uniform Real Property Electronic Recording Act (765 ILCS 33/1 through 33/7), which establishes a 15-member commission to set standards for electronic recording in the state. The law also stipulates: "A requirement that a document or a signature associated with a document be notarized, acknowledged, verified, witnessed, or made under oath is satisfied if the electronic signature of the person authorized to perform that act, and all other information required to be included, is attached to or logically associated with the document or signature. A physical or electronic image of a stamp, impression, or seal need not accompany an electronic signature" (765 ILCS 33/3[c]).

NOTARY RECORDS

"There is no requirement in Illinois that a notary public keep a log book or journal. However, a notary may keep a journal for his or her own record keeping" (NPH).

Must Keep Record of Fees

Statute does require Illinois Notaries to keep a record of the fees they charge for notarial services provided: "Failure to ... keep records that can be presented as evidence of no wrongdoing shall be construed as a presumptive admission of allegations raised in complaints against the notary for violations related to accepting prohibited fees" (5 ILCS 312/3-104[d]).

'Notarial Record' for Cook County Conveyances

Under a four-year pilot program in effect from June 1, 2009, through June 30, 2013, Illinois Notaries must create — but not keep — a separate "Notarial Record," which includes a thumbprint, each time a notarization is performed on certain conveyances for residential real property in Cook County. Depending on the circumstances, each Notarial Record must then be surrendered to the Notary's employer or to the Cook County Recorder of Deeds — see "Pilot Program for Cook County Conveyances" above, under "Notary Powers."

AUTHENTICATION OF NOTARIAL ACTS

County Clerks

Locally, an authenticating certificate ("certificate of authority") for an Illinois Notary may be obtained for a fee of $2 at the office of the county clerk where the Notary's appointment has been recorded (5 ILCS 312/3-106). The county clerk keeps a record of the Notary's appointment and of the time the appointment expires (5 ILCS 312/2-106).

Secretary of State

Certificates of authority for Notaries, including apostilles, are also issued by the Illinois Secretary of State's office (5 ILCS 312/3-106), as are authenticating certificates ("certificates of incumbency") for county clerks, circuit clerks and local registrars (website, "Certifying Official Documents for Foreign Use").

Fees: $2 per document, including an apostille, payable to "Secretary of State" (5 ILCS 312/3-106).

Springfield Address:
Office of Secretary of State
Index Department
Notary Public Division
111 East Monroe Street
Springfield, IL 62756

Telephone: 1-217-782-7017

Chicago Address:
Office of Secretary of State
Index Department
17 N. State St., Rm. 1030
Chicago, IL 60602

Telephone: 1-312-814-2067

Procedure: Mail to the Springfield office or present in person at either office the original notarized document(s), along with the appropriate fee. If submitting the document(s) by mail, include a written request indicating the country to which the document will be sent. Also include an addressed, stamped return envelope, which may be addressed to a third party. Prepaid Express Mail, Priority Mail, Federal Express, UPS or Airborne Express envelopes also are accepted. Normal processing time for a document mailed to the Springfield office is five to seven business days. (On the Secretary of State's "Notary Services" web page, click "Download Notary Public Forms," then "Certifying Official Documents for Foreign Use.")

COMMISSIONING AND ADMINISTRATION

The Illinois Secretary of State appoints, commissions, and maintains records on the state's Notaries, through the Secretary's Index Department (5 ILCS 312/2-101 and website, "Notary Public Application Checklist").

"Notary public applications and appointments are public records and available to any interested person for examination or copying" (NPH).

Applying for Commission

Qualifications: An applicant for appointment as an Illinois Notary must: (a) be a U.S. citizen or an alien lawfully admitted for permanent residence, (b) be an Illinois resident for at least 30 days or a resident of a qualifying bordering state who has been employed in Illinois for at least 30 days, (c) be at least 18 years old, (d) be able to read and write English, (e) have not ever been convicted of a felony and (f) have not had a Notary commission revoked or suspended in the past 10 years (5 ILCS 312/2-102[d] through [i]).

No Course or Test: There is no requirement that applicants take a course of instruction or an examination on their duties.

Application: "Every applicant for appointment and commission as a notary shall complete an application form furnished by the Secretary of State to be filed with the Secretary of State" (5 ILCS 312/2-102). Application forms may be downloaded from the website.

The required $5,000 bond must accompany the application (5 ILCS 312/2-105), and the signature of an authorized representative and the corporate seal of the surety company must be affixed on the bond (website, "Notary Public Application Checklist"). "The Secretary of State determines the effective date of your commission, not the bonding company.... Notify your bonding company of the effective date of your commission after you have registered with the county clerk. The bond will expire when your commission does" (NPH). The applicant's signature on the "Notarial Oath" on the application must be notarized (5 ILCS 312/2-104). The application must be accompanied by a legible copy of the applicant's driver's license or state ID card (website, "Notary Public Application Checklist"), as well as the commissioning fee of $10, payable to "Secretary of State" (5 ILCS 312/2-103).

For renewals, the application process is the same (5 ILCS 312/5-101). Applications submitted more than six months before commission expiration will not be accepted (NPH).

Filing after Commissioning: The Secretary of State forwards a newly appointed Notary's commission to the clerk of the county in which the Notary resides or is employed. The county clerk notifies the Notary to appear within 30 days to receive and record the commission. The Notary may satisfy this requirement in person or by mail, If done in person, the fee to the county clerk is $5; if done by mail, $10. If the applicant fails to appear within 60 days, the commission will be returned to the Secretary of State and then cancelled. The county clerk will keep a record of the Notary's appointment and its date of expiration (5 ILCS 312/2-106).

Non-Residents: Residents of states bordering Illinois may be commissioned as Illinois Notaries for a one-year term if they have had a place of work or business in the state for at least 30 days preceding their application, but only if the laws of the bordering state they reside in permit Illinois residents to become Notaries in that state (5 ILCS 312/2-101). Currently, the bordering states of Iowa, Kentucky, Missouri and Wisconsin offer such reciprocation, but the state of Indiana does not. A special non-resident application packet must be used (website, "Non-Resident Notary Public Application Checklist").

Online Search: The "Notary Public Search" index was created to assist in verifying current or past Notary commissions. The index may be searched by the Notary's name, commission number, city or zip code. Information available on listed Notaries includes: city and zip code, county, employer (if any), commission number, current and original commission starting date, length of term and information regarding the Notary's bond (website, "Notary Public Search").

Changes of Status

<u>If Notary Changes Name or Moves</u>: "When any notary public legally changes his or her name or moves from the county in which he or she was commissioned or, if the notary public is a resident of a state bordering Illinois, no longer maintains a principal place of work or principal place of business in the same county in Illinois in which he or she was commissioned, the commission ceases to be in effect and should be returned to the Secretary of State. These individuals who desire to again become a notary public must file a new application, bond, and oath with the Secretary of State" (5 ILCS 312/4-101).

<u>If Notary Moves Out of County</u>: "If you move out of the county (from which you were appointed), or if you are a non-resident notary who changes employment to another county, you must resign your commission…. You can then apply for a new appointment" (NPH).

<u>If Notary Moves Within County</u>: "If you move or change employers and your new residence or place of employment is within the boundaries of the county from which you were appointed, you merely report the change of address to the Secretary of State" (NPH). A card is provided for this purpose in the back of the "Illinois Notary Public Handbook."

COUNTY CLERKS

To contact an Illinois county clerk to obtain an authenticating certificate for a Notary, or to seek assistance in locating a given Notary, telephone long-distance information — 1-XXX-555-1212 — using the following area codes. More information pertaining to Illinois county clerks may be accessed on the Secretary of State's website.

County	City/Town	Area Code
Adams	Quincy	(217)
Alexander	Cairo	(618)
Bond	Greenville	(618)
Boone	Belvidere	(815)
Brown	Mt. Sterling	(217)
Bureau	Princeton	(815)
Calhoun	Hardin	(618)
Carroll	Mt. Carroll	(815)
Cass	Virginia	(217)
Champaign	Urbana	(217)
Christian	Taylorville	(217)
Clark	Marshall	(217)
Clay	Louisville	(618)
Clinton	Carlyle	(618)
Coles	Charleston	(217)
Cook	Chicago	(312)
Crawford	Robinson	(618)
Cumberland	Toledo	(217)
DeKalb	Sycamore	(815)
DeWitt	Clinton	(217)
Douglas	Tuscola	(217)
DuPage	Wheaton	(630)
Edgar	Paris	(217)
Edwards	Albion	(618)
Effingham	Effingham	(217)
Fayette	Vandalia	(618)
Ford	Paxton	(217)
Franklin	Benton	(618)
Fulton	Lewistown	(309)
Gallatin	Shawneetown	(618)
Greene	Carrollton	(217)
Grundy	Morris	(815)
Hamilton	McLeansboro	(618)
Hancock	Carthage	(217)
Hardin	Elizabethtown	(618)
Henderson	Oquawka	(309)
Henry	Cambridge	(309)
Iroquois	Watseka	(815)
Jackson	Murphysboro	(618)
Jasper	Newton	(618)
Jefferson	Mt. Vernon	(618)
Jersey	Jerseyville	(618)
Jo Daviess	Galena	(815)
Johnson	Vienna	(618)
Kane	Geneva	(630)
Kankakee	Kankakee	(815)
Kendall	Yorkville	(630)
Knox	Galesburg	(309)
Lake	Waukegan	(847)
LaSalle	Ottawa	(815)
Lawrence	Lawrenceville	(618)
Lee	Dixon	(815)
Livingston	Pontiac	(815)

Illinois

County	City/Town	Area Code
Logan	Lincoln	(217)
Macon	Decatur	(217)
Macoupin	Carlinville	(217)
Madison	Edwardsville	(618)
Marion	Salem	(618)
Marshall	Lacon	(309)
Mason	Havana	(309)
Massac	Metropolis	(618)
McDonough	Macomb	(309)
McHenry	Woodstock	(815)
McLean	Bloomington	(309)
Menard	Petersburg	(217)
Mercer	Aledo	(309)
Monroe	Waterloo	(618)
Montgomery	Hillsboro	(217)
Morgan	Jacksonville	(217)
Moultrie	Sullivan	(217)
Ogle	Oregon	(815)
Peoria	Peoria	(309)
Perry	Pinckneyville	(618)
Piatt	Monticello	(217)
Pike	Pittsfield	(217)
Pope	Golconda	(618)
Pulaski	Mound City	(618)
Putnam	Hennepin	(815)
Randolph	Chester	(618)
Richland	Olney	(618)
Rock Island	Rock Island	(309)
Saline	Harrisburg	(618)
Sangamon	Springfield	(217)
Schuyler	Rushville	(217)
Scott	Winchester	(217)
Shelby	Shelbyville	(217)
Stark	Toulon	(309)
St. Clair	Belleville	(618)
Stephenson	Freeport	(815)
Tazewell	Pekin	(309)
Union	Jonesboro	(618)
Vermilion	Danville	(217)
Wabash	Mt. Carmel	(618)
Warren	Monmouth	(309)
Washington	Nashville	(618)
Wayne	Fairfield	(618)
White	Carmi	(618)
Whiteside	Morrison	(815)
Will	Joliet	(815)
Williamson	Marion	(618)
Winnebago	Rockford	(815)
Woodford	Eureka	(309)

OTHER NOTARIAL OFFICERS

Officers for Oaths, Affidavits, Depositions

"All courts, and judges, and the clerks thereof, the county clerk, deputy county clerk, the Secretary of State, notaries public, and persons certified under the Illinois Certified Shorthand Reporters Act of 1984 may administer all oaths of office and all other oaths authorized or required of any officer or other person, and take affidavits and depositions concerning any matter or thing, process or proceeding commenced or to be commenced, or pending in any court or before them, or on any occasion wherein any affidavit or deposition is authorized or required by law to be taken" (5 ILCS 255/2).

QUICK FACTS

Notary Jurisdiction

Statewide, as long as the Notary continues to reside in the same county in which commissioned or, in the case of an out-of-state resident, continues to maintain a principal place of work or business in the same county (5 ILCS 312/3-105).

Notary Term Length

Four years (5 ILCS 312/2-101), expiring at midnight on the commission expiration date (NPH).

<u>One-Year Term for Non-Residents</u>: Residents of some bordering states may qualify for an Illinois Notary commission but only for a one-year term (5 ILCS 312/2-101).

Notary Bond

$5,000, with a surety qualified to write surety bonds in the state (5 ILCS 312/2-105).

<u>Employer May Be Liable</u>: ""The employer of a notary public is also liable to the persons involved for all damages caused by the notary's official misconduct, if: (a) the notary public was acting within the scope of the notary's employment at the time the notary engaged in the official misconduct; and (b) the employer consented to the notary public's official misconduct" (5 ILCS 312/7-102).

Editors' Note: On the following page is a sample "Notarial Record" form — see "Pilot Program for Cook County Conveyances" above, under "Notary Powers."

Illinois

Space Above Reserved for Employer or Cook County Recorder of Deeds

NOTARIAL RECORD — RESIDENTIAL REAL PROPERTY TRANSACTIONS

PROPERTY The undersigned grantor(s) hereby certifies(y) that the residential real property identified in this notarial record is residential real property as defined in the Illinois Notary Public Act.

Type or Name of Document of Conveyance   PIN Number of Residential Real Property

Common Street Address of Residential Real Property   City   State   ZIP

Date of Notarization   Notary Fee   Additional Comments

NOTARY

Notary Printed Name   Notary Phone Number

Notary Commission Expiration Date   Notary Signature

Notary Residential Street Address   City   State   ZIP

Notary's Employer or Principal and Business Street Address   City   State   ZIP

GRANTOR #1   **GRANTOR #2**

Grantor (Signer) #1 Printed Name   Grantor (Signer) #2 Printed Name

Grantor (Signer) #1 Signature   Grantor (Signer) #2 Signature

Grantor (Signer) #1 Residential Street Address   Grantor (Signer) #2 Residential Street Address

City   State   ZIP   City   State   ZIP

Grantor (Signer) #1 Means of Identification   Right Thumbprint of Grantor/Signer #1 — Top of thumb here   Grantor (Signer) #2 Means of Identification   Right Thumbprint of Grantor/Signer #2 — Top of thumb here

Description of Print if not Right Thumb   Description of Print if not Right Thumb

Additional Comments   Additional Comments

Printed by authority of the State of Illinois. May 2009 — 1 — I 212

Indiana

NOTARY SEAL

An Indiana Notary must attest to all official acts with a seal of office, and the seal's format must be as follows (IC 33-42-2-4):

Kind

Inked Stamp or Embosser: "The notary public's seal shall either be a seal press or a rubber stamp.... If a seal press is used, the impression must be inked or blackened so that it may be photocopied" (website, "Frequently Asked Questions").

Shape/Size

Not specified.

Components

1. Name of Notary (preferred but optional);
2. "Notary Public";
3. "State of Indiana" or "Indiana";
4. "Seal";
5. Optional: commission expiration date.

Examples

The above typical, actual-size examples of Notary seals are allowed by Indiana law. Formats other than these may also be permitted.

NOTARY ADMINISTRATION

Office of Secretary of State
Notary Department   1-317-232-6542
State House, Room 201
200 W. Washington St.
Indianapolis, IN 46204

Website: www.in.gov/sos/business/2378.htm

NOTARY RULES

IC — INDIANA CODE

Most Notary rules are in the Indiana Code, Title 33, Article 42 ("Notaries Public").

"A notary may not act until the notary has procured a seal that will stamp upon paper a distinct impression, in words or letters, sufficiently indicating the notary's official character, to which may be added any other device as the notary may choose .... All notarial acts not attested by a seal as described (above) are void" (IC 33-42-2-4).

The Notary Department directs Notaries to include the word "Seal" in any seal, particularly inked stamps, so that it will not be confused with other devices that may be used to affix the Notary's name or commission expiration date.

Commission Expiration Date Must Appear

The Notary's commission expiration date must appear on every notarial certificate (IC 33-42-3-1). A Notary's failure to comply is a Class C infraction (IC 33-42-3-2).

Printed Name and County of Residence

"(a) A notary, in addition to affixing the notary's name, expiration date, and seal, shall:

"1. print or type the notary's name immediately beneath the notary's signature on a certificate of acknowledgment, jurat, or other official document, unless the notary's name appears:

"A. in printed form on the document; or

"B. as part of the notary's stamp in a form that is legible when the document is photocopied; and

"2. indicate the notary's county of residence on the document.

"(b) Failure to comply with subsection (a) does not affect the validity of any document notarized before July 1, 1982" (IC 33-42-2-9).

Must Sign Commissioned Name

A Notary may not "use any other name or initial in signing acknowledgments, other than that by which the notary has been commissioned" (IC 33-42-2-2[a][1]).

Township Trustee Must Affix Seal

An Indiana township trustee has the same powers as a Notary (IC 33-42-5-1) and "the trustee must obtain a seal that can stamp upon paper a distinct impression that indicates the trustee's official character, along with any other information that the trustee chooses. A notarial act of a trustee that is not attested by a seal is void" (IC 33-42-5-2). The trustee must also append his or her date of election (IC 33-42-5-3).

Employer May Not Keep Seal

"A notary commission is personal to the notary public. The stamp and commission belong to the notary public and must be safeguarded by the notary in order to prevent forgeries and other misuse. Even if an employer pays for the notary commission, the employer cannot convert the stamp and journal" (website, "Frequently Asked Questions").

NOTARY POWERS

Indiana Notaries are authorized to perform the following notarial acts (IC 33-42-2-5):
1. Take acknowledgments* and proofs**;
2. Administer oaths and affirmations***;
3. Take affidavits**** and depositions;
4. "(D)o all acts that by common law, and the custom of merchants, notaries are authorized to do."

* Acknowledgments: A Notary may not take an acknowledgment of a document "unless the person who executed the instrument: (i) signs the instrument before the notary; or (ii) affirms to the notary that the signature on the instrument is the person's own" (IC 33-42-2-2[a]).

An acknowledgment is a "formal declaration before a notary public that the instrument presented is the free and voluntary act of the party executing it and the signatures on the document are genuine" (website, "Definition of Terms").

** Proofs by Subscribing Witness: "A deed may be proved according to the rules of common law before any officer who is authorized to take acknowledgments. A deed that is proved in the manner provided in this section is entitled to be recorded" (IC 32-21-2-6).

*** Affirmations: An affirmation is an "oral or written declaration made by a person who has an objection to taking oaths certifying that under penalty of perjury the declarations are true" (website, "Definition of Terms").

**** Affidavits: A Notary may not execute an affidavit "unless the affiant acknowledges the truth of the statements in the affidavit" (IC 33-42-2-2[a]).

Identifying Document Signers

"In the event a notary public does not know the person presenting the instrument for notarization, the notary should do the following:

"1. Ask the person for identification (driver's license), or

"2. Have another person identify the party requesting notarization.

"3. If neither option is available or satisfactory, the notary may ask the person to take an oath as to his/her identity.

"4. If these attempts at identification are unsuccessful, the notary may refuse service for his/her own protection" (website, "Duties and Responsibilities").

Determining Competence

"Although there are differing opinions on whether a notary public has a duty to determine the person's competency, many experts recommend that the notary make a limited inquiry into the person's ability to understand the contents of the document that the person is signing. The notary can make a quick assessment by asking the person if he or she understands the document. Clearly, a notary should refuse to notarize the signature of a person who unquestionably has no ability to understand the document (unconscious, mentally disabled)" (website, "Frequently Asked Questions").

Nonetheless, the Notary is required by law not to notarize for a person known by the Notary to have been "adjudged mentally incompetent by a court" and to be under a guardianship under IC 29-3 at the time of notarization (IC 33-42-2-2[a]).

Notary May Read Document to Signer

"Before taking acknowledgment or oath of any person, the notary public shall ascertain whether the person executing the instrument knows the contents of the instrument. If the person does not know the contents, the notary shall take steps to ensure the person knows the contents before taking the oath or acknowledgment" (website, "Duties and Responsibilities").

Requirements for Recorded Documents

"When notarizing documents for the purpose of recording, the notary public must ensure the following:

"1. The name of each person (typed, printed, or stamped) executing the instrument is immediately beneath the signature.

"2. That the person's name written in the body of the instrument matches the signature.

"3. That the name of each witness (typed, printed, or stamped) is beneath the signature.

"4. That the name of the notary (typed, printed, or stamped) is beneath the signature" (website, "Duties and Responsibilities").

NOTARY DON'TS

An Indiana Notary may (IC 33-42-2-2[a] and website, "Prohibited Acts"):

1. NOT notarize for someone whom the Notary knows has been adjudged mentally incompetent by a court and is under the guardianship of another person;
2. NOT notarize for someone under a guardianship under IC 29-3;
3. NOT take the acknowledgment of a blind person without first reading the document to that person;
4. NOT take the acknowledgment of a person who does not speak or understand English, "unless the nature and effect of the instrument to be notarized is translated into a language which the person does speak or understand";
5. NOT affix his or her signature to a blank form of affidavit or certificate of acknowledgment and deliver that form to another person with fraudulent intent that it be filled in by someone else later, since this is a Class D felony (IC 33-42-4-2[1]);
6. NOT notarize a notarial certificate containing untrue statements (website, "Frequently Asked Questions");
7. NOT postdate or antedate any document or certificate.

Disclosure Required in Notary Ads

A non-attorney may not advertise in any medium services as a Notary, Notario "or any other term indicating in English or a language other than English that a person is a notary public" without conspicuously posting the following disclosure: "I AM NOT AN ATTORNEY LICENSED TO PRACTICE LAW IN INDIANA, AND I MAY NOT GIVE LEGAL ADVICE OR ACCEPT FEES FOR LEGAL ADVICE" (IC 33-42-2-10).

A person who knowingly advertises as a Notary without the disclosure in the ad and on the person's business card and letterhead, or who advertises or claims to be an expert on immigration matters without being a designated entity as defined under 8 CFR 245a1(1), or accepts payment for providing legal advice commits "notario publico deception," a Class A misdemeanor. Conviction for this offense permanently revokes a Notary's commission (IC 33-42-2-2[d]).

Signer's Presence Is Mandatory

"The most serious error made by notaries is failure to require the person to appear before the notary before notarizing the document. The person who signed the document must always appear in person. Failure to observe this requirement can result in criminal and civil liability and the loss of the notary's commission....

"(N)ever notarize a document outside the presence of the person.... The notary cannot take a notarization over the telephone (because the person has not appeared in person before the notary). The notary cannot notarize a document just because someone else assures the notary that the signature is genuine. The notary cannot take an acknowledgment just because the notary recognizes the person's signature" (website, "Frequently Asked Questions").

Disqualifying Interests

An Indiana Notary may not "acknowledge (sic) any instrument in which the notary's name appears as a party to the transaction" (IC 33-42-2-2[a][2]);

"A notary public can never notarize his or her own signature, whether signing for themselves or for a corporation" (website, "Frequently Asked Questions").

Not Disqualified: The following Notaries are not excluded from notarizing for the organization with which they are employed or associated:

1. Notaries who are managers, officers or employees of any federal land bank association located in Indiana (IC 33-42-6-1);
2. Notaries who are stockholders or officers of any cemetery association, in taking acknowledgments for the sale of lots, as long as they are not beneficiaries (IC 33-42-7-1).

Notaries Are Impartial, Unbiased: "Notaries are expected to be impartial, unbiased, and without financial interest in the documents they notarize" (website, "General Information").

Family Members: "A notary public may not notarize his or her own signature, but may notarize the signatures of his or her spouse, children, parents or other relatives" (website, "Frequently Asked Questions").

NOTARY SIGNING AGENTS

Indiana law requires that any person, including a Notary Signing Agent, who conducts a real estate closing on behalf of a title insurance producer or company in which a title insurance policy is to be issued must be a licensed title insurance producer (Indiana Department of Insurance Bulletin 135, "Title Insurance Licensing Requirements: Insured Closing Services"). These rules define "to conduct a real estate closing" as to "determine proper execution, acknowledgment and delivery of all conveyances, mortgage documents and other title instruments necessary to consummate a transaction."

In order to conduct home loan signings in Indiana, Notary Signing Agents must take an approved 10-hour pre-licensing course through the Indiana Land Title Association and apply to become a title insurance producer. In addition to these licensing requirements, licensees must complete 14 hours of continuing education during the four-year license term.

NOTARY FEES

"The maximum fee of a notary public is two dollars ($2) for each notarial act" (IC 33-42-8-1).

No Charge by Official

"A person who is a public official, or a deputy or appointee acting for or serving under a public official, may not make any charge for services as a notary public in connection with any official business of that office, or of any other office in the governmental unit in which the person serves, unless the charges are specifically authorized by a statute other than the statute that establishes generally the fees and charges of notaries public" (IC 33-42-2-7[b]).

NOTARY CERTIFICATES

The following notarial certificates are prescribed by the Indiana Code:

Acknowledgment by Individual (IC 32-21-2-7):

State of Indiana
               SS:
County of _____

Before me, _____ (name of Notary or other officer), this _____ day of _____, 20__, _____ (name of signer), acknowledged the execution of the annexed deed (or mortgage, as the case may be).

_____ (Notary's signature)   (SEAL)
_____ (Printed /typed name), Notary Public

My commission expires: _____
County of residence: _____

Acknowledgment by Person in Armed Forces (IC 32-21-9-1):

With the Armed Forces (or other component part) of the United States at _____SS:

The foregoing instrument was acknowledged this ____ day of _____, 20___, by _____, (serving in the Armed Forces of the United States) (as a merchant seaman outside the limits of the United States) (as a person not in the Armed Forces, but outside the limits of the United States by permission, assignment or direction of a department of the United States Government in connection with activity pertaining to the prosecution of the war), before me, a commissioned officer in the active service of the (Army of the United States) (United States Marine Corps) (United States Navy) (United States Coast Guard) (or equivalent rank in any other component part of the Armed Forces).

_____ *(Signature of officer)*
_____ *(Rank and branch of service)*

NOTES: "In the event that military considerations preclude disclosure of the place of execution or acknowledgment the words 'an undisclosed place' may be supplied in lieu of the appropriate city or county, state, and country …

"If (the document is signed) by a natural person or persons, insert name or names; if by a person acting in a representative or official capacity or as attorney-in-fact, then insert name of the person acknowledging the instrument, followed by an accurate description of the capacity in which he acts including the name of the person, corporation, or other entity represented."

The military officer taking the acknowledgment must be an ensign or a second lieutenant or higher.

Certificate Is Presumptive Evidence

"The official certificate of a notary public, attested by the notary's seal, is presumptive evidence of the facts stated in cases where, by law, the notary public is authorized to certify the facts" (IC 33-42-2-6).

Certificate Type Not Notary's Choice

"(I)f a document does not contain a notarial certificate, the notary public cannot advise as to the proper type of notarization. An attorney should be consulted as to the proper notarization that is required for the document (acknowledgment, witnessing or verification).… The determination whether a document is required to be notarized cannot be made by the notary public" (website, "Frequently Asked Questions").

Venue Required

"The beginning of each notarial certificate should include jurisdictional information that indicates where the document was notarized, similar to the following: State of _____), County of _____)" (website, "Frequently Asked Questions").

ELECTRONIC NOTARIZATIONS

The state of Indiana has not yet adopted statutes or regulations expressly establishing rules, definitions and procedures for electronic notarization.

UETA Recognizes Notary's eSignature

Indiana has adopted an amended version of the Uniform Electronic Transactions Act (IC 26-2-8), including the following provision related to electronic notarization, thereby recognizing the legal validity of electronic signatures used by Notaries:

"If a law requires that a signature be notarized, the requirement is satisfied with respect to an electronic signature if an electronic record includes, in addition to the electronic signature to be notarized, the electronic signature of a notary public together with all other information required to be included in a notarization by other applicable law" (IC 26-2-8-110).

NOTARY RECORDS

"There is no statutory requirement in Indiana that a notary public keep a log book or journal. However, it is recommended that a notary public keep one for his or her own records and protection from liability" (website, "Frequently Asked Questions").

Employer May Not Keep Journal

"Even if an employer pays for the notary commission, the employer cannot (keep) the stamp and journal" (website, "Frequently Asked Questions").

AUTHENTICATION OF NOTARIAL ACTS

County Clerks

Locally, a certificate authenticating the act of a given Notary may be issued by the clerk of the circuit court of the county in which the Notary resides. ("Upon request of the clerk of the circuit court of a county, the secretary of state shall furnish to the clerk a list of all commissioned notaries public residing in that county" [IC 33-42-2-8][a].)

A document acknowledged in one Indiana county for recording in another must be authenticated by the circuit court clerk of the county in which the notarizing officer resides — unless this officer uses an official seal, in which case no such authentication is required (IC 32-21-2-4).

Secretary of State

Certificates authenticating the acts of Notaries, including apostilles, are also issued by the Indiana Secretary of State, as are certificates authenticating the acts of county clerks.

Fees: No charge.

Address:
Office of Secretary of State
Authentication Department
302 W. Washington St., Room E-018
Indianapolis, IN 46204

Telephone: 1-317-232-2677

Procedure: Mail or present in person the original notarized document, which must have an original signature and seal/stamp of a Notary. An accompanying cover letter must indicate the nation to which the document(s) will be sent, a daytime phone number for questions about the document(s), and where the document(s) should be mailed after processing. A postage-paid envelope should be included. "All apostille requests should be mailed. For documents delivered in person, the office cannot guarantee a prompt turnaround due to high volume. If you are requesting more than fifteen (15) documents, you must come in and drop off for the following turnaround times: Requests received by noon will be completed by noon the following business day; Filings received after noon will be completed by noon in two business days" (website, "Apostilles").

COMMISSIONING AND ADMINISTRATION

Though the Governor nominally appoints and commissions Indiana's Notaries (IC 33-42-2-1[b]), it is the office of the Secretary of State that administers the commissioning process and directly regulates and maintains records on Notaries (IC 33-42-2-2[c]).

"All notary public applications and appointments are required to be open to public inspection pursuant to Indiana law and available in the Notary Public database" (website, "Frequently Asked Questions").

Applying for Commission

Qualifications: An applicant for appointment as an Indiana Notary Public must: (a) be at least 18 years old, (b) be a legal resident of Indiana (IC 33-42-2-1), (c) not hold a lucrative public office or appointment under the government of the United States or the state of Indiana, though civil, school, city and town officials of Indiana may serve as Notaries with certain limitations (IC 33-42-2-7) and (d) not have been convicted of a crime for which the sentence exceeds six months of imprisonment (IC 5-8-3-1).

No Course or Test: No course or test is required to become a Notary in Indiana.

Application: A person should not apply using initials for both the first and middle names, but may either 1) spell out both these names, 2) spell out the first name and use a middle initial, or 3) use an initial for the first name and spell out the middle name (website, "Procedure for Becoming a Notary Public").

Applicants for a Notary commission must use the Indiana Secretary of State's Online Notary Portal to initiate the application process. The applicant must obtain a $5,000 bond. The application fee is $5. The application may be submitted electronically (IC 5-14-3-2) through the Secretary of State's website and its Online Notary Portal.

There is an online bulk application process that may be used by companies with multiple Notaries on staff, or by a service or bonding company assisting customers applying to become Notaries; however, each applicant must have already accessed the state's Online Notary Portal application and completed the pre-qualification, training, and oath agreement.

There is no automatic reappointment in Indiana. A notary public must apply for appointment and follow the same procedures required for a new appointment. Application should be made sufficiently prior to expiration to ensure uninterrupted authority. The Secretary of State's online portal will accept filings up to sixty (60) days prior to expiration (website, "Frequently Asked Questions").

<u>Non-Residents</u>: Non-residents of Indiana may not become a Notary in the state.

<u>Online Search</u>: The Indiana Notary Public database may be searched online by commission number, name, county and zip code for both active and inactive Notaries at www.in.gov/apps/sos/notary/sos_notary. Available online information about a given Notary includes the Notary's commission number and expiration date, street address and bonding agent.

Changes of Status

<u>If Notary Changes Name or County</u>: "If a notary public changes the notary's: (1) name; or (2) county of residence; during the term of the notary's commission, the notary public shall notify the secretary of state in writing of the change .... The secretary of state shall process a revised commission to reflect any change of name or county. A revised commission under this subsection is valid for the unexpired term of the original commission" (IC 33-42-2-8). The change should be reported to the Secretary of State using the online service on the website (website, "Frequently Asked Questions"). The fee for a name or county change is $5.

COUNTY CLERKS

To contact an Indiana county clerk of the circuit court to obtain an authenticating certificate for a Notary, or to seek assistance in locating a given Notary, telephone long-distance information — 1-XXX-555-1212 — for the following area codes:

County	City/Town	Area Code
Adams	Decatur	(260)
Allen	Fort Wayne	(260)
Bartholomew	Columbus	(812)
Benton	Fowler	(765)
Blackford	Hartford City	(765)
Boone	Lebanon	(765)
Brown	Nashville	(812)
Carroll	Delphi	(765)
Cass	Logansport	(574)
Clark	Jeffersonville	(812)
Clay	Brazil	(812)
Clinton	Frankfort	(765)
Crawford	English	(812)
Daviess	Washington	(812)
Dearborn	Lawrenceburg	(812)
Decatur	Greensburg	(812)
Dekalb	Auburn	(260)
Delaware	Muncie	(765)
Dubois	Jasper	(812)
Elkhart	Goshen	(574)
Fayette	Connersville	(765)
Floyd	New Albany	(812)
Fountain	Covington	(765)
Franklin	Brookville	(765)
Fulton	Rochester	(574)
Gibson	Princeton	(812)
Grant	Marion	(765)
Greene	Bloomfield	(812)
Hamilton	Noblesville	(317)
Hancock	Greenfield	(317)
Harrison	Corydon	(812)
Hendricks	Danville	(317)
Henry	New Castle	(765)
Howard	Kokomo	(765)
Huntington	Huntington	(260)
Jackson	Brownstown	(812)
Jasper	Rensselaer	(219)
Jay	Portland	(260)
Jefferson	Madison	(812)
Jennings	Vernon	(812)
Johnson	Franklin	(317)
Knox	Vincennes	(812)
Kosciusko	Warsaw	(574)
Lagrange	Lagrange	(260)
Lake	Crown Point	(219)
La Porte	La Porte	(219)
Lawrence	Bedford	(812)
Madison	Anderson	(765)
Marion	Indianapolis	(317)
Marshall	Plymouth	(574)
Martin	Shoals	(812)
Miami	Peru	(765)
Monroe	Bloomington	(812)
Montgomery	Crawfordsville	(765)
Morgan	Martinsville	(765)
Newton	Kentland	(219)
Noble	Albion	(260)
Ohio	Rising Sun	(812)
Orange	Paoli	(812)
Owen	Spencer	(812)
Parke	Rockville	(765)

Indiana

County	City/Town	Area Code
Perry	Tell City	(812)
Pike	Petersburg	(812)
Porter	Valparaiso	(219)
Posey	Mount Vernon	(812)
Pulaski	Winamac	(574)
Putnam	Greencastle	(765)
Randolph	Winchester	(765)
Ripley	Versailles	(812)
Rush	Rushville	(765)
Scott	Scottsburg	(812)
Shelby	Shelbyville	(317)
Spencer	Rockport	(812)
Starke	Knox	(574)
Steuben	Angola	(260)
St. Joseph	South Bend	(574)
Sullivan	Sullivan	(812)
Switzerland	Vevay	(812)
Tippecanoe	Lafayette	(765)
Tipton	Tipton	(765)
Union	Liberty	(765)
Vanderburgh	Evansville	(812)
Vermillion	Newport	(765)
Vigo	Terre Haute	(812)
Wabash	Wabash	(260)
Warren	Williamsport	(765)
Warrick	Boonville	(812)
Washington	Salem	(812)
Wayne	Richmond	(765)
Wells	Bluffton	(260)
White	Monticello	(574)
Whitley	Columbia City	(260)

OTHER NOTARIAL OFFICERS

Besides Notaries, the following officers may take acknowledgments and administer oaths in their respective jurisdictions (IC 33-42-4-1):
1. Judges and justices of courts;
2. Mayors, clerks, and clerk-treasurers of towns and cities, and township trustees;
3. Clerks of circuit courts;
4. County master commissioners;
5. Judges, commissioners of U.S. district courts;
6. A precinct election officer and an absentee voter board member for any purpose authorized under IC 3;
7. County auditors;
8. A member of the Indiana Election Commission, a co-director of the Election Division, or an employee of the Election Division;
9. The clerk of the Indiana Supreme Court.

In addition, members of the Indiana General Assembly and the Secretary of State may notarize any document anywhere in the state.

Township Trustees May Notarize

"A township trustee may perform any act that a notary public may perform in Indiana. Acknowledgments to deeds or other instruments taken by a trustee shall be recorded as if they had been acknowledged before a notary public" (IC 33-42-5-1). When notarizing, a township trustee must use a seal (IC 33-42-5-2), append the trustee's date of election (IC 33-42-5-3), and not charge a fee (IC 33-42-5-4). "A trustee may not perform an act that is prohibited to a notary public" (IC 33-42-5-5).

QUICK FACTS

Notary Jurisdiction

Statewide (IC 33-42-2-1[b] and 33-42-1-1). "The jurisdiction of a notary public is statewide, but no notary public can be compelled to act outside of the notary's home county" (website, "Functions of a Notary").

Notary Term Length

Eight years (IC 33-42-2-1[b]), expiring at midnight on the commission expiration date.

Notary Bond

$5,000, "with freehold or corporate security, to be approved by the secretary of state" (IC 33-42-2-1[e]). With a freehold bond, someone other than the Notary and holding land worth at least $5,000 serves as the surety.

"(Even) if the employer paid for the notary's bond, the employer cannot cancel the bond" (website, "Frequently Asked Questions").

Iowa

NOTARY SEAL

Effective January 1, 2002, an Iowa Notary, as well as any other person empowered to perform notarial acts under Iowa law, must affix a seal of office on all documents notarized, and the seal's format must be as shown below (IC 9E.6A).

EXCEPTIONS: Seals for notarial acts are not required in the following instances: "a. A notarial act performed by a judicial officer as defined in section 602.1101, if the notarial act is performed in accordance with state or federal statutory authority. b. A certification by a chief officer or a chief officer's designee of a peace officer's verification of a uniform citation and complaint pursuant to section 805.6, subsection 3, paragraph 'c'. c. The administration of oaths and the acknowledgment of signatures by a peace officer pursuant to section 80.9A, subsection 3, or by a certified law enforcement officer pursuant to section 817.3" (IC 9E.6A[3]).

Examples

The above typical, actual-size examples of Notary seals are allowed by Iowa law. Formats and sizes other than these may also be permitted.

NOTARY ADMINISTRATION

Office of Secretary of State
Notary Division   1-515-281-5204
Lucas Building, 1st Floor
321 East 12th Street
Des Moines, IA 50319

Website: www.sos.state.ia.us/notaries/index.html

NOTARY RULES

IC — IOWA CODE
PB — POCKETBOOK FOR IOWA NOTARIES PUBLIC

Most Notary rules are in the Iowa Code:

a. Chapter 9E, called the "Iowa Law on Notarial Acts"*;

   * Much of the chapter is drawn from the *Uniform Law on Notarial Acts* of 1982.

b. Title XIV, Subtitle 2, Chapter 558, "Conveyances."

Other helpful guidelines for Notaries are in the "Pocketbook for Iowa Notaries Public," issued by the Secretary of State and available on the website

Kind

There are four Notary seal options, with the latter two available by computer (website, "Notary Stamp and Seal Information"):

1. Inked stamp.

2. Embosser.

3. Adhesive label: "Notaries public can create their own labels containing the appropriate information and attach them to the notarial certificate.... Simply use the label creating function on your word processor."

4. Computer-Printed Certificates: "Because the law allows you to attach a notarial certificate to the document being notarized, you can create

your own certificates." The seal information would appear on an electronic notarial certificate and this form would then be printed out on paper, completed by the Notary and attached to the document. The website provides this sample seal format for such a certificate:

> Notary Name
> Iowa Notarial Seal
> Commission Number: XXXXX
> My Commission Expires: XXXXX

Shape/Size

Not specified.

Components

<u>Notary Commissioned by Secretary of State</u>:
1. "Notarial Seal" and "Iowa";
2. Notary's name exactly as on commission;
3. "Commission Number" followed by Notary's commission number;
4. "My Commission Expires" followed by:
   a. Commission expiration date; or
   b. Blank line on which Notary prints commission expiration date by hand.

<u>Other Officers with Notarial Powers</u>:
1. "Notarial Seal" and "Iowa";
2. Officer's name;
3. Title under which officer is empowered to perform notarial acts under IC 9E.10.

NOTARY POWERS

Iowa Notaries are authorized to perform the following notarial acts (IC 9E.2[2] and 558.31):
1. Take acknowledgments* and proofs**;
2. Administer oaths and affirmations;
3. Take verifications (jurats***) upon oath or affirmation;
4. Witness or attest**** signatures;
5. Certify or attest copies of documents or other items*****;
6. Note protests of negotiable instruments.

* <u>Acknowledgments</u>: "An Acknowledgment is a formal declaration made before the notary that the person signing the document did so freely, voluntarily, and for the purpose stated in the document. The document does not have to be signed in the notary's presence, but the signer must personally appear before the notary at the time of notarization to acknowledge he signed it" (PB).

In an acknowledgment, the signer must: (a) personally appear before the Notary, (b) be positively identified by the Notary and (c) acknowledge having willingly signed the document (website, "Notary Forms").

"'Acknowledgment' means a declaration by a person that the person has executed an instrument for the purposes stated in the document and, if the instrument is executed in a representative capacity, that the person signed the instrument with proper authority and executed it as the act of the person or entity represented and identified in the document" (IC 9E.2[1]).

** <u>Proofs by Subscribing Witness</u>: "Proof of the due and voluntary execution and delivery of a deed or other instrument may be made before any officer authorized to take acknowledgments, by one competent person other than the vendee or other person to whom the instrument is executed, in the following cases: 1. If the grantor dies before making the acknowledgment. 2. If the grantor's attendance cannot be procured. 3. If, having appeared, the grantor refuses to acknowledge the execution of the instrument" (IC 558.31).

"An officer having power to take the proof hereinbefore contemplated may issue the necessary subpoenas, and compel the attendance of witnesses residing within the county, in the manner provided for the taking of depositions" (IC 558.33).

*** <u>Jurats</u>: "A verification (jurat) contains the words 'signed and sworn (or affirmed) before me….' When this language is used, you must verbally administer an oath to the signer prior to the execution of the document. An oath can be administered as follows: 'Do you swear that the statements in this document are true?' When a person is unable to 'swear' due to personal or religious beliefs, the following oath may be used: 'Do you affirm that the statements contained in this document are true?'

"To notarize the jurat without administering the oath can affect the validity of the document" (PB).

In a jurat: (a) the signer must personally appear before the Notary, (b) the Notary must watch the signer sign the document, (c) the signer must be positively identified by the Notary and (d) the Notary must administer an oral oath or affirmation (website, "Notary Forms").

"'Verification upon oath or affirmation' means a declaration that a statement is true, made by a person upon oath or affirmation" (IC 9E.2[5]).

**** Attesting Signatures: "In witnessing or attesting a signature, the notarial officer must determine, either from personal knowledge or from satisfactory evidence, that the signature is that of the person appearing before the officer and named on the document" (IC 9E.9[3]).

Based on the wording of the statutory short-form certificate for witnessing or attesting a signature (IC 9E.15[4]), the signature must be affixed to the document in the Notary's presence.

***** Certifying Copies: "In certifying or attesting a copy of a document or other item, the notarial officer must determine that the copy is a full, true, and accurate transcription or reproduction of that which was copied" (IC 9E.9[4]).

In a copy certification, the Notary: (a) makes (or supervises the making of) a photocopy of the original document, (b) makes sure the copy is an exact replica of the original document, (c) positively identifies the signer and (d) attaches the certificate to the copy (website, "Notary Forms").

"Copy certification is an act where the notary determines a photocopy is a full, true and accurate reproduction of an original, privately held document. The typical types of documents for copy certification are business documents, diplomas, passports, and copies of letters. The notary should supervise the photocopying of the document. Notaries must avoid certifying copies of documents that are public records, such as birth/death certificates, court records and deeds" (PB).

"Only certify copies of privately held documents..." (website, "Notary Forms").

Identifying Document Signers

For acknowledgments, verifications upon oath or affirmation (jurats) and for witnessing or attesting a signature, positive identification of the signer through "satisfactory evidence" is required (IC 9E.9).

"You must have satisfactory evidence that a person is the individual whose true signature is on the document. Identity may be proven through: personal knowledge, identification documents (i.e., driver's license), or the sworn word of a credible identifying witness" (PB).

'Satisfactory Evidence' Defined: "A notarial officer has satisfactory evidence that a person is the person whose true signature is on a document in any of the following circumstances: a. The person is personally known to the notarial officer. b. The person is identified upon the oath or affirmation of a credible witness personally known to the notarial officer. c. The person is identified on the basis of identification documents" (IC 9E.9[6]).

Reliable IDs: "The best forms will include a picture, a physical description, a signature for you to compare and be issued by a government agency. A valid driver's license, passport, school or work identification can all be used. You may request as much identification as you feel necessary to verify the person's identity" (PB).

Notarizing for the Disabled

"A person who cannot sign a document due to a physical disability may request that you or another person sign their name to the document. A rubber stamp, a mark, or a facsimile of the disabled person's signature or mark may also be used. The person who signs the document or affixes the facsimile must be in the presence of the disabled person at the time of the notarization" (PB).

Notary Musts

According to the "Pocketbook for Iowa Notaries Public," Notaries must abide by these rules, in addition to other express requirements:

1. "All document signers must personally appear before you."

2. "Assess whether each document signer is competent."

3. "While not responsible for the content of a document, alert the signer to any blanks."

Determining Awareness: "Do not notarize the document if you have a reasonable belief that the person signing the document is not aware of the significance of the transaction" (PB).

Determining Volition: "Make sure the signer is not being forced to sign the document. If you suspect coercion, it is best to refuse to notarize" (PB).

Skimming for Blanks: "When notarizing, skim the document for blanks. If the blanks are intended to be left unfilled, the signer needs to line through each space or write 'not applicable.' Also, be sure all signatures are original and made in ink" (PB).

NOTARY DON'TS

Customer-Only Policy Is Prohibited

"A notary public may exercise reasonable discretion in performing or declining to perform notarial services, but a notary shall not condition the performance of notarial services upon the requirement that the person served be a customer or client of the establishment by which the notary is employed.

"The employer of a notary public shall not condition the performance of notarial services upon the requirement that the person served be a customer or client of the establishment by which the notary is employed" (IC 9E.8).

Notary Disqualifications

"The notary's duties are confined to those of an impartial witness. A notary who acts as impartial witness and as advocate or agent in connection with the same transaction can be accused of unduly influencing and/or coercing the signer.

"If the notary stands to make a financial gain by notarizing such a document or is a party or a representative of a party to the document, they should refer it to another notary and avoid the risk of a lawsuit based upon the financial interest in the agreement" (PB).

Corporate Notarizations: "The validity of a notarial act shall not be affected or impaired by the fact that the notarial officer performing the notarial act is an officer, director, or shareholder of a corporation that may have a beneficial interest or other interest in the subject matter of the notarial act" (IC 9E.10A).

NOTARY SIGNING AGENTS

Currently, there are no statutes, regulations or rules expressly governing, prohibiting or restricting the operation of Notary Signing Agents within the state of Iowa.

NOTARY FEES

The statutory schedule of fees for notarial acts was repealed in 1989. The rationale was that very few Iowa Notaries charged for their services.

"A notary in Iowa may charge a reasonable fee for their services. However, a notary cannot refuse to perform services because a person is not a client/customer nor may the notary's employer restrict the notary from providing services because a person is not a client/customer of the employer" (PB).

NOTARY CERTIFICATES

"When notarizing a document, you must complete and sign a notarial certificate. It indicates the procedure followed in performing the notarization. The certificate includes:

"1. a place at the top to fill in the jurisdiction ('State of _____' and 'County of _____'). This is the location where your 'feet are planted' at the time the document is notarized.

"2. a place to include the title 'Notary Public' under your signature; not your title at work" (PB).

The short-form certificates provided below from IC 9E.15 are taken virtually verbatim from the Uniform Law on Notarial Acts of 1982.

Short Form Acknowledgment by Individual (IC 9E.15[1]):

State of _____)
) ss.
County of _____)

This instrument was acknowledged before me on _____ (date) by _____ (name[s] of person[s]).

_____ (Signature)   (Stamp or Seal)
Notary Public (or title/rank of other officer)

Format of Notarial Certificate

"1. A notarial act must be evidenced by a certificate signed and dated by a notarial officer. The certificate must include identification of the jurisdiction in which the notarial act is performed and the title of the office of the notarial officer and shall include the official stamp or seal of the office. If the notarial officer is a commissioned officer on active duty in the military service of the United States, the certificate must also include the officer's rank.

"2. A certificate of a notarial act is sufficient if it meets the requirements of subsection 1, and is in any of the following forms:

"a. The short form set forth in section 9E.15.

"b. A form otherwise prescribed by the law of this state, including those forms set out in chapter 558.

"c. A form prescribed by laws or regulations applicable in the place in which the notarial act was performed.

"d. A form which sets forth the actions of the notarial officer and those are sufficient to meet the requirement of the designated notarial act" (IC 9E.14).

'Loose' Certificates Authorized

"Iowa notarial law allows a notary public to attach a notarial certificate to a document. In other words, the wording of the notarial certificate is not required to be a part of the original text of the document....Simply type in the information required for the stamp, print the certificate out, complete the notarial certificate by supplying the appropriate information, and attaching it to the document you are notarizing" (website, "Notary Stamp and Seal Information").

Short Form Acknowledgment in a Representative Capacity* (IC 9E.15[2]):

State of _____)
) *ss.*
County of _____)

This instrument was acknowledged before me on _____ *(date) by* _____ *(name[s] of person[s]) as* _____ *(type of authority, e.g., officer, trustee, etc.) for* _____ *(name of party on behalf of whom instrument was executed).*

_____ *(Signature)*   *(Stamp or Seal)*
Notary Public (or title/rank of other officer)

* 'Representative Capacity' Defined: "Representative capacity" means any of the following: (a) representative on behalf of a corporation, partnership, trust or other entity as an authorized officer, agent, partner, trustee or other representative; (b) public officer, personal representative, guardian or other representative in the capacity recited in the instrument; (c) attorney in fact for a principal; (d) any other capacity as an authorized representative of another (IC 9E.2[4]).

Short Form for Verification Upon Oath or Affirmation (Jurat) (IC 9E.15[3]):

State of _____)
) *ss.*
County of _____)

Signed and sworn to (or affirmed) before me on _____ *(date) by* _____ *(name[s] of person[s] making statement).*

_____ *(Signature)*   *(Stamp or Seal)*
Notary Public (or title/rank of other officer)

Short Form for Witnessing or Attesting Signature (IC 9E.15[4]):

State of _____)
) *ss.*
County of _____)

Signed or attested before me on _____ *(date) by* _____ *(name[s] of person[s]).*

_____ *(Signature)*   *(Stamp or Seal)*
Notary Public (or title/rank of other officer)

Short Form Copy Certification (IC 9E.15[5]):

State of _____)
) *ss.*
County of _____)

I certify that this is a true and correct copy of a document in the possession of _____.

Dated _____

_____ *(Signature)*   *(Stamp or Seal)*
Notary Public (or title/rank of other officer)

Contents of Proof of Execution Certificate

"The certificate endorsed by the officer upon a deed or other instrument thus proved must state:

"1. The title of the officer taking the proof.

"2. That it was satisfactorily proved that the grantor was dead, or that for some other reason the grantor's attendance could not be procured in order to make the acknowledgment, or that, having appeared, the grantor refused to acknowledge the same.

"3. The name of the witness by whom proof was made, and that it was proved by the witness that the instrument was executed and delivered by the person whose name is thereunto subscribed as a party" (IC 558.32).

Defective Certificate Cured after 10 Years

"An instrument in writing to which is attached a defective certificate of acknowledgment attached by a notary public more than ten years earlier is valid, legal, and binding as if the instrument had been properly acknowledged by the notary public" (IC 9E.9A).

ELECTRONIC NOTARIZATIONS

The state of Iowa has not yet adopted statutes or regulations expressly establishing rules, definitions and procedures for electronic notarization.

UETA Recognizes Notary's eSignature

Iowa has adopted its own version of the Uniform Electronic Transactions Act (IC 554D.101 through 554D.125), including the following provision on electronic notarization, thereby recognizing the legal validity of electronic signatures used by Notaries:

"If a law requires a signature or record to be notarized, acknowledged, verified, or made under oath, the requirement is satisfied if the electronic signature of the person authorized to perform those acts, together with all other information required to be included by other applicable law, is attached to or logically associated with the signature or record" (IC 554D.113).

NOTARY RECORDS

"Although Iowa law does not require notaries to keep a journal, it is strongly recommended. A journal serves as a permanent record of notarizations you perform" (PB). Particularly when using a loose certificate, "it is highly recommended you keep a journal to document the fact that a notarial certificate was attached" (website, "Certificates").

Making Journal Entries

"When making journal entries:
"1. Complete the entry in ink; do not use a pencil.
"2. Enter the data before the notarial certificate is complete to prevent the signer from leaving before all data is recorded.
"3. Record all notarizations — even the requests for notarization that you have refused" (PB).

Recommended Entries

The "Pocketbook" and website further recommend that the Notary journal contain the following information for each notarization:
1. Date and time of day of the notarization;
2. Type of notarization;
3. Date of the document;
4. Type of document being notarized;
5. Name and address of the signer;
6. Description of how the signer was identified, including any ID's issuing agency, serial number and issuance or expiration date;
7. Any additional pertinent information;
8. Signature of the document signer.

AUTHENTICATION OF NOTARIAL ACTS

Secretary of State

Authenticating certificates for Notaries, including apostilles, are issued only by the Iowa Secretary of State's office (IC 9E.16[3] and Secretary of State's website, "Business Services").

Fees: $5 per certification, including apostille.

Address:
Office of Secretary of State
Attention: Business Services
Lucas Building, 1st Floor
321 East 12th Street
Des Moines, IA 50319

Telephone: 1-515-281-5204

Procedure: To avoid loss of the original notarized document, the Secretary of State's office requires only that a copy or fax of the original be submitted, along with the $5 fee. If the document is submitted by mail, the fee should be in the form of a check or money order made payable to the Secretary of State; if submitted by fax, the fee may be paid by credit card over the phone.

A letter of request should accompany the document. The letter should indicate: the name, address, phone number and email address of the requesting party; the name and commission number of the Notary; the date of notarization; and the country of destination.

COMMISSIONING AND ADMINISTRATION

The Iowa Secretary of State appoints, commissions, regulates and maintains records on the state's Notaries (IC 9E.3).

On the "Application for Appointment as a Notary Public," the instructions state that "(r)ecords of Iowa notaries are stored on microfilm and in computer databases. These records are available to the public." However, the application offers applicants the option to shield their personal (home) contact information from display on the Secretary of State's website (website, "Notary Forms").

Applying for Commission

Qualifications: An applicant for a commission as an Iowa Notary Public must: (a) be at least 18 years old, (b) be a resident of Iowa or a resident of a bordering state who has a place of work or business in Iowa and (c) not be disqualified from voting either due to conviction for a felony or having been adjudged mentally incompetent (IC 9E.3 and 48A.6).

No Course or Test: No course of instruction or test is required of Notary commission applicants in Iowa.

Application: On the application form, applicants have the option of providing an email address and being placed on a list of bilingual notaries (website, "Notary Forms").The application fee is $30 (IC 9E.6).

Commissions may be renewed online. "The secretary of state shall, two months preceding the expiration of a commission, notify the notary public of the expiration date and furnish a blank application for reappointment" (IC 9E.5).

Non-Residents: A resident of a state bordering Iowa may become a Notary if that person's place of work or business is within the state. Such a commission expires if the person ceases to work or maintain a business in the state (IC 9E.3[3]).

Online Search: The Iowa Secretary of State's website provides a "Search Notaries" capability, allowing search for Notaries by name, business name, city, zip code and language proficiency. (Notaries may indicate any bilingual ability on the commission application form.) Considerable information may then be provided on each Notary, including commission expiration date and status (active or inactive), and home and business postal and email addresses and phone numbers.

Changes of Status

For any change of status, the Notary should submit a "Notary Public Change/Amendment to Application" form, which is available on the Secretary of State's website under "Notary Forms."

If Notary Moves: "If you move, inform the (Secretary of State's) office of your new home address. If you change employers, notify the office of your new employer and new address" (PB).

If Notary Changes Name: "If you change your name, you may use your new name or continue using your former name through the end of your term. If you use your new name, inform the Secretary of State's office immediately of the change" (PB).

If Anything on Application Changes: The instructions on the commission application state that, "(i)f information on this application changes during the duration of your notary appointment, you must notify this office" (website, "Notary Forms"). This particularly includes a change of name by the Notary; a change of home address or phone; a change of employer's name, address or phone; and a change of where the state is to send official mail (home or business).

COUNTY CLERKS

In the state of Iowa, county clerks are not involved in the Notary-commissioning process, nor do they issue authenticating certificates for notarial acts.

OTHER NOTARIAL OFFICERS

Besides Notaries, the following officers are authorized to perform notarial acts in Iowa (IC 9E.10[1]):

1. A judge, clerk or deputy clerk of a court of Iowa;

2. A registrar of vital statistics or the registrar's designee;

3. A person authorized by the law of Iowa to administer oaths;

4. Any other person authorized to perform the specific act by Iowa law.

Members of the General Assembly may also be appointed as Notaries, upon request (IC 9E.3[2]).

QUICK FACTS

Notary Jurisdiction

Statewide. "Iowa notaries may notarize anywhere within the geographical boundaries of the State of Iowa" (PB).

Notary Term Length

Three years for an Iowa resident, and one year for a resident of a state bordering Iowa who works or has a place of business within Iowa (IC 9E.4).

For a member of the Iowa General Assembly, the commission term is the member's legislative term of office (IC 9E.4).

Notary Bond

Not required by law (PB).

Kansas

NOTARY SEAL

A Kansas Notary must authenticate all official acts with a seal of office, and the seal's format must be as follows (KSA 53-105):

Kind

Inked Rubber Stamp or Embosser: "The seal of every notary public shall be either a seal press and the impression thereof inked or blackened or a rubber stamp to be used with permanent ink so that any such seal may be legibly reproduced by photographic process. No notary public shall use either such seal unless an impression thereof has been filed in the office of secretary of state" (KSA 53-105).

Shape/Size

Not specified.

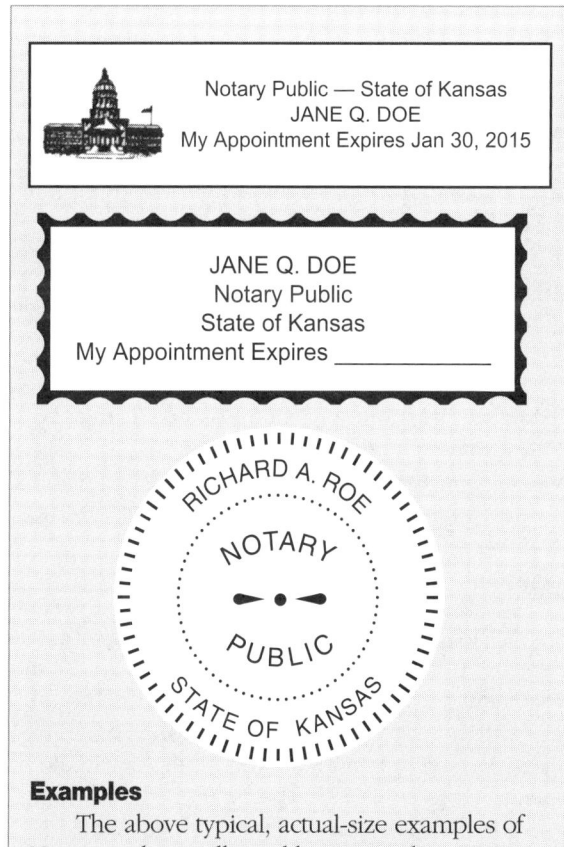

Examples

The above typical, actual-size examples of Notary seals are allowed by Kansas law. Formats other than these may also be permitted.

NOTARY ADMINISTRATION

Office of Secretary of State
Notary Clerk   1-785-296-2239
Memorial Hall, 1st Floor
120 S.W. 10th Ave.
Topeka, KS 66612-1594

Website: www.kssos.org/business/
business_notary.html

NOTARY RULES

KSA — Kansas Statutes Annotated
KAR — Kansas Administrative Regulations
NPH — Kansas Notary Public Handbook

Most Notary rules are in the Kansas Statutes Annotated, Chapter 53, "Notaries Public and Commissioners":

a. Article 1, "Notaries Public";

b. Article 5, "Uniform Law on Notarial Acts."*

  * This is the *Uniform Law on Notarial Acts* of 1982, adopted virtually intact as KSA 53-501 through 53-511.

Rules for electronic notarization are in the Kansas Administrative Regulations, Agency 7 ("Secretary of State"), Article 43 ("Electronic Notarization").

Other guidelines for Notaries are in the "Kansas Notary Public Handbook," published by the Kansas Secretary of State and available on the website.

Components

1. Name of Notary (exactly as it appears on application for appointment);
2. "Notary Public";
3. "State of Kansas" or words of like import indicating statewide authority, approved by Secretary of State;
4. OPTIONAL: appointment expiration date; picture of the Kansas Capitol building.

Blank Space Allowed: Because a seal impression must be affixed to each application for a Kansas Notary commission, a blank space may be left in the seal for the yet-to-be-assigned expiration date, with the date later written in by hand for each notarial act. Or the applicant may pick an expiration date sufficiently in the future to allow commission processing and have that date made part of the seal. Or, as indicated above, no expiration date at all is needed in the seal. "(S)ince the date is assigned by the secretary of state after the application is filed, we recommend that the expiration date be left blank" (website, "Become a Notary").

Appointment Expiration Date Must Appear

"Every notary public shall add to such notary's official signature the date of expiration of appointment as a notary public" (KSA 53-105). This expiration date may be included in the seal.

"If any notary public shall willfully neglect or refuse to attach to the notary's official signature the date of expiration of appointment, as provided in KSA 53-105, the notary shall be deemed guilty of a class C misdemeanor" (KSA 53-106). "Failure to attach the date of expiration also may be grounds for revocation of the notary's appointment (KSA 53-118)" (NPH, "Guidelines for Notaries Public").

"If the officer is a notary public, the certificate must also indicate the date of expiration, if any, of the commission of office, but omission of that information may subsequently be corrected" (KSA 53-508[a]).

Name Change Requires Seal Change

Notaries who legally change their names must get a seal with the new name and, before notarizing and within 30 days after the name change, mail or deliver notice of the change to the Secretary of State (on a "Notary Public Change of Status" form provided by the Secretary) that includes an impression of the new seal (KSA 53-114[a]). A Notary who gets a new seal for any reason must likewise report the change to the Secretary of State and include an impression within 30 days (KSA 53-114[b]).

Employer Cannot Keep Seal

"A notary commission is personal to the notary public. The stamp and journal belong to the notary public and must be safeguarded by the notary in order to prevent forgeries and other misuse. Even if an employer pays for the notary commission, the employer cannot convert the stamp and journal" (NPH, "Frequently Asked Questions").

NOTARY POWERS

Kansas Notaries are authorized to perform the following notarial acts (KSA 53-107 and 53-502):
1. Take acknowledgments*;
2. Administer oaths** and affirmations***;
3. Take verifications upon oath or affirmation;
4. Witness or attest signatures****;
5. Certify or attest copies*****;
6. Note protests of negotiable instruments******;
7. "(P)erform any other act permitted by law."

* Acknowledgments: "'Acknowledgment' means a declaration by a person that the person has executed an instrument for the purposes stated therein and, if the instrument is executed in a representative capacity, that the person signed the instrument with proper authority and executed it as the act of the person or entity represented and identified therein" (KSA 53-502[b]).

** How to Administer Oath: "All oaths shall be administered by laying the right hand upon the Holy Bible or by the uplifted right hand" (KSA 54-102). "All oaths shall commence and conclude as follows: 'You do solemnly swear,' etc.; 'So help you God.'" (KSA 54-104).

The oath-of-office wording for all officers elected or appointed under any law of the state of Kansas is as follows (KSA 54-106): "I do solemnly swear (or affirm, as the case may be) that I will support the constitution of the United States and the constitution of the state of Kansas, and faithfully discharge the duties of _____, so help me God."

*** How to Administer Affirmation: An affirmation is a "(s)poken promise that the contents of the document are true, without requirement of swearing under oath to God. An affirmation is made by a person having conscientious or religious objections to oaths" (NPH, "Glossary of Terms").

"Affirmations shall commence and conclude as follows: 'You do solemnly, sincerely and truly declare and affirm,' etc.; 'And this you do under the pains and penalties of perjury.'" (KSA 54-104).

**** Witnessing or Attesting Signatures: "If the document requires witnessing or attesting, the person must personally appear before you and sign the document in your presence" (NPH).

"In witnessing or attesting a signature, the notarial officer must determine, either from personal knowledge or from satisfactory evidence that the signature is that of the person appearing before the officer and named in the instrument" (KSA 53-503[c]).

***** Certified Copies: "In certifying or attesting a copy of a document or other item, the notarial officer must determine that the proffered copy is a full, true, and accurate transcription or reproduction of that which was copied" (KSA 53-503[d]).

"The notary public must be presented with the original document and make the copy so as to ensure that the copy is in fact a true copy of the original. This procedure should not be used for publicly recorded documents as the notary public cannot obtain the original. Original documents on file with an office/entity must be certified by that entity (i.e., court documents are certified by the court clerk who retains the originals; corporation documents filed with the Secretary of State's office are certified by the Secretary of State; birth/death certificates are certified by the Kansas Department of Health and Environment, Office of Vital Statistics, which maintains the original records, etc.)" (NPH, "Duties of Notaries Public").

****** Protests: For rules on execution of protests, see KSA Chapter 84 ("Uniform Commercial Code"), Article 3 ("Negotiable Instruments"), Part 5 ("Dishonor"). "A protest is a certificate of dishonor made by a notary public or other person authorized by the law where dishonor occurs. The protest must identify the instrument and certify either that presentment has been made or, if not made, the reason why it was not made, and that the instrument has been dishonored by nonacceptance or nonpayment. The protest also may certify that notice of dishonor has been given to some or all parties" (NPH, "Duties of Notaries Public").

Unsworn Declaration Substitute for Oath

"(W)henever a law of this state or any rules and regulations, order or requirement adopted or issued thereunder requires or permits a matter to be supported, evidenced, established or proved by the sworn written declaration, verification, certificate, statement, oath or affidavit of a person, such matter may be supported, evidenced, established or proved with the same force and effect by the unsworn written declaration, verification, certificate or statement dated and subscribed by the person as true, under penalty of perjury .... (These) provisions ... do not apply to the following oaths:

"(1) An oath of office.

"(2) An oath required to be taken before a specified official other than a notary public.

"(3) An oath of a testator or witnesses as required for wills, codicils, revocations of wills and codicils and republications of wills and codicils ..." (KSA 53-601).

For wording, see "Unsworn Declarations," under "Notary Certificates," below.

Identifying Signers

The following identification requirements from the Uniform Law on Notarial Acts apply to acknowledgments, verifications upon oath or affirmation and witnessing or attesting signatures:

"A notarial officer has satisfactory evidence that a person is the person whose true signature is on a document if that person is (1) personally known to the notarial officer, (2) identified upon the oath or affirmation of a credible witness personally known to the notarial officer or (3) identified on the basis of identification documents" (KSA 53-503[f]).

"Proper 'identification' should include a photograph on a reliable identification card such as a driver's license" (NPH, "Frequently Asked Questions").

Representative Capacity: "If the person signs in a representative capacity (i.e., John Smith as President of ABC Corporation), the notary public is not required to check the person's authority, meaning the notary does not check to see if John Smith is in fact president of ABC Corporation. Notaries only must verify the person's legal name as it is the only fixed means of identifying the person; titles come and go. The notary should ensure that the notarial block (certificate) indicates that the person is signing in a representative capacity for the principal....

"An agent authorized by power of attorney to sign for a principal is not required to show the POA at the time of notarization. The notary does not check the person's authority to sign, but merely checks the identity of the agent signing. The document should be signed with the principal's name and the agent's name, with disclosure of the relationship ("by POA" or "as Attorney-in-Fact). The notary should ensure that the notarial block (certificate) indicates that the person is signing in a representative capacity for the principal" (NPH, "Helpful Hints for Notaries Public").

Signature Must Agree with Identification:
"Q. A person whose identification indicates a first name of 'Robert' has asked me to take his acknowledgment on a document he has signed as 'Bob.' Should I insist that he sign as 'Robert?'

"A. Not necessarily. As long as the name that is printed on the document matches the name that is printed on the identification of the signer, the signature does not have to be legible or identical to the printed name" (NPH, "Frequently Asked Questions").

Must Notary Determine Competence?

"Although there are differing opinions on whether a notary public has a duty to determine the person's competency, many experts recommend that the notary make a limited inquiry into the person's ability to understand the contents of the document that the person is signing. The notary can make a quick assessment by asking the person if he or she understands the document. Clearly, a notary should refuse to notarize the signature of a person who unquestionably has no ability to understand the document (unconscious, mentally disabled, etc.)" (NPH, "Frequently Asked Questions").

Conditions for Proof of Execution

"If the grantor dies before acknowledging the deed, or if for any other reason the grantor's attendance cannot be procured, in order to make the acknowledgment, or if, having appeared, the grantor refuses to acknowledge it, proof of the due execution and delivery of the deed may be made by any competent testimony" (KSA 58-2214).

"The certificate endorsed upon the deed thus proved must state: First. The title of the court or office taking the proof. Second. That it was satisfactorily proved that the grantor was dead, or that, for some other cause, the grantor's attendance could not be procured, in order to make the acknowledgement, or that, having appeared, he or she refused to acknowledge the deed.

Third. The names of the witnesses by whom the proof was made, and that it was proved by them that the instrument was executed by the person whose name is thereunto subscribed as a party" (KSA 58-2216).

NOTARY DON'TS

Kansas Notaries may (NPH):
1. NOT notarize their own signatures;
2. NOT notarize an unsigned document;
3. NOT sign a notarial certificate containing false statements;
4. NOT take an acknowledgment over the telephone;
5. NOT take an acknowledgment "because someone else assures you that the signature is genuine";
6. NOT take an acknowledgment "just because you recognize the person's signature."

Signer Must Appear in Person

"The most serious error made by notaries is failure to require the person to appear before the notary before notarizing the document. The person who signed the document must always appear in person. Failure to observe this requirement can result in criminal and civil liability and the loss of the notary's commission" (NPH, "Frequently Asked Questions").

"Never notarize a document outside the presence of the signing party. A notary is required to properly identify the person to ensure that he or she signed the document; the only was to perform this duty is to have the person appear before the notary" (NPH, "Guidelines for Notaries Public").

Notary May Not Select Notarization Type

"Unless the notary also is an attorney, the notary cannot act as a legal advisor and cannot prepare legal documents. For example, if a document does not contain a notarial certificate, the notary public cannot advise as to the proper type of notarization. An attorney should be consulted as to the proper notarization that is required for the document (acknowledgment, witnessing or verification)" (NPH, "Frequently Asked Questions").

"The type of notarization should be evident from the notary block on the document. If the notary block is not already on the document, the signing party or the party drafting/providing the document should instruct the notary public what notarial block is required (acknowledgment, witnessing or verification)....The notary should not make the determination as to what notarization type is appropriate as this could constitute the unlawful practice of law. However, the notary should know the correct language to be used when the person explains what type of notarization is needed" (NPH, "Guidelines for Notaries Public").

Foreign-Language Advertising Restrictions

"(a) A notary public who is not admitted to the practice of law in this state and who advertises notarial services in a language other than English shall include, in any advertisement, notice, letterhead or sign, a statement prominently displayed, in the same language in which such notarial services are offered, as follows: 'I am not authorized to practice law and have no authority to give advice on immigration law or other legal matters.'

"(b) A notary public who is not admitted to the practice of law in this state shall not use the term 'notario publico' or any equivalent non-English term in any business card, advertisement, notice or sign unless it complies with the requirements of subsection (a)" (KSA 53-121).

Violation of the above subsection constitutes a class B misdemeanor, as well as a deceptive act or practice under KSA 50-626 that is subject to the penalties and remedies provided by the Kansas Consumer Protection Act.

Disqualifying Interests for Notary

A Notary who has a direct financial or beneficial interest in a transaction must not notarize in connection with that transaction, as when the Notary (KSA 53-109):

1. With respect to a financial transaction, is named, individually, as a principal to the transaction; or

2. With respect to real property, is named, individually, as a grantor, grantee, mortgagor, mortgagee, trustor, trustee, beneficiary, vendor, vendee, lessor or lessee, to the transaction.

"If there is a question of a direct financial or beneficial interest, it would be advisable for a disinterested notary public to notarize the document" (NPH).

"In general, if a notary is named in a document, or is signing a document, he or she should not notarize it" (website, "Responsibilities and Duties").

No Disqualifying Interest: "For purposes of this act, a notary public has no direct financial or beneficial interest in a transaction when the notary public acts in the capacity of an agent, employee, insurer, attorney, escrow agent or lender for a person having a direct financial or beneficial interest in the transaction" (KSA 53-109[c]).

Notarizing for Family Members: "A notary public may not notarize his or her own signature, but may notarize the signatures of his or her spouse, children, parents or other relatives. However, the power is limited by the provisions of KSA 53-109" (NPH, "Frequently Asked Questions").

May Not Be Both Witness and Notary on Will

"A notary may not serve as both a witness and a notary public on a will. KSA 59-606 requires the notary public to notarize the signature of the testator and the witnesses. Because a notary cannot witness and notarize his or her own signature, a notary may not serve as both a witness and the notary on a will executed in Kansas" (NPH, "Helpful Hints for Notaries Public").

NOTARY SIGNING AGENTS

Currently, there are no statutes, regulations or rules expressly governing, prohibiting or restricting the operation of Notary Signing Agents within the state of Kansas.

NOTARY FEES

Notary fees are not specified by law. "There is no statutory fee schedule in Kansas that a notary public must follow, nor is there a prohibition against a notary public charging a fee. Therefore, a notary public may charge a reasonable fee for the performance of a notarial act" (NPH, "Frequently Asked Questions").

NOTARY CERTIFICATES

Kansas has adopted the *Uniform Law on Notarial Acts*, including the short-form certificates (KSA 53-509) for:

1. Acknowledgment by individual;
2. Acknowledgment by representative;
3. Verification upon oath or affirmation;
4. Witnessing or attesting signature;
5. Attesting copy of document.

For the text of these certificates, see "Uniform Law on Notarial Acts (1982)", Section 8, in Appendix 2.

Requirements for Any Notarial Certificate

"(a) A notarial act must be evidenced by a certificate signed and dated by a notarial officer. The certificate must include identification of the jurisdiction in which the notarial act is performed and the title of the office of the notarial officer and may include the official stamp or seal of office, but omission of that information may subsequently be corrected. If the officer is a commissioned officer on active duty in the military service of the United States, it must also include the officer's rank.

"(b) A certificate of a notarial act is sufficient if it meets the requirement of subsection (a) and it:

"(1) Is in the short form set forth in (KSA 53-509);

"(2) Is in a form otherwise prescribed by the law of this state;

"(3) Is in a form prescribed by the laws or regulations applicable in the place in which the notarial act was performed; or

"(4) Sets forth the actions of the notarial officer and those are sufficient to meet the requirements of the designated notarial act" (KSA 53-508).

<u>'Notarial Block' Requirements</u>: According to the "Kansas Notary Public Handbook," a so-called "notarial block" — also known as the notarial certificate — must contain the following components:

1. Venue ("State of Kansas, County of _____");
2. Declarative wording that provides the signer's name, describes the type of notarial act, and states the date of notarization;
3. Notary's signature;
4. Notary's stamp/seal;
5. Commission expiration date.

Unsworn Declarations (KSA 53-601):

If Executed Outside Kansas:

I declare (or verify, certify or state) under penalty of perjury under the laws of the state of Kansas that the foregoing is true and correct. Executed on (date).

_____ *(Signature)*

If Executed Inside Kansas:

I declare (or verify, certify or state) under penalty of perjury that the foregoing is true and correct. Executed on (date).

_____ *(Signature)*

Correcting Notarial Certificates

"The notary can cross through any incorrect information and write in the correction. The notary should place his or her initials by the correction. White-out should not be used, as the receiving party may reject the notarized document if it contains white-out. White-out raises questions as to what information was deleted, whereas simply crossing through the incorrect information allows the receiving party to see what information has been altered" (NPH, "Frequently Asked Questions").

ELECTRONIC NOTARIZATIONS

Kansas has adopted the Uniform Electronic Transactions Act (KSA 16-1601 through 16-1620), including the provision on notarization and acknowledgment, which has been amended to authorize the Kansas Secretary of State to set rules for electronic notarization. The Act recognizes the legal validity of electronic signatures used by Notaries:

"(a) If a law requires a signature or record to be notarized, acknowledged, verified or made under oath, the requirement is satisfied if the electronic signature of the person authorized to perform those acts, together with all other information required to be included by other applicable law, is attached to or logically associated with the signature or record."

"(b) The secretary of state is hereby authorized to promulgate rules and regulations establishing procedures for an electronic notarization" (KSA 16-1611).

Secretary Sets eNotary Rules

Effective December 30, 2005, the Kansas Secretary of State has set regulations for electronic notarization in the state, by authority of KSA 16-1611(b). These eNotarization rules are contained in the Kansas Administrative Regulations (KAR), Agency 7 ("Secretary of State"), Article 43 ("Electronic Notarization"). "Currently, we are in the pilot stage of issuing e-notary commissions" (website, "E-Notary").

eNotary Registration Requirements

"'Electronic notary public,' 'electronic notary,' and 'e-notary' mean a notary public who has registered with the secretary of state and who provides electronic notarial acts using a digital certificate authorized by the secretary of state" (KAR 7-43-1[c]).

"Each individual who wants to become an electronic notary shall meet the following requirements:

"a. Complete a course of instruction approved by the secretary of state;

"b. pass an examination approved by the secretary of state on the course of instruction specified in subsection (a);

"c. obtain a digital certificate authorized by the secretary of state;

"d. register with the secretary of state on a form prescribed by the secretary of state, which shall include providing proof of compliance with subsections (a), (b), and (c); and

"e. pay an information and services fee of $20" (KAR 7-43-2).

Electronic Notarization Requirements

"a. Each electronic notary shall use a digital signature when performing any electronic notarization. Before performing any electronic notarization, each electronic notary shall take reasonable steps to ensure that the digital certificate used to create the digital signature is valid and has not expired, been revoked, or been terminated by its registered certification authority.

"b. When performing any electronic notarization, each electronic notary shall complete a notarial certificate, which shall be attached to, or logically associated with, the electronic document" (KAR 7-43-3).

Obtaining Digital Signature: "Kansas administrative regulations…require a notary public to obtain a Kansas digital signature issued through the Kansas Secretary of State for purposes of electronic notarization (KAR 7-43-1 et seq.)" (NPH, "Electronic Notarizations").

Personal Appearance: "Notwithstanding any security measures used in performing any electronic notarization, an electronic notary public shall not perform any electronic notarial act if the principal does not appear in person before the electronic notary at the time of notarization" (KAR 7-43-4).

"As with all notarizations, the signature must still physically take place in front of the notary. This (electronic) commission does not allow a notary to notarize a document that was previously signed and then electronically submitted to the notary" (website, "E-notary").

Remote "notarizations" by webcam are not allowed (NPH, "Test Your Notary Knowledge").

Other Notary Statutes Apply: "Except as otherwise provided in these regulations, the provisions of KSA 53-101 et seq., and amendments thereto, governing notaries public and KSA 16-1601 et seq., and amendments thereto, governing electronic transactions shall apply to each electronic notary public" (KAR 7-43-6).

Authentication: If authentication of an electronically notarized document is required by another state or nation, an electronic authenticating certificate will be attached or logically associated by the Kansas Secretary of State in conformance with pertinent current treaties and conventions" (KAR 7-43-5).

Certificate, Signature, Seal Defined

"'Notarial certificate' means the portion of a notarized document that is completed by the notary, bears the notary's signature and seal, and states the facts attested by the notary in a particular notarized" (KAR 7-43-1[i]).

"'Electronic signature' means an electronic sound, symbol or process attached to or logically associated with a record and executed or adopted by a person with the intent to sign the record" (KSA 16-1602[i]).

"'Electronic notary seal' means the information within a notarized electronic document that includes the notary's name, jurisdiction of appointment, and expiration date of the appointment" (KAR 7-43-1[f]).

URPERA Does Not Address Seal Image

Kansas adopted the Uniform Real Property Electronic Recording Act (URPERA) in 2006 (KSA 58-4401 through 58-4407), but without its standard provision removing any requirement that a physical image of a Notary seal be affixed to an electronic document. This provision was omitted at the request of the Secretary of State out of concern that it could conflict with a provision in the state's Uniform Electronic Transactions Act directing the Secretary to promulgate rules for electronic notarization.

NOTARY RECORDS

"There is no statutory requirement in Kansas that a notary public keep a log book or a journal. However, it is recommended that a notary public keep one for his or her own records and protection from liability" (NPH, "Frequently Asked Questions"). "(K)eeping a journal ensures that the notary has an accurate record of all transactions that could protect the notary if any action is ever questioned" (website, "Responsibilities and Duties").

Recommended Entries

"The notary public should record the name of the person signing, the date of the signature and the type of document notarized. The notary should have the signing party sign the notebook so that the notary has an example of his or her signature" (NPH, "Helpful Hints for Notaries Public").

Employer May Not Keep Journal

"Can my employer keep my journal or notary stamp after I leave my job? — No. A notary commission is personal to the notary public. The stamp and journal belong to the notary public and must be safeguarded by the notary in order to prevent forgeries and other misuse. Even if an employer pays for the notary commission, the employer cannot convert the stamp and journal" (NPH, "Frequently Asked Questions").

AUTHENTICATION OF NOTARIAL ACTS

Secretary of State

Authenticating certificates for Notaries, including apostilles, are issued only by the Kansas Secretary of State's office (KSA 53-401).

Fees: $7.50 per document for a regular authenticating certificate or an apostille.

Address:
Office of Secretary of State
Notary Clerk
Memorial Hall, 1st Floor
120 S.W. 10th Ave.
Topeka, KS 66612-1594

Telephone: 1-785-296-2239

Procedure: Mail or present in person the original notarized document(s), along with the appropriate fee. Mailed requests must include an addressed, stamped envelope. Indicate the nation to which the document(s) will be sent and how many certifications or apostilles are needed. "We will return documents through an expedited mail company as long as the fees are prepaid" (website, "Certifications"). Notarial errors may prevent authentication of the document(s), according to the website.

COMMISSIONING AND ADMINISTRATION

The Kansas Secretary of State appoints and maintains records on the state's Notaries (KSA 53-101). "All notary public applications and appointments are open records and subject to public inspection pursuant to the Kansas Open Records Act" (NPH, "Frequently Asked Questions").

Applying for Commission

Qualifications: An applicant for a Kansas Notary Public commission must (KSA 53-101): (a) be at least 18 years of age, (b) be a citizen of the United States and (c) be a resident of Kansas or of a bordering state who is regularly employed in or carries on a business or profession in Kansas. Persons who have been convicted of a felony or have had a professional license revoked do not qualify for a Notary commission (website, "Become a Notary").

No Course or Test: No course of instruction or test is required to become a Notary Public in Kansas — although a course must be taken in order to register as an electronic notary (KAR 7-43-2[a]). A "pop-quiz" with answers provided is included in the "Kansas Notary Public Handbook" ("Test Your Notary Knowledge") as a self-examination on notarial procedures.

Application: A Notary seal must be obtained before submitting the application and an impression of this seal must be affixed on the form (KSA 53-102); if the applicant opts to use more than one seal, an impression of each must be affixed. A section of the application must be completed by the surety for the $7,500 Notary bond (KSA 53-102); an insurance company must affix a corporate seal or attach its power of attorney. The application must be sworn to before another Notary, then submitted to the Secretary of State with a $25 fee. "The expiration date is determined by the date that the Secretary of State's office files the application, not the date on the bond or the date the application is submitted to our office" (website, "Become a Notary").

"Once the Secretary of State's office has received and accepted the application a certificate, wallet card and handbook will be mailed to the home address on the application. Until receipt of the certificate and wallet card, the applicant cannot notarize any documents" (website, "Become a Notary" and KSA 53-105).

The renewal process is the same as for initial application (KSA 53-117). "Application should be made sufficiently prior to expiration to ensure uninterrupted authority, generally one month prior to the expiration of the current commission" (NPH, "Frequently Asked Questions").

Non-Residents: Any resident of a bordering state who regularly works or carries on a business or profession in Kansas may become a Kansas Notary (KSA 53-101).

Changes of Status

"If at any time while commissioned the name, address, phone number or stamp of a notary changes, he or she must file a 'Change of Status' form with the Secretary of State's office" (website, "Become a Notary"). This form may be downloaded from the website ("Filings & Forms").

If Notary Changes Name: Notaries who legally change their names must get a seal with the new name and, before notarizing and within 30 days after the name change, mail or deliver notice of the change to the Secretary of State (on a "Notary Public Change of Status" form provided by the Secretary) that includes an impression of the new seal (KSA 53-114). A Notary who gets a new seal for any reason must likewise report the change to the Secretary of State and include an impression within 30 days. A name change also requires obtaining a rider for the Notary bond.

If Notary Moves: Any change of address by the Notary must be reported to the Secretary of State on a "Notary Public Change of Status" form (NPH, "Frequently Asked Question").

If Notary Resigns: "If a notary public no longer desires to be a notary public in this state, the notary shall send immediately by mail or deliver to the secretary of state a letter informing the secretary of state of the notary's desire to resign as a notary public in the state of Kansas. The appointment of the notary shall thereupon cease to be in effect" (KSA 53-116).

COUNTY CLERKS

In Kansas, Notaries do not file oaths, bonds and seal/signature samples at the county level, and, thus, county officials do not issue authenticating certificates for, nor keep records on, Notaries.

OTHER NOTARIAL OFFICERS

Besides Notaries, the following officers can notarize in Kansas (KSA 53-504):
   1. A judge, clerk or deputy clerk of any court in the state;
   2. A county clerk or deputy county clerk;
   3. An election commissioner or assistant election commissioner.

Registers of Deeds

County registers of deeds are authorized to take acknowledgment of instruments conveying or affecting real estate within Kansas (KSA 58-2211).

Kansas

QUICK FACTS

Notary Jurisdiction

Statewide (KSA 53-101). "(A Notary's) authority extends no further than the geographic boundaries of Kansas. You cannot perform one part of a notarial act outside the state and the other part inside the state. Both parts must be executed at the same time and the same place inside Kansas" (NPH, "Frequently Asked Questions").

Notary Term Length

Four years (KSA 53-101), expiring at midnight on the commission expiration date.

Notary Bond

$7,500, with an insurance company licensed in Kansas (KSA 53-102). A surety may cancel a Notary's bond after giving 14 days' written notice to the Secretary of State (KSA 53-115). "(I)f the employer provided the notary's bond, the employer can cancel the bond" (NPH, "Frequently Asked Questions").

Three-Year Statute of Limitations: "No suit shall be instituted against any such notary or his or her securities more than three years after the cause of action accrues" (KSA 53-113).

Kentucky

NOTARY SEAL

A Kentucky Notary Public is not required by law to use a seal of office.

Optional Seal Guidelines

"Kentucky notary statutes ... do not require the notary to use a seal. Notarizations in Kentucky are regularly performed without a stamp or seal. However, if a Notary wishes to obtain a seal of office, it should contain name and notary public title such as 'Notary Public — State at Large' or 'Notary Public — Special Commission'" (NPH).

Examples

Above are actual-size examples of typical Notary seals allowed by Kentucky law. Formats other than these may also be permitted.

NOTARY ADMINISTRATION

Office of Secretary of State
Administrative Services
Notary Branch   1-502-564-3490
P.O. Box 821
700 Capital Ave., Suite 86
Frankfort, KY 40601

Website: www.sos.ky.gov/adminservices/notaries

NOTARY RULES

KRS — *Kentucky Revised Statutes*
NPH — *Commonwealth of Kentucky Notary Public Handbook*

Most Notary rules are in the Kentucky Revised Statutes, Chapter 423, "Notaries Public and Commissioners of Foreign Deeds" including the "Uniform Recognition of Acknowledgments Act."*

* This is the *Uniform Recognition of Acknowledgments Act* of 1968, adopted virtually intact as KRS Sections 423.110 through 423.190.

Other guidelines for Notaries are in the "Commonwealth of Kentucky Notary Public Handbook" (Rev. January 2011) issued by the Secretary of State and available on the website.

Kind
Inked seal or embosser not specified.

Shape/Size
Not specified.

Components
1. Name of Notary;
2. "Notary Public — State at Large" or "Notary Public — Special Commission";
3. "Kentucky".

Commission Expiration Date Must Appear
Every notarial certificate must state the commission expiration date of the Notary Public (KRS 423.010).

Notary Public — Special Commission

Residents or non-residents of Kentucky may be appointed by the Governor to notarize documents, inside or outside the state, that will be recorded in Kentucky (KRS 423.110[6]). Such Notaries must use the following signature format (NPH):

> I, _____, a Kentucky Notary Public Special Commission, for acts performed in or outside Kentucky for recordation in Kentucky; my commission expires: _____.

NOTARY POWERS

Kentucky Notaries are authorized to perform the following notarial acts (KRS 423.110):
1. Take acknowledgments* and proofs**;
2. Administer oaths*** and affirmations;
3. Attest documents;
4. Take depositions****;
5. Execute protests (KRS 423.030 through 423.050).

* Identifying Acknowledgers: "An acknowledgment is a verification that the person whose signature appears on the document is the person who appears before the notary and whose identity the notary took reasonable steps to verify" (NPH).

"The person taking an acknowledgment shall certify that: (1) The person acknowledging appeared before him and acknowledged he executed the instrument; and (2) The person acknowledging was known to the person taking the acknowledgment or that the person taking the acknowledgment had satisfactory evidence that the person acknowledging was the person described in and who executed the instrument" (KRS 423.130).

"An acknowledgment authenticates a signature. An acknowledgment proves that the signer personally appeared before a notary; the notary identified the signer; and the signature on the document matches the signature on the identification which the signer presented to the notary and to the signature in (the) journal" (NPH).

** Proof by Two Subscribing Witnesses: Proofs must be made by two subscribing witnesses, or by one subscribing witness who also proves the attestation of the other (KRS 382.130[2]). There are also procedures for when one or both of the subscribing witnesses are dead or out of the state (KRS 382.130[3] and [4]).

"Where a deed is proved by persons other than the subscribing witnesses, the officer shall state the name and residence of each person in his certificate" (KRS 382.160[2]).

*** Official Oaths: "The official oath of any officer, may be administered by: (1) Any state or federal judge, with Kentucky jurisdiction; or (2) Any county judge/executive, notary public, clerk of a court, or justice of the peace, within his district or county" (KRS 62.020).

"A Kentucky notary public is empowered to administer most types of oath. These fall into two categories: (1) oaths of office and (2) oaths of testimony.

"State law sets forth the form of the oath of office for most public officials. Some oaths of office must be administered by a specific official other than a notary.

"The oath of testimony is used to swear a person to the truthfulness of her/his statement (written or oral). The oath is familiar: 'Do you solemnly swear to tell (or write) the truth, the whole truth and nothing but the truth, so help you God?' or 'Do you swear or affirm to tell (or write) the truth, the whole truth and nothing but the truth?' Depositions, affidavits, hearings and government documents are common occasions for the use of the oath of testimony" (NPH).

Jurat: "A jurat authenticates a signature made under oath or affirmation. A jurat proves that the signer personally appeared before the notary; the signer was positively identified by the notary; the notary placed the signer under oath; and the notary watched the signature being made.

"In a jurat, the notary does have to see the signer sign the document and the notary must place the signer under oath before the signer signs the document" (NPH).

**** Depositions: "Depositions taken in this state, to be used in its courts, shall be taken before an examiner; a judge, clerk, commissioner or official reporter of a court; a notary public; or before such other persons and under such circumstances as shall be authorized by law" (Ky. Rules of Civil Proc., Rule 28.01).

Identifying Document Signers

"A notary first identifies the signer to be the person whose name is signed to the document. The identification can be made through personal knowledge or through appropriate credentials such as a driver's license" (NPH).

"A notary should examine the I.D. for three features:

"1. A photo of the bearer; and

"2. Accurate physical description of the bearer; and

"3. Signature of the bearer" (NPH).

Date of Notarization

"If the notary is signing a certificate of acknowledgment, the document's date of signing does not have to match the certificate date. The document could have been signed several months earlier.

"If the notary is signing a jurat, the document's date must always be the same date of the date of the notarization, since the affiant must always sign the document in the notary's presence" (NPH).

NOTARY DON'TS

No Backdating

"The date of the notarization should always be the date the notarization was made, which should be the day the signer actually appeared in person for the notarial act. A notary should not backdate notarizations" (NPH).

Disqualifying Interests

Notarizing with Financial Interest: "This is not specifically prohibited, but is definitely a bad practice. By notarizing a document in which a notary has a financial interest, a notary is simply increasing the chances that the document, and the underlying transaction, might be challenged. Therefore, the practice should be avoided" (NPH).

Notarizing for Oneself: "Though self-notarization is not specifically prohibited by statute, the practice would defeat the entire purpose of a certificate of acknowledgment, which is to obtain independent, reliable confirmation of the act of signing a document" (NPH).

Notarizing for Family: "There is no specific prohibition against notarizing for a family member. A notary should probably avoid the practice, however, to avoid any possible challenges based upon allegations of bias, conflict of interest or other impropriety" (NPH).

Savings and Loan Notaries: A Notary who is a member or employee of a savings and loan association may notarize for that association (KRS 286.5–241).

NOTARY SIGNING AGENTS

Currently, there are no statutes, regulations or rules expressly governing, prohibiting or restricting the operation of Notary Signing Agents within the state of Kentucky.

Influential Kentucky Supreme Court Ruling

Notary Signing Agents may operate freely in the Commonwealth of Kentucky due to a 2003 Kentucky Supreme Court ruling in the case of *Countrywide Home Loans v. Kentucky Bar Association*, 2000-SC-0206-KB (Ky. 8-21-2003). Countrywide had asked the Supreme Court to review the Kentucky Bar's Advisory Opinion U-58, which declared that performance of a real estate closing by a lay closing agent is the unauthorized practice of law, reversing a previous Bar advisory, U-31, that allowed laypersons to conduct real estate closings subject to certain limitations. The Court concluded:

"We do not deny that there are some portions of the residential real estate transaction that do constitute the practice of law, i.e., the title commitment letter and the preparation of deeds and mortgages, but this case has not asked us to deal with those matters attendant to the real estate closing itself. What we have been concerned with today is merely the thin slice at the end of the real estate transaction that we refer to as the closing. Certainly, we do not doubt that legal issues arise at some real estate closings. We do not, however, believe that the rate at which these issues arise requires that only attorneys or persons under their immediate supervision conduct real estate closings. Stated otherwise, although a layperson may not dispense legal advice anywhere — not the golf course, not in line at the grocery, not while fishing on a lake somewhere, and certainly not at a real estate closing — we do not believe that a real estate closing is a setting so fraught with the potential for unauthorized practice that U-58's blanket prohibition against lay closing agents is warranted as a prophylactic measure. Thus, we vacate U-58. In doing so, we recognize that U-31 properly states the law on real estate closings in Kentucky: laypersons may conduct real estate closings on behalf of other parties, but they may not answer legal questions that arise at the closing or offer any legal advice to the parties. If they do answer such questions, they are then engaged in the unauthorized practice of law."

NOTARY FEES

The maximum fees for notarial acts are (KRS 64.300[1]):
1. Taking an acknowledgment: 50 cents;
2. Administering an oath or affirmation, with a certificate: 20 cents;
3. Executing a protest, 50 cents; each notice of protest, 25 cents;
4. Recording each protest, attestation or acknowledgment in a book to be kept for that purpose, 75 cents (KRS 423.030).

No Fee for Veterans' Benefit Papers

"No fee or compensation shall be allowed or paid for affixing the jurat of a notary public to any application, affidavit, certificate or other paper necessary to be filed in support of any claim for the benefits of federal legislation for any person or his dependents who has served as a member of the Army, Navy, or Marine Corps of the United States" (KRS 64.300[2]).

NOTARY CERTIFICATES

Kentucky has adopted the *Uniform Recognition of Acknowledgments Act*, including the five short-form certificates (KRS 423.160) for:
1. Acknowledgment by individual;
2. Acknowledgment by corporation;
3. Acknowledgment by partnership;
4. Acknowledgment by attorney in fact;
5. Acknowledgment by public officer, trustee, or personal representative.

For the text of these certificates, see "Uniform Recognition of Acknowledgments Act (1968)," Section 6, in Appendix 3.

Form of Acknowledgment Certificate

"The form of a certificate of acknowledgment used by a person whose authority is recognized under (Uniform Recognition of Acknowledgments Act, Section 1) shall be accepted in this state if:
"1. The certificate is in a form prescribed by the laws or regulations of this state;
"2. The certificate is in a form prescribed by the laws or regulations applicable in the place in which the acknowledgment is taken;
"3. The certificate contains the words 'acknowledged before me,' or their substantial equivalent" (KRS 423.140).

Certificates of Acknowledgment or Proof

"1. Where the acknowledgment of a deed is taken by an officer of this state or by an officer residing out of this state, he may simply certify that it was acknowledged before him, and when it was done.
"2. Where a deed is proved by persons other than the subscribing witnesses, the officer shall state the name and residence of each person in his certificate" (KRS 382.160).

ELECTRONIC NOTARIZATIONS

The state of Kentucky has not yet adopted statutes or regulations expressly establishing rules, definitions and procedures for electronic notarization.

UETA Recognizes Notary's E-Signature

Effective August 1, 2000, Kentucky adopted the Uniform Electronic Transactions Act (KRS 369.101 through 369.120), including the provision on notarization, thereby recognizing the legal validity of electronic signatures used by Notaries:
"If a law requires a signature or record to be notarized, acknowledged, verified, or made under oath, the requirement is satisfied if the electronic signature of the person authorized to perform those acts, together with all other information required to be included by other applicable law, is attached to or logically associated with the signature or record" (KRS 369.111).

NOTARY RECORDS

"Although many states require (keeping a Notary journal) by law, this is not the case in Kentucky. However, it is advisable to keep a record book of official acts because a journal provides documentation of the notary's personal knowledge of performance of the notarization ....

"The journal should be bound with pre-numbered pages to deter unauthorized removal of pages. There should be entry space to record all pertinent information. The journal should be completed before the notarization" (NPH).

Recommended Entries

"The Commonwealth of Kentucky Notary Public Handbook" recommends that the following data be recorded in the journal for each notarial act:

1. Document signer's signature;
2. Date and time of notarization;
3. Date of document;
4. Type of notarization performed and type of document notarized;
5. Document signer's address;
6. Statement on how the Notary verified the signer's identity;
7. Fee, if any, charged for the notarial act;
8. Special comments about the transaction.

Record of Protest Required

"The notaries public shall record in a well bound and properly indexed book, kept by them for that purpose, all protests made by them for the nonacceptance or nonpayment of all bills of exchange, checks or promissory notes placed on the footing of bills of exchange, and on which a protest is required by law, or of which protest is evidence of dishonor" (KRS 423.030).

"For each failure to record his protest as required by KRS 423.030, a notary public shall forfeit all his fees and shall be fined five dollars ($5)" (KRS 423.990).

County Clerk Keeps Notary Records

"Upon the resignation of a notary public or the expiration of his term of office if he is not reappointed, he shall place his record book in the office of the county clerk in the county in which he was appointed, and if a notary dies, his representative shall deposit the record book with the clerk aforesaid. A copy of such record certified by the clerk in whose office it is filed shall be evidence in all the courts of this state" (KRS 423.050).

AUTHENTICATION OF NOTARIAL ACTS

County Clerk

Locally, authenticating certificates for Notaries are available from the office of the county clerk where a particular Notary has filed a signature and commissioning certificate (KRS 423.020[2]).

Secretary of State

Certificates authenticating the acts of Notaries, including apostilles, are also issued by the Kentucky Secretary of State's office, as are certificates authenticating the acts of county clerks.

Fees: $5 per document for a certificate of authentication or an apostille. Payable to "Kentucky State Treasurer."

Mailing Address:
Office of Secretary of State
Authentications and Apostilles
P.O. Box 718
Frankfort, KY 40602-0718

Telephone: 1-502-564-3490

Courier or Personal Delivery:
Office of Secretary of State
State Capitol
700 Capital Ave., Suite 156
Frankfort, KY 40601

Procedure: Mail or present in person the original notarized document(s), along with the appropriate fee. A county clerk's authentication is required first, even for an apostille. The document(s) should be submitted with a completed "Request for Apostille or Authentication" form, downloadable from the Secretary's website ("Apostilles").

COMMISSIONING AND ADMINISTRATION

The Kentucky Secretary of State appoints and maintains records on the commonwealth's Notaries (KRS 423.010).

There are two different kinds of Kentucky Notary Public commission and the same individual may qualify for either or both. A Special Commission Notary is a resident or non-resident of Kentucky who is appointed by the Governor of Kentucky to perform notarial acts inside or outside of the state for documents to be recorded in Kentucky only (KRS 423.110[6]). A Notary Public State at Large is a resident or non-resident of Kentucky who is appointed to perform notarial acts only within the state for documents that may be recorded inside or outside Kentucky (KRS 423.010).

Applying for Commission

Qualifications: An applicant for appointment as a Kentucky Notary must (KRS 423.010): (a) be at least 18 years old, (b) for a State at Large commission, be a Kentucky resident who lives or is employed in the county where applying, or a non-resident of Kentucky principally employed in the county where applying, or for a Special commission, be a resident of the county from which applying or a non-resident of Kentucky, (c) be of good moral character (i.e., not be a convicted felon unless civil rights have been restored by executive order) and (d) be capable of discharging the duties of a Notary.

No Course or Test: No course of instruction or examination is required to become a Notary Public in Kentucky.

Application: Each application for a Notary appointment (including for a Notary Public — Special Commission) must be approved and endorsed by "the Circuit Judge, circuit clerk, county judge/executive, county clerk, justice of the peace (magistrate), or a member of the General Assembly of the county of the residence of the applicant or in the county in which the applicant's principal place of employment is located" (KRS 423.010). The "Certificate of Approval" that must be signed by one of the above officials is part of the application. The commissioning fee is $10.

Renewing Notaries should not send in an application earlier than four weeks before commission expiration.

Filing for Notary Public — State at Large: After the application has been sent to the Secretary of State, a "Certificate of Appointment" as a Kentucky Notary Public — State at Large is sent by the Secretary to the county clerk in the county of application, and at the same time a written notice is sent to the new Notary. Within 30 days of receiving this notice, the Notary must go to the county clerk's office to (a) post a bond, (b) take the oath of office and (c) file and record the Notary commission.

Filing for Notary — Special Commission: After the application has been sent to the Secretary of State, a "Notice of Appointment" is sent directly to the applicant. This Notice includes an oath-of-office form. The oath of office must be taken within 30 days of receiving the Notice before any judge, county judge/executive, Notary, clerk of court or justice of the peace (magistrate) in the applicant's district or county. The oath-of-office form must be signed by both the applicant and the official administering the oath, after which it must be returned to the Secretary of State within 30 days of the date on the Notice (KRS 62.010). At that point, the Governor of Kentucky, through the Secretary of State, will issue a commission to the applicant, who need not post a bond.

Non-Residents: Commuting out-of-state residents may apply for a State at Large commission from the county in which they are principally employed, with an endorsement from an official (see above) of that county (KRS 423.010). Non-resident applicants for a Special commission are not required to be principally employed in a given Kentucky county; they may choose the county of application.

May Be Appointed as Both Kinds of Notary: "A person may be appointed both a Notary Public — Special Commission and a Notary Public State at Large. Two different applications must be submitted; two different filing fees are required" (NPH).

Online Search: Using the Kentucky Secretary of State's "Notary Portal," the roster of Kentucky Notaries may be searched from 1996 to the present at http://apps.sos.ky.gov/adminservices/notaries/.

Changes of Status

If Notary Changes Name: A Notary with a changed name should continue to use the "old" name as stated on the commission certificate, though the new name may be put in parentheses, if desired (NPH).

COUNTY CLERKS

To contact a Kentucky county clerk to obtain an authenticating certificate for a Notary, or to seek assistance in locating a given Notary, telephone long-distance information — 1-XXX-555-1212 — using the following area codes:

County	City/Town	Area Code
Adair	Columbia	(270)
Allen	Scottsville	(270)
Anderson	Lawrenceburg	(502)
Ballard	Wickliffe	(270)
Barren	Glasgow	(270)
Bath	Owingsville	(606)
Bell	Pineville	(606)
Boone	Burlington	(859)
Bourbon	Paris	(859)
Boyd	Catlettsburg	(606)
Boyle	Danville	(859)
Bracken	Brooksville	(606)
Breathitt	Jackson	(606)
Breckinridge	Hardinsburg	(270)
Bullitt	Shepherdsville	(502)
Butler	Morgantown	(270)
Caldwell	Princeton	(270)
Calloway	Murray	(270)
Campbell	Newport	(859)
Carlisle	Bardwell	(270)
Carroll	Carrollton	(502)
Carter	Grayson	(606)
Casey	Liberty	(606)
Christian	Hopkinsville	(270)
Clark	Winchester	(859)
Clay	Manchester	(606)
Clinton	Albany	(606)
Crittenden	Marion	(270)
Cumberland	Burkesville	(270)
Daviess	Owensboro	(270)
Edmonson	Brownsville	(270)
Elliott	Sandy Hook	(606)
Estill	Irvine	(606)
Fayette	Lexington	(859)
Fleming	Flemingsburg	(606)
Floyd	Prestonsburg	(606)
Franklin	Frankfort	(502)
Fulton	Hickman	(270)
Gallatin	Warsaw	(859)
Garrard	Lancaster	(859)
Grant	Williamstown	(859)
Graves	Mayfield	(270)
Grayson	Leitchfield	(270)
Green	Greensburg	(270)
Greenup	Greenup	(606)
Hancock	Hawesville	(270)
Hardin	Elizabethtown	(270)
Harlan	Harlan	(606)
Harrison	Cynthiana	(859)
Hart	Munfordville	(270)
Henderson	Henderson	(270)
Henry	New Castle	(502)
Hickman	Clinton	(270)
Hopkins	Madisonville	(270)
Jackson	McKee	(606)
Jefferson	Louisville	(502)
Jessamine	Nicholasville	(859)
Johnson	Paintsville	(606)
Kenton	Covington	(859)
Knott	Hindman	(606)
Knox	Barbourville	(606)
Larue	Hodgenville	(270)
Laurel	London	(606)
Lawrence	Louisa	(606)
Lee	Beattyville	(606)
Leslie	Hyden	(606)
Letcher	Whitesburg	(606)
Lewis	Vanceburg	(606)
Lincoln	Stanford	(606)
Livingston	Smithland	(270)
Logan	Russellville	(270)
Lyon	Eddyville	(270)
McCracken	Paducah	(270)
McCreary	Whitley City	(606)
McLean	Calhoun	(270)
Madison	Richmond	(859)
Magoffin	Salyersville	(606)
Marion	Lebanon	(270)
Marshall	Benton	(270)
Martin	Inez	(606)
Mason	Maysville	(606)
Meade	Brandenburg	(270)
Menifee	Frenchburg	(606)
Mercer	Harrodsburg	(859)
Metcalfe	Edmonton	(270)
Monroe	Tompkinsville	(270)
Montgomery	Mt. Sterling	(859)
Morgan	West Liberty	(606)
Muhlenberg	Greenville	(270)
Nelson	Bardstown	(502)
Nicholas	Carlisle	(859)
Ohio	Hartford	(270)
Oldham	LaGrange	(502)
Owen	Owenton	(502)

County	City/Town	Area Code
Owsley	Booneville	(606)
Pendleton	Falmouth	(859)
Perry	Hazard	(606)
Pike	Pikeville	(606)
Powell	Stanton	(606)
Pulaski	Somerset	(606)
Robertson	Mt. Olivet	(606)
Rockcastle	Mt. Vernon	(606)
Rowan	Morehead	(606)
Russell	Jamestown	(270)
Scott	Georgetown	(502)
Shelby	Shelbyville	(502)
Simpson	Franklin	(270)
Spencer	Taylorsville	(502)
Taylor	Campbellsville	(270)
Todd	Elkton	(270)
Trigg	Cadiz	(270)
Trimble	Bedford	(502)
Union	Morganfield	(270)
Warren	Bowling Green	(270)
Washington	Springfield	(859)
Wayne	Monticello	(606)
Webster	Dixon	(270)
Whitley	Williamsburg	(606)
Wolfe	Campton	(606)
Woodford	Versailles	(859)

OTHER NOTARIAL OFFICERS

County Clerk Has Notarial Powers

"A county clerk shall have the powers of a notary public in the exercise of the official functions of the office of clerk within his county, and the official actions of the county clerk shall not require the witness or signature of a notary appointed pursuant to subsection (1) of this section" KRS 423.010[2]).

Commissioner of Foreign Deeds

"The Governor may appoint and commission one (1) or more commissioners of deeds in each state of the United States for a term of two (2) years. Before entering on the duties of his office, each commissioner shall make and subscribe an affidavit, before an officer authorized to administer an oath, to well and truly execute and perform all the duties of his office. The affidavit must be filed in the office of the Secretary of State of this state" (KRS 423.070).

"Any commissioner of deeds appointed and qualified pursuant to KRS 423.070 may take the acknowledgment or proof of any instrument of writing, except wills, which instrument is required by the laws of this state to be recorded. The examination, acknowledgment or proof of any such instrument taken by a commissioner, and certified under his official seal, in the manner required by the laws of this state, shall authorize the instrument to be recorded in the proper office. A commissioner of deeds may administer any oath or take any affirmation necessary to discharge his official duties, and may take and certify depositions to be read on the trial of any action or proceeding in any of the courts of this state" (KRS 423.080).

QUICK FACTS

Notary Jurisdiction

Notary — State at Large: A Notary Public — State at Large may notarize anywhere within the borders of Kentucky and the notarized document may be recorded inside or outside Kentucky. Previous to October 15, 1996, countywide-only commissions were also issued, but these have all expired (KRS 423.010).

Notary — Special Commission: A Notary Public — Special Commission may notarize inside or outside the state documents that will be recorded in Kentucky (KRS 423.110[6]).

Notary Term Length

Four years for both State at Large and Special Commissions (KRS 423.010[1]).

Notary Bond

Varies from county to county (KRS 423.010). $1,000 in Jefferson County.
The posting of a bond is not required for a Notary Public — Special Commission (NPH).

Louisiana

NOTARY SEAL

A Louisiana Notary is not required by law to use a seal of office, though some Notaries do opt to use seals.

"A Louisiana notary's signature is his seal. A notary is not required to have a particular style of seal to give authenticity to his copies. See *Flemming v. Richardson & Smith*, 13 La. Ann. 414 (1858)" (website, "Notary Quick Facts").

Examples of Optional Seals

Many Notaries elect to use seals of office. The above actual-size examples of optional Notary seals are typical.

NOTARY ADMINISTRATION

Office of Secretary of State
Notary Division   1-225-922-0507
P.O. Box 94125
Baton Rouge, LA 70804-9125

Physical Address:
8585 Archives Ave.
Baton Rouge, LA 70809

Website: www.sos.la.gov/notary

NOTARY RULES

RS — Louisiana Revised Statutes

Most Notary regulations are in the Louisiana Revised Statutes, Title 35, "Notaries Public and Commissioners."

Notary Name, ID Number Must Appear

"The notary shall type, print, or stamp his or her name as it appears on his or her commission" (RS 35:12[A][2]).

"B. Every document notarized in this state shall bear the notary identification number assigned by the secretary of state, except that if the notary is an attorney licensed to practice law in this state, he may use his Louisiana state bar roll number in lieu of his notary identification number. The number shall be typed or printed legibly and placed next to the typed, printed, or stamped name of the notary as required by Subsection A of this Section.

"C. No person other than a regularly commissioned notary public shall use the title 'Notary Public'. Every person, other than a regularly commissioned notary, who is otherwise given notarial powers or authorized as a notary ex officio, shall clearly indicate his actual position or title from which his authority to notarize is derived, in addition to his notary identification number" (RS 35:12).

Recorded Documents Need Notary ID

"1. Any document notarized in this state on or after January 1, 2005, submitted for filing or recording in the office of notarial records, register of conveyances, or recorder of mortgages in and for the parish of Orleans, or in the office of any clerk of court or recorder of mortgages or conveyances may be refused by the clerk or his employee if the document fails to contain the notary identification or attorney bar roll number and the typed, printed, or stamped name of the notary and the witnesses. However, documents filed in the civil or criminal suit records of any court shall not be subject to the provisions of this Subsection.

"2. Except as otherwise provided in this Section, no state office, agency, department, or political subdivision shall accept, file, or record any document notarized in this state on or after January 1, 2005, unless the document contains the notary identification or attorney bar roll number and the typed, printed, or stamped name of the notary and the witnesses.

"3. No office, agency, department, or political subdivision, or any officer or employee thereof, refusing to accept, file, or record any notarized document pursuant to the provisions of this Section shall be liable for any damages resulting from the refusal to accept, file, or record a notarized document for its failure to comply with the provisions of this Section" (RS 35:12[D]).

NOTARY POWERS

Louisiana Notaries are unique in the United States. Deriving their authority from statutes based on the French Napoleonic Code, they have broad powers to prepare documents and execute "authentic acts." Among their authorized official powers are the following (RS 35:2[A][1] and 35:3):
1. Take acknowledgments;
2. Administer oaths*;
3. Make inventories, appraisements, and partitions;
4. "Receive wills**, make protests, matrimonial contracts, conveyances, and generally, all contracts and instruments of writing";
5. Hold family meetings and meetings of creditors;
6. Make affidavits of correction***;
7. "Affix the seals upon the effects of deceased persons and...raise the same";
8. Certify copies****.

* Oaths: "(E)ach notary public of this state shall have authority to administer oaths in any parish of the state, to swear in persons who appear to give testimony at a deposition before a general reporter or free-lance reporter certified under the provisions of R.S. 37:2551 et seq., and to verify interrogatories and other pleadings to be used in the courts of record of this state" (RS 35:2[B]).

Notaries also have the power to swear in public officials: "The oath of all officers of the state may be administered by the governor, any judge, justice of the peace, notary public, or clerk of court, and shall be subscribed to by the party taking it, and certified in his commission by the person administering it. This oath or affirmation shall be deposited in the office of the secretary of state and recorded by him. The oath or affirmation of all parish officers shall also be recorded in the clerk of court's office of the parish where the same may have been administered, to be recorded by the clerk of court in a book kept for that purpose" (RS 42:162[A]).

** Receiving Wills: "Notwithstanding any provision in the law to the contrary, a notary public shall have power, within the parish or parishes in which he is authorized ... to receive wills in which he is named as administrator, executor, trustee, attorney for the administrator, attorney for the executor, attorney for the trustee, attorney for a legatee, attorney for an heir, or attorney for the estate" (RS 35:2[A][3]).

*** Affidavit of Correction: "A clerical error in a notarial act affecting movable or immovable property or any other rights, corporeal or incorporeal, may be corrected by an act of correction executed by the notary or one of the notaries before whom the act was passed, or by the notary who actually prepared the act containing the error. The act of correction shall be executed in compliance with this Section shall be given retroactive effect to the date of recordation of the original act. However, the act of correction shall not prejudice the rights acquired by any third person before the act of correction is recorded where the third person reasonably relied on the original act. The act of correction shall not alter the true agreement and intent of the parties" (RS 35:2.1).

**** Certifying Copies: "Every qualified notary public is authorized to certify true copies of any authentic act or any instrument under private signature hereafter or heretofore passed before him or acknowledged before him, and to make and certify copies, by any method, of any certificate, research, resolution, survey or other document annexed to the original of any authentic acts passed before him, and may certify such copies as true copies of the original document attached to the original passed before him" (RS 35:2[C]).

Authentic Acts

"A. An authentic act is a writing executed before a notary public or other officer authorized to perform that function, in the presence of two witnesses, and signed by each party who executed it, by each witness, and by each notary public before whom it was executed. The typed or hand printed name of each person shall be placed in a legible form immediately beneath the signature of each person signing the act.

"B. To be an authentic act, the writing need not be executed at one time or place, or before the same notary public or in the presence of the same witnesses, provided that each party who executes it does so before a notary public or other officer authorized to perform that function, and in the presence of two witnesses and each party, each witness, and each notary public signs it. The failure to include the typed or hand printed name of each person signing the act shall not affect the validity or authenticity of the act.

"C. If a party is unable or does not know how to sign his name, the notary public must cause him to affix his mark to the writing" (Civil Code Article 1833, "Authentic act").

According to Alan Jennings, editor of "Louisiana Notary" and author of the official study guide for the statewide Notary exam, "The authentic act is Louisiana's 'gold standard' for proof of an agreement between parties. It binds the parties and their heirs and successors as much as any law. An authentic act is, under Louisiana law, afforded the presumption of accuracy and is directly admissible into evidence in a court of law without further proof. La. C.C. art 1835."

NOTARY DON'TS

When Notary May Not Act

A Louisiana Notary may not exercise any notarial function in the state during any period when the Notary: (a) has a commission which has been statutorily or judicially suspended or revoked; (b) is no longer validly commissioned in Louisiana; (c) has elected to place his or her commission in retirement status; (d) no longer possesses the office from which his or her notarial authority was derived; (e) has been convicted of a felony and has not been pardoned; (f) is not authorized by law to exercise a particular notarial function (RS 35:602[A]).

Bank and Corporate Notaries

A Notary who is an employee, officer, stockholder or director of a bank or other corporation may notarize for that bank or corporation, unless the Notary is a party to the instrument, either individually or as a representative of the bank or corporation (RS 35:4).

NOTARY SIGNING AGENTS

In recent years, much conflicting information has circulated about whether Louisiana Notaries may lawfully conduct mortgage closings without the presence of a licensed attorney. Some corporate sources have claimed that Louisiana Notaries are not authorized to act by themselves at real estate closings. They argue that closings must be conducted by attorneys and corporate title agents and that the role of the Notary is limited to authenticating the signatures on certain documents.

Clarification by Alan Jennings

Information on this matter has been provided by Alan Jennings, editor of "Louisiana Notary" and author of the official study guide for the statewide Notary exam. According to Jennings, the role of the Louisiana Notary is to preside in the closing of any written contract where the parties desire the highest standard of legal authenticity. "In fact," he said, "a lawyer in Louisiana may not preside over the execution of a notarial act unless he or she is also a notary."

Jennings pointed out that in Louisiana title to real estate is transferred, and mortgages are established, by the contract between the parties, and Louisiana Notaries are authorized by law to make "generally, all contracts and instruments of writing" (RS 35:2). He said the law provides for the sale or mortgage of real property in the state to be memorialized by an instrument of writing, and its proper execution before a Notary and witnesses establishes the authentic evidence for the title or "deed." (See discussion under "Authentic Acts," above.)

"That does not diminish the role or importance of the lawyer's involvement in Louisiana real estate transactions," Jennings said. "In fact, it elevates it considerably. The lawyer's role is that of title examiner, whereby the lawyer examines the public record and issues his or her opinion as to the merchantability of the title and whether any existing mortgage outranks the mortgage contemplated by the lender. This title opinion is issued in advance of the closing, and the signing will take place only when the lender has the assurances necessary that his or her security interest ranks first in the event of the borrower's default.

"Louisiana's civil law system establishes broad powers for its notaries — for example, the power to prepare notarial instruments. Such powers are reserved for attorneys in other states — that is, in states that operate under a common law rather than a civil law system. Louisiana notaries may also administer oaths and take acknowledgments of instruments 'under private signature,' just like notaries in the common law states."

According to Jennings, whether a mortgage finance transaction is considered an "authentic act" or an "act under private signature" depends somewhat on the wording of the mortgage instrument, but the essence of the difference is whether the parties make their signatures privately or in the presence of the Notary.

Notary's Role in Recording Mortgages

Louisiana Notaries have the additional responsibility of recording "all acts of sale ... and mortgage of immovable property passed before them" with the recorder of the local parish unless the Notary has been expressly directed in writing by all parties to refrain from such recordation or to deliver the documents to one of the parties or to another person (RS 35:199[A] and [D]). For transfer of immovable property in Orleans Parish, such an act must be registered with the office of the clerk, as the recorder for the parish, within 48 hours. Notaries in the rest of the country are not required to record mortgages and property transfers.

Ex Officio May Not Oversee Closing

The numerous personnel for public agencies who by law have "ex officio" notarial powers are not authorized to oversee closings for the general public, because they may only execute oaths, jurats and acknowledgments for their governmental agencies.

NOTARY FEES

Louisiana statute prescribes no schedule of fees for Notaries.

NOTARY CERTIFICATES

"An act under private signature is regarded prima facie as the true and genuine act of a party executing it when his signature has been acknowledged… An act under private signature may be acknowledged by a party to that act by recognizing the signature as his own before a court, or before a notary public, or other officer authorized to perform that function, in the presence of two witnesses" (Louisiana Civil Code Art. 1836).

Acknowledgment by Individual (RS 35:511[1]):

State of Louisiana
Parish of _____

On this ____ day of _____, 20____, before me personally appeared _____ (name[s] of signer[s]), to me known to be the person (or persons) described in and who executed the foregoing instrument, and acknowledged that he/she/they executed it as his/her/their free act and deed.

(NOTARY'S SIGNATURE, TITLE AND TYPED, PRINTED OR STAMPED NAME AND IDENTIFICATION NUMBER)

Acknowledgment by Attorney in Fact (RS 35:511[2]):

State of Louisiana
Parish of _____

On this ____ day of _____, 20____, before me personally appeared _____ (name of attorney in fact), to me known to be the person who executed the foregoing instrument in behalf of _____ (name of principal signer), and acknowledged that he/she executed it as the free act and deed of said _____ (name of principal signer).

(NOTARY'S SIGNATURE, TITLE AND TYPED, PRINTED OR STAMPED NAME AND IDENTIFICATION NUMBER)

Acknowledgment by Corporation or Joint Stock Association (RS 35:511[3]):

*State of Louisiana
Parish of _____*

On this _____ day of _____, 20____, before me appeared _____ (name of corporate signer), to me personally known, who, being by me duly sworn (or affirmed) did say that he/she is the president (or other officer or agent of the corporation or association), of _____ (describing the corporation or association), and that the seal* affixed to said instrument is the corporate seal of said corporation (or association) and that the instrument was signed (and sealed) in behalf of the corporation (or association) by authority of its Board of Directors (or trustees) and that _____ (name of corporate signer) acknowledged the instrument to be the free act and deed of the corporation (or association).

(NOTARY'S SIGNATURE, TITLE AND TYPED, PRINTED OR STAMPED NAME AND IDENTIFICATION NUMBER)

* In case the corporation or association has no corporate seal, omit the words "the seal affixed to said instrument is the corporate seal of the corporation (or association), and that" and add, at the end of the affidavit clause, the words "and that the corporation (or association) has no corporate seal."

Acknowledgment by Individual outside United States (RS 35:552):

"Every certificate of acknowledgment, made without the United States, shall contain the name or names of the person or persons making the acknowledgment, the date when and the place where made, a statement of the fact that the person or persons making the acknowledgment knew the contents of the instrument, and acknowledged it to be his, her or their act; the certificate shall also contain the name of the person before whom made, his official title, and be sealed with his official seal and may be substantially in the following form":

*_____ (name of country)
_____
(name of city, province or
other political subdivision)*

Before the undersigned _____ (naming the officer and designating his official title), duly commissioned (or appointed) and qualified, this day personally appeared at the place above named _____ (naming the person or persons acknowledging) who declared that he/she/they knew the contents of the foregoing instrument, and acknowledged it to be his/her/their act.

Witness my hand and official seal this _____ day of _____, 20____.

*_____ (name of officer)   (SEAL)**
_____ (official title)*

** "When the seal affixed shall contain the names or the official style of the officer, any error in stating, or failure to state otherwise the name or the official style of the officer, shall not render the certificate defective."

Rules Regarding Signers' Names

"A. 1. Notaries shall insert in their acts the Christian names and surnames of the parties in full and not their initial letters alone or the full names of the parties and not their initial letters alone, together with the permanent mailing addresses of the parties, and shall print or type the full names of the witnesses and of themselves under their respective signatures.

"2. For the purposes of this Section, a full name or a name in full shall include at least one given name and other initials in addition to the surname. It may be any combination of first name and middle initial or initials, if any, and the surname; or the first initial and at least one middle name and the surname; or the complete first and middle name or names and the surname. The notary shall type, print, or stamp his or her name as it appears on his or her commission" (RS 35:12[A]).

Marital Status Must Be Noted by Notary

"Whenever notaries pass any acts they shall give the marital status of all parties to the act, viz: If either or any party or parties are men, they shall be described as single, married, or widower.

If married or widower the Christian and family name of wife shall be given. If either or any party or parties are women, they shall be described as single, married or widow. If married or widow, their Christian and family name shall be given, adding that she is the wife of or widow of _____ the husband's name" (RS 35:11[A]).

Foreign Acknowledgments
"A certificate of acknowledgment of a deed or other instrument acknowledged without the United States before any officer mentioned in RS 35:551 shall also be valid if in the same form as now is or hereafter may be required by law, for an acknowledgment within this state" (RS 35:553).

ELECTRONIC NOTARIZATIONS

The state of Louisiana has not yet adopted statutes or regulations expressly establishing rules, definitions and procedures for electronic notarization.

UETA Recognizes Notary's eSignature
Louisiana has adopted the Uniform Electronic Transactions Act (RS 9:2601 through 2620), including the provision on notarization, thereby recognizing the legal validity of electronic signatures used by Notaries:

"If a law requires a signature or record to be notarized, acknowledged, verified, or made under oath, the requirement is satisfied if the electronic signature of the person authorized to perform those acts, together with all other information required to be included by other applicable law, is attached to or logically associated with the signature or record" (RS 9:2611).

NOTARY RECORDS

"(A)ll regularly commissioned non-attorney notaries shall file an annual report with the secretary of state on or before the anniversary date of his commission on the form developed and mailed, or provided by electronic means, by the secretary of state pursuant to R.S. 35:191.2(2)(a), together with payment of the filing fee established by the secretary of state pursuant to R.S. 35:191.2(3). The annual report shall be completed in full and signed by the notary" (RS 35:202[A]).

"Annual reports are being mailed to notaries sixty (60) days prior to the anniversary date of their commission ... (T)he annual report shall be completed in full, signed by the notary and returned with payment of the $10 filing fee. The completed annual report and fee must be returned by the anniversary date of their commission to avoid a late fee or suspension" (website, "Annual Reports").

Failure to File Annual Report on Time
"The commission of any notary who fails to timely file his fully completed annual report within sixty days after its due date as provided in Subsection A of this Section shall be automatically suspended, and the notary shall have no authority to exercise any of the duties or functions of a notary public until a current required annual report has been filed, and the notary has paid all accrued fees and late charges for a period not to exceed three years in connection with the suspension of his commission" (RS 35:202[C]).

Annual Reports for Ex Officio Notaries
In regard to ex officio Notaries and other persons other than regularly commissioned Notaries who have notarial powers, on July 1 of each year, all offices, agencies, departments and political subdivisions of the state must file an annual report showing all the persons currently appointed with such powers (RS 35:202[D]).

Recording Acts Affecting Immovables
"A. Notaries public shall record all acts of sale, exchange, donation, and mortgage of immovable property passed before them, together with all resolutions, powers of attorney, and other documents annexed to or made part of the acts, in their proper order, and after first making a careful record of the acts in record books to be kept for that purpose as follows:

"1. If the immovable is located in this state outside of the parish of Orleans, the notary shall record the instrument within fifteen days after they are passed, with the appropriate recorder of the parish or parishes in which the immovable property is situated.

"2. (a) If the immovable is situated within the parish of Orleans, the notary shall file the instrument in the office of the custodian of notarial records for the parish of Orleans and record the instrument with the register of conveyances or recorder of mortgages or both.

"(b) If the instrument is an act of sale or any other act evidencing a transfer of immovable property situated in the parish of Orleans, it shall be the duty of the notary to cause the act to be registered with the clerk as the recorder for the parish of Orleans, within forty-eight hours after the passage of the act.

"(c) The original of every authentic act, except chattel mortgages and acts relating to immovable property outside of Orleans Parish, passed before a notary public in Orleans Parish, and also every act, contract, and instrument except money judgments and chattel mortgages filed for record in the offices of either the recorder of mortgages or the registrar of conveyances for the parish of Orleans, shall, as a condition precedent to such filing in the office of the recorder of mortgages or the register of conveyances for the parish of Orleans, be first filed in the notarial archives of the parish of Orleans.

"B. The provisions of Subsection A of this Section shall not be applicable to instruments affecting cemetery plots and shall not be so construed as embracing inventories or partitions or any other act required by law to be performed by notaries or parish recorders under any order of court, but the original of all such acts, without being recorded, shall be returned to the court from which the order is issued ...

"D. A notary public shall be relieved of his obligations under Paragraph (A)(1) and Subparagraph (A)(2)(a) of this Section when he has been expressly directed in writing by all parties to the instrument to defer or refrain from such recordation or to deliver the instruments to one of the parties or to another person" (RS 35:199).

Any violation of the above is subject to a fine of $200 (RS 35:199[C]).

AUTHENTICATION OF NOTARIAL ACTS

Secretary of State

The office of the Secretary of State issues authenticating certificates, including apostilles, for Notaries, clerks and deputy clerks of court, ex officio Notaries, judges, justices of the peace and the Registrar of Vital Records.

Fees: $20 per certificate, but only $10 if for an adoption document, in authenticating the act of a Notary or a parish clerk of court, including an apostille. Payable to "Secretary of State."

Mail:
Louisiana Secretary of State
Commissions Division
P.O. Box 94125
Baton Rouge, LA 70804-9125

In Person:
Louisiana Secretary of State
Commissions Division
8585 Archives Ave.
Baton Rouge, LA 70809

Telephone: 1-225-922-0330

Procedure: Mail or present in person the original notarized document, along with the appropriate fee. Indicate the nation to which the document will be sent and a daytime telephone number.

"The document with an original signature (with name printed underneath) must be sent to our office. We do not accept photocopies of birth certificates or death certificates. Always use our physical address when using FedEx, UPS, DHL, etc....A pre-paid mailing envelope or a completed return label with the customer's account number must be provided for us to have the certified documents returned by courier. Walk-in customers may call 225-922-0330 for more information" (website, "Apostille and Authentication Certificates").

COMMISSIONING AND ADMINISTRATION

Though the Governor commissions Notaries "with the advice and consent of the Senate" (RS 35:1), the Secretary of State administers the Notary application, qualification and examination process, and maintains records on Notaries (RS 35:201[B]).

Applying for Commission

Qualifications: An applicant for a commission as a Louisiana Notary Public must (RS 35:191[A][1]): (a) be at least 18 years old, (b) be a resident citizen or alien lawfully residing in the state, (c) read, write, speak and be sufficiently knowledgeable of the English language, and (d) not be "under interdiction or incapable of serving as a notary because of mental infirmity."

Statewide Notary Exam: Applicants must take and pass the statewide Notary examination (RS 35:191.1), but are exempted if they are attorneys licensed to practice law in Louisiana. The examination is given twice a year on the first Saturday in June and December. The exam is in three parts (scenario, research and multiple-choice components, all of which must be passed) and lasts about five hours. It is administered at regional test centers. To help applicants prepare for the exam, "The Fundamentals of Louisiana Notarial Law and Practice: The Louisiana Notary Public Examination Official Study Guide" (2011 Edition) is available through the Secretary of State's office at a cost of $90. "No course or class is required by law in order for you to take the examination, but we suggest you take a good course or join a good study group" (website, "How to Become a Louisiana Notary" and "Examinations"). All exam preparation providers must register with the Secretary of State's office and are listed on its Provider Registry. Any questions about the exam administration or content may be directed to the LSU Office of Assessment and Evaluation at 1-225-578-1145.

Application: After completing the "Application to Qualify for Appointment as Notary Public," which must be notarized and includes a $25 application fee, non-attorney applicants may register to take the statewide Notary exam by completing the "Notary Public Examination Registration Form," which includes a $75 examination fee. The "Application to Qualify" and the "Examination Registration Form," with their separate respective fees, must be submitted together to the Secretary of State no later than 45 days prior to the exam (RS 35:191[C] and website, "How to Become a Louisiana Notary").

Applicants who have taken and passed the exam will receive a Notary commission when they have submitted the following items to the Secretary of State's office: (a) two properly executed original oaths of office, one for the Secretary of State and the other to be filed with the clerk of court in the applicant's parish of residency; (b) an official signature page; (c) in the amount of $10,000, a Notary surety bond or a personal surety bond approved by the parish clerk of court or an errors and omissions policy; and (e) a $35 commission filing fee, payable to the Secretary of State. Attorneys do not have to file a bond, but must submit a certificate of good standing issued from the Louisiana Supreme Court within 30 days prior to application to become a Notary (website, "How to File"; RS 35:71[A], RS 35:72, RS 35:201[A] and 201[B]).

Application for Ex Officio Powers: Any sheriff may appoint deputies, any municipal police chief may appoint officers, and any mayor in a municipality of less than 15,000 population may appoint employees to serve the municipal police department and the office of the mayor, as ex officio Notaries (RS 33:1464[A] and RS 35:407[A]).

According to the Secretary of State's website, each sheriff, police chief or mayor must file the following items with the Secretary: (a) a letter of appointment, which must be signed by the sheriff, police chief or mayor and designate a particular deputy, officer or employee for appointment, and (b) an oath of office (RS 35:391[7]), which must be properly executed but a second copy of which does not need to be filed with the parish clerk of court (RS 35:392[C]). Sheriffs who appoint deputies as ex officio Notaries also must file a Notary bond or errors and omissions insurance in the amount of $10,000 (RS 35:391[6] and RS 33:1464[B]), which must be signed by the parish clerk of court; members of the Louisiana Sheriff's Association Risk Management Program are exempt from this requirement. Ex officio Notaries must wait until they receive an ex officio Notary ID card from the Secretary of State before they begin notarizing.

Dual Commissions: "(A) person validly appointed notary public in the parish of his residence may exercise any and all of the functions of a notary public in an adjacent parish which has a population of less than thirty-five thousand and in which he maintains an office, without additional bonding or further application or examination, but shall file with the Office of the Secretary of State an affidavit giving the location of his office. Additionally, the applicant shall obtain a dual commission by complying with the procedures established by the office of the Secretary of State" (RS 35:191[A][2]).

Non-Residents: Non-residents of Louisiana are not qualified to receive a Notary commission in the state.

Online Search: The Louisiana Secretary of State's "Notary Database" may be searched online for information about a given Notary. Information available includes a Notary's identification number, address, parish, status as attorney or non-attorney, telephone, commission starting and expiration dates, and whether the Notary is in good standing.

Changes of Status

If Notary's Name Changes: For a name change, the Notary must submit to the Secretary of State's office a notarized name-change affidavit stating the name on the current commission, the name on the requested commission and the reason for the change. The Notary also must file the following items, using the new name, with the Secretary of State's office: (a) two properly executed original oaths of office, one for the Secretary and the other to be filed with the clerk of court in the applicant's parish of residency, (b) an official signature page, (c) a Notary surety bond or a personal surety bond approved by the parish clerk of court or an errors and omissions policy in the amount of $10,000, and (e) a $35 commission filing fee, payable to the Secretary of State. Attorneys do not have to file a bond, and non-attorney Notaries have the option of filing a rider for an existing surety bond that changes the name on the bond and that has been signed by the parish clerk of court (website, "How to File Name Changes").

If Notary Moves: For a change of residential or mailing address, the Notary must inform the Secretary of State's office by mail, fax or e-mail within 60 days after the date of change (RS 35:191.3[A] and website, "Frequently Asked Questions").

If Notary Moves to New Parish: In changing a parish of residence, both attorney and non-attorney Notaries must transfer their commission to the new parish, even if the parish is within a reciprocal group (website, "Frequently Asked Questions"). To transfer a commission to a new parish, the Notary must submit to the Secretary of State's office a new "Application to Qualify," along with a $25 application fee. The Notary must also file the following items: (a) two properly executed original oaths of office, one for the Secretary of State and the other to be filed with the clerk of court in the applicant's new parish of residency, (b) an official signature page, (c) a Notary surety bond or a personal surety bond approved by the parish clerk of court or an errors and omissions policy in the amount of $10,000, and (e) a $35 commission filing fee, payable to the Secretary of State. Attorneys do not have to file a bond, and non-attorney Notaries have the option of filing a rider for an existing surety bond that changes the parish on the bond and that has been signed by the parish clerk of court (website, "How to File: Parish Changes").

However, any person who has been a Notary in one parish for five years or who took and passed the statewide exam on or after June 13, 2005, may, upon changing residence to another parish, be given a notarial commission by the Governor without the advice and consent of the Senate and without passing an examination (RS 35:191[E][1]).

Bond Renewed Every Five Years: Notary bonds are renewable every five years with "any surety company authorized to do business in the state," except when a Notary is bonded by a personal surety, in which case the bond is renewed upon the death of the surety. A personal surety must be approved by the presiding judge of the parish for which the Notary is commissioned (RS 35:71[D][1] and RS 35:75). The bond of an Orleans Parish applicant must be certified by the custodian of notarial records (RS 35:192[A] and RS 35:392[A]).

The fee for renewing the bond or errors and omissions policy with the Notary Division is $20 (website, "How to File").

If Notary Resigns: "Any notary may resign his or her commission by signing a letter of resignation and forwarding it to (the Notary Division). After resigning, the notary shall not exercise any duties or functions of a notary public and may become an active notary again only by completing the application process of his parish, including the exam if applicable" (website, "How to File").

Leave of Absence: "Leaves of absence will now be handled administratively on behalf of the governor by the secretary of state. If you're going to be out of the state for an extended period, a leave of absence will enable you to maintain a valid commission. Requirements that a notary on leave must appoint a substitute have been repealed" (website, "Recent Legislation"). Leaves of absence may not exceed 36 months (RS 35:131), except when the absence is for military service (RS 35:133).

Retirement: "A regularly commissioned non-attorney notary who is seventy years of age or older shall be permitted to elect a special commission status upon retirement from active service as a notary public by filing with the secretary of state a written request for such status along with an affidavit attesting to such status and certifying that he will no longer exercise the duties and functions of a notary public during such time as such status is in effect. A notary with such inactive status shall not be required to maintain a bond or file an annual report. However, a notary granted inactive status shall notify the secretary of state of any change of address to ensure the accuracy of information contained in the notary database maintained by the secretary of state. A notary may resume active commission status by filing a current annual report with the required fees with the secretary of state and posting bond in the amount then required by law" (RS 35:202[G]).

PARISH CLERKS

To contact a Louisiana parish clerk of court to seek assistance in locating a given Notary, telephone long-distance information — 1-XXX-555-1212 — and ask for the phone number of the appropriate parish using the area codes listed below. The numbers in parentheses following the parish names refer to reciprocal agreements with other parishes, as explained in "Reciprocity Among Parishes," below.

Parish	City/Town	Area Code
Acadia (1)(2)	Crowley	(337)
Allen (3)	Oberlin	(337)
Ascension (4)	Donaldsonville	(225)
Assumption (5)	Napoleonville	(985)
Avoyelles (6)	Marksville	(318)
Beauregard (3)	DeRidder	(337)
Bienville (7)(8)(15)	Arcadia	(318)
Bossier (7)	Benton	(318)
Caddo (7)	Shreveport	(318)
Calcasieu (3)	Lake Charles	(337)
Caldwell (8)	Columbia	(318)
Cameron (3)	Cameron	(337)
Catahoula (9)	Harrisonburg	(318)
Claiborne (7)	Homer	(318)
Concordia (9)	Vidalia	(318)
DeSoto (8)	Mansfield	(318)
East B. Rouge (4)	Baton Rouge	(225)
East Carroll (8)	Lake Providence	(318)
East Feliciana (4)	Clinton	(225)
Evangeline (1)	Ville Platte	(337)
Franklin (8)	Winnsboro	(318)
Grant (6)	Colfax	(318)
Iberia (10)(11)	New Iberia	(337)
Iberville (4)	Plaquemine	(225)
Jackson (8)	Jonesboro	(318)
Jefferson (12)	Gretna	(504)
Jeff. Davis (3)	Jennings	(337)
Lafayette (2)(13)	Lafayette	(337)
Lafourche (5)	Thibodaux	(985)
LaSalle (0)	Jena	(318)
Lincoln (8)	Ruston	(318)
Livingston (4)(14)	Livingston	(225)
Madison (8)	Tallulah	(318)
Morehouse (8)	Bastrop	(318)
Natchitoches (15)	Natchitoches	(318)
Orleans (12)	New Orleans	(504)
Ouachita (8)	Monroe	(318)
Plaquemines (12)	Belle Chasse	(504)
Pointe Coupee (4)	New Roads	(225)
Rapides (6)	Alexandria	(318)
Red River (15)	Coushatta	(318)
Richland (8)	Rayville	(318)
Sabine (15)	Many	(318)
St. Bernard (12)	Chalmette	(504)
St. Charles (0)	Hahnville	(985)
St. Helena (14)	Greensburg	(225)
St. James (0)	Convent	(225)
St. Jn. the Baptist (0)	La Place	(985)
St. Landry (1)(13)	Opelousas	(337)
St. Martin (10)	St. Martinville	(337)
St. Mary (5)(10)	Franklin	(337)
St. Tammany (0)	Covington	(985)
Tangipahoa (14)	Amite	(985)
Tensas (0)	St. Joseph	(318)
Terrebonne (5)	Houma	(985)
Union (8)	Farmerville	(318)
Vermilion (2)(11)	Abbeville	(337)
Vernon (3)(15)	Leesville	(337)
Washington (0)	Franklinton	(985)
Webster (7)	Minden	(318)
West B. Rouge (4)	Port Allen	(225)
West Carroll (7)	Oak Grove	(318)
W. Feliciana (4)	St. Francisville	(225)
Winn (15)	Winnfield	(318)

Reciprocity Among Parishes

Reciprocity exists within each of the following 15 groups of parishes, and a non-attorney Notary commissioned for any parish within one of these groups may notarize in any other parish within that same group — without additional bonding or examination (RS 35:191 [D] through [U]):

1. Acadia, Evangeline and St. Landry
2. Acadia, Lafayette and Vermilion
3. Allen, Beauregard, Calcasieu, Cameron, Jefferson Davis and Vernon
4. Ascension, East Baton Rouge, East Feliciana, Iberville, Livingston, Pointe Coupee, West Baton Rouge and West Feliciana
5. Assumption, Lafourche, St. Mary and Terrebonne
6. Avoyelles, Grant and Rapides
7. Bienville, Bossier, Caddo, Claiborne, DeSoto and Webster
8. Bienville, Caldwell, East Carroll, Franklin, Jackson, Lincoln, Madison, Morehouse, Ouachita, Richland, Union and West Carroll
9. Catahoula and Concordia
10. Iberia, St. Martin and St. Mary
11. Iberia and Vermilion
12. Jefferson, Orleans, Plaquemines and St. Bernard
13. Lafayette and St. Landry
14. Livingston, St. Helena and Tangipahoa
15. Sabine, Bienville, Natchitoches, Red River, Vernon and Winn

OTHER NOTARIAL OFFICERS

Ex Officio Notarial Powers

Designated personnel for the following public agencies have ex officio notarial powers:

1. Department of Public Safety and Corrections (RS 35:393 and RS 35:393.1);
2. Louisiana State Police (RS 35:393[B]);
3. Department of Justice (RS 35:394);
4. Department of State (RS 35:395);
5. Governor's Consumer Protection Division (RS 35:396);
6. Louisiana State Racing Commission (RS 35:397);
7. District attorney offices (RS 35:398);
8. U.S. Forest Service (RS 35:400);
9. Sabine River Authority (RS 35:401);
10. State Registrar of Vital Records (RS 35:402 and RS 40:46.2);
11. Hospital Service district hospitals (RS 35:403);
12. Office of Financial Institutions (RS 35:404);
13. Levee district police (RS 35:405);
14. Adult Protection Agency (RS 35:406);
15. Municipal police departments (RS 35:407);
16. Crescent City Connection Police Department (RS 35:408);
17. University police departments (RS 35:409);
18. Louisiana Agricultural Finance Authority or Department of Agriculture and Forestry (RS 35:410);
19. Office of Coastal Protection and Restoration (RS 35:411);
20. Sheriffs' departments (RS 33:1464);
21. Commissioner of Alcoholic Beverage Control (RS 26:78[C] and RS 26:278[D]).

Only Act for Purposes of Agency: Typically the ex officio Notaries designated by the above public agencies may only execute oaths, jurats and acknowledgments for matters within the official function of their agencies. They may not charge for their notarial acts. Their notarial powers terminate upon separation from the agencies. However, ex officio Notaries who are clerks of court or deputy clerks of court may notarize vehicle titles or take acknowledgment of signatures for authentic acts even if this is not done in the course and scope of their employment (RS 35:392.1[B]).

Non-Resident Attorneys Are Ex Officio: In addition to the ex officio Notaries designated by the 21 agencies listed above, as of August 15, 2010, any non-resident individual licensed to practice law in Louisiana is designated as an ex officio Notary Public, is authorized to perform notarial acts in any parish in which he or she maintains an office to practice law, and is required to post the bond or insurance required under RS 35:71 (RS 35:412).

QUICK FACTS

Notary Jurisdiction

Statewide for attorneys (RS 35:191[P][1][a]), but parish-wide for non-attorneys. However, any commissioned non-attorney Notary in and for any parish in the state who passes the statewide written examination on or after June 13, 2005, may also exercise his or her notarial authority statewide (RS 35:191[P][1][b]). Failure to pass the exam has no effect on the status of the existing commission of the non-attorney Notary (RS 35:191[P][2]). See also "Dual Commissions" and "Reciprocity Among Parishes," above.

Notary Term Length

Lifetime, provided the Notary remains in good standing and is not removed from office for due cause. "A Louisiana notary's commission does not expire until his death. See Louisiana Attorney General Opinion 1940-42, p. 2346" (website, "Quick Facts"). See also "Leave of Absence" and "Retirement," above.

Notary Bond

Non-attorney Notaries and ex officio Notaries must be bonded for $10,000 or maintain a minimum of $10,000 in errors and omissions insurance coverage (RS 35:71[A], RS 35:201[A][3] and 35:391[6]). The bond must be signed by the parish clerk of court. Notaries who are licensed attorneys are not required to post a bond (RS 35:72). Ex officio Notaries who are state employees, municipal police officers or members of the Louisiana Sheriff's Association Risk Management Program need not be bonded (RS 35:392[A], RS 35:407[C]). See also "Bond Renewed Every Five Years," above.

Maine

NOTARY SEAL

For Maine Notaries, seals of office are optional (4 MRSA 951). If a seal is used, however, the format must be as follows:

Kind

Inked Stamp or Embosser: The law does not specify. "It is optional for Notaries Public in the State of Maine to own or use an embossing or ink seal or a stamp with their name and expiration date" (NPH). The Notary embosser is traditional and widely seen in the state. "The Secretary of State recommends that a seal be used on documents that will be leaving Maine" (NPH).

Shape/Size

The law does not specify, but a circular seal is traditional and widely seen.

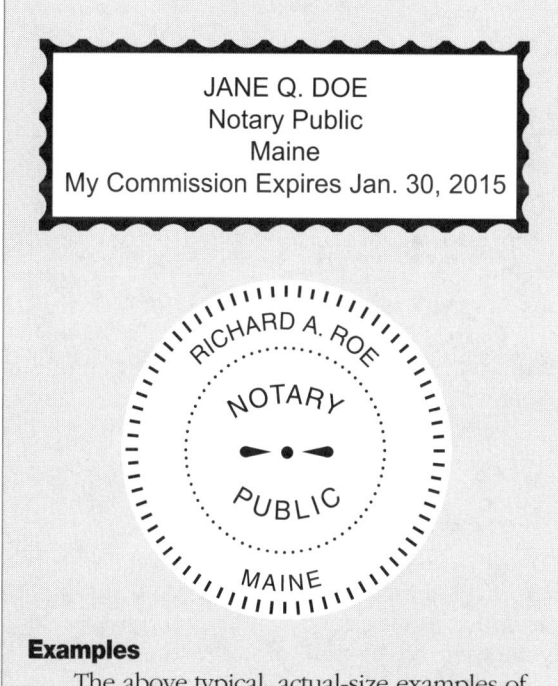

Examples

The above typical, actual-size examples of optional Notary seals are allowed by Maine law. Formats other than these may also be permitted.

NOTARY ADMINISTRATION

Department of Secretary of State
Bur. of Corporations, Elections & Commissions
Division of Corporations, UCC & Commissions
Notary Public Section   1-207-624-7752
101 State House Station
(111 Sewall St., 4th Floor)
Augusta, ME 04333-0101

Website: www.maine.gov/sos/cec/notary/notaries.html

NOTARY RULES

MRSA — MAINE REVISED STATUTES ANNOTATED
SS RULES — CODE OF MAINE RULES FOR SECRETARY OF STATE
NPH — NOTARY PUBLIC HANDBOOK AND RESOURCE GUIDE

Most Notary rules are in the Maine Revised Statutes Annotated:

a. Title 4, Chapter 19, "Notaries Public";

b. Title 4, Chapter 22, "Uniform Recognition of Acknowledgments Act."*

* This is the *Uniform Recognition of Acknowledgments Act* of 1968, adopted virtually intact.

c. Title 5, Chapter 5, "Secretary of State."

The Code of Maine Rules (CMR) for the Secretary of State's Bureau of Corporations, Elections & Commissions (29-250), Chapter 700 ("Rules Governing the Eligibility and Procedures for Appointment and Renewal of Commissions of Notaries Public"), also set requirements.

Other guidelines for Notaries are in the "Notary Public Handbook and Resource Guide," issued by the Secretary of State and available on the website.

Components

Any embossing seal used must contain the following elements (4 MRSA 951):

1. Name of Notary exactly as on commission;

2. "Notary Public";
3. "Maine" or "ME," either as individual words or within "the arms of state or such other device as the notary public chooses."*

* "The Secretary of State recommends the use of the words rather than the Great Seal, as it is easier to identify the state of the notary public commission" (NPH).

Notary's Name Printed or Typed

"In addition to the signature of the Notary Public and in order for a document to be self-authenticating on its face …, the Notary Public must print or type the name (as it appears on the records of the Secretary of State's office) and the commission expiration date directly beneath their signature" (NPH). The following example is offered:

John V. Doe
Notary Public, State of Maine
My Commission expires on January 24, 2013

"This information does not need to be handwritten, to the contrary, the Secretary of State recommends purchasing a stamp that includes this information so that it is legible to read" (NPH).

Placement of Seal

"When affixing the seal, embossed or inked, the Notary Public should use care as to not obstruct information on the document. The seal should be affixed next to the Notary Public's signature" (NPH).

Destruction of Seal

"When a notary public who has obtained a seal of office resigns, or the notary public's commission is revoked or expires, the notary public or heirs shall destroy the official seal or send it to the Secretary of State for destruction" (4 MRSA 951).

Notary Signature Must Be Original

"The signature of the Notary Public must match the name and signature that is on file with the Secretary of State and must be originally signed. The use of a rubber stamped signature is not permitted under Maine law" (NPH).

"When performing a notarization, a notary public must sign by producing that notary public's official signature by hand in the same form as indicated on the notary public's commission. For the purposes of this section, the notary public's official signature is the signature that appears on the notary public's most recent oath of office or most recent application for a notary public commission…. If the official signature of a notary public changes during the term of the notary public's commission, the notary public shall immediately provide the Secretary of State with a new sample of the notary public's official signature" (4 MRSA 951-A).

NOTARY POWERS

Maine Notaries are authorized to perform the following notarial acts:
1. Take acknowledgments* and proofs (4 MRSA 1011);
2. Administer oaths** and affirmations** (4 MRSA 951 and 1011);
3. Certify affidavits with a jurat*** (NPH);
4. Execute protests (4 MRSA 952 and 953 and 11 MRSA 3-1505);
5. Solemnize marriages**** (19-A MRSA 655);
6. Certify copies of private documents***** (NPH);
7. Witness election petitions and absentee ballots****** (21-A MRSA 335, 336, 354, 355, 754-A and 901);
8. Issue subpoenas and call meetings******* (16 MRSA 101, 23 MRSA 3101, 30-A MRSA 2521, 37-B MRSA 427, 38 MRSA 851).

* <u>Acknowledgments</u>: "An acknowledgment is a formal admission made in person before a proper officer by someone who has executed an instrument. The person must state that the instrument was personally and freely executed" (NPH).

In an acknowledgment, the Notary must: (a) require the signer to personally appear before the Notary, (b) verify the identity of the signer and (c) require the signer to acknowledge that he or she signed the document (NPH).

** <u>Oath/Affirmation Wording and Ceremony</u>: "When a Notary Public takes a sworn statement, an oath must be administered to each person sworn and must, in effect, ask each person 'do you swear' to the truth of the statement? It is important to note that there must be a verbal response from the oath taker in the presence of the Notary Public" (NPH).

The following sample oaths appear in the

Maine Secretary of State's "Notary Public Handbook and Resource Guide":

"Do you (swear/affirm) under penalty of law that what you are about to say will be true (so help you God)?"

"Do you (swear/affirm) under penalty of law that you have read and understood _____ and that to the best of your knowledge and belief it is true (so help you God)?"

"Do you (swear/affirm) under penalty of law that you have executed this _____ and that it is your free act and deed (so help you God)?"

"When administering an oath or affirmation, the Notary Public should require the signer to raise their right hand — we have all seen this done on television and in movies — and repeat the required oath or affirmation" (NPH).

*** Jurats: A jurat is a "notarial statement that certifies the signer's personal appearance, (and that the Notary) witnesses the signer signing the document, administers an oath, and positively identifies the signer" (NPH).

"The jurat requires both the physical signing of the document in the presence of the Notary Public and administration of an oath or affirmation by the Notary Public to the signer stating the facts of the document" (NPH).

In a jurat, the Notary must: (a) require the signer to personally appear before the Notary, (b) verify the identity of the signer, (c) administer an oath or affirmation to the signer and (d) watch the signer sign the document physically and manually (NPH).

**** Marriages: "Maine Notaries like those in Florida and South Carolina, can officiate at wedding ceremonies. Unfortunately, there is no reciprocity with other states — this means that out-of-state Notaries or Justices of the Peace cannot obtain permission to officiate at marriage ceremonies in Maine" (website, "Notaries").

"If questions should arise concerning any aspect of the marriage process or marriage laws in the State of Maine, the Department of Human Services, Office of Data, Research and Vital Statistics is the state agency that handles information for this particular area. The contact telephone number for this office is (207) 287-3181.

"There are mandated rules for civil marriage ceremonies. Couples planning to be married often write their own ceremonies. As long as the activities are lawful, there is no reason not to conduct a ceremony as they have planned it" (NPH).

***** Certifying Copies: Though certifying copies is not expressly stated as a statutory power of Maine Notaries, there are numerous references in statute to this notarial duty. For example, 4 MRSA 568 gives clerks of courts authority to charge the same fees for copy certification as Notaries; and 7 MRSA 53-B refers to a Notary certifying that a copy is "true and accurate."

The Maine Secretary of State's "Notary Public Handbook and Resource Guide" instructs Notaries not to certify copies of birth certificates or of other documents issued by government agencies: "Only the issuing governmental agency can certify a document's authenticity. In order to obtain a certified copy, the individual must obtain it from the agency that controls the original document. (For school diplomas and transcripts, a notarized sworn statement or acknowledgment from a school official stating the document is a true copy is acceptable.)"

****** Election Petitions, Absentee Ballots: "The (election) petition is an important part of the political process in Maine, and every petition must be taken to a Notary Public before it may be filed with the Department of the Secretary of State.

"The duty of the Notary Public is to administer the oath as printed on the petition form and witness the signature of the person who circulated the petition. That person must verify to the Notary Public that the petition was circulated according to law. There is a space on every petition form where the circulator must swear and sign in the presence of a Notary Public that the petition was circulated by the individual appearing before the Notary Public" (NPH).

In addition, a Notary is one of the officials authorized to witness absentee ballots. The voter, before marking the ballot, must show it to the Notary, who must examine it to ensure that it is unmarked. While the voter is marking the ballot, there must be no communication between the voter and the Notary. The voter must then seal the ballot in its return envelope and complete the affidavit on the envelope in the presence of the Notary, who must sign the witness certification. A Notary who is unfamiliar with Maine's election laws (21-A MRSA) should not undertake the execution of absentee ballots.

******* Issue Subpoenas, Call Meetings: Throughout Maine statute, Notaries are authorized to issue subpoenas for witnesses for various purposes. "(N)otaries public may issue subpoenas for witnesses to attend before any court or before persons authorized to examine witnesses, to give evidence concerning any pending matter" (16 MRSA 101).

Notaries may also call town meetings in towns without selectmen, on petition of any three voters; or in towns with selectmen, on petition of 10% of the voters (30-A MRSA 2521).

Identifying Document Signers

"The person taking an acknowledgment shall certify that ... (t)he person acknowledging was known to the person taking the acknowledgment or that the person taking the acknowledgment had satisfactory evidence that the person acknowledging was the person described in and who executed the instrument" (4 MRSA 1013).

"Identification credentials must have a photograph to properly identify the signer. The Secretary of State strongly encourages Notaries Public to accept only government issued credentials. All credentials accepted by Notaries Public for identification purposes should still be valid. For example, do not accept a driver's license that has expired. Other non-governmental issued credentials may be easily falsified and might impact the validity of the transaction.

"Credit cards or social security cards are not 'good' forms of identification, as these items do not contain physical descriptions of the holder" (NPH).

"(T)he Secretary of State suggests that a Notary Public only use (the) credible or subscribing witness process with a witness that is personally known to the Notary Public. The Notary Public should unconditionally trust this person to take their word on the identity of another. This would not be the first option to exercise by the Notary Public; instead, if appropriate, require the signer to acquire proper identification, for example. If a Notary Public uses this witness process, the notarial certificate should reflect that a credible or subscribing witness was used in the language of the notarial certificate" (NPH).

Disabled Signers

In addition to the normal notarial procedures used with any signer, the "Notary Public Handbook and Resource Guide" recommends these special accommodations for signers with disabilities:

For a signer by mark, the Notary must observe the individual affix his or her mark or signature stamp to the document.

For a visually impaired signer, it is recommended that the Notary read the document to the signer, without explaining the contents.

For a hearing-impaired signer, it is recommended that the Notary find someone fluent in American Sign Language (ASL) to assist in communication. Notaries fluent in ASL may be located on the Secretary of State's website using the Notary search feature (website, "Notary/Dedimus Search").

Foreign-Language Documents

"There are certain risks associated with signing a notarial statement when the Notary Public does not understand the overall content. A Notary Public should never sign a notarial certificate on a document that has been written in a language that is not understandable by the Notary Public. So, if the document is in another language and cannot be translated into English, what should occur? The Secretary of State would advise referring the customer to another Notary Public fluent in that language.

"The Secretary of State maintains information on Notaries Public who are fluent in many languages. If a customer is looking for a Notary Public who is fluent in Spanish, for example, the customer can go to the Secretary of State website ... to use the Notary/Dedimus Search feature to locate a Notary Public that is fluent in Spanish" (NPH).

Notary Musts

According to the Maine Secretary of State's "Notary Public Handbook and Resource Guide," a Notary must:

1. "Require personal appearance."

2. "Make certain the signers of the document have an understanding of what they are signing."

3. "Make sure no blanks exist which could possibly be filled in at a later time."

4. "Never use 'white out' products to alter a document."

Personal Appearance: "Personal appearance is required by Maine law. To perform a notarization, the signer must personally and physically appear before the Notary Public.... Never deviate from this requirement of personal appearance. No exceptions. A notarization cannot be done via video conferencing or similar video technology" (NPH).

Determining Awareness: "While competency is both a complex medical and legal issue, it is incumbent upon a Notary Public to have a strong belief that the person understands the consequences of signing the document.... If the signer is unsure, confused or is possibly being unduly influenced to sign, the Notary Public should not act; instead referring the signer to an attorney or other professional to assist them would be appropriate and in the best interest of the signer" (NPH).

Skimming for Blanks: "There is no need for the Notary Public to read or know every item contained in the document.... Because blanks may affect the validity of a document, Notaries Public should advise the signer of the document to carefully understand the consequences of leaving blanks in a document and its impact on the validity of the document. Ultimately, the signer must make the final decision in this area. If blanks are left, the Notary Public should note such in the record book" (NPH).

Making Corrections: "If (document) language needs to be altered, the signer should cross out or line through the language and initial all altered areas in the document" (NPH).

NOTARY DON'TS

Disqualifying Interests

"A Notary Public must not act in any official capacity if there is any interest which may affect impartiality.... (O)ne may not act if one is a 'party to the instrument'.... A Notary Public is a 'party to the instrument' in any transaction if the completion of the transaction will directly benefit the Notary Public, whether financially or in any other way" (NPH).

Corporate Notaries: A Notary who is an employee, stockholder, director or officer of a bank or other corporation may notarize for that bank or corporation, unless the Notary is a party to the transaction, either individually or as a representative of the bank or corporation (4 MRSA 954).

Notarizing for Relatives: "A Notary Public shall not perform any notarial act for any person if that person is the Notary Public's spouse, parent, sibling, child, spouse's parent, spouse's sibling, spouse's child or child's spouse, except that a Notary Public may solemnize the marriage of the Notary Public's parent, sibling, child, spouse's parent, spouse's sibling or spouse's child. Additionally, the intention of this law also includes those relationships formed by virtue of remarriage and not by blood, commonly described by using the prefix 'step' or 'half'..." (NPH and 4 MRSA 954-A).

Formerly, in order to solemnize the marriage of a family member, an unrelated second Notary had to be present to sign the marriage license as one of the two required witnesses. This no longer is necessary.

Domestic Partners

"In 2004, Maine law (see Title 22, Section 2710) created a new relationship called a registered domestic partner. Although not considered a spouse under this law, registered domestic partners have similar rights as married persons under the law. Therefore, the Secretary of State believes that Notaries Public cannot perform notarial acts for registered domestic partners and the relationships to the registered domestic partners" (NPH).

Notary May Not Be Witness

"As a general guideline, the Office of the Attorney General has advised ... that a Notary should not act both as a witness and as a Notary for the same transaction" (NPH).

No Discrimination

"In the course of conducting the duties as a Notary Public, the Notary Public must never discriminate because of a person's race, color, sex, sexual orientation, physical or mental disability, religion, creed, age, ancestry or national origin" (NPH).

Foreign-Language Ads

A non-attorney Notary who advertises notarial services in a language other than English — including business cards, brochures and notices — must include in the ad (a) information on the fees the Notary may charge and (b) the statement, "I AM NOT AN ATTORNEY LICENSED TO PRACTICE LAW IN MAINE AND MAY NOT GIVE LEGAL ADVICE ABOUT IMMIGRATION OR ANY OTHER LEGAL MATTER OR ACCEPT FEES FOR LEGAL ADVICE." The words in (a) and (b) must be in both English and the language of the ad and be in letters of a conspicuous size. If the ad is on radio, television or other audio medium, it must include substantially the same information (4 MRSA 960[1] and [2]).

Further: "An advertisement for notary services may not include a literal translation of the phrase 'Notary Public' into any language other than English if the literal translation implies that the notary public is an attorney licensed to practice in the State or in any jurisdiction of the United States. For purposes of this subsection, 'literal translation' means the translation of a word or phrase without regard to the true meaning of the word or phrase in the language that is being translated" (4 MRSA 960[3]).

A violation of the above constitutes a civil violation for which a fine of not more than $5,000 may be imposed (4 MRSA 960[4]). In addition, a civil action may be brought for injunctive relief, or damages or both, and the state Attorney General may initiate an action in Superior Court (4 MRSA 960[5] and [6]).

NOTARY SIGNING AGENTS

Currently, there are no statutes, regulations or rules expressly governing, prohibiting or restricting the operation of Notary Signing Agents within the state of Maine.

NOTARY FEES

There is no schedule of fees for notarial acts. The only reference to fees in statute states, "For each protest of a bill or note, notifying parties, making his certificate thereof in due form and recording his proceedings, a notary public shall receive $1.50" (NPH and 4 MRSA 958).

No Unreasonable Fees

"For other services, the Notary Public may determine the fees to be charged. Given the fact the citizens of the State of Maine are placing trust in Notaries Public when seeking their services, it would be most inappropriate to charge fees which are unreasonable or unfair" (NPH).

Notary Should Set Fee Schedule

"If a Notary Public charges for services, the Notary Public should establish a fee structure or schedule so that persons seeking their services will have some predictability or assurance on the fee" (NPH).

NOTARY CERTIFICATES

Maine has adopted the *Uniform Recognition of Acknowledgments Act*, including the short-form certificates (4 MRSA 1016) for:

1. Acknowledgment by individual;
2. Acknowledgment by corporation;
3. Acknowledgment by partnership;
4. Acknowledgment by attorney in fact;
5. Acknowledgment by public officer, trustee or personal representative.

For the text of these certificates, see "Uniform Recognition of Acknowledgments Act (1968)," Section 6, in Appendix 3.

Specifically for real-estate transactions, the following certificates are prescribed by statute:

Acknowledgment by Individual (33 MRSA 775[12]):

State of Maine
County of _____, ss _____ (date)

Then personally appeared the above named A. (and B.) and (severally) acknowledged the foregoing instrument to be his/her/their free act and deed.
Before me,

_____ *(signature of Notary)*
_____ *(printed name of Notary)*
Notary Public, State of Maine
My commission expires: _____

Acknowledgment by Attorney (33 MRSA 775[13]):

State of Maine
County of _____, ss _____ (date)

Then the above named _____, who signed the foregoing instrument as the attorney of the above named _____ (grantor), personally appeared and acknowledged the same to be his/her free act and deed.
Before me,

_____ *(signature of Notary)*
_____ *(printed name of Notary)*
Notary Public, State of Maine
My commission expires: _____

Acknowledgment by Corporate Officer (33 MRSA 775[14]):

State of Maine
County of _____, *ss* _____ *(date)*
Then personally appeared the above named _____ *(name of officer who signed the deed, with his/her title), and acknowledged the foregoing instrument to be his/her free act and deed in his/her said capacity and the free act and deed of said corporation.*
Before me,

_____ *(signature of Notary)*
_____ *(printed name of Notary)*
Notary Public, State of Maine
My commission expires: _____

Acknowledgment by Executor, Administrator, Trustee, Guardian, Conservator, Receiver or Commissioner (33 MRSA 775[15]):

State of Maine
County of _____, *ss* _____ *(date)*

Then personally appeared the above named A. (and B.) in his/her/their said capacity and (severally) acknowledged the foregoing instrument to be his/her/their free act and deed.
Before me,

_____ *(signature of Notary)*
_____ *(printed name of Notary)*
Notary Public, State of Maine
My commission expires: _____

Format for Acknowledgment Certificate

"The form of a certificate of acknowledgment used by a person whose authority is recognized under section 1011 shall be accepted in this State if:
"1. Laws of the State. The certificate is in a form prescribed by the laws or regulations of this State;
"2. Laws of state where acknowledged. The certificate is in a form prescribed by the laws or regulations applicable in the place in which the acknowledgment is taken; or
"3. Certain words. The certificate contains the words 'acknowledged before me,' or their substantial equivalent" (4 MRSA 1014).

Out-of-State Forms: "For the purposes of section 1014, subsection 2, a certificate of acknowledgment taken in a state other than Maine shall be presumed to be in a form prescribed by the laws or regulations applicable in the place in which the acknowledgment is taken if upon that certificate appears, in stamped, printed, or embossed form, either separately or together:
"1. Notary public. The words 'notary public;'
"2. Name. The name of the notary public; and
"3. State. The name of the state, or an abbreviation of the name of the state, in which the acknowledgment was taken" (4 MRSA 1014-A).

Attaching the Certificate: "A certificate of acknowledgment should be written on the same document as the instrument acknowledged. If this is not possible, the certificate should fully and accurately describe the instrument acknowledged and should be securely attached to that instrument…. (A) number of Notaries have found it more convenient to have a stamp with the form of the acknowledgment on it, thereby having only to fill in the county, date, name of the person acknowledged, their own signature and their own date of commission expiration" (NPH).

Jurat for Affidavit (NPH):

State of Maine
County of _____

I, _____ *(name of person making affidavit), do swear (affirm), under penalty of perjury, and state (insert facts to be affirmed).*
_____ *(signature of person making affidavit)*

Sworn to and subscribed before me this ____ *day of* _____, *20*____.

_____ *(signature of Notary)*
_____ *(printed name of Notary)*
Notary Public, State of Maine
My commission expires: _____

Affidavit by Document Custodian (NPH):

I, _____ (name of custodian appearing before Notary), do swear that this is a true and exact copy of the _____ (type of document) and that the original _____ (type of document) remains in my possession.

_____ (signature of custodian)
_____ (printed name of custodian)
Sworn to and subscribed before me this ____ day of _____, 20____, by _____ (name of custodian).

_____ (signature of Notary)
_____ (printed name of Notary)
Notary Public, State of Maine
My commission expires: _____

Additional Requirements

The Maine Secretary of State's "Notary Public Handbook and Resource Guide" states that Notaries must print, type or stamp on each certificate the Notary's name, the words "Notary Public, State of Maine" and the commission expiration date.

Certificate Mandatory: "A document that needs to be notarized may be invalid without some statement by the Notary Public. A Notary Public must never sign a document without some notarial statement of the action taken" (NPH).

ELECTRONIC NOTARIZATIONS

The state of Maine has not yet adopted statutes or regulations expressly establishing rules, definitions and procedures for electronic notarization.

UETA Recognizes Notary's eSignature

Maine has adopted the Uniform Electronic Transactions Act (10 MRSA 9401 through 9419), including the provision on notarization, thereby recognizing the legal validity of electronic signatures used by Notaries:

"If a law requires a signature or record to be notarized, acknowledged, verified or made under oath, the requirement is satisfied if the electronic signature of the person authorized to perform those acts, together with all other information required to be included by other applicable law, is attached to or logically associated with the signature or record" (10 MRSA 9411).

NOTARY RECORDS

"Effective July 14, 1994, pursuant to 4 MRSA Section 955-B, Notaries Public commissioned in and for the State of Maine were no longer required to maintain or keep records of all acts they performed while acting in their capacity as Notaries Public. However, a Notary Public is required to keep and make a record of all marriages performed (see 19-A MRSA, Section 654). The Secretary of State strongly recommends that Notaries Public maintain a record of all notarial acts. Not only is it a good way to keep track of individual acts; it also provides protection for both the Notary Public and the person requesting the notarial service. Additionally, a detailed record of the notarial transaction is useful in the event a Notary Public may be asked to provide documentation to a competent authority (a court of law for example)….

"When the Notary Public is removed or resigns from office, the records may be sent to the Secretary of State" (NPH).

Formerly, Maine Notaries commissioned on or after November 1, 1991, were required to keep a record of their notarial acts and, upon resignation or removal from office, to deposit these records with the clerk of the judicial court in the county for which they were appointed.

Format of Record

"A notarial journal of a Notary Public may be in any form that meets the following physical requirements:

"a. The cover and pages inside the cover shall be bound together by any binding method that is designed to prevent the insertion or removal of the cover or a page;

"b. Each page shall be consecutively numbered from the beginning to the end of the journal. If a journal provides two pages on which to record the required information about the same notarial act, then both pages may be numbered with the same number or each page may be numbered with a different number. A page number shall be preprinted;

"c. A notarial journal of a Notary Public should contain on the inside of the front cover or on the first page the following information in any order: 1) The name of the Notary Public; 2) The Notary Public's commission expiration date; 3) The Notary Public's residence or business street or mailing address; 4) The earliest date the journal may be destroyed, which shall be seven years after expiration of the last commission in which entry was made in the journal; and 5) That, in the event of the death of the Notary Public, the journal must be delivered or mailed to the Secretary of State;

"d. The meaning of any not commonly abbreviated word or symbol used in recording a notarial act in the notarial journal;

"e. The signature of the notary public;

"f. At the respective time of entry, the dates of the first and last notarial acts recorded in the notarial journal" (NPH).

Contents of Record

"If a record book (also referred to as a notarial register or journal) is used, each notarial act should be recorded with at least the following:

"a. the date and time of day of the notarial act;

"b. the type of notarial act;

"c. the type, title, or a description of the document or proceeding;

"d. the signature, printed name, and address of each principal;

"e. the evidence of identity of each principal, in the form of either: 1) a statement that the person is 'personally known' to the notary public; 2) a notation of the type of identification document, its issuing agency, its serial or identification number, and its date of issuance or expiration; or 3) the signature, printed name and address of each credible witness swearing or affirming to the person's identity. If the credible witnesses are not personally known to the notary public, a description of identification documents relied on by the notary public;

"f. the fee, if any, charged for the notarial act;

"g. the address where the notarization was performed if not the notary public's business address; and

"h. any other information that the notary public deems to be necessary to fulfill the requirements under this section.... The Secretary of State also strongly recommends that a Notary Public record in the journal any time that the Notary Public refused to act and the circumstances surrounding that refusal" (NPH).

Do Not Record: "(T)o protect private information, a Notary Public must not record a Social Security or credit card number in the journal" (NPH).

"Maine law does not allow nor does it require, as some other states do, a Notary Public to record a finger or thumb print in a notarial record book or journal. The Secretary of State strongly recommends that Notaries Public do not undertake finger printing in any way until Maine law determines the need for this process as part of standard notarial practice" (NPH).

Notary Has Exclusive Custody

"The Secretary of State shall recommend that every notary public keep and maintain records of all notarial acts performed. The notary shall safeguard and retain exclusive custody of these records. The notary may not surrender the records to another notary or to an employer. The records may be inspected in the notary's presence by any individual whose identity is personally known to the notary or is proven on the basis of satisfactory evidence and who specifies the notarial act to be examined" (4 MRSA 955-B).

"The notarial seal, stamp and record book/journal (are) the property of the Notary Public ... without regard to who paid for these notarial supplies or commission — including an employer" (NPH).

Illegal Destruction or Concealment

"Whoever knowingly destroys, defaces or conceals such (Notary) record forfeits not less than $200 nor more than $1,000, and is liable for damages to any person injured in a civil action" (4 MRSA 957).

AUTHENTICATION OF NOTARIAL ACTS

Secretary of State

Authenticating certificates for Notaries, including apostilles, are issued by the office of Maine's Secretary of State (website, "Authentications/Apostilles).

Fees: $10 per signed document for an authenticating certificate, including an apostille, payable to the "Secretary of State."

Mailing Address:
Secretary of State
Div. of Corporations, UCC & Commissions
101 State House Station
Augusta, ME 04333-0101

Courier Delivery or in Person:
Secretary of State
111 Sewall St., 4th Flr.
Augusta ME 04330

Telephone: 1-207-624-7736

Procedure: Download and complete a "Request for Authentications/Apostilles," available on the Secretary of State's website. Mail or present in person the original notarized document(s), the completed request form and the appropriate fee.

County Clerks

A law enacted in 1991 eliminated the requirement that the Maine Secretary of State inform the register of probate and clerks of judicial courts of new Notary commissions in their counties. (Such notification appears to have been discontinued around 1981, when the original office of justice of the peace was merged with that of Notary.) Thus, county officials no longer issue authenticating certificates for Notaries.

COMMISSIONING AND ADMINISTRATION

Maine's Notaries are appointed, commissioned and regulated by the Secretary of State, who maintains records on them (5 MRSA 82).

Applying for Commission

Qualifications: An applicant for a commission as a Maine Notary Public must: (a) be at least 18 years old, (b) be a resident of Maine or a resident of an adjacent state who is regularly employed or carries on a trade or business in Maine, (c) demonstrate proficiency in English, (d) not have had a Notary commission revoked for official misconduct in Maine or any other jurisdiction in the five years preceding the date of application and (e) not have been convicted of a crime punishable by imprisonment for one year or more, or of a lesser offense incompatible with the duties of a Notary as defined by rule of the Secretary of State, during the 10 years preceding application for a new or renewed commission (5 MRSA 82[1]).

Test Required: The application form provides a written, open-book examination that must be completed and passed by the applicant (5 MRSA 82[1][F] and [3]). The testing process is different for renewals — see "Renewal Process Is Different," below.

Application: There are separate application forms for Maine and New Hampshire residents. These forms may be downloaded from the Secretary of State's website. The form must be signed and sworn to in the presence of another Notary, who may affix a seal. In addition, the local municipal clerk and/or registrar of voters must certify on the form that the applicant is a resident of the municipality listed, signing and affixing the municipal seal; and a registered Maine voter, who may not be the Notary who notarized the form, must endorse the appointment of the applicant on the form. Non-English language fluencies may be indicated on the form. The completed application must be submitted with a $50 fee. Non-residents must also submit an affidavit, as described below under "Non-Residents."

"Once the application has been processed by the Secretary of State, the certificate of office and the certificate of qualification will be mailed to the applicant. From the date of appointment, as listed on the certificate of qualification, the applicant has 30 calendar days to be sworn into office by a Dedimus Justice, and 45 days from the date of appointment to return the completed certificate of qualification to the Secretary of State" (SS Rules, Sect. 2E).

Dedimus Justices are appointed for life by the Governor strictly to administer oaths of office (website, "Dedimus Justice"). Dedimus Justices are listed in the "Maine Register," available in most town offices and libraries. They are also all listed by town on the Secretary of State's website (website, "Notary/Dedimus Search"). Most county clerks of court are Dedimus Justices.

Renewal Process Is Different: The application process for renewals is different.

"The Secretary of State sends a notice of renewal approximately six weeks before a commission expires. The notice is sent either by regular mail or to the email address of record" (NPH).

Starting May 2008, all persons seeking to renew a Notary commission must use the online renewal process, including passage of a 30-question exam and responding to questions about criminal convictions. The application fee is $50 but payable only by credit card. Go to the Secretary of State's website to link to the online renewal application (NPH and website, "Total Notary Solution").

"At the end of the online process, the renewal application, the Oath of Office form and a document providing instructions to complete the renewal process will be available ... to download" (NPH).

To complete the renewal, the applicant must (a) have the municipal clerk or registrar of voters validate the application for residency, (b) have the form notarized, (c) appear before a Dedimus Justice to take the oath of office and (d) return the application and "Certificate of Qualification" (oath of office) to the Secretary of State's office by the deadline (NPH).

Non-Residents: Residents of the adjacent state of New Hampshire who are regularly employed or carry on a trade or business in Maine may become Notaries in the state. Applicants must use the application for New Hampshire residents. Self-employed applicants must submit with the application a notarized affidavit stating that their business is physically located in Maine and is licensed, authorized or registered to do business in the state. Employed applicants must submit a notarized affidavit stating that they are employed in Maine, and the applicant's employer must submit a notarized affidavit stating that the business employing the applicant is physically located in Maine and is licensed, authorized or registered to do business in the state (5 MRSA 82[2]). Non-residents may qualify for only a four-year, rather than a seven-year, term (5 MRSA 82[4][B]).

Online Search: On the website maintained by the Secretary of State, under "Notary/Dedimus Search," information on any of Maine's Notaries or Dedimus Justices may be looked up by submitting a name, town, county or language spoken. The Notary's or Justice's name, town, county, home phone, work phone and (for Notaries) commission expiration date are then provided.

Changes of Status

"If a Notary Public changes his or her name or address, the Notary Public must notify the Secretary of State within 10 days of the date of the change" (SS Rules, Sec. 4)

Notaries may update their contact information (including changes in name, addresses, telephone numbers, language fluency, etc.) at any time through the Secretary of State's website.

There is no fee to update this information (website, "Total Notary Solution").

If Notary's Name Changes: "If the Notary Public does not notify the Secretary of State of a change in name, the new name should not be used in notary transactions. If the Notary Public uses a name not on file with the Secretary of State and a certification of the Notary Public for an authentication or apostille is later sought from the Secretary of State, the certification of the Notary Public could not be completed, thus defeating the function of the Notary Public" (SS Rules, Sec. 4).

"If a Notary Public maintains an embossing or ink seal or stamp with the commission name and expiration date, they must be replaced to reflect the change of name" (NPH).

COUNTY CLERKS

In the state of Maine, county clerks have no involvement in the administration of the Notary Public program nor in the authentication of notarial acts.

OTHER NOTARIAL OFFICERS

Attorneys

"Attorneys have 'all of the powers of' and are 'authorized to do all acts which may be done by' Notaries Public (4 MRSA Section 1056). However, attorneys may apply for Notary Public commissions if they wish to officially hold the office of Notary Public. If an attorney does not apply, an attorney is not authorized to sign using the title 'Notary Public'" (NPH).

Judges and Clerks of Court

Judges and clerks of the district court are ex officio Notaries (4 MRSA 158). Acknowledgment of deeds and other written instruments, before recording, may be taken by any clerk of a court of record having a seal (33 MRSA 203).

Commissioners of Deeds

The Governor of Maine may appoint commissioners of deeds to serve in any U.S. jurisdiction or foreign nation and notarize documents for use or recording in Maine. Commissioners' powers include taking acknowledgments and proofs, administering oaths, and taking and certifying depositions (33 MRSA 251 and 253).

Justice of Peace Office Changed

"Beginning in 1981, the office of Justice of the Peace, as it was traditionally known, was phased into the office of Notary Public under the title Notary Public. The process was completed in 1988" (NPH).

An office called Justice of the Peace still exists in Maine, but these officers no longer share any powers with Notaries Public (website, "Justices of the Peace").

Dedimus Justices

"Dedimus Justices perform a single function under Maine statute, that of swearing in various public officials, including Notaries Public. The office is a lifetime appointment by the Governor" (website, "Dedimus Justice").

County Jail Employees

Under very specific circumstances, a county-jail employee may take an acknowledgment: "If a court issues an order that a defendant in custody be released, pending trial, on personal recognizance or upon execution of an unsecured appearance bond ..., an employee of the county jail having custody of the defendant, if authorized to do so by the Sheriff, may, without fee, prepare the personal recognizance or bond and take the acknowledgment of the defendant" (15 MRSA 1025-A).

QUICK FACTS

Notary Jurisdiction
Statewide (5 MRSA 82[5]).

Notary Term Length
Seven years for a resident, four years for a New Hampshire resident (5 MRSA 82[4]).

Notary Bond
Not required by law.

Maryland

NOTARY SEAL

A Maryland Notary must authenticate official acts with a seal of office, and the seal's format must be as follows (ACM St. Gov. 18-108):

Kind

Embosser or Inked Rubber Stamp: "The seal must be either an embosser which makes a raised impression in the paper or a rubber stamp which makes an ink impression upon the paper. Both are in general use throughout the State" (HNP).

Shape/Size

Not specified.

Components

1. Name of Notary (as it appears on commission);
2. "Notary Public";
3. Name of county or "City of Baltimore"

Examples

The above typical, actual-size examples of Notary seals are allowed by Maryland law. Formats other than these may also be permitted.

NOTARY ADMINISTRATION

Office of Secretary of State
Notary Division   1-410-974-5520
State House
Annapolis, MD 21401

Website: www.sos.state.md.us/Notary/Notary.aspx

NOTARY RULES

ACM — Annotated Code of Maryland
CMR — Code of Maryland Regulations
HNP — Handbook for Maryland Notaries Public

Most Notary rules are in the Annotated Code of Maryland, under "State Government," Titles 18 and 19:

a. "Notaries Public," Sections 18-101 through 18-114;

b. "Acknowledgments," including "Maryland Uniform Acknowledgment Acts,"* Sections 19-101 through 19-114.

* The *Uniform Acknowledgment Act* of 1939 is included here. Most sections are adopted verbatim, but there are significant deviations in Sections 2, 3, 9 and 10 of the Act (see Appendix 4).

Rules regarding Notary fees are in the Code of Maryland Regulations:

c. Title 01 ("Executive Department"), Subtitle 02 ("Secretary of State"), Chapter 08 ("Notary Public Fees").

Other guidelines for Notaries are in the "Handbook for Maryland Notaries Public" (2008) issued by the Maryland Secretary of State and available online.

where Notary resides or was qualified;
4. OPTIONAL: symbol or device chosen by the Notary.

Expiration Date, Printed Name Must Appear

"Every notary shall include on each act, instrument, or attestation the expiration date of the notary's commission as a notary public" (ACM St. Gov. 18-108[c]).

"The certificate of the acknowledging officer shall be completed by his signature, his official seal if he has one, the title of his office, and if he is a notary public, the date his commission expires" (ACM St. Gov. 19-108).

"A notary must include on each document the notary's printed name, signature, date of notarization, and expiration date of his or her commission. In addition, the notary must affix his or her notary seal or stamp to the document" (website, "Duties & Responsibilities ...").

'A Public Seal'

"It is a public seal, even though the notary public purchased it. The notary public should use great care to see that it is not lost, stolen, or misused" (HNP).

NOTARY POWERS

Maryland Notaries are authorized to perform the following notarial acts (ACM At. Gov. 18-105, 106, 107 and 113):

1. Take acknowledgments*;
2. Administer oaths** and affirmations;
3. "Make protests and declarations"***;
4. Take depositions**** (NPH);
5. Certify copies of notarial records*****;
6. Witness signings******.

* <u>Identifying Acknowledgers</u>: "'Acknowledgement' means a declaration by an individual that he or she has executed an instrument for the purposes stated therein and, if the instrument is executed in a representative capacity, that the individual signed the instrument with proper authority, and executed it as the act of the person or entity represented and identified therein" (CMR, Chapt. 08, Sec. .01B).

"An acknowledgment is a statement by a person who has executed a document that the document is his or her act and deed. An acknowledgment is made to the notary public, but it is not an oath or affirmation of the truth — it is a statement that a certain person did something of his or her own fee will" (NPH).

"The officer taking the acknowledgment shall know or have satisfactory evidence that the person making the acknowledgment is the person described in and who executed the instrument" (ACM St. Gov. 19-105).

In regard to satisfactory evidence, "(a) good rule for a notary public to follow would be to require such proof of identification as he or she would require to cash a very large check for that person" (HNP).

"If asked to take an acknowledgment, you must ask: 'Does this document constitute your own act and deed?' or 'Are you signing this document of your own free will?'" (website, "Duties & Responsibilities ...").

** <u>Oaths and Affirmations</u>: "A notary public should ordinarily require a person taking an oath or affirmation to hold up his or her hand. If this is not practical (for instance, when the person making the oath is injured or an amputee), the notary public should direct the person taking the oath to do some other act which shows recognition of the solemnity of the occasion. The notary public may also permit the person making the oath to do some other act if it appears to the notary that another act will be more binding upon the conscience of the swearer" (HNP).

"The form of oath administered for oral testimony is: Do you solemnly swear or affirm under the penalties of perjury that the responses given and statements made will be the whole truth and nothing but the truth" (HNP).

"For an oath or affirmation, you ask: 'Do you solemnly affirm under the penalties of perjury and upon personal knowledge that the contents of the document are true?'" (website, "Duties & Responsibilities ...").

<u>For Affidavit Required by Rule of Law</u>: "Do you solemnly affirm, under the penalties of perjury (and upon personal knowledge), that the contents of the foregoing paper, (here the Notary should refer to the document to which the person is making an affidavit), are true (to the best of your knowledge, information, and belief)?" (Select the applicable italicized phrase, but not both.) (HNP)

<u>For Affidavit Not Required by Rule of Law</u>: When the affiant wishes to appeal to a divine being: "In the presence of Almighty God, do you solemnly swear, under the penalties of perjury (and upon personal knowledge), that the contents of the foregoing paper, (here the Notary

should refer to the document to which the person is making an affidavit), are true (to the best of your knowledge, information, and belief)?" (Select the applicable italicized phrase, but not both.) (HNP)

For Oral Testimony, Such as in Deposition: "Do you solemnly swear or affirm under the penalties of perjury that the responses given and statements made will be the whole truth and nothing but the truth?" (HNP).

For Mortgagee Secured by Deed of Trust: "Do you solemnly affirm under the penalties of perjury and upon personal knowledge that (you are an officer/agent/executor of the mortgagee/person secured by the foregoing mortgage/deed of trust and that) the consideration recited in the mortgage/deed of trust is true and bona fide as therein set forth?" (HNP).

*** Protests: "Protest is not required except upon dishonor of a draft which on its face appears to be either drawn or payable outside of the United States and its territories, and the District of Columbia" (HNP).
"It shall not be lawful for any notary public to sign and issue any protest except in the form prescribed by the Comptroller" (ACM. St. Gov. 18-110).
"Matters regarding protest are found in Commercial Law, Title 3, Subtitle 5, Sections 3-501 through 3-514, Annotated Code of Maryland" (HNP).

**** Depositions: "A notary public may take a deposition unless the notary is (a) a relative, employee, or attorney of any party to the case, (b) a relative or employee of any attorney in the case or (c) financially interested in the case.
"However, every notary public is warned that because all that occurs during a deposition must be accurately recorded and the rules relating to the taking and filing of a deposition are very complex, no one should undertake to act as a notary at a deposition unless he or she has had the special training necessary to such practice" (HNP).
"By written agreement of the parties or by court order, a deposition may be taken by telephone. The law provides that the officer before whom such a deposition is taken may administer the oath by telephone" (HNP).

***** Certifying Copies: "A notary public is required to provide a certified copy of any record in his or her office upon demand and upon payment of the $2.00 fee. Ordinarily this would mean a certified copy of a record in his or her fair register of official acts" (HNP).
"A notary public has no authority to certify a copy of a public record, a publicly recorded document, a school record or diploma, a professional license, or any other public or private document or record which does not pertain to the notary public's official acts" (HNP).
"A notary in the State of Maryland does not have the power to certify the authenticity of any document — official or unofficial — other than the notary's registry. For example, a notary cannot notarize a passport, birth certificate, school transcript, or other document" (website, "Duties & Responsibilities ...").

****** Witnessing Signatures: If a document presented for notarization does not contain a notarial certificate reflecting the taking of an oath or acknowledgment, a Notary may witness the signing of the document in the Notary's official capacity through the following steps (HNP and ACM St. Gov. Sec. 18-113):
1. Obtain satisfactory proof of the identity of the person signing the document;
2. Observe the signing of the document;
3. Date, sign and seal or stamp the document;
4. Note on the document the date on which the notary's commission expires; and
5. Record the notarization in the Notary's register of official acts" (NPH and ACM St. Gov. 18-113).

Satisfactory Proof of Identity
"Satisfactory proof is that amount of proof which is sufficient to convince the notary public that the person making the acknowledgment is the person described in the document, and the one who executed it. A good rule for a notary public to follow would be to require such proof of identification as he or she would require to cash a very large check for that person" (HNP).

Notary Should Serve All
"As a public officer, a notary should perform any notarial power (for) any individual who makes a reasonable and lawful request for notarization. A notary may, however, refuse to notarize

a document if the notarization would result in an illegal or improper act or the notary knows that the transaction is fraudulent.

"Generally, a notary should not refuse to notarize a document solely because the individual requesting notarization is not a client or customer of the notary or the notary's employer. Because the notary is a public official, a notary public should be available to perform notarial services for the public at large" (website, "Frequently Asked Questions").

Maryland Power of Attorney Act

Under Maryland's General and Limited Power of Attorney Act (ACM 17-101 through 17-204), a power of attorney must be acknowledged before a Notary and witnessed by two witnesses, one of whom may be the Notary.

NOTARY DON'TS

May Not Confirm Affidavit Facts

"(A) notary public has no right to investigate or pass upon any facts sworn to by another person. A notary public only has power to administer an oath or affirmation, and the certificate he or she issues shows only the facts were sworn to before the notary. However, a notary public should never act in a situation where the notary knows, or has reason to believe, that a person is making a false oath or affirmation, since this may render the notary public guilty as a conspirator or an accomplice of the perjurer" (HNP).

Advertising under Trade Name

"Because notaries public are civil officers, they should not advertise their notarial services under a trade name. The public is entitled to know the name of the officer to whom it is going for the services given by a notary public" (HNP).

Disqualifying Interests

"As a general rule, a notary public should not perform any official act with regard to any matter in which the notary is personally involved, whether that involvement is direct or indirect. Notaries are prohibited from notarizing their own signature, and to minimize personal involvement, notaries should refrain from performing official acts for members of their immediate families, even though not ordinarily under a legal duty to refrain" (HNP). A Notary with a "beneficial interest" in a transaction should not notarize in that transaction (HNP).

Corporate or Bank Notaries: A Notary who is a stockholder, director, officer or employee of a bank or other corporation may notarize for that corporation, unless a party to the document (ACM St. Gov. 18-111).

NOTARY SIGNING AGENTS

In order to lawfully operate in the state of Maryland, a Notary Signing Agent must either: (a) be licensed by the state (i.e., Maryland Insurance Agency) as a Title Insurance Producer (TIP), as defined in ACM, Insurance Article, Sec. 10-101(i), which requires surety and fidelity bonding and continuing education; or (b) operate as a Title Insurance Producer Independent Contractor (TIPIC) under the supervision of a duly licensed and bonded TIP. The TIP thereby assumes all liability for the actions of the TIPIC.

Any mortgage or deed of trust executed in a transaction in which a TIPIC is acting on behalf of a Title Insurance Producer must include the name, address and license number of the TIPIC and title insurance producer for which the TIPIC is acting.

The Secretary of State's "Handbook for Maryland Notaries Public" provides the following clarification about Notaries and real estate closings:

"According to the Maryland Insurance Administration, 'a notary who merely attends a real estate closing or settlement that is conducted by another person or entity and who merely witnesses signatures in consideration of the statutory fees that a notary is permitted to charge does not, in the view of the MIA, fall within the scope of (Insurance Article) § 10-101(i) and is not required to secure a title producer's license in order to perform such services. However, if the notary is the only individual other than the buyer who is present at the closing and the notary is presenting documents for signature which may result in the issuance of title insurance, collecting escrow funds, or otherwise performing a duty other than the witnessing of a signature, the notary must also be licensed as a title insurance producer.' Bulletin from MIA to Title Insurers, Property & Casualty 03-18, December 1, 2003" (HNP).

NOTARY FEES

A Notary may demand and receive a fee of $2 for any "original notarial act" (ACM St. Gov. 18-112 and CMR, Chapt. 08, Sec. .03A).

Copies of Same Document

"When a notary public is requested to notarize more than one copy of the same document, where the copy or copies have been signed at the same time by the same person or persons, the notary may demand and receive $2.00 for notarizing each signature on the original or first copy of the document, and may demand and receive not more than $1.00 for each signature on each additional copy of the same document" (CMR, Chapt. 08, Sec. .03B).

"A notary public may also charge $2.00 for certifying a copy of an entry in the notary's register of official acts" (CMR, Chapt. 08, Sec. .03E).

Reproductions of Notarized Document

"When a notary public is requested to make reproductions of a notarized document by photocopying or other means, the notary may demand and receive not more than $1.00 for each copy furnished" (CMR, Chapt. 08, Sec. .03C).

Mileage

The Notary may also charge a mileage reimbursement of 31 cents per mile for travel required for the performance of a notarial act plus a flat travel fee of up to $5 (ACM St. Gov. 18-112[b]).

NOTARY CERTIFICATES

Maryland has adopted the *Uniform Acknowledgment Act*, including the certificates (ACM St. Gov. 19-107) for:

1. Acknowledgment by individual;
2. Acknowledgment by corporation;
3. Acknowledgment by attorney in fact;
4. Acknowledgment by any public officer or deputy thereof, or by any trustee, administrator, guardian or executor.

The Notary's seal and commission expiration date must be added to each of these certificates, as required by Maryland law.

For the text of the certificates, see "Uniform Acknowledgment Act (1939, amended 1960)," Section 7, in Appendix 4.

In the Secretary of State's "Notary Public Handbook" (NPH), the following certificates are also prescribed — some based on the forms in the Uniform Acknowledgment Act.

Acknowledgment by Private Individual(s) — Option 1 (NPH and ACM St. Gov. 19-107[a]):

State of Maryland
County of _____ (or City of Baltimore)

On this _____ day of _____ (month), 20____, before me, the undersigned officer, personally appeared _____ (name[s] of person[s] who make acknowledgment), known to me (or satisfactorily proven) to be the person(s) whose name(s) is/are subscribed to the within instrument and acknowledged that he/she/they executed the same for the purposes therein contained.

(For mortgage or deed of trust, here insert additional wording indicated below and administer oath to lender/mortgagee.)*

In witness hereof I hereunto set my hand and official seal.

(SEAL, SIGNATURE AND TYPEWRITTEN OR PRINTED NAME OF NOTARY)

Notary Public
My Commission expires _____

* For Mortgage or Deed of Trust (NPH):

Wording if oath made by lender:

At the same time, also appeared _____ (name of person making oath/affirmation), (one of) the mortgagee(s) named in the foregoing mortgage (or one of the persons secured by the foregoing deed of trust), and made oath/affirmation in due form of law that the consideration recited in said mortgage/ deed of trust is true and bona fide as therein set forth.

Wording if oath made by agent, executor or corporate officer:

At the same time, also appeared _____ (name of person making oath/affirmation), (one of) the _____ (agent[s], executor[s], or corporate officer[s]) of the said mortgagee/ person and made oath/affirmation in due form of law that he/she is an _____ (agent, executor or officer) of the mortgagee/person secured by the foregoing mortgage/deed of trust and that the consideration recited in said mortgage/deed of trust is true and bona fide as therein set forth.

Acknowledgment by Private Individual — Option 2 (HNP):

State of Maryland, _____ County (or City of Baltimore)

I hereby certify, that on this _____ day of _____ (month), in the year 20____, before the subscriber, a Notary Public of the State of Maryland, in and for _____ (name of county or "City of Baltimore," as the case may be, for which Notary is appointed), personally appeared _____ (name[s] of person[s] who make acknowledgment) and acknowledged the foregoing _____ (type of instrument, e.g., deed, mortgage, lease, or whatever) to be his/her act (or their respective) act.

(For mortgage or deed of trust, here insert additional wording indicated above and administer oath to lender/mortgagee.)*

(SEAL, SIGNATURE AND TYPEWRITTEN OR PRINTED NAME OF NOTARY)

*Notary Public
My Commission expires _____*

Acknowledgment by Corporation (HNP and ACM St. Gov. 19-107[b]):

*State of Maryland
County of _____ (or City of Baltimore)*

On this _____ day of _____ (month), 20____, before me, the undersigned officer, personally appeared _____ (name[s] of person[s] who made acknowledgment on behalf of corporation), who acknowledged himself/ herself/themselves to be the _____ (title of corporate officer or other description of legal capacity) of _____ (name of corporation), a corporation, and that he/she/they, as such _____ (title of corporate officer or other description of legal capacity), being authorized so to do, executed the foregoing instrument for the purposes therein contained, by signing the name of the corporation by himself/herself/ themselves as _____ (title of corporate officer or other description of legal capacity).

(For mortgage or deed of trust, here insert additional wording indicated above and administer oath to lender/mortgagee.)*

In witness whereof I hereunto set my hand and official seal.

(SEAL, SIGNATURE AND TYPEWRITTEN OR PRINTED NAME OF NOTARY)

*Notary Public
My Commission expires _____*

Acknowledgment by Attorney in Fact (HNP and ACM St. Gov. 19-107[c]):

*State of Maryland
County of _____ (or City of Baltimore)*

On this _____ day of _____ (month), 20____, before me, the undersigned officer, personally appeared _____ (name[s] of person[s] who made acknowledgment), known to me (or satisfactorily proven) to be the person(s) whose name(s) is/are subscribed as attorney(s) in fact for _____ (name of person[s] for whom the attorney in fact is appearing), and acknowledged that he/she/they executed the same as the act of his/her/their principal for the purposes therein contained.

(For mortgage or deed of trust, here insert additional wording indicated above and administer oath to lender/mortgagee.)*

In witness whereof I hereunto set my hand and official seal.

(SEAL, SIGNATURE AND TYPEWRITTEN OR PRINTED NAME OF NOTARY)

*Notary Public
My Commission expires _____*

Acknowledgment by Public Officer, Trustee, Administrator, Guardian or Executor (HNP and ACM St. Gov. 19-107[d]):

State of Maryland
County of _____ (or City of Baltimore)

On this _____ day of _____(month), 20____, before me, the undersigned officer, personally appeared _____ (name[s] of person[s] who made acknowledgment), of the State (county or city as the case may be) of _____, known to me (or satisfactorily proven) to be the person(s) described in the foregoing instrument, and acknowledged that he/she/they executed the same in the capacity therein stated and for the purposes therein contained.

(For mortgage or deed of trust, here insert additional wording indicated above and administer oath to lender/mortgagee.)*

In witness whereof I hereunto set my hand and official seal.

(SEAL, SIGNATURE AND TYPEWRITTEN OR PRINTED NAME OF NOTARY)

Notary Public
My Commission expires _____

Acknowledgment Before Commissioned Military Officer by Person Serving with U.S. Armed Forces (ACM St. Gov. 19-111):

"(A)ny person serving in or with the armed forces of the United States and their respective spouses or dependents, may acknowledge ... wherever located before any commissioned officer in active service of the armed forces of the United States with the rank of second lieutenant or higher in the Army, Air Force, or Marine Corps, or ensign or higher in the Navy or United States Coast Guard. The instrument shall not be rendered invalid by the failure to state therein the place of execution or acknowledgment. No authentication of the officers' certificate of acknowledgment shall be required but the officer taking the acknowledgment shall endorse thereon or attach thereto a certificate substantially in the following form."

On this the _____ day of _____, 20____, before me, _____, the undersigned officer, personally appeared _____ (name and serial number, if any), known to me (or satisfactorily proven) to be serving in or with the armed forces of the United States (or the spouse of or a dependent of _____ [name and serial number, if any], a person serving in or with the armed forces of the United States) and to be the person whose name is subscribed to the within instrument and acknowledged that he/she/they executed the same for the purpose therein contained. And the undersigned does further certify that he/she is at the date of this certificate a commissioned officer of the rank stated below and is in the active service of the armed forces of the United States.

(OFFICER'S SIGNATURE, RANK, SERIAL NUMBER, AND COMMAND TO WHICH ATTACHED)

Certificate for Oath or Affirmation (HNP):

State of Maryland
County of _____
(or City of Baltimore), to wit:

I hereby certify that on the _____day of _____ (month), 20____, before me, the subscriber, a Notary Public for the State of Maryland, in and for _____ (here insert name of county or City of Baltimore for which Notary is appointed), personally appeared _____ (name[s] of person[s] swearing) and made oath (or affirmation) in due form of law that the matters and facts set forth in the _____ (here describe document to which the person[s] is/are swearing) are true.
As witness, my hand and notarial seal.

(SEAL, SIGNATURE AND TYPEWRITTEN OR PRINTED NAME OF NOTARY)

Notary Public
My Commission expires _____

Short Form Certificate for Oath or Affirmation (HNP):

State of Maryland
County of _____ (or City of Baltimore)

Sworn and subscribed to before me this _____ day of _____ (month), 20____.

(SEAL, SIGNATURE AND TYPEWRITTEN OR PRINTED NAME OF NOTARY)

*Notary Public
My Commission expires _____*

Certificate to Certify Copy of Notary Register (HNP):

*State of Maryland
County of _____ (or City of Baltimore)*

On this _____ day of _____ (month), 20____, I hereby certify that the attached document is a true copy made by me from a record in my fair register of official acts.

In witness whereof I hereunto set my hand and official seal.

(SEAL, SIGNATURE AND TYPEWRITTEN OR PRINTED NAME OF NOTARY)

*Notary Public
My Commission expires _____*

Certificate Not Necessary for Witnessing

Effective October 1, 1996, Maryland law allows Notaries to certify the witnessing of a signature merely by signing, sealing and dating the document, without certificate wording. See "Witnessing Signatures" under "Notary Powers," above.

Certificate of Protest

"The protest (certificate) must: (a) Identify the negotiable instrument; (b) Certify that due presentment has been made or the reason why presentment is excused; and (c) Certify that the instrument has been dishonored (i) By nonacceptance or (ii) By nonpayment. The protest may also certify that notice of dishonor has been given to all parties or to specified parties ....

"The protest need not be in a particular form, so long as it certifies the matters stated (above)" (HNP).

Notary Should Not Draft Certificates

"(E)xcept to certify a record in his or her fair register, a notary should only complete a certificate which has already been prepared. These certificates are ordinarily printed or typewritten at the end of a document" (HNP).

ELECTRONIC NOTARIZATIONS

The state of Maryland has not yet adopted statutes or regulations expressly establishing rules, definitions and procedures for electronic notarization.

UETA Recognizes Notary's eSignature

Maryland has adopted the Uniform Electronic Transactions Act (ACM Comm. Law Art. 21, Secs. 101 through 120) in substantially amended form, including the provision on notarization, thereby recognizing the legal validity of electronic signatures used by Notaries:

"If a law requires a signature or record to be notarized, acknowledged, verified, or made under oath, the requirement is satisfied if the electronic signature of the person authorized to perform those acts, together with all other information required to be included by other applicable law, is attached to or logically associated with the signature or record" (ACM Comm. Law 21-110).

NOTARY RECORDS

"A notary public shall keep a fair register of all protests and other official acts done by the notary in virtue of the notary's office and shall, when required, give a certified copy of any record in the notary's office to any person applying for the record on payment of the usual fees for the certified copy by the person applying for it" (ACM St. Gov. 18-107).

Components of Each Entry

According to the Maryland Secretary of State (HNP), a fair register includes at least:

1. Name and address of each person appearing before the Notary;
2. Date on which the person(s) appeared;
3. Method by which each person was identified;
4. Type of notarial act;
5. Type of document;
6. Fee charged;
7. Signature(s) of person(s) signing document.

Register Kept Five Years

"Registries should be retained for at least five years" (website, "Duties & Responsibilities ...").

AUTHENTICATION OF NOTARIAL ACTS

County Clerks

Whether or not a notarized document requires an apostille from the Maryland Secretary of State, an authenticating certificate from a circuit court clerk must first be obtained. This is the county office where the Notary has qualified after commissioning.

Secretary of State

Authenticating certificates for clerks of the circuit court, and apostilles, are issued by the Maryland Secretary of State.

Fees: $5 per document, covering authentication for a circuit court clerk, or an apostille. Payable to "Secretary of State."

Mailing and Walk-In Address:
Office of Secretary of State
16 Francis St.
Jeffrey Building, 1st Floor
Annapolis, MD 21401

Telephone: 1-410-974-5521

Procedure: After securing an authenticating certificate from a circuit court clerk, mail or present in person the original notarized document(s), along with the appropriate fee. In a cover letter, indicate the country the document(s) will be sent to, and include a daytime telephone number or e-mail address for questions, as well as a stamped, addressed return envelope. A cover letter form may be printed out from the Secretary of State's website ("Certification").

COMMISSIONING AND ADMINISTRATION

Though the Governor appoints and commissions Maryland's Notaries (ACM St. Gov. 18-101[a]), the Secretary of State regulates and maintains records on them (ACM St. 18-103). These records are open to public inspection, including the Notary's home address and home and business telephone numbers (ACM St. Gov. 10-617).

Applying for Commission

Qualifications: An applicant for a commission as a Maryland Notary Public must: (a) be at least 18 years old, (b) be of known good character, integrity and abilities and (c) live or work in the state of Maryland.

No Course or Test: No course of instruction or test is required to become a Notary Public in Maryland.

Application: In completing the application, the would-be Notary must cite two character references who are not family members and preferably Maryland residents. Applicants must also indicate their state senator or, in the case of non-residents, the county (or Baltimore City) in which they wish to be commissioned. The completed application must then be sent to the Notary Division with a $20 fee.

The Division will forward the application to the respective state senator for endorsement. The senator may contact the character references.

Taking Oath, Picking up Commission: Upon the application's approval by the senator, the Secretary of State issues a commission and sends it to the clerk of the circuit court in the applicant's county of residence (or Baltimore City), or to the clerk of the county indicated by a non-resident applicant. A postcard will also be sent directing the applicant to appear at the clerk's office within 30 days to take an oath of office and pick up the new commission. A total fee of $11 is paid to the county clerk at that time.

Renewal of Commission: Approximately two months before commission expiration, a form to renew the commission will be sent to the Notary by the office of the Secretary of State.

Non-Residents: Out-of-state residents who work in Maryland may become Notaries (ACM St. Gov. 18-101). However, only residents of states which reciprocally allow Maryland residents to become Notaries may qualify as Maryland Notaries.

Online Search: The state's database of Notaries may be searched by entering any part of a last or first name or the name of a county. The online Notary roll may be accessed through www.sos.state.md.us/Notary/NotarySearch.aspx.

Changes of Status

If Notary Changes Name or Address: "Whenever the name of a notary is changed, the notary may continue to perform official acts under the name in which the notary was commissioned, until the expiration of commission. However, it is preferable to use the form "(New Name), commissioned as (Prior Name)." The notary shall, within 30 days after a change of name or address notify the Secretary of State and the Clerk of the Circuit Court of the County, or Baltimore City, depending upon where the notary received the commission.

"A notary who wishes to obtain a commission in a new name may do so by requesting a name change application from the Secretary of State, which is to be completed and returned, along with the old commission. The notary must appear before the Clerk to be sworn in and pay an administrative fee of $8.00. When a new commission is issued because of a change of name, the previous commission held in the old name is canceled" (website, "Frequently Asked Questions").

If Married Notary Uses Maiden Name: "The Attorney General has issued an opinion that a married woman may use her maiden or married name on her notary commission and seal. The name chosen must agree, on the commission, on the seal, and as she signs her name on the certification. She may choose either name, but whichever she chooses, the use must be consistent. That is, her name as used as a notary public, should be the same one used for other purposes: business, professional, or personal. Based upon an earlier court case, the opinion stated that 'a married female may retain her given birth name by using it exclusively, consistently, and non-fraudulently'" (HNP).

COUNTY CLERKS

To contact a Maryland clerk of the court of the county to obtain an authenticating certificate for a Notary, or to seek assistance in locating a given Notary, telephone long distance information — 1-XXX-555-1212 — and ask for the number of "the clerk of the circuit court" in the following cities or towns:

County	City/Town	Area Code
Allegany	Cumberland	(301)
Anne Arundel	Annapolis	(410)
Baltimore (City)	Baltimore	(410)
Baltimore (County)	Towson	(410)
Calvert	Prince Frederick	(410)
Caroline	Denton	(410)
Carroll	Westminster	(410)
Cecil	Elkton	(410)
Charles	La Plata	(301)
Dorchester	Cambridge	(410)
Frederick	Frederick	(301)
Garrett	Oakland	(301)
Harford	Bel Air	(410)
Howard	Ellicott City	(410)
Kent	Chestertown	(410)
Montgomery	Rockville	(240)
Prince George's	Upper Marlboro	(301)
Queen Anne's	Centreville	(410)
St. Mary's	Leonardtown	(301)
Somerset	Princess Anne	(410)
Talbot	Easton	(410)
Washington	Hagerstown	(301)
Wicomico	Salisbury	(410)
Worcester	Snow Hill	(410)

OTHER NOTARIAL OFFICERS

Besides Notaries Public, the following officers have statewide powers to take acknowledgments (ACM St. Gov. 19-102):

1. A judge of a court of record;
2. A clerk or deputy clerk of a court having a seal;
3. A master in chancery.

QUICK FACTS

Notary Jurisdiction
Statewide (ACM St. Gov. 18-109).

Notary Term Length
Four years (ACM St. Gov. 18-103[c]).

Notary Bond
Not required by law.

Massachusetts

NOTARY SEAL

A Massachusetts Notary Public must keep "an official notarial seal or stamp" (EO Sec. 5[c]).

Kind

Black-Inked Stamp or Embosser: "Each new notarial seal that uses ink shall, after the date of this Executive Order, use black ink" (EO Sec. 5[c][3]).

Shape/Size

Not specified by law.

Components

The following five components must appear in either a seal (embosser) or a stamp (inking device) (EO Sec. 5[c][2]), or in a seal and a stamp which, when used together, include all of the components (EO Sec. 5[c][4]):

Examples

The above typical, actual-size examples of Notary seals are allowed by Massachusetts law. Formats other than these may also be acceptable.

NOTARY ADMINISTRATION

In Massachusetts, the Secretary of the Commonwealth and the Governor are both involved with the administration of the Notary program. The Governor appoints Notaries with the advice and consent of the Executive Council, while the Secretary maintains records on the appointees and authenticates their acts.

A. Office of Secretary of Commonwealth
   Public Records Division 1-617-727-2832
   Commissions Section
   McCormack Building, Room 1719
   One Ashburton Place
   Boston, MA 02108

Website: www.sec.state.ma.us/pre/
   prenot/notidx.htm

B. Office of the Governor
   Notary Public Office 1-617-725-4016
   State House, Room 184
   Boston, MA 02133

Website: www.mass.gov/

NOTARY RULES

EO — Governor's Executive Order No. 455 (04-04)
GL — Massachusetts General Laws
GNP — Guidelines for the Notary Public

Executive Order No. 455 (03-13), signed by Governor Mitt Romney on December 19, 2003, extensively supplemented the state's statutory rules for Notaries. This Order was later amended and superseded by Romney's Revised Executive Order No. 455 (04-04), effective May 15, 2004.

Other Notary rules are in the Massachusetts General Laws:

a. Chapter 222, "Justices of the Peace, Notaries Public and Commissioners";

b. Chapter 183, "Alienation of Land."

Some still helpful tips for Notaries are in "Guidelines for the Notary Public," a pamphlet formerly issued by the Secretary of the Commonwealth.

1. Name of Notary exactly as on commission;
2. "Notary Public";
3. "Commonwealth of Massachusetts" or "Massachusetts";
4. "My commission expires on _____ (date)" or "My commission expires _____ (date)" or "Commission expires _____ (date)";
5. Facsimile of Great Seal of Commonwealth of Massachusetts.

Seal Not to Be Used by Another

"A notary shall keep an official notarial seal or stamp that is the exclusive property of the notary, which may not be used by any other person" (EO Sec. 5[c]).

Commission Expiration Date Must Appear

"A justice of the peace or notary public, when taking acknowledgment of any instrument provided by law to be recorded, shall print or type his name directly below his signature and affix thereto the date of the expiration of his commission in the following language: 'My commission expires _____.' Failure to comply with this section shall not affect the validity of any instrument, or the record thereof" (GL 222, Sec. 8).

Notary's Name Printed or Typewritten

"A justice of the peace, notary public or other person duly authorized, when taking an acknowledgment or administering an oath with relation to an instrument filed in a proceeding in the probate court shall print or type his name directly below his signature thereon. Failure to comply with this section shall not affect the validity of any instrument or the record thereof" (GL 222, Sec. 8[A]).

When New Seal Is Required

"A notary public shall obtain a new seal or stamp if the notary public renews his or her commission, receives a new commission, or changes his or her name" (EO Sec. 5[c][1]).

Seal of Commissioner

Though the Governor may appoint commissioners to perform notarial acts in other U.S. states, territories, districts and dependencies, such officers are rarely appointed, according to state officials. However, the seal of any such commissioner must contain the following (GL 222, Sec. 5):

1. Name of commissioner;
2. "Commissioner for Massachusetts";
3. Name of state, territory, district or dependency, and town or county where residing.

"In each case, a certificate of the commissioner's oath of office and his signature and an impression of his official seal shall be forthwith transmitted to and filed in the office of the State Secretary."

Disposition of Seal

"When a notary commission expires, is resigned, or is revoked, the notary shall ... as soon as reasonably practicable, destroy or deface all notary seals and stamps so that they may not be used ..." (EO Sec. 13[a]).

Smeared Seal

"What if I smear my seal on the document? — If there is room, affix a second impression nearby. It is not necessary to cross out the original seal impression or write an explanation on the document; the reason for the second impression will be obvious. If there is no room for a second impression, attach a separate certificate with the same wording, signature and a clear seal impression. Line through the original notarial wording and draw a line specifically through your seal and signature. Near that old certificate wording, write 'See Attached Certificate'" (Governor's Legal Counsel website, "Frequently Asked Questions").

Signature of Notary

"In completing a notarial act, a notary shall sign his or her name exactly as it appears on the notary's commission" (EO Sec. 5[b]).

"The notary should use a dark colored ink such as blue or black. Rarely, some receiving agencies may require the certificate to be filled out in a particular color. If so, the notary should comply" (Governor's Legal Counsel website, "Frequently Asked Questions").

NOTARY POWERS

Massachusetts Notaries are authorized to perform the following notarial acts (EO Sec. 5[a]):

1. Take acknowledgments*;
2. Administer oaths** and affirmations***;
3. Execute jurats****;
4. Witness signatures*****;
5. Certify copies******;
6. Issue summonses for witnesses as set forth in GL, Chapter 233, Sec. 1;
7. Issue subpoenas as provided by law;
8. Witness opening of bank safe, vault or box as set forth in GL, Chapter 167, Sec. 32.

* <u>Acknowledgment</u>: In an acknowledgment, an individual must, at a single time and place, (a) appear in person before a Notary and present a document, (b) be identified by the Notary through satisfactory evidence of identity, and (c) indicate to the Notary "that the signature on the document was voluntarily affixed by the individual for the purposes stated within the document and, if applicable, that the individual had authority to sign in a particular representative capacity" (EO Sec. 2).

** <u>Oath Wording</u>: An oath is a notarial act, or part thereof, which is legally equivalent to an affirmation and in which an individual, at a single time and place, (a) appears in person before the Notary, (b) is identified by the Notary through satisfactory evidence of identity, and (c) "makes a vow of truthfulness or fidelity under the pains and penalties of perjury by invoking a deity" (EO Sec.2).

The oath wording for an affidavit may be as follows (GNP): "Do you solemnly swear that the statements contained herein are true, so help you God?"

*** <u>Affirmation Wording</u>: An affirmation is a notarial act, or part thereof, that is legally equivalent to an oath and in which an individual, at a single time and place, (a) appears in person before the Notary, (b) is identified by the Notary through satisfactory evidence of identity, and (c) "makes a vow of truthfulness or fidelity under the pains and penalties of perjury without invoking a deity" (EO Sec. 2).

The affirmation wording for an affidavit may be as follows (GNP): "Do you solemnly affirm, under the penalties of perjury, that the statements made herein are true?"

**** <u>Jurat</u>: In a jurat, an individual must, at a single time and place, (a) appear in person before a Notary and present a document, (b) be identified by the Notary through satisfactory evidence of identity, (c) sign the document in the presence of the Notary, and (d) take an oath or affirmation before the Notary vouching for the truthfulness or accuracy of the signed document (EO Sec. 2). "(E)ven though it may not be a statutory requirement that the notary positively identify a signer for a jurat, it is always a good idea to do so" (Governor's Legal Counsel website, "Frequently Asked Questions").

***** <u>Signature Witnessing</u>: In a signature witnessing, an individual must, at a single time and place, (a) appear in person before a Notary and present a document, (b) be identified by the Notary through satisfactory evidence of identity, and (c) sign the document in the presence of the Notary (EO Sec. 2).

****** <u>Copy Certification</u>: In a copy certification, a Notary (a) is presented with a document, (b) copies or supervises the copying of the document using a photographic or electronic copying process, (c) compares the document to the copy, and (d) determines that the copy is accurate and complete (EO Sec. 2).

A Notary may certify a copy of a passport or driver's license (Governor's Legal Counsel website, "Frequently Asked Questions").

"A notary should not certify a copy of a birth or death certificate since cities and towns have their own procedures for certifying birth and death certificates. Refer the person instead to the state Bureau of Vital Statistics or county clerk's office in the county where the birth occurred. For foreign birth certificates, refer the person to the consulate of the country of origin" (Governor's Legal Counsel website, "Frequently Asked Questions").

Depositions

"Yes, notaries public are authorized to take a deposition. When a notary is called upon to do this, the proper procedure can be found in Rules 27 through 33 of the Massachusetts Rules of Civil Procedure" (GNP).

Protests

"A protest is a certificate of dishonor made under the hand and seal of certain individuals, including notaries, who are authorized to certify dishonor. The need to protest commercial paper was greatly diminished by the Uniform Commercial Code (UCC) which became effective in Massachusetts on October 1, 1958. Occasionally, however, it is still necessary for a notary to perform this highly technical service" (GNP). For specifics on executing protests, see GL 106, Secs. 3-501 through 3-505.

Proofs Not Taken by Notaries

In Massachusetts, proofs by at least one subscribing witness may only be taken by a judge, clerk or register of any court of record (GL 183, Secs. 34 and 40), in cases where the grantor has died or moved from the state — but not by Notaries. There are also proof procedures for when the subscribing witness(es) are dead or out of the state (Sec. 35) or when the grantor refuses to acknowledge (Sec. 36).

Satisfactory Evidence of Identity

In executing an acknowledgment, a jurat or a signature witnessing, or in administering an oath or affirmation, the Notary must identify the principal through "satisfactory evidence of identity" (EO Sec. 2).

"'Satisfactory evidence of identity' shall mean identification of an individual based on at least one current document issued by a Federal or State government agency bearing the photographic image of the individual's face and signature; or on the oath or affirmation of a credible witness unaffected by the document or transaction who is personally known to the notary and who personally knows the individual; or identification of an individual based on the notary public's personal knowledge of the identity of the principal" (EO Sec. 2).

"For a person who is not a United States citizen, 'satisfactory evidence of identity' shall mean identification of an individual based on a valid passport, or another government-issued document evidencing the individual's nationality or residence, that bears a photographic image of the individual's face and signature" (EO Sec. 2).

'Personal Knowledge' Defined: "'Personal knowledge of identity' shall mean familiarity with an individual resulting from interactions with that individual over a period of time sufficient to ensure beyond doubt that the individual has the identity claimed" (EO Sec. 2).

'Credible Witness' Defined: "'Credible witness' means an honest, reliable, and impartial person who personally knows an individual appearing before a notary and takes an oath or affirmation from the notary to vouch for that individual's identity" (EO Sec. 2).

"The word of a credible identifying witness is satisfactory evidence of identity and equivalent to personal knowledge. A credible identifying witness, often called simply 'a credible witness,' is like a human ID card that identifies the document signer .... By definition, a credible identifying witness is a believable person. Credible identifying witnesses should be honest, competent and impartial to the matter at hand. This means that the credible identifying witness should neither have a financial interest in a notarized document nor be named in it" (Governor's Legal Counsel website, "Frequently Asked Questions").

Due Cause for Refusal to Notarize

A Notary must perform any notarial act described in Section 5(a) of the Governor's Executive Order for any person requesting such an act who tenders the appropriate fee set forth in GL Chapter 262, Section 41, unless (EO Sec. 7):

1. The notary knows or has good reason to believe that the notarial act or associated transaction is unlawful;

2. The principal has a demeanor causing the Notary to have a "compelling doubt" about whether the principal knows the consequences of the transaction or document requiring the notarial act;

3. The act is prohibited by the Governor's Executive Order or other applicable law;

4. The number of notarial acts requested "practically precludes completion of all acts at once, in which case the notary public shall arrange for later completion of the remaining acts."

Customer-Only Policy Prohibited: "Can I limit my notarial services to customers? To people I know personally? To business associates?

"No. As public officials, notaries must serve anyone who makes a lawful (and) reasonable request for notarization. Notarial services may be limited to transactions related to the place of employment; however, these provisions do not allow the notary to refuse services based on the status of a signer" (Governor's Legal Counsel website, "Frequently Asked Questions and Answers").

"Notaries public cannot decline to notarize a document solely because a person is not conducting business at the notary public's employer. For example, if the notary public works in a bank, the notary public cannot decline to notarize a document because a person is not a client of that bank" (Governor's Legal Counsel website, "Find a Notary Public").

Foreign-Language Documents

"There is no law which says you cannot notarize a document written in a foreign language. However, there are numerous potential problems including the fact that the term 'notary public,' when translated into other languages, can refer to a markedly different office, imbued with far greater authority than in the United States .... A notary who has questions about a document written in another language is encouraged to find another notary who understands the document (perhaps at a Consulate)" (Governor's Legal Counsel website, "Frequently Asked Questions").

Signature by Mark

A Notary may certify the affixation of a signature by mark on a document presented for notarization if (EO Sec. 5[h]):

1. The principal affixes the mark in the presence of the Notary and two witnesses unaffected by the document;
2. Both witnesses sign their own names beside the mark;
3. The Notary writes below the mark: "Mark affixed by (name of signer by mark) in the presence of (names and addresses of two witnesses) and undersigned Notary pursuant to Executive Order No. 455"; and
4. The Notary notarizes the signature by mark through an acknowledgment, jurat, or signature witnessing.

Signing for Principal Unable to Sign

A Notary may sign the name of a principal who is physically unable to sign or make a mark on a document presented for notarization if (EO Sec. 5[i]):

1. The principal directs the Notary to do so in the presence of two witnesses unaffected by the document;
2. The principal does not have a demeanor that causes the Notary to have a "compelling doubt" about whether the principal knows the consequences of the transaction requiring the notarial act;
3. In the Notary's judgment, the principal is acting of his or her own free will;
4. The Notary signs the principal's name in the presence of the principal and two witnesses;
5. Both witnesses sign their own names beside the signature;
6. The Notary writes below the signature: "Signature affixed by Notary Public in the presence of (names and addresses of principal and two witnesses)";
7. The Notary notarizes the signature through an acknowledgment, jurat or signature witnessing.

NOTARY DON'TS

According to the Governor's Executive Order, a Massachusetts Notary may:

1. NOT act unless the principal is in the Notary's presence at the time of the notarization (Sec. 6[a][1]);
2. NOT act unless the principal is identified by the Notary through satisfactory evidence of identity (Sec. 6[a][2]);
3. NOT act if the principal "has a demeanor that causes the notary public to have a compelling doubt about whether the principal knows the consequences of the transaction or document requiring the notarial act" (Sec. 6[a][3]);
4. NOT proceed if, in the Notary's judgment, the principal is not acting of his or her own free will (Sec. 6[a][4]).

False Certificates

"A notary public shall not execute a certificate containing information known or believed by the notary public to be false" (EO Sec. 6[d]).

"A notary public shall not perform any official act with the intent to deceive or defraud" (EO Sec. 6[h]).

Incomplete Documents and Certificates

"A notary public shall not affix an official signature or seal on a notarial certificate that is incomplete" (EO Sec. 6[e]).

"A notary public shall not notarize a signature on a blank or incomplete document" (EO Sec. 6[g]).

"A prudent notary should skim the document for blanks and ask the document signer to fill them in: If they are intended to be left blank, then the signer can line through them or write 'N/A'" (Governor's Legal Counsel website, "Frequently Asked Questions").

Fax Signature May Not Be Notarized

"A photocopy or fax may be notarized, but only if it bears an original signature. That is, the copy must have been signed with an ink pen. A photocopied or faxed signature may never be notarized" (Governor's Legal Counsel website, "Frequently Asked Questions").

Issuing Unattached Notarial Certificates

"A notary public shall not provide or send a signed or sealed notarial certificate to another person with the understanding that it will be completed or attached to a document outside of the notary public's presence" (EO Sec. 6[f]). "If it were fraudulently or mistakenly attached to another document, the notary would be in an indefensible position" (Governor's Legal Counsel website, "Frequently Asked Questions"). Exception: "In connection with a commercial non-consumer transaction, a notary public may deliver a signed, sealed, or signed and sealed, notarial certificate to an attorney with the understanding that: (i) the attorney will attach the certificate to a document outside of the notary's presence; (ii) the attorney will hold such notarial certificate in escrow; and (iii) the attorney informs the notary public that the attorney will obtain the approval of the principal, or principals, involved before attaching the certificate to the document" (EO Sec. 6 [f][1]).

Improper Advertising by Notary

"A notary public shall not claim to have powers, qualifications, rights, or privileges that the office of notary public does not provide, including the power to counsel on immigration matters" (EO Sec. 6[i]).

Non-English Language Ads: "A non-attorney notary public who advertises notarial services in a language other than English shall include in the advertisement, notice, letterhead, or sign the following, prominently displayed in the same language the statement: 'I am not an attorney and have no authority to give advice on immigration or other legal matters'" (EO Sec. 10).

"A notary public shall not use the term 'notario' or 'notario publico' or any equivalent non-English term in any business card, advertisement, notice, or sign" (EO Sec. 6[j]).

Unauthorized Practice of Law

A non-attorney Notary must not assist another person in "drafting, completing, selecting, or understanding a document or transaction requiring a notarial act, rendering legal advice, or otherwise engage in the practice of law" (EO Sec. 9[a]).

However, the above subsection does not prevent a Notary who is duly qualified, trained or experienced in a particular industry or professional field from selecting, drafting, completing or advising on a document or certificate related to a matter within that industry or field (EO Sec. 9[b]).

Unsupervised Notary Can't Do Closing: "A notary public who is not an attorney licensed to practice law in Massachusetts, or who is not directly supervised by an attorney, shall not conduct a real estate closing and shall not act as a real estate closing agent. A notary public who is employed by a lender may notarize a document in conjunction with the closing of his or her employer's real estate loans" (EO Sec. 9[c]).

Notary Not Concerned with Text: "A notary public has neither the duty nor the authority to investigate, ascertain, or attest to the lawfulness, propriety, accuracy, or truthfulness of a document or transaction involving a notarial act" (EO Sec. 8[a]).

Breach of Impartiality

Refusal to Notarize: "A notary public shall not refuse to perform a notarial act solely based on the principal's race, advanced age, gender, sexual orientation, religion, national origin, health, disability, or status as a non-client or non-customer of the notary public or the notary public's employer" (EO Sec. 6[b]).

"A notary public is a public servant performing a public duty. If a notary public is performing notarizations at a place of business, the notary public may not decline to notarize a document for a person who is not conducting business with the notary public's employer. For example, if the notary public works at a bank, the notary public may not decline to notarize a document solely because a person is not a client of that bank" (Massachusetts Notary application form).

"As public officials, notaries must serve anyone who makes a lawful or reasonable request for notarization. Notarial services may be limited to transactions related to the peace of employment; however these provisions do not allow the notary to refuse services based on the status of a signer" (Governor's Legal Counsel website, "Frequently Asked Questions").

Influencing Signer: "A notary public shall not influence a person either to enter into or avoid a transaction involving a notarial act by the notary public, except that the notary public may provide advice relating to a transaction if section 9(b) applies" (EO Sec. 6[c]). Section 9(b) refers to a "duly qualified, trained, or experienced" Notary being authorized to select, draft, complete or advise on a document or certificate within the industry or field of expertise.

Disqualifying Interests

A Notary must not perform a notarial act if:

1. The Notary is a party to or is named in the document that is to be notarized, "except that a notary public may notarize a document if the notary public is named in the document for the sole purpose of receiving notices relating to the document and except that a notary public who is licensed as an attorney in the Commonwealth of Massachusetts and is named as an executor, trustee or in any fiduciary capacity in a document or employees of such attorney may perform notarial acts concerning such document" (EO Sec. 6[a][5]);

2. The Notary "will receive as a direct result of the notarial act any commission, fee, advantage, right, title, interest, cash, property, or other consideration exceeding in value the fees set forth in section 41 of chapter 262 of the General Laws or has any financial interest in the subject matter of the document. For example, this section shall not preclude a notary public who is licensed as an attorney in the Commonwealth of Massachusetts or any employee of such attorney from notarial acts concerning any document where the attorney receives a legal fee for professional legal services rendered in connection with such document" (EO Sec. 6[a][6]).

May Not Notarize for Relatives: A Notary may not notarize if the Notary "is a spouse, domestic partner, parent, guardian, child, or sibling of the principal, including in-law, step, or half relatives, except where such persons witness a will or other legal document prepared by the notary public who is an attorney licensed in the Commonwealth of Massachusetts" (EO Sec. 6[a][7]).

Notarization of Photos Unauthorized

"For individuals needing a photograph notarized, a Notary Public may not certify nor authenticate a photograph. However, a Notary Public may notarize a statement by the principal regarding the photograph. That notarization does not authenticate or certify the photograph, it only verifies that the individual making the statement signed the statement" (Secretary of Commonwealth's pamphlet, "Apostilles and Certificates of Appointment").

NOTARY SIGNING AGENTS

"A notary public who is not an attorney licensed to practice law in Massachusetts, or who is not directly supervised by an attorney, shall not conduct a real estate closing and shall not act as a real estate closing agent. A notary public who is employed by a lender may notarize a document in conjunction with the closing of his or her employer's real estate loans" (EO Sec. 9[c]).

"Conducting a real estate closing involves the practice of law in Massachusetts. Thus, non-attorney notaries public may not conduct real estate closings. A notary public who is employed by a bank may notarize a document in conjunction with the closing of his or her employer's real estate loans. Also, a non-attorney notary public who works for a bank may notarize bank documents relating to an equity line of credit or a refinance mortgage, absent other violation of the Executive Order" (Governor's Legal Counsel website, "Frequently Asked Questions").

REBA Opposes Signing Agents

In recent years, the Real Estate Bar Association (REBA) for Massachusetts, Inc. has been active in filing suit not only to prevent Notary Signing Agents from notarizing at closings without an attorney present, but also to prevent Massachusetts attorneys from being present at closings only in the role of a Notary without "control or supervision over the other activities that might be undertaken to ensure that the real estate interest is properly conveyed" (REBA Ethics Committee Opinion of October 11, 2006).

REBA contends that closings by non-attorneys have been designated as the unauthorized practice of law by Massachusetts Supreme Court decisions since 1935. "Out-of-state closing companies are getting around the requirements of these decisions. In order to appear to comply with Massachusetts law, many engage attorneys to participate in the settlement of a residential real estate transaction while divesting them of virtually all responsibility for the conveyance. In these 'witness only' closings, the attorneys do nothing more than witness the execution of the closing documents, acting not as attorneys but as notaries" (REBA Press Release of November 8, 2006).

"(A) 'notary only' closing, in which the conveyance of real property is controlled and supervised by a non-lawyer and the attorney's participation is restricted to notarizing documents, is not permitted under Massachusetts law" (REBA pleading in The Real Estate Bar Association for *Massachusetts, Inc. v. National Real Estate Information Services, Inc.* of 2006).

NOTARY FEES

In Massachusetts, there is no statutory fee schedule for acknowledgments, oaths, and affirmations. However, the Secretary of the Commonwealth cautions Notaries (GNP): "As a notary, you are a public servant and should be available to perform a public service at a reasonable cost. Excessive charges could result in complaints to the Governor's Council."

Attorney-Notary May Charge More

"Can attorneys charge for their legal work drafting a document that they also notarize?

"Yes. Notaries can charge no more than the statutory amount set forth in General Laws chapter 262, section 41. (For example, the cost of noting, including recording and notices, shall not exceed $1.25.) However, an attorney or other professional may still charge a separate fee for document preparation or other professional services that are provided in conjunction with a document that is being notarized" (Governor's Legal Counsel website, "Frequently Asked Questions").

Protests

The law does prescribe the following fees for protests (GL 262, Sec. 41):

1. Protesting for non-acceptance or non-payment:
   a. If amount $500 or more: $1;
   b. If amount less than $500: 50 cents;
2. Recording protest: 50 cents;
3. Noting non-acceptance or non-payment: 75 cents;
4. For each notice of non-acceptance or non-payment given to person liable for payment thereof: 25 cents.

However, the whole cost of protest, including necessary notices and the record, must not exceed $2 if the contested amount is $500 or more; nor exceed $1.50 if the amount is less than $500; and the whole cost of noting, including recording and notices, must not exceed $1.25 in any case.

NOTARY CERTIFICATES

Massachusetts has adopted acknowledgment certificates from the *Uniform Acknowledgments Act* of 1892 (GL 183, Sec. 42):

1. Acknowledgment by individual;
2. Acknowledgment by attorney in fact;
3. Acknowledgment by corporation or joint-stock association.

For the text of these three certificates, see "Uniform Acknowledgments Act (1892)," Section 1, in Appendix 6.

The Notary's commission expiration date and printed or typed name should be added to each of these certificates (GL 222, Sec. 8 and 8[A]).

If other forms are not prescribed — see "When Other Forms May Be Used," below — certificates in "substantially the following form" (EO Sec. 5) must be used by the Notary to complete the following four respective notarial acts:

All-Purpose Acknowledgment (EO Sec. 5[d]):

Commonwealth of Massachusetts
County of _____

On this ____ day of _____, 20___, before me, the undersigned Notary Public, personally appeared _____ (name of document signer), proved to me through satisfactory evidence of identification, which were _____ (description of satisfactory evidence relied on), to be the person whose name is signed on the preceding or attached document and acknowledged to me that he/she signed it voluntarily for its stated purpose(.)

(as partner for _____, a partnership.)

(as _____ for _____, a corporation.)

(as attorney in fact for _____, the principal.)

(as _____ for _____, (a) (the) _____.)

_____
(Official Signature and Seal of Notary)
My commission expires_____

Jurat (EO Sec. 5[e]):

Commonwealth of Massachusetts

County of _____

On this _____ day of _____, 20____, before me, the undersigned Notary Public, personally appeared _____ (name of document signer), proved to me through satisfactory evidence of identification, which were _____ (description of satisfactory evidence relied on), to be the person who signed the preceding or attached document in my presence, and who swore or affirmed to me that the contents of the document are truthful and accurate to the best of his/her knowledge and belief.

_____
(Official Signature and Seal of Notary)
My commission expires_____

Signature Witnessing (EO Sec 5[f]):

Commonwealth of Massachusetts
County of _____

On this _____ day of _____, 20____, before me, the undersigned Notary Public, personally appeared _____ (name of document signer), proved to me through satisfactory evidence of identification, which were _____ (description of satisfactory evidence relied on), to be the person whose name was signed on the preceding or attached document in my presence.

_____
(Official Signature and Seal of Notary)
My commission expires_____

Certified Copy Certificate (EO Sec. 5[g]):

Commonwealth of Massachusetts
County of _____

On this _____ day of _____, 20____, I certify that the preceding/following/attached document is a true, exact, complete, and unaltered copy made by me of _____ (description of original document), presented to me by _____.

_____
(Official Signature and Seal of Notary)
My commission expires_____

When Other Forms May Be Used

"This section does not require a notary public to use the forms set forth above if the form of an acknowledgment, jurat, signature witnessing, or copy certification is required or allowed by the provisions of any court rule or court forms; a Massachusetts General Law, including but not limited to, chapter 183, section 42 or the forms set forth in the appendix thereto, or chapter 192, section 2; any Federal statute; or any regulation adopted pursuant to any such Massachusetts or Federal statute" (EO Sec. 5[j]).

Form from Another State: "This section does not require a notary public to use the forms set forth above if the form of acknowledgment, jurat, signature witnessing, or copy certification (in) a document contains an alternative form from another State if the document is to be filed or recorded in, or governed by the laws of, that other State" (EO Sec. 5[k]).

Alteration Prohibited: "This section does not require a notary public to use the forms set forth above if the form of acknowledgment, jurat, signature witnessing, or copy certification appears on a printed form that contains an express prohibition against altering that form" (EO Sec. 5[l]).

If Certificate Is Deficient

"Failure of a document to contain the forms of acknowledgment, jurat, signature witnessing, or copy certification, or otherwise comply with the requirements set forth in this Executive Order shall not have any effect on the validity of the underlying document" (EO Sec. 8[b]).

"Failure of a document to contain the forms of acknowledgment, jurat, signature witnessing, or copy certification set forth in this Executive Order should not be the basis of refusal to accept the document for filing, recordation, registration, or acceptance by a third party" (EO Sec. 8[c]).

ELECTRONIC NOTARIZATIONS

The Commonwealth of Massachusetts has not yet adopted statutes or regulations expressly establishing rules, definitions and procedures for electronic notarization.

UETA Recognizes Notary's eSignature

Massachusetts has enacted the Uniform Electronic Transactions Act (GL, Chapter 110G), including the provision on notarization, thereby recognizing the legal validity of electronic signatures used by Notaries:

"If a law requires a signature or record to be notarized, acknowledged, verified, or made under oath, the requirement is satisfied if the electronic signature of the person authorized to perform those acts, together with all other information required to be included by other applicable law, is attached to or logically associated with the signature or record" (Sec. 11).

NOTARY RECORDS

"A notary shall keep, maintain, protect, and provide for lawful inspection a chronological official journal of notarial acts that is a permanently bound book with numbered pages, except as otherwise provided in this section" (EO Sec. 11[a]). "A journal that has entries that are sequentially numbered will satisfy this requirement as well" (Governor's Legal Counsel website, "Frequently Asked Questions").

Only One Active Journal

"A notary public shall keep no more than one active journal at the same time" (EO Sec. 11[b]).

Attorneys and Their Employees Exempted

"A journal shall be recommended as the best practice, but not required, for a notary public who is an attorney licensed to practice law in the Commonwealth of Massachusetts or employed by such attorney. This Executive Order shall not be construed in any way to impair or infringe in any way on the attorney-client privilege or the attorney work product doctrine" (EO Sec. 11[f]).

"Notwithstanding any general law, rule, regulation or order to the contrary, attorneys-at-law and counselors-at-law as well as paralegals, legal secretaries and other legal staff, who by virtue of their employment perform notarial duties shall be exempt from maintaining a journal of their notary transactions" (GL 222, Sec. 12).

Journal Entries

For every notarial act, except for the issuance of summons or subpoenas, or the administration of an oral oath, the notary must record in the journal at the time of notarization the following (EO Sec. 11[c]):

1. Date and time of the notarial act, proceeding, or transaction;
2. Type of notarial act;
3. Type, title, or a description of the document or proceeding, but "(i)f multiple documents are signed by the same principal in the course of a transaction during a single date (i.e. real estate closings, mortgage, discharges, state laboratory drug analysis certificates, etc.), a single journal entry shall be sufficient";
4. Signature, printed name, and address of each principal and witness, but "(i)f a principal or witness tells the notary that he or she is a battered person, the notary shall make a note in the journal that the person's address shall not be subject to public inspection";
5. Description of the type of satisfactory evidence of identity presented by each principal whose signature is notarized, including: a notation of the type of identification document, its issuing agency, its serial or ID number, and its date of issuance or expiration, but "(i)f the identification number on the document is the person's Social Security number, instead of including the number, write in the words "Social Security number' or the acronym 'SSN'"; or a notation either that the Notary identified the individual based on the oath or affirmation of a credible witness, or based on the Notary's personal knowledge of the individual's identity;
6. The fee, if any, charged for the notarial act;
7. The address where the notarization was performed.

"A notary public shall record in the journal the circumstances for not completing a notarial act" (EO Sec. 11[e]).

No SSN or Credit Card Number: "A notary public shall not record a Social Security or credit card number in the journal" (EO Sec. 11[d]).

Multiple Documents: "Section 11(c)(3) of the Executive Order specifically states that you may record as a single journal entry a transaction or proceeding that involves multiple documents signed by the same principal in the course of that transaction occurring on the same day. For example, if you notarize multiple documents at a corporate closing, you may include a single entry that describes the proceeding — 'ABC and

XYZ merger' — followed by the other information that is required by the Executive Order" (Governor's Legal Counsel website, "Frequently Asked Questions").

Law Enforcement Inspection

"The journal may be examined without restriction by a law enforcement officer in the course of an official investigation, subpoenaed by court order, or surrendered at the direction of the Governor's Office. Nothing in this section shall prevent a notary public from seeking appropriate judicial protective orders" (EO Sec. 12[a]).

Copy of Journal Entry

"I had a call requesting a photocopy of my journal entry. Do I have to comply?

"Yes, you should comply if the following procedure is met. A person who wants to inspect or copy an entry in your journal must (1) demonstrate his or her identity through satisfactory evidence, (2) affix a signature in the journal in a separate, dated entry, and (3) specify the month, year, type of document, and name of the person for the notarial act or acts sought. The person may be shown only the entry or entries specified. However, if you have a reasonable belief that a person bears a criminal or harmful intent in requesting the information, you may refuse to provide access to any entry and be able to substantiate your belief" (Governor's Legal Counsel website, "Frequently Asked Questions").

Safeguarding Journal

"A notary public shall safeguard the journal and all other notarial records and surrender or destroy them only by rule of law, by court order, or at the direction of the Governor's Office" (EO Sec. 12[b]).

"When not in use, the journal shall be kept in a secure area under the exclusive control of the notary public, and shall not be used by any other notary nor surrendered to an employer upon termination of employment" (EO Sec. 12[c]).

Disposition of Journal

"When a notary commission expires, is resigned, or is revoked, the notary shall ... retain the notarial journal and records for seven years after the date of expiration, resignation, or revocation" (EO Sec. 13[b]).

Law Protects Notarial Records

The law states (GL 222, Sec. 10): "Whoever knowingly destroys, defaces or conceals the records or official papers of a notary public shall forfeit not more than one thousand dollars and be liable for damages to any person injured thereby."

AUTHENTICATION OF NOTARIAL ACTS

Secretary of Commonwealth

Authenticating certificates for Notaries, including apostilles, are issued by the office of Massachusetts' Secretary of Commonwealth.

Fees: $6 per document for any authenticating certificate, including an apostille, payable to "Commonwealth of Massachusetts." Credit cards are not accepted as pre-payment for express mail service.

Address:
Secretary of Commonwealth
Public Records Division
Commissions Section
One Ashburton Place, Room 1719
Boston, MA 02108

Telephone: 1-617-727-2836

Procedure: Mail or present in person the original notarized document, along with the appropriate fee. Photocopied signatures cannot be certified. Indicate the country of destination and include a prepaid return envelope (with a billing account number if an express delivery firm is used). For more information, see the pamphlet "Apostilles and Certificates of Appointment," available on the Secretary's website.

Authenticating School Transcript or Diploma: Before a transcript or diploma from an in-state school may be authenticated by the Secretary of the Commonwealth, the school registrar must first certify the record in the presence of a Notary, who will notarize the signature of the registrar (Secretary's pamphlet, "Apostilles and Certificates of Appointment").

Regional Offices: Authenticating certificates, including apostilles, may also be issued at the following regional offices of the Secretary. The turnaround times and number of documents accepted will vary — contact the office for details.

SOUTHEASTERN DISTRICT OFFICE:
Secretary of the Commonwealth
218 South Main St., Suite 206
Fall River, MA 02721

Telephone: 1-508-646-1374

WESTERN DISTRICT OFFICE:
Secretary of the Commonwealth
436 Dwight St., Room 102
Springfield, MA 01103

Telephone: 1-413-784-1376

Superior Court Clerks

An authenticating certificate for a Notary may also be issued by a clerk of the superior court if the Notary has filed with that official — but such filing is not mandatory.

COMMISSIONING AND ADMINISTRATION

Though Massachusetts' Notaries are appointed by the Governor, with the advice and consent of the Executive Council, it is the Public Records Division in the office of the Secretary of the Commonwealth that maintains records on them.

Applying for Commission

Qualifications: An applicant for a commission as a Massachusetts Notary Public must (EO Sec. 3[a]): (a) be at least 18 years old and (b) reside legally or conduct business on a regular basis within Massachusetts.

Application: An "up-to-date resume" and, if available, a business card must be stapled to the four-page application form, which must be notarized by another Notary. The application must also be endorsed by four persons residing in the state, one of whom must be a Massachusetts attorney in good standing. The $60 commissioning fee is not included with the application, but is paid after the applicant has been commissioned.

Renewal applications are automatically sent out to every Notary five weeks before commission expiration.

Taking Oath of Office: After appointment, the applicant has three months to take an oath of office before two "Commissioners to Qualify Public Officers" (GL 30, Sec. 12); they will inform the Public Records Division in writing that the appointee took the oath of office. The oath may also be taken in the Secretary of the Commonwealth's office. A wallet ID card showing the commission expiration date is issued to each appointee.

Non-Residents: "A person residing outside of the Commonwealth of Massachusetts may apply for a notary commission if they work or do business in Massachusetts. However, notarial services must be conducted only within the borders of Massachusetts" (Governor's Legal Counsel website, "Frequently Asked Questions and Answers ...").

Changes of Status

If Notary Moves or Changes Name: "Within 10 days after the change of a notary public's residence, business, mailing address, or name, the notary shall send to the Office of the Secretary of State (Division of Public Records) a signed notice of the change, giving both the old and new information" (Gov. Exec. Order, Sec. 14).

"While moving out of Massachusetts does not automatically void a notary public commission, notaries should be aware that they may notarize documents only within the boundaries of the Commonwealth. A notary commission is renewable for a person who has moved outside the state if he continues to work or conduct business (and notarizes only) in the Commonwealth" (Governor's Legal Counsel website, "Frequently Asked Questions").

A Notary with a name change may continue to notarize with the former name until commission expiration. "However, if you intend to notarize using your new name, while in the term of your maiden name, you must register it with the Secretary of State, using a re-registration form which can be obtained from the Division of Public Records (617-727-2836). Do not notarize any document in your new name until the re-registration certificate is issued to you. If you have notarized documents under your new name prior to receiving this certificate, these notarial acts must be validated by the Secretary of State..." (Governor's Legal Counsel website, "Frequently Asked Questions").

A form to register a change of address or name may be obtained online at www.sec.state.ma.us.

If Notary Resigns: "When a notary resigns or his or her commission expires or is revoked, the notary shall: (a) as soon as reasonably practicable, destroy or deface all notary seals and stamps so that they may not be used; and (b) retain the notarial journal and records for seven years after the date of expiration, resignation, or revocation" (Governor's Legal Counsel website, "Frequently Asked Questions").

SUPERIOR COURT CLERKS

Massachusetts superior court clerks are not administratively involved in the Commonwealth's Notary program, either in the issuance of certificates of authority for notarial acts, a duty performed by the office of the Secretary of the Commonwealth, or in administering oaths of office to newly commissioned Notaries. Massachusetts Notaries do not take their oaths of office before a superior court clerk but before two "Commissioners to Qualify Public Officers," who are appointed by the Governor (GL 222 Sec. 3). One commissioner must administer the oaths and the other must witness the oath-taking. Both commissioners will sign the commission certificate and inform the Public Records Division in writing that the appointee appeared before them and took the oaths of office.

OTHER NOTARIAL OFFICERS

Justices of the Peace

Under Chapter 222 of the Massachusetts General Laws ("Justices of the Peace, Notaries Public and Commissioners"), justices of the peace generally have the same notarial powers as Notaries Public and may act throughout the state.

Commissioners Rarely Appointed

"The governor, with the advice and consent of the council, may appoint commissioners in the states, territories, districts and dependencies of the United States, and one or more commissioners in every foreign country, to hold office for three years from the date of their respective appointments" (GL 222, Sec. 4). Such officers are rarely appointed.

Such commissioners may "in (their) state, territory, district, dependency or country, administer oaths and take depositions, affidavits and acknowledgments of deeds and other instruments, to be used or recorded in this commonwealth, and the proof of such deeds, if the grantor refuses to acknowledge the same, all of which shall be certified by him under his official seal" (GL 222, Sec. 6).

QUICK FACTS

Notary Jurisdiction
Statewide (GL 222, Sec. 1).

Notary Term Length
Seven years (EO Sec. 4). "Whoever presumes to act as a justice of the peace or notary public after the expiration of his commission, and after receiving notice of such expiration, shall be punished by a fine of not less than one hundred nor more than five hundred dollars" (GL 222, Sec. 9).

Notarizing after Expiration: "Should you inadvertently notarize a document (after your commission has expired), the Secretary of the Commonwealth can validate such an act to protect the integrity of your client's document by issuing a validation certificate from the Public Records Division" (Governor's Legal Counsel website, "Frequently Asked Questions").

Notary Bond
Not required by law.

M

Michigan

NOTARY SEAL

While Michigan Notaries are not required by law to use a seal of office, they may affix a seal to fulfill the requirement to "print, type, stamp, or otherwise imprint mechanically or electronically sufficiently clear and legible to be read by the secretary and in a manner capable of photographic reproduction" certain information. This information must be affixed "immediately near the notary public's signature, as is practical" (MCL 55.287[2]).

"Michigan law does not require notaries to use an embossed seal or rubber stamp on a document. However, documents sent out of state may require an embossed notary seal" (website, "Notarization of Document(s)").

Kind

Inked Stamp or Electronic Process: "A notary public may use a stamp, seal, or electronic process that contains all of the information required by MCL 55.287(2). However, the stamp, seal, or electronic process shall not be used in a manner that renders anything illegible on the record being notarized" (MCL 55.287[3]).

Embosser Not to Be Used Alone: "An embosser alone or any other method that cannot be reproduced shall not be used" (MCL 55.287[3]).

Size/Shape

Not specified.

```
JANE Q. DOE
Notary Public, State of Michigan
County of Ogemaw
My Commission expires Jan. 30, 2018
```

Examples

The above is a typical, actual-size example of a Notary seal used in Michigan. Formats other than this may also be seen.

NOTARY ADMINISTRATION

Michigan Department of State
Office of the Great Seal   1-888-767-6424
7064 Crowner Drive
Lansing, MI 48918

(Richard H. Austin Bldg., 1st Floor
430 W. Allegan St.)

Website: www.michigan.gov/sos/
(Click on "Notary & Document Certification")

NOTARY RULES

MCL — MICHIGAN COMPILED LAWS

Most Notary regulations are in the Michigan Compiled Laws:

a. "Michigan Notary Public Act," as amended (2003 PA 238) (MCL 55.261, et seq.).

b. "Uniform Recognition of Acknowledgments Act," as amended (1969 PA 57) (MCL 565.261, et seq.).

* This is the *Uniform Recognition of Acknowledgments Act* of 1968.

Components

The following information may be affixed by any Notary seal used, or this information must be printed, typed, stamped or otherwise mechanically or electronically imprinted in a photographically reproducible manner (MCL 55.287[2]):

1. Name of Notary exactly as on the application for commission;
2. "Notary Public, State of Michigan, County of _____ (name of county).";
3. "My commission expires _____ (date).";
4. If notarizing elsewhere in Michigan other than the county of commission, "Acting in the County of _____ (county where notarial act was performed).";
5. Date notarial act was performed.

Illegibility Does Not Invalidate: "The illegibility of the statements required in subsection (2) does not affect the validity of the transaction or record that was notarized" (MCL 55.287[4]).

Notary's Signature

"A notary public shall place his or her signature on every record upon which he or she performs a notarial act. The notary public shall sign his or her name exactly as his or her name appears on his or her application for commission as a notary public" (MCL 55.287[1]).

"'Signature' means a person's written or printed name or electronic signature as that term is defined in the uniform electronic transactions act, 2000 PA 305, MCL 450.831 to 450.849, or the person's mark attached to or logically associated with a record including, but not limited to, a contract and executed or adopted by the person with the intent to sign the record" (MCL 55.267[b]).

NOTARY POWERS

Michigan Notaries are authorized to perform the following notarial acts (MCL 55.285[1]):
1. Take acknowledgments* and proofs;
2. Administer oaths** and affirmations;
3. Take verifications upon oath or affirmation***;
4. Witness or attest signatures****.

* Acknowledgments: "An acknowledgment does not require that a record be signed in the notary's presence. An acknowledgment merely confirms the identity of the signer, who acknowledges that he or she signed the record. When taking an acknowledgment, a notary public must determine that the individual appearing before the notary and making the acknowledgment is the person whose signature is on the record. Again, a personal appearance before the notary is required" (website, "Notarization of Document(s)" and MCL 55.285[2]).

** Oath Ceremony and Wording: The following wording for an oath and for an affirmation was recommended in the "Notary Manual," a pamphlet formerly prepared by the State Bar of Michigan, Young Lawyers Section and distributed to Notaries around the state:

An example of oath wording: "Do you solemnly swear that what you are about to say is true, so help you God?" Answer: "I do."

An example of affirmation wording: "Do you solemnly affirm that what you have said or are about to say is true under the pains and penalty of perjury?" Answer: "I do."

*** Verification Upon Oath or Affirmation: "'Verification upon oath or affirmation' means the declaration by oath or affirmation that a statement is true" (MCL 55.267[d]).

"In taking a verification upon oath or affirmation, the notary public shall determine, either from personal knowledge or from satisfactory evidence, that the person in the presence of the notary public and making the verification is the person whose signature is on the record being verified" (MCL 55.285[3]).

"In all matters where the notary public takes a verification upon oath or affirmation ... the notary public shall require that the person sign the record being verified ... in the presence of the notary public" (MCL 55.285[5]).

A jurat is the type of certificate wording completed by a Notary in executing a verification upon oath or affirmation. "'Jurat' means a certification by a notary public that a signer, whose identity is personally known to the notary public or proven on the basis of satisfactory evidence, has made in the presence of the notary public a voluntary signature and taken an oath or affirmation vouching for the truthfulness of the signed record" (MCL 55.265[a]).

"If no other wording is prescribed in a given instance, a notary may use the following language for an affidavit or deposition: Do you solemnly swear that the contents of this affidavit (or deposition, document, etc.) subscribed (signed) by you are correct and true, so help you God? Or, do you solemnly, sincerely and truly declare and affirm that the statements made by you are true and correct? When administering oaths, parties should raise their right hands. The left hand may be used in cases of disability" (website, "Jurat vs. Acknowledgments...").

**** Witnessing or Attesting Signatures: "In witnessing or attesting to a signature, the notary public shall determine, either from personal knowledge or from satisfactory evidence, that the signature is that of the person in the presence of the notary public and is the person named in the record" (MCL 55.285[4]).

"In all matters where the notary public ... witnesses or attests to a signature, the notary public shall require that the person sign the record being verified, witnessed, or attested in the presence of the notary public" (MCL 55.285[5]).

Identifying Signers

In taking an acknowledgment or verification upon oath or affirmation, or in witnessing or attesting to a signature, the signer must be identified by the Notary through personal knowledge or satisfactory evidence of identity (MCL 55.285).

"A notary public has satisfactory evidence that a person is the person whose signature is on a record if that person is any of the following:

"(a) Personally known to the notary public.

"(b) Identified upon the oath or affirmation of a credible witness personally known by the notary public and who personally knows the person.

"(c) Identified on the basis of a current license, identification card, or record issued by a federal or state government that contains the person's photograph and signature" (MCL 55.285[6])."

Notary May Refuse to Act

"A notary public may refuse to perform a notarial act" (MCL 55.285[8]).

May Both Notarize and Act as Witness

"A notary public may act as a witness to and notarize the same instrument" (website, "Notarization of Document(s)").

Signature by Mark

"A notary public may take the acknowledgment of a person who cannot sign his or her own name. Such a person should sign the instrument by marking an 'X' in the presence of two witnesses, one of whom may be a notary public" (website, "Jurat vs. Acknowledgments..."). An example of the signing format would be as follows:

In the presence of:

_____
Jane Doe   his
               JOHN   X   JONES
                         mark

Notary May Sign for Disabled

"A notary public may sign the name of a person whose physical characteristics limit his or her capacity to sign or make a mark on a record presented for notarization under all of the following conditions:

"(a) The notary public is orally, verbally, physically, or through electronic or mechanical means provided by the person and directed by that person to sign that person's name.

"(b) The person is in the physical presence of the notary public.

"(c) The notary public inscribes beneath the signature: 'Signature affixed pursuant to section 33 of the Michigan notary public act'" (MCL 55.293).

Notarizing Foreign-Language Documents

"Notaries are not prohibited legally from notarizing a document written in a foreign language. However, there are numerous potential problems, including the fact that the term notary public, when translated into other languages, can refer to a markedly different office, with far greater authority than in the United States. A notary public should not proceed to notarize any document with which they are not comfortable doing so. The notary may recommend using a notary public familiar with the language in which the document is written" (website, "Foreign Language Documents").

NOTARY DON'TS

Notary May Not Certify True Copy

A Michigan Notary may not certify or notarize that a document is either an original or a true copy of another document (MCL 55.291[1]).

"Michigan notaries public lack the authority to certify on a copy of a document that it is a true copy of an original document. In Michigan, only the person or agency that issued the document, or the person or agency to whom the document was issued, can certify that a copy of the original document is true and accurate.

"For example, an official from the school that issued a diploma can certify that a duplicate is a true copy of the original diploma. Or the person named on the diploma can make a true copy of the original diploma" (From the official pamphlet "Notaries Public Guide," formerly issued by the Michigan Department of State).

Notary Does Not Decide Type of Act

"A notary should not decide which type of notarial act a document requires. The customer must know and tell the notary. However, if the jurat indicates that the document was 'sworn to before me,' then an oath must be administered" (website, "Jurat vs. Acknowledgments...").

Advertising by Notary

False Claims: "A notary public shall not claim to have powers, qualifications, rights, or privileges that the office of notary does not provide, including the power to counsel on immigration matters" (MCL 55.291[3]).

Implying Notary Is Attorney: "A notary public shall not, in any document, advertisement, stationery, letterhead, business card, or other comparable written material describing the role of the notary public, literally translate from English into another language terms or titles including, but not limited to, notary public, notary, licensed, attorney, lawyer, or any other term that implies the person is an attorney" (MCL 55.291[4]).

Non-English Ads: "A notary public may not use the term 'notario publico' or any equivalent non-English term in any business card, advertisement, notice, or sign" (MCL 55.291[6]).

"A notary public who is not a licensed attorney and who advertises notarial services in a language other than English shall include in the document, advertisement, stationery, letterhead, business card, or other comparable written material the following, prominently displayed in the same language:

"(a) The statement: 'I am not an attorney and have no authority to give advice on immigration or other legal matters'.

"(b) The fees for notarial acts as specified by statute" (MCL 55.291[5]).

Disqualifying Interests

May Not Notarize Own Signature: "A notary public shall not do any of the following:

"(a) Perform a notarial act upon any record executed by himself or herself.

"(b) Notarize his or her own signature.

"(c) Take his or her own deposition or affidavit" (MCL 55.291[2]).

Conflict of Interest: "A notary public shall not perform any notarial act in connection with a transaction if the notary public has a conflict of interest. As used in this subsection, 'conflict of interest' means either or both of the following:

"(a) The notary public has a direct financial or beneficial interest, other than the notary public fee, in the transaction.

"(b) The notary public is named, individually, as a grantor, grantee, mortgagor, mortgagee, trustor, trustee, beneficiary, vendor, vendee, lessor, or lessee or as a party in some other capacity to the transaction" (MCL 55.291[7]).

"For purposes of subsection (7), a notary public has no direct financial or beneficial interest in a transaction where the notary public acts in the capacity of an agent, employee, insurer, attorney, escrow, or lender for a person having a direct financial or beneficial interest in the transaction" (MCL 55.291[10]).

Relatives: "A notary public shall not perform a notarial act for a spouse, lineal ancestor, lineal descendent, or sibling including in-laws, steps, or half-relatives" (MCL 55.291[8]). A "lineal ancestor" is an individual in the direct line of ascent, including but not limited to a parent or grandparent; a "lineal descendant" is an individual in the direct line of descent, including but not limited to a child or grandchild (MCL 55.265).

Notarizing as Employee or Stockholder: A Notary who is a stockholder, director, officer or employee of a bank or other corporation may notarize documents executed by that corporation, or administer oaths to any of its agents, unless the Notary is named as a party to the document, either individually or as a representative of the corporation (MCL 55.291[9]).

Penalties for Violation of Notary Act

Effective January 1, 2012, "(A) person who violates this act is guilty of a misdemeanor punishable by a fine of not more than $5,000 or by imprisonment for not more than 1 year, or both" (MCL 55.309[1]).

"If a person knowingly violates this act when notarizing any document relating to an interest in real property or a mortgage transaction, a felony punishable by a fine of not more than $5,000 or by imprisonment for not more than 4 years, or both, may be imposed" (MCL 55.309[2]).

In addition, any person convicted for the crime of "residential mortgage fraud" may face a fine of up to $500,000 and/or imprisonment of up to 20 years (MCL 750.249[d]).

NOTARY SIGNING AGENTS

Currently, there are no statutes, regulations or rules expressly governing, prohibiting or restricting the operation of Notary Signing Agents within the state of Michigan. However, the

Office of the Great Seal does offer the following cautionary note:

"Notary signing agents are employed by private companies, and are not certified or qualified by the State of Michigan beyond the normal notary application process. A notary signing agent has no special powers, and must adhere to Michigan notary law in all transactions. It is illegal for a notary or a notary signing agent to give legal advice, explain legal documents or aid customer(s) in completing legal or immigration forms. Otherwise, unauthorized practice of law charges may result" (website, "Notary Signing Agents").

NOTARY FEES

"The fee charged by a notary public for performing a notarial act shall not be more than $10.00 for any individual transaction or notarial act" (MCL 55.285[7]).

Post Sign or Advise

"A notary public shall either conspicuously display a sign or expressly advise a person concerning the fee amount to be charged for a notarial act before the notary public performs the act" (MCL 55.285[7]).

Travel Fee

"Before the notary public commences to travel in order to perform a notarial act, the notary public and client may agree concerning a separate travel fee to be charged by the notary public for traveling to perform the notarial act" (MCL 55.285[7]).

Duplicate Certificates

"It was the intent of the legislature, we believe, that the notary should be paid for every certificate of acknowledgment which he executes and since instruments acknowledged in duplicate call for duplicate certificates, it is our opinion that a notary may charge the statutory fee for each certificate of acknowledgment executed by him" (Michigan Attorney General Opinion No. 1815 of September 14, 1954).

NOTARY CERTIFICATES

Michigan has adopted the *Uniform Recognition of Acknowledgments Act*, including the five short-form certificates (MCL 565.267) for:

1. Acknowledgment by individual;
2. Acknowledgment by corporation;
3. Acknowledgment by partnership;
4. Acknowledgment by attorney in fact;
5. Acknowledgment by public officer, trustee or personal representative.

For the text of these certificates, see "Uniform Recognition of Acknowledgments Act (1968)," Section 6, in Appendix 3.

Format of Acknowledgment Certificate

"The person taking an acknowledgment shall certify that the person acknowledging appeared before him and acknowledged he executed the instrument; and the person acknowledging was known to the person taking the acknowledgment or that the person taking the acknowledgment had satisfactory evidence that the person acknowledging was the person described in and who executed the instrument" (MCL 565.264).

"The form of a certificate of acknowledgment ... shall be accepted in this state if 1 of the following is true:

"a. The certificate is in a form prescribed by the laws or regulations of this state;

"b. The certificate is in a form prescribed by the laws applicable in the place in which the acknowledgment is taken;

"c. The certificate contains the words 'acknowledged before me', or their substantial equivalent" (MCL 565.265).

Secretary Shall Prescribe Forms

"The secretary (of state) shall prescribe the form that a notary public shall use for a jurat, the taking of an acknowledgment, the administering of an oath or affirmation, the taking of a verification upon oath or affirmation, the witnessing or attesting to a signature, or any other act that a notary public is authorized to perform in this state" (MCL 55.285[9]).

Acknowledgment by Individual (website):

Acknowledged by _____ before me on the _____ day of _____, 20____.

_____ (Notary signature)
_____ (Notary printed name)

Notary Public, State of Michigan,
County of _____
My commission expires
_____

(If notarizing outside the county of commission:
Acting in the County of _____ *)*

Jurat (website):

Subscribed and sworn to by _____
before me on the _____ *day of* _____,
20___.

_____ *(Notary signature)*
_____ *(Notary printed name)*

Notary Public, State of Michigan,
County of _____
My commission expires
_____

(If notarizing outside the county of commission:
Acting in the County of _____ *)*

Content of Notarial Certificate

"When performing a notarial act, you should…(c)omplete the notarial certificate. This must include all of the following: the date of notarization; your name; the county of appointment; the expiration date of your commission; and if performing a notarial act in a county other than your county of commission, the statement 'Acting in the County of _____.' Always sign your name exactly as it appears on your application for commission as a notary public, including middle name or initial(s) if used.

"The county of notarization (or 'venue') is essential as it determines the legal jurisdiction in the event the notarization is challenged in a court of law. This is not the notary's county of residence or commission, although it may be the same" (website, "Notarization of Document(s)").

ELECTRONIC NOTARIZATIONS

The state of Michigan has not yet adopted statutes or regulations expressly establishing rules, definitions and procedures for electronic notarization: "Michigan does not participate in E-Notarization. Michigan notaries public must verify the signature and identity of the person(s) that signed the document. The signer(s) must physically be in their presence and all signatures must be an original to obtain notarization" (website, "E-Notarization").

UETA Recognizes Notary's eSignature

Michigan has adopted the Uniform Electronic Transactions Act (2000 PA 305) (MCL 450.831, et seq.), including the provision on notarization, thereby recognizing the legal validity of electronic signatures used by Notaries:

"If a law requires a signature or record to be notarized, acknowledged, verified, or made under oath, the requirement is satisfied if the electronic signature of the person authorized to perform those acts, together with all other information required to be included by other applicable law, is attached to or logically associated with the signature or record" (MCL 450.841).

URPERA Does Not Require Seal Image

In 2010, Michigan enacted the Uniform Real Property Electonic Recording Act (Public Act 123, Enrolled Senate Bill 791), including the following provision:

"A requirement that a document or a signature associated with a document be notarized, acknowledged, verified, witnessed, or made under oath is satisfied if the electronic signature of the person authorized to perform that act, and all other information required to be included, is attached to or logically associated with the document or signature. A physical or electronic image of a stamp, impression, or seal need not accompany an electronic signature."

NOTARY RECORDS

"A notary public is not required to keep a journal, ledger, list, etc., but many notaries find these to be effective methods for keeping records. If you keep a record of your notarizations, it is recommended that you record the signer's name, identification presented, date, type of document and other information you deem pertinent to the transaction.… However the law does not describe the type of record that must be kept or what must be included in a record" (website, "Record Keeping").

Records Kept for Five Years

"A person, or the personal representative of a person who is deceased, who both performed a notarial act and created a record of the act performed while commissioned as a notary public under this act shall maintain all the records of that notarial act for at least 5 years after the date of the notarial act" (MCL 55.313).

Because certain crimes of real estate and mortgage fraud may be prosecuted up to 10 years after the offense was committed or the pertinent document was recorded (MCL 767.24[5]), prudent Notaries may wish to keep and safeguard their records at least 10 years.

Inspection of Records by State

Upon written or electronic request by the Secretary of State, a Notary must comply within 15 days by providing a copy or permitting inspection of the specified records of the Notary, but only if such records are kept by that Notary (MCL 55.295). For failure to comply, the Secretary may indefinitely suspend the Notary's commission.

AUTHENTICATION OF NOTARIAL ACTS

County Clerks

Authenticating certificates for Michigan Notaries are available from the office of the county clerk where a particular Notary has filed an oath and bond. The fee is $10 per notarial act certified (MCL 55.285[10]).

Secretary of State

Authenticating certificates for Notaries, including apostilles, are also issued by the Michigan Secretary of State's office, as are authenticating certificates for county clerks.

Fees: $1 per authentication for a "certificate of authority" or an apostille, payable to "State of Michigan."

Mailing Address:
Michigan Department of State
Office of the Great Seal
7064 Crowner Drive
Lansing, MI 48918

Telephone: 1-888-767-6424

In Person:
Office of the Great Seal
420 W. Allegan St.
Lansing

Other Walk-In Authentication Sites:
Capital Area Super!Center
3315 E. Michigan Ave.
Lansing

Clinton Township Super!Center
37015 Gratiot Avenue
Clinton Township

Detriot New Center Super!Center
Cadillac Place Building
3046 West Grand Blvd., Suite L650
Downtown Detroit

Flint Area Super!Center
5512 Fenton Road
Flint

Grand Rapids Super!Center
Centerpoint Mall 6-B, 3665 28th Street, S.E.
Grand Rapids

Livonia Area Super!Center
17176 Farmington Road
Livonia

Marquette County PLUS
2025 U.S. 41 West
Marquette

Oakland County Super!Center
1608 North Perry Road
Pontiac

Procedure: Mail or present in person the original notarized document(s), along with the appropriate fee. Indicate the country of destination and provide an addressed, stamped return envelope. "If you like your documents returned via courier service, please remember to include a pre-paid air bill, showing yourself as the sender. If may take as long as 1-2 weeks before your documents are returned, depending on the mail delivery and processing time" (website, "Document Certification").

Authentication of School Records: "A Michigan Notary Public cannot make a 'true copy' statement on copies of any records. Only a School Official, the person named in the document or a parent or guardian of a dependent student can make a 'true copy' statement on copies of a diploma, transcript or other school records" (website, "Certification Criteria").

This statement (e.g., "This is a true copy of my diploma... etc.") may then be signed before a Notary, notarized and authenticated by the state.

COMMISSIONING AND ADMINISTRATION

Michigan's Secretary of State (Office of the Great Seal) administers the Notary program and maintains records on Notaries (MCL 55.271[1]). All information contained in Notary commission applications is subject to disclosure under the Freedom of Information Act (MCL 15.231 et seq.).

Applying for Commission

Qualifications: An applicant for a commission as a Michigan Notary Public must: (a) be at least 18 years old, (b) be a resident of Michigan or maintain a place of business in the state, (c) be a U.S. citizen or possess proof of legal presence in the United States, (d) be a resident of the county from which a commission is sought, or, for a non-resident of Michigan, show that his or her principal place of business is located in the county in which an appointment is sought, (e) read and write the English language, (f) be free of any felony convictions within the past 10 years, (g) not be currently imprisoned in any state, county or federal correctional facility and (h) not have been convicted of two or more misdemeanors for violating the Michigan Notary Public Act within a 12-month period while commissioned, or of three or more such violations within a five-year period regardless of being commissioned.

No Course or Test: No course of instruction or test is required of Notary commission applicants in Michigan. However: "Before a notary public performs any notarial act, the notary public shall obtain and read a copy of all the current statutes of this state that regulate notarial acts" (MCL 55.283).

Application: Within 90 days before submitting an application to the state, a would-be Notary must obtain a $10,000 surety bond and file it with the county clerk in the county where the Notary resides or, for an out-of-state resident, where the Notary's principal place of business is located (MCL 55.273[1]). The completed application should also be presented to the clerk at that time. (The county filing fee is $10, though it may be higher in some counties.) The clerk will administer an oath of office and fill out the designated part of the application, verifying that the applicant has completed all the requirements. The applicant must then sign the form. Licensed Michigan attorneys are not required to file a surety bond as of April 1, 2007 (MCL 55.271), but they must still file an oath with the county.

The completed application, along with a $10 fee payable to the "State of Michigan" must then be submitted by the applicant to the Office of the Great Seal. If issued, the commission — in the form of a blue, wallet-sized card — will be sent directly to the Notary's residence address.

The renewal process is the same as for the original commission. Current Notaries seeking renewal must apply for a new commission no earlier than 60 days before expiration. Licensed Michigan attorneys whose commission was issued on or after April 1, 2007, will receive a reappointment application 90 days prior to expiration.

There are special application rules for Michigan Department of Corrections Employees only: "MDOC employees who are required as a condition of employment to perform notarial services must process their application in accordance with specific guidelines as directed by MDOC" (website, "Michigan Department of Corrections Employees Only").

Non-Residents: An out-of-state resident with a principal place of business in Michigan may become a Michigan Notary (MCL 55.271[1]). The applicant must show that his or her principal place of business is located in the county in which an appointment is sought and that he or she is likely to be asked to perform notarial acts.

Online Search: The state's roster of Notaries may be searched by name, county or expiration date through the "Michigan Notary Public Search" function (website, "Online Services"). Information provided describes a Notary's current status, including county of commission, appointment date and commission expiration date.

Changes of Status

If Notary Moves or Changes Name: If there is a change in the Notary's name, residence address or business address, the Notary must immediately apply to the Secretary of State, "in a format prescribed by the secretary," for a corrected Notary commission (MCL 55.281[1]). (A "Michigan Notary Public Request for Duplicate/Notice of Change" form is available for this purpose and downloadable on the website.) This also applies if the commission contains an error in the person's name, birth date, county or other pertinent information, reflecting a change in factual information in the person's application.

"Please note that you are required to update your driver's license (or personal identification card) prior to correcting your notary public commission. After your commission has been corrected, you will receive a new certificate in the mail. Be sure to change your address at this time if applicable" (website, "FAQs").

"The secretary shall notify the county clerk of the applicant's appointment when a corrected commission is issued by the secretary" (MCL 55.281[3]).

If Data in Application Changes: "A notary public shall immediately notify both the secretary and the county clerk of his or her appointment, in a format prescribed by the secretary, upon any change in the factual information stated in the notary public's application for appointment" (MCL 55.281[2]).

COUNTY CLERKS

To contact a Michigan county clerk to obtain an authenticating certificate for a Notary, or to seek assistance in locating a given Notary, telephone long-distance information — 1-XXX-555-1212 — for the following cities and towns:

County	City/Town	Area Code
Alcona	Harrisville	(989)
Alger	Munising	(906)
Allegan	Allegan	(269)
Alpena	Alpena	(989)
Antrim	Bellaire	(231)
Arenac	Standish	(989)
Baraga	L'Anse	(906)
Barry	Hastings	(269)
Bay	Bay City	(989)
Benzie	Beulah	(231)
Berrien	St. Joseph	(616)
Branch	Coldwater	(517)
Calhoun	Marshall	(269)
Cass	Cassopolis	(269)
Charlevoix	Charlevoix	(231)
Cheboygan	Cheboygan	(231)
Chippewa	Sault Ste. Marie	(906)
Clare	Harrison	(989)
Clinton	St. Johns	(989)
Crawford	Grayling	(989)
Delta	Escanaba	(906)
Dickinson	Iron Mountain	(906)
Eaton	Charlotte	(517)
Emmet	Petoskey	(231)
Genesee	Flint	(810)
Gladwin	Gladwin	(989)
Gogebic	Bessemer	(906)
Grand Traverse	Traverse City	(231)
Gratiot	Ithaca	(989)
Hillsdale	Hillsdale	(517)
Houghton	Houghton	(906)
Huron	Bad Axe	(989)
Ingham	Mason	(517)
Ionia	Ionia	(616)
Iosco	Tawas City	(989)
Iron	Crystal Falls	(906)
Isabella	Mt. Pleasant	(517)
Jackson	Jackson	(517)
Kalamazoo	Kalamazoo	(269)
Kalkaska	Kalkaska	(231)
Kent	Grand Rapids	(616)
Keweenaw	Eagle River	(906)
Lake	Baldwin	(231)
Lapeer	Lapeer	(810)
Leelanau	Leland	(231)
Lenawee	Adrian	(517)
Livingston	Howell	(517)
Luce	Newberry	(906)
Mackinac	St. Ignace	(906)
Macomb	Mt. Clemens	(586)
Manistee	Manistee	(231)
Marquette	Marquette	(906)
Mason	Ludington	(231)
Mecosta	Big Rapids	(231)
Menominee	Menominee	(906)
Midland	Midland	(989)
Missaukee	Lake City	(231)
Monroe	Monroe	(734)
Montcalm	Stanton	(989)
Montmorency	Atlanta	(989)
Muskegon	Muskegon	(231)
Newaygo	White Cloud	(231)
Oakland	Pontiac	(248)
Oceana	Hart	(231)
Ogemaw	West Branch	(517)
Ontonagon	Ontonagon	(906)
Osceola	Reed City	(231)

County	City/Town	Area Code
Oscoda	Mio	(989)
Otsego	Gaylord	(989)
Ottawa	Grand Haven	(616)
Presque Isle	Rogers City	(989)
Roscommon	Roscommon	(989)
St. Clair	Port Huron	(810)
St. Joseph	Centreville	(616)
Saginaw	Saginaw	(989)
Sanilac	Sandusky	(810)
Schoolcraft	Manistique	(906)
Shiawassee	Corunna	(989)
Tuscola	Caro	(517)
Van Buren	Paw Paw	(269)
Washtenaw	Ann Arbor	(734)
Wayne	Detroit	(313)
Wexford	Cadillac	(231)

OTHER NOTARIAL OFFICERS

Besides Notaries, the following officials may take acknowledgment of deeds (MCL 565.8): a judge or a clerk of a court of record.

QUICK FACTS

Notary Jurisdiction
Statewide (MCL 55.269[2]).

Notary Term Length
Expiring on the Notary's birthday not less than six years nor more than seven years from the date of appointment (MCL 55.269[2]).

Notary Bond
$10,000, with "a surety licensed to do business in this state ... The county clerk shall not accept the personal assets of an applicant as security for a surety bond under this act" (MCL 55.273[2]). A surety may cancel the bond 60 days after notifying the Notary, Secretary of State and county clerk.

Attorneys Exempted: Effective April 1, 2007, licensed Michigan attorneys applying for a new commission are exempted from the Notary surety bond requirement (MCL 55.271).

Employer May Also Be Liable: In addition to the Notary, the Notary's employer may be liable for damages if the Notary was acting within the scope of employment and the employer had knowledge of and consented to or permitted the Notary's misconduct (MCL 55.297[1]).

Minnesota

NOTARY ADMINISTRATION

Office of Secretary of State
Retirement Systems Bldg.   1-651-296-2803
60 Empire Drive, Suite 100   1-877-551-6767
St. Paul, MN 55103

Website: https://notary.sos.state.mn.us

NOTARY RULES

MS — MINNESOTA STATUTES
NCG — NOTARY COMMISSION GUIDE

Most Notary regulations are in the Minnesota Statutes:

a. Chapter 359, "Notaries Public";

b. Chapter 358*, "Seals, Oaths, Acknowledgments."

* *The Uniform Law on Notarial Acts* of 1982 is included virtually intact as MS Sections 358.41 through 358.49.

Other guidelines for Notaries are in the "Notary Commission Guide," also referred to on the Secretary of State's website as the "Notary Guide" and the "Notary Public Brochure." It is published by the Secretary and available on the website.

NOTARY SEAL

Every Minnesota Notary, and every ex officio Notary as defined in MS 358.15, must authenticate all official acts on paper documents with a physical "stamp" of office, and this stamp's format must be as follows:

Kind

Inked Stamp: Only a stamp that can be "reproduced in any legibly reproducible manner" is allowed (MS 359.03[3]). For notarial acts on paper documents, this means an inking stamp.

Shape/Size

Rectangular, not more than ³/₄ inch vertically by 2¹/₂ inches horizontally (MS 359.03[3]).

Border

Must have "a serrated or milled edge border" (MS 359.03[3]).

Components

Notary Commissioned by Secretary of State:
1. Name of Notary exactly as on commission;
2. "Notary Public";
3. Minnesota state seal;
4. "My commission expires _____ (commission expiration date)" (MS 359.03[3]).

Ex Officio Officers with Notarial Powers:
1. Name of officer;
2. Office title and jurisdiction, "Minnesota";
3. "Notarial Officer (ex officio notary public)";
4. Minnesota state seal;
5. "My commission (term) expires _____ (term expiration date)" or, where applicable, "My term is indeterminate" (MS 359.03[3]).

Examples

The above typical, actual-size examples of mandatory inked stamps are allowed by Minnesota law.

Electronic Affixation of Stamp

In performing electronic notarial acts, a duly registered, electronically-capable Minnesota Notary must use an electronic Notary stamp. A Notary's electronic stamp must contain the same information required for a physical stamp, which information "shall be logically and securely affixed or associated with the electronic record being notarized" (MS 359.03[4]). See also "Electronic Notarizations" later in this chapter.

Notary Stamp a 'Seal' for Court Purposes

"The official notarial stamp required by this section, whether applied to the record physically or electronically, is deemed to be a 'seal' for purposes of the admission of a document in court" (MS 359.03[2][b]).

New Stamp Required

Because the commission expiration date is a required component on the official notarial stamp, when Notaries renew their commission, they must obtain a new stamp with the new commission expiration date on it (website, "Frequently Asked Questions").

Stamp Belongs to Notary

"The official notarial stamp ... (is) the personal property of the notary and (is) exempt from execution" (MS 359.03[1]).

Stamp Disposition on Removal from Office

"(U)pon removal from office by the commissioner of commerce, a notary public shall deliver the notary's official notarial stamp to the commissioner of commerce" (MS 359.12).

Smeared Notary Stamp

"What if I smear my notarial stamp on the document? — If there is room, affix a second stamp nearby. It is not necessary to cross out the original stamp or write an explanation on the document; the reason for the second stamp will be obvious. If there is no room for a second stamp, attach a separate certificate with the same wording, signature, and legible stamp. Line through the original notarial wording and draw a line specifically through your stamp and signature. Near the old certificate wording, write 'See Attached Certificate'" (website, "Frequently Asked Questions").

No Room for Stamp

"There is no room on the notarial certificate for my stamp impression. What do I do? — A stamp is required so attach a loose notarial certificate" (website, "Frequently Asked Questions").

Other Official Stamps

"Every member of the legislature, while in office and residing in the district from which elected, may have an official notarial stamp, in the form provided in section 358.03, with which to authenticate official acts provided for in section 358.15(a)" (MS 358.028).

"Upon every seal of a court or officer authorized or required to have a seal there shall be engraved the same device that is engraved on the seal of the state, and the name of the court or office in which it is to be used" (MS 358.03).

"When any court of record is unprovided with a seal, the judge thereof may authorize the use of any temporary seal, or of any device by way of seal, until one is provided" (MS 358.04).

Private Seals Abolished

"Private seals are abolished, and all written instruments formerly required by law to be sealed shall be equally effective for all purposes without a seal; but nothing herein shall apply to the use of corporate seals" (MS 358.01).

Original Signature for Real Estate

"Unless otherwise provided by law, an instrument affecting real estate that is to be recorded as provided in this section or other applicable law must contain the original signatures of the parties who execute it and of the notary public or other officer taking an acknowledgment" (MS 507.24[2][a]).

Notary's Signature May Differ

While Minnesota law requires the Notary's name on the notarial stamp to exactly match the name on the commission certificate (MS 359.03[3]), in the "Notary Commission Guide" and on the Secretary of State's website ("Notary Commission Application" and "Frequently Asked Questions"), Notaries are told that they should use their "normal signature" when signing notarial certificates, even if that signature is different from the name on their stamp and commission. This policy is supported by MS 359.061, Subd. 1, which provides for both the full and the normal signature to be filed with the county.

NOTARY POWERS

Minnesota Notaries are authorized to perform the following notarial acts (MS 359.04 and 358.41[1]):
1. Take acknowledgments*;
2. Administer oaths** and affirmations**;

3. Take verifications*** (jurats) upon oath or affirmation;
4. Take depositions****;
5. Witness or attest signatures*****;
6. Certify or attest copies******;
7. Receive, make out and record protests (MS 336.3-505).

* Acknowledgments: "'Acknowledgment'" means a declaration by a person that the person has executed an instrument or electronic record for the purposes stated therein and, if the instrument or electronic record is executed in a representative capacity, that the person signed the instrument with proper authority and executed it as the act of the person or entity represented and identified therein" (MS 358.41[2]).

"In taking an acknowledgment, the notarial officer must determine, either from personal knowledge or from satisfactory evidence, that the person appearing before the officer and making the acknowledgment is the person whose true signature is on the instrument or electronic record" (MS 358.42[a] and 359.085[1]).

"Providing acknowledgments … means certifying that the signature already appearing on the document is genuine. If individuals have signed on behalf of another person or an organization, they must also demonstrate their authority to do so" (NCG).

** Oath/Affirmation Wording: The following wording is prescribed by statute for the Notary in executing an affidavit:

For an oath on an affidavit: "You do swear that the statements of this affidavit, by you subscribed, are true. So help you God" (MS 358.07[10]).

For an affirmation on an affidavit: "You do affirm that the statements of this affidavit, by you subscribed, are true, and this you do under the penalties of perjury" (MS 358.08).

In either case, the affiant customarily answers, "I do."

For oaths taken by trustees, referees, executors, administrators, guardians, arbitrators, viewers, assessors, appraisers, grand and petit jurors, witnesses, interpreters and attorneys, wording is prescribed in MS 358.06 and 358.07.

"The mode of administering an oath commonly practiced in the place where it is taken shall be followed, including, in this state, the ceremony of uplifting the hand" (MS 358.09).

*** Verifications upon Oath or Affirmation: "'Verification upon oath or affirmation' means a declaration that a statement is true made by a person upon oath or affirmation" (MS 358.41[3]).

"In taking a verification upon oath or affirmation, the notarial officer must determine, either from personal knowledge or from satisfactory evidence, that the person appearing before the officer and making the verification is the person whose true signature is made in the presence of the officer on the statement verified" (MS 358.42[b] and 359.085[2]).

**** Power to Compel for Deposition: "In taking depositions, the notary shall have the power to compel the attendance of and to punish witnesses for refusing to testify as provided by statute or court rule. All sheriffs shall serve and return all process issued by any notary in taking depositions" (MS 359.11).

***** Witness or Attest Signatures: "In witnessing or attesting a signature the notarial officer must determine, either from personal knowledge or from satisfactory evidence, that the signature is that of the person appearing before the officer and named therein. When witnessing or attesting a signature, the officer must be present when the signature is made" (MS 358.42[c] and 359.085[3]).

****** Certify or Attest Copies: "In certifying or attesting a copy of a document, electronic record, or other item, the notarial officer must determine that the proffered copy is a full, true, and accurate transcription or reproduction of that which was copied" (MS 358.42[d] and 359.085[4]).

"Attesting to copies of documents. Notaries evaluate copied documents to determine that they are complete and correct reproductions of the original documents" (NCG).

"Do not notarize if … (t)he document is an original birth, death or marriage certificate. Certified copies should (in that case) be obtained from the MN Department of Health or the County" (NCG).

Personal Appearance Is Required

The individual acknowledging a signature must appear in person before the Notary at the time of acknowledgment (MS 358.42[a] and 359.085[1]).

The individual making a verification upon oath or affirmation must appear before the

Notary and must affix his or her signature on the statement verified in the presence of the Notary (MS 358.42[b] and 359.085[2]).

The individual having his or her signature witnessed or attested must appear before the Notary and must affix his or her signature on the document in the presence of the Notary (MS 358.42[c] and 359.085[3]).

The Secretary of State's office stresses the importance of this statutory requirement:

"All document signers must personally appear before you" (website, "Notary Duties").

"You may only perform notarial acts if … the document signer appears in person before you…. Do not notarize if … (t)he document signer or oath-taker does not personally appear before you" (NCG).

"Personal appearance by all individuals requesting notarization is required at the time of notarization in ALL instances" (website, "Notary Handbook").

Identifying Document Signers

"Do not notarize if … (t)he document signer does not provide satisfactory evidence that he or she is the person whose true signature appears on the document" (NCG).

"A notarial officer has satisfactory evidence that a person is the person whose true signature is on a document or electronic record if that person (i) is personally known to the notarial officer, (ii) is identified upon the oath or affirmation of a credible witness personally known to the notarial officer, or (iii) is identified on the basis of identification documents" (MS 358.42[f] and MS 359.085[6]).

In statute, the preceding identification requirements apply specifically to acknowledgments, to verifications upon oath or affirmation and to witnessing or attesting signatures.

Determining Willingness and Awareness

<u>Willingness</u>: "Notarization … requires the Notary to ensure the signer's identity and willingness to sign,…. Make sure the signer is not being forced to sign the document. If you suspect coercion, it is best to refuse to notarize" (website, "Notary Handbook").

"Verify a document signer's willingness to sign the document" (NCG).

<u>Awareness</u>: "Assess whether each document signer is competent" (website, "Notary Duties").

"Do not notarize the document if you have a reasonable belief that the person signing the document is not aware of the significance of the transaction" (website, "Notary Handbook").

Notarizing for Disabled Signers

"(a) A notary public may certify as to the subscription or signature of an individual when it appears that the individual has a physical limitation that restricts the individual's ability to sign by writing or making a mark, pursuant to the following: (1) the name of an individual may be signed, or attached electronically in the case of an electronic record, by another individual other than the notary public at the direction and in the presence of the individual whose name is to be signed and in the presence of the notary public. The signature may be made by a rubber stamp facsimile of the person's actual signature, mark, or a signature of the person's name or mark made by another and adopted for all purposes of signature by the person with a physical limitation; and (2) the words "Signature written by" or "Signature attached by" in the case of an electronic record, "(name of individual directed to sign or directed to attach) at the direction and in the presence of (name as signed) on whose behalf the signature was written" or "attached electronically" in the case of an electronic record, or words of substantially similar effect must appear under or near the signature.

"(b) A notary public may use signals or electronic or mechanical means to take an acknowledgment from, administer an oath or affirmation to, or otherwise communicate with any individual in the presence of such notary public when it appears that the individual is unable to communicate verbally or in writing" MS 359.091).

NOTARY DON'TS

A Minnesota Notary Public should (NCG):
1. NOT notarize if the signer or oath-taker is not in the Notary's presence;
2. NOT notarize if the signer or oath-taker is not willing or if coercion is suspected;
3. NOT notarize if the Notary is the signer of the document to be notarized;
4. NOT notarize if the notarial certificate has blank spaces or is incomplete;
5. NOT notarize if the Notary will profit or gain from the transaction;

6. NOT notarize if there is the potential for a conflict of interest, such as when notarizing for a spouse or family member;
7. NOT notarize if the Notary believes the document or transaction is false, deceptive or fraudulent;
8. NOT notarize if the Notary does not have adequate time to ensure the notarial act is carried out properly.

Declining to Notarize

"When may I decline to perform a notarization? — If you know or suspect that the signer doesn't understand the transaction or is being coerced, if the signer cannot be satisfactorily identified, if the document is dated later than the notarization, if the document is incomplete, if the signer is not present" (website, "Frequently Asked Questions").

False Certificates

"Whoever, when acting or purporting to act as a notary public or other public officer, certifies falsely that an instrument has been acknowledged or that any other act was performed by a party appearing before the actor or that as such notary public or other public officer the actor performed any other official act may be sentenced as follows:

"1. If the actor so certifies with intent to injure or defraud, to imprisonment for not more than three years or to payment of a fine of not more than $5,000, or both; or

"2. In any other case, to imprisonment for not more than 90 days or to payment of a fine of not more than $1,000, or both" (MS 609.65).

Blank Spaces in Document

"While not responsible for the content of a document, (the Notary should) alert the signer to any blanks" (website, "Duties of a Notary").

"Can I notarize a document with blank spaces? — This may be prohibited by law in Minnesota. Even if not addressed in statute, a prudent Notary should skim the document for blanks and ask the document signer to fill them in. If they are intended to be left blank, then the signer can line through them or write N/A" (website, "Frequently Asked Questions").

No Date on Document: "Can I notarize an undated document? — If there is a space for a date it should be filled in with the correct date or lined through by the document signer. If the document simply doesn't have a date, it is acceptable to notarize it and record in your journal that the document has no date" (website, "Frequently Asked Questions").

Notarizing Faxes

"Can I notarize a fax or a photocopy? — A photocopy or fax may be notarized, but only if it bears an original signature. That is, the copy must have been signed with pen and ink. A photocopied or faxed signature may never be notarized" (website, "Frequently Asked Questions").

Health Care Directive Prohibitions

"a. A health care agent or alternate health care agent appointed in a health care power of attorney may not act as a witness or notary public for the execution of the health care directive that includes the health care power of attorney.

"b. At least one witness to the execution of the health care directive must not be a health care provider providing direct care to the principal or an employee of a health care provider providing direct care to the principal on the date of execution. A person notarizing a health care directive may be an employee of a health care provider providing direct care to the principal" (MS 145C.03[3]).

Non-English Advertising by Notaries

"(a) A notary public who is not an attorney who advertises the services of a notary public in a language other than English, whether by radio, television, signs, pamphlets, newspapers, or other written communication, with the exception of a single desk plaque, shall post or otherwise include with the advertisement a notice in English and the language in which the advertisement appears. This notice must be of a conspicuous size, if in writing, and must state: 'I AM NOT AN ATTORNEY LICENSED TO PRACTICE LAW IN MINNESOTA AND MAY NOT GIVE LEGAL ADVICE OR ACCEPT FEES FOR LEGAL ADVICE.' If the advertisement is by radio or television, the statement may be modified but must include substantially the same message.

"(b) A notary public who violates this section is guilty of a misdemeanor" (MS 359.062).

Disqualifying Interests

"A notarial officer may not acknowledge, witness or attest to the officer's own signature, or take a verification of the officer's own oath or affirmation" (MS 359.085[7]).

"Can I notarize a document in which I am named? — 359.12 prohibits the dishonest and unfaithful discharge of notary duties and Bank of Benson v. Hove, 47 N.W. 449 (1890), involving a deed to a horse, declared that, 'Undoubtedly the policy of the law forbids that the acknowledgment should be taken before a party to the deed…' This policy extends to other documents in which the notary is named" (website, "Frequently Asked Questions").

<u>Corporate Notaries May Notarize</u>: A Notary who is an officer, director or stockholder of a corporation may notarize for that corporation (MS 358.25).

Notarizing for Family Members

"Can I notarize for a family member? — Most state laws do not expressly prohibit notarizing for a relative. However, Notaries who do so in many instances will violate statutes prohibiting a direct beneficial interest. For instance, if a Notary is asked to witness her husband's signature on a loan document for the purchase of a home they will share, she will directly benefit from the transaction and should disqualify herself. The likelihood of a direct beneficial interest is usually greater with immediate family members — spouse, mother, father, son, daughter, sister or brother — than with non-immediate (family) such as in-laws, cousins, nieces, nephews, aunts and uncles. The matter of interest in an inheritance is more often a consideration with lineal descendants (children, grandchildren, etc.) and ascendants (parent, grandparents, etc.) than with nonlineal relatives. In many instances, a Notary will have no beneficial interest in notarizing for a relative and will not be prevented by law from doing so. However, to avoid later questioning of the Notary's impartiality, as well as accusations of undue influence, it is always safest for a signer to find a Notary who is not related" (website, "Frequently Asked Questions").

Do Not Invade Signer's Privacy

"Respect the privacy of each signer and do not divulge or use personal or proprietary information disclosed during execution of a notarial act for other than an official purpose" (NCG).

NOTARY SIGNING AGENTS

Currently, there are no statutes, regulations or rules expressly governing, prohibiting or restricting the operation of Notary Signing Agents within the state of Minnesota.

NOTARY FEES

The maximum fees allowed for notarial acts are (MS 357.17):
1. Taking an acknowledgment: $1;
2. Administering an oath: $1;
3. Notarizing any affidavit or paper not otherwise specified: $1 per folio, plus 20 cents per folio for copies;
4. For executing a protest, with copy: $1; for making and serving every notice of nonpayment or nonacceptance, with copy: $1.

Penalty for Overcharging

For the offense of charging more than allowed by Minnesota statute, a Notary Public may be removed from office and become thereby ineligible for a future Notary Public commission: "Every notary who shall charge or receive a fee or reward for any act or service done or rendered as a notary greater than the amount allowed by law … is subject to the penalties imposed pursuant to section 45.027. A notary may be removed from office only by the governor, the district court or the commissioner of commerce" (MS 359.12).

NOTARY CERTIFICATES

Minnesota has adopted the *Uniform Law on Notarial Acts*, including the short-form certificates (MS 358.48) for:
1. Acknowledgment by individual;
2. Acknowledgment by representative;
3. Verification upon oath or affirmation;
4. Witnessing or attesting signature;
5. Attesting copy of document.

For the text of these certificates, see "Uniform Law on Notarial Acts (1982)," Section 8, in Appendix II. In the certificates, the words "Seal, if any" have been replaced by the single word "Stamp," indicating that Minnesota Notaries and ex officio Notaries are required to use an inking stamp as their official seal.

In addition, the following certificate is offered as an alternative when a Notary administers a verbal oath that is also in written form:

Jurat for a Written Oath (MS 358.09):

State of Minnesota
County of _____

Subscribed and sworn to before me this ____ *day of* _____, 20___.

(SIGNATURE AND STAMP OF NOTARY)

Description of Spouses on Certificate

"(I)f husband and wife join in and acknowledge the execution of any instrument, they shall be described in the certificate of acknowledgment as husband and wife; and, if they acknowledge it before different officers, or before the same officer at different times, each shall be described in the certificate as the spouse of the other" (MS 358.14).

Format for Notarial Certificate

"(a) A notarial act must be evidenced by a certificate physically or electronically signed and dated by a notarial officer in a manner that attributes such signature to the notary public. The notary's name as it appears on the official notarial stamp and on any jurat or certificate of acknowledgment and in the notary's commission must be identical. The certificate must include identification of the jurisdiction in which the notarial act is performed and the title of the office of the notarial officer and must include the official notarial stamp, pursuant to section 359.03. If the officer is a commissioned officer on active duty in the military service of the United States, it must also include the officer's rank.

"(b) A certificate of a notarial act is sufficient if it is in English and meets the requirements of subsection (a) and it:

"(1) is in the short form set forth in section 358.48;

"(2) is in a form otherwise prescribed by the law of this state;

"(3) is in a form prescribed by the laws or regulations applicable in the place in which the notarial act was performed; or

"(4) sets forth the actions of the notarial officer and those are sufficient to meet the requirements of the designated notarial act ..." (MS 358.47).

ELECTRONIC NOTARIZATIONS

Effective July 1, 2006, Minnesota Statutes Chapters 358 and 359 were revised to reflect the fact that "a notary public may perform a notarial act by electronic means" (MS 358.41[1]).

Notary Must Register e-Capability

"Before performing electronic notarial acts, a notary public shall register the capability to notarize electronically with the secretary of state. Before performing electronic notarial acts after recommissioning, a notary public shall reregister with the secretary of state" (MS 359.01[5]).

Upon registration with the Secretary of State, the Notary will be issued an "E-Notarization Authorization Certificate." If the Notary subsequently changes county of residence or renews the commission or if the commission expires, reregistration will be necessary (website, "E-Notarization Authorization Application").

Electronic Signature and Record Defined

Borrowing from the Uniform Electronic Transactions Act, Minnesota's electronic notarization law defines "electronic signature" and "electronic record" as follows:

"'Electronic signature' means an electronic sound, symbol, or process attached to or logically associated with a record and executed or adopted by a person with the intent to sign the record" (MS 358.41[6]).

"'Electronic record' means a record created, generated, sent, communicated, received, or stored by electronic means" (MS 358.41[7]).

Electronic Stamp Requirements

"The information required by this section may be affixed electronically and shall be logically and securely affixed or associated with the electronic record being notarized" (MS 359.03[4]).

UETA Recognizes Notary's eSignature

Minnesota has adopted the Uniform Electronic Transactions Act (MS 325L.01 through 325L.19), including the provision on notarization and acknowledgment, thereby recognizing the legal validity of electronic signatures used by Notaries:

"If a law requires a signature or record to be notarized, acknowledged, verified, or made under oath, the requirement is satisfied if the electronic signature of the person authorized to perform those acts, together with all other information required to be included by other applicable law, is attached to or logically associated with the signature or record" (MS 325L.11).

Digital Certificate Equates to Acknowledgment

The Minnesota Electronic Authentication Act (MS 325K.001 through 325K.27) equates use of a digital certificate with acknowledgment before a Notary:

"Unless otherwise provided by law or contract, a certificate issued by a licensed certification authority satisfies the requirement for an acknowledgment pursuant to section 358.41 of a digital signature verified by reference to the public key listed in the certificate, regardless of whether words of an express acknowledgment appear with the digital signature and regardless of whether the signer physically appeared before the certification authority when the digital signature was created, if that digital signature is:

"(1) verifiable by that certificate; and

"(2) affixed when that certificate was valid" (MS 325K.23[1]).

Certification Authority Has Notary's Liability: "If the digital signature is used as an acknowledgment, then the certification authority is responsible to the same extent as a notary up to any limit on liability stated in the certification authority's certification practice statement for failure to satisfy the requirements for an acknowledgment. The certification authority may not disclaim or limit, other than as provided in section 325K.17, the effect of this section" (MS 325K.23[2]).

URPERA Permits Notary's eSignature

Effective July 1, 2008, the state enacted the Minnesota Real Property Electronic Recording Act (MS 507.0941 through 507.0949), its version of the Uniform Real Property Electronic Recording Act (URPERA). The Act enables Minnesota county recorders to record land records in electronic format and authorizes Notaries to use electronic signatures in notarizing such electronic land records:

"(a) If a law requires, as a condition for recording, that a document be an original, on paper or another tangible medium, or in writing, the requirement is satisfied by an electronic document satisfying sections 507.0941 to 507.0948. If a law requires or refers to something related to tangible media including, without limitation, book, certificate, floor plan, page, volume, or words derived from them, the requirement or reference is satisfied by an electronic document satisfying sections 507.0941 to 507.0948.

"(b) If a law requires, as a condition for recording, that a document be signed, the requirement is satisfied by an electronic signature.

"(c) A requirement that a document or a signature associated with a document be attested, acknowledged, verified, witnessed, or made under oath is satisfied if the electronic signature of the person authorized to perform that act, and all other information required to be included, is attached to or logically associated with the document or signature. A physical or electronic image of a stamp, impression, or seal need not accompany an electronic signature" (MS 507.0943).

Pilot e-Recording Program Repealed: Beginning in the year 2000, Minnesota had allowed electronic recording of real property documents under a pilot program enacted by the Minnesota Legislature. Several counties participated in the pilot. The enactment of URPERA repealed this pilot program. However, the new law states that documents electronically recorded under standards of the pilot program nonetheless satisfy the new electronic recording requirements (MS 507.24).

NOTARY RECORDS

The only mention in Minnesota law is that "the notary's official journal (is) the personal property of the notary and (is) exempt from execution" (MS 359.03[1]). Prior to 2010, this statute also stipulated that, upon the Notary's death, resignation or removal from office, the journal was to be deposited with the court administrator of the district court of the Notary's county.

A Recommended Prudent Practice

Although keeping a journal is not required by law, the Secretary of State's office strongly encourages Minnesota Notaries to do so:

"The process of notarization involves three critical steps that a Notary Public should always follow…." One of these critical steps is to "(m)ake a journal entry…. Although having a journal is not required in Minnesota, we highly recommend you have a journal and make a journal entry of all notarial activity, whether you notarize the document or you refuse to notarize it. Provide enough detail that might be relevant, in case of fraud" (website, "Notary Handbook").

"While Minnesota Law does not require a journal, it is prudent of a notary public to keep one. The journal is to record all notarial acts performed, which could include the date and time of the act, the type of act, a description of the document, signature of each principal and circumstances for not completing a notarial act" (website, "Frequently Asked Questions").

Components of Journal Entry

"State law does not require a notary to keep records of their official acts. However, it is recommended that you keep a journal to assist in recalling what you have done, if needed or if legally challenged. You should record the following information:
 "1. Date
 "2. Type of notarial act
 "3. A description of the document
 "4. The signature, printed name and address of each document signer
 "5. How the signer proved their identity
 "6. County
 "7. Fee charged, if any" (NCG).

Journal Belongs to Notary

"The ... notary's official journal (is) the personal property of the notary and (is) exempt from execution" (MS 359.03[1]).

Journal Must Be Safeguarded

"Safeguard your journal because it serves as an important public record" (NCG).

AUTHENTICATION OF NOTARIAL ACTS

County Registrars

Locally, authenticating certificates for Minnesota Notaries are issued for a fee of $5 by the registrar of the county in which the Notary filed his or her commission (MS 359.061[4]).

Secretary of State

Authenticating certificates ("certificates of office") and apostilles are also issued by the Minnesota Secretary of State's office.

Fees: $5 per certificate or apostille, with check or money order payable to "Minnesota Secretary of State."

Address:
Minnesota Secretary of State
Attention: Certification
Retirement Systems Bldg.
60 Empire Drive, Suite 100
St. Paul, MN 55103

Telephone: 1-651-296-2803
 1-877-551-6767

Procedure: Mail or present in person the original notarized document(s) or an original certified copy from the county, along with the appropriate fee and a cover letter indicating the country of destination. "You may enclose a prepaid FedEx or UPS label which will speed up the return of the document being delivered back to you (this is not required)" (website, "Authentications and Apostilles").

COMMISSIONING AND ADMINISTRATION

Though Minnesota's Governor nominally appoints and commissions the state's Notaries, they are in fact commissioned through the Secretary of State's office, which maintains records on them (MS 359.01[1]).

Before July 1, 2005, the state Department of Commerce, through its Licensing Division, administered Minnesota's Notary program. The Department of Commerce is still responsible for investigating complaints and allegations of misconduct against Notaries Public through their Market Assurance Division at www.commerce.state.mn.us (website, "File a Complaint).

Applying for Commission

Qualifications: An applicant for a commission as a Minnesota Notary Public must: (a) be at least 18 years of age and (b) be either a Minnesota resident or a resident of Iowa, North Dakota, South Dakota or Wisconsin (MS 359.01[1] and [2]).

No Course or Test: No course of instruction or test is required of an applicant for a

Minnesota Notary commission, though it is recommended: "Seek additional training and education (optional)" (NCG). Further, new Notaries are directed to "(r)eview Minnesota Statutes 357, 358 and 359 at www.leg.state.mn.us to familiarize yourself with notary requirements" (NCG).

Application: The application fee is $120 (MS 359.01[3]). Those applying for a new Notary commission or renewing a commission that has expired must apply by mail. Those renewing an unexpired commission may apply either online or by mail (website, "Notaries").

Renewal applications may be filed up to six months before commission expiration (MS 359.02). Since all commissions expire on January 31 of the fifth year following the year the commission was issued, Notaries may begin the renewal process any time after August 1 of the year before their commission expires (website, "Notaries").

Registration with County: After commissioning or renewal, the commission of every resident Notary must be "recorded in the office of the local registrar of the notary's county of residence" (MS 359.061).

In the case of a non-resident Notary, "the person designates the Minnesota county in which the person's notary commission will be recorded …" (MS 359.01[2]).

The fee for county registration of the commission is $20 (MS 357.021).

Online Search: Information on all Minnesota Notaries may be obtained online through the Secretary of State's website ("Find a Notary"). Notaries can be located by name, commission number, county or status (active or inactive) (website, "Notaries"). These details, as well as the address the Notary designates when he or she applies for a commission, are public information (website, "Notary Commission Application").

Changes of Status

If Notary Moves: Any address change must be reported to the Secretary of State within 30 days of the change (MS 359.071). A "Notification of Address Change for Notary Public" form may be downloaded from the Secretary's website, or the address change may be done online. There is no fee for an address change. If the move is to a new county, the Notary must reregister the commission in the new county (website, "Notary Commission Application" and "Change Name Or Address").

If Notary Changes Name: Any name change must be reported to the Secretary of State within 30 days of the change (MS 359.071). The Notary must submit his or her current commission certificate and a new commission application using the new name. A copy of the legal document changing the name (e.g., marriage certificate, divorce decree, court order) must be attached. There is no fee for a change of name. A new stamp must be obtained, and the Notary must register again with the local registrar (website, "Notary Commission Application" and "Change Name Or Address").

If Notary Resigns: "To cancel your commission, email the office of the Secretary of State at notary.sos@state.mn.us or call us at 651-296-2803 or toll-free at 1-877-551-6767 and press option #3" (NCG).

COUNTY REGISTRARS

To contact a Minnesota county registrar to obtain an authenticating certificate for a Notary, telephone long-distance information — 1-XXX-555-1212 — using the following area codes and ask for the phone number of the registrar for the appropriate county.

County	City/Town	Area Code
Aitkin	Aitkin	(218)
Anoka	Anoka	(763)
Becker	Detroit Lakes	(218)
Beltrami	Bemidji	(218)
Benton	Foley	(320)
Big Stone	Ortonville	(320)
Blue Earth	Mankato	(507)
Brown	New Ulm	(507)
Carlton	Carlton	(218)
Carver	Chaska	(952)
Cass	Walker	(218)
Chippewa	Montevideo	(320)
Chisago	Center City	(651)
Clay	Moorhead	(218)
Clearwater	Bagley	(218)
Cook	Grand Marais	(218)
Cottonwood	Windom	(507)
Crow Wing	Brainerd	(218)
Dakota	Hastings	(651)
Dodge	Mantorville	(507)
Douglas	Alexandria	(320)
Faribault	Blue Earth	(507)

County	City/Town	Area Code	County	City/Town	Area Code
Fillmore	Preston	(507)	Stearns	St. Cloud	(320)
Freeborn	Albert Lea	(507)	Steele	Owatonna	(507)
Goodhue	Red Wing	(651)	Stevens	Morris	(320)
Grant	Elbow Lake	(218)	Swift	Benson	(320)
Hennepin	Minneapolis	(612)	Todd	Long Prairie	(320)
Houston	Caledonia	(507)	Traverse	Wheaton	(320)
Hubbard	Park Rapids	(218)	Wabasha	Wabasha	(651)
Isanti	Cambridge	(763)	Wadena	Wadena	(218)
Itasca	Grand Rapids	(218)	Waseca	Waseca	(507)
Jackson	Jackson	(507)	Washington	Stillwater	(651)
Kanabec	Mora	(320)	Watonwan	St. James	(507)
Kandiyohi	Willmar	(320)	Wilkin	Breckenridge	(218)
Kittson	Hallock	(218)	Winona	Winona	(507)
Koochiching	International Falls	(218)	Wright	Buffalo	(763)
Lac qui Parle	Madison	(320)	Yellow Medicine	Granite Falls	(320)
Lake	Two Harbors	(218)			
Lake of the Wds	Baudette	(218)			
Le Sueur	Le Center	(507)			
Lincoln	Ivanhoe	(507)			
Lyon	Marshall	(507)			
Mahnomen	Mahnomen	(218)			
Marshall	Warren	(218)			
Martin	Fairmont	(507)			
McLeod	Glencoe	(320)			
Meeker	Litchfield	(320)			
Mille Lacs	Milaca	(320)			
Morrison	Little Falls	(320)			
Mower	Austin	(507)			
Murray	Slayton	(507)			
Nicollet	St. Peter	(507)			
Nobles	Worthington	(507)			
Norman	Ada	(218)			
Olmsted	Rochester	(507)			
Otter Tail	Fergus Falls	(218)			
Pennington	Thief River Falls	(218)			
Pine	Pine City	(320)			
Pipestone	Pipestone	(507)			
Polk	Crookston	(218)			
Pope	Glenwood	(320)			
Ramsey	St. Paul	(651)			
Red Lake	Red Lake Falls	(218)			
Redwood	Redwood Falls	(507)			
Renville	Olivia	(320)			
Rice	Faribault	(507)			
Rock	Luverne	(507)			
Roseau	Roseau	(218)			
Roseau	Roseau	(218)			
St. Louis	Duluth	(218)			
Scott	Shakopee	(952)			
Sherburne	Elk River	(763)			
Sibley	Gaylord	(507)			

OTHER NOTARIAL OFFICERS

Besides Notaries, the following officers may perform a notarial act in Minnesota: a judge, a court administrator or a deputy court administrator of any court in the state (MS 358.43[a]).

"The signature and title of a person performing a notarial act are prima facie evidence that the signature is genuine and that the person holds the designated title" (MS 358.43[c]).

Ex Officio Notaries

The following officers also have the ex officio powers of a Notary within the state (MS 358.15):

1. Every member of the Legislature while still residing in the district from which elected, but no fee may be received. (The form of the official signature would be: "John Doe, Representative [or Senator], _____ District, Minnesota, Ex Officio Notary Public. My term expires January 1, _____.");

2. Clerks or recorders of towns and cities. (The form of the official signature would be: "John Doe, (official title), _____ County, Minnesota, Ex Officio Notary Public. My term expires _____" or, where applicable, "My term is indeterminate.");

3. Court commissioners, county recorders, and county auditors, and their several deputies, and county commissioners, all within their respective counties. (The form of the official signature would be the same as for town or city clerks or recorders);

4. Peace officers licensed under Section 626.845 for the purpose of administering oaths in criminal proceedings. (The form of the official signature would be: "John Doe, Peace Officer License Number _____, _____ County, Minnesota. My license expires June 30, _____.")

QUICK FACTS

Notary Jurisdiction

Statewide (MS 359.04).

Notary Term Length

Five years (MS 359.02). "A notary ... holds office until January 31 of the fifth year following the year the commission was issued" (MS 359.02)

"Any notary who shall exercise the duties of office after the expiration of a term, or when otherwise disqualified, shall be guilty of a misdemeanor" (MS 359.08).

Notary Bond

Not required by statute. However, Notaries commissioned before January 1, 1990, were required to have a $10,000 bond.

Mississippi

NOTARY ADMINISTRATION

Office of Secretary of State
Business Services Division
Notary Section   1-601-359-1615
P.O. Box 1020
(700 North Street)
Jackson, MS 39215-1020

Website: www.sos.ms.gov/business_
services_notaries.aspx

NOTARY RULES

MCA — *Mississippi Code Annotated*
MAC — *Mississippi Administrative Code*

Most Notary rules are in the Mississippi Code Annotated:

a. Sections 25-33-1 through 25-33-23 (Title 25, Chapter 33, "Notaries Public");

b. Sections 89-3-1 through 89-3-15 (Title 89, Chapter 3, "Acknowledgments").

Comprehensive changes to the *Mississippi Administrative Code* based on the NNA's Model Notary Act of 2002 took effect July 1, 2007, to complement the statutes:

c. Title 01, Part III ("Secretary of State of Mississippi"), Chapter 14 ("Notaries Public"), Sections 100-999.

NOTARY SEAL

Mississippi Notaries must authenticate their official acts on paper documents with a seal of office, and the seal's format must be as described below (MCA 25-33-3 and MAC Sect. 403.01[2]). The seal rules set by the Mississippi Administrative Code (MAC) apply to Notary commissions issued on or after July 1, 2007.

Kind

Inked Stamp: "Near the notary's official signature on the notarial certificate of a paper document, the notary shall affix a sharp, legible,

Examples

The above typical, actual-size examples of Notary seals are allowed by Mississippi law. Formats other than these may also be permitted.

permanent, and photographically reproducible image of the official seal ..." (MAC Sect. 403.02[1]). Both black and blue ink are mentioned as acceptable in a "Model Notary Seals" sheet distributed by the Notary Section.

"An embossed seal impression that is not photographically reproducible may be used in addition to but not in lieu of the seal described in Subsection (1)" (MAC Sect. 403.02[3]).

Shape/Size

Circular: The border must be "in a circular shape with a diameter no less than one and one-half inches and no larger than two and one-half inches, surrounding the required words" (MAC Sect. 403.02[1][e]). "Each seal shall have the name of the county of the notary's residence with that of the state and his own name on the margin thereof, and the words 'notary public' across the center ..." (MCA 25-33-3).

Components

On the Margin:
1. Name of Notary;
2. "State of Mississippi";
3. Name of county where Notary resides.

Across the Center:
4. "Notary Public";
5. Identification number of commission;
6. "Commission expires _____ (date)".

Commission Expiration Date Must Appear

To every acknowledgment certificate, a Notary must affix his or her "written or printed" commission expiration date, in addition to the Notary's official seal and signature (MCA 25-33-13).

"The failure of such notary public to affix such recital of date at which his commission expires shall not invalidate the acknowledgment of such instrument or such certificate of acknowledgment, or otherwise affect the validity or recording of any instrument." However, it may result in revocation of the Notary's commission.

Seal Affixed at Time of Notarization

"An image of the seal shall be affixed only at the time the notarial act is performed" (MAC Sect. 403.01[3]).

Non-Conforming Seals

"The failure of such seal to conform to the provisions of this section shall not invalidate any official act or certificate of such notary public" (MCA 25-33-3).

Illegible Data in Seal

"Illegible information within a seal impression may be typed or printed legibly by the notary adjacent to but not within the impression" (MAC Sect. 403.02[2]).

Notarial Seal of County Circuit Court

"The board of supervisors of every county shall provide a notarial seal, with the inscription 'notary public' around the margin and the image of an eagle in the center, which seal shall be kept in the office of the clerk of the circuit court; and all ex-officio notaries public may at all times have access to and use such seal for the authentication of any notarial act necessary to be so authenticated" (MCA 25-33-19 and 25-33-17).

Seal Is Exclusive Property of Notary

"A notary shall keep an official seal that is the exclusive property of the notary. The seal shall not be possessed or used by any other person, nor surrendered to an employer upon termination of employment" (MAC Sect. 403.01[1]).

"When not in use, the seal shall be kept secure and accessible only to the notary" (MAC Sect. 403.01[4]).

Stolen or Lost Seal

"Within 10 days after the seal of a notary is stolen, after informing the appropriate law enforcement agency, or lost, the notary shall notify the Secretary of State by submitting an Application for Replacement Commission, SOS Form NP 006. The notary shall also provide a copy or number of any pertinent police report. Upon receipt of such notice the Secretary of State shall issue to the notary a replacement commission with a new Notary Identification Number" (MAC Sect. 403.01[5]).

Disposition of Seal

"As soon as reasonably practicable after resignation, revocation, or expiration of a notary commission or death of the notary, the seal shall be destroyed or defaced so that it may not be misused" (MAC Sects. 403.01[6], 602 and 603).

Notary's Official Signature

"In notarizing a paper document, a notary shall:

"1. sign by hand on the notarial certificate exactly and only the name indicated on the notary's commission;

"2. not sign using a facsimile stamp or an electronic or other printing method; and

"3. affix the official signature only at the time the notarial act is performed" (MAC Sect. 402).

NOTARY POWERS

Mississippi Notaries are authorized to perform the following notarial acts (MCA 25-33-11 and 25-33-9; MAC Sect. 201):

1. Take acknowledgments* and proofs;
2. Administer oaths** and affirmations***;
3. Execute jurats****;
4. Perform signature witnessings*****;
5. Take affidavits (MCA 25-7-29[d]);
6. "(P)erform all other duties required of notaries by commercial usage …."

* Acknowledgments: "'Acknowledgment' means a notarial act in which an individual at a single time and place:
"1. appears in person before the notary and presents a document;
"2. is personally known to the notary or identified by the notary through satisfactory evidence; and
"3. indicates to the notary that the signature on the document was voluntarily affixed by the individual for the purposes stated within the document and, if applicable, that the individual had due authority to sign in a particular representative capacity" (MAC Sect. 101.01).

** Oaths: "'Oath' means a notarial act, or part thereof, which is legally equivalent to an affirmation and in which an individual at a single time and place:
"1. appears in person before the notary;
"2. is personally known to the notary or identified by the notary through satisfactory evidence; and
"3. makes a vow of truthfulness or fidelity on penalty of perjury while invoking God or using any form of the word 'swear'" (MAC Sect. 101.13).

*** Affirmations: "'Affirmation' means a notarial act, or part thereof, which is legally equivalent to an oath and in which an individual at a single time and place:
"1. appears in person before the notary;
"2. is personally known to the notary or identified by the notary through satisfactory evidence; and
"3. makes a vow of truthfulness or fidelity on penalty of perjury, based on personal honor and without invoking God or using any form of the word 'swear'" (MAC Sect. 101.02).

**** Jurats: "'Jurat' means a notarial act in which an individual at a single time and place:
"1. appears in person before the notary and presents a document;
"2. is personally known to the notary or identified by the notary through satisfactory evidence;
"3. signs the document in the presence of the notary; and
"4. takes an oath or affirmation from the notary vouching for the truthfulness or accuracy of the signed document" (MAC Sect. 101.08).

***** Signature Witnessings: "'Signature witnessing' means a notarial act in which an individual at a single time and place:
"1. appears in person before the notary and presents a document;
"2. is personally known to the notary or identified by the notary through satisfactory evidence; and
"3. signs the document in the presence of the notary" (MAC Sect. 101.21).

Methods to Establish Identity
Any document signer or principal must be identified by the Notary through personal knowledge or satisfactory evidence of identity (MAC Sect. 201[2][b]).

Personal Knowledge: "'Personal knowledge of identity' and 'personally knows' means familiarity with an individual resulting from interactions with that individual over a period of time sufficient to dispel any reasonable uncertainty that the individual has the identity claimed" (MAC Sect. 101.16).

Personal Appearance: "'Appears in person before the notary' means that the principal and the notary are physically close enough to see, hear, communicate with, and give identification documents to each other" (MAC Sect. 101.03).

Satisfactory Evidence: "'Satisfactory evidence of identity' means identification of an individual based on:
"1. at least one current document issued by a federal, state, or tribal government agency bearing the photographic image of the individual's face and signature and a physical description of the individual, though a properly stamped passport without a physical description is acceptable; or
"2. the oath or affirmation of one credible witness unaffected by the document or transaction who is personally known to the notary and who personally knows the individual, or of 2 credible witnesses unaffected by the document or transaction who each personally knows the

individual and shows to the notary documentary identification as described in Subparagraph (1) of this section" (MAC Sect. 101.19).

Credible Witness: "'Credible witness' means an honest, reliable, and impartial person who personally knows an individual appearing before a notary and takes an oath or affirmation from the notary to vouch for that person's identity" (MAC Sect. 101.05).

Proof When Signer, Witness Dead or Absent

"If the grantor and witness or witnesses of any instrument of writing be dead or absent, so that personal attendance of neither can be had, it may be established by the oath of a person who, on examination before an officer competent to take acknowledgments, can prove the handwriting of the deceased or absent witness or witnesses; or when such proof cannot be had, then the handwriting of the grantor may be proved, and the officer before whom such proof is made shall certify accordingly, and such certificate shall be deemed equivalent to an acknowledgment by the grantor or proof by a subscribing witness, and entitle the instrument to be recorded" (MCA 89-3-15).

Signing by Mark or Unable to Sign

"Certificates may be used for signers by mark or persons physically unable to sign or make a mark if:

"1. for a signer by mark, the notary and 2 witnesses unaffected by the document observe the affixation of the mark, both witnesses sign their own names beside the mark, and the notary writes below the mark 'Mark affixed by (name of signer by mark) in presence of (names and addresses of 2 witnesses) and undersigned notary'; or

"2. for a person physically unable to sign or make a mark, the person directs the notary to sign on his or her behalf in the presence of the person and 2 witnesses unaffected by the document, both witnesses sign their own names beside the signature, and the notary writes below the signature: 'Signature affixed by notary in presence of (names and addresses of person and 2 witnesses)'" (MAC Sect. 501).

A signature by mark may be notarized through an acknowledgment, jurat or signature witnessing (MAC Sect. 201[3][d]).

NOTARY DON'TS

Notary May Not

A Mississippi Notary Public may (MAC Sect. 201[2]):

1. NOT notarize if the principal is not in the Notary's presence at the time of notarization;
2. NOT notarize if the principal is not personally known to the Notary or identified by the Notary through satisfactory evidence;
3. NOT notarize if the principal shows a demeanor which causes the notary to have compelling doubt about whether the principal knows the consequences of the transaction requiring a notarial act;
4. NOT notarize if, in the Notary's judgment, the principal is not acting of his or her own free will.

Disqualifications

"A notary is disqualified from performing a notarial act if the notary:

"1. is a party to or named in the document that is to be notarized;

"2. is a spouse, ancestor, descendant, or sibling of the principal, including in-law, step, or half relatives and other persons residing in the same household;

"3. will receive as a direct or indirect result any commission, fee, advantage, right, title, interest, cash, property, or other consideration exceeding in value the fees specified in this Chapter;

"a. an employee notary is not disqualified from performing a notarial act solely by virtue (of) the employee/employer relationship, participation in an employee stock ownership plan (ESOP), or a qualified retirement plan.

"b. an attorney notary is not disqualified from performing a notarial act solely by virtue of the attorney/client relationship.

"c. a shareholder notary is not disqualified solely by virtue of a corporation/shareholder relationship" (MAC Sect. 202).

Corporate Notaries Not Disqualified: Notaries who are stockholders, directors, officers or employees of a bank or other corporation may notarize for that bank or corporation, unless they are parties to the transaction, either individually or as a representative (MCA 25-33-21).

May Not Copy-Certify Certain Records

A Notary who is not an employee of the issuing government agency may not certify or authenticate a copy of any official government document, including but not limited to: (a) a birth certificate, (b) a death certificate, (c) a driver's license, (d) a passport, (e) a Social Security card and (f) any official government-issued identity card (MAC Sect. 206[3]).

However, "(n)othing in this section shall prohibit a Notary from notarizing a signature on a document which has a copy of an official government document embedded or attached as an exhibit."

Improper Documents

A Notary may not notarize a signature (a) on a blank or incomplete document or (b) on a document without notarial certificate wording (MAC Sect. 206[1]).

"A notary shall neither certify nor authenticate a photograph" (MAC Sect. 206[2]).

Refusal to Notarize

"1. A notary shall not refuse to perform a notarial act based on the principal's race, advanced age, gender, religion, national origin, health or disability.

"2. A notary shall perform any notarial act described in this Chapter for any person requesting such an act who tenders the appropriate fee, unless:

"a. the notary knows or has good reason to believe that the notarial act or the associated transaction is unlawful;

"b. the act is prohibited under this Chapter;

"c. the number of notarial acts requested practicably precludes completion of all acts at once, in which case the notary shall arrange for later completion of the remaining acts; or

"3. A notary may but is not required to perform a notarial act outside the notary's regular workplace or business hours" (MAC Sect. 203).

Avoidance of Influence

"1. A notary shall not influence a person either to enter into or avoid a transaction involving a notarial act by the notary, except that the notary may advise against a transaction if Section 201(2)(c) or (d) of this Chapter applies. (These subsections prohibit notarizing if the signer shows a demeanor causing the Notary to have a compelling doubt about whether the signer knows what he or she is doing, or if the signer appears not to be acting of his or her own free will.)

"2. A notary has neither the duty nor the authority to investigate, ascertain, or attest the lawfulness, propriety, accuracy, or truthfulness of a document or transaction involving a notarial act" (MAC Sect. 204).

Improper Certificates

"1. A notary shall not execute a certificate containing information known or believed by the notary to be false.

"2. A notary shall not affix an official signature or seal on a notarial certificate that is incomplete.

"3. A notary shall not provide or send a signed or sealed notarial certificate to another person with the understanding that it will be completed or attached to a document outside of the notary's presence" (MAC Sect. 205).

Intent to Deceive

"A notary shall not perform any official action with the intent to deceive or defraud" (MAC Sect. 207).

Testimonials

"A notary shall not use the official notary title or seal to endorse, promote, denounce, or oppose any product, service, contest, candidate, or other offering" (MAC Sect. 208).

Unauthorized Practice of Law

"1. If notarial certificate wording is not provided or indicated for a document, a non-attorney notary shall not determine the type of notarial act or certificate to be used.

"2. A non-attorney notary shall not assist another person in drafting, completing, selecting, or understanding a document or transaction requiring a notarial act.

"3. This section does not preclude a notary who is duly qualified, trained, or experienced in a particular industry or professional field from selecting, drafting, completing, or advising on a document or certificate related to a matter within that industry or field.

"4. A notary shall not claim to have powers, qualifications, rights, or privileges that the office of notary does not provide, including the power to counsel on immigration matters" (MAC Sect. 209).

Preventing Abuse of Immigrants

The following statutory provisions were

enacted to prevent exploitation of immigrants who do not understand the Notary's role in the U.S. legal system:

Not Advertise as Immigration Consultant: "A notary public who is not an attorney licensed to practice law is prohibited from representing or advertising that the notary public is an immigration consultant, immigration paralegal or expert on immigration matters unless the notary public is an accredited representative of an organization recognized by the board of immigration appeals pursuant to 8 CFR Section 292, 2 (a-e) or any subsequent federal law" (MCA 25-33-27).

Notice that Notary Is Not Attorney: "A notary public who is not an attorney licensed to practice law in this state and, who advertises in any language the person's services as a notary public by radio, television, signs, pamphlets, newspapers, telephone directory or other written or oral communication, or in any other advertisement, shall include with such advertisement the notice set forth in this section in English and/or in any other languages used in the advertisement. The notice shall be of conspicuous size and shall state: 'I AM NOT AN ATTORNEY LICENSED TO PRACTICE LAW IN THE STATE OF MISSISSIPPI AND I MAY NOT GIVE LEGAL ADVICE OR ACCEPT FEES FOR LEGAL ADVICE.'

"An advertisement on radio or television must include substantially the same message" (MCA 25-33-25).

The Mississippi Administrative Code (MAC Sect. 209[5]) prescribes slightly different rules for non-English ads for notarial services: (a) the prominently displayed statement in the foreign language must read: "I am not an attorney and have no authority to give advice on immigration or other legal matters"; (b) the fees for notarial acts must also be stated in the foreign language; and the term "notario publico" or any equivalent non-English term may not be used.

Exceptions: "The provisions of Sections 25-33-25 through 25-33-31 shall not apply to:

"(a) Notary services offered by a state or national bank trust company, savings and loan association, savings bank or by any affiliate or subsidiary of such state or national bank, trust company, savings and loan association, or savings bank or any agent or employee thereof; or

"(b) Any offering of notary services or listing of fees for notary services as a part of the closing of any loan transaction, extension of credit, security instrument or transfer of title" (MCA 25-33-29).

NOTARY SIGNING AGENTS

Currently, there are no statutes, regulations or rules expressly governing, prohibiting or restricting the operation of Notary Signing Agents within the state of Mississippi.

NOTARY FEES

"Notaries public may charge a fee in an amount of not less than two dollars ($2.00) nor more than five dollars ($5.00) for services rendered ..." (MCA 25-7-29). This is to be applied per signature notarized, per affiant sworn or per individual notarial act executed.

Maximum Fees
The maximum fees that may be charged by a Mississippi Notary for performing notarial acts are (MAC Sect. 302[1]):
1. Taking an acknowledgment: $5 per signature;
2. Administering an oath or affirmation without a signature: $5 per person;
3. Executing a jurat: $5 per signature;
4. Witnessing a signature: $5 per signature.

Minimum Fee
While "a notary may charge the maximum fee specified in Section 302, charge less than the maximum fee, or waive the fee" (MAC Sect. 301), according to the office of the Secretary of State, if a fee is charged for a notarial act, it must be no less than $2 (MCA 25-7-29).

Travel Fee
"A notary may charge a travel fee when traveling to perform a notarial act if: (a) the notary and the person requesting the notarial act agree upon the travel fee in advance of the travel; and (b) the notary explains to the person requesting the notarial act that the travel fee is both separate from the notarial fee ... and neither specified nor mandated by law" (MAC Sect. 302[2]).

Payment Prior to Act
A Notary may require payment of fees for notarization and for travel prior to performance

of a notarial act (MAC Sect. 303). These fees are non-refundable if: (a) the act was completed or (b) in the case of travel fees, the act was not completed for reasons stated in Sections 201 through 206 after the Notary had traveled to meet the principal.

Fees of Employee Notary

"An employer may prohibit an employee who is a notary from charging for notarial acts performed on the employer's time" (MAC Sect. 304).

Notice of Fees

"Notaries who charge for their notarial services shall conspicuously display in their places of business, or present to each principal outside their places of business, an English-language schedule of fees for notarial acts, as specified in Section 302" (MAC Sect. 305).

Discriminatory Charging

"A notary shall not discriminatorily condition the fee for a notarial act on the attributes of the principal as delineated in Section 203, though a notary may waive or reduce fees for humanitarian or charitable reasons" (MAC Sect. 301[2]).

NOTARIAL CERTIFICATES

Notary May Not Draft Certificate

"The party drafting a document for notarization is responsible for the form of the certificate, its wording and legal sufficiency. A notary public is not required to draft, edit or amend a certificate where the document presented does not contain an acceptable certificate; the notary shall instead, refuse to notarize the document pursuant to Rule 206" (MAC Sect. 500). Note: Rule 206 prohibits notarization of a document without notarial certificate wording.

Acknowledgment by Individual (MCA 89-3-7[a]):

STATE OF _____
COUNTY OF _____

Personally appeared before me, the undersigned authority in and for the said county and state, on this _____ day of _____, 20__, within my jurisdiction, the within named _____, who acknowledged that he/she/they executed the above and foregoing instrument.

_____ (NOTARY PUBLIC)
My commission expires: _____ (Seal)

Acknowledgment by Corporation (MCA 89-3-7[b]):

STATE OF _____
COUNTY OF _____

Personally appeared before me, the undersigned authority in and for the said county and state, on this _____ day of _____, 20__, within my jurisdiction, the within named _____, who acknowledged that he/she is _____ of _____, a _____ corporation, and that for and on behalf of the said corporation, and as its act and deed he/she executed the above and foregoing instrument, after first having been duly authorized by said corporation so to do.

_____ (NOTARY PUBLIC)
My commission expires: _____ (Seal)

Acknowledgment by Corporate General Partner of Limited Partnership (MCA 89-3-7[c]):

STATE OF _____
COUNTY OF _____

Personally appeared before me, the undersigned authority in and for the said county and state, on this _____ day of _____, 20__, within my jurisdiction, the within named _____, who acknowledged that (he)(she) is _____ of _____, a _____ corporation and general partner of _____, a _____ limited partnership, and that for and on behalf of said corporation as general partner of said limited partnership, and as the act and deed of said corporation as general partner of said limited partnership, and as the act and deed of said limited partnership, (he)(she) executed the above and foregoing instrument, after first having been duly authorized by said corporation and said limited partnership so to do.

_____ (NOTARY PUBLIC)
My commission expires: _____ (Seal)

Acknowledgment by Corporate Member of Member-Managed Limited Liability Company (MCA 89-3-7[d]):

STATE OF _____
COUNTY OF _____

Personally appeared before me, the undersigned authority in and for the said county and state, on this ____ day of _____, 20__, within my jurisdiction, the within named _____, who acknowledged that (he)(she) is _____ of _____, a _____ corporation and member of _____, a _____ member-managed limited liability company, and that for and on behalf of said corporation as member of said limited liability company, and as the act and deed of said corporation as member of said limited liability company, and as the act and deed of said limited liability company, (he)(she) executed the above and foregoing instrument, after first having been duly authorized by said corporation and said limited liability company so to do.

_____(NOTARY PUBLIC)
My commission expires: _____ (Seal)

Acknowledgment by Corporate Manager of Manager-Managed Limited Liability Company (MCA 89-3-7[e]):

STATE OF _____
COUNTY OF _____

Personally appeared before me, the undersigned authority in and for the said county and state, on this ____ day of _____, 20__, within my jurisdiction, the within named _____, who acknowledged that (he)(she) is _____ of _____, a _____ corporation and manager of _____, a _____ manager-managed limited liability company, and that for and on behalf of said corporation as manager of said limited liability company, and as the act and deed of said corporation as manager of said limited liability company, and as the act and deed of said limited liability company, (he)(she) executed the above and foregoing instrument, after first having been duly authorized by said corporation and said limited liability company so to do.

_____(NOTARY PUBLIC)
My commission expires: _____ (Seal)

Acknowledgment by Representative (MCA 89-3-7[f]):

STATE OF _____
COUNTY OF _____

Personally appeared before me, the undersigned authority in and for the said county and state, on this ____ day of _____, 20__, within my jurisdiction, the within named _____, who acknowledged that he/she is _____ of _____ and that in said representative capacity he/she executed the above and foregoing instrument, after first having been duly authorized so to do.

_____(NOTARY PUBLIC)
My commission expires: _____ (Seal)

Proof by Subscribing Witness (MCA 89-3-7[g]):

STATE OF _____
COUNTY OF _____

Personally appeared before me, the undersigned authority in and for the said county and state, on this ____ day of _____, 20__, within my jurisdiction, _____ (name of subscribing witness 1), one of the subscribing witnesses to the above and foregoing instrument, who, being first duly sworn, states that he/she saw the within (or above) named _____ (name of principal signer), whose name is subscribed thereto, sign and deliver the same to _____ (name of subscribing witness 2) (or that he/she heard _____ [name of principal signer] acknowledge that he/she signed and delivered the same to _____ [name of subscribing witness 2]); and that the affiant (i.e., subscribing witness 1) subscribed his/her name as witness thereto in the presence of _____ (name of principal signer).

_____ (Signature of subscribing witness 1)

_____(NOTARY PUBLIC)
My commission expires: _____ (Seal)

Acknowledgement by Any Business Organization, Foreign or Domestic (MCA 89-3-7[h]):

*STATE OF _____
COUNTY OF _____*

Personally appeared before me, the undersigned authority in and for the said county and state, on this _____ day of _____, 20__, within my jurisdiction, _____ the within named _____, who proved to me on the basis of satisfactory evidence to be the person(s) whose name(s) is/are subscribed in the above and foregoing instrument and acknowledged that he/she/they executed the same in his/her/their representative capacity(ies), and that by his/her/their signature(s) on the instrument, and as the act and deed of ther person(s) or entity(ies) upon behalf of which he/she/they acted, executed the above and foregoing instrument, after first having been duly authorized so to do.

_____ *(NOTARY PUBLIC)*
My commission expires: _____ *(Seal)*

Certificate of U.S. Military Officer

The notarial acts of U.S. commissioned military officers are recognized, as follows (MCA 25-33-23):

"In the taking of acknowledgments and the performing of other notarial acts requiring certification, a certificate endorsed upon or attached to the instrument or documents, which shows the date of the notarial act and which states, in substance, that the person appearing before the officer acknowledged the instrument as his act or made or signed the instrument or document under oath, shall be sufficient for all intents and purposes. The instrument or document shall not be rendered invalid by the failure to state the place of execution or acknowledgment.

"If the signature, rank, and branch of service or subdivision thereof, of any such commissioned officer appear upon such instrument or document or certificate, no further proof of the authority of such officer so to act shall be required ...."

Correcting Notarial Certificate

"If an attestation of a notary public is questioned as to its authenticity or correctness of language, the notary public may file an affidavit regarding the truth of the attestation in question along with any corrected language and may file such with the land records in the office of the Chancery Clerk where such land is located, properly indexed, if such authenticity or correctness of language affects real property. Such affidavit shall be a rebuttable presumption that the attestation is true and correct" (MCA 25-33-9).

Curative Law for Imperfect Certificates

"1. Concerning an interest in land, whenever an instrument of conveyance (including but not limited to a deed of trust or assignment), release, termination or cancellation which contains a defective acknowledgment has been of record seven (7) years or more in the land records of the county in which the said land is located, the acknowledgment shall be good without regard to the form of the certificate of acknowledgment.

"2. Any such instrument which has been of record for ten (10) years and which bears no acknowledgment shall likewise be treated as if properly acknowledged" (MCA 89-5-13).

ELECTRONIC NOTARIZATIONS

The state of Mississippi has not yet adopted statutes or regulations expressly establishing rules, definitions and procedures for electronic notarization.

UETA Recognizes Notary's eSignature

Mississippi has adopted the Uniform Electronic Transactions Act (MCA 75-12-1, et seq.), including the provision on notarization and acknowledgment, thereby recognizing the legal validity of electronic signatures used by Notaries:

"If a law requires a signature or record to be notarized, acknowledged, verified, or made under oath, the requirement is satisfied if the electronic signature of the person authorized to perform those acts, together with all other information required to be included by other applicable law, is attached to or logically associated with the signature or record" (MCA 75-12-21).

URPERA Permits eSignature by Notary

Mississippi has adopted the Uniform Real Property Electronic Recording Act, permitting a Notary to use an electronic signature to notarize a recordable electronic document without affixing an image of the Notary's official physical seal. As long as the information within the seal is "attached to or logically associated with the document or signature," a Notary is not required to place an image of a Notary seal on the electronic document (MCA 89-3-1, 89-5-1 and 89-5-3).

NOTARY RECORDS

"A notary shall keep, maintain, protect, and provide for lawful inspection a chronological official journal of notarial acts (in) a permanently bound book with numbered pages .... A notary shall keep no more than one active journal at the same time" (MAC Sect. 401.01). "'Journal of notarial acts' and 'journal' mean a device for creating and preserving a chronological record of notarizations performed by a notary" (MAC Sect. 101.07).

Required Entries

"For every notarial act, the notary shall record in the journal at the time of notarization at least the following: (a) the date and time of day of the notarial act; (b) the type of notarial act; (c) the type, title, or a description of the document or proceeding; (d) the printed name and address of each principal; (e) the fee, if any, charged for the notarial act; (f) the address where the notarization was performed if not the notary's business address; and (g) if the principal is not personally known ... the notary may require, the signature of the principal and the evidence of identity of each principal, in the form of either: a notation of the type of identification document, its issuing agency, its serial or identification number, and its date of issuance or expiration" (MAC Sect. 401.02[1]).

"A notary shall not record a Social Security or credit card number in the journal" (MAC Sect. 401.02[2]).

"A notary shall record in the journal the circumstances for not completing a notarial act" (MAC Sect. 401.03[3]).

"As required in Section 401.03, a notary shall record in the journal the circumstances of any request to inspect or copy an entry in the journal, including the requester's name, address, signature, and evidence of identity. The reasons for refusal to allow inspection or copying of a journal entry shall also be recorded" (MAC Sect. 401.02[4]).

Record of Protests

"When any notary public, justice of the peace, or clerk shall protest any bill of exchange or promissory note, he shall make a full and true record in his register or book kept for that purpose of all his proceedings in relation thereto, and shall note thereon whether demand of the sum of money therein mentioned was made, of whom, when, and where; whether he presented such bill or note; whether notices were given, to whom, and in what manner; where the same was mailed, and when and to whom and where directed; and of every other fact touching the same" (MCA 25-33-15).

Inspection and Copying of Journal

"Every notary public shall keep a fair register of all his official acts, and shall give a certified copy of his record, or any part thereof, to any person applying for it and paying the legal fees therefor" (MCA 25-33-5).

"In the notary's presence, any person may inspect an entry in the official journal of notarial acts during regular business hours, but only if: (a) the person's identity is personally known to the notary or proven through satisfactory evidence; (b) the person affixes a signature in the journal in a separate, dated entry; (c) the person specifies the month, year, type of document, and name of the principal for the notarial act or acts sought; and (d) the person is shown only the entry or entries specified" (MAC Sect. 401.03[1]).

"Upon complying with a request under Subsection (1), the notary shall provide a copy of a specified entry or entries in the journal at a cost of not more than five dollars ($5.00) per copy; other entries on the same page shall be masked" (MAC Sect. 401.03[4]).

When Access May Be Denied: "If the notary has a reasonable and explainable belief that a person bears a criminal or harmful intent in requesting information from the notary's journal, the notary may deny access to any entry or entries" (MAC Sect. 401.03[2]).

Unrestricted Examination: "The journal may be examined without restriction by a law enforcement officer in the course of an investigation, subpoenaed by court order, or surrendered at the direction of the Secretary of State" (MAC Sect. 401.03[3]).

Safeguarding the Journal

"A notary shall safeguard the journal and all other notarial records and surrender or destroy them only by rule of law, by court order, or at the direction of the Secretary of State" (MAC Sect. 401.03[5]).

"When not in use, the journal shall be kept in a secure area under the exclusive control of the notary, and shall not be used by any other notary nor surrendered to an employer upon termination of employment" (MAC Sect. 401.03[6]).

Stolen, Lost, Damaged Journal

"Within 10 days after the journal is stolen, lost, destroyed, damaged, or otherwise rendered unusable or unreadable as a record of notarial acts, the notary after informing the appropriate law enforcement agency in the case of theft or vandalism, shall notify the Secretary of State by any means providing a tangible receipt or acknowledgment, including certified mail and electronic transmission, and also provide a copy or number of any pertinent police report" (MAC Sect. 401.03[7]).

Disposition of Journal

"In the case of the death, resignation, disqualification or expiration of the term of office of any notary public, his registers and other public papers shall, within thirty (30) days, be lodged in the office of the clerk of the circuit court of the county of his residence; and the clerk of that county may maintain an action for them" (MCA 25-33-7).

"A former notary who intends to apply for a new commission and whose previous commission or application was not revoked or denied by this State, need not deliver the journal and records within 30 days after commission expiration, but must do so within 6 months after expiration unless recommissioned within that period" (MAC Sect. 602.[2]).

AUTHENTICATION OF NOTARIAL ACTS

Secretary of State

Certificates authenticating the acts of all Mississippi Notaries, including apostilles, are issued by the Secretary of State.

Fees: $2 per document for a certificate authenticating the act of a Notary or other public official, including an apostille. Checks or money orders payable to "Secretary of State."

Address:
Office of Secretary of State
P.O. Box 136
Jackson, MS 39205-0136
Attention: Notary/Apostille/Authentication

For Delivery Services:
Office of Secretary of State
700 North Street
Jackson, MS 39202

Telephone: 1-601-359-1615

Procedure: Mail or present in person the original document(s) notarized by a Mississippi Notary Public or bearing the signature of a Mississippi Public official, along with the $2 fee(s). For mail-ins, an "Apostille Certification Request" form should be sent that includes a name, address and daytime telephone, and indicates the country of destination. This form is available on the website and may be completed by computer before it is printed out.

"NOTE: If you elect to use Federal Express or UPS to send your documents to the Secretary of State's office and would like the same in return, you MUST include in your original Federal Express/ UPS envelope, an additional PREPAID completed Federal Express/UPS return envelope to return your documents to the desired destination. Please be aware that if you do not include a return Federal Express/UPS pre-paid envelope your documents will be returned by regular mail" (website, "Apostilles and Authentications").

COMMISSIONING AND ADMINISTRATION

While the Governor nominally appoints Mississippi's Notaries (MCA 25-33-1), the Secretary of State oversees the application process and maintains records on these Notaries.

Applying for Commission

Qualifications: An applicant for a Mississippi Notary commission must: (a) be at least 18 years old, (b) be a citizen or a permanent legal resident of the United States, (c) have resided in the state of Mississippi for at least 30 days prior to the application, (d) read and write the English language, (e) not be convicted of a felony (unless pardoned by the Governor or had voting rights restored by the state Legislature) and not be currently incarcerated, on probation or parole and (f) meet any other requirements the Secretary of State may set by rule (MCA 25-33-1 and MAC Sect. 102).

No Course or Test: There is no requirement that applicants take a course of instruction or a test on their duties.

Application: The application must be notarized by another Notary before it is submitted to the Secretary of State. The commission fee is $25. An electronic application form (11NP001) is available on the website that may be completed by computer before it is printed out for signing and notarization.

Filing After Pre-Commissioning: The following instructions appeared in the "Mississippi Notary Public Reference Guide," formerly published by the Secretary of State: "If the application is complete and accompanied by the fee, the Secretary of State transmits it to the Governor. If the Governor approves the application, a pre-commission certificate is mailed to the applicant. The applicant is not a notary at this point.

"After receiving the pre-commission certificate, the applicant must obtain the proper $5,000 surety bond and oath. The bond should not be obtained prior to receiving the pre-commission certificate. The applicant should make certain he or she signed the bond as principal, and signed the oath in the presence of a notary. The surety bond and oath should be mailed to the Mississippi Secretary of State's office.

"The law requires that the surety bond be approved by the insurance commissioner and the governor before a commission can be issued. Once both officials have approved the bond, the Secretary of State's office will mail the applicant his or her original Commission Certificate.

"Once the applicant has received his or her Commission Certificate, he or she should obtain a legally suitable notarial seal. Only after being properly commissioned, bonded, and obtaining his or her seal should the notary perform notarial acts."

To renew the commission, within 60 days prior to expiration of the current commission, the Notary must file a new application and, when approved, submit a new bond (website, "Frequently Asked Questions," and MAC Sect. 110).

Non-Residents: A non-resident of Mississippi may not become a Notary in the state.

Online Search: Online search of the current Mississippi Notary roll by name, city, employer and county of residence is available at www.sos.ms.gov/business_services_notaries3.aspx.

Through this search, a Notary's telephone, employment address, county, identification number, and commission expiration date are available.

Changes of Status

If Notary Moves: "Within 30 days after the change of a notary's residence, business, or mailing address, the notary shall send to the Secretary of State a signed notice of the change, giving both old and new addresses on SOS Form NP 004, Application for Notary Public Change of Address" (MAC Sect. 601.01). This form is available on the website and may be completed by computer before it is printed out and signed. There is a $20 fee for an address change.

A new seal or stamp must be obtained that show the Notary's new county of residence.

If Notary Changes Name: Within 30 days after the change of Notary's name by court order or marriage, the Notary must send the Secretary of State a signed notice of the change, giving both former and new names and a copy of any official authorization (marriage license, etc.), on SOS Form NP 005, "Application for Notary Public Change of Name" (MAC Sect. 601.02). This form is available on the website and may be completed by computer before it is printed out and signed. There is a $20 fee for a name change.

A Notary with a new name must continue using the former name in performing notarial acts until the following steps have been completed: (a) the notice described above has been delivered or transmitted, (b) a "Confirmation of Notary's Name" has been received from the Secretary of State and a replacement commission issued, (c) a new seal bearing the new name exactly as in the replacement commission has been obtained and (d) the surety for the notary's bond has been informed in writing (MAC Sect. 601.02[2]).

Resignation: A Notary who resigns a commission must send a signed notice to the Secretary of

State, indicating the effective date of resignation on SOS Form NP 007, "Notice of Notary Resignation or Death" (MAC Sect. 601.03[1]). This form is available on the website and may be completed by computer before it is printed out and signed. There is no fee for a resignation.

A Notary who ceases to reside in or to maintain a regular place of work or business in the state, or who becomes permanently unable to perform notarial duties, must resign his or her commission (MAC Sect. 601.03[2]).

Death of Notary: If a Notary dies during the commission term before disposing of the seal and journal as prescribed in MAC Sect. 602, the Notary's personal representative must: (a) notify the Secretary of State in writing using the SOS Form NP 007 cited above under "Resignation" (no fee is required), (b) destroy or deface all Notary seals so that they may not be misused, as soon as reasonably practicable and (c) within six months after death, send the journal and any other notarial records to the respective county circuit court clerk (MAC Sect. 603).

COUNTY CLERKS

Effective July 1, 1988, each new Notary files an oath and duplicate original bond with the Secretary of State, rather than with the county clerk, as before when Notaries had only county-wide authority. Thus, county clerks now have no record of local Notaries and no longer may authenticate their acts.

County Clerks Keep Notary Registers

Notary registers of notarial acts must be surrendered to the clerk of the county in which the Notary resides within 30 days of the Notary's death, resignation, disqualification or commission expiration (MCA 25-33-7).

To track down the records of a particular Notary at the office of a county clerk, telephone long-distance information — 1-XXX-555-1212 — using one of the area codes below:

County (Code)*	City/Town	Area Code
Adams (1)	Natchez	(601)
Alcorn (2)	Corinth	(662)
Amite (3)	Liberty	(601)
Attala (4)	Kosciusko	(662)
Benton (5)	Ashland	(662)
Bolivar (6)	Rosedale	(601)
	Cleveland	(662)
Calhoun (7)	Pittsboro	(662)
Carroll (8)	Carrollton	(662)
Chickasaw (9)	Houston	(662)
Choctaw (10)	Ackerman	(662)
Claiborne (11)	Port Gibson	(601)
Clarke (12)	Quitman	(601)
Clay (13)	West Point	(662)
Coahoma (14)	Clarksdale	(662)
Copiah (15)	Hazlehurst	(601)
Covington (16)	Collins	(601)
DeSoto (17)	Hernando	(662)
Forrest (18)	Hattiesburg	(601)
Franklin (19)	Meadville	(601)
George (20)	Lucedale	(601)
Greene (21)	Leakesville	(601)
Grenada (22)	Grenada	(662)
Hancock (23)	Bay St. Louis	(228)
Harrison (24)	Biloxi	(228)
	Gulfport	(228)
Hinds (25)	Jackson	(601)
Holmes (26)	Lexington	(662)
Humphreys (27)	Belzoni	(662)
Issaquena (28)	Mayersville	(662)
Itawamba (29)	Fulton	(662)
Jackson (30)	Pascagoula	(228)
Jasper (31)	Bay Springs	(601)
Jefferson (32)	Fayette	(601)
Jefferson Davis (33)	Prentiss	(601)
Jones (34)	Laurel	(601)
	Ellisville	(601)
Kemper (35)	De Kalb	(601)
Lafayette (36)	Oxford	(662)
Lamar (37)	Purvis	(601)
Lauderdale (38)	Meridian	(601)
Lawrence (39)	Monticello	(601)
Leake (40)	Carthage	(601)
Lee (41)	Tupelo	(662)
Leflore (42)	Greenwood	(662)
Lincoln (43)	Brookhaven	(601)
Lowndes (44)	Columbus	(662)
Madison (45)	Canton	(601)
Marion (46)	Columbia	(601)
Marshall (47)	Holly Springs	(662)
Monroe (48)	Aberdeen	(662)
Montgomery (49)	Winona	(662)
Neshoba (50)	Philadelphia	(601)
Newton (51)	Decatur	(601)

County (Code)*	City/Town	Area Code
Noxubee (52)	Macon	(662)
Oktibbeha (53)	Starkville	(662)
Panola (54)	Batesville	(662)
Pearl River (55)	Poplarville	(601)
Perry (56)	New Augusta	(601)
Pike (57)	Magnolia	(601)
Pontotoc (58)	Pontotoc	(662)
Prentiss (59)	Booneville	(662)
Quitman (60)	Marks	(662)
Rankin (61)	Brandon	(601)
Scott (62)	Forest	(601)
Sharkey (63)	Rolling Fork	(662)
Simpson (64)	Mendenhall	(601)
Smith (65)	Raleigh	(601)
Stone (66)	Wiggins	(601)
Sunflower (67)	Indianola	(662)
Tallahatchie (68)	Charleston	(662)
Tate (69)	Senatobia	(662)
Tippah (70)	Ripley	(662)
Tishomingo (71)	Iuka	(662)
Tunica (72)	Tunica	(662)
Union (73)	New Albany	(662)
Walthall (74)	Tylertown	(601)
Warren (75)	Vicksburg	(601)
Washington (76)	Greenville	(662)
Wayne (77)	Waynesboro	(601)
Webster (78)	Walthall	(662)
Wilkinson (79)	Woodville	(601)
Winston (80)	Louisville	(662)
Yalobusha (81)	Water Valley	(662)
	Coffeeville	(601)
Yazoo (82)	Yazoo City	(662)

* County codes are occasionally used in filling out Notary and UCC forms.

OTHER NOTARIAL OFFICERS

Ex Officio Notaries

Ex officio, the following officials have the same powers as Notaries and, when acting, "may authenticate all their acts, instruments and attestations by the common seal of office" (MCA 25-33-17):

1. Justice court judges and clerks;
2. Circuit and chancery court clerks;
3. Assistant secretaries of state.

May Take Acknowledgments and Proofs

Power to take acknowledgment or proof of recordable documents is also given to the following officials (MCA 89-3-3):

1. U.S. court judges;
2. State supreme court judges;
3. Circuit court judges;
4. Chancellors;
5. Judges of county courts;
6. Clerks of courts of record;
7. Justices of the peace;
8. Police justices;
9. Mayors of any city, town or village;
10. Clerks of a municipality;
11. Members of board of supervisors.

QUICK FACTS

Notary Jurisdiction
Statewide (MCA 25-33-1). However, before July 1, 1988, when Chapter 456, Laws of 1988, took effect, jurisdiction was only countywide in one or more counties.

Notary Term Length
Four years (MCA 25-33-1), expiring at midnight on the commission expiration date. "The (starting) date of the commission shall be the date the completed application was received by the Secretary of State; however, an applicant may not perform notarial acts prior to the actual issuance of the notary commission" (MAC Sect. 109).

Notary Bond
$5,000, with the surety licensed by the Mississippi Department of Insurance (MCA 25-33-1).

Missouri

NOTARY SEAL

A Missouri Notary Public must "provide, keep, and use" an official seal (RSMo 486.285), and the seal's format must be as follows:

Kind

Black-Inked Rubber Stamp or Embosser: The seal must be "either an engraved embosser seal or a black inked rubber stamp seal" (RSMo 486.285[1]).

Shape/Size

State officials recommend that any inking seal be rectangular, though a circular inking seal is lawful. The embosser traditionally is circular. No size is specified for either.

Minimum Type Size: The wording within a Notary seal must be affixed "in print not smaller than eight-point type" (RSMo 486.285[1]).

Examples

The above typical, actual-size examples of rubber stamp and embossing Notary seals are allowed by Missouri law. Other formats may also be permitted.

NOTARY ADMINISTRATION

Office of Secretary of State
Commissions Division 1-573-751-2783
Kirkpatrick State 1-866-223-6535
Info Center
P.O. Box 784
(600 W. Main St., Room 322)
Jefferson City, MO 65102-0784

Website: www.sos.mo.gov/business/commissions

NOTARY RULES

RSMo — Revised Statutes of Missouri
NPH — Notary Public Handbook

Most Notary regulations are in the Revised Statutes of Missouri 1986, Title XXXII, Chapter 486, "Commissioners of Deeds and Notaries Public."

Other guidelines are in the "Missouri Notary Handbook" (revised May 2011), issued by the Secretary of State and available on the website.

Components

Black-Inked Rubber Stamp: A rectangular inking seal must have the following information (RSMo 486.280 and 486.285[1] and MNH):

1. Notary's name, exactly as it appears on the commission;
2. "Notary Public";
3. "Notary Seal";
4. "State of Missouri";
5. Name of county where Notary is commissioned (or "St. Louis City");
6. "My commission expires _____ (date)";
7. Notary's assigned commission number (required for commissions issued on or after August 28, 2004).

NOTE: "The Great Seal of the State of Missouri cannot be used on the notary stamp" (MNH).

Embosser: An embossing seal must contain the following information (RSMo 486.285[1]):

1. Notary's name, exactly as it appears on the commission;
2. "Notary Seal";
3. "Notary Public";
4. Notary's assigned commission number (required for commissions issued on or after August 28, 2004);
5. "State of Missouri."

Additional Information with Embosser: If an embosser seal is used, the Notary additionally must rubber stamp, typewrite or print "clearly and legibly, in print not smaller than eight-point type …, so that it is capable of photographic reproduction," the following data on the notarial certificate portion of each document (RSMo 486.280):
6. Notary's name, exactly as it appears on the commission;
7. "Notary Public";
8. "State of Missouri";
9. Name of county where Notary is commissioned (or "St. Louis City");
10. "My commission expires _____ (date)";
11. Notary's assigned commission number (required for commissions issued on or after August 28, 2004).

The following is an example of a stamp format for the additional information required above:

Richard A. Roe
Notary Public – State of Missouri
Mississippi County
My Commission Expires Jan 30, 2015
Commission # 12345678

Seal May Not Overlap Text

"The indentations made by the seal embosser or printed by the black inked rubber stamp seal shall not be applied on the notarial certificate or document to be notarized in a manner that will render illegible or incapable of photographic reproduction any of the printed marks or writing on the certificate or document" (RSMo 486.285[2]).

Illegibility of Certificate

The illegibility of any information described above does not affect the validity of a transaction (RSMo 486.290).

Lost or Stolen Seal

"If the notary's notary seal has been stolen, the notary shall immediately notify the secretary of state in writing to report the theft. Upon receipt of the written documentation, the secretary of state shall issue the notary a new commission number for the notary to order a new seal. The secretary of state may post notice on the secretary of state's website notifying the general public that the notary seal of such notary with the stolen commission number is invalid and is not an acceptable notary commission number" (RSMo 486.396).

"Any notary public who loses or misplaces his … official seal shall forthwith mail or deliver notice of the fact to the secretary of state" (RSMo 486.305).

"The date the seal … was lost or stolen should be noted in the notary records. The notary may also want to contact their local police department and see if they require a police report to be filed for stolen goods" (MNH).

Unlawful Possession of Seal

"Every notary shall keep an official notarial seal that is the exclusive property of the notary and the seal may not be used by any other person or surrendered to an employer upon termination of employment" (RSMo 486.285[3]).

"Any person who unlawfully possesses a notary's … official seal … is guilty of a misdemeanor and is punishable upon conviction by a fine not exceeding five hundred dollars" (RSMo 486.380).

Official Signature of Notary

"At the time of notarization a notary public shall sign his official signature on each notary certificate" (RSMo 486.275).

NOTARY POWERS

Missouri Notaries are authorized to perform the following notarial acts (RSMo 486.250 and 486.340):
1. Take acknowledgments* and proofs**;
2. Administer oaths and affirmations***;
3. Certify true copies****;
4. "Perform any other act permitted by law."

* Identifying Acknowledgers: No acknowledgment of a document affecting real estate may be taken unless the notarizing officer either (a) personally knows the acknowledger, or (b) bases the identification on at least two credible witnesses (RSMo 442.200). The names and places of residence of these credible witnesses must be inserted on the certificate (RSMo 442.210).

The state allows Missouri Notaries to rely on ID cards as a means to achieve the personal knowledge mentioned above in (a).

** Proof by Executing Witness: While taking a proof from an executing witness is not listed as a notarial duty in RSMo 486.250, this notarial power is recognized in other parts of the law. Under RSMo 486.340, an executing witness (also known as a subscribing witness in other states) may prove by an affidavit signed and sworn to before a Notary that a document was signed by another person not present before the Notary at the time of notarization. The executing witness may not be named individually as a party to the transaction or be related by blood or marriage to the principal signer (RSMo 486.340).

Absentee ballot forms may not be witnessed through an executing witness (Missouri Attorney General Opinion No. 114-83).

*** Affirmation Wording: A spoken affirmation may be worded as follows (RSMo 486.335[2]): "You do solemnly affirm, under the penalty of perjury, that the testimony you shall give in the matter in issue, pending between ____ and ____, shall be the truth, the whole truth, and nothing but the truth."

**** Certifying Copies: "A notary public may certify a facsimile of a document if he or she receives a signed written request stating that a certified copy or facsimile, preparation of a copy, or certification of a copy of the document does not violate any state or federal law.... Each notary public shall retain a facsimile of each document he or she has certified as a facsimile of another document, together with other papers or copies relating to his or her notarial acts" (RSMo 486.345[1] and [2]).

"DO NOT CERTIFY ANY COPIES OF DOCUMENTS WHICH STATE ON THE FACE OF THE DOCUMENT THEY CANNOT BE REPRODUCED. Copies of birth certificates, death certificates, marriage licenses and divorce decrees cannot be certified. Certified copies of these documents should be obtained from the issuing agency" (MNH).

"Birth and death certificates should be obtained from the Missouri Department of Health and Senior Services, Bureau of Vital Records.... Vital Records will issue a certified copy of these MISSOURI records.... Marriage licenses can sometimes be obtained from the county recorder of deeds offices where they have been recorded for public record. Divorce decrees can sometimes be obtained from the circuit clerk where they have been filed. The recorder of deeds or circuit clerk will issue and sign the copy of the original document" (MNH).

Journal Copies: "Each notary public, upon written court order, shall furnish facsimiles of entries made in his journal of notarial acts or any other papers or copies relating to his notarial acts, upon receipt of a fee of one dollar per $8\frac{1}{2}$ x 11-inch page or part of a page" (RSMo 486.270).

Forms of Identification

"The best form of identification is one that includes a photograph and signature. A valid driver's license is a good source of identification. The person can also be personally known to the notary or can be identified by an individual personally known to the notary" (MNH).

NOTARY DON'TS

Disqualifying Interests

A Notary individually named as a party to a transaction may not notarize for that transaction (RSMo 486.255).

"A notary cannot notarize his or her own signature. A notary is to be an impartial witness" (MNH).

Notarizing for Relatives: "Missouri law does not forbid notaries from notarizing the signatures of relatives. However, if the notarized document was ever the subject of a court suit, a judge might determine the notary was not an impartial witness to the signing of the document. The Office of Secretary of State suggests that a notary not notarize documents for a spouse, parent, grandparent, brother, sister, niece, nephew, aunt, uncle, child or grandchild" (MNH).

False Advertising

A Notary may not use "false or misleading advertising wherein he or she represents or implies, by virtue of the title of notary public, that he or she has qualifications, powers, duties, rights, or privileges that he or she does not possess by law" (RSMo 486.385[1][5]).

Foreign-Language Documents

"Notarizing a foreign language document is not illegal. CAUTION should be used as the notary is dependent upon the signer to explain the contents.... You may want to suggest to your constituent to find a notary who speaks the language.... If you are requested to notarize a document in another language you will want to note this in your journal. You may want to complete an English language notary certificate... (so) you will know what you have notarized because this can be stated in your certificate" (MNH).

No Executing Witness for Absentee Ballot

"On October 27, 1983, the attorney general issued Opinion No. 114-83, which states 'An executing witness, as provided for in Section 486.340, RSMo, is neither a notary public nor an officer authorized by law to administer oaths with the scope of Section 115.291.1, RSMo.' Therefore, the affidavit of a person voting an absentee ballot may not be subscribed and sworn to before an executing witness" (MNH).

NOTARY SIGNING AGENTS

Currently, there are no statutes, regulations or rules expressly governing, prohibiting or restricting the operation of Notary Signing Agents within the state of Missouri.

NOTARY FEES

The maximum fees that a Missouri Notary may charge for a notarial act are (RSMo 486.350 and 486.270):

1. Notarizing a signature, whether by acknowledgment or jurat: $2 per signature;
2. Administering an oath or affirmation, apart from a jurat: $1 per person;
3. Certifying a copy: $2 per 8½-by-11-inch page ($1 per page if Notary journal copy requested by court order);
4. Any other notarial act: $1.

Travel Fees

"A notary public may charge a travel fee, not to exceed the approved federal mileage rate and may charge an expedited convenience service charge not to exceed twenty-five dollars when traveling to perform a notarial act, provided that:

"1. The notary explains to the person requesting the notarial act that the travel fee is separate from the notarial fee and is not specified or mandated by law; and

"2. The notary and the person requesting the notarial act agree upon his or her fees in advance of the notary affixing his or her official seal" (RSMo 486.350[6]).

Absentee Ballot

No fee is allowed for notarizing an absentee ballot or absentee voter registration form (RSMo 486.350[4]).

NOTARY CERTIFICATES

Certificates for notarial acts authorized by Missouri law must be "in print not smaller than eight-point type" (RSMo 486.330) and in substantially the following forms, any of which may be used for real estate transactions:

Acknowledgment by Individual (RSMo 486.330[1]):

State of Missouri,
County (and/or City) of _____

On this ____ day of _____ in the year 20__ before me, _____ (name of Notary), a Notary Public in and for said state, personally appeared _____ (name of individual), known to me to be the person who executed the within _____ (type of document), and acknowledged to me that he/she executed the same for the purposes therein stated.

(NOTARY'S SIGNATURE, SEAL AND PHOTOCOPIABLE DATA THAT IS RUBBER-STAMPED, TYPED OR PRINTED)

Acknowledgment by Individual (RSMo 442.210[1]):

The following certificate may be used for documents affecting real estate, with the names and residences of any credible witnesses also noted on the certificate:

State of Missouri,
County (and/or City) of _____

On this _____ day of _____, 20__, before me personally appeared _____ (name of signer[s]), to me known to be the person (or persons*) described in and who executed the foregoing instrument, and acknowledged that he/she/they executed the same as his/her/their free act and deed.

(NOTARY'S SIGNATURE, SEAL AND PHOTOCOPIABLE DATA THAT IS RUBBER-STAMPED, TYPED OR PRINTED)

* If Married Woman Acknowledging: "When a married woman unites with her husband in the execution of any … instrument, and acknowledges the same in one of the forms in (RSMo 442.210), she shall be described in the acknowledgment as his wife, but in all other respects her acknowledgment shall be taken and certified as if she were sole; and no separate examination … shall be required" (RSMo 442.210.[4]).

Acknowledgment through Affidavit of Executing Witness (RSMo 486.340):

"The affidavit of executing witness for acknowledgment by an individual who does not appear before a notary shall be in type not smaller than eight-point and in substantially the following form" (RSMo 386.340):

State of Missouri,
County (and/or City) of _____

I, _____ (name of executing witness), do solemnly affirm under the penalty of perjury, that _____ (name of person who does not appear before a Notary), personally known to me, has executed the within _____ (type of document) in my presence, and has acknowledged to me that he/she executed the same for the purposes therein stated and requested that I sign my name on the within document as an executing witness.

_____ (signature of executing witness)

Subscribed and affirmed before me this _____ day of _____, 20__.

(NOTARY'S SIGNATURE, SEAL AND PHOTOCOPIABLE DATA THAT IS RUBBER-STAMPED, TYPED OR PRINTED)

Acknowledgment by Partner (RSMo 486.330[2]):

State of Missouri,
County (and/or City) of _____

On this _____ day of _____ in the year 20__ before me, _____ (name of Notary), a Notary Public in and for said state, personally appeared _____ (name of partner) of _____ (name of partnership), known to me to be the person who executed the within _____ (type of document) in behalf of said partnership and acknowledged to me that he/she executed the same for the purposes therein stated.

(NOTARY'S SIGNATURE, SEAL AND PHOTOCOPIABLE DATA THAT IS RUBBER-STAMPED, TYPED OR PRINTED)

Acknowledgment by Corporation (RSMo 486.330[3]):

State of Missouri,
County (and/or City) of _____

On this _____ day of _____ in the year 20__ before me, _____ (name of Notary), a Notary Public in and for said state, personally appeared _____ (name of officer), _____ (title of officer: president, vice president, etc.), _____ (name of corporation), known to me to be the person who executed the within _____ (type of document) in behalf of said corporation and acknowledged to me that he/she executed the same for the purposes therein stated.

(NOTARY'S SIGNATURE, SEAL AND PHOTOCOPIABLE DATA THAT IS RUBBER-STAMPED, TYPED OR PRINTED)

Acknowledgment by Corporation or Joint Stock Association (RSMo 442.210[3]):

The following certificate may be used for documents affecting real estate, with the names and residences of credible witnesses also noted on the certificate:

State of Missouri,
County (and/or City) of _____

On this _____ day of _____, 20__, before me appeared _____, to me personally known, who, being by me duly sworn (or affirmed) did say that he/she is the president (or other officer or agent of the corporation or association), of _____ (describing the corporation or association), and that the seal* affixed to the foregoing instrument is the corporate seal of said corporation (or association), and that said instrument was signed and sealed in behalf of said corporation (or association) by authority of its board of directors (or trustees), and said _____ acknowledged said instrument to be the free act and deed of said corporation (or association).

(NOTARY'S SIGNATURE, SEAL AND PHOTOCOPIABLE DATA THAT IS RUBBER-STAMPED, TYPED OR PRINTED)

* If No Corporate Seal: If the corporation or association has no corporate seal, omit the words "the seal affixed to the foregoing instrument is the corporate seal of said corporation (or association), and that" and the words "and sealed," and add at the end of the affidavit clause the words "and that said corporation (or association) has no corporate seal" (RSMo 442.210[2]).

Acknowledgment by Attorney in Fact for Principal or Surety (RSMo 486.330[4]):

State of Missouri,
County (and/or City) of _____

On this _____ day of _____ in the year 20__ before me, _____ (name of Notary), a Notary Public in and for said state, personally appeared _____ (name of attorney in fact), Attorney In Fact for _____ (name of principal or surety), known to me to be the person who executed the within _____ (type of document) in behalf of said principal (or surety), and acknowledged to me that he/she executed the same for the purposes therein stated.

(NOTARY'S SIGNATURE, SEAL AND PHOTOCOPIABLE DATA THAT IS RUBBER-STAMPED, TYPED OR PRINTED)

Acknowledgment by Public Officer, Deputy, Trustee, Administrator, Guardian or Executor (RSMo 486.330[5]):

State of Missouri,
County (and/or City) of _____

On this _____ day of _____ in the year 20__, before me, _____ (name of Notary), a Notary Public in and for said state, personally appeared _____ (name of person), _____ (person's official title), known to me to be the person who executed the within _____ (type of document) in behalf of _____ (public corporation, agency, political subdivision or estate) and acknowledged to me that he/she executed the same for the purposes therein stated.

(NOTARY'S SIGNATURE, SEAL AND PHOTOCOPIABLE DATA THAT IS RUBBER-STAMPED, TYPED OR PRINTED)

Acknowledgment by U.S. Citizen Outside United States (RSMo 486.330[6]):

(Description or location of place where acknowledgment is taken)

On this _____ day of _____, in the year 20__, before me, _____ (name and title of person acting as a Notary, with reference to law or authority granting power to act as a Notary), personally appeared _____ (name of citizen), known to me to be the person who executed the within _____ (type of document) and acknowledged to me that he/she executed the same for the purposes therein stated.

(NOTARY'S SIGNATURE AND SEAL, WITH REFERENCE TO LAW OR AUTHORITY GRANTING POWER TO NOTARIZE)

Acknowledgment by Individual Who Cannot Write Name (RSMo 486.330[7]):

State of Missouri,
County (and/or City) of _____

On this _____ day of _____ in the year 20__, before me, _____ (name of Notary), a Notary Public in and for said state, personally appeared _____ (name of individual), known to me to be the person who, being unable to write his/her name, made his/her mark in my presence.

I signed his/her name at his/her request and in his/her presence on the within _____ (type of document) and he/she acknowledged to me that he/she made his/her mark on the same for the purposes therein stated.

(NOTARY'S SIGNATURE, SEAL AND PHOTOCOPIABLE DATA THAT IS RUBBER-STAMPED, TYPED OR PRINTED)

Acknowledgment by Manager or Member of Limited Liability Company (RSMo 486.330[8]):

State of Missouri,
County (and/or City) of _____

On this _____ day of _____ in the year 20__, before me, _____ (name of Notary), a Notary Public in and for said state, personally appeared _____ (name of manager or member) of _____ (name of limited liability company), known to me to be the person who executed the within _____ (type of document) in behalf of said limited liability company and he/she acknowledged to me that he/she executed the same for the purposes therein stated.

(NOTARY'S SIGNATURE, SEAL AND PHOTOCOPIABLE DATA THAT IS RUBBER-STAMPED, TYPED OR PRINTED)

Acknowledgment before Commissioned Military Officer (RSMo 442.160[3]):

With the Armed Forces)
of the United States) ss
at _____)

On this _____ day of _____, A.D. 20__, before me, a commissioned officer of the armed forces of the United States, on active duty therewith, personally appeared _____, a member of the armed forces of the United States, on active duty therewith, (and _____, [his wife, her husband],) to me known to be the person described in and who executed the foregoing instrument, and acknowledged that _____ executed the same as _____ free act and deed. (The said _____ declared _____ to be single and unmarried.)

IN TESTIMONY WHEREOF, I have hereunto set my hand and grade (serial number, branch of service, and permanent mailing address).

_____ (Signature & Serial Number)
(Grade) (Branch of Service: Army, Navy, etc.)
(Permanent mailing address)

Jurat (MNH):

State of Missouri
County of _____

Subscribed and sworn to before me this ____ day of _____, in the year 20__.

(NOTARY'S SIGNATURE, SEAL AND PHOTOCOPIABLE DATA THAT IS RUBBER-STAMPED, TYPED OR PRINTED)

Affirmation in Writing (RSMo 486.335[1]):

"Affirmations shall be in type not smaller than eight-point and in substantially the following form" (RSMo 486.335[1]):

State of Missouri
County (and/or City) of _____

Subscribed and affirmed before me this ____ day of _____, 20__.

(NOTARY'S SIGNATURE, SEAL AND PHOTOCOPIABLE DATA THAT IS RUBBER-STAMPED, TYPED OR PRINTED)

Certification of Facsimile (RSMo 486.345[3]):

"The certification of a facsimile shall be in type not smaller than eight-point and in substantially the following form" (RSMo 486.345[3]):

State of Missouri,
County (and/or City) of _____

I, _____ (name of Notary), a Notary Public in and for said state, do certify that *on _____ (date) I carefully compared the attached facsimile of _____ (type of document) and the facsimile I now hold in my possession. They are complete, full, true and exact facsimiles of the document they purport to reproduce.*

(NOTARY'S SIGNATURE, SEAL AND PHOTOCOPIABLE DATA THAT IS RUBBER-STAMPED, TYPED OR PRINTED)

ELECTRONIC NOTARIZATIONS

The state of Missouri has not yet adopted statutes or regulations expressly establishing rules, definitions and procedures for electronic notarization.

UETA Recognizes Notary's eSignature

Repealing its former Digital Signatures Act, Missouri in 2003 adopted the Uniform Electronic Transactions Act (RSMo 432.200 through 432.295), including the section on notarization (RSMo 432.250), and thereby recognized the legal validity of electronic signatures used by Notaries:

"If a law requires a signature or record to be notarized, acknowledged, verified or made under oath, the requirement is satisfied if the electronic signature of the person authorized to perform those acts, together with all other information required to be included by other applicable law, is attached to or logically associated with the signature or record."

NOTARY RECORDS

Every Missouri Notary must "provide and keep a permanently bound journal of his or her notarial acts containing numbered pages" (RSMo 486.260). This must be "a true and perfect record of his or her official acts." An entry must be made for each act, with the exception of those connected with judicial proceedings or "for whose public record the law provides and the public record as defined in section 610.010 is publicly filed within ninety days of execution" (RSMo 486.265).

Required Entries

The following entries are required for each notarial act (RSMo 486.260):
1. The month, day and year of notarization;
2. The type of notarization (e.g., acknowledgment or jurat);
3. The type of document notarized;
4. The name, signature and address of the signer;
5. The identification used to identify the signer;
6. The fee charged for the notarization.

<u>Retain Copy of Facsimile Certification</u>: The Notary must keep a copy of each facsimile certified (RSMo 486.345[2]), in addition to recording a journal entry for the certification (MNH).

<u>Foreign-Language Document</u>: "If you are requested to notarize a document in another language, you will want to note this in your journal" (MNH).

Copies upon Court Order

"Each notary public, upon written court order, shall furnish facsimiles of entries made in his journal of notarial acts or any other papers or copies relating to his notarial acts, upon receipt of a fee of one dollar per $8\frac{1}{2}$-x-11-inch page or part of a page" (RSMo 486.270).

Lost or Stolen Journal

"Any notary public who loses or misplaces his journal of notarial acts … shall forthwith mail or deliver notice of the fact to the secretary of state" (RSMo 486.305).

"The date the … journal was lost or stolen should be noted in the notary records. The notary may also want to contact their local police department and see if they require a police report to be filed for stolen goods" (MNH).

Unlawful Possession

"The journal is the exclusive property of the notary" (RSMo 486.265).

"Any person who unlawfully possesses a notary's journal … is guilty of a misdemeanor and is punishable upon conviction by a fine not exceeding five hundred dollars" (RSMo 486.380).

AUTHENTICATION OF NOTARIAL ACTS

Secretary of State

Certificates authenticating the acts of Notaries (including apostilles) are issued only by the

Commissions Division of the Secretary of State's office (RSMo 486.395).

Fee: $10 per certificate; payable to the "Director of Revenue." A law effective August 28, 2002, "limits the state's allowable fee for processing certain adoption documents to $100 per child per adoption, or per multiple children adopted at the same time" (website, "Certificates and Apostilles").

Address:
Office of Secretary of State
Commissions Office
P.O. Box 784
Jefferson City, MO 65102-0784

In Person or Express Mail:
Office of Secretary of State
Commissions Office
Kirkpatrick State Info Center
600 W. Main St., Room 322
Jefferson City, MO 65101

Telephone: 1-573-751-2783

Procedure: Mail or present the original notarized document, along with the fee. Indicate the country to which the notarized document will be sent. Include a return address and a contact phone number and email address. Documents will be returned by regular mail unless there is a prepaid envelope with an addressed airbill included with the documents.

"The Secretary of State's office is pleased to forward documents directly to a third party if a stamped addressed envelope to the third party is enclosed with the letter of request. If the third party is a consulate or embassy for the country requiring the documents, it is practical to include a letter of instruction to them with their fees" (MNH).

Branch Offices: Authenticating certificates (including apostilles) for a Missouri Notary can also be obtained at any of the Secretary of State's three branch offices (MNH):

1. Office of Secretary of State
   815 Olive St., Suite 210
   St. Louis, MO 63101
   Telephone: 1-314-340-7490

2. Office of Secretary of State
   615 E. 13th St., Room 513
   Kansas City, MO 64106
   Telephone: 1-816-889-2925

3. Office of Secretary of State
   149 Park Central Sq., Suite 624
   Springfield, MO 65806
   Telephone: 1-417-895-6330

Authentication of School Documents: "The face of a diploma should not be altered by the registrar or notary.

"The registrar or other authority of the school must sign a statement, which is typed on the BACK of the diploma or transcript. The wording in this statement says that the diploma or transcript is either the original record issued by the school or a copy of the original document issued by the school and the date it was issued.

"The signature of the school official is witnessed by a notary public. The notary states that he/she saw the school official sign the document.

"If the school does not issue a diploma for foreign students, a notarized letter from the registrar or other school authority must be given to the student. The letter must state that the student has completed the requirements for graduation from that school, but the school does not issue diplomas for foreign students. The letter is notarized in the same manner as other notarized school documents" (MNH).

COMMISSIONING AND ADMINISTRATION

The Missouri Secretary of State appoints, commissions, regulates and maintains records on the state's Notaries (RSMo 486.205).

A Notary's bond, signature and oath are permanently retained by the Secretary of State. These items are mailed to this office within 30 days of receipt by the county clerk (RSMo 486.245).

Applying for Commission

Qualifications: An applicant for a commission as a Missouri Notary Public must: (a) be at least 18 years old, (b) be a registered voter of the county in which the applicant seeks to be commissioned, or a permanent resident alien of the United States, (c) legally reside in the county in which the applicant seeks to be commissioned, (d) be able to read and write the English language and (e) not have had a commission revoked within the past 10 years (RSMo 486.220[1]). A non-resident applicant, in addition, must be employed in Missouri, use the Notary seal only in the course of employment, have a work address in the county in which commissioning is sought and authorize the Missouri Secretary of State to accept services of process or other legal notifications on their behalf (RSMo 486.220[2]).

"According to Missouri law, a person convicted of a felony may not be able to become a notary public" (NPH).

Training Required: Prior to submitting an application, the applicant must "read the Missouri notary public handbook and complete a computer-based notary training or other notary training in a manner prescribed by the secretary of state" (RSMo 486.225[6]). This also applies to reapplications.

Application: The completed application must be submitted to the Secretary of State with a $25 fee, a certificate showing completion of state-approved Notary training and, if the applicant is a permanent resident alien, a copy of the applicant's green card (RSMo 28.160[3] and 486.225[1], [2] and [6]; website, "Application for Commission as a Notary Public").

Reapplications should be submitted no earlier than six weeks prior to commission expiration (MNH).

Appearance before County Clerk: The Secretary of State will mail the new commission to the appropriate county clerk (RSMo 486.230). The new Notary will be notified by mail that he or she has 90 days to appear in person before this clerk (RSMo 486.240). When the Notary appears, he or she must present a $10,000 surety bond, take the oath of office, and submit a signature specimen, after which the county clerk will present the commission to the Notary (RSMo 486.235). The county clerk will then forward the bond, oath and signature specimen to the Secretary of State (RSMo 486.245).

Within the City of St. Louis, the circuit clerk performs the functions of a county clerk in regard to Notaries (RSMo 486.200[2]); within the County of St. Charles, it is the office of the county registrar.

Non-Residents: Persons residing in other states but working in Missouri may become Missouri Notaries. For further details, see "Qualifications," above.

"If the notary is presently commissioned as a non-resident notary public and they move into Missouri, the notary may immediately be appointed and commissioned as a notary upon becoming a resident. The notary will need to return their nonresident notary certificate with a request to cancel that commission, along with a completed reapplication as a resident, proof of training and the $25 fee for issuing another commission" (MNH).

Online Search: A search of Missouri's list of current Notaries may be conducted on the Secretary of State's website. Searches may be done by Notary name (last name and at least the first letter of the first name), county or both (website, "Search for a Notary Public").

Changes of Status

If Notary Changes Residence Address: For any change of residence address, in or out of the county in which the Notary is commissioned, a Notary must inform the Secretary of State within 30 days of the change. If the change of address is within the Notary's county, the Notary must submit a completed "Application for Notary Change of Address in Same County." In the case of a change in county, the Notary must be issued an amended commission and must submit a completed "Application for Amended Commission as a Notary Public: Change of Name or Change of County." Along with the application, the Notary must submit the current commission certificate and a $5 fee (RSMo 486.295 and 486.315).

For a county change, "(t)he notary must be a registered voter in their new county before submitting the application.... The notary will need to check with the entity that issued their bond as to whether they will need a rider. If a rider is needed, a copy of that rider must be sent to (the Secretary of State's) office.... If the notary is using a seal containing the county name, a new seal reflecting the new county of residence must be purchased and used" (MNH).

If Notary Changes Employer Address: Out-of-state residents who are Notaries must inform the Secretary of State of a change in their employer and/or county of employment within 30 days. As applicable, the Notary must submit either a completed "Application for Change of Employer:

Non-Resident Notaries (Same County of Employment)" or a completed "Application for Amended Commission as a Notary Public: Change of Employer County (Non-Resident Notaries Only)." If there is a change of county, the Notary must submit the current commission certificate and a $5 fee with the application (MNH).

If Notary Changes Name: Notaries who change their legal name must, within 30 days of the change, obtain a rider for their bond (if required) and notify the Secretary of State. Such Notaries must be issued an amended commission and therefore must submit a completed "Application for Amended Commission as a Notary Public: Change of Name or Change of County." Along with the application, the Notary must submit any required bond rider, the current commission certificate and a $5 fee. The Secretary of State will notify the appropriate county clerk of the name change. The Notary must also obtain a new seal (stamp and/or embosser) with the new name on it (RSMo 486.300 and MNH).

If Notary Resigns: Notaries who resign their commissions must notify the Secretary of State in writing (RSMo 486.310). They also must surrender their commission certificate. "The notary is not required to state a reason for resigning" (MNH).

COUNTY CLERKS

Though Missouri county clerks maintain a register of local Notaries that lists the name and address of each person to whom a commission was awarded (RSMo 486.245), anyone seeking proof of the authority of a Missouri Notary Public should contact the Commissions Division.

OTHER NOTARIAL OFFICERS

Court Officers
Judges, justices and clerks of a court having a seal may take acknowledgments and proofs (RSMo 442.150[1]) and may administer oaths and affirmations (RSMo 492.010).

Shorthand Reporters
Certified court and shorthand reporters have authority to administer oaths and affirmations in performing their duties (RSMo 492.010).

Commissioners of Deeds
The Governor of Missouri may appoint and commission commissioners of deeds to operate in other states, territories, districts and countries in order to notarize documents to be used or recorded in Missouri. Their powers include administering oaths and taking and certifying depositions and interrogatories. They also have power "to certify to the official character, signature or seal of any officer within their district, who is authorized to take acknowledgments or declarations under oath." They may collect the same fees as clerks of courts of record (RSMo 486.100 through 486.140).

No Automatic Notary Powers for Attorneys
Though a statute effective in August of 2005 redefines the term Notary Public as "any person appointed and commissioned to perform notarial acts, including any attorney licensed to practice in this state" (RSMo 486.200[5]), this provision is not currently interpreted by the Missouri Secretary of State to give attorneys automatic notarial powers. Just like any other person seeking a Notary commission, attorneys must formally make application to the Secretary of State and comply with all qualifying requirements, including the requirement to take a course of instruction on notarial duties (website, "Attorneys as Notaries Public").

QUICK FACTS

Notary Jurisdiction
Statewide (RSMo 486.210).

Limited Jurisdiction for Non-Residents: Missouri Notaries who are non-residents may notarize only in the course of their employment in Missouri (RSMo 486.220[2][2]).

Notary Term Length
Four years (RSMo 486.215).

Acting After Commission Expiration: "Any person who acts as ... a notary public while not lawfully appointed and commissioned ... is guilty of a misdemeanor and punishable upon conviction by a fine ... or by imprisonment ... or both" (RSMo 486.375).

Notary Bond
$10,000, with a company qualified to write surety bonds in Missouri (RSMo 486.235).

Employer May Be Liable: "The employer of a notary public is ... liable to the persons involved for all damages proximately caused by the notary's official misconduct, if: (1) The notary public was acting within the scope of his employment at the time he engaged in the official misconduct; and (2) The employer consented to the notary public's official misconduct" (RSMo 486.360).

Montana

NOTARY SEAL

A Montana Notary must authenticate all official acts with a seal of office, and the seal's format must be as follows (MCA 1-5-416[1]):

Kind

Inked Stamp/Seal: Notaries who receive a new or renewal commission on or after October 1, 2009, must use "an official ink stamp and seal prescribed by the secretary of state" (MCA 1-5-416[1][d]) — see requirements below.

Notaries holding current commissions on October 1, 2009, "may continue to use the seals they presently use … until the end of their current term as long as they are compliant with the requirements for the notary seal …" (NPH) — see "Components of Seal" below. This provision applies to both embossers and inked-stamp seals. However, starting October 1, 2013, no embossers or Notary stamp and seal designs at variance with the Secretary of State's prescription will be permitted (NPH).

Ink Color: The Notary's official stamp/seal and official signature "must be in blue or black ink" (MCA 1-5-416[e]).

JANE Q. DOE
NOTARY PUBLIC for the
State of Montana
Residing at Helena, Montana
My Commission Expires
January 30, 2014

Example

For any Montana Notary with a commission expiration date of October 1, 2013, or later, the Secretary of State prescribes this combination seal-stamp unit, containing both a circular seal and certain other information required by statute. A Notary with a commission expiration date before October 1, 2013, need not use such a "combined unit" but may instead separately affix the seal and the other required information until expiration of the current commission (NPH).

NOTARY ADMINISTRATION

Office of Secretary of State
Notary and Certification Services
P.O. Box 202801   1-406-444-5379
(1236 6th Avenue)   1-406-444-1877
Helena, MT 59620-2801

Website: http://sos.mt.gov/Notary/index.asp

NOTARY RULES

MCA — MONTANA CODE ANNOTATED
NPH — MONTANA NOTARY PUBLIC HANDBOOK

Most Notary laws are in the Montana Code Annotated, Title 1, Chapter 5 ("Proof and Acknowledgment of Instruments Notaries Public"), which includes the "Uniform Law on Notarial Acts."*

* This is the *Uniform Law on Notarial Acts* of 1982, adopted with modifications as MCA Sections 1-5-601 through 1-5-611.

Other directions for Notaries are in the "Montana Notary Public Handbook" (November 2010), issued by the Secretary of State and available on the website.

Shape/Size of Seal-Stamp

The combination seal-stamp unit prescribed by the Montana Secretary of State has an outer rectangular border of approximately 1 inch by $2^{1}/_{2}$ inches, and the seal contained within is circular (NPH).

Components of Seal

Only the following information may appear within the circular seal, with anything additional rendering the image invalid as an official seal (NPH):

1. Name of Notary exactly as it appears on the commission;
2. "Notarial Seal" or "Notary Public";
3. "State of Montana".

Other Information Must Appear

In addition to the official seal, the following information must appear below the Notary's signature on every notarized document (MCA 1-5-416[1][e] and [f]):

1. Typed, stamped or legibly printed name of Notary exactly as it appears on the commission;
2. "Notary Public for the State of Montana";
3. "Residing at _____ (city or town where Notary lives)";
4. Commission expiration date, expressed as month/day/four-digit year.

Although the law does not require specific language for the commission expiration date, all illustrations of acceptable seal-stamp formats, both on the Secretary of State's website and in the "Montana Notary Public Handbook," use the words, "My commission expires" followed by the date as required in statute, e.g., "August 2, 2014."

Prior to October 1, 2009, the information in items 1 through 4 above had to be added below the Notary's signature on every notarized document. The Secretary of State now mandates that this information be included in the combination seal-stamp unit required for Notaries commissioned on or after October 1, 2009. Notaries who use the new seal-stamp format do not need to add this information below their signatures (NPH).

Seal Must Be Destroyed

"A notary public, upon resignation or removal from office or at the expiration of the notary public's term if the notary public is not reappointed, or, in the case of the notary public's death, the notary public's legal representative shall ... destroy the notary's official stamp and seal" (MCA 1-5-419[1][b]).

For a knowing failure to destroy the seal, the offender is liable for damages to any person injured by the failure (MCA 1-5-419[2]).

Notary's Signature May Not Be Facsimile

All notarized documents must bear the Notary's "original signature, which must be in blue or black ink, as it appears on the notary's certificate of commission" (MCA 1-5-416[1][e]). A facsimile signature is not allowed.

NOTARY POWERS

Montana Notaries are authorized to perform the following notarial acts (MCA 1-5-416[1][a] through [c] and 1-5-603[1] through [5]):

1. Take acknowledgments*;
2. Administer oaths** and affirmations**;
3. Take verifications*** upon oath or affirmation (jurats);
4. Witness or attest signatures****;
5. Certify or attest copies***** (MCA 1-5-603[4] and 1-5-416[1][c];
6. Take depositions****** and affidavits*******, but only "if the notary is knowledgeable of the applicable legal requirements" (MCA 1-5-416[1][b]);
7. Execute protests********.

* Acknowledgments: "'Acknowledgment'" means a declaration by a person that the person has executed an instrument for the purposes stated in the instrument and, if the instrument is executed in a representative capacity, that the person signed the instrument with proper authority and executed it as the act of the person or entity represented and identified in the instrument" (MCA 1-5-602[1]).

"Although this process requires the signer to appear before the notary, it does not require the notary to witness the act of signing…. In most cases, the requirement will be met if the signer acknowledges before the notary that he/she signed the document, and the notary then merely attests to the fact that the signer personally acknowledged the signature in the presence of the notary and that the notary has determined the identity of the signer as otherwise required" (NPH).

An acknowledgment is "(a) notarial act which requires the person who has already signed a document to personally appear before the notary and … acknowledge that he/she willingly signed the document for the purposes for which it was intended. The notary does not have to actually see the person sign the document …" (NPH).

** Oath or Affirmation Wording: "An oath or affirmation in an action or proceeding may be administered by the person who swears or affirms expressing that person's assent when addressed with, 'You do solemnly swear (or affirm, as the case may be) that the evidence you will give in this issue (or matter), pending between _____ and _____, is the truth, the whole truth, and nothing but the truth, so help you God'" (MCA 1-6-102).

The Notary may "vary the mode of swearing or affirming to accord with the witness's beliefs whenever ... satisfied that the witness has a distinct mode of swearing or affirming" (MCA 1-6-103).

"Montana statutes do not specify the wording the notary should use for an oath, but generally the person taking the oath should respond affirmatively to the question, 'Do you swear that the information contained in this document is the truth to the best of your knowledge and ability?'

"Or, in the case of a Credible Witness, 'Do you swear that the person you have identified to me as _____ is, in fact, that person?'" (website, "Powers and Duties of a Notary").

*** Verifications upon Oath or Affirmation: "'Verification upon oath or affirmation' means a declaration that a statement is true made by a person upon oath or affirmation" (MCA 1-5-602[5]).

"The notary not only witnesses the signature which must be made in his/her presence and must authenticate the identity of the signer, but he/she must also administer an oath (or affirmation) and affix a jurat to reflect that the signer swore or affirmed the truth of the document signed. A jurat includes an oath by the signer that the statements in the document are true" (NPH).

**** Witnessing Signatures: "Witnessing or attesting a signature is probably the most common of notarial acts requiring the notary to witness the signature by the signer who appears in person before the notary to do the signing. The notary also must authenticate the identity of the signer by approved methods" (NPH).

***** Certifying Copies: "In certifying or attesting a copy of a document or other item, the notarial officer shall determine that the proffered copy is a full, true, and accurate transcription or reproduction of that which was copied" (MCA 1-5-603[4]).

"A notary public shall ... whenever requested and upon payment of the required fees, make and give a certified copy of any record kept or that originated in the notary public's place of employment ..." (MCA 1-5-416[1][c]).

"A notary public may not ... certify a document issued by a public entity, such as a birth, death, or marriage certificate, unless the notary is employed by the entity issuing or holding the original version of that document" (MCA 1-5-416[2][c]).

"A Montana Notary Public may not certify a document issued by a public entity, such as a birth, death, or marriage certificate, unless the notary is employed by the entity issuing or holding the original version of that document.... The originals (or official copy) of those documents are maintained by the issuing authority, and they issue 'certified copies' under the seal of the issuing authority.

"Not all publically issued documents fall into this category, however. Drivers' licenses, passports, and school diplomas are examples of documents issued by public entities, but, because the owner has the original document, a Montana notary can make a copy and certify it to be a 'true and exact copy' as contemplated under 1-5-603(4)....

"A Montana Notary Public may certify or attest that a copy of a document is a full, true, and accurate transcription or reproduction of that which was copied, upon making such a determination.... In order to do this, the notary must see the original document. It is recommended that the notary make the photocopy, rather than accepting a copy made by the person requesting the notarization.

"The Montana Notary could also notarize the signature and oath of the individual swearing that the copy is a true and correct copy of another document. This is called 'copy certification by document custodian'. The Notary would then only be charged with determining the true identity of the signer, not the accuracy of the copy. Technically, this would not be a certified copy under the definition below, but often is sufficient for many purposes.

"The definition of a certified copy in Black's Law Dictionary (seventh Edition, 1999) is 'A duplicate of an original (usually official) document, certified as an exact reproduction usually by the officer responsible for issuing or keeping the original.' Certified copy is what is intended by 1-5-416(2)(c) ..., not 1-5-603(4).... A Montana notary would be wise to determine if an individual needs a certified copy, in which case the attestation to a true and correct copy should not be done" (NPH).

****** Depositions: "A written statement used in legal matters that is transcribed from oral testimony given under oath or affirmation and is usually signed by the person giving the oath or affirmation" (NPH).

"The statute reserves the taking of depositions to notaries who are specifically knowledgeable in that process. Unless you have training as a court reporter, legal secretary, paralegal or other legal professional, the statute does not bestow this duty to a notary" (website, "Powers and Duties of a Notary").

******* Affidavits: Effective October 1, 2011, the term "affidavit" has been redefined throughout the Montana Code Annotated as follows: "'Affidavit' means a sworn written declaration made before an officer authorized to administer oaths or an unsworn written declaration made under penalty of perjury ..." (MCA 1-1-203[1]). Affidavits dated after October 1, 2011, and signed and sworn under penalty of perjury therefore do not require notarization.

******* Protests: "This notarial act is rarely used for legitimate business transactions these days. Unless you are specifically aware of the requirements for a proper use of this act, please contact a lawyer before agreeing to issue a protest of (an) instrument" (website, "Powers and Duties of a Notary").

Personal Appearance Required

"(O)ne of the notary's greatest responsibilities is to be able to unequivocally testify that they did in fact witness the act they claimed to have notarized. In other words, the person whose signature, oath, or acknowledgment is being notarized MUST appear in front of the notary at the time the act takes place. There are no exceptions to this requirement. Failure to conclusively establish the identity of the person requesting a notarization places the notary at risk of being sued for negligence or malfeasance in office" (NPH).

"There is one absolute: The person whose signature, acknowledgement, or oath is being notarized MUST be in your physical presence when the notarization takes place. ALWAYS. EVERY TIME. NO EXCEPTIONS — EVER" (NPH).

Identifying Document Signers

In taking an acknowledgment or a verification upon oath or affirmation, or in witnessing or attesting a signature, a Notary must identify the signer "either from personal knowledge or from satisfactory evidence" (MCA 1-5-603[1] through [3]).

Satisfactory evidence means that the signer is either (a) personally known to the Notary, (b) identified upon the oath or affirmation of a credible witness personally known to the Notary, or (c) identified on the basis of current identification documents that show a photograph and a signature of the bearer (MCA 1-5-603[6]).

"Montana law views personal knowledge as the best form of identification, and thus requires no further proof of identity. However, if the notary does not know the person, it is most prudent for the notary to request current, signed, and pictured ID before performing a notarization. Acceptable forms of identification include a driver's license, a military or student ID, a passport, or a government issued ID. If there is any doubt as to the person's identity, the only safe practice is to refuse to notarize any signature, oath, or acknowledgment....

"When determining the identity of an unknown individual, a notary should request current, signed, and pictured ID.... Birth certificates, social security cards, green cards, and other documents which do not have a current picture and signature of the bearer are of no use in identifying an individual. Credit cards and other privately issued documents may not have required an adequate level of identification for issuance and should not be relied upon" (NPH).

Determining Representative Capacity: "Note: When notarizing a document that is being signed by someone other than the person or entity designated as the signer, the notary should determine: 1.) the identity of the person who is actually signing the document, 2.) the capacity of the person to sign on behalf of the person or entity, and 3.) the authority to sign for that person or entity in this particular transaction" (NPH).

Competence and Willingness of Signer

Competence refers to someone's "ability to understand. A notary should be comfortable that all parties understand what they are signing or affirming....

"A notary should refuse to notarize a signature or acknowledgment unless all parties are willingly involved" (NPH).

Motor Vehicle Title Notarizations

The signature(s) of the seller(s) on a Montana motor vehicle title must be notarized. "Once notarized, the title becomes a 'negotiable instrument' and ownership is ready transferred to the person holding the title. For this reason, Montana notaries are urged to be particularly conscientious when asked to notarize a title", (NPH):

1. On most Montana motor vehicle titles, the preprinted notarial certificate — what the Secretary of State calls the "notarial block" — does not contain all nine elements required by Montana law — see "Components of 'Notarial Block'" below. For example, the venue ("State of Montana, County of _____") is missing on most existing titles. Any required information that is missing must be added by the Notary.

2. "If there are two or more owners listed on a title, they need not have their signatures notarized at the same time or by the same notary. The sellers sign and print their names on the lines provided on the title; the first notary should use the 'preprinted block' and be sure to specify whose signature was notarized ('Signed and sworn before me by John Doe (only)'). The subsequent notary completes a full notarial block either on the title (in the lien holder's section, if there is enough room) or on a separate piece of paper.

3. "The Montana Department of Motor Vehicles will not accept a title with information that has been in any way corrected or crossed out. If an error is made by the signers or the notary, a Statement of Fact will have to be completed and filed with the Title….

4. "Notaries may place their seals in the lien holder section, just to the left of the signature in the notarial block" (NPH).

Open Titles: Versions of the Montana motor vehicle title dating from 2006 to the present bear wording forbidding notarization unless the title contains the name(s) of the purchaser(s). Titles without this information are considered "open."

As of October 2010, the Montana Motor Vehicle Division (MVD) is in the process of redesigning the motor vehicle title, in part "to remove the admonition about notarizing an open title" (NPH). Until the new title format is implemented, the MVD advises as follows:

"(C)onsistent with the upcoming change, a notary may disregard the open title admonition on the current title … and proceed with notarization of the vehicle owner's (seller's) signature — even though the purchaser's name and address is not entered in section 1 of the title — if the notary has properly identified the signatory in accordance with the requirements of their commission. The notary is not required to interpret and/or enforce Montana title laws when acknowledging signatures on a Montana title document" (NPH).

Electronic Signatures: Effective March 25, 2011, Montana law permits the use of electronic signatures on a certificate of title or on a limited power of attorney assigning ownership of a motor vehicle, trailer, semitrailer, pole trailer, camper, motorboat, personal watercraft, sailboat or snowmobile. If an electronic signature is used, the requirement of acknowledgment before a Notary is waived (MCA 61-3-205).

Mark Does Not Require Witnesses

According to the Secretary of State's office, affixation of a mark does not require witnesses, because Montana statute defines a "mark" as a signature:

"A signature is made: (a) manually or by means of a device or machine; and (b) by use of any name, including any trade or assumed name, or by any word, mark, or symbol executed or adopted by a person with present intention to authenticate a writing" (MCA 30-3-401[2]).

NOTARY DON'TS

Notary May Not Refuse to Serve

"It is the duty of all notaries to serve the public, and a notary may not unreasonably refuse to perform a notarial act for any member of the public who pays the statutory fee and meets all requirements prescribed by statute" (NPH).

Signing and Sealing Is Not Sufficient

"Simply affixing your seal and signing your name does not constitute a proper notarization in the state of Montana…. A notary will be held personally responsible for improper, negligent, or fraudulent actions" (NPH).

Notary's Disqualifying Interests

A Montana Notary may (MCA 1-5-416[2][a] and [b]):
1. NOT notarize the Notary's own signature;
2. NOT "notarize a document in which the notary is individually named or has an interest from which the notary will directly benefit by a transaction involving the document."

Notarizing for Family: "Q. Can I notarize my spouse's or other family member's signature?

"A. Yes as long as you are not named in, or a direct beneficiary of, the transaction referenced in the document being signed," as per MCA 1-5-416[2][b]) (NPH).

Corporate Notaries: A Notary who is a stockholder, director, officer, employee or agent of a bank or other corporation may notarize for that bank or corporation, unless the Notary is named in the instrument or signs it as a representative of the bank or corporation (MCA 1-5-417[1] and [2]).

NOTARY SIGNING AGENTS

Currently, there are no statutes, regulations or rules prohibiting or restricting the operation of Notary Signing Agents within the state of Montana.

"A 'Signing Agent' is a notary public who specializes in the process of obtaining and notarizing the signatures of the party(ies) involved on real estate loan documents for the purpose of closing a real estate loan transaction. Montana statutes do no specifically reference this term….

"Montana statutes do not currently regulate signing agents per se. A Montana Notary is acting on behalf of the State of Montana regardless of the type of notarial act being performed" (NPH).

NOTARY FEES

The fees Montana Notaries may charge for notarial acts are as follows (MCA 1-5-418[1] through [5]):
1. Taking an acknowledgment: $5 for the first signature and $1 for each additional signature of the same person;
2. Administering an oath or affirmation: $5;
3. Taking a verification upon oath or affirmation, including oath: $5;
4. Taking a deposition, affidavit or other paper for which a maximum fee is not otherwise specified: $3.50 per page.

Mileage

For traveling to and/or from the place of a notarial act, a Notary may charge "the amount provided by law for state employees when using the same mode of travel and traveling on state business" (MCA 1-5-418[6]). This rate currently is 34.5 cents per mile (website, "Notary Fees").

NOTARY CERTIFICATES

Montana has adopted the *Uniform Law on Notarial Acts*, including the short-form certificates (MCA 1-5-610) for:
1. Acknowledgment by individual;
2. Acknowledgment by representative;
3. Verification upon oath or affirmation;
4. Witnessing or attesting signature;
5. Attesting copy of document.

For the text of these certificates, see "Uniform Law on Notarial Acts (1982)," Section 8, in Appendix 2.

In addition, the following certificates are prescribed in the "Montana Notary Public Handbook":

Acknowledgment by Individual Signing before Notary (NPH):

State of Montana
County of _____

Signed and acknowledged before me on _____ (date) by _____ (name of person signing document).

(NOTARY SEAL)   _____
                    (Signature of Notary)

[IF FOLLOWING DOES NOT APPEAR ON SEAL-STAMP:]

_____ (Printed name of Notary)

Notary Public for the State of Montana (Title)

Residing at _____ (City/town where Notary lives)

My Commission Expires _____ (Month/day/4-digit year)

Acknowledgment by Individual Not Signing before Notary (NPH):

State of Montana
County of _____

This instrument was acknowledged before me on _____ (date) by _____ (name of person signing document).

(NOTARY SEAL) _____
                    (Signature of Notary)

[IF FOLLOWING DOES NOT APPEAR ON SEAL-STAMP:]

_____ (Printed name of Notary)

Notary Public for the State of Montana (Title)

Residing at _____ (City/town where Notary lives)

My Commission Expires _____ (Month/day/4-digit year)

Acknowledgment (or Jurat) by Representative (NPH):

State of Montana
County of _____

This instrument was (signed and sworn to) (acknowledged) before me on _____ (date) by _____ (name of person coming before Notary) as _____ (type of authority — officer, trustee, attorney-in-fact, etc.) of _____ (name of party or entity on behalf of whom document was executed).

(NOTARY SEAL) _____
                    (Signature of Notary)

[IF FOLLOWING DOES NOT APPEAR ON SEAL-STAMP:]

_____ (Printed name of Notary)

Notary Public for the State of Montana (Title)

Residing at _____ (City/town where Notary lives)

My Commission Expires _____ (Month/day/4-digit year)

Verification upon Oath or Affirmation Certificate, i.e., Jurat (NPH):

State of Montana
County of _____

Signed and sworn to (or affirmed) before me on _____ (date) by _____ (name of person making statement).

(NOTARY SEAL) _____
                    (Signature of Notary)

[IF FOLLOWING DOES NOT APPEAR ON SEAL-STAMP:]

_____ (Printed name of Notary)

Notary Public for the State of Montana (Title)

Residing at _____ (City/town where Notary lives)

My Commission Expires _____ (Month/day/4-digit year)

Copy Certification by Notary (NPH):

State of Montana
County of _____

I certify that this is a true and correct photocopy of _____ (document description) in the possession of _____ (name of person), made by me on _____ (date).

(NOTARY SEAL) _____
                    (Signature of Notary)

[IF FOLLOWING DOES NOT APPEAR ON SEAL-STAMP:]

_____ (Printed name of Notary)

Notary Public for the State of Montana (Title)

Residing at _____ (City/town where Notary lives)

My Commission Expires _____ (Month/day/4-digit year)

Copy Certification by Document Custodian (NPH):

This is a true and exact copy of _____ (document description) in my possession on _____ (date).

_____
(Signature of Custodian)

State of Montana
County of _____

Signed and sworn to (or affirmed) before me on _____ *(date) by* _____ *(name of person signing document).*

(NOTARY SEAL) _____
                        (Signature of Notary)

[IF FOLLOWING DOES NOT APPEAR ON SEAL-STAMP:]

_____ *(Printed name of Notary)*

Notary Public for the State of Montana (Title)

Residing at _____ *(City/town where Notary lives)*

My Commission Expires _____ *(Month/day/4-digit year)*

Format for Notarial Certificate

"1. A notarial act must be evidenced by a certificate signed and dated by a notarial officer. The certificate must include identification of the jurisdiction in which the notarial act is performed, the date on which the notarial act is performed, the type of notarial act being performed, and the title of the office of the notarial officer and must include the official seal of office. If the officer is a Montana notary public, the certificate must also indicate the place of the notarial officer's residence and the date of expiration of the commission of office, but omission of that place or date may subsequently be corrected. If the officer is a commissioned officer on active duty in the military service of the United States, it must also include the officer's rank.

"2. A certificate of a notarial act is sufficient if it meets the requirements of subsection (1) and it:

"a. is in the short form set forth in 1-5-610;

"b. is in a form otherwise prescribed by the law of this state;

"c. is in a form prescribed by the laws or regulations applicable in the place in which the notarial act was performed; or

"d. sets forth the actions of the notarial officer and those are sufficient to meet the requirements of the designated notarial act" (MCA 1-5-609[1] and [2]).

Components of 'Notarial Block' (Certificate): To clarify the requirements set forth in MCA 1-5-609[1], the "Montana Notary Public Handbook" offers the following list of nine elements that must appear on every notarial certificate — what the Secretary of State calls the "notarial block" — completed by a Montana Notary:

1. Venue (state and county where notarial act is performed);
2. Date of notarization;
3. Declaration describing type of notarial act performed;
4. Notary's original official signature;
5. Notary's official name clearly typed, stamped or printed (under the signature and in addition to the Notary's name in the seal);
6. Notary's title: "Notary Public for the State of Montana";
7. Words "Residing at _____ (city or town where Notary lives)";
8. Commission expiration date (month/day/4-digit year);
9. Notary's official seal.

If a preprinted notarial certificate does not contain all nine elements above, then the Notary must add any information that is missing.

The combination seal-stamp unit required for Notaries commissioned on or after October 1, 2009, contains the information in items 5 through 9 above. Its use meets the statutory requirement for those items to appear on every notarial certificate.

If No Room for 'Notarial Block' (Certificate)

"If there is absolutely no room for the notarial block near the signature, the next best place is on the reverse of the document. If that is not possible, a notarial block may be placed on a separate sheet of paper, but it is very important that the notary very clearly identify the type of document, the date of the document and any other pertinent data, as well as the name of the person whose signature is being notarized, so that there is no possibility of the notarization being applied to a different document. That paper should then be attached to the document. This is referred to as a 'loose certificate'" (NPH).

ELECTRONIC NOTARIZATIONS

The state of Montana has not yet adopted statutes or regulations expressly establishing rules, definitions and procedures for electronic notarization.

UETA Recognizes Notary's eSignature

Effective July 1, 2001, Montana adopted with amendments the Uniform Electronic Transactions Act (MCA 30-18-101 through 30-18-118), including its standard provision on notarization and acknowledgment, thereby recognizing the legal validity of electronic signatures used by Notaries:

"If a law requires a signature or record to be notarized, acknowledged, verified, or made under oath, the requirement is satisfied if the electronic signature of the person authorized to perform those acts, together with all other information required to be included by other applicable law, is attached to or logically associated with the signature or record" (MCA 30-18-110).

NOTARY RECORDS

Effective October 1, 2009, a Montana Notary Public must "keep and maintain an official notary journal recording the details of each notarial act performed" (MCA 1-5-416[1][g]).

Bound Book Required

"'An official notary journal' is a bound book designed specifically for this purpose…. There are different formats available; you may choose whichever you prefer as long as the pages are numbered and the book is designed in such a way as to prohibit any alteration or modification of the pages. You may not use a loose-leaf notebook, or any kind of electronic record" (NPH).

Mandatory Entries

For each notarial act, the Notary must make an entry in the journal that includes (MCA 1-5-416[1][g] and NPH):
 1. The date of the notarization;
 2. The type of notarial act;
 3. The type of document;
 4. The date of the document;
 5. The name, address and signature of the person for whom the notarization was performed;
 6. The type of identification relied on by the Notary;
 7. Any other information prescribed by the Secretary of State and/or any additional non-private information deemed relevant by the Notary.

Forbidden Entries: "The information that Montanan notaries are required to keep in the journal should not be of a nature to violate the privacy rights of the signers. Specific information unique to the identity of the signer, such as (driver's) license numbers, social security numbers, or birthdates should never be entered into the notary journal" (NPH).

Journals Surrendered to County

"A notary public, upon resignation or removal from office or at the expiration of the notary public's term if the notary public is not reappointed, or, in case of the notary public's death, the notary public's legal representative shall … transfer in a timely manner all the journals kept by the notary public to the office of the county clerk and recorder of the county in which the notary public was a resident …" (MCA 1-5-419[1][a]).

For a knowing failure to surrender the journal(s) in this manner, the offender is liable for damages to any person injured by the failure (MCA 1-5-419[2]).

County Clerk Shall Provide Copies: "It is the duty of each county clerk and recorder to receive and safely keep all such records and papers of the notary in the case described in 1-5-419 and to give attested copies of them under a seal. The county clerk and recorder may charge the fees allowed by law to the notaries, and the copies have the same effect as if certified by the notary" (MCA 1-5-420).

AUTHENTICATION OF NOTARIAL ACTS

Secretary of State

Authenticating certificates for Notaries, including apostilles, are issued by the Montana Secretary of State's office (MCA 1-5-407).

Fees: $10 per document for an authentication, including an apostille, payable to "Montana Secretary of State." No credit cards accepted.

Address:
Office of Secretary of State
Notary and Certification Services
P.O. Box 202801
(1236 6th Avenue)
Helena, MT 59620-2801

For Courier Service:
Office of Secretary of State
Notary and Certification Services
1301 6th Avenue
Helena, MT 59601

Telephone: 1-406-444-1877 or 1-406-444-5379

Procedure: Mail or present in person the original notarized document(s), along with the appropriate fee and a stamped, addressed return envelope. The document must be properly notarized or it may not be authenticated by the state. Provide contact information and indicate the country of destination for the document(s). The Secretary of State's office will determine whether an apostille or an ordinary authenticating certificate is needed. A special "State Certification — Apostille or Authentication Request Form" may be downloaded from the website for this purpose (NPH).

Official School Records: In order for a certified copy of a school transcript or grade report to be authenticated by the state, an authorized school official (e.g., principal, registrar) must certify the document, and then that official's signature must be notarized. The following sample wording may be used above the Notary's certificate (NPH):

For School Official Certifying Original Document:

On _____ (date), I the undersigned, do hereby certify that this is a true and original _____ (type of document) issued by _____ (name of school).

_____
(signature of school official)

_____
(printed name and official title)

(Notary's certificate)

For School Official Certifying Copy of Original:

On _____ (date), I the undersigned, do hereby certify that this is a true and unaltered copy of the original _____ (type of document) issued by _____ (name of school).

_____
(signature of school official)

_____
(printed name and official title)

(Notary's certificate)

COMMISSIONING AND ADMINISTRATION

The Montana Secretary of State appoints and commissions the state's Notaries (MCA 1-5-401), regulating their activities and maintaining records on them, including each Notary's current business and residence addresses and telephone numbers (MCA 1-5-409[1]).

Applying for Commission

Qualifications: An applicant for appointment as a Montana Notary Public must: (a) have been a resident of Montana for at least 30 days preceding appointment (effective July 1, 2010), (b) be at least 18 years old, (c) not be a convicted felon and (d) not have had a Notary commission revoked in Montana or any other state (MCA 1-5-402[3] and NPH).

Course Required: Effective July 1, 2010, an applicant must satisfactorily complete a training program certified by the Secretary of State (MCA 1-5-402[1]). In addition, renewal applicants must take this same training "if at any time during the notary's term a complaint has been filed against the notary or the secretary of state's office has received evidence of improperly notarized documents by the notary" (MCA 1-5-402[2]).

The "Montana Notary Public Handbook" offers additional clarification: "All persons applying for appointment to a new commission must satisfactorily complete a training program certified by the Secretary of State…. A commission is considered new if the person has never held a notary commission in the state of Montana prior to making application or if a previous commission was not renewed within thirty days after the expiration of the previous commission...."

Application: New applicants must complete an "Application for Appointment as a Notary Public." The applicant's "Statement & Oath of Office" on the application must be signed and sworn to before another Notary. The original application, a $10,000 Notary surety bond and a filing fee of $25 must be submitted to the Secretary of State. The application materials must be submitted within 30 days (before or after) of the effective date of the bond (MCA 1-5-405 and NPH).

The renewal process is the same as for first-time applicants, except that renewing Notaries must submit an "Application for Reappointment as a Notary Public," which requests information on the Notary's current commission (NPH). Renewing Notaries "must submit the required paperwork no more than thirty days prior to (the) current commission expiration date or thirty days after (the) current commission expires" (website, "How to Renew Your Commission").

Non-Residents: Non-residents of Montana may not become Notaries in the state. However, Notaries commissioned by certain other states may operate in Montana — see "Notary Jurisdiction" below, under "Quick Facts."

Changes of Status

If Notary Changes Name: When a Notary's name is changed due to divorce, marriage or other circumstance, the Notary must contact his or her bonding company and request a rider for the Notary bond. Once the Notary receives the rider, he or she must sign it using the new signature and then send the signed bond rider to the Secretary of State along with a completed "Contact Information Update" form, available on the Secretary of State's website. The Secretary of State will then send the Notary a certificate reflecting the change of name, at which point the Notary can replace his or her official seal-stamp (MCA 1-5-409[2] and NPH).

If Notary Moves: Notaries who change their residence or business address or telephone number during their term of commission must notify the Secretary of State of the change in writing by submitting a completed "Contact Information Update" form, available on the Secretary of State's website.

If the Notary's city of residence changes, the Notary also must contact his or her bonding company and request a rider for the Notary bond. Once the Notary receives the rider, he or she must send it to the Secretary of State. The Secretary of State will then send the Notary a certificate reflecting the change of city of residence, at which point the Notary can replace his or her official seal-stamp (MCA 1-5-409[1] and NPH).

Moving from the state vacates the Notary's office and is equivalent to resignation (MCA 1-5-402[3]).

COUNTY CLERKS

To contact a Montana county clerk to find the journal of a former Notary (MCA 1-5-419 and -420), telephone information at 1-406-555-1212 and ask for the phone number of the county clerk or recorder for the appropriate county listed below.

County	City/Town
Beaverhead	Dillon
Big Horn	Hardin
Blaine	Chinook
Broadwater	Townsend
Carbon	Red Lodge
Carter	Ekalaka
Cascade	Great Falls
Chouteau	Ft. Benton
Custer	Miles City
Daniels	Scobey
Dawson	Glendive
Deer Lodge	Anaconda
Fallon	Baker
Fergus	Lewistown
Flathead	Kalispell
Gallatin	Bozeman
Garfield	Jordan
Glacier	Cut Bank
Golden Valley	Ryegate
Granite	Philipsburg
Hill	Havre
Jefferson	Boulder
Judith Basin	Stanford
Lake	Polson
Lewis and Clark	Helena
Liberty	Chester
Lincoln	Libby
Madison	Virginia City

County	City/Town
McCone	Circle
Meagher	White Sulphur Springs
Mineral	Superior
Missoula	Missoula
Musselshell	Roundup
Park	Livingston
Petroleum	Winnett
Phillips	Malta
Pondera	Conrad
Powder River	Broadus
Powell	Deer Lodge
Prairie	Terry
Ravalli	Hamilton
Richland	Sidney
Roosevelt	Wolf Point
Rosebud	Forsyth
Sanders	Thompson Falls
Sheridan	Plentywood
Silver Bow	Butte
Stillwater	Columbus
Sweet Grass	Big Timber
Teton	Choteau
Toole	Shelby
Treasure	Hysham
Valley	Glasgow
Wheatland	Harlowton
Wibaux	Wibaux
Yellowstone	Billings

QUICK FACTS

Notary Jurisdiction
Statewide (MCA 1-5-415).

May Act in Bordering State: "A Montana notarial officer may perform a notarial act in a bordering state if the state recognizes the officer's authority within the state" (MCA 1-5-605[1]). At present, Wyoming and North Dakota provide such recognition (MCA 1-5-605[2]).

Notary Term Length
Four years (MCA 1-5-403).

Notary Bond
$10,000, with the bond approved by the Secretary of State (MCA 1-5-405).

OTHER NOTARIAL OFFICERS

Besides Notaries Public, the following officers have statewide power to perform notarial acts: judges, clerks and deputy clerks of any court of the state (MCA 1-5-604[1]).

"The signature and title of a person performing a notarial act are prima facie evidence that the signature is genuine and that the person holds the designated title" (MCA 1-5-604[4]).

Reciprocity of Notarial Acts: "A notarial act performed in Montana by a notarial officer of a bordering state (i.e., Idaho, Wyoming, South Dakota, North Dakota) has the same effect under Montana law as if the act were performed by a Montana notarial officer, provided that the bordering state grants Montana's notarial officers similar authority within the bordering state" (MCA 1-5-605[2]). At present, Wyoming and North Dakota provide such reciprocity.

Nebraska

NOTARY SEAL

A Nebraska Notary must authenticate all official acts with a seal of office, and the seal's format must be as follows (RSN 64-210):

Kind

Inked Stamp: "Each notary public, before performing any duties of his or her office, shall provide himself or herself with an official ink stamp seal ..." (RSN 64-210). "Hand drawn representations of Notary Seals are not allowed" (ONPH).

Shape/Size

A rectangular shape with a size of 2 inches by $\frac{1}{2}$ inch, or a shape like the geographic form of the state of Nebraska is suggested by the Notary Section.

"Round seals are discouraged as there may NOT be enough space allowed on a document to properly affix a round seal" (ONPH).

Components

1. Name of Notary exactly as on commission;
2. "State of Nebraska";
3. "General Notary" or "General Notarial";
4. Commission expiration date.*

* Effective for all commissions issued after August 31, 2007, a Notary seal must include an expiration date. Formerly, this date was optional in the seal. "Notaries may not cross through and insert a new date or use correction fluid to change information on their Notary seal" (ONPH).

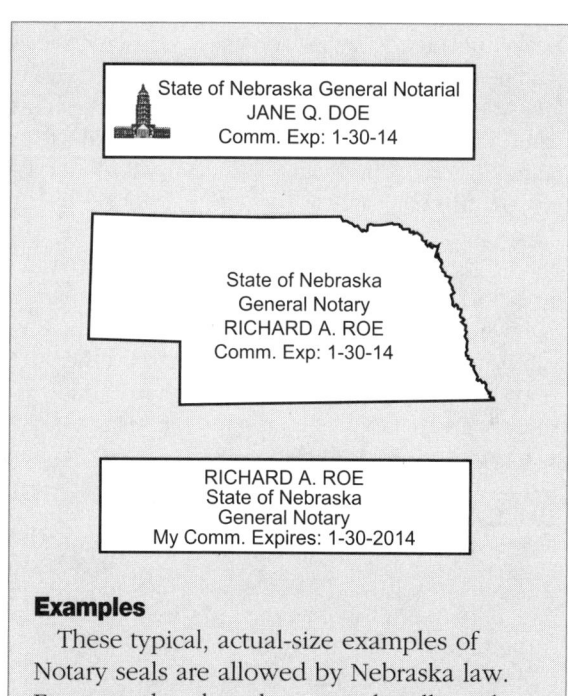

Examples

These typical, actual-size examples of Notary seals are allowed by Nebraska law. Formats other than these may be allowed.

NOTARY ADMINISTRATION

Office of Secretary of State
Business Services Division, Notary Section
State Capitol, Room 1301   1-402-471-2558
1445 "K" St.
P.O. Box 95104
Lincoln, NE 68509-5104

Website: www.sos.state.ne.us/business/notary/

NOTARY RULES

RSN — REVISED STATUTES OF NEBRASKA
ONPH — NEBRASKA OFFICIAL NOTARY PUBLIC HANDBOOK
NB — NOTARY BULLETIN NEWSLETTER
NLS — NEBRASKA NOTARY LAW SEMINAR

Most Notary rules are in the Revised Statutes of Nebraska, Chapter 64 ("Notaries Public").*

* The *Uniform Recognition of Acknowledgments Act* of 1968 is included virtually intact in this chapter as Article 2, Sections 64-201 through 64-210.

Other guidelines are in the "Nebraska Official Notary Public Handbook" (Revised Jan. 2, 2008) issued by the Secretary of State and available online. Editions of the Secretary's "Notary Bulletin" quarterly email newsletter are also available on the website, as is the Secretary's Power Point presentation, "Nebraska Notary Law Seminar: Charting the Changes of LB 315."

Must Fill in Expiration Date

"If a Notary's Seal contains their commission expiration date and there is a blank space on the document to write in the commission expiration date, (the Notary) must write in the date in addition to affixing your Notary Seal" (ONPH).

Seal, Signature Must Not Overprint

"The seal and signature of the Notary may NOT be affixed over printed wording or other signatures on the document" (ONPH).

Seal Not Retained by Employer

"Employers who pay for the Notary Commission fees for their employees should not retain the Notary Seal or Certificate of the employee upon the employee's removal from their employ as a Notary. A Commission is issued to a person, not the company who paid the fees" (ONPH).

Defective Seal Wording

"No deed, mortgage, affidavit, power of attorney or other instrument in writing shall be invalidated because of any defects in the wording of the seal of the notary public attached thereto" (RSN 76-217.01).

Commission Certificate for Seal Purchase

In order to purchase an official Notary ink stamp seal, the Notary should present his or her Commission Certificate to the vendor.

Notary's Signature

"The Notary's signature must be a written signature as a Notary may not use a rubber stamp to affix their name when notarizing a document .... When notarizing, the Notary must sign their name exactly as commissioned" (ONPH).

NOTARY POWERS

Nebraska Notaries are authorized to perform the following notarial acts (RSN 64-107):

1. Take acknowledgments and proofs*;
2. Administer oaths and affirmations**;
3. Execute jurats for signings by mark (RSN 64-105.02[1][d]);
4. Execute signature witnessings for signings by mark (RSN 64-105.02[1][d]);
5. Take depositions***;
6. Issue summons and command presence of witnesses for depositions in civil lawsuits, when directed to do so (RSN 64-108);
7. Execute protests;
8. "Exercise and perform such other powers and duties as by the law of nations, and according to commercial usage, or by the laws of the United States, or of any other state or territory of the United States, or of any other government or country, may be exercised and performed by notaries public."

* Taking Proofs: "If the grantor dies before acknowledgment, or if for any cause his attendance cannot be procured in order to make the same, or having appeared, he refused to acknowledge it, proof of the execution and delivery of the deed may be made by any competent subscribing witness thereto before any officer authorized to take acknowledgments. The witness must state, upon oath, his own place of residence, that he set his name to the deed as witness, that he knew the grantor in such deed, and saw him sign or heard him acknowledge he had signed the same. Such proof shall not be taken unless the officer is personally acquainted with such subscribing witness, or has satisfactory evidence that he is the same person who was a subscribing witness to such deed" (RSN 76-228).

** Affirmations: An affirmation is a "solemn declaration made by persons who conscientiously decline taking an oath. An affirmation is equivalent to an oath and is just as binding. If a person has religious or conscientious scruples against taking an oath, the Notary Public should have the person affirm" (ONPH).

*** Depositions: A deposition is the "testimony of a witness taken out of court or other hearing proceeding, under oath or by affirmation, before a Notary Public or other person, officer, or commissioner before whom such testimony is authorized by law to be taken, which is intended to be used at the trial or hearing" (ONPH).

Identifying Document Signers

"1. A notary public shall not perform any notarial act ... if the principal:

"a. Is not in the presence of the notary public at the time of the notarial act; and

"b. Is not personally known to the notary public or identified by the notary public through satisfactory evidence.

"2. For purposes of this section:

"a. Identified by the notary public through satisfactory evidence means identification of the individual based on:

"i. At least one document issued by a government agency that is current and that bears the photographic image of the individual's face and signature and a physical description of the individual, except that a properly stamped passport without a physical description is satisfactory evidence; or

"ii. The oath or affirmation of one credible witness unaffected by the document or transaction to be notarized who is personally known to the notary public and who personally knows the individual, or the oaths or affirmations of two credible witnesses unaffected by the document or transaction to be notarized who each personally knows the individual and shows to the notary public documentary identification as described in subdivision (a)(i) of this subsection; and

"b. Personal knowledge of identity or personally known means familiarity with an individual resulting from interactions with that individual over a period of time sufficient to dispel any reasonable uncertainty that the individual has the identity claimed" (RSN 64-105).

Representative Status Need Not Be Proven: If someone signs as president of a corporation, trustee of a trust, etc., the Notary does not need to ask for proof of official capacity (website, "Frequently Asked Questions").

Identifying Minors: "(M)inors may not sign or enter into contracts; however, there are certain situations where a minor's signature may need to be notarized… If the parents are not personally known to you, ask them for proper identification to prove their identity; have the minor and/or parents sign the (document) in your presence; and proceed to properly notarize…" (website, "Frequently Asked Questions").

Personal Appearance before Notary Essential

In the "Nebraska Notary Law Seminar "given by the Secretary of State's office to explain the statutory changes that took effect July 16, 2004, the importance of each signer's personal appearance before the Notary at the time of notarization is stressed:

"Administering an oath over the phone or by video conference is not administering an oath in the presence of the notary.

"Putting your notary seal and signature on a document that was signed 'just a few minutes ago in the office next door' is not performing a notarial act in the presence of the principal.

"The principal and the notary must be in the same room or location and able to effectively communicate by hearing and/or writing at the time the notarial act is performed."

Consider Demeanor of Signer

"Do consider the capacity and demeanor of the principal. If the principal does not seem to be coherent, understand the proceedings around them, or not have the capacity to enter into binding agreements because of age or disability do not notarize the document" (NLS).

Power to Issue Summons

When directed by a court or by a party in a pending civil lawsuit, the Notary may issue a summons to a witness for a deposition (RSN 64-108).

Correcting Notary Certificates

"If information in the document is incorrect or an error is made when completing the attestation clause, the error may be crossed through and the new information inserted. Correction fluid should never be used to correct or remove an error" (ONPH).

Predating and Postdating: "The date in the attestation clause must match the date the principal affixes (or acknowledges) their signature (because) a Notary may not pre-date or post-date when performing the Notarial Act" (ONPH).

Blank Spaces

"Prior to notarizing, the Notary should look over the document to be notarized to be sure there are no blank lines or spaces in the document. Blank lines or spaces should be: a) completed by the principal(s) or b) crossed through by the principal(s) prior to notarization. Failure to do so, leaves the document open to easy alteration after the notarial act is performed" (ONPH).

Signature by Mark

"The principal's signature may not be a rubber stamp" (ONPH). Instead, the Secretary of State's "Handbook" advises, if the principal is physically unable to write a signature, the procedures for a signing by mark or for having the Notary sign on the principal's behalf should be used.

"A notary public may certify the affixation of a signature by mark on a document presented for notarization if:

"a. The mark is affixed in the presence of the notary public and of two witnesses unaffected by the document;

"b. Both witnesses sign their own names beside the mark;

"c. The notary public writes below the mark: 'Mark affixed by (name of signer by mark) in presence of (names and addresses of witnesses) and undersigned notary public';

"d. The notary public notarizes the signature by mark through an acknowledgment, jurat, or signature witnessing." (RSN 64-105.02[1])

Signing for Person Unable to Sign

"A notary public may sign the name of a person physically unable to sign or make a mark on a document presented for notarization if:

"a. The person directs the notary public to do so in the presence of two witnesses unaffected by the document;

"b. The notary public signs the person's name in the presence of the person and the witnesses;

"c. Both witnesses sign their own names beside the signature;

"d. The notary public writes below the signature: 'Signature affixed by notary public in the presence of (names and addresses of person and two witnesses)'; and

"e. The notary public notarizes the signature through an acknowledgment, jurat, or signature witnessing" (RSN 64-105.02[2]).

NOTARY DON'TS

According to instructions in the "Nebraska Official Notary Public Handbook," a Notary Public may:
1. NOT notarize his or her own signature;
2. NOT "certify or copy certify that a government record is valid or authentic";
3. NOT "copy certify, authenticate, or notarize pictures, photographs, artwork, scripts, and the like as it serves no legal purpose nor has any force or effect";
4. NOT "notarize signatures for minor children"; however there are exceptions.

Notary May Not Act Like an Attorney

"1. A notary public who is not an attorney shall not engage in the unauthorized practice of law as provided in this section.

"2. If notarial certificate wording is not provided or indicated for a document, a notary public who is not an attorney shall not determine the type of notarial act or certificate to be used.

"3. A notary public who is not an attorney shall not assist another person in drafting, completing, selecting, or understanding a document or transaction requiring a notarial act.

"4. A notary public who is not an attorney shall not claim to have powers, qualifications, rights, or privileges that the office of notary public does not provide, including the power to counsel on immigration matters.

"5. A notary public who is not an attorney and who advertises notarial services in a language other than English shall include in any advertisement, notice, letterhead, or sign a statement prominently displayed in the same language as follows: 'I am not an attorney and have no authority to give advice on immigration or other legal matters.'

"6. A notary public who is not an attorney may not use the term notario publico or any equivalent non-English term in any business card, advertisement, notice, or sign.

"7. This section does not preclude a notary public who is duly qualified, trained, or experienced in a particular industry or professional field from selecting, drafting, completing, or advising on a document or certificate related to a matter within that industry or field.

"8. A violation of any of the provisions of this section shall be considered the unauthorized practice of law and subject to the penalties provided in section 7-101" (RSN 64-105.03).

Notary Should Not Read Document: "[A] Notary should not read in detail the document they have been asked to notarize or offer advice about the content or legality of the document; however, a notary should look for blank spaces or blank signature lines on the document. Blank lines should either be completed or crossed through by the principal(s) prior to notarization" (website, "Frequently Asked Questions").

Disqualifying Interests

A Notary who is:

1. An attorney, an employer or associate of an attorney, or a stockholder, officer or employee of a professional law corporation may notarize for the professional activities of that attorney or corporation (RSN 64-211[1]);

2. A real estate salesman or broker, or an employee or associate of such, may notarize for clients (RSN 64-211[2]);

3. An employee, member, shareholder, officer, agent or director of an insurance company, cooperative credit association or credit union may notarize for the company, association or union (RSN 64-212 and 64-213);

4. A stockholder, officer or director of a bank may notarize for the bank (RSN 64-214);

5. An employee, shareholder, director, agent or officer of a savings and loan association or industrial loan and investment company may notarize for the association or company (RSN 64-215).

Simply Signing, Stamping Insufficient

"(T)here should be some sort of attestation clause when a notarial act is performed, simply signing as notary public, dating, and stamping the seal is not a proper notarial act" (NLS). See also RSN 64-203.

Denial of Notarial Services

"Notaries are not required to perform requested notarial acts (however, discrimination in offering services is prohibited under appropriate federal, state or local law)" (NLS).

Notarizing for Relatives

"A notary public is disqualified from performing a notarial act ... if the notary is a spouse, ancestor, descendant, or sibling of the principal, including in-law, step, or half relatives" (RSN 64-105.01).

On the website ("Frequently Asked Questions"), it was clarified that Nebraska Notaries may notarize for their own aunts, uncles, nieces, nephews and cousins, but they may not notarize for their own parents, grandparents, children, grandchildren, husbands, wives, brothers and sisters, nor for such in-laws, step or half relatives as their own mother-in-law, step sister or half brother.

NOTARY SIGNING AGENTS

The Nebraska Secretary of State issued the following notice to all Notaries in the state on August 17, 2009 (updated January 1, 2010):

"The Nebraska Secretary of State's Office continues to urge notaries to exercise caution in considering 'signing agent' or 'mobile notary' offers.

"The fees a notary may charge are set by law. See Neb. Rev. Stat § 33-133 (Reissue 2008). Current law provides that notaries may charge $5.00 for taking acknowledgment of deed or other instrument. In addition to the $5.00 fee, the only other fee a notary is allowed by law to charge when taking acknowledgment of deed or other instrument is mileage at the current statutory rate of 51 cents per mile traveled.

"Further, current law provides that notaries may not act as real estate closing agents. Only persons (or their employees) licensed or regulated by one of the following regulating entities may act as real estate closing agents: the Department of Insurance, Supreme Court, Real Estate Commission, Federal Deposit Insurance Corporation, Federal Office of Thrift Supervision, Federal Farm Credit Administration, or National Credit Union Administration. If you are acting as a real estate closing agent, in violation of the law, you should be aware that this action would constitute a Class V misdemeanor."

An earlier communication from the Nebraska Secretary of State to all Notaries (March 14, 2003) is also instructive: "If a bank or mortgage company wants to employ a notary to perform notary services, act as a 'signing agent' or 'mobile notary officer' and wants to pay more than the statutory rate, that is up to them. However, the fee a notary may charge for their services is set forth in law... Neither the notary nor a third party changing notary fees as part of the services they provide should exceed the statutory fees in charging for notary services."

NOTARY FEES

The maximum fees a Nebraska Notary may charge are (RSN 33-133):
1. Taking an acknowledgment: $5;
2. Administering an oath or affirmation: $2;
3. Taking an affidavit, with jurat and seal: $2;
4. Executing a protest: $1, plus $2 for recording and $2 for each notice of protest.

Travel Fees for Protest

For each mile traveled in serving notice of protest, a Notary may charge at the rate provided in NRS 81-1176 for state employees (RSN 33-133). The current rate is 51 cents per mile, according to officials in the Notary Section.

Fees of County Officers

All fees for notarial acts received by Notaries who are acting officially as county officers, or as deputies or employees of such officers, must be reported to the county board and paid into the county treasury (RSN 33-153).

No Fee for State Employee

"An employee of the state or its political subdivisions may not charge the fees prescribed in this section if his or her governmental employer paid the commission and bonding fees required of notaries public" (RSN 33-133).

NOTARY CERTIFICATES

Nebraska has adopted the *Uniform Recognition of Acknowledgments Act* virtually intact, including the short-form certificates (RSN 64-206) for:

1. Acknowledgment by individual;
2. Acknowledgment by corporation;
3. Acknowledgment by partnership;
4. Acknowledgment by limited liability company*;
5. Acknowledgment by attorney in fact;
6. Acknowledgment by public officer, trustee or personal representative.

* The short-form certificate for a limited liability company is not in the Act in Appendix 3. It is reproduced below.

The Notary's official seal must be added to each short-form certificate prescribed by the Act (RSN 64-210).

For the text of the above certificates, see "Uniform Recognition of Acknowledgments Act (1968)," Section 6, in Appendix 3.

Acknowledgment by Limited Liability Company (RSN 64-206[4]):

State of _____
County of _____

The foregoing instrument was acknowledged before me this _____ *(date) by* _____ *(name of acknowledging member or agent), member (or agent) on behalf of* _____ *(name of limited liability company), a limited liability company.*

(Signature of Person Taking Acknowledgment)
(Title or Rank)
(Serial Number, if any)   *(Seal)*

Format for Acknowledgment Certificate

"The form of a certificate of acknowledgment used by a person whose authority is recognized under (Uniform Recognition of Acknowledgments Act, Section 1) shall be accepted in this state if:

"1. The certificate is in a form prescribed by the laws or regulations of this state;

"2. The certificate is in a form prescribed by the laws or regulations applicable in the place in which the acknowledgment is taken;

"3. The certificate contains the words acknowledged before me; or their substantial equivalent" (RSN 64-204).

If No Certificate Wording Provided

"Nebraska Statute § 64-105.03[2] states ... (i)f notarial certificate wording is not provided or indicated for a document, a Notary Public who is not an attorney shall not determine the type of notarial act or certificate to be used ...

"If you, as a Notary, are presented with a document to be notarized that does not have an attestation clause, you should suggest to the principal:

"1. That the document does not have an attestation clause, and a Notary merely signing the document and affixing their seal does not constitute a proper notarial act.

"2. That the principal may want to have an attorney review the document and affix a proper attestation clause, or

"3. If the principal chooses not to use an attorney and is comfortable making the decision himself or herself, you may show the acknowledgments (in RSN 64-206) and ask the principal if one of these Acknowledgments would work for their document. If the principal selects one of the Acknowledgments, you may then fill out the wording in the Acknowledgment; have the principal sign (after being properly identified); proceed to notarize the document; and then attach the Acknowledgment to the document" (website, "Sample Acknowledgment Forms").

Acknowledgment by Signer by Mark (website):

Mark affixed by _____ *(name of principal), in the presence of the following two*

witnesses and undersigned Notary Public:

_____ _____ *(printed names of two witnesses)*
_____ _____ *(street addresses of two witnesses)*
_____ _____ *(city/state/zips of two witnesses)*
_____ _____ *(signatures of two witnesses)*

State of Nebraska
County of _____

Acknowledged before me on this _____ day of _____, 20 ____, by _____ (name of principal acknowledging).

(SEAL, SIGNATURE OF NOTARY)

Acknowledgment by Person Directing Notary to Sign (website):

Signature affixed by _____ (name of Notary), in the presence of the following two witnesses:

_____ _____ *(printed names of two witnesses)*
_____ _____ *(street addresses of two witnesses)*
_____ _____ *(city/state/zips of two witnesses)*
_____ _____ *(signatures of two witnesses)*

State of Nebraska
County of _____

Acknowledged before me on this _____ day of _____, 20 ____, by _____ (name of person acknowledging who directed Notary to sign on his or her behalf).

(SEAL, SIGNATURE OF NOTARY)

ELECTRONIC NOTARIZATIONS

The state of Nebraska has not yet adopted statutes or regulations expressly establishing rules, definitions and procedures for electronic notarization.

UETA Recognizes Notary's eSignature

Effective July 13, 2000, Nebraska adopted the Uniform Electronic Transactions Act (RSN 86-612 through 86-643), including the provision on notarization and acknowledgment, thereby recognizing the legal validity of electronic signatures used by Notaries:

"If a law requires a signature or record to be notarized, acknowledged, verified, or made under oath, the requirement is satisfied if the electronic signature of the person authorized to perform those acts, together with all other information required to be included by other applicable law, is attached to or logically associated with the signature or record" (RSN 86-638).

NOTARY RECORDS

Maintenance of a record of the Notary's official acts is not specifically required by statute, though Notaries are directed to "faithfully discharge the duties pertaining to said office and keep records according to law" (RSN 64-101[7]).

Recommended by Secretary of State

"Journals are optional under Nebraska law but are recommended by our office" (website, "Advisory on Notary Associations"). "The Secretary of State strongly recommends the use of notary journals …. Many complaints filed with the Secretary of State's Office could be quickly settled if a complete notary journal entry were recorded at the time of the notarial act" (NLS).

Recommended Journal Entries: A sample journal format with entry instructions is provided on the Secretary of State's website ("Sample Notary Journal").

The recommended journal entries are:
1. Date on document;
2. Date notarial act performed;
3. Type of document;
4. Type of ID presented by principal(s);
5. Printed name of principal(s);
6. Printed address of principal(s);
7. Signature of principal(s).

AUTHENTICATION OF NOTARIAL ACTS

Secretary of State

Authenticating certificates for acts by Notaries, including apostilles, are issued only by the Nebraska Secretary of State's office.

Fees: $10 per document for any certificate of authentication for a Notary, including an apostille.

Address:
Office of Secretary of State
Business Services Division, Notary Section
P.O. Box 95104
Lincoln, NE 68509

In Person or Delivery:
Office of Secretary of State
Business Services Division, Notary Section
State Capitol, Room 1301
1445 "K" Street
Lincoln, NE 68509

Telephone: 1-402-471-2558

Procedure: Mail or present in person the original notarized document(s), along with the appropriate fee, and instructions as to the country of destination, as well as where the certification should be sent and a telephone number for any questions. Documents are processed and mailed out on the day they are received. "Documents are mailed by first class mail. If you want express mail then you will need to provide a pre-paid addressed airbill" (website, "Apostilles and Authentication").

COMMISSIONING AND ADMINISTRATION

Effective July 16, 2004, the Secretary of State replaced the Governor as the Notary appointing and commissioning official for the state of Nebraska (RSN 64-101[1]). The Secretary appoints and commissions one class of Notaries — "General Notaries Public" — with statewide jurisdiction.

Applying for Commission

Qualifications: An applicant for a commission as a Nebraska Notary Public must (RSN 64-101, NLS): (a) be at least 19 years old, (b) be a resident of Nebraska, (c) be able to read and write English and (d) not have been convicted of a felony or a crime involving fraud or dishonesty. (Applicants no longer need be endorsed by 25 registered voters of their county.)

Take-Home Test Required: A first-time applicant must pass a written, open-book, "take-home" examination (RSN 64-101.01) before submitting an application. The test is available only from the Secretary of State's office via regular mail. Renewing Notaries need not take the exam, but those who let their commissions expire must do so. There are 20 multiple-choice or true-false questions on the test; an applicant may miss no more than three questions. The applicant must take an oath that he or she was not assisted during the test by another person. Any person failing the test may take it once more within 60 days; if failing a second time, the person must wait six months before retaking it. The applicant is given only three attempts to pass the exam.

Application: The Notary "application packet" — including an application form with instructions, a bond form and the "Nebraska Official Notary Public Handbook" — may be sent to the applicant with the test or downloaded from the Notary Division website; the applicant should first receive written notice of test passage before submitting the application packet.

A $15,000 Notary surety bond must be submitted with the application (RSN 64-102), along with the $30 application fee. Renewals should be sent in within 30 days of the commission expiration date (RSN 64-104). There are different application forms for first-time and for renewing Notaries — for both, the "Notarial Oath" must be taken by the applicant before another Notary. The Notary oath of office on the "General Notary Public Bond Form," which accompanies the application, must also be notarized. As a result of enactment of Legislative Bill 403, which took effect October 1, 2009, a United States Citizenship Attestation Form is required for any new or renewing applicant (RSN 4-108 through 4-114).

Bilingual applicants may authorize their names to be placed on a list of bilingual Notaries maintained in the Secretary's office.

Non-Residents: Out-of-state residents may not apply to become Nebraska Notaries, even if they are employed in Nebraska.

Changes of Status

If Notary Changes Name: "Any person, whose name is legally changed after a commission as a notary public is issued to him or her, may continue to act as such notary public and use the original commission, seal, and name until the expiration or termination of such commission. The bond given by such notary public shall continue in effect, regardless of such legal change of name of such notary public, if the notary public uses the name under which the commission is issued" (RSN 64-114).

The Notary also has the option of applying for a new commission using the new name. This will entail filling out a new application, obtaining a new bond in the new name, submitting an explanation of the reason for the name change, and paying the $30 application fee. Upon receipt of these items, a new commission will be issued (website, "Frequently Asked Questions").

If Notary Moves: A Notary must notify the Secretary of State of any change of residence within 45 days of the change, using a form prescribed by the Secretary, available on the website (RSN 64-105.04).

If Notary Moves from State: "Every notary public removing from the State of Nebraska shall notify the Secretary of State of such removal. Such a removal shall terminate the term of his office" (RSN 64-112).

COUNTY OFFICES

In the state of Nebraska, county officials have no role in the administration of the state Notary program, nor in the authentication of notarial acts.

QUICK FACTS

Notary Jurisdiction
Statewide (RSN 64-101[2]). Effective July 16, 2004, there is one class of Notaries in the state, "General Notaries Public," with statewide jurisdiction.

Notary Term Length
Four years (RSN 64-101[8]).

Notary Bond
$15,000, with an incorporated surety company licensed in the state. The bond is filed with the Secretary of State (RSN 64-102 and 64-109).

N

Nevada

NOTARY SEAL

A Nevada Notary must authenticate all official acts with an inked stamp (NRS 240.1655[1][d]. The stamp's format must be as follows (NRS 240.040):

Kind

Rubber or Other Mechanical Stamp: The seal must be "imprinted in indelible, photographically reproducible ink with a rubber or other mechanical stamp ... As used in this section, 'mechanical stamp' includes an imprint made by a computer or other similar technology" (NRS 240.040[1][a] and [5]).

In Nevada, the Notary's official imprinting device is generally referred to as the "Notary stamp," which typically is a rubber inking stamp. The term "Notary seal" is reserved for embossers, which Notaries in the state were required to use prior to July 1, 1965 (NRS 240.040[2]).

Shape/Size

Rectangular, not larger than 1 inch by 2½ inches. A border for the stamp is optional (NRS 240.040[3][a]).

Components

The required components for the stamp are as follows (NRS 240.040[1][b]):
1. Notary's name;
2. "Notary Public, State of Nevada";
3. Appointment expiration date;

JANE Q. DOE
Notary Public, State of Nevada
Appointment No. 1234567
My Appt. Expires Jan 30, 2018

Examples

The above typical, actual-size example of a Notary stamp is allowed by Nevada law. Formats other than this may also be permitted. The Great Seal and border are optional.

NOTARY ADMINISTRATION

Office of Secretary of State
Notary Division   1-775-684-5708
101 N. Carson Street, Suite 3
Carson City, NV 89701

Website: www.nvsos.gov/index.aspx?page=165

NOTARY RULES

NRS — Nevada Revised Statutes

Most Notary regulations are in the Nevada Revised Statutes:

a. Chapter 240, "Notaries Public and Commissioned Abstracters" including the "Uniform Law on Notarial Acts"*;

b. Chapter 111, "Estates in Property; Conveyancing and Recording."

* This is the *Uniform Law on Notarial Acts* of 1982, adopted with certain omissions.

4. Number on Notary's certificate of appointment;
5. "Nonresident" if Notary resides in adjoining state;
6. OPTIONAL: Great Seal of the State of Nevada.

Stamp, Signature Must Not Overprint

"A notary public shall not affix his stamp over printed material" (NRS 240.040[4]).

"A notarial officer shall not affix his signature over printed material" (NRS 240.1655[6]).

"Your signature and stamp by themselves do not constitute a complete notarization. You also need to complete the notarial wording" (website, "FAQs").

"The notary stamp must be readable, and the 1997 law prohibits placing your notary stamp or your signature over printed material. You may use the back of the document or use an attached sheet. Note on the document that a notarial certificate is attached and note on the notarial certificate the kind of document to which it is attached" (website, "FAQs").

Conditions for Manufacturing Stamp

"A person or governmental entity shall not make, manufacture or otherwise produce a notary's stamp unless the notary public presents his original or amended certificate of appointment or a certified copy of his original or amended certificate of appointment to that person or governmental entity" (NRS 240.045[3]).

<u>More Than One Stamp Allowed</u>: A Notary may obtain and use more than one stamp (website, "FAQs").

Lost or Damaged Stamp

"1. If the stamp of a notary public is lost, the notary public shall, within 10 days after the stamp is lost, submit to the secretary of state a request for an amended certificate of appointment, on a form provided by the secretary of state, and obtain a new stamp …

"2. If the stamp is destroyed, broken, damaged or otherwise rendered inoperable, the notary public shall immediately notify the secretary of state of that fact and obtain a new stamp …" (NRS 240.045).

Stamp Must Be Kept Secure

"A notary public shall keep his or her stamp in a secure location during any period in which the notary public is not using the stamp to perform a notarial act" (NRS 240.040[5]).

New Stamp for Amended Certificate

After securing an amended certificate of appointment due to a change of address, signature or name, the Notary must destroy the old stamp and obtain a new one with the new information (NRS 240.036[5][a]).

Employer May Not Withhold Stamp

"It is unlawful for a person who comes into possession of the official stamp, journal or certificate of appointment of a notary public to withhold such an item from the notary public, whether or not the person provided the notary public with the money to acquire the item." Such items are considered the "personal property" of the Notary (NRS 240.143).

Notary's Resignation or Death

Upon the resignation or death of a current Notary, the Notary — or the executor of the Notary's estate — must notify the Secretary of State and destroy the official stamp (NRS 240.051[1]). "The stamp must be destroyed immediately" (website, "FAQs").

NOTARY POWERS

Nevada Notaries are authorized to perform the following notarial acts (NRS 240.004):
1. Take acknowledgments* and proofs**;
2. Administer oaths and affirmations***;
3. Execute jurats****;
4. Certify copies*****;
5. Make or note protests of negotiable instruments******.
6. Perform other duties as prescribed by a specific statute

* <u>Acknowledgments</u>: "The document signer must present the document to you, the notarial officer, and acknowledge or declare (state) that he or she previously signed the document, or the document signer can sign the document in your presence. If the document is signed in a representative capacity — for example, the person is an officer of a corporation — the person must declare (state) to you that he or she signed the document with proper authority and executed it as the act of the person or entity represented" (website, "Duties").

** <u>Proofs by Subscribing Witness</u>: NRS 111.265 authorizes Notaries, justices of the peace, and judges and clerks of courts having a seal to take acknowledgments and proofs.

"No proof by a subscribing witness shall be taken unless the witness shall be personally known to the person taking the proof to be the person whose name is subscribed to the conveyance as witness thereto, or shall be proved to be such by the oath or affirmation of a credible witness" (NRS 111.120).

"If a document signer cannot personally appear before a notary, a subscribing witness may bring the document to the notary and swear or affirm that the signature is that of the document signer. The subscribing witness had to be present when the document was signed … Only documents requiring an acknowledgment can be notarized through a subscribing witness. Any document requiring an oath or affirmation (like an affidavit) cannot be notarized in this manner.

"To guard against fraud, you must personally know the subscribing witness.

"You give the subscribing witness an oath in which he or she swears or affirms that the signature is that of the document signer's and then you complete a subscribing witness jurat. The subscribing witness then signs the jurat in your presence ..." (website, "Duties").

There are provisions for a proof by handwriting in the event that a subscribing witness is dead or cannot be found (NRS 111.135 through 111.150).

*** Oaths and Affirmations: "The individual taking the oath or affirmation raises (his or her) right hand while you, the notarial officer, state the words of the oath or affirmation. The oath taker then repeats these words back to you. In some cases a written statement must then be signed, and the notarial officer completes the document as required" (website, "Duties").

**** Jurats: "In executing a jurat, (a notarial officer shall) administer an oath or affirmation to the affiant and determine, from personal knowledge or satisfactory evidence, that the affiant is the person named in the document. The affiant shall sign the document in the presence of the notarial officer. The notarial officer shall administer the oath or affirmation required pursuant to this paragraph in substantially the following form: Do you (solemnly swear, or affirm) that the statements in this document are true, (so help you God)?" (NRS 240.1655[2][e]).

"Be sensitive to people who, for religious reasons, do not take an oath by swearing. If such a person appears before you, substitute the word 'affirm' for 'swear' and do not add the phrase 'so help you God.' The person then signs the document in your presence, and you complete the jurat" (website, "Duties").

***** Certifying Copies: "In certifying a copy of a document, (a notarial officer shall) photocopy the entire document and certify that the photocopy is a true and correct copy of the document that was presented to the notarial officer" (NRS 240.1655[2][c]). However, Notaries may not certify photocopies of a certificate of birth, death or marriage, or a divorce decree (NRS 240.075[5] and 440.175[2]). "When a notary public certifies that a document is a certified or true copy of an original document, the certification shall not be deemed to be evidence that the notary public knows the contents of the document" (NRS 240.063[2]).

"The notarial wording used to certify a copy does not indicate that you are certifying to an original document" (website, "FAQs").

"If you are asked to certify a copy (written in a foreign language), you should make the photocopy yourself rather than try to compare two copies" (website, "FAQs").

****** Protests: "In making or noting a protest of a negotiable instrument, (a notarial officer shall) verify compliance with the provisions of subsection 2 of NRS 104.3505" (NRS 240.1655[2][d]).

"A notary public shall not... (m)ake or note a protest of a negotiable instrument unless the notary public is employed by a depository institution and the protest is made or noted within the scope of that employment. As used in this subsection, 'depository institution' has the meaning ascribed to it in NRS 657.037" (NRS 240.075[10]).

"A protest is a declaration in writing made by — among others — a notary public, on behalf of the holder of a bill or note, indicating that acceptance or payment has been refused. The notarial officer must determine the matters set forth in NRS 104.3505, so knowledge of banking and commercial paper is a prerequisite of performing this service. The law does not provide a suggested format or wording" (website, "Duties").

Identifying Signers

In taking an acknowledgment, in executing a jurat, or in administering an oath or affirmation, a Notary must identify the principal "from personal knowledge or satisfactory evidence" (NRS 240.1655[2]).

"A notary public who is appointed pursuant to (Chapter 240) shall not willfully notarize the signature of a person unless the person is in the presence of the notary public and:

"(a) Is known to the notary public; or

"(b) If unknown to the notary public, provides documentary evidence of identification to the notary public." A Notary who violates this provision, or any person who abets a Notary in violating this provision, is guilty of a gross misdemeanor (NRS 240.155).

Satisfactory Evidence Defined: Satisfactory evidence means that the signer is either (a) personally known to the Notary, or (b) identified on the oath or affirmation of a credible witness who "is known personally to the signer of the document and the notarial officer," or (c) identified through an identifying document which contains a signature and a photograph, or (d) identified through a consular identification card issued by a foreign consulate located within Nevada, or (e) identified on the oath or affirmation of a subscribing witness personally known to the Notary or (f) in the case of a person 65 years of age or older and without recourse to identification methods (a) through (e) above, is identified by an ID card issued by a governmental agency or a senior citizen center (NRS 240.1655[4] and [8] and 240.0025[2]).

Credible Witness Requirements: "If a credible witness is used, that person must also sign your journal…. The credible witness needs to be present" (website, "FAQS").

An oath or affirmation administered by a Notary to a credible witness must be in substantially the following form: "Do you (solemnly swear, or affirm) that you personally know _____ (name of person who signed the document) (so help you God)?" (NRS 240.1655[5]).

Determining Comprehension Not Obligatory

"Must I determine if the person signing before me understands what he or she is signing? – You are not obligated to make this determination. If you are not comfortable performing a notarial service, you may refuse…" (website, "FAQs").

Signature by Mark

"In order that a signature by mark may be acknowledged or may serve as the signature to any sworn statement, it must be witnessed by two persons who must subscribe their own names as witnesses thereto." The name of the person making the mark must be written near the mark (NRS 52.305).

A person using a mark in the state may register the mark with the Nevada Secretary of State (NRS 600.340).

Signature Stamp Use Due to Disability

Under NRS Chapter 426, a person who is unable to write a signature due to a physical disability may use a signature stamp to affix a signature "any time that a signature is required by law":

"A person, government, governmental agency and political subdivision of a government must treat each signature affixed by (such a person) through the use of a signature stamp in the same manner as it treats a signature made in writing" (NRS 426.257).

Notarize A Blank Document?

"What if I am asked to notarize a signature that is on a blank piece of paper (no text)? — You must ask your customer to write an explanation as to why they want their signature notarized…This statement may be as simple as: 'I have been asked to have my signature notarized for verification'" (website, "FAQs").

Foreign-Language Document

"Can I notarize a document that is written in a foreign language? — In most instances, yes. All you need is a title to put in your journal, and you can use the title the person gives you. However, you may not be able to witness a signature because you must be able to tell if that person is named in the document. If you are asked to certify a copy, you should make the photocopy yourself rather than try to compare two copies. You may need to check with an interpreter as to the type, or title, of the document. If this document is false or endorses or promotes a product, you will not know that. Finally, if the document is written in a language you can not read, you must add the notarial wording in English" (website, "FAQs").

Steps to Proper Notarization

"There is a correct order of steps to follow when notarizing signatures. Never change or streamline the process. It may cause an incomplete notarization resulting in a violation of Nevada Notary law.

"Print and use the following Quick Reference Procedure to prevent errors in notarizing" (website, "Notarial Wording"):

1. Read notarial wording.
2. Examine signer's ID.
3. Document signer signs journal.
4. Complete journal entry.
5. Document signer signs document, if unsigned.
6. Complete notarial wording.
7. Sign and stamp the document.

Notary Availability to Public

"May I set aside certain hours to notarize documents for the general public and limit notarization to those hours? (Example: 1 p.m. to 2 p.m. only) – This is a business decision to be made by each notary. The law does not prohibit such a practice" (website, "FAQs").

"Do I have to declare that I am a notary if a person off the street asks, 'Where can I find a notary?' – No. The law simply states that a 'notary public may, during normal business hours, perform notarial acts in lawful transactions for a person who requests the act and tenders the appropriate fee' (see NRS 240.060)" (website, "FAQs").

NOTARY DON'TS

A Nevada Notary may:
1. NOT willingly notarize for an individual unless that person is in the presence of the Notary and is known to the Notary or produces a credible witness or documentary evidence of identification (NRS 240.155[1]);
2. NOT influence a person to enter or not enter into a lawful transaction involving a notarial act performed by that Notary (NRS 240.075[1]);
3. NOT "certify an instrument containing a statement known by (the Notary) to be false" (NRS 240.075[2]);
4. NOT perform any act as a Notary with intent to deceive or defraud, "including, without limitation, altering the journal that he is required to keep" (NRS 240.075[3]);
5. NOT endorse or promote any product, service, or offering if the Notary's title or stamp is used in the endorsement or promotional statement (NRS 240.075[4]);
6. NOT certify photocopies of a certificate of birth, death or marriage, or of a divorce decree (NRS 240.075[5]);
7. NOT allow any other person to use the Notary's stamp (NRS 240.075[6]);
8. NOT allow any other person to sign the Notary's name in a notarial capacity (NRS 240.075[7]);
9. NOT notarize a document that contains only a signature (NRS 240.075[8]);.
10. NOT notarize a document "including a form that requires the signer to provide information within blank spaces, unless the document has been filled out completely and has been signed" (NRS 240.075[9]);
11. NOT reproduce a signed Notary certificate for use in a mailing to endorse, promote, or sell any product, service, or offering (NRS 240.145[1]);
12. NOT, as a non-attorney, advertise notarial services in a language other than English, except in a single desk plaque, without including with the ad in the foreign language and in a conspicuous size the following statement: "I AM NOT AN ATTORNEY IN THE STATE OF NEVADA. I AM NOT LICENSED TO GIVE LEGAL ADVICE. I MAY NOT ACCEPT FEES FOR GIVING LEGAL ADVICE." (NRS 240.085[1]);
13. NOT, as a non-attorney, "use the term 'notario,' 'notario publico' or any other non-English term in any form of communication that advertises his services as a notary public including, without limitation, a business card, stationery, notice, and sign" (NRS 240.085[2]).

Notaries No Longer Take Depositions

"The authority to take a deposition was removed from the list of notarial acts in the law by the 1995 Legislature." Certified court reporters now exclusively take depositions (website, "FAQs").

Disqualifying Interests

Nevada Notaries may not notarize a document if they (NRS 240.065[1]):

1. Signed the document or are named in it;
2. Have received or will receive as a direct result any "commission, fee, advantage, right, title, interest, property, or other consideration in excess of the fee authorized pursuant to NRS 240.100 for the notarial act";
3. Are a relative of the signer by marriage or blood.

<u>'Relative' Defined</u>: As used above in NRS 240.065[1], "relative" includes (NRS 240.065[3]):

   a. A spouse, parent, grandparent or stepparent;
   b. A natural born child, stepchild or adopted child;
   c. A grandchild, brother, sister, half brother, half sister, stepbrother or stepsister;
   d. A grandparent, parent, brother, sister, half brother, half sister, stepbrother or stepsister of the Notary's spouse; and

e. A natural born child, stepchild or adopted child of a sibling or half sibling of the Notary or of a sibling or half sibling of the Notary's spouse.

Attorneys Exempted: "A notary public who is an attorney licensed to practice law in this State may perform a notarial act on an instrument or pleading if he has (received) or will receive directly from a transaction relating to the instrument or pleading a fee for providing legal services in excess of the fee authorized pursuant to NRS 240.100 for the notarial act" (NRS 240.065[2]).

Notarizing False Title Documents

Legislation that took effect July 1, 2011, defines the new crime of "making a false representation concerning title" and makes it a category C felony (NRS 205.395). This crime applies when any person "(e)xecutes or notarizes a document purporting to create an interest in, or a lien or encumbrance against, real property, that is recorded in the office of the county recorder in which the real property is located and who knows or has reason to know that the document is forged or groundless, contains a material misstatement or false claim or is otherwise invalid…"

NOTARY SIGNING AGENTS

Notary Signing Agents may operate within the state of Nevada, but they are cautioned by the state to adhere strictly to the statutory schedule of fees for notarial acts and for travel, as outlined immediately below.

NOTARY FEES

The maximum fees for notarial acts are (NRS 240.100[1]):
1. For taking an acknowledgment, $5.00 for the first signature of each signer, plus $2.50 for each additional signature of each signer;
2. For administering an oath or affirmation without a signature, $2.50;
3. For executing a jurat, $5.00 per signature;
4. For certifying a copy, $2.50.

Travel Fees

Notaries may charge an additional fee for traveling to perform a notarial act if (a) they are asked to travel by the person requesting the notarial act, (b) they explain to the person requesting the act that the fee is in addition to the statutory fee and not required by law, (c) there is agreement in advance upon the hourly rate to be charged for the travel, and (d) the fee does not exceed $10 per hour for travel between 6 a.m. and 7 p.m. or $25 per hour for travel between 7 p.m. and 6 a.m. "The notary public may charge a minimum of 2 hours for such travel and shall charge on a pro rata basis after the first 2 hours" (NRS 240.100[3]).

A Notary is entitled to the travel fee agreed upon in advance if (a) the person requesting the notarization cancels the request after the Notary has begun the requested travel, or (b) the Notary "is unable to perform the requested notarial act as a result of the actions of the person who requested the notarial act or any other person who is necessary for the performance of the notarial act" (NRS 240.100[4]).

In addition, the website ("FAQs") states: "if a travel fee is going to be assessed, pursuant to NRS 240.100(3)(d)(1)(2), full disclosure of the travel fee must be made in advance of the travel and be agreed upon by the person requesting the service."

The travel fee must be noted in the Notary's official journal, along with the "date and time that the notary public began and ended such travel" (NRS 240.100[5]).

Payable in Advance

All fees are payable in advance, if demanded (NRS 240.100[2]).

No Unauthorized Fees

"A notary public shall not charge a fee to perform a service unless he is authorized to charge a fee for such a service pursuant to this chapter" (NRS 240.130).

"The statute doesn't require that you charge a fee. But if you charge one person and not another, other laws such as those prohibiting discrimination may be applicable. Check with an attorney" (website, "FAQs").

Employer May Prohibit Fees

"A person who employs a notary public may prohibit the notary public from charging a fee for a notarial act that the notary public performs within the scope of his employment. Such a person shall not require the notary public whom he employs to surrender to him all or part of a fee charged by the notary public for a notarial act performed outside the scope of his employment" (NRS 240.100[6]).

"The statutes state that the notary can charge a fee. The issue of who keeps the fee (notary or employer) can be negotiated between you and your employer" (website, "FAQs").

Fees Must Be Posted

All Notaries who charge for notarizing must conspicuously post a table of fees for notarial acts in their offices, using no smaller than ½-inch type (NRS 240.110).

NOTARY CERTIFICATES

Nevada has adopted much of the *Uniform Law on Notarial Acts*, including the short-form certificates (NRS 240.166, 240.1665, 240.167 and 240.168, respectively) for:

1. Acknowledgment by individual;
2. Acknowledgment by representative;
3. Jurat ("verification upon oath or affirmation");
4. Certifying copy of document.

For the text of these certificates, see "Uniform Law on Notarial Acts (1982)," Section 8, in Appendix 2.

Nevada also has adopted certificates for an acknowledgment by a signer who is identified by a credible witness, for an acknowledgment by an attorney in fact, for the jurat of a subscribing witness, and for an oath or affirmation of office (NRS 240.169, 240.1667, 240.1685 and 240.1663, respectively). The text of these certificates appears below.

Specifically for the acknowledgment of a durable power of attorney for either finances or health care, effective October 1, 2009, Nevada has adopted the Uniform Power of Attorney Act (NRS Chapter 162A). This Act stipulates specific wording for the Notary certificate on such documents (NRS 162A.620). The text of this certificate also appears below.

On all these Nevada certificates, the "title and rank" of the notarial officer are indicated as "optional," since this information appears within the Notary's mandatory stamp.

Requirements for Any Notarial Certificate

"1. A notarial act must be evidenced by a certificate that:

"(a) Identifies the county, including, without limitation, Carson City, in this state in which the notarial act was performed in substantially the following form:

"State of Nevada
"County of _____

"(b) Except as otherwise provided in this paragraph, includes the name of the person whose signature is being notarized. If the certificate is for certifying a copy of a document, the certificate must include the name of the person presenting the document. If the certificate is for the jurat of a subscribing witness, the certificate must include the name of the subscribing witness.

"(c) Is signed and dated in ink by the notarial officer performing the notarial act.

"(d) If the notarial officer performing the notarial act is a notary public, includes the statement imprinted with the stamp of the notary public, as described in NRS 240.040.

"(e) If the notarial officer performing the notarial act is not a notary public, includes the title of the office of the notarial officer and may include the official stamp or seal of that office. If the officer is a commissioned officer on active duty in the military service of the United States, the certificate must also include the officer's rank" (NRS 240.1655[1]) ....

"3. A certificate of a notarial act is sufficient if it meets the requirements of subsections 1 and 2 and it:

"(a) Is in the short form set forth in NRS 240.166 to 240.169, inclusive;

"(b) Is in a form otherwise prescribed by the law of this state;

"(c) Is in a form prescribed by the laws or regulations applicable in the place in which the notarial act was performed; or

"(d) Sets forth the actions of the notarial officer and those are sufficient to meet the requirements of the designated notarial act" (NRS 240.1655[3]).

Notarial Certificate Wording: "If you are notarizing a document that was created without the notarial wording or only has part of the required wording then you will need to handwrite, type or stamp it on the document.

"It is up to the document signer to select the type of notarial wording you add" (website, "Notarial Wording").

If No Room for Notarial Certificate

"When there is no room for the notarial certificate (such as on many DMV documents), may I use my stamp on the back or attach one on another piece of paper? How should I indicate that this is what I have done? — The notary stamp must be readable, and the 1997 law prohibits placing your notary stamp or your signature over printed material. You may use the back of the document or use an attached sheet. Note on the document that a notarial certificate is attached and note on the notarial certificate the kind of document to which it is attached" (website, "FAQs").

Acknowledgment by Signer Identified by Credible Witness (Short Form) (NRS 240.169):

State of Nevada
County of _____

This instrument was acknowledged before me on _____ *(date) by* _____ *(name of person), who personally appeared before me and whose identity I verified upon the oath of* _____ *(name of credible witness), a credible witness personally known to me and to the person who acknowledged this instrument before me.*

(Stamp) _____
(Signature of notarial officer)

_____
(Title and rank [optional])

Acknowledgment by Attorney in Fact (Short Form) (NRS 240.1667):

State of Nevada
County of _____

This instrument was acknowledged before me on _____ *(date) by* _____ *(name of attorney in fact), as attorney in fact for* _____ *(name of principal/person named in the document).*

(Stamp) _____
(Signature of notarial officer)

_____
(Title and rank [optional])

Jurat of Subscribing Witness (Short Form) (NRS 240.1685):

State of Nevada
County of _____

On _____ *(date),* _____ *(name of subscribing witness) personally appeared before me, whom I know to be the person who signed this jurat of a subscribing witness while under oath, and swears that he/she was present and witnessed* _____ *(name of principal signer) sign his/her name to the above document.*

_____ *(Signature of subscribing witness)*

Signed and sworn before me on _____ *(date) by* _____ *(name of subscribing witness).*

(Stamp) _____
(Signature of notarial officer)

_____
(Title and rank [optional])

Jurat of Person Taking Oath or Affirmation of Office (NRS 240.1663):

State of Nevada
County of _____

I, _____ *(name of person taking oath or affirmation of office), do solemnly swear (or affirm) that I will support, protect and defend the Constitution and Government of the United States and the Constitution and Government of the State of Nevada against all enemies, whether domestic or foreign, and that I will bear true faith, allegiance and loyalty to the same, any ordinance, resolution or law of any state not withstanding, and that I will well and faithfully perform all the duties of the office of* _____ *(title of office), on which I am about to enter; (if an oath) so help me God; (if an affirmation) under the pains and penalties of perjury.*

_____
(Signature of person taking oath or affirmation of office)

Signed and sworn to (or affirmed) before me on _____ (date) by _____ (name of person taking oath or affirmation of office).

(Stamp) _____
(Signature of notarial officer)

_____
(Title and rank [optional])

Acknowledgment for Durable Power of Attorney for Finances or Health Care (NRS 162A.620):

*State of Nevada
County of _____*

On this _____ day of _____ in the year, before me _____ (name of Notary), personally appeared _____ (name of principal), personally known to me (or proved to me on the basis of satisfactory evidence) to be the person whose name is subscribed to this instrument, and acknowledged that he or she executed it. I declare under penalty of perjury that the person whose name is subscribed to this instrument appears to be of sound mind and under no duress, fraud or undue influence.

(Stamp) _____
(Signature of notarial officer)

_____
(Title and rank [optional])

Notarial Wording Required

"Your signature and stamp by themselves do not constitute a complete notarization. You also need to complete the notarial wording" (website, "FAQs").

ELECTRONIC NOTARIZATIONS

Effective July 1, 2009, Nevada enacted the Electronic Notary Public Authorization Act, which regulates Electronic Notaries and electronic notarization in the state. The Act was part of Senate Bill 92 and added the sections described below to NRS Chapter 240.

Online Notarization Prohibited

The following "Customer Alert" appeared prominently on the Nevada Secretary of State's website: "Online webcam notarizations are not permitted in the State of Nevada. A person seeking a notarization is required to personally appear before a notary public and sign the document in the presence of the notary. Appearance via a webcam or other electronic medium such as Skype does not meet Nevada's law governing personal appearance. Please be aware of any online notarization service being offered by a private company. If you have any questions, please contact the Notary Division at 775-684-5708."

eNotary Appointment Requirements

The Electronic Notary Public Authorization Act empowers the Nevada Secretary of State to appoint electronic Notaries, who will be authorized to notarize electronic documents. Appointment as an Electronic Notary is separate and distinct from a standard Notary appointment. To become an Electronic Notary, the applicant must have held a standard Notary appointment in Nevada for at least four years prior to applying and must retain that appointment throughout his or her term as an Electronic Notary. (NRS 240.196).

Applicants for an Electronic Notary appointment must:

1. Submit an application which contains no substantial or material misstatement or omission of fact and which includes the applicant's electronic signature and a description of the technology or device approved by the Secretary of State that the applicant used to create that signature;

2. Pay an application fee of $50;

3. Take a state-approved, three-hour course and an exam on electronic notarization, notarial law and ethics, technology and procedures;

4. Submit proof of successful completion of the mandatory course of study;

5. File a $10,000 Notary bond, specifically for the Electronic Notary appointment, with the clerk of the county in which the applicant resides or, if the applicant is a resident of an adjoining state, with the clerk of the county in which the applicant is employed;

6. Submit a certificate of filing issued by the clerk of the county in which the bond is filed;

7. Take the oath of office.

The initial term of appointment as an Electronic Notary is two years. Each successive term is four years. If an Electronic Notary's standard Notary appointment expires or is revoked or suspended, the electronic Notary appointment is suspended.

Electronic Notarization Requirements

A Nevada Electronic Notary may only perform electronic notarizations involving acknowledgments, jurats and oaths and affirmation. Electronic copy certifications and protests are not authorized. Electronic notarizations may not be performed on a will, codicil or testamentary trust or on any transaction governed by certain provisions of the Uniform Commercial Code (NRS 240.199).

Fee: "An electronic notary public may charge the following fees and no more:

"(a) For taking an acknowledgment, for each signature $10;

"(b) For executing a jurat, for each signature $10;

"(c) For administering an oath or affirmation without a signature $10" (240.197[1]).

"An electronic notary public may charge an additional fee for traveling to perform an electronic notarial act if:

"(a) The person requesting the electronic notarial act asks the electronic notary public to travel;

"(b) The electronic notary public explains to the person requesting the electronic notarial act that the fee for travel is in addition to the fee authorized in subsection 1 and is not required by law;

"(c) The person requesting the electronic notarial act agrees in advance upon the hourly rate that the electronic notary public will charge for the additional fee for travel; and

"(d) The additional fee for travel does not exceed: (1) If the person requesting the electronic notarial act asks the electronic notary public to travel between the hours of 6 a.m. and 7 p.m., $10 per hour. (2) If the person requesting the electronic notarial act asks the electronic notary public to travel between the hours of 7 p.m. and 6 a.m., $25 per hour.

"The electronic notary public may charge a minimum of 2 hours for such travel and shall charge on a pro rata basis after the first 2 hours" (NRS 240.197[4]).

Device Must Be Approved: The Electronic Notary Public Authorization Act requires the Nevada Secretary of State to approve the technology or device used by an Electronic Notary to create his or her electronic signature.

Notary Journal: For each electronic notarial act performed, an Electronic Notary must create a journal entry that conforms to the requirements of NRS 240.120 (NRS 240.201).

Other Notary Statutes Apply: An Electronic Notary must comply with all provisions in NRS Chapter 240 that pertain to Notaries Public.

Authentication: The Nevada Secretary of State must issue a certificate of authentication or apostille, as appropriate, certifying that an Electronic Notary's signature is genuine and that the Electronic Notary holds an appointment to perform electronic notarial acts (NRS 240.205).

Electronic Signature, Seal and Certificate

Each electronic notarial act must be evidenced by the electronic signature and seal of the Electronic Notary and the appropriate notarial certificate wording. The signature, seal and certificate wording must be attached to or logically associated with the electronic document, and they must be immediately perceptible and reproducible (NRS 240.199).

An Electronic Notary's electronic signature and seal may only be used for the purposes of performing electronic notarizations (NRS 240.202[1]).

An Electronic Notary must take reasonable steps to ensure that the technology or device used to create the Notary's electronic signature has not been recalled, revoked, terminated or otherwise rendered ineffective or unsecure. Upon learning that the technology or device has been rendered ineffective or unsecure, an Electronic Notary must cease performing electronic notarizations with that technology or device until a new one has been acquired and registered with the Secretary of State (NRS 240.202[2][a]).

Change of Name, Address or Technology: Within 10 days after a change of the Electronic Notary's name, e-mail address, county of residence or employment, or technology or device used to create an electronic signature, the Notary must notify the Secretary of State by creating an electronic document containing the new information and signing it with the approved electronic signature submitted on the Notary's application for appointment. The fee is $10 (NRS 240.203).

If Notary Resigns or Dies: Upon the resignation or death of an Electronic Notary, the Notary — or the executor of the Notary's estate — must notify the Secretary of State and erase, delete, destroy or otherwise render ineffective the technology or device used to create the Notary's electronic signature (NRS 240.203[1]).

"A former electronic notary public whose previous appointment as an electronic notary public was not revoked and whose previous application for appointment as an electronic notary public was not denied is not required to erase, delete, destroy or otherwise render ineffective the technology or device used to create his or her electronic signature if the former electronic notary public renews his or her appointment, using the same electronic signature, within 3 months after the expiration of his or her previous appointment as an electronic notary public" (NRS 240.203[3]).

Penalties and Prohibitions
"1. An electronic notary public shall not willfully electronically notarize the signature or electronic signature of a person unless the person is in the presence of the electronic notary public at the time of notarization and: (a) Is known to the electronic notary public; or (b) If unknown to the electronic notary public, provides a credible witness or documentary evidence of identification to the electronic notary public.

"2. A person who: (a) Violates the provisions of subsection 1; or (b) Aids and abets an electronic notary public to commit a violation of subsection 1, is guilty of a gross misdemeanor.

"3. An electronic notary public shall not electronically notarize any electronic document related to the following: (a) A will, codicil or testamentary trust; and (b) Any transaction governed by the Uniform Commercial Code other than NRS 104.1306, 104.2101 to 104.2725, inclusive, and 104A.2101 to 104A.2532, inclusive.

"4. An appointment as an electronic notary public pursuant to NRS 240.181 to 240.206, inclusive, does not authorize the electronic notary public to perform notarial acts in another state" (NRS 240.198).

UETA Recognizes Notary's eSignature
Nevada has adopted the Uniform Electronic Transactions Act (NRS 719.010 through 719.350), including the provision on notarization and acknowledgment. The Act recognizes the legal validity of electronic signatures used by Notaries:

"If a law requires a signature or record to be notarized, acknowledged, verified or made under oath, the requirement is satisfied if the electronic signature of the person authorized to perform those acts, together with all other information required to be included by other applicable law, is attached to or logically associated with the signature or record" (NRS 719.280).

Nevada statute gives the Secretary of State authority to establish "procedures for the notarization of digital or electronic signatures" (NRS 240.017[1][b]).

URPERA Does Not Require Seal Image
Nevada enacted the Uniform Real Property Electronic Recording Act in 2007 (NRS 111.366 through 111.3697), including the following:

"A requirement that a document or a signature associated with a document be notarized, acknowledged, verified, witnessed or made under oath is satisfied if the electronic signature of the person authorized to perform that act, and all other information required to be included, is attached to or logically associated with the document or signature. A physical or electronic image of a stamp, impression or seal need not accompany an electronic signature" (NRS 111.3685[3]).

Digital Signature as Acknowledgment
"The secretary of state shall adopt regulations regarding digital signatures, including, without limitation, regulations pertaining to … (t)he use of a digital signature as an acknowledgment, as that term is defined in NRS 240.002 …" (NRS 720.150[5]).

"1. Except as otherwise provided by specific statute, regulation or contract, a digital signature that is verifiable with reference to the public key set forth in a valid certificate shall be deemed to satisfy the requirements for an acknowledgment, regardless of whether the person who executed the digital signature appeared before the certification authority or a person who is authorized to take acknowledgments in this state, if:

"(a) The digitally signed message includes a statement that the digital signature is intended as an acknowledgment;

"(b) The digital signature is verified by the public key set forth in the certificate;

"(c) The certificate was a valid certificate when the digital signature was affixed; and

"(d) The certificate provides that the digital signature satisfies the requirements for an acknowledgment.

"2. If a certificate provides that a digital signature satisfies the requirements for an acknowledgment, the certification authority who issued the certificate is liable for the digital signature to the same extent as if the certification authority was a notary public who had acknowledged the signature, except that his liability must not exceed any recommended limit of reliance set forth in the certificate. No certification authority may waive, disclaim or otherwise limit by agreement the provisions of this subsection.

"3. As used in this section, 'acknowledgment' has the meaning ascribed to it in NRS 240.002" (Nevada Administrative Code 720.770).

NOTARY RECORDS

A Nevada Notary Public must keep a journal of notarial acts "in a bound volume with preprinted page numbers" (NRS 240.120[6][b]). Two or more Notaries may not share the same journal (website, "FAQs").

Required Journal Entries

"1. Except as otherwise provided in subsection 2, each notary public shall keep a journal in his office in which he shall enter for each notarial act performed, at the time the act is performed:

"a. The fees charged, if any;

"b. The title of the document;

"c. The date on which he performed the service;

"d. Except as otherwise provided in subsection 3, the name and signature of the person whose signature is being notarized;

"e. Subject to the provisions of subsection 4, a description of the evidence used by the notary public to verify the identification of the person whose signature is being notarized;

"f. An indication of whether he administered an oath; and

"g. The type of certificate used to evidence the notarial act, as required pursuant to NRS 240.1655.

"2. A notary public may make one entry in the journal which documents more than one notarial act if the notarial acts documented are performed:

"a. For the same person and at the same time; and

"b. On one document or on similar documents.

"3. When taking an acknowledgement for a person, a notary public need not require the person to sign the journal if the notary public has performed a notarial act for the person within the previous 6 months and the notary public has personal knowledge of the identity of the person.

"4. If, pursuant to subsection 3, a notary public does not require a person to sign the journal, the notary public shall enter 'known personally' as the description required to be entered into the journal pursuant to paragraph (e) of subsection 1" (NRS 240.120).

Travel Fees: Any travel fee charged must be noted in the journal, along with the "date and time that the notary public began and ended such travel" (NRS 240.100[5]).

Open to Public Inspection

The Nevada Notary's journal must be open to public inspection and, upon payment of the fee set in NRS 240.100, the Notary must provide a certified copy of any requested entry in the journal (NRS 240.120[6] and [7]).

Any person may inspect the Notary's journal during the time that the Notary "would normally be at work" (website, "FAQs").

Lost or Stolen Journal

"A notary public shall file a report with the secretary of state and the appropriate law enforcement agency if his journal is lost or stolen" (NRS 240.120[10]).

Journal Kept Seven Years

"A notary public shall retain each journal that he has kept pursuant to this section until 7 years after the date on which he ceases to be a notary public" (NRS 240.120[9]). "Notify the Secretary of State (in) writing as to the location of the journal..." (website, "FAQs").

Secure Location Required

"A notary public shall keep his or her journal in a secure location during any period in which the notary public is not making an entry or notation in the journal pursuant to this section" (NRS 240.120.1[8]).

No Journal for Ex Officio Notary

"The provisions of this section do not apply to a person who is authorized to perform a notarial act pursuant to paragraph (b), (c) or (d) of subsection 1 of NRS 240.1635" (NRS 240.120[11]). Such persons include a justice of the peace and a judge, clerk or deputy clerk of any Nevada court.

Altering with Intent to Deceive

Altering the journal with intent to deceive or defraud is expressly prohibited by Nevada law (NRS 240.075[3]).

Employer May Not Withhold Journal

"It is unlawful for a person who comes into possession of the official stamp, journal or certificate of appointment of a notary public to withhold such an item from the notary public, whether or not the person provided the notary public with the money to acquire the item." Such items are considered the "personal property" of the Notary (NRS 240.143).

Destruction, Defacing, Concealing Unlawful

"It is unlawful for a person to knowingly destroy, deface or conceal a notarial record" (NRS 240.147).

AUTHENTICATION OF NOTARIAL ACTS

Secretary of State

Authenticating certificates for Notaries, including apostilles, are issued only by the Nevada Secretary of State's office, as are authenticating certificates for county clerks.

No Authentication of Improper Act: "The Secretary of State shall not issue an authentication ... if:

"(a) The document has not been notarized in accordance with the provisions of (Chapter 240); or

"(b) The Secretary of State has reasonable cause to believe that the document may be used to accomplish any fraudulent, criminal or unlawful purpose" (NRS 240.1657[2]).

Fees: There is a fee of $20 per authenticating certificate or apostille (NRS 240.1657[1]).

Address:
Office of Secretary of State
Notary Division
101 N. Carson St., Suite 3
Carson City, NV 89701

Telephone: 1-775-684-5708

Procedure: Mail or present in person the original notarized document, along with the fee. An "Apostille/Certification Order Instructions" form, downloadable from the website, may be used — any request submitted without this form will be returned. "(I)t is necessary to provide an email address, a return address or self-addressed, stamped envelope AND the name of the country in which the authentication will be used.... All documents are returned by First Class Mail, regardless if the document is expedited. If you want your documents returned using a special handling company please include a pre-paid self addressed mailing envelope" (website, "Apostilles").

COMMISSIONING AND ADMINISTRATION

The Nevada Secretary of State appoints, regulates and maintains records on the state's Notaries (NRS 240.010).

Generally, all information filed with or obtained by the Secretary of State — except that relating either to investigations of alleged notarial misconduct or to the appointment of someone previously convicted of certain crimes — is public information and available for public examination (NRS 240.007[1] through [3] and 240.010[2]). However, Notaries are not required to submit a residential address or telephone number on any application document that will become available to the public (NRS 240.030[3]).

Applying for Commission

Qualifications: An applicant for appointment as a Nevada Notary Public must (NRS 240.015[1]): (a) be a U.S. citizen or a lawfully admitted permanent resident alien, (b) be at least 18 years old, (c) be a resident of Nevada and (d) possess his or her civil rights, since a convicted felon whose civil rights have not been restored cannot become a Notary. A 2011 law gives the Nevada Secretary of State discretion and authority to require fingerprinting of Notary commission applicants and to charge a fee for their processing (NRS 240.030[1][e]).

Course of Instruction Required: A first-time applicant for a Notary commission must pass an approved four-hour course of instruction, as must a person renewing an appointment as a Notary if the commission has been expired for more than one year or if the person was fined for failure to comply with Notary law in the preceding four years (NRS 240.018.[3]). The Nevada Secretary of State's office is the official provider of Notary training classes. There is a $45 fee for the class.

Application: The first step in the application process is to obtain a $10,000 surety bond, which must be filed in the applicant's county of residence with the county clerk, who will administer the oath of office (if it is not administered by another Notary). The county clerk will then issue a "Filing Notice" to the applicant. Along with the application, proof of course completion (if course required) and a $35 fee, this Notice is submitted to the office of the Secretary of State (NRS 240.030[1] and [4]). Non-U.S. citizens must also include a completed "Document Verification Request Form," downloadable on the website.

Non-Residents: Residents of bordering states (i.e., Arizona, California, Idaho, Oregon, Utah) may become Nevada Notaries if they maintain a licensed place of business or are employed by a licensed employer in Nevada (NRS 240.015[3]). Such non-resident applicants must include with their applications a notarized "Nonresident Notary Public Affidavit." Non-resident applicants who are employed by a licensed employer must also submit a notarized "Affidavit of Applicant's Employer" and a copy of the employer's business license(s); applicants who are self-employed must also submit a notarized "Affidavit of Self-Employed Applicant" and a copy of the applicant's business license(s). The applicant's bond and oath must be filed in his or her county of employment (NRS 240.030[1], [2] and [4]).

"A notary public who is a resident of an adjoining state shall submit to the secretary of state annually, within 30 days before the anniversary date of his appointment as a notary public, a copy of the state business license of his place of employment in the State of Nevada..., a copy of any license required by the local government where the business is located and the information required pursuant to subsection 2 of NRS 240.030" (NRS 240.031).

Changes of Status

If Notary Moves: Within 30 days after changing a mailing address or county of residence, the Notary must apply for an amended certificate of appointment with the Secretary of State. The same applies if the Notary is an out-of-state resident and changes a place of business or employment. The cost is $10 (NRS 240.036[1]).

If Notary Changes Name, Signature: Within 30 days after changing a signature or a name with the intention to use the new name in performing notarial duties, the Notary must apply for an amended certificate of appointment with the Secretary of State. The cost is $10 (NRS 240.036[1] and [3]).

COUNTY CLERKS

To contact a Nevada county clerk for assistance in locating a given Notary, telephone long-distance information — 1-XXX-555-1212 — using the appropriate area code listed below and ask for the phone number of the clerk for the pertinent county:

County	City/Town	Area Code
Carson City*	Carson City	(775)
Churchill	Fallon	(775)
Clark	Las Vegas	(702)
Douglas	Minden	(775)
Elko	Elko	(775)
Esmeralda	Goldfield	(775)
Eureka	Eureka	(775)
Humboldt	Winnemucca	(775)
Lander	Battle Mountain	(775)
Lincoln	Pioche	(775)
Lyon	Yerington	(775)
Mineral	Hawthorne	(775)
Nye	Tonopah	(775)
Pershing	Lovelock	(775)
Storey	Virginia City	(775)
Washoe	Reno	(775)
White Pine	Ely	(775)

* This municipality, the state capital, has its own courthouse.

OTHER NOTARIAL OFFICERS

Besides Notaries, the following officials are authorized to perform notarial acts within the state (NRS 111.265 and 240.1635):
1. A judge, clerk or deputy clerk of a court;
2. A justice of the peace.

Court Reporters May Administer Oaths

Legislation that took effect July 1, 2007, gives Nevada court reporters automatic power to administer oaths and affirmations in the course of taking depositions without the need to apply for a commission as a limited-power Notary, as was the case prior to that date (NRS 656.315). All such limited-power Notary commissions became null and void on the law's effective date. The powers of these former Notaries had been limited solely to administering oaths and affirmations; they did not have to post a bond or keep a journal.

QUICK FACTS

Notary Jurisdiction
Statewide (NRS 240.020).

Notary Term Length
Four years (NRS 240.020) expiring at midnight on the appointment expiration date.

Term Starts on Bond Date: "(T)he term of a notary public commences on the effective date of the bond ... A notary public shall not perform a notarial act after the effective date of the bond unless he has been issued a certificate of appointment" (NRS 240.030[6]).

Notary Bond
$10,000, with a state-licensed surety company (NRS 240.030[1]).

Employer May Be Liable: Along with the Notary, the employer of a Notary "may be assessed a civil penalty by the Secretary of State of not more than $2,000 for each violation". The Employer may also be liable for any damages proximately caused by the Notary's misconduct if the "notary public was acting within the scope of his employment at the time he engaged in the misconduct; and ... (t)he employer of the notary public consented to the misconduct of the notary public" (NRS 240.150[2]).

N

New Hampshire

NOTARY ADMINISTRATION

Office of Secretary of State
State House, Room 204   1-603-271-3242
107 North Main Street
Concord, NH 03301

Website: www.sos.nh.gov/notary.html

NOTARY RULES

RSA — NEW HAMPSHIRE REVISED STATUTES
       ANNOTATED
NPJP — NOTARY PUBLIC AND JUSTICE OF THE
       PEACE MANUAL

Most Notary regulations are in the New Hampshire Revised Statutes Annotated, Title 42:

a. Chapter 455, "Notaries Public and Commissioners";

b. Chapter 456-B, "Uniform Law on Notarial Acts."*

* This is the *Uniform Law on Notarial Acts* of 1982, adopted with modifications as RSA 456-B:1 through 456-B:11, effective January 1, 2006.

Other guidelines for Notaries are in the "Notary Public and Justice of the Peace Manual" (Aug. 2009), jointly issued by the Office of the Attorney General and the Department of State, pursuant to RSA 455:17.

NOTARY SEAL

New Hampshire statute requires Notaries to affix a seal or stamp of office when executing acknowledgments (RSA 455:3). In addition, a joint directive from the Office of the Attorney General and the Department of State extends this requirement to all notarizations: "All of a Notary Public's certifications must either be under an official seal or carry the legible imprint of an official rubber stamp" (NPJP).

Kind

Embosser or Inked Rubber Stamp: "All acknowledgments made by a notary public shall be either under an official seal (embosser) or shall carry the legible imprint of an official rubber stamp stating the name of the notary, the words 'notary public, New Hampshire' and the expiration date of the notary public's commission" (RSA 455:3).

Prior to January 1, 1996, only an embosser was authorized for New Hampshire Notaries. Prior to October 1, 1988, Notaries were not required to use seals.

Shape/Size

Not specified by law. For embossers, a circular seal is customary. Most rubber Notary stamps are manufactured in a rectangular shape.

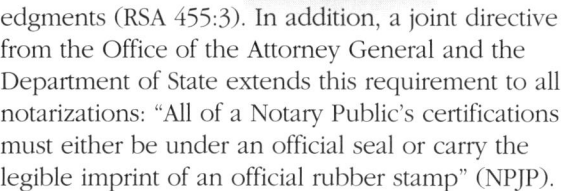

Examples

The above typical, actual-size examples of Notary seals are allowed by New Hampshire law. Formats other than these may also be permitted.

Components

Embosser:
1. Name of Notary;
2. "Notary Public";
3. "New Hampshire".

"If the notary uses an official seal (embosser), he or she must also have a separate rubber stamp that has the expiration date of the Notary Public's commission on it" (NPJP).

Inked Rubber Stamp:
1. Name of Notary;
2. "Notary Public";
3. "New Hampshire";
4. Commission expiration date.

Seals of Notaries and Justices of Peace

"The signature, official seal or the legible imprint of an official rubber stamp stating the name of the notary, and the words 'notary public, New Hampshire' and the expiration date of the notary public's commission of a person performing a notarial act or for a justice of the peace the name of the justice and the expiration date of his or her commission typed, printed, or stamped on the document are prima facie evidence that the signature is genuine and that the person holds the designated title" (RSA 456-B:3 III).

Justice Need Not Use Seal: "Unlike a Notary Public, a Justice of the Peace is not required to have a seal. When signing any document or instrument a Justice of the Peace must: (1) Type, print, or stamp his or her name; and, (2) State the expiration date of his or her commission. Failure to meet these requirements does not invalidate the legal effect of the notarial act" (NPJP).

If Expiration Date Omitted

If the expiration date is omitted inadvertently from the Notary's certificate, RSA 456:B-7 I allows it to be subsequently added.

Destruction of Seal

According to the office of the Secretary of State, the seals of persons no longer holding a New Hampshire Notary commission, through resignation or other cause, must no longer be deposited with the Secretary — effective January 1, 2006. Instead, the seals should be destroyed.

Notary Must Consider Adequacy of Stamp

"While state law permits notaries public to use a rubber stamp, it may not be sufficient for certain purposes. For example, federal passport regulations may require a raised seal. A Notary Public should consider whether the rubber stamp is sufficient for the type of notarial act being performed" (NPJP).

Recent History of Notary Seals

Prior to October 1, 1988, Notary seals were not required by statute on any document, though use of embosser seals by Notaries was common. On that date, embosser seals became mandatory for Notaries executing acknowledgments (Chapter 121, Laws of 1988).

Effective January 1, 1996, New Hampshire Notaries may use either an embosser or an inked rubber stamp (Chapter 74, Laws of 1995).

NOTARY POWERS

New Hampshire Notaries are authorized to perform the following notarial acts (RSA 455:3 and 456-B:1):

1. Take acknowledgments*;
2. Administer oaths** and affirmations**;
3. Take verifications upon oath or affirmation (jurats)***;
4. Witness or attest signatures****;
5. Certify or attest copies*****;
6. Take depositions****** (RSA 517:2);
7. Execute protests (RSA 455:4 and 382-A:3-505):
8. Observe opening of safe deposit box for which rent has not been paid (NPJP).

* Acknowledgments: "An acknowledgment is a notarial act in which a Notary certifies having positively identified a document signer who personally appeared and who admitted having signed the document freely" (website, "Certificates of Notarial Acts"). The website also details the following steps in performing an acknowledgment: (1) the signer personally appears before the Notary; (2) the Notary scans the document to make sure there are no blank spaces; (3) the Notary positively identifies the signer; (4) the Notary asks the signer to acknowledge executing the document and sign the document if it has not been signed; and (5) the Notary completes certificate wording for an acknowledgment and affixes the official signature and seal.

"The Notary Public should request the signer to raise his or her right hand and ask, 'Do you swear and acknowledge that the signing of this document is your voluntary act and deed?' The signer must give an affirmative response before the Notary Public can complete the certification" (NPJP).

** Oaths and Affirmations: "An oath is a spoken, solemn promise to a Supreme Being that is made before a Notary…. An affirmation is a spoken, solemn promise on one's personal honor, with no reference to a Supreme Being, that is made before a Notary…" (website, "Certificates of Notarial Acts"). When administering an oath or affirmation, no particular ceremony is necessary other than that the declarant hold up his or her right hand …. A notary must accommodate any person who, due to disability, cannot hold up his or her right hand, and may use any reasonable means of ensuring the person taking the oath understands the seriousness of the act ….

"When swearing in a witness during court proceedings, … (i)f the witness objects to raising his or her hand, he or she may be permitted to use any other form or ceremony, so long as he or she 'professes to believe (it) more binding upon the conscience'" (NPJP).

The language generally used for swearing in a witness or signer under oath or affirmation in New Hampshire is as follows (NPJP):

FOR OATH: "Please raise your right hand. Do you swear to tell the truth, the whole truth and nothing but the truth, so help you God?" or "Do you solemnly swear that the contents of this (name of document) signed by you are true and correct, so help you God?"

FOR AFFIRMATION: "Please raise your right hand. Do you under the pains and penalties of perjury affirm to tell the truth, the whole truth and nothing but the truth?" or "Do you swear and affirm that the contents of this (name of document) signed by you are true and correct?"

*** Executing Jurats: A jurat is a "notarial act in which a Notary certifies having witnessed the signing of a document by a signer who swears or affirms that the document is truthful; also called verification upon oath or affirmation" (website, "Certificates of Notarial Acts"). The website also details the following steps in the execution of a jurat: (1) the signer personally appears before the Notary; (2) the Notary scans the document to make sure there are no blanks spaces; (3) the Notary positively identifies the signer; (4) the Notary administers an oath or affirmation to the signer (see wording below); (5) the Notary completes certificate wording for a jurat and affixes the official signature and seal. Suggested oath wording: "Do you solemnly swear that the statements in this document are true, so help you God?" Suggested affirmation wording: "Do you affirm that the statements in this document are true?"

**** Witnessing or Attesting Signatures: "The act of witnessing a signature differs from an acknowledgment in that the party relying on the document may know for certain that the document was signed on the same date that the Notary affixed the official seal and signature to the document….The act of witnessing a signature differs from a jurat in that the signer is merely signing the document, not swearing or affirming that the contents of the document are true" (website, "Certificates of Notarial Acts"). The website also details the following steps in witnessing or attesting a signature: (1) the signer personally appears before the Notary, (2) the Notary scans the document to make sure there are no blank spaces; (3) the Notary positively identifies the signer; (4) the Notary asks the signer to sign the document in his or her presence; and (5) the Notary completes certificate wording for a signature witnessing and affixes the official signature and seal.

***** Certifying Copies: "In certifying or attesting a copy of a document or other item, the notarial officer must determine that the proffered copy is a full, true, and accurate transcription or reproduction of that which was copied" (RSA 456-B:2 IV). Examples of "other items" that may be copy certified include maps, diagrams, graphs, etc. (NPJP).

The website ("Certificates of Notarial Acts") details the following steps in performing a copy certification: (1) the document custodian personally appears before the Notary; (2) the Notary positively identifies the custodian; (3) the Notary makes the photocopy; (4) the Notary completes certificate wording for a copy certification and affixes the official signature and seal; and (5) the Notary affixes the certificate to the first page of the copy.

"As a practical matter, for long or complex documents, it will typically be necessary for the copy to be made in the presence of the notary using equipment the notary reasonably believes to make accurate copies. Otherwise, it would be necessary to make a word for word comparison of the original to the copy before a notary could certify that the copy is a true copy. Even where the notary makes or personally witnesses a copy being made by standard copying equipment, the notary should conduct a visual page by page comparison and inspection of each page to ensure that the copy is complete and accurate" (NPJP).

Documents that may not be copy-certified by a Notary are (NPJP): (a) vital records (pertaining to birth, adoption, death, fetal death, marriage, divorce, legal separation and civil annulments) though such records may be photocopied; (b) apostilles, particularly when they are attached to a notarized document; (c) U.S. naturalization and citizenship certificates, since copies of these documents may only be certified by the U.S. Citizenship and Immigration Service; and (d) recordable instruments, such as real property deeds, which may only be copy-certified by the county register of deeds.

******Depositions: "A deposition is a written record of a witness's out-of-court testimony that is reduced to writing for later use in court or for discovery purposes in a legal action. In New Hampshire, depositions must be taken before a Notary public, or other authorized notarial officer....

"A notary may issue a notice for witnesses to appear before himself or herself, or any other justice or notary, to give depositions in any matter in which a deposition may be lawfully taken. A notice of deposition must be in writing and must contain the day, hour, and place of taking the deposition. The notice must be signed by the Notary public. RSA 517:4....

"Prior to the start of the deposition, the deponent must take an oath or affirmation that his or her testimony will be truthful. The Notary Public may administer this oath or affirmation in the same manner as a witness is sworn during court proceedings.... Since any person admitted to the practice of law in New Hampshire may administer an oath or affirmation for the purpose of taking an oral testimony, an attorney present at a deposition could also administer the oath or affirmation to the deponent. RSA 456-B:3, IV.... After completing the review, the deponent must sign the deposition under oath. The wording of this oath is provided for by law. The deponent is required to swear that the deposition: '(C)ontains the truth, the whole truth and nothing but the truth relative to the cause for which it was taken.' A Notary Public or other authorized notarial officer must take the written oath for the transcript of the deposition. Members of the bar who (are) not also notarial officers are not permitted to take this oath because they are limited to taking oaths for oral testimony only. RSA 456-B:3, IV, 517:7" (NPJP).

Identifying Document Signers

In taking an acknowledgment or a verification upon oath or affirmation, or in witnessing or attesting a signature, a Notary must identify the signer "from personal knowledge or from satisfactory evidence."

Satisfactory evidence means that the signer is either (a) personally known to the Notary, (b) identified upon the oath or affirmation of a credible witness personally known to the Notary or (c) identified on the basis of identification documents (RSA 456-B:2 VI).

Personal Knowledge: "Personal knowledge does not require extensive knowledge of the individual or his or her history. If the notary could testify under oath in a court of law as to the identity of the individual without using an identification or reference document, then the notary has personal knowledge of the individual's identity" (NPJP).

Credible Witness: "The key here is that the witness must be someone that the notary personally knows and who is credible. It cannot be a person that the notary has just met or someone the notary knows to be dishonest. The witness must also personally know the signer who is appearing before the notary. For example, a person appearing before the notary could be identified under oath or affirmation by an acquaintance of the notary who personally knows the signer of the document" (NPJP).

Identification Documents: "While the notary statutes do not define identification documents, New Hampshire's election law statutes provide a list of identification documents that may be used in determining a person's identity. See RSA 654:12. Acceptable documents for election law purposes include a photo driver's license issued by any state or the federal government, a United States passport, armed services identification, or other photo identification issued by the United States government, or a photo identification issued by a local or state government. Id. The election law also allows use of other photo identification, such as an employee photo identification card issued by a local employer where the official is familiar with the appearance of a legitimate employee ID from that employer and knows that the employer exercises reasonable care in issuing employee identification cards. Id. Because the notary law does not provide a list of acceptable identification documents, good practice would include consulting this elections law list when deciding whether an identification document is acceptable" (NPJP).

No Duty to Determine Representative Status: "The notary must still determine the identity of the person appearing before him or her for acknowledgments made in a representative capacity. The notary is certifying that the person represented him or herself to the notary as having authority to act in the representative capacity. The notary does not have a duty to determine if the person in fact and law does have authority to represent the other person or entity" (NPJP). However, the "Manual" does recommend as a "best practice" that the Notary require a person signing as attorney in fact to present the authorizing power of attorney.

Proof of Execution by Handwriting

"If any grantor or lessor shall die, become insane, or go out of the state before the acknowledgment of a deed or lease, proof of due execution of such deed or lease may be made by the oath of 2 witnesses acquainted with the handwriting of the grantor or lessor that the deed or lease was signed by said grantor or lessor" (RSA 477:12). The same applies to a grantor or lessor who refuses to acknowledge a signed deed or lease (RSA 477:13).

Signing by Mark

"A Notary Public may still perform a notarial act for a person who is unable to sign his or her name due to physical disability or other inability to write .... Best practice would be to permit the person to sign the document by marking an 'X' or other symbol on the signature line. If the person is unable to make any mark at all and has a signature stamp, this may also be permitted. The Notary Public should exercise considerable caution in making sure the signature, whether a symbol or stamp, is the true signature of the person before him or her. Having a witness in addition to the notary is recommended.

"If another person needs to make the mark or signature for the person, the notary should add a statement to the notarial certificate stating what actually occurred at the notarization. For example if a notary is notarizing a document for John Doe, who is a quadriplegic, and Jane Doe, his wife, signs his name after he communicates to the notary his intent that the document be signed, the notary could write: 'Notarized in the presence of John Doe, who was unable to sign his name due to a disability. Mr. Doe communicated his intent to sign this document and his wife Jane Doe signed his name in my presence'" (NPJP).

NOTARY DON'TS

Civil Penalties for Misconduct

Among the acts of misconduct that a Notary Public or justice of the peace may be subject to a civil penalty of up to $1,000 for are (RSA 455:16):

1. Negligently or recklessly making a notarial act that is false;

2. Negligently or recklessly notarizing for an unknown person without requiring that person to establish his or her identity;

3. Negligently or recklessly purporting to have witnessed a person's signing of a document, or to have administered an oath or affirmation to a person, without actually doing so.

Signer's Physical Presence Is Mandatory

"A person must be physically in the presence of the notarial officer for any notarial act to be performed in that person's name. It is not sufficient that the notarial officer know the person and his or her signature on the document to be notarized. It is not sufficient that the person verify by telephone that it is his or her signature. The law does not currently permit a notarial officer to witness an act through video conference or other electronic means where the person making the act is at a physical location different from the notarial officer or otherwise not in the physical presence of the notarial officer. Even where a notarial officer may work with and perform notarial acts regularly for another person, there are no exceptions to the legal requirement that the person be in the physical presence of the notary for each and every notarial act" (NPJP).

Blank Document or Certificate

"(A) Notary Public may not sign a blank document or jurat" (NPJP).

Disqualifying Interests

"No person acting in the capacity of notary public shall notarize his or her own signature" (RSA 455:2-a).

"All notarial officers ... have both a statutory and common law duty to avoid conflicts of interest in the performance of their duties .... In general, a public official must never act in his or her own interest in performing notarial acts, official acts must always be done solely in the interest of the public" (NPJP).

No Money for Endorsement: "(N)o public servant may solicit, accept, or agree to accept money or any other pecuniary benefit as compensation for his or her endorsement of any person for a position as a public servant (RSA 640:7). This provision is particularly applicable to notarial officers, who may be asked to endorse an applicant to be a Notary Public or Justice of the Peace" (NPJP).

"(A)s a public servant, a notarial officer is required by statute to report to a law enforcement officer any conduct by another designed to improperly influence the notarial officer's official action, decision, opinion, recommendation, nomination, vote or other exercise of discretion (RSA 640:3 I[c])" (NPJP).

Corporate Notaries Not Disqualified: Notaries who are employees, stockholders, directors or officers of a bank or other corporation may notarize for that bank or corporation as long as they are not parties to the document, either individually or as a representative (RSA 455:2-a).

NOTARY SIGNING AGENTS

Currently, there are no statutes, regulations or rules expressly governing, prohibiting or restricting the operation of Notary Signing Agents within the state of New Hampshire.

NOTARY FEES

"Notaries public shall be entitled to a fee of up to $10 for each oath, witness, service or certification with the following exceptions (RSA 455:11):

"I. For services related to the taking of depositions, the notary public shall be entitled to the same fees as justices (of the peace) are entitled to receive pursuant to RSA 517:19." ("For services related to the taking of depositions, a Justice of the Peace is entitled to a fee of at least five dollars but no more than fifty dollars. The Justice of the Peace can vary the fee depending upon the amount the Justice of the Peace feels is sufficient payment for the deposition services. In addition to the fee, a Justice of the Peace is entitled to twenty cents per mile as mileage to swear witnesses" [NPJP]).

Deposition Fees

"For depositions, a fee of $5.00 but not more than $50.00 may be collected. The fee is based upon the amount that the notary feels is sufficient payment for his services. The notary is also entitled to .20/mile when traveling to swear in witnesses" (website, "Notaries Public").

No Fees for Oaths of Town Officers

"No fees shall be allowed for administering and certifying oaths of office for town officers" (RSA 455:11).

Travel Fees

"In addition to the fees (for notarial acts), when a Notary Public travels to swear witnesses, he or she is entitled to twenty cents per mile as mileage" (NPJP).

NOTARY CERTIFICATES

New Hampshire has adopted the *Uniform Law on Notarial Acts*, including the short-form certificates (RSA 456-B:8) for:

1. Acknowledgment by individual;
2. Acknowledgment by representative;
3. Verification upon oath or affirmation;
4. Witnessing or attesting signature;
5. Attesting copy of document.

For the text of these certificates, see "Uniform Law on Notarial Acts (1982)," Section 8, in Appendix 2.

Requirements for Any Notarial Certificate

"I. A notarial act must be evidenced by a certificate signed and dated by a notarial officer. The certificate must include identification of the jurisdiction in which the notarial act is performed and the title of the office of the notarial officer and may include the official stamp or seal of office. If the officer is a notary public, the certificate must also indicate the date of expiration, if any, of the commission of office, but omission of that information may subsequently be corrected. If the officer is a commissioned officer on active duty in the military service of the United States, it must also include the officer's rank.

"II. A certificate of a notarial act is sufficient if it meets the requirements of paragraph I and it:

"(a) Is in the short form set forth in RSA 456-B:8;

"(b) Is in a form otherwise prescribed by the law of this state;

"(c) Is in a form prescribed by the laws or regulations applicable in the place in which the notarial act was performed; or

"(d) Sets forth the actions of the notarial officer and those are sufficient to meet the requirements of the designated notarial act" (RSA 456-B:7).

ELECTRONIC NOTARIZATIONS

The state of New Hampshire has not yet adopted statutes or regulations expressly establishing rules, definitions and procedures for electronic notarization.

UETA Recognizes Notary's eSignature

Effective September 11, 2001, New Hampshire adopted the Uniform Electronic Transactions Act (RSA 294-E:1 through 294-E:20), including its provision on notarization and acknowledgment, thereby recognizing the legal validity of electronic signatures used by Notaries:

"If a law requires a signature or record to be notarized, acknowledged, verified, or made under oath, the requirement is satisfied if the electronic signature of the person authorized to perform those acts, together with all other information required to be included by other applicable law, is attached to or logically associated with the signature or record" (RSA 294-E:11).

NOTARY RECORDS

"While not required by law, it is recommended that a Notary Public maintain a journal of all notarial acts performed. Good practice would dictate including in the journal, at a minimum, the following information:

"1. The notarial act performed;

"2. The date of the notarial act;

"3. The identifying information of the person appearing before the Notary Public; and

"4. Any other details the Notary Public believes would be useful in referring back to the act.

"A journal will provide a record of the details of each notarial act that the Notary Public can refer to if called upon to verify the act" (NPJP).

Misuse of Information

"A notarial officer is ... forbidden by statute from misusing information he or she acquires by virtue of his or her office or from another public servant. Misuse of information includes:

"1. Acquiring or divesting himself or herself of a pecuniary interest in any property, transaction or enterprise which may be affected by such action or information; or

"2. Speculating or making a wager on the basis of such action or information; or

"3. Knowingly aiding another to do any of the foregoing" (NPJP).

Journal Disposition Provisions Repealed

Effective January 1, 2006, all former statutory provisions regarding the disposition of a Notary's official records were repealed by Chapter 118, Laws of 2005 (Senate Bill 672). These provisions, which were quite detailed, comprised the former RSA sections 455:5 through 455:10, which are reprinted below, for reference:

REPEALED, EFFECTIVE JANUARY 1, 2006: "Whenever a notary shall remove from the state, resign or from any cause cease to act in that capacity, he shall, within 3 months thereafter, deposit all his notarial records and all papers filed in his office in the office of the secretary of state" (RSA 455:5). "If a notary shall die or become insane, it shall be the duty of his administrator, executor or guardian to deposit his records and papers in the manner aforesaid" (RSA 455:6).

REPEALED, EFFECTIVE JANUARY 1, 2006: "The secretary of state may demand and receive any such records and papers of any person in whose possession the same may be" (RSA 455:7). "If any person in whose possession any such records or papers may be shall neglect or refuse to deliver the same to the secretary of state, or upon his order on demand, or shall knowingly destroy or conceal any such records, he shall be guilty of a misdemeanor if a natural person, or guilty of a felony if any other person, and shall also be liable for damages to any person injured in an action on the case" (RSA 455:8).

REPEALED, EFFECTIVE JANUARY 1, 2006: "All notarial records and papers shall be kept by the secretary of state safely and in such manner that reference thereto may easily be had for a period of 3 years. These records shall be open to the examination of any person interested therein" (RSA 455:9). "The secretary of state shall make out and certify copies of any such records and papers, upon payment or tender of the fees therefor, and his certificate shall have the same validity as if made by such notary himself" (RSA 455:10).

AUTHENTICATION OF NOTARIAL ACTS

Secretary of State

Authenticating certificates for Notaries, including apostilles, are issued by the New Hampshire Secretary of State's office.

"This office cannot certify signatures of town and city clerks, county or state registrars or other state officials. The signatures must be those of a Notary Public or Justice of the Peace for the State of New Hampshire" (website, "Apostilles and Certificates").

Fees: $10 for an authenticating certificate, including an apostille. Check or cash payable to "State of New Hampshire."

Address:
Office of Secretary of State
State House, Room 204
107 North Main Street
Concord, NH 03301

Telephone: 1-603-271-3242

Procedure: Mail or present in person the original notarized document, along with the required fee. Mailings should include a letter indicating the country of destination and a telephone number in case there are any questions. An addressed, postage-paid return envelope should also be included. "Each document must have an original Notary Public or Justice of the Peace signature witnessing the signature of the author of the document. If signed by a notary, the notary's seal must be included in order to be certified by this office" (website, "Apostilles and Certificates").

NOTE: "Once an apostille has been attached to a document, a notary public cannot copy certify it" (NPJP).

County Clerks

Since a Notary, upon commissioning, must file an index card with the clerk of the superior court of the county in which the Notary resides, these clerks may also issue authenticating certificates for Notaries.

COMMISSIONING AND ADMINISTRATION

While New Hampshire's Governor, "with the advice and consent of the executive council," appoints the state's Notaries (RSA 455:1), it is the Secretary of State who directly regulates and maintains records on them.

Applying for Commission

Qualifications: An applicant for a commission as a New Hampshire Notary must (RSA 455:2): (a) be at least 18 years old, (b) be a New Hampshire resident and (c) be endorsed by two New Hampshire Notaries and a person registered to vote in the state. "The endorsement by two New Hampshire Notaries and a person registered to vote requires more than just the endorsers' signatures on the application. The endorsement referred to in the statute requires that the endorser actually give his or her approval and support to the applicant. Such approval requires that the endorser, at a minimum, personally knows the applicant and believe that he or she is of a character consistent with the honesty and integrity required of a Notary Public" (NPJP). In addition to the above qualifications, it is within the discretion of the

Governor and Executive Council to find particular criminal convictions as disqualifying (NPJP). Accordingly, "(t)he applicant must sign a written statement under oath as to whether he/she has ever been convicted of a crime that has not been annulled by a court, other than minor traffic violations" (website, "Notaries Public").

Application: The completed application, with its three endorsements, must be sent to the Secretary of State, along with a fee of $75 (payable to "Treasurer, State of New Hampshire") and a "State Police Records Check Form." The application must be signed in the presence of a Notary (not the applicant) or justice of the peace. The State Police Records Check Form will be forwarded to the Department of Safety. It should be kept in mind that any person who negligently or recklessly makes a material false statement on the application form is subject to a civil penalty of up to $1,000 per violation (NPJP). The review of this application by the Governor and Executive Council takes eight to 10 weeks.

Applications for reappointment are mailed to each Notary about three months prior to commission expiration. Renewal applications are not available online. The renewal process is otherwise the same as for the initial application.

"Any person who holds the title of notarial officer shall be able to produce, upon request of a person seeking notarization services, a copy of his or her commission signed by the Governor, evidencing that he or she is a notarial officer" (NPJP).

Taking the Oath: A newly appointed Notary will be mailed the new commission along with the oath of office and an index card. The oath of office must be signed and taken before either two Notaries Public or two justices of the peace or one Notary and one justice of the peace — each of whom must sign both the oath form and the Notary's commission. (Alternately, one or two members of the Governor's Executive Council may perform the oath administration.) The new Notary must then keep the signed commission and return the oath form as soon as possible to the Secretary of State. After the oath of office is taken, the Notary fills out the index card (i.e., name, address, date of birth and signature) and mails it to the clerk of the Superior Court of the county in which the Notary resides. A Notary may not notarize until the oath of office has been taken (RSA 92:2).

Non-Residents: Non-residents of New Hampshire may not become Notaries in the state.

Changes of Status

If Notary Changes Name: A Notary must notify the Secretary of State's office of any name change during the term of commission and request a new commission reflecting the new name (NPJP). The fee for a new commission is $5. "If the Notary Public is within six months of the end of his or her five-year commission, it is the practice of the Secretary of State's office to permit the Notary Public to continue to sign official documents using both the old and new names rather than requesting a new commission. For example, if Jane Smith's name changes to Jane Jones she could still sign as Jane (Smith) Jones" (NPJP).

If Notary Moves: Notaries who move are asked to notify the New Hampshire Secretary of State's office (NPJP). "If you move during the 5 years of your commission, and do not notify the secretary of state's office, your renewal form will not reach you" (website, "Notaries Public").

COUNTY CLERKS

To contact a New Hampshire county clerk of the superior court to obtain an authenticating certificate for a Notary, or for help in locating a particular Notary, telephone long-distance information — 1-603-555-1212 — and ask for the phone number of the appropriate county clerk for the following cities and towns.

County	City/Town
Belknap	Laconia
Carroll	Ossipee
Cheshire	Keene
Coos	Lancaster
Grafton	North Haverhill
Hillsborough-No.	Manchester
Hillsborough-So.	Nashua
Merrimack	Concord
Rockingham	Exeter
Strafford	Dover
Sullivan	Newport

OTHER NOTARIAL OFFICERS

Besides Notaries, the following officials are authorized to perform notarial acts in New Hampshire (RSA 456-B:3):

1. A judge, marital master, clerk, deputy clerk, register of probate or deputy register of probate of any court of this state;
2. A justice of the peace.

Justice of the Peace

New Hampshire justices of the peace enjoy certain of the same powers as Notaries, including the authority to administer oaths of office and take depositions. Their fees and term length are the same as Notaries', but they are not required to use a seal in taking acknowledgments; however, effective January 1, 2000, they must type, print or stamp their name and commission expiration date on each document. Unlike Notaries, justices of the peace may perform marriages (website, "Justices of the Peace").

Commissioner of Deeds

A New Hampshire commissioner of deeds is a non-resident of New Hampshire who is appointed by the Governor of New Hampshire to perform certain notarial acts (i.e., administer oaths, take depositions and affidavits, take acknowledgements) in designated U.S. and foreign jurisdictions on documents that will be filed or used in New Hampshire. The commissioner is entitled to the same fees as a Notary and has the same term length of five years. The commissioner's official rubber stamp and embosser are similar to the Notary's except that the term "Commissioner of Deeds" replaces "Notary Public" (RSA 455:12 – 455:14).

"Commissioners may also be appointed by the Supreme or Superior Court (of New Hampshire) or any justice thereof. Commissioners so appointed have the same power as justices of the peace to administer oaths and affirmations, to issue writs of summons to a witness, to proceed against a witness who fails to appear and give a deposition, and in all proceedings under his commission" (NPJP).

Court Reporters

Effective July 1, 2007, licensed court reporters have statutory authority to perform a limited notarial function. They may place any person under oath in the performance of their court reporting duties without having been designated a Notary, justice of the peace or commissioner of deeds (RSA 310-A:181).

Attorneys

"Any person admitted to the practice of law in this state may administer an oath or affirmation for the purpose of taking oral testimony" (RSA 456-B:3 IV).

QUICK FACTS

Notary Jurisdiction
Statewide.

Notary Term Length
Five years (RSA 455:1), expiring at midnight on the commission expiration date.

Notary Bond
Not required by law.

New Jersey

NOTARY SEAL

A New Jersey Notary is not required by law to use a seal of office:

"The seal of the officer taking the acknowledgment or proof need not be affixed to the certificate stating that acknowledgment or proof" (NJSA 46:14-2.1[d]).

"It shall not be necessary to the validity or sufficiency of any oath, affirmation or affidavit, made or taken before any of the persons named in section 41:2-1 of this title (which includes Notaries and commissioners of deeds), that the same shall be certified under the official seal of the officer before whom made" (NJSA 41:1-7).

> JANE Q. DOE
> Notary Public
> State of New Jersey
> My Commission Expires on Jan 30, 2014

Examples

The above are typical, actual-size examples of non-mandatory Notary seals used in New Jersey. The rectangular seal at top may also serve to affix the legally required imprint of the Notary's name and commission expiration date.

NOTARY ADMINISTRATION

Department of Treasury
Division of Revenue
Business Support Services Bureau
Notary Public Unit   1-609-633-8258
P.O. Box 452
Trenton, NJ 08646-0452

(33 West State St., 5th Floor
Trenton, NJ 08608-1214)

Website: http://www.state.nj.us/treasury/
revenue/dcr/ programs/notary.
shtml

NOTARY RULES

NJSA — NEW JERSEY STATUTES ANNOTATED
NPM — NEW JERSEY NOTARY PUBLIC MANUAL

Most Notary rules are in the New Jersey Statutes Annotated:

a. Title 52, Chapter 7 ("Notaries Public"), also known as the "Notaries Public Act of 1979";

b. Title 46, Chapter 14 ("Acknowledgments and Proofs").

Other guidelines for Notaries are in the "New Jersey Notary Public Manual (Rev. Mar. 21, 2003)" issued by the Division of Revenue and available on the website.

Seals Are Widely Used

Though Notary seals of office are not required by law, many Notaries elect to use seals, according to the Notary Public Unit.

Signature, Name, Expiration Date Required

"Each notary public, in addition to subscribing his autograph signature to any jurat upon the administration of any oath or the taking of any acknowledgment or proof, shall affix thereto his name in such a manner and by such means, including, but not limited to, printing, typing, or impressing by seal or mechanical stamp, as will enable the Secretary of State easily to read said name" (NJSA 52:7-19).

The "New Jersey Notary Public Manual" requires Notaries "to sign, date and stamp" their notarial certificates: "The ink stamp should include the date on which the Notary's commission expires. The stamp should be placed next to, but not over, the Notary's signature. (If the Notary does not have an ink stamp, his/her name and commission expiration date must be printed or typed on the certificate....)"

If a Notary elects to use an inking Notary seal as shown above, this seal could serve as both the means to affix the Notary's commission expiration date, as required by the "New Jersey Notary Public Manual," and the means to affix the Notary's name, as required by statute.

NOTARY POWERS

New Jersey Notaries are authorized to perform the following notarial acts (NJSA 22A:4-14 and NPM):
  1. Take acknowledgments* and proofs**;
  2. Administer oaths and affirmations***;
  3. Execute jurats****;
  4. Execute protests*****.

* Acknowledgments: "To acknowledge a deed or other instrument the maker of the instrument shall appear before an officer specified in R.S. 46:14-6.1 and acknowledge that it was executed as the maker's own act. To acknowledge a deed or other instrument made on behalf of a corporation or other entity, the maker shall appear before an officer specified in R.S. 46:14-6.1 and state that the maker was authorized to execute the instrument on behalf of the entity and that the maker executed the instrument as the act of the entity" (NJSA 46:14-2.1[a]).

"An acknowledgment formally documents the following: ... That the signer of a document appeared before the Notary, ... That the Notary positively identified the signer, and ... That the signer both acknowledged the signature as his/hers, and that the signature was made willingly" (NPM).

For an acknowledgment, the Notary should additionally "(e)nsure that the signer understands the title of the document and is signing freely and willingly. By obtaining positive ID and asking brief questions as to the title and basic substance of the document, the Notary can make these determinations" (NPM).

** Proofs: "To prove a deed or other instrument, a subscribing witness shall appear before an officer specified in R.S. 46:14-6.1 and swear that he or she witnessed the maker of the instrument execute the instrument as the maker's own act,. To prove a deed or other instrument executed on behalf of a corporation or other entity, a subscribing witness shall appear before an officer specified in R.S. 46:14-6.1 and swear that the representative was authorized to execute the instrument on behalf of the entity, and that he or she witnessed the representative execute the instrument as the act of the entity" (NJSA 46:14-2.1[b]).

"A proof of execution (proof) is a declaration by a subscribing witness that he/she knows the person who signed the document being presented, and was present for its signing or acknowledgment by the signer. The subscribing witness must sign (subscribe) the same document. A proof is taken when the signer cannot be present. A proof may be taken only when the subscribing witness appears before the Notary. The Notary must personally know the witness. Further, the Notary must administer an oath or affirmation (at no extra fee) to the witness to compel truthfulness. In all other respects, the procedural components of and fee for a proof are the same as for an acknowledgment.

"Note: State law indicates that a proof may be taken for a deed. There is no specific guidance with respect to taking a proof for another instrument. Therefore, it would be advisable to limit this particular notary service to deeds" (NPM).

If a document cannot be acknowledged or proved for any reason, it may be proved by handwriting in superior court (NJSA 46:14-4.1).

*** Oaths and Affirmations: "An oath is a spoken pledge, given by a person appearing before the Notary, that his/her attestation or promise is made under an immediate sense of responsibility to a Supreme Being for the truthfulness of a specific statement or statements, or the faithful performance of a specific duty or function.

"An affirmation is a solemn declaration without oath. Whenever the law requires an oath, an affirmation may be taken instead. This accommodates persons who have conscientious objections against taking an oath.

"Notaries may administer oaths and affirmations to public officials and officers of various organizations. They may also administer oaths and affirmations in order to execute jurats for affidavits/verifications, and to swear in witnesses" (NPM).

The "New Jersey Notary Public Manual" prescribes the following wording for an oath to be administered to the signer of an affidavit or other sworn document: "Do you swear that the information presented in this document, entitled _____, which you have signed before me, is the truth, so help you God?" For an affirmation, it prescribes: "Do you solemnly affirm that the information presented in this document, entitled _____, which you have signed before me, is the truth, and this you affirm under the pains and penalties of perjury?" For both oaths and affirmations, the signer must answer affirmatively.

"The process of administering oaths and affirmations could be formalized by gestures — e.g., asking the signer to raise his/her hand and/or place his/her hand on a holy book such as the Holy Bible, Old Testament, Koran, etc." (NPM).

Statute prescribes two wording alternatives for oaths and affirmations: "I, _____, do declare, in the presence of Almighty God, the witness of the truth of what I say …," and, "I, _____, do solemnly, sincerely and truly declare and affirm …," (e)ither of which forms shall be as good and effectual in law, as an oath taken in the usual form. In the affirmation or declaration, the words 'so help me God', at the close of the usual oath, shall be omitted" (NJSA 41:1-6).

**** Jurats: "A jurat … is designed to compel truthfulness on the part of the signer. The jurat is completed during the execution of an affidavit or other form of verification and is generally written at the foot of an affidavit stating when, where, and before whom such affidavit was sworn.

"The jurat shares several of the basic elements of the acknowledgment. However, there are two additional requirements: 1) the signer must sign the document before the Notary; and 2) the signer must take an oath or affirmation regarding the truthfulness of the statements in the documents" (NPM).

***** Protests: "Protests for non-payment/non-acceptance occur within complex and specialized financial and commercial contexts. Therefore, Notaries are advised to consult the State's Uniform Commercial Code (NJSA 12:A) and if applicable, their employers for further technical guidance on providing this particular service" (NPM).

"The certificate of a notary public of this state or any other state of the United States, under his hand and official seal accompanying any bill of exchange or promissory note which has been protested by such notary for nonacceptance or nonpayment, shall be received in all the courts of this state as competent evidence of the official character of such notary, and also of the facts therein certified as to the presentment and dishonor of such bill or note and of the time and manner giving or sending notice of dishonor to the parties to such bill or note" (NJSA 2A:82-7).

Identifying Signers

For both acknowledgments and jurats, the Notary must identify the signer. The "New Jersey Notary Public Manual" instructs that signers present "at least one form of identification (ID) that provides a physical description of the signer — e.g., driver's license. Note: Identification documents are not required if: 1) the signer is personally known to the Notary; or 2) a credible witness, known to both the signer and Notary, swears to the identity of the signer."

Ensuring Comprehension and Volition

"Ensure that the signer understands the title of the document and is signing freely and willingly. By obtaining positive ID and asking brief questions as to the title and basic substance of the document, the Notary can make these determinations" (NPM).

Reviewing Documents for Completeness

"Review the document presented for completeness. This is not a formal legal review, such as would be performed by an accountant or an attorney. Rather, it is a review to ensure that there are no blanks in the document. Should blanks be discovered, the signer must either fill them in or strike them out by drawing a line or 'X' through them" (NPM).

NOTARY DON'TS

The "New Jersey Notary Public Manual" stipulates that a Notary should:
1. NOT predate a notarial certificate prior to the document's date of signing;

2. NOT "lend a journal, stamp, or other personalized Notary equipment to another individual";
3. NOT "prepare a legal document or give advice on legal matters or matters pertaining to land titles";
4. NOT "in the capacity of Notary Public, appear as a representative of another person in a legal proceeding";
5. NOT "in the capacity of Notary Public, act for others in the collection of delinquent bills or claims."

Disqualifying Interests

"Notaries should refrain from notarizing documents in which they have a personal interest, including documents they have prepared for a fee" (NPM).

Corporate Notaries: "a. A notary public who is a stockholder, director, officer, employee or agent of a financial institution or other corporation may administer an oath to any other stockholder, director, officer, employee or agent of the corporation.

"b. A notary public employed by a financial institution may follow directions or policies of the employer which provide that during the hours of the notary public's employment by the financial institution the notary public shall not administer oaths except in the course of the business of the employer.

"As used in this section, 'financial institution' means a State or federally chartered bank, savings and loan association or credit union" (NJSA 41:2-3).

Protest by Corporate Notary: A Notary who is a stockholder, director, officer, employee or agent of a bank or other corporation may execute a protest for the bank or corporation unless the Notary is individually a party to the instrument at issue (NJSA 7:5-6).

NOTARY SIGNING AGENTS

Currently, there are no statutes, regulations or rules expressly governing, prohibiting or restricting the operation of Notary Signing Agents within the state of New Jersey. However, the statutory maximum fees for notarizations performed in real property transfers and mortgage finance transactions should be noted — see "Real Estate Transactions" under "Notary Fees," below.

NOTARY FEES

New Jersey law authorizes the following fees for notarial acts (NJSA 22A:4-14):
1. Taking an acknowledgment: $2.50;
2. Taking proof of a deed: $2.50;
3. Executing a jurat: $2.50;
4. Administering an oath/affirmation: $2.50.

No Fee for Witness

"There is no fee for swearing in a witness in conjunction with an acknowledgment" (NPM).

When performing a proof of execution by subscribing witness, "the Notary must administer an oath or affirmation (at no extra fee) to the witness ..." (NPM).

Real Estate Transactions

"For administering oaths, taking affidavits, taking proofs of a deed, and taking acknowledgments of the grantors in the transfer of real estate, regardless of the number of such services performed in a single transaction to transfer real estate, (the fee is) $15.00.

"For administering oaths, taking affidavits and taking acknowledgments of the mortgagors in the financing of real estate, regardless of the number of such services performed in a single transaction to finance real estate, (the fee is) $25.00" (NJSA 22A:4-14).

NOTARY CERTIFICATES

The "New Jersey Notary Public Manual" offers the following notarial certificates as samples, not disallowing use of other appropriate certificate wording:

Acknowledgment by Individual (NPM):

State of New Jersey)
*   ) ss*
County of _____   )

On _____, 20___, before me, _____, Notary Public in and for said county, personally appeared _____ (name[s] of signer[s/witness[es]), who has/have satisfactorily identified himself/ herself/themselves as the signer(s)/witness(es) to the above-referenced document.

_____ (Notary's signature) _____ (Date)

(Notary's printed, typed or stamped name and commission expiration date)

Proof of Execution (NPM):

State of New Jersey)
) ss
County of _____)

On _____, 20____, before me, _____, Notary Public in and for said county, personally appeared _____ (name[s] of subscribing witness[es]), personally known to me (or proved to me on the oath of _____ [name of credible witness]) to be the person(s) whose name(s) is/are subscribed on the attached document as witness(es) thereto, and who, being duly sworn by me, say(s) that he/she/they saw _____ (name of absent principal) sign the attached document, and that said affiant(s) subscribed his/her/their name(s) to the attached document at the request of _____ (name of absent principal again).

_____ (Notary's signature) _____ (Date)

(Notary's printed, typed or stamped name and commission expiration date)

Jurat for Affidavit (NPM):

State of New Jersey)
) ss
County of _____)

I, _____ (name of affiant), being duly sworn, make this my affidavit and state:

xxxxxxxxxxxxxxxxxxxxxxxxxxxxxxxxx.

_____ (Affiant's signature) _____ (Date)

Subscribed and sworn to before me on _____, 20____, by _____ (affiant's name).

_____ (Notary's signature) _____ (Date)

(Notary's printed, typed or stamped name and commission expiration date)

Content of Notarial Certificate

"The officer taking an acknowledgment or proof shall sign a certificate stating that acknowledgment or proof. The certificate shall also state:

"(1) that the maker or the witness personally appeared before the officer;

"(2) that the officer was satisfied that the person who made the acknowledgment or proof was the maker of or the witness to the instrument;

"(3) the jurisdiction in which the acknowledgment or proof was taken;

"(4) the officer's name and title;

"(5) the date on which the acknowledgment was taken" (NJSA 46:14-2.1[c]).

"The seal of the officer taking the acknowledgment or proof need not be affixed to the certificate stating that acknowledgment or proof" (NJSA 46:14-2.1[d]).

ELECTRONIC NOTARIZATIONS

The state of New Jersey has not yet adopted statutes or regulations expressly establishing rules, definitions and procedures for electronic notarization.

Online Notarization Not Allowed

The following warning regarding webcam or video notarizations may be viewed by clicking "Notice Concerning Online Notary Services" in the drop-down menu on the Division of Revenue's homepage:

"The Division of Revenue requested legal guidance concerning the practice of online notarization services utilizing a webcam or other video in lieu of a personal appearance in front of a valid New Jersey Notary. It has been determined that New Jersey's statutes do not allow for this type of notarization."

UETA Recognizes Notary's eSignature

New Jersey has adopted the Uniform Electronic Transactions Act (NJSA 12A:12-1 through 12A:12-26), including the provision on notarization, thereby recognizing the legal validity of electronic signatures used by Notaries:

"If a law requires a signature or record to be notarized, acknowledged, verified, or made under oath, the requirement is satisfied if the electronic signature of the person authorized to perform those acts, together with all other information required to be included by other applicable law, is attached to or logically associated with the signature or record" (NJSA 12A:12-11).

NOTARY RECORDS

Statute provides that "each notary public shall take and subscribe an oath before the clerk of the county in which he resides, faithfully and honestly to discharge the duties of his office, and that he will make and keep a true record of all such matters as are required by law ..." (NJSA 52:7-14[a]).

"Note: Journals should be bound to prevent tampering" (NPM).

Components of Entry

In the "New Jersey Notary Public Manual," the Division of Revenue recommends a journal entry for each notarial act: "Make a journal entry. The journal entry provides evidence and an audit trail, thereby protecting both the Notary and the general public. Required information includes: 1) date and time of notary act, 2) type of act (i.e., acknowledgment), 3) title of document, 4) date document was signed, 5) signature, printed name and address of each signer, and if applicable, each witness, and 6) form of ID — e.g., identification document, personal knowledge, or credible witness."

Record of Protest

"Every notary public, upon protesting any bill of exchange or promissory note, shall record in a book to be kept for that purpose the time when, place where and upon whom, demand of payment was made, with a copy of the notice or nonpayment, how and when served; or if sent, in what manner and the time when; and if sent by post, to whom the same was directed, at what place, and when the same was put into such post office, to which record he shall sign his name" (NJSA 7:5-3). Upon the Notary's death or departure from the state, this record must be surrendered to the clerk of the county in which the Notary last resided (NJSA 7:5-5).

"When a notary public or any other person authorized to protest instruments under the laws of this state is called upon to testify concerning a protest made by him, he may, to refresh his memory, refer to the record thereof kept by him as required by law" (NJSA 2A:82-5).

AUTHENTICATION OF NOTARIAL ACTS

County Clerks

Certificates authenticating the acts of a New Jersey Notary are obtained from county clerks in counties where the Notary has qualified:

"A Notary may request from the State Treasurer, or clerk of the county in which he/she was sworn, copies of his/her commission and qualification certificates for filing in other counties in this State. Upon receipt of the copies, the Notary may present the same along with an autograph copy of his/her signature, to any county clerk in this State for filing" (NPM). See also NJSA 52:7-15[b].

"The county clerk of the county in which a notary public resides or the county clerk of any county where such notary public shall have filed his autograph signature and certificate (of commission and qualification) ... shall, upon request, subjoin to any certificate of proof, acknowledgment or affidavit signed by the notary public, a certificate under the clerk's hand and seal stating that the notary public was at the time ... duly commissioned and sworn and residing in this State, and was as such an officer of this State duly authorized to take and certify said proof, acknowledgment or affidavit ...; that full faith and credit are and ought to be given to the official acts of the notary public; and that the county clerk is well acquainted with the handwriting of the notary public and believes the signature to the instrument to which the certificate is attached is his genuine signature" (NJSA 52:7-16).

"County clerks may only provide certifications for Notaries who reside in their respective counties or Notaries who have filed copies of their commission/qualification certificates and autograph signatures" (NPM).

Department of Treasury

Apostilles for Notaries and certificates authenticating the acts of county clerks may be obtained from the New Jersey Department of the Treasury's Notary Public Unit (website, "Apostilles and Notary Certifications").

In the event that an authenticating certificate for a Notary cannot be obtained from the county clerk of a county in which that Notary is qualified, "(t)he State Treasurer may provide certifications relating to any Notary in this State" (NPM).

Fee: $5 per certificate, including an apostille, if the document relates to adoption of a child; otherwise, $25 per certificate. Payable to "Treasurer, State of New Jersey" (website, "Apostilles and Notary Certifications"). Expedited service, add $15 per certificate (in-person or via overnight courier); for in-person requests only, add $100 per certificate for same-day service, $500 per certificate for two-hour service, $1,000 per certificate for one-hour service (website, "Fees").

Address:
New Jersey Division of Revenue
Notary Public Unit
P.O. Box 452
Trenton, NJ 08646-0452

Courier Delivery:
New Jersey Division of Revenue
Notary Public Unit
33 West State St., 5th Floor
Trenton, NJ 08608-1214

Telephone: 1-609-633-8257

Procedure: Mail or present in person the original notarized document, along with the appropriate fee. In a cover letter, indicate the nation to which the document will be sent and whether the transaction involves an adoption. Mail-in requests typically require 15 days for processing. Paying for expedited service ensures a processing time of 8-1/2 business hours, not including return delivery. All documents will be returned by regular mail unless other arrangements are made (website, "Apostilles and Notary Certifications").

COMMISSIONING AND ADMINISTRATION

While the Secretary of State nominally appoints and commissions New Jersey Notaries (NJSA 52:7-11[a]), the state Department of the Treasury's Notary Public Unit is responsible for processing Notary commissions, as well as for providing certificates (including apostilles) to authenticate the acts of individual Notaries. The Unit also processes and records any changes of status of individual Notaries (NPM).

Applying for Commission

Qualifications: An applicant for a commission as a New Jersey Notary Public must: (a) be at least 18 years old, (b) be a resident of New Jersey or a resident of an adjoining state who maintains or is regularly employed in an office in New Jersey and (c) not have been convicted of a crime under the laws of any state or of the United States for an offense involving dishonesty, or a crime of the first or second degree (NPM and NJSA 52:7-12, 52:7-13, 52:7-20 and 52:7-21).

No Course or Test: No course of instruction or test is required of applicants for a New Jersey Notary commission.

Application: An application for a Notary commission must be endorsed by a state Senator or Assemblyman or by the Secretary of State or Assistant Secretary of State (NJSA 52:7-11[b]). The application must be submitted to the Notary Public Unit, along with a filing fee of $25, payable to "Treasurer, State of New Jersey" (NJSA 52:7-11[c] and website, "Application Instructions"). Non-residents must additionally submit an affidavit setting forth the address of their residence and of their place of employment in New Jersey (NJSA 52:7-13).

Upon approval of the application, the Notary Public Unit returns to the applicant a "Commission Certificate" and "Oath Qualification Certificate." Within three months of receiving the certificates, the Notary must take them to the clerk of the county in which the Notary resides or, in the case of non-residents, is employed. The county clerk will administer an oath of office to the Notary, collect a filing fee and return the completed "Oath Qualification Certificate" to the state Notary Public Unit (NJSA 52:7-14, NPM and website, "Application Instructions:).

"Under normal operating conditions, the State sends out a renewal package three months prior to the commission expiration date" (website, "Application Instructions"). The renewal process is the same as that for an initial commission (NJSA 52:7-11[b]).

Non-Residents: Residents of adjoining states (New York, Pennsylvania, Delaware) may become New Jersey Notaries if they maintain or are regularly employed in an office in the state. "Any such nonresident notary public shall file with the Secretary of State a certificate showing any change of residence or of his office or place of employment address in this State" (NJSA 52:7-13). This certificate now must be filed with the Department of the Treasury's Notary Public Unit (website, "Application Instructions").

<u>Online Search</u>: New Jersey's "Notary Public Search" service may be accessed by clicking "Look Up Active NJ Notaries Public" in the drop-down menu on the Division of Revenue's homepage. Notaries may be searched by last name, city or zip code. Search results include the Notary's full name, city, zip code and commission expiration date.

Changes of Status

<u>If Notary Changes Name</u>: "Whenever a Notary Public adopts a different name, before notarizing any documents, he/she must notify the State Treasurer and clerk of the county in which he/she resides by submitting a form furnished by the State Treasurer. Change request forms are available online, from the Business Services Customer Information Center, P.O. Box 452, Trenton, NJ 08646 or from the telephone forms line — (609) 292-9292, option #2 on the voice menu" (NPM). See also NJSA 52-7:18.

There is a $25 fee for a name change (website, "Fees").

<u>If Notary Moves</u>: Notification of the State Treasurer's Division of Revenue should be made for any change of address by the Notary, using the same form described above for a change of name (NPM).

There is a $25 fee for an address change (website, "Fees").

Notary May File in Additional Counties

"Any notary public, after having been duly commissioned and qualified, shall, upon request, receive from the clerk of the county where he has qualified, as many certificates of his commission and qualification as he shall require for filing with the other county clerks of this State, and upon receipt of such certificates the notary public may present the same, together with his autograph signature, to such county clerks as he may desire, for filing" (NJSA 52:7-15[b]).

COUNTY CLERKS

To contact a New Jersey county clerk to obtain an authenticating certificate for a notarial act, or to seek assistance in locating a given Notary, telephone long-distance information — 1-XXX-555-1212 — using the following area codes, and ask for the appropriate county clerk.

County	City/Town	Area Code
Atlantic	Mays Landing	(609)
Bergen	Hackensack	(201)
Burlington	Mount Holly	(609)
Camden	Camden	(856)
Cape May	Cape May Crt. Hse.	(609)
Cumberland	Bridgeton	(856)
Essex	Newark	(973)
Gloucester	Woodbury	(856)
Hudson	Jersey City	(201)
Hunterdon	Flemington	(908)
Mercer	Trenton	(609)
Middlesex	New Brunswick	(732)
Monmouth	Freehold	(732)
Morris	Morristown	(973)
Ocean	Toms River	(732)
Passaic	Paterson	(973)
Salem	Salem	(856)
Somerset	Somerville	(908)
Sussex	Newton	(973)
Union	Elizabeth	(908)
Warren	Belvidere	(908)

OTHER NOTARIAL OFFICERS

Besides Notaries, the following officers may take acknowledgments and proofs in New Jersey (NJSA 46:14-6.1[a]):

1. An attorney at law;
2. A clerk or deputy clerk of any county;
3. A surrogate or deputy surrogate of any county;
4. A register or deputy register of deeds and mortgages of any county.

Foreign Commissioners of Deeds

The Secretary of State may appoint "Foreign Commissioners of Deeds" for three-year terms to notarize documents in the U.S. state, territory, or district where they reside (NJSA 52:6-12 and 52:6-13). Such commissioners must attest their official acts with an official seal and file a seal impression with the Secretary of State (NJSA 52:6-18). A resident of New Jersey may be appointed a Foreign Commissioner of Deeds with authority to act in a state adjoining New Jersey (NJSA 52:6-15).

QUICK FACTS

Notary Jurisdiction
Statewide (NJSA 52:7-15[a]).

Notary Term Length
Five years (NJSA 52:7-11[a]).

Notary Bond
Not required by law.

N

New Mexico

NOTARY SEAL

New Mexico Notaries must authenticate their official acts with a seal of office, and the format must be as follows (NMSA 14-12A-18):

Kind

Embosser or Inked Stamp: If a stamp is used, the law specifies that it be rubber.

Shape/Size

"Rubber stamps cannot have a signature line, and a round rubber stamp is not acceptable" (NPH). The required arrangement of the five components within the inking stamp (see below) suggests a rectangular shape for the stamp.

Examples

The above typical, actual-size examples of Notary seals are allowed by New Mexico law. The circular example shown above is a metal embosser.

NOTARY INFORMATION

Office of Secretary of State
Business Services
Notary Division   1-505-827-3600
State Capitol North Annex 1-800-477-3632
325 Don Gaspar, Suite 300
Santa Fe, NM 87503

Website: www.sos.state.nm.us/sos-notary.html

NOTARY RULES

NMSA — NEW MEXICO STATUTES ANNOTATED
NMAC — NEW MEXICO ADMINISTRATIVE CODE
NPH — NEW MEXICO NOTARY PUBLIC HANDBOOK

Most Notary rules are in the New Mexico Statutes Annotated, Chapter 14:

a. Article 12A, "Notary Public"

b. Article 14, Uniform Law on Notarial Acts*

   * This is the *Uniform Law on Notarial Acts* of 1982, adopted virtually intact, as NMSA 14-14-1 through 14-14-11.

Rules for electronic notarization are provided in the *New Mexico Administrative Code*, Title 12, Chapter 9, Part 2.

Other guidelines are in the *New Mexico Notary Public Handbook*, issued by the Secretary of State.

Components

Embosser:
1. Name of Notary;*
2. "Notary Public – State of New Mexico".

Inked Stamp:
1. "Official Seal";
2. Name of Notary;*
3. "Notary Public – State of New Mexico";
4. "My Commission Expires _____ (date)";**
5. New Mexico state seal.

* The Notary's name consists of a "surname and one given name, plus an initial or additional name if the (Notary) so desires, or surname and at least two initials" (NMSA 14-12A-4[C]).

** The commission expiration date may be written in by hand.

The above five components must be arranged within the stamp as shown below:

```
            (1)
   (5)      (2)
            (3)
            (4)
```

Signature Rules

"Rubber stamps (i.e., Notary seals) cannot have a signature line" (NPH). On any notarized document, the Notary must not affix the official signature within the seal.

"In notarizing a paper document, a notary public shall … not sign using a facsimile stamp or an electronic or other printing method …" (NMSA 14-12A-17). Notaries must sign by hand "exactly and only" the name on the seal and "only at the time the notarial act is performed."

Commission Expiration Date Must Appear

"Upon performance of any notarial act, the notary public shall, immediately opposite or following the notary public's signature, endorse the date of the expiration of commission. The endorsement may be legibly written, stamped or printed upon the instrument and shall be substantially in the following form:

"'My commission expires (stating date of expiration of commission)'" (NMSA 14-12A-19).

It is sufficient for this statement to appear within a Notary's inked stamp, according to state officials.

Seal Affixed Only at Time of Act

"An impression or image of the seal or stamp shall be affixed only at the time the notarial act is performed" (NMSA 14-12A-18[D]).

Seal Exclusive Property of Notary

"A notary public shall keep an official seal or stamp that is the exclusive property of the notary public. The seal or stamp shall not be possessed or used by any other person or surrendered to an employer upon termination of employment" (NMSA 14-12A-18[A]).

"When not in use, the seal or stamp shall be kept secure and accessible only to the notary public" (NMSA 14-12A-18[E]).

Seal Stolen, Lost or Damaged

"Within 10 days after the seal or stamp of a notary public is stolen, lost, damaged, or otherwise rendered incapable of affixing a legible impression or image, the notary public, after informing the appropriate law enforcement agency in the case of theft or vandalism, shall notify the secretary of state by any means providing a tangible receipt or acknowledgment, including certified mail and electronic transmission, and also provide a copy of any pertinent police report" (NMSA 14-12A-18[F]).

Seal Destroyed or Defaced

"As soon as reasonably practicable after resignation, revocation, change of name, expiration of a commission or death of the notary public, the seal or stamp shall be destroyed or defaced so that it may not be misused" (NMSA 14-12A-18[G]).

NOTARY POWERS

New Mexico Notaries are authorized to perform the following notarial acts (NMSA 14-12A-7[A] and 14-14-1[A]):

1. Take acknowledgments*;
2. Administer oaths** and affirmations***;
3. Take jurats (verifications upon oath or affirmation)****;
4. Certify copies*****;
5. Any other act so authorized by state law. (NOTE: Witnessing or attesting a signature and noting a protest of a negotiable instrument are listed as authorized notarial powers in New Mexico's Uniform Law on Notarial Acts [NMSA 14-14-1].)

* Acknowledgments: "'(A)cknowledgment' means a notarial act in which a person at a single time and place:

"(1) appears in person before the notary public and presents a document;

"(2) is personally known to the notary public or identified by the notary public through satisfactory evidence; and

"(3) indicates to the notary public that the signature on the document was voluntarily affixed by the person for the purposes stated within the document and, if applicable, that the person had due authority to sign in a particular representative capacity …" (NMSA 14-12A-2[A]).

See also Uniform Law on Notarial Acts, NMSA 14-14-1[B] and 14-14-2[A].

** Oath Procedure: "(A)ny person administering the oath shall do so in the following form, viz: the person swearing shall, with his right hand uplifted, follow the words required in the oath as administered, beginning: I do solemnly swear, and closing: so help me God" (NMSA 14-13-1).

"'(O)ath' means a notarial act that is legally equivalent to an affirmation and in which a person at a single time and place:

"(1) appears in person before the notary public;

"(2) is personally known to the notary public or identified by the notary public through satisfactory evidence; and

"(3) makes a vow of truthfulness or fidelity on penalty of perjury while invoking a deity or using any form of the word 'swear'" (NMSA 14-12A-2[J]).

*** Affirmation Procedure: "Whenever any person is required to take or subscribe an oath and shall have conscientious scruples against taking the same, he shall be permitted, instead of such oath, to make a solemn affirmation, with uplifted right hand, in the following form, viz: you do solemnly, sincerely and truly declare and affirm, and close with: and this I do under the pains and penalties of perjury …" (NMSA 14-13-2).

"'(A)ffirmation' means a notarial act that is legally equivalent to an oath and in which a person at a single time and place:

"(1) appears in person before a notary public;

"(2) is personally known to the notary public or identified by the notary public through satisfactory evidence; and

"(3) makes a vow of truthfulness or fidelity on penalty of perjury, based on personal honor and without invoking a deity or using any form of the word 'swear'…" (NMSA 14-12A-2[B]).

**** Jurats: "'(J)urat' means a notarial act in which a person at a single time and place:

"(1) appears in person before the notary public and presents a document;

"(2) is personally known to the notary public or identified by the notary public through satisfactory evidence;

"(3) signs the document in the presence of the notary public; and

"(4) takes an oath or affirmation from the notary public that the person is voluntarily affixing his signature and vouching for the truthfulness or accuracy of the signed document ..." (NMSA 14-12A-2[F]).

See also Uniform Law on Notarial Acts, NMSA 14-14-1[C] and 14-14-2[B].

***** Certifying Copies: "In certifying or attesting a copy of a document or other item, the notarial officer shall determine that the proffered copy is a full, true and accurate transcription or reproduction of the one that was copied" (NMSA 14-14-2[D]).

"'(C)opy certification' means a notarial act in which a notary public:

"(1) is presented with a document that is neither a vital record, a public record, nor publicly recordable;

"(2) copies or supervises the copying of the document using a photographic or electronic copying process;

"(3) compares the document to the copy; and

"(4) determines that the copy is accurate and complete ..." (NMSA 14-12A-2[D]).

"Examples of public documents include birth certificates, death certificates, marriage licenses, divorce decrees, and school transcripts" (website, "Apostille Information").

Identifying Document Signers

The following identification requirements apply to acknowledgments, verifications upon oath or affirmation and to witnessing or attesting signatures:

"A notarial officer has satisfactory evidence that a person is the person whose true signature is on a document if that person is:

"(1) personally known to the notarial officer;

"(2) identified upon the oath or affirmation of a credible witness personally known to the notarial officer; or

"(3) identified on the basis of identification documents" (NMSA 14-14-2[F]).

"'(S)atisfactory evidence of identity' means identification of an individual based on:

"(1) at least one current document issued by a federal, state or tribal government agency bearing the photographic image of the person's face and signature and a physical description of the person, though a properly stamped passport without a physical description is acceptable; or

"(2) the oath or affirmation of one credible witness unaffected by the document or transaction who is personally known to the notary public and who also personally knows the person, or of two credible witnesses unaffected by the document or transaction who each personally knows the person and shows to the notary public documentary identification as described in subparagraph (1) of this subsection" (NMSA 14-12A-2[O]).

"'(C)redible witness' means an honest, reliable and impartial person who personally knows the person appearing before a notary public and takes an oath or affirmation from the Notary to vouch for that individual's identity ..." (NMSA 14-12A-2[E]).

"'Personally known' means familiarity with a person resulting from interactions with that person over a period of time sufficient to dispel any reasonable uncertainty that the person has the identity claimed ..." (NMSA 14-12A-2[M]).

<u>Personal Appearance Allows ID Exchange</u>: "'(P)ersonal appearance' and 'appears before the notary' mean that the principal and the notary public are physically close enough to see, hear, communicate with and give identification documents to each other" (NMSA 14-12A-2[L]).

<u>Verifying Willingness, Competence</u>: "A notarization provides verification of a document signer's willingness to sign, his competence to sign, and that the signer is, indeed, the person identified by the signature" (website, "Reminders').

"You are not responsible for the contents of the document, however you should be satisfied that there is no compelling doubt about whether the signer is aware of what he/she is signing.... A Notary must not notarize a document if the Notary suspects that the signer is not acting on his/her own free will" (website, "How to Perform a Notarization").

Signature by Mark
A New Mexico Notary may certify the affixation of a signature by mark on a document presented for notarization if (NMSA 14-12A-7[C]):

"(1) the mark is affixed in the presence of a notary public and of two credible witnesses unaffected by the document;

"(2) both witnesses sign their own names beside the mark;

"(3) the notary public writes below the mark: 'Mark affixed by (name of signer of mark) in presence of (names of witnesses) and undersigned notary public pursuant to subsection C of section 7 of the Notary Public Act'; and

"(4) the notary public notarizes that signature by mark through an acknowledgment or jurat."

Notary Signing for Disabled
A New Mexico Notary may sign the name of a person physically unable to sign or make a mark on a document presented for notarization if (NMSA 14-12A-7[D]):

"(1) the person directs the notary public to do so in the presence of two credible witnesses unaffected by the document;

"(2) the notary public signs the person's name in the presence of the person and the witnesses;

"(3) both witnesses sign their own names beside the signature;

"(4) the notary writes below the signature: 'Signature affixed by notary public in the presence of (names and addresses of person and two witnesses) pursuant to subsection D of section 7 of the Notary Public Act'; and

"(5) the notary public notarizes the signature through an acknowledgment or jurat."

Alternative to Photo Certification
"For individuals needing a photograph notarized, a Notary Public may not certify nor authenticate a photograph pursuant to Section 14-12A-12 NMSA ... However, a Notary Public may notarize a statement by the principal regarding the photograph. That notarization does not authenticate or certify the photograph, it only verifies that the individual making the statement signed the statement" (website, "Apostilles ...").

NOTARY DON'TS

A New Mexico Notary may:
1. NOT "certify nor authenticate a photograph" but see "Alternative to Photo Certification" above (NMSA 14-12A-12[B]);
2. NOT make a testimonial by using "the official notary public title or seal to endorse, promote, denounce or oppose any product, service, contest, candidate or other offering" (NMSA 14-12A-14);
3. NOT "claim to have powers, qualifications,

rights or privileges that the office of notary public does not provide, including the power to counsel on immigration matters" (NMSA 14-12A-15[D]);
4. NOT "use the term 'notario publico' or any equivalent non-English term in any business card, advertisement, notice or sign" (NMSA 14-12A-15[E]);
5. NOT notarize "(d)ocuments which have been changed or altered with correction fluid or correction tape" (website, "Precautions");
6. NOT "notarize his own signature" (website, "Precautions");
7. NOT notarize a "signature affixed to a document by a rubber stamp" (website, "Reminders");
8. NOT notarize a vital record, a public record, nor a publicly recordable document (NMSA 14-12A-2);
9. NOT predate or postdate a notarial certificate (website, "How To Perform a Notarization").

Conditions Prohibiting Notarial Act

A New Mexico Notary may not notarize when the principal (NMSA 14-12A-7[B]):

(1) is not in the Notary's presence at the time of notarization (see definition of "personal appearance" below);
(2) is not personally known to the Notary or identified by the Notary on the basis of satisfactory evidence;
(3) shows a demeanor that causes the Notary "to have a compelling doubt about whether the principal knows the consequences of the transaction requiring a notarial act"; or
(4) in the Notary's judgment, is not acting of his or her own free will.

"A notarization provides verification of a document signer's willingness to sign, his competence to sign, and that the signer is, indeed, the person identified by the signature" (website, "Reminders").

Personal Appearance Defined: "'Personal appearance' means that the principal and the notary public are physically close enough to see, hear, communicate with and give identification documents to each other" (NMSA 14-12A-2[L]).

"A Notary must never notarize a signature that was not signed or acknowledged in the Notary's presence! This is the most important rule to protect a Notary from legal liability" (website, "Reminders").

"A notary who notarizes a document without the person appearing before him or her may be charged with a misdemeanor and, if convicted, may be punished by imposition of a fine of not more than $1,000.00 or imprisonment for not more than six months, or both" (website, "Notary Tips").

Refusal to Notarize

"A notary public shall not refuse to perform a notarial act based on the principal's race, age, gender, sexual orientation, religion, national origin, health or disability or status as a non-client or non-customer of the notary public or the notary public's employer" (NMSA 14-12A-8).

If a person requests a notarial act and "tenders the appropriate fee," the Notary must perform the act unless (NMSA 14-12A-8[B]):

(1) the Notary knows or has good reason to believe that the act or associated transaction is unlawful;
(2) the act is prohibited; or
(3) "the number of notarial acts requested practically precludes completion of all acts at once, in which case the notary shall arrange for later completion of the remaining acts."

Lawful, Reasonable Requests Honored: "A Notary is to serve any person who makes a lawful and reasonable request for notarization" (website, "Reminders").

Avoidance of Influence

"A notary public shall not influence a person either to enter into or avoid a transaction involving a notarial act by the notary public, except that the notary public may advise against a transaction if the notary public knows or has good reason to believe that the notarial act or the associated transaction is unlawful" (NMSA 14-12A-10[A]).

"A notary public has neither the duty nor the authority to investigate, ascertain, or attest the lawfulness, propriety, accuracy, or truthfulness of a document or transaction involving a notarial act" (NMSA 14-12A-10[B]).

Incomplete Certificates and Documents

"A notary public shall not affix an official signature or seal on a notarial certificate that is incomplete" (NMSA 14-12A-11[B]).

"A notary public shall not provide or send a signed or sealed notarial certificate to another person with the understanding that it will be completed or attached to a document outside of the notary public's presence" (NMSA 14-12A-11[C]).

"A notary public shall not notarize a signature:
"(1) on a blank or incomplete document; or
"(2) on a document without notarial certificate wording" (NMSA 14-12A-12).

False Certificates or Actions

"If a notary public, or any other officer authorized by law to make or give a certificate or other writing makes or delivers as true a certificate or writing containing statements which he knows to be false, or appends his official signature to acknowledgments or other documents when the principals executing the document have not appeared in person before him, is guilty of a misdemeanor and upon conviction shall be punished by a fine not exceeding one thousand dollars ($1,000), or by imprisonment for a period not exceeding six months, or both" (NMSA 14-12A-11[A]).

"A notary public shall not perform any official action with the intent to deceive or defraud (NMSA 14-12A-13).

Disqualifying Interests

"Notaries should not notarize documents in which they are a signer or in which they are named ...

"Notaries should not notarize documents or transactions to which the notary is a personal beneficiary (this does not include notaries acting in the scope of their employment for their employer, such as a secretary or an office clerk)" (website, "Precautions").

Family Members: "Because of the notary's need to be impartial, he should avoid notarizing for family members or in any other circumstances when his impartiality can be questioned or challenged" (website, "Precautions").

Professional Clients: "Notaries may notarize documents when acting in a professional capacity, such as a professional advisor, counselor, agent, or attorney" (website, "Precautions").

Corporate Employees: "It is unlawful for any Notary Public to take the acknowledgment of an instrument by or to a bank or other corporation of which the Notary is a stockholder, director, officer, or employee, where such Notary is a party to such instrument, either individually or as a representative of such corporation. It is also unlawful for a Notary to protest any negotiable instrument owned or held for collection by a corporation of which the Notary is a stockholder, director, officer, or employee, where such Notary is individually a party to the instrument" (website, "Information for Notary Public").

Acting with Expired Commission

"A person exercising the duties of a Notary Public with the knowledge that his commission has expired, or that he is otherwise disqualified from serving as a Notary Public, is guilty of a misdemeanor and, upon conviction, shall be punished by imposition of a fine of $500 and removed from office by the governor" (website, "Information for Notary Public").

NOTARY SIGNING AGENTS

Currently, there are no statutes, regulations or rules expressly governing, prohibiting or restricting the operation of Notary Signing Agents within the state of New Mexico.

NOTARY FEES

Notaries are entitled to collect the following fees for notarial acts (NMSA 14-12A-16[D]):
1. Taking an acknowledgment: $5;
2. Administering an oath or affirmation, without a signature: $5 per person;
3. Executing a jurat: $5;
4. Certifying a copy: 50 cents per page, with a minimum total charge of $5.

Travel Fee: "A notary public may charge a travel fee not to exceed thirty cents ($.30) per mile when traveling to perform a notarial act if: 1. the notary public and the person requesting the notarial act agree upon the travel fee in advance of the travel; and 2. the notary public explains to the person requesting the notarial act that the travel fee is separate from the notarial fees and not mandated by law" (NMSA 14-12A-16[E]).

Need Not Charge: "For performing a notarial act, a notary public may charge the maximum fee specified in this section, charge less than the maximum fee or waive the fee" (NMSA 14-12A-16[A]).

No Discrimination in Fees: "A notary public shall not discriminate by conditioning the fee for a notarial act on the attributes of the principal" (NMSA 14-12A-16[B]).

"An employer shall not establish fees for notarial services that are in excess of those specified ..." (website, "Reminders").

Electronic Notarization Fees: A maximum fee of $10 may be collected by a registered, electronically enabled Notary for the electronic performance of an acknowledgment, a jurat or an oath or affirmation (NMAC 12.9.2.12). A Notary may charge less than this maximum or waive the fee altogether. An employer may not compel the Notary to change more than the stipulated maximum fee for an electronic notarial act.

NOTARY CERTIFICATES

New Mexico has adopted the *Uniform Law on Notarial Acts*, including the short-form certificates (NMSA 14-14-8) for:
1. Acknowledgment by individual;
2. Acknowledgment by representative;
3. Verification upon oath or affirmation (jurat);
4. Witnessing or attesting signature;
5. Attesting copy of document.

For the text of these certificates, see Uniform Law on Notarial Acts (1982), Section 8, in Appendix 2.

The certificates described above from the *Uniform Law on Notarial Acts* are printed below in the Spanish language for use on notarized documents that will be sent to Spanish-speaking jurisdictions (website, "Sample Notarial Certificates"):

Acknowledgment by Individual — Spanish Language (NMSA 14-14-8[A]):

Estado de Nuevo México
Condado de _____

*Este documento fue reconocido ante mi en*_____ *(fecha) por* _____
(nombre de la persona o de las personas).

(Sello, si existe)

_____ *(Firma del oficial notarial)*
_____ *(Título y Cargo)*
[Mi comisión vence: _____*]*

Acknowledgment by Representative — Spanish Language (NMSA 14-14-8[B]):

Estado de Nuevo México
Condado de _____

Este documento fue reconocido ante mi en _____ *(fecha) por* _____ *(nombre/s de la persona o personas) en su capacidad de* _____ *(tipo de autoridad de la persona, e.j., oficial, fideicomisario, etc.) por* _____ *(nombre de la persona de parte de quien el documento fue firmado).*

(Sello, si existe)

_____ *(Firma del oficial notarial)*
_____ *(Título y Cargo)*
[Mi comisión vence: _____*]*

Verification upon Oath or Affirmation (Jurat) — Spanish Language (NMSA 14-14-8[C]):

Estado de Nuevo México
Condado de _____

Firmado bajo juramento (o afirmado) ante mi en _____ *(fecha) por* _____ *(nombre de la persona o de las personas que ha declara/n).*

(Sello, si existe)

_____ *(Firma del oficial notarial)*
_____ *(Título y Cargo)*
[Mi comisión vence: _____*]*

Witnessing or Attesting Signature — Spanish Language (NMSA 14-14-8[D]):

Estado de Nuevo México
Condado de _____

Firmado o atestiguado ante mi en _____ *(fecha) por* _____
(nombre de la persona o de las personas).

(Sello, si existe)

_____ (Firma del oficial notarial)
_____ (Título y Cargo)
[Mi comisión vence: _____]

Copy Certification — Spanish Language (NMSA 14-14-8[E]):

Estado de Nuevo México
Condado de _____

Yo certifico que esta es copia fiel de un documento en la posesión de _____ *(nombre). Fechado* _____.

(Sello, si existe)

_____ *(Firma del oficial notarial)*
_____ *(Título y Cargo)*
[*Mi comisión vence:* _____]

Form of Notarial Certificate

"A. A notarial act shall be evidenced by a certificate signed and dated by a notarial officer. The certificate shall include identification of the jurisdiction in which the notarial act is performed and the title of the office of the notarial officer and may include the official stamp or seal of office. If the officer is a notary public, the certificate shall also indicate the date of expiration, if any, of the commission of office, but omission of that information may subsequently be corrected. If the officer is a commissioned officer on active duty in the military service of the United States, it shall also include the officer's rank.

"B. A certificate of a notarial act is sufficient if it meets the requirements of Subsection A of this section and it:

"1. is in the short form set forth in Section 8 of the Uniform Law on Notarial Acts;

"2. is in a form otherwise prescribed by the law of this state;

"3. is in a form prescribed by the laws or regulations applicable in the place in which the notarial act was performed; or

"4. sets forth the actions of the notarial officer and those are sufficient to meet the requirements of the designated notarial act …" (NMSA 14-14-7).

Shall Not Select Nor Advise on Certificates

"If notarial certificate wording is not provided or indicated for a document, a non-attorney notary public shall not determine the type of notarial act or certificate to be used" (NMSA 14-12A-15[A]).

"A non-attorney notary public shall not assist another person in drafting, completing, selecting, or understanding a document or transaction requiring a notarial act" (NMSA 14-12A-15[B]).

"This section does not preclude a notary public who is duly qualified, trained or experienced in a particular industry or professional field from selecting, drafting, completing or advising on a document or certificate related to a matter within that industry or field" (NMSA 14-12A-15[C]).

"You may refuse to notarize a document when the document does not have notarial language. You may suggest to the signer that he return the document to the issuing agency, the receiving agency or the individual that indicated it was necessary and ask that the proper notarial certificate be placed on the document, so that it may be notarized" (website, "Notary Tips").

Notarial Form for Signature of School Registrar (Web site, 'Apostilles...'):

I, _____ the registrar of _____ (name of school, college), hereby certify that this is a true and original transcript/diploma for _____ (name of student).

_____ (Signature of Registrar)

State of New Mexico
County of _____

Signed or attested before me on _____ (date) by _____.

_____ (Signature of Notary Public)

(Notary Seal)

Commission expiration: _____

ELECTRONIC NOTARIZATIONS

Through adoption of Title 12, Chapter 9, Part 2 ("Performing Electronic Notarial Acts") of the New Mexico Administrative Code, effective May 30, 2008, the New Mexico Secretary of State established rules for eNotarization.

Registration Required

Under these rules, an "electronically enabled notary public" must register with the Secretary of State the capability to perform electronic notarial acts (NMAC 12.9.2.7D),

In registering, the applicant, who must be an active New Mexico Notary Public, must provide "proof of successful completion of a course of instruction on electronic notarization offered through an educational provider approved by the United States department of education (ACCET) accrediting council for continuing education and training" (NMAC 12.9.2.9B[3]).

The Notary must also include in registering: a description of the electronic technology(ies) that the Notary will use in attaching an electronic signature and an electronic notarial certificate to an electronic document; exemplars of the Notary's electronic signature and electronic seal, "which shall contain the notary's name and any necessary instructions or techniques that allow the notary's electronic signature or official electronic seal to be read"; and the name, address and phone number of the New Mexico-registered vendor issuing the electronic Notary seal, among other required information (NMAC 12.9.2.9B).

Performing Electronic Notarizations

The following notarial acts may be performed electronically: acknowledgments, jurats, and oaths or affirmations (NMAC 12.9.2.10).

Notary Electronic Signature: "'Notary electronic signature' means those forms of electronic signature, which have been approved by the secretary of state as an acceptable means for an electronic notary to affix the notary's official signature to an electronic record that is being notarized" (NMAC 12.9.2.7H).

"When performing an electronic notarial act, a notary public shall apply an electronic signature, which shall be attached to or logically associated with the electronic document such that removal or alteration of such electronic signature is detectable and will render evidence of alteration of the document containing the notary certificate which may invalidate the electronic notarial act" (NMAC 12.9.2.11A).

The Notary's electronic signature is deemed to be reliable if it is unique to the Notary, capable of independent verification, retained under the Notary's sole control, attached to or logically associated with the electronic document, and "linked to the data in such a manner that any subsequent alterations to the underlying document's electronic notarial certificate are detectable and may invalidate the electronic notarial act" (NMAC 12.9.2.11C).

"The notary public's electronic signature and with the electronic notary seal shall be used only for the purpose of performing electronic notarial acts" (NMAC 12.9.2.11G).

Electronic Notary Seal: "'Electronic notary seal'" and 'official electronic seal' mean information within a notarized electronic document that includes the notary public's name, jurisdiction of appointment, commission expiration date and generally corresponds to data in notary public seals used on paper documents" (NMAC 12.9.2.7E).

"When performing an electronic notarial act, a notary public shall apply an electronic seal, when required by law, which shall be attached to or logically associated with the electronic document such that removal or alteration of such official electronic seal is detectable and will render evidence of alteration of the document containing the notary certificate which may invalidate the electronic notarial act" (NMAC 12.9.2.11D).

The Notary's electronic seal is deemed to be reliable if it is unique to the Notary, capable of independent verification, retained under the Notary's sole control, is attached to or logically associated with the electronic document, and "linked to the data in such a manner that any subsequent alterations to the underlying document or electronic notarial certificate are detectable and may invalidate the electronic notarial act" (NMAC 12.9.2.11E).

"An electronic image of a seal need not accompany an electronic signature" (NMAC 12.9.2.11F).

Electronic Notarial Certificate: "'Electronic notarial certificate' means the portion of a notarized document that is completed by a notary public and contains the notary public's electronic signature or official electronic seal, official title, commission expiration date, and any required information concerning the date and place of the electronic notarization, and states the facts attested to or certified by the notary public in a particular electronic notarization" (NMAC 12.9.2.7G).

"When performing an electronic notarial act, a notary public shall complete an electronic notarial certificate, which shall be attached to or logically associated with the electronic document such that removal or alteration of the electronic notarial certificate is detectable and will render evidence of alteration of the document containing the notary certificate which may invalidate the electronic notarial act" (NMAC 12.9.2.11B).

Electronic Signer Must Appear in Person: "A notary public shall not perform an electronic notarial act if the document signer does not appear in person before the notary public at the time of notarization. Under no circumstances shall a notary public base identification merely upon familiarity with a signer's electronic signature or an electronic verification process that authenticates the signer's electronic signature when the signer is not in the physical presence of the notary public" (NMAC 12.9.2.8A).

"The methods for identifying document signers for an electronic notarization shall be the same as the methods required for a paper-based notarization" (NMAC 12.9.2.8B).

Fees for Electronic Notarization: A maximum fee of $10 may be collected by the Notary for the electronic performance of an acknowledgment, a jurat or an oath or affirmation (NMAC 12.9.2.12). A Notary may charge less than this maximum or waive the fee altogether. An employer may not compel the Notary to charge more than the maximum fee.

UETA Recognizes Notary's eSignature

New Mexico has enacted the Uniform Electronic Transactions Act (NMSA 14-16-1 through 14-16-19) and its provision on notarization and acknowledgment, thereby recognizing the legal validity of electronic signatures used by Notaries:

"If a law requires a signature or record to be notarized, acknowledged, verified or made under oath, the requirement is satisfied if the electronic signature of the person authorized to perform those acts, together with all other information required to be included by other applicable law, is attached to or logically associated with the signature or record" (NMSA 14-16-11).

URPERA Does Not Require Seal Image

In 2007, New Mexico adopted the Uniform Real Property Electronic Recording Act (Chapter 2007-261), including the following provision:

"A requirement that a document or a signature associated with a document be notarized, acknowledged, verified, witnessed or made under oath is satisfied if the electronic signature of the person authorized to perform that act and all other information required to be included is attached to or logically associated with the document or signature. A physical or electronic image of a stamp, impression or seal need not accompany an electronic signature."

NOTARY RECORDS

Prior to July 1, 2003, New Mexico statute (NMSA 14-12-12) required that Notaries keep a record of their protests, but this was repealed by enactment of Chapter 286, 2003 Laws.

Notary Journal Is Recommended

"Although it is not required by law, it is recommended that the Notary Public keep a journal of his notarial acts containing at a minimum the date, type of document, and name(s) and signature(s) of the person(s) whose signature(s) were notarized by him" (website, "Information for Notary Public").

"New Mexico law does not require that notaries keep a journal, however we strongly encourage you to do so. Journals can be used to jog your memory about a notarization that took place earlier in the year and can be used as evidence in a court of law" (website, "How To Perform A Notarization").

Bound Journal Is Preferred: "The best way of keeping a record of all your notarial acts, is by purchasing a bound notary journal (record book or log), not a loose leaf notebook....We encourage you to complete your journal (entry) before you perform your notarization, so that all information in your journal is complete before the signer has left your presence" (website, "How To Perform A Notarization").

Journal Must Be Safeguarded: "Your journal is your personal property and should not be surrendered to an employer even if you have left their employment. Always safeguard your journal by keeping it in a locked area" (website, "How To Perform A Notarization").

AUTHENTICATION OF NOTARIAL ACTS

Secretary of State

Authenticating certificates for Notaries, including apostilles, are issued only by the New Mexico Secretary of State's office (NMSA 14-12A-22).

Fees: $3 per document notarized for any certificate of authentication ("certificate of appointment") for a Notary, including an apostille. Payable to: "Secretary of State" or "New Mexico Secretary of State."

Address:
Office of Secretary of State
325 Don Gaspar, Suite 300
Santa Fe, NM 87503

Telephone: 1-800-477-3632

Procedure: Mail or present in person the original notarized document(s), along with the appropriate fee. Indicate the country to which the document will be sent and include a stamped, addressed return envelope. "(P)lease provide a telephone number in the event that we need to contact you regarding your request. If delivery other than first class mail is needed, you must enclose a pre-addressed, pre-paid airbill with your request" (website, "Apostille Information").

COMMISSIONING AND ADMINISTRATION

While New Mexico's Governor nominally appoints the state's Notaries, it is the office of the Secretary of State that regulates their activities, screening applicants and maintaining records (NMSA 14-12A-5).

Applying for Commission

Qualifications: An applicant for appointment as a New Mexico Notary Public must: (a) be a resident of New Mexico, (b) be at least 18 years old, (c) be able to read and write the English language, (d) not have pled guilty or nolo contendere to a felony or have been convicted of a felony and (e) not have had a Notary commission revoked within the past five years.

No Course or Test: Neither education nor testing is mandated for Notary commission applicants in New Mexico.

Application: Prior to submitting the application, which must be in black ink, the applicant must obtain a Notary seal (rubber stamp or embosser) and affix an impression on the form, which must be notarized (oath of office) and bear the character endorsement of two New Mexico residents. A notarized $10,000 Notary surety bond must be sent with the application (including a power of attorney from the insurance company, with the name of the company officer who signed the bond), along with the $20 application fee.

A Notary may be reappointed by applying in the same manner as for the original commission (NMSA 14-12A-6).

Non-Residents: Non-residents of New Mexico may not qualify for a Notary commission in the state.

Changes of Status

If Notary Moves: Within 10 days of a change of the Notary's residence, business or mailing address, the Notary must inform the Secretary of State and the bond surety in writing (NMSA 14-12A-21[A]). The "Notary Public Change of Address" form on the website may be used. No fee is required.

A Notary may be removed from office by the Governor if the Notary ceases to be a New Mexico resident (website, "Information for Notary Public").

If Notary Changes Name: A Notary with a changed name must within 10 days apply to the Secretary of State for issuance of a corrected commission, for a fee of $3. A "Notary Public Name Change Application" form, available on the Web site, must be used. The Application must bear an impression of the Notary's new seal. The Secretary will then issue a corrected commission that shows the Notary's new name and expires on the same date as the certificate it replaced. The Notary must also notify his or her bond surety company within 10 days in order to receive a bond rider (NMSA 14-12A-20).

If Notary Dies: If a Notary dies during the term of commission or before destroying or defacing his or her official seal, the Notary's personal representative must notify the Secretary of State about the death in writing and "as soon as reasonably practicable, destroy or deface all notary seals and stamps so that they may not be misused" (NMSA 14-12A-24[B]).

COUNTY CLERKS

In the state of New Mexico, county clerks are not involved with administration of the state's Notary program, nor do they authenticate the official acts of Notaries.

OTHER NOTARIAL OFFICERS

Besides Notaries, the following officers are authorized to perform notarial acts within the state (NMSA 14-14-3):
1. A judge, clerk or deputy clerk of any court of the state; or
2. A person authorized by the law of the state to administer oaths.

Oath-Administering Officers

"The Secretary of State of New Mexico, county clerks, clerks of probate courts, clerks of district courts, clerks of magistrate courts if the magistrate has a seal, and all duly commissioned and acting notaries public, are hereby authorized and empowered to administer oaths and affirmations in all cases where magistrates and other officers within the state authorized to administer oaths may do so, under existing laws, and with like effect" (NMSA 14-13-3).

QUICK FACTS

Notary Jurisdiction
Statewide (NMSA 14-12A-5).

Notary Term Length
Four years (NMSA 14-12A-5), expiring at midnight on the commission expiration date.
Knowingly notarizing with an expired commission is a misdemeanor punishable by a $500 fine and commission revocation (NMSA 14-12A-25).

Notary Bond
$10,000, executed by a licensed surety company (NMSA 14-12A-9[A]).

New York

NOTARY SEAL

A New York State Notary Public is not required by law to use a seal of office.

If Seal Is Used

"The laws of the State of New York do not require the use of seals by notaries public. If a seal is used, it should sufficiently identify the notary public, his authority and jurisdiction. It is the opinion of the Department of State that the only inscription required is the name of the notary and the words 'Notary Public for the State of New York'" (NPLL).

Must Print, Typewrite or Stamp

On every notarial certificate, a Notary must "print, typewrite, or stamp beneath his signature in black ink" the following (EL 137):
1. Notary's name;
2. "Notary Public State of New York" or, if applicable and preferred, "Attorney and Counselor at Law State of New York";

JANE Q. DOE
Notary Public - State of New York
No. 12-3456789
Qualified in Bronx County
My Commission Expires _____.

Examples

Above are typical examples of an optional embossing Notary seal (bottom) and of the information that must be printed, typewritten or stamped beneath the Notary's signature in black ink, whether or not appearing in a seal. Formats other than these may also be seen.

NOTARY ADMINISTRATION

Department of State
Div. of Licensing Services 1-518-474-4429
Alfred E. Smith Building
P.O. Box 22001
Albany, NY 12201-2001

(80 South Swan St., 10th Floor
Albany, NY 12210)

Website: www.dos.state.ny.us/licensing/

NOTARY RULES

EL — NEW YORK EXECUTIVE LAW
POL — NEW YORK PUBLIC OFFICERS LAW
RPL — NEW YORK REAL PROPERTY LAW
NPLL — NOTARY PUBLIC LICENSE LAW

Most Notary rules are in the:

a. Executive Law, Sections 130 through 138;

b. Public Officers Law, Sections 3, 67, 69, 534;

c. Real Property Law, Sections 298 through 333.

Pertinent statutes and other guidelines for Notaries are compiled and issued by the (June 2011) Department of State in its "Notary Public License Law" publication, also available on the website.

3. Name of county where Notary originally qualified for commission;
4. Notary's commission expiration date;
5. Wherever required, name of county in which Notary's certificate of official character is filed, using the words, "Certificate filed … County".

Numbers Required within New York City

"A notary public who has qualified or who has filed a certificate of official character in the office of the clerk in a county or counties within the city of New York must also affix to each instrument his official number or numbers in black ink, as given to him by the clerk or clerks of such county or counties at the time such notary qualified in such county or counties and, if the instrument is to be recorded in an office of the register of the City of New York in any county within such city and the notary has been given a number or numbers by such register or his predecessors in any county or counties, when his autographed signature and certificate are filed in such office or offices pursuant to this chapter, he shall also affix such number or numbers. No official act of such notary public shall be held invalid on account of the failure to comply with these provisions" (EL 137).

Notary's Married or Religious Name

"When a woman marries during the term of office for which she was appointed, she may continue to use her maiden name as notary public. However, if she elects to use her marriage name, then for the balance of her term as a notary public she must continue to use her maiden name in her signature and seal when acting in her notarial capacity, adding after her signature her married name, in parentheses" (NPLL).

A person known within a religious order by a name other than a legal name may be commissioned as a Notary in the religious name (NPLL).

NOTARY POWERS

New York Notaries are authorized to perform the following notarial acts (EL 135):
1. Take acknowledgments* and proofs**;
2. Administer oaths*** and affirmations****;
3. Take affidavits and depositions*****;
4. Demand acceptance or payment of foreign and inland bills of exchange, promissory notes and obligations in writing.

* Identifying Acknowledgers: "An acknowledgment must not be taken by any officer unless he knows or has satisfactory evidence, that the person making it is the person described in and who executed such instrument" (RPL 303).

** Identifying Subscribing Witnesses: "When the execution of a conveyance is proved by a subscribing witness, such witness must state his own place of residence, and if his place of residence is in a city, the street and street number, if any thereof, and that he knew the person described in and who executed the conveyance. The proof must not be taken unless the officer is personally acquainted with such witness, or has satisfactory evidence that he is the same person, who was a subscribing witness to the conveyance" (RPL 304). The witness' place of residence must be indicated on the Notary's certificate (RPL 306).

*** Oath Wording: "An oath or affirmation shall be administered in a form calculated to awaken the conscience and impress the mind of the person taking it in accordance with his religious or ethical beliefs" (Civil Practice Law and Rules 2309[b]).

"The person taking the oath must personally appear before the notary; an oath cannot be administered over the telephone (*Matter of Napolis*, 169 App. Div. 469), and the oath must be administered in the form required by the statute (*Bookman v. City of New York*, 200 NY 53, 56)" (NPLL).

"When an oath is administered, the person taking the oath must express assent to the oath repeated by the notary by the words 'I do' or some other words of like meaning" (NPLL).

"The simplest form in which an oath may be lawfully administered is: 'You do solemnly swear that the contents of this affidavit subscribed by you is correct and true?' (*Bookman v. City of New York*, 200 N.Y. 53,56)" (NPLL).

There must be "an unequivocal and present act by which the affiant consciously took upon himself the obligation of an oath; his silent delivery of a signed affidavit to the notary for his certificate, is not enough .... When an oath is administered the person taking the oath must express assent to the oath repeated by the notary by the words 'I do' or some other words of like meaning" (NPLL).

**** Affirmation Wording: Affirmation wording might be: "You do solemnly, sincerely, and truly declare and affirm that the statements made by you are true and correct?" (NPLL).

***** Depositions: Rule 3113 of the Civil Practice Law and Rules authorizes a deposition to be taken before a Notary Public in a civil proceeding (NPLL).

Other Powers

For use in another jurisdiction, a New York Notary may also "exercise such other powers and duties as by the laws of nations and according to commercial usage, or by the laws of any other government or country may be exercised and performed by notaries public, provided that when exercising such powers he shall set forth the name of such other jurisdiction" (EL 135).

Witness Safe Deposit Box Openings

New York Notaries have power to witness the opening and inventorying of safe deposit boxes. For further information on this notarial act, see Section 335 of the New York Banking Law.

NOTARY DON'TS

According to the "Notary Public License Law," Notaries may:
1. NOT issue certified copies. ("A notary public has no authority to issue certified copies.");
2. NOT authenticate documents filed with foreign consular offices;
3. NOT take an affidavit known to be false by the Notary, upon penalty of commission revocation;
4. NOT take the acknowledgment of a blank document (New York Attorney General Opinion of February 2, 1939);
5. NOT perform marriage ceremonies, because New York Notaries have no authority to solemnize marriages;
6. NOT take the acknowledgment of parties and witnesses to a written marriage contract (Domestic Relations Law 11);
7. NOT take an acknowledgment for the execution of a will, since such acknowledgment is not equivalent to an attestation clause accompanying a will;
8. NOT take acknowledgments and affidavits without the presence of the signer (*Matter of Napolis*, 169 App. Div. 469, 472);
9. NOT refer persons to lawyers with whom the Notary has a business relationship or from whom the Notary is receiving money or other consideration;
10. NOT advertise falsely "in any manner, any paper or advertisement, or say to anyone that he has any powers or rights not given to the notary by the laws under which the notary was appointed";
11. NOT refuse to perform a lawful notarial act (Penal Law 195 and *People v. Brooks*, 1 Den. 457).

Blank or Incomplete Documents

"No one would question the utter impropriety of a notary taking the acknowledgment of a person who had affixed his signature to a blank piece of paper. It is no less improper to take an acknowledgment where the signature is affixed to a printed form which is obviously and entirely incomplete. The opportunities for fraud and deceit inherent in such a procedure are boundless ....

"Conveyances which were acknowledged before the grantee's name was inserted have, under certain circumstances, been upheld in this State (2409 *Broadway Corp. v. Lange*, 128 Misc. 118; *Van Decar v. Streeter*, 136 Misc. 206); such instruments are probably of doubtful validity unless it clearly appears that the omission was supplied expressly by the act of the grantor. In any event, the practice is not to be commended ....

"(I)t is my opinion that it is improper for a notary public or a commissioner of deeds to take the acknowledgment of a paper or a form which is executed entirely in blank. Before authenticating the notary's signature, it is undoubtedly the duty of the County Clerk to see that the acknowledgment or proof of execution complies with the law and contains all of the requirements of the statute. Consequently, (the Clerk) should properly decline to attach (a) certificate of authentication under such circumstances.

"Manifestly, I cannot particularize the circumstances under which a notary public should refuse to act where the paper or instrument is not entirely in blank, but does have omissions or is otherwise incomplete" (New York Attorney General Opinion of February 2, 1939).

Issuing False Certificates

"A person is guilty of issuing a false certificate when, being a public servant authorized by law to make or issue official certificates or other official written instruments, and with intent to defraud, deceive or injure another person, he issues such an instrument, or makes the same with intent that it be issued, knowing that it contains a false statement or false information.

"Issuing a false certificate is a class E felony" (Penal Law 175.40).

According to the "Notary Public License Law," a notary public who knowingly makes a false certificate that a deed or other written instrument was acknowledged by a party thereto is guilty of forgery in the second degree, which is punishable by imprisonment for a term not exceeding seven years. See Penal Law 170.10 and 70.00(2)(d).

No Telephone Acknowledgments

"Taking an acknowledgment over the telephone is illegal and a notary public is guilty of a misdemeanor in so acting. In the certificate of acknowledgment a notary public declares: 'On this ____ day of _____, 20____, before me came _____, to me known,' etc. Unless the person purporting to have made the acknowledgment actually and personally appeared before the notary on the day specified, the notary's certificate that he so came is palpably false and fraudulent (*Matter of Brooklyn Bar Assoc.*, 225 App.Dir.680)" (NPLL).

Immigration Ad Restrictions

No provider of immigration assistance services shall "assume, use or advertise the title of lawyer or attorney at law, or equivalent terms in the English language, or any other language, or represent or advertise other titles or credentials, including but not limited to 'notary public,' 'accredited representative of the board of immigration appeals' or 'immigration consultant,' that could cause a customer to believe that the person possesses special professional skills or is authorized to provide advice on an immigration matter; provided that a notary public licensed by the secretary of state may use the term 'notary public'" (General Business Law, 460-E[2]).

Specific Ad Limits for Notaries: A law taking effect March 21, 2012, sets specific limits for ads by non-attorney Notaries (EL 135-b):

"2. A notary public who advertises his or her services as a notary public in a language other than English shall post with such advertisement a notice in such other language (containing) the following statement: 'I am not an attorney licensed to practice law and may not give legal advice about immigration or any other legal matter or accept fees for legal advice.'

"3. A notary public shall not use terms in a foreign language in any advertisement for his or her services as a notary public that mean or imply that the notary public is an attorney licensed to practice in the state of New York or in any jurisdiction of the United States. The secretary shall designate by rule or regulation the terms in a foreign language that shall be deemed to mean or imply that a notary public is licensed to practice law in the state of New York and the use of which shall be prohibited by notary publics who are subject to this section.

"4. For purposes of this section, 'advertisement' shall mean and include material designed to give notice of or to promote or describe the services offered by a notary public for profit and shall include business cards, brochures, and notices, whether in print or electronic form.

"5. Any person who violates any provision of this section or any rule or regulation promulgated by the secretary may be liable for civil penalty of up to one thousand dollars. The secretary of state may suspend a notary public upon a second violation of any of the provisions of this section and may remove from office a notary public upon a third violation of any of the provisions of this section, provided that the notary public shall have been served with a copy of the charges against him or her and been given an opportunity to be heard. The civil penalty provided for by this subdivision shall be recoverable in an action instituted by the attorney general on his or her own initiative or at the request of the secretary.

"6. The secretary may promulgate rules and regulations governing the provisions of this section, including the size and type of statements that a notary public is required by this section to post."

Disqualifying Interests

"(I)f the notary is a party to or directly and pecuniarily interested in the transaction, the person is not capable of acting in that case. For example, a notary who is a grantee or mortgagee in a conveyance or mortgage is disqualified to take the acknowledgment of the grantor or mortgagor; likewise a notary who is a trustee in a deed of trust; and, of course, a notary who is the grantor could not take his own acknowledgment. A notary beneficially interested in the conveyance by way of being secured thereby is not competent to take the acknowledgment of the instrument. In New York the courts have held an acknowledgment taken by a person financially or beneficially interested in and a party to a conveyance or instrument of which it is a part to be a nullity; and that the acknowledgment of an assignment of a mortgage before one of the assignees is a nullity; and that an acknowledgment by one of the incorporators of the other incorporators who signed a certificate was of no legal effect" (NPLL).

Armstrong v. Combs, 15 App. Div. 246, held that the Notary shouldn't take an acknowledgment of a document to which the Notary is a party in interest.

Thus, grantors and grantees cannot notarize their own conveyances; mortgagees and assignees cannot notarize their own mortgages; trustees cannot notarize their own deeds of trust; incorporators cannot notarize in their own corporation for other incorporators; and so on (NPLL).

No Disqualifying Interest: Attorneys admitted to practice in New York State may, at their discretion, notarize for clients (EL 135);

Corporate stockholders, directors, officers and employees may notarize for other stockholders, directors, officers or employees if the notarizing officer is not a party to the transaction, either individually or as a representative of the corporation (EL 138).

Validation of Imperfect Notarial Acts

"1. Except as provided in subdivision three of this section, the official certificates and other acts heretofore or hereafter made or performed of notaries public and commissioners of deeds heretofore or hereafter and prior to the time of their acts appointed or commissioned as such shall not be deemed invalid, impaired or in any manner defective, so far as they may be affected, impaired or questioned by reason of defects described in subdivision two of this section.

"2. This section shall apply to the following defects:

"(a) ineligibility of the notary public or commissioner of deeds to be appointed or commissioned as such;

"(b) misnomer or misspelling of name or other error made in his appointment or commission;

"(c) omission of the notary public or commissioner of deeds to take or file his official oath or otherwise qualify;

"(d) expiration of his term, commission or appointment;

"(e) vacating of his office by change of his residence, by acceptance of another public office, or by other action on his part;

"(f) the fact that the action was taken outside the jurisdiction where the notary public or commissioner of deeds was authorized to act.

"3. No person shall be entitled to assert the effect of this section to overcome a defect described in subdivision two if he knew of the defect or if the defect was apparent on the face of the certificate of the notary public or commissioner of deeds; provided however, that this subdivision shall not apply after the expiration of six months from the date of the act of the notary public or commissioner of deeds.

"4. After the expiration of six months from the date of the official certificate or other act of the commissioner of deeds, subdivision one of this section shall be applicable to a defect consisting in omission of the certificate of a commissioner of deeds to state the date on which and the place in which an act was done, or consisting of an error in such statement.

"5. This section does not relieve any notary public or commissioner of deeds from criminal liability imposed by reason of his act, or enlarge the actual authority of any such officer, nor limit any other statute or rule of law by reason of which the act of a notary public or commissioner of deeds, or the record thereof, is valid or is deemed valid in any case" (EL 142-a).

NOTARY SIGNING AGENTS

Currently, there are no statutes, regulations or rules expressly governing, prohibiting or restricting the operation of Notary Signing Agents within the state of New York.

NOTARY FEES

The maximum fees that a New York Notary may charge for a notarial act are (EL 136):
1. Taking an acknowledgment or proof: $2 per person, plus $2 for each witness sworn in;
2. Administering an oath or affirmation including, as applicable, any jurat certificate: $2 per person (except where another fee is specifically prescribed by statute);
3. Executing a protest: 75 cents per protest and 10 cents per notice of protest, not exceeding five notices (EL 135).

No Fee for Oath of Office

A Notary may not charge a fee for administering an oath of office to any public officer or employee, or to a military officer (POL 69).

Free in County Office

"Each county clerk shall designate from among the members of his or her staff at least one notary public to be available to notarize documents for the public in each county clerk's office during normal business hours free of charge. Each individual appointed by the county clerk to be a notary public pursuant to this section shall be exempt from the examination fee and application fee required by § 131 of the Executive Law" (County Law, 534).

NOTARY CERTIFICATES

Uniform Acknowledgment for Signer of Any Capacity within New York State (RPL 309-a):

On September 1, 1999, the following certificate, or any substantially similar form, became mandatory for all acknowledgments taken within the state on any document — including those signed by corporations — affecting real property located within the state:

State of New York   )
*   ) ss.:*
County of _____)

On the _____ day of _____ in the year 20_____, before me, the undersigned, personally appeared _____, personally known to me or proved to me on the basis of satisfactory evidence to be the individual(s) whose name(s) is (are) subscribed to the within instrument and acknowledged to me that he/she/they executed the same in his/her/their capacity(ies), and that by his/her/their signature(s) on the instrument, the individual(s), or the person* upon behalf of which the individual(s) acted, executed the instrument.

(SIGNATURE AND OFFICE OF PERSON TAKING ACKNOWLEDGMENT, ALONG WITH REQUIRED PRINTED, TYPED OR STAMPED DATA)

* 'Person' Defined: "For the purposes of this section, the term 'person' means any corporation, joint stock company, estate, general partnership (including any registered limited liability partnership or foreign liability partnership), limited liability company (including a professional service limited liability company), foreign limited liability company (including a foreign professional service limited liability company), joint venture, limited partnership, natural person, attorney in fact, real estate investment trust, business trust or other trust, custodian, nominee or any other individual or entity in its own or any representative capacity" (RPL 309-a[4]).

Uniform Proof by Subscribing Witness within New York State (RPL 309-a):

On September 1, 1999, the following certificate, or any substantially similar form, became mandatory for all proofs of execution taken within the state on any document affecting real property located within the state:

State of New York   )
*   ) ss.:*
County of _____)

On the _____ day of _____ in the year 20_____, before me, the undersigned, personally appeared _____, the subscribing witness to the foregoing instrument, with whom I am personally acquainted, who, being by me duly sworn, did depose and say that he/she/they reside(s) in _____ (if the place of residence is in a city, include the street and street number, if any thereof); that he/she/they know(s) _____ to be the individual described in and who executed the foregoing instrument; that said subscribing witness, was present and saw said _____ execute the same; and that said witness at the same time subscribed his/her/their name(s) as witness thereto.

(SIGNATURE AND OFFICE OF PERSON TAKING PROOF, ALONG WITH REQUIRED PRINTED, TYPED OR STAMPED DATA)

Address of Subscribing Witness: The certificate for a proof of execution must state the address of the subscribing witness' residence, including city, street and street number, if applicable (RPL 304 and 306).

Uniform Acknowledgment for Signer of Any Capacity outside New York State (RPL 309-b):

For acknowledgments taken outside New York State, the following certificate may be used on documents affecting real property located within New York State, not excluding use of other forms authorized in the place where the acknowledgment is taken:

State, District of Columbia, Territory, Possession or Foreign Country _____) ss.:

On the ____ day of _____ in the year 20____ before me, the undersigned, personally appeared _____, personally known to me or proved to me on the basis of satisfactory evidence to be the individual(s) whose name(s) is (are) subscribed to the within instrument and acknowledged to me that he/she/they executed the same in his/her/their capacity(ies), and that by his/her/their signature(s) on the instrument, the individual(s), or the person upon behalf of which the individual(s) acted, executed the instrument.*

(SIGNATURE AND OFFICE OF PERSON TAKING ACKNOWLEDGMENT, ALONG WITH ANY REQUIRED SEAL OR PRINTED, TYPED OR STAMPED DATA)

* "The inclusion within the body (other than a jurat) of a certificate of acknowledgment or proof made under this section of the city or other political subdivision and the state or country or other place the acknowledgment was taken shall be deemed a non-substantial variance from the form of a certificate authorized by this section."

Uniform Proof by Subscribing Witness outside New York State (RPL 309-b):

For a proof of execution by subscribing witness taken outside New York State, the following certificate may be used on documents affecting real property located within New York State, not excluding use of other forms authorized in the place where the proof is taken:

State, District of Columbia, Territory, Possession or Foreign Country _____) ss.:

On the ____ day of _____ in the year 20____ before me, the undersigned, personally appeared _____, the subscribing witness to the foregoing instrument, with whom I am personally acquainted, who, being by me duly sworn, did depose and say that he/she resides in _____ (if the place of residence is in a city, include the street and street number, if any, thereof); that he/she knows _____ to be the individual described in and who executed the foregoing instrument; that said subscribing witness was present and saw said _____ execute the same; and that said witness at the same time subscribed his/her name as a witness thereto.*

(SIGNATURE AND OFFICE OF PERSON TAKING PROOF, ALONG WITH ANY REQUIRED SEAL OR PRINTED, TYPED OR STAMPED DATA)

* See note with acknowledgment form immediately above.

Acknowledgment by Corporation without Seal Not Affecting Real Property (RPL 309):

Starting September 1, 1999, the following certificate may be used on documents signed by any corporation without a seal that do not affect real property located within the state:

State of New York   )
*   ) ss.:*
County of _____   )

On the ____ day of _____ in the year 20____ before me personally came _____ to me known, who, being by me duly sworn, did depose and say that he/she/they reside(s) in _____ (if the place of residence is in a city, include the street and street number, if any, thereof); that he/she/they is (are) the _____ (president or other officer or director) of the _____ (name of corporation), the corporation described in and which executed the above instrument; and that he/she/they signed his/her/their name(s) thereto by order of the board of directors of said corporation.

(SIGNATURE AND OFFICE OF PERSON TAKING ACKNOWLEDGMENT, ALONG WITH REQUIRED PRINTED, TYPED OR STAMPED DATA)

Acknowledgment by Corporation with Seal Not Affecting Real Property (RPL 309):

Starting September 1, 1999, the following certificate may be used on documents signed by any corporation with a seal that do not affect real property located within the state:

State of New York   )
*   ) ss.:*
County of _____)

On the _____ day of _____ in the year 20_____ before me personally came _____ to me known, who, being by me duly sworn, did depose and say that he/she/they reside(s) in _____ (if the place of residence is in a city, include the street and street number, if any, thereof); that he/she/they is (are) the _____ (president or other officer or director) of the _____ (name of corporation), the corporation described in and which executed the above instrument; that he/she/they know(s) the seal of said corporation; that the seal affixed to said instrument is such corporate seal; that it was so affixed by order of the board of directors of said corporation, and that he/she/they signed his/her/their name(s) thereto by like authority.

(SIGNATURE AND OFFICE OF PERSON TAKING ACKNOWLEDGMENT, ALONG WITH REQUIRED PRINTED, TYPED OR STAMPED DATA)

Acknowledgment by Corporation

"The acknowledgment of a conveyance or other instrument by a corporation, must be made by an officer or attorney in fact duly appointed, or in case of a dissolved corporation, by an officer, director or attorney in fact duly appointed thereof authorized to execute the same by the board of directors of said corporation" (EL 309).

Instructions from Department of State

Instructions from the Counsel's Office of the New York Department of State (website, "Legal Memorandum LI03") provide the following directions regarding use of notarial certificates:

"The new uniform acknowledgment and the new uniform proof (RPL 309-a) are to be used (1) only on documents relating to a conveyance or other instruments with respect to real property located in New York State, and (2) only for acknowledgments or proofs taken within the State of New York.

"In all other cases, use a form acknowledgment or proof that has been acceptable in the past. For example, the section 309 forms for corporations or a traditional form of acknowledgment or proof for individuals, representatives and other entities may be used."

For Notarial Acts outside New York State: The instructions further specify that, for acknowledgments and proofs executed outside New York State for any principals except corporations, "Use any form that has been acceptable in the past under New York law or a form that conforms to the law of the place where the acknowledgment (or proof) is taken." Forms provided by RPL 309-b may be used when real property in New York State is involved.

The instructions additionally specify that, for acknowledgments and proofs executed outside New York State by corporations, "Use the Real Property Law, Section 309, form or a form that conforms to the law of the place where the acknowledgment (or proof) is taken."

In instances where a certificate of acknowledgment or proof from another jurisdiction is used, a "certificate of conformity" attesting to the form's compliance with the law of that other jurisdiction may need to be attached if the notarized document affects real property and is to be recorded in New York State.

For questions about notarial certificate selection, call the Department's Office of General Counsel at (518) 474-6740.

ELECTRONIC NOTARIZATIONS

The state of New York has not yet adopted statutes or regulations expressly establishing rules, definitions and procedures for electronic notarization.

Recording of Notarized Electronic Documents

A law taking effect September 23, 2012, puts in place statutory provisions that enable the recording of electronic documents, largely based on the Uniform Real Property Electronic Recording Act (URPERA). It includes this provision:

"(W)here a law, rule or regulation requires, as a condition of recording, that an instrument affecting real property or a signature associated with such an instrument be notarized, acknowledged, verified, witnessed or made under oath, the signature requirement is satisfied if: (i) the digitized image of a wet signature of the person authorized to perform that act and any stamp, impression or seal required by law to be included, appears on a digitized paper document of such instrument; or (ii) the electronic signature of the person authorized to perform that act, and all other information required to be included, is attached to or logically associated with an electronic record of such instrument, provided, however that no physical or electronic image of a stamp, impression or seal shall be required to accompany such electronic signature" (RPL 291-i[c]).

NOTARY RECORDS

New York Notaries Public are not required by law to keep a record of the notarial acts they perform.

AUTHENTICATION OF NOTARIAL ACTS

County Clerk

Authenticating certificates for a Notary are obtained at the office of the county clerk where the Notary's commission is filed (EL 134).

For a given Notary, an authenticating certificate may additionally be available in other counties, if the Notary has filed a certificate of official character and a sample signature in those other county clerks' offices. "Notaries who expect to sign documents regularly in counties other than that of their residence may elect to file a certificate of official character with the other New York State county clerks" (NPLL).

Fee: $3.

Secretary of State

Certificates authenticating the county clerk forms that authenticate notarial acts are issued by the Department of State at the Albany and New York City locations listed below.

Fee: $10 for an authenticating certificate, including an apostille, payable to "New York State Department of State."

Albany Address: Mail & Hand Delivery
New York Department of State
Div. of Corporations/State Records
   and Uniform Commercial Code
99 Washington Ave., 6th Flr.
Albany, NY 12231

Telephone: 1-518-473-1001

New York City Address: Hand Delivery Only
New York Department of State
Division of Licensing Services
123 William St., 19th Flr.
New York, NY 10038

Telephone: 1-212-417-5747

Procedure: After obtaining a county clerk's certificate, needed even for an apostille, mail or present in person the original notarized document, along with the clerk's certificate, the appropriate fee and an "Apostille/Certificate of Authentication Request" form, downloadable on the website noted below. To expedite, include an addressed, stamped envelope. "The processing of documents submitted by mail is usually completed within 4 business days. The processing of documents submitted in person is usually completed while you wait" (www.dos.state.ny.us/corps/apostille.html).

Education Documents: "Educational documents submitted to the New York Department of State for an Apostille or Certificate of Authentication must first be certified by an official at the educational institution attesting that the document is an official record or a true copy of the original document. The official's signature then must be notarized by a notary public. The notary public's signature must then be certified by the County Clerk in the county where the notary public is qualified to certify" (see website noted above).

COMMISSIONING AND ADMINISTRATION

New York State Notaries are appointed, commissioned, and regulated by the Secretary of State, who maintains records on them (EL 130).

Applying for Commission

Qualifications: An applicant for a commission as a New York Notary Public must: (a) be at least 18 years old, (b) be a person of good moral character, (c) be a resident of New York State or have an office or place of business in the state, (d) have the equivalent of a "common school education" and (e) not have been convicted of a felony or of certain misdemeanors, unless an executive pardon or a parole board certificate of good conduct has been received. In addition, "(e)very person appointed as notary public must, at the time of his or her appointment, be a citizen or permanent resident alien of the United States..." (website, "Frequently Asked Questions").

Proctored Test Required: Every applicant must take a proctored, closed-book, one-hour examination, regularly scheduled at different sites around the state. All test takers will be thumbprinted. A score of at least 70 percent is required to pass. The examination fee is $15. A "pass slip" will be mailed to every successful test taker, along with an application form. (The application is not suitable for downloading from the state website.) Current licensed New York attorneys are exempted from the exam, as are court clerks of the Unified Court System.

Application: The completed application form, along with the original exam pass slip and a $60 application fee, must be submitted to the Department of State's Division of Licensing Services. The application includes an oath of office, which must be sworn to and notarized.

After its approval and issuance by the Secretary of State, the new commission is mailed to the respective county clerk, along with the new Notary's signature and original oath of office. "The public may then access this record and verify the 'official' signature of the notary at the county clerk's office" (NPLL). Within four to six weeks of application, the new Notary will receive an identification card indicating the Notary's name, address, county and commission term (EL 131[4]).

A renewal application form will be sent to the Notary about three months prior to commission expiration. Renewals must be submitted, with the $60 fee (payable to the county clerk's office), to the county clerk rather than to the Department of State (EL 131[7]), as was the case with the original application. "A reappointed notary will receive a replacement identification card for the Department of State within six to eight weeks of the date the county clerk receives his or her renewal application" (website, "Frequently Asked Questions").

Notaries May File in Additional Counties: A New York Notary may file a "certificate of official character" and a sample signature with the county clerk or registrar of any county in the state for a fee of $10; authenticating certificates for that Notary would then be available in those counties (EL 132-134). (A certificate of official character may be issued by the Secretary of State for a fee of $10, or by the clerk of the county where the Notary originally qualified for a fee of $5.)

Non-Residents: Persons residing in other states but having an office or place of business in New York State may become New York State Notaries; these individuals have thereby authorized the New York Secretary of State to accept processes on their behalf (EL 130). The oath of office and signature of such Notaries must be filed in the New York State county where their office or place of business is located (NPLL). "Attorneys, residing out of State, who are admitted to practice in the State and who maintain a law office within the State are deemed to be residents of the county where the office is maintained" (NPLL).

Online Search: The New York Department of State's Index of Licensees and Registrants may be searched by the Notary's name or ID number to determine any current Notary's commission expiration date and business name and address. The Index is available on the Department of State's home page through "Search Licensees and Registrants."

Changes of Status

If Notary Moves Out of State: A Notary resident of New York State who moves out of state but still maintains a place of business in the state may remain a Notary; otherwise, the office of Notary is thereby vacated (EL 130). A Notary non-resident who ceases to have an office or place of business in New York State thereby vacates the office of Notary.

Name or Address Change: Upon receipt of fee of $10 and a change-of-name or address form, the Secretary of State will correct the public record to reflect a Notary's change of name and/or address (EL 131[12]). "The $10 fee is not required if the individual name change is the result (of a) change of marital status" (website, "Frequently Asked Questions"). It is not mandatory to immediately notify the Division of Licensing Services of a name change or a change of address within the state.

<u>If Notary Marries, Changes Name</u>: Notaries who change their name through marriage may: (a) continue using the former name when functioning as a Notary; or (b) use the former name in the official signature and stamp, adding the new name in parentheses after the signature. Upon renewing the commission, however, the Notary must select one or the other name and use that name exclusively in performing notarizations (NPLL). "If you are changing or have changed your name, you should use your new name when signing your renewal application" (website, "Frequently Asked Questions").

"You must provide proof of your name change, e.g. a copy of one of the following: court order changing your name; marriage certificate; driver's license, or a non-driver's ID card; valid passport; or immigration documents. A change in the business name requires re-application" (website, "Frequently Asked Questions").

COUNTY CLERKS

To contact a New York State county clerk to obtain an authenticating certificate for a Notary, or to seek assistance in locating a given Notary, telephone long-distance information — 1-XXX-555-1212 — using the following area codes:

County	City/Town	Area Code
Albany	Albany	(518)
Allegany	Belmont	(585)
Bronx	Bronx	(718)
Broome	Binghamton	(607)
Cattaraugus	Little Valley	(716)
Cayuga	Auburn	(315)
Chautauqua	Mayville	(716)
Chemung	Elmira	(607)
Chenango	Norwich	(607)
Clinton	Plattsburgh	(518)
Columbia	Hudson	(518)
Cortland	Cortland	(607)
Delaware	Delhi	(607)
Dutchess	Poughkeepsie	(845)
Erie	Buffalo	(716)
Essex	Elizabethtown	(518)
Franklin	Malone	(518)
Fulton	Johnstown	(518)
Genesee	Batavia	(585)
Greene	Catskill	(518)
Hamilton	Lake Pleasant	(518)
Herkimer	Herkimer	(315)
Jefferson	Watertown	(315)
Kings	Brooklyn	(347)
Lewis	Lowville	(315)
Livingston	Geneseo	(585)
Madison	Wampsville	(315)
Monroe	Rochester	(585)
Montgomery	Fonda	(518)
Nassau	Mineola	(516)
New York	New York	(646)
Niagara	Lockport	(716)
Oneida	Utica	(315)
Onondaga	Syracuse	(315)
Ontario	Canandaigua	(585)
Orange	Goshen	(845)
Orleans	Albion	(585)
Oswego	Oswego	(315)
Otsego	Cooperstown	(607)
Putnam	Carmel	(845)
Queens	Jamaica	(718)
Rensselaer	Troy	(518)
Richmond	Staten Island	(718)
Rockland	New City	(845)
St. Lawrence	Canton	(315)
Saratoga	Ballston Spa	(518)
Schenectady	Schenectady	(518)
Schoharie	Schoharie	(518)
Schuyler	Watkins Glen	(607)
Seneca	Waterloo	(315)
Steuben	Bath	(607)
Suffolk	Riverhead	(631)
Sullivan	Monticello	(845)
Tioga	Owego	(607)
Tompkins	Ithaca	(607)
Ulster	Kingston	(845)
Warren	Lake George	(518)
Washington	Fort Edward	(518)
Wayne	Lyons	(315)
Westchester	White Plains	(914)
Wyoming	Warsaw	(585)
Yates	Penn Yan	(315)

OTHER NOTARIAL OFFICERS

In addition to Notaries Public, the following officers have power to take acknowledgments and proofs for conveyances of real property situated in the state (RPL 298):

Statewide Jurisdiction
1. State supreme court justice;
2. Official title examiner;
3. Official referee;

District-Wide Jurisdiction
4. County clerk or other county recording officer;
5. City mayor or recorder;
6. Judge or clerk of any court of record;
7. Surrogate, special surrogate or special county judge;
8. Commissioner of deeds of New York City within the five city counties;
9. Commissioner of deeds outside New York City;

Free Services at County Clerk Office: Each county clerk must make available at least one staff member to notarize for the public free of charge during normal business hours (County Law, 534).

Countywide Jurisdiction
10. Justice of the peace;
11. Town councilmember;
12. Village police justice;
13. Judge of any court of inferior local jurisdiction.

QUICK FACTS

Notary Jurisdiction
Statewide (EL 130).

Notary Term Length
Four years (EL 130), effective July 18, 2001, pursuant to Chapter 171 of the laws of 2000. Formerly, the term of office for a New York Notary was two years.

Notary Bond
Not required by law.

North Carolina

NOTARY SEAL

A North Carolina Notary must use a seal of office to attest to all notarizations of paper documents (GS 10B-37) and the seal's format must be as follows:

Kind

Inked Stamp or Embosser: "A North Carolina notary may use either a seal that makes an impression or a stamp that uses ink, provided the image is clear and legible...The notary must ensure that a seal by impression (i.e., an embosser) will be reproducible. When using a stamp that leaves ink, the notary should be careful not to place it where it will obscure any of the document's text or the certificate's contents" (NPG 3.5.2)

Shape/Size

"The notary seal may be either circular or rectangular in shape. Upon receiving a commission

```
JANE Q. DOE
Notary Public
Wake Co., North Carolina
My Commission Expires Jan. 30, 2017
```

Examples

The above typical, actual-size examples of Notary seals are allowed by North Carolina law. Formats other than these may also be permitted.

NOTARY ADMINISTRATION

Department of Secretary of State
Notary Public Section   1-919-807-2219
AND
Electronic Notary Public Section
P.O. Box 29626
Raleigh, NC 27626-0626

Website: www.secretary.state.nc.us/notary/
AND
www.secretary.state.nc.us/enotary/

NOTARY RULES

GS — NORTH CAROLINA GENERAL STATUTES
NCAC — NORTH CAROLINA ADMINISTRATIVE CODE
NPG — NOTARY PUBLIC GUIDEBOOK FOR NORTH CAROLINA

Most Notary rules are in the North Carolina General Statutes:

a. Chapter 10B, "Notaries," consisting of Article 1 ("Notary Public Act") and Article 2 ("Electronic Notary Act");

b. Chapter 47, "Probate and Registration."

Effective Jan. 1, 2007, the North Carolina Administrative Code contains rules for electronic notarization, implementing GS Chapters 10B (Article 2) and 47 (Article 1A, "Uniform Real Property Electronic Recording Act"):

c. Title 18, Subchapter 07C ("Electronic Notary Standards"), Sections .0100 through .0600.

Other guidance for Notaries is in the "Notary Public Guidebook for North Carolina" (10th Ed., July 2006), published by the School of Government at the University of North Carolina at Chapel Hill.

or a recommission on or after October 1, 2006, a notary shall not use a circular seal that is less than $1\frac{1}{2}$ inches, nor more than 2 inches in diameter. The rectangular seal shall not be over 1 inch high and 2½ inches long. The perimeter of the seal shall contain a border that is visible when impressed" (GS 10B-37[c]).

Components

A Notary's official seal must include all of the following components (GS 10B-37[b]):

1. Name of Notary exactly as it appears on commission;
2. "Notary Public";
3. Name of county in which commissioned, including the word "County" or "Co.";
4. "North Carolina" or "NC".
5. OPTIONAL: Commission expiration date.*

* NOTE: "the law permits but does not require a notary's commission date to be included (on the seal), either permanently imprinted or typed or handwritten in space allocated for that purpose (GS 10B-37[d]). So that the device may be used for more than one term, the Department of the Secretary of State advises against including the commission expiration date on the seal or stamp" (NPG 3.5.2).

Placement of Seal

"A notary shall affix the notary's official seal near the notary's official signature on the notarial certificate of a record" (GS 10B-37[a]). "The notary shall place the image or impression of the seal near the notary's signature on every paper record notarized. The seal and the notary's signature shall appear on the same page of a record as the text of the notarial certificate" (GS 10B-36[b]).

Alterations to Seal Prohibited

"Alterations to any information contained within the seal as embossed or stamped on the record are prohibited" (GS 10B-37[c1]).

Noncompliance Is Not Invalidating

"The failure of a notarial seal to comply with the requirements of this section shall not affect the sufficiency, validity, or enforceability of the notarial certificate, but shall constitute a violation of the notary's duties" (GS 10B-37[f]).

Seal Affixed after Act Performed

"The seal shall be affixed only after the notarial act is performed" (GS 10B-36[b]).

Signature, Name, Expiration Date to Appear

"A notarial act shall be attested by all of the following:

"1. The signature of the notary, exactly as shown on the notary's commission.

"2. The legible appearance of the notary's name exactly as shown on the notary's commission. The legible appearance of the name may be ascertained from the notary's typed or printed name near the notary's signature or from elsewhere in the notarial certificate or from the notary's seal if the name is legible.

"3. The clear and legible appearance of the notary's stamp and seal.

"4. A statement of the date the notary's commission expires. The statement of the date that the notary's commission expires may appear in the notary's stamp or seal or elsewhere in the notarial certificate" (GS 10B-20[b]).

Must Sign by Hand: "When notarizing a paper record, a notary shall sign by hand in ink on the notarial certificate. The notary shall comply with the requirements of GS 10B-20(b)(1) and (b)(2). The notary shall affix the official signature only after the notarial act is performed. The notary shall not sign a paper record using the facsimile stamp or an electronic or other printing method" (GS 10B-35).

Erroneous Date: "An erroneous statement of the date that the notary's commission expires shall not affect the sufficiency, validity, or enforceability of the notarial certificate or the related record if the notary is, in fact, lawfully commissioned at the time of the notarial act" (GS 10B-67).

Seal Acceptance by Register of Deeds

"The acceptance of a record for registration by the register of deeds shall give rise to a presumption that, at the time the record was presented for registration, a clear and legible image of the notary's official seal was affixed or embossed on the record near the notary's official signature. This presumption applies regardless of whether the image is legible or photographically reproduced in the records maintained by the register of deeds. A register of deeds may not refuse to accept a record for registration because a notarial seal does not satisfy the requirements of GS 10B-37" (GS 47-14).

Curing Certain Seal Defects

"All documents bearing a notarial seal and which contain any of the following errors are validated and given the same legal effect as if the errors had not occurred:

"1. The date of the expiration of the notary's commission is stated, whether correctly or erroneously.

"2. The notarial seal does not contain a readable impression of the notary's name, contains an incorrect spelling of the notary's name, or does not bear the name of the notary exactly as it appears on the commission, as required under GS 10B-37.

"3. The notary's signature does not comport exactly with the name on the notary commission or on the notary seal, as required by GS 10B-20.

"4. The notarial seal contains typed, printed, drawn, or handwritten material added to the seal, fails to contain the words 'North Carolina' or the abbreviation 'NC', or contains correct information except that instead of the abbreviation for North Carolina contains the abbreviation for another state" (GS 10B-65[b]).

"This section applies to notarizations performed on or before February 1, 2004" (GS 10B-65[e]).

If No Seal on Out-of-State Document

"If the proof or acknowledgment of any instrument is had before a notary public of any state other than North Carolina and the instrument does not show the seal or stamp of the notary public and the expiration date of the commission of the notary public, the certificate of proof or acknowledgment made by such notary public shall be accompanied by the certificate of the county official before whom the notary qualifies for office, stating that such notary public was at the time his certificate bears date an acting notary public of such state, and that such notary's genuine signature is set to his certificate. The certificate of the official herein provided for shall be under his hand and official seal" (GS 47-2.2).

Seal Exclusive Property of Notary

"A notary shall keep an official seal or stamp that is the exclusive property of the notary. The notary shall keep the seal in a secure location. A notary shall not allow another person to use or possess the seal, and shall not surrender the seal to the notary's employer upon termination of employment" (GS 10B-36[a]).

Stolen, Lost or Damaged Seal

"A notary shall do the following within 10 days of discovering that the notary's seal has been lost or stolen: (1) Inform the appropriate law enforcement agency in the case of theft or vandalism. (2) Notify the appropriate register of deeds and the Secretary in writing and signed in the official name in which he or she was commissioned" (GS 10B-36[c]).

Disposition of Seal

"As soon as is reasonably practicable after resignation, revocation, or expiration of a notary commission, or death of the notary, the seal shall be delivered to the Secretary for disposal" (GS 10B-36[d]).

"a. When a notary commission is resigned or revoked, the notary shall deliver the notary's seal to the Secretary within 45 days of the resignation or revocation. Delivery shall be accomplished by certified mail, return receipt requested. The Secretary shall destroy any seal received under this subsection.

"b. A notary whose commission has expired and whose previous commission or application was not revoked or denied by this State, is not required to deliver the seal to the Secretary as provided under subsection (a) of this section if the notary intends to apply to be recommissioned and is recommissioned within three months after the notary's commission expires.

"c. If a notary dies while commissioned or before fulfilling the disposition of seal requirements in this section, the notary's estate shall, as soon as is reasonably practicable and no later than the closing of the estate, notify the Secretary in writing of the notary's death and deliver the notary's seal to the Secretary for destruction" (GS 10B-55).

Misuse of Seal

"Any person who without authority obtains, uses, conceals, defaces, or destroys the seal or notarial records of a notary is guilty of a Class I felony" (GS 10B-60[f]).

NOTARY POWERS

North Carolina Notaries are authorized to perform the following notarial acts (GS 10B-20[a]):

1. Take acknowledgments*;
2. Administer oaths** and affirmations***;
3. Execute verifications or proofs****.

* Acknowledgments: An acknowledgment is "(a) notarial act in which a notary certifies that at a single time and place all of the following occurred: (a) An individual appeared in person before the notary and presented a record. (b) The individual was personally known to the notary or identified by the notary through satisfactory evidence. (c) The individual did either of the following: (i) Indicated to the notary that the signature on the record was the individual's signature. (ii) Signed the record while in the physical presence of the notary and while being personally observed signing the record by the notary" (GS 10B-3[1]).

"Any attempted acknowledgment by telephone, telegraph, mail, or any other means that does not bring the acknowledger physically before the official who takes the acknowledgment is invalid" (NPG 3.2.1).

** Oaths: An oath is "(a) notarial act which is legally equivalent to an affirmation and in which a notary certifies that at a single time and place all of the following occurred: (a) An individual appeared in person before the notary. (b) The individual was personally known to the notary or identified by the notary through satisfactory evidence. (c) The individual made a vow of truthfulness on penalty of perjury while invoking a deity or using any form of the word 'swear'" (GS 10B-3[14]).

"Whenever the law prescribes an oath without specifying the officer before whom it must be taken, a notary public may administer the oath ... (A) North Carolina notary acting within North Carolina may administer any oath authorized or required under the laws of the United States, including oaths of office for all federal offices" (NPG 3.6).

"The statute (GS 11-2)…provides that the person administering the oath 'shall…require the party to be sworn to lay his hand upon the Holy Scriptures'…The words 'Holy Scriptures' can be interpreted as referring specifically to the Christian Bible as the only book on which the oath-taker's hand is to be placed…(T)he North Carolina Supreme Court recognized the validity of an oath based on another book considered sacred by the oath-taker. The statute can be construed consistent with this principle by interpreting the phrase 'Holy Scriptures' more broadly to include all books sacred to various religions, which for Christians would be the New Testament or the Bible, for Jews the Torah or the Old Testament, for Muslims the Koran, for Hindus the Bhagavad-Gita, and so forth…The person making an affirmation is not required to place his or her hand on any book or document" (NPG 3.6).

*** Affirmations: An affirmation is "(a) notarial act which is legally equivalent to an oath and in which a notary certifies that at a single time and place all of the following occurred: (a) An individual appeared in person before the notary. (b) The individual was personally known to the notary or identified by the notary through satisfactory evidence. (c) The individual made a vow of truthfulness on penalty of perjury, based on personal honor and without invoking a deity or using any form of the word 'swear'" (GS 10B-3[2]).

**** Verifications or Proofs: A verification or proof is "(a) notarial act in which a notary certifies that all of the following occurred: (a) An individual appeared in person before the notary. (b) The individual was personally known to the notary or identified by the notary through satisfactory evidence. (c) The individual was not a party to or beneficiary of the transaction. (d) The individual took an oath or gave an affirmation and testified to one of the following: (i) The individual is a subscribing witness and the principal who signed the record did so while being personally observed by the subscribing witness. (ii) The individual is a subscribing witness and the principal who signed the record acknowledged his or her signature to the subscribing witness. (iii) The individual recognized either the signature on the record of the principal or the signature on the record of the subscribing witness and the signature was genuine" (GS 10B-3[28]).

A subscribing witness is "(a) person who signs a record for the purpose of being a witness to the principal's execution of the record or to the principal's acknowledgment of his or her execution of the record. A subscribing witness may give proof of the execution of the record as provided in subdivision (28) of this section" (GS 10B-3[26]).

"(T)he execution of any instrument required or permitted by law to be registered, which has been witnessed by one or more subscribing witnesses, may be proved for registration before any official authorized by law to take proof of such an instrument, by a statement under oath of any such subscribing witness that the maker either signed the instrument in his presence or acknowledged to him the execution thereof" (GS 47-12).

Ordinarily, any signature whose execution may be acknowledged by the original signer also may be proved by a subscribing witness. Vehicle titles are one exception to this rule: "Motor vehicle title forms require acknowledgments; proofs are not acceptable" (NPG 4.9).

The subscribing witness, who must either be personally known to the Notary or have his identity proven through satisfactory evidence, must be put under oath (NPG 3.1). An oath such as the following might be used: "Do you swear (or affirm) that the information you give concerning this writing is the truth, so help you God?"

A subscribing witness may not be a grantee or beneficiary of the document that is notarized (GS 47-12.2).

If a subscribing witness is unavailable, incompetent, or there is no subscribing witness, proof of execution by handwriting is provided for (GS 47-12.1, 47-13 and 47-13.1).

Determining Competence and Volition

"(B)y making or giving a notarial certificate, whether or not stated in the certificate, a notary certifies to all of the following: ... If the notarial certificate is for an acknowledgment or the administration of an oath or affirmation, the person whose signature was notarized did not appear in the judgment of the notary to be incompetent, lacking in understanding of the nature and consequences of the transaction requiring the notarial act, or acting involuntarily, under duress, or undue influence" (GS 10B-40[a2]).

Identifying Document Signers

"A notary shall be guilty of a Class 1 misdemeanor if the notary does any of the following:... (3) Takes an acknowledgment or administers an oath or affirmation without personal knowledge or satisfactory evidence of the identity of the principal. (4) Takes a verification or proof without personal knowledge or satisfactory evidence of the identity of the subscribing witness" (GS 10B-60[c]).

Need Not Determine Representative Status: "In performing a notarial act ... a notary is under no duty to verify whether the individual acted in a representative capacity or fiduciary capacity or, if so, whether the individual was duly authorized so to do" (GS 10B-40[h]).

'Personal Knowledge' Defined: Personal knowledge or personally known means "(f)amiliarity with an individual resulting from interactions with that individual over a period of time sufficient to eliminate every reasonable doubt that the individual has the identity claimed" (GS 10B-3[17]).

'Satisfactory Evidence' Defined: Satisfactory evidence means identification of an individual based on either of the following: (a) at least one current document issued by a federal, a state, or a federal or state-recognized tribal government agency, bearing the photographic image of the individual's face and either the signature or a physical description of the individual, or (b) the vouching under oath or affirmation of one credible witness who personally knows the individual seeking to be identified (GS 10B-3[22]).

'Credible Witness' Defined: A credible witness is an individual who is personally known to the notary and to whom both of the following also apply: (a) the notary believes the individual to be honest and reliable for the purpose of confirming to the notary the identity of another individual, and (b) the notary believes the individual is not a party to or beneficiary of the transaction (GS 10B-3[5]).

Notarizing for Disabled

Persons unable to write may sign by mark or have their name signed for them by another person, provided that certain rules are observed. The resulting mark or proxy signature may be notarized.

Signature by Mark: "A notary may certify the affixation of a signature by mark on a record presented for notarization if:

"1. The mark is affixed in the presence of the notary;

"2. The notary writes below the mark: 'Mark affixed by (name of signer by mark) in presence of undersigned notary'; and

"3. The notary notarizes the signature by performing an acknowledgment, oath or affirmation, jurat, or verification or proof" (GS 10B-20[d]).

Principal Physically Unable to Sign: "If a principal is physically unable to sign or make a mark on a record presented for notarization, that

North Carolina

principal may designate another person as his or her designee, who shall be a disinterested party to sign on the principal's behalf pursuant to the following procedure:

"1. The principal directs the designee to sign the record in the presence of the notary and two witnesses unaffected by the record;

"2. The designee signs the principal's name in the presence of the principal, the notary, and the two witnesses;

"3. Both witnesses sign their own names to the record near the principal's signature;

"4. The notary writes below the principal's signature: 'Signature affixed by the designee in the presence of (names and addresses of principal and witnesses)'; and

"5. The notary notarizes the signature through an acknowledgment, oath or affirmation, jurat, or verification or proof" (GS 10B-20[e]).

Non-English Ads by Notaries

"A notary public who is not an attorney licensed to practice law in this State who advertises the person's services as a notary public in a language other than English, by radio, television, sign, pamphlets, newspapers, other written communication, or in any other matter, shall post or otherwise include with the advertisement the notice set forth in this subsection in English and in the language used for the advertisement. The notice shall be of conspicuous size, if in writing, and shall state: 'I AM NOT AN ATTORNEY LICENSED TO PRACTICE LAW IN THE STATE OF NORTH CAROLINA, AND I MAY NOT GIVE LEGAL ADVICE OR ACCEPT FEES FOR LEGAL ADVICE.' If the advertisement is by radio or television, the statement may be modified but must include substantially the same message" (GS 10B-20[i]).

"A notary public required to comply with the provisions of subsection (i) of this section shall prominently post at the notary public's place of business a schedule of fees established by law, which a notary public may charge. The fee schedule shall be written in English and in the non-English language in which the notary services were solicited and shall contain the notice required in subsection (i) of this section, unless the notice is otherwise prominently posted at the notary public's place of business" (GS 10B-20[l]).

NOTARY DON'TS

A North Carolina Notary may:
1. NOT notarize if the principal or subscribing witness is not in the Notary's presence at the time of notarization — see definition of "personal appearance" below — "(h)owever, nothing in this Chapter shall require a notary to complete the notarial certificate attesting to the notarial act in the presence of the principal or subscribing witness" (GS 10B-20[c][1]);
2. NOT notarize if the principal or subscribing witness is not personally known to the notary or identified by the notary through satisfactory evidence (GS 10B-20[c][2]);
3. NOT notarize if the credible witness is not personally known to the Notary (GS 10B-20[c][2a]);
4. NOT execute a notarial certificate containing information known or believed by the Notary to be false (GS 10B-22[a]);
5. NOT execute a notarial certificate this is not written in the English language (GS 10B-22[b]).

'Personal Appearance' Defined

"Personal appearance" and "appear in person" mean that "(a)n individual and a notary are in close physical proximity to one another so that they may freely see and communicate with one another and exchange records back and forth during the notarization process" (GS 10B-3[16]).

"What is the penalty for notarizing a document without the personal appearance of the principal? — In addition to losing the notarial commission, a notary who performs a notarial act without the principal personally appearing before the notary is guilty of a Class 1 misdemeanor. If the notary performs the notarial act without the principal's personal appearance with the intent to commit fraud, the notary is guilty of a Class I felony" (Notary website, "Frequently Asked Questions" and GS 10B-60[c] and [d]).

Telephone Oaths Unlawful: "Appearance of a witness by telephone does not comply with the definition of 'personal appearance' and 'appear in person before a notary' found in GS § 10B-3(16); 'personal appearance' and 'appear before a notary' are defined as 'an individual and a notary are in close physical proximity to one another so that they may freely see and communicate with one another and exchange records back and forth during the notarization process'" (Memorandum of Deputy Secretary Haley Haynes, September 9, 2008).

The Memorandum continues: "A WORD OF CAUTION: A notary is committing a CRIME when administering an oath without the person appearing before them (GS §10B-60[c][1]). Furthermore, a person who solicits, coerces, or in any material way influences a notary to administer an oath without the person appearing in person before them also commits a crime (GS §10B-60[i])."

Neither may an acknowledgment be taken by phone or fax (Notary website, "Frequently Asked Questions").

Notary May Not Certify Copies

"May a notary certify a true copy of a document? — No, a notary is not authorized to certify any document to be a true copy, however, a notary public may notarize an affidavit in regard to a document" (Notary website, "Frequently Asked Questions").

Notary May Not Certify Photographs

"A notary shall neither certify, notarize, nor authenticate a photograph. A notary may notarize an affidavit regarding and attached to a photograph" (GS 10B-23[b]).

Immigration Consultant Restrictions

A non-attorney Notary may not represent himself or herself as an "immigration consultant" or expert on immigration matters unless the Notary is an accredited representative of an organization recognized by the Board of Immigration Appeals (GS 10B-20[j]).

Unauthorized Law Practice Prohibited

"A nonattorney notary shall not assist another person in drafting, completing, selecting, or understanding a record or transaction requiring a notarial act" (GS 10B-20[k]).

"If notarial certificate wording is not provided or indicated for a record, a notary who is not also a licensed attorney shall not determine the type of notarial act or certificate to be used. This does not prohibit a notary from offering the selection of certificate forms recognized in this Chapter or as otherwise authorized by law" (GS 10B-20[m]).

"A notary shall not claim to have powers, qualifications, rights, or privileges that the office of notary does not provide, including the power to counsel on immigration matters" (GS 10B-20[n]).

Not Act as Notary and Witness

"If a notary notarizes a document, may he or she also act as a witness to that document? — No" (Notary website, "Frequently Asked Questions").

Testimonials Using Seal, Title Prohibited

"A notary shall not use the official notary title or seal in a manner intended to endorse, promote, denounce, or oppose any product service, contest, candidate, or other offering. This section does not prohibit a notary public from performing a notarial act upon a record executed by another individual" (GS 10B-24).

Disqualifying Interests

"A notary shall not perform a notarial act if any of the following apply: ...

"The notary is a signer of, party to, or beneficiary of the record, that is to be notarized. However, a disqualification under this subdivision shall not apply to a notary who is named in a record solely as the trustee in a deed of trust, the drafter of the record, the person to whom a registered document should be mailed or sent after recording, or the attorney for a party to the record, so long as the notary is not also a party to the record individually or in some other representative or fiduciary capacity ...

"The notary will receive directly from a transaction connected with the notarial act any commission, fee, advantage, right, title, interest, cash, property, or other consideration exceeding in value the fees specified in G.S. 10B-31, other than fees or other consideration paid for services rendered by a licensed attorney, a licensed real estate broker or salesperson, a motor vehicle dealer, or a banker" (GS 10B-20[c][5] and [6]).

Notarizing for Spouse: "May a notary notarize an assignment or a reassignment of a vehicle title for his or her spouse? — Yes, if the notary is not a named party on the title or does not directly benefit from the transaction. The Department highly recommends, however, that notaries not perform notarial acts for relatives" (Notary website, "Frequently Asked Questions").

NOTARY SIGNING AGENTS

The operation of Notary Signing Agents and "Mobile Notaries" has been strongly discouraged by the North Carolina Department of the Secretary of State, which maintains that the only fees Notaries may lawfully charge for their services are the statutory fees for notarial acts set forth in GS 10B-31. Notaries are even discouraged from charging travel fees. The Department has gone so far as to revoke the commission of a Notary who declared herself a "Mobile Notary," though this revocation was reversed as groundless in 2007 by an administrative law judge.

Legislation was sponsored in the state General Assembly in 2007 by the North Carolina Bar to codify in statute the principle that an attorney must be present at every real estate closing — though this bill was defeated, due in no small part to the efforts of the National Notary Association. The Bar has issued a legal opinion on this matter (Authorized Practice Advisory Opinion 2002-1), available on its website at www.ncbar.com.

A relatively small number of Notaries do continue to operate as Signing Agents in the state, but their professional existence remains open to official challenge.

NOTARY FEES

Maximum Fees Set by Statute

North Carolina Notaries are allowed no more than the following fees for notarial acts (GS 10B-31):
1. For acknowledgments, jurats, verifications or proofs: $5 per principal's signature;
2. For oaths or affirmations without a signature (except when given to a credible witness vouching for the identity of a principal or a subscribing witness): $5 per person.

Fees Not Mandatory

"Nothing in this Chapter shall compel a notary to charge a fee" (GS 10B-30[c]).

No Discrimination with Fees

"A notary shall not discriminatorily condition the fee for a notarial act on any attribute of the principal that would constitute unlawful discrimination" (GS 10B-30[b]).

No Travel Fees

The North Carolina Department of the Secretary of State strongly discourages the charging of travel fees by Notaries. See discussion above, under "Notary Signing Agents."

Ex Officio Notaries

When acting as ex officio Notaries, county registers of deeds and clerks of the superior court, their duly trained assistants and deputies, and the director of the state's Notary Section may charge for performing notarial acts but must give the fees to their employing agency (GS 10B-21[d]).

Fees Must Be Posted

"Notaries who charge for their notarial services shall conspicuously display in their places of business, or present to each principal outside their places of business, an English-language schedule of fees for notarial acts. No part of any notarial fee schedule shall be printed in smaller than 10-point type" (GS 10B-32).

A non-attorney Notary who advertises notarial services in a language other than English must prominently post in his or her place of business a fee schedule in English and in the foreign language, including the notice required by GS 10B-20(i), unless this notice is already prominently posted (GS 10B-20[l]).

Fees for Electronic Acts

In performing electronic notarizations, the maximum fees that may be charged by an Electronic Notary for acknowledgments, jurats, verifications or proofs, and oaths or affirmations are $10 per signature (GS 10B-118).

NOTARY CERTIFICATES

Certificate May Not Be Omitted

"A notary shall not notarize a signature on a record without a notarial certificate indicating what type of notarial act was performed" (GS 10B-23[a]).

Old or New Forms May Be Used

"In 2005 and 2006 the Notary Act was substantially revised and it now provides simplified general purpose certificate forms that are consistent with the laws and practices of most other states. Although various special-purpose certificate forms can be found in other statutes such as those pertaining to real estate instruments, estate planning, and corporate conveyances, the revised and simplified Notary Act forms are now sufficient for notarial acts performed in North Carolina and may be used in circumstances in which neither law nor custom requires that special information be included in the certificate. The forms described in the other statutes have not been repealed, however, and may continue to be used" (NPG 4.1).

Choice Is Not Notary's: "In any event, it is not the notary's responsibility to give advice about which certificate is most appropriate for a specific purpose; rather, the notary is to ensure that the certificate he or she completes contains the minimum elements required by law for a particular notarial act" (NPG 4.2).

Crossing Out Blank Spaces in Certificates

"Before signing a notarial certificate and except as provided in this subsection, a notary shall cross out or mark through all blank lines or spaces in the certificate. However:

"1. Notwithstanding the provisions of this section, a notary shall not be required to complete, cross out, or mark through blank lines or spaces in the notary certificate form provided for in G.S. 47-43 indicating when and where a power of attorney is recorded if that recording information is not known to the notary at the time the notary completes and signs the certificate;

"2. A notary's failure to cross out or mark through blank lines or spaces in a notarial certificate shall not affect the sufficiency, validity, or enforceability of the certificate or the related record; and

"3. A notary's failure to cross out or mark though blank lines or spaces in a notarial certificate shall not be grounds for a register of deeds to refuse to accept a record for registration" (GS 10B-20[o]).

Certificate Must Be in English Language

"A notary shall not execute a certificate that is not written in the English language. A notary may execute a certificate written in the English language that accompanies a record written in another language, which record may include a translation of the notarial certificate into the other language. In those instances, the notary shall execute only the English language certificate" (GS 10B-22[b]).

Acknowledgment Certificate Components

"A notarial certificate for the acknowledgment taken by a notary of a principal who is an individual acting in his or her own right or who is an individual acting in a representative or fiduciary capacity is sufficient and shall be accepted in this State if it is substantially in the form set forth in GS 10B-41, if it is substantially in a form otherwise prescribed by the laws of this State, or if it includes all of the following:

"1. Identifies the state and county in which the acknowledgment occurred.
"2. Names the principal who appeared in person before the notary.
"3. Indicates that the principal appeared in person before the notary and the principal acknowledged that he or she signed the record.
"4. States the date of the acknowledgment.
"5. Contains the signature and seal or stamp of the notary who took the acknowledgment.
"6. States the notary's commission expiration date" (GS 10B-40[b]).

Acknowledgment by Individual or Representative (GS 10B-41[a]):

"When properly completed by a notary, a notarial certificate that substantially complies with the following form may be used and shall be sufficient under the law of this State to satisfy the requirements for a notarial certificate for the acknowledgment of a principal who is an individual acting in his or her own right or who is an individual acting in a representative or fiduciary capacity. The authorization of the form in this section does not preclude the use of other forms."

_____ *County, North Carolina*

I certify that the following person(s) personally appeared before me this day, each acknowledging to me that he or she signed the foregoing document: _____
(name[s] of principal[s]).*

Date: _____

(Official Seal)

_____ *(Official signature of Notary)*
_____, *Notary Public*
(Notary's printed or typed name)
My commission expires: _____

* Following the name of the principal, a phrase may be added to indicate the principal's representative or fiduciary capacity (e.g., "…Mary S. Jones, as President of XYZ Corporation"). Other common types of representative or fiduciary capacity include other officers of a corporation, a general partner on behalf of a partnership or limited partnership, a manager on behalf of a limited liability company, and a trustee on behalf of a trust or association. Execution by an ecclesiastical officer such as a minister or bishop is done in the same manner, with the capacity indicated. An individual using an assumed or "doing business as" name may also adapt this form. (See NPG 4.2.1.3.)

Verification or Proof Certificate Components

"A notarial certificate for the verification or proof of the signature of a principal by a subscribing witness taken by a notary is sufficient and shall be accepted in this State if it is substantially in the form set forth in GS 10B-42, if it is substantially in a form otherwise prescribed by the laws of this State, or if it includes all of the following:

"1. Identifies the state and county in which the verification or proof occurred.

"2. Names the subscribing witness who appeared in person before the notary.

"3. (Repealed by Session Laws 2006-59, s. 18, effective October 1, 2006.)

"4. Names the principal whose signature on the record is to be verified or proven.

"5. Indicates that the subscribing witness certified to the notary under oath or by affirmation that the subscribing witness is not a party to or beneficiary of the transaction, signed the record as a subscribing witness, and either (i) witnessed the principal sign the record, or (ii) witnessed the principal acknowledge the principal's signature on the record.

"6. States the date of the verification or proof.

"7. Contains the signature and seal or stamp of the notary who took the verification or proof.

"8. States the notary's commission expiration date" (GS 10B-40[c]).

Verification or Proof Certificate (GS 10B-42[a]):

"When properly completed by a notary, a notarial certificate in substantially the following form may be used and shall be sufficient under the law of this State to satisfy the requirements for a notarial certificate for the verification or proof of the signature of a principal by a subscribing witness. The authorization of the form in this section does not preclude the use of other forms."

_____ *County, North Carolina*

I certify that _____ (name of subscribing witness) personally appeared before me this day and certified to me under oath or by affirmation that he or she is not a grantee or beneficiary of the transaction, signed the foregoing document as a subscribing witness, and either (i) witnessed _____ (name of principal) sign the foregoing document or (ii) witnessed _____ (name of principal) acknowledge his or her signature on the already-signed document.

Date: _____

(*Official Seal*)

_____ (*Official signature of Notary*)
_____, *Notary Public*
(*Notary's printed or typed name*)
My commission expires: _____

Proof by Nonsubscribing Witness

"A notarial certificate for the verification or proof of the signature of a principal or a subscribing witness by a nonsubscribing witness taken by a notary is sufficient and shall be accepted in this State if it is substantially in the form set forth in GS 10B-42.1, if it is substantially in a form otherwise prescribed by the laws of this State, or if it includes all of the following:

"1. Identifies the state and county in which the verification or proof occurred.

"2. Names the nonsubscribing witness who appeared in person before the notary.

"3. Names the principal or subscribing witness whose signature on the record is to be verified or proven.

"4. Indicates that the nonsubscribing witness certified to the notary under oath or by affirmation that the nonsubscribing witness is not a party to or beneficiary of the transaction and that the nonsubscribing witness recognizes the signature of either the principal or the subscribing witness and that the signature is genuine.

"5. States the date of the verification or proof.

"6. Contains the signature and seal or stamp of the notary who took the verification or proof.

"7. States the notary's commission expiration date" (GS 10B-40[c1]).

Nonsubscribing Witness Certificate (GS 10B-42.1[a]):

"When properly completed by a notary, a notarial certificate in substantially the following form may be used and shall be sufficient under the law of this State to satisfy the requirements for a notarial certificate for the verification or proof of the signature of a principal or subscribing witness by a nonsubscribing witness. The authorization of the form in this section does not preclude the use of other forms."

_____ *County, North Carolina*

I certify _____ (name of nonsubscribing witness) personally appeared before me this day and certified to me under oath or by affirmation that he or she is not a grantee or beneficiary of the transaction, that _____ (name of nonsubscribing witness) recognizes the signature of _____ (name of principal or subscribing witness) and that the signature is genuine.

Date: _____

(Official Seal)

_____ (Official signature of Notary)
_____, Notary Public
(Notary's printed or typed name)
My commission expires: _____

Oath/Affirmation Certificate Components

"A notarial certificate for an oath or affirmation taken by a notary is sufficient and shall be accepted in this State if it is substantially in the form set forth in GS 10B-43, if it is substantially in a form otherwise prescribed by the laws of this State, or if it includes all of the following:

"1. (Repealed by Session Laws 2006-59, s. 18, effective October 1, 2006.)

"2. Names the principal who appeared in person before the notary unless the name of the principal otherwise is clear from the record itself.

"3. (Repealed by Session Laws 2006-59, s. 18, effective October 1, 2006.)

"4. Indicates that the principal who appeared in person before the notary signed the record in question and certified to the notary under oath or by affirmation as to the truth of the matters stated in the record.

"5. States the date of the oath or affirmation.

"6. Contains the signature and seal or stamp of the notary who took the oath or affirmation.

"7. States the notary's commission expiration date" (GS 10B-40[d]).

Oath/Affirmation Certificate (GS 10B-43[a]):

"When properly completed by a notary, a notarial certificate that substantially complies with either of the following forms may be used and shall be sufficient under the law of this State to satisfy the requirements for a notarial certificate for an oath or affirmation. The authorization of the forms in this section does not preclude the use of other forms."

_____ *County, North Carolina*

Signed and sworn to (or affirmed) before me this day by _____ (name* of principal).

(OR)

Sworn to (or affirmed) and subscribed before me this day by _____ (name* of principal).

Date: _____

(Official Seal)

_____ (Official signature of Notary)
_____, Notary Public
(Notary's printed or typed name)
My commission expires: _____

* "The name of the principal may be omitted if the name of the principal is located near the jurat, and the principal who so appeared before the notary is clear from the record itself" GS 10B-43(d)(1).

ADDITIONAL FORMS: The following additional certificates are some of the many prescribed by Chapter 47 of the General Statutes for real estate documents, but "any statute that permits or requires the use of a notarial certificate contained within Chapter 47 of the General Statutes may also be satisfied by the use of a notarial certificate permitted by this Part (i.e., GS 10B-40 through 10B-43)" (GS 10B-40[g], GS 47-37.1 and NPG 4.1):

Acknowledgment by Individual or Representative (GS 47-38):

The following certificate is suitable for taking the acknowledgment of "one or more individuals acting on behalf of an unincorporated association, as an officer or director of a corporation, as a partner of a general or limited partnership, as a manager or member of a limited liability company, as the trustee of a trust, as the personal representative of a decedent's estate, as an agent or attorney in fact for another, as the guardian of a minor or an incompetent, or as a public official."

North Carolina,
_____ County.

I, _____ (here give the name of the official and his official title), do hereby certify that _____ (here give the name of the individual whose acknowledgment is being taken) personally appeared before me this day and acknowledged the due execution of the foregoing instrument (or attached document _____[description of document]).

WITNESS my hand and (where an official seal is required by law) official seal this the _____ day of _____ (month/year).

_____ (Signature of officer taking acknowledgment)
_____ (Official title of officer taking acknowledgment)

(Official seal)
My commission expires _____

Proof of Execution by Subscribing Witness (GS 47-43.2):

State of North Carolina
_____ County

I, _____ (name of officer taking proof), a _____ (official title of officer taking proof) of _____ COUNTY, NORTH CAROLINA, certify that _____ (name of subscribing witness) personally appeared before me this day, and being duly sworn, stated that in his/her presence _____ (name of maker) signed the foregoing instrument (or acknowledged the execution of the foregoing instrument).

WITNESS my hand and official seal, this the _____ day of _____ (month), 20____ (year).

_____ (Signature of officer taking proof)
_____ (Official title of officer taking proof)

(Official seal)
My commission expires _____

Proof by Handwriting of Signer (GS 47-43.3):

State of North Carolina
_____ County

I, _____ (name of officer taking proof), a _____ (official title of officer taking proof) of _____ COUNTY, NORTH CAROLINA, certify that _____ (name of person familiar with maker's handwriting) personally appeared before me this day, and being duly sworn, stated that he knows the handwriting of _____ (name of maker) and that the signature to the foregoing instrument is the signature of _____ (name of maker).

WITNESS my hand and official seal, this the _____ day of _____ (month), 20____.

_____ (Signature of officer taking proof)
_____ (Official title of officer taking proof)

(Official seal)
My commission expires _____

Acknowledgment by Attorney in Fact (GS 47-43):

North Carolina,
_____ County.

I, _____ (here give name of the official and his official title), do hereby certify that _____ (here give name of attorney in fact), attorney in fact for _____ (here give name of parties who executed the instrument through attorney in fact), personally appeared before me this day, and being by me duly sworn, says that he/she executed the foregoing and annexed instrument for and in behalf of _____ (here give names of parties who executed the instrument through attorney in fact), and that his/her authority to execute and acknowledge said instrument is contained in an instrument duly executed, acknowledged, and recorded in the office of _____ (here insert name of official in whose office power of attorney is recorded, and the county and state of recordation), on the _____ (day of month, month, and year of recordation), and that this instrument was executed under and by virtue of the authority given by said instrument granting him/her power of attorney; that the said _____ (here give name of attorney in fact) acknowledged the due execution of the foregoing and annexed instrument for the purposes therein expressed for and in behalf of the said _____ (here give names of parties who executed the instrument through attorney in fact).

WITNESS my hand and official seal, this _____ day of _____, 20____.

_____ *(Signature of officer taking acknowledgment)*
_____ *(Official title of officer taking acknowledgment)*

(Official seal)
My commission expires _____

ADDITIONAL CORPORATE FORMS: For acknowledgments by a corporation in different circumstances, the following three "alternative" certificates may be used. "Some forms include a reference to a corporate seal. These seals are no longer required for real estate conveyances (GS 39-6.5), and the phrase 'sealed with its corporate seal' should be omitted from a certificate if the seal of the corporation has not been affixed to the instrument being acknowledged" (NPG 4.4).

1. Acknowledgment by Corporation (GS 47-41.01[c]):

For deeds and other documents conveying an interest in real estate that are executed by a corporation, if the deed or other instrument is executed by an officer of the corporation, signing the name of the corporation in his or her official capacity, then the form below may be used. If the officer of the corporation is its chairman, president, chief executive officer, vice president, assistant vice president, treasurer or chief financial officer (GS 47-41.01[d][4]), there is no need for attestation by another corporate officer, and a corporate seal is not required.

North Carolina, _____ County

I, _____ (name of officer taking acknowledgment), a _____ (official title of officer taking acknowledgment), certify that _____ (name of corporate officer) personally came before me this day and acknowledged that he/she is _____ (title of corporate officer) of _____, a corporation, and that he/she, as _____ (title of officer), being authorized to do so, executed the foregoing on behalf of the corporation.

WITNESS my hand and official seal, this _____ day of _____, 20____.

_____ *(Signature of officer taking acknowledgment)*
_____ *(Official title of officer taking acknowledgment)*

(Official seal)
My commission expires _____

2. Acknowledgment by Corporation (GS 47-41.01[b]):

For deeds and other documents conveying an interest in real estate that are executed by a corporation, if the deed or other instrument is executed by an officer of the corporation, signing the name of the corporation in his or her official capacity, is sealed with its common or corporate seal, and is attested by another person who is an attesting officer of the corporation, then the form below may be used. The officer of the corporation could be its chairman, president, chief executive officer, vice president, assistant vice president, treasurer or chief financial officer (GS 47-41.01[d][4]). The attesting officer of the corporation is its secretary or assistant secretary, trust officer, assistant trust officer, associate trust officer, or in the case of a bank, its secretary, assistant secretary, cashier or assistant cashier (GS 47-41.01[d][5]). Only this attesting officer need appear before the Notary.

North Carolina, _____ County

I, _____ (name of officer taking acknowledgment), a _____ (official title of officer taking acknowledgment), certify that _____ (name of attesting corporate officer) personally came before me this day and acknowledged that he/she is _____ (title of attesting corporate officer) of _____, a corporation, and that by authority duly given and as the act of the corporation, the foregoing instrument was signed in its name by its _____ (title of absent corporate officer), sealed with its corporate seal, and attested by himself/herself as its _____ (title of attesting corporate officer).

· WITNESS my hand and official seal, this the _____ day of _____, 20____.

_____ (Signature of officer taking acknowledgment)
_____ (Official title of officer taking acknowledgment)

(Official seal)
My commission expires _____

3. Acknowledgment by Corporation (GS 47-41.02[d]):

For deeds and other documents conveying an interest in real estate that are executed by a corporation, if the deed or other instrument is executed by the signature of the president, vice president, presiding member or trustee of the corporation, sealed with its common seal and attested by its secretary or assistant secretary, then the form below may be used.

North Carolina, _____ County

This _____ day of _____, 20____, personally came before me, _____ (name and official title of officer taking acknowledgment), _____ (name of corporate officer), who, being by me duly sworn, says that he/she is _____ (president, vice president, presiding member or trustee) of the _____, a corporation, and that the seal affixed to the foregoing (or annexed) instrument in writing is the corporate seal of said corporation, and that said writing was signed and sealed by him/her in behalf of said corporation by its authority duly given. And the said _____ (corporate officer) acknowledged the said writing to be the act and deed of said corporation.

WITNESS my hand and official seal, this _____ day of _____, 20____.

_____ (Signature of officer taking acknowledgment)
_____ (Official title of officer taking acknowledgment)

(Official seal)
My commission expires _____

ADDITIONAL SAMPLE FORMS: The following two certificate samples for an affidavit and a will are provided on the Department of the Secretary of State's website for Notaries ("Sample Documents"):

Sample Affidavit Certificate (Notary website):

North Carolina
County of _____

_____ (name of principal), appearing before the undersigned Notary and being duly sworn, says that:

1. _____
_____
2. _____
_____

_____ (Signature of principal)

Sworn to (or affirmed) and subscribed before me this the _____ day of _____, 20___.

(Official Seal)

_____ (Official signature of Notary)
_____, Notary Public
(Notary's printed or typed name)
My commission expires: _____

Sample Certificate for Will Already Executed and Attested (Notary website):

State of North Carolina
County/City of _____

Before me, the undersigned authority, on this day personally appeared _____, _____, and _____, known to me to be the testator and the witnesses, respectively, whose names are signed to the attached or foregoing instrument, and all of these persons being by me first duly sworn. The testator declared to me and to the witnesses as his free and voluntary act for the purposes therein expressed; or that the testator signified that the instrument was his instrument by acknowledging to them his signature previously affixed thereto.

The said witnesses stated before me that the foregoing will was executed and acknowledged by the testator as his last will in the presence of said witnesses who, in his presence and at his request, subscribed their names thereto as attesting witnesses and that the testator, at the time of the execution of said will, was over the age of 18 years and of sound and disposing mind and memory.

_____ (Signature of testator)

_____ (Signature of witness)

_____ (Signature of witness)

Subscribed, sworn to and acknowledged before me by:

_____, the testator,

_____, as a witness, and

_____, as a witness.

Witness my hand and official seal, this the ____ day of _____, 20___.

(Official Seal)

_____ (Official signature of Notary)
_____, Notary Public
(Notary's printed or typed name)
My commission expires: _____

Out-of-State Certificates and Filings

"Any notarial certificate made in another jurisdiction shall be sufficient in this State if it is made in accordance with federal law or the laws of the jurisdiction where the notarial certificate is made" (GS 10B-40[e]).

"Any electronic document filed in the Mecklenburg County Register of Deeds office that purports to be notarized in the Commonwealth of Virginia and that contains the typed name of a Virginia notary together with the notary's expiration date (sic) shall be given the same legal effect as if the person performed a lawful notarization in Virginia" (GS 10B-70[b]).

"On records to be filed, registered, recorded, or delivered in another state or jurisdiction of the United States, a North Carolina notary may complete any notarial certificate that may be required in that other state or jurisdiction" (GS 10B-40[f]).

Certificate Defects Cured

"Technical defects, errors, or omissions in a notarial certificate shall not affect the sufficiency, validity, or enforceability of the notarial certificate or the related instrument or document. This subsection applies to notarial certificates made on or after December 1, 2005" (GS 10B-68[a]).

ELECTRONIC NOTARIZATIONS

The state of North Carolina in 2005 became the first in the nation ever to enact a comprehensive and detailed code that integrates paper-based and electronic notarial acts, while embracing such traditional principles of notarization as the requirement that the document signer appear in person before the Notary at the time of notarization.

Drawing extensively from the National Notary Association's *Model Notary Act* of 2002, North Carolina's sweeping new notarial code was enacted as Session Law 2005-391 (Senate Bill 671), effective December 1, 2005. This legislation repealed Chapter 10A of the General Statutes, replacing it with a new Chapter 10B, which has two parts: Article 1, "Notary Public Act," and Article 2, "Electronic Notary Act."

Effective January 1, 2007, North Carolina published permanent administrative rules implementing GS 10B, Article 2, and also GS 47, Article 1A, "Uniform Real Property Electronic Recording Act" (URPERA). The new rules are laid out in 18 NCAC 07C.

Becoming an Electronic Notary

Before performing electronic notarial acts, a North Carolina Notary must register his or her capability to notarize electronically with the Secretary of State. There are 10 basic steps to the registration process (eNotary website, "How to Become an Electronic Notary" and "Frequently Asked Questions"; GS 10B-105 through 108; 18 NCAC 07C.0200 and .0300).

1. Hold or obtain a North Carolina Notary Commission.

2. Register to take the three-hour Electronic Notarization Course at a local community college. The course and test are developed by the Department of the Secretary of State.

3. Take the Course and pass the exam with a score of 80% or better. Purchase of the state's "Electronic Notarization Manual" is essential.

4. Complete the registration form online at www.secretary.state.nc.us/enotary/enotaryhowto.aspx.

5. Print out and sign the registration form and have it notarized.

6. Send or bring the notarized registration form to the Department of the Secretary of State, with a $50 registration fee.

7. Obtain the Electronic Notary Oath Notification Letter from the Department.

8. Present valid identification and take the Electronic Notary oath of office at the local county Register of Deeds office within 45 days of the issue date of the Electronic Notary commission.

9. Obtain the Electronic Notary Certificate to Perform Electronic Notarizations from the Register of Deeds.

10. To purchase an Electronic Notary signature and seal, present the Electronic Notary Certificate to Perform Electronic Notarizations to an authorized Electronic Notary Solution Provider. A list of approved Providers is available online at www.secretary.state.nc.us/enotary/enotarysp.aspx

"Please note that authorization of an electronic notary solution by the Department of the Secretary of State is NOT an endorsement by the State. Authorization means that the solution has met our technical and legal standards" (eNotary website, "Frequently Asked Questions" and 18 NCAC 07C.0502).

The Electronic Notary's registration will expire on the same date as the commission, and both may be renewed at the same time (GS 10B-106[b] and [c]).

Performing Electronic Notarizations

The following types of notarial act may be performed electronically (GS 10B-115):

1. Acknowledgments;
2. Jurats;
3. Verifications or proofs; and
4. Oaths or affirmations.

Fees: The maximum fee that a North Carolina Notary may charge for electronic notarial acts is $10 per signature for acknowledgments, jurats, verifications or proofs, and oaths or affirmations (eNotary website, "Frequently Asked Questions").

Personal Appearance Required: "When an electronic notary performs an electronic notarization, the principal and the electronic notary shall be in each other's physical presence during the entire electronic notarization so that the principal and the electronic notary can see, hear, communicate with, and give identification documents to each other without the use of electronic devices such as telephones, computers, video cameras, or facsimile machines ... Electronic notaries must require face to face personal appearance for every electronic notarization, just as they do for a paper-based notarial act" (eNotary website, "Frequently Asked Questions"; GS 10B-116; 18 NCAC 07C.0403).

Electronic Notary Signature: "The electronic notary signature is a unique, independently verifiable image of the electronic notary's handwritten signature, that is retained under the electronic notary's sole control and is attached or logically associated with the document, linking the data in such a manner that any subsequent alterations to the underlying document or electronic notary certificate are observable through visual examination" (eNotary website, "Frequently Asked Questions"; GS 10B-101[7]; 18 NCAC 07C.0401). "An image of the electronic notary's handwritten signature shall appear on any visual or printed representation of an electronic notary certificate regardless of the technology being used to affix the electronic notary's electronic signature" (18 NCAC 07C.0401[e]).

Electronic Notary Seal: "The electronic notary seal is a unique, independently verifiable image with a border containing the electronic notary's name exactly as commissioned, the words 'Electronic Notary Public', the words 'North Carolina' or 'N.C.', and the county of commission including the word 'County' or 'Co.'. The physical appearance of the seal replicates the appearance of an inked seal on paper and shall appear on any visual or printed representation of the electronic notary certificate. The electronic notary seal is attached or logically associated with the document, linking the data in such a manner that any subsequent alterations to the underlying document or electronic notary certificate are observable through visual examination. The seal must also be retained under the electronic notary's sole control" (eNotary website, "Frequently Asked Questions"; GS 10B-101[5]; 18 NCAC 07C.0402).

Protected Access: "Access to electronic notary signatures and electronic notary seals shall be protected by the use of a password, token, biometric, or other form of authentication approved by the Department ..." (18 NCAC 07C.0604).

Notarial Components of e-Document: "In performing an electronic notarial act, all of the following components shall be attached to, or logically associated with, the electronic document by the electronic notary, all of which shall be immediately perceptible and reproducible in the electronic record to which the notary's electronic signature is attached:

"1. The notary's name, state, and county of commissioning exactly as stated on the commission issued by the Secretary;

"2. The words 'Electronic Notary Public';

"3. The words 'State of North Carolina';

"4. The expiration date of the commission;

"5. The notary's electronic signature; and

"6. The completed wording of one of the following notarial certificates: (a) Acknowledgment; (b) Jurat; (c) Verification or proof; or (d) Oath or affirmation" (GS 10B-117).

Record of Electronic Act: "The Secretary may require an electronic notary to create and to maintain a record, journal, or entry of each electronic notarial act as of June 1, 2007. However, it is strongly recommended as a 'best practice' that all notaries voluntarily keep a journal to record all official notarial acts" (eNotary website, "Frequently Asked Questions").

Security Measures: "When not in use, the notary shall keep the notary's electronic signature, electronic seal, and all other notarial records secure, under the exclusive control of the notary, and shall not allow them to be used by any other notary or any other person" (GS 10B-126[b]).

UETA Recognizes Notary's eSignature

North Carolina has adopted its own version of the Uniform Electronic Transactions Act (GS 66-311 through 66-330), including the provision on notarization, thereby recognizing the legal validity of electronic signatures used by Notaries:

"If a law requires a signature or record relating to a transaction to be notarized, acknowledged, verified, or made under oath, the requirement is satisfied if the electronic signature of the person authorized to perform those acts, together with all other information required to be included by other applicable law, is attached to or logically associated with the signature or record" (GS 66-321).

NOTARY RECORDS

North Carolina Notaries Public are not required by law to keep a record of the notarial acts they perform.

Keeping Journal Is Recommended

"Notaries should...consider the benefits, both to themselves and to those who rely on them, of keeping a journal. A journal could prove to be invaluable for reconstructing the events related to a notarial act if the act's validity is later challenged. Memories, especially those about the details of one of many similar events, fade over time, and a journal can become an important historic source. A journal also can confirm a notary's adherence to statutory requirements and good practices. Finally, a journal can be a kind of checklist for notaries, reminding them about each step they must take with every notarial act. Even the most experienced notary can use reminders about careful practices" (NPG 3.8).

Format of Journal

"A journal should be permanently bound with sequentially numbered pages and entries made without blank spaces, to prevent removal or insertion of pages or entries" (NPG 3.8).

Journal Entries

For each notarial act, the following entry components are described in the "Notary Public Guidebook for North Carolina" (3.8):

1. Date and brief description of each document notarized;
2. Date of notarization;
3. Type of notarial act (acknowledgment, verification, etc.);
4. Location where the notarial act was performed;
5. Name and address of each principal and subscribing witness;
6. How the principal or subscribing witness was identified (a general description, not specific ID numbers, but include names and addresses of any credible witnesses);
7. Fees received by the Notary.

Record of Electronic Acts

"The Secretary may require an electronic notary to create and to maintain a record, journal, or entry of each electronic notarial act" (GS 10B-126[e]).

Misuse of Journal

"Any person who without authority obtains, uses, conceals, defaces, or destroys the seal or notarial records of a notary is guilty of a Class I felony" (GS 10B-60[f]).

AUTHENTICATION OF NOTARIAL ACTS

Registers of Deeds

The register of deeds in the county in which a Notary qualified may issue certificates authenticating the signature of that Notary (GS 10B-20[h]).

Secretary of State

Authenticating certificates for North Carolina Notaries, including apostilles, are also issued by the office of the Secretary of State (GS 66-270).

Fees: $10 per document. For adoptions only, there is a processing fee of $5 for duplicate originals. Checks or money orders are payable to "N.C. Secretary of State."

Mailing Address:
Department of Secretary of State
Authentication Office
P.O. Box 29622
Raleigh, NC 27626-0622

Telephone: 1-919-807-2140

Email: authen@sosnc.com

In Person or Overnight Mail:
Department of Secretary of State
Authentication Office
2 South Salisbury Street
Raleigh, NC 27601-2903

Procedure: "Submit documents to the NC Authentication Office with a cover letter, money order or check, the original document(s) with all certifications attached and a return paid carrier envelope. Should you wish the documents to be directed to a third party, please include that information and the paid carrier envelope addressed to the third party. Any documents received without a paid return envelope and/or a third party address will be delivered by regular mail to the person submitting the documents" (Secretary of State website, "Authentication Section"). Cover letters for submitting notarized documents to the Authentication Office are available in several languages on the Secretary of State's website.

COMMISSIONING AND ADMINISTRATION

North Carolina's Notaries are appointed and commissioned by the Secretary of State, whose office regulates and maintains records on them (GS 10B-5). Most documents kept by the Secretary's office are public records and subject to disclosure, but the following information, required on a commission application, is considered confidential and is not subject to disclosure: the applicant's date of birth, addresses (email, physical and mailing) and phone number and the last four digits of a Social Security number (GS 10B-7[b]).

Applying for Commission

Qualifications: An applicant for a commission

as a North Carolina Notary Public must (GS 10B-5[b]): (a) be at least 18 years old or legally emancipated as defined in Article 35 of Chapter 7B of the General Statutes, (b) reside or have a regular place of work or business in the state, (c) reside legally in the United States, (d) speak, read and write the English language, (e) possess a high school diploma or the equivalent and (f) purchase and keep as a reference the most recent manual approved by the Secretary of State that describes the duties and authority of Notaries. (The current manual, "Notary Public Guidebook for North Carolina" is available through the Publications Office of the University of North Carolina's School of Government at 1-919-966-4119 or www.sog.unc.edu/pubs. The cost of the current edition is $20.)

"According to GS 10B-5(d)(2), the Department may deny an application for commission or recommission based on '(t)he applicant's conviction or plea of admission or nolo contendere to a felony or any crime involving dishonesty or moral turpitude. In no case may a commission be issued to an applicant within 10 years after release from prison, probation, or parole, whichever is later'" (Notary website, "Frequently Asked Questions"). There are other disqualifications based on misconduct in an applicant's past — see NPG 1.3.1).

Course and Exam Required: Each first-time applicant must complete a six-hour course of instruction on Notary duties. Approved courses are offered by all community colleges and certain other institutions. All applicants, both first-time and renewing, must pass a written examination with a score of 80% or better. Attorneys licensed to practice in North Carolina are exempt from both the education and exam requirements (GS 10B-8 and NPG 1.3.2). The exam requirement does not apply "if the notary has been continuously commissioned in North Carolina since July 10, 1991, and has never been disciplined by the Secretary" (GS 10B-11[b]). Any non-attorney applicant must apply for a commission within three months of successfully completing the mandatory course and exam (GS 10B-8[a]).

Application: The applicant's signature on the completed application must be notarized and sent to the Notary Public Section with a $50 fee and, for non-citizens, a copy of the I-551 permanent resident card (Notary website, "Initial Application for NC Notary Public"; GS 10B-5[b][8] and GS 10B-13). First-time applicants must have their course instructor sign and date the application to indicate successful completion of the course. First-time applicants must also obtain an endorsement from a local elected official, such as a mayor, councilman, court clerk, register of deeds, sheriff, etc. If the course instructor is also a register of deeds or a court clerk, he or she may sign the application in both capacities (NPG 1.3.2 and 1.3.4). Applicants in counties with more than 5,250 active Notaries are exempt from the requirement for an endorsement from an elected official (GS 10B-5[b][9]).

For Notaries seeking reappointment, online reappointment is offered for a total fee of $52, which includes a nonrefundable $2 electronic transaction fee. Applicants for reappointment are not required to get an elected official's endorsement. They are required to take the exam and may do so online at the Department's Notary website. Applications should not be made earlier than 10 weeks before commission expiration.

Oath of Office at Register of Deeds: Upon commissioning, the new Notary will be notified by mail to go to the local office of the register of deeds to pick up the commission and take the required oaths of office, for a $10 fee. This must be done within 45 days (Notary website, "Initial Application for NC Notary Public"; GS 10B-10[a] and [b]).

Non-Residents: Non-residents of North Carolina may qualify as Notaries if they have a regular place of work or business in the state (GS 10B-5[c]). "(A) nonresident is commissioned in the county in North Carolina where he or she is regularly employed or maintains a place of business" (NPG 1.3.1). Non-resident applicants for a North Carolina Notary commission must submit a proof-of-employment statement from their employer on company letterhead.

Changes of Status

If Notary's Name Changes: Within 45 days of a legal name change, the Notary must inform the Secretary by fax, email or certified mail, return receipt requested, and must include both the old and the new name. The Notary may continue to use the old name in notarizing until: (a) receiving a confirmation from the Secretary; (b) obtaining a new seal with the new name; and (c) requalifying with the county register of deeds in the new name (GS 10B-51).

If a name change occurs at the same time as a move to a new county, the Notary must apply for a new commission within 45 days of the name change, but may continue to notarize using the old name and seal until: (a) receiving a new appointment from the Secretary; (b) obtaining a new seal with the new name and county; and (c) qualifying with the register of deeds in the new county within 45 days of commissioning (GS 10B-53).

If Notary Moves: "Within 45 days after the change of a notary's residence, business, or any mailing address or telephone number, the notary shall send to the Secretary by fax, email, or certified mail, return receipt requested, a signed notice of the change, giving both old and new addresses or telephone numbers" (GS 10B-50).

If the move is to another county in the state, the Notary need not get a new seal. However, if recommissioned in the new county, then the Notary must get a new seal bearing the new county's name and must register in the new county (GS 10B-52).

If Notary Resigns Commission: A Notary who resigns the commission must notify the Secretary of the date of resignation by fax, email or certified mail, return receipt requested. "Notaries who cease to reside in or maintain a regular place of work or business in this State, or who become permanently unable to perform their notarial duties, shall resign their commissions…" Within 45 days of resignation, Notaries must deliver their seal to the Secretary by certified mail, return receipt requested" (GS 10B-54 and GS 10B-55[a]).

COUNTY REGISTERS

To contact a North Carolina county register of deeds to obtain an authenticating certificate for a Notary, or to seek assistance in locating a given Notary, telephone long-distance information — 1-XXX-555-1212 — using the area code from the listing below, and ask for the phone number for the register in the appropriate jurisdiction:

County	City/Town	Area Code
Alamance	Graham	(336)
Alexander	Taylorsville	(828)
Alleghany	Sparta	(336)
Anson	Wadesboro	(704)
Ashe	Jefferson	(336)
Avery	Newland	(828)
Beaufort	Washington	(252)
Bertie	Windsor	(252)
Bladen	Elizabethtown	(910)
Brunswick	Bolivia	(910)
Buncombe	Asheville	(828)
Burke	Morganton	(828)
Cabarrus	Concord	(704)
Caldwell	Lenoir	(828)
Camden	Camden	(252)
Carteret	Beaufort	(252)
Caswell	Yanceyville	(336)
Catawba	Newton	(828)
Chatham	Pittsboro	(919)
Cherokee	Murphy	(828)
Chowan	Edenton	(252)
Clay	Hayesville	(828)
Cleveland	Shelby	(704)
Columbus	Whiteville	(910)
Craven	New Bern	(252)
Cumberland	Fayetteville	(910)
Currituck	Currituck	(252)
Dare	Manteo	(252)
Davidson	Lexington	(336)
Davie	Mocksville	(336)
Duplin	Kenansville	(910)
Durham	Durham	(919)
Edgecombe	Tarboro	(252)
Forsyth	Winston-Salem	(336)
Franklin	Louisburg	(919)
Gaston	Gastonia	(704)
Gates	Gatesville	(252)
Graham	Robbinsville	(828)
Granville	Oxford	(919)
Greene	Snow Hill	(252)
Guilford	Greensboro	(336)
Halifax	Halifax	(252)
Harnett	Lillington	(910)
Haywood	Waynesville	(828)
Henderson	Hendersonville	(828)
Hertford	Winton	(252)
Hoke	Raeford	(910)
Hyde	Swan Quarter	(252)
Iredell	Statesville	(704)
Jackson	Sylva	(828)
Johnston	Smithfield	(919)

County	City/Town	Area Code
Jones	Trenton	(252)
Lee	Sanford	(919)
Lenoir	Kinston	(252)
Lincoln	Lincolnton	(704)
Macon	Franklin	(828)
Madison	Marshall	(828)
Martin	Williamston	(252)
McDowell	Marion	(828)
Mecklenburg	Charlotte	(704)
Mitchell	Bakersville	(828)
Montgomery	Troy	(910)
Moore	Carthage	(910)
Nash	Nashville	(252)
New Hanover	Wilmington	(910)
Northampton	Jackson	(252)
Onslow	Jacksonville	(910)
Orange	Hillsborough	(919)
Pamlico	Bayboro	(252)
Pasquotank	Elizabeth City	(252)
Pender	Burgaw	(910)
Perquimans	Hertford	(252)
Person	Roxboro	(336)
Pitt	Greenville	(252)
Polk	Columbus	(828)
Randolph	Asheboro	(336)
Richmond	Rockingham	(910)
Robeson	Lumberton	(910)
Rockingham	Wentworth	(336)
Rowan	Salisbury	(704)
Rutherford	Rutherfordton	(828)
Sampson	Clinton	(910)
Scotland	Laurinburg	(910)
Stanly	Albemarle	(704)
Stokes	Danbury	(336)
Surry	Dobson	(336)
Swain	Bryson City	(828)
Transylvania	Brevard	(828)
Tyrrell	Columbia	(252)
Union	Monroe	(704)
Vance	Henderson	(252)
Wake	Raleigh	(919)
Warren	Warrenton	(252)
Washington	Plymouth	(252)
Watauga	Boone	(828)
Wayne	Goldsboro	(919)
Wilkes	Wilkesboro	(336)
Wilson	Wilson	(252)
Yadkin	Yadkinville	(336)
Yancey	Burnsville	(828)

OTHER NOTARIAL OFFICERS

Officers of General Court of Justice

Besides Notaries, the following officials may take acknowledgment or proof of any recordable document: justices, judges, magistrates, clerks, assistant clerks, and deputy clerks of the General Court of Justice (GS 47-1).

Registers of Deeds, Superior Court Clerks

Superior Court Clerks: "The clerks of the superior court may act as notaries public in their several counties by virtue of their offices as clerks and may certify their notarial acts only under the seals of their respective counties. Assistant and deputy clerks of superior court, by virtue of their offices, may perform the following notarial acts and may certify these notarial acts only under the seals of their respective courts: (1) Oaths and affirmations. (2) Verifications or proofs.

"Upon completion of the course of study provided for in G.S. 10B-5(b), assistant and deputy clerks of superior court may, by virtue of their offices, perform all other notarial acts and may certify these notarial acts only under the seals of their respective courts. A course of study attended only by assistant and deputy clerks of superior court may be taught at any mutually convenient location agreed to by the Secretary and the Administrative Office of the Courts" (GS 10B-21[a]).

Registers of Deeds: "Registers of deeds may act as notaries public in their several counties by virtue of their offices as registers of deeds and may certify their notarial acts only under the seals of their respective offices. Assistant and deputy registers of deeds, by virtue of their offices, may perform the following notarial acts and may certify these notarial acts only under the seals of their respective offices: (1) Oaths and affirmations. (2) Verifications or proofs.

"Upon completion of the course of study provided for in G.S. 10B-5(b), assistant and deputy registers of deeds may, by virtue of their offices, perform all other notarial acts and may certify these notarial acts only under the seals of their respective offices. A course of study attended only by assistant and deputy registers of deeds may be taught at any mutually convenient location agreed to by the Secretary and the North Carolina Association of Registers of Deeds" (GS 10B-21[b]).

Fees: All such ex officio Notaries may act only in the performance of their official duties unless regularly commissioned as a Notary under GS 10B-5 (GS 10B-21[e]). These ex officio Notaries may charge fees, which are payable to the governmental entity employing them (GS 10B-21[d]).

Division Director May Notarize

The Director of the Secretary of State's Notary Public Section has ex officio power to notarize and may certify notarial acts under the seal of the Secretary (GS 10B-21[c]). A fee may be changed but it is payable to the Department of the Secretary of State (GS 10B-21[d]).

QUICK FACTS

Notary Jurisdiction
Statewide (GS 10B-9).

Notary Term Length
Five years (GS 10B-9), expiring at midnight on the day preceding the fifth anniversary of the effective date (NPG 1.4).

Curative Provision: "Any acknowledgment taken and any instrument notarized by a person...whose notary commission has expired, is hereby validated. The acknowledgment and instrument shall have the same legal effect as if the person qualified as a notary public at the time the person performed the act" (GS 10B-65[a]). This applies to notarial acts performed on or before May 1, 2008 (GS 10B-65[e]).

Notary Bond
Not required by law.

North Dakota

NOTARY SEAL

A North Dakota Notary who performs a notarial act involving a tangible record must affix an official seal to each notarial certificate at the time of notarization (NDCC 44-06.1-14[2] and 44-06.1-23[8]). For seal requirements for notarial acts involving electronic records, see "Electronic Notarizations" below.

When used on a tangible record, the seal's format must be as follows:

Kind

Stamping Device: Effective August 1, 2011, "a notary seal/stamp is now referred to as an official notary stamping device" (NN, July 2011). Neither North Dakota statute nor the Secretary of State's website stipulates what type of stamp a Notary must use.

In reference to tangible (rather than electronic) records, statute defines stamping device as a "physical device capable of affixing to a tangible record an official stamp" (NDCC 44-06.1-01[12]) and defines official stamp as "a physical image affixed to a tangible record" (NDCC 44-06.1-01[8]).

Statute also stipulates that the stamp "must be designed to leave a clear impression (and) be photographically reproducible" (NDCC 44-06.1-16[1]) and states that "(t)he official stamp of a notary public must ... (b)e capable of being copied together with the record to which it is affixed or attached ..." (NDCC 44-06.1-15[2]).

When the record to be stamped is tangible

Examples

The above typical, actual-size examples of official Notary stamping devices are allowed by North Dakota law. Formats other than these may also be permitted.

NOTARY ADMINISTRATION

Office of Secretary of State
Administrative/Licensing Division
600 E. Boulevard Ave. 1-701-328-2901
Department 108 1-800-352-0867
Bismarck, ND 58505-0500

Website: www.nd.gov/sos/notaryserv/

NOTARY RULES

NDCC — NORTH DAKOTA CENTURY CODE
NN — NOTARY NOTES NEWSLETTER

Most Notary rules are in the North Dakota Century Code:

a. Title 44, Chapter 44-05, "Administration of Oaths";

b. Title 44, Chapter 44-06.1, "Revised Uniform Law on Notarial Acts"*;

c. Title 44, Chapter 44-08, "Miscellaneous Provisions";

d. Title 47, Chapter 47-19, "Record Title."

* This is the *Revised Uniform Law on Notarial Acts* of 2010, adopted with modifications, effective August 1, 2011.

Other guidelines for Notaries are in the "Notary Notes" newsletter published by the North Dakota Secretary of State and available on the website.

(rather than electronic), an inking stamp meets all statutory requirements.

Embosser Disallowed: Effective August 1, 2003, issuance of embossing Notary seals was disallowed in favor of photocopiable inking stamps. A six-year phase-in for Notaries with unexpired commissions permitted use of embossers that were "smudged" in order to be photocopiable. Effective August 1, 2009, all embossing seals were outlawed.

Shape/Size

Circular, $1^5/_8$ inches (41.28 millimeters) in diameter; or rectangular, up to or equal to $^7/_8$ inch (22.23 millimeters) vertically by $2^5/_8$ inches (66.68 millimeters) horizontally (NDCC 44-06.1-16[1]).

Components

The following components must be surrounded by a border (NDCC 44-06.1-16[1]):
1. Name of Notary, exactly as on the commission;
2. "Notary Public";
3. "State of North Dakota";
4. Commission expiration date.

Great Seal and Other Symbols Prohibited: The stamp "may not contain any other words, numbers, symbols, or a reproduction of the great seal of the state" (NDCC 44-06.1-16[1]).

Stamp Affixed at Time of Notarization

"A notarial act must be evidenced by a certificate. The certificate must ... (b)e executed contemporaneously with the performance of the notarial act ... (and) the notary public's official stamp must be affixed to the certificate" (NDCC 44-06.1-14[1] and [2]). As a result of this statute, Notaries may not pre-stamp notarial certificates prior to performing a notarial act.

Stamp Should Not Obscure Text

"A notary's seal/stamp should not obscure text nor overlap any written or typed text. The impression of the seal/stamp on the document must be clear and legible" (NN, December 2006).

Validation of Imperfect Seal or Stamp

"All certificates of acknowledgment by notaries public on all documents filed for record with a recorder in the state, notwithstanding any defects or irregularities with the notary seal, are hereby validated, ratified, approved, and confirmed. Notwithstanding section 44-08-06, all seals of a court or officer of this state are binding, legal, and enforceable. The provisions of this section relating to validation of acknowledgments are applicable to all documents filed with any county recorder in the state after July 1, 1987" (NDCC 44-08-06.1).

Authorization Needed to Purchase Stamp

"The secretary of state, upon receipt of the proper fee, oath, and bond, shall issue a certificate of authorization with which the notary public may obtain an official notary stamping device. A notary stamp vendor may provide a notary with an official stamping device only upon presentation by the notary of a certificate of authorization" (NDCC 44-06.1-16).

New Stamp for Name Change: See "If Notary Changes Name" later in this chapter for procedures on issuance of a new stamp after a name change by the Notary.

Notary Responsible for Stamp

"A notary public is responsible for the security of the notary public's stamping device and may not allow another individual to use the device to perform a notarial act" (NDCC 44-06.1-16[2])

Stamp Belongs Exclusively to Notary

"An official stamping device is the property of the notary only and may not be retained or used by any other person, including an employer of a notary even if the employer purchased or paid for the notary's stamping device. An official stamping device must remain in the direct and exclusive control of the notary at all times during a notary's commission" (NDCC 44-06.1-16[4]).

Disposal of Stamp

"On resignation from, or the revocation or expiration of, the notary public's commission, or on the expiration of the date set forth in the stamping device, if any, the notary public shall disable the stamping device by destroying, defacing, damaging, erasing, or securing it against use in a manner that renders it unusable.

"On the death or adjudication of incompetency of a notary public, the notary public's personal representative or guardian or any other individual knowingly in possession of the stamping device shall render it unusable by destroying, defacing, damaging, erasing, or securing against use in a manner that renders it unusable" (NDCC 44-06.1-16[2]).

Lost, Stolen or Damaged Stamp

"If a notary public's stamping device is lost or stolen, the notary public or the notary public's personal representative or guardian shall notify promptly the secretary of state on discovering that the device is lost or stolen" (NDCC 44-06.1-16[3]).

The Secretary of State further instructs the Notary to "(s)end the Secretary of State a letter explaining what happened and, if applicable, photocopies of a police report…. If the seal/stamp was lost or stolen, obtaining a different type of seal/stamp is suggested" (website, "Notary Public Seal/Stamp").

Requirements for Other Public Officers

"An officer taking and certifying an acknowledgment or proof of an instrument for record must authenticate the officer's certificate by affixing thereto:

"1. The officer's signature followed by the name of the officer's office; and

"2. The officer's seal of office, if … the officer is required to have an official seal.

"A judge or clerk of a court of record must authenticate that officer's certificate by affixing thereto the seal of the judge's or clerk's court. A mayor of a city must authenticate that officer's certificate by affixing thereto the seal of the mayor's city" (NDCC 47-19-32).

"Except as otherwise provided by law relating to notary stamps, upon every seal of a court or officer of this state required or authorized to have a seal, there must be engraved the words 'State of North Dakota' and the name of the court or office in which the seal is to be used. All such seals, except the great seal, must be surrounded by a border" and have the same dimensions as those of the Notary stamps described above (NDCC 44-08-06).

"When any court of record is unprovided with a seal, the judge thereof may authorize the use of any temporary seal, or of any device by way of seal, until a permanent seal is provided" (NDCC 44-08-07).

NOTARY POWERS

North Dakota Notaries are authorized to perform the following notarial acts:

1. Take acknowledgments* and proofs** (NDCC 44-06.1-01[5] and 47-19-21);
2. Administer oaths and affirmations (NDCC 44-05-01[4] and 44-06.1-01[5]);
3. Take verifications*** (jurats) on oath or affirmation (NDCC 44-06.1-01[5]);
4. Witness or attest signatures (NDCC 44-06.1-01[5]);
5. Certify or attest copies**** (NDCC 44-06.1-01[5]);
6. Execute protests (NDCC 44-06.1-01[5]).

* <u>Acknowledgments</u>: "'Acknowledgment' means a declaration by an individual before a notarial officer that the individual has signed a record for the purpose stated in the record and, if the record is signed in a representative capacity, that the individual signed the record with proper authority and signed it as the act of the individual or person identified in the record" (NDCC 44-06.1-01[1]).

"The acknowledgment of an instrument must not be taken unless the officer taking it knows or has satisfactory evidence (or) the oath or affirmation of a credible witness that the person making the acknowledgment is the individual who is described in and who executed the instrument, or if executed by a corporation or limited liability company, that the officer or manager making such acknowledgment is authorized to make it as provided in section 47-10-05.1" (NDCC 47-19-20).

"An acknowledgment is the simple authentication of a signature which may or may not have been signed in front of a notary. It proves … that the signer personally appeared before the notary, was identified, and that the individual declared that he or she signed the document for the purpose stated in the document. It acts as a safeguard against forgery and undue influence" (NN, July 2011).

"To make an acknowledgment, the document signer must personally appear before the notary public, and declare that he/she has executed and signed the document voluntarily…. The notary may want to ask the signer 'Do you acknowledge that this is your signature and that you are executing this document of your own free will?' If yes, the notary should complete a certificate that states the signer acknowledged the document" (website, "Certifications").

In lieu of acknowledgment before a Notary or other authorized officer, a document transferring title to personal property may be signed by the transferor in the presence of two witnesses, who must also sign the document (NDCC 47-19-50).

** Proofs of Execution: "Proof of the execution of an instrument when not acknowledged may be made:

"1. By the party executing it;

"2. By a subscribing witness; or

"3. By other witnesses in cases mentioned in sections 47-19-23 and 47-19-24" (NDCC 47-19-21).

"If proof of the execution of an instrument is made by a subscribing witness, such witness must be known personally to the officer taking the proof to be the person whose name is subscribed to the instrument as a witness or must be proved to be such by the oath of a credible witness" (NDCC 47-19-22).

"Officers authorized to take the proof of instruments are authorized in such proceedings:

"1. To administer oaths or affirmations;

"2. To employ and swear interpreters; and

"3. To issue subpoenas, obedience to which may be enforced as provided by title 28" (NDCC 47-19-36).

Proof of the execution of a document may be established by handwriting in certain cases, such as when the principals and all subscribing witnesses are deceased, reside out of state or at an unknown location or refuse to cooperate (NDCC 47-19-23 and 47-19-24).

The notarial certificate for a proof of execution by a subscribing witness must include the names and places of residence of all witnesses and "the substance of the evidence given by witnesses" (NDCC 47-19-25).

*** Verifications on Oath or Affirmation: "'Verification on oath or affirmation' means a declaration, made by an individual on oath or affirmation before a notarial officer, that a statement in a record is true" (NDCC 44-06.1-01[13]).

"Jurats are the authentication of a signature made under oath or affirmation. An oath or affirmation is administered to a document signer when the signer is required to make a sworn statement about certain facts. The signer personally appears before the notary to swear (or affirm) to the notary, an officer duly appointed to administer oaths, that the information contained in the document is true. A person who makes a false oath or affirmation is subject to criminal charges for perjury" (website, "Certifications").

A verification or jurat "should begin with the administration of an oath or affirmation. The notary may want to ask the signer 'Do you swear (or affirm) that the information contained in this document is true?' After receiving an affirmative answer and a signature on the document, the notary completes a proper notarial certificate indicating that an oath or affirmation was taken. A jurat is attached to an affidavit or other sworn statement which must be signed by the individual in front of the notary" (NN, July 2011).

**** Copy Certification: "A notarial officer who certifies or attests a copy of a record or an item that was copied shall determine that the copy is a full, true, and accurate transcription or reproduction of the record or item" (NDCC 44-06.1-04[4]).

"Copy certifications prove the notary compared the copy of a document with the original and the copy is a true, correct and complete copy of the original. Notaries are not authorized to certify a copy of a 'recordable document' such as birth and death certificates, recorded titles to property, college transcripts or anything bearing an official government seal" (website, "Certifications").

"A notary public may not make or purport to make any certified copy of a vital record, a recordable instrument, or a public record containing an official seal …" (NDCC 44-06.1-23[7]).

Identifying Document Signers

In taking an acknowledgment or a verification on oath or affirmation, or in witnessing or attesting a signature, a Notary "shall determine, from personal knowledge or satisfactory evidence of the identity of the individual, that the individual appearing before the officer … has the identity claimed" (NDCC 44-06.1-04[1] through [3]).

"1. A notarial officer has personal knowledge of the identity of an individual appearing before the officer if the individual is personally known to the officer through dealings sufficient to provide reasonable certainty that the individual has the identity claimed.

"2. A notarial officer has satisfactory evidence of the identity of an individual appearing before the officer if the officer can identify the individual:

"a. By means of: (1) A passport, driver's license, or government-issued nondriver identification card that is currently valid or expired not more than three years before performance of the notarial act; or (2) Another form of government identification issued to an individual that is currently valid or expired not more than three years before performance of the notarial act, contains the individual's signature or a photograph of the individual, and is satisfactory to the officer; or

"b. By a verification on oath or affirmation of a credible witness personally appearing before the officer and known to the officer or whom the officer can identify on the basis of a passport, driver's license, or government-issued nondriver identification card that is currently valid or expired not more than three years before performance of the notarial act" (NDCC 44-06.1-06).

"A notary's primary responsibility is to take necessary steps to verify a signer's identity before notarizing a signature. A notary public may not notarize a signature unless the notary personally knows, or has satisfactory evidence, that the person whose signature is to be notarized is the individual who is described in and who is executing the instrument. There are three ways to verify a signer's identity:

"Personal knowledge is the safest and best verification of a person's identity. It requires no witnesses or identification cards. It means having an acquaintance, derived from association with the individual, which establishes the individual's identity with at least a reasonable certainty.

"Credible witness is a third person that personally knows the document signer, and verifies the signer's identity. (Credible witness is for the purpose of identifying people who do not have identification. This does not replace the 'presence' requirement. The person whose signature is being notarized must be present at the time of notarization.)

"Identification card or papers are necessary in verifying the signer's identity. The notary should examine the photograph, accurate physical description, and signature of the bearer. Asking for two forms of ID can further assure the signer's identity.

"If a notary is uncomfortable or suspicious of any identification, the notary should not notarize for that person" (website, "Notary Responsibilities").

Notarizing Health Care Directives

"1. To be legally sufficient in this state, a health care directive must:
"a. Be in writing;
"b. Be dated;
"c. State the principal's name;
"d. Be executed by a principal with capacity to do so with the signature of the principal or with the signature of another person authorized by the principal to sign on behalf of the principal;
"e. Contain verification of the principal's signature or the signature of the person authorized by the principal to sign on behalf of the principal, either by a notary public or by witnesses as provided under this chapter; and
"f. Include a health care instruction or a power of attorney for health care, or both.

"2. A health care directive must be signed by the principal and that signature must be verified by a notary public or at least two or more subscribing witnesses who are at least eighteen years of age. A person notarizing the document may be an employee of a health care or long-term care provider providing direct care to the principal. At least one witness to the execution of the document must not be a health care or long-term care provider providing direct care to the principal or an employee of a health care or long-term care provider providing direct care to the principal on the date of execution. The notary public or any witness may not be, at the time of execution, the agent, the principal's spouse or heir, a person related to the principal by blood, marriage, or adoption, a person entitled to any part of the estate of the principal upon the death of the principal under a will or deed in existence or by operation of law, any other person who has, at the time of execution, any claims against the estate of the principal, a person directly financially responsible for the principal's medical care, or the attending physician of the principal. If the principal is physically unable to sign, the directive may be signed by the principal's name being written by some other person in the principal's presence and at the principal's express direction" (NDCC 23-06.5-05).

The certificate to be used by the Notary in such declarations is as follows (NDCC 23-06.5-17):

STATE OF NORTH DAKOTA   )
County of _____   )

In my presence on _____ (date), _____ (name of declarant) acknowledged the declarant's signature on this document or acknowledged that the declarant directed the person signing this document to sign on the declarant's behalf.

(NOTARY'S SIGNATURE AND STAMP)

Signature by Mark

"On rare occasions, a notary public may have to notarize the signature of a person who signs by way of mark.... The notary laws do not require any additional procedures for notarizing in these situations. However, some notaries prefer to take extra precautions by ... (questioning) the signer to make sure that they understand the nature and effect of the document to be signed. If the person is illiterate, read the document to him/her. If the person does not understand, do not notarize....

"Before the person signs the document, print their (first) name at the beginning of the signature line and the last name at the end of the line. Just below the line, print the words 'His Mark' or 'Her Mark'.... Then, ask the person to make his/her mark on the designated line.

"Complete the notarial certificate. When filling in the person's name whose signature is being notarized, (you) may want to indicate the person signed by way of mark.

"It is also recommended that (one or more) uninterested person(s) witness the signing of the document and the notarization and that their names and addresses be clearly printed under their signatures" (website, "Notary Responsibilities").

The website offers sample acknowledgment and jurat certificates for a signature by mark:

John   X   Doe
His Mark

(Signature of witness)
(Printed name and address of witness)

(Signature of witness)
(Printed name and address of witness)

STATE OF NORTH DAKOTA)
County of _____)

The foregoing instrument was acknowledged / sworn to (or affirmed) and subscribed before me this _____ day of _____, 20___, by John Doe, who signed by way of mark in the presence of this/these witness(es).

(NOTARY'S SIGNATURE AND STAMP)

Signing for Disabled Person

"If an individual is physically unable to sign a record, the individual may direct an individual other than the notarial officer to sign the individual's name on the record. The notarial officer shall insert 'Signature affixed by (insert name of other individual) at the direction of (insert name of individual)' or words of similar import" (NDCC 04-06.1-08).

"A notary public may ... be asked to notarize the signature of an individual with a disability who may direct another person to sign on their behalf.... A notary public may notarize this signature, but should indicate the unusual circumstances in the notarial certificate. Although notary laws do not provide specific guidelines for this situation, the notary may want to take precautions to prevent any problems" (website, "Notary Responsibilities").

The precautions suggested on the website include the following:

1. "Question the person to make sure they understand the nature and effect of the document to be signed. If the person is blind, read the entire document to them. If the person does not understand, do not notarize."

2. "Ask for proper identification from the person with the disability. It is not necessary to require identification from the designated signer."

3. Have "(t)he designated person ... sign the signature of the person with the disability at the direction of and in the presence of that person."

4. On the notarial certificate, "(w)hen stating whose signature is being notarized, it would be best to indicate the special circumstances."

5. "It is also recommended that (one or more) person(s), with no interest in the transaction, witness the signing of the document and the notarization and that (their) name(s) and address(es) be clearly printed below their signature(s)."

The website offers sample acknowledgment and jurat certificates for a signature by mark:

(Signature of person with disability)
By (name of person signing on
behalf of person with disability)

(Signature of witness)
(Printed name and address of witness)

(Signature of witness)
(Printed name and address of witness)

STATE OF NORTH DAKOTA)
County of _____)

The foregoing instrument was acknowledged / sworn to (or affirmed) before me this _____ day of _____, 20___, by (name of person with disability) and subscribed by (name of person signing on behalf of person with disability) in the presence and at the direction of (name of person with disability) and in the presence of this/these witness(es).

(NOTARY'S SIGNATURE AND STAMP)

Foreign-Language Documents

"If a notary is asked to notarize a document written in a foreign language, it must be accompanied by a permanently affixed and accurate written English translation…. Both documents must be properly notarized …" (NN, July 2011). Additionally, "both documents need to be signed and notarized in English" (NN, July 2010).

Advertising Notarial Services

Non-attorney Notaries who advertise or represent in any fashion that they offer notarial services — whether orally or in writing, including broadcast media, print media and the internet — must include the following statement, or an alternate statement authorized or required by the Secretary of State, in the advertisement or representation: "I am not an attorney licensed to practice law in this state. I am not allowed to draft legal records, give advice on legal matters, including immigration, or charge a fee for those activities."

The statement must appear prominently and in each language used in the advertisement or representation. If the form of advertisement or representation is not broadcast media, print media or the internet, and if it does not permit the inclusion of the statement because of size, then the statement must be prominently displayed at the Notary's place of business or otherwise provided to anyone requesting a notarial act before the act is performed (NDCC 44-06.1-23[4]).

Notary Musts

According to North Dakota statute and the Secretary of State, Notaries must abide by these rules, in addition to other express requirements:

1. Require the signer to personally appear before you (NN, July 2011).
2. Make sure the signer understands the document (website, "Certifications").
3. Make sure the signer has not been coerced into signing (website, "Certifications").
4. Never just sign and stamp a document (NN, July 2008).
5. Always scan the document for blanks (NN, July 2010).
6. Have a current commission posted before notarizing (NN, July 2010).

Personal Appearance: "If a notarial act relates to a statement made in or a signature executed on a record, the individual making the statement or executing the signature shall appear personally before the notarial officer" (NDCC 44-06.1-05).

Willingness and Awareness: "A notarial officer may refuse to perform a notarial act if the officer is not satisfied that: (a) The individual executing the record is competent or has the capacity to execute the record; or (b) The individual's signature is knowingly and voluntarily made" (NDCC 44-06.1-07[1]).

"The notary should ensure that the signer understands the document and has not been coerced into signing. If there is any question about the signer's willingness to execute the document or his/her understanding of the terms of the document, a notary should refuse to notarize" (website, "Certifications").

Signing and Stamping: "A notary should not just sign and affix his or her notary stamp to a document. It does not mean anything…. To have a complete legally recognized notarial act, (certificate wording) is required along with a venue. Without them, it does not establish when and where the notarization occurred and whether the notary had the authority to act in the place in which it occurred" (NN, July 2008).

If a venue and certificate wording "is not on the document being notarized, the notary is responsible for either writing or typing the information on the document. To just sign and stamp a document and consider it notarized could result in disciplinary action" (NN, July 2007).

Scanning for Blanks: North Dakota Notaries are now statutorily forbidden to notarize documents which have no text or have blank spaces in their text: "A notary public may not notarize a signature on a document if … (t)he signature is on a blank or incomplete document" (NDCC 44-06.1-23[6][h]).

"Always scan your document to be sure there are no blanks" (NN, July 2010).

Commission Posted: The Notary's commission must be posted in a "conspicuous place" in the Notary's office or place of employment (NDCC 44-06,1-20[5]).

Will May Be Acknowledged before Notary

An amendment to North Dakota's probate statutes that took effect August 1, 2009 — House Bill 1072 — permits a will to be acknowledged before a Notary or other officer authorized to take acknowledgments as an alternative to witnessing of the will by two persons (NDCC 30.1-08.02).

NOTARY DON'TS

A North Dakota Notary should (NDCC 44-06.1-23):
1. NOT assist in drafting legal records, give legal advice, practice law in any other way, advertise or represent that he or she is qualified to do so or receive compensation for doing so, unless the Notary is an attorney licensed to practice law in North Dakota;
2. NOT act as an immigration consultant or expert on immigration matters, represent someone in a judicial or administrative proceeding relating to immigration, advertise or represent that he or she is qualified to do so or receive compensation for doing so;
3. NOT engage in false or deceptive advertising;
4. NOT use the term "Notario" or "Notario Publico," unless the Notary is an attorney licensed to practice law in North Dakota;
5. NOT withhold access to or possession of any original record provided by an individual who seeks performance of a notarial act by that Notary;
6. NOT make or purport to make a certified copy of a vital record, a recordable instrument or a public record containing an official seal;
7. NOT use a false date of notarization;
8. NOT notarize a signature on a blank or incomplete document;
9. NOT notarize a non-English document unless an English translation is permanently affixed to the document.

Disqualifying Interests

No Conflict of Interest: A North Dakota Notary may not notarize a signature on a document if:
1. The name of the Notary or of the Notary's spouse appears on the document as a party to the transaction;
2. The Notary is a member of a partnership that is a party to the transaction;
3. The Notary or the Notary's spouse has a direct beneficial interest in the document;
4. The signature on the document is that of the Notary or of the Notary's spouse;
5. The Notary or the Notary's spouse is a signatory on an election petition under NDCC 1-01-50.

A notarial act performed in violation of any of the above is invalid or voidable (NDCC 44-06.1-23[6][b] and [c] and 47-19-33).

Since Notaries serve as impartial witnesses, they "must ask themselves two questions before notarizing a document:

"1. 'Am I a party to the transaction?' Or, 'Am I named in the document?'

"2. 'Do I have any financial or beneficial interest in this transaction?'

"If the answer to both of these questions is no, the notary is an impartial witness" (website, "What is a Notary Public?").

Should Not Notarize for Close Family: "A Notary should not notarize a document for close family members. Notarizing documents for parents, siblings, spouses, and other relatives opens an ethical can of worms for the Notary. In many cases, a close family relationship with a signer automatically brings beneficial interest ... (I)t is best to refer close family members to another Notary in order to avoid even the slightest appearance of bias" (NN, July 2008).

Corporate Status Not Disqualification: "No person otherwise qualified or authorized by law to take and receive the proof or acknowledgment of an instrument or affidavit and to certify thereto shall be disqualified by reason of being an officer, director, employee, or stockholder of any corporation or a manager, governor, employee, or member of any limited liability company which is a party to such instrument ..." (NDCC 47-19-34).

NOTARY SIGNING AGENTS

Currently, there are no statutes, regulations or rules expressly governing, prohibiting or restricting the operation of Notary Signing Agents within the state of North Dakota.

NOTARY FEES

"A notary public is entitled to charge and receive not more than five dollars per notarial act. A notary who charges a fee exceeding that amount is guilty of an infraction. It is an infraction for any person other than the notary public to impose or collect any monetary fee, charge, or commission in connection with the notarization of any document" (NDCC 44-06.1-28).

"Any officer authorized by law to take and certify acknowledgment of a deed or other instrument is entitled to charge and receive not more than five dollars" (NDCC 44-05-03).

Travel Fee Allowed

"A notary may charge a travel fee when traveling to perform a notarial act if:

"1. The notary and the person requesting the notarial act agree upon the travel fee in advance of the travel; and

"2. The notary explains to the person requesting the notarial act that the travel fee is both separate from the notarial fee and neither specified nor mandated by law" (NDCC 44-06.1-28).

NOTARY CERTIFICATES

North Dakota has adopted the *Revised Uniform Law on Notarial Acts*, including the short-form certificates (NDCC 44-06.1-19) for:
1. Acknowledgment by individual;
2. Acknowledgment in a representative capacity;
3. Verification on oath or affirmation;
4. Witnessing or attesting a signature;
5. Certifying a copy of a record.

For the text of these certificates, see "Revised Uniform Law on Notarial Acts (2010)," Section 16, in Appendix 1B.

North Dakota law additionally prescribes the following certificates:

Acknowledgment by Individual (NDCC 47-19-27):

STATE OF NORTH DAKOTA)
County of _____)

On this _____ day of _____, in the year 20___ before me personally appeared _____, known to me (or proved to me on oath of _____) to be the person(s) who is/are described in and who executed the within instrument, and acknowledged to me that he/she/they executed the same.

(NOTARY'S SIGNATURE AND STAMP)

Acknowledgment by Corporation (NDCC 47-19-28):

STATE OF NORTH DAKOTA)
County of _____)

On this _____ day of _____, in the year 20___ before me _____ (here insert the name and quality of the notarial officer), personally appeared _____, known to me (or proved to me on oath of _____) to be the president (or other officer or person) of the corporation that is described in and that executed the within instrument, and acknowledged to me that such corporation executed the same.

(NOTARY'S SIGNATURE AND STAMP)

Acknowledgment by Limited Liability Company (NDCC 47-19-28.1):

STATE OF NORTH DAKOTA)
County of _____)

On this _____ day of _____, in the year 20___ before me _____ (here insert the name and quality of the notarial officer), personally appeared _____, known to me (or proved to me on oath of _____) to be the president (or other manager or person) of the limited liability company that is described in and that executed the within instrument, and acknowledged to me that such limited liability company executed the same.

(NOTARY'S SIGNATURE AND STAMP)

Acknowledgment by Attorney in Fact (NDCC 47-19-29):

STATE OF NORTH DAKOTA)
County of _____)

On this _____ day of _____, in the year 20___ before me _____ (here insert the name and quality of the notarial officer), personally appeared _____, known to me (or proved to me on the oath of _____) to be the person who is described in and whose name is subscribed to the within instrument as the attorney in fact of _____, and acknowledged to me that he/she subscribed the name of _____ thereto as principal and his/her own name as attorney in fact.

(NOTARY'S SIGNATURE AND STAMP)

Acknowledgment by Deputy Sheriff (NDCC 47-19-30):

STATE OF NORTH DAKOTA)
County of _____)

On this _____ day of _____, in the year 20___ before me, a _____ in and for said county, personally appeared _____, known to me to be the person who is described in and whose name is subscribed to the within instrument as deputy sheriff of said county, and acknowledged to me that he/she subscribed the name of _____ thereto as sheriff of said county and his/her own name as deputy sheriff.

(NOTARY'S SIGNATURE AND STAMP)

Copy Certification (website, "Certifications"):

STATE OF NORTH DAKOTA)
County of _____)

On this _____ day of _____, 20___, I certify that the preceding/attached document is a true, exact. complete and unaltered photocopy made by _____ (custodian of original document or other person who made copy) of _____ (description of original document).

(NOTARY'S SIGNATURE AND STAMP)

Format for Notarial Certificate

"1. A notarial act must be evidenced by a certificate. The certificate must:

"a. Be executed contemporaneously with the performance of the notarial act;

"b. Be signed and dated by the notarial officer and, if the notarial officer is a notary public, be signed in the same manner as on file with the secretary of state;

"c. Identify the jurisdiction in which the notarial act is performed;

"d. Contain the title of office of the notarial officer; and

"e. Indicate the date of expiration, if any, of the notarial officer's commission, if the officer is a notary public.

"2. If a notarial act is performed by a notary public regarding a tangible record, the notary public's official stamp must be affixed to the certificate....

"3. A certificate of a notarial act is sufficient if it meets the requirements of subsections 1 and 2 and:

"a. Is in a short form set forth in section 44-06.1-19;

"b. Is in a form otherwise permitted by the law of this state;

"c. Is in a form permitted by the law applicable in the jurisdiction in which the notarial act was performed; or

"d. Sets forth the actions of the notarial officer and the actions are sufficient to meet the requirements of the notarial act as provided in sections 44-06.1-04, 44-06.1-05, and 44-06.1-06 or other law" (NDCC 44-06.1-14).

For certificate format for notarial acts involving electronic records, see "Electronic Notarizations" below.

Additional Requirements

"A notarial officer may not affix the officer's signature to ... a certificate until the notarial act has been performed....

"If a notarial act is performed regarding a tangible record, a certificate must be part of, or securely attached to, the record ..." (NDCC 44-06.1-14). The reference to a "securely attached" certificate means that so-called loose certificates are permitted in North Dakota.

"(T)he date of the notary commission's expiration date ... is on the official stamping device and ... does not have to be written separately on the (certificate) even if there is a space for it" (NN, July 2011).

For certificate requirements for notarial acts involving electronic records, see "Electronic Notarizations" below.

Notary Obeys Certificate Wording

"A notary is accountable for every word in the notarial certificate. A notary shall not notarize any document which does not have a complete notarial certificate on the document or on an attachment to the document.

"A notary should never assume a preprinted certificate complies with law, nor is it accurate or truthful. A notary should scrutinize the preprinted certificate for legality, accuracy and truthfulness.

"Notary certificates need not be typed or printed in order to be valid. They may be hand written in ink. The notary certificates need not be on the same page as the signature being notarized. If necessary, the notary should prepare the certificate on a separate page and attach it to the document on which the notarized signature appears. If the certificate is on a separate page (the notary) may want to add additional wording for extra security.

'This notary certificate is prepared on a separate page and is attached to the document entitled _____, containing _____ pages and is attached to that document by means of _____ (staple, glue, tape).'" (website, "Certifications").

Notary Does Not Select Certificate

"Even if the requester does not know what type of certificate of a notarial act is required, the notary should never, on behalf of the signer, select the notarial wording to be used.... (T)he notary may present the different types of statutory short forms available in NDCC § 44-06.1-19 and let the signer choose from among them. Or, the requester could be directed to contact the issuing or receiving agency or his or her attorney for further instructions" (NN, July 2011).

Correcting Certificates

"Do not permit anyone else to make corrections to a notarial certificate. Some companies and agencies, anticipating mistakes on a document, ask notaries to sign a statement giving them permission to correct errors made by the notary in completing the notarial certificate. While this may appear to be convenient, it is also dangerous and generally illegal" (NN, July 2007).

"If any line in the notarization block (the notarial certificate) is pre-filled, be sure to cross out any incorrect information, fill in the correct information and initial" (NN, July 2010).

"When the acknowledgment or proof of execution of an instrument is made properly but is defectively certified, any party interested may institute an action in the district court to obtain a judgment correcting the certificate" (NDCC 47-19-38).

Imperfect Acknowledgments Validated

"The execution, acknowledgment, filing, and recording of all deeds, leases, mortgages, assignments, satisfactions, and other written instruments affecting the title to real property in this state, in good faith made, taken, or certified, and which have been filed or recorded in the proper counties of this state for a period of five years or more, are declared to be legal and valid for all purposes, anything in the laws of this state, or of any other state, territory, or country at the time of execution, acknowledgment, filing, or recording to the contrary notwithstanding" (NDCC 1-04-01).

ELECTRONIC NOTARIZATIONS

With the passage of the *Revised Uniform Law on Notarial Acts* (RULONA), the state of North Dakota has adopted certain rules, definitions and procedures for electronic notarization in NDCC Chapter 44-06.1, which are not effective until August 1, 2013.

UETA Recognizes Notary's eSignature

North Dakota has adopted the Uniform Electronic Transactions Act (NDCC Title 9, Chapter 16, "Electronic Transactions"), including its standard provision on notarization and acknowledgment, thereby recognizing the legal validity of electronic signatures used by Notaries:

"If a law requires a signature or record to be notarized, acknowledged, verified, or made under oath, the requirement is satisfied if the electronic signature of the person authorized to perform those acts, together with all other information required to be included by other applicable law, is attached to or logically associated with the signature or record" (NDCC 9-16-10).

One or More Tamper-Evident Technologies

Effective August 1, 2013, Section 44-06.1-18 of the RULONA states:

"1. A notary public may select one or more tamper-evident technologies to perform notarial acts with respect to electronic records. An individual may not require a notary public to perform a notarial act with respect to an electronic record with a technology that the notary public has not selected.

"2. Before a notary public performs the notary public's initial act with respect to an electronic record, a notary public shall notify the secretary of state that the notary public will be performing notarial acts with respect to electronic records and identify the technology the notary public intends to use. If the secretary of state has established standards for approval of technology pursuant to section 44-06.1-25, the technology must conform to the standards. If the technology conforms to the standards, the secretary of state shall approve the use of the technology."

Electronic Notary Certificate Requirements

"If a notarial act is performed regarding an electronic record, the certificate must be affixed to, or logically associated with, the electronic record. If the secretary of state has established standards pursuant to section 44-06.1-25 for attaching, affixing, or logically associating the certificate, the process must conform to those standards" (NDCC 44-06.1-14[6]).

An electronic certificate of a notarial act is sufficient if it meets the requirements of NDCC 44-06.1-14(3) — see "Notary Certificates" above.

NOTE: The electronic provisions of Chapter 44-06.1 are effective August 1, 2013.

Electronic Notary Stamp Requirements

In reference to electronic records, statute defines stamping device as an "electronic device or process capable of attaching to or logically associating with an electronic record an official stamp" and defines official stamp as "an electronic image attached to or logically associated with an electronic record" (NDCC 44-06.1-01).

If an official electronic stamp is used, it must contain the same information as a physical stamp and "(b)e capable of being copied together with the record … with which it is logically associated" (NDCC 44-06.1-15).

NOTE: The electronic provisions of Chapter 44-06.1 are effective August 1, 2013.

Electronic Notary Signature Requirements

Statute defines electronic signature as "an electronic symbol, sound, or process attached to or logically associated with a record and executed or adopted by an individual with the intent to sign the record" (NDCC 44-06.1-01[3]).

"A notarial officer may not … logically associate (the officer's signature) with a certificate until the notarial act has been performed" (NDCC 44-06.1-14[5]).

NOTE: The electronic provisions of Chapter 44-06.1 are effective August 1, 2013.

NOTARY RECORDS

Journal Recommended by State

"A notary public is not required by law to maintain a notary journal. However, a notary journal does protect the notary and document signer from accusations of wrong doing and it prevents the notary from engaging in wrong doing.

"The journal documents that the notary took reasonable steps to verify the signer's identity. Every journal entry is legally presumed to be truthful and it constitutes the notary's personal knowledge of the notarization performed.

"If a notarized document is lost or altered, or if certain facts about the transaction are later challenged, the journal becomes valuable evidence that can both protect the rights of property owners and help notaries defend themselves against false accusations….

"If a notary decides to use a journal, the notary should use one that is permanently bound with pre-numbered empty spaces" (website, "Notary Journal").

Components of Entry

The Secretary of State recommends the following components for a journal entry recording the performance of a notarial act (website, "Notary Journal"):

1. The document signer's signature;
2. The date and time of notarization;
3. The date of the document;
4. The type of notarization performed;
5. The type of document notarized;
5. The document signer's address;
6. A statement on how the signature was verified (i.e., how the signer was identified);
7. Any comments about the transaction.

"The journal should be completed before notarizing each document. A new entry should be made in the notary journal for every notary service provided" (website, "Notary Journal").

Disposition of Notary's Records

"Whenever the office of any notary public becomes vacant, the record of the notary together with all papers relating to the office must be deposited in the office of the secretary of state...."

"Any notary public who, on resignation or removal from office, or any executor or personal representative of the estate of any deceased notary public who neglects to deposit the records and papers as aforesaid for the space of three months, or any person who knowingly destroys, defaces, or conceals any records or papers of any notary public, shall forfeit and pay a sum of not less than fifty dollars nor more than five hundred dollars, and that person also is liable in a civil action for damages to any party injured" (NDCC 44-06.1-17).

Records Go to Notary, Not Employer: "(A)ll of the notary's records ... follow the notary and must never be retained by an employer" (NN, July 2007).

AUTHENTICATION OF NOTARIAL ACTS

Secretary of State

Authenticating certificates for Notaries, including apostilles, are issued only by the North Dakota Secretary of State's office.

Fees: $10 per certificate or apostille.

Address:
Office of Secretary of State
Administrative/Licensing Division
600 E. Boulevard Avenue
Dept. 108, First Floor
Bismarck, ND 58505-0500

Telephone: 1-701-328-2901

Procedure: Mail or present in person the original notarized document, along with the fee. Include a letter indicating the country to which the document will be sent. The authenticated document will be returned by first class mail unless a prepaid and preaddressed envelope for expedited service is included. Persons wishing to verify the accuracy of a notarized document prior to submitting it should email or fax a copy of the document(s) to the Secretary of State at sosadlic@nd.gov or 701-328-1690 (website, "Notary Services").

COMMISSIONING AND ADMINISTRATION

The North Dakota Secretary of State appoints, commissions and maintains records on the state's Notaries (NDCC 44-06.1-01[7], 44-06.1-20 and 44-06.1-21).

Applying for Commission

Qualifications: An applicant for appointment as a North Dakota Notary Public must: be at least 18 years of age; be a citizen or permanent legal resident of the United States; either be a resident of North Dakota, have a place of employment or practice in North Dakota or reside in a county that borders North Dakota and that is in a state that extends reciprocity to Notaries who reside in such a North Dakota border county; be able to read and write English; and not be disqualified to receive a commission under NDCC 44-06.1-21(1) (NDCC 44-06.1-20[2]).

No Course or Test: No course of instruction or examination is required to become a Notary Public in North Dakota.

Application: On the application form, the applicant's signature on the "Affidavit of Qualifications and Oath of Office" must be notarized. The application must include a six-year $7,500 Notary bond "or its functional equivalent" and a $36 filing fee. On the bond form, the signatures of both the applicant and a representative of the surety company must be notarized. All forms related to the application process are available on the Secretary of State's website.

After receipt of the application, oath, bond and fee, the Secretary of State will issue to an applicant a certificate of authorization, which must be presented to a Notary stamp vendor in order to obtain an official Notary stamping device. The Notary must affix an impression of the new stamp on the certificate of authorization and then return it to the Secretary of State. After the certificate is approved and filed, a Notary commission will be issued to the applicant (NDCC 44-06.1-16). No notarizations may be performed until receipt of the commission and until the beginning date on the commission certificate (website, "How to Become a Notary Public").

"An impression of the stamping device must be received in the Secretary of State's office on or before the month and day listed in the authorization letter. The impression must be received in the Secretary of State's office before a certificate of commission can be issued. (The impression) cannot be accepted past the month and day listed in the authorization letter. Otherwise, a new authorization must be obtained and the applicant must purchase a new official notary stamping device with a new commission expiration date." The stamp impression may be mailed, faxes or scanned and emailed (NN, July 2010).

To initiate the renewal process, the Secretary will notify each Notary by mail at least 30 days before the Notary's term of office expires (NDCC 44-06.1-20[8]). According to the July 2010 edition of "Notary Notes," the Secretary of State's office sends renewal information to Notaries two months prior to their commission expiration date.

Non-Residents: If a North Dakota Notary resides out of state in a county bordering North Dakota, "that person by applying for a commission in this state appoints the secretary of state as the agent for service of process, for all purposes relating to notarial acts, including the receipt of correspondence relating to notarial acts" (NDCC 44-06.1-20[2]).

Changes of Status

If Notary Moves: "Each notary public issued a commission shall notify the secretary of state by mail within sixty days of any change of address," upon penalty of a $10 late fee (NDCC 44-06.1-20[9]).

Notaries who change their business or residence address to another location within North Dakota must submit a "Notary Change of Address/Resignation" form, which is available on the Secretary of State's website.

Notaries who change their residence address to a county bordering North Dakota in a state that extends reciprocity to such Notaries must also submit a "Notary Change of Address/Resignation" form.

Notaries who change their residence address to a location outside of North Dakota and its bordering counties and who do not maintain a place of employment or practice in North Dakota must resign their commission within 60 days. To do so, they may submit a "Notary Change of Address/Resignation" form (website, "Notary Address and/or Name Change").

If Notary Changes Name: "A notary who has legally changed the notary's name shall submit to the secretary of state a rider to the notary's surety bond stating both the old and new names, the effective date of the new name, and a ten dollar fee within sixty days of the name change. Upon receipt of the rider and fee the secretary of state shall issue a certificate of authorization that a notary public may use to obtain a new stamping device. Once the authorization is on file, the secretary of state shall issue a commission with the notary's new name. After notification to the secretary of state of the name change and until a new stamping device is obtained, the notary may continue to use the old stamping device but must sign any notarial certificate substantially as follows:

Notary public North Dakota
Formerly known and commissioned as
_____

My commission expires _____
Notary Seal" (NDCC 44-06.1-27).

In addition to the bond rider and $10 fee, Notaries who change their names must submit a "Notary Name Change/Notary Seal/Stamp Change" form, which is available on the Secretary of State's website. If a Notary fails to notify the Secretary of State of a name change within 60 days, a late fee of $10 may be imposed (website, "Notary Address and/or Name Change").

COUNTY CLERKS

In the state of North Dakota, county clerks have no involvement in the administration of the Notary Public program nor in the authentication of notarial acts.

OTHER NOTARIAL OFFICERS

Statewide Jurisdiction

Besides Notaries, the following officers have statewide jurisdiction to perform all authorized notarial acts: a judge, clerk or deputy clerk of any court of this state (NDCC 44-06.1-09[1][b]).

Limited Jurisdiction

Oaths and Affirmations: The following officers

may only administer oaths and affirmations and may do so only under the indicated circumstances, if any (NDCC 44-05-01):

1. The county auditor, the recorder and the deputy of each such officer within that officer's county;
2. The county commissioner and public administrator within that officer's county;
3. The city auditor, municipal judge and township clerk within that officer's city or township;
4. The sheriff and deputy sheriff within the sheriff's county in the cases prescribed by law.

Acknowledgments and Proofs: The following officers may only take acknowledgments and proofs and may do so only within the districts for which they were elected or appointed (NDCC 47-19-14):

1. A mayor of a city;
2. A recorder;
3. A county justice;
4. A U.S. commissioner;
5. A county auditor;
6. A township clerk or city auditor

When any of the above officers are authorized by law to appoint deputies, "the acknowledgment or proof may be taken by such deputy in the name of his principal as deputy, or by such deputy as deputy" (NDCC 47-19-18).

"The signature and title of an individual performing a notarial act in this state are prima facie evidence that the signature is genuine and that the individual holds the designated title" (NDCC 44-06.1-09[2]).

QUICK FACTS

Notary Jurisdiction
Statewide (NDCC 44-05-01[4] and 47-19-13).

May Act in Other States: A North Dakota Notary may perform a notarial act in another state if that state recognizes the Notary's authority within that state (NDCC 47-19-55 and 44.06.1-20[7]).

Notary Term Length
Six years (NDCC 44-06.1-20[5]), expiring at midnight on the commission expiration date (NN, July 2011).

Notary Bond
$7,500, with a surety or other entity licensed or authorized to do business in the state. This "assurance" must be in the form of a surety bond "or its functional equivalent" (NDCC 44-06.1-20[4]). The surety must inform the Secretary of State of any claim against the Notary's bond.

N

Northern Marianas

NOTARY SEAL

A Commonwealth Notary must authenticate all official acts with a seal of office (4 CMC 3322[a]), and the seal's format must be as follows (AGR 3-101[10] and 4-203[a]):

Kind

Rubber Stamp or Embosser: "Every notary public shall keep a seal of office, which may be a rubber stamp or impression seal ..." (4 CMC 3322[a]).

"Near the notary's official signature on a notarial certificate, the notary shall affix in black ink a sharp, legible, and photographically reproducible impression of the notarial seal or stamp ..." (AGR 4-203[a][4]).

Shape/Size

Rectangular; or circular, no larger than 2 inches. The border must surround all required wording (AGR 4-203[a][4]).

Components

The Notary's official seal of office must contain the following (4 CMC 3322[a]):

1. Name of Notary exactly as on commission;
2. "Notary Public";
3. "Commonwealth of the Northern Mariana Islands";
4. Address of Notary's business or residence*;
5. "My commission expires _____ (commission expiration date)"*.

* Required by AGR 4-203(a)(2) and (3) but not by 4 CMC 3322.

```
JANE Q. DOE
NOTARY PUBLIC
Commonwealth of the
Northern Mariana Islands
1234 Main St., Saipan, MP 96950
My Commission Expires Jan. 30, 2014
```

Example

The above typical, actual-size example of a rectangular inking seal is allowed by Commonwealth law. Formats other than this, including circular formats, may also be permitted.

Embosser May Additionally Be Used

"An embossed seal impression that is not photographically reproducible may be used in addition to but not in lieu of the seal or stamp described in subsection (a)" (AGR 4-203[c]).

Illegible Information in Seal

"Illegible information within a seal impression may be typed or printed legibly by the notary adjacent to but not within the impression" (AGR 4-203[b]).

NOTARY ADMINISTRATION

Commonwealth of Northern Mariana Islands
Office of Attorney General 1-670-664-2341
Administration Bldg., Box 10007
Capital Hill
Saipan, MP 96950

Website: www.cnmigov.mp/government.php

NOTARY RULES

CMC — COMMONWEALTH OF MARIANAS CODE
AGR — ATTORNEY GENERAL REGULATIONS

Most Notary rules are in:

a. Commonwealth of Marianas Code, Title 4, Div. 3, Chapter 3, "Notaries Public";

b. Attorney General Regulations, published in Commonwealth Register, Vol. 14. No. 09, September 15, 1992, and adopted pursuant to 4 CMC 3312*.

* The Regulations are the National Notary Association's *Model Notary Act* of 1984, adopted with minor modifications.

Seal May Not Be Surrendered

"A notary shall keep an official notarial seal or stamp that is the exclusive property of the notary and that may not be used by any other person nor may it be surrendered to an employer upon termination of employment" (AGR 4-202[b]).

Obtaining a Seal

A Notary seal vendor may not provide a seal to a Notary unless the Notary presents a photocopy of the commission and a notarized declaration (or a copy of a "Confirmation of Notary's Name Change" from the Attorney General), which the vendor must retain for five years (AGR 4-204). A vendor's failure to follow these rules may result in a $100 civil penalty.

Seal Impression Must Be Filed

"Each person appointed and commissioned a notary public shall forthwith file a literal or photostatic copy of his or her commission, an impression of his or her seal and a specimen of his official signature with the clerk of the Commonwealth Superior Court and the Attorney General" (4 CMC 3314[a]).

Wrongful Possession of Seal

"Any person who knowingly obtains, conceals, defaces, or destroys the seal, journal, or official records of a notary is guilty of a crime as set out in 4 CMC 3317" (AGR 6-302).

Loss or Theft of Seal

"Within 10 days after the loss, destruction or theft of an Official Journal or seal, the notary shall deliver to the Attorney General by hand delivery, certified mail or other means providing a receipt, a signed affidavit of loss, destruction or theft, and inform the appropriate law enforcement agency in the case of theft" (AGR 7-103).

Upon Resignation, Expiration or Removal

"Upon resignation, death, expiration of term of office, removal from or abandonment of office, or change in residence from the Commonwealth, the notary public shall immediately deliver his or her seal to the Attorney General, who shall deface or destroy it. By failing for 60 days to comply with the above requirement, the notary public, or the notary's executor or administrator, shall forfeit to the Commonwealth not more than $500, in the discretion of the court, to be recovered in an action to be brought by the Attorney General on behalf of the Commonwealth" (4 CMC 3322[b]).

Official Signature

"In completing a notarial act, a notary shall sign on the notarial certificate exactly and only the name indicated on the notary's commission and seal" (AGR 4-201).

NOTARY POWERS

Commonwealth Notaries are authorized to perform the following notarial acts (4 CMC 3321 and AGR 3-101):

1. Take acknowledgments* and proofs;
2. Administer oaths and affirmations;
3. Execute jurats**;
4. Certify copies***;
5. Take depositions and affidavits****;
6. Present and protest commercial paper.

* <u>Acknowledgments</u>: An acknowledgment is "a notarial act in which a notary certifies that a signer, whose identity is personally known to the notary or proven on the basis of satisfactory evidence, has admitted, in the notary's presence, having signed a document voluntarily for its stated purpose" (AGR 1-105[1]).

** <u>Jurats</u>: A jurat is "a notarial act in which a notary certifies that a signer, whose identity is personally known to the notary or proven on the basis of satisfactory evidence, has made, in the notary's presence, a voluntary signature and taken an oath or affirmation vouching for the truthfulness of the signed document" (AGR 1-105[4]).

*** <u>Copy Certifications</u>: A copy certification "is a notarial act in which a notary certifies having made a photocopy of a document that is neither a public record nor publicly recordable" (AGR 1-105[3]).

"A notary is empowered ... when requested and upon payment of their fees therefor, to make and give a certified copy of any record in their office" (AGR 3-101[8]).

"Every notary public shall record in a book of records all acts, protests, depositions, and other things noted or done in his or her official capacity. All copies or certificates granted by the notary public shall be under the notary's hand and seal, and shall be received as evidence of the transactions" (4 CMC 3323).

**** Failure to Administer Affidavit Oath: "No notary public shall certify to the affidavit of a person without personally administering the oath or affirmation to such person. Such act shall constitute grounds for removal from office by the Attorney General. A notary public so removed from office shall be ineligible for a subsequent appointment" (AGR 3-107).

Identifying Signers

Personal knowledge of identity "means familiarity with an individual resulting from interactions with that individual over a period of time sufficient to eliminate every reasonable doubt that the individual has the identity claimed" (AGR 1-105[10]).

Satisfactory evidence of identity "means identification of an individual based on: (i) at least 2 current documents, including those issued by a government with the individual's photograph, signature and physical description, and the other by an institution, business entity, or federal or state government with at least the individual's signature; or (ii) the oath or affirmation of a credible person who is personally known to the notary and who personally knows the individual" (AGR 1-105[11]).

Proof by Subscribing Witness Banned

Though 4 CMC 3321 specifies "receiv(ing) proof" as a notarial power, the Notary's authority to take proofs through a subscribing witness was intentionally omitted from the Regulations by the Attorney General, who noted, "(W)e agree that notarizations of absent party signatures by way of a subscribing witness are inherently unreliable and should not be authorized in these regulations.

"The proper procedure in case of proof of the signature of an absent party would be for the subscribing witness to sign a declaration or affidavit under penalty of perjury, attesting to the validity of his or her own signature if subscribed on the document in question, or to the validity of the absent person and setting forth facts supporting this assertion. Such a declaration, if properly notarized, could be separately recorded. In the case of land transactions, the public will now be able to make its own assessment of the validity of the absent person's signature and will place on the subscribing witness possible liability for slander of title. This modification of the proposed regulations frees the notary from unintentional involvement in absent party signature fraud by requiring that notaries only attest to signatures of persons actually appearing before them" (Commonwealth Register, Vol. 14, No. 09, Page 9640, September 15, 1992).

NOTARY DON'TS

Notary May Not

A Notary of the Commonwealth of the Northern Mariana Islands may:

1. NOT influence a person to enter into or not enter into a lawful transaction involving a notarial act by the Notary (AGR 3-103[a]);
2. NOT refuse to notarize in a lawful transaction for any person who tenders the appropriate fee (AGR 3-103[b]);
3. NOT execute any certificate containing a statement known by the Notary to be false, or execute any certificate, form or document which is not completely filled out, including the proper date and signatures, or perform any official act with intent to deceive or defraud (AGR 3-104);
4. NOT endorse or promote any product, service, contest or other offering if the Notary's title or seal is used in the endorsement or promotional statement (AGR 3-105);
5. NOT make representations to have powers, qualifications, rights or privileges that the office of Notary does not possess, including the power to counsel on immigration or other legal matters (AGR 3-106[c]);
6. NOT advertise or use the term "Notary Public" or any equivalent non-English term in any business card, advertisement, notice or sign in any manner that is misleading, deceptive, fraudulent or untrue (AGR 3-106[e]);
7. NOT advertise notarial services in a language other than English without including in the ad, notice or sign in addition to an English-language translation the following, in the same foreign language: the statutory maximum fees for notarial acts specified in Section 3-201(a) and the statement, prominently displayed: "I am not an attorney and have no authority to give advice on immigration or other legal matters" (AGR 3-106[d]).

Unauthorized Practice of Law

"A non-attorney notary may complete but may not select notarial certificates, and may not assist another person in drafting, completing, selecting, or understanding a document or transaction requiring a notarial act .... This section does not preclude a notary who is duly qualified in a particular profession from giving advice relating to matters in that professional field and charging separate professional fees for advice unrelated to his notarial services" (AGR 3-106).

Disqualifications

A Notary is disqualified from performing a notarial act if the Notary (AGR 3-102):

1. Is a signer of or named in the document that is to be notarized;

2. Will receive directly or indirectly from a transaction connected with the notarial act any commission, fee, advantage, right, title, interest, cash, property or other consideration exceeding in value the statutory maximum fees specified in Section 3-201;

3. Is related to the person whose signature is to be notarized as a spouse, brother, sister, parent or child.

<u>Attorneys May Notarize for Clients</u>: "Nothing in subsection 3-102(2) shall prevent any attorney who is a notary, from performing any notarial act done in the course and scope of the attorney's practice of law or the employee's employment, and nothing in this subsection shall prevent an attorney from collecting attorneys fees in any transaction in which the attorney or employee also provides notarial services, provided that no notarial act shall be valid if the notary has a direct or indirect personal monetary interest, other than for attorneys fees and costs, in the subject matter or proceeds of the transaction" (AGR 3-102[4]).

NOTARY SIGNING AGENTS

Currently, there are no statutes, regulations or rules expressly governing, prohibiting or restricting the operation of Notary Signing Agents within the Commonwealth of the Northern Mariana Islands.

NOTARY FEES

The following are maximum fees for notarial acts (4 CMC 3325 and AGR 3-201):

1. Taking an acknowledgment: $2 for each person signing; plus $2 for affixing a certificate to each duplicate original;

2. Administering an oath or affirmation, including certificate: $2; plus $1 for affixing a certificate of oath or affirmation to each duplicate original;

3. Executing a deposition or an official certificate: $2 each;

4. Certifying a copy: $2 per certificate;

5. Noting protest of mercantile paper: $2; each notice and certified copy of protest of mercantile paper: $2; noting a protest of other than mercantile paper: $4; each notice and certified copy of other than mercantile paper: $4.

Photocopies of Journal

A Notary may charge no more than 50 cents per photocopy for requested copies of journal entries (AGR 4-104). For a certified copy of journal information, the Notary may charge $2 per certificate (AGR 3-201).

Travel Fee

A Notary may charge a "reasonable" travel fee when traveling within the Commonwealth to perform a notarial act if: a) the Notary first explains to the person requesting the notarial act that the travel fee is separate from the notarial fee and is neither specified nor mandated by law; and b) the Notary and the person requesting the notarial act agree upon the travel fee in advance (AGR 3-201).

No Contingent or Percentage Fee

"A notary may not request, seek or receive any contingent fee or, as a notary fee, any amount based on a percentage of the value of any transaction which he is authenticating" (AGR 3-201).

No Fee by Government Notary

No fees may be charged by Notaries commissioned for and employed by government agencies when their bond and commissioning fees are waived (AGR 2-301).

"A notary public who is also a paid employee of the United States, or the Commonwealth government who is permitted to perform services as a notary public during working hours may not demand or receive any fees for services performed as a notary public during such hours, or for such services performed at any other time which are in connection with or in aid of his or her regular employment" (4 CMC 3326).

Overcharging

A Notary's overcharging constitutes official misconduct and is grounds for removal from office by the Attorney General (AGR 3-108[a]).

"(F)or violations of Section 3325, the Attorney General may, on findings of guilt based on a preponderance of the evidence and after a hearing, impose a fine not to exceed $500, plus the amount of the overcharge" (4 CMC 3317[c]).

Fees Must Be Posted

"Notaries shall maintain and have available for inspection an English language schedule of fees for notarial acts, as specified in Section 3-201(a). No part of any displayed notarial fee schedule may be printed in smaller than 10-point type" (AGR 3-202).

No Fees in Certain Commonwealth Offices

Under 4 CMC 3327, Commonwealth residents have access to free notarial services in certain offices of the Commonwealth government: (a) Saipan Higher Education Financial Assistance Board; (b) CNMI Scholarship Office; (c) Marianas Hawaii Liaison Office; (d) CNMI Liaison Office, Guam; (e) Rota Municipal Scholarship Foundation Office; (f) Office of the Tinian and Aguiguan Municipal Scholarship Board; and (g) United States House Representative for the CNMI in Washington, D.C.

NOTARY CERTIFICATES

A Notary must use a certificate in substantially the following form in notarizing the signature or mark of persons acknowledging for themselves or as partners, corporate officers, attorneys in fact or in other representative capacities.

General Acknowledgment (AGR 5-101):

Commonwealth of the Nor. Mariana Islands (Island)

On this _____ day of _____, 20___, before me, the undersigned Notary, personally appeared _____, (personally known to me) (proved to me through government-issued documentary evidence in the form of _____) (proved to me on the oath or affirmation of _____, who is personally known to me,) to be the person(s) whose name(s) (is) (are) signed on the preceding or attached document, and acknowledged to me that (he)(she)(they) signed it voluntarily for its stated purpose(.)

(as partner for _____, a partnership.)
(as _____ for _____, the principal.)
(as _____ for _____, a/the _____.)
(by mark before _____ and _____, subscribing witnesses.)

(OFFICIAL SIGNATURE AND SEAL OF NOTARY)

Certified Copy Certificate (AGR 5-104):

Commonwealth of the Nor. Mariana Islands (Island)

On this _____ day of _____, 20___, I certify that the preceding or attached are true, exact, complete, and unaltered photocopies made by me of _____ (description of document), (presented to me by the document's custodian, _____,) (held in my custody as a notarial record,) and that, to the best of my knowledge, the photocopied document is neither a public record nor a publicly recordable document, certified copies of which are available from an official source other than a Notary.

(OFFICIAL SIGNATURE AND SEAL OF NOTARY)

ELECTRONIC NOTARIZATIONS

The Commonwealth of the Northern Mariana Islands has not yet adopted statutes or regulations expressly establishing rules, definitions and procedures for electronic notarization.

Online Webcam Notarization Is Illegal

On July 7, 2011, the Attorney General of the Commonwealth issued a warning that "online webcam notarization" is invalid and illegal in the Northern Marianas Islands.

The AG warned that a private company sent out misleading information and made false claims to CNMI Notaries about a new purported online notarization service. The web-based platform is claimed to allow a document signer to submit copies of identification over the Internet and to use a webcam in lieu of personal appearance before the Notary.

The Attorney General pointed out that CNMI law requires a signer to be physically present before the Notary at the time of the notarial act, and that a video image or other non-physical representation does not constitute personal appearance.

NOTARY RECORDS

"Every notary public shall record in a book of records all acts, protests, depositions, and other things noted or done in his or her official capacity" (4 CMC 3323). "A notary shall keep, maintain, protect as a public record, and provide for lawful inspection a chronological, permanently bound official journal of notarial acts, containing numbered pages" (AGR 4-101).

Required Entries

For every notarial act, the Notary must record in the journal at the time of notarization at least the following information (AGR 4-102):

1. Date and time of day of notarial act;
2. Type of notarial act;
3. Description of document or proceeding;
4. Signature, printed name and address of each person for whom notarial act is performed (AGR 4-103[1]);
5. Evidence of identity of above person(s), in the form of either: "personally known"; or description of ID card, with its issuing agency, serial number and date of issuance or expiration; or name, signature and address of a credible witness swearing or affirming to person's identity (AGR 4-103[2]);
6. Fee charged, if any;
7. Address where notarization was performed, if not Notary's business address;
8. If applicable, circumstances of Notary's refusal to perform or complete a notarial act;
9. If applicable, signature of two witnesses to signing by mark (AGR 4-103[4]).

Inspection, Copying of Journal

"A journal of notarial acts is an official public record that may be inspected in the notary's presence by any individual whose identity is personally known to the notary or proven on the basis of satisfactory evidence, who specifies the notarial act sought, and who signs the notary's journal" (AGR 4-104[a]).

"All copies or certificates granted by the notary public shall be under the notary's hand and seal, and shall be received as evidence of the transactions" (4 CMC 3323).

"Upon request in compliance with subsection (a), the notary shall provide a photocopy of an entry in the journal at a cost of not more than fifty ($.50) cents per photocopy. If a certified copy is requested, the additional cost is as specified in Section 3-201" (AGR 4-104[b]).

Journal Must Be Safeguarded

"A notary shall safeguard the journal and all other notarial records as valuable public documents and never destroy them, except at the direction of the Office of the Attorney General" (AGR 4-104[c]).

"The journal must be kept in the exclusive custody of the notary, and may not be used by any other notary or surrendered to an employer upon termination of employment" (AGR 4-104[d]).

Loss or Theft of Journal

"Within 10 days after the loss, destruction or theft of an Official Journal or seal, the notary shall deliver to the Attorney General by hand delivery, certified mail or other means providing a receipt, a signed affidavit of loss, destruction or theft, and inform the appropriate law enforcement agency in the case of theft" (AGR 7-103).

<u>Wrongful Possession</u>: "Any person who knowingly obtains, conceals, defaces, or destroys the seal, journal, or official records of a notary is guilty of a crime as set out in 4 CMC 3317" (AGR 6-302).

Disposal of Journal

"The records of each notary public shall be deposited with the Attorney General each year on June 30 and upon the resignation, death, expiration of term of office, removal from or abandonment of office, or change of residence from the Commonwealth" (4 CMC 3324). For failing to comply with this section within 60 days, the Notary or his or her executor or administrator may be fined $100 to $500.

"Upon resignation, revocation, or expiration of a notarial commission, or death of the notary, the notarial journal and records must be delivered by hand delivery, certified mail or other means providing a receipt to the Office of the Attorney General in accordance with these Regulations. Failure to do so may result in a civil penalty assessment of a maximum of two hundred ($200.00) dollars to the former notary or his estate" (AGR 4-104[e]). Delivery of the journal and records must be made within 60 days after the effective date of the resignation, revocation or expiration (AGR 7-105[a] and 4 CMC 3322[b]).

"A former notary who intends to apply for a new commission and whose previous commission or application was not revoked or denied need not deliver the journal and records within 30 days after commission expiration, but must do so within 3 months after expiration unless recommissioned within that period" (AGR 7-105[b]).

AUTHENTICATION OF NOTARIAL ACTS

Clerk of Commonwealth Trial Court

"Each person appointed and commissioned a notary public shall forthwith file a literal or photostatic copy of his or her commission, an impression of his or her seal and a specimen of his official signature with the clerk of the Commonwealth Superior Court and the Attorney General. Thereafter, the Attorney General, when so requested, shall certify to the official character and acts of any notary public whose commission, impression of seal and specimen of official signature is filed in the Office of the Attorney General" (4 CMC 3314[a]).

Attorney General

Authenticating certificates for Notaries, including apostilles, are issued by the Commonwealth Attorney General's office (AGR 8-101, 8-102 and 8-103).

Fee: None.

Address:
Commonwealth of the Northern
 Mariana Islands
Office of Attorney General
Administration Bldg., Box 10007
Capital Hill
Saipan, MP 96950

Telephone: 1-670-664-2341

Procedure: Commonwealth officials indicate that authentication may be requested only by walk-ins and not through the mail. They say there is no charge if the document is brought in during normal business hours.

COMMISSIONING AND ADMINISTRATION

The office of the Attorney General appoints, commissions, regulates and keeps records on the Commonwealth's Notaries (4 CMC 3311 and 1 CMC 2153).

Applying for Commission

Qualifications: An applicant for a commission as a Northern Marianas Notary Public must (4 CMC 3313[a]): (a) be at least 18 years old, (b) be of good character and (c) be a resident of the Commonwealth or a U.S. citizen who is a resident of and employed by the U.S. government in the Commonwealth or employed by a contractor engaged in work for the U.S. government in the Commonwealth.

No Course or Test: No course of instruction or test is required of applicants for a Notary Public commission in the Commonwealth of the Northern Marianas.

Application: The application to the Attorney General must be accompanied by two letters of recommendation and an application fee in an amount set by regulation by the Attorney General (4 CMC 3313[a]). The fee set by such regulation is $25 (AGR 2-204).

Oath Must Be Taken, Signed, Filed: Every person appointed as a notary public shall, before acting in that capacity, take and subscribe to an oath for the faithful discharge of his or her duties. The oath may be taken before the Attorney General, a judge, a clerk of courts or other official authorized to administer oaths. This oath shall be executed in duplicate. The original shall be filed in the office of the Attorney General and a duplicate original filed in the office of the clerk of court for the Commonwealth Superior Court" (4 CMC 3313[b]).

"Each person appointed and commissioned a notary public shall forthwith file a literal or photostatic copy of his or her commission, an impression of his or her seal and a specimen of his official signature with the clerk of the Commonwealth Superior Court and the Attorney General" (4 CMC 3314[a]).

"The Office of the Attorney General shall charge a fee of fifty dollars for filing each certificate of authentication. The clerk of the Superior

Court shall charge a fee of one dollar for filing a copy of a commission" (4 CMC 3314[b]).

Governmental Employee Notaries: "The Attorney General may commission any number of governmental employees to act as notaries, but notaries so empowered may perform notarial acts only in service of their respective governmental agencies" (AGR 2-301). (Note: If pending legislation, HB 16-268, is enacted in 2010, all Notaries – even government-employed Notaries – would have to provide notarial services to any member of the public upon request.) Government-employed Notaries are commissioned for a two-year term, carry no bond, charge no fees and are commissioned at the Commonwealth's expense. Their commission application must include "a written declaration signed by the applicant's governmental employer stating that the commissioning is in the public interest"; the signer of this declaration may have knowledge of the Notary's whereabouts.

Changes of Status

If Notary Moves: "Within 30 days after the change of a notary's business or residence address, the notary shall deliver to the Attorney General by hand delivery, certified mail or other means providing a receipt, a signed notice of the change, giving both old and new addresses" (AGR 7-101).

"Upon any change in office, occupation or employment, a notary shall forthwith report the change to the Attorney General" (4 CMC 3311[c]).

If Notary Changes Name: The Notary must notify the Attorney General in writing of any name change, and may only begin notarizing using the new name upon receiving a "Confirmation of Notary's Name Change" and obtaining a new seal (AGR 7-102).

If Notary Resigns: The Notary who resigns must notify the Attorney General in writing, indicating an effective date of resignation (AGR 7-104). "Notaries who cease to reside or work in, or for, this Commonwealth or who become physically incapacitated such that they are unable to read or write shall resign their commissions."

If Notary Dies: If a Notary dies, an heir or personal representative, "as soon as reasonably practicable," must notify the Attorney General in writing, also delivering the seal, journal and records (AGR 7-106).

QUICK FACTS

Notary Jurisdiction
All islands and waters of the Commonwealth (AGR 2-102 and 4 CMC 3321).

Notarizing outside Islands: "A notary has no authority and may not perform any notarial act outside the geographical territory of the Commonwealth. Any notarial act so performed shall be null, void and of no effect" (AGR 3-203).

Notary Term Length
Two years (4 CMC 3311[b] and AGR 2-102).

Notarizing beyond Expiration Date: "A person who has been appointed and commissioned as a Notary Public and who performs any act as such after expiration of his term of office shall be ineligible for a subsequent appointment, unless the Attorney General is satisfied that such act was inadvertent or otherwise explainable" (AGR 2-105).

Notary Bond
$1,000, with a licensed surety and filed with the Attorney General (4 CMC 3315 and AGR 2-103). No bond is required for government employee Notaries (AGR 2-301).

Employer's Liability: "An employer of a notary is liable to any person for all damages proximately caused that person by the notary's official misconduct in performing a notarization related to the employer's business, if the employer directed, encouraged, consented to, or approved the notary's misconduct, either in the particular transaction or, impliedly, by previous actions in at least one similar transaction subject to similar employer conduct" (AGR 6-101[c]).

Ohio

NOTARY SEAL

Before performing any notarial act, an Ohio Notary is required to have a seal of office (ORC 147.04). The seal's format must be as follows:

Kind

Inked Stamp or Embosser: "The seal may be of either a type that will stamp ink onto a document or one that will emboss it" (ORC 147.04).

Shape/Size

Circular with, in the center, the state coat of arms within a circle 1 inch in diameter, surrounded by the required wording (ORC 147.04). The state coat of arms is described in ORC 5.04.

Examples

The above typical, actual-size examples of Notary seals are allowed by Ohio law. Formats other than these may also be allowed.

NOTARY ADMINISTRATION

The Ohio Secretary of State is the appointing, commissioning and record-keeping authority for Ohio's Notaries. However, Notary application procedures and disciplinary standards are still largely set and enforced by the county courts of common pleas, which screen and endorse each qualified Notary commission applicant in their respective counties. In many counties, the local bar association also plays a role in commissioning Notaries.

Office of Secretary of State
Ohio Notary Commission   1-614-644-4559
P.O. Box 1658   1-614-466-2566
Columbus, OH 43216-1658

(180 E. Broad St., Suite 103
Columbus, OH 43215)

Website: www.sos.state.oh.us/SOS/
recordsIndexes/Notary.aspx

NOTARY RULES

ORC — Ohio Revised Code
INCN — Information for Newly Commissioned Notaries Public
HNP — A Handbook and Notarial Journal for Notaries Public

Most Notary rules are in the Ohio Revised Code, Title 1, Chapter 147 ("Notaries Public"), which includes the "Uniform Recognition of Acknowledgments Act."*

* This is the *Uniform Recognition of Acknowledgments Act* of 1968, adopted as ORC Sections 147.51 through 147.58.

"Information for Newly Commissioned Notaries Public" is published by the Secretary of State and may be downloaded from the Secretary's website.

Other guidelines for Ohio Notaries are in "A Handbook and Notarial Journal for Notaries Public" (Jan. 2008), published by the Franklin County Common Pleas Court and Columbus Bar Association and referred to around the state. Bar groups and courts of other counties may also issue guidebooks for local Notaries and/or have pertinent information available on their websites.

Components

1. State coat of arms within a 1-inch diameter circle surrounded by the following words:
2. "Notary Public" or "Notarial Seal" or words to that effect;
3. Name of Notary*;
4. "State of Ohio."

* "The name of the notary public may, instead of appearing on the seal, be printed, typewritten, or stamped in legible, printed letters near (the notary public's) signature on each document signed by (the notary)" (ORC 147.04).

Commission Expiration Date Must Appear

"(T)he notary must ... write, type or stamp the expiration date of his or her commission on each document notarized. Most notaries satisfy (all) the above requirements by purchasing a stamp containing their name, the words 'Notary Public, State of Ohio' and the expiration date of their commission" (HNP, p. 10). Below is an example of such a stamp.

Richard A. Roe
Notary Public, State of Ohio
My Commission Expires Jan. 30, 2016

Seal Placement on Recorded Documents

Strict formatting rules for documents that will be recorded with Ohio county recorders went into effect July 1, 2009. On such documents, margins on pages other than the first must be 1 inch on the sides and bottom of the page and 1$\frac{1}{2}$ inches on the top of the page. For any failure to adhere to these rules, the recorder may charge an additional fee of $20 per document. An impression of a Notary's official seal and/or other commission-related information that protrudes into the margin could result in such a fee (ORC 317.114[A][6], [7] and [9] and 317.114[B][1]).

Failure to Affix Notary Seal

"A notary public is an officer of the State of Ohio and has the authority and the duty to use an official seal. Ohio law provides that a notary public must have a notary public seal before performing notarial acts, and it is common practice for notaries to use a seal when performing their duties. However, an instrument which has been notarized without a seal being affixed is still valid, provided that all of the other requirements are met" (HNP, p. 9). See also ORC 5301.071(B) concerning instruments that convey real estate or an interest therein.

Seal of Veterans' Affairs Commissioners

The seal of a veterans' affairs commissioner is identical to the Notary seal, except it bears the words "Commissioner of the State of Ohio for Veterans' Affairs" instead of "Notary Public" and "State of Ohio." This seal should only be affixed on documents used in connection with or before the veterans' administration (ORC 147.32).

NOTARY POWERS

Ohio Notaries are authorized to perform the following notarial acts:

1. Take acknowledgments* (ORC 147.07 and 147.51);
2. Administer oaths** and affirmations (ORC 147.07 and 147.51);
3. Take affidavits*** (ORC 147.08 and 147.14);
4. Take depositions**** (ORC 147.07);
5. Receive, make and record protests (ORC 147.07 and 147.09).

* Acknowledgments: "The person taking an acknowledgment shall certify that: (A) The person acknowledging appeared before him (or her) and acknowledged he (or she) executed the instrument; (B) The person acknowledging was known to the person taking the acknowledgment, or that ... the person taking the acknowledgment had satisfactory evidence that the person acknowledging was the person described in and who executed the instrument" (ORC 147.53).

"(T)he person acknowledging the signature on a document must personally appear before the notary. An acknowledgment may not ... be taken over the telephone. Nor can a notary certify a document which is brought to the notary by a third person. Therefore, although a person may sign a document outside the presence of the notary, that person must personally appear before the notary to acknowledge that signature for the notary to certify the acknowledgment" (HNP, p. 23).

If the person acknowledging is acting in a representative capacity (e.g., a corporate or public officer, partner, attorney in fact, trustee or other personal representative), that person must acknowledge to the Notary that he or she signed the document in that capacity and had the authority to do so (ORC 147.541[C][2] through [5]).

** Oaths: "To be a proper oath the declaration must be substantiated by an appeal to God to witness the sincerity of the statement accompanied by some outward act demonstrating the appeal such as raising the right hand or placing it on the Bible. Example: 'Do you solemnly swear that what you are about to say is true, so help you, God?' 'I do'" (HNP, p. 15).

*** Affidavits: "In certifying to an affidavit, the notary must do the following:

"(1) Adequately identify the affiant (the person signing the affidavit);

"(2) Administer an oath or affirmation to the affiant whereby the affiant is asked to state that the facts set forth in the affidavit are true …;

"(3) Have the affiant sign the affidavit in the presence of the notary;

"(4) Complete and execute the certification on the instrument, below the signature of the affiant" (HNP, p. 16).

"No notary public shall certify to the affidavit of a person without administering the appropriate oath or affirmation to the person. A notary public who violates this section shall be removed from office by the court of common pleas of the county in which a conviction for a violation of this section is had. The court shall certify the removal to the secretary of state. The person so removed shall be ineligible to reappointment for a period of three years" (ORC 147.14). This person may also be fined not more than $100 or imprisoned for 30 days, or both (ORC 147.99[B]).

Sample wording: "Do you swear that the facts set forth in this affidavit are true, so help you God?" or "Do you affirm that the facts set forth in this affidavit are true?" (HNP, p. 16).

**** Depositions: "In taking depositions, (notaries) shall have the power that is by law vested in judges of county courts to compel the attendance of witnesses and punish them for refusing to testify. Sheriffs and constables are required to serve and return all processes issued by notaries public in the taking of depositions" (ORC 147.07).

"The subpoena is served on the witness by the sheriff or constable. The subpoena may also include a clause directing the witness to bring with him/her any book, writing or other thing under his/her control which he/she may be compelled to produce as evidence" (HNP, p. 17).

Any Signer Must Be Identified

The effect of the case of *Keck v. Keck*, 54 Ohio App. 2d 128 (1977) is that a Notary must positively identify any document signer, whether for an acknowledgment or a jurat.

"The notary must either know the person seeking notarial services or must obtain satisfactory evidence that he/she is the person described in, and who executed the document" (HNP, p. 11).

"If the signer is not known to the notary, proof of the individual's identity must be presented. This proof is often satisfied by examination of a driver's license or other identification card (preferably one with a picture). Proof may also include introduction of the individual by a third person whom the notary knows and trusts. A court has held that the failure of a notary public to obtain some evidence of identification independent of a stranger's representation is negligence as a matter of law" (HNP, p. 12).

Signature by Mark

"A notary may take the acknowledgment of a person who cannot sign his/her name. Such person executes the instrument by marking an 'X' in the presence of two witnesses, one of whom may be the notary" (HNP, p. 13). In the example below, the notarial certificate would follow the signatures:

(Signature of first witness)
(Printed name of first witness)

(Signature of second witness)
(Printed name of second witness)

(Mark of signer)
"Mark of *(printed name of signer)*"

NOTARY DON'TS

Blank Documents

"A notary … need not concern him/herself with the specific contents of the instrument. This does not mean, however, that a notary may acknowledge (sic) a signature on a blank or partly blank piece of paper. The notary should insist that all blanks be filled in. Blank spaces not used in a legal instrument should have a line in ink drawn through them, so that no one can add to the terms of the instrument after it is signed" (HNP, p. 13).

Disqualifying Interests

"A notary cannot take the acknowledgment to an instrument in which the notary has an interest, for example, a deed of real estate either to or from the notary. A notary may take the acknowledgment of a relative, even a wife or husband, if the notary has no interest in the transaction" (HNP, p. 13).

"A notary may not certify his/her own affidavit or any affidavit in which he/she is a party. For example, a notary who signs the certificate of title to his car as the seller cannot certify either his own affidavit (e.g., the odometer affidavit on the top of the form) or the affidavit of the buyer (on the bottom of the form). A notary may certify affidavits of the notary's family if the notary has no interest in the subject of the affidavit" (HNP, pp. 16-17).

Curative Provisions

No recorded document affecting real estate shall be invalidated by the failure to affix an official seal, by the fact that the certificate of acknowledgment is not on the same sheet of paper as the document or by the fact that an executor, administrator, guardian, assignee or trustee signed individually instead of in a representative or official capacity (ORC 5301.071).

NOTARY SIGNING AGENTS

Currently, there are no statutes, regulations or rules expressly governing, prohibiting or restricting the operation of Notary Signing Agents within the state of Ohio.

NOTARY FEES

Ohio Notaries may charge no more than the following fees:
1. Taking an acknowledgment: $2 (ORC 147.08[C] and 2303.20[N]);
2. Administering an oath or affirmation: $2 (HNP, p. 20; see also 2320.20[D]);
3. Taking and certifying an affidavit including oath: $1.50 (ORC 147.08[D]);
4. Protesting a bill or note: $1 plus "actual necessary expenses in going beyond the corporate limits of a municipal corporation to make presentment or demand" (ORC 147.08[A]);
5. Recording any document required to be recorded by a Notary: 10 cents per 100 words (ORC 147.08[B]);
6. Taking a deposition: fees should not exceed those that are usual and customary in a given community, unless higher fees were agreed upon ahead of time (ORC 2319.27).

"For taking and certifying acknowledgment of deeds, mortgages, liens, powers of attorney, and other instruments of writing, and for taking and certifying depositions, administering oaths, and other official services, (a notary public is entitled to) the same fees as are allowed by Section 2319.27 of the Revised Code or by law to clerks of the courts of common pleas for like services" (ORC 147.08[C]).

Fees Are Not Cumulative

"The maximum fee that a notary currently may charge for administering an oath or certifying an acknowledgment is two dollars. However, a notary may charge only up to $1.50 for certifying an affidavit. The fee includes the fee for administering the oath to the affiant before the affidavit is signed. The fees are not cumulative! For example, a notary who administers an oath and certifies the signature of the seller or buyer on a car title may not charge $2.00 for the oath plus $1.50 for the certification of the signature" (HNP, p. 20).

Overcharging

A Notary who overcharges may be removed from office by the local court of common pleas. A person so removed is ineligible for reappointment as a Notary (ORC 147.13 and HNP, p. 20).

Veterans' Organizations

Representatives of veterans' organizations who are specially commissioned to notarize papers submitted to the Veterans' Administration under ORC 147.32 may not charge for their notarial services.

NOTARY CERTIFICATES

Ohio has adopted the *Uniform Recognition of Acknowledgments Act*, including the short-form certificates (ORC 147.55) for:

1. Acknowledgment by individual;
2. Acknowledgment by corporation;
3. Acknowledgment by partnership;
4. Acknowledgment by attorney in fact;
5. Acknowledgment by public officer, trustee or personal representative.

For the text of these certificates, see "Uniform Recognition of Acknowledgments Act (1968)," Section 6, in Appendix 3.

The Notary's seal and other required information (either included in the seal or separately printed, typed or stamped by the Notary) must be affixed to each of these certificates (ORC 147.04).

"Information for Newly Commissioned Notaries Public" (INCN), issued by the Secretary of State, provides the following example of a "common acknowledgment":

Acknowledgment by Individual(s) (INCN):

State of Ohio   )
*   ) ss.*
County of _____)

Before me, a Notary Public for the State of Ohio, appeared the above named _____ and _____, who acknowledged and signed the foregoing instrument and their signing was their free act.

IN TESTIMONY WHEREOF, I have hereunto subscribed my name and affixed my seal this ____ day of _____, 20____.

_____ (Notary's Signature)
_____ (Name printed or typed)   (Seal)
Notary Public, State of Ohio
My commission expires _____
Recorded in _____ County (if applicable)

In addition to the short forms above, the following certificates are cited as acceptable in "A Handbook and Notarial Journal for Notaries Public" (HNP), published by the Columbus Bar Association:

Acknowledgment by Individual — 1 (HNP):

State of Ohio   )
*   ) ss.*
County of _____)

Before me, a Notary Public in and for said state, personally appeared the above named _____, who acknowledged before me that he/she/they did sign the foregoing instrument and that the same is his/her/their free act and deed.

IN TESTIMONY WHEREOF, I have hereunto affixed my name and official seal at _____, Ohio, this ____ day of _____, 20____.

_____ (Notary's Signature)
_____ (Name printed or typed)   (Seal)
Notary Public, State of Ohio
My commission expires _____

Acknowledgment by Individual — 2 (HNP):

State of Ohio   )
*   ) ss.*
County of _____)

On this the ____ day of _____, 20____, before me, _____, the undersigned Notary Public, personally appeared _____, proved to me on the basis of satisfactory evidence to be the person(s) whose name(s) was/were subscribed to the within instrument, and acknowledged that he/she/they executed it.

WITNESS my hand and official seal.

_____ (Notary's Signature)
_____ (Name printed or typed)   (Seal)
Notary Public, State of Ohio
My commission expires _____

Acknowledgment of Signer-by-Mark (HNP):

State of Ohio   )
*   ) ss.*
County of _____)

On this the ____ day of _____, 20____, before me, _____, the undersigned Notary Public, personally appeared _____, personally known to me (proven to me on the basis of satisfactory evidence) to be the person who made and acknowledged his/her mark on the within instrument in my presence and in the presence of the two persons indicated below who have signed the within instrument as witnesses, one of whom, _____, also wrote the name of the signer by mark near the mark.

WITNESS my hand and official seal.

_____ *(Notary's Signature)*
_____ *(Name printed or typed)* (Seal)
Notary Public, State of Ohio
My commission expires _____

Acknowledgment by Attorney in Fact (HNP):

State of Ohio)
) ss.
County of _____)

On this the _____ day of _____, 20___, before me, a Notary Public, personally appeared _____, known to me to be the person who is described in and whose name is subscribed to the within instrument, as the attorney in fact of _____, and acknowledged to me that he/she subscribed the name of _____ thereto as principal and his/her own name as attorney in fact.

WITNESS my hand and official seal.

_____ *(Notary's Signature)*
_____ *(Name printed or typed)* (Seal)
Notary Public, State of Ohio
My commission expires _____

Acknowledgment by a Corporation (HNP):

State of Ohio)
) ss.
County of _____)

On _____, 20___, before me, the undersigned, a Notary Public in and for the said state, personally appeared _____, personally known to me or proved to me on the basis of satisfactory evidence to be the person who executed the within instrument as the _____ of _____, a corporation, and acknowledged to me that such corporation executed the within instrument pursuant to its by-laws or a resolution of its board of directors, and that the seal that is affixed to the within instrument is the corporate seal of said corporation.

WITNESS my hand and official seal.

_____ *(Notary's Signature)*
_____ *(Name printed or typed)* (Seal)
Notary Public, State of Ohio
My commission expires _____

Form of Acknowledgment Certificate

"The form of a certificate of acknowledgment used by a person whose authority is recognized under section 147.51 of the Revised Code shall be accepted in this state if: (A) The certificate is in a form prescribed by the laws or regulations of this state; (B) The certificate is in a form prescribed by the laws or regulations applicable in the place in which the acknowledgment is taken; or (C) The certificate contains the words 'acknowledged before me,' or their substantial equivalent" (ORC 147.54).

Subscribing Witness Certificate (HNP):

State of Ohio)
) ss.
County of _____)

Before me, a Notary Public, on this day personally appeared _____, personally known to me (or proved to me on the oath of _____) to be the person whose name is subscribed as a witness to the foregoing instrument, and who, after being duly sworn by me, stated on oath that he/she saw _____, the person who executed the foregoing instrument, subscribe the same (acknowledge in his/her presence having executed the same) for the purposes and considerations therein expressed, and that he/she had signed the same as a witness at the request of the person who executed the same.

Given under my hand and seal of office this _____ day of _____, A.D., 20___.

_____ *(Notary's Signature)*
_____ *(Name printed or typed)* (Seal)
Notary Public, State of Ohio
My commission expires _____

Affidavit Certificate (INCN):

State of Ohio)
) ss.
County of _____)

Being duly sworn, _____ says as follows:

(AFFIANT'S STATEMENT)

_____ *(Affiant's signature)*
_____ *(Name printed or typed)*

Sworn to and subscribed in my presence this ____ day of _____, 20____.

_____ *(Notary's Signature)   (Seal)*
_____ *(Name printed or typed)*
Notary Public, State of Ohio
My commission expires _____
Recorded in _____ County (if applicable)

Affidavit Certificate (HNP):

State of Ohio   )
) ss.
County of _____)

Before me, a Notary Public in and for said state, personally appeared _____, who being by me duly sworn (or affirmed) deposes and says that _____. Further affiant sayeth naught.

_____ *(Affiant's signature)*

Sworn to (or affirmed) before me and signed in my presence this ____ day of _____, 20____.

_____ *(Notary's Signature)*
_____ *(Name printed or typed)   (Seal)*
Notary Public, State of Ohio
My commission expires _____

ELECTRONIC NOTARIZATIONS

The state of Ohio has not yet adopted statutes or regulations expressly establishing rules, definitions and procedures for electronic notarization.

UETA Recognizes Notary's eSignature

Ohio has adopted its own version of the Uniform Electronic Transactions Act (ORC 1306.01 through 1306.23), including the following provision on notarization and acknowledgment, thereby recognizing the legal validity of electronic signatures used by Notaries:

"If a law requires a signature or record to be notarized, acknowledged, verified, or made under oath, the requirement is satisfied if the electronic signature of the person authorized to perform those acts, together with all other information required to be included by other applicable law, is attached to or logically associated with the signature or record" (ORC 1306.10).

'Online Webcam Notarization' Invalid in Ohio

The following "Scam Alert" was posted on the state's website by Ohio Attorney General Mike DeWine on July 25, 2011:

"'Online webcam notarization' is invalid in Ohio, but at least one company is claiming to provide a web-based notary service to consumers throughout the U.S.

"Under Ohio law, if you need to get a document notarized to verify your signature on the document, you must be physically present with the notary public at the time you sign the document.

"If you are not physically present (in person) with the notary public at the time of signing, the notarization is invalid and the document itself may become invalid."

NOTARY RECORDS

"(A) notary public shall … provide himself (or herself) with an official register in which shall be recorded a copy of every certificate of protest and copy of note, which seal and record shall be exempt from execution. Upon the death, expiration of term without reappointment, or removal from office of any notary public, his (or her) official register shall be deposited in the office of the county recorder of the county in which he (or she) resides" (ORC 147.04).

"(I)t is not necessary to obtain a registry unless, and until a notary is called upon to make a notarial protest" (HNP, p. 10).

Recommended Entries in Register

Section VI of "A Handbook and Notarial Journal for Notaries Public" (HNP), published by the Columbus Bar Association, prints sample journal pages with the following entry spaces for each notarial act:

1. Date;

2. Name of person(s);
3. Fee paid;
4. Type of notarization;
5. ID used;
6. Other/Comments.

AUTHENTICATION OF NOTARIAL ACTS

County Clerks of Court of Common Pleas

Certificates authenticating the signatures and seals of non-attorney Notaries are issued by the clerk of the court of common pleas in each Notary's county of residence (website, "Apostilles & Authentications"). Depending on the document's ultimate destination, the clerk of court's signature and seal may require authentication by the Ohio Secretary of State.

Fees: County fees for authenticating certificates for non-attorney Notaries range from $1 to $3 per certificate.

Ohio Secretary of State

Authenticating certificates for attorney Notaries who are admitted to the practice of law in Ohio and for county clerks of the court of common pleas are issued by the Ohio Secretary of State. If an attorney notarized a document, that document may be submitted directly to the Secretary of State without authentication by a county clerk. If a non-attorney notarized a document, authentication by the county clerk is first required, even for apostilles (website, "Apostilles & Authentications").

Fees: The Secretary of State's fee is $5 per authentication of the signature of an attorney-Notary or of a clerk of a court of common pleas, whether by a "gold seal certificate" or an apostille. Payable to "Ohio Secretary of State" (website, "Apostilles & Authentications").

Address:
Ohio Secretary of State
Client Service Center
(Continental Plaza)
180 E. Broad St., Suite 103
Columbus, OH 43215

Telephone: 1-614-728-9200
1-877-767-6446

Procedure: Authenticating certificates come in the form of either an apostille or a "gold seal certificate." To obtain an authenticating certificate, mail or present in person the attorney-notarized document(s) or the non-attorney-notarized document(s) with county clerk's certificate(s), along with the appropriate fee. For walk-ins, no appointments are necessary and the documents are authenticated while you wait. For mailings, include a cover letter (form available on the website) indicating the country to which the document(s) will be sent, and provide a daytime telephone number. A prepaid addressed envelope or airbill is required for return of the document(s).

Photocopies of marriage licenses or certificates, divorce decrees, probated wills and judgments may be authenticated by the Secretary of State's office if they are "notarized by a notary public ... and then certified by the county Clerk of Courts or notarized by an attorney notary." Alternatively, these documents may be certified by the state or county official responsible for keeping the respective records.

Birth and death certificates must be certified copies from the Ohio Department of Health or Vital Statistics. Notarized photocopies of these records are not eligible for authentication (website, "Apostilles & Authentication").

COMMISSIONING AND ADMINISTRATION

Effective July 1, 2001, the Ohio Secretary of State appoints, commissions and maintains minimal records on the state's Notaries (ORC 147.01[A] and [C] and 147.05[B]). More comprehensive background information on non-attorney Notaries may be kept by the county in which the Notary resides. The Secretary of State also maintains certain records on attorney Notaries.

Applying for Commission

Qualifications: An applicant for a commission as an Ohio Notary Public must: (a) be at least 18 years old and (b) be an Ohio resident or a resident of another state who is an attorney admitted to the practice of law in Ohio and who has a principal place of business or a primary practice in Ohio (ORC 147.01[B]).

No Statewide Course or Test: Statewide, no course of instruction or testing is required of applicants for an Ohio Notary Public commission. However, testing may be imposed by a local judge of the court of common pleas or a local county bar association screening committee — see immediately below.

Application: Applications for a new or renewed Notary commission are handled through the respective counties, and each county has a slightly different process. Applicants for a Notary commission must be endorsed by a "certificate of qualifications" from a local judge of the court of common pleas, court of appeals or supreme court (ORC 147.02[A]). "No judge or justice shall issue a certificate … until the judge or justice is satisfied from personal knowledge that the applicant possesses the qualifications necessary to a proper discharge of the duties of the office or until the applicant has passed an examination under any rules that the judge or justice may prescribe" (ORC 147.02[B]). When applicable, the judge's certificate must additionally certify that the applicant is an attorney admitted to the practice of law in Ohio, either as a resident of the state or as a non-resident whose principal place of business or primary practice is in Ohio (ORC 147.02[C] and [D]).

To assist the judge or justice in screening applicants, a court may appoint a screening committee involving the county clerk or a local bar association; Franklin County, for example, has such a committee. A test may be required of applicants.

A judge's certificate of qualifications for an applicant is forwarded to the Secretary of State with the applicant's $15 processing fee (ORC 147.37). Additional processing fees may have been charged by the county clerk's office (ORC 147.05[A]) or the local county bar association.

Recording Commission and Oath with Clerk: Upon being commissioned by the state, new and renewing Notaries must record their commissions, with the oath endorsed thereon, with the clerk of the court of common pleas in the county in which the Notary resides (ORC 147.03 and 147.05[A]).

"A notary public who violates the oath of office required by this section shall be removed from office by the court of common pleas of the county in which the notary public resides, upon complaint filed and substantiated in the court, and the court, upon removing a notary public from office, shall certify the removal to the secretary of state. The person so removed shall be ineligible for reappointment to the office of notary public" (ORC 147.03).

Non-Residents: Only those non-residents who are attorneys admitted to practice law in Ohio and whose principal place of business or primary practice is in Ohio may become Notaries in the state (ORC 147.01[B][2][c]).

Online Search: On the Secretary of State's website under "Search Notaries," Ohio's roster of active and inactive Notaries may be searched by first and last name, zip code and county. Information provided will include the Notary's full name, address, county, commission number, commission type (Notary, attorney or police officer) and commission starting and expiration dates. "Notaries are placed into the database daily after the Notary Commission receives applications from county clerks of court or bar associations" (website, "Search Notaries").

Changes of Status

If Notary Changes Name or Address: Within 30 days, a name or address change must be reported to the appropriate clerk of courts and, at the address below, to the Notary Commission Clerk in the Secretary of State's office, using an "Application for Amendment of Notary Public Information" (ORC 147.05[C] and website, "Amending Notary Public Information"):

Ohio Notary Commission
Client Service Center
180 E. Broad St.
Columbus, OH 43215
Attention: Amendment Form

The application must be notarized. "There is no fee for this change of record; however, there is a $2.00 fee assessed for the revised commission when a name change of the record is granted (R.C. 147.371). Once the revised commission is received, it must be recorded at the county clerk of the courts of common pleas office (R.C. 147.05 A).

"When the change of address places a notary public in another county, the notary public must record their notary commission with the clerk of courts of common pleas in the new county (R.C. 147.05 A).

"Once the amendment application is approved, the commission's current expiration date will not be adjusted" (website, "Amending Notary Public Information").

"Notaries whose names have changed during

their tenure of office and who have not obtained a commission in their new names may continue to perform duties as a notary. Each must, however, indicate the name in which the commission was issued in parentheses after the new name on each document notarized" (HNP, p. 8).

If Notary Resigns: A Notary, other than an attorney, who resigns a Notary commission must deliver to the Secretary of State a written notice indicating the effective date of resignation (ORC 147.05[D])

COUNTY CLERKS

To contact a Ohio county clerk of the court of common pleas to obtain an authenticating certificate for a Notary, or to seek assistance in locating a given Notary, telephone long-distance information — 1-XXX-555-1212 — using the area code listed below and ask for the phone number of the clerk for the appropriate county:

County	City/Town	Area Code
Adams	West Union	(937)
Allen	Lima	(419)
Ashland	Ashland	(419)
Ashtabula	Jefferson	(440)
Athens	Athens	(740)
Auglaize	Wapakoneta	(419)
Belmont	St. Clairsville	(740)
Brown	Georgetown	(937)
Butler	Hamilton	(513)
Carroll	Carrollton	(330)
Champaign	Urbana	(937)
Clark	Springfield	(937)
Clermont	Batavia	(513)
Clinton	Wilmington	(937)
Columbiana	Lisbon	(330)
Coshocton	Coshocton	(740)
Crawford	Bucyrus	(419)
Cuyahoga	Cleveland	(216)
Darke	Greenville	(937)
Defiance	Defiance	(419)
Delaware	Delaware	(740)
Erie	Sandusky	(419)
Fairfield	Lancaster	(740)
Fayette	Washington Ct. Hse.	(740)
Franklin	Columbus	(614)
Fulton	Wauseon	(419)
Gallia	Gallipolis	(740)

County	City/Town	Area Code
Geauga	Chardon	(440)
Greene	Xenia	(937)
Guernsey	Cambridge	(740)
Hamilton	Cincinnati	(513)
Hancock	Findlay	(419)
Hardin	Kenton	(419)
Harrison	Cadiz	(740)
Henry	Napoleon	(419)
Highland	Hillsboro	(937)
Hocking	Logan	(740)
Holmes	Millersburg	(330)
Huron	Norwalk	(419)
Jackson	Jackson	(740)
Jefferson	Steubenville	(740)
Knox	Mount Vernon	(740)
Lake	Painesville	(440)
Lawrence	Ironton	(740)
Licking	Newark	(740)
Logan	Bellefontaine	(937)
Lorain	Elyria	(440)
Lucas	Toledo	(419)
Madison	London	(740)
Mahoning	Youngstown	(330)
Marion	Marion	(740)
Medina	Medina	(330)
Meigs	Pomeroy	(740)
Mercer	Celina	(419)
Miami	Troy	(937)
Monroe	Woodsfield	(740)
Montgomery	Dayton	(937)
Morgan	McConnelsville	(740)
Morrow	Mount Gilead	(419)
Muskingum	Zanesville	(740)
Noble	Caldwell	(740)
Ottawa	Port Clinton	(419)
Paulding	Paulding	(419)
Perry	New Lexington	(740)
Pickaway	Circleville	(740)
Pike	Waverly	(740)
Portage	Ravenna	(330)
Preble	Eaton	(937)
Putnam	Ottawa	(419)
Richland	Mansfield	(419)
Ross	Chillicothe	(740)
Sandusky	Fremont	(419)
Scioto	Portsmouth	(740)
Seneca	Tiffin	(419)
Shelby	Sidney	(937)
Stark	Canton	(330)
Summit	Akron	(330)
Trumbull	Warren	(330)

County	City/Town	Area Code
Tuscarawas	New Philadelphia	(330)
Union	Marysville	(937)
Van Wert	Van Wert	(419)
Vinton	McArthur	(740)
Warren	Lebanon	(513)
Washington	Marietta	(740)
Wayne	Wooster	(330)
Williams	Bryan	(419)
Wood	Bowling Green	(419)
Wyandot	Upper Sandusky	(419)

OTHER NOTARIAL OFFICERS

Besides Notaries, the following officers in Ohio have authority to take the acknowledgment of a deed, mortgage, land contract or lease of any interest in real property (ORC 5301.01[A]):
1. Judge of a court of record;
2. Clerk of a court of record;
3. County auditor;
4. County engineer;
5. Mayor.

Veterans' Affairs Commissioners: Representatives of congressionally chartered veterans' organizations (American Legion, VFW, Disabled American Veterans, etc.) may be appointed as Ohio commissioners of veterans' affairs, with a term of three years and power to affix a seal in notarizing documents used in connection with or before the veterans' administration. They may not charge fees (ORC 147.32).

QUICK FACTS

Notary Jurisdiction
Statewide (ORC 147.07).

Notary Term Length
Five years (ORC 147.03) for non-attorney Notaries. However, an attorney admitted to practice law in Ohio "shall hold office as a notary public as long as the attorney is a resident of this state or has the attorney's principal place of business or primary practice in this state, the attorney is in good standing before the Ohio supreme court, and the commission is not revoked" (ORC 147.03). The term of office for a specially commissioned police officer is three years (website, "Forms and Fees").

Notarizing after Expiration: For knowingly notarizing after commission expiration, a Notary must forfeit not more than $500 and becomes ineligible for reappointment (ORC 147.11). However, an official act done by a Notary after expiration of the Notary's term of office is as valid as if done during the term of office (ORC 147.12).

Notary Bond
Not required by law.

O-R

Oklahoma

NOTARY SEAL

An Oklahoma Notary must authenticate all official acts with a seal of office, and the seal's format must be as follows (49 OS 5 and 16 OS 35):

Kind

Inked Rubber Stamp or Metal Embosser: "This seal may be either a metal seal which leaves an embossed impression or a rubber stamp used in conjunction with a stamp pad and ink" (49 OS 5 and OAC 655:25-5-2[b]).

Shape/Size

Not specified.

Components

1. Notary's name;
2. "Notary Public";
3. "State of Oklahoma".

JANE Q. DOE Com. No. 1234567890
Notary Public
State of Oklahoma
My Commission Expires Jan 30, 2014

Examples

The above typical, actual-size examples of Notary seals are allowed by Oklahoma law. Formats other than these may also be permitted.

NOTARY ADMINISTRATION

Office of Secretary of State
Notary Public Services   1-405-521-2516
2300 N. Lincoln Blvd., Room 101
Oklahoma City, OK 73105-4897

Website: www.sos.state.ok.us/notary/notary_welcome.htm

NOTARY RULES

OS — Oklahoma Statutes
OAC — Oklahoma Administrative Code
NPG — Notary Public Guide

Most Notary rules are in the Oklahoma Statutes:

a. Title 49, "Notaries Public";*

b. Title 16, "Conveyances."

* The *Uniform Law on Notarial Acts* of 1982 is included as Sections 49-111 through 49-121.

Supplementary Notary regulations are in the Oklahoma Administrative Code, Title 655 ("Secretary of State"), Chapter 25 ("Notary Public").

Other guidelines for Notaries are in the "Notary Public Guide" issued by the Oklahoma Secretary of State and available on the website.

OPTIONAL: Notary's commission number and/or commission expiration date.

Commission Number and Expiration Date

"Each notary ... shall add to the notary's official signature, the commission number of the notary and the date of expiration of the commission of the notary. Failure to add the commission number or the date of expiration of the commission shall not affect the recordability of the instrument or the notice given by such recording. This date and commission number may be a part of the stamp or seal. If any notary public shall neglect or refuse to attach to the notary's official signature the date of expiration of the notary's commission, the notary shall be deemed guilty of a misdemeanor, and upon conviction thereof shall be fined in any sum not exceeding Fifty Dollars ($50.00)" (49 OS 5).

"If the officer is a notary public, the certificate must also indicate the date of expiration, if any, of the commission of office, but omission of that information may subsequently be corrected" (49 OS 118).

Seal Specimen Filed with Secretary

Before starting to notarize, the newly commissioned Notary must file an impression of the Notary's official seal with the Secretary of State (49 OS 2A).

Seal Not Surrendered to Employer

According to Oklahoma Attorney General Opinion 00-28 of May 11, 2000: "While Oklahoma does not prohibit an employer from paying for the notarial seal, the seal is evidence of the notary's ministerial office. Since the seal is acquired in the notary's name, the employer may not require the notary to surrender the seal."

However, the opinion points out, "(a)n employment agreement could require the employee to reimburse the employer for such expenditures."

Seal Is Notary's Exclusive Property: "A notary shall keep an official notarial seal that is the exclusive property of the notary and that may not be used by any other person. At the end of a notary's employment, an employer may not require the notary to surrender the seal" (OAC 655:25-5-2[a]).

No New Seal for Change of County

"If a notary's resident address changes, the notary must inform the Secretary of State in writing within thirty (30) days of such change. The notary is not required to file a new bond or obtain another seal if the notary moves from one county to another" (49 OS 11A).

New Name Need Not Mean New Seal

"If a name change occurs in the middle of a term, the notary has two options:

"1. The notary may continue to use the former name as issued on the existing commission until it expires; or

"2. The notary may use the notary's new name by completing and filing an application with the Secretary of State with a fee of Twenty-five Dollars ($25.00). A new commission expiration date will be established. It will be necessary for the notary to purchase a new seal and obtain a new bond for filing with the court clerk." (49 OS 11B).

Lost or Stolen Seal

"Within ten (10) days after the loss of the seal, the notary shall deliver to the Secretary of State a written notice of the loss or theft and the date the seal was first discovered missing. In addition, the notary should notify the appropriate law enforcement agency in the case of theft" (NPG).

"When purchasing a new seal, it is advisable to add a symbol on the new seal to identify it from the lost or stolen one. Such as a star or an asterisk. Include this information in the notification letter to the Secretary of State" (website, "Frequently Asked Questions …").

Notification to the Secretary of State about a lost or stolen seal must be within 10 days; notification that a replacement has been obtained must also be within 10 days of the replacement (OAC 655:25-5-3).

Seal to Be Destroyed

"The notary seal should be destroyed upon (the Notary's) resignation or death" (NPG). This is to be done as soon as reasonably practicable after death by the Notary's heirs or personal representative (OAC 655:25-3-3).

"When a notarial commission is revoked, the notary shall…destroy the official seal…" (OAC 655:25-3-1[b]).

NOTARY POWERS

Oklahoma Notaries are authorized to perform the following notarial acts (49 OS 112 and 113):

1. Take acknowledgments and proofs (49 OS 6[A]);
2. Administer oaths and affirmations;
3. Take verifications upon oath or affirmation;
4. Witness or attest signatures;
5. Certify or attest copies of documents* or other items;
6. Execute protests (49 OS 6);
7. "(E)xercise such other powers and duties

as by law of nations and commercial usage may be performed by notaries public" (49 OS 6).

* Certifying Copies: "(T)he notarial officer must determine that the proffered copy is a full, true, and accurate transcription or reproduction of that which was copied. In the case of official records, only the custodian of the official records may issue an official certified copy" (49 OS 113[D]).

Identifying Document Signers

The following definition of "satisfactory evidence" applies to acknowledgments, verifications upon oath or affirmation and to witnessing or attesting signatures (49 OS 113[F]):

"A notarial officer has satisfactory evidence that a person is the person whose true signature is on a document if that person is personally known to the notarial officer, is identified upon the oath or affirmation of a credible witness personally known to the notarial officer or is identified on the basis of identification documents."

"Proper 'ID' should include a photograph and signature such as a driver's license or passport" (website, "Frequently Asked Questions ...").

Employer May Limit Notary's Acts

"An employer, in setting terms and conditions of employment, may limit the notarial acts performed by the notary during employment hours. For example, the employer could prohibit the notary from performing notarial acts for anyone other than the employer while at work. The employer, however, may not prohibit the notary, as a ministerial officer, from performing lawful notarial acts, as set forth in 49 O.S. 1991, § 6, outside employment hours. Courts have generally held that employers cannot restrict employees from pursuing outside employment as long as such employment does not interfere with duties owed to the employer" (Oklahoma Attorney General Opinion 00-28 of May 11, 2000).

NOTARY DON'TS

Oklahoma Notaries Public may:
1. NOT notarize their own signatures (49 OS 6);
2. NOT notarize without personal appearance of signer (In re Initiative Petition No. 142, State Question No. 205, 176 Okl.155, 55 P.2d 455);
3. NOT act in a double capacity as attorney and Notary when the notarized document will be used in a case involving one of the attorney's clients (Crawford v. Ferguson, 5 Okl.Cr. 377, 115 P. 278, 45 L.R.A., N.S., 519).

No Disqualification

1. A Notary who is a stockholder, director, officer or employee of a bank may notarize for that bank, unless the Notary is a party to the document, either individually or as a representative (6 OS 904).
2. A Notary who is an officer, trustee, member or shareholder of a cooperative may take acknowledgment of documents executed in favor of that cooperative or to which it is a party (18 OS 438.28).

Notarizing for Relatives: "The law does not forbid notaries from notarizing the signatures of relatives. However, if the notarized document was ever the subject of a court suit, a judge might determine the notary was not an impartial witness" (website, "Frequently Asked Questions ...").

Absentee Ballots

"The ballot shall not be notarized by any person whose name appears on the ballot as a candidate or by any campaign chairperson or campaign treasurer for a candidate whose name appears on the ballot" (26 OS 14-108). The Notary may not charge a fee for the notarization.

Immigration Assistance Restrictions

"No notary public, except those who are licensed attorneys or otherwise authorized by law to represent persons on immigration or citizenship matters, shall hold himself or herself out as having expertise in providing legal advice on any proceeding, filing or action affecting the immigration or citizenship status of another person" (49 OS 6[B]).

Nonlegal Immigration Assistance: "Any notary public who provides nonlegal assistance on any proceeding, filing or action affecting the immigration or citizenship status of another person shall give the following notice to that person verbally and in writing: 'I am not a licensed attorney or representative of any government agency with authority over immigration or citizenship and, therefore, cannot offer legal advice about immigration or any other legal matters'" (49 OS 6[B]). If the Notary operates a business or advertises notarial or nonlegal immigration services in a language other than English, the above notice must be given in both English and the other language(s). Further, use of the term notario publico or notario in such business or ads is prohibited.

NOTARY SIGNING AGENTS

Currently, there are no statutes, regulations or rules expressly governing, prohibiting or restricting the operation of Notary Signing Agents within the state of Oklahoma.

NOTARY FEES

"The maximum fee a notary may charge and collect for each notarial act is Five Dollars ($5.00)" (49 OS 5).

"Notaries are not required to charge a fee. If a fee is charged, it is recommended that it be recorded in the notary's official records" (website, "Frequently Asked Questions …").

Absentee Ballots

The Notary may not charge a fee for notarizing an absentee ballot (26 OS 14-108).

NOTARY CERTIFICATES

Oklahoma has adopted the *Uniform Law on Notarial Acts*, including the short-form certificates (49 OS 119) for:
1. Acknowledgment by individual;
2. Acknowledgment by representative;
3. Verification upon oath or affirmation;
4. Witnessing or attesting signature;
5. Attesting copy of document.

The Notary's commission number and commission expiration date must be added to each certificate, if this information does not appear in the Notary's seal.

For the text of these certificates, see "Uniform Law on Notarial Acts (1982)," Section 8, in Appendix 2.

Requirements for Notarial Certificate

"A. A notarial act must be evidenced by a certificate signed and dated by a notarial officer. The certificate shall include identification of the jurisdiction in which the notarial act is performed and the title of the office of the notarial officer and may include the official stamp or seal of office. If the officer is a notary public, the certificate must also indicate the date of expiration, if any, of the commission of office, but omission of that information may subsequently be corrected. If the officer is a commissioned officer on active duty in the military service of the United States, it must also include the rank of the officer.

"B. A certificate of a notarial act is sufficient if it meets the requirements of subsection A of this section and it:

"1. is in the short form set forth in Section (49 OS 119) of this act;

"2. is in a form otherwise prescribed by the law of this state;

"3. is in a form prescribed by the laws or regulations applicable in the place in which the notarial act was performed; or

"4. sets forth the actions of the notarial officer and those are sufficient to meet the requirements of the designated notarial act" (49 OS 118).

Acknowledgment by Individual (16 OS 33):

An acknowledgment by an individual affecting real estate must be substantially in the following form:

State of Oklahoma,)
) ss.
_____ County.)

Before me, a _____ in and for said county and State, on this ____ day of _____, 20__, personally appeared _____ and _____, to me known to be the identical person(s) who executed the within and foregoing instrument, and acknowledged to me that he/she/they executed the same as his/her/their free and voluntary act and deed for the uses and purposes therein set forth.

(NOTARY'S SIGNATURE, SEAL AND COMMISSION EXPIRATION DATE)

Acknowledgment by Corporation (16 OS 95):

An acknowledgment by a corporation affecting real estate must be substantially in the following form:

State of Oklahoma,)
*   ) ss.*
_____ County.   )

Before me, a _____ in and for said county and State, on this ____ day of _____ 20__, personally appeared _____, to me known to be the identical person who subscribed the name of the maker thereof to the foregoing instrument as its _____ (attorney in fact, president, vice-president, chair or vice-chair of the board of directors, or mayor, as the case may be) and acknowledged to me that he/she executed the same as his/her free and voluntary act and deed, and as the free and voluntary act and deed of such corporation, for the uses and purposes therein set forth.

(NOTARY'S SIGNATURE, SEAL AND COMMISSION EXPIRATION DATE)

Certificate for Signature by Mark

"When real estate is conveyed or encumbered by an instrument in writing by a person who cannot write his name, he shall execute the same by his mark, and his name shall be written near such mark by one of two persons who saw such mark made, who shall write their names on such instrument as witnesses. In case such instrument is acknowledged, then the officer taking the acknowledgment shall, in addition to the other necessary recitals in the acknowledgment, state that the grantor executed the instrument, by inserting in the ordinary form of acknowledgment by individuals after the words 'foregoing instrument' the words 'by his mark, in my presence and in the presence of _____ and _____ as witnesses'" (16 OS 34).

ELECTRONIC NOTARIZATIONS

The state of Oklahoma has not yet adopted statutes or regulations expressly establishing rules, definitions and procedures for electronic notarization.

UETA Recognizes Notary's eSignature

Effective November 1, 2000, Oklahoma adopted the Uniform Electronic Transactions Act (12A OS 15-101 through 120), including the provision on notarization and acknowledgment, thereby recognizing the legal validity of electronic signatures used by Notaries:

"If a law requires a signature or record to be notarized, acknowledged, verified, or made under oath, the requirement is satisfied if the electronic signature of the person authorized to perform those acts, together with all other information required to be included by other applicable law, is attached to or logically associated with the signature or record" (12A OS 15-111).

No Seal Image for Electronic Recording

Oklahoma has adapted the Uniform Real Property Electronic Recording Act (URPERA) — see 16 OS 86.1 through 16 OS 86.7 — including the following provision related to the Notary's seal:

"A requirement that a document or a signature associated with a document be notarized, acknowledged, verified, witnessed, or made under oath is satisfied if the electronic signature of the person authorized to perform that act, and all other information required to be included, is attached to or logically associated with the document or signature. A physical or electronic image of a stamp, impression or seal need not accompany an electronic signature" (16 OS 86.3).

Electronic Submission Okay with Safeguards

"The Office of Administrative Hearings (OAH) may allow electronic transmittals of documents and electronic signatures if safeguards are in place to protect against unauthorized use. If a law requires a signature or record to be notarized, acknowledged, verified, or made under oath when filed with OAH, the requirement is satisfied if the electronic signature of the person authorized to perform those acts, together with all other information required to be included by other applicable law, is attached to or logically associated with the signature or record" (56 OS 237.9a).

The state's Commission for Human Services is tasked with promulgating rules for such electronic filings.

Online Notary Services Outlawed

According to a news release issued July 13, 2011, by Oklahoma Attorney General Scott

Pruitt's Public Protection Unit, "Online notaries are illegal and should not be used by Oklahoma consumers. A document must be notarized in person by a notary public with a valid state commission number."

Pruitt warned against electronic notarization service providers offering "an online notary via webcam that bypass(es) the need to appear in person to receive notarization."

NOTARY RECORDS

Effective June 4, 2001, Oklahoma Notaries need no longer keep a "fair record" of their official acts (Laws of 201, Chapter 406). Prior to that date, all Notaries had to maintain a log, which was delivered to the county clerk within 30 days after their resignation, disqualification, removal from the county or death.

Log of Official Acts Recommended
"State law does not require a notary to keep records of their official acts. However, it is recommended that a notary maintain a log of his/her official acts to assist in recalling past notarial acts, if needed, or if legally challenged. If a notary is called upon to testify in court, a log may become evidence to help establish what actually took place. Information to be retained in the notary log should include the following:
"1. Date of notarial act
"2. Type of notarial act performed
"3. A description of the document
"4. The signature and printed name and address of each person for whom a notarial act was performed
"5. A description of the form of identification provided (i.e. driver's license or photo identification) or a statement that the person was 'personally known' to the notary
"6. The location where the notarization was performed
"7. The amount of fee charged, if any
"8. Personal notes" (NPG).

Record of Protests: "In cases of protests for banks, notaries shall keep a register thereof in a book provided for that purpose by the bank, and the notary shall not be required to deliver such register to the county clerk, but shall leave the same in the possession of such bank" (49 OS 7).

AUTHENTICATION OF NOTARIAL ACTS

Secretary of State
Authenticating certificates for Notaries, including apostilles, are issued by the Oklahoma Secretary of State's office, as are authenticating certificates for the state's county court clerks.

Fees: For each notarial act or certified document, $20 for an authenticating certificate ("Certificate of Signature"); $25 for an apostille; $10 for any apostille for international adoption (28 OS 111.10). Payable to "Secretary of State." Personal checks not accepted.

Address:
Office of Secretary of State
Certification Department
2300 N. Lincoln Blvd., Room 101
Oklahoma City, OK 73105-4897

Telephone: 1-405-521-4211

Procedure: Mail or present in person the original notarized document(s), along with the appropriate fee. Indicate the nation to which the document(s) will be sent and whether an adoption is involved. If mailed in, provide a daytime telephone number and a return address.

County Court Clerks
Effective November 1, 2004, Oklahoma Notaries no longer file their oaths and bonds with the local county clerk (Laws 2004, Chapter 101); instead these are now filed with the Secretary of State. As a result, county clerks no longer perform the function of authenticating the acts of local Notaries — a function now solely done by the Secretary of State.

COMMISSIONING AND ADMINISTRATION

The Oklahoma Secretary of State appoints, commissions, regulates and maintains records on the state's Notaries (49 OS 1).

Applying for Commission
Qualifications: An applicant for an Oklahoma Notary Public commission must (49 OS 1): (a) be a citizen of the United States, (b) be a legal

resident of Oklahoma or an out-of-state resident who is employed within Oklahoma and (c) be 18 years of age or older. "A felony conviction shall be grounds for removal of a person from the office of notary public. If you have been convicted of a felony you should not apply for appointment as an Oklahoma notary public" ("Instructions for Completing Application").

No Course or Test: No course of instruction or examination is required of an applicant for an Oklahoma Notary commission.

Application: Online or by mail, the completed application form (49 OS 2) must be submitted to the Secretary of State with a $25 fee for first-time applicants or applicants with an expired commission, or a $20 fee for renewing Notaries (49 OS 1); "same day filing" costs an additional $25. Upon commissioning, the new Notary will be sent a $1,000 bond form, which includes an oath of office and a loyalty oath; the bond and both oaths require notarization before another Notary. An impression of the new Notary's seal must be affixed on this bond form, which is to be completed and returned to the Secretary of State, along with a $10 filing fee. The bond must bear the same dates as the Notary commission (NPG).

"Before entering upon the duties of his or her office every notary public so appointed and commissioned shall file in the office of the Secretary of State, the notary's oath of office, the notary's loyalty oath, the notary's official signature, an impression of the notary's official seal, and a good and sufficient bond to the State of Oklahoma, in the sum of One Thousand Dollars ($1,000.00), to be approved by the Secretary of State, conditioned for the faithful performance of the duties of the notary's office" (49 OS 2A).

A renewal application will not be accepted earlier than six weeks prior to expiration of the Notary's current commission, nor will it be accepted after the expiration date (OAC 655:25-1-2). An application received after commission expiration will be processed as a new appointment ($25 fee) with a new commission number and expiration date (NPG).

Non-Residents: Out-of-state residents may become Notaries if they are employed in Oklahoma.

Online Search: The Secretary of State's website ("Notary Search") enables an online search of the state's roster of Notaries by name, commission number, county and city. Information available includes the Notary's commission number, active or inactive status, commission expiration date and address (website, "Notary Search").

Changes of Status

If Notary Changes Name: "If a name change occurs in the middle of a term, the notary has two options:

"1. The notary may continue to use the former name as issued on the existing commission until it expires; or

"2. The notary may use the notary's new name by completing and filing an application with the Secretary of State with a fee of Twenty-five Dollars ($25.00). A new commission expiration date will be established. It will be necessary for a notary to purchase a new seal and obtain a new bond ..." (49 OS 11B).

If Notary Moves: "If a notary's resident address changes, the notary must inform the Secretary of State in writing within thirty (30) days of such change. The notary is not required to file a new bond or obtain another seal if the notary moves from one county to another" (49 OS 11A).

"A notary who ceases to reside or work in Oklahoma must resign their commission" (NPG).

If Notary Resigns: "A notary who resigns his/her notarial commission shall deliver to the Secretary of State a notice of resignation and the effective date of such resignation" (NPG). Notaries who cease to reside or work in the state must resign their commission (OAC 655:25-3-2[b]). "When a notarial commission is resigned, the notary shall destroy the official seal (OAC 655:25-3-2[c]).

Death of Notary: "If a notary dies during the term of commission, the notary's heirs or personal representative, as soon as reasonably practicable after death, shall deliver a signed notice of the date of death to the Secretary of State" (NPG).

COUNTY CLERKS

Effective November 1, 2004, Oklahoma Notaries no longer file their oaths and bonds with the local county clerk (Laws 2004, Chapter 101); instead these are filed with the Secretary of State. As a result, county clerks no longer perform the function of authenticating the acts of local Notaries — a function now solely done by the Secretary of State.

Prior to June 4, 2001, Oklahoma Notaries had to keep a record of their official acts and deliver this record to the local county clerk within 30 days after termination of their commission. These notarial records may still be retained in some counties. To contact an Oklahoma county court clerk to seek assistance in finding and reviewing such records, telephone long-distance information — 1-XXX-555-1212 — using the following area codes and ask for the phone number of the court clerk for the appropriate jurisdiction:

County	City/Town	Area Code
Adair	Stilwell	(918)
Alfalfa	Cherokee	(580)
Atoka	Atoka	(580)
Beaver	Beaver	(580)
Beckham	Sayre	(580)
Blaine	Watonga	(580)
Bryan	Durant	(580)
Caddo	Anadarko	(405)
Canadian	El Reno	(405)
Carter	Ardmore	(580)
Cherokee	Tahlequah	(918)
Choctaw	Hugo	(580)
Cimarron	Boise City	(580)
Cleveland	Norman	(405)
Coal	Coalgate	(580)
Comanche	Lawton	(580)
Cotton	Walters	(580)
Craig	Vinita	(918)
Creek	Sapulpa	(918)
Custer	Arapaho	(580)
Delaware	Jay	(918)
Dewey	Taloga	(580)
Ellis	Arnett	(580)
Garfield	Enid	(580)
Garvin	Pauls Valley	(405)
Grady	Chickasha	(405)
Grant	Medford	(580)
Greer	Mangum	(580)
Harmon	Hollis	(580)
Harper	Buffalo	(580)
Haskell	Stigler	(918)
Hughes	Holdenville	(405)
Jackson	Altus	(580)
Jefferson	Waurika	(580)
Johnston	Tishomingo	(580)
Kay	Newkirk	(580)
Kingfisher	Kingfisher	(405)
Kiowa	Hobart	(580)
Latimer	Wilburton	(918)
LeFlore	Poteau	(918)
Lincoln	Chandler	(405)
Logan	Guthrie	(405)
Love	Marietta	(580)
Major	Fairview	(580)
Marshall	Madill	(580)
Mayes	Pryor	(918)
McClain	Purcell	(405)
McCurtain	Idabel	(580)
McIntosh	Eufaula	(918)
Murray	Sulphur	(580)
Muskogee	Muskogee	(918)
Noble	Perry	(580)
Nowata	Nowata	(918)
Okfuskee	Okemah	(918)
Oklahoma	Oklahoma City	(405)
Okmulgee	Okmulgee	(918)
Osage	Pawhuska	(918)
Ottawa	Miami	(918)
Pawnee	Pawnee	(918)
Payne	Stillwater	(405)
Pittsburg	McAlester	(918)
Pontotoc	Ada	(580)
Pottawatomie	Shawnee	(405)
Pushmataha	Antlers	(580)
Roger Mills	Cheyenne	(580)
Rogers	Claremore	(918)
Seminole	Wewoka	(405)
Sequoyah	Sallisaw	(918)
Stephens	Duncan	(580)
Texas	Guymon	(580)
Tillman	Frederick	(580)
Tulsa	Tulsa	(918)
Wagoner	Wagoner	(918)
Washington	Bartlesville	(918)
Washita	Cordell	(580)
Woods	Alva	(580)
Woodward	Woodward	(580)

OTHER NOTARIAL OFFICERS

Besides Notaries, the following officials are authorized to perform notarial acts in Oklahoma: a judge, or a secretary-bailiff of a judge; a clerk or deputy clerk of any court of this state; and a judge advocate or legal officer of the state military forces in performance of official duties for military personnel and their dependents. "The signature and title of a person performing a notarial act are prima facie evidence that the signature is genuine and that the person holds the designated title" (49 OS 114).

Certified Shorthand Reporters

"Certified shorthand reporters shall be authorized to issue affidavits in respect to their regular duties, to subpoena witnesses for depositions, administer oaths and affirmations, and to take depositions or other sworn statements, with authority equal to that of a notary public" (Oklahoma Reporter Certification Law, Section 1508).

QUICK FACTS

Notary Jurisdiction
Statewide (49 OS 6).

Notary Term Length
Four years (49 OS 1), expiring at midnight on the commission expiration date.

Notary Bond
$1,000, as approved by the Secretary of State, with the bond signed by either: an insurance agent licensed by the state of Oklahoma; an attorney in fact on behalf of an insurance company, with a power of attorney attached; or one or more individual sureties who are property owners in the Notary's county of residence or employment (49 OS 2A).

Cancellation Can't Be Forced: "At the conclusion of a notary's employment, an employer may neither require the notary to surrender the seal nor cancel the surety bond; however, the employer is not required to pay any remaining premium or fee which may be due on the bond" (Oklahoma Attorney General Opinion 00-28 of May 11, 2000).

Statute of Limitations: "No suit shall be instituted against any such notary or his securities more than three (3) years after the cause of action accrues" (49 OS 10).

O-R

Oregon

NOTARY SEAL

An Oregon Notary must affix an official seal of office on every document notarized (ORS 194.031[3] and OAR 160-100-0110[1] and [2]) and that seal's format must be as follows:

Kind

Inked Stamp: "The official seal of a notary public shall be a stamp made of rubber or some other substance capable of making a legible imprint on paper in black ink. The imprint must legibly reproduce under photographic methods" (ORS 194.031[1]). Use of any other object in lieu of the prescribed seal is prohibited (OAR 160-100-0110[7] and 160-100-0130[7]).

Examples

The above typical, actual-size examples of inked and embossing Notary seals are allowed by Oregon law. The embossing seal may be used in addition to — but not in place of — the inked stamp.

NOTARY ADMINISTRATION

Office of Secretary of State
Corporation Division
Notary Public Section   1-503-986-2200
255 Capitol St. N.E., Suite 151
Salem, OR 97310-1327

Website: www.filinginoregon.com/notary/index.htm

NOTARY RULES

ORS — OREGON REVISED STATUTES
OAR — OREGON ADMINISTRATIVE RULES
NPG — OREGON NOTARY PUBLIC GUIDE

Most Notary rules are in:

a. Oregon Revised Statutes, Chapter 194, "Notaries Public"*:

b. Oregon Administrative Rules, Chapter 160, Division 100, "Notaries Public."

* The *Uniform Law on Notarial Acts* of 1982 is included nearly verbatim as sections 194.505 through 194.595.

Other helpful directions for Notaries are in the "Oregon Notary Public Guide" available on the website. Bulletins on law and rule changes are available on "Notary News," a free email subscription service of the Secretary of State.

"The imprint of an official seal of a notary public shall be made with permanent black ink" (OAR 160-100-0100[2]).

Components

An Oregon Notary Public's official inked-stamp seal must contain the following elements, which must be "reasonably legible" when stamped on a document (OAR 160-100-0100[1]):

1. Oregon state seal, as described in ORS 186.020;
2. The following words, in descending

order, centered to the right of the Oregon state seal:
a. "Official Seal";
b. Name of Notary;
c. "Notary Public — Oregon";
d. "Commission No." immediately followed by the commission number;
e. "My Commission Expires" immediately followed by the Notary's commission expiration date (month-day-year), e.g., November 03, 2012, with the month spelled out completely, two digits used for the date, and the year unabbreviated, using four digits.

Embosser May be Used in Addition

In addition to the inked-stamp seal — but not in place of it — a Notary may use an embossing seal on notarized documents (ORS 194.031[7] and OAR 160-100-0130[1] and [2]). The format for the embosser must be as follows:

Circular: "An official seal embosser of a notary public shall be two concentric circles each formed by a continuous solid or intermittent line. The circle shall measure not less than one and one half inches and not more than two inches in diameter" (OAR 160-100-0120[1]).

Components: The components of the embosser seal must be as follows, the printing of which must be legible when embossed on a document (OAR 160-100-0120[2]):
1. Name of Notary centered at the top between the two circles;
2. "STATE OF OREGON" centered at the bottom between the two circles;
3. The word "NOTARY" above the word "PUBLIC" both centered within the inner circle.

Rules for Using Notary Seals

The following rules apply to both inked-stamp seals and embossing seals:

1. A Notary must not place a stamp impression or an embossment over a signature in a document or notarial certificate, or over any writing in a notarial certificate (ORS 160-100-0110[3] and 160-100-0130[3]).

2. When a notarial certificate is on a separate piece of paper attached to the document to be notarized, or when there are attachments to the document to be notarized, a Notary may use an additional stamp impression or embossment to mark for identification the document or attachment, as long as the impression or embossment does not make any part of the document or attachment illegible (OAR 160-100-0110[4] and 160-100-0130[4]).

3. "An embosser is especially useful to guard against fraudulent certificate use.... Affix the impression so that it rests half on the certificate and half on the signer's page. Make sure a whole impression is also on the certificate so that an auditor can compare the divided impression to the whole. You can use the (inked-stamp) notary seal in the same manner, but make sure that the seal (impression) does not obscure anything on either paper" (NPG).

4. "Do not put the seal over the abbreviation 'LS.' Even though 'LS' stands for place of the seal, placing the seal there could obscure some of the words or obliterate some writing" (NPG).

5. "If your seal is smudged so that it is illegible, or is obscured by lines or other graphics on the page, initial the first attempt and re-stamp your seal as close as possible to the certificate" (NPG).

6. A Notary's official seal — whether an inking stamp or an embosser — must not be used for any purpose other than to perform a notarial act (OAR 160-100-0110[5] and 160-100-0130[5]). "A notary may not indorse or promote any product, service, contest or other offering if the notary's title or seal is used in the indorsement or promotional statement" (ORS 194.158[2]).

7. A Notary must not permit any other person to use the Notary's official seal — whether an inking stamp or an embosser — for any purpose (OAR 160-100-0110[6] and 160-100-0130[6]).

8. A Notary must not use any other Notary's official seal — whether an inking stamp or an embosser — to perform a notarial act (OAR 160-100-0110[7] and 160-100-0130[7]).

Omitting Seal on Mylar Plat Maps

Plastic-surfaced plat maps may be notarized without affixation of the Notary seal, as long as the following information appears below the Notary's signature (ORS 194.031[4]):
1. Printed name of Notary;
2. "NOTARY PUBLIC — OREGON";
3. "COMMISSION NO." immediately followed by Notary's commission number;
4. "MY COMMISSION EXPIRES" immediately followed by the Notary's commission

expiration date, "expressed in terms of the month, by name not abbreviated, two-digit date and complete year."

Use of Improper Seal

For use of an improper Notary seal not conforming to ORS 194.031 or the rules of the Oregon Secretary of State, a Notary commission may be revoked, suspended or denied (ORS 194.166[14]).

Seal Imprint Filed with Secretary of State

The Oregon Secretary of State sends each newly commissioned Notary a "Certificate of Authorization," which the Notary must present to a vendor as proof of commissioning when purchasing a seal (ORS 194.010[2]). Within 10 days after obtaining a new seal, the Notary must file this Certificate, completed by the vendor and bearing the imprint of the new seal, with the Secretary of State (OAR 160-100-0140 and ORS 194.031[5]).

Locking Up Seal

"The notary needs to make sure that their journal and seal are secure at all times" (NPG).

"Common examples of misconduct include … not securing the notary … seal" (NPG).

Seal Belongs to Notary, Not Employer

"An individual, not an employer, is commissioned as a notary public. It does not matter who paid for the notarial commission, official notary seal, and notarial journal — they belong to the notary public" (NPG).

"Any person who knowingly obtains, conceals, defaces or destroys the official seal … of a notary public is guilty of a Class B misdemeanor (ORS 194.990[1][c]).

Lost, Destroyed, Damaged Notary Seal

If a Notary's seal is lost, misplaced, destroyed, broken, damaged or otherwise rendered unworkable, the Notary must deliver a sworn, written explanation to the Secretary of State within 10 days (OAR 160-100-0160[1] and [2]), whereupon a new Certificate of Authorization will be issued to the Notary to allow purchase of a new seal (ORS 194.031[6]). Within 10 days after obtaining a new seal, the Notary must file this Certificate, completed by the vendor and bearing the imprint of the new seal, with the Secretary of State (OAR 160-100-0140[3] and ORS 194.031[5]).

Seal on Attached Certificate

"When using an attachment certificate, a complete imprint of your official seal must be on the attachment certificate. A second imprint may overlap the document and the certificate as a protection device. OAR 160-100-0110(2)" (NPG).

Disposition of Seal

Expiration: When a Notary's commission expires normally, the Notary must destroy the official seal(s) immediately (ORS 194.154[1][a] and OAR 160-100-0301[4]). "It must be defaced so that the stamp becomes illegible and unusable" (NPG).

"To destroy the seal, peel off the rubber strip with the tip of your scissors, cut (it) up, and then throw it away" (website, "Notary Commissions").

Death: If a Notary dies in office, an heir or personal representative must surrender the official seal(s) to the Secretary of State within 30 days of the Notary's death (ORS 194.156[1] and OAR 160-100-0340[3]).

Resignation: If a Notary resigns, the Notary must surrender the official seal(s) to the Secretary of State within 30 days after the date of resignation (ORS 194.154[1][a] and OAR 160-100-0320[4]).

Revocation: If a Notary's commission is revoked, the Notary must surrender the official seal(s) to the Secretary of State within 30 days after the date of revocation (ORS 194.154[1][a] and [2] and OAR 160-100-0330[3]).

NOTARY POWERS

Oregon Notaries are authorized to perform the following notarial acts (ORS 194.505[3]):

1. Take acknowledgments*;
2. Administer oaths** and affirmations**;
3. Take verifications upon oath or affirmation***;
4. Witness or attest signatures****;
5. Certify or attest copies***** of documents or other items;
6. Make or note protests of negotiable instruments****** (ORS 73.0505 and 194.070).

* Acknowledgments: "An 'acknowledgment' is a statement by a person that the person has executed an instrument for the purposes stated therein and, if the instrument is executed

in a representative capacity, that the person signed the instrument with proper authority and executed it as the act of the person or entity represented and identified therein" (ORS 194.505[1]).

** Oaths and Affirmations: "'Oath' and 'affirmation' mean a notarial act or part thereof in which a notary certifies that a person made a vow in the presence of the notary on penalty of perjury" (ORS 194.505[5]).

*** Verifications upon Oath or Affirmation: "A 'verification upon oath or affirmation' is a statement by a person who asserts it to be true and makes the assertion upon oath or affirmation" (ORS 194.505[6]).

**** Witnessing or Attesting Signature: "Witnessing or attesting a signature is like an acknowledgment, except that the signer must sign before the notary" (NPG).

***** Certifying or Attesting Copies: "In certifying or attesting a copy of a document or other item, the notarial officer must determine that the proffered copy is a full, true and accurate transcription or reproduction of that which was copied" (ORS 194.515[4]).

"It is vital that the notary make the copy or carefully oversee its making…. "Notaries should not copy public records…. Certified copies are available from the agencies in charge of these records. If an individual wishes you to certify a copy of his or her articles of incorporation, for example, refer him or her to the Corporation Division, which has them on record. It is illegal to make copies, or to certify to copies, of Oregon birth or death certificates and marriage or divorce decrees. According to Oregon Revised Statutes, Chapter 432.210 and Oregon Administrative Rule 333-011-101, only the Oregon Center for Health Statistics may make copies of those records" (NPG).

****** Protests: Effective January 1, 2010, "a notary public may protest commercial paper if the notary public is: (a) An officer or employee of a financial institution as defined in ORS 706.008 or an investment company, or a person serving under the direct supervision of the officer of employee; or (b) An active member of the Oregon State Bar, or a person serving under the direct supervision of an active member of the Oregon State Bar…. A notary public may not protest any commercial paper owned or held for collection by a financial institution or investment company if the notary is individually a party to the commercial paper" (ORS 194.070[1] and [3]).

BACKGROUND: This law was enacted to restrict the performance of protests to Notaries who meet certain qualifications. In Oregon and in many other states, Notary protests have been used in recent years to harass public officials, including judges, corrections officers and law-enforcement personnel. Further, certain individuals have illegally attempted to eliminate valid debt obligations on mortgages and the security interest on real property of mortgage-lending institutions by filing fraudulent documents containing protests. In these scams, Notaries either knowingly or unknowingly served as "Notary Acceptors" on "claims of default" requiring a protest. This law attempts to counteract such unlawful uses of the notarial act of protest by limiting who may perform such acts.

Use of Subscribing Witness

"Q – May I use a subscribing witness when doing a notarization?

"A – No, not according to notary law. There is a special provision in Real Estate law which allows for a subscribing witness in a limited number of real estate transactions. Should this come up, the notary public would need to consult with legal counsel" (website, "FAQs").

Identifying Document Signers

In taking an acknowledgment or a verification upon oath or affirmation, or in witnessing or attesting a signature, a Notary must identify the signer "either from personal knowledge or from satisfactory evidence" (ORS 194.515[1] through [3]).

Personal Knowledge Defined: Personal knowledge "means familiarity with a person resulting from interactions with that person over a period of time sufficient to eliminate every reasonable doubt that the person has the identity claimed" (ORS 194.515[7]).

Satisfactory Evidence Defined: Satisfactory evidence means either that the signer: "(a) Is personally known to the notarial officer; (b) Is identified upon the oath or affirmation of a credible witness personally known to the notarial officer; or (c) Is identified on the basis of identification documents" (ORS 194.515[6]).

Identification Documents: In regard to identification documents, "satisfactory evidence" means that the person produces a current: (a) driver's license or ID card issued by any state; (b) United States passport or officially recognized passport of a foreign country; (c) United States military ID card; or (d) ID card issued by a federally recognized Indian tribe. Alternatively, the person may produce "at least one current document, other than a document described in paragraphs (a) to (d) of this subsection, issued by the federal government or a state, county, municipal or other local government and containing the person's photograph, signature and physical description" (ORS 194.515[8]).

"For the purposes of 194.515: (1) 'Current' means not expired. (2) 'United States passport' means a U.S. passport and a U.S. passport card issued by the U.S. Department of State" (OAR 160-100-0700).

Credible Witness: To use a credible witness to identify a signer, the Notary must personally know the witness and the witness must personally know the signer. A credible witness should be "honest, competent, and impartial," should sign the Notary's journal and must take an oath or affirmation from the Notary, such as "Do you swear (or affirm) that you personally know this document signer to be the individual he/she claims to be (so help you God)?" (NPG).

Signer in Correctional Facility: A signer who is confined in a correctional facility may be "positively identified through examination or comparison of official government documents or records" (ORS 194.515[8][f]).

Ascertaining Willingness, Awareness

"The notary, by the act of notarizing, declares that the signer did so freely and willingly. This can be especially important when people who are easily victimized must sign legal documents; i.e., minors, the infirm, and non-English speaking individuals.

"The notary must make a judgment that the signer is aware of what they are signing. If the notary is questioning the awareness of the signer, the notary can engage in normal conversation with the individual. After a few minutes, it should be apparent if he or she is incoherent, disoriented, or otherwise incapacitated. When in doubt, the notary can get the opinion of a doctor or an attorney" (NPG).

Refusal to Provide Notary Services

"(Y)ou must be careful not to pick and choose whom you will notarize for, or you may be subject to a civil action for discrimination. At this time, notaries may be required by their employer to notarize only for customers of that employer, if that is the employer's consistent policy and is not discriminating against a protected class" (NPG).

Notarizing for Customers Only: "(A)n employer may limit access to employee notaries public during work hours. For example, a bank may only allow its employees to notarize documents involving bank business or documents for people with accounts at that bank. Such a policy should be carefully reviewed by legal staff, however, to protect the employer from lawsuits based on protected class considerations....

"Although an Attorney General's Opinion (DOJ 165-300-0093) states, '... the notary public may, under the notaries public laws, either serve the entire public which desires notary services, a portion of the public (such as customers of a business or fellow employees) or no one at all,' notaries may be seen as having an obligation to respond to any reasonable request for a notarization, and employers may wish to uphold that duty. Restriction of notary services must be carefully crafted, so that the possibility of lawsuits based on perceived discrimination is minimized" (NPG).

Blank Spaces in Document

Notaries should point out blank spaces in documents. If they are intended to be left blank, Notaries should encourage signers to fill them in with "N/A" or something similar. The Notary may not otherwise tell the signer how to fill any blank. The Notary may refuse to notarize if the signer refuses to fill in the blanks (NPG).

"Common sense would prevent most notaries from notarizing a signature on a completely blank sheet of paper, knowing that a fraudulent document could be created on the blank sheet" (NPG).

Foreign-Language Documents

"A notary public who fluently reads and writes a language may notarize the signature on a document written in that language.... (T)he notary should note the foreign language factor in the notarial journal.... A notary public may use a certificate written in a foreign language, if he or she can read and write the language on the certificate, and the certificate meets the minimum requirements of Oregon statute.... When in doubt, a notary can always refuse to notarize and refer the customer to a bilingual notary" (NPG).

Disabled Signer May Use Stamp

"(a) A person who is blind, a person with a visual impairment or a person with a disability who is unable to sign any document because of the disability may use a signature stamp whenever the signature of the person is required on any document presented for notarization;

"(b) In performing any notarial act involving the signature of a person described in paragraph (a) of this subsection, a notarial officer, in the manner prescribed by the Secretary of State by rule, shall witness the use of the signature stamp and accept the stamp in lieu of the signature of the person; and

"(c) The notarial certificate of an act signed with a signature stamp shall contain the phrase 'signed by stamp before me' or words to that effect" (ORS 194.578[2]).

As used above, "person who is blind" and "person with a visual impairment" are defined in ORS 346.110 (ORS 194.578[1]).

Signature by Mark

"There must be two witnesses in addition to the notary, who of course must be present when the signer makes an 'X' on the signature line. One witness then writes the signer's name next to the mark or symbol. Each witness signs the document as a witness to the signature.

"Witnesses should be without financial or other beneficial interest in the transaction. It is preferable that they not be related to the signer ....

"Witnesses ... should be identified and they must sign the journal" (NPG).

Notarizing Photographs

"Although a photograph itself may not be notarized, the notary public may notarize a statement about the photograph. If the customer has a statement on the back of the photograph (For example: I certify that this is an actual photograph of myself), and the customer asks the notary public to witness his or her signature on that statement, the notary public may (if there is room on the photo for the notarial certificate, notary public signature and official notary seal) notarize the photograph.

"For smaller photographs the customer may make a statement about the photograph on a piece of paper referring to 'the attached photo.' As long as the notary public is just witnessing the customer's signature per the customer's instruction, the notary public may notarize.

"After the notarial certificate is complete (venue, statement, official notary seal, and signature), use the official notary seal a second time so that it overlaps the photograph and the paper it is attached to (be careful not to cover the face on the photo). This is a protection device which allows the receiving agency to know that the photograph is the one attached to the document at the time of notarization (website, "FAQs").

Notarizing for Minor

"A minor must provide acceptable ID just as an adult would (or be personally known or have a credible witness) ORS 194.515(6).

"Have the minor put his or her age next to the signature so that the receiving party realizes that they are dealing with a minor. Note the age of the minor in the notary journal.

"Minors must be competent when signing. Ask questions of the minor such as 'What kind of document are you signing?' 'What will the document do?' 'Do you want to sign the document?' If the notary public is not comfortable with the answers the minor gives, he or she should refuse to notarize, noting why in the notary journal, and advise the customer to seek legal advice" (website, "FAQs").

NOTARY DON'TS

Disqualifying Interests

"A notary public may not perform a notarial act if the notary is a signer of or named in the document that is to be notarized" (ORS 194.158[1]). "A notary public cannot notarize his or her own signature" (website, "FAQs").

Relatives: "The law does not forbid notaries from notarizing the signatures of relatives, but it is not a good practice. If the document was ever taken to court, a judge might determine that the notary public was not impartial, or had influenced a relative in the signing of the document. ORS 194.158" (website, "FAQs").

Corporate Employees, Officers: A Notary who

is an employee, officer, director or stockholder of a bank, trust company or other corporation may notarize for that organization as long as the Notary is not a party to the particular transaction, either individually or as a representative of the corporation (ORS 194.100).

A Notary who is an officer or employee of a financial institution or investment company, and who meets the criteria laid out in ORS 194.070(1), may protest any commercial paper owned or held for collection by that organization as long as the Notary is not a party to the commercial paper (ORS 194.070[1] and [3]).

No Telephone Oaths

"Oaths cannot be given over the telephone. The oath-taker must be in the physical presence of the notary" (NPG).

Non-English Advertising

"A notary who is not licensed to practice law in this state and who advertises notarial services in a language other than English shall include in the advertisement, notice or sign, in the same language and in English, the following … statement, prominently displayed: 'I am not licensed to practice law in the State of Oregon and I am not permitted to give legal advice on immigration or other legal matters or accept fees for legal advice.'" (ORS 194.162[3][a]). This notice must be conspicuously displayed in the Notary place of business (ORS 194.162[4]).

"A person may not use the term 'notario publico' or any equivalent non-English term, in any business card, advertisement, notice, sign or in any other manner that misrepresents the authority of a notary public" (ORS 194.162[5]).

NOTARY SIGNING AGENTS

Currently, there are no statutes, regulations or rules expressly governing, prohibiting or restricting the operation of Notary Signing Agents within the state of Oregon.

NOTARY FEES

The maximum fees for notarial acts are (OAR 160-100-0400 and ORS 194.164[1]):
1. For taking an acknowledgment, $10;
2. For administering an oath or affirmation without a signature, $10;
3. For taking a verification upon oath or affirmation, $10;
4. For witnessing or attesting a signature, $10;
5. For certifying a copy of a document, $10;
6. For protesting commercial paper, $10 (except a check drawn on an insolvent financial institution, in which case there is no fee).

Travel Fee

A Notary Public may charge an additional fee for traveling to perform a notarial act if: (a) the Notary explains to the person requesting the notarial act that the fee is in addition to the allowed statutory fee and is not required by law, and (b) the person requesting the notarial act agrees in advance upon the amount of this additional fee (ORS 194.164[2]).

Fees Must Be Posted

Notaries must display in their place of business an English-language schedule of fees for notarial acts (ORS 194.164[3]). Any non-English ads for notarial services must include a schedule of fees, both in the language of the ad and in English (ORS 194.162[3][b]).

The schedule of fees must be posted in a conspicuous location in the Notary's place of business. Alternatively, a copy of the schedule of fees must be handed to each signer to read before the notarization is performed (OAR 160-100-0410).

Fees Can Be Waived

A Notary may file with the Secretary of State a statement waiving the statutory fees, in which case the office of Notary is considered non-lucrative. In this case, a Notary must not charge a fee for any notarial service, and a list of fees must not be displayed (ORS 194.010[5] and OAR 160-100-0420[1] and [2]).

"If a waiver is filed the notary shall not charge, attempt to charge or receive any notary fee for a notarial act performed after the date the notary filed the statement of waiver…. To begin charging, the notary public must send the Secretary of State Corporation Division a letter rescinding the waiver of fees" (NPG).

Fee Agreement with Employer

"Oregon statutes and rules do not address the

collection of notary fees by employers, but a written agreement about notary fees is advisable. The statute gives only the notary public the right to charge notary fees, but an employer often includes a notary charge to the customer when notarization takes place. The fees must not be more than established by Oregon Administrative Rule, and the agreement should make it clear that the notary gives the employer the right to collect and retain the appropriate revenue. The notary public, however, should be allowed to keep fees collected when notarizations are not connected to his/her employment. The employer's legal counsel should draw up an appropriate agreement" (NPG).

"A notary public who is employed by a private entity may enter into an agreement with the entity under which fees collected by the notary under this section are collected by and accrue to the entity…. (A) public body as defined in ORS 174.109 may collect the fees ,,, for notarial acts performed in the course of employment by notaries public who are employed by the public body" (ORS 194.164[4] and [5]).

Notary Employees of Secretary of State

"The Secretary of State shall collect $10 per notarial act performed by a notary public employed by the Secretary of State (Corporation Division) during the course of that person's employment. Notarial acts performed by the employee outside of the course of employment shall be subject to OAR 160-100-0400 through 0420" (OAR 160-005-0008).

NOTARY CERTIFICATES

Oregon has adopted the *Uniform Law on Notarial Acts*, including the short-form certificates (ORS 194.575) for:
1. Acknowledgment by individual;
2. Acknowledgment by representative;
3. Verification upon oath or affirmation;
4. Witnessing or attesting signature;
5. Attesting copy of document.

For the text of these certificates, see "Uniform Law on Notarial Acts (1982)," Section 8, in Appendix 2.

"Although the Oregon Short Form Certificate does not appear to require it, it is usually best to see some confirmation of the person's representative capacity, such as the power of attorney, company annual report (stating officers), official minutes, partnership agreement, etc." (NPG).

In addition the following certificates are prescribed as samples in the "Oregon Notary Public Guide":

Acknowledgment by Attorney in Fact (NPG):

State of OREGON
County of _____

On this _____ day of _____, 20__, before me personally appeared _____, (proved to me on the basis of satisfactory evidence) (personally known to me) to be the person whose name is subscribed to the within instrument (type of document: _____) as the attorney in fact of: _____, and acknowledged that (he)(she) subscribed the name of _____ thereto as principal, and (his)(her) own name as attorney in fact.

_____   (Seal)
Notary Public — State of Oregon

Acknowledgment by Signer by Mark (NPG):

State of OREGON
County of _____

On this _____ day of _____, 20__, before me personally appeared _____, (proved to me on the basis of satisfactory evidence) (personally known to me) to be the person who made and acknowledged (his)(her) mark on the within instrument (type of document: _____) in my presence and in the presence of the two persons who have signed the within instrument as witnesses, one of whom, _____, also wrote the name of the signer by mark near the mark.

_____   (Seal)
Notary Public — State of Oregon

Witness Affidavit for Signing by Mark (NPG):

According to the "Oregon Notary Public Guide," the following form should be attached to the document:

State of OREGON
County of _____

_____ *and* _____, *after first (being by me duly sworn) (affirming to me), declare that: We saw* _____, *the person who executed the foregoing instrument (type of document:* _____), *subscribe the same for the purposes and considerations therein expressed, and that we signed the same as witnesses at the request of the person who executed the same.*

_____ _____
Signature   Date   Signature   Date

Subscribed and (sworn) (affirmed) before me by _____ *and* _____ *this* _____ *day of* _____, *20*__.

_____   (Seal)
Notary Public — State of Oregon

Requirements for Any Notarial Certificate

"(1) A notarial act must be evidenced by a certificate signed and dated by a notarial officer. The certificate must include identification of the jurisdiction in which the notarial act is performed and the title of the office the notarial officer holds and may include the official stamp or seal of office. If the officer is a notary public, the certificate must also indicate the date of expiration, if any, of the commission of office, but omission of that information may subsequently be corrected. If the officer is a commissioned officer on active duty with the military services of the United States, it must also include the officer's rank.

"(2) A certificate of a notarial act is sufficient if it meets the requirements of subsection (1) of this section and it:

"(a) Is in the short form set forth in ORS 194.575;

"(b) Is in a form otherwise prescribed by the law of this state;

"(c) Is in a form prescribed by the laws or regulations applicable in the place in which the notarial act was performed; or

"(d) Sets forth the actions of the notarial officer and those are sufficient to meet the requirements of the designated notarial act" (ORS 194.565[1] and [2]).

AG Opinion on Selecting Certificates

"(T)he notary public should not advise any party concerning which notarial certificate to select. That action is very likely the practice of law....

"The job of the notary public is to assure that a certificate is complete and contains the required information. ORS 194.565. The notary public cannot execute any certificate which contains a statement known to be false. ORS 194.166(13). However, if neither of these two concerns are present, and the notary still believes that the certificate is not the proper one for that type of document, the most the notary public should do is recommend that the person reexamine the document and consult with an attorney. If the person insists that this is the correct certification, then the notary should complete the notarial act as requested, or decline to provide the notarial service. The notary public should not take it upon himself or herself to select or substitute a certificate on behalf of the person. In addition to the risk that the notary public may be found to be unlawfully practicing law, there is also some possibility that the notary public may become involved in litigation if the document is later found not to accomplish what was intended by the parties, and the problem is with a certificate that the notary public selected....

"If the certificate is clearly incorrect, then the notary public must refuse to perform the notarial act and request that the party have the document corrected so that the certificate is not false. The notary public should advise that if the person is uncertain as to the correct certificate to include, the person should consult with an attorney....

"The notary public may point out ORS 194.565 and the required elements of the certificate, and may suggest that the person consider using one of the 'short forms' in ORS 194.575. However, the notary public should not select a form of certificate for the person or otherwise draft a certificate for the person....

"In conclusion, I advise that the Corporation Division should not assist notaries public with the selection of proper certificates, and should further advise notaries public that they should not be recommending or selecting notarial certificates for persons requesting notarial certificates. So long as nothing in the certificate is false, and the necessary information is included, the notary public may complete the certificate. If the notary public has a concern about whether a particular certificate is correct, the notary public should recommend that the person seek legal advice before selecting another certificate" (Oregon Attorney General Opinion, November 12, 1993).

Notwithstanding the above, Oregon law does state: "A notary public may select notarial certificates pursuant to ORS 194.005 to 194.200 and 194.505 to 194.595" (ORS 194.162[1]).

Protecting 'Loose' Certificates

"Because a loose certificate is not an integral part of a document, it is very important to guard against its fraudulent use. The object is to make sure that the certificate may be used with one, and only one, particular document" (NPG). The following seven protective steps are suggested by the state in the "Oregon Notary Public Guide":

1. Any notarial wording on the document itself that the certificate is replacing should be crossed out and the following words should be typed or printed on the page: "SEE ATTACHED NOTARIAL CERTIFICATE."

2. Attach the certificate to the left-hand margin using staples or other fasteners that will make holes if detached.

3. The certificate should be attached on the signature page "directly over the signature so that a recorder can easily film the certificate in sequence with the signature that goes with it."

4. On the certificate itself, the document's date, type and signer should be noted, as well as the number of pages.

5. A notation should be made in the Notary's journal, such as "attached loose certificate to document."

6. A Notary seal embossment may be affixed half on the certificate and half on the signature page. "Make sure a whole impression is also embossed on the certificate so that an auditor can compare the divided impression to the whole. You can use the (inked-stamp) notary seal in the same manner, but make sure the seal (impression) does not obscure anything on either paper."

7. "Attach the certificate yourself, don't allow someone else to do it. Sometimes a client will call later and ask for a 'corrected certificate.' If there is a mistake, the document, and often the signer, will have to reappear before you. An unattached certificate is like a blank check; you are liable."

Correcting Certificates

"Q – May I correct a mistake I made in a notary certificate several days after it was executed?

"A — Yes, corrections can be made. Only the notary public may make corrections that are needed, and the corrections must be made on the original document, i.e. the notary public cannot send a new attachment certificate, the original must be corrected" (website, "FAQs").

"Any corrections must be noted in your journal.... Don't use white-out" (NPG).

ELECTRONIC NOTARIZATIONS

The state of Oregon has not yet adopted statutes or regulations expressly establishing rules, definitions and procedures for electronic notarization.

Online Notarization Not Legal

The following announcement appears on the Secretary of State's website:

"Online webcam notarization is invalid and illegal in the State of Oregon.

"A private company claims to have the first online notarization website and has false claims concerning a new online notarization service. The web-based platform purports to allow a person to submit copies of identification over the Internet and to use a webcam in lieu of a personal appearance in front of a notary public. Appearance via webcam does not meet the requirements for notarization in Oregon.

"Oregon notaries public are not authorized under current law to perform electronic notarizations. Even if they were, Oregon law requires a person to appear personally before a notary public to obtain notarial acts like acknowledgments or oaths. This means the party must be physically present before the notary public. A video image or other form of non-physical representation is not a personal appearance in front of a notary public under current state or federal laws. The technology solution offered by this private company does not comply with Oregon law.

"It is important that Oregon notaries do not participate in this scheme. Clearly, Oregon notaries public who notarize in this fashion are breaking the law, and are subject to administrative and possibly criminal and civil sanctions. It is unclear if notarizations of Oregon citizens done remotely by notaries that are not in Oregon will be upheld in court" (website, "Notary News").

UETA Recognizes Notary's eSignature

Oregon has adopted its own version of the Uniform Electronic Transactions Act (ORS 84.001 through 84.061), including the provision on notarization and acknowledgment, thereby recognizing the legal validity of electronic signatures used by Notaries:

"If a law requires a signature or record to be notarized, acknowledged, verified or made under oath, the requirement is satisfied if the electronic signature of the person authorized to perform those acts, together with all other information required to be included by other applicable law, is attached to or logically associated with the signature or record" (ORS 84.031).

Notary's Use of Electronic Signature

"(1) As used in this section 'electronic signature' has the meaning given that term in ORS 84.004.

"(2) Notwithstanding any provision of ORS 194.005 to 194.200 or 194.505 to 194.595:

"(a) A person may use an electronic signature in the manner prescribed by the Secretary of State by rule whenever the signature of the person is required on any electronic document presented for notarization;

"(b) In performing any notarial act involving an electronic signature of a person described in paragraph (a) of this subsection, a notarial officer, in the manner prescribed by the Secretary of State by rule, shall accept the electronic signature of the person; and

"(c) In addition to the requirements of ORS 194.505 to 194.595, the notarial certificate of an act signed with an electronic signature shall be attached electronically by the notarial officer in the manner prescribed by the Secretary of State by rule and shall contain the phrase 'signed by electronic signature' or words to that effect.

"(3) The Secretary of State shall adopt rules necessary to implement this section" (ORS 194.582)

NOTARY RECORDS

"Each notary public shall provide, keep, maintain and protect one or more chronological journals of notarial acts performed by the notary public" (ORS 194.152[1]).

No More Than One Active Journal

"(A) notary public may not have more than one journal in active use.... All entries of notarizations shall comply with chronologically consecutive entries in the format outlined by the rules of this chapter" (OAR 160-100-0200[6]). "A notary public may not keep more than one journal at a time" (NPG).

Recording Certain Acts Is Optional

Recording the following acts is optional: (a) oaths and affirmations, (b) copy certifications, (c) affidavits, (d) billing statements for media advertising, (e) protests of commercial paper and (f) verifications upon oath or affirmation (OAR 160-100-0230). "However, the Secretary of State recommends all notarial acts be recorded in the journal" (NPG).

Recording Protests Is Mandatory

"A notary public shall maintain a record of information about each protest of commercial paper performed by the notary public consisting of copies of source originals" (OAR 160-100-0240). These copies are considered "competent evidence to prove notice of dishonor for purposes of ORS 73.0505" (ORS 194.090).

Format of Journal

The Notary's journal should be "bound together by any binding method that is designed to prevent the insertion or removal of the cover or a page" (OAR 160-100-0200[1]). The pages must be consecutively numbered from the beginning to the end of the journal, and the page numbers must be preprinted. The entry lines must be consecutively numbered from the beginning to the end of each page, and the line numbers must be preprinted (OAR 160-100-0200[2] and [3]).

Electronic Journals Not Authorized: "May I use an electronic journal? — No, an Oregon notary public must use a paper-bound journal. No electronic journals have been approved for use in Oregon. Before you purchase one, please contact the Secretary of State" (NPG).

Data Required Inside Journal

On the journal's inside front cover or first page, certain information must appear, in any order (OAR 160-100-0200[4]): the Notary's name, address, signature, commission number and commission expiration date; the dates of the first and last notarial act entered in the journal; and the "earliest date the journal may be destroyed, which shall be seven years after expiration of the last commission in which entry was made in the journal" (OAR 160-100-0200[4][e]).

Journal Disposition Indicated: In this same location, the Notary also must indicate the appropriate disposition of the journal in the event of the Notary's death: either surrendered to the Secretary of State or, if the Notary has entered into the relevant agreement with his or her employer, surrendered to the Notary's employer. In the latter case, the Notary must include the date of the agreement and the name and address of the employer (OAR 100-160-0200[4][f]).

Data Must Be Updated: If any of this information changes during the period in which the particular journal is in use, the Notary must update it by drawing a single line through the old information and writing the new information to the side of the old (OAR 160-100-0200[5]).

Abbreviations: "The notary public may wish to create abbreviations of terms to use when recording entries in the notarial journal. If abbreviations are created, put a glossary of abbreviations in the front of the notarial journal. (For example: Ack for Acknowledgment)" (NPG). See also OAR 160-100-0200(4)(g).

New Commission Indicated: "If the notary public is renewing ... (t)he notary public should indicate where the new notarial commission begins on the next notarial journal entry line" (NPG).

Required Entries

For each notarial act that must be recorded in the journal, the Notary must enter (OAR 160-100-0210):

1. Date and time;
2. Type of notarial act;
3. Date of document notarized;
4. Type of document notarized;
5. Printed name of person whose statement, signature, or document was notarized;
6. Signature of person mentioned above;
7. Description of how that person was identified: "personally known" or "personal knowledge"; or the name and residence address of a credible witness, in that order; or the issuing agency of the ID document, the type of ID and the ID's expiration date, in that order;
8. Any other information considered pertinent by the Notary.

According to the "Oregon Notary Public Guide," journal entries also should include any fees collected and any "(u)nusual circumstances, such as power of attorney, reason for refusal to notarize; corrections made to notarial certificate; representative authority (example: President of ABC Company); etc."

Notaries "should not keep copies of the documents they notarize. Your journal entry is sufficient evidence for the purpose of recording a notarial act.... (Notaries) should not keep copies of identification that they use to identify the signer. Your journal entry is sufficient evidence for the purpose of recording how you identified the signer" (NPG).

Journal Entry Shortcuts: Journal entry shortcuts are prescribed for duplicate originals or multiple documents presented by the same person (OAR 160-100-0220).

"If a notary public notarizes duplicate originals of a single statement or document for the same person on the same date, the notary public may fill out one journal entry indicating how many originals (were) notarized....

"If a notary notarizes different statements or documents for the same person on the same date, the notary public may fill out one journal entry, indicating the different notarial acts, document dates, and document types ... (or) ... the notary public may fill out separate journal entries and, where the information is the same, may use ditto marks to indicate the same information that is carried over.... The notary may draw a horizontal line across the signature area and have the signer sign on the line....

"If a notary public notarizes more than one statement, signature or document for the same person but not on the same date, the notary public may refer to previous journal entries in regards to the signer's address and how the notary identified the signer" (NPG).

Locking Up Journal

"The notary needs to make sure that their journal and seal are secure at all times" (NPG).

"Common examples of misconduct include … not securing the notary journal" (NPG).

Unauthorized Handling of Journal

"If any person knowingly destroys, defaces, materially alters or conceals any record or paper of a notary public, that person shall forfeit not more than $500, and shall be liable to an action for damages by the party injured" (ORS 194.130[2]).

"Any person who knowingly obtains, conceals, defaces or destroys the official … journal or official records of a notary public is guilty of a Class B misdemeanor" (ORS 194.990[1][c]).

Journal Belongs to Notary, Not Employer

"It does not matter who paid for the notarial commission, official notary seal, and notarial journal — they belong to the notary public. During a notarial commission term, a notary public may change employers several times, and the notarial commission, official notary seal, and notarial journal move with the notary.... The only exception would be if there is a signed journal agreement with the employer. The notary public would then purchase a new notarial journal for use with the new employer" (NPG).

May Be Public or Private Record

"Because the notary public is an officer of the state and is responsible to the public, the notary journal falls under the public record disclosure laws if the journal resides with the Secretary of State, or if the notary public is a public official or public employee. If the Secretary of State deems that it is in the public interest not to disclose such information, then the journal is kept private.

"Every other notary is exempt from being required to disclose the journal contents, unless requested by the Secretary of State or under subpoena. Normally, it will be in the notary's interest to cooperate with an investigation to avoid being named in a suit" (NPG). See also ORS 194.152(4).

'Fishing Expeditions' Disallowed: "Notaries should not allow 'fishing expeditions,' or malicious attempts to view private information, such as addresses or signatures. There is no reason to allow someone just to browse through your journal" (NPG).

"It is reasonable for a customer to see his or her own entry recorded in the notary journal, but the entries above and below should be covered to protect the privacy of those individuals" (website, "FAQs").

Disposition of Journal

The Notary whose commission is terminated must "dispose of the notarial journal and records pursuant to rules adopted by the Secretary of State within 30 days …" (ORS 194.154[2]). With the exception of records of protests of commercial paper (see below), these rules vary according to the reason for which the Notary's commission is terminated:

Commission Expiration or Resignation: "A notary public whose commission was terminated because of expiration, and who has not applied for a new commission within 30 days after the date of termination, shall arrange for the storage of his/her notarial records …, in any form and at any location. The records or any reproduction of the records must be readable and the notary public must be able to obtain possession of such records within 15 days of receipt of a request for such records" (OAR 160-100-0301[1]). A Notary whose commission was terminated due to resignation must follow the same procedure within 30 days of the resignation (OAR 160-100-0320[1]). In either case, the Notary must inform the Secretary of State in writing of the location of the records within 10 days of storing them (OAR 160-100-0301[2] and 160-100-0320[2]).

"A notary public shall store such records for a period of seven years after the date of commission expiration (or resignation). After the seven-year period, the notary public may destroy such records" (OAR 160-100-0301[3] and OAR 160-100-0320[3]). "However, because it is the only record of the notarization and because the statute of limitations is uncertain, the Secretary of State encourages permanent storage" (NPG).

"A former notary who intends to apply for a new commission need not dispose of the notarial journal and records within 30 days after commission expiration, but must do so within three months after expiration unless newly commissioned within that period" (ORS 194.154[3]). See also OAR 160-100-0310.

Commission Revocation or Death of Notary: Within 30 days after the revocation of a Notary's commission or after the Notary's death, the Notary's journal and records must be surrendered to the Secretary of State. The Secretary must store the records for seven years, after which they may be destroyed (ORS 194.154[2], OAR 160-100-0330[1] and [4] and OAR 160-100-0340[1] and [4]).

Agreement with Employer: A Notary may enter into a written agreement with an employer whereby the notarial records are retained by the employer upon termination of the Notary's employment. The employer then becomes responsible for disposing of the records according to law (ORS 194.152[3]). "If there is an employer agreement ..., the journal stays with the employer upon termination of the employee. The employer must follow the same rules as the notary would" (NPG). The Notary must retain a copy of this written agreement and allow it to be examined by the Secretary of State (OAR 160-100-0360).

If the Notary had entered into a written agreement with his or her employer and the Notary dies while still employed by that employer, the records may be retained by the Notary's employer (OAR 160-100-0340[1]).

Record of Protests: Should the Notary's office become vacant for any reason, the Notary's separate record of protests must be filed with the Secretary of State within 30 days. The Secretary must store the records for seven years, after which they may be destroyed (OAR 160-100-0350[1] and [3] and ORS 194.130).

AUTHENTICATION OF NOTARIAL ACTS

Secretary of State

Authenticating certificates for Notaries, including apostilles, are issued only by the Oregon Secretary of State's office (ORS 194.040[1]).

"Even though the counties (of Oregon) can, by statute, issue certificates, it saves much time and trouble to go directly to our office (i.e., Secretary of State, Corporation Division), because we hold the notary records and the county cannot issue state level certificates required by some foreign governments" (website, "Authentication of Notarizations").

Fees: $10 for a certificate authenticating the Notary's status, including an apostille, payable to "State of Oregon" or "Corporation Division" (OAR 160-100-0040[1] and [2] and website, "Request for Apostille/Authentication: Notary").

Address:
Office of Secretary of State
Corporation Division
Notary Public Section
255 Capitol St. N.E., Suite 151
Salem, OR 97310-1327

Telephone: 1-503-986-2593

Procedure: Mail or present in person the original notarized document, along with the fee and a completed "Request for Apostille/Authentication: Notary" form, available for download on the Secretary of State's website. The form includes all the information needed to process the request. If return by mail is desired, either a stamped, addressed envelope or, for expedited delivery, a prepaid airbill should be included (website, "How to Get an Apostille or Authentication" and "Request for Apostille/Authentication: Notary").

Unauthorized Certificates: "The Secretary of State may not certify a signature of a notary public on a document: (a) Regarding allegiance to a government or jurisdiction; (b) Relating to the relinquishment or renunciation of citizenship, sovereignty, in itinere status or world service authority; or (c) Setting forth or implying a claim of immunity for the bearer from the laws of this state or nation" (ORS194.040[2]).

COMMISSIONING AND ADMINISTRATION

The Oregon Secretary of State appoints, commissions, regulates and maintains records on the state's Notaries (ORS 194.010[1] and 194.040[1]).

Applying for Commission

Qualifications: An applicant for a commission as an Oregon Notary Public must: (a) be at least 18 years old, (b) be a resident of Oregon or be a resident of an adjacent state (i.e., California, Idaho, Nevada or Washington) and regularly employed or carrying on a trade or business in Oregon, (c) be able to read and write English, (d) be of good moral character, (e) not have had a Notary commission revoked for official misconduct during the previous five years and (f) not have been convicted of a felony or a lesser offense incompatible with the duties of a Notary during the previous 10 years (ORS 194.022[1][a] through [f]).

Course and Test Required: A mandatory three-hour class must be taken before submitting an application. All first-time applicants and all current Notaries whose commissions will expire before renewal must take the class. Current Notaries who apply before commission expiration are exempted. Authorized classes are conducted by the Secretary of State's office as well as by approved education providers. A list of approved providers is available on the Secretary's website (OAR 160-100-1110) The application includes a mandatory open-book test; no more than three questions may be missed on the 20-question test (ORS 194.022[1][g] and [h] and 194.028 and website, "Notary Training" and "Notary Public Application").

Application: The applicant must bring the application to another Notary to take the oath of office and have his or her signature notarized (ORS 194.014). A $40 fee is submitted with the application (ORS 194.020).

Notary commissions are not automatically renewed. The renewal process is identical to the initial application process, except that current Notaries who apply for renewal before their commission expires are exempted from the three-hour training class (ORS 194.063{1} and [2]). "Due to budget limitations, the Corporation Division will no longer send courtesy commission renewal notices prior to the commission expiration. Notaries are responsible for tracking and renewing their own commission. Renewal applications received after the commission expiration are subject to the 3-hour mandatory training requirement in ORS 194" (website, "Notary News"). Renewal applications and exams should be submitted no earlier than two-and-one-half months prior to commission expiration (NPG).

After receipt of a new commission and a "Certificate of Authorization," the Notary must use the Certificate to obtain an official seal and then affix an imprint of the seal on the Certificate and return it to the Secretary of State (website, "Commission Application/Renewal").

Non-Residents: Out-of-state residents of adjacent states (California, Nevada, Idaho, Washington) may become Oregon Notaries if they are regularly employed in Oregon or carry on a trade or business within the state (ORS 194.022[1][b]).

Online Search: The "Notary Search" function allows anyone to search for a Notary by location (county and city), by language(s) spoken and/or by name. Information available on listed Notaries includes: city and zip code, county, contact information, languages spoken, commission expiration date and whether the Notary has an embossing seal as well as the mandatory inked-stamp seal (website, "Notary Search").

Changes of Status

If Notary Moves: Within 30 days of changing a residence or business address, a Notary must notify the Secretary of State in writing (ORS 194.047).

If Notary Changes Name: A Notary whose name has changed must either: (a) notify the Secretary of State in writing within 30 days, if he or she wishes to use the old name until commission expiration; or (b) file for an amended commission, using a "Change of Name" form and including the required fee for the amendment, if he or she wishes to begin using the new name immediately (ORS 194.052). The fee "for processing a request to change the notary public's name on the notary public's written commission" is $10 (OAR 160-100-0040[6]).

If Notary Resigns: If a Notary no longer wishes to hold a Notary commission, ceases to live or work in Oregon or becomes unable to read or write, he or she must notify the Secretary of State in writing (ORS 194.063[3]). A resignation form, available for download on the Secretary of state's website, must be submitted. The Notary must tell the state where the journal will be stored for the next seven years, and the seal must be destroyed (website, "Notary Commissions").

COUNTY CLERKS

Oregon Notaries no longer file their commissions and signature and seal samples with the county clerk, and a law enacted in 2005 (Chapter 68) repealed the statutory authority for county clerks to certify a Notary's status.

OTHER NOTARIAL OFFICERS

In addition to Notaries, the following officers have authority to perform notarial acts in Oregon:

judges, clerks and deputy clerks of any court of the state (ORS 194.525[1][b]).

Tribal Officers Have Notarial Powers
"(1) A notarial act has the same effect under the law of this state as though performed by a notarial officer of this state if performed anywhere by any of the following persons under authority granted by a federally recognized American Indian tribal government located within the United States:

"(a) A notary public of the tribal government.

"(b) A judge, clerk or deputy clerk of any court of the tribal government.

"(c) Any other person authorized by the law of the tribal government to perform notarial acts.

"(2) The signature and title of a person performing a notarial act under this section are prima facie evidence that the signature is genuine and that the person holds the designated title.

"(3) The signature and title of an officer listed in subsection (1)(a) or (b) of this section conclusively establish the authority of a holder of that title to perform a notarial act" (ORS 194.558).

QUICK FACTS

Notary Jurisdiction
Statewide (ORS 194.043).

Notary Term Length
Four years (ORS 194.012).

Notary Bond
Not required.

Liability of Employer: "An employer of a notary is liable to the notary for all damages recovered from the notary as a result of official misconduct that was coerced by threat of the employer, if the threat, such as that of demotion or dismissal, was made in reference to the particular notarization" (ORS 194.200[3]).

Pennsylvania

NOTARY SEAL

A Pennsylvania Notary must authenticate all official acts with a seal of office and the format must be as follows (57 PS 158):

Kind

Inked Rubber Stamp: "The seal shall be a rubber stamp and shall show clearly in the following order: the words 'Notarial Seal'; the name and surname of the notary and the words 'Notary Public'; the name of the municipality and county in which the notary maintains an office; and the date the notary's commission expires" (57 PS 158[a]).

'Commonwealth of Pennsylvania': "(S)ince Act 151 of 2002 does not require the rubber stamp seal to contain a reference to the state of Pennsylvania following the name of the municipality and county in which the notary public

Commonwealth of Pennsylvania

NOTARIAL SEAL
Jane Q. Doe, Notary Public
City of Harrisburg, Dauphin County
My commission expires Jan 30, 2016

Examples

The above typical, actual-size examples of a mandatory rubber stamp and an optional embosser seal are allowed by law. Formats other than these may also be permitted. The optional words "Commonwealth of Pennsylvania" by law are not currently allowed within the border of the rubber stamp seal.

NOTARY ADMINISTRATION

Department of State
Bur. of Commissions, Elections and Legis.
Division of Legislation
  and Notaries   1-717-787-5280
210 North Office Building
Harrisburg, PA 17120-0029

Website: www.dos.state.pa.us/notaries

NOTARY RULES

PS — Pennsylvania Statutes
NPP — Notaries Public in Pennsylvania

Most Notary regulations are in the Pennsylvania Statutes:

a. Title 57, Chapter 7, "Notary Public Law of 1953" (Sections 57 PS 147 through 57 PS 169) as amended by Public Law 1269, Act No. 151-2002, effective July 1, 2003;

b. Title 21, Chapter 1, "Uniform Acknowledgment Act,"* Sections 21 PS 291.1 through 21 PS 291.13.

* This is the *Uniform Acknowledgment Act* of 1939, adopted with amendments.

Other guidelines for Notaries are in the "Notaries Public in Pennsylvania" (Rev. Aug. 2005) booklet issued by the Department of State and also available on the website.

maintains an office, the notary public may wish to exercise the option of using an embosser in conjunction with the seal or add the preprinted words 'Commonwealth of Pennsylvania' outside the top of the plain border of the seal" (website, "General Information and Equipment").

Embosser Is Optional Addition: Pennsylvania Notaries retain the option of using an embosser seal in addition to the mandatory rubber stamp seal (website, "Notary Public Equipment"). There is no prescribed format.

Shape/Size

Rectangular, with a maximum height of 1 inch and maximum width of $3^{1}/_{2}$ inches, "with a plain border" (57 PS 158[b]).

Components

Within the plain border, the components of the seal must appear in the following order (57 PS 158[a]):
1. "Notarial Seal";
2. Name and surname of Notary;
3. "Notary Public";
4. Name of municipality (city/town) and county in which Notary maintains office;
5. Commission expiration date.

Placement of Seal

"(The seal) shall be stamped in a prominent place on the official notarial certificate near the notary's signature in such a manner as to be capable of photographic reproduction" (57 PS 158[b]).

Unauthorized Use, Possession of Seal

"The notary public seal is the exclusive property of the notary to whom it is issued and a notary shall be responsible at all times for maintaining custody and control of the seal. No notary public shall permit the use of the seal by another person" (57 PS 158[c]).

"The use of a notary public seal by a person who is not the notary public named on the seal shall be deemed an impersonation of a notary public under and shall be subject to the penalties set forth in 18 Pa.C.S. § 4913 (relating to impersonating a notary public)" (57 PS 158[d]).

Noncompliant Seals

"The seal of any notary public appointed after the effective date (in 1953) of the act to which this act is a supplement, and prior to the effective date of this act (July 1, 2003), on which seal there is engraved the name, surname, the words 'Notary Public,' and the location of the office of the notary using the same, shall be a valid and legal seal during the term for which he or she was reappointed, notwithstanding the fact that in addition thereto it has engraved thereon the arms of this Commonwealth; and all the acts, instruments and attestations of such notary authenticated by such seal shall be as valid and binding as though the arms of this Commonwealth were not thereon" (57 PS 31a).

Disposal of Seal

"Should an application or renewal be rejected, or should a commission be revoked or recalled for any reason, or should a notary public resign, the applicant or notary shall deliver the seal of office to the Department of State within ten (10) days after notice from the department or from the date of resignation, as the case may be" (57 PS 168.1[a]). Any person failing to do so may be guilty of a summary offense, punishable by a fine not exceeding $300 or imprisonment not exceeding 90 days, or both.

"Upon the death of a notary public, the notary's personal representative shall deliver the seal of office to the Department of State within ninety (90) days of the date of the notary's death" (57 PS 168.1[b]).

Electronic Image of Seal Not Required

"(A) notary public is not required to use an electronic seal for the notarization, acknowledgment or verification of electronic records and electronic signatures, provided that, in any event, the following information is attached to or logically associated with the electronic signature or electronic record being notarized, acknowledged, or verified:

"1. The full name of the notary along with the words 'Notary Public.'

"2. The name of the municipality and the county in which the notary maintains an office.

"3. The date the notary's commission is due to expire" (57 PS 158[f]).

Notary's Signature

"In acting as a notary public, a notary shall sign the notary's name exactly and only as it appears on the commission, or otherwise execute the notary's electronic signature in a manner that attributes such signature to the notary public identified in the commission .... A county may permit notaries to register their electronic signatures" (57 PS 155[c] and [d]).

NOTARY POWERS

Pennsylvania Notaries are authorized to perform the following notarial acts (57 PS 162):
1. Take acknowledgments and proofs*;
2. Administer oaths** and affirmations;
3. Take depositions***, affidavits and verifications;

4. Certify copies****;
5. Execute protests;
6. Perform certain functions related to motor vehicle titles*****.

* Proof by Attorney at Law: Statute prescribes a certificate for a proof by a subscribing witness who is a member of the Pennsylvania bar — see below under "Notary Certificates" (21 PS 291.7[5]).

** Oath Wording: The following oath wording is suggested for (a) affidavits and for (b) oral testimony (website, "Sample Notary Statements"):

a. "Do you solemnly swear that the statements contained in this affidavit are true to the best of your knowledge and belief?";

b. "Do you solemnly swear that the testimony that you are about to give will be the truth, the whole truth, and nothing but the truth?"

*** Depositions: "In taking a deposition, the notary should first make sure the witness is sworn in. The notary should then personally record or supervise the recording of the testimony of the witness. After the testimony is transcribed the notary should let the witness read and sign the transcribed copy of the deposition. The notary then certifies that the witness was sworn and that this document is a true record of the witness' testimony. The deposition should be sealed in an envelope and filed with the court or sent to the prothonotary for filing.

"If a videotaped deposition is requested, the notary should make sure the witness is sworn. However, it is unnecessary to have a stenographic transcript and the witness' signature. The videotape should be given to the attorney for the party requesting the deposition" (NPP).

**** Certifying Copies: "In certifying a copy of a document or other item, a notary public shall determine that the proffered copy is a full, true and accurate transcription or reproduction of that which was copied" (57 PS 158.1[b]).

Birth and death certificates, marriage records and articles of incorporation are excluded from copy certification since "(o)nly the agencies where these records are filed may certify copies, because they alone hold the original documents or records" (website, "Sample Notary Statements").

"To make a certified copy of a record in the register, the notary public reproduces the page in its entirety and attaches a certificate stating 'this is a true and correct copy from my official register, showing that'" (NPP).

***** Motor Vehicle Attestations: The role of Pennsylvania Notaries who are qualified to process paperwork related to the title and transfer of motor vehicles is beyond the scope of this publication. Notaries interested in performing such duties may inquire with the Pennsylvania Department of Transportation in Harrisburg.

Identifying Signers

"The officer notarizing the instrument shall know through personal knowledge or have satisfactory evidence that the person appearing before the notary is the person described in and who is executing the instrument. For the purposes of this act and section 5 of the act of July 24, 1941 (P.L. 490, No. 188), known as the Uniform Acknowledgment Act, 'personal knowledge' means having an acquaintance, derived from association with the individual in relation to other people and based upon a chain of circumstances surrounding the individual, which establishes the individual's identity, and 'satisfactory evidence' means the reliance on the presentation of a current, government-issued identification card bearing a photograph, signature or physical description and serial or identification number, or the oath or affirmation of a credible witness who is personally known to the notary and who personally knows the individual" (57 PS 158.1[a]).

NOTARY DON'TS

Disqualifying Interests

Direct or Pecuniary Interest: "No notary public may act as such in any transaction in which he is a party directly or pecuniarily interested. For the purpose of this section, none of the following shall constitute a direct or pecuniary interest:

"1. being a shareholder in a publicly traded company that is a party to the notarized transaction;

"2. being an officer, director or employee of a company that is a party to the notarized transaction, unless the director, officer or employee personally benefits from the transaction other than as provided in clause (3); or

"3. receiving a fee that is not contingent upon the completion of the notarized transaction" (57 PS 165[e]).

May Not Notarize Own Signature: "A notary cannot notarize his or her own signature" (website, "Powers of a Notary Public").

District Justice May Be Disqualified: "No district justice, holding at the same time the office of notary public, shall have jurisdiction in cases arising on papers or documents containing acts by him done in the office of notary public" (57 PS 165[d]).

May Not Perform Marriages

"Notaries public in Pennsylvania may not take an application for a marriage license, issue a marriage license, or perform a civil marriage ceremony" (website, "Powers of a Notary Public").

Powers May Not Be Delegated

"Since a notary commission is granted to a particular individual, a notary public cannot delegate notarial authority to another person. A notary public's commission is not transferable, even on a temporary basis. It is prohibited to permit another person to use your notary public commission and you must safeguard your seal at all times" (website, "Powers of a Notary Public").

Voluntary Compliance on Non-English Ads

"(T)he Department is…asking that commissioned Pennsylvania notaries public, who are not licensed attorneys and who advertise their notarial services in any language other than English, to make it clear to customers and the general public that the notary may not offer legal advice or services in Pennsylvania and most other States" (website, "Voluntary Compliance…").

Disclaimer Must Be Posted: "Every notary public, who is 1) not an attorney or 2) not an Accredited Immigration Representative with a Board of Immigration Appeals Recognized Organization entitled to represent applicants before the United States Citizenship and Immigration Services, and 3) advertises the services of a notary public in a language other than English, should include in, post or otherwise attach to said advertisement, a written or verbal notice, in English and in every other language used, which sets forth the following disclaimer: 'I am not an attorney licensed to practice law in the Commonwealth of Pennsylvania and I may not give any legal advice or accept fees for legal advice. I cannot explain or interpret the contents of any document for you, instruct you on how to complete a document or direct you in the advisability of signing a particular document'" (website, "Voluntary Compliance…"). The disclaimer should include the Notary fee schedule fixed by 4 Pa. Code 161.1.

If the foreign-language ad is written, the disclaimer should be translated into each foreign language used and placed in a separate notice or sign of a conspicuous size. "The disclaimer should be posted either 1) in a location, the notaries' place of business, where it will be visible to customers and at a minimum, each notice or sign should be at least 8-1/2 inches by 14 inches or 2) adjacent to the advertisement. If the foreign language advertisement is verbal, the required disclaimer above should be immediately translated in each language used" (website, "Voluntary Compliance…").

Use of Term 'Notario' Discouraged: "Literal translation of the phrase 'notary public' into Spanish, as 'notario publico' or 'notario,' or into any other foreign language, that conveys terms or titles including but not limited to, licensed attorney, lawyer, or any other term that implies the notary is an attorney is strongly discouraged, unless used with the required disclaimer above" (website, "Voluntary Compliance…").

NOTARY SIGNING AGENTS

Currently, there are no statutes, regulations or rules expressly governing, prohibiting or restricting the operation of Notary Signing Agents within the Commonwealth of Pennsylvania.

NOTARY FEES

The fees for Notaries are set by the Secretary of the Commonwealth with the approval of the Attorney General (57 PS 167). The fees listed below became effective August 6, 2005 (4 Pa. Code 161.1):

1. Taking an acknowledgment: for the first signature: $5; for each additional signer: $2;
2. Administering an oath, per person: $5;
3. Executing an affidavit, no matter how many signatures: $5;
4. Executing a verification: $5;
5. Taking a deposition, per page: $3;

6. Making a protest, per page: $3;
7. Executing a certificate, per certified copy: $5.

Fees Must Be Displayed

"The fees of notaries public shall be displayed in a conspicuous location in the notary's place of business or be provided upon request to any person utilizing the services of the notary. The fees of the notary shall be separately stated" (57 PS 167[c]).

Fees May Be Waived

"A notary public may waive the right to charge a fee, in which case the requirements ... regarding the display or provision of fees shall not apply" (57 PS 167[c]).

Bank Employee Keeps Fees

"The fee for any notary public employed by a bank, banking institution or trust company shall be the property of the notary and in no case belong to or be received by the corporation for whom the notary is employed" (57 PS 167[d]).

Clerical Fees

"Notaries public may charge a clerical or administrative fee for services they have provided in addition to the notarization of a document such as copying documents, postage, phone calls or completing forms. These clerical fees are not set by statute. Customers should be informed if a clerical fee is being charged in addition to to the notary public fees prior to the notarization of a document. The customer's receipt should itemize these fees. Besides notary fees, a notary may also charge a customer clerical and travel fees. These fees should not be recorded in the notarial register. Clerical and travel fees should be recorded in a separate record or receipt book" (NPP).

NOTARY CERTIFICATES

Pennsylvania has adopted the *Uniform Acknowledgment Act*, including the certificates (21 PS 291.7) for:

1. Acknowledgment by individual;
2. Acknowledgment by corporation;
3. Acknowledgment by attorney in fact;
4. Acknowledgment by any public officer or deputy thereof or by any trustee, administrator, guardian or executor.

Pennsylvania has added a fifth certificate to its version of the *Uniform Acknowledgment Act* — a "Proof of Execution by Attorney at Law," printed below.

The Notary's inked seal must be affixed to each certificate.

For the text of these certificates, see "Uniform Acknowledgment Act (1939, amended 1960)," Section 7, in Appendix 4.

In addition, Pennsylvania statute prescribes the following certificates:

Acknowledgment of Deed by Individual(s) (21 PS 81):

COMMONWEALTH OF PENNSYLVANIA)
) SS:
COUNTY OF _____)

On this ____ day of _____ A.D. 20____, before me, a _____ in and for _____, came the above named _____ and acknowledged the foregoing deed to be his/her/their act and deed, and desired the same to be recorded as such.

Witness my hand and _____ seal, the day and year aforesaid.

_____ (Signature)
_____
(Official character)

(NOTARY'S STAMP)

My commission expires _____

Acknowledgment by Individual (21 PS 291.7[1] and website, "Sample Notary Statements"):

COMMONWEALTH OF PENNSYLVANIA)
) SS:
COUNTY OF _____)

On this, the ____ day of _____, 20____, before me, _____, a Notary Public, the undersigned officer, personally appeared _____, known to me (or satisfactorily proven) to be the person(s) whose name(s) is/are subscribed to the within instrument and acknowledged that he/she/they executed the same for the purposes therein contained.

In witness whereof, I hereunto set my hand and official seal.

_____
Notary Public

(NOTARY'S STAMP)

Proof of Execution by Attorney at Law (21 PS 291.7[5]):

*State of Pennsylvania
County of _____*

On this, the ____ day of _____, 20___, before me, _____, the undersigned officer, personally appeared _____, known to me (or satisfactorily proven) to be a member of the bar of the highest court of said state and a subscribing witness to the within instrument, and certified that he/she was personally present when _____, whose name(s) is/are subscribed to the within instrument executed the same, and that said person(s) acknowledged that he/she/they executed the same for the purposes therein contained.

In witness whereof, I hereunto set my hand and official seal.

_____ *(Signature)*
_____
Title of Officer

(NOTARY'S STAMP)

Acknowledgment Certificate Requirements

"The certificate of the acknowledging officer shall be completed by his signature, his official seal, if he has one, the title of his office, and, if he is a notary public, the date his commission expires" (21 PS 291.8).

Out-of-State Acknowledgment Certificates

"Notwithstanding any provision of this act contained, the acknowledgment of any instrument without this State in compliance with the manner and form prescribed by the laws of the place of its execution, if in a state, a territory or insular possession of the United States, or in the District of Columbia, verified by the official seal of the officer before whom it is acknowledged or authenticated ... shall have the same effect as an acknowledgment in the manner and form prescribed by the laws of this State for instruments executed within the State" (21 PS 291.10).

Certified Copy Certificate (website, "Sample Notary Statements"):

COMMONWEALTH OF PENNSYLVANIA)
) SS:
COUNTY OF _____)

I certify that the attached copy of a _____ dated _____ is a true, correct and complete copy of the original _____.

In witness whereof, I hereunto set my hand and official seal.

_____
Notary Public

(NOTARY'S STAMP)

Affidavit (website, "Sample Notary Statements"):

COMMONWEALTH OF PENNSYLVANIA)
) SS:
COUNTY OF _____)

Before me, the undersigned notary public, this day, personally appeared _____, to me known, who being duly sworn according to law, deposes the following:

(Affiant's Statement)
_____ *(Affiant's Signature)*

Subscribed and sworn to before me this ____ day of _____, 20___.

_____
Notary Public

(NOTARY'S STAMP)

Deposition (website, "Sample Notary Statements"):

COMMONWEALTH OF PENNSYLVANIA)
) SS:
COUNTY OF _____)

I, _____ (name of officer), a _____ (title), do hereby certify that, pursuant to _____ (specify the stipulation, notice or order of court under which the deposition was taken), the deposition of _____ (name of witness) was duly taken at _____ (place) on _____ (date) at _____ o'clock __ m. before me. The said _____ (name of witness) was first duly sworn (or affirmed) by me according to law to tell the truth and thereupon did testify as set forth in the above transcript of testimony. The testimony was taken down in my presence stenographically by _____ (name of stenographer) under my direction.

I do further certify that the above deposition is a full, complete and true record of all the testimony given by the said witness.

_____
Officer

(NOTARY'S STAMP)

ELECTRONIC NOTARIZATIONS

"The Electronic Notarization Initiative was established on January 20, 2006, to enhance economic development in Pennsylvania, and was the first of its kind in the nation. E-Notarization allows qualified Pennsylvania notaries public to perform notarizations electronically, in compliance with provisions of the amended Notary Public Law and the Uniform Electronic Transactions Act" (website, "Electronic Notarization"). The Initiative is overseen by the Pennsylvania Department of State through its Electronic Notarization Program.

'More Accessible' eNotarization Is Aim

"The Department is now accepting applications for the electronic notarization program...."

"The Department of State has taken new steps to make e-Notarization more accessible to Pennsylvania's approximately 80,000 notaries public.

"1. Starting January 30, 2008, the Department (began) the transition to a multi-vendor system, to increase the opportunities and choices for Pennsylvania notaries to electronically notarize electronic documents.

"2. The Department (eliminated) the $40.00 fee for electronic notarization applications submitted and received after January 30, 2008" (website, "Electronic Notarization").

Electronic Notarization Initiative

The Electronic Notarization Initiative authorizes and enables qualified Pennsylvania Notaries to perform electronic notarizations on electronic documents that are then recorded electronically by participating Pennsylvania recorders of deeds. Initially the participating counties were Chester, Lancaster, Philadelphia and Westmoreland. Currently, the following counties participate in the program: Allegheny, Berks, Blair, Bucks, Centre, Chester, Forest, Lackawanna, Lancaster, Lebanon, Lehigh, Luzerne, Montgomery, Northampton and Philadelphia (website, "Approved Electronic Notary Solution Vendors").

In regard to the completion of a notarial certificate, the in-person screening of each signer and the making of a journal entry for each official act, electronic notarizations in Pennsylvania are essentially the same as paper-based notarial acts. The maximum fees that may be charged are also the same. The five major components for valid paper-and-ink notarizations also apply to eNotarizations: personal appearance of the signer before the Notary; identification of the signer by the Notary; acknowledgment of the signature by the signer; lack of duress on the part of the signer; and the signer's evident awareness of the transaction (website, "Electronic Notarization"/"Frequently Asked Questions").

Commissioning of Electronic Notary

There are eight steps to becoming an electronic notary:

1. "The duly appointed and commissioned notary public… who holds a current and unrestricted commission commission completes the Electronic Notary Public Application and submits it to the Department of State's Bureau of Commissions, Elections and Legislation…"

2. "If approved to act as an electronic notary, the applicant will be notified by mail with an Electronic Notary Approval Letter from the Department of State,.. The notary has 45 days from the date of the Approval Letter to complete the process for obtaining an electronic notary solution or the approval becomes null and void…"

3. "The approved electronic notary appears in-person before a participating county Recorder

of Deeds and presents the Electronic Notary Approval Letter and satisfactory evidence of identity to the Recorder…"

4. "The approved electronic notary is notified via e-mail to log onto the Department of State's website to select an approved electronic notary solution provider. The approved electronic notary may select more than one approved electronic notary solution provider at this time…"

5. "The Department of State provides information to the selected electronic notarization solution provider(s) that the Pennsylvania notary is authorized to receive an electronic notary solution…"

6. "The electronic notary and the selected electronic notary solution provider will work together directly to pay for and obtain an electronic notary solution. Contact information for the approved electronic notary solution providers may be found at http://www.dos.state.pa.us/notaries…"

7. "Once an electronic notary solution has been issued by the approved electronic notary solution provider to the notary, notification will be made to the Department of State and the electronic notary's record will be updated showing that an electronic notary solution has been issued to that notary…"

8. "The approved electronic notary may now use his/her electronic notary solution until the end of the notary's current four-year commission as a notary public or for a lesser period of time as necessitated by the particular electronic notary solution, whichever is shorter" (website, "Eight Steps…").

No Additional Education Requirement: "There is no additional notary education required to become an electronic notary under the Electronic Notarization Program. However, the Department of State strongly suggests continuing notary education for all notaries with basic and advanced course content that includes electronic notarization" (website, "Frequently Asked Questions").

Approved Electronic Notary Solution Provider
A Pennsylvania Electronic Notary must select an Electronic Notary Solution Provider approved by the Department of State that will enable the Notary to use an electronic signature in performing electronic notarial acts — see Step 4 above.

"An approved solution provider must comply with the technical specifications… that govern electronic notarization processes and procedures in Pennsylvania, such that the electronic notary seal must be: (a) unique to the notary public; (b) capable of independent verification; (c) retained under the notary's sole control; (d) attached to or logically associated with the electronic document; and (e) linked to the data in such a manner that any subsequent alterations to the underlying document or electronic notarial certificate are detectable (website, "Frequently Asked Questions").

Act Recognizes Notary's eSignature
Pennsylvania has adopted an amended version of the Uniform Electronic Transactions Act (Act No. 69 of 1999), called the Electronic Transactions Act, including the following provision on notarization, thereby recognizing the validity of electronic signatures used by Notaries:

"If a law requires a signature or record to be notarized, acknowledged, verified or made under oath, the requirement is satisfied if the electronic signature of the person authorized to perform those services, together with all other information required to be included by other applicable law, is attached to or logically associated with the signature or record" (73 PS 2260.307).

Electronic Image of Seal Not Required: "Notwithstanding other provisions of this section, in accordance with the act of December 16, 1999 (P.L. 971, No. 69), known as the 'Electronic Transactions Act,' a notary public is not required to use an electronic seal for the notarization, acknowledgment or verification of electronic records and electronic signatures, provided that, in any event, the following information is attached to or logically associated with the electronic signature or electronic record being notarized, acknowledged or verified:

"1. The full name of the notary along with the words 'Notary Public.'

"2. The name of the municipality and the county in which the notary maintains an office.

"3. The date the notary's commission is due to expire" (57 PS 158[f])."

'Commonwealth of Pennsylvania': "This information can be displayed in different and customized ways, depending on the software manufacturer and the document preparation software used. As with the rubber stamp seal, the Department recommends that the notary public add the words 'Commonwealth of Pennsylvania' near the above-cited information" (website, "Electronic Notarization").

NOTARY RECORDS

"Every notary public shall keep and maintain custody and control of an accurate chronological register of all official acts by that notary done by virtue of that notary's office, and shall, when thereunto required, give a certified copy of the register in the notary's office to any person applying for same" (57 PS 161[a]).

Required Entries

"Each register shall contain the date of the act, the character of the act, and the date and parties to the instrument, and the amount of fee collected for the service. Each notarization shall be indicated separately" (57 PS 161[a]).

Separate Book for Clerical, Travel Fees: "Besides notary fees, a notary may also charge a customer clerical and travel fees. These fees should not be recorded in the notarial register. Clerical and travel fees should be recorded in a separate record or receipt book" (NPP).

Being Careful with Confidential Data

"When required, each notary public must give a certified copy of the register in the notary public's office in its entirety to any person requesting it. Therefore, given that the notary register is a public document, a notary may wish to take care not to include any entries (particularly, confidential identifying information about the signer, such as Social Security numbers) in their register that are not explicitly required by the Notary Public Law" (NPP).

Certifying Copy of Register

"To make a certified copy of a record in the register, the notary public reproduces the page in its entirety and attaches a certificate stating, 'this is a true and correct copy from my official register, showing that.' The reproduction should be a photocopy of the entire register page containing the entry in question. However, the notary public may wish to cover the other entries on the page to protect the confidentiality of the other entries" (website, "Powers of a Notary Public").

Register Is Exclusive Property of Notary

"The register and other public records of such notary shall not in any case be liable to be seized, attached or taken in execution for debt or for any demand whatsoever" (57 PS 161[b]).

"A notary public register is the exclusive property of the notary public, may not be used by any other person and may not be surrendered to any employer of the notary upon termination of employment" (57 PS 161[c]).

Records Delivered to Recorder

"Upon a notary public's resignation, death or disqualification, or upon the revocation or expiration of a commission, unless the notary public applies for a commission within thirty (30) days of the expiration of the prior commission, the notary public's register shall be delivered to the office of the recorder of deeds of the proper county within thirty (30) days of such event" (57 PS 161[d]).

"Even if he/she ceases to be a notary public because of, for example, resignation or commission expiration, it is recommended that the individual permanently retain a copy of the register for his/her own protection from possible future findings of liability" (website, "General Information and Equipment").

AUTHENTICATION OF NOTARIAL ACTS

County Prothonotaries

Locally, an authenticating certificate for a given Notary may be issued by the prothonotary (clerk of the court of common pleas) in whose office the Notary has filed an official signature. The prothonotary maintains a "Notary Register" containing the signatures of Notaries who keep an office within the county (57 PS 155).

In Allegheny County, the clerk of the court may authenticate the acts of local Notaries, since they are required to register in that office. In the several counties that have eliminated the office of prothonotary, Notaries instead register their signatures with the clerk of courts, the clerk of records, or the equivalent; these offices may then issue authenticating certificates.

Secretary of Commonwealth

Authenticating certificates for Notaries, including apostilles, are also issued by the office of the Secretary of the Commonwealth.

Fees: $15 per certificate issued, including issuance of any needed apostille. Check or money order payable to "Commonwealth of Pennsylvania."

Address:
Pennsylvania Department of State
Bureau of Commissions, Elections
   and Legislation
210 North Office Building
Harrisburg, PA 17120-0029

Telephone: 1-717-787-5280

Procedure: Present in person or mail the original notarized document(s), along with the appropriate fee. If mailed, include a cover letter, indicating the nation to which the document will be sent. A "Request for Legalization of Documents" form is available online. Include an addressed, stamped envelope, or a prepaid air bill; FedEx and DHL are no longer accepted. "Diplomas, transcripts and criminal record checks must be notarized prior to requesting an apostille or certification. Birth Certificates do not need to be and should not be notarized…Photocopies of notarized or certified documents may not be certified by the Secretary of the Commonwealth" (website, "Certifications, Apostilles, and the Authentication of Documents"). County documents must be signed by the clerk in charge of the county office. Documents will not be accepted if they are signed by an assistant or deputy clerk.

COMMISSIONING AND ADMINISTRATION

The Secretary of the Commonwealth appoints, commissions, regulates and maintains records on Pennsylvania's Notaries (57 PS 148, 168).

Applying for Commission

Qualifications: An applicant for a commission as a Pennsylvania Notary Public must: (a) be at least 18 years old, (b) be a resident of or employed within the Commonwealth (i.e., maintain an actual physical business address in the state rather than merely a post office box), (c) be of good character, integrity and ability, (d) not have been convicted of or pled guilty or nolo contendere to a felony or lesser offense incompatible with the duties of a Notary in the past five years and (e) not have had a Notary commission revoked in Pennsylvania or any other state in the past five years. The following persons are not eligible to become a Notary: any holder of a judicial office in the Commonwealth, except a magisterial district justice; any member of the U.S. Congress or holder of an office or appointment of profit or trust under the legislative, executive or judiciary departments of the U.S. government for which a salary, fees or perquisites are received; and any member of the Pennsylvania General Assembly (website, "Become a Notary").

Course of Instruction Required: Each applicant must complete a three-hour, approved Notary course of instruction within six months preceding application. Applicants for reappointment must also take the course. The course may be comprised of either interactive or classroom instruction (website, "Mandatory Education Requirement"). A list of "Notary Education Providers" is available on the website. (Permanently exempted from the course requirement is any applicant for reappointment who had been appointed as a Notary on or before July 1, 2003, and whose commission was in effect on that date — see *Tritt v. Cortés*, 851 A.2d 903 [Pa. 2004].)

"In order to ensure that notaries public conduct themselves in a professional manner, the Department of State encourages the attendance of notary public courses beyond the required mandatory education. These courses will assist the notary public in maintaining a high level of excellence and professionalism in serving their customers as a commissioned public official" (website, "Education Providers").

Application: The application must be endorsed by the state senator of the district in which the applicant resides or (if a non-resident) is employed. A photocopy of the course completion certificate must accompany the application, along with a $40 fee payable to the "Commonwealth of Pennsylvania." Online application is available in which case the completed application will be sent electronically to the applicant's state senator for endorsement.

Applicants for reappointment, who must meet all of the same requirements, should file at least two to three months prior to commission expiration.

Filing with County Recorder of Deeds: The new commission is sent to the recorder of deeds in the county where the Notary maintains an office. Within 45 days after appointment, the Notary must obtain a $10,000 bond, register a signature with the prothonotary of the county, take and subscribe an oath of office, and record the bond, commission and oath with the county recorder of deeds. (In the several counties that have eliminated the office of prothonotary, the Notary's signature is filed instead with the clerk of courts, clerk of records or the like.) In counties of the "second class" (i.e., Allegheny County), the Notary's signature must also be registered in the clerk of court's office.

After this is done, Notaries who wish to be able to process certain Pennsylvania Department of Transportation (PennDOT) documents, such as titles, registrations and tags, must register with the Regulated Client Services Section of PennDOT's Dealer Agent Services Unit — 1101 S. Front St., Harrisburg, PA 17104, telephone (717) 787-7207.

Non-Residents: A non-resident employed at an actual physical business address in the Commonwealth may qualify to become a Pennsylvania Notary. "(A)ny nonresident notary public in Pennsylvania irrevocably appoints the Secretary of the Commonwealth as the person's agent upon whom may be served any summons, subpoena, order or other process" (website, "What is a Notary").

Notary Search: The Department of State's database of Notaries is searchable by the Notary's name or commission ID number, or the street and general location of the Notary. Notaries may register to be able personally to update their own information. See website, "Notary Searchable Database & eServices").

Changes of Status

If Notary Moves: A Notary who changes an office address must provide written or electronic notice to both the Secretary of the Commonwealth and the recorder of deeds in the county of original appointment within five days of the change (57 PS 153). If the move is to another Pennsylvania county, the Notary must register with the prothonotary of the new county within 30 days (57 PS 155). "In counties of the second class (i.e., Allegheny County), such signature shall also be registered in the clerk of courts' office within said period" (57 PS 155). "A change of address of a notary public may be submitted by letter to the Bureau of Commissions, Elections and Legislation, 210 North Office Building, Harrisburg, PA 17120-0029, or by using the online [form]" on the website (website, "Update Your Information").

"If a notary public neither resides nor works in the Commonwealth, that notary public shall be deemed to have resigned from the office of notary public as of the date the residency ceases or employment within the Commonwealth terminates. A notary public who resigns that notary's commission in accordance with this subsection shall notify the Secretary of the Commonwealth in writing of the effective date of the resignation" (57 PS 153[b]).

If Name of Notary Changes: A Notary whose name changes may continue to notarize in the original name until commission expiration, whereupon any application for a new commission must be made in the new name (57 PS 156). Within 30 days of any name change, however, the Notary must inform the Secretary of the Commonwealth and the recorder of deeds of the county in which the Notary maintains an office. The Notary may opt to use the new name when notarizing but only after so notifying the recorder of deeds, registering the new signature with the prothonotary, purchasing a new rubber stamp seal and informing the Department of State in writing (NPP). A name change form is available on the website.

If Notary Resigns: "A notary public who resigns his/her commission must notify the Secretary of the Commonwealth of the effective date of the resignation or of a change of address which effects residency or employment within the Commonwealth in a letter to [the Department of State].

"Resigning notaries public, pursuant to 57 PS § 161, must deliver their register and all other public papers to the office of the recorder of deeds of the county in which they maintain their business address within 30 days pursuent to 57 PS § 168.1. The notary public must deliver the rubber stamp seal to the Department of State, Bureau of Commissions, Elections and Legislation within 10 days after the date of resignation..." (website, "Update Your Information"). A printable resignation form is available on the website.

Death of Notary: Notification of the death of a Notary should be mailed or faxed to the Department of State's Bureau of Commissions, Elections and Legislation. Within 30 days, the Notary's register and all public papers should be delivered to the recorder of deeds of the county in which the Notary maintained a business address, and the rubber stamp seal should be delivered to the Department of State within 90 days after the death (website, "Update Your Information").

COUNTY OFFICES

To contact a Pennsylvania county prothonotary or recorder to obtain an authenticating certificate for a Notary, telephone long-distance information — 1-XXX-555-1212 — and ask for the phone number of the appropriate official from the following jurisdictions:

County	City/Town	Area Code
Adams	Gettysburg	(717)
Allegheny	Pittsburgh	(412)
Armstrong	Kittanning	(724)
Beaver	Beaver	(724)
Bedford	Bedford	(814)
Berks	Reading	(610)
Blair	Hollidaysburg	(814)
Bradford	Towanda	(570)
Bucks	Doylestown	(215)
Butler	Butler	(724)
Cambria	Ebensburg	(814)
Cameron	Emporium	(814)
Carbon	Jim Thorpe	(570)
Centre	Bellefonte	(814)
Chester	West Chester	(610)
Clarion	Clarion	(814)
Clearfield	Clearfield	(814)
Clinton	Lock Haven	(570)
Columbia	Bloomsburg	(570)
Crawford	Meadville	(814)
Cumberland	Carlisle	(717)
Dauphin	Harrisburg	(717)
Delaware	Media	(610)
Elk	Ridgway	(814)
Erie	Erie	(814)
Fayette	Uniontown	(724)
Forest	Tionesta	(814)
Franklin	Chambersburg	(717)
Fulton	McConnellsburg	(717)
Greene	Waynesburg	(724)
Huntingdon	Huntingdon	(814)
Indiana	Indiana	(724)
Jefferson	Brookville	(814)
Juniata	Mifflintown	(717)
Lackawanna	Scranton	(570)
Lancaster	Lancaster	(717)
Lawrence	New Castle	(724)
Lebanon	Lebanon	(717)
Lehigh	Allentown	(610)
Luzerne	Wilkes-Barre	(570)
Lycoming	Williamsport	(570)
McKean	Smethport	(814)
Mercer	Mercer	(724)
Mifflin	Lewistown	(717)
Monroe	Stroudsburg	(570)
Montgomery	Norristown	(610)
Montour	Danville	(570)
Northampton	Easton	(610)
Northumberland	Sunbury	(570)
Perry	New Bloomfield	(717)
Philadelphia	Philadelphia	(215)
Pike	Milford	(570)
Potter	Coudersport	(814)
Schuylkill	Pottsville	(570)
Snyder	Middleburg	(570)
Somerset	Somerset	(814)
Sullivan	Laporte	(570)
Susquehanna	Montrose	(570)
Tioga	Wellsboro	(570)
Union	Lewisburg	(570)
Venango	Franklin	(814)
Warren	Warren	(814)
Washington	Washington	(724)
Wayne	Honesdale	(570)
Westmoreland	Greensburg	(724)
Wyoming	Tunkhannock	(570)
York	York	(717)

OTHER NOTARIAL OFFICERS

In addition to Notaries, the following officials may take acknowledgments within Pennsylvania (21 PS 291.2):
1. A judge of a court of record;
2. A clerk, deputy clerk, prothonotary or deputy prothonotary of a court having a seal;
3. A recorder of deeds or deputy recorder of deeds;
4. A justice of the peace, magistrate or alderman.

May Also Take Oaths

"Whenever any act has provided that an oath shall be administered by a notary public, the same hereafter may also be administered by a magistrate, alderman or a justice of the peace" (57 PS 55).

Commissioner of Deeds Laws Repealed

The various laws providing for appointment of commissioners of deeds have been repealed and, effective July 1, 2003, no additional commissioners of deeds will be appointed by the Commonwealth. According to the Department of State, those commissions already appointed may continue in that capacity until the end of their five-year terms.

QUICK FACTS

Notary Jurisdiction
Statewide (57 PS 148).

Notary Term Length
Four years (57 PS 148).

Notary Bond
$10,000, with "a duly authorized surety company or two sufficient individual sureties, to be approved by the Secretary of the Commonwealth ..." (57 PS 154).

O-R

PUERTO RICO

NOTARY SEAL

The Notaries of Puerto Rico must authenticate their official acts with a seal of office (4 LPRA 2021). The seal's customary format is as follows:

Kind
Inked stamp or embosser.

Shape/Size
Shape and size are not specified by law, but circular seals are virtually universal. They generally vary in diameter from 1 inch to 2 inches.

Components
The following seal components are customary:
1. Name of Notary as registered with the Clerk of the Supreme Court of Puerto Rico;
2. "Abogado-Notario" (meaning Attorney-Notary);
3. "Puerto Rico" or "Isla de Puerto Rico" (Island of Puerto Rico) appears in many seals;
4. Any icon* of the Notary's choice.

* The composition of the seal is left to the discretion of the Notary. Reproducing the full Seal of Puerto Rico is prohibited, though using parts of that Seal is not. Actual seal icons include such disparate objects as flowers, birds, native artifacts and the face of an Indian.

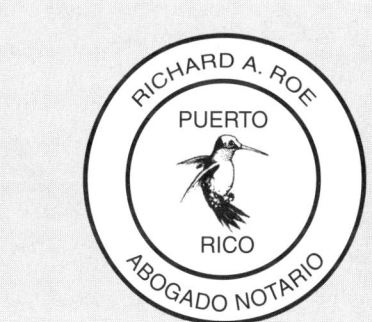

Examples
The above two seals exemplify the diversity of the seals of the Notaries of Puerto Rico. Formats and sizes other than these may also be permitted.

NOTARY ADMINISTRATION

Supreme Court of Puerto Rico
Office of Notarial
   Inspection   1-787-763-8816
Judicial Center (3rd Floor)
Muñoz Rivera Ave.
P.O. Box 190860
San Juan, PR 00919-0860

Website: www.ramajudicial.pr/odin/index.htm
AND
www.lexjuris.com/lexnotaria.htm

NOTARY RULES

LPRA — Laws of Puerto Rico Annotated
NR — Notarial Regulations of Puerto Rico

Most Notary rules are in:

a. Laws of Puerto Rico Annotated, Title 4, Part VI, Chapter 101, Sections 2001 through 2143, called the Puerto Rico Notarial Act of 1987; and Chapter 102, Sections 2155 through 2166, called the Non-Contentious Notarial Matters Act;

b. Notarial Regulations of Puerto Rico, adopted by the Puerto Rico Supreme Court on August 1, 1995 (for Chapter 101), and supplemented effective February 1, 2012 (for Chapter 102).

Seal and Flourish Must Be Registered

Each Notary's "signature, sign, seal and flourish" must be registered with the Clerk of the

Supreme Court of Puerto Rico (4 LPRA 2011).

The flourish, also called a paraph, is a distinctive handwritten design at the end of a signature used as a deterrent to forgery.

NOTARY POWERS

Because of the island's Spanish heritage, Puerto Rico's Notaries have the same general powers as civil-law Notaries in other Latin nations. Since they are both legal professionals and public officials, they must be lawyers (*abogados*) as well as Notaries (*notarios*). Puerto Rico Notaries do not, however, serve any one client in a given transaction. Rather, they serve the public trust, and impartiality is their byword. In any transaction, Notaries represent both the public and the law, and they perform multiple functions. They may offer legal advice, act as legal arbiters, prepare legal documents (including those they will notarize) and record the completed instruments related to the acts they perform.

"The notary is a legal professional who practices a public function, authorized to attest and authenticate pursuant to the laws the juridical business and other acts and extrajudicial events executed before him, without prejudice of what is provided in the special laws. His function is to receive and interpret the will of the parties giving it a legal format, draft the notarial documents and deeds for such purpose and confer authority to them. The notary's public faith is complete with regard to the facts carried out and corroborated by him in the exercise of his functions, and also with regard to the manner, place, date and time of the execution" (4 LPRA 2002). See also NR Rule 2.

Even though only attorneys may become Notaries, in Puerto Rico the practice of notarial law is distinct from the regular practice of law. One of the most important differences is that the ethical duty of Notaries is to serve as impartial observers and guarantors of the authenticity of the legal acts they certify, rather than to represent the interests of any one client (NR Rule 4). For situations in which a Notary may and may not act as both Notary and attorney for the same party, see NR Rule 5.

Specifically, the powers of the Notary office in Puerto Rico include:

1. Drafting and authorizing deeds* (4 LPRA 2006);
2. Certifying copies** (4 LPRA 2006 and 2091);
3. Administering oaths and affirmations*** (4 LPRA 882);
4. Issuing affidavits, testimonies, declarations or statements of authenticity and maintaining a register of same**** (4 LPRA 2091 and 2094);
5. Compiling and maintaining protocols and indices***** (4 LPRA 2006, 2023 and 2031a);
6. Serving as depository of documents, securities, and sums that any parties may wish to deposit with the Notary to secure their contracts (4 LPRA 2006 and NR Rule 17).

* Deeds: "The original deed is the one that the notary shall write regarding the contract or act submitted for his authorization signed by the grantors, by the attesting witnesses or those having knowledge of the facts of his case, signed, marked, sealed and flourished by the notary himself" (4 LPRA 2031). See also NR Rule 19.

The Notary must include the following information when authorizing a public deed (4 LPRA 2033[a] though [e]):

1. The deed's protocol number, written in letters at the beginning of the document;
2. The type of act or contract, using its legally recognized name unless it does not have one;
3. The Notary's name, residence address, and the location of his or her office;
4. The day, month, year and place of execution, the latter being that in which the last of the grantors signed the document if there were no attesting witnesses;
5. The name and surname(s), age, civil status, profession and residence address of the executors;
6. The name(s) and circumstances of the witnesses, if any;
7. If any of the executors is married and the appearance of the spouse was not necessary, the name and surname(s) of the spouse, even though the latter did not appear at the execution;
8. The Notary's attestation that (a) he or she identified the grantors according to statutory requirements (see "Identifying Signers," below), (b) in the Notary's judgment the grantors had the necessary legal capacity to execute the act or contract concerned and (c) the Notary read the deed to the grantors (and, if applicable, the witnesses), the Notary allowed them to read it themselves or they waived their right to do so.

"The grantors and witnesses shall sign the deed and shall also affix the initials of their name and surname or surnames to the margin of each one of the pages of the document which shall be flourished and sealed by the notary" (4 LPRA 2034). See also NR Rule 34.

"Any additions, annotations, interlineations, erasures and crossouts in the public deeds shall be held as valueless unless they are certified after the last line, with the express approval and signature of those who must sign the document. However, the mistaken words may be placed within parentheses followed by the words 'I say' ('I mean') to make it clear that they should not be read" (4 LPRA 2050). See also "Correcting Errors in Public Documents," below.

Notaries must attach and cancel on every original deed they grant, as well as on any certified copies thereof, a series of stamps: internal revenue stamps, issued by the Secretary of the Treasury; Society for Legal Assistance stamps, issued by the Society; and notarial tax stamps, issued by the Puerto Rico Bar Association. In most cases, the fees represented by these stamps will vary depending on the value represented by the document (LPRA 851 and 2021).

"The deed or certified copies of it shall be voidable or ineffective if the corresponding stamps are not attached to it or if any method established by the Secretary of the Treasury in substitution of the affixing of the seals required by law is not observed" (4 LPRA 2021). See also NR Rule 45.

A Notary who fails to affix and cancel the stamps required by law is subject to sanctions and disciplinary action (NR Rule 14 commentary). See also 4 LPRA 2106.

** Certified Copies: "A certified copy is the literal, total or partial transcript of a document executed before a notary that is issued by him or the person officially in charge of his protocol, with a certificate regarding the truth of the contents, and the number of folios of the document as well as the signature, sign and flourish, and the seal and flourish of the attesting notary on every page" (4 LPRA 2061). See also NR Rule 49.

"At the request of a party the notary may issue partial copies of documents found in his protocol, stating under his responsibility that there is nothing which broadens, restricts, modifies or conditions the excerpt in what is issued" (4 LPRA 2062). A Notary may refuse to issue a partial copy if, in the Notary's judgment, the copy does not meet the criteria just stated (NR Rule 50).

"When issuing a certified copy the notary shall consign in the main deed, by means of a signed annotation, the name of the person to whom it is issued, the date and the number corresponding to the copy according to those already issued. These data shall (also) appear in the copies" (4 LPRA 2063). The signed annotation must be placed in the margin of the pages of the original deed or, if there is not sufficient room in the margin, at the bottom or on the back of the page. The annotation may be typed, stamped, printed, handwritten or in any other legible format, but always must be signed by the Notary (NR Rule 51).

The certificate issued by the Notary must state the number of sheets in the document, including any attachments; pages with text on both sides count as one sheet. It must indicate that the original document included: the signature(s) and initials of the person(s) who signed; the signature, sign, flourish and seal of the Notary; and cancellation of the internal revenue and notarial tax stamps. The certificate also must indicate the place and date of its execution and the name(s) of the person(s) for whom the copy was made. If the copy is a partial one, the certificate must state that the omitted material does not impact the authenticity of the excerpt (NR Rule 49).

"The notary is hereby empowered to issue certified photographic copies, or copies reproduced by any other electronic means, of original deeds which once they are certified by the notary shall be deemed valid for all legal purposes" (4 LPRA 2067).

Notaries must attach and cancel on certified copies of deeds the same stamps that they are required to attach and cancel on the original, and any failure to do so has the same result, both for the document and the Notary; see "Deeds" above for details and relevant laws and rules.

Notaries may also issue uncertified copies of deeds in their protocols, "but without a guaranteed transcription of the document. These copies shall not be signed, sealed or flourished, nor shall a marginal note of its certified copy be placed on the original deed" (4 LPRA 2068). On such copies the Notary may, however, include a note below his or her signature and seal, indicating that the copy is uncertified (NR Rule 46).

*** Oaths and Affirmations: "All oaths, affidavits and affirmations shall be administered in the mode most binding upon the conscience of the individual taking the same, and shall be taken subject to the pains and penalties of perjury" (4 LPRA 881).

Verbal oaths or affirmations that Notaries administer in depositions or similar proceedings do not need to be recorded in writing (NR Rule 65 commentary). Compare with "Affidavits and Registers" and "Protocols and Indices," below.

**** Affidavits and Registers: "Testimony or statement of authenticity is the document through which a notary ... may notarize a non-original document" (4 LPRA 2091). See also NR Rule 65.

With an affidavit, testimony, declaration or statement of authenticity, a Notary may certify any of the following: the legality of signatures on non-original or private documents; having taken a sworn statement in writing; that a translation from one language to another is true and exact (provided the Notary has knowledge of both languages); that a document is a true and exact copy of a document not in the Notary's protocol; and "in general ... the identity of any object or thing" (4 LPRA 2091). See also NR Rules 66, 69 (translations) and 70 (objects or things).

When the Notary authenticates a signature, the signer must sign the document in the Notary's presence. The Notary may or may not need to administer an oath or affirmation (NR Rule 67). Although "(t)he notary does not assume any responsibility for the contents of the private document whose signature he/she authenticates" (4 LPRA 2091), if the Notary knows that the document contains a falsehood and/or that the signer is swearing to or affirming a falsehood, he or she must refuse to authenticate the signature (NR Rule 67 commentary).

When the Notary certifies a copy as true and exact, the certification may appear at the foot of the document, on its back or on an attachment. The Notary must record a description of the document copied and who presented it in both the certificate and the register of affidavits (see below). The Notary must affix his or her seal and flourish to each page of the copy (NR Rule 70).

"It shall be the duty of every notary to cancel a stamp in the amount of three dollars ($3), that shall be adopted and issued by the Legal Aid Society, for each sworn statement or affidavit that he issues" (4 LPRA 896). See also NR Rules 9 and 72.

"Notaries shall keep a register of the affidavits in which they intervene" (4 LPRA 2094). Affidavits must be numbered consecutively, and the number on the affidavit must correspond to the number in the register (4 LPRA 2093). Registers must be retained by the Notary for 30 years after the date of the last affidavit in the register. At that point, the register must be examined and approved by an inspector of protocols, after which the Director of the Office of Notarial Inspection will authorize the Notary to destroy the register. Registers of affidavits are not retained in the notarial archives (4 LPRA 2111).

Notaries also must send monthly and annual indices of all their notarial activities to the Office of Notarial Inspection; see "Protocols and Indices," below.

"Any affidavit or declaration not recorded in the Registry, or not included in the corresponding index shall be null" (4 LPRA 894). "Any testimony not included in the index that does not have the executing notary's signature or has not been recorded in the registry of affidavits shall be null" (4 LPRA 2095). See also NR Rule 73.

Many officials are authorized to issue affidavits and declarations, but "only notaries may authorize such affidavits and declarations when they have reference to facts, acts or contracts of a purely private nature." In towns where there is no Notary with an open office, district judges and justices of the peace may take affidavits related to matters not exceeding $2,500 in value (4 LPRA 890). See "Other Notarial Officers," below.

***** Protocols and Indices: "The protocol is the orderly collection of original deeds and acts executed during a calendar year by the notary, as well as the documents included therein.

"The protocol shall be secret and shall only be examined according to the provisions of this chapter or by judicial order issued pursuant to the provisions of this chapter" (4 LPRA 2071).

"The protocols belong to the State. Notaries shall conserve them in accordance with the provisions of this chapter and shall be responsible for their integrity" (4 LPRA 2072). Protocols must be kept in a fireproof office or container (4 LPRA 2078). If they are lost or damaged, they must be reconstructed as much as possible by contacting the pertinent parties (4 LPRA 2079). If they are lost or damaged due to neglect, the Notary may be sanctioned (4 LPRA 2072).

Protocols must not be moved from the office where they are kept except by judicial decree or by authorization of the Office of Notarial Inspection (4 LPRA 2077). In the event of an emergency that threatens their integrity, protocols and registers of affidavits may be moved without prior authorization. In such cases, the Notary must immediately notify the Director of the Office of Notarial Inspection, either in person or by certified mail with return receipt, indicating the nature of the emergency and the new location of the records (NR Rule 58).

Notaries must send a monthly index of their notarial activities to the Office of Notarial Inspection. The index must be submitted no later than the tenth calendar day of the month following the month being reported. In this index, Notaries must state "with respect to the original deeds and affidavits authorized by them during the preceding month, the numerical order of the same, the name of the appearing parties, the date, the subject of the instrument or testimony, the amount of each instrument and the name of the witnesses, if any appeared" (4 LPRA 2023). See also NR Rule 15.

The monthly index also must include the Notary's name, number, postal, physical and email addresses, telephone and fax numbers; the month and year covered by the index; the total number of items in the index, broken down by category (public instruments or deeds; affidavits, testimonies, declarations or statements of authenticity; and non-contentious matters); and, if the Notary is employed by a public entity, the name and address where he or she is employed (NR Rule 12).

Notaries also must submit to the Office of Notarial Inspection an annual statistical report on the documents they authorized during the preceding year. The annual report must be submitted no later than the last day of February in the year following the year being reported (4 LPRA 2031a).

The annual report must be formatted as follows: "The protocols of the preceding year together with the corresponding index of the contents of each volume shall be bound by the third month of each year. Said protocols shall be indexed by order of instrument and shall include the full name of the parties appearing, the name of the person represented, should that be the case, and the date and place of execution, the juridical business transacted and the number of the folios included therein" (4 LPRA 2076). Each volume comprising the annual report may contain a maximum of 500 pages, and all pages of each individual instrument within each volume must be included: Instruments may not be split across volumes (NR Rule 57).

"When the notary is an employee of a public instrumentality which allows him/her to engage in notarial private practice outside working hours, the notary shall separate the notarial work performed as notary of the public body from the work performed in private practice in the required (annual) report" (4 LPRA 2031a). The same requirement holds true for the monthly indices (NR Rule 12).

When a Notary ceases for any reason to be a Notary (e.g., resignation, termination, permanent disability, permanent appointment to a conflicting public office, death), the Notary's protocols and registers of affidavits must be surrendered within 30 days to the Office of Notarial Inspection. Once they have been examined and approved, they will be given to the general custodian of notarial protocols of the corresponding local district (4 LPRA 2104 and 2106); see "Notarial Districts" below for a listing of these 13 districts.

The Director of the Office of Notarial Inspection may authorize the destruction of registers of affidavits whose last affidavit is dated more than 30 years earlier. In contrast, protocols are retained by the district custodian for 60 years, after which they are transferred to the General Archives of Puerto Rico, and copies of these may be issued by the notarial custodian for the District of San Juan (4 LPRA 2111).

'Non-Contentious Notarial Matters': Effective July 31, 2000, the Non-Contentious Notarial Matters Act grants Puerto Rico Notaries certain powers in addition to those granted by the Puerto Rico Notarial Act (4 LPRA 2155):

1. Managing testate and intestate proceedings, including issuance of declarations of heirship and of letters testamentary to an executor by a Notary other than the one who handled the original will;
2. Certification and registration of holographic wills;
3. Statements of simple absence;
4. Perpetuation of facts in civil procedures in which no controversy is stated, that will not result in prejudice of a person and that are not intended to confer the identity of a person;
5. Correction of records in the Demographic Record and changes of names and surnames.

For further details, see 4 LPRA 2155 through 2166.

Identifying Signers

If the Notary does not personally know a deed signer (grantor), the signer may be identified through (4 LPRA 2035 and NR Rules 29 and 30):

1. The word of an individual who knows the grantor and is personally known by the Notary;
2. The word of another party to the document who is personally known by the Notary;
3. An identification document with a photograph and signature issued by a competent public authority of Puerto Rico, a U.S. state or the U.S. federal government; or a passport duly issued by a foreign authority.

In any affidavit, testimony, declaration or statement of authenticity, Notaries must certify "that they personally know the signers or the attesting witness, or … supplemented (their) personal knowledge in the manner indicated in §2035 of this title" (4 LPRA 2092). See also NR Rule 67.

'Personal Knowledge' Defined: In order to certify that he or she "personally knows" a signer, the Notary does not necessarily need to have met the signer prior to the date of the document's execution. A Notary may attest to personal knowledge of a signer's identity based on the Notary's critical judgment during his or her interactions with and observation of the signer during the preliminary stages of the notarial act and on the Notary's conviction that the signer is who he or she claims to be (NR Rule 29 and commentary).

Failure to Identify Signer: "Public instruments in which the notary fails to attest to his cognizance of the grantors or does not supplement this deficiency in the form established by §2035 of this title shall be voidable" (4 LPRA 2053).

Signer's Representative Capacity: "Every grantor who appears in representation of another person shall always validate his designation before the notary with authenticating documents, except when there is the expressed agreement of the grantors" (4 LPRA 2037). The Notary must record in the deed the type of authenticating document presented; if requested by any party to the transaction, the Notary may also attach a copy of the authenticating document to the deed. If the necessary document is not available at the time of the notarization, all parties must agree to allow the transaction to go forward, and the Notary must note this fact in the deed (NR Rule 28).

"Public officials legally authorized to represent the Commonwealth of Puerto Rico, municipalities, instrumentalities or corporations shall not have to validate their powers before the notary" (4 LPRA 2037).

Determining Competence

When authorizing a public deed, the Notary must attest that, in his or her judgment, the grantors had the necessary legal capacity to execute the act or contract concerned (4 LPRA 2033[e]). See also NR Rule 2[B].

Attesting and Identifying Witnesses

"The intervention of attesting witnesses shall not be necessary in the execution of deeds, except when required by the authorizing notary or any of the parties, or when one of the grantors does not know how to or cannot read or sign.

"Attesting witnesses shall be present at the act of reading, consenting, signing and execution of the public document. Likewise, they may be identifying witnesses who, in turn, may be attestors if they meet the applicable legal requirements" (4 LPRA 2038). See also NR Rule 31.

"The witnesses, including those as to identity, shall be of legal age, competent and know how to read and write and sign" (4 LPRA 2040). Identifying witnesses must be present before the Notary at the time the party being identified signs the deed. When attesting witnesses are used, all parties — signers and witnesses — must appear together and sign the document in the presence of the Notary. In both cases, the Notary must record the use of the witness(es) in the deed (4 LPRA 2042 and NR Rules 35 and 36).

All parties to the transaction must agree on who serves as an attesting witness (4 LPRA 2041).

An identifying witness may be a relative or employee of the Notary or a relative of the party being identified; an attesting witness may not. For details, see "Disqualifying Interests," below.

Public Document Rules

"Those persons who sign a public instrument on any account, shall do so by signing at the end and affixing the initials of their name and surname or surnames in the margin of all folios, in the manner they usually do and the notary shall do so after them, flourishing, signing and sealing it" (4 LPRA 2046). See also NR Rule 34. Public instruments which lack the required initials or, where necessary due to disability, fingerprints of any signer are null (NR Rule 45).

"If there are no attesting witnesses, it shall not be necessary for those appearing to sign the document together in the presence of the notary, but he/she may personally receive their signatures at any time within the same calendar day of the execution" (4 LPRA 2046). If there are attesting witnesses, however, unity of action is essential: All parties must appear together and sign the document in the presence of the Notary (4 LPRA 2042 and NR Rules 35 and 36).

"Public notarial documents shall be written on sheets of paper or folios fourteen inches (14) long by eight and a half inches (8½) wide, and on the side by which they are to be bound they shall have a blank margin of twenty millimeters (20mm) plus another on the left side of the deed of sixty millimeters (60mm) and on the right a strip or margin of three millimeters (3mm)" (4 LPRA 2055).

Correcting Errors in Public Documents

"If the notary fails to record any data or circumstance provided by this chapter, or if it concerns an error in the statement as to the facts witnessed by the notary which is his duty to consign, they may be corrected by the executing notary at his own expense, on his own initiative or by petition of any of the parties, through a notarial certificate that shows the error or defect, its cause and the statement that corrects it…. (T)he notary shall indicate the fact of the correction in the margin of the original document under his signature and seal, and shall indicate the deed or notarial certificate in which they were made" (4 LPRA 2047). See also NR Rule 39, which provides additional procedural details as well as examples of the types of errors that may and may not be corrected by means of this method.

Illiteracy or Disability of Signer

"When any of the grantors does not know how to, or cannot read, the (public) document in question shall be read out loud twice, once by the notary and another by the witness designated by the grantor, all of which shall be attested to by the notary.

"When any of the grantors is deaf or blind who does not know how to read and sign, he must designate a witness who upon his request shall read or sign the public document for him or both. The notary shall record these circumstances" (4 LPRA 2039). See also NR Rule 32.

The same norms apply for private documents (4 LPRA 2092 and NR Rule 67).

Signature by Mark: "Whenever any of the grantors does not know how to, or cannot sign, the notary shall require that they affix their two (2) thumb prints. If they do not have thumbs, any other fingers, next to the witness' signature who signs at his or their request, and on the margin of the rest of the document's folios, all which the notary shall attest to in the deed. If the grantor or grantors have no fingers, the notary shall state this circumstance and two (2) attesting witnesses shall sign at their request" (4 LPRA 2043). See also NR Rule 32.

The same procedures are to be used for private documents (4 LPRA 2092 and NR Rule 67).

Notary May Appoint Substitute

"The notary may appoint another notary to substitute for him/her when he/she is absent from his/her office for any nonpermanent cause, for a maximum initial period of three (3) months. Said period may be extended … in exceptional cases and when there is a just cause, up to a maximum term of six (6) months" (4 LPRA 2013).

The substitute is responsible for custody of the Notary's protocols and registers of affidavits and may issue certified copies of documents in the protocols. The substitute may not, however, authorize deeds or original documents or issue affidavits, testimonies, declarations or statements of authenticity in the substituted Notary's name (4 LPRA 2013 and NR Rule 18).

Notarial Practice Certificate to Be Displayed

"The Clerk of the Supreme Court shall issue a certificate to the notary attesting to the name and number of the notary, his/her membership number, the date on which the Supreme Court authorized him/her to practice as a notary, the date on which he/she registered his/her signature, flourish, sign and seal as a notary and the facsimile of his/her signature, sign, seal and flourish, as registered. It shall be the obligation of the notary to display the certificate on one of the walls of his/her office" (4 LPRA 2012).

Wills

The Office of Notarial Inspection maintains a registry of wills (4 LPRA 2121).

"(N)otaries shall remit to the Director of the Notarial Inspection Office, the next day after its execution … a notice authorized by them of each master deed granting, modifying, revoking or extending a will or recording of a holographic or sealed will ..." (4 LPRA 2123). See also NR Rule 62. The notification may be made in person, by certified mail with return receipt or by whatever electronic means has been authorized by the Director (NR Rule 60).

"The Court of First Instance shall not admit or process any petition of declaration of heirship whatsoever that is not filed with a negative certification from the Office of Notarial Inspection" (4 LPRA 2125).

More generally, see also 4 LPRA 2121 through 2125 and NR Rules 59B, 60 and 63.

Powers of Attorney

The Office of Notarial Inspection maintains a registry of powers of attorney (4 LPRA 921).

"It shall be the duty of every notary before whom a deed to constitute, modify, extend, substitute, renounce, revoke or renew a power of attorney is executed, to send to the Notarial Inspection Office, within the next three (3) days following the execution thereof ... a notice ..." (4 LPRA 922). See also NR Rule 61. The notification may be made in person, by certified mail with return receipt or by whatever electronic means has been authorized by the Director (NR Rule 60).

More generally, see 4 LPRA 922 through 927, 4 LPRA 2126 and NR Rules 59A, 60 and 63.

NOTARY DON'TS

Disqualifying Interests

"No notary may authorize documents he is a party to, or which include provisions in his favor. Neither may he authorize them if any one of the executing parties is related to him within the fourth degree of consanguinity or the second degree of affinity, except when he appears in the document as a representative.... The provisions in favor of relatives of the notary who authorized the public document in which they were made within the fourth degree of consanguinity or the second degree of affinity shall have no effect" (4 LPRA 2005). These same restrictions apply to affidavits, testimonies, declarations or statements of authenticity (4 LPRA 2091).

Additionally, Notaries may not authorize any public instrument or authenticate any document that involves a corporation in which the Notary and/or the Notary's spouse hold more than 50% of the shares or voting rights (NR Rule 7).

"Employees of the executing notary, his relatives or those of the interested parties within the fourth degree of consanguinity or the second of affinity shall not be attesting witnesses" (4 LPRA 2040). In contrast, an identifying witness may be an employee of the Notary or a relative of the Notary or the party being identified, regardless of the degree of consanguinity or affinity (NR Rules 30 and 33).

"Public instruments shall be null: (1) That include any provision in favor of the notary who executes it; (2) Where the (attesting) witnesses are relatives of the interested parties in the degree prohibited by §2040 of this title, the relatives or employees of the notary himself" (4 LPRA 2052). See also NR Rule 33.

Blank Spaces

Blank spaces may not be left in the text of a public document (4 LPRA 2045). Blank spaces in excess of 10 millimeters and those that occur at the end of a line that precedes a new article, paragraph, or section must be filled in with a line or a dash (NR Rule 22 and 4 LPRA 2050).

Spaces of less than 10 millimeters are not considered blank spaces if they occur (a) at the end of a line that does not precede a new article, paragraph, or section; or (b) between words in the text of an instrument created on a computer or word processor that justifies left and right margins (NR Rule 22).

NOTARY FEES

Notaries are authorized to charge the following fees for their notarial services (4 LPRA 2131):

1. For notarizing public instruments* concerning valuables not exceeding $10,000 in value: $150;
2. For notarizing public instruments* concerning valuables between $10,000 and $5,000,000 in value: fee fixed by agreement between the parties and the Notary but never more than 1% or less than 0.5% of the value, and never less than $250;
3. For notarizing public instruments* concerning valuables exceeding $5,000,000 in value: same fee as above plus the fee fixed by agreement between the parties and the Notary on the amount exceeding

$5,000,000;
4. For notarizing public instruments concerning nonvaluables: fee fixed by agreement between the parties and the Notary but never less than $150;
5. For notarizing testimonies and sworn statements and for authenticating signatures or affidavits: fee fixed by agreement between the parties and the Notary;
6. For issuing certified copies of deeds: fee based on document's amount, excluding costs, expenses and disbursements, as follows: from $0 to $10,000 — $15; from $10,001 to $500,000 — $25; over $500,000 — $40.

* Specifically for notarizations dealing with mortgage cancellations, newly constructed housing, and refinancings in which more than one instrument is executed by a single party before the same Notary in the same transaction, notarial fees are governed by additional rules (4 LPRA 2131[e] and [f]).

Uncertified Copies: When issuing uncertified copies, Notaries may charge a fee sufficient to cover their costs (NR Rule 52).

Additional Fees for Lawyer Services: "The fees fixed above for executing the documents shall not impair or limit the notary from charging the fees he believes reasonable and prudent in accordance with Canon 24 of Professional Ethics for the fixing of fees, for his prior and preparatory efforts, including the subsequent ones, such as background and titles, studies, consultations, opinions, preparation of certificates and compensated powers of attorney in which the notary renders an additional service as a lawyer" (4 LPRA 2132).

U.S. Government Exempt: The U.S. government and its agencies are generally exempt from paying notarial fees (30 LPRA 1770[a]).

Overcharging

"A notary shall not charge or receive for notarial services compensation other than that established in this chapter, be it through the reimbursement of fees, granting of discounts or privileges, or through any other method used to reduce the fees herein established. This prohibition does not include the rendering of services gratuitously when the notary deems and considers it necessary, provided it does not become a customary practice in business or a subterfuge to violate the purpose of this chapter" (4 LPRA 2131[4][a]).

CERTIFICATES

The various and complex formats for the deeds of sale, contracts, leases, mortgages and other documents drafted by the Attorney-Notaries of Puerto Rico are beyond the scope of this manual.

NOTARY RECORDS

Rather than maintain a journal or register of notarial acts as do many Notaries in the U.S. states that have a common-law heritage, the civil-law Notaries of Puerto Rico keep the public documents they draft and certify in a "protocol." They also keep a register of their affidavits. For further information, see "Protocols and Indices" and "Affidavits and Registers" above, under "Notary Powers."

Copies and Inspection of Records

"In addition to the grantors, their representatives and assigns, any person entitled to some right as a result of the deed, whether directly, or already acquired through a different deed, and who, in the judgment of the notary or the Notarial Registrar concerned, establishes a legitimate interest in the document, except for wills executed prior to the death of the testator, shall be entitled to obtain copies at any time. All persons entitled to obtain copies may conduct said transaction through legal or voluntary representation provided the right for so doing is vouched for by the notary or the Notarial Registrar concerned, and that the latter states in writing under his/her signature, the full name of the person being represented and the basis whereby he/she deems that the person thus represented is entitled, per se, to obtain the copy being requested" (4 LPRA 2065). See also NR Rule 47.

"The notary shall allow the contents of documents of his protocol to be read by those who, in his judgment, show a legitimate interest as provided in §2065 of this title" (4 LPRA 2068).

AUTHENTICATION OF NOTARIAL ACTS

"Deeds and other instruments affecting land situate in the District of Columbia, or any other territory or possession of the United States, may be acknowledged in Puerto Rico before any notary public appointed therein by proper authority, or any officer therein who has ex officio the powers of a notary public. The certificate by such notary shall be accompanied by the certificate of the executive secretary of Puerto Rico to the effect that the notary taking such acknowledgment is in fact such notarial officer" (48 United States Code 742).

Documents Executed outside Puerto Rico

"In order for it to be valid as a public instrument, every notarial document executed outside Puerto Rico must be previously protocolized, with the notary being bound to cancel the same fees as if it had been originally executed in Puerto Rico.

"The protocolization of certifications of resolutions adopted by a Board of Directors of a banking entity, corporation or trust, issued outside Puerto Rico shall not be necessary; but they must be duly attested before a notary and the notary's signature authenticated" (4 LPRA 2056). See also NR Rule 41.

AUTHORIZATION AND ADMINISTRATION

"Only those presently authorized to practice the notarial profession and those attorneys who in the future are admitted to practice the (legal) profession (and who) are thereafter authorized to practice as notaries by the Supreme Court of Puerto Rico, shall practice the notarial profession in Puerto Rico" (4 LPRA 2011). See also NR Rule 2.

Puerto Rico Notaries "enjoy full autonomy and independence ... and (are) under the administrative direction of the Supreme Court of Puerto Rico, through the Office of Notarial Inspection" (4 LPRA 2003). See also NR Rule 4.

Qualification Process

Besides meeting all requirements for the practice of law in Puerto Rico (i.e., being over 21 years of age and of good moral character, having approved baccalaureate and law degrees, passing the General Bar Examination), would-be Notaries must also pass a Notarial Law Examination prepared and offered by the Board of Bar Examiners; see "Rules for the Admission of Applicants to the Practice of Law and the Notarial Profession," issued by the Supreme Court of Puerto Rico's Board of Bar Examiners, and NR Rule 8.

Upon securing a bond and taking an oath of office, the Notary must register a "signature, sign, seal and flourish" with the Clerk of the Supreme Court of Puerto Rico in a special register, which includes the Notary's residential and mailing address and the location of his or her notarial office (4 LPRA 2011).

Changes of Status

If Notary Moves: The Notary must notify the Clerk of the Supreme Court and the Director of the Office of Notarial Inspection of any change in his or her residential or mailing address or in the location of the Notary's office. Notification must be made within five days of the change (4 LPRA 2011 and NR Rule 11).

NOTARIAL DISTRICTS

The Commonwealth is divided into 13 notarial districts, corresponding to the demarcations of the Courts of First Instance. The notarial districts are:

Aguadilla	Guayama
Aibonito	Humacao
Arecibo	Mayaguez
Bayamon	Ponce
Caguas	San Juan
Carolina	Utuado
Fajardo	

In each district except San Juan, a general custodian of notarial protocols maintains the surrendered protocols of Notaries from that district. In the San Juan district, this function is performed by the Director of the Office of Notarial Inspection. Each custodian "may issue literal, full or partial, handwritten, typewritten, photographic or photostatic copies reproduced by any other electronic means designed to obtain an exact reproduction of an original, of the notarial deeds in his custody.... The copies thus issued of any deed duly certified by the General Custodian of the District, or by the Director of the Office of

Notarial Inspection in the case of the San Juan Notarial District Archives, shall be admissible in evidence" (4 LPRA 2107).

OTHER NOTARIAL OFFICERS

Besides Notaries, the following officers are authorized to perform the acts indicated:

"All oaths, affidavits and affirmations, that are necessary or convenient, or required by law, may be administered within Puerto Rico, and certificates given thereof, by any judge of the Supreme Court, or of the Circuit Court of Appeals, of the Court of First Instance, or any clerk of the said courts…, or any Commissioner of the United States for the District of Puerto Rico" (4 LPRA 882).

"All … Supreme Court justices, judges of the Court of First Instance, municipal judges, prosecutors, justices of the peace, the Secretary of State, the heads of the departments and the municipal treasurers shall authorize affidavits or declarations. …" (4 LPRA 890).

QUICK FACTS

Notary Jurisdiction
Entire Commonwealth of Puerto Rico including its two island municipalities (4 LPRA 2003 and NR Rule 3).

Notary Term Length
Indefinite. Puerto Rican Notaries may remain in office as long as they are in good standing with the Supreme Court and the Bar Association of the Commonwealth.

Notary Bond
$15,000, either a mortgage bond or a bond posted by an insurance company licensed in Puerto Rico or by the Office of the Insurance Commissioner, which must be renewed by the Notary and reviewed for sufficiency by the Supreme Court annually (4 LPRA 2011). See also NR Rule 10.

O-R

Rhode Island

NOTARY SEAL

"Although not required by The Rhode Island General Laws, it is prudent for a notary public to use a seal when notarizing documents" (EO Sec. 3[d]).

Seal Use Is Recommended

"Although Rhode Island does not require notaries to put seals on documents, it is generally prudent for a Notary Public to do so. Some other states require notaries to use a seal, as do certain corporations or government agencies. Documents to be used in foreign countries always need to be sealed. Since a Notary Public will not always know how or where an instrument he or she is notarizing is to be used, it is always safer to use a seal" (website, "Frequently Asked Questions").

Examples

The above are typical, actual-size examples of Notary seals that may be used in Rhode Island. Formats other than these may also be seen.

NOTARY ADMINISTRATION

Office of Secretary of State
Division of Business Services
Notary Public Section   1-401-222-3040
148 W. River St.
Providence, RI 02904-2615

Website: http://sos.ri.gov/business/notary/

NOTARY RULES

GI — RHODE ISLAND GENERAL LAWS
EO — EXECUTIVE ORDER 09-08

Many Notary rules are in the Rhode Island General Laws:

a. Title 42, Chapter 30, "Notaries Public and Justices of the Peace";

b. Title 34, Chapter 12, "Acknowledgments and Notarial Acts."

Executive Order 09-08, "Standards of Conduct for Notaries Public in the State of Rhode Island and Providence Plantations," issued by the Rhode Island Governor April 8, 2009, and amended Oct. 15 and Nov. 18, 2009, prescribes best practices for Notaries. "All notaries public should adhere to the 'Standards'.... These standards will be considered by the Governor in the appointment, reappointment, and removal of notaries public from their commissions" (EO Sec. 1[a]). This Order and other guidance from the Secretary of State is available on the website.

Legislator Need Not Use Seal: During open session on the floor of the Rhode Island General Assembly, a Notary who is a member of the General Assembly may notarize signatures on documents without using a seal (EO Sec. 3[d]).

Kind

Inked Stamp or Embosser: Rhode Island Notaries may use an inked stamp or an embosser as a seal (website, "Purchasing a Notary Seal"). Traditionally, embosser seals have been widely used.

"Your seal should produce a sharp, legible, embossed or printed image that legibly reproduces under photographic methods" (website, "Purchasing a Notary Seal").

Shape/Size
Not specified by law or Executive Order.

Components
"The seal (embosser) should include the notary's name exactly as it appears on his or her commission and the words 'NOTARY PUBLIC' and 'RHODE ISLAND'" (EO Sec. 3[d]).

"A stamp may have additional information such as your (commission) expiration date, 'signed before me' or other useful phrases" (website, "Frequently Asked Questions").

State Seal May Not Appear: "No seal manufacturer has permission from the Secretary of State to reproduce the State Seal of the State of Rhode Island as an element of the notary public seal" (website, "Purchasing a Notary Seal").

Signature, Title, ID Number, Expiration Date
"In completing a notarial act, a notary public should sign his or her name exactly as it appears on the notary's commission, write the title 'Notary Public' after his or her signature, list his or her commission expiration date and list his or her notary identification number" (EO Sec. 3[b]).

Seal Is Notary's Exclusive Property
"A notary's seal is the exclusive property of the notary; it may not be used by any other person" (EO Sec. 3[d]).

"You should make every effort to secure your seal and protect it from unauthorized use" (website, "Purchasing a Notary Seal").

Lost Seal
"Any notary public whose seal is lost, misplaced, destroyed, broken, damaged, stolen or otherwise unworkable should immediately deliver written notice of that fact to the Office of the Secretary of State. If and when the notary's seal is recovered or replaced, written notice of the recovery or replacement should also be delivered immediately to the Office of the Secretary of State" (EO Sec. 8[b]).

Seal Should Be Destroyed or Defaced
When a Notary's commission expires, is resigned or is revoked, or if a Notary dies during the term of his or her commission, the Notary or the Notary's personal representative should, "(a)s soon as reasonably practicable, destroy or deface all notary seals or stamps so that they may not be used" (EO Sec. 9[c] and 10[a]).

Name Printed or Typed Beneath Signature
The Notary's name must be printed or typed beneath or next to his or her signature on every acknowledgment of signatures on a deed that is to be recorded. Failure to do so will increase the recording fee, although it will not invalidate the transaction: "The signatories and notaries public to all deeds, mortgages, transfers, assignments, and discharges of mortgages, leases, rental agreements, rescissions or assignments thereof, and contracts for the sale of land shall have their names typed or printed immediately beneath or adjacent to their signatures. Failure to comply herewith shall not affect the validity of any such instrument, but the recording fee for the instrument shall be increased by two dollars ($2.00)" (GL 34-11-1.1).

NOTARY POWERS

Rhode Island Notaries are authorized to perform the following notarial acts (EO Sec. 3[a]):

1. Take acknowledgments* (GL 34-12-2[1] and 42-30-8);
2. Administer oaths and affirmations** (GL 36-2-1);
3. Execute jurats*** (GL 9-18-1 and GL 42-30-8);
4. Witness signatures****;
5. Certify copies*****;
6. Issue subpoenas to summon witnesses****** (GL 9-17-3);
7. Execute protests******* (GL 6A-3-505[b] and 42-30-8).

* Acknowledgments: "'Acknowledgment' shall mean a notarial act in which an individual, at a single time and place:

"1. appears in person before the notary public and presents a document;

"2. is personally known to the notary public or is identified by the notary through satisfactory evidence of identity; and

"3. indicates to the notary public that the signature on the document was voluntarily affixed by the individual for the purposes stated within the document and, if applicable, that the individual had authority to sign in a particular representative capacity" (EO Sec. 2[a]).

** Oaths and Affirmations: "'Oath' shall mean a notarial act, or part thereof, which is legally equivalent to an affirmation, and in which an individual, at a single time and place:

"1. appears in person before the notary public;

"2. is personally known to the notary public or is identified by the notary through satisfactory evidence of identity; and

"3. makes a vow of truthfulness or fidelity under the pains and penalties of perjury by invoking a deity or using any form of the word 'swear'" (EO Sec. 2[k]).

"'Affirmation' shall mean a notarial act, or part thereof, that is legally equivalent to an oath in which an individual, at a single time and place:

"1. appears in person before the notary public;

"2. is personally known to the notary public or is identified by the notary through satisfactory evidence of identity; and

"3. makes a vow of truthfulness or fidelity under the pains and penalties of perjury based on personal honor and without invoking a deity or using any form of the word 'swear'" (EO Sec. 2[b]).

*** Jurats: "'Jurat' means a notarial act in which an individual, at a single time and place:

"1. appears in person before the notary public and presents a document;

"2. is personally known to the notary public or is identified by the notary through satisfactory evidence of identity;

"3. signs the document in the presence of the notary public; and

"4. takes an oath or affirmation before the notary public vouching for the truthfulness or accuracy of the signed document" (EO Sec. 2[g]).

A jurat is an essential component of affidavits and depositions. While a Notary by law may also "take" (i.e., transcribe) an affidavit or deposition, normally only Notaries who are trained shorthand reporters do so. "Any justice of the supreme or superior or family court, justice of the peace or notary public may take the deposition of any witness, to be used in the trial of any civil suit, action, petition or proceeding, in which he is not interested, nor counsel, nor the attorney of either party, and which shall then be commenced or pending in this state, or in any other state or in the District of Columbia, or in any territory, government or country" (GL 9-18-1).

**** Witnessing Signatures: "'Signature witnessing' shall mean a notarial act in which an individual, at a single time and place:

"1. appears in person before the notary public and presents a document;

"2. is personally known to the notary public or is identified by the notary through satisfactory evidence of identity; and

"3. signs the document in the presence of the notary public" (EO Sec. 2[r]).

***** Copy Certifications: "'Copy certification' shall mean a notarial act in which a notary public:

"1. is presented with a document that is neither a vital record, a public record nor publicly recordable; and

"2. copies or supervises the copying of the document using a photographic or electronic copying process; or

"3. compares the document to the copy; and

"4. determines that the copy is accurate and complete; and

"5. applies an acknowledgment to the document owner's signature attesting to the above listed facts" (EO Sec. 2[d]).

"A notary public should not perform a notarial act if … the document presented for certification is a vital record, a public record or a publicly recordable document that is available as a certified copy from an official source other than a notary public" (EO Sec. 4[a][3]). "(P)ublic records are available as certified copies from the public offices that issued them originally" (website, "Frequently Asked Questions").

****** Subpoenas to Summon Witnesses: "(J)ustices of the peace and notaries public may issue subpoenas to witnesses in any case, civil or criminal, before any court, and in any matter before any body or person authorized by law to summon witnesses" (GL 9-17-3).

******* Protests: "A protest is a certificate of dishonor made by a United States consul or vice consul, or a notary public or other person authorized to administer oaths by the law of the place where dishonor occurs. It may be made upon information satisfactory to that person. The protest must identify the instrument and certify either that presentment has been made or, if not made, the reason why it was not made, and that the instrument has been dishonored by nonacceptance or nonpayment. The protest may also certify that notice of dishonor has been given to some or all parties" (GL 6A-3-505[b]).

Executive Order Doesn't Supersede Laws

"Nothing in these 'Standards of Conduct for Notaries Public in the State of Rhode Island and Providence Plantations' supersedes the provisions of any court rule, including court forms; The Rhode Island General Laws, including but not limited to Title 42, Chapter 30; any Federal statute; or any regulation adopted pursuant to The Rhode Island General Laws or Federal statute" (EO Sec. 1[b]).

Identifying Document Signers

"'Satisfactory evidence of identity' shall mean identification of an individual based on at least one current document issued by a Federal or State or tribal government agency bearing the photographic image of the individual's face and signature; or on the oath or affirmation of a credible witness unaffected by the document or transaction who is personally known to the notary public and who personally knows the individual; or identification of an individual based on the notary's personal knowledge of the identity of the principal. For a person who is not a United States citizen, 'satisfactory evidence of identity' shall mean identification of an individual based on a valid passport, or another government-issued document evidencing the individual's nationality or residence, that bears a photographic image of the individual's face and signature" (EO Sec. 2[q]).

Credible Witness: "'Credible witness' means an honest, reliable, and impartial person who personally knows an individual appearing before a notary public and takes an oath or affirmation from the notary to vouch for that individual's identity"(EO Sec. 2[e]).

Personal Knowledge: "'Personal knowledge of identity' shall mean familiarity with an individual resulting from interactions with that individual over a period of time sufficient to dispel any reasonable uncertainty that the individual has the identity claimed" (EO Sec. 2[n]).

Notary's 'Standard Operating Procedure'

"Each notary public should develop and adhere to his or her own 'standard operating procedure' when notarizing instruments. This will benefit the notary if he or she is ever required to testify as to how a particular instrument was notarized" (EO Sec. 3[e]).

Notary May Certify Signature by Mark

"A notary public may certify the affixation of a signature by mark on a document presented for notarization if:

"1. the principal affixes the mark in the presence of the notary public and of 2 witnesses unaffected by the document;

"2. both witnesses sign their own names beside the mark;

"3. the notary public writes below the mark: 'Mark affixed by (name of signer by mark) in the presence of (names and addresses of witnesses) and undersigned notary'; and

"4. the notary public notarizes the signature by mark through an acknowledgment, jurat or signature witnessing" (EO Sec. 3[g]).

Notary May Sign on Behalf of Principal

"The notary public may sign the name of a principal who is physically unable to sign or make a mark on a document presented for notarization if:

"1. the principal directs the notary public to do so in the presence of 2 witnesses who are unaffected by the document;

"2. the principal does not have a demeanor that causes the notary public to have a compelling doubt about whether the principal knows the consequences of the transaction requiring the notarial act;

"3. in the notary public's judgment, the principal is acting of his or her own free will;

"4. the notary public signs the principal's name in the presence of the principal and the witnesses;

"5. both witnesses sign their own names beside the signature;

"6. the notary public writes below the signature: 'Signature affixed by notary public in the presence of (names and addresses of principal and 2 witnesses)'; and

"7. the notary public notarizes the signature through an acknowledgment, jurat or signature witnessing" (EO Sec. 3[h]).

Acting as Witness and Notary

The following information appeared in the 2007 edition of the "Notary Public Guide," formerly published and distributed to Notaries by the Rhode Island Secretary of State:

"Under most circumstances, an individual may act as both a witness and a notary to the same instrument. A Notary Public who is acting only as a witness should sign as an individual and should not include the words 'Notary Public' after his or her signature.

"There are instances, however, where a Notary Public cannot act as both witness and notary. For example, if an individual acts as a witness to a will, he or she may be asked to sign a 'self-proving affidavit' to the will in which he or she swears that the formalities of execution were adhered to. In such a case, a Notary Public could not complete the jurat to the affidavit with respect to his or her own oath as a witness. A Notary Public could, however, sign the jurat with respect to the other witness to the will.

"It is prudent to get into the habit of acting as either a witness or a Notary Public to a given instrument but not as both" (NPG).

Notarizing Wills

Unless a Notary is working under the instruction of an attorney or has had extensive estate-planning experience, he or she should be cautious in notarizing a will. A will can be a complex document and an improperly prepared or notarized will can have far-reaching consequences. A Notary should never give legal advice about a will, whether or not he or she has had estate-planning experience, unless the Notary is also an attorney (website, "Frequently Asked Questions").

Health Care Powers of Attorney

In 2006, the statutory form for a durable power of attorney for health care was amended to allow its acknowledgment before a Notary as an alternative to being witnessed by, or acknowledged before, two adult witnesses. Neither the Notary nor the two witnesses may be the designated health-care agent or the alternative agent, a health-care provider or the employee of such, or the operator of a community care facility or the employee of such (GL 23-4.10-2).

See "Certificate for Durable Power of Attorney for Health Care" under "Notary Certificates," below.

NOTARY DON'TS

A Rhode Island Notary Public should:
1. NOT notarize without the principal's personal appearance before the Notary at the time of notarization (EO Sec. 4[a][1]), with personal appearance meaning "that the principal and the notary public are physically close enough to see, hear, communicate with and hand identification documents to each other" (EO Sec. 2[m]);
2. NOT notarize unless the principal is personally known to the Notary or identified through satisfactory evidence (EO Sec. 4[a][2]);
3. NOT complete a notarial certificate with information known or believed by the Notary to be false (EO Sec. 4[d]);
4. NOT sign or affix a seal on a notarial certificate that is incomplete (EO Sec. 4[e]).

Fraud or Deceit by Notary

The Executive Order states that Notaries should "not perform any official act with the intent to deceive or defraud" (EO Sec. 4[h]). "A notary public, who in the exercise of the powers, or in the performance of the duties of such office, shall practice any fraud or deceit, the punishment for which is not otherwise provided by law, shall be guilty of a misdemeanor and fined not more than one thousand dollars ($1,000) or imprisoned not more than one year or both" (GL 42-30-16). See also EO Sec. 13.

Principal's Awareness and Free Will Essential

"A notary public should not perform a notarial act if … the principal has a demeanor that causes the notary public to have a compelling doubt about whether the principal knows the consequences of the transaction or document requiring the notarial act; (or) in the notary public's judgment, the principal is not acting of his or her own free will" (EO Sec. 4[a][4] and [5]).

"You should not notarize a document for someone who appears confused about what he or she is signing or appears to be coerced into signing" (website, "Frequently Asked Questions").

Notarizing a Fax or Photocopy

"A photocopy or fax may be notarized only if it bears an original signature. That is, the copy must have been signed with an ink pen. A photocopied or faxed signature may never be notarized" (website, "Frequently Asked Questions").

Disqualifying Interests and Exceptions

A Notary should not perform a notarial act if:
1. "(T)he notary public is a party to or is named in the document that is to be notarized, except that a notary may notarize a document if

the notary is named in the document for the sole purpose of receiving notices relating to the document and except that a notary who is licensed as an attorney in the State of Rhode Island and is named as an executor, trustee or in any fiduciary capacity in a document, or employees of such attorney, may perform notarial acts concerning such document" (EO Sec. 4[a][6]); or

2. "(T)he notary public will receive as a direct result of the notarial act any commission, fee, advantage, right, title, interest, cash, property or other consideration exceeding in value the fees set forth in section 42-30-13 of The Rhode Island General Laws or has any financial interest in the subject matter of the document. This section shall not preclude (notarization by) a notary who is licensed as an attorney in the State of Rhode Island or any employee of such attorney where the attorney receives a legal fee for professional legal services rendered in connection with such document" (EO Sec. 4[a][7]).

Notarizing for Self or Relatives

"A notary public should not perform a notarial act if … the notary public is a spouse, domestic partner, parent, guardian, child or sibling of the principal, including in-law, step, or half relatives, except where such persons witness a will or other legal document prepared by the notary who is an attorney licensed in the State of Rhode Island" (EO Sec. 4[a][8]).

"It is inadvisable for a Notary Public to notarize a document for a close relative. The purpose of a notary is to be an independent witness to the signing of a document. If there were to be a dispute involving the document, the validity of the notarization could be called into question. Additionally, you may not notarize your own signature" (website, " Frequently Asked Questions").

Refusing to Notarize

"A notary public should not refuse to perform a notarial act solely based on the principal's race, advanced age, gender, sexual orientation, religion, national origin, health or disability" (EO Sec. 4[b]).

<u>Causes for Refusing to Act</u>: "A notary public should perform any notarial act for any person requesting such an act who tenders the fee set forth in section 42-30-13 of The Rhode Island General Laws unless:

"1. the notary public knows or has good reason to believe that the notarial act or the associated transaction is unlawful;

"2. the principal has a demeanor that causes the notary public to have a compelling doubt about whether the principal knows the consequences of the transaction or document requiring the notarial act;

"3. the act is prohibited by other applicable law; or

"4. the number of notarial acts requested practicably precludes completion of all acts at once, in which case the notary public shall arrange for later completion of the remaining acts" (EO Sec. 5).

Influencing Principal

A Notary should not influence a person either to enter into or avoid a transaction involving a notarial act by the Notary, except in two situations:

1. The Notary may provide advice relating to that transaction if he or she is "duly qualified, trained or experienced in a particular industry or professional field" (EO Sec. 4[c]).

2. The Notary may advise against a transaction if he or she "knows or has good reason to believe that the associated transaction is unlawful" (EO Sec. 4[k]).

Incomplete Document or Certificate

"A notary public should not notarize a signature on a blank or incomplete document" or "provide or send a signed or sealed notarial certificate to another person with the understanding that it will be completed or attached to a document outside of the notary's presence," except that "in connection with a commercial, non-consumer transaction, a notary public may deliver a signed, sealed or signed and sealed notarial certificate to an attorney with the understanding that:

"(i) the attorney will attach the certificate to a document outside of the notary's presence; and

"(ii) the attorney will hold such notarial certificate in escrow; and

"(iii) the attorney informs the notary that the attorney will obtain the approval of the principal, or principals, involved before attaching the certificate to the document" (EO Sec. 4[f] and [g]).

Claiming Unauthorized Powers

"A notary public should not claim to have powers, qualifications, rights or privileges that the office of notary does not provide, including the power to counsel on immigration matters" (EO Sec. 4[i]). See also "Advertising Disclaimer Required" below, under "Practicing Law."

'Notario' and Equivalents Discouraged: "A notary public should not use the term 'notario' or 'notario publico' or any equivalent non-English term in any business card, advertisement, notice or sign. It is recommended to use only the commission title of 'Notary Public.' Any equivalent non-English term may imply to the general public that legal services are being rendered" (EO Sec. 4[j]).

Practicing Law

"A non-attorney notary public should not assist a non-attorney in drafting, completing, selecting or understanding a document or transaction requiring a notarial act, rendering legal advice or otherwise engage in the practice of law" (EO Sec. 6[a]).

However, a Notary who is duly qualified, trained or experienced in a particular industry or professional field may select, draft, complete, or give advice on a document or certificate related to a matter in that industry or field (EO Sec. 6[b]).

May Not Certify Legality: "A notary public has neither the duty nor the authority to investigate, ascertain or attest to the lawfulness, propriety, accuracy or truthfulness of a document or transaction involving a notarial act" (EO Sec. 3[c]).

Advertising Disclaimer Advised: "A non-attorney notary public who advertises notarial services in any language should include in the advertisement, notice, letterhead or sign the following, prominently displayed in the same language the statement: 'I am not an attorney and have no authority to give advice on immigration or other legal matters.'" (EO Sec. 7).

NOTARY SIGNING AGENTS

Currently, there are no statutes, regulations or rules expressly governing, prohibiting or restricting the operation of Notary Signing Agents within the state of Rhode Island.

NOTARY FEES

Rhode Island Notaries may charge the following fees for notarial acts (GL 42-30-13):
1. Taking an acknowledgment: $1;
2. Taking an affidavit: 25 cents;
3. Noting a marine protest, $1; drawing, extending and recording a marine protest, $1.50;
4. Recording a protest* for nonacceptance or nonpayment, if amount involved is $500 dollars or more, $1; if less than $500, 50 cents; noting nonacceptance or nonpayment, 25 cents; for each notice given to a party liable for payment, 25 cents.

* "(T)he whole cost of protest, including necessary notices and the record, shall not exceed two dollars ($2.00), and the whole cost of noting, including notices, shall in no case exceed one dollar and twenty-five cents ($1.25)" (GL 42-30-13[8]).

Travel Fee

Notaries may charge 10 cents per mile for traveling to perform a notarial act (GL 42-30-13[4]).

NOTARY CERTIFICATES

Acknowledgment by Individual for Self or as Representative (EO Sec. 3[f]):

"A notary public should take the acknowledgment of the signature or mark of persons acknowledging for themselves or in any representative capacity by using substantially the following form:"

State of Rhode Island
County of _____

On this ____ day of _____, 20__, before me, the undersigned Notary Public, personally appeared _____ (name of document signer), personally known to the Notary or proved to the Notary through satisfactory evidence of identification, which was _____ (description of satisfactory evidence), to be the person whose name is signed on the preceding or attached document,

and acknowledged to the Notary that (he)(she) signed it voluntarily for its stated purpose(.)
(as partner for _____, a partnership.)
(as _____ for _____, a corporation.)
(as attorney in fact for _____, the principal.)
(as _____ for _____, (a) (the) _____.)

_____
(Signature of Notary)   (Notary Seal)

_____, *Notary Public*
(Printed Name of Notary)
Commission Number: _____
My commission expires: _____

Form of Acknowledgment

"Acknowledgment of any instrument hereafter made need not be in any set form, but shall be made by all the parties executing the instrument and the certificate thereof shall express the ideas that the parties were each and all known to the magistrate taking the acknowledgment, and known by the magistrate to be the parties executing the instrument, and that they acknowledge the instrument to be their free act and deed; provided, however, that in case of any such instrument executed without this state, and within the limits of the United States or of any dependency thereof, if the instrument is acknowledged or proved in the manner prescribed by the law of the state, District of Columbia, territory or such dependency, where executed, it shall be deemed to be legally executed, and acknowledged and shall have the same effect as if executed and acknowledged in the mode above prescribed, including an acknowledgment by less than all parties if made in a jurisdiction the laws of which permit acknowledgments in such manner; provided however, that instruments requiring acknowledgments by parties having opposing interests must be acknowledged by at least one party of each interest" (GL 34-12-1).

Acknowledgments by Attorneys in Fact

This useful information appeared in the 2007 edition of the "Notary Public Guide," formerly distributed to Notaries by the Rhode Island Secretary of State:

"An attorney-in-fact can act on behalf of an incompetent principal only if the power of attorney contains proper statutory language that it is not affected by competency. In order for its validity to be unaffected, the power of attorney must specifically state that it will not be invalidated by incompetency.

"Before a Notary Public takes the acknowledgment of an attorney-in-fact, he or she should ask to see the power of attorney or obtain some other proof of the attorney-in-fact's power to act. While a Notary Public has no duty to inquire into the reasons for the attorney-in-fact's appointment, he or she should try to make sure the power of attorney is valid. If a Notary Public has any questions as to the validity of a power of attorney, he or she may wish to contact a lawyer.

"An individual signing an instrument as an attorney-in-fact for another will generally sign his or her own name along with his or her title and the name of the principal. For example, the signature might read: 'Jane Smith as attorney-in-fact for Mary Smith,' or 'Jane Smith power of attorney for Mary Smith.' Both names should appear in the acknowledgment form and the Notary Public should be sure that the words 'attorney-in-fact' appear after the name of the attorney-in-fact and that the acknowledgment contains the language that the signing is the free act and deed of the principal" (NPG).

Jurat (EO Sec. 3[f]):

"A notary public should use a jurat certificate in substantially the following form in notarizing a signature or mark on an affidavit or other sworn or affirmed written declaration:"

State of Rhode Island
County of _____

On this ____ *day of* _____, *20*__, *before me, the undersigned Notary Public, personally appeared* _____ *(name of document signer), personally known to the Notary or proved to the Notary through satisfactory evidence of identification, which was* _____ *(description of satisfactory evidence), to be the person who signed the preceding or attached document in my presence, and who swore or affirmed to the Notary that the contents of the document are truthful and accurate to the best of (his)(her) knowledge and belief.*

_____
(Signature of Notary)   (Notary Seal)
_____, Notary Public
(Printed Name of Notary)
Commission Number: _____
My commission expires: _____

Certificate for Witnessing Signature (EO Sec. [3][f]):

"A notary public should witness a signature in substantially the following form in notarizing a signature or mark to confirm that it was affixed in the notary's presence without administration of an oath or affirmation:"

State of Rhode Island
County of _____

On this ____ day of _____, 20__, before me, the undersigned Notary Public, personally appeared _____ (name of document signer), personally known to the notary or proved to the notary through satisfactory evidence of identification, which was _____ (description of satisfactory evidence), to be the person whose name was signed on the preceding or attached document in my presence.

_____
(Signature of Notary)   (Notary Seal)

_____, Notary Public
(Printed Name of Notary)
Commission Number: _____
My commission expires: _____

Certificate for Witnessing Signature on School Transcript/Diploma/Degree (website, "Apostilles and Authentications: Examples of Public Documents"):

I, _____ (name of school officer), the (school principal/registrar) of _____ (name of school), hereby certify that this is a true and original (transcript/diploma/degree) of _____ (name of student).

_____   Date: _____
(Signature of School Officer)

State of Rhode Island
County of _____

On this ____ day of _____, 20__, before me personally appeared _____ (name of school officer), (school principal/registrar), and signed the above statement.

_____
(Signature of Notary)   (Notary Seal)

_____, Notary Public
(Printed Name of Notary)
Commission Number: _____
My commission expires: _____

Certificate for Certified Copy (EO Sec. [3][f]):

"A notary public should certify a copy by using substantially the following form:"

State of Rhode Island
County of _____

On this ____ day of _____, 20__, I certify that the (preceding) (following) (attached) document is a true, exact, complete, and unaltered copy made by me of _____ (description of the original document), presented to me by _____, and to the best of my knowledge the copied document is neither a vital record nor a publicly recordable document, certified copies of which may be available from an official source other than a Notary.

_____
(Signature of Notary)   (Notary Seal)

_____, Notary Public
(Printed Name of Notary)
Commission Number: _____
My commission expires: _____

When Above Forms Not to Be Used

"The forms of certificates for notarial acts set forth in this section are not intended to replace or supersede the existing forms commonly used in conveyances of real estate or in other legal documents within the State of Rhode Island, and in particular, those forms of certificates for notarial acts approved by any committee of the Rhode Island Bar Association" (EO Sec. 3[k]).

If Form from Another State: "This section does not require a notary public to use the forms set forth above if the form of acknowledgment, jurat, signature witnessing or copy certification of a document contains an alternative form from another State (and) if the document is to be filed or recorded in, or governed by the laws of, that other State" (EO Sec. 3[i]).

If Other Form May Not Be Altered: "This section does not require a notary public to use the forms set forth above if the form of acknowledgment, jurat, signature witnessing or copy certification appears on a printed form that contains an express prohibition against altering that form" (EO Sec. 3[j]).

Certificate for Durable Power of Attorney for Health Care (GL 23-4.10-2):

State of Rhode Island
County of _____

I declare under penalty of perjury that the person who signed or acknowledged this document is personally known to me to be the principal, that the principal signed or acknowledged this durable power of attorney in my presence, that the principal appears to be of sound mind and under no duress, fraud, or undue influence, that I am not a health care provider, an employee of a health care provider, the operator of a community care facility, nor an employee of an operator of a community care facility.

_____, *Notary Public*
(Signature of Notary)
(Notary Seal)

_____ Date: _____
(Printed Name of Notary)
Commission Number: _____
My commission expires: _____

I further declare under penalty of perjury that I am not related to the principal by blood, marriage, or adoption, and, to the best of my knowledge, I am not entitled to any part of the estate of the principal upon the death of the principal under a will now existing or by operation of law.

_____   _____
(Signature of Notary)   (Printed Name of Notary)

Contents of Military Officer Certificate

"In the taking of acknowledgments and the performing of other notarial acts requiring certification, a certificate endorsed upon or attached to the instrument or documents, which shows the date of the notarial act and which states, in substance that the person appearing before the (military) officer acknowledged the instrument as his act or made or signed the instrument or document under such oath, shall be sufficient for all intents and purposes. The instrument or document shall not be rendered invalid by the failure to state the place of execution or acknowledgment" (GL 34-12-7). If such officers affix their signature, rank and branch of service or subdivision thereof upon the certificate or document, no further proof of authority is needed (GL 34-12-8).

ELECTRONIC NOTARIZATIONS

The state of Rhode Island has not yet adopted statutes or regulations expressly establishing rules, definitions and procedures for electronic notarization.

UETA Recognizes Notary's eSignature

Effective July 13, 2000, Rhode Island adopted the Uniform Electronic Transactions Act (GL 42-127.1-1 through 42.127.1-20), including the provision on notarization and acknowledgment, thereby recognizing the legal validity of electronic signatures used by Notaries:

"If a law requires a signature or record to be notarized, acknowledged, verified, or made under oath, the requirement is satisfied if the electronic signature of the person authorized to perform those acts, together with all other information required to be included by other applicable law, is attached to or logically associated with the signature or record" (GL 42-127.1-11).

Webcam 'Notarizations' Unauthorized

The following appears in an "Alert" that has been prominently posted on the Secretary of State's website:

"An individual completing an acknowledgment must do so 'before' a person authorized to take acknowledgments under Rhode Island law, including Notaries Public. The Governor of the State of Rhode Island and the Rhode Island

Secretary of State have further set forth, by Executive Order, the requirement that the person completing an acknowledgment or seeking other services from the Notary Public must 'appear in person' before the Notary Public. Other electronic means of appearance, such as web cam and Skype, do not comply with the requirements of state law and the Executive Order" (website, Notary Public homepage).

NOTARY RECORDS

While a journal is not required by statute in Rhode Island, the Governor's Executive Order recommends keeping one as a part of the Notary's "standard operating procedure": "A notary may find the use of a 'journal of notarial acts' to be a beneficial tool," which "will benefit the notary if he or she is ever required to testify as to how a particular instrument was notarized" (EO Sec. 3[e]).

Permanently Bound Book

A proper journal is "a permanently bound book that creates and preserves a chronological record of notarizations performed by a notary public" (EO Sec. 2[f]).

Recommended Journal Entries

"Notaries electing to use a 'journal of notarial acts' should as a matter of good practice record the following:

"1. the date and time of the notarial act, proceeding or transaction;

"2. the type of notarial act;

"3. the type, title or a description of the document, transaction or proceeding. If multiple documents are signed by the same principal in the course of a transaction or during a single date (i.e., real estate closings, mortgage discharges, state laboratory drug analysis certificates, etc.), a single journal entry shall be sufficient;

"4. the signature, printed name and address of each principal and witness;

"5. description of the satisfactory evidence of identity of each person, including: (i) a statement that the person is 'personally known to me;' or (ii) a notation of the type of identification document, the issuing agency, its serial or identification number and its date of issuance or expiration …; or (iii) a notation if the notary public identified the individual on the oath or affirmation of a credible witness …;

"6. the fee, if any, charged for the notarial act; and

"7. the address where the notarization was performed" (EO Sec. 3[e]).

Record Reason for Any Incompletion: "A notary public should record in the journal the circumstances for not completing a notarial act" (EO Sec. 3[e][8]).

Don't Record SSN or Credit Card: "A notary public should not record a Social Security or credit card number in the journal" (EO Sec. 3[e]).

"If the identification number on the document is the person's Social Security number, instead of including the number, write in the words 'Social Security number' or the acronym 'SSN'" (EO Sec. 3[e][5][ii][1]).

Journal Kept for Seven Years

When the commission of a Notary who elected to use a journal of notarial acts expires, is resigned or is revoked, "the notary should retain the journal and records for seven years after the date of expiration, resignation or revocation" (EO Sec. 10[b]). If a Notary dies during the term of his or her commission, the Notary's personal representative should comply with this section of the Executive Order (EO Sec. 9[c]).

Not Required for Attorney

"A Journal is recommended as best practice, but not required, for a notary public who is an attorney licensed to practice law within the State of Rhode Island. These Standards of Conduct shall not be construed to impair or infringe in any way on the attorney-client privilege or the attorney work product doctrine" (EO Sec. 3[e]).

AUTHENTICATION OF NOTARIAL ACTS

Secretary of State

Authenticating certificates for Notaries, including apostilles, are issued primarily by the Rhode Island Secretary of State's office (GL 42-30-15).

Fee: $5 per authentication. "A fee of no more than one hundred fifty dollars ($150.00) shall be charged and collected by the secretary of state for the authentication or certification of the signature(s) of a notary public on all relevant documents filed at one time which pertain to the same matter or transaction" (GL 42-30-15). Fee payable to "R.I. Secretary of State" (website, "Apostilles and Authentications: How to Obtain").

Address:
Office of Secretary of State
Division of Business Services
Authentication/Certification Section
148 W. River St.
Providence, RI 02904-2615

Telephone: 1-401-222-1487

Procedure: Mail or present in person the original notarized document(s) or a certified copy of the document(s), along with the fee. If five documents or less are being presented in person, there is no need to phone or complete any paperwork ahead of time. If more than five documents are being presented in person, first phone the office, then download and complete an In-Person Authentication Request Form, then fax the form to the office at 1-401-222-1309. If documents are being mailed, download and complete a Mail Authentication Request Form, then mail the completed form with the document(s). "Mailed requests are processed daily. A mailed request will be returned to you by first class mail. A self-addressed/stamped envelope will help expedite delivery time. If overnight service is required, a pre-addressed, pre-paid airbill must be included with the request" (website, "Apostilles and Authentications: How to Obtain").

School Transcripts/Diplomas/Degrees: "Many foreign exchange students need to provide their home countries with certified records of their school transcripts, diplomas or degrees. Most often the school record is certified to in the presence of a notary, who then notarizes that statement. Often it is the record officer of the school who certifies to the record in the presence of a notary public. The notarized transcript, diploma or degree is sent to the Secretary of State's office for authentication" (website, "Apostilles and Authentications: Examples of Public Documents"). See "Certificate for Witnessing Signature on School Transcript/Diploma/Degree" above, under "Notary Certificates."

Court Clerks

"It shall be the duty of the secretary of state to make a list of all notaries public and justices of the peace appointed by the governor and duly qualified, and send a copy thereof to each of the clerks of the supreme, superior, and family courts and to the clerks of the district courts for the second, third, fourth, ninth, tenth, eleventh and twelfth judicial districts, to be kept in the files of those courts, and the clerks shall, upon application, issue certificates of office to the person entitled thereto, and shall receive a fee of one dollar ($1.00) for every certificate" (GL 42-30-9).

NOTE: According to several sources, in general only the superior courts are prepared to issue authenticating certificates for Notaries.

COMMISSIONING AND ADMINISTRATION

Rhode Island's Notaries are appointed by the Governor (GL 42-30-3), who will consider the standards of conduct in Executive Order 09-08 in the appointment, reappointment and removal from their commissioned office of Notaries Public (EO Sec. 1[a]). The office of the Secretary of State directly regulates and maintains records on Rhode Island Notaries.

Applying for Commission

Qualifications: An applicant for a commission as a Rhode Island Notary Public must be: (a) a registered voter in Rhode Island; or (b) an attorney who is a member of the Rhode Island Bar (GL 42-30-5[a] and [c]).

Application: The application must be signed by a member or staff of the board of canvassers and registration or by the city or town clerk in the applicant's city or town of residence. This endorsement certifies that the applicant is a registered voter in that city or town. An attorney is not required to get this certification but must include with the application a copy of his or her current Rhode Island Bar card or a certified copy of his or her Certificate of Admission to the Rhode Island Bar. On the application, the applicant's signature on the "Certificate of Engagement" must be notarized by a Rhode Island Notary or Justice of the Peace. The application filing fee is $80, payable to the "Secretary of State" (GL 42-30-5 and website, "Application for Appointment as Notary Public or Justice of the Peace").

Prior to commission expiration, a renewal notice will be sent out to the Notary by the

Secretary of State's Notary Public Section (website, "Frequently Asked Questions".

Non-Resident Notaries: Out-of-state residents who are members of the Rhode Island Bar may qualify to become Notaries (GL 42-30-5[c]).

Online Search for Notaries: The full name, city or town, commission expiration date and Notary ID number of any Rhode Island Notary may be obtained online by entering the Notary's ID number or name on the "Notary Database Look-Up" page of the Secretary of State's website.

Changes of Status

If Notary's Address or Name Changes: "Within 10 days after the change of a notary public's residence or name, the notary should file with the Office of the Secretary of State, Notary Public Section, a Change of Address or Change of Name form," which may be obtained either by download from the website or by calling (401) 222-1487 (EO Sec. 8[a]). There is no charge for the change.

The Notary's signature on the "Change of Name Form" must be notarized by another Notary.

Resignation or Death of Notary: When a Notary ceases to be a qualified voter in Rhode Island or a member of the Rhode Island Bar, or when a Notary becomes permanently unable to perform his or her notarial duties, that Notary should resign his or her commission (EO Sec. 9[a]).

A Notary who resigns his or her commission should send the Office of the Secretary of State a signed notice indicating the effective date of the resignation. The notice may be sent "by any means that provides a tangible receipt or acknowledgment, including certified mail and electronic transmission" (EO Sec. 9[b]).

In addition, the resigning Notary should "destroy or deface all notary seals or stamps so that they may not be used" (EO Sec. 10[a]). If the Notary used a journal of notarial acts, the Notary should retain the journal and records for seven years from the date of resignation (EO Sec. 10[b]).

If a Notary Public dies during the term of his or her commission, the Notary's personal representative should notify the Secretary of State's office of the death in writing as soon as reasonably practical after the death (EO Sec. 9[c]). The Notary's personal representative should also destroy or deface all notary seals or stamps so that they are unusable and should retain any journal(s) of notarial acts and records for seven years (EO Sec. 9[c] and 10).

Revocation of Commission: A Notary Public's commission may be revoked for official misconduct, for cause by the Governor at his or her discretion, or if the Notary is convicted of a felony and incarcerated (GL 42-30-10; EO Sec. 11 and 12). Official misconduct is "a notary's public performance of any act prohibited, or failure to perform any act mandated by any law, in connection with a notarial act; or … a notary's public performance of an official act in a manner found to be grossly negligent or against the public interest" (EO Sec. 2[l]).

When the Notary's commission is revoked, he or she should destroy or deface all seals or stamps so that they are unusable but should retain any journal of notarial acts and records for seven years (EO Sec. 10).

COUNTY AND DISTRICT CLERKS

"It shall be the duty of the secretary of state to make a list of all notaries public and justices of the peace appointed by the governor and duly qualified, and send a copy thereof to each of the clerks of the supreme, superior and family courts and to the clerks of the district courts for the second, third, fourth, ninth, tenth, eleventh and twelfth judicial districts, to be kept in the files of those courts, and the clerks shall, upon application, issue certificates of office to the person entitled thereto, and shall receive a fee of one dollar ($1.00) for every certificate" (GL 42-30-9).

Superior Courts

Providence Superior Court*:
Licht Judicial Complex
250 Benefit Street
Providence, RI 02903
1-401-222-3250

Kent County Superior Court:
Leighton Judicial Complex
222 Quaker Lane
Warwick, RI 02886
1-401-822-6900

Washington County Superior Court:
McGrath Judicial Complex
4800 Tower Hill Road
Wakefield, RI 02879
1-401-782-4121

Newport County Superior Court:
Murray Judicial Complex
45 Washington Square
Newport, RI 02840
1-401-841-8330

* Superior Court administration and central offices are located in the Providence office.

District Courts

Second Division:
Murray Judicial Complex
45 Washington Square
Newport, RI 02840-2913
1-401-841-8350
Serving: Jamestown, Little Compton, Middletown, Newport, Portsmouth and Tiverton

Third Division:
Noel Judicial Complex
222 Quaker Lane
Warwick, RI 02886-0107
1-401-822-6750
Serving: Coventry, Cranston, East Greenwich, Foster, Glocester, Johnston, Lincoln, North Kingstown, North Providence, North Smithfield, Scituate, Smithfield, Warwick, West Greenwich and West Warwick

Fourth Division:
McGrath Judicial Complex
4800 Tower Hill Road
Wakefield, RI 02879-2239
1-401-782-4131
Serving: Charlestown, Exeter, Hopkinton, Narragansett, New Shoreham, Richmond, South Kingstown and Westerly

Sixth Division:
Garrahy Judicial Complex
One Dorrance Plaza
Providence, RI 02903-2719
1-401-458-5400
Serving: Barrington, Bristol, Burrillville, Central Falls, Cumberland, East Providence, Pawtucket, Providence, Warren and Woonsocket

OTHER NOTARIAL OFFICERS

The following officers have the power to act as Notaries Public in Rhode Island (GL 42-30-14):
1. State senators and representatives;
2. Clerks and the registrar of the board of canvassers;
3. Members of city or town councils;
4. Municipal clerks;
5. Chief clerks, deputy clerks and assistant clerks of any state court;
6. Clerks of worker's compensation courts;
7. Two police officers from each state and local police department, as identified in writing by the chief of police.

To exercise their authority to act as Notaries, the officers listed above must file a "certificate of engagement" with the Secretary of State (GL 42-30-4[a]). As long as they are reappointed or continued in office, they need not file a new engagement (GL 42-30-12).

Acknowledgments Only: The following officers are authorized to take acknowledgments in Rhode Island (GL 34-12-2[1]):
1. Justices of the peace;
2. Judges;
3. Clerks and assistant clerks of the superior court;
4. Mayors;
5. Town clerks;
6. Recorders of deeds.

Unqualified Officials: "Any acknowledgment made in good faith before a person claiming to be one of the foregoing officials authorized to take acknowledgments within the respective jurisdictions as above (in 34-12-2[1]), shall be valid, although the official before whom the same is made was not duly qualified in such office; but every person who shall, within this state, willfully take and certify to the taking of any such acknowledgment, without being lawfully qualified thereunto, shall be liable in a criminal proceeding to a fine not exceeding fifty dollars ($50.00), one-half (½) to the use of the complainant and the other half thereto to the use of this state" (GL 34-12-3).

Commissioners

"The governor may appoint, in any foreign

country and in any state of the United States and in any territory of the United States and in the District of Columbia, one or more commissioners, under the seal of the state, to continue in office for the period of five (5) years" (GL 42-31-1).

"The commissioners may administer oaths and take depositions and affidavits to be used in this state; and may also take the acknowledgment of any deed or other instrument to be used or recorded in this state" (GL 42-31-3).

Military Officers

Any commissioned officer in the active service of the U.S. armed forces may perform notarial acts anywhere in the world for military personnel and dependents (GL 34-12-5 and 34-12-6). The notarized document need not state the place of execution or acknowledgment in order to be valid (GL 34-12-7), nor does it require further authentication if the officer's signature, rank and branch of service (or subdivision thereof) appears on the document or certificate (GL 34-12-8).

QUICK FACTS

Notary Jurisdiction
Statewide (GL 42-30-3 and 36-2-1).

Notary Term Length
Four years (GL 42-30-3 and 42-30-4[b]).

Thirty-Day 'Grace' Period: "Every justice of the peace and notary public appointed by the governor and not reappointed, may continue to officiate for a space of thirty (30) days after the day on which his or her commission expires" (GL 42-30-11).

Notary Bond
Not required by law.

O-R

South Carolina

NOTARY SEAL

A South Carolina Notary is required by law to "have" a seal of office but is not required to affix it on notarized documents if the Notary's official title ("Notary Public") is affixed instead (SCC 26-1-60):

"Each notary public shall have a seal of office, which shall be affixed to his instruments of publications and to his protestations. He shall indicate below his signature the date of expiration of his commission. But the absence of such seal or date prior to and after May 30, 1968 shall not render his acts invalid if his official title be affixed thereto."

Any of the following suffices as an official title for a Notary (NPRM): "Notary Public for South Carolina"; "SC Notary Public"; or "Notary Public for SC."

The "South Carolina Notary Public Reference Manual" unreservedly endorses the Notary's employment of a seal for every notarial act: "Use of a notary seal/stamp is strongly recommended."

Example

The above typical, actual-size examples of Notary seals are allowed by South Carolina law. Formats other than these may also be permitted.

NOTARY ADMINISTRATION

Office of Secretary of State
Notary Public Division   1-803-734-2512
1205 Pendleton Street, Suite 525
Columbia, SC 29201

Website: www.scsos.com/Notaries_and_Apostilles

NOTARY RULES

SCC — SOUTH CAROLINA CODE
NPRM — SOUTH CAROLINA NOTARY PUBLIC REFERENCE MANUAL

Most Notary rules are in the South Carolina Code:

a. Title 26, Chapter 1, "Notaries Public";

b. Title 26, Chapter 3, "Uniform Recognition of Acknowledgments Act."*

* This is the *Uniform Recognition of Acknowledgments Act* of 1968, adopted virtually intact as Sections 26-3-10 through 26-3-90.

Other directives for Notaries are in the Secretary of State's "South Carolina Notary Public Reference Manual" (2010), which is also available on the website.

Kind

Embosser or Inking Stamp: "A notarial embossing seal or rubber ink stamp can be purchased and personalized…" (NPRM).

Shape/Size

"If using a rubber stamp, it may be in a circular or rectangular format" (NPRM).

Components

"The seal or stamp should have the notary's name, title and state (John Doe, Notary Public, South Carolina). The expiration may be included but is optional" (NPRM).

Commission Expiration Date Must Appear

Below the Notary's signature on each notarial certificate the commission expiration date must appear, but the absence of this date will not affect the validity of the act if the Notary's official title is affixed (SCC 26-1-60).

Unsealed Documents Valid

"Any instrument heretofore or hereafter recorded in this state, which does not have affixed the impressed seal of the authorized officer who administered the oath or affirmation contained therein, shall be valid and constitute notice as though such impressed seal were affixed" (SCC 30-5-60).

"Whenever it shall appear from the attestation clause or from the other parts of any instrument in writing that it was the intention of the party or parties thereto that such instrument should be a sealed instrument, such instrument shall be construed to be, and shall have the effect of, a sealed instrument, although no seal be actually attached thereto" (SCC 27-7-30).

No Seal on Marriage License

In the performance of a marriage ceremony, when witnessing the signature of the bride and groom on a marriage license, the Notary does not affix the seal on the license (NPRM).

NOTARY POWERS

South Carolina Notaries are authorized to perform the following notarial acts (SCC 26-1-90 and 26-3-20):

1. Take acknowledgments* and proofs**;
2. Administer oaths and affirmations;
3. Take depositions and affidavits***;
4. Execute protests;
5. Solemnize marriages (SCC 20-1-20);
6. Take renunciations of dower****.

* Identifying Acknowledgers: "The person taking an acknowledgment shall certify that: (1) The person acknowledging appeared before him and acknowledged he executed the instrument; and (2) The person acknowledging was known to the person taking the acknowledgment or that the person taking the acknowledgment had satisfactory evidence that the person acknowledging was the person described in and who executed the instrument" (SCC 26-3-40).

** Taking Proofs of Execution: "Except as otherwise provided by statute, before any deed or other instrument in writing can be recorded in this State:

"1. The execution of the deed or other instrument must be first proved by the affidavit of a subscribing witness to the instrument, taken before some officer within this State competent to administer an oath ...

"2. The Uniform Recognition of Acknowledgments Act must be complied with; or

"3. The person executing it shall submit an affidavit subscribed to before a person authorized to perform notarial acts herein or by the Uniform Recognition of Acknowledgments Act that the signature on the deed or other instrument is his signature and that the instrument was executed for the uses and purposes stated in the instrument" (SCC 30-5-30).

If a subscribing witness is unavailable because of "death, insanity or absence from the state," there is provision for a proof of execution based on recognition of the handwriting of all parties (SCC 30-5-60).

*** Taking Affidavits: The following wording for an oath or affirmation is prescribed by the "South Carolina Notary Public Reference Manual": "Do you solemnly swear (or affirm under penalty of perjury) that the statements in the document you have asked me to notarize are the truth, the whole truth, and nothing but the truth (so help you God)?" The signer should be asked to raise his or her right hand.

**** Taking Renunciations of Dower: This is "a wife's act of waiving, upon her husband's death, a right to a life estate in one-third of the land that he owned in fee. This is an antiquated law that only applies to the dower rights of wives whose husbands died on or before May 22, 1984" (NPRM).

Scanning for Originality and Blank Spaces

"A notary public must first examine the document to ensure that it is an original, not a photocopy. The document should also be complete, with no blanks to be filled in, and should not appear to be fraudulent in nature." (NPRM).

Steps in a Proper Notarization

"Before any signing can take place, the notary must require the personal appearance of the signer and evidence of identification from the signer. This can be in the form of: a valid driver's license; a valid state identification; a valid military identification card; a valid passport; personal knowledge by the notary public; and verification by a credible witness. A credible witness is someone who personally knows the signer. Notarization must include the name of the credible witness and type of identification provided" (NPRM).

Signer Must Be Competent and Willing: "As notary, you must also determine to the best of your ability that the signer is competent and not under the influence of drugs or alcohol; not suffering from dementia; understands what he/she is doing; shows a willingness to sign the document without force or duress; and has the capacity to sign the document" (NPRM).

Representative Status Must Be Verified: A Notary "should require documentation verifying that the signer has authority to sign on behalf of the (corporation)" (NPRM).

Likewise, the Notary should require presentation of an authorizing power of attorney before notarizing for an attorney in fact signing on behalf of an absent principal (NPRM). In addition, acknowledgment certificates for signings by public officers, personal representatives and trustees — see below under "Notary Certificates" — dictate that proof of representative status be presented to the Notary.

NOTARY DON'TS

A South Carolina Notary may (NPRM):
1. NOT notarize his/her own signature;
2. NOT certify copies of documents;
3. NOT notarize blank or incomplete documents;
4. NOT offer legal advice as a non-attorney;
5. NOT notarize without identifying the signer;
6. NOT notarize for absent people;
7. NOT postdate or predate notarizations;
8. NOT certify vital records;
9. NOT notarize outside South Carolina.

May Not Certify Copies

"You cannot certify documents as 'true and accurate' copies of the original. If the person who owns the document says it is a true and accurate copy of the original, you may notarize his/her signature, but not the document itself. This procedure is not applicable to documents where certified copies are available from an official source" (NPRM).

As an alternative to a Notary-certified copy, a "Verification of Copy by Document Holder" — see below under "Notary Certificates" — is often acceptable.

May Not Certify Incomplete Documents

"You are not expected to know or understand the contents of the document but are expected to act prudently. Be sure the document is complete and appears to have a legitimate nature" (NPRM)

May Not Certify Vital Records

"It is unlawful for anyone other than the country, state or county to certify vital records. The country, state office or county where the vital record originated and is filed must certify the document. Vital records are birth certificates, marriage licenses, death certificates or divorce decrees" (NPRM).

False Certification by Notary

"A notary public who, in his official capacity, falsely certifies to affirming, swearing, or acknowledging of a person or his signature to an instrument, affidavit, or writing is guilty of a misdemeanor and, upon conviction, must be fined not more than two hundred dollars or imprisoned not more than thirty days. A notary public convicted under the provisions of this section shall forfeit his commission and shall not be issued another commission" (SCC 26-1-95).

Disqualifying Interests

Notary's Own Signature: "You may notarize documents for anyone but yourself as long as you are not a party to the document and will not benefit directly or indirectly from the transaction" (NPRM).

Notarizing for Family Members: "Notarizing documents such as wills, living wills, advance directives, powers-of-attorney, or property transactions for family members is not recommended. Notaries are impartial witnesses and must use prudent judgment when notarizing for family members. Notarizing sensitive documents such as those listed above often causes undue stress between family members" (NPRM).

Attorney May Notarize: "Any attorney at law who is a notary public may exercise all his powers as a notary notwithstanding the fact that he may be interested as counsel or attorney at law in any matter with respect to which he may so exercise any such power and may probate in any court in this State in which he may be counsel" (SCC 26-1-110).

Employee, Officer, Director or Stockholder: A Notary who is an employee, officer, director or stockholder of a corporation may notarize for that corporation, unless the Notary individually is a party to the transaction (SCC 26-1-120).

Foreign-Language Documents and Signers

Notarizing Document in Foreign Language: "The Secretary of State's Office cautions you against this practice. Although you are not expected to know or understand the contents of the document, you are expected to act prudently. Advise the document owner that a notary who is fluent in the language should notarize the document. You may also suggest that they contact the local college/university language division; they may have someone who can assist them" (NPRM).

Notarizing for Foreign-Speaking Person: "The Secretary of State's Office cautions you against this practice. Attempting to assist the holder of a document in understanding the contents could be perceived as practicing law. If you are not an attorney this would be considered the unauthorized practice of law. You should suggest that the document holder contact the local college/university language division; they may have someone who can assist them" (NPRM).

Immigration Assistance Limitations

Under the "Registration of Immigration Assistance Service Act," effective June 17, 2008, the following notarial service is defined as one of 11 separate types of "immigration assistance service" that may be performed by a non-attorney but that is therefore subject to certain requirements and restrictions:

"(N)otarizing signatures on government agency forms if the person performing the service is a notary public commissioned in the State of South Carolina and is lawfully present in the United States" (SCC 40-83-30[A][6]).

The requirements and restrictions include:
1. Posting signs visible to customers in one's place of business – with separate signs in English and in every other language in which immigration assistance services such as notarization of immigration documents are provided, at least 12-by-17 inches in size, and stating: "I AM NOT AN ATTORNEY LICENSED TO PRACTICE LAW AND MAY NOT GIVE LEGAL ADVICE OR ACCEPT FEES FOR LEGAL ADVICE" (SCC 40-83-30[E]).

2. In any advertisement for immigration notarial services in a language other than English (with the exception of a single desk plaque), including the above statement ("I AM NOT AN ATTORNEY...etc.") in a conspicuous size. "If an advertisement is by radio or television, the statement may be modified but must include substantially the same information (SCC 40-83-30[F]).

3. Not literally translating "from English into another language any document, advertisement, stationery, letterhead, business card, or other comparable written material terms or titles including, but not limited to, notary public, notary, licensed attorney, lawyer, or another term that implies the person is an attorney" (SCC 40-83-30[G]).

4. Not representing or advertising oneself in connection with immigration matters through use of titles or credentials, including but not limited to "notary public" or "immigration consultant," that could cause a customer to believe that one holds special skills or can give advice on immigration – though a commissioned Notary may use the term "Notary Public" if accompanied by the statement that the person is not an attorney. "The term 'notary public' may not be translated into another language" (SCC 40-83-30[H][3]).

NOTARY SIGNING AGENTS

In regard to the closing of real estate transactions, South Carolina is regarded as an "attorney-only" state, and, by judicial rule, Notary Signing Agents and other non-attorneys are not permitted by themselves to act at a closing. In its rulings over the years, the South Carolina Supreme Court has identified at least five steps related to a real estate transaction which it labels the practice of law, including: performing a title search, preparing loan documents, presiding at a closing, disbursing loan funds and recording documents. At least two of these functions are performed by Notary Signing Agents and thus, arguably, constitute the unauthorized practice of law in the state.

Online 'Notice' of Secretary

The following "Notice" appears on the Secretary of State's website ("Notaries and Apostilles"): "The handling of real estate closings by notaries public constitutes the unauthorized practice of law in South Carolina. Offering advice to clients, preparing deeds, notes, mortgages, and any other documents related to the transfer of property do not fall within the duties of a notary public. (Exception: An attorney who is also a notary public.) Real estate and mortgage loan closings must be conducted by attorneys in South Carolina."

'Fee Causes Unauthorized Practice'

In one notable South Carolina Supreme Court case — *South Carolina v. Buyers Service Company*, 357S.E.2d 15 (S.C. 1987) — the Court reversed a lower appellate decision permitting a commercial title company to conduct real estate closings, provided that it gave no legal advice. Agreeing in theory with the lower court, the Supreme Court nonetheless stated, "there is in practice no way of assuring that lay persons conducting a closing will adhere to the restrictions. One handling a closing might easily be tempted to offer a few words of explanation, however innocent, rather than risk losing a fee for his or her employer."

NOTARY FEES

The fees of Notaries must be as follows (SCC 8-21-140):
1. Executing every notarial certificate, with seal: 50 cents;
2. Administering an oath for an affidavit: 25 cents;
3. Taking a deposition and swearing witnesses: 25 cents per document sheet;
4. Duplicating a deposition, protest and certificate: 10 cents per document sheet of 100 words;
5. Executing every protest, 50 cents plus the cost of postage for sending the notice; for each attendance upon any person for proving any matter and certifying the same, 50 cents;
6. Taking a renunciation of dower or inheritance: $1.

NOTARY CERTIFICATES

South Carolina has adopted the *Uniform Recognition of Acknowledgments Act*, including the short-form certificates (SCC 26-3-70) for:
1. Acknowledgment by individual;
2. Acknowledgment by corporation;
3. Acknowledgment by partnership;
4. Acknowledgment by attorney in fact;
5. Acknowledgment by public officer, trustee or personal representative.

The Notary's seal and commission expiration date must be added to each certificate, but their inadvertent omission is not invalidating if the Notary's official title (e.g., "SC Notary Public") is affixed (SCC 26-1-60).

For the text of these certificates, see "Uniform Recognition of Acknowledgments Act (1968)," Section 6, in Appendix 3.

Acknowledgment by Grantor or Maker (SCC 30-5-30[C]):

South Carolina,
_____ County

I, _____(name and title of official taking acknowledgment), do hereby certify that _____(name of grantor or maker), personally appeared before me this day and acknowledged the due execution of the foregoing instrument.

Witness my hand and (where an official seal is required by law) official seal this the ____ day of _____, 20__.

_____ (Seal, if necessary)
(Signature of Officer)

Affidavit with Jurat (NPRM):

State of South Carolina
County of _____

_____ personally appears before me, the undersigned officer duly authorized by the laws of South Carolina to administer oaths, and now on this____ day of _____, in the year 20___ at _____ p.m./a.m. of said day, being by me first duly sworn on his/her oath/

affirmation, deposes and says:

_____
_____
_____
_____*(Signature of Affiant)*
_____*(Printed name of Affiant)*

Sworn/affirmed to and subscribed before me on this ____ day of _____, 20___. Personally known [ ] or produced identification [ ]. Type of identification produced: ____
_____.

_____*(Signature of Notary) (Notary Seal)*
_____*(Printed name of Notary), Notary Public*
_____ *County, South Carolina*
My commission expires _____

Acknowledgment by Natural Person (NPRM):

State of South Carolina
County of _____

On this ____ day of _____, 20___, before me personally appeared _____, who provided satisfactory evidence of his/her identification to be the person whose name is subscribed to this instrument, and he/she acknowledged that he/she executed the foregoing instrument.

_____*(Signature of Notary) (Notary Seal)*
_____*(Printed name of Notary), Notary Public*
_____ *County, South Carolina*
My commission expires _____

Acknowledgment by Corporate Officer (NPRM):

State of South Carolina
County of _____

On this ____ day of _____, 20___, before me personally appeared _____, _____(title of corporate office: president, treasurer, etc.) of _____(name of corporation), who provided satisfactory evidence of his/her identification to be the person whose name is subscribed to this instrument, and he/she acknowledged that he/she executed the foregoing instrument.

_____*(Signature of Notary) (Notary Seal)*
_____*(Printed name of Notary), Notary Public*
_____ *County, South Carolina*
My commission expires _____

Acknowledgment by Partner (NPRM):

State of South Carolina
County of _____

On this ____ day of _____, 20___, before me personally appeared _____, a partner in the firm of _____(name of partnership), and who provided satisfactory evidence of his identification to be the person whose name is subscribed to this instrument, and he acknowledged that he executed the foregoing instrument.

_____*(Signature of Notary) (Notary Seal)*
_____*(Printed name of Notary), Notary Public*
_____ *County, South Carolina*
My commission expires _____

Acknowledgment by Attorney in Fact (NPRM):

State of South Carolina
County of _____

On this ____ day of _____, 20___, before me personally appeared _____, attorney in fact for _____(name of principal), as demonstrated by the power of attorney executed by _____(name of principal), dated _____(date), appointing _____(name of attorney in fact)) as his/her attorney in fact, and who provided satisfactory evidence of his/her identification to be the person whose name is subscribed to this instrument, and he/she acknowledged that he/she executed the foregoing instrument.

_____*(Signature of Notary) (Notary Seal)*
_____*(Printed name of Notary), Notary Public*
_____ *County, South Carolina*
My commission expires _____

Acknowledgment by Public Officer (NPRM):

State of South Carolina
County of _____

On this ____ day of _____, 20___, before me personally appeared _____(name of public officer), _____(title of public officer and name of public entity represented, e.g., Mayor, City of Charleston), as demonstrated by _____(documentation proving the officer's authority), and who provided satisfactory evidence of his/her identification to be the person whose name is subscribed to this instrument, and he/she acknowledged that he/she executed the foregoing instrument.

*_____(Signature of Notary)   (Notary Seal)
_____(Printed name of Notary), Notary Public
_____ County, South Carolina
My commission expires _____*

Acknowledgment by Personal Representative (NPRM):

*State of South Carolina
County of _____*

On this ____ day of _____, 20___, before me personally appeared _____, personal representative of the estate of _____(name of individual represented), as demonstrated by _____(documentation proving authority to represent, e.g., letters testamentary issued by a probate court) and who provided satisfactory evidence of his/her identification to be the person whose name is subscribed to this instrument, and he/she acknowledged that he/she executed the foregoing instrument.

*_____(Signature of Notary)   (Notary Seal)
_____(Printed name of Notary), Notary Public
_____ County, South Carolina
My commission expires _____*

Acknowledgment by Trustee (NPRM):

*State of South Carolina
County of _____*

On this ____ day of _____, 20___, before me personally appeared _____, trustee of the _____(name of trust), as demonstrated by the _____(documentation proving status as trustee) and who provided satisfactory evidence of his/her identification to be the person whose name is subscribed to this instrument, and he/she acknowledged that he/she executed the foregoing instrument.

*_____(Signature of Notary)   (Notary Seal)
_____(Printed name of Notary), Notary Public
_____ County, South Carolina
My commission expires _____*

Recording Requirements

Before any deed or other document may be recorded in South Carolina, it must first be witnessed in one of two ways (SCC 30-5-30):

1. Acknowledgment before a Notary or other officer authorized to administer oaths, in the presence of at least two witnesses, one of whom may be the Notary;

2. Proof of execution before a Notary or other officer authorized to administer oaths, by the affidavit of a subscribing witness.

Form of Acknowledgment Certificate

"The form of a certificate of acknowledgment used by a person whose authority is recognized under (the Uniform Recognition of Acknowledgments Act, Section 1) shall be accepted in this State if:

"1. The certificate is in a form prescribed by the laws or regulations of this State;

"2. The certificate is in a form prescribed by the laws or regulations applicable in the place in which the acknowledgment is taken; or

"3. The certificate contains the words 'acknowledged before me,' or their substantial equivalent" (SCC 26-3-50).

Verification of Photocopy by Document Holder (NPRM):

Because South Carolina Notaries may not certify copies, the following "Verification of Copy by Document Holder" form is sometimes an acceptable alternative.

*State of South Carolina
County of _____*

On this ____ day of _____, 20___, I, _____(name of document holder), holder of _____(description of photocopy), consisting of ___(number of pages) pages, attest that it is a true, exact, complete and unaltered photocopy of the original. To the best of my knowledge and belief, the photocopied document is not a public record of which certified copies are available from an official source. Each page has been embossed or stamped with the Notary's official seal.

_____(Name of person making oath)

Sworn to before me this ___ day of _____, 20___.

_____(Signature of Notary)   (Notary Seal)
_____(Printed name of Notary), Notary Public
_____ County, South Carolina
My commission expires _____

ELECTRONIC NOTARIZATIONS

The state of South Carolina has not yet adopted statutes or regulations expressly establishing rules, definitions and procedures for electronic notarization.

UETA Recognizes Notary's eSignature

South Carolina has adopted the Uniform Electronic Transactions Act (SCC 26-6-10 through 26-6-210), including the following provision on notarization, thereby recognizing the legal validity of electronic signatures used by Notaries:

"A law requiring a signature or record to be notarized, acknowledged, verified, or made under oath is satisfied if the electronic signature of the person authorized to perform those acts, together with all other information required to be included by other applicable law, is attached to or logically associated with the signature or record" (SCC 26-6-110).

No Seal Image for Electronic Recording

South Carolina has adopted the Uniform Real Property Electronic Recording Act (URPERA) — see SCC 30-6-10 through 30-6-70 — including the following provision related to the Notary's seal:

"A requirement that a document or signature associated with a document be notarized, acknowledged, verified, witnessed, or made under oath is satisfied if the electronic signature of the person authorized to perform that act, and all other information required to be included, is attached to or logically associated with the document or signature. A physical or electronic image of a stamp, impression, or seal need not accompany an electronic signature" (SCC 30-6-30[c]).

NOTARY RECORDS

South Carolina law does not require Notaries to keep records of their official acts, but the practice of recordkeeping is encouraged by the Secretary of State. "Although not required, it is a prudent practice to keep a journal as it is beneficial if you are called to testify to past notarizations" (NPRM).

AUTHENTICATION OF NOTARIAL ACTS

County Clerks

Locally, an authenticating certificate for a given Notary may be obtained at the office of the county clerk of court where the Notary presented his or her commission within 15 days after commissioning (SCC 26-1-50).

Secretary of State

Authenticating certificates for Notaries, including apostilles, are also issued by the office of South Carolina's Secretary of State.

"Documents will not be certified that appear to be contrary to state or federal law, interest, or policy.

"All documents that are notarized in a foreign language must be accompanied by an English translation signed by the translator with the translator's signature notarized....

"School transcripts, report cards or letters MUST be signed by a school official and the official's signature MUST be notarized" (NPRM).

Fees: $2 for each document authenticated, including an apostille, payable to "SC Secretary of State."

Mail or in Person:
Office of Secretary of State
Notary Public Division
1205 Pendleton St., Suite 525
Columbia, SC 29201

Telephone: 1-803-734-2512

Procedure: Mail or present in person the original notarized document(s), along with the fee. If mailed, an explanatory cover letter indicating the country of destination is needed — a "South Carolina Authentications Cover Letter" is available on the website). A return envelope with postage or a pre-paid shipping label is required. "A public copier is not available in our office. Please make copies before submitting originals for apostille or certification" (NPRM).

COMMISSIONING AND ADMINISTRATION

Though South Carolina's Notaries are appointed by the Governor, it is the office of the Secretary of State that regulates and maintains records on them (SCC 26-1-10).

Applying for Commission

<u>Qualifications</u>: An applicant for a commission as a South Carolina Notary Public must be a registered voter. In order to become a registered voter, one must (NPRM): (a) be a United States citizen; (b) be at least 18 years old on or before the next election; (c) be a resident of South Carolina, declaring a county and precinct; (d) not be under a court order declaring mental incompetence; (e) not be serving a term of imprisonment resulting from a conviction of a crime; and (f) never have been convicted of a felony or offense against the election laws, or, if previously convicted, have served an entire sentence including probation or parole, or have received a pardon for the conviction.

<u>No Course or Test</u>: No course of instruction or test is required of applicants. However, as a public service the Secretary of State's office regularly conducts Notary seminars around the state, and registration is done through the Secretary's website. "Once commissioned as a notary public, it is the responsibility of the notary to maintain a level of training necessary to perform the duties of the position as required by law. These seminars will address state laws governing the duties and responsibilities of notaries. The unauthorized practice of law will also be addressed in a joint session with a representative from the South Carolina Bar" (website, "Media/News Releases").

<u>Application</u>: The top portion of the application for a Notary commission must be completed and its oath then signed in the presence of a Notary who is not the applicant. It must include the applicant's voter registration number, which may be obtained from the local county voter registration office or election commission. Next, the bottom portion of the application must be mailed to the office of the local county legislative delegation and endorsed by at least one-half of the delegates to the state legislature from the applicant's county, or by the state senator and representative from the district in which the applicant resides (SCC 26-1-20), or by the chairman or secretary of the county legislative delegation signing on a local legislator's behalf (SCC 26-1-25). (If this is not possible, it must be forwarded to the South Carolina House of Representatives [P.O. Box 11867, Columbia SC 29211-1867].) The mailed application must include the $25 commissioning fee (SCC 26-1-30), payable to "SC Secretary of State." The county delegation office will then forward the endorsed application and the fee to the Secretary of State's office, which will mail out the commission certificate within a week after a typical four to six weeks of total processing time.

The commission will be sent to the new Notary, who has 15 days to register it with the local county clerk (SCC 26-1-50). The county recording fee is $5.

A wallet card is issued as part of the commission certificate. This card can be detached and laminated (NPRM).

The renewal process is the same as for the initial application. Check "Renew" at the top of the application form instead of "New." Renewal should be started at least one month prior to commission expiration.

<u>Non-Residents</u>: Persons who do not reside in South Carolina may not become a Notary in the state.

<u>Online Search</u>: The South Carolina Secretary of State's Notary Public database allows the public to obtain certain information about Notaries (e.g., commission expiration date). Updates are uploaded every 48 hours (website, "Notary Search"). Information about commissioned Notaries is also available by telephoning the Notary Public Division at 1-803-734-2512.

Changes of Status

<u>If Notary Changes Name</u>: "Any notary public whose name is legally changed during his term of office may apply to the Secretary of State in such manner as may be prescribed by him, and the Secretary of State may change the name of the notary upon proper application and upon payment of a fee of ten dollars. The term expires at the same time as the original term" (SCC 26-1-70).

A name-change form is available on the website. This form must be notarized and accompanied by the $10 fee.

The Notary Public Division advises that a name change must be filed before notarizing in a new name, and that the Notary must continue notarizing in the former name until the name change is made.

If Notary Moves: If the Notary relocates to a new address in South Carolina, the Notary Public Division must be informed. There is no charge for this notification. "If you move out of South Carolina and register to vote in another state, you should resign your commission in South Carolina. Please return via US mail your commission certificate and enclose a letter resigning your position as a notary public in South Carolina" (NPRM).

COUNTY CLERKS

To contact a South Carolina county clerk to obtain an authenticating certificate for a Notary, or to seek assistance in locating a given Notary, telephone long-distance information — 1-XXX-555-1212 — using the following area codes and ask for the phone number of the clerk for the appropriate county. Further information is available on the South Carolina Association of Counties' website: www.sccounties.org

County	City/Town	Area Code
Abbeville	Abbeville	(864)
Aiken	Aiken	(803)
Allendale	Allendale	(803)
Anderson	Anderson	(864)
Bamberg	Bamberg	(803)
Barnwell	Barnwell	(803)
Beaufort	Beaufort	(843)
Berkeley	Moncks Corner	(843)
Calhoun	Saint Matthews	(803)
Charleston	Charleston	(843)
Cherokee	Gaffney	(864)
Chester	Chester	(803)
Chesterfield	Chesterfield	(843)
Clarendon	Manning	(803)
Colleton	Walterboro	(843)
Darlington	Darlington	(843)
Dillon	Dillon	(843)
Dorchester	Saint George	(843)
Edgefield	Edgefield	(803)
Fairfield	Winnsboro	(803)
Florence	Florence	(843)
Georgetown	Georgetown	(843)
Greenville	Greenville	(864)
Greenwood	Greenwood	(864)
Hampton	Hampton	(803)
Horry	Conway	(843)
Jasper	Ridgeland	(843)
Kershaw	Camden	(803)
Lancaster	Lancaster	(803)
Laurens	Laurens	(864)
Lee	Bishopville	(803)
Lexington	Lexington	(803)
Marion	Marion	(843)
Marlboro	Bennettsville	(843)
McCormick	McCormick	(864)
Newberry	Newberry	(803)
Oconee	Walhalla	(864)
Orangeburg	Orangeburg	(803)
Pickens	Pickens	(864)
Richland	Columbia	(803)
Saluda	Saluda	(864)
Spartanburg	Spartanburg	(864)
Sumter	Sumter	(803)
Union	Union	(864)
Williamsburg	Kingstree	(843)
York	York	(803)

OTHER NOTARIAL OFFICERS

Designated Military Personnel

Certain designated military personnel have the general powers of a Notary in serving persons in or with the armed forces, in accordance with Title 10, U.S. Code, Section 1044a, including (SCC 25-1-630[C]):

1. Judge advocates, including those in the reserve and in the South Carolina National Guard, when not in a duty status;

2. Civilian attorneys serving as legal assistance officers;

3. Adjutants, assistant adjutants and personnel adjutants, including those in the reserve and in the South Carolina National Guard, when not in a duty status.

Signature and Title Sufficient: "The signature of any person acting as a notary under the authority of Title 10, United States Code, Section

1044a or of this section, together with the title of that person's offices, is prima facie evidence that the signature is genuine, that the person holds the designated title, and that the person is authorized to perform a notarial act" (SCC 25-1-630[E]).

QUICK FACTS

Notary Jurisdiction
Statewide (SCC 26-1-80).

Notary Term Length
Ten years (SCC 26-1-10).

Notary Bond
Not required by law.

S-U

South Dakota

NOTARY SEAL

A South Dakota Notary must have an official seal "which shall be used for the purpose of acknowledging documents" and the seal's format must be as follows (SDCL 18-1-3.1 and NPH):

Kind

Inked Stamp or Embosser: "The Secretary of State's website indicates that any of three types of Notary seal are acceptable — "the embossing seal, the rubber stamp and the perma-stamp." The "perma-stamp" is a type of self-inking seal. "If a rubber stamp is used the word 'Seal' must be included on the stamp" (website, "Getting a Notary Seal"). A border must surround the imprint of the seal (SDCL 18-1-3.1).

Shape/Size

Not specified.
(Embossers customarily are circular, while many inked seals are rectangular or circular, according to the office of the Secretary of State.)

Examples

Above are actual-size examples of typical Notary seals allowed by South Dakota law (inking seal on top, embosser below). Formats other than these may also be permitted.

NOTARY ADMINISTRATION

Office of Secretary of State
Notary Administrator   1-605-773-3537
State Capitol, Suite 204
500 East Capitol Ave.
Pierre, SD 57501

Website: http://sdsos.gov/content/viewcontent.aspx?cat=adminservices&pg=/adminservices/notaries.shtm

NOTARY RULES

SDCL — *South Dakota Codified Laws*
NPH — *South Dakota Notary Public Handbook*

Most Notary rules are in the South Dakota Codified Laws, Title 18:

a. Chapter 18-1 ("Notaries Public");

b. Chapter 18-4 ("Acknowledgment and Proof of Instruments");

c. Chapter 18-5 ("Uniform Acknowledgment Law").*

 * This is the *Uniform Acknowledgment Act* of 1939, adopted with amendments.

Other helpful guidelines for Notaries are in the "South Dakota Notary Public Handbook" (2009), published by the Secretary of State and available on the website.

Components

The seal must contain at least the following components, surrounded in all cases by a border (SDCL 18-1-3.1):

1. Name of Notary, exactly as on commission;
2. "Notary Public";
3. "South Dakota";
4. FOR INKED STAMPS: "Seal".
OPTIONAL: Commission expiration date.

Commission Expiration Must Appear

"If a seal is used by a notary public, the notary public shall write, or print by a device made for such printing, below the seal's imprint or print and if not provided by the form, the words 'my commission expires', and shall provide a date therefor" (SDCL 18-1-3.1).

The commission expiration date must be in the form of month, day and year and may be included in the Notary's seal. Additionally, "if the words are printed on the form, the notary need not duplicate them" (NPH).

Seal Impression Filed with State

"Every notary public before entering upon the duties of his office, shall provide an official seal and file an impression of the same, together with his oath and bond, in the office of the secretary of state" (SDCL 18-1-3). "The official notary seal imprint on your Application, Oath and Bond is the only Seal imprint to be used when notarizing documents. If you find it necessary to have a different type of notary seal, you must first submit an imprint to our office before using a different notary seal." (NPH).

Because a seal imprint is required on the commission application form, an applicant must purchase a Notary seal before being commissioned (website, "How to Become a Notary").

Using a "Notary Public Request to Change Record" form, a Notary may replace a current seal or add and use a second seal along with the current one. The form is obtained from and filed with the Secretary of State; it may be downloaded from the Secretary's website.

Lost or Stolen Seal

A Notary seal's loss or theft must be reported immediately to the office of the Secretary of State so that a notation can be made on the Notary's record (website, "Lost or Stolen Seal"). The Notary may then either (1) obtain an identical or different type of seal as a replacement, filing a new seal impression with the Secretary of State or (2) request that the present commission be cancelled and that a new commission with a different expiration date be issued. If the second option is taken, the Notary must follow the normal application procedure.

"In addition to whatever option is taken, the Notary may also wish to change the name on his/her Notary Commission and Seal. (Example: Elizabeth B. Jackson could be changed to Elizabeth Jackson or E.B. Jackson or Liz B. Jackson.) The new impression of the Notary's Seal would have to correspond exactly to the way the name is signed and recorded with the Office of the Secretary of State" (NPH).

Seal Must Be Kept Secure

"The notary journal and seal should always be kept in a safe and secure place" (website, "Glossary of Terms").

"Don't ... (p)ermit others to use your official seal or stamp" (website, "Dos & Don'ts").

Title and Legibly Printed Name Required

"The certificate of the acknowledging officer shall be completed by his signature and immediately following his signature and immediately preceding his official description, he shall endorse thereon his name with a typewriter or print the same legibly with a stamp or with pen and ink, his official seal, if he has one, the title of his office, and if he is a notary public, the date his commission expires. Failure of an acknowledging officer to endorse his name on an instrument as required herein shall not render such instrument invalid, but a recording officer may refuse to accept such instrument for record until such endorsement is made" (SDCL 18-5-13).

Facsimile Signature Allowed for Bond: "Notwithstanding any provision in this chapter, a facsimile of the original signature and notarization may be used in lieu of an original signature when acknowledging a fidelity or surety bond in a form as required herein" (SDCL 18-5-13).

Signature of Notary with New Name

A Notary whose name changes may add to the signature an appropriate notation such as "presently" or "now" and the new surname. Example: "Sally Smith, presently Sally Jones" but the Notary's seal and commission would continue to carry the name "Sally Smith" (NPH). See other options for a Notary name change below under "Commissioning and Administration."

NOTARY POWERS

South Dakota Notaries are authorized to perform the following notarial acts:
1. Take acknowledgments* and proofs** (SDCL 18-4-1);

2. Administer oaths and affirmations*** (SDCL 18-3-1);
3. Execute jurats on affidavits**** and other sworn documents.

* Identifying Acknowledgers: "The acknowledgment of an instrument must not be taken unless the officer taking it knows or has satisfactory evidence on the oath or affirmation of a credible witness, that the person making such acknowledgment is the individual who is described in and who executed the instrument; or, if executed by a corporation, that the person making such acknowledgment is an officer of the corporation authorized to execute the instrument" (SDCL 18-4-10). See also SDCL 18-5-5.

According to the "South Dakota Notary Public Handbook" ("Frequently Asked Questions"), the following types of documentary identification are sufficient when notarizing: a driver's license or non-driver's ID card; a U.S. passport; and an ID issued by any branch of the U.S. armed forces; and an ID card issued by the USCIS, such as the Resident Alien card.

"In a typical acknowledgment ceremony ... (t)he document, declaration or avowal is signed in the presence of the notary. 'Do you acknowledge the execution of this (name the document — deed, mortgage, etc.) to be your free act and deed?' The acknowledger says, 'Yes,' and the notary completes the certificate" (website, "Glossary of Terms").

"Notaries are encouraged to utilize a 'credible witness' when in doubt about a person's identity. A 'credible witness' is any person who personally knows the signer of a document. The notary should likewise personally know the credible witness. The credible witness may, under oath from the notary, attest to the identity of the document signer. Remember, the credible witness should be impartial to the transaction being notarized" (website, "Seven Concepts").

** Proofs of Execution: "If proof of the execution of an instrument is made by a subscribing witness, such witness must be personally known to the officer taking the proof to be the person whose name is subscribed to the instrument as a witness or must be proved to be such by the oath of a credible witness" (SDCL 18-4-18).

"Officers authorized to take the proof of instruments are authorized in such proceedings:
"1. To administer oaths or affirmations;
"2. To employ and swear interpreters;
"3. To issue subpoenas and to punish for contempt as provided in Title 19 in regard to the means of producing witnesses" (SDCL 18-4-21).

Provision is made for a proof of execution by handwriting when the principal(s) and/or subscribing witnesses are dead, out of state, at an unknown location or uncooperative (SDCL 18-4-19 and 18-4-20).

*** Affirmation Wording: "A person who objects to swearing may make an affirmation. In such a case, the notary would ask, 'Do you solemnly and sincerely affirm under the penalties of perjury that the statements contained in this affidavit are true?' The notary would change the jurat to show that the affiant affirmed rather than swore" (website, "Glossary of Terms").

**** Affidavit Procedure: "In most states it is not necessary for a notary to request identification of a person making an affidavit because he does not vouch for his identity in any way ... However, there is nothing wrong with asking for identification, and it might in fact be a good idea to do so. Properly an affidavit should be taken in the following manner: the notary and the affiant should stand facing each other with raised right hand and the notary should then say, 'Do you solemnly swear that the statements contained in this affidavit are the truth, so help you, God?' However, the essential thing is that the affiant be made to realize that he or she is taking an oath. This fact should be impressed upon the affiant" (website, "Glossary of Terms").

Notarization Verifies Volition, Competence

"A notarization provides verification of a document signer's willingness to sign, his competence to sign, and that the signer is, indeed, the person identified by the signature" (website, "Seven Concepts").

Commission Must Be Conspicuously Posted

"The secretary of state shall issue a commission to each notary public which shall be posted in a conspicuous place in the notary's office for public inspection" (SDCL 18-1-4).

NOTARY DON'TS

The South Dakota Secretary of State recommends that a Notary (website, "Seven Concepts," "Dos & Don'ts"):

1. NOT notarize his or her own signature;
2. NOT draft legal documents for clients (unless the Notary is an attorney);
3. NOT notarize a blank or incomplete document;
4. NOT take an acknowledgment or administer an oath over the telephone;
5. NOT permit others to use the official Notary seal;
6. NOT refuse "to serve any person who makes a lawful and reasonable request for a notarization";
7. NOT notarize the signature of a person who is not present, which is a Class 2 misdemeanor (SDCL 18-1-11).

False Certification Is Forgery

"If any officer authorized to take the acknowledgment or proof of any conveyance of real property or of any other instrument which by law may be recorded, knowingly and falsely certifies that any such conveyance or instrument was acknowledged by any party thereto or was proved by any subscribing witness, when in truth such conveyance or instrument was not proved as certified, he is guilty of forgery" (SDCL 18-4-25).

Disqualifying Interest

<u>Notary Cannot Be Party to Transaction</u>: "It is a Class 1 misdemeanor for a person to affix a signature to a document as a notary public when the person has also signed the document as a party to the transaction proceeding" (SDCL 18-1-12.2).

A Notary may not notarize for a transaction in which he or she is a principal party (SDCL 18-1-7):

"A notary public who is personally interested directly or indirectly, or as a stockholder, officer, agent, attorney, or employee of any person or party to any transaction concerning which he is exercising any function of his office as such notary public, may make any certificates, take any acknowledgments, administer any oaths, or do any other official acts as such notary public with the same legal force and effect as if he had no such interest except that he cannot do any of such things in connection with any instrument which shows upon its face that he is a principal party thereto."

<u>Notarizing for Relatives</u>: "Obviously a notary can not appear before himself or take his own affidavit. While it is not illegal for a notary to take a relative's affidavit, it is not advisable to do so. If the subject matter is something that would benefit the notary or a relative, it is not considered a good business practice. Still (it) is not illegal for a notary to witness the signatures of close friends and relatives. There are, however, federal and state courts which do have special rules governing the taking of depositions for use in court" (website, "Glossary of Terms").

NOTARY SIGNING AGENTS

Currently, there are no statutes, regulations or rules expressly governing, prohibiting or restricting the operation of Notary Signing Agents within the state of South Dakota.

NOTARY FEES

"Notaries public may charge and receive a fee not to exceed ten dollars for each instrument notarized, except that no notary public may charge a fee for notarizing a request for an absentee ballot" (SDCL 18-1-9).

No Fees for Certain Oaths

"No fee for the administering of oaths shall be charged or taxed as costs against any person by any official authorized to administer oaths when the oath so administered is in connection with some official duty of said officer essential to the administration of his office" (SDCL 18-3-6).

NOTARY CERTIFICATES

South Dakota has adopted much of the *Uniform Acknowledgment Act,* including the certificates (SDCL 18-5-8 through 18-5-11) for:
1. Acknowledgment by individual;
2. Acknowledgment by corporation;
3. Acknowledgment by attorney in fact;
4. Acknowledgment by any public officer or deputy thereof, or by any trustee, administrator, guardian, conservator or executor.

The Notary's seal, commission expiration date and legibly typed, stamped or printed name must be added to each certificate prescribed by the Act (SDCL 18-5-13).

For the text of the certificates, see "Uniform Acknowledgment Act (1939, amended 1960)," Section 7, in Appendix 4. An additional certificate for an acknowledgment by a partner (SDCL 18-5-12) is included below.

South Dakota law additionally prescribes the following certificates:

Acknowledgment by Individual (SDCL 18-4-12):

Territory of _____ or State of _____
County of _____ ss

On this ____ day of _____, in the year 20__, before me personally appeared _____, known to me (or proved to me on the oath of _____) to be the person who is described in, and who executed the within instrument and acknowledged to me that he/she (or they) executed the same.

(NOTARY'S SIGNATURE; LEGIBLY TYPED, STAMPED OR PRINTED NAME; TITLE; SEAL; AND COMMISSION EXPIRATION DATE)

Acknowledgment by Partner (SDCL 18-5-12):

State of South Dakota
County of _____

On this the ____ day of _____, 20__, before me, _____, the undersigned officer, personally appeared _____, who acknowledged himself/herself to be one of the partners of _____, a partnership, and that he/she, as such partner, being authorized so to do, executed the foregoing instrument for the purposes therein contained, by signing the name of the partnership by himself/herself as a partner.
In witness whereof I hereunto set my hand and official seal.

_____
_____
Title of officer

(NOTARY'S SIGNATURE; LEGIBLY TYPED, STAMPED OR PRINTED NAME; TITLE; SEAL; AND COMMISSION EXPIRATION DATE)

Acknowledgment by Corporation (SDCL 18-4-13):

Territory of _____ or State of _____
County of _____ ss

On this ____ day of _____, in the year 20__, before me, _____, personally appeared _____, known to me (or proved to me on the oath of _____) to be the _____ of the corporation that is described in and that executed the within instrument and acknowledged to me that such corporation executed the same.

(NOTARY'S SIGNATURE; LEGIBLY TYPED, STAMPED OR PRINTED NAME; TITLE; SEAL; AND COMMISSION EXPIRATION DATE)

Acknowledgment by Attorney in Fact (SDCL 18-4-14):

Territory of _____ or State of _____
County of _____ ss

On this ____ day of _____, in the year 20__, before me personally appeared _____, known to me (or proved to me on the oath of _____) to be the person who is described in and whose name is subscribed to the within instrument as the attorney in fact of _____, and acknowledged to me that he/she subscribed the name of _____ thereto as principal and his/her own name as attorney in fact.

(NOTARY'S SIGNATURE; LEGIBLY TYPED, STAMPED OR PRINTED NAME; TITLE; SEAL; AND COMMISSION EXPIRATION DATE)

Acknowledgment by Deputy Sheriff (SDCL 18-4-15):

Territory of _____ or State of _____
County of _____ ss

On this ____ day of _____, in the year 20__, before me personally appeared _____, known to me (or proved to me on the oath of _____) to be the person who is described in and whose name is subscribed to the within instrument as deputy sheriff of said county and acknowledged to me that he/she

South Dakota

subscribed the name of _____ thereto as sheriff of said county and his/her own name as deputy sheriff.

(NOTARY'S SIGNATURE; LEGIBLY TYPED, STAMPED OR PRINTED NAME; TITLE; SEAL; AND COMMISSION EXPIRATION DATE)

Acknowledgment before Military Officer (SDCL 18-4-7):

"No authentication of the officer's certificate of acknowledgment ... shall be required but the officer taking the acknowledgment shall endorse thereon or attach thereto a certificate substantially in the following form ...":

On this the _____ day of _____, 20__, before me, _____, the undersigned officer, personally appeared _____, known to me (or satisfactorily proven) to be serving in or with the armed forces of the United States and to be the person whose name is subscribed to the within instrument and acknowledged that he/she executed the same for the purposes therein contained. And the undersigned does further certify that he/she is at the date of this certificate a commissioned officer of the rank stated below and is in the active service of the armed forces of the United States.

_____ *(Signature of officer)*
_____
(Rank of officer and command to which attached)

("The instrument shall not be rendered invalid by the failure to state therein the place of execution or acknowledgment" [SDCL 18-4-6].)

Acknowledgments in Black or Blue Ink

"Any real estate document recorded with the register of deeds, except for plats, shall . . . (2) Be printed, typewritten, or computer generated in black ink and the print type of the document may not be smaller than 10-point type. However, dates, notarial acknowledgments, signatures, and other items may be completed in black or blue ink if the document is predominantly completed in black ink and if the items that are completed in blue ink are sufficiently dark to meet the (legibility) requirements of subdivision (6)" (SDCL 43-28-23).

Jurat before Military Officer (SDCL 18-3-3):

Subscribed and sworn to before me this _____ day of _____, 20__, by _____, to me well known to be in the military service of the United States, and who stated to me that his home post office address is as follows: _____.

_____
Signature of officer

_____
Title and unit

Jurat (website, 'Glossary of Terms'):

State of South Dakota
County of _____

Subscribed and sworn to (or affirmed) before me this _____ day of _____, 20__.

(NOTARY'S SIGNATURE; LEGIBLY TYPED, STAMPED OR PRINTED NAME; TITLE; SEAL; AND COMMISSION EXPIRATION DATE)

Content of Certificate of Proof

"An officer taking proof of the execution of an instrument must in his certificate endorsed thereon or attached thereto set forth all the matters required by law to be done or known by him or proved before him on the proceeding, together with the names of all the witnesses examined before him, their places of residence respectively, and the substance of their evidence" (SDCL 18-4-22).

ELECTRONIC NOTARIZATIONS

The state of South Dakota has not yet adopted statutes or regulations expressly establishing rules, definitions and procedures for electronic notarization.

UETA Recognizes Notary's eSignature

Effective July 1, 2000, South Dakota enacted its own version of the Uniform Electronic Transactions Act (Title 53, Chapter 12, "Electronic Transactions," Sections 53-12-1 through 53-12-50), including the following provision on notarization, thereby recognizing the legal validity of electronic signatures used by Notaries:

"If a law requires a signature or record to be notarized, acknowledged, verified, or made under oath, the requirement is satisfied if the electronic signature of the person authorized to perform those acts, together with all other information required to be included by other applicable law, is attached to or logically associated with the signature or record" (SDCL 53-12-24).

NOTARY RECORDS

"While South Dakota law no longer requires a register be kept by a notary, it would certainly be to the advantage of the notary to do so. Most lawsuits against notaries could be avoided if the notary kept a record" (website, "Glossary of Terms").

Journal is Legal Protection for Notary

"The notary journal serves as an excellent form of legal protection for the notary for two important reasons:

"1. If a notarization certificate is lost or damaged, a notary can refer to the journal entry to verify prior existence and purpose.

"2. If a notary is called upon to testify in a legal proceeding about a notarization, the journal provides the ideal reminder of the facts and circumstances" (website, "Glossary of Terms").

Recommended Entries

At a minimum, the following journal notations are suggested by the "South Dakota Notary Public Handbook": date and time of notarization; type of document notarized; name and address of persons whose signatures are notarized; and the signatures of the signing parties.

"There are other details which might be included such as land description, kinds of identification presented, number of pages to document, etc."

Journal Must Be Kept Secure

"The notary journal and seal should always be kept in a safe and secure place" (website, "Glossary of Terms").

AUTHENTICATION OF NOTARIAL ACTS

Secretary of State

Authenticating certificates for Notaries, including apostilles, are issued only by the South Dakota Secretary of State's office.

Fees: $5 per document for any certificate of authentication for a Notary, including an apostille, payable to "Secretary of State." Check, money order, cash, Visa, and MasterCard are accepted.

Address:
Office of Secretary of State
Notary Administrator
State Capitol, Suite 204
500 East Capitol Ave.
Pierre, SD 57501-5070

Telephone: 1-605-773-3537

Procedure: Mail or present in person — appointments should be made — the original notarized document, along with the $5 per document fee. If mailed, a cover letter should be included that states the country of destination, a daytime telephone number for questions and information on where the document(s) should be mailed after processing. Documents will be returned by first-class mail. "If you want to track your documents and/or want them mailed in a different manner, you must enclose a pre-paid self-addressed envelope for that service" (website, "Apostilles & Authentications").

COMMISSIONING AND ADMINISTRATION

The South Dakota Secretary of State appoints, commissions and maintains records on the state's Notaries (SDCL 18-1-1 and 18-1-4).

Applying for Commission

Qualifications: An applicant for a South Dakota Notary Public commission must be a permanent resident of the state as defined in SDCL 12-1-4, or a resident of a county bordering South Dakota who works or has a place of business in the state. Any person who has been convicted of a felony may not be appointed as a Notary (SDCL 18-1-1).

No Course or Test: No course of instruction or test is required to become a Notary in South Dakota.

Application: The "Notary Public Application, Oath & Bond" form must be completed and submitted to the Secretary of State, with the $30 filing fee (SDCL 18-1-1). However, a Notary seal must first be obtained and an imprint of this seal affixed in the box in the upper left corner of the application (SDCL 18-1-3). In addition, a bond must be obtained and the bond portion of the application filled out with the name of the surety company and signed by both the applicant and the bond agent; if a personal surety is used, the signatures of both the applicant and the personal surety must be notarized on the "Personal Surety Form" on the back of the application The oath part of the application is not notarized (SDCL 18-1-2).

The process for renewing a commission is the same as for the initial application: "If you wish to renew your Notary Public commission and would like to keep the same commission date and expiration date (month and day), you may do so by completing and mailing to the Office of the Secretary of State the Application-Oath and Bond form in advance of the expiration of the commission. If you would like a different expiration date than your previous commission, please indicate the date on which you wish to have your next six-year term begin. We must receive the Application prior to the date you have selected. We cannot back date an application…" (website, "Renewal").

Non-Residents: A non-resident may become commissioned as a South Dakota Notary if the person resides in a county bordering South Dakota and has a place of work within the state (SDCL 18-1-1).

Online Search: Through the Secretary of State's online Information Access System, the list of South Dakota Notaries with current commissions may be accessed by submitting a name, city or county. The information available for each listed Notary includes name, commission expiration date, county, city and address (website, "Search Notary Database").

Changes of Status

If Notary Moves: Notaries are asked to notify the Secretary of State of any change of address (website, "What If I Move?"). A "Notary Public Request to Change Record" form may be downloaded from the Secretary's website.

If Notary Changes Name: Notaries who change their name have three options (NPH):
1. Continue signing the former name; or
2. Continue signing the former name, but add "presently" or "now" and then the new name; or
3. Obtain a "Notary Public Request to Change Record" form from the Secretary of State; after purchasing a new seal bearing the new name, placing the imprint on the form, and submitting the form to the Secretary, a "Certificate of Correction" will be issued without any additional filing fee.

COUNTY CLERKS

In South Dakota, Notaries no longer file commissions and seal/signature samples at the county level, nor do they any longer submit their notarial records to the county, and, thus, county officials do not issue authenticating certificates for Notaries nor retain Notary journals.

OTHER NOTARIAL OFFICERS

Statewide Jurisdiction

Besides Notaries, the following officers have statewide authority to take acknowledgments and proofs (SDCL 18-4-1, 18-4-2 and 18-5-2), using the court seal to authenticate their acts (SDCL 18-4-23):
1. A justice or clerk of the Supreme Court;
2. A judge of the circuit court;
3. A clerk or deputy clerk of the circuit court;
4. A magistrate of the circuit court;
5. A U.S. magistrate;
6. A register of deeds.

Authentication of County Magistrate's Act: If a county magistrate's act of proof or acknowledgment is to be used outside the magistrate's county, it must be authenticated by the county clerk of courts (SDCL 18-4-24).

Limited Jurisdiction

Within their county or municipality, the following officers have authority to take proofs and acknowledgments (SDCL 18-4-2):
1. A county auditor;
2. A county register of deeds;
3. A mayor;
4. A municipal finance officer.

Native American Agents

"Indian agents or superintendents are authorized to take acknowledgments or proofs of deeds or other instruments in writing, in Indian country …. To qualify for taking such acknowledgments or proofs, such Indian agent or superintendent shall file for record in the office of the register of deeds of the county in which he is stationed …a certificate signed by the secretary of the interior of the United States showing his appointment and authority as such Indian agent or superintendent" (SDCL 18-4-3).

Commissioners Appointed by Governor

South Dakota's Governor may appoint commissioners in any U.S. state or territory to take acknowledgments and proofs for documents that will be used or recorded back in South Dakota (SDCL 18-2-1). Each such commissioner "shall have an official seal on which shall be engraved the words 'Commissioner of South Dakota,' with his surname at length and at least the initials of his Christian name; also the name of the state or territory in which he has been commissioned to act, which seal must be so engraved as to make a clear impression" (SDCL 18-2-2). Such officers may also administer oaths and take depositions (SDCL 18-2-4).

Military Officers

Persons serving in or with the U.S. armed forces may acknowledge a signature anywhere in the world before a U.S. military officer with the rank of second lieutenant or ensign or higher (SDCL 18-4-6). "The instrument shall not be rendered invalid by the failure to state therein the place of execution or acknowledgment."

QUICK FACTS

Notary Jurisdiction
Statewide (SDCL 18-1-1).

Notary Term Length
Six years (SDCL 18-1-1), expiring at midnight on the commission expiration date.
"It is a Class 2 misdemeanor for any notary public to exercise the duties of his office after the expiration of his commission or when he is otherwise disqualified" (SDCL 18-1-12).

Notary Bond
$5,000, to be approved by the state Attorney General (SDCL 18-1-2). The bond may be purchased from an insurance company or posted by a personal surety, who may not be a company, business or organization. A personal surety may be a friend, relative, spouse or co-worker (website, "How to Become a Notary").

S-U

Tennessee

NOTARY SEAL

A Tennessee Notary must attest to all official acts with a seal of office (TCA 8-16-112 and 66-22-110), and the seal's format must conform to the following design prescribed by the Secretary of State (TRR 1360-7-2-.01):

Kind

Inked Stamp: "The seal of office may be imprinted by a rubber or other type stamp. Such stamp shall imprint the seal of office in any color other than black or yellow, provided the color used to imprint the seal shall be clearly legible and appear as black when photocopied on a non-color copier" (TCA 8-16-114[a]).

Prior to May 12, 2003, and enactment of Chapter 106 (2003 Tennessee Public Acts), an embosser also was allowed as an official Notary seal.

"Nothing in this subsection (a) shall be construed to require a notary public to procure such a rubber or other stamp or to use a particular color ink with the stamp prior to the expiration of the notary's term of office, and all impression notary seals shall be valid for use until the end of the notary's term of office. Notwithstanding any other provision of law or provision of this subsection (a) to the contrary, the use of an embossed notary seal after May 12, 2003, shall not render such an acknowledgment defective. No person shall incur any civil or criminal liability for failure to imprint the seal of office in a color required by this subsection (a) nor shall any document or title imprinted with a seal of the wrong color be invalid because of such failure" (TCA 8-16-114[a]).

Shape/Size

Circular, with two concentric circles (TRR 1360-7-2-.01).

Components

If Commissioned on or after July 1, 2004: Current Notary seals must adhere to the following format (TRR 1360-7-2-.01):

Examples

Above is an actual-size example of a Tennessee Notary seal, in accordance with specifications of the Secretary of State. Circular formats other than this may also be acceptable.

NOTARY ADMINISTRATION

Tennessee Department of State
Division of Business Services
Notary Commission
Services   1-615-741-3699
312 Rosa L. Parks Blvd.
William R. Snodgrass Tower, 6th Floor
Nashville, TN 37243

Website: www.state.tn.us/sos/bus_svc/notary.htm

NOTARY RULES

TCA — TENNESSEE CODE ANNOTATED
NPH — TENNESSEE NOTARY PUBLIC HANDBOOK
NCS — NOTARY COMMISSION SERVICES BROCHURE
TRR — TENNESSEE RULES AND REGULATIONS

Most Notary regulations are in the Tennessee Code Annotated:

a. Title 8, Chapter 16, "Notaries Public";

b. Title 66, Chapter 22, "Acknowledgment of Instruments."

Other guidelines for Notaries are in the "Tennessee Notary Public Handbook" (March 2006) and in the "Notary Commission Services Brochure" (Jan. 2008), both available on the website.

1. AT TOP: name of Notary exactly as it appears on the commission;
2. IN MIDDLE: "State of Tennessee Notary Public" or "Tennessee Notary Public";
3. AT BOTTOM: name of Notary's county of election.

If Commissioned before July 1, 2004: Notaries were allowed to use the prior seal design until the end of their current term of office (TRR 1360-7-2-.01[2]):
1. AT TOP: name of Notary exactly as it appears on the commission;
2. IN MIDDLE: "Notary Public at Large";
3. AT BOTTOM: name of Notary's county, "Tennessee."

Expiration Date May Not Appear in Seal

The Notary's commission expiration date must appear on every acknowledgment certificate (TCA 8-16-112 and 66-22-110). According to the Department of State's prescribed seal design, however, it may not appear in the seal.

Failure to include the Notary's commission expiration date will not invalidate the notarization (TCA 8-16-115).

"However, where the true date of expiration shows the commission has expired, the certificate of acknowledgment is invalid. *Haynes v. State*, 374 S.W.2d 394 (Tenn. 1964)" (NPH).

Seal Available through County Clerk

"At the notary public's request, the county clerk may obtain an official seal or any part thereof for the notary public. Any county clerk providing this service may charge a fee not to exceed twenty percent (20%) of the cost of the seal or part obtained for the notary public" (TCA 8-16-114[c]).

Seal Surrendered to County

"Every notary public shall … procure a seal of office, which the notary shall surrender to the county legislative body when the notary resigns, or at the expiration of such notary public's term of office, and which such notary's representatives, in case of such notary's death, shall likewise surrender, to be cancelled" (TCA 8-16-114[b]).

The seal is surrendered to the county legislative body through the county clerk (NPH).

Signature of Notary

"(T)he notary public shall sign … documents in ink by the notary's own hand unless otherwise provided by law" (TCA 8-16-112).

NOTARY POWERS

Tennessee Notaries are authorized to perform the following notarial acts (TCA 8-16-112):
1. Take acknowledgments* (TCA 66-22-102) and proofs** (TCA 66-22-101);
2. Administer oaths and affirmations;
3. Take depositions*** and affidavits****;
4. "Qualify parties to bills (complaints) in chancery (court)".

* Acknowledgments: "An acknowledgment … is a declaration by a person who has executed or signed a deed or other document, that he or she has in fact executed such document.… An acknowledgment may be made before a notary, who then certifies to the fact either at the end of that document or on a separate paper that is attached" (NPH).

Identifying Acknowledgers: Identification may be made either through personal knowledge or satisfactory evidence (TCA 8-16-112).

"Personal Knowledge" Defined: "For purposes of this chapter, 'know' or 'personally acquainted with' means having an acquaintance, derived from association with the individual in relation to other people and based upon a chain of circumstances surrounding the individual, which establishes the individual's identity with at least reasonable certainty" (TCA 66-22-106[b]).

In addition, the ruling in *Figuers v. Fly*, 137 Tenn. 358, 193 S.W. 117 (1916), may be helpful: "The phrase 'with whom I am personally acquainted' in … a (notarial) certificate means a knowledge independent and complete in itself, and existing without other information, and it imports more than a slight or superficial knowledge."

"Satisfactory Evidence" Defined: "For the purposes of this chapter 'satisfactory evidence' means the absence of any information, evidence, or other circumstances which would lead a reasonable person to believe that the person making the acknowledgment is not the individual he or she claims to be and any one (1) of the following:

"1. The oath or affirmation of a credible

witness personally known to the officer that the person making the acknowledgment is personally known to the witness.

"2. Reasonable reliance on the presentation to the officer of any one of the following, if the document is current or has been issued within five (5) years:

"A. An identification card or driver's license issued by the department of safety; or

"B. A passport issued by the United States department of state.

"3. Reasonable reliance on the presentation of any one (1) of the following, if the document is current or has been issued within five (5) years and contains a photograph and description of the person named on it, is signed by the person, bears a serial or other identifying number, and, in the event that the document is a passport, has been stamped by the United States immigration and naturalization service:

"A. A passport issued by a foreign government;

"B. A driver's license issued by a state other than Tennessee;

"C. An identification card issued by a state other than Tennessee; or

"D. An identification card issued by any branch of the armed forces of the United States" (TCA 66-22-106[c]).

** Proof by Two Subscribing Witnesses: In lieu of acknowledgment, proof of execution may be made by at least two subscribing witnesses (TCA 66-22-101).

*** Depositions: "A deposition is the testimony of a witness taken by interrogatories, not in open court, but by a person commissioned to take the testimony issued by a court, or according to general law, and reduced to writing and duly authenticated, and intended to be used upon the trial of an action in court or a written declaration under oath, made after notice to the adverse party to enable cross-examination or upon written interrogatories.

"The taking of depositions in this state is governed by Rules 27 through 32 of the Tennessee Rules of Civil Procedure (TRCP), which must be strictly followed. Any officer authorized to administer oaths by federal, state, or territorial law is authorized to take depositions. TRCP 28.01. No deposition shall be taken before a person who is a party to the action, or a relative, employee or attorney of one of the parties, or someone with a financial interest in the action or its outcome. 'Employee' includes a person with a contractual relationship with a person or entity interested in the outcome of the litigation. Taking a deposition in violation of these provisions is a Class C misdemeanor. TCA § 24-9-136" (NPH).

"The deposition of a notary may be taken, whether a suit be pending or not, on ten (10) days' notice to the opposite party, if resident in the state, and forty (40) days' notice out of the state, to be read as evidence between the same parties in any suit then or afterward depending, should the notary die or leave the state before the trial" (TCA 8-16-117).

**** Affidavits: "An affidavit is a sworn statement made by a person called an affiant. The affiant makes oath before a notary public that the facts contained in the affidavit are true. The affidavit consists of the venue, body, affiant's signature, and jurat. Venue indicates the place where the affidavit is made or taken and must be a place where the notary is empowered to act. The body of the affidavit ... contains the facts the affiant swears are true. The affiant's signature is subscribed at the end of the affidavit.... The jurat, also known as the notary's certificate, is the concluding statement that the affidavit was sworn to before the notary on a certain date. Immediately beneath the jurat appears the signature of the notary before whom the oath is taken, and the notary's commission (expiration date)" (NPH).

"The notary public need not be concerned with the truthfulness of the facts stated by the affiant (other than in regard to the identity of the affiant). If the facts are willfully misstated, the affiant is guilty of perjury. The notary, of course, cannot know the truth of the statements and is under no duty to investigate the facts" (NPH).

NOTARY DON'TS

Signer Must Appear in Person

"A notary should under no circumstances take the acknowledgment of a person who does not appear before the notary since the statute by express language 'personally appeared before me' demands actual appearance. If identification as statutorily defined ... is not produced, the notary should refuse to take the acknowledgment" (NPH).

"A notary may not take the affidavit of a person who does not appear before the notary" (NPH).

Advertising Restrictions on Notaries

"A notary who is not an attorney licensed to practice law in Tennessee who advertises his or her services as a notary public is required by law to include the following notice in the advertisement:

"'I AM NOT AN ATTORNEY LICENSED TO PRACTICE LAW IN THE STATE OF TENNESSEE, AND I MAY NOT GIVE LEGAL ADVICE OR ACCEPT FEES FOR LEGAL ADVICE.'

"The foregoing disclaimer must be included in any advertisement, whether by radio, television, signs, pamphlets, newspapers, telephone directory, or other written or oral communication, or in any other matter. It must be in English and in the language used in the advertisement, if different. In a written advertisement the statement must be of conspicuous size. An advertisement on radio or television must include substantially the same message. TCA § 8-16-401(a)" (NPH).

In addition, a nonattorney Notary is prohibited from:

1. "Advising or assisting in selecting or completing forms affecting or related to a person's immigration status" (TCA 8-16-401[b]); or

2. "Representing or advertising that the notary public is an immigration consultant, immigration paralegal or expert on immigration matters" unless the Notary is an accredited representative of an organization recognized by the Board of Immigration Appeals under Title 8, Part 292, Section 2(a-3) of the Code of Federal Regulations (TCA 8-16-402).

Violations of the above constitute "unfair" or "deceptive" acts under TCA 47-18-104, but the above restrictions do not apply to Notaries employed by banks, trust companies and savings and loan associations, nor to Notaries engaged in the closing of loans, the extension of credit or the transfer of title or security instruments (TCA 8-16-403 and 8-16-404).

Disqualifying Interests

"A notary should not acknowledge his or her own signature nor notarize any signature if he or she is a party to the transaction or an agent of a party taking an acknowledgment" (NPH).

NOTARY SIGNING AGENTS

Currently, there are no statutes, regulations or rules expressly governing, prohibiting or restricting the operation of Notary Signing Agents within the state of Tennessee.

NOTARY FEES

"Notaries public are entitled to demand and receive the following fees and compensation for services:

"1. For recording in a well-bound book, to be kept by the notary for that purpose, each attestation, protestation, and other instrument of publication…$1.00

"2. For the protestation of negotiable instruments, for each instrument protested, without regard to the number of parties on each instrument…$1.50

"3. For every acknowledgment or probate of deed, or other instrument of writing, with seal attached, the same as county clerks.*

"4. For every acknowledgment of notes for advances on tobacco…$0.25

"5. For each deposition taken…$1.00

"6. For any other service legally performed by the notary, the same fees allowed other officers for like services" (TCA 8-21-1201).

* "(C)ounty clerks are entitled to demand and receive for … certifying a copy of a document or taking an acknowledgment or affixing a seal … $5.00" (TCA 8-21-701[11]).

Fees for Other Services: "If it is necessary for the notary to prepare the affidavit for the affiant's signature and oath, an additional fee for that service is allowable, depending on the nature of the service. If additional services are stenographic in nature, a stenographer's fee, or if said additional services are performed by an attorney and are legal in nature, an attorney's fee may be appropriate" (NPH).

NOTARY CERTIFICATES

Form of Acknowledgment Certificate

"Any certificate clearly evidencing intent to authenticate, acknowledge or verify a document shall constitute a valid certificate of acknowledgment for purposes of this chapter and for any other purpose for which such certificate may be used under the law. It is the legislative intent that no specific form or wording be required in such certificate and that the ownership of property, or the determination of any other right or obligation, shall not be affected by the inclusion or omission of any specific words" (TCA 66-22-114[b]).

"Although the certificate of acknowledgment need not include the 'magic words' contained in the statutory form, it must nevertheless contain language to satisfy the substance of the certificate of acknowledgment" (NPH).

Acknowledgment by Individual (Alternative 1) (TCA 66-22-107[a]):

State of Tennessee   )
County of _____)

Personally appeared before me, _____ (name of clerk, deputy clerk or Notary), clerk (or deputy clerk or Notary) of this county, _____ (bargainor's name), the within named bargainor, with whom I am personally acquainted (or proved to me on the basis of satisfactory evidence), and who acknowledged that he/she executed the within instrument for the purposes therein contained.

Witness my hand, at office, this _____ day of _____, 20____.

(SIGNATURE, SEAL, TITLE AND COMMISSION EXPIRATION DATE OF NOTARIZING OFFICER)

Acknowledgment by Individual (Alternative 2) (TCA 66-22-107[b]):

State of Tennessee   )
County of _____)

On this _____ day of _____, 20____, before me personally appeared _____, to me known to be the person (or persons) described in and who executed the foregoing instrument, and acknowledged that he/she/they executed the same as his/her/their free act and deed.

(SIGNATURE, SEAL, TITLE AND COMMISSION EXPIRATION DATE OF NOTARIZING OFFICER)

Acknowledgment by Corporation (Alternative 1) (TCA 66-22-108[a]):

State of Tennessee   )
County of _____)

Before me, _____, of the state and county mentioned, personally appeared _____, with whom I am personally acquainted (or proved to me on the basis of satisfactory evidence), and who, upon oath, acknowledged himself/herself to be president (or other officer authorized to execute the instrument) of _____, the within named bargainor, a corporation, and that he/she as such _____, executed the foregoing instrument for the purpose therein contained, by personally signing the name of the corporation by himself/herself as _____

Witness my hand and seal, this _____ day of _____, 20___.

(SIGNATURE, SEAL, TITLE AND COMMISSION EXPIRATION DATE OF NOTARIZING OFFICER)

Acknowledgment by Corporation or Association (Alternative 2) (TCA 66-22-108[a]):

State of Tennessee   )
County of _____)

On this _____ day of _____, 20____, before me appeared _____, to me personally known (or proved to me on the basis of satisfactory evidence), who, being by me duly sworn (or affirmed) did say that he/she is the president (or other officer or agent of the corporation or association) of _____ (describing the corporation or association), and that the seal* affixed to the instrument is the corporate seal of the corporation (or association), and that the instrument was signed and sealed in behalf of the corporation (or association), by authority of its Board of Directors (or Trustees) and _____ acknowledged the instrument to be the free act and deed of the corporation (or association).

(SIGNATURE, SEAL, TITLE AND COMMISSION EXPIRATION DATE OF NOTARIZING OFFICER)

* In case the corporation or association has no corporate seal omit the words "the seal affixed

to the instrument is the corporate seal of the corporation or association and that," and add at the end of the affidavit clause, the words "and that the corporation (or association) has no corporate seal."

Acknowledgment by Partnership (TCA 66-22-108[b][1]):

State of Tennessee)
County of _____)

Before me, _____, of the state and county aforementioned, personally appeared _____, with whom I am personally acquainted (or proved to me on the basis of satisfactory evidence), and who, upon oath, acknowledged himself/herself to be a partner of _____, the within named bargainor, a partnership, and that he/she, as such partner, executed the foregoing instrument for the purpose therein contained, by signing the name of the partnership by himself/herself as partner.

Witness my hand and seal, this _____ day of _____, 20____.

(SIGNATURE, SEAL, TITLE AND COMMISSION EXPIRATION DATE OF NOTARIZING OFFICER)

Acknowledgment by Attorney in Fact (TCA 66-22-107[c]):

State of Tennessee)
County of _____)

On this _____ day of _____, 20____, before me personally appeared _____, to me known (or proved to me on the basis of satisfactory evidence) to be the person who executed the foregoing instrument in behalf of _____, and acknowledged that such person executed the same as the free act and deed of _____.

(SIGNATURE, SEAL, TITLE AND COMMISSION EXPIRATION DATE OF NOTARIZING OFFICER)

All-Purpose Acknowledgment (TCA 66-22-114[a]):

State of Tennessee)
County of _____)

Personally appeared before me, _____ (name of notarizing officer), _____ (official capacity of notarizing officer), _____ (name of the natural person executing the instrument), with whom I am personally acquainted, and who acknowledged that he/she executed the within instrument for the purposes therein contained (the following to be included only where the natural person is executing as agent), and who further acknowledged that he/she is the _____ (identification of the agency position of the natural person executing the instrument, such as "attorney in fact" or "president" or "general partner") of the maker or a constituent of the maker and is authorized by the maker or by its constituent, the constituent being authorized by the maker, to execute this instrument on behalf of the maker.

Witness my hand, at office, this _____ day of _____, 20____.

(SIGNATURE, SEAL, TITLE AND COMMISSION EXPIRATION DATE OF NOTARIZING OFFICER)

Affidavit (NPH):

(CAPTION, IF FOR LEGAL PROCEEDING)

State of Tennessee)
County of _____)

_____, *being duly sworn, makes oath as follows:*

(Recite facts to be sworn by affiant)

_____
(Affiant's Signature)

Sworn to and subscribed before me this _____ day of _____, 20____.

(SIGNATURE, SEAL, TITLE AND COMMISSION EXPIRATION DATE OF NOTARIZING OFFICER)

Copy Certification of Electronic Document by Attorney or Custodian (TCA 66-24-101[d][3]):

I, _____ (name of attorney or custodian), do hereby make oath that I am a licensed attorney and/or the custodian of the electronic version of the attached document tendered for registration herewith and that this is the true and correct copy of the original document executed and authenticated according to law.

_____ *(Signature of attorney or custodian)*

State of Tennessee   )
County of _____)

Personally appeared before me, _____ (name of Notary), a Notary Public for this county and state, _____ (name of attorney or custodian making certification), who acknowledges that this certification of an electronic document is true and correct and whose signature I have witnessed.

_____ *(Notary's signature)*

MY COMMISSION EXPIRES: _____

Notary's Seal (if on paper)

ELECTRONIC NOTARIZATIONS

The state of Tennessee has not yet adopted statutes or regulations expressly establishing rules, definitions and procedures for electronic notarization.

UETA Recognizes Notary's eSignature

Tennessee has adopted the Uniform Electronic Transactions Act (TCA 47-10-101 through 47-10-123), including the provisions on notarization, thereby recognizing the legal validity of electronic signatures used by Notaries:

"If a law requires a signature or record to be notarized, acknowledged, verified, or made under oath, the requirement is satisfied if the electronic signature of the person authorized to perform those acts, together with all other information required to be included by other applicable law, is attached to or logically associated with the signature or record" (TCA 47-10-111).

URPERA Allows Digitized Wet Signature

Effective July 1, 2007, Tennessee has adopted its own version of the Uniform Real Property Electronic Recording Act (TCA 66-24-201 through 66-24-206), including the following provision:

"A requirement that a document or a signature associated with a document be notarized, acknowledged, verified, witnessed, or made under oath is satisfied if the electronic signature or a digitized image of a wet signature of the person authorized to perform that act, and all other information required to be included, is attached to or logically associated with the document or signature. A physical or electronic image of a stamp, impression, or seal need not accompany an electronic signature" (TCA 66-24-203[c]).

Two Types of eDocument May Be Recorded: "(1) The county register may register a copy of an electronic document if the writing is otherwise eligible for registration and the electronic document is certified as a true and correct copy of the original as required in subdivision (d)(3).

"(2) For purposes of this section, an electronic document is defined as one of the following:

"(A) A writing created or retained as an electronic record in accordance with the Uniform Electronic Transactions Act (UETA) … or the Uniform Real Property Electronic Recording Act (URPERA) …, as codified in this state or a substantially similar law of another state as defined in the URPERA, and transmitted to the county register electronically, or a paper copy of such an electronic record; or

"(B) A writing that is a digitized image of a paper document (electronic copy) that is transmitted to the county register electronically.

"(3) The certification of an electronic document shall be made by either a licensed attorney or the custodian of the electronic version of the document and the signature of that person shall be acknowledged by a notary public. The certification shall be transmitted with the electronic document and shall be recorded by the county register as a part of the document being registered" (TCA 66-24-101[d]).

For the required certificate wording, see "Copy Certification of Electronic Document by Attorney or Custodian," above.

NOTARY RECORDS

"In order to charge the statutory fee, a notary must keep a record in a well-bound book of his or her attestations, protestations, and other instruments of publication. A record of fees received should also be kept for income tax records" (NPH).

Recommended Recordbook Entries

The "Tennessee Notary Public Handbook" recommends that the following information be kept for each act of the Notary:

1. The date of acknowledgments, affidavits and other transactions;
2. The name of the person whose signature is being notarized;
3. The name of the person or entity to whom the instrument is being executed;
4. A description, including the date, of the instrument;
5. Whether the person whose signature was notarized was a personal acquaintance or what other proof of identity was shown;
6. What fee, if any, the Notary received.

AUTHENTICATION OF NOTARIAL ACTS

County Clerks

The authentication process begins by first submitting the notarized document to the clerk of the county which elected a particular Notary to office and in which that Notary resides or maintains a principal place of business. The county clerk will issue a certificate authenticating the Notary's signature (Secretary of State's website, "Other Services").

Department of State

Notarized documents that will be sent out of state or abroad may be certified — through an apostille or other authenticating certificate — by the Tennessee Department of State. Such documents must already bear the authenticating certificate of a county clerk.

"The Division of Business Services can issue an apostille or authentication only for documents bearing the signature, seal and position of a Tennessee County Clerk, Tennessee State Registrar, or the Tennessee Secretary of State" (Secretary of State's website, "Other Services").

Fees: $2 per apostille or other authenticating certificate. Checks or money orders payable to "Tennessee Secretary of State."

Address:
Tennessee Department of State
Division of Business Services, NTS Unit
312 Rosa L. Parks Blvd.
William R. Snodgrass Tower, 6th Floor
Nashville, TN 37243

Telephone: 1-615-741-3699

Procedure: Mail or present in person the original(s) of the notarized document(s), with the certificate(s) from the county clerk attached to the document(s), along with the appropriate fee. Faxed documents are not accepted.

If documents are mailed, include a cover letter indicating the country of destination and whether an apostille or other authentication is needed (Secretary of State's website, "Other Services").

COMMISSIONING AND ADMINISTRATION

Though the Governor of Tennessee signs commissions for the state's Notaries (TCA 8-16-102), the Secretary of State coordinates the issuance of these commissions with the county clerks (TCA 8-16-106) and sets certain rules for Notaries regarding the official seal (TCA 8-16-114).

Applying for Commission

Qualifications: An applicant for a commission as a Tennessee Notary Public must: (a) be at least 18 years old, (b) be a resident of or maintain a principal place of business in a Tennessee county, and (c) be a United States citizen or a legal permanent resident alien (TCA 8-16-101[a] and 8-18-101).

No one may serve as a Notary who: (a) has been convicted of bribery, larceny or certain other offenses unless restored to citizenship, (b) has any unpaid judgments owing to the U.S. government, to Tennessee or to any Tennessee county, or (c) is a defaulter to the Tennessee treasury at the time of application. Nor may a Notary be: (a) a member of the regular U.S. armed forces, (b) a member of Congress, or (c) a person holding any office of profit or trust under any foreign power, other state or the U.S. government (TCA 8-18-101).

No Course or Test: No statewide course of instruction or test is required of applicants for a Tennessee Notary commission.

Application: According to the "Tennessee Notary Public Handbook" and the "Notary Commission Services Brochure," the application process for a Tennessee Notary is as follows:

1. The applicant obtains a commission

application from the county clerk in the county in which the applicant, at the time of application, resides or maintains his or her principal place of business.

2. The applicant completes the application. On the application, the applicant must certify under penalty of perjury before a Notary that he or she has never: (a) been removed from office as a Notary for official misconduct, (b) had a notarial commission revoked or suspended, or (c) been found by a court to have engaged in the unauthorized practice of law (TCA 8-16-101[c]).

3. The applicant submits to the county clerk the completed, signed, and notarized application and the application fee of $12, of which $7 is for the county clerk and $5 is for the Secretary of State (TCA 8-16-106).

4. The county legislative body in the county in which the applicant, at the time of election, resides or maintains his or her principal place of business elects the applicant as a Notary (TCA 8-16-101[a]). "A county legislative body member is not prohibited from serving as a notary public; however, such member may not vote on his or her appointment as a notary" [NPH].

5. The county clerk certifies the election of the applicant and forwards the certification and the $5 fee to the Secretary of State. The Secretary of State prepares, records and forwards to the county clerk the Notary commission, signed by the Governor and the Secretary of State. The county clerk records the commission and notifies the applicant that the commission has been received (TCA 8-16-106).

6. The applicant secures a $10,000 bond, either executed by some surety company authorized to do business in Tennessee or with two or more personal sureties approved by the county legislative body. The applicant then files the bond with the county clerk (TCA 8-16-104).

7. The county clerk administers the oath of office (TCA 8-16-105) and then delivers the commission to the new Notary (TCA 8-16-107).

Renewal: The Notary commission renewal process is the same as for an original commission (NPH).

Non-Residents: A person with a principal place of business in any Tennessee county may be elected a Notary in that county even though the person's residence is in another state (TCA 8-16-101).

Online Search: By using the online "Notary Commission Search" feature of the Department of State's website and submitting a last name, the following are available: the full name, county of election and commission expiration date of every Notary with that last name. The database reflects all unexpired Notary commissions issued by the Tennessee Secretary of State as of three working days prior to the date of search. Expired Notary commissions are removed from the database monthly.

NOTE: While the online database reflects information about commissions issued by the Secretary of State, it does not reflect whether the commissionees have thereafter taken the oath of office and executed the bond required. For full information regarding the current status of a particular commissionee, the appropriate county clerk's office should be contacted (website, "Notary Commission Search").

Changes of Status

If Notary Moves or Changes Name: "If a notary public's surname changes, or if a notary public moves such notary's residence or principal place of business out of the county from which the notary was elected and commissioned to another county in Tennessee, the notary shall notify the county clerk of the county from which the notary was elected and commissioned and shall pay to such county clerk a fee of seven dollars ($7.00). The county clerk shall thereupon notify the secretary of state of the change of address or name change and forward to the secretary of state two dollars ($2.00) of the seven dollar ($7.00) fee received from the notary" (TCA 8-16-109).

When a Notary reports a surname change, it does not change the Notary's name of record as it appears on a previously issued Notary commission. "A Notary whose name has been legally changed can obtain a new commission by submitting to the Division of Business Services (through the County Clerk) the original commission, a statement from the County Clerk indicating that the legal name has changed and identifying the former and current names, and payment of a $5 fee to the Secretary of State. The new commission will be forwarded to the County Clerk for delivery to the Notary" (website, "Notary Commission Services Brochure").

"If a notary public moves such notary's residence or principal place of business out of the state of Tennessee, such notary is no longer qualified to act as a Tennessee notary public and shall surrender such notary's commission. It is an offense for any person who has been commissioned as a Tennessee notary public to take acknowledgments or otherwise act in an official capacity after moving out of the state of Tennessee. A violation of this section is a Class C misdemeanor" (TCA 8-16-110).

COUNTY CLERKS

To contact a Tennessee county clerk to obtain an authenticating certificate for a Notary, or to seek assistance in locating a given Notary, telephone long-distance information — 1-XXX-555-1212 — using one of the following area codes and ask for the phone number for the clerk of the appropriate county listed below.

County	City/Town	Area Code
Anderson	Clinton	(865)
Bedford	Shelbyville	(931)
Benton	Camden	(731)
Bledsoe	Pikeville	(423)
Blount	Maryville	(865)
Bradley	Cleveland	(423)
Campbell	Jacksboro	(423)
Cannon	Woodbury	(615)
Carroll	Huntingdon	(731)
Carter	Elizabethton	(423)
Cheatham	Ashland City	(615)
Chester	Henderson	(731)
Claiborne	Tazewell	(423)
Clay	Celina	(931)
Cocke	Newport	(423)
Coffee	Manchester	(931)
Crockett	Alamo	(731)
Cumberland	Crossville	(931)
Davidson	Nashville	(615)
Decatur	Decaturville	(731)
De Kalb	Smithville	(615)
Dickson	Charlotte	(615)
Dyer	Dyersburg	(731)
Fayette	Somerville	(901)
Fentress	Jamestown	(931)
Franklin	Winchester	(931)
Gibson	Trenton	(731)
Giles	Pulaski	(931)
Grainger	Rutledge	(865)
Greene	Greeneville	(423)
Grundy	Altamont	(931)
Hamblen	Morristown	(423)
Hamilton	Chattanooga	(423)
Hancock	Sneedville	(423)
Hardeman	Bolivar	(731)
Hardin	Savannah	(731)
Hawkins	Rogersville	(423)
Haywood	Brownsville	(731)
Henderson	Lexington	(731)
Henry	Paris	(731)
Hickman	Centerville	(931)
Houston	Erin	(931)
Humphreys	Waverly	(931)
Jackson	Gainesboro	(931)
Jefferson	Dandridge	(865)
Johnson	Mountain City	(423)
Knox	Knoxville	(865)
Lake	Tiptonville	(731)
Lauderdale	Ripley	(731)
Lawrence	Lawrenceburg	(931)
Lewis	Hohenwald	(931)
Lincoln	Fayetteville	(931)
Loudon	Loudon	(865)
McMinn	Athens	(423)
McNairy	Selmer	(731)
Macon	Lafayette	(615)
Madison	Jackson	(731)
Marion	Jasper	(423)
Marshall	Lewisburg	(931)
Maury	Columbia	(931)
Meigs	Decatur	(423)
Monroe	Madisonville	(423)
Montgomery	Clarksville	(931)
Moore	Lynchburg	(931)
Morgan	Wartburg	(423)
Obion	Union City	(731)
Overton	Livingston	(931)
Perry	Linden	(931)
Pickett	Byrdstown	(931)
Polk	Benton	(423)
Putnam	Cookeville	(931)
Rhea	Dayton	(423)
Roane	Kingston	(865)
Robertson	Springfield	(615)
Rutherford	Murfreesboro	(615)
Scott	Huntsville	(423)
Sequatchie	Dunlap	(423)
Sevier	Sevierville	(865)
Shelby	Memphis	(901)
Smith	Carthage	(615)
Stewart	Dover	(931)

County	City/Town	Area Code
Sullivan	Blountville	(423)
Sumner	Gallatin	(615)
Tipton	Covington	(901)
Trousdale	Hartsville	(615)
Unicoi	Erwin	(423)
Union	Maynardville	(865)
Van Buren	Spencer	(931)
Warren	McMinnville	(931)
Washington	Jonesboro	(423)
Wayne	Waynesboro	(931)
Weakley	Dresden	(731)
White	Sparta	(931)
Williamson	Franklin	(615)
Wilson	Lebanon	(615)

OTHER NOTARIAL OFFICERS

Besides Notaries, the following officers may take acknowledgments within Tennessee (TCA 66-22-102):

1. County clerk or deputy county clerk;
2. Clerk and master of chancery court of a county.

Also, probate judges may take acknowledgment of deeds and other instruments within their counties (TCA 66-22-105).

Licensed Court Reporters

Effective July 1, 2010, licensed court reporters are authorized to administer oaths, to swear in witnesses and to record any deposition, court proceeding, administrative law proceeding or any other proceeding, without benefit of a Notary commission. Further, transcripts taken and submitted by a licensed court reporter do not require notarization.

These rules do not apply to court reporting services paid for by a federal agency or other instrumentality of the United States, nor to court reporting services provided pursuant to criminal matters under Title 40 of the TCA (TCA 29-9-603).

QUICK FACTS

Notary Jurisdiction
Statewide (TCA 8-16-112). Prior to July 1, 1993, there were two kinds of Notary: at-large Notaries with statewide powers, and Notaries with only countywide authority. On that date, however, all Tennessee Notaries became Notaries Public for the State of Tennessee, with authority to notarize in any county of the state (TCA 8-16-113).

Notary Term Length
Four years, beginning on the date the commission is issued by the Governor (TCA 8-16-103).

It is a Class C misdemeanor for a person to act as a Notary after the expiration of a commission (TCA 8-16-120).

Notary Bond
$10,000, executed with a licensed surety or with two or more personal sureties approved by the county (TCA 8-16-104).

Liability of Notary: "Tennessee statutes provide that if a notary who takes acknowledgment of a deed or other instrument fails or refuses to comply with and discharge the duties required of a notary, he or she shall forfeit and pay the sum of $100 for the use of the county of the notary's residence and shall, moreover, be liable to the party injured for all damages, including costs, the party may sustain by the notary's failure or refusal to discharge the statutory duties. TCA 66-22-113. Such action can be based on the negligence or misconduct of the notary" (NPH).

S-U

Texas

Texas

NOTARY SEAL

A Texas Notary Public must authenticate all official acts with a seal of office, and the seal's format must be as follows (GC 406.013):

Kind

Inked Stamp or Embosser: "The seal must be affixed by a seal press or stamp that embosses or prints a seal that legibly reproduces the required elements of the seal under photographic methods. An indelible ink pad must be used for

Examples

The above typical, actual-size examples of rectangular and circular seals are allowed by Texas law. Formats other than these may also be permitted.

NOTARY ADMINISTRATION

Office of Secretary of State
Statutory Documents Section
Notary Public Unit 1-512-463-5705
P.O. Box 13375
Austin, TX 78711-3375

Website: www.sos.state.tx.us/statdoc/index.shtml

NOTARY RULES

GC — TEXAS GOVERNMENT CODE
CPRC — TEXAS CIVIL PRACTICE & REMEDIES CODE
TAC — TEXAS ADMINISTRATIVE CODE
EI – NOTARY PUBLIC EDUCATIONAL INFORMATION

Most Notary rules are in:

a. Texas Government Code, Title 4, Chapter 406, "Notary Public; Commissioner of Deeds";

b. Texas Civil Practices and Remedies Code, Title 6, Chapter 121, "Acknowledgments and Proofs of Written Instruments";

c. Texas Administrative Code, Title 1, Chapter 87, "Secretary of State," and Title 28, Chapter 252, "State Risk Management."

Guidelines for Notaries are in the "Notary Public Educational Information" available on the website, also offering a specialized version for non-bonded Notaries employed by state agencies.

affixing by a stamp the impression of a seal ..." (GC 406.013[c]).

Shape/Size

Circular, not more than 2 inches in diameter; or rectangular, not more than 1 inch wide and 2 1/2 inches long (GC 406.013[b]).

Border

The seal must have "a serrated or milled edge border" containing the following components (GC 406.013[b]):

Components

1. "Notary Public, State of Texas"*;
2. Star of five points;
3. Name of Notary;
4. Commission expiration date.

* The words "Notary Public, State of Texas" must appear around the five-pointed star.

Seal of 'Notary Without Bond'

An employee or officer of the state of Texas who is a Notary Public and who is exempted from the surety bond requirement (GC 653.002 through 653.005 and 635.012) must include the words "Notary Without Bond" with the Notary's inking seal imprint on every notarized document. These words must appear below the border of the inking rectangular seal used by such Notaries (28 TAC 252.505) — see example below.

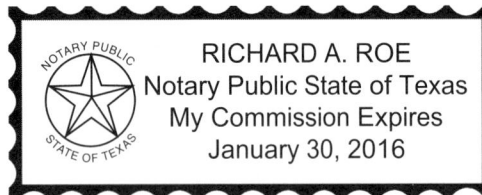

Notary Without Bond

Electronically Transmitted Documents

"The application of an embossed seal is not required on an electronically transmitted certificate of an acknowledgment" (CPRC 121.004[d]).

"Subsection (c) (of Section 406.013, which requires stamping or embossing a photographically reproducible seal impression) does not apply to an electronically transmitted authenticated document, except that an electronically transmitted authenticated document must legibly reproduce the required elements of the seal" (GC 406.013[d]).

Is the image of the five-pointed star an "element" of the seal that must be reproduced? The answer to this question is confused by the following section of the Texas Uniform Real Property Electronic Recording Act (Property Code, Chapter 15), which states: "A physical or electronic image of a stamp, impression, or seal need not accompany an electronic signature" (PC 15.004[c]).

Commissioner of Deeds' Seals

Commissioners of deeds are appointed by the Texas Governor to notarize documents within a designated jurisdiction outside the state of Texas, when these documents will be filed or used within Texas. "A commissioner of deeds shall provide a seal with a star of five points in the center and the words 'Commissioner of the State of Texas' engraved on the seal. The seal shall be used to certify all official acts of the commissioner of deeds. An instrument that does not have the impression of the seal, or an act of the commissioner of deeds that is not certified by the impression of the seal, is not valid in this state" (GC 406.054).

Omission of Out-of-State Seal

"The failure of a notary public to attach an official seal to a certificate of an acknowledgment or proof of a written instrument made outside this state but inside the United States or its territories renders the acknowledgment or proof invalid only if the jurisdiction in which the certificate is made requires the notary public to attach the seal" (CPRC 121.004 and Property Code 12.001).

"The secretary of state annually shall compile a list of those states or territories within the United States that require a notary public to validate a certificate of an acknowledgment, proof of a written instrument, or a jurat by attaching an official seal …. The secretary of state shall send the list to each of the county clerks of this state before January 1 of each year …. The secretary of state shall amend the list and immediately send the amended list to the county clerks of this state if the secretary learns that a state or territory has changed its requirements relating to a notary public in a manner that requires it to be added to or deleted from the list" (GC 405.019).

Report Lost Seal

"Every commissioned notary public has a duty to safeguard his/her notary materials. However, if your notary seal or record book has been misplaced or lost, send a letter to this office detailing the circumstances in which the materials went missing, the last time you used it, and any other relevant information. If any of your notary materials have been stolen, you should file a report with your local law enforcement office and enclose a copy of that report with your letter to this office. Send the letter to the Legal Support Unit, P.O. Box 13550, Austin, Texas 78711-3550…. (Y)ou must get a new seal if your seal is lost or stolen, as notaries are required to affix their seals to all official acts they perform" (website, "Frequently Asked Questions").

Notary's Signature

"A notary must sign the notarial certificate using the same name that is listed on the commission issued by the secretary of state. However, as long as the name matches, the signature of the notary may be printed, written, typed, stamped, etc." (website, "Frequently Asked Questions").

NOTARY POWERS

Texas Notaries have the same authority as a county clerk to perform the following notarial acts (GC 406.016):

1. Take acknowledgments* and proofs**;
2. Administer oaths and affirmations;
3. Take depositions;
4. Certify copies of documents not recordable in the public record***;
5. Execute protests.

* <u>Identifying Acknowledgers</u>: "An officer may not take the acknowledgment of a written instrument unless the officer knows or has satisfactory evidence that the acknowledging person is the person who executed the instrument and is described in it. An officer may accept, as satisfactory evidence of the identity of an acknowledging person, only: (1) the oath of a credible witness personally known to the officer; (2) a current identification card or other document issued by the federal government or any state government that contains the photograph and signature of the acknowledging person; or (3) with respect to a deed or other instrument relating to a residential real estate transaction, a current passport issued by a foreign country" (CPRC 121.005).

** <u>Taking Proof</u>: "To prove a written instrument for recording, at least one of the witnesses who signed the instrument must personally appear before an officer who is authorized by this chapter to take acknowledgments or proofs and must swear:

(1) either that he saw the grantor or person who executed the instrument sign it or that that person acknowledged in the presence of the witness that he executed the instrument for the purposes and consideration expressed in it; and (2) that he signed the instrument at the request of the grantor or person who executed the instrument" (CPRC 121.009[a]).

"The officer may take the testimony of a witness only if the officer personally knows or has satisfactory evidence on the oath of a credible witness that the individual testifying is the person who signed the instrument as a witness. If evidence is used to identify the witness who signed the instrument, the officer must note the use of the evidence in the certificate of acknowledgment" (CPRC 121.009[c]).

In certain cases of taking a proof, a Notary may be authorized to issue subpoenas to require attendance of a witness, and to "employ and swear interpreters" (CPRC 121.003[3] and 121.013).

There are procedures for a proof by handwriting in cases where the signer or witnesses of a document are dead, out of the state, in an unknown location, incompetent or uncooperative (CPRC 121.011).

"In a proceeding to prove a written instrument, an officer authorized by this chapter to take an acknowledgment or a proof of a written instrument is also authorized to:

"1. administer oaths;

"2. employ and swear interpreters; and

"3. issue subpoenas" (CPRC 121.003).

*** <u>Certifying Copies</u>: "May I make a certified copy of a birth certificate or a marriage license? — No. Birth certificates and marriage licenses are recordable documents. Recordable documents are recorded with some specific governmental entity, such as the secretary of state's office, a court of law, a county clerk, or the Bureau of Vital Statistics. A certified copy of a recordable document may be obtained by contacting the recording entity. A notary cannot make certified copies of recordable documents.

"A notary may, however, make a certified copy of a non-recordable document. A non-recordable document is one that cannot be recorded with any type of governmental entity. For instance, a letter is not recorded with anyone, but there are times the sender of the letter would like to maintain a certified copy of that letter for his or her file" (website, "Frequently Asked Questions").

According to officials in the Texas Notary Public Unit, Notaries may not certify a copy of a passport because it is a potentially recordable document.

Notary May Sign for Disabled

"(a) A notary may sign the name of an individual who is physically unable to sign or make a mark on a document presented for notarization if directed to do so by that individual, in the presence of a witness who has no legal or equitable interest in any real or personal property that is the subject of, or is affected by, the document being signed. The notary shall require identification of the witness in the same manner as from an acknowledging person under Section 121.005, Civil Practice and Remedies Code.

"(b) A notary who signs a document under this section shall write, beneath the signature, the following or a substantially similar sentence: "'Signature affixed by notary in the presence of (name of witness), a disinterested witness, under Section 406.0165, Government Code.'

"(c) A signature made under this section is effective as the signature of the individual on whose behalf the signature was made for any purpose. A subsequent bona fide purchaser for value may rely on the signature of the notary as evidence of the individual's consent to execution of the document.

"(d) In this section, 'disability' means a physical impairment that impedes the ability to sign or make a mark on a document" (GC 406.0165).

Signature by Mark

"The individual signing the document may sign in whatever manner he/she chooses. The name or manner of signing by the signor is not the responsibility of the notary public. However, the notary public does have a responsibility to make sure that the information contained in the notarial certificate is accurate. For example if John Doe appears before a notary public and signs the instrument with an 'X' the notary public should still state in the notarial certificate that John Doe personally appeared on a given date" (website, "Frequently Asked Questions").

"'Signed' includes any symbol executed or adopted by a person with present intention to authenticate a writing" (GC 311.005[6]).

NOTARY DON'TS

Under Texas law, Notaries may:
1. NOT notarize a document without the signer being in the Notary's presence at the time of notarization (EI);
2. NOT notarize the Notary's own signature (EI);
3. NOT issue an identification card (GC 406.016[c]);
4. NOT as a non-attorney advertise notarial services in a foreign language without, in that language and in English, also stating the statutory fees and the following, in a conspicuous size: "I AM NOT AN ATTORNEY LICENSED TO PRACTICE LAW IN TEXAS AND MAY NOT GIVE LEGAL ADVICE OR ACCEPT FEES FOR LEGAL ADVICE" (GC 406.017);
5. NOT use the term "notario" or "notario publico" in any advertisement of notarial services (GC 406.017);
6. NOT take an acknowledgment over the phone (website, "Frequently Asked Questions");
7. NOT use "false or misleading advertising of either an oral or written nature, whereby the notary public has represented or indicated that he or she has duties, rights, powers, or privileges that are not possessed by law" (1 TAC 87.11);
8. NOT advertise "in any manner whatsoever that the notary public is an immigration specialist, immigration consultant, or any other title or description reflecting an expertise in immigration matters" (1 TAC 87.11);
9. NOT execute "any certificate as a notary public containing a statement known to the notary public to be false" (1 TAC 87.11).

Refusing to Notarize

"A notary public is a public servant. It is fundamental that a public servant cannot refuse to execute a duty imposed on him or her by law. In accepting a notary commission, a notary public accepts the burdens and obligations of that office. The public has a right to expect a notary to perform the duties attached to that office. However, a notary can execute those duties at such reasonable time that is consistent with the other duties imposed on the notary by reason of his or her particular employment" (website, "Frequently Asked Questions").

A Texas Notary may refuse a request for notarial services "only after careful deliberation" and never on the basis of the sex, age, religion, race, ethnicity or national origin of the requesting party (1 TAC 87.30). A Notary is authorized to refuse to perform a notarial act if: (a) the Notary has reasonable grounds to believe that the signer is acting under coercion or undue influence, (b) the Notary reasonably believes the document may be used for an unlawful or improper purpose, (c) the Notary has concerns about the ability of the signer to understand the contents of the document, or (d) the Notary is not familiar with the type of notarization requested (1 TAC 87.30).

Government Employees: "The Texas Attorney General's office issued a letter opinion in 1988 indicating that a notary public who is employed by a governmental body may refuse to take acknowledgments for the general public and must refuse when doing so would interfere with the employee's discharge of his or her duties as a public employee. Tex. Atty. Gen. Op. LO-88-34" (website, "Frequently Asked Questions").

"A notary who is employed by a governmental body shall not perform notarial services that interfere with the notary's discharge of the notary's duties as a public employee" (1 TAC 87.30[b]).

Employer May Restrict Employee-Notary: "The Texas Attorney General's office has issued an opinion supporting the authority of a private employer to limit or prohibit the notarial activities of its employees during work hours. Tex. Atty. Gen. Op. GA-0723" (website, "Frequently Asked Questions").

Disqualifying Interests

"(N)otarizations should not be performed by a notary public who is a party to the instrument or financially or beneficially interested in the transaction. The facts in each situation will determine whether the notary's action was proper" (website, "Frequently Asked Questions").

Notarizing for Relatives: "There is no specific prohibition against notarizing a spouse's or relative's signature or notarizing for a spouse's business" (website, "Frequently Asked Questions").

Corporate Interest Not Disqualifying: A Notary is NOT disqualified from taking an acknowledgment or proof when the Notary is (CPRC 121.002):
  1. An employee of a corporation and the corporation has an interest in the notarized document; or
  2. An officer who is a shareholder in a corporation and the corporation has an interest in the notarized document, unless:
    a. The corporation has 1,000 or fewer shareholders, and
    b. The officer owns more than one-tenth of one percent of the issued and outstanding stock.

In addition, a Notary is NOT disqualified from notarizing solely because of the Notary's ownership of stock or participation in or employment by a state trust company that has an interest in the underlying transaction (Texas Finance Code 199.002).

Notary May Not Decide Certificate

"A notary public who is not an attorney should only complete a notarial certificate which is already on the document, or type or attach a certificate of the maker's choosing. If a notary public were presented with a document that did not contain a certificate and decided which certificate to attach, that notary public would be 'practicing law.' Instead, the notary may allow the person for whom the notarization is performed to choose among the sample certificates provided to the notary with the notary's commission" (website, "Frequently Asked Questions").

May Not Certify Form I-9

"Although the United States Citizenship and Immigration Services (USCIS) would allow a notary public to fill out Form I-9 on the behalf of an employer, Texas notaries public are not provided this authority under Texas law. Therefore, if an employer requests that you complete any portion of a Form I-9 in your capacity as a notary public, you should refuse" (website, "Frequently Asked Questions").

NOTARY SIGNING AGENTS

Notary Signing Agents may lawfully operate within the state of Texas. However, because Texas law dictates that a lender may not force a home sale to recover a loan debt if the loan was closed at a location other than the office of the lender, an attorney at law or a title company, in many cases lenders will not authorize loan closings in a borrower's home. See explanation immediately below.

Notarizing at Home of Borrower

A measure passed by the 77th Texas Legislature and approved by the voters amended Section 50, Article 16 of the Texas Constitution to add a subsection that states a homestead is protected from a forced sale for the payment of debt for an extension of credit unless such extension of debt is closed at the offices of the lender, an attorney at law, or a title company. This change does not specifically preclude the execution of the closing documents at other locations. However, an extension of credit where the closing is performed at such other locations is subject to the homestead protection, which prevents a forced sale of the homestead. Thus, lenders who furnish extension of credit, secured by a lien on a homestead, may instruct notaries public not to acknowledge a borrower's signature at other locations, such as the borrower's home.

NOTARY FEES

The maximum fees that a Texas Notary may charge for a notarial act are (GC 406.024):

1. Taking an acknowledgment or proof: $6 for the first signature and $1 for each additional signature;
2. Administering an oath or affirmation, with or without a certificate/seal: $6;
3. Providing a copy of a record or paper kept in the Notary's office: 50 cents per page;
4. Taking a deposition: $6 for the oath and certificate, plus 50 cents per 100 words;
5. Protesting for nonacceptance or non-payment, $4; protest certificate/seal, $4; each notice of protest, $1;
6. Performing any other lawful notarial act: $6.

Lesser Fee May Be Charged

"A lesser fee is allowed or no fee at all may be charged. Excessive fees are grounds for disciplinary action" (website, "Frequently Asked Questions").

Fees Must Be Posted

"A county judge, clerk of a district or county court, sheriff, justice of the peace, constable, or notary public shall keep posted at all times in a conspicuous place in the respective offices a complete list of fees the person may charge by law" (GC 603.008).

Itemization of Fees

A Notary must itemize or be prepared to itemize in writing any fees charged (GC 603.007).

Fee Book

"An officer who by law may charge a fee for a service shall keep a fee book and shall enter in the book all fees charged for services rendered" (GC 603.006).

NOTARY CERTIFICATES

Upon issuing a Notary commission, the Texas Secretary of State must supply the Notary with "sample forms for an acknowledgment, jurat, and verification and for the administering of an oath, protest, and deposition" (GC 406.008). Accordingly, the Secretary of State currently directs that Texas Notaries use the following forms, based closely upon certificates prescribed by CPRC 121.007 and 121.008(b):

Acknowledgment by Individual ('Ordinary Certificate of Acknowledgment') (CPRC 121.007 and EI):

The State of Texas,
County of _____,

Before me, _____ (here insert the name and character of the notarizing officer), on this day personally appeared _____, known to me (or proved to me on the oath of _____ or through _____ [description of identity card or other document]) to be the person whose name is subscribed to the foregoing instrument and acknowledged to me that he/she executed the same for the purposes and consideration therein expressed.

Given under my hand and seal of office this ____ day of _____, 20__.

_____   (SEAL)
(Notary Public Signature)

Short Form Acknowledgment by Individual (Natural Person) (CPRC 121.008 and EI):

State of Texas
County of _____

This instrument was acknowledged before me on _____ (date) by _____ (name or names of person or persons acknowledging).

_____   (SEAL)
(Notary Public Signature)

Short Form Acknowledgment by Attorney in Fact Acting for Natural Person (CPRC 121.008 and EI):

State of Texas
County of _____

This instrument was acknowledged before me on _____ *(date) by* _____ *(name of attorney in fact) as attorney in fact on behalf of* _____ *(name of principal).*

_____ *(SEAL)*
(Notary Public Signature)

Short Form Acknowledgment by Partnership (CPRC 121.008 and EI):

State of Texas
County of _____

This instrument was acknowledged before me on _____ *(date) by* _____ *(name of acknowledging partner or partners), partner(s) on behalf of* _____ *(name of partnership), a partnership.*

_____ *(SEAL)*
(Notary Public Signature)

Short Form Acknowledgment by Corporation (CPRC 121.008 and EI):

State of Texas
County of _____

This instrument was acknowledged before me on _____ *(date) by* _____ *(name of corporate officer),* _____ *(title of corporate officer) of* _____ *(name of corporation acknowledging), a* _____ *(state of incorporation) corporation, on behalf of said corporation.*

_____ *(SEAL)*
(Notary Public Signature)

Short Form Acknowledgment by Public Officer, Trustee, Executor, Administrator, Guardian or Other Representative (CPRC 121.008 and EI):

State of Texas
County of _____

This instrument was acknowledged before me on _____ *(date) by* _____ *(name of representative) as* _____ *(title of representative) of* _____ *(name of entity or person represented).*

_____ *(SEAL)*
(Notary Public Signature)

Acknowledgment Certificate Format

"Except in a short form certificate of acknowledgment authorized by Section 121.008, the officer must note in the certificate of acknowledgment that: (1) he personally knows the acknowledging person; or (2) evidence of a witness or an identification card or other document was used to identify the acknowledging person" (CPRC 121.005).

"An acknowledgment form provided by this chapter may be altered as circumstances require. The authorization of a form does not prevent the use of other forms. The marital status or other status of the acknowledging persons may be shown after the person's name" (CPRC 121.006).

Jurat (EI):

State of Texas
County of _____

Sworn to and subscribed before me on the _____ *day of* _____, *20__, by* _____ *(name of principal signer).*

_____ *(SEAL)*
(Notary Public Signature)

Unsworn Declaration in Lieu of Jurat

Under Texas statute (CPRC 132.001), an unsworn written declaration signed on penalty of perjury may be used in lieu of any written and sworn or affirmed declaration, verification, certification, oath or affidavit required by law or rule to be made before a Notary or other oath-administering official.

This unsworn declaration must include a certificate substantially in the form below (CPRC 132.001[d]); a separate certificate is provided for an inmate in custody (CPRC 132.001[e]).

My name is _____ *(first, middle, last names), my date of birth is* _____, *and my address is _____ (street, city, state, zip) and _____ (county). I declare under penalty of perjury that the foregoing is true and correct.*

Executed in _____ County, State of ____, on the _____ day of _____, 20___.

_____, Declarant

Proof by Subscribing Witness (CPRC 121.010 and EI):

*The State of Texas,
County of _____*

Before me, _____ (here insert the name and character of the notarizing officer), on this day personally appeared _____, known to me (or proved to me on the oath of _____) to be the person whose name is subscribed as a witness to the foregoing instrument of writing, and after being duly sworn by me stated on oath that he/she saw _____, the grantor or person who executed the foregoing instrument, subscribe the same (or that the grantor or person who executed such instrument of writing acknowledged in his/her presence that he/she had executed the same for the purposes and consideration therein expressed), and that he/she had signed the same as a witness at the request of the grantor (or person who executed the same).

Given under my hand and seal of office this _____ day of _____, A.D., 20__.

(OFFICER'S SIGNATURE AND SEAL)

Certified Copy of Notarial Record (EI):

*State of Texas
County of _____*

On this _____ day of _____, 20__, I certify, pursuant to Tex. Gov't Code § 406.014(c), that the preceding or attached document is a true, exact, complete, and unaltered copy made by me of _____ (description of notarial record), the original of which is held in my custody as a notarial record.

*_____   (SEAL)
(Notary Public Signature)*

Certified Copy of Non-Recordable Document (EI):

*State of Texas
County of _____*

On this _____ day of _____, 20__, I certify that the preceding or attached document, and the duplicate retained by me as a notarial record, are true, exact, complete, and unaltered photocopies made by me of _____ (description of document), presented to me by the document's custodian, _____, (or, held in my custody as a notarial record) and that, to the best of my knowledge, the photocopied document is neither a public record nor a publicly recordable document, certified copies of which are available from an official source other than a Notary.

*_____   (SEAL)
(Notary Public Signature)*

Verification (Form 1) (EI):

*State of Texas
County of _____*

_____, personally appeared before me, and being first duly sworn declared that, he/she signed this application in the capacity designated, if any, and further states that, he/she has read the above application, and the statements therein contained are true.

*_____   (SEAL)
(Notary Public Signature)*

Verification (Form 2) (EI):

*State of Texas
County of _____*

Before me, a Notary Public, on this day personally appeared _____, known to me to be the person whose name is subscribed to the foregoing document and, being by me first duly sworn, declared that the statements therein contained are true and correct.

*_____   (SEAL)
(Notary Public Signature)*

Oath or Affirmation of Office (EI):

State of Texas
County of _____

I _____ (person taking office), do solemnly swear (or affirm) that I will faithfully execute the duties of the office of _____ of the State of Texas, and will to the best of my ability preserve, protect, and defend the Constitution and laws of the United States and of this State (so help me God).

_____
(Signature of person taking office)

Sworn to and subscribed before me by _____ (person taking office) on this _____ day of _____, 20____.

_____   (SEAL)
(Notary Public Signature)

Certificate to Deposition upon Written Questions (EI):

State of Texas
County of _____

(Plaintiff)   ) In the _____ Court
v.   ) of _____ County, Texas
(Defendant)   ) Cause No. _____

I hereby certify that the foregoing answers of _____, the witness forenamed, were signed and sworn to before me on _____ (date), by said witness.

_____   (SEAL)
(Notary Public Signature)

Certificate of Protest (EI):

(HERE INSERT BILL, NOTE OR COPY THEREOF)

United State of America
State of Texas
County of _____

Be it known that on the _____ day of _____, 20____ (year), at the request of _____ (name), of _____, I, _____ (Notary Public's name), a Notary Public duly commissioned and sworn, residing in _____ County, Texas, did present the original (instrument) _____, hereto attached, for $_____, with accrued interest thereon of $_____, dated _____, and demanded payment (or acceptance) thereof, which was refused.

Whereupon I, at the request of the aforesaid _____, did protest, and by these presents do protest, as well against the drawer, maker, endorsers, and acceptors of said instruments as against all others whom it may concern, for exchange, costs, charges, damages, and interest already incurred and hereinafter to be incurred by reason of nonpayment thereof. I further certify that on (date) _____, notice in writing of the foregoing presentment, demand, refusal and protest was given by (persons and status) _____ by deposing notices thereof in the post office at _____, Texas, postage paid, directed as follows: _____. I further certify that notices were left as follows:

Notice left for _____ at _____
Notice left for _____ at _____

Each of the named places the reputed place of residence of the person for whom the notice was left.

In testimony whereof I have hereunto set my hand and affixed my self of office at _____, Texas, on _____ day of _____, 20____ (year).

_____   (SEAL)
(Notary Public Signature)

Selecting Notarial Certificates

"A notary public who is not an attorney should only complete a notarial certificate which is already on the document or type a certificate of the maker's choosing. If a notary public is brought a document without a certificate and decides which certificate to attach, that notary public would be 'practicing law.' However, a notary public is provided copies of sample notarial certificates with his or her notary commission. The person for whom the notarization is performed may choose the certificate, and the notary may add such certificate to the document" (website, "Frequently Asked Questions ...").

Private Seal or Scroll

"A private seal or scroll may not be required on a written instrument other than an instrument made by a corporation" (CPRC 121.015).

ELECTRONIC NOTARIZATIONS

"Any Texas notary may perform an electronic notarization. An electronic notarization must meet all of the requirements of any other notarization, such as the requirement that the signer personally appear before the notary to acknowledge the document. In addition, the notary's electronic seal must reproduce the required elements of the notary seal" (website, "Frequently Asked Questions").

UETA Recognizes Notary's eSignature

Effective January 1, 2002, Texas adopted the Uniform Electronic Transactions Act (Business & Commerce Code [BCC], Chapter 322), including the following provision on notarization, thereby recognizing the legal validity of electronic signatures used by Notaries:

"If a law requires a signature or record to be notarized, acknowledged, verified, or made under oath, the requirement is satisfied if the electronic signature of the person authorized to perform those acts, together with all other information required to be included by other applicable law, is attached to or logically associated with the signature or record" (BCC 322.011).

Seal Image Not Needed on eDocument

In addition, effective September 1, 2005, Texas adopted the Uniform Real Property Electronic Recording Act (Property Code, Chapter 15), including:

"A requirement that a document or a signature associated with a document be notarized, acknowledged, verified, witnessed, or made under oath is satisfied if the electronic signature of the person authorized to perform that act, and all other information required to be included, is attached to or logically associated with the document or signature. A physical or electronic image of a stamp, impression, or seal need not accompany an electronic signature" (PC 15.004[c]).

Seal Elements Must Be Reproduced: "The application of an embossed seal is not required on an electronically transmitted certificate of an acknowledgment" (CPRC 121.004[d]).

"Subsection (c) does not apply to an electronically transmitted authenticated document, except that an electronically transmitted authenticated document must legibly reproduce the required elements of the seal" (GC 406.013). Subsection (c) requires stamping or embossing a photographically reproducible seal impression.

Is the image of the five-pointed star an "element" of the seal that must be reproduced? The answer to this question is confused by the following section of the Texas Uniform Real Property Electronic Recording Act, which states: "A physical or electronic image of a stamp, impression, or seal need not accompany an electronic signature" (PC 15.004[c]).

Electronic Journal Authorized

Effective September 1, 2005, through enactment of Senate Bill 220, Texas Notaries may maintain their required notarial records "electronically in a computer or other storage device" (GC 406.014[e]).

NOTARY RECORDS

Whether or not fees are charged for notarial services, a Notary must keep in a book, in a computer or in another storage device, a record of each document notarized (GC 406.014 and CPRC 121.012).

Required Entries

For each notarization performed, the Notary must record the following (GC 406.014):

1. The date of each document notarized;
2. The date of the notarization;
3. The name of the signer, grantor or maker;
4. The signer's, grantor's or maker's residence address;
5. Whether the signer, grantor or maker was personally known by the Notary; was identified by an ID card issued by a governmental agency, or by a U.S. passport; or was introduced to the Notary and, if so, the name and residence address of the introducer;
6. If the document is proved by a subscribing witness, whether the witness was personally known by the Notary or introduced, and, if introduced, the name and residence address of the introducer;
7. The name and residence address of the grantee;

8. If land is conveyed or charged by the document, the name of the original grantee and the county where the land is located;

9. A brief description of the document.

"The person for whom a notarization is performed is not required to sign the record book" (website, "Frequently Asked Questions").

<u>Retain Duplicate of Certified Copy</u>: In addition, Notaries are required to retain in their records a duplicate of any copy certified (EI).

Certain Oaths Exempted from Entry

"A notary public who administers an oath pursuant to Article 45.019 of the Code of Criminal Procedure is exempt from the requirement of recording that oath in the notary public's record book" (EI).

ID Numbers May Not Be Entered

"1 TAC § 87.40 prohibits a notary from recording in the notary's book of record the identification number that was assigned by the governmental agency or by the United States to the signer, grantor or maker and that is set forth on the identification card or passport; or any other number that could be used to identify the signer, grantor or maker of the document. Section 87.40 does not prohibit a notary from recording a number related to the residence or alleged residence of the signer, grantor or maker of the document or instrument" (EI).

According to the state Notary Public Unit, these regulations do not require purging of ID numbers from journal entries made before these regulations took effect in April of 2007, though Notaries may do so if they wish. However, if a Notary is asked to provide a photocopy of a journal entry made before the rule change took effect, the Notary must remove or obscure any ID numbers on the photocopy provided — see also 1 TAC 87.42.

Electronic Journal Authorized

Effective September 1, 2005, through enactment of Senate Bill 220, Texas Notaries may maintain their required notarial records "electronically in a computer or other storage device" (GC 406.014[e]).

"A notary may maintain the notary record book electronically in a computer or other storage device so long as the records from that book are adequately backed-up and are capable of being printed in a tangible medium when requested" (1 TAC 87.41).

Repeal of Signature and Bound Book

A law that took effect September 1, 1989, eliminated the requirement that the Notary record book be "well-bound" and that each document signer affix a signature in the journal. Another law, effective June 14, 1989, specifies that oaths administered pursuant to the Texas Code of Criminal Procedure, Article 45.01, need not be recorded in the Notary's book (GC 406.014[d]). Fee Book: Section 603.006 of the Texas Government Code requires Notaries to keep a fee book recording all fees charged for official services.

Public Inspection

Entries in the Notary's book are "public information," and upon payment of the fees allowed by law, the Notary must provide a certified copy of any notarial record to any person requesting the copy (GC 406.014 and 1 TAC 87.42).

"Failure to respond to a request for public information may be good cause for suspension or revocation of a notary commission or other disciplinary action against the notary" (1 TAC 87.43).

The Secretary of State suggests that all requests for copies of entries in a Notary's record book be made in writing through a certified letter to the Notary's official address on file (website, "Frequently Asked Questions").

County Clerk Keeps Records

"If the office of a notary public becomes vacant due to resignation, removal, or death, the county clerk of the county in which the notary public resides shall obtain the record books and public papers belonging to the office of the notary public and deposit them in the county clerk's office" (GC 406.022). The clerk may then certify copies of these records with the same authority as if certified by the Notary (GC 406.015).

Report Lost Journal

"(I)f your notary…record book has been misplaced or lost, send a letter to this office detailing the circumstances in which the materials went missing, the last time you used it, and any other relevant information. If any of your notary materials have been stolen, you should file a report with your local law enforcement office and enclose a copy of that report with your letter to this office. Send the letter to the Legal Support

Unit, P.O. Box 13550, Austin, Texas 78711-3550.

"Remember that you have a duty to record every notarial act in your record book. Therefore, if your notary record book is lost or stolen, you must get a new book before you resume providing notarial services" (website, "Frequently Asked Questions").

If Employer Won't Release Record

"The employer is not the owner of a notary's record book or seal, even if the employer paid for the materials. Tex. Atty. Gen. Op. GA-0723... The record book is public information and a notary is required to produce copies of the book upon request. Therefore, the book and seal should remain in the possession of the notary at all times" (website, "Frequently Asked Questions").

Retention of Journal by Notary

"A notary shall retain, in a safe and secure manner, copies of the records of notarization performed for the longer of the term of commission in which the notarization occurred or three years following the date of notarization" (1 TAC 87.44).

AUTHENTICATION OF NOTARIAL ACTS

Secretary of State

Authenticating certificates for Texas Notaries, including apostilles, are issued only by the Notary Public Unit of the Secretary of State's office.

Fee: $15 per certificate or apostille, with check or money order payable to the "Secretary of State of Texas." However, only $10 may be charged "for the issuance of an apostille requested for use in proceedings related to the adoption of a child in another country, provided that the total fees charged for apostilles issued in connection with the adoption of one child may not exceed $100" (GC 405.031).

Mailing Address:
Office of Secretary of State
Authentications Unit
P.O. Box 13550
Austin, TX 78711-3550

In Person or Overnight Mail:
James Earl Rudder Office Bldg., B-05
1019 Brazos
Austin, TX 78701

Telephone: 1-512-463-5705

Procedure: The complete and original notarized document(s) must be forwarded along with the fee and a written request including the country of destination, the Notary's name and commission expiration date, and the date of notarization (website, "Apostilles/Authentication of Documents"). Form 2102, "Request for Official Certificate or Apostille," may be used — available on the website. For adoptions, use Form 2103. Persons paying by credit card should include Form 2101. In addition, a self-addressed, stamped envelope or a pre-paid overnight airbill/envelope should be included.

School Transcripts and Diplomas: "A school transcript or diploma may only be certified by the educational institution that issued the transcript or diploma. The certifying official for the institution must complete the certification before a Texas notary public....You may obtain an official certificate or apostille on a document notarized by a Texas notary public from the Authentications Unit..." (website, "Frequently Asked Questions ").

COMMISSIONING AND ADMINISTRATION

The Texas Secretary of State appoints, commissions, regulates and maintains records on the state's Notaries (GC 406.001 through 406.012).

"All records concerning the appointment and qualification of the notary public shall be kept in the office of the secretary of state. The records are public information" (GC 406.012).

Applying for Commission

Qualifications: An applicant for a Texas Notary Public commission must (GC 406.004): (a) be a legal resident of the state of Texas, (b) be at least 18 years old and (c) not have been convicted of a felony or crime of moral turpitude that has not been dismissed or discharged by law. Applicants are subject to background investigations. As a result of legislation passed in 2009 (Senate Bill 2073), escrow agents who are residents of a state adjacent to Texas may qualify as Texas Notaries without meeting the Texas residency requirements; such individuals must apply using the special Form 2301-E.

No Course or Test: No course of instruction or testing is required of an applicant for a Texas Notary commission. However, as required by law (GC 406.008[b]), "Notary Public Educational Information" is made available for Notaries to study, including special "Notary Public Information for State Employees" — see the website. "This information should be kept for reference throughout your four-(4) year term. Please read through this information at least once before you begin to perform your notarial duties." Several pertinent Power Point presentations are available through the Secretary of State's website, including one on apostilles.

Application: The application (Form 2301) contains a section to be filled out by a representative of the surety firm providing the required $10,000 Notary bond (GC 406.005).

Applicants who are state employees must complete Form 2301-NB and Form SORM-203, "State Employee Notary Acknowledgment Form." Employees and officers of the state of Texas are not required to secure a Notary bond; instead, public protection for their acts is provided through the State Office of Risk Management (28 TAC 252.501).

The filing fee for an application is $21. Applicants who provide an email address on the application will have their "e-commission" returned to them by email.

A renewal application should be submitted no earlier than 90 days before commission expiration (website, "Frequently Asked Questions").

Non-Residents: The only non-residents who are eligible for appointment as a Texas Notary are licensed Texas escrow officers residing in an adjacent state (i.e., Louisiana, Arkansas, Oklahoma, New Mexico). They must apply using Form 2301-E.

Online Search: A searchable database of Texas Notaries is available on the Secretary of State's website, allowing users to locate Notary services in their area or verify that a commission is current or expired. The search engine is activated by entering the Notary's name, ID number, zip code or county. Searchers have the option of looking through records of past or present Notaries. Results provided include the Notary's name, address, surety company, county and commission dates.

To search for a Notary, go to https://direct.sos.state.tx.us/notaries/NotarySearch.asp.

Changes of Status

If Notary Moves: Notaries who change their address must notify the Secretary of State no later than the 10th day after the change (GC 406.019) by letter or using a "Notary Public Change of Address Form" (Form 2302). Notaries who move their residence from Texas automatically vacate the office (GC 406.020).

State employee Notaries without a bond must notify the State Office of Risk Management when moving to a new state agency or terminating employment at a state agency.

If Notary Changes Name: A Notary may change the name on his or her commission by sending the Secretary of State an "Application for Change of Name as Texas Notary Public" (Form 2305 or Form 2305-NB for a Notary without a bond), the current commission, if applicable a rider or endorsement from the surety firm showing the name change, and a $20 filing fee (website, "Frequently Asked Questions"). Name change notification is optional; the Notary may continue to use the name on the commission until the commission expires.

COUNTY CLERKS

The notarial records of Notaries who resign, are removed from office or die must be deposited in the local county clerk's office (GC 406.022). The clerk may then certify copies of these records with the same authority as if certified by the Notary (GC 406.015), since the "secretary of state may provide for the appointment of county clerks as deputy custodians for the limited authentication of notary public records deposited in the clerks' offices" (GC 406.023[c]).

To contact a Texas county clerk to obtain access to a former Notary's official records, telephone long-distance information — 1-XXX-555-1212 — using one of the area codes listed below and ask for the phone number of the clerk for the appropriate county.

County	City/Town	Area Code
Anderson	Palestine	(903)
Andrews	Andrews	(432)
Angelina	Lufkin	(936)
Aransas	Rockport	(361)

Texas

County	City/Town	Area Code	County	City/Town	Area Code
Archer	Archer City	(940)	Culberson	Van Horn	(432)
Armstrong	Claude	(806)	Dallam	Dalhart	(806)
Atascosa	Jourdanton	(830)	Dallas	Dallas	(214)
Austin	Bellville	(979)	Dawson	Lamesa	(806)
Bailey	Muleshoe	(806)	Deaf Smith	Hereford	(806)
Bandera	Bandera	(830)	Delta	Cooper	(903)
Bastrop	Bastrop	(512)	Denton	Denton	(940)
Baylor	Seymour	(940)	Dewitt	Cuero	(361)
Bee	Beeville	(361)	Dickens	Dickens	(806)
Bell	Belton	(254)	Dimmit	Carrizo Springs	(830)
Bexar	San Antonio	(210)	Donley	Clarendon	(806)
Blanco	Johnson City	(830)	Duval	San Diego	(361)
Borden	Gail	(806)	Eastland	Eastland	(254)
Bosque	Meridian	(254)	Ector	Odessa	(432)
Bowie	New Boston	(903)	Edwards	Rocksprings	(830)
Brazoria	Angleton	(979)	Ellis	Waxahachie	(972)
Brazos	Bryan	(979)	El Paso	El Paso	(915)
Brewster	Alpine	(432)	Erath	Stephenville	(254)
Briscoe	Silverton	(806)	Falls	Marlin	(254)
Brooks	Falfurrias	(361)	Fannin	Bonham	(903)
Brown	Brownwood	(325)	Fayette	La Grange	(979)
Burleson	Caldwell	(979)	Fisher	Roby	(325)
Burnet	Burnet	(512)	Floyd	Floydada	(806)
Caldwell	Lockhart	(512)	Foard	Crowell	(940)
Calhoun	Port Lavaca	(361)	Fort Bend	Richmond	(281)
Callahan	Baird	(325)	Franklin	Mount Vernon	(903)
Cameron	Brownsville	(956)	Freestone	Fairfield	(903)
Camp	Pittsburg	(903)	Frio	Pearsall	(830)
Carson	Panhandle	(806)	Gaines	Seminole	(432)
Cass	Linden	(903)	Galveston	Galveston	(409)
Castro	Dimmitt	(806)	Garza	Post	(806)
Chambers	Anahuac	(409)	Gillespie	Fredericksburg	(830)
Cherokee	Rusk	(903)	Glasscock	Garden City	(432)
Childress	Childress	(940)	Goliad	Goliad	(361)
Clay	Henrietta	(940)	Gonzales	Gonzales	(830)
Cochran	Morton	(806)	Gray	Pampa	(806)
Coke	Robert Lee	(325)	Grayson	Sherman	(903)
Coleman	Coleman	(325)	Gregg	Longview	(903)
Collin	McKinney	(972)	Grimes	Anderson	(936)
Collingsworth	Wellington	(806)	Guadalupe	Seguin	(830)
Colorado	Columbus	(979)	Hale	Plainview	(806)
Comal	New Braunfels	(830)	Hall	Memphis	(806)
Comanche	Comanche	(325)	Hamilton	Hamilton	(254)
Concho	Paint Rock	(325)	Hansford	Spearman	(806)
Cooke	Gainesville	(940)	Hardeman	Quanah	(940)
Coryell	Gatesville	(254)	Hardin	Kountze	(409)
Cottle	Paducah	(806)	Harris	Houston	(713)
Crane	Crane	(432)	Harrison	Marshall	(903)
Crockett	Ozona	(325)	Hartley	Channing	(806)
Crosby	Crosbyton	(806)	Haskell	Haskell	(940)

County	City/Town	Area Code	County	City/Town	Area Code
Hays	San Marcos	(512)	Marion	Jefferson	(903)
Hemphill	Canadian	(806)	Martin	Stanton	(432)
Henderson	Athens	(903)	Mason	Mason	(915)
Hidalgo	Edinburg	(956)	Matagorda	Bay City	(979)
Hill	Hillsboro	(254)	Maverick	Eagle Pass	(830)
Hockley	Levelland	(806)	McCulloch	Brady	(325)
Hood	Granbury	(817)	McLennan	Waco	(817)
Hopkins	Sulphur Springs	(903)	McMullen	Tilden	(361)
Houston	Crockett	(936)	Medina	Hondo	(830)
Howard	Big Spring	(432)	Menard	Menard	(325)
Hudspeth	Sierra Blanca	(915)	Midland	Midland	(432)
Hunt	Greenville	(903)	Milam	Cameron	(254)
Hutchinson	Stinnett	(806)	Mills	Goldthwaite	(325)
Irion	Mertzon	(325)	Mitchell	Colorado City	(325)
Jack	Jacksboro	(940)	Montague	Montague	(940)
Jackson	Edna	(361)	Montgomery	Conroe	(936)
Jasper	Jasper	(409)	Moore	Dumas	(806)
Jeff Davis	Fort Davis	(432)	Morris	Daingerfield	(903)
Jefferson	Beaumont	(409)	Motley	Matador	(806)
Jim Hogg	Hebbronville	(361)	Nacogdoches	Nacogdoches	(936)
Jim Wells	Alice	(361)	Navarro	Corsicana	(903)
Johnson	Cleburne	(817)	Newton	Newton	(409)
Jones	Anson	(325)	Nolan	Sweetwater	(325)
Karnes	Karnes City	(830)	Nueces	Corpus Christi	(361)
Kaufman	Kaufman	(972)	Ochiltree	Perryton	(806)
Kendall	Boerne	(830)	Oldham	Vega	(806)
Kenedy	Sarita	(361)	Orange	Orange	(409)
Kent	Jayton	(806)	Palo Pinto	Palo Pinto	(940)
Kerr	Kerrville	(830)	Panola	Carthage	(903)
Kimble	Junction	(325)	Parker	Weatherford	(817)
King	Guthrie	(806)	Parmer	Farwell	(806)
Kinney	Brackettville	(830)	Pecos	Fort Stockton	(432)
Kleberg	Kingsville	(361)	Polk	Livingston	(936)
Knox	Benjamin	(940)	Potter	Amarillo	(806)
Lamar	Paris	(903)	Presidio	Marfa	(432)
Lamb	Littlefield	(806)	Rains	Emory	(903)
Lampasas	Lampasas	(512)	Randall	Canyon	(806)
La Salle	Cotulla	(830)	Reagan	Big Lake	(325)
Lavaca	Hallettsville	(361)	Real	Leakey	(830)
Lee	Giddings	(979)	Red River	Clarksville	(903)
Leon	Centerville	(903)	Reeves	Pecos	(432)
Liberty	Liberty	(936)	Refugio	Refugio	(361)
Limestone	Groesbeck	(254)	Roberts	Miami	(806)
Lipscomb	Lipscomb	(806)	Robertson	Franklin	(979)
Live Oak	George West	(361)	Rockwall	Rockwall	(972)
Llano	Llano	(325)	Runnels	Ballinger	(325)
Loving	Mentone	(432)	Rusk	Henderson	(903)
Lubbock	Lubbock	(806)	Sabine	Hemphill	(409)
Lynn	Tahoka	(806)	San Augustine	San Augustine	(936)
Madison	Madisonville	(936)	San Jacinto	Coldspring	(936)

County	City/Town	Area Code
San Patricio	Sinton	(361)
San Saba	San Saba	(325)
Schleicher	Eldorado	(325)
Scurry	Snyder	(325)
Shackelford	Albany	(325)
Shelby	Center	(936)
Sherman	Stratford	(806)
Smith	Tyler	(903)
Somervell	Glen Rose	(254)
Starr	Rio Grande City	(956)
Stephens	Breckenridge	(254)
Sterling	Sterling City	(325)
Stonewall	Aspermont	(940)
Sutton	Sonora	(325)
Swisher	Tulia	(806)
Tarrant	Fort Worth	(817)
Taylor	Abilene	(325)
Terrell	Sanderson	(432)
Terry	Brownfield	(806)
Throckmorton	Throckmorton	(940)
Titus	Mount Pleasant	(903)
Tom Green	San Angelo	(325)
Travis	Austin	(512)
Trinity	Groveton	(936)
Tyler	Woodville	(409)
Upshur	Gilmer	(903)
Upton	Rankin	(432)
Uvalde	Uvalde	(830)
Val Verde	Del Rio	(830)
Van Zandt	Canton	(903)
Victoria	Victoria	(361)
Walker	Huntsville	(936)
Waller	Hempstead	(979)
Ward	Monahans	(432)
Washington	Brenham	(979)
Webb	Laredo	(956)
Wharton	Wharton	(979)
Wheeler	Wheeler	(806)
Wichita	Wichita Falls	(940)
Wilbarger	Vernon	(940)
Willacy	Raymondville	(956)
Williamson	Georgetown	(512)
Wilson	Floresville	(830)
Winkler	Kermit	(432)
Wise	Decatur	(940)
Wood	Quitman	(903)
Yoakum	Plains	(806)
Young	Graham	(940)
Zapata	Zapata	(956)
Zavala	Crystal City	(830)

OTHER NOTARIAL OFFICERS

Besides Notaries, the following officials may take acknowledgments and proofs within Texas (CPRC 121.001) and are required to keep a record book of these acts (CPRC 121.012):

1. Clerk of a district court;
2. Judge or clerk of a county court;
3. County tax assessor-collector, or an employee of such, if the document is to be filed in the assessor-collector's office;
4. Employee of a personal bond office, if the document is required or authorized by Art. 17.04, Code of Criminal Procedure.

Commissioners of Deeds

Outside the state, commissioners of deeds may be appointed for two-year terms by the Texas Governor to take acknowledgments and proofs, administer oaths and take depositions that will be used or recorded in the state (GC 406.051–406.055). The oath of a commissioner of deeds is filed with the Texas Secretary of State.

QUICK FACTS

Notary Jurisdiction
Statewide (GC 406.003).

Notary Term Length
Four years (GC 406.002), expiring at midnight on the commission expiration date.

Notary Bond
$10,000, with a solvent surety company authorized to do business in the state (GC 406.010).

State Employees: Effective September 1, 2002, employees and officers of state agencies may be exempted from the Notary bond requirement if the State Office of Risk Management makes other arrangements to protect the public (Labor Code 412.011 and GC 653.002 through 653.005 and 653.012).

Utah

NOTARY SEAL

A Utah Notary Public must affix an impression of an official seal "near the notary's official signature on a notarial certificate." The seal's format must be as follows (UCA 46-1-16):

Kind

Purple-Inked Stamp: It must affix "a sharp, legible, and photographically reproducible ink impression" (UCA 46-1-16[3][c]). Each Notary stamp obtained on or after July 1, 2003, must use purple ink (UCA 46-1-16[2][c]).

Additional Embosser Allowed: "An embossed seal impression that is not photographically reproducible may be used in addition to, but not in place of, the photographically reproducible seal required in this section" (UCA 46-1-16[4]).

Examples

The above typical, actual-size examples of inking and embossing Notary seals are allowed by Utah law. The embossing seal may be used in addition to, but not in place of, the inking seal. Formats other than these may also be permitted.

NOTARY ADMINISTRATION

Office of Lieutenant Governor
Notary Office, Suite 220   1-801-538-1041
Utah State Capitol Complex
P.O. Box 142325
Salt Lake City, UT 84114-2325

Website: http://notary.utah.gov/

NOTARY RULES

UCA – Utah Code Annotated
NPSG – Notary Public Study Guide

Most Notary regulations are in the *Utah Code Annotated*:

a. Title 46, Chapter 1 ("Notaries Public Reform Act");

b. Title 57, Chapters 2 ("Acknowledgments") and 2a ("Recognition of Acknowledgments Act").

Th "Notary Public Study Guide" (2010) created by the Lieutenant Governor's office for use "before and during" the mandatory test for Notary applicants sets forth important rules and guidelines.

According to state officials, this "generic" seal need only contain the Notary's name and the words "Notary Public" and "State of Utah."

Shape/Size

Rectangular, no larger than 1 inch by $2\frac{1}{2}$ inches surrounding the required words and Seal.

Components

1. Notary's name, exactly as on the commission;
2. "Notary Public";
3. "State of Utah";
4. "My commission expires on (commission expiration date)";
5. Commission number, exactly as on Notary's commission (for seals issued on or after July 1, 2008);
6. Facsimile of Great Seal of Utah.

Where to Affix Seal

"The notarial seal shall be affixed in a manner that does not obscure or render illegible any information or signatures contained in the document or in the notarial certificate" (UCA 46-1-16[5]).

It should "be affixed near the Notary's official signature on a notarial certificate" (UCA 46-1-16[3]).

No Seal Needed on Plat Map

No Notary seal need be affixed on an acknowledgment form on a synthetic-surface plat map if: (a) the Notary signs the acknowledgment in permanent ink and (b) the following appear below or immediately adjacent to the Notary's signature: the Notary's full name and commission number exactly as they appear on the commission, the Notary's commission expiration date, and the words, "A Notary Public commissioned in Utah" (UCA 46-1-16[6]).

No Seal Sale Without Commission

A vendor may not provide an inking or embossing Notary seal to a person claiming to be a Notary unless that person presents a copy of the notarial commission, attached to a notarized declaration, for the vendor's inspection (UCA 46-1-17). A vendor who violates this section is guilty of a Class B Misdemeanor.

Security of Seal

The seal "is the exclusive property of the notary public and ... may not be used by any other person" (UCA 46-1-16[2]). "Upon the resignation, revocation, or expiration of a notarial commission, the seal shall be destroyed."

New Seal for New Commission or Name

"A new seal shall be obtained for any new commission or recommission. ... A new seal shall be obtained if the notary changes the notary's name of record at any time during the notary's commission" (UCA 46-1-16[3]). The old seal must be destroyed (UCA 46-1-20).

Notary's Signature

"In completing a notarial act, a notary shall sign on the notarial certificate exactly and only the name indicated on the notary's commission" (UCA 46-1-16[1]).

NOTARY POWERS

Utah Notaries are authorized to perform the following notarial acts (UCA 46-1-6):
1. Take acknowledgments* and proofs**;
2. Administer oaths*** and affirmations**** (UCA 46-1-2[8]);
3. Execute jurats*****;
4. Take affidavits (UCA 78-26-5);
5. Certify photocopies of documents that are neither public records nor publicly recorded (UCA 46-1-2[3]).

* Acknowledgments: "'Acknowledgment' means a notarial act in which a notary certifies that a signer, whose identity is personally known to the notary or proven on the basis of satisfactory evidence, has admitted, in the presence of the notary, to voluntarily signing a document for the document's stated purpose" (UCA 46-1-2[1]).

** Proof in Lieu of Acknowledgment: A real estate conveyance may be executed through a proof by a subscribing witness, who must be either personally known to the Notary or identified on the oath or affirmation of a credible witness who is personally known to the Notary (UCA 57-2-11).

In the event a subscribing witness is dead or cannot be found, there are procedures for a proof through handwriting (UCA 57-2-10[2], 57-2-14 and 57-2-15).

There are also procedures authorizing notarial officers to issue subpoenas requiring the appearance of a subscribing witness, or providing for a proof through handwriting if the witness does not appear (UCA 57-2-16 and 57-2-17).

NOTE: Because proofs of execution by subscribing witness are not generally accepted by Utah county recorders, Utah Notaries are discouraged from performing this type of notarial act on instruments that will be presented for recording within the state.

*** Oath Form: An oath for a judicial proceeding may be in the following form (UCA 78-24-17): "You do solemnly swear that the evidence you shall give in this issue (or matter) pending between _____ and _____ shall be the truth, the whole truth and nothing but the truth, so help you God."

"Whenever the court before which a person is offered as a witness is satisfied that he has a peculiar mode of swearing, connected with or in addition to the usual form, which in his opinion is more solemn or obligatory, the court may in its discretion adopt that mode. If a person who is sworn believes in any other than the Christian religion, he may be sworn according to the peculiar ceremonies of his religion, if there are any" (UCA 78-24-19).

**** Affirmation Form: An affirmation for a judicial proceeding may be in the following form (UCA 78-24-18): "You do solemnly affirm (or declare) that the evidence you shall give in this issue (or matter) pending between _____ and _____ shall be the truth, the whole truth and nothing but the truth, under the pains and penalties of perjury."

***** Jurats: "'Jurat' means a notarial act in which a notary certifies that a signer, whose identity is personally known to the notary or proven on the basis of satisfactory evidence, has made in the notary's presence, a voluntary signature and taken an oath or affirmation vouching for the truthfulness of the signed document" (UCA 46-1-2[5]).

Identifying Document Signers

For both acknowledgments and jurats, the identity of the document signer must be personally known to the Notary or proven on the basis of satisfactory evidence (UCA 46-1-2[1] and [4]).

Personal Knowledge: *Personal knowledge of identity* "means familiarity with an individual resulting from interactions with that individual over a period of time sufficient to eliminate every reasonable doubt that the individual has the identity claimed" (UCA 46-1-2[11]).

Satisfactory Evidence: *Satisfactory evidence of identity* "means identification of an individual based on: (i) valid personal identification with the individual's photograph, signature, and physical description issued by the United States government, any state within the United States, or a foreign government; (ii) a valid passport issued by any nation; or (iii) the oath or affirmation of a credible person who is personally known to the notary and who personally knows the individual" (UCA 46-1-2[12][a]).

"'Satisfactory evidence of identity' does not include: (i) a driving privilege card under Subsection 53-3-207(10); or (ii) another document that is not considered valid for identification" (UCA 46-1-2[12][b]). A driving privilege card "means the evidence of the privilege granted and issued ... to drive a motor vehicle to a person whose privilege was obtained without providing evidence of lawful presence in the United States" (UCA 53-3-102 [13]). "A governmental entity may not accept a driving privilege card as proof of personal identification" (UCA 53-3-207[10]).

Notarization Confirms Willingness

"A notarization provides verification of a document signer's willingness to sign and that the signer is, indeed, the person identified by the signature" (website, "Cautions for Notaries").

NOTARY DON'TS

A Utah Notary may:
1. NOT influence a person to enter into or not enter into a lawful transaction involving a notarial act by the Notary (UCA 46-1-8);
2. NOT endorse or promote any product, service, contest or other offering if the Notary's title or seal is used in the endorsement or promotional statement (UCA 46-1-10);
3. NOT execute a certificate known by the Notary to be "false or materially incomplete," nor perform any official action with intent to deceive or defraud (UCA 46-1-9);
4. NOT refuse to notarize in any lawful transaction for a person who offers the appropriate fee (UCA 46-1-8) — see "Notaries Serve Customers and Non-Customers," below.

Signer Must Be Present

"The signer must always appear before the notary. Title 46 does not allow for variation on this matter. Many fraud cases begin with stories of why the signer cannot personally appear: 'He is too ill to come into the office'; 'The signer is my grandmother and she asked me to get this notarized'; 'You've been my friend for years — you know I wouldn't lie to you.' As convincing as these statements can be, none of them justify notarizing the signature without the signer personally present" (NPSG, "Top Ten Mistakes of Notaries Public").

Notary Serves Customers and Non-Customers

"According to law, a notary may not refuse to enter into a lawful transaction involving a notarial act (i.e., UCA 46-1-8)... Some employers have expressed concern over this law. It is true, employers often carry the burden in finding a balance that complies with the law and, at the same time, allows for reasonable limits to protect the notary's time and liability. Regardless all policies should be carefully created while keeping in mind the notary's main purpose to serve the public — not just the company.

"Reasonable limits may and should be in place to prevent abuse from members of the public who would demand immediate service regardless of the notary's workload and availability" (NPSG, "Top Ten Mistakes of Notaries Public").

Employee Do's and Don'ts: According to the Utah "Notary Public Study Guide," the following are do's and don'ts for employers of Notaries:

1. Employers may determine the hours when a Notary employee is available to serve the public, but only during work hours — not when a Notary is "off duty."

2. Employers may set a policy that a Notary employee only notarize company documents during work hours — but not restrict a Notary's notarial services to the workplace.

3. Employers may limit a Notary employee to serving the public at designated times during work hours, but may not "pick and choose" which documents or customers will be served.

Document Content or Type Not Limiting: According to the Utah Lieutenant Governor's "Notary Public Study Guide," the content or type of document may not in itself be cause for refusing to notarize:

"Many have asked 'can I notarize a will?' The answer should be 'yes,' unless there is some other reason as found in Title 46 that would categorize the transaction as unlawful. Company policies 'override' the law that requires service on lawful transactions.

"What about documents in another language? You should not be reading the document anyway — even if it is in English. However, you must communicate sufficiently with the signer to ensure the signer signed voluntarily."

Notary's Disqualifying Interest

A Notary may not perform a notarization if the Notary has signed or is named in the document that is to be notarized, except in the case of a self-proved will (UCA 75-2-504) or in the case where a lawyer Notary is named in the document but only as representing a signer or another person named in the document (UCA 46-1-7[1]).

Further, a Notary may not notarize when the Notary will directly profit from: (a) a financial transaction in which the Notary is named individually as "a grantor, grantee, mortgagor, mortgagee, trustor, trustee, beneficiary, vendor, vendee, lessor, or lessee" (UCA 46-1-7[2] and [3]).

Foreign-Language Advertising

"Literal translation of the phrase 'Notary Public' into any language other than English is prohibited if the literal translation implies that the notary is a licensed attorney ... '(L)iteral translation' means the translation of a word or phrase without regard to the true meaning of the word or phrase in the language that is being translated" (46-1-11[2][c]).

A nonattorney Notary who advertises notarial services in any language other than English must include in the ad a notice that the Notary is not an attorney, as follows verbatim: "I am not an attorney licensed to practice law in Utah and may not give legal advice about immigration or any other legal matter or accept fees for legal advice." The notice must also include the maximum fees that Notaries may charge under UCA 46-1-12. The notice must be both in English and the language of the ad and "in letters of a conspicuous size." A radio or television ad may be modified but must include substantially the same message (UCA 46-1-11[2]).

NOTARY SIGNING AGENTS

In the past, the Utah Department of Insurance had required any Notary or Notary Signing Agent who notarized real estate title and escrow settlement documents to be licensed by the Department as a title escrow producer.

In July of 2006, the Department of Insurance changed its policy to allow Notaries who are merely obtaining signatures and notarizing those signatures on settlement documents to be exempted from the need for a title escrow producer insurance license. However, in a July 13, 2006, letter to the Utah Notary Public and Authentications Office, the Department emphasized that limitations still remained in the Notary's role in the settlement process:

"Obtaining and notarizing title and escrow settlement documents may not include explaining the content or purpose of a document being signed or the handling of an escrow settlement monies, or any other duties performed by a title escrow producer. If a notary is asked to do anything other than obtain and notarize signatures on title and escrow settlement documents, a title escrow producer license will be required."

May Not Handle Checks

Subsequent discussions between the National Notary Association and the Utah Department of Insurance have clarified that Notaries who are not licensed title escrow producers may perform courier services to deliver documents, but they may not handle settlement checks. Thus, Notary Signing Agents who accept assignments in Utah will need to inform the contracting companies of these limitations so that other arrangements may be made for the delivery of any settlement checks.

NOTARY FEES

The maximum fees that a Utah Notary may charge for notarial acts are (UCA 46-1-12):
1. Taking an acknowledgment or proof: $5 per signature;
2. Administering an oath or affirmation, without a signature: $5 per person;
3. Executing a jurat: $5 per signature;
4. Certifying a copy: $5 per page certified.

Travel Fees

A Notary may charge a travel fee, not to exceed the approved federal mileage rate, when traveling to perform a notarial act if: (a) the Notary explains to the person requesting the notarial act that the travel fee is separate from the notarial fee allowed by law for an acknowledgment, jurat or other act, and (b) the Notary and the person requesting the notarial act agree upon the travel fee in advance (UCA 46-1-12[2]).

Fees Do Not Apply to Attorneys

A Notary's total fee must not exceed $5 per individual for each set of forms for any services, notarial or non-notarial, relating to a change of that individual's immigration status, but this does not apply to a licensed attorney rendering professional services on immigration matters (UCA 46-1-12[4]).

Fee Schedule Must Be Posted

"A Notary shall display an English-language schedule of fees for notarial acts and may display a non English-language schedule of fees" (UCA 46-1-12[3]).

Employers May Not Compel Added Fee

An employer of a Notary may not require the Notary to charge more than $5 per signature notarized (NPSG, "Top Ten Mistakes of Notaries Public").

NOTARY CERTIFICATES

Utah prescribes the following notarial certificates without excluding the use of other forms:

Acknowledgment by Individual or Representative ('Statutory Short Form') (UCA 57-2a-7):

State of Utah   )
*   SS.*
County of _____)

The foregoing instrument was acknowledged before me this _____ (date) by _____ (person acknowledging, title or representative capacity, if any).

_____
(Signature of Person Taking Acknowledgment)
Title: _____   SEAL
*My commission expires: _____
*Residing at: _____

* (The phrases "My commission expires _____" and "Residing at _____" may be omitted if this information is included in the seal.)

Acknowledgment by Individual Whose Identity Proved by Satisfactory Evidence (NPSG, 'Sample Certificates'):

State of Utah   )
*   SS.*
County of _____)

On this ____ day of _____, in the year 20__, before me, _____ (Notary's name), a Notary Public, personally appeared _____ (signer's name), proved on the basis of satisfactory evidence to be the person(s) whose name(s) is/are subscribed to this instrument, and acknowledged he/she/they executed the same.

Witness my hand and official seal.

SEAL   _____
             Notary Public

Acknowledgment by Attorney in Fact (website, 'Notary Test'):

State of Utah   )
*   SS.*
County of _____)

On this ____ day of _____, 20__, personally appeared before me _____, who being by me duly sworn/affirmed, did say that he/she is the attorney in fact* of _____, and that said instrument was signed on behalf of said _____ and acknowledged to me that he/she as such attorney in fact executed the same.

SEAL   _____
             Notary Public

* (The Notary must require a person signing in the capacity of attorney in fact to present the original power of attorney as satisfactory evidence of authority to sign. The attorney in fact would sign the principal's name on the document and then his or her own signature as attorney in fact.)

Acknowledgment by Corporation (website, 'Notary Test'):

State of Utah   )
*   SS.*
County of _____)

On this ____ day of _____, 20__, personally appeared before me _____, whose identity is personally known to me (or proven on the basis of satisfactory evidence) and who by me duly sworn/affirmed, did say that he/she is the _____ (title of office) of _____ (name of corporation*) and that said document was signed by him/her in behalf of said corporation by authority of its bylaws (or resolution of its board of directors), and said _____ acknowledged to me that said corporation executed the same.

SEAL   _____
             Notary Public

* (In addition to a corporation, this certificate may also be used when a partnership, trust, limited liability company or other entity is represented by an authorized signing officer, agent, partner, trustee, member or other representative. The Notary must require such a signer to present satisfactory evidence of authority and administer an oath or affirmation.)

Acknowledgment by Individual Whose Identity Proved by Credible Witness (website, 'Notary Test'):

State of Utah   )
*   SS.*
County of _____)

On this ____ day of _____, 20__, personally appeared before me _____, satisfactorily proved to me to be the signer of the above document by the oath of _____, who is personally known to me and is a competent and credible witness* for that purpose, by me duly sworn, and he/she acknowledged that he/she executed the same.

SEAL   _____
             Notary Public

* ("A credible witness must be an impartial person who personally knows both the notary and the document signer. This credible witness is a walking, talking ID card that personally vouches for the identity of an unknown document signer without an ID card. The notary must administer an oath to the credible witness attesting to the signer's identity.")

Proof by Subscribing Witness (UCA 57-2-10 through 57-2-13):

State of Utah, County of _____

On this _____ day of _____, 20__, before me personally appeared _____, personally known to me (or satisfactorily proved to me by the oath of _____, a competent and credible witness for that purpose, by me duly sworn) to be the same person whose name is subscribed to the above instrument as a witness thereto, who, being by me duly sworn, deposed and said that he/she resides in _____, county of _____, and state of Utah; that he/she was present and saw _____, personally known to him/her to be the signer of the above instrument as a party thereto, sign and deliver the same, and heard him/her acknowledge that he/she executed the same, and that he/she, the deponent, thereupon signed his/her name as a subscribing witness thereto at the request of said _____.

SEAL   _____
          Notary Public

NOTE: According to state officials in the Lietenant Governor's office, Utah county recorders will not accept notarial certificates for a proof of execution by subscribing witness.

Form of Acknowledgment Certificate

"The form of a certificate of acknowledgment … shall be accepted if:

"(1) the certificate is in a form prescribed by the laws or rules of this state;

"(2) the certificate is in a form prescribed by the laws or regulations applicable in the place where the acknowledgment is taken; or

"(3) the certificate contains the words 'acknowledged before me,' or their substantial equivalent" (UCA 57-2a-6).

Jurat (website, 'Notary Test'):

State of Utah   )
                    SS.
County of _____)

Subscribed and sworn to before me on this _____ day of _____, in the year 20__, by _____.

SEAL   _____
          Notary Public

Copy Certification (website, 'Notary Test'):

State of Utah   )
                    SS.
County of _____)

On this _____ day of _____, in the year 20__, I certify that the preceding or attached document is a true, exact, complete and unaltered photocopy made by me of _____(describe document), presented to me by the document's custodian, _____, and that, to the best of my knowledge, the photocopied document is neither a public record nor a publicly recorded document, certified copies of which are available from an official source other than a Notary.

SEAL   _____
          Notary Public

Certificate Language Must Be Included

"Never just stamp and sign. Make sure the proper language, with all necessary material information, is included in the written description of the notarial act (also called 'certificate')…. The (Notary's) stamp and signature are the 'finishing touches' to a certificate, but they do not stand alone" (NPSG, "Top Ten Mistakes of Notaries Public").

ELECTRONIC NOTARIZATIONS

Uniform Electronic Transactions Act

In 2000, Utah passed its own version of the Uniform Electronic Transactions Act (UCA 46-4-101 through 46-4-503), including the following provisions regarding execution of electronic documents:

"(1) If a law requires a signature or record to be notarized, acknowledged, verified, or made under oath, the requirement is satisfied by following the procedures and requirements of Subsection 46-1-16(7).

"(2) The electronic signature of the person authorized to perform the acts under subsection (1), and all other information required to be included by other applicable law, shall be attached to or logically associated with the signature or record" (UCA 46-4-205).

Notary Seal Imprint Unnecessary: "A notary acknowledgment on an electronic message or document is considered complete without the imprint of the notary's seal if the following information appears electronically within the message:

"(a) the notary's full name and commission number appearing exactly as indicated on the notary's commission; and

"(b) the words 'notary public,' 'state of Utah,' and 'my commission expires on (date)'" (UCA 46-1-16[7]).

Signer's Physical Presence Still Required

"Notarization of an electronic signature requires personal appearance and certification of a voluntary signature just the same as any other signature. Notarization of an electronic signature does NOT mean by phone, fax, email or video conference. For electronic notarization, the signer is in the presence of the notary using a computer instead of pen and paper. The rule of personal appearance is not affected by the definition of "Electronic Signature" (NPSG, "Top Ten Mistakes of Notaries Public").

NOTE: "'Electronic signature' means an electronic sound, symbol, or process attached to or logically associated with a record and executed or adopted by a person with the intent to sign the record" (UCA 46-4-102[8]).

Utah Digital Signature Act Repealed

Effective May 1, 2006, legislation repealed the Utah Digital Signature Act, one of the nation's first comprehensive state laws implementing public key technology (PKI). Also repealed were certain provisions in the state's Notary code that authorized a Notary's performance of an acknowledgment without the presence of the acknowledger, provided there was a reliable audio-visual link between Notary and acknowledger; these provisions never proved workable.

The Utah Digital Signature Act was undermined by enactment in 2000 of Utah's Uniform Electronic Transactions Act and of the federal Electronic Signatures in Global and National Commerce Act ("E-Sign"), also in 2000. The technological neutrality stance of these two laws undercut the Digital Signature Act's commitment to PKI technology.

NOTARY RECORDS

"A notary may keep, maintain, and protect as a public record, and provide for lawful inspection a chronological, permanently bound official journal of notarial acts, containing numbered pages" (UCA 46-1-13).

Journal Entries Specifed

"For every notarial act, the notary may record the following information in the journal at the time of notarization:

"(a) the date and time of day of the notarial act;

"(b) the type of notarial act;

"(c) a description of the document or proceeding;

"(d) the signature and printed name and address of each person for whom a notarial act is performed;

"(e) the evidence of identity of each person for whom a notarial act is performed, in the form of:

"(i) a statement that the person is 'personally known' to the notary;

"(ii) a description of the identification document, its issuing agency, its serial or identification number, and its date of issuance or expiration; or

"(iii) the signature and printed name and address of a credible witness swearing or affirming to the person's identity; and

"(f) the fee, if any, charged for the notarial act" (UCA 46-1-14).

The law specifies that the Notary may also record in the journal the circumstances in refusing to perform or complete a notarial act.

Journal Must be Safeguarded

"If a notary maintains a journal, the notary shall:

"(1) safeguard the journal and all other notarial records as valuable public documents and may not destroy the documents; and

"(2) keep the journal in the exclusive custody of the notary, not to be used by any other notary or surrendered to an employer upon termination of employment" (UCA 46-1-15).

AUTHENTICATION OF NOTARIAL ACTS

Lieutenant Governor

Certificates authenticating the acts of Utah

Notaries are issued by the office of Utah's Lieutenant Governor.

Fee: $15 per document for an apostille or other certificate authenticating a notarial act; payable to "State of Utah."

Same-day (2 hours) service or shipping is $65 per document. Next-business-day service (24 hours) is $40 per document.

Address:
Utah State Capitol Complex
Office of Lieutenant Governor
Notary Office, Suite 220
(350 N. State Street)
Salt Lake City, UT 84114

Telephone: 1-801-538-1041

Procedure: Mail or present in person the original notarized document and the appropriate fee. Enclose a "cover sheet" or letter ("Document Authentication or Apostille Request Form" available online) indicating the country of intended use and full name, address and a daytime telephone number in case clarification is needed; also provide a stamped, addressed envelope. See the website for further information — http://www.authetications.utah.gov/. Apart from the expedited service (same-day or next-day), processing normally takes three to five business days. Walk-ins should allow two hours for processing. Persons requesting expedited service by mail should contact the Notary Office on the day the document is expected to arrive; failure to confirm the document's arrival may delay the response.

Proper Notarization Necessary: The following statute section took effect May 12, 2010 (UCA 67-1a-13):

"The lieutenant governor may not certify a signature of a notary or county recorder on: (1) a document that is not properly notarized, if notarization is required; or (2) a document regarding: (a) allegiance to a government or jurisidiction; (b) sovereignty; (c) in itinere status or world service authority; or (d) a claim similar to a claim listed in Subsections (2) (a) through (c)."

Above, subparagraph (2) addresses the spate of spurious documents that have been generated in recent years by the so-called sovereign citizen movement.

Handling of Notarized Documents: The Utah Lieutenant Governor's "Authentications" webpages also contain instructions on the pre-authentication handling of these types of notarized document: powers of attorney, survival certificates, certificates of free sale, Utah Department of Agriculture forms, county/city police forms, medical letters, photos, employment letters, FBI fingerprint cards, copy certifications, I-171H forms, passport photos, professional licenses, corporation documents, and private school documents.

COMMISSIONING AND ADMINISTRATION

The Lieutenant Governor commissions, regulates and maintains records on the state's Notaries (UCA 46-1-3).

Applying for Commission

Qualifications: An applicant for appointment as a Utah Notary must: (a) be at least 18 years old, (b) be a resident of Utah for at least 30 days preceding appointment and maintain residency in Utah thereafter, (c) if not a Utah resident, have permanent resident status under Section 245 of the Immigration and Nationality Act, and (d) be able to read, write, speak and understand English.

Test Required: To take the online Notary test, applicants must first create a Utah.gov account and log in with a username and password. "The notary test has 35 questions totaling 65 points. A passing score is 61 or higher. Ten questions are heavily weighted (4 points each) to ensure a basic understanding of notary law. You will fail the test if you miss more than one of the weighted questions, so you will want to become familiar with the Top Ten Mistakes of Notaries Public (in the "Notary Public Study Guide"). All other questions on the test are 1 point each…. While each test will have the same 10 fundamental (4-point) questions, the remaining 25 1-point questions are pulled randomly from sections in the bank of questions" (website, "Notary Test").

The test is open-book and not timed. However, if a test-taker's browser "times out" (i.e., sits idle too long), progress will be lost and the test taker will have to start over.

Both the $30 testing fee and the $45 application fee are paid together by credit card at the end of the online test. Once the credit card payment is processed, the test is automatically submitted. Results are immediate. Applicants who want a record, may print out and save their answers. Once the applicant logs out or leaves the page displaying the questions or answers, all will be lost except for the score, which will be saved in the database. If the test is passed, an application may be printed out. See website, "Process."

Application: Upon passage of the online test, the applicant must obtain a $5,000 surety bond and submit it along with the completed application. The application requires endorsement by two permanent Utah residents from different households who are over the age of 18. The Notary bond must be signed and the oath of office signed and notarized prior to the application package's submission to the Lieutenant Governor. Applicants who are state employees require a "risk bond" that is executed by the state Office of Risk Management.

Upon commissioning, the new Notary will be sent a "Certificate of Authority of Notary Public," a copy of which must be presented to a seal manufacturer before a seal of office may be made. The original Certificate must be signed by the Notary in the presence of another Notary.

The process for "renewing" a Notary commission is essentially the same as for obtaining an initial commission, including testing.

Non-Residents: Non-residents of Utah do not qualify for a commission in the state. In order to qualify, an applicant must be a resident of Utah for at least 30 days preceding appointment.

Changes of Status

If Notary Moves or Changes Name: Notaries who move or change their name during their four-year commission term must notify the Lieutenant Governor's office within 30 days, including a copy of any official name change documents (UCA 46-1-20). For a name change, they must obtain a bond rider from the surety company and forward it to the state with a $5 fee, along with the original "Certificate of Authority of Notary Public." They must also obtain a new seal bearing the new name and destroy the old one. An address change, which requires no fee or bond rider, may be communicated by mail, email or fax.

COUNTY CLERKS

In Utah, county clerks have no administrative involvement with Notaries.

OTHER NOTARIAL OFFICERS

Judge, Clerk or Recorder

Besides Notaries Public, the following officers have power to take acknowledgments and proofs: a judge or a clerk of a court having a seal and a county clerk or recorder (UCA 57-2a-3).

No More Commissioners of Deeds

In 2001, the Utah Legislature repealed all statutory provisions relating to the office of commissioner of deeds.

QUICK FACTS

Notary Jurisdiction
Statewide (UCA 46-1-3[4]).

Notary Term Length
Four years (UCA 46-1-3[4]), expiring at midnight on the commission expiration date. The commissions of Notaries employed by a Utah state office or agency are cancelled upon termination of employment.

Notary Bond
$5,000, with a licensed surety (UCA 46-1-4). For Notaries employed by a state office or agency, the bond may be executed by the state Office of Risk Management.

Vermont

NOTARY SEAL

"Vermont law does not require the use of a notary seal. This requirement was repealed by the VT legislature in 1984 (Act #194, 1983 Adj. Sess.)" (website, "Frequently Asked Questions").

Acknowledgments, Oaths Do Not Need Seals

"Deeds and other conveyances of lands, or of an estate or interest therein, shall be signed by the party granting the same and acknowledged by the grantor ... and recorded at length in the clerk's office of the town in which such lands lie. Such acknowledgment before a notary public shall be valid without an official seal being affixed to his or her signature" (27 VSA 341[a]).

"(A) notary public need not affix his official seal to a certificate of an oath administered by him" (12 VSA 5854).

Examples

The above are typical, actual size examples of optional Notary seals used in Vermont. Formats other than these may also be seen.

NOTARY ADMINISTRATION

While Vermont Notaries are appointed by county superior court assistant judges, it is the office of the Vermont Secretary of State that maintains a centralized record of all Notary appointments in the state:

Office of Secretary of State
Vermont State Archives &
   Records Admin.   1-802-828-3287
1078 U.S. Rte. 2, Middlesex
Montpelier, VT 05633-7701

Website: http://vermont-archives.org/notary/

NOTARY RULES

VSA — *Vermont Statutes Annotated*
GNP — *Short Guide for Vermont Notaries Public*

Vermont's statutes set relatively few requirements for Notaries. Most Notary rules are in the Vermont Statutes Annotated, particularly:

a. Title 24, Chapter 5, Subchapter 9 "Notaries Public";

b. Title 27, Chapter 5, "Conveyance of Real Estate."

Other guidelines for Notaries are in the "Short Guide for Vermont Notaries Public," issued by the Secretary of State in printed form and available on the Web site.

Seal Use on Documents Sent Out of State

"Some states require the use of the notary seal and documents destined for those states may be rejected if a seal is not used. However, documents remaining in Vermont do not require a seal for recording" (website, "Frequently Asked Questions").

Embosser Customary

A circular embosser is the type of optional

Notary seal most often seen, though inked stamps are not prohibited.

NOTARY POWERS

Vermont Notaries are authorized to perform the following notarial acts (24 VSA 445):
1. Take acknowledgments*;
2. Administer oaths** and affirmations (12 VSA 5852 and 5854);
3. Take affidavits (12 VSA 5854) and depositions*** (Vermont Rules of Civil Procedure 28[a]);
4. Certify true copies**** (24 VSA 445);
5. Issue protests***** (9A VSA 3-509);
6. Issue subpoenas****** (VRCP 45[a]).

* Acknowledgments: "Acknowledgment means to admit, declare, testify, avow, confess or own as geniune. Notaries as notaries do not acknowledge; they take acknowledgments, meaning that they certify that an individual has acknowledged that an act of signing a document is his or her free act and deed" (website, "Responsibilities of a Notary Public").

"Any document may be acknowledged, but many do not require acknowledgment. Among these are wills, which are attested to by three or more credible witnesses in the presence of the testator and of each other. 14 VSA 5. Similarly, corporate charters are not required to be acknowledged under Vermont law" (GNP).

** Oaths And Affirmations: "(I)n the administration of an oath, the word 'swear' may be omitted, and the word 'affirm' substituted, when the person to whom the obligation is administered is religiously scrupulous of swearing, or taking an oath in the prescribed form; and, in such case, the words 'so help you God' may be omitted, and the words 'under the pains and penalties of perjury' substituted; and a person so affirming shall be considered, for every legal purpose or privilege, qualification or liability, as having been duly sworn" (12 VSA 5851)....

"A notary may also administer the voter's oath to applicants to a town checklist. The notary administers the oath, which appears on the voter application form, and after the applicant signs, the notary subscribes his or her name and title on the application. It is the applicant's duty to deliver the completed application to the town clerk. 17 VSA 2124.

"There is no requirement in Vermont that a Bible be used in the administration of oaths or affirmations, and no legal prohibition against administration on a Sunday. Asking an individual to raise his or her right hand is also not technically required by law, but the practice is so ingrained in tradition that is is advisable.

"A notary may examine a person to see if he or she comprehends the meaning of the oath or affirmation, and may decline to administer if not satisfied.

"Oaths and affirmations may not be administered over the telephone or by proxy. It is good practice to keep a record of all oaths and affirmations administered, as well as information on the date, time and place of these official acts, for future reference" (GNP).

In addition: "State law permits notaries to administer oaths and affirmations of office. 12 VSA 5851. A notary may administer an oath or affirmation to any state or local officer. Local offices requiring oaths or affirmations include justices of the peace, listers, grand jurors and fence viewers. 24 VSA 831; 4 VSA 491. Copies of these oaths or affirmations should be filed, with the signature of the officer and the notary, in the town clerk's office" (GNP).

*** Affidavits and Depositions: "Notarization of affidavits and depositions is within the authority of notaries public in Vermont, but these duties are more likely to be handled by notaries who are also attorneys, or paralegals or those who have specialized training" (GNP).

"An affidavit is a sworn or affirmed written statement or declaration of facts made voluntarily by an individual (affiant). The oath or affirmation that confirms the truth of an affidavit may be taken before a notary public in Vermont. 12 VSA 5854" (GNP).

The oath required of a deponent is: "You solemnly swear (or affirm) that the evidence you shall give, relative to the cause now under consideration, shall be the whole truth and nothing but the truth, (if an oath) so help you God (if an affirmation) under the pains and penalties of perjury" (GNP).

In addition: "The Rules of Civil Procedure (Rule 30[f]) require that the notary certify on the deposition that the witness was duly sworn by him or her, and that the deposition is a true record of the testimony given by the witness. Then, unless the court orders something else to be done, the notary should securely seal the deposition in an envelope indorsed with the title of the action and marked 'Deposition of (name of witness here)' and promptly file it with the court or send it by registered or certified mail to the clerk of that court" (GNP).

**** Certified Copies: "A notary may certify that a copy of an original document is a true copy. 24 VSA 445. This applies to any document of a personal nature. It does not apply to vital records, such as birth, marriage, death or divorce records" (GNP).

"Can I certify a copy of my friend's birth certificate as a true copy? — No, you may not. Certified copies of vital records (birth, marriage and death) may be obtained only from the custodian of those records (website, "Frequently Asked Questions").

"Certified copies of vital records (birth, marriage and death) may be obtained only from the custodian of those records. In Vermont, the custodian would be the town or city clerk where the person was born, married or died. Certified copies may also be issued from the VT Department of Health (last five years only) and the Vital Records section of the Vermont State Archives and Records Administration" (website, "Apostilles/Authentication").

***** Protests: "(Protests are) rarely used today, and then almost exclusively in the case of foreign drafts.

"Under Vermont law, a protest must identify the instrument and certify either that due presentment had been made or the reason why it is excused and that the instrument has been dishonored by nonacceptance or nonpayment. It may also certify that notice of dishonor has been given to all parties or to specified parties. 9A VSA 3-509.

"Again, notaries who are unfamiliar with protests should proceed with extreme caution into this field" (GNP).

****** Issuance Of Subpoenas By Notaries: Under the Vermont Rules of Civil Procedure, a Notary is allowed to issue subpoenas for attendance of witnesses, production of documentary evidence and for taking depositions (VRCP 45[a]).

Identifying Document Signers

"If you don't know the person to be who he or she claims to be, you have three choices. You may refuse to act. You may rely on a credible witness who is personally known to you. Or, to be most prudent, you can insist that a credible witness personally known to you takes and signs a written oath, administered by you as a notary, that he or she personally knows the signer .... This oath could be satisfied by the following language: 'I (the witness) do solemnly swear (or affirm) that I know this person (the signer) to be (place signer's name here).' You should then complete a jurat following this oath ..." (GNP).

Proof Only before Judge

"When a grantor or lessor dies or leaves the state without acknowledging his deed, the execution thereof may be proved by the testimony of a subscribing witness thereto before a justice of the supreme court, a superior judge or a judge of the superior court. If all the subscribing witnesses to such deed are dead or out of the state, the same may be proved before the supreme or superior court by proving the handwriting of the grantor or lessor and of a subscribing witness or adducing other evidence to the satisfaction of such court. Such evidence entered in such deed or annexed thereto shall be equivalent to the grantor's or lessor's acknowledgment thereof" (27 VSA 371).

In addition, there are procedures for a proof of execution when the grantor or lessor refuses to acknowledge (27 VSA 372-375).

A curative provision validates instruments that were imperfectly sealed, witnessed or acknowledged if they have been recorded for 15 years (27 VSA 348).

NOTARY DON'TS

Disqualifying Interests

"Although the administration of an oath is a ministerial act, it has been generally held that, whether ministerial or quasijudicial in nature, public policy forbids it to be done by one who has either a financial or a beneficial interest in the proceeding" (*Schirmer v. Myrick*, 111 Vt. 255 [1940]). The court included among its list of disqualifying interests the acknowledgment of a deed by one with a beneficial interest in the conveyance.

Notary Must Be Impartial, Disinterested: "In order for the notary public to ethically perform the duties of office, it is essential that the notary public be an impartial party or 'disinterested' in the act or transaction. Therefore, you may not take your own acknowledgment or administer an oath or affirmation to yourself. You should neither gain nor lose from the result of the transaction. If you are a party to a transaction or have a financial interest in the transaction, you must decline to officiate" (website, "Frequently Asked Questions").

"Avoid raising the issue of a conflict of interest. If you have any doubt about your beneficial or financial interest in a transaction to which you are being asked to exercise notarial powers, decline" (GNP).

Notarizing for Relatives: "We highly recommend you avoid performing notarial services for any relative, by blood or marriage, in order to avoid potential, unforeseen conflicts of interest" (website, "Frequently Asked Questions").

Exception for Corporation: Vermont law allows a Notary who is a duly qualified stockholder, officer or employee of a corporation to take acknowledgment of an instrument to which the corporation is a party (11 VSA 231).

NOTARY SIGNING AGENTS

In regard to the closing of real estate transactions, Vermont is regarded as an "attorney-only" state and Notary Signing Agents and other non-attorneys are not permitted to act by themselves when a loan or other real estate transaction is finalized.

NOTARY FEES

Vermont Notaries are entitled to collect the following fees for notarial acts (32 VSA 1759):
1. Each certificate under seal: 50 cents;
2. Each protest under seal and the notices: $2.00.

No Fee Allowed for Ex Oficio Notary

Ex officio Notaries who are town clerks, state police officers, fish and game wardens, motor vehicle inspectors or justices of the peace may not charge fees for notarial services (32 VSA 1403[b]).

NOTARY CERTIFICATES

Vermont law does not prescribe particular forms for notarial certificates. The Secretary of State cites the following certificates as typical in the official booklet "A Short Guide for Vermont Notaries Public":

Acknowledgment by Individual (GNP):

STATE OF VERMONT   )
COUNTY OF _____)

On this _____ day of _____, 20__, before me personally appeared _____ (name of person acknowledging), to me known to be the person who executed the foregoing instrument, and he/she thereupon duly acknowledged to me that he/she executed the same to be his/her free act and deed.

(NOTARY'S SIGNATURE
AND, IF DESIRED, SEAL)

Jurat for Affidavit (GNP):

STATE OF VERMONT   )
COUNTY OF _____)

(TEXT OF AFFIDAVIT)
(SIGNATURE OF AFFIANT)

Subscribed and sworn to before me this _____ day of _____, 20__.

(NOTARY'S SIGNATURE
AND, IF DESIRED, SEAL)

Copy Certification (GNP):

STATE OF VERMONT   )
COUNTY OF _____)

This will certify that the attached document(s) is/are (a) true copy/copies of _____ (description of document[s] copied, including number of pages).

Certified this _____ day of _____, 20__.

_____ (Notary's Signature)   (SEAL, IF ANY)
Notary Public

ELECTRONIC NOTARIZATIONS

The state of Vermont has not yet adopted statutes or regulations expressly establishing rules, definitions and procedures for electronic notarization.

UETA Recognizes Notary eSignature

Effective January 1, 2004, Vermont adopted the Uniform Electronic Transactions Act (9 VSA Chapter 20), including the provision on notarization and acknowledgment, thereby recognizing the legal validity of electronic signatures used by Notaries (9 VSA 280):

"If a law requires a signature or record to be notarized, acknowledged, verified, or made under oath, the requirement is satisfied if the electronic signature of the person authorized to perform those acts, together with all other information required to be included by other applicable law, is attached to or logically associated with the signature or record" (9 VSA 280).

NOTARY RECORDS

"Keeping a journal of your notarial acts is…not required by Vermont law, as it is in many other states, but it is a good idea. Buy a notebook or journal, and enter the date, names of the parties who sign the documents, the type of document and the time and have the signers sign their names in your book as well, for your greatest protection as a notary" (GNP).

"It is good practice to keep a record of all oaths and affirmations administered, as well as information on the date, time and place of these official acts, for future reference" (GNP).

"(G)ood recordkeeping of notarial acts will always repay the time it takes to note down what you did as a notary on a particular day" (GNP).

AUTHENTICATION OF NOTARIAL ACTS

County Clerks

Locally, an authenticating certificate for a Vermont Notary may be obtained at the office of the county clerk in the county in which the Notary was appointed.

Secretary of State

Authenticating certificates for Notaries, including apostilles, are also issued by the Vermont Secretary of State's office, as are authenticating certificates for county clerks (24 VSA 183).

Fees: $2 per document, covering authentication for a Notary or county clerk, or an apostille; payable to "Vermont Secretary of State."

Address:
Office of Secretary of State
Vermont State Archives & Records
 Administration
1078 U.S. Rte. 2, Middlesex
Montpelier, VT 05633-7701
Attention: Kathy Watters

Telephone: 1-802-828-3287

Procedure: Mail or present in person the original notarized document(s), along with the appropriate fee. Indicate the nation to which the document will be sent. Generally, there is a one-day turnaround.

"Please include a letter or note indicating the country of destination, mailing instructions, if any, and contact information for yourself in the event additional information is needed or we need to contact you …. If you wish us to return your documents via special means such as Federal Express or any other courier service, you must provide a prepaid air bill. Unless otherwise instructed, we will mail documents back to you via first class mail" (website, "Apostilles/Authentication").

"Should you have a deed or like instrument that requires multiple signatures, please obtain certified copies of the original so that we can authenticate that notary's signature" (website, "Apostilles/Authentication").

COMMISSIONING AND ADMINISTRATION

While Vermont Notaries are appointed by assistant judges of the 14 county superior courts, "(t)he secretary of state's office is the only location in the state where all Vermont notary public certifications may be found" (GNP).

"Complaints against Vermont notaries public must be referred to the appointing judges of the Superior Court. The Secretary of State has no jurisdiction or disciplinary authority over notaries" (website, "Frequently Asked Questions").

"A notary public takes office on the day the certificate of appointment is recorded in the office of the county clerk and serves until 10 days after the expiration of the term of office of the judges of the Superior Court (24 VSA 441). "Although rarely exercised, there is presumably an inherent right within the office of the judges of the Superior Court to revoke this appointment at any time" (GNP).

NOTE: A law that took effect July, 2010, transfered responsibility for appointing Vermont Notaries from judges of the Superior Court to assistant judges, also called "side judges." Under the new law, the judicial roles of elected assistant judges — non-lawyers who historically have joined law-trained judges in hearing cases in Traffic, Probate and Superior Court — were reduced.

Applying for Commission

Qualifications: The only qualification for the Notary Public office set by law is being at the age of majority or older (24 VSA 441[c]). Vermont's Superior Court judges otherwise have discretion to appoint Notaries.

No Course or Test: There is no statewide course of instruction or test for Notary commission applicants. However, for those interested in training, the state does offer four to six seminars annually.

Application: An applicant for a commission as a Vermont Notary Public must apply to the Superior Court of the county in which the applicant resides. Even ex officio officers who derive their notarial powers from a particular governmental position (and lose those powers upon leaving their position) must first apply to the Superior Court and take the oath of office, though the application fee is waived. (See listing of ex officio Notaries at the end of this chapter under "Other Notarial Officers.")

The application form — available online at the Secretary of State's website or at www.vermontjudiciary.org/eforms — is submitted to the local county clerk (who is also a Superior Court clerk) in person or by mail, along with the $30 fee, but the oath of office in the form must first be signed and taken before another Notary or a justice of the peace or other oath-administering officer.

"Immediately after the appointment of a notary public, the county clerk shall send to the secretary of state a certificate of such appointment, on blanks furnished by the secretary, containing the name, signature, and legal residence of the appointee, and the term of office of each notary public. The secretary shall cause such certificates to be bound in suitable volumes and to be indexed. Upon request, the secretary may certify the appointment, qualification, and signature of a notary public on tender of his or her legal fees" (24 VSA 183).

"Reapplication is your responsibility; no notice will be sent to you to remind you of the renewal date" (website, "Term of Office").

Non-Residents: Residents of Massachusetts, New Hampshire and New York who are regularly employed in a place of business in Vermont may become Notaries (24 VSA 441a). They are appointed by the Superior Court assistant judges in the counties of their places of business, and must inform the courts of any change of residence or place of employment.

Online Search: The "Notary Database" may be accessed by entering a name, city or county. Any requested Notary's term of office, address and status (resident or non-resident, active or inactive, ex officio or regular) will be provided. The Database is accessible at: http://vermont-archives.org/notary/notary.asp.

Changes of Status

If Notary Changes Name or Address: There are no Vermont laws or regulations requiring Notaries resident in the state to report a change of name or address. "Resident aliens may become Vermont Notaries. However, they must notify the county clerk of any changes in status or address" (website, "Frequently Asked Questions").

Revocation: "A notary public takes office on the day the certificate of appointment is recorded in the office of the county clerk and serves until ten days after the expiration of the term of office of the judges of the Superior Court. 24 VSA § 441. Although rarely exercised, there is presumably an inherent right within the office of the judges of the Superior Court to revoke the appointment at any time" (website, "Term of Office").

Immigration Status: "Resident aliens may become Vermont notaries. However, they must notify the county clerk of any change in status or address" (website, "Frequently Asked Questions").

COUNTY CLERKS

To contact a Vermont county clerk to obtain an authenticating certificate for a Notary, or to seek assistance in locating a given Notary, telephone 1-802-555-1212 and ask for the number for the clerk of the appropriate counties listed below:

County	City/Town
Addison	Middlebury
Bennington	Bennington
Caledonia	Saint Johnsbury
Chittenden	Burlington
Essex	Guildhall
Franklin	Saint Albans
Grand Isle	North Hero
Lamoille	Hyde Park
Orange	Chelsea
Orleans	Newport
Rutland	Rutland
Washington	Montpelier
Windham	Newfane
Windsor	Woodstock

OTHER NOTARIAL OFFICERS

Ex Officio Notaries

The following officers who apply for notarial powers are designated as "ex officio Notaries," since their notarial powers terminate upon leaving their governmental office: clerk of the supreme court, county clerk, superior court clerk, deputy superior court clerk, town clerk and the clerk's assistants, and justice of the peace (24 VSA 441).

In addition, state police officers, municipal police officers, fish and game wardens, motor vehicle inspectors, liquor inspectors and sheriffs and deputy sheriffs may apply to be ex officio Notaries (32 VSA 1403[b]).

Officers Taking Acknowledgments

Besides Notaries, the following officers may take acknowledgments (27 VSA 341[a]):
1. Town clerk;
2. Master in chancery;
3. County clerk;
4. County judge;
5. Register of probate.

Military Officers

"(U)nder Vermont law, any officer of the armed forces of the United States of the rank of captain or of superior rank is authorized to administer oaths of office, oaths to an affidavit, deposition or other written instrument or an acknowledgment of a deed, lease, conveyance, release or other written instrument.

"In performing these acts, the officer must state his or her rank or title and authority. 12 VSA 5855. No notary appointment is necessary in this case. Notarial acts by these officers are not necessarily limited to services performed for military personnel" (website, "Ex-Officio Notaries Public").

Vermont

QUICK FACTS

Notary Jurisdiction

Statewide (24 VSA 441[a]), in spite of the fact that Notaries are appointed by county judges.

Notarizing outside Vermont: "In 1994, 27 VSA 379 was added to provide that 'Acknowledgments for deeds and other conveyances, and powers of attorney for the conveyance of lands, which are taken out of state before a proper officer of this state, shall be valid as if taken within the state.' This applies only to documents that will be returned to Vermont for recording and is the only case where your notary commission may cross state lines" (GNP).

Notary Term Length

"Vermont notaries are commissioned to four year terms providing they sign up between February 1 and February 10 of the year of expiration (of their previous commissions). All Vermont notary commissions expire on the same date (February 10, every four years). The current commission expires 2/10/15. The next 2/10/2019, and so on" (website, "Frequently Asked Questions").

"Notaries taking office on February 1, 2011 will serve full four-year terms. The law then allows a ten-day grace period before a notary is automatically removed from office by law on February 10, 2015. There is no prohibition against reapplying for further terms, however" (GNP).

Ex officio Notaries lose their notarial powers upon leaving their governmental office.

Notary Bond

Not required by law.

Virginia

NOTARY SEAL

A Virginia Notary Public must affix an official seal on every notarized paper or electronic document (COV 47.1-16[C]).

Notary Must Affix Seal

"Near the notary's official signature on the notarial certificate of a paper document, the notary shall affix a sharp, legible, permanent, and photographically reproducible image of the official seal, or, to an electronic document, the notary shall attach an official electronic seal" (COV 47.1-16[C]).

"Care should be taken not to obscure the signatures or other parts of the document" (HNP).

Kind

Inked Stamp or Embosser: "Compliance with the new legislation can also occur by using an existing embossment-type Notary seal and simply darkening the seal embossment with ink so it

```
JANE Q. DOE
Notary Public
Commonwealth of Virginia
123456
My Commission Expires Jan. 30, 2015
```

Examples

The above are typical, actual-size example of acceptable Notary seals. Formats other than these may also be permitted.

NOTARY ADMINISTRATION

Office of the Secretary of the Commonwealth
Notary Public Division 1-804-786-2441
P.O. Box 1795
Richmond, VA 23218-1795

Website: www.commonwealth.virginia.gov/OfficialDocuments/Notary/notary.cfm

NOTARY RULES

COV — CODE OF VIRGINIA
HNP — A HANDBOOK FOR VIRGINIA NOTARIES PUBLIC

Most Notary rules are in the Code of Virginia:

a. Title 47.1, "Notaries and Out-of-State Commissioners," which may be cited as the "Virginia Notary Act" of 1980;

b. Title 55, "Property and Conveyances," Sections 55-118.1 through 55-118.9, which comprise the "Uniform Recognition of Acknowledgments Act."*

* This is the *Uniform Recognition of Acknowledgments Act* of 1968, adopted virtually intact.

Other guidelines for Notaries are in "A Handbook for Virginia Notaries Public" (Updated July 1, 2011) issued by the Secretary of the Commonwealth and available on the website.

will meet the standard of being 'photographically reproducible'" (Joint statement by Secretary of Commonwealth and National Notary Association, June 13, 2007).

Shape/Size

Not specified.

Components

While on paper documents only the first three components listed below are specifically required in the seal by the Secretary of the Commonwealth (HNP), the fourth and fifth components are also acceptable and widely seen. "Any information included on the notary's seal/stamp must be accurate. The notary cannot strike through or white-out an area to make a change" (HNP).

1. Name of Notary exactly as on commission;
2. "Notary Public";
3. "Commonwealth of Virginia";
4. "My commission expires _____ (date)";
5. Notary registration number*.

* "(T)here is no requirement that the 'registration number' be part of the seal, although it can be under the new law. Your notary registration number must appear on each notarial certificate in order for your notarization to be valid. If you acquire a new seal, we strongly recommend that the notary registration number be part of the new notary seal" (Joint statement by Secretary of Commonwealth and the NNA, June 13, 2007).

IMPORTANT NOTE: For an electronic Notary seal, all five of the components listed above are required — see "Electronic Notarizations" section in the middle of this chapter.

Notary Registration Number Must Appear

If the registration number assigned to the Notary by the state does not appear in the seal, it must appear elsewhere on the notarial certificate. "Registration numbers became an official part of the notarial act on July 1, 2007. Documents notarized before this date were not required to have the notary's registration number" (HNP).

Commission Expiration Date Must Appear

"Upon every writing which is the subject of a notarial act, the notary shall, after his certificate, state the date of the expiration of his commission in substantially the following form: 'My commission expires the _____ day of _____, 20__'" (COV 47.1-16[C]). This information may appear in the Notary seal.

The date of expiration is required and generally appears after the signature of the notary in this form: 'My commission expires, _____, 20___.'" (HNP).

If Seal Missing Prior to July 1, 1995

"When a certificate of acknowledgment was made prior to July 1, 1995, to any instrument in writing required by this chapter to be acknowledged and the notary or other official whether of this or some other state taking same failed to affix his official seal to such certificate of acknowledgment when a seal was necessary, the certificate of acknowledgment shall be as valid for all purposes as if such seal had been affixed, and the deed shall be, and shall since such date have been, notice to all persons as effectually as if such seal had been affixed, provided that such acknowledgment was in other respects sufficient" (COV 55-123).

Certificate Reflects Name Change

A Notary who changes a name is directed by the state to continue using the seal issued in the old name until commission expiration (HNP).

"Any notary ... who shall legally change his name during his term of office as a notary shall, after such change of name, when performing any notarial act, have written or printed in or annexed to each certificate the words: 'I was commissioned notary as _____,' or the equivalent" (COV 47.1-17). The name change must be reported to the Secretary of the Commonwealth. However, an electronic Notary must apply for a new electronic commission in the new name within 90 days.

Notary's Signature

"A notarial act requires the original signature of the notary. Signature stamps and other facsimiles or photocopies do not satisfy this requirement" (HNP).

No Seal Image Needed on e-Document

According to Virginia's Uniform Real Property Electronic Recording Act, "A physical or electronic image of a stamp, impression, or seal is not required to accompany an electronic signature" (COV 55-142.11).

"Virginia law requires a (traditional and electronic) notary to use a stamp or seal on every document they notarize....In the case of an electronic notary, the attached seal must be capable of independent verification. Any subsequent changes or modifications to the electronic document must be evident" (HNP).

Disposition of the Seal

"It is the responsibility of the notary to dispose of or destroy the notary seal once the notary ceases to be a notary" (HNP).

NOTARY POWERS

Virginia Notaries are authorized to perform the following notarial acts (COV 47.1-12 and 55-118.1):
1. Take acknowledgments* and proofs**;
2. Administer oaths and affirmations***;
3. Certify true copies**** of any document other than a document in the custody of a court;
4. Certify affidavits and depositions;
5. Perform verification of fact*****;
6. "(P)erform such other acts as may be specifically permitted by law."

* <u>Acknowledgments</u>: "'Acknowledgment' means a notarial act in which an individual at a single time and place (i) appears in person before the notary and presents a document; (ii) is personally known to the notary or identified by the notary through satisfactory evidence of identity; and (iii) indicates to the notary that the signature on the document was voluntarily affixed by the individual for the purposes stated within the document and, if applicable, that the individual had due authority to sign in a particular representative capacity" (COV 47.1-2).

** <u>Proof by Two Subscribing Witnesses</u>: Though taking proof of execution by subscribing witness is not mentioned as a notarial duty in COV 47.1-12 ("Powers and Duties"), it is mentioned as one of the "acts which the laws and regulations of this State authorize notaries public of this State to perform" in COV 55-118.1 ("'Notarial act' defined ...").

A proof of execution certificate is prescribed by COV 55-113(3) for use by out-of-state commissioners appointed by the Virginia Governor and by notarial officers in other U.S. jurisdictions.

Two subscribing witnesses are specified by COV 55-113(3).

*** <u>Oaths and Affirmations</u>: Virginia Notaries are oath-administering officers who may also administer certain state-required oaths of office (e.g., for elected members of the General Assembly). In addition, Notaries may administer oaths of office to U.S. military personnel on active duty and to civilians deployed by the U.S. Department of Defense (COV 49-3).

"'Affirmation' means a notarial act, or part thereof, that is legally equivalent to an oath and in which an individual at a single time and place (i) appears in person before the notary and presents a document; (ii) is personally known to the notary or identified by the notary through satisfactory evidence of identity; and (iii) makes a vow of truthfulness or fidelity on penalty of perjury" (COV 47.1-2).

**** <u>Certifying Copies</u>: "'Copy certification' means a notarial act in which a notary (i) is presented with a document that is not a public record; (ii) copies or supervises the copying of the document using a photographic or electronic copying process; (iii) compares the document to the copy; and (iv) determines that the copy is accurate and complete" (COV 47.1-2).

"Virginia notaries are not authorized to certify true copies of birth, death, or marriage certificates. Only the Division of Vital Records/Statistics may perform such a certification. Virginia notaries are not authorized to certify true copies of court issued documents. Virginia notaries are also not authorized to perform marriage ceremonies" (HNP).

***** <u>Verification of Fact</u>: 'Verification of fact' means a notarial act in which a notary reviews public or vital records to (i) ascertain or confirm facts regarding a person's identity, identifying attributes, or authorization to access a building, database, document, network, or physical site or (ii) validate an identity credential on which satisfactory evidence of identity may be based" (COV 47.1-2).

"The Commonwealth of Virginia is the first state in the country to authorize the verification of fact as a notarial power. This involves a notary directly accessing public or vital records to confirm or validate a signer's identity credentials or to confirm facts about an individual's identity or authorization. A notary may also access public records to confirm facts about such matters as corporate status, date of birth, or date of marriage" (HNP). This notarial power became effective July 1, 2011.

Identifying Document Signers

"A notary shall exercise reasonable care in the performance of his duties generally. He shall exercise a high degree of care in ascertaining the identity of any person whose identity is the subject of a notarial or electronic notarial act ...Unless such person is personally known by the notary, identity shall be ascertained upon presentation of satisfactory evidence of identity as defined in this title" (COV 47.1-14).

Personal Knowledge of Identity: "'Personal knowledge of identity' or 'personally knows' means familiarity with an individual resulting from interactions with that individual over a period of time sufficient to dispel any reasonable uncertainty that the individual has the identity claimed" (COV 47.1-2).

Satisfactory Evidence of Identity: "'Satisfactory evidence of identity' means identification of an individual based on (i) examination of one or more of the following documents bearing a photographic image of the individual's face and signature: a United States Passport, a certificate of United States citizenship, a certificate of naturalization, an unexpired foreign passport, an alien registration card with photograph, a state issued driver's license or a state issued identification card or a United States military card or (ii) the oath or affirmation of one credible witness unaffected by the document or transaction who is personally known to the notary and who personally knows the individual or of two credible witnesses unaffected by the document or transaction who each personally knows the individual and shows to the notary documentary identification as described in clause (i)" (COV 47.1-2).

Effective July 1, 2012, see the expanded definition of "satisfactory evidence of identity" that accommodates so-called "remote" or "online" notarization, using video conference technology, in the "Electronic Notarizations" section of this chapter, further below.

Credible Witness: "'Credible witness' means an honest, reliable, and impartial person who personally knows an individual appearing before a notary and takes an oath or affirmation from the notary to confirm that individual's identity" (COV 47.1-2).

May Decline to Notarize

"A notary may decline to notarize a document" (COV 47.1-15).

NOTARY DON'TS

Notary Shall Not

A Virginia Notary Public shall (COV 47.1-15):

1. NOT notarize a document if the signer is not in the presence of the Notary at the time of notarization, "unless (i) in the case of an electronic notarization, satisfactory evidence of the identity of the signer is established in accordance with § 47.1-2 or (ii) otherwise authorized by law to do so";
2. NOT use the official Notary title or seal to endorse, promote, denounce or oppose any product, service, contest, candidate or other offering;
3. NOT notarize a signature on a document without notarial certificate wording on the same page as the signature unless the certificate includes the name of each person whose signature is being notarized;
4. NOT affix an official Notary seal or signature on a notarial certificate that is incomplete;
5. NOT perform any official act with the intent to deceive or defraud.

No Assistance in Drafting

"A nonattorney notary shall not assist another person in drafting, completing, selecting, or understanding a document or transaction requiring a notarial act. This section does not preclude a notary who is duly qualified, trained, or experienced in a particular industry or professional field from selecting, drafting, completing, or advising on a document or certificate related to a matter within that industry or field or prevent a notary from adding a notarial certificate or electronic notarial certificate to a paper or electronic document at the direction of a principal or lawful authority" (COV 47.1-15).

Disqualifying Interests

"No notary shall perform any notarial act with respect to any document, writing, or electronic document to which the notary or his spouse is a party, or in which either of them has a direct beneficial interest, or where the notary is a signatory or is named in the document to be notarized. A notary nominated as a fiduciary in a will shall not for that reason alone, be deemed a party to the will or to have a direct beneficial interest therein.

"Any notary who violates the provisions of this section shall be guilty of official misconduct.

"A notarial act performed in violation of this section shall not automatically be void for such reason, but shall be voidable in the discretion of any court of competent jurisdiction upon the motion of any person injured thereby" (COV 47.1-30).

However, acknowledgments taken by an officer prior to July 1, 1995, when the acknowledger is the spouse of the officer, may not necessarily be invalid (COV 55-131).

"Regardless of whether any beneficial or other interests exist, a notary may never take his or her own acknowledgment, oath, affidavit or deposition" (HNP).

Campaign Employee May Not Notarize: "(N)o notary who is a paid employee of a political campaign, including a referendum or petition effort, shall perform a notarial act in regard to petitions for that campaign" (HNP).

May Not Notarize as Beneficiary: "Notaries should not notarize any document when there is any possibility that the contents of the document will benefit them or their spouse. Notaries may notarize wills in which the notary is fiduciary. Notaries must NEVER notarize wills in which they are named beneficiaries" (HNP and COV 47.1-30).

Corporate Notaries: Notaries who are corporate stockholders or officers, or both, may notarize documents for the corporation, provided the Notary has no personal interest or is not signing on the corporation's behalf (COV 55-121).

NOTARY SIGNING AGENTS

Under Virginia's Consumer Real Estate Settlement Protection Act (CRESPA), any person conducting a settlement in a real property transaction, including Notary Signing Agents, must be a licensed title insurance agent for the Commonwealth. According to the Virginia Bureau of Insurance, the handling of settlement funds, including the passing of a check for settlement costs from a borrower to a Notary Signing Agent, requires a title insurance license and an appointment from a title insurance company. Only attorneys, real estate brokers, financial institutions authorized to do business in Virginia under Title 55 or under federal law, or licensed title insurance companies and agents may perform real estate closings (COV 55-525.19).

Requirements for a title insurance license include: a minimum $250,000 of coverage through an errors and omissions or malpractice insurance policy; a minimum $100,000 of coverage through a blanket fidelity bond or employee dishonesty insurance policy; and a surety bond of not less than $200,000.

Since the Virginia Bar Association has expressed no formal opposition to "witness closings," some Notary Signing Agents do manage to operate in the Commonwealth without a title insurance license, but only in transactions that do not require them to handle settlement checks. If closing checks are involved, some signing services even instruct their Signing Agents to give overnight express envelopes to borrowers so that the borrowers themselves may forward a required settlement check without it being "handled" by the Signing Agent.

NOTARY FEES

In notarizing paper documents, the maximum fee allowed for taking and certifying an acknowledgment, administering and certifying an oath, certifying a true copy, or certifying an affidavit or deposition is $5 (COV 47.1-19[A]). The Notary may charge a fee less than $5 for performing a notarial act, or may charge no fee at all.

For other services, a Notary may charge the same as would a circuit court clerk for the same services (COV 47.1-19[B]).

"A notary or other officer returning affidavits or depositions of witnesses and a commissioner returning a report shall state at the foot thereof the fees therefor, to whom charged and, if paid, by whom" (COV 17.1-270).

Fee for Electronic Act

The maximum fee for an electronic notarial act is $25 (COV 47.1-19[B]).

Officers Who May Not Charge

"Any person appointed as a member of an electoral board or a general registrar shall be prohibited from collecting any fee as a notary during the term of such appointment. Any person appointed as an assistant registrar or officer of election shall be prohibited from collecting a fee as a notary for services relating to the administration of elections or the election laws" (COV 47.1-19[C]).

May Not Require Fee Split

"Any employer, as a condition of employment of a person who is a notary, may require the employee to perform notarial acts in the course of or in connection with such employment without charging the fee allowed by law for the performance of such acts .... It shall not be lawful for any employer to require a notary in his employment to surrender to such employer a fee, if charged, or any part thereof" (COV 47.1-20).

Travel Fee

"(A) notary may recover, with the agreement of the person to be charged, any actual and reasonable expense of traveling to a place where a notarial act is to be performed if it is not the usual place in which the notary performs his office" (COV 47.1-19[D]).

NOTARY CERTIFICATES

Virginia has adopted the *Uniform Recognition of Acknowledgments Act*, including the short-form certificates (COV 55-118.6) for:

1. Acknowledgment by individual;
2. Acknowledgment by corporation;
3. Acknowledgment by partnership;
4. Acknowledgment by attorney in fact;
5. Acknowledgment by public officer, trustee or personal representative.

The Notary's commission expiration date must be added to each certificate (COV 47.1-16[C]), as well as the Notary's registration number, if not within the seal.

For the text of the above certificates, see "Uniform Recognition of Acknowledgments Act (1968)," Section 6, in Appendix 3.

Form for Acknowledgment Certificate

"The form of a certificate of acknowledgment used by a person whose authority is recognized under (Uniform Recognition of Acknowledgments Act, Section 1) shall be accepted in this State if:

"1. The certificate is in a form prescribed by the laws or regulations of this State;

"2. The certificate is in a form prescribed by the laws or regulations applicable in the place in which the acknowledgment is taken; or

"3. The certificate contains the words 'acknowledged before me,' or their substantial equivalent" (COV 55-118.4).

Seven Components of Any Certificate

"Every notarial act must contain seven items of TRADITIONAL information:

"1. Notarial statement

"2. The date of the notarial act

"3. The place of the notarial act

"4. The expiration date of the notary's commission

"5. Notary's signature

"6. Notary's registration number

"7. Photographically reproducible notary seal/stamp

"Each of these items is required by law and is extremely important. The notary must be accurate in providing this information" (HNP).

Must Include Date and County or City: "Every notarization shall include the date upon which the notarial act was performed, and the county or city and state in which it was performed (COV 47.1-16[A]).

"Usually, the language of a notarial act contains a place for [the date]. When it does not, the best place to put the date is immediately above the place where the notary will sign" (HNP), using language such as (COV 55-120):

"Given under my hand this _____ day of _____, 20__."

If Certificate Not in Proper Form: "A writing that is not properly notarized in accordance with the laws of the Commonwealth shall not invalidate the underlying document, however, any such writing shall not be in proper form for recordation. All writings admitted to record shall be presumed to be in proper form for recording after having been recorded, and conclusively presumed to be in proper form for recording after having been recorded for a period of three years, except in cases of fraud" (COV 55-106.2).

'Loose' Certificates: "A notary shall not... (n)otarize a signature on a document without notarial certificate wording on the same page as the signature unless the notarial certificate includes the name of each person whose signature is being notarized...Any document notarized prior to July 1, 2008, which does not have the notarial certificate wording on the same page as the signature, but otherwise appears on its face to be properly notarized, shall be deemed validly notarized" (COV 47.1-15).

Virginia

Acknowledgment by Corporation or Representative (COV 55-120):

"When any writing purports to have been signed in behalf or by authority of any person or corporation, or in any representative capacity whatsoever, the certificate of the acknowledgment by the person so signing the writing shall be sufficient for the purposes of this and Sections 55-106, 55-113, 55-114, and 55-115, and for the admission of such writing to record as to the person or corporation on whose behalf it is signed, or as to the representative character of the person so signing the same, as the case may be, without expressing that such acknowledgment was in behalf or by authority of such other person or corporation or was in a representative capacity. In the case of a writing signed in behalf or by authority of any person or corporation or in any representative capacity a certificate to the following effect shall be sufficient" (COV 55-120):

State (or territory or district) of _____, county (or corporation) of _____, to wit:

I, _____, a _____ (here insert the official title of the person certifying the acknowledgment) in and for the State (or territory or district) and county (or corporation) aforesaid, do certify that _____, (here insert the name or names of the persons signing the writing on behalf of the person or corporation, or the name of the person signing the writing in a representative capacity), whose name (or names) is (or are) signed to the writing above, bearing date on the _____ day of _____, 20__, has (or have) acknowledged the same before me in my county (or corporation) aforesaid.
Given under my hand this _____ day of _____, 20__.

(NOTARY'S SIGNATURE, SEAL, REGISTRATION NO. AND COMMISSION EXPIRATION DATE)

Proof of Execution by Two Subscribing Witnesses (COV 55-113[3]):

State (or territory, or district) of _____; county (or corporation) of _____, to wit:

I, _____, clerk (or deputy clerk, or a commissioner in chancery) of the _____ court, (or a notary public) for the county (or corporation) aforesaid, in the State (or territory or district) of _____ (or a commissioner appointed by the Governor of the State of Virginia for said State, or territory, or district of _____), do certify that the execution of the writing above (or hereto annexed) bearing date on the _____ day of _____, 20__, by _____ (name of signer or signers), whose name (or names) is (or are) signed thereto, was proved before me in my county (or corporation, or State) aforesaid, by the evidence on oath of _____ (names of two subscribing witnesses), subscribing witnesses to said writing.
Given under my hand this _____ day of _____, 20__.

(NOTARY'S SIGNATURE, SEAL, REGISTRATION NO. AND COMMISSION EXPIRATION DATE)

Acknowledgment before U.S. Military Officer (COV 55-114.1 and 55-115):

Anywhere in the world, commissioned U.S. military officers may take the acknowledgment of military personnel on active duty or their consorts using a certificate substantially as follows:

In the Army (or Navy, etc.) of the United States. I, _____, a commissioned officer of the Army (or Navy, Marine Corps, Coast Guard or other branch of service) of the United States with the rank of lieutenant (or ensign or other appropriate rank) whose home address is _____, do certify that _____ (name of signer or signers), whose name (or names) is (or are) signed to the writing above (or hereby annexed), bearing date on the _____ day of _____, 20__, and who, or whose consort, is a private (corporal, seaman, captain or other grade or rank) in the Army (or Navy, etc.) of the United States, and whose home address is _____, has (or have) acknowledged the same before me.
Given under my hand this _____ day of _____, 20__.

(OFFICER'S SIGNATURE AND COMMISSION NUMBER)

Jurat (HNP):

*City/County of _____
Commonwealth of Virginia*

The foregoing instrument was subscribed and sworn before me this ____ day of _____, 20__, by _____ (name of affiant).

(NOTARY'S SIGNATURE, SEAL, REGISTRATION NO. AND COMMISSION EXPIRATION DATE)

Copy Certification (HNP):

*County/City of _____
Commonwealth of Virginia*

I certify this to be a complete, full, true and exact reproduction of the original document. Certified this ____ day of _____, 20__.

(NOTARY'S SIGNATURE, SEAL, REGISTRATION NO. AND COMMISSION EXPIRATION DATE)

ELECTRONIC NOTARIZATIONS

Originally effective July 1, 2008, legislation was enacted by the Virginia General Assembly which set statutory rules for electronic notarization (House Bill 2058, signed into law as Chapter 269), while at the same time making across-the-board revisions, effective July 1, 2007, to the rules for notarizing paper documents. However, the Virginia Governor cancelled the effective date of July 1, 2008, and indefinitely postponed implementation of the electronic notarization provisions, based on concerns of the Attorney General and the Virginia Information Technology Authority that the lack of pertinent technical standards in place would make eNotarization inherently prone to fraud. The Governor asked the General Assembly to provide a remedy.

In response, the General Assembly enacted Virginia Senate Bill 833, effective March 16, 2009, authorizing the Secretary of the Commonwealth to develop standards for electronic notarization in consultation with the Virginia Information Technology Authority. The creation and maintenance of these electronic notarization standards are exempted from the Administrative Process Act (COV 47.1-6.1).

As of the publication of this *Manual*, the signer of an electronic document must be in the physical presence of the Notary for any electronic notarial act. On July 1, 2012, however, Virginia laws authorizing so-called "remote, online" eNotarization through video-conferencing take effect. The exact rules for this process are still under development. See "Remote, Online eNotarization," below.

Electronic Notarization Defined

"Electronic notarization is a process whereby a notary affixes an electronic notary signature and seal information to an electronic document (such as a PDF or Word document). Once affixed to the electronic document, the document is rendered tamper evident such that unauthorized attempts to alter the document will be evident to relying parties. The Electronic Notary also must keep an electronic register of each act performed. … While the signer must still appear personally before an Electronic Notary, beginning July 1, 2012, an approved Virginia Electronic Notary may perform acts online using audio-video conference technology" (website, "Frequently Asked Questions about Becoming a Virginia Electronic Notary").

Types of eNotarization: The following types of notarial acts may be performed electronically: acknowledgments, oaths and affirmations (e.g., jurats), certification of affidavits or depositions, certification of copies, and verifications of fact (website, "Frequently Asked Questions…").

"'Verification of fact' means a notarial act in which a notary reviews public or vital records to (i) ascertain or confirm facts regarding a person's identity, identifying attributes, or authorization to access a building, database, document, network, or physical site or (ii) validate an identity credential on which satisfactory evidence of identity may be based" (COV 47.1-2).

Pertinent Other Definitions

Electronic Notary Public: "'Electronic notary public' or 'electronic notary' means a notary public who has been commissioned by the Secretary of the Commonwealth with the capability of performing electronic notarial acts under § 47.1-7 and has been sworn in by the clerk of the circuit court under § 47.1-9" (COV 47.1-2).

Electronic Signature: "'Electronic signature' means an electronic sound, symbol, or process attached to or logically associated with an electronic document and executed or adopted by a person with the intent to sign the document" (COV 47.1-2).

Electronic Notary Seal: "'Electronic notary seal' or 'electronic seal' means information within a notarized electronic document that contains the notary's name, jurisdiction and commission expiration date and generally corresponds to data in notary seals used on paper documents" (COV 47.1-2). "The notary's electronic seal is simply text that appears on an electronic document and that must include, at minimum, the notary's name as it appears on his commission, the notary's jurisdiction (i.e., the Commonwealth of Virginia), the notary's registration number, and the notary's commission expiration date . … The notary's electronic signature and seal must be independently verifiable — such that relying parties can determine the validity of the signature and seal independent of the notary – and must be tamper evident such that subsequent and unauthorized changes or modifications to the electronic document will be evident to relying parties through visual examination of the electronic document." (website, "Frequently Asked Questions about Becoming a Virginia Electronic Notary").

Electronic Notarial Certificate: "'Electronic notarial certificate' means the portion of a notarized electronic document that is completed by the notary public, bears the notary public's signature, title, commission expiration date, and other required information concerning the date and place of the electronic notarization, and states the facts attested to or certified by the notary public in a particular notarization" (COV 47.1-2).

Remote, Online eNotarization

"Effective July 1, 2012, the Commonwealth of Virginia (becomes) the first state to authorize a principal signer to be in a remote location and have a document notarized electronically. Remote electronic notarization incorporates strict federal standards for determining the identity of the signer and requires the notary to keep a record of the video conference for each notarial act, which is not required in paper notarizations" (HNP).

It should be kept in mind that the above described law permits but does not require Virginia Notaries to perform remote online notarizations. "A Notary may decline to notarize a document" (COV 47.1-15).

Video-Audio Conference Technology Used: "In the case of an electronic notarization, 'satisfactory evidence of identity' may be based on video and audio conference technology, in accordance with the standards for electronic video and audio communications set out in subdivisions B 1, B 2, and B 3 of § 19.2-3.1, that permits the notary to communicate with and identify the principal at the time of the notarial act, provided that such identification is confirmed by (a) personal knowledge, (b) an antecedent in-person identity proofing process in accordance with the specifications of the Federal Bridge Certification Authority, or (c) a valid digital certificate accessed by biometric data or by use of an interoperable Personal Identity Verification card that is designed, issued, and managed in accordance with the specifications published by the National Institute of Standards and Technology in Federal Information Processing Standards Publication 201-1, 'Personal Identity Verification (PIV) of Federal Employees and Contractors,' and supplements thereto or revisions thereof, including the specifications published by the Federal Chief Information Officers Council in "Personal Identity Verification Interoperability for Non-Federal Issuers" (COV 47.1-2).

"The two-way live teleconferencing capability must meet the following performance criteria for establishing personal appearance:
"1) The persons communicating must simultaneously see and speak to one another;
"2) The signal transmission must be live, real time; and,
"3) The signal transmission must be secure from interception through lawful means by anyone other than the persons communicating" (HNP).

Antecedent Identity Proofing: One of the three identification options for online notarization mentioned above is "(r)eliance on prior in-person identity proofing by a third party such as an employer, a law firm, or a bank. Otherwise known as antecedent proofing, this security standard relies upon a prior trust relationship having been created between the signer and a third party" (HNP).

Jurisdiction Defined for eNotary

"All electronic notarial acts performed by Virginia electronic notaries are deemed to have been performed within the Commonwealth of Virginia and are governed by Virginia law. This reflects the reality that electronic documents may not be physically stored in Virginia. In fact, the network-based digital economy has no geographic boundaries and is, therefore, borderless. Thus, regardless of the physical location of the electronic document, Virginia law governs the electronic notarial act.

"Virginia electronic notaries also have limited extraterritorial powers. An electronic notary public may perform any authorized notarial act outside of the Commonwealth for any writing intended to be used in the Commonwealth of Virginia or by the United States government. Please note the remote notarial act is not extraterritorial because it is deemed to have been performed within the Commonwealth of Virginia at the place where the electronic notary is located" (HNP).

Becoming an Electronic Notary

In order to become an Electronic Notary, the applicant must first be a commissioned Virginia Notary Public. "Prior to submitting an electronic notary application, the applicant must purchase an electronic seal from an electronic notary seal provider. The electronic seal is a required item on the electronic notary application" (HNP).

"Federal employees authorized to perform notarial acts pursuant to federal laws and who would like to perform electronic notarizations in accordance with Virginia law are not required to become commissioned electronic notaries in Virginia" (website, "Electronic Notary Application Instructions").

Application Form: "A. An applicant shall submit a registration form ("Electronic Notary Application")established by the Secretary for registering and being commissioned as an electronic notary public, which shall include:

"1. The applicant's full legal and official notary names;

"2. A general description of the technology or technologies the registrant will use to create an electronic signature in performing official acts;

"3. Certification of compliance to the Secretary of the Commonwealth with electronic notary standards developed in accordance with Section 47.1-6.1; and

"4. The electronic mail address of the registrant.

"B. The registration form shall (i) be signed by the applicant using the electronic signature described in the form; (ii) include any decrypting instructions, codes, keys, or software that allow the registration to be read; and (iii) be transmitted electronically to the Secretary.

"C. Nothing herein shall be construed to prevent an electronic notary from using updated technology or technologies during the term of the commission; however, the electronic notary shall notify the Secretary electronically within 90 days of installation or use of such updated technology or technologies and provide a brief description thereof" (COV 47.1-7).

No Additional Education: "There is no additional notary education required to become an electronic notary. However, the Secretary of the Commonwealth strongly suggests that you read and understand the Handbook for Virginia Notaries Public…" (website, "Frequently Asked Questions…").

Fee for eNotary Commission: The fee for issuing a commission to an Electronic Notary public is $35 (COV 2.2-409). In addition, a "technology fee" of $10 will be charged, for a total fee of $45. The fee is to be paid electronically and emailed as an attachment to the "Electronic Notary Application" (website, "Electronic Notary Application Instructions").

Receive Commission from Court Clerk: As with recipients of regular Notary commissions, a person appointed as an Electronic Notary must appear before the circuit court clerk within 60 days to take the oath of office and receive the new commission (COV 47.1-9).

Term of Electronic Commission: "The electronic notary commission will expire on the same date the notary's regular commission expires. The electronic notary commission will need to be renewed at the same time the notary commission is renewed" (website, "Frequently Asked Questions…").

Electronic Record and Backup to Be Kept

"A notary performing electronic notarial acts shall keep, maintain, protect, and provide for lawful inspection an electronic record of notarial acts that contains at least the following for each notarial act performed: (i) the date and time of the day of the notarial act; (ii) the type of notarial act; (iii) the type, title, or description of the document or proceeding; (iv) the printed name and address of each principal; (v) the evidence of identity of each principal in the form of either a statement that the person is personally known to the notary, a notation of the type of identification document, which may be a copy of the driver's license or other photographic image of the individual's face, or the printed name and address of each credible witness swearing or affirming to the person's identity, and, for credible witnesses who are not personally known to the notary or electronic notary, a description of the type of identification documents relied on by the notary; and (vi) the fee, if any, charged for the notarial act. If video and audio conference technology authorized under § 47.1-2 is the basis for satisfactory evidence of identity and the principal's identity has been ascertained upon presentation of such satisfactory evidence of identity, the electronic notary shall keep a copy of the recording of the video and audio conference and a notation of the type of any other identification used. The electronic notary shall ... maintain a backup for his electronic record of notarial acts, and ... ensure protection of such backup records from unauthorized use" (COV 47.1-14[C]).

Record Maintained Five Years: "The electronic record of an electronic notarial act shall be maintained for a period of at least five years from the date of the transaction" (COV 47.1-14[C]).

Security Obligations of eNotary

"The electronic notary shall take reasonable steps to ... ensure the integrity, security, and authenticity of electronic notarizations ..." (COV 47.1-14[C]).

"A notary performing electronic notarial acts shall take reasonable steps to ensure that any registered device used to create an electronic signature is current and has not been revoked or terminated by its issuing or registering authority" (COV 47.1-14[D]).

"A notary performing electronic notarial acts shall keep his record, electronic signature, and physical and electronic seals secure under his exclusive control and shall not allow them to be used by any other notary or any other person" (COV 47.1-14[E]).

"A notary performing electronic notarial acts shall use the notary's electronic signature only for the purpose of performing electronic notarial acts" (COV 47.1-14[F]).

"A notary performing electronic notarial acts, immediately upon discovering that the notary's record, electronic signature, or physical or electronic seal has been lost, stolen, or may by otherwise used by a person other than the notary, shall (i) inform the appropriate law-enforcement agency in the case of theft or vandalism and (ii) notify the Secretary in writing and signed in the official name in which he was commissioned" (COV 47.1-14[G]).

Attachment of Certificate, Signature, Seal

"A notarial act shall be evidenced by a notarial certificate or electronic notarial certificate signed by a notary in a manner that attributes such signature to the notary public identified on the commission" (COV 47.1-16[B]).

"The notary shall attach the official electronic signature and seal to the electronic notarial certificate of an electronic document in a manner that is capable of independent verification and renders any subsequent changes or modifications to the electronic document evident" (COV 47.1-16[D]).

Fee for eNotarization

"A notary may, for taking and certifying the acknowledgment of any electronic document, or administering and certifying an oath or affirmation, or certifying electronic affidavits and depositions of witnesses, or certifying that a copy of an electronic document is a true copy thereof, charge a fee not to exceed $25" (COV 47.1-19[B]).

Authentication of Electronic Acts

"On a notarized electronic document transmitted to another state or outside of the United States, electronic evidence of the authenticity of the official signature and seal of an electronic notary of the Commonwealth of Virginia, if required, shall be attached to or logically associated with the document and shall be in the form of an electronic certificate of authority signed by the Secretary that is independently verifiable, will be invalidated if the underlying document is improperly modified, and is in conformance with any current and pertinent international treaties, agreements and conventions subscribed to by the government of the United States" (COV 47.1-11.1).

Termination of eNotary Commission

"Every electronic notary who wishes to resign his commission or who ceases to be a notary pursuant to this section shall forthwith erase, delete, or destroy the coding, disk, certificate, card, software, or password that enables electronic affixation of the notary's official electronic signature or seal and so certify to the Secretary" (COV 47.1-22[E]).

"A former electronic notary, whose previous commission or application was not revoked or denied need not erase, delete, or destroy the coding, disk, certificate, card, software, or password that enables electronic affixation of the notary's electronic signature or seal if he is recommissioned and reregistered as an electronic notary using the same electronic signature and seal within three months after commission expiration" (COV 47.1-22[F]).

Misuse of Electronic Signature, Seal

"The Secretary may revoke the commission of any notary who .... (f)ails to keep the official physical seal, journal, or device, coding, disk, certificate, card, software, or passwords used to affix the notary's official electronic signature or seal under the exclusive control of the notary when not in use" (COV 47.1-23[10]).

"Any person who knowingly obtains, conceals, damages, or destroys the certificate, disk, coding, card, program, software, or hardware enabling an electronic notary to affix an official electronic signature or seal, without authority, shall be guilty of a Class 1 misdemeanor" (COV 47.1-29.1).

UETA Recognizes Notary's eSignature

Effective July 1, 2000, Virginia adopted its own version of the Uniform Electronic Transactions Act (COV 59.1-479 through 59.1-497), including the provision on notarization and acknowledgment, thereby recognizing the legal validity of electronic signatures used by Notaries:

"If a law requires a signature or record to be notarized, acknowledged, verified, or made under oath, the requirement is satisfied if the electronic signature of the person authorized to perform those acts, together with all other information required to be included by other applicable law, is attached to or logically associated with the signature or record" (COV 59.1-489).

Electronic Filing and Recording

The following statutory provisions relate to filing and recording of notarized electronic documents:

Filing of Notarized Electronic Documents: "A clerk of a circuit court may establish a system for electronic filing in civil or criminal actions that shall be governed by Rule 1:17 of the Rules of Supreme Court of Virginia. The circuit court clerk shall enter into an agreement with each person whom the clerk authorizes to file documents electronically, specifying the electronic filing procedures to be followed, including, but not limited to, security procedures, as defined in the Uniform Electronic Transactions Act, for transmitting notarized documents." (COV 17.1-258.3).

"A. If the electronically filed document contains an electronic signature pursuant to the Uniform Electronic Transactions Act (Section 59.1-479 et seq.), any statutory requirement for original signature shall be deemed to be satisfied.

"B. Any statutory requirement for a document to be notarized shall be deemed satisfied by the appropriately executed electronic signature of such notary" (COV 17.1-258.4).

Real Property Electronic Recording Act: "A. If a law requires, as a condition for recording, that a land record be an original, on paper or other tangible medium, or in writing, an electronic land records document satisfying this Act satisfies the law.

"B. If a law requires, as a condition for recording, that a land record be signed, an electronic signature satisfies the law.

"C. A requirement that a land records document or a signature associated with a land records document be notarized, acknowledged, verified, witnessed, or made under oath is satisfied if the electronic notarization of the person authorized to perform that act, and all other information required to be included, is attached to or logically associated with the land records document or signature. A physical or electronic image of a stamp, impression, or seal is not required to accompany an electronic signature" (COV 55-142.11).

NOTARY RECORDS

Only for electronic notarial acts is a Virginia Notary currently required to keep a record — see "Electronic Record and Backup to Be Kept," above under "Electronic Notarizations." An electronic record must be maintained for at least five years from the date of the transaction (COV 47.1-14[C]).

Secretary Recommends Journal

"A traditional notary is not required to keep a notary journal. However, the Office of the Secretary of the Commonwealth recommends that each notary maintain a journal that provides a record of all notarial acts performed so as to provide evidence for resolving future disputes over authenticity of signatures and documents. The journal may also provide proof that the notary has lawfully performed his or her notarial duties" (HNP).

'Record of Notarial Acts' Definition

Virginia statute does provide a definition of "record of notarial acts" that appears to apply to both electronic and paper records: "'Record of notarial acts' means a device for creating and preserving a chronological record of notarizations performed by a notary" (COV 47.1-2).

AUTHENTICATION OF NOTARIAL ACTS

Circuit Court Clerk

An authenticating certificate for a Notary may be obtained at the office of the circuit court clerk where the Notary filed an oath.

Secretary of Commonwealth

Authenticating certificates for Notaries, including apostilles, are also issued by the office of Virginia's Secretary of the Commonwealth.

Fees: $10 per document for authentication of a Notary's or a circuit court clerk's signature. "If there are several documents signed by the same public official (notary public, deputy clerk, etc...) on the same date for the same country; the fee is $10.00 for the first document and $5.00 for each additional document" (website, "Authentications"). Payable to "Secretary of the Commonwealth."

Address:
Secretary of the Commonwealth's Office
Authentication Division
1111 East Broad Street, 1st Floor
Richmond, VA 23219

Telephone: 1-804-692-2536

Procedure: "Before documents are sent to the Authentication Office, they must have the proper signatures (original signatures only) and/or certificates attached. ... All documents for Authentication must be less than one year old... On all documents signed by a notary, Deputy Clerk, or any other Virginia official, that signing must have taken place less than one year from the day processed" (website, "Authentications").

The Authentication Office requests that documents be mailed for processing. Include the appropriate fee and a cover letter with a contact name, daytime phone number and the country of destination. (An "Authentication Request" form is available.) Also include an addressed, postage-paid return envelope or prepaid shipping label. "The Secretary of the Commonwealth's Office is a scheduled 'Air Delivery' pick-up location for FedEx and UPS. The office is also a scheduled 'Ground Delivery' pick-up for UPS" (website, "Authentications").

Documents that must be dropped off for processing should be accompanied by the appropriate fee and a cover letter with a daytime phone number. A person must have a valid photo ID in order to enter the building. The Drop-Off/Pick-Up schedule is posted on the "Authentications" page of the website.

COMMISSIONING AND ADMINISTRATION

Although Virginia's Notaries are commissioned by the Governor (COV 47.1-3), it is the office of the Secretary of the Commonwealth that maintains records on and reviews complaints against Notaries (COV 47.1-8).

"The Secretary shall ... be required to retain the completed applications of persons seeking appointment as notary public for a period of three months after their receipt; provided, however, that he shall retain the applications of persons refused appointment for not less than four years" (COV 47.1-10).

"Anyone may request the address and telephone number of a notary by submitting a letter of request stating the name of the notary and the reason for request to the Office of the Secretary of the Commonwealth" (website, "Official Documents"). For all active and expired commissions dating back to 1998, the Secretary of the Commonwealth may provide a formal letter stating any commission starting and expiration date.

Applying for Commission

Qualifications: An applicant for a commission

as a Virginia Notary Public must (COV 47.1-4): (a) be at least 18 years old, (b) be able to read and write the English language and (c) never have been convicted of a felony in Virginia or any other state unless pardoned, had rights restored or had the conviction vacated. Though the statute also stipulates U.S. citizenship for applicants, this is not enforced due to the 1984 U.S. Supreme Court decision in *Bernal v. Fainter*.

No Course or Test: No course of instruction or test is required of applicants for a Virginia Notary Public commission.

Application: The completed application form must be acknowledged and sworn to before another Notary or before a circuit court clerk or deputy clerk. The application fee is $45, payable to the "Treasurer of Virginia." The Secretary has discretion to accept applications by electronic means. (Applications are available on the website or at the local circuit court.)

For renewals, a reminder notice will not be sent by the state. The renewal process is the same as for the original commission. "(I)f you are a notary whose commission expires in January, submit your application in January. Applications received prior to January will be processed in a way wherein your commission will expire one year earlier than anticipated" (website, "Official Documents"). An electronic signature may be submitted on an application for recommissioning: "For persons already commissioned as notaries public or electronic notaries public . . . the Secretary may accept electronic signatures, authorized by the Uniform Electronic Transactions Act (§ 59.1-479 et seq.), as confirmation that the application has been signed and sworn pursuant to § 47.1-5" (COV 47.1-5.1).

Take Oath, Claim Commission from Clerk: The new Notary commission is sent to the designated circuit court clerk and a notice is also sent to the new Notary, who then has 60 days to appear before the clerk, take the oath and claim the commission for a fee of $10 (COV 47.1-9). The clerk has 14 days to certify the fact of the Notary's qualification with the Secretary of the Commonwealth. "An applicant, who has not received notice within four weeks of mailing their application to the Office of the Secretary of the Commonwealth, should call the Clerk of Court to verify if the commission has been received. If it has not, the applicant should contact the Office of the Secretary ..." (HNP).

Non-Residents: A non-resident of Virginia may be appointed as a Notary "only if he is regularly employed in this Commonwealth and if such appointment will be necessary or useful to him in such employment" (COV 47.1-4). "A nonresident notary who ceases to be regularly employed in Virginia must surrender his or her commission" (HNP). Persons in the U.S. armed services may also be appointed.

Changes of Status

If Contact Information Changes: For any change of contact information (address, phone, business address and phone, etc.) the Notary must notify the office of the Secretary of the Commonwealth. A "Change of Contact Information" form is available on the website.

For a change of residence, the Notary must inform the Secretary of the Commonwealth in writing (COV 47.1-18). Likewise, a Notary who is a non-resident must inform the Secretary of any change in the place of employment.

"Any notary who ceases to be a resident of the Commonwealth of Virginia shall, from that time, cease to be a notary; provided, however, that such notary may retain his commission with the written consent of the Secretary if he meets the qualifications for nonresident appointment under § 47.1-4" (COV 47.1-22[B]).

"Any nonresident notary who ceases to be employed in this Commonwealth shall forthwith cease to be a notary" (COV 47.1-22[C]).

If Notary Changes Name: "Any notary ... who shall legally change his name during his term of office as a notary shall, after such change of name, when performing any notarial act, have written or printed in or annexed to his certificate the words: 'I was commissioned a notary as _____,' or the equivalent" (COV 47.1-17).

If Notary Resigns: "A notary who wishes to resign may do so by sending a letter of resignation and his or her commission to the Secretary of the Commonwealth" (HNP).

CIRCUIT COURT CLERKS

To contact a Virginia county (or city) circuit court clerk to obtain an authenticating certificate for a Notary, or to seek assistance in locating a given Notary, telephone long-distance information — 1-XXX-555-1212 — using one of the area codes below:

County	City/Town	Area Code
Accomack	Accomac	(757)
Albemarle	Charlottesville	(434)
Alleghany	Covington	(540)
Amelia	Amelia	(804)
Amherst	Amherst	(434)
Appomattox	Appomattox	(434)
Arlington	Arlington	(703)
Augusta	Staunton	(540)
Bath	Warm Springs	(540)
Bedford	Bedford	(540)
Bland	Bland	(276)
Botetourt	Fincastle	(540)
Brunswick	Lawrenceville	(434)
Buchanan	Grundy	(276)
Buckingham	Buckingham	(434)
Campbell	Rustburg	(434)
Caroline	Bowling Green	(804)
Carroll	Hillsville	(276)
Charles City	Charles City	(804)
Charlotte	Charlotte Ct. Hse.	(434)
Chesterfield	Chesterfield	(804)
Clarke	Berryville	(540)
Craig	New Castle	(540)
Culpeper	Culpeper	(540)
Cumberland	Cumberland	(804)
Dickenson	Clintwood	(276)
Dinwiddie	Dinwiddie	(804)
Essex	Tappahannock	(804)
Fairfax	Fairfax	(703)
Fauquier	Warrenton	(540)
Floyd	Floyd	(540)
Fluvanna	Palmyra	(434)
Franklin	Rocky Mount	(540)
Frederick	Winchester	(540)
Giles	Pearisburg	(540)
Gloucester	Gloucester	(804)
Goochland	Goochland	(804)
Grayson	Independence	(276)
Greene	Stanardsville	(434)
Greensville	Emporia	(434)
Halifax	Halifax	(434)
Hanover	Hanover	(804)
Henrico	Richmond	(804)
Henry	Martinsville	(276)
Highland	Monterey	(540)
Isle of Wight	Isle of Wight	(757)
James City	Williamsburg	(757)
King & Queen	King & Queen C.H.	(804)
King George	King George	(540)
King William	King William	(804)
Lancaster	Lancaster	(804)
Lee	Jonesville	(276)
Loudoun	Leesburg	(703)
Louisa	Louisa	(540)
Lunenburg	Lunenburg	(434)
Madison	Madison	(540)
Mathews	Mathews	(804)
Mecklenburg	Boydton	(434)
Middlesex	Saluda	(804)
Montgomery	Christiansburg	(540)
Nelson	Lovingston	(434)
New Kent	New Kent	(804)
Northampton	Eastville	(757)
Northumberland	Heathsville	(804)
Nottoway	Nottoway	(434)
Orange	Orange	(540)
Page	Luray	(540)
Patrick	Stuart	(276)
Pittsylvania	Chatham	(434)
Powhatan	Powhatan	(804)
Prince Edward	Farmville	(434)
Prince George	Prince George	(804)
Prince William	Manassas	(703)
Pulaski	Pulaski	(540)
Rappahannock	Washington	(540)
Richmond	Warsaw	(804)
Roanoke	Salem	(540)
Rockbridge	Lexington	(540)
Rockingham	Harrisonburg	(540)
Russell	Lebanon	(276)
Scott	Gate City	(276)
Shenandoah	Woodstock	(540)
Smyth	Marion	(276)
Southampton	Courtland	(757)
Spotsylvania	Spotsylvania	(540)
Stafford	Stafford	(540)
Surry	Surry	(757)
Sussex	Sussex	(434)
Tazewell	Tazewell	(276)
Warren	Front Royal	(540)
Washington	Abingdon	(276)
Westmoreland	Montross	(804)
Wise	Wise	(276)
Wythe	Wytheville	(276)
York	Yorktown	(757)

Virginia is unique in having a great number of "independent cities," each with its own court system and, in most cases, record depositories. These independent cities have essentially the same authority as counties, particularly in regard to Notaries:

Independent City	Area Code
Alexandria	(703)
Bedford[1]	(540)
Bristol	(276)
Buena Vista	(540)
Charlottesville	(434)
Chesapeake	(757)
Clifton Forge	(540)
Colonial Heights	(804)
Covington	(540)
Danville	(434)
Emporia[2]	(434)
Fairfax[3]	(703)
Falls Church[4]	(703)
Franklin[5]	(757)
Fredericksburg	(540)
Galax[6]	(276)
Hampton	(757)
Harrisonburg[7]	(540)
Hopewell	(804)
Lexington[8]	(540)
Lynchburg	(434)
Manassas[9]	(703)
Manassas Park[10]	(703)
Martinsville	(276)
Newport News	(757)
Norfolk	(757)
Norton[11]	(540)
Petersburg	(804)
Poquoson[12]	(757)
Portsmouth	(757)
Radford	(540)
Richmond	(804)
Roanoke	(540)
Salem	(540)
South Boston[13]	(434)
Staunton	(540)
Suffolk	(757)
Virginia Beach	(757)
Waynesboro	(540)
Williamsburg[14]	(757)
Winchester	(540)

1. Bedford City records kept by Bedford County.
2. Emporia City records kept by Greensville County.
3. Fairfax City records kept by Fairfax County.
4. Falls Church City records kept by Arlington County.
5. Franklin City records kept by Southampton County.
6. Galax City records kept by Carroll County.
7. Harrisonburg City records kept by Rockingham County.
8. Lexington City records kept by Rockbridge County.
9. Manassas City records kept by Prince William County.
10. Manassas Park City records kept by Prince William County.
11. Norton City records kept by Wise County.
12. Poquoson City records kept by York County.
13. S. Boston City records kept by Halifax County.
14. Willamsburg City records kept by James City County.

OTHER NOTARIAL OFFICERS

District Court Clerks and Deputies

Clerks and deputy clerks of general district courts "may take affidavits and administer oaths and affirmations, take and certify depositions in the same manner as a notary public, perform such other notarial acts as allowed under § 47.1-12, take acknowledgments to deeds or other writings for the purposes of recordation, and issue all other legal processes which may be issued by the judge of such court and exercise such other powers and perform such other duties as are conferred or imposed upon them by law…" (COV 16.1-69.40).

"The clerk of the circuit court of any jurisdiction shall be immune from suit arising from any acts or omissions relating to providing official certificates and certified records in digital form of any document maintained by the clerk pursuant to this section unless the clerk was grossly negligent or engaged in willful misconduct" (COV 17.1-258.3:2).

Federal Employees

"An employee of the federal government

authorized to perform notarial acts may perform notarial acts (in Virginia) in accordance with this chapter" (COV 47.1-13[C]).

QUICK FACTS

Notary Jurisdiction
Statewide for any document (COV 47.1-13[A]) and worldwide for any document intended to be used in Virginia or by the U.S. government (COV 47.1-13[B]).

Notary Term Length
Four years. "The term of a notary public shall expire in the fourth calendar year after issuance of his commission on the last day of the month in which the notary was born" (COV 47.1-21).

"Acting under an expired commission may constitute a criminal offense" (HNP).

Notary Bond
Not required by law.

<u>Employer's Liability</u>: "The employer of a notary public shall also be liable for all damages proximately caused by the official misconduct by such notary if:

"1. The notary public was acting within the scope of his employment at the time such damages were caused; and

"2. The employer had actual knowledge of, or reasonably should have known of, such notary's misconduct" (COV 47.1-27).

V–W

U.S. Virgin Islands

NOTARY SEAL

A Notary of the U.S. Virgin Islands must affix an official seal on every document notarized, and the seal's format must be as follows (3 VIC 776):

Kind

Embosser: "Each notary public shall keep an official impression seal bearing his name, date of expiration of commission, and judicial division.... The notary public must affix his impression seal to each document ..." (3 VIC 776).

An inking stamp that prints the Notary's name, commission expiration date and commission number may be used in addition to but not in place of the official embosser (NPH).

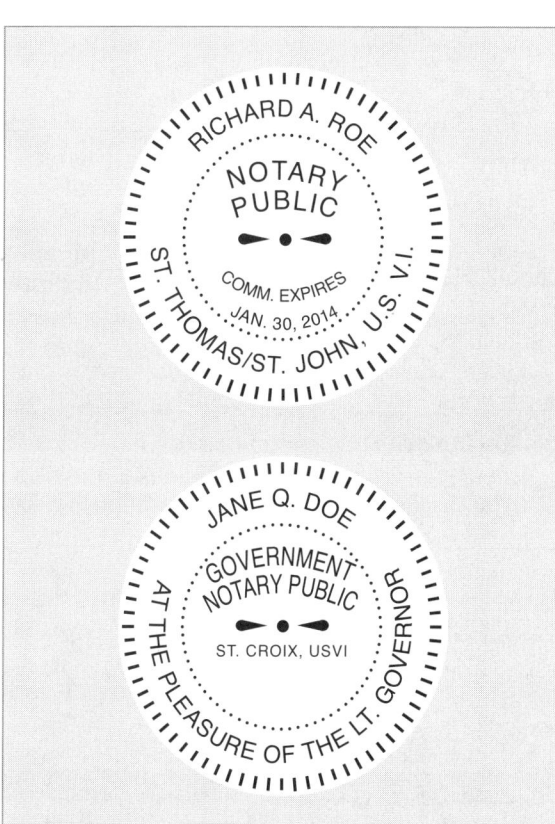

Examples

The above actual-size embosser seals are allowed by law in the U.S. Virgin Islands for regular Notaries (top) and for special government employee Notaries (bottom). Other formats may also be permitted.

NOTARY ADMINISTRATION

Office of the Lieutenant Governor
18 Kongens Gade   1-340-774-2991
Charlotte Amalie, St. Thomas, VI 00802

Office of the Lieutenant Governor
Division of Banking   1-340-773-6459
and Insurance
1131 King Street, Suite 101
Christiansted, St. Croix, VI 00820

Website: www.ltg.gov.vi/notary-public.html

NOTARY RULES

NPH — Notary Public Handbook
VIC — Virgin Islands Code

Most Notary rules are in the *Virgin Islands Code:*

a. Title 3, Chapter 29, Sections 771 through 778 ("Notaries Public"); and Sections 801 through 805 ("Special Notaries Public");

b. Title 28, Chapter 5, Sections 81 through 93 ("Recognition of Acknowledgments")*.

* This is largely the *Uniform Recognition of Acknowledgments Act* of 1968.

Other guidelines for Notaries are in the "Notary Public Handbook" (n.d.) published by the Office of the Lieutenant Governor and available on the website.

Shape/Size

Not specified.

Components

Notary seals must include the following information (NPH):
1. Name of Notary;
2. "Notary Public";
3. Commission expiration date;
4. Name of judicial division* in which Notary resides;
5. "U.S. Virgin Islands" or "USVI".

* There are two judicial divisions: St. Thomas/St. John (STT/STJ) and St. Croix (STX).

Seal of Government Notary

Notaries who are employed by the government of the U.S. Virgin Islands or of the United States under 3 VIC 801 "shall keep an official impression seal which shall be furnished by the respective department" (3 VIC 804). In addition to including the components for a Notary seal listed above (without the commission expiration date, if not applicable), the seal for a government employee Notary must specify that the person is a "Government Notary Public" and must include the phrase "at the pleasure of the Lt. Governor".

Seal Imprint to Lt. Governor

According to the "Notary Public Commissioning Instructions," an imprint of the newly commissioned Notary's seal must be forwarded to the Lieutenant Governor's office before the Notary may begin notarizing.

Notary's Name Must Be Legible

"The notary public must affix his impression seal to each document and either write, print or stamp his or her name in a legible fashion on the document .... A document is not properly notarized until both the seal has been impressed thereon and the name of the notary public has been affixed thereto" (3 VIC 776).

Surrendering Seal

"Upon the expiration of the term of office, the notary public's official record and seal shall be filed in the Office of the Lieutenant Governor, in the judicial division of his or her residence, for a period of five years. The Lieutenant Governor shall make an impression of such seal and keep such impression with the records of the notary public" (3 VIC 775[c]).

"A notary public shall not be eligible for a renewal of office unless there is presented with the application for renewal a receipt showing the deposit of official records and seal with the Lieutenant Governor" (3 VIC 775[e]).

NOTARY POWERS

A Notary of the U.S. Virgin Islands may perform the following notarial acts (3 VIC 777), provided that government employee Notaries notarize only for government business (3 VIC 805):
1. Take acknowledgments* and proofs**;
2. Administer oaths and affirmations;
3. "Perform such other acts as may be authorized by law."

* Acknowledgments: "The person taking an acknowledgment shall certify that the person acknowledging appeared before him and acknowledged he executed the instrument; and the person acknowledging was known to the person taking the acknowledgment or that the person taking the acknowledgment has satisfactory evidence that the person acknowledging was the person described in and who executed the instrument" (28 VIC 84).

** Proofs of Execution: According to 28 VIC 82, a proof of execution by a subscribing witness may be taken by a Notary of the U.S. Virgin Islands, though no certificate is prescribed.

"Proof of the execution of any conveyance may be made before any officer authorized to take acknowledgment of deeds and shall be made by a subscribing witness thereto who shall state his own place of residence and that he knows the person described in and who executed the conveyance. Such proof shall not be taken unless the officer is personally acquainted with the subscribing witness or has satisfactory evidence that he is the same person who was a subscribing witness to the instrument" (28 VIC 43).

Identifying and Qualifying Signers

"Each notary public shall administer the oath or inquire of each person executing a document as to the truth and authenticity of such document; and shall request identification of the person(s) requiring his or her notarial services. Failure to do so shall subject the notary public to an administrative fine of $100.00 or to revocation of his or her commission, or both, by and in the discretion of the Lieutenant Governor" (3 VIC 777[c]).

Forms of Identification: "The best form of identification is one which includes a photograph and signature. A valid driver's license is a good source of identification. The person can also be personally known to the notary" (NPH).

Two Witnesses for Property Deeds

According to the Lieutenant Governor's website — under "Recorder of Deeds," see "Frequently Asked Questions" — two witnesses are needed if a real property deed is notarized in the U.S. Virgin Islands.

NOTARY DON'TS

Disqualifying Interests

"No notary public shall certify, attest or take an oath or acknowledgment for or to an instrument to which he is an interested party" (3 VIC 777[b]).

Impartiality: "A notary cannot notarize his or her own signature. A notary is to be an impartial witness. The law does not forbid notaries from notarizing the signature of relatives. However, it is not a good practice to notarize relatives' signatures because if the notarized document was ever the subject of a court suit, a judge might determine the notary was not an impartial witness to the signing of the document. We suggest that you do not notarize documents for a spouse, grandparent, parent, brother, sister, niece, nephew, aunt, uncle, child or grandchildren" (NPH).

NOTARY SIGNING AGENTS

Currently, there are no statutes, regulations or rules expressly governing, prohibiting or restricting the operation of Notary Signing Agents within the U.S. Virgin Islands.

NOTARY FEES

"Each notary public may charge and retain a fee not to exceed $5.00 for each document notarized or for each time his or her seal is affixed to a document" (3 VIC 778[a]).

Fees for protests of notes and bills of exchange are specified in 4 VIC 519.

Government Notaries May Not Charge

The 40 or fewer Notaries who are employees of the government of the Virgin Islands or United States and commissioned under 3 VIC 801 may not charge for their notarial services, which are restricted to government business only (3 VIC 805[a]).

However, no more than four government Notaries on the island of St. John, no more than two for the area of Cruz Bay, and two for the area of Coral Bay, may be allowed to notarize in non-government business; they must charge fees, which are to be deposited in the General Fund of the Treasury (3 VIC 805[b]).

NOTARY CERTIFICATES

The following short-form acknowledgment certificates, adapted from the Uniform Recognition of Acknowledgments Act, may be used in the U.S. Virgin Islands, not precluding use of other forms:

Acknowledgment by Individual (28 VIC 87[b]):

Territory of the Virgin Islands
Judicial Division of _____

The foregoing instrument was acknowledged before me this _____ *(date) by* _____ *(name of person acknowledging).*

(Signature of person taking acknowledgment)
(Title or rank)
(Serial number, if any)   *(SEAL)*

Acknowledgment by Corporation (28 VIC 87[c]):

Territory of the Virgin Islands
Judicial Division of _____

The foregoing instrument was acknowledged before me this _____ *(date) by* _____ *(name of officer or agent, title of officer or agent) of* _____ *(name of corporation acknowledging), a* _____ *(state or place of incorporation) corporation, on behalf of the corporation.*

(Signature of person taking acknowledgment)
(Title or rank)
(Serial number, if any)   *(SEAL)*

Acknowledgment by Partnership (28 VIC 87[d]):

Territory of the Virgin Islands
Judicial Division of _____

The foregoing instrument was acknowledged before me this _____ *(date) by*

_____ (name of acknowledging partner or agent), partner (or agent) on behalf of _____ (name of partnership), a partnership.

(Signature of person taking acknowledgment)
(Title or rank)
(Serial number, if any) (SEAL)

Acknowledgment by Attorney in Fact (28 VIC 87[e]):

Territory of the Virgin Islands
Judicial Division of _____

The foregoing instrument was acknowledged before me this _____ (date) by _____ (name of attorney in fact) as attorney in fact on behalf of _____ (name of principal).

(Signature of person taking acknowledgment)
(Title or rank)
(Serial number, if any) (SEAL)

Acknowledgment by Any Public Officer, Trustee or Personal Representative (28 VIC 87[f]):

Territory of the Virgin Islands
Judicial Division of _____

The foregoing instrument was acknowledged before me this _____ (date) by _____ (name and title of person acknowledging).

(Signature of person taking acknowledgment)
(Title or rank)
(Serial number, if any) (SEAL)

Acknowledgment by Person Serving with U.S. Armed Forces (28 VIC 91):

"Any person serving in or with the armed forces of the United States may acknowledge (a document) wherever located before any commissioned officer in active service of the armed forces of the United States with the rank of Second Lieutenant or higher in the Army, Air Force, or Marine Corps, or Ensign or higher in the Navy or United States Coast Guard. The instrument shall not be rendered invalid by the failure to state therein the place of execution or acknowledgment. No authentication of the officer's certificate of acknowledgment shall be required but the officer taking the acknowledgment shall indorse thereon or attach thereto a certificate substantially in the following form:"

On this the _____ day of _____, 20 ____, before me, _____, the undersigned officer, personally appeared _____, known to me (or satisfactorily proven) to be serving in or with the armed forces of the United States and to be the person(s), whose name(s) is/are subscribed to the within instrument, acknowledged that he/she/they executed the same for the purposes therein contained. And the undersigned does further certify that he/she is at the date of this certificate a commissioned officer of the rank stated below and is in the active service of the armed forces of the United States.

_____ (Signature of officer)
_____ (Rank of officer and command to which attached)

Form of Acknowledgment

"The form of a certificate of acknowledgment used by a person whose authority is recognized under section 82 of this chapter shall be accepted in the Virgin Islands if one of the following is true:
"(a) The certificate is in a form prescribed by the laws or regulations of the Virgin Islands;
"(b) The certificate is in a form prescribed by the laws applicable in the place in which the acknowledgment is taken; or
"(c) The certificate contains the words 'acknowledged before me,' or their substantial equivalent" (28 VIC 85).

ELECTRONIC NOTARIZATIONS

The U.S. Virgin Islands has not yet adopted statutes or regulations expressly establishing rules, definitions and procedures for electronic notarization.

UETA Recognizes Notary's eSignature

The U.S. Virgin Islands has adopted the Uniform Electronic Transactions Act (11 VIC 101 through 120), including the following provision on notarization, thereby recognizing the legal validity of electronic signatures used by Notaries:

"If a law requires a signature or record to be notarized, acknowledged, verified or made under oath, the requirement is satisfied if the electronic signature of the person authorized to perform those acts, together with all other information required to be included by other applicable law, is attached to or logically associated with the signature or record" (11 VIC 111).

NOTARY RECORDS

"Each notary public shall keep an official record in which a memorandum of all official acts shall be noted" (3 VIC 775[a] and 3 VIC 802). This record is a protection against possible lawsuits (NPH).

Required Entries in Record

"The records kept by the notary public shall include, among other information, the date of the document, the nature or name of the document, the consideration named in the document, if any, the parties making the oath and such other information as the Lieutenant Governor, may by regulation, deem necessary" (3 VIC 775[d]). According to the "Notary Public Handbook," Notaries should keep a record of the date and time the document was notarized, the type of notarization completed, the signature of the person(s), the address and identification of person, and the notary fee, if any.

Inspection and Copying of Records

"The Lieutenant Governor may inspect the official record of any notary public at any time" (3 VIC 775[b]).

"Every citizen of this Territory shall have the right to examine all public records and to copy such records …. The right to copy records shall include the right to make photographs or photographic copies while the records are in the possession of the lawful custodian of the records. All rights under this section are in addition to the right to obtain certified copies of records under section 882 herein" (33 VIC 881[b]).

Supervision Required: "Such examination and copying shall be done under the supervision of the lawful custodian of the records or his authorized designee. The lawful custodian may adopt and enforce reasonable rules and regulations regarding such work and the protection of the records against damage or disorganization. The lawful custodian shall provide a suitable place for such work, but if it is impracticable to do such work in the office of the lawful custodian, the person desiring to examine or copy shall pay any necessary expenses for providing a place for such work. All expenses of such work shall be paid by the person desiring to examine or copy. The lawful custodian may charge a reasonable fee for the services of the lawful custodian or his authorized deputy in supervising the records during such work" (33 VIC 881[c]).

During Customary Office Hours: "The rights of citizens under this chapter may be exercised at any time during the customary office hours of the lawful custodian of the records. However, if the lawful custodian does not have customary office hours of at least thirty hours per week, such right may be exercised at any time from nine o'clock a.m. to noon and from one o'clock p.m. to four o'clock p.m., Monday through Friday, excluding legal holidays, unless the citizen exercising such right and the lawful custodian agree on a different time" (33 VIC 881[d]).

Filing Records

"Upon the expiration of the term of office, the notary public's official record and seal shall be filed in the Office of the Lieutenant Governor, in the judicial division of his or her residence, for a period of five years. The Lieutenant Governor shall make an impression of such seal and keep such impression with the records of the notary public" (3 VIC 775[c]).

"A notary public shall not be eligible for a renewal of office unless there is presented with the application for renewal a receipt showing the deposit of official records and seal with the Lieutenant Governor" (3 VIC 775[e]).

AUTHENTICATION OF NOTARIAL ACTS

Lieutenant Governor

The offices of the Lieutenant Governor provide authenticating certificates ("certificates of authenticity") and apostilles for documents notarized in the U.S. Virgin Islands (3 VIC 778[b]).

Fees: $25 per certificate. Money orders and

checks are payable to the "Government of the Virgin Islands."

> Addresses and Telephones:
> Office of the Lieutenant Governor
> 18 Kongens Gade
> Charlotte Amalie
> St. Thomas, VI 00802
> 1-340-774-2991
>
> OR
>
> Office of the Lieutenant Governor
> Division of Banking and Insurance
> 1131 King Street, Suite 101
> Christiansted, St. Croix, VI 00820
> 1-340-773-6459

COMMISSIONING AND ADMINISTRATION

The Lieutenant Governor may appoint and regulate no more than 600 Notaries for the U.S. Virgin Islands, exclusive of ex officio Notaries and attorneys who are members of the Virgin Islands Bar (3 VIC 771[a]).

Applying for Commission

Qualifications: An applicant for a commission as a U.S. Virgin Islands Notary Public must: (a) be at least 21 years old, (b) be a citizen of the United States, (c) be a resident of the Virgin Islands for at least five years, except for attorneys in the Virgin Islands Bar, (d) be a graduate of an accredited high school or have passed the high school equivalency exam and (e) not have been convicted of any crime within or outside the Virgin Islands (3 VIC 772). "Any person admitted to practice law in the Virgin Islands as a member of the Virgin Islands Bar shall upon application and showing of his membership be issued a commission for a period of four years" (3 VIC 771[a]).

No Course or Exam: No course of instruction or examination is required of applicants for a Notary commission in the U.S. Virgin Islands. However, the application instructions clearly state: "You are responsible for reading the law and making yourself familiar with its provisions and your duties as a Notary Public…"

Application: The application process has three phases. First, an application form is submitted along with the following "package" of documents: (a) an affidavit in which the applicant declares certain facts, notarized by another Notary; (b) a signed consent for a criminal background check; (c) two letters of character reference, with the return addresses and daytime contact numbers of the authors; (d) proof of U.S. citizenship, with photo ID; and (e) for attorneys only, a certificate of good standing from the Superior Court of the U.S. Virgin Islands.

Second, after the application package has been reviewed and the applicant deemed eligible for appointment, the applicant must submit a $5,000 bond, with the forms properly notarized, along with a $100 commission fee. "Each notary public shall pay to the Treasury of the Virgin Islands an initial fee of $100.00 for the commission and thereafter, on the 1st day of January of each year, an annual fee of $25.00" (3 VIC 773[a]).

Third, after the bond is approved by the Superior Court, a Notary commission will be issued to the applicant, whereupon the Notary submits a signed and notarized oath of office and an imprint of the Notary's official seal. At that point, the new Notary may begin notarizing.

"A notary public may, at the expiration of his or her term of office, apply for a renewal of the commission by the filing of an application accompanied with a new bond and a renewal fee of $75.00, and such application shall, if all other qualifications are in order, be given priority over other applications, provided it is postmarked no later than 60 days after the term ends" (3 VIC 773[d]). A renewal application should be submitted no earlier than 60 days before commission expiration (NPH).

"A notary public shall not be eligible for a renewal of office unless there is presented with the application for renewal a receipt showing the deposit of official records and seal with the Lieutenant Governor" (3 VIC 775[e]) — see "Filing the Records," under "Notary Records," above.

Non-Residents: The five-year residency requirement will not be waived. A Virgin Islands Attorney General Opinion (V.I. Op.A.G. 285) stipulated that even a person who had been a Notary in the United States for more than five years and was permanently located in the Islands could not have the five-year residency requirement waived because he was not an attorney.

Government Notaries: In addition to the 600 Notaries mentioned above, the Lieutenant

Governor may appoint and regulate no more than 40 Notaries who are employees of the government of the Virgin Islands or of the United States (3 VIC 801). They may only act on matters of official government business, and may not charge fees for their services (3 VIC 805[a]).

Changes of Status

If Notary Moves: A Notary who moves within the Virgin Islands must send a letter with both old and new addresses to the Lieutenant Governor's office, requesting a change in the official records. In addition, the Notary must execute an affidavit affirming under oath that he or she continues to meet the requirements to be a Notary in the Virgin Islands (NPH).

If Notary Leaves Islands: A Notary's move from the Virgin Islands automatically vacates the Notary office and is equivalent to a resignation (3 VIC 772).

If Notary's Name Changes: A Notary who intends to use a new name must apply for an amended commission with the new name. The Notary should submit a new application form and letter to the office of the Lieutenant Governor with supporting documents (i.e., marriage certificate, divorce decree, order changing name etc.). The Notary will need to purchase a rider to change the name on his or her Notary Public bond and a new die for the seal. The commission with the new name will be mailed directly to the Notary. There is no fee for issuing an amended commission (NPH).

If Notary Resigns: "To resign your commission as a notary public, return your original commission, seal and journal to the Office of the Lieutenant Governor, #18 Kongens Gade, Charlotte Amalie, St. Thomas, VI 00802, along with a letter of resignation" (NPH).

OTHER NOTARIAL OFFICERS

In addition to Notaries, the following officers may take acknowledgments in the U.S. Virgin Islands (28 VIC 81):
1. A judge, clerk or deputy clerk of any court of record having a seal;
2. A commissioner or recorder of deeds.

Special Government Employee Notaries

"In addition to the notaries public provided for in subchapter I of this chapter, the Lieutenant Governor may authorize and empower employees of the Government of the United States Virgin Islands or of the United States, not exceeding 40 in number, to take acknowledgment of deeds and administer oaths and affirmations, and such employees shall be appointed and commissioned as notaries public with terms of office at the pleasure of the Lieutenant Governor" (3 VIC 801).

Such special government employee Notaries are not required to pay commissioning fees or to post a bond (3 VIC 803). They must keep an official record of all official acts (3 VIC 802) and use "an official impression seal which shall be furnished by the respective department" (3 VIC 804[a]).

Special government employee Notaries "shall not be permitted to take acknowledgments of deeds and administer oaths and affirmations except on matters of official business of the Government of the United States, and no fees for such acknowledgments and oaths or affirmations shall be charged" (3 VIC 805[a]). However, special government employee Notaries in the following geographic areas are not restricted to notarizing just for government business and must charge for their services, with the fees deposited in the General Fund of the Treasury: no more than four Notaries commissioned for the island of St. John; no more than two for the area of Cruz Bay; and no more than two for the area of Coral Bay (3 VIC 805[b]).

Ex Officio Notaries

In the U.S. Virgin Islands, the following officers have ex officio notarial powers (3 VIC 771[a]):
1. The Executive Secretary of the Legislature;
2. Each official court reporter and assistant court reporter of the Superior and District Courts;
3. Each official reporter of the Legislature;
4. The Registrar and Deputy Registrars of Vital Statistics of the Department of Health.

Two Notarial Offices Disallowed: A governmental ex officio Notary of the U.S. Virgin Islands may not at the same time become commissioned as a Notary (NPH).

List of Ex Officio Notaries: "Chief clerks of the United States District Court for the Virgin Islands and the Territorial Court of the Virgin Islands shall submit, at least once a year, to and for the information of the Office of the Lieutenant Governor, a list of all persons authorized as ex officio notaries public" (3 VIC 804[b]).

Attorney Statement Same as Affidavit
"The statement of an attorney authorized by law and admitted to the practice in the Courts of the Virgin Islands, who is not a party to an action, when subscribed and affirmed by him to be true under the penalties of perjury, may be served or filed in an action in lieu of and with the same force and effect as an affidavit duly notarized" (5 VIC 699).

QUICK FACTS

Notary Jurisdiction
The islands and waters of the U.S. Virgin Islands (3 VIC 771), including islands of St. Croix, St. John and St. Thomas.

Notary Term Length
Four years (3 VIC 771[a]), expiring at midnight on the commission expiration date.
The term of office of a special government employee Notary is set "at the pleasure of the Lieutenant Governor" (3 VIC 801).

Notary Bond
$5,000, with any insurance/bonding company authorized to do business in the Virgin Islands, or with two resident sureties who are owners of real property within the Virgin Islands with a value of $10,000 over and above any encumbrances (3 VIC 773[b]). The bond must be approved by the presiding judge of the Superior Court.
No bond is required of Notaries commissioned as employees of the government of the Virgin Islands or United States (3 VIC 803).

Washington

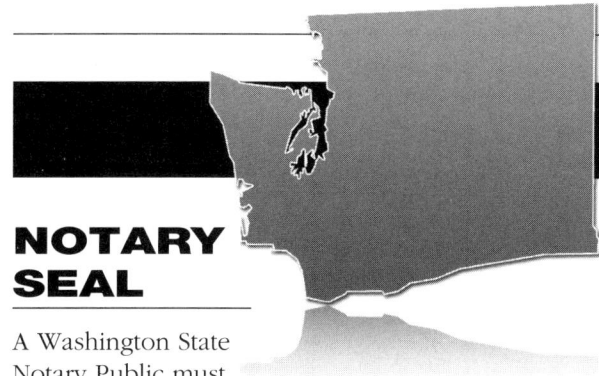

NOTARY SEAL

A Washington State Notary Public must affix an "official seal or stamp" on the certificate portion of every document notarized (RCW 42.44.090). However, the seal or stamp may be omitted in certifying an oath for use in any court in Washington. The format must be as follows (RCW 42.44.050 and WAC 308-30-010):

Kind

Inked Stamp or Embosser ("Seal"):

INKED STAMP:
1. The type must be a minimum of 8 points in size;
2. Only indelible ink may be used;
3. The stamp must contain permanently affixed letters and numbers, and not be preprinted on the document or certificate.

Examples

The above typical, actual-size examples of Notary stamp and embosser seals are allowed by Washington state law. Formats other than these may also be permitted.

NOTARY ADMINISTRATION

Department of Licensing
Business and Professional Licenses
Notaries Public Unit
PO Box 9027
Olympia, WA 98507-9027

405 Black Lake Blvd., SW
Olympia, WA 98502

Website: www.dol.wa.gov/business/notary/

NOTARY RULES

RCW — Revised Code of Washington
WAC — Washington Administrative Code

Most Notary rules are in:

a. Revised Code of Washington, Chapter 42.44, "Notaries Public" and Chapter 64.08, "Acknowledgments";

b. Washington Administrative Code, Chapter 308-30, "Notaries Public."

EMBOSSER:
1. No minimum seal type size is specified, but 8-point or larger is required of type on recordable documents (RCW 65.04.045);
2. Impressions must be "smudged" on recordable documents to be "capable of being imaged" (RCW 65.04.045).

Shape/Size

INKED STAMP: The law states that a circular inked stamp must have a minimum diameter of $1^{5}/_{8}$ inches; and a rectangular inked stamp a minimum respective width and length of 1 inch and $1^{5}/_{8}$ inches.

EMBOSSER: The law states that an embosser seal must be a minimum of $1^{5}/_{8}$ inches in diameter, indicating that the embosser must be circular.

Components

1. "Notary Public";
2. "State of Washington";
3. Notary's name (surname and at least the initials of both first and middle names);

4. Notary's appointment expiration date.

STATE SEAL PROHIBITED: Reproduction of the Washington state seal within the Notary stamp or embosser seal is prohibited (WAC 308-30-010[5]).

Notary's Signature

"Upon completion of a notarial act, the notary must sign the notary certification using his/her name exactly as it appears on the notary certificate of appointment and the stamp or seal. The notary's name must be legibly printed or stamped directly below their signature" (WAC 308-30-120).

Seal, Signature May Intrude into Margin

Recording laws allow "a minor portion of a notary seal, incidental writing, or minor portion of a signature" to extend into the mandatory one-inch margin at the top, bottom and sides of all pages of a recorded document (three-inch mandatory margin at the top of the first page) (RCW 65.04.045).

Omitted or Expired Date

"If the notarial officer is a notary public, the certificate shall also indicate the date of expiration of such notary public's appointment, but omission of that information may subsequently be corrected" (RCW 42.44.090).

Use of a Notary seal or stamp with an expired date is prohibited (WAC 308-30-130).

Notary Seal Sale without Certificate

"A vendor may not provide a notarial seal, or stamp, either inking or embossing, to a person claiming to be a notary, unless the person presents a photocopy of the person's Notary Certificate" (WAC 308-30-010[6]).

"It is unlawful for any person intentionally to manufacture, give, sell, procure or possess a seal or stamp evidencing the current appointment of a person as a notary public until the director (of licensing) has delivered a certificate evidencing the appointment as provided for in RCW 42.44.040" (RCW 42.44.050). (NOTE: RCW 42.44.040 was repealed in 2003.)

Name Change: "A notary applying for a seal or stamp as a result of a name change shall present a copy to the vendor of the certificate evidencing that notary's name change from the director (of licensing)" (WAC 308-30-010[7]).

Seal Is Exclusive Property of Notary

A Notary seal or stamp belongs exclusively to the Notary and may not be used by any other person, nor surrendered to an employer upon termination of employment, regardless of whether the employer paid for the seal or stamp or for the Notary's bond or appointment fees (RCW 42.44.090[4]).

Lost or Stolen Seals

When a Notary seal or stamp is lost or stolen, the Department of Licensing must be notified by certified mail through a written statement signed by the Notary before a replacement can be obtained. Any new seal or stamp must contain some variance, such as a different border, from the original (WAC 308-30-050). If the original is then recovered, it must be surrendered to the Department.

Seal Surrendered to Licensing Department

"If a notary public voluntarily resigns his or her notary appointment or if the notary appointment is revoked, suspended or restricted, the notary public must mail or deliver his or her notary stamp or seal to the department of licensing (Notaries Public Unit). No voluntary resignation of a notary appointment shall be effective until the notary seal or stamp is mailed or delivered to the notary section" (WAC 308-30-040).

Seal or Stamp Is Prima Facie Evidence

"The signature and seal or stamp of a notary public are prima facie evidence that the signature of the notary is genuine and that the person is a notary public" (RCW 42.44.080[9]).

NOTARY POWERS

Washington State Notaries are authorized to perform the following notarial acts (RCW 42.44.010 and 42.44.080):

1. Take acknowledgments*;
2. Administer oaths and affirmations;
3. Take verifications upon oath or affirmation;
4. Witness or attest signatures;
5. Certify or attest copies** of documents or other items;
6. Certify that "an event has occurred or an act has been performed"***;
7. Make or note the protest of a negotiable instrument according to RCW 62A.3-509.

* <u>Taking Acknowledgments</u>: "'Acknowledgment' means a statement by a person that the person has executed an instrument as the person's free and voluntary act for the uses and purposes stated therein and, if the instrument is executed in a representative capacity, a statement that the person signed the document with proper authority and executed it as the act of the person or entity represented and identified therein" (RCW 42.44.010[4]).

** <u>Certifying Copies</u>: "In certifying or attesting a copy of a document or other item, a notary public must determine that the proffered copy is a full, true, and accurate transcription or reproduction of that which was copied" (RCW 42.44.080[5]).

*** <u>Occurrence of Event, Performance of Act</u>: "In certifying that an event has occurred or an act has been performed, a notary public must determine the occurrence or performance either from personal knowledge or from satisfactory evidence based upon the oath or affirmation of a credible witness personally known to the notary public" (RCW 42.44.080[7]).

However, a Notary "may not endorse or promote any service, contest, or other offering if the notary's seal or title is used in the endorsement or promotional statement" (WAC 308-30-160).

Identifying Document Signers

For all acknowledgments — as well as for verifications upon oath or affirmation and for witnessing or attesting a signature — the Notary must positively identify the document signer through either personal knowledge or satisfactory evidence (RCW 42.44.080).

<u>Satisfactory Evidence</u>. "A notary public has satisfactory evidence that a person is the person described in a document if that person: (a) is personally known to the notary public; (b) is identified upon the oath or affirmation of a credible witness personally known to the notary public; or (c) is identified on the basis of identification documents" (RCW 42.44.080[8]).

Identification documents must be "(c)urrent documents issued by a federal or state government with the individual's photograph, signature and physical description" (WAC 308-30-155[1]). A credible witness must personally know the identified individual (WAC 308-30-155[2]).

Notary May Sign for Disabled

Persons who are mentally competent but unable to sign their name or make a mark may orally direct a Washington State Notary (or other authorized notarial officer) to sign for them (RCW 42.44.080[2] and 64.08.100). The Notary must determine that the person is unable to sign or make a mark and is otherwise capable, based on personal knowledge or satisfactory evidence.

"The notary public shall include in the acknowledgment a statement that the signature in the acknowledgment was obtained under the authority of RCW 64.08.100."

Illegibility Does Not Invalidate

"The illegibility of any wording, writing, or marking required under this chapter does not in and of itself affect the validity of a document or transaction" (RCW 42.44.110).

NOTARY DON'TS

Non-Attorneys May Not Select Certificates

"A nonattorney notary may complete notarial certificates, and may not assist another person in drafting, completing, selecting, or understanding a document or transaction requiring a notarial act. This does not preclude a notary who is duly qualified in a particular profession from giving advice relating to matters in that professional field" (WAC 308-30-090[2]).

Proof of Execution Not Authorized

A proof of execution by subscribing witness is not an act authorized for Notaries by Washington law (RCW 42.44.010 and 42.44.080).

False Certificate

"A notary public commits official misconduct when he or she signs a certificate evidencing a notarial act, knowing that the contents of the certificate are false. Official misconduct also constitutes unprofessional conduct for which disciplinary action may be taken....A notary public who commits an act of official misconduct shall be guilty of a gross misdemeanor" (RCW 42.44.160).

No Testimonials

"A notary may not endorse or promote any service, contest, or other offering if the notary's seal or title is used in the endorsement or promotional statement" (WAC 308-30-160).

Notary's Disqualifying Interest

A Notary is disqualified from performing a notarial act when the Notary is a signer of the document that is to be notarized (RCW 42.44.080[10]).

Notarizing for Relatives: "Can I notarize my relative's or spouse's signature? — Yes, a notary is only disqualified from notarizing their own signature. However, notarizing a relative's or spouse's signature may be seen as a conflict of interest" (website, "Frequently Asked Questions").

NOTARY SIGNING AGENTS

Currently, there are no statutes, regulations or rules expressly governing, prohibiting or restricting the operation of Notary Signing Agents within the state of Washington.

NOTARY FEES

The maximum fees that a Washington State Notary may charge for a notarial act are (WAC 308-30-020[1]):

1. Taking an acknowledgment, or a verification upon oath or affirmation: $10 per signature;
2. Administering an oath or affirmation: $10 per person;
3. Witnessing or attesting a signature: $10 per signature;
4. Certifying or attesting a copy: $10 per copy certified;
5. Certifying that an event has occurred or an act has been performed: $10 per certification;
6. Receiving or noting a protest of a negotiable instrument: $10;
7. Being present at demand, tender or deposit of a protest and noting same: $10;
8. Copying any document or record: actual cost.

Fees Need Not Be Charged

A Notary need not charge fees for notarial services (RCW 42.44.120[2] and WAC 308-30-020).

Travel Fee May Be Charged

"A notary may charge a travel fee when traveling to perform a notarial act if:

"a. The notary and the person requesting the notarial act agree upon the travel fee in advance of the travel; and

"b. The notary explains to the person requesting the notarial act that the travel fee is in addition to the notarial fee in subsection (1) of this section and is not required by law" (WAC 308-30-020[4]).

Fees Must Be Posted or Presented

"A notary who chooses to charge for notarial acts shall conspicuously display in their place of business, or present to each customer outside of their business, an English-language schedule of fees for notarial acts. No part of the displayed notarial fee schedule may be printed in smaller than 10-point type" (WAC 308-30-020[2]).

NOTARY CERTIFICATES

Form of Certificate

"1. A notarial act by a notary public must be evidenced by a certificate signed and dated by a notary public. The certificate must include the name of the jurisdiction in which the notarial act is performed and the title of the notary public or other notarial officer and shall be accompanied by an impression of the official seal or stamp. It shall not be necessary for a notary public in certifying an oath to be used in any of the courts in this state, to append an impression of the official seal or stamp. If the notarial officer is a notary public, the certificate shall also indicate the date of expiration of such notary public's appointment, but omission of that information may subsequently be corrected.

"2. A certificate of notarial act is sufficient if it meets the requirements of subsection (1) of this section and it:

"a. Is in the short form set forth in RCW 42.44.100;

"b. Is in a form otherwise permitted or prescribed by the laws of this state;

"c. Is in a form prescribed by the laws or regulations applicable in the place in which the notarial act was performed; or

"d. Is in a form that sets forth the actions of the notary public and the described actions are sufficient to meet the requirements of the designated notarial act.

"If any law of this state specifically requires a certificate in a form other than that set forth in RCW 42.44.100 in connection with a form of document or transaction, the certificate required by such law shall be used for such document or transaction...." (RCW 42.44.090).

Attached Notary Forms Must Be Page-Size

Effective September 1, 1997, state recording requirements stipulate that the Notary seal must be photocopiable and that attached notarial certificates must be the same size as the other document pages and with a one-inch margin. Stapled, taped or glued "Notary blocks" smaller than page size will be rejected:

"All pages of the document shall be on sheets of paper of a weight and color capable of producing a legible image that are not larger than fourteen inches long and eight and one-half inches wide with text printed or written in eight point type or larger. All text within the document must be of sufficient color and clarity to ensure that when the text is imaged all text is readable. Further, all pages presented for recording must have at minimum a one-inch margin on the top, bottom, and sides for all pages except page one, except that an instrument may be recorded if a minor portion of the notary seal, incidental writing, or minor portion of a signature extends beyond the margins, be prepared in ink color capable of being imaged, and have all seals legible and capable of being imaged. No attachments, except firmly attached bar code or address labels, may be affixed to the pages" (RCW 65.04.045).

Acknowledgment by Individual (RCW 64.08.060 and 64.08.050):

State of Washington)
County of _____)

On this day personally appeared before me _____ (here insert the name of grantor or grantors), to me known to be the individual or individuals described in and who executed the within and foregoing instrument, and acknowledged that he/she/they signed the same as his/her/their free and voluntary act and deed, for the uses and purposes therein mentioned.

Given under my hand and official seal this ____ day of _____, 20___.

(SIGNATURE AND SEAL/STAMP OF OFFICER)

For Notaries only, the following statement must follow the Notary's signature:

Notary Public in and for the state of Washington, residing at _____ (giving place of residence).

Certificates Only Suggested

"The forms in RCW 42.44.100 are only suggested certificates with the sufficient information included. These forms may be used; however, when a specific form is required by a specific statute, the required form shall be used" (WAC 308-30-090).

Short Form Acknowledgment by Individual (RCW 42.44.100[1]):

State of Washington
County of _____

I certify that I know or have satisfactory evidence that _____ (name of signer) is the person who appeared before me, and said person acknowledged that he/she signed this instrument and acknowledged it to be his/her free and voluntary act for the uses and purposes mentioned in the instrument.

Dated: _____
_____ (Signature)
_____ (Title)   (Seal or stamp)
My appointment expires _____

Acknowledgment by Person Unable to Sign Authorizing Notary to Sign on His or Her Behalf (RCW 42.44.080[2]) and 64.08.100):

State of Washington
County of _____

I certify that I know or have satisfactory evidence that _____ (name of person unable to sign) is the person who appeared before me and that said person was unable to write his/her name or to make a mark and is otherwise capable, and said person orally directed me to write his/her signature on this instrument on his/her behalf under authority of RCW 64.08.100, and acknowledged it to be his/her free and voluntary act for the uses and purposes mentioned in the instrument.

Washington

Dated: _____
_____ (Signature)
_____ (Title)   (Seal or stamp)
My appointment expires _____

Illegible Writing

The illegibility of any wording, writing or marking required by Chapter 42.44, "Notaries Public," does not in itself affect the validity of a document or transaction (RCW 42.44.110).

Acknowledgment by Corporation (RCW 64.08.070 and 64.08.050):

State of Washington)
County of _____)

On this ____ day of _____, 20____, before me personally appeared _____ (name of individual signing), to me known to be the _____ (president, vice president, secretary, treasurer, or other authorized officer or agent, as the case may be) of the corporation that executed the within and foregoing instrument, and acknowledged said instrument to be the free and voluntary act and deed of said corporation, for the uses and purposes therein mentioned, and on oath stated that he/she was authorized to execute said instrument and that the seal affixed is the corporate seal of said corporation.

In Witness Whereof I have hereunto set my hand and affixed my official seal the day and year first above written.

(SIGNATURE AND SEAL/STAMP OF OFFICER)

Notary Public in and for the state of Washington, residing at _____ (giving place of residence).

Short Form Acknowledgment by Corporate Officer, Attorney in Fact, Partner, Trustee, Guardian, Agent or Other Representative (RCW 42.44.100[2] and 42.44.010[6]):

State of Washington
County of _____

I certify that I know or have satisfactory evidence that _____ (name of person signing) is the person who appeared before me, and said person acknowledged that he/she signed this instrument, on oath stated that he/she was authorized to execute the instrument and acknowledged it as the _____ (type of authority, e.g., officer, trustee, etc.) of _____ (name of party on behalf of whom instrument was executed) to be the free and voluntary act of such party for the uses and purposes mentioned in the instrument.

Dated: _____
_____ (Signature)
_____ (Title)   (Seal or stamp)
My appointment expires _____

Short Form Verification Upon Oath or Affirmation (RCW 42.44.100[3]):

State of Washington
County of _____

Signed and sworn to (or affirmed) before me on _____ (date) by _____ (name of person making statement).

Dated: _____
_____ (Signature)
_____ (Title)   (Seal or stamp)
My appointment expires _____

Short Form Witnessing or Attesting of Signature (RCW 42.44.100[4]):

State of Washington
County of _____

Signed or attested before me on _____ (date) by _____ (name of signer or attestor).

Dated: _____
_____ (Signature)
_____ (Title)   (Seal or stamp)
My appointment expires _____

Short Form Attesting Copy of Document (RCW 42.44.100[5]):

State of Washington
County of _____

I certify that this is a true and correct copy of a document in the possession of _____ as of this date.

Dated: _____
_____ *(Signature)*
_____ *(Title)* *(Seal or stamp)*
My appointment expires _____

Short Form Certifying Occurrence of Event or Performance of Act (RCW 42.44.100[6]):

State of Washington
County of _____

I certify that the event or act described in this document has occurred or been performed.

Dated: _____
_____ *(Signature)*
_____ *(Title)* *(Seal or stamp)*
My appointment expires _____

ELECTRONIC NOTARIZATIONS

The state of Washington has not yet adopted statutes or regulations expressly establishing rules, definitions and procedures for electronic notarization.

Digital Certificate Same as Acknowledgment

Under the "Washington Electronic Authentication Act" (Chapter 19.34 RCW), a digital certificate issued by a certification authority may satisfy the requirements of a Notary's acknowledgment certificate:

"1. Unless otherwise provided by law or contract, if so provided in the certificate issued by a licensed certification authority, a digital signature verified by reference to the public key listed in a valid certificate issued by a licensed certification authority satisfies the requirements for an acknowledgment under RCW 42.44.010(4) and for acknowledgment of deeds and other real property conveyances under RCW 64.04.020 if words of an express acknowledgment appear with the digital signature regardless of whether the signer personally appeared before either the certification authority or some other person authorized to take acknowledgments of deeds, mortgages, or other conveyance instruments under RCW 64.08.010 when the digital signature was created, if that digital signature is:

"a. Verifiable by that certificate; and
"b. Affixed when that certificate was valid.

"2. If the digital signature is used as an acknowledgment, then the certification authority is responsible to the same extent as the notary up to the recommended reliance limit for failure to satisfy the requirements for acknowledgment. The certification authority may not disclaim or limit, other than as provided in RCW 19.34.280, the effect of this section" (RCW 19.34.340).

Certificates from Certification Authorities

Under the "Administrative Rules for Implementation of the Washington Electronic Authentication Act" (WAC 434-180) specifications for electronic acknowledgment certificates are as prescribed:

"1. Certificates issued by licensed certification authorities shall follow the Basic Certificate Field Standards specified in standard X.509, part one, section 4.1. Certificate data extension fields are optional. If certificate extension fields are used, usage must conform to the required guidelines referenced in X.509 section 4.1.2.1, section 4.2, and may be displayed on the certificate.

"2. Any certificate issued by a licensed certification authority that is to be used as an acknowledgment, as provided in RCW 19.34.340, shall include a certificate data extension field that specifies the reliance limit, if any, and a certificate data extension field that states that the certificate may be used as an acknowledgment" (WAC 434-180-300).

No Seal Image for Electronic Recording

Washington has adopted the Uniform Real Property Electronic Recording Act (URPERA) — see Title 65, Chapter 65.24 of the Revised Code of Washington — including the following provision related to the Notary's seal:

"A requirement that a document or a signature associated with a document be notarized, acknowledged, verified, witnessed, or made under oath is satisfied if the electronic signature of the person authorized to perform that act, and all other information required to be included, is attached to or logically associated with the document or signature. A physical or electronic image of a stamp, impression, or seal need not accompany an electronic signature" (RCW 65.24.020).

NOTARY RECORDS

Washington State law does not require Notaries to keep journals of notarial acts.

"Is a notary required to keep a journal? — No. It is not a requirement in Washington. However, it would be to your advantage to keep one" (website, "Frequently Asked Questions").

AUTHENTICATION OF NOTARIAL ACTS

Secretary of State

While state law (RCW 42.44.180[1][a]) gives both the Director of Licensing and the Secretary of State authority to issue authenticating certificates for notarial acts, such certificates (including apostilles) are currently issued only by the Washington Secretary of State (website, "Apostilles and Certificates of Authority"). The pertinent website for the Secretary of State is: www.sos.wa.gov/corps/apostilles/.

Fee: $15 per document (WAC 308-30-100), payable to "Secretary of State."

Mailing Address:
Washington Secretary of State
Corporations Division
Apostille and Certification Program
801 Capitol Way South
P.O. Box 40228
Olympia, WA 98504-0228

Telephone: 1-360-725-0344
1-360-725-0345

Procedure: Mail or present the original notarized document(s), along with the appropriate fee. If the document is mailed, a cover letter must include the name of the nation to which the document will be sent; a return name and address; and a daytime telephone number for any questions that may arise.

County Clerks No Longer Authenticate

See below, "County Clerks," indicating that county clerks no longer keep records of Notaries and, thus, are unable to authenticate their acts.

COMMISSIONING AND ADMINISTRATION

The Director of the Department of Licensing appoints, regulates and maintains records on Washington State's Notaries (RCW 42.44.020).

Most information in an application for a Notary appointment is a public record and subject to public disclosure provisions in RCW 42.17.

Applying for Appointment

Qualifications: An applicant for appointment as a Washington State Notary Public must (RCW 42.44.020[1]): (a) be at least 18 years old, (b) be able to read and write the English language and (c) reside in Washington or reside in Oregon or Idaho and be regularly employed or carry on business in Washington.

No Course or Test: No course of instruction or test is required of applicants for a Notary appointment in Washington. "Although you aren't required to complete an education course to become a notary in Washington State, we feel it's extremely beneficial because you'll learn how to perform notarial acts correctly" (website, "Education").

Application: The application form (WAC 308-30-030) must be endorsed by three persons, not relatives, who are 18 years of age or older and eligible to vote in Washington and who must write in their addresses (RCW 42.44.020[2]), but these endorsements are not required for reappointment if the application is made before appointment expiration (RCW 42.44.070), nor is completing the "Declaration of Applicant" before a Notary. Along with the $30 fee (RCW 42.44.020[3]), a copy of a $10,000 Notary surety bond must accompany the application. The name and signature on the application form must be identical.

Non-Residents: An applicant for a Notary appointment may reside in an adjoining state (Oregon or Idaho) if regularly employed or conducting business in Washington (RCW 42.44.020[1]).

Online Search: The Department's system for online search of business and professional licenses (https://fortress.wa.gov/business/check-status.html) allows access to certain licensing data, including that of Notaries. Information available about a given Washington Notary includes: city and zip code, license number, active or inactive status and commission expiration date.

Changes of Status

If Notary Moves: Notaries who move must notify the Department of Licensing in writing

(WAC 308-30-060). Notification by email at intnotarie@dol.wa.gov is allowed. The name as shown on the certificate of appointment, along with date of birth, and previous and new addresses, must be included. There is no fee for an address change.

If Notary Changes Name: Notaries who change their name must notify the Department of Licensing in writing, submitting a rider from the bonding company and $15 for a new certificate of appointment, and then notarize using the new name (WAC 308-30-060).

If Notary Resigns: No voluntary resignation of a Notary appointment is effective until the Department of Licensing is notified in writing and the Notary seal or stamp is mailed or delivered to the Department (WAC 308-30-040). A Notary who moves from the state or ceases to be employed in the state must resign the commission (WAC 308-30-150).

If a Notary is found to be incompetent by a court, the Notary's guardian or conservator must mail or deliver a letter of resignation within 30 days of the judicial finding (RCW 42.44.170[1]).

Notification of Conviction, Lawsuit: "The notary must notify the department of licensing of any conviction against him or her of official misconduct, and/or civil or criminal charges. Notification must be submitted within thirty days of such happening" (WAC 308-30-140).

COUNTY CLERKS

County clerk records related to the appointing and commissioning of Notaries were transferred to the Department of Licensing on or before December 31, 1985 (RCW 42.44.200).

OTHER NOTARIAL OFFICERS

Besides Notaries Public, the following officers have power to take acknowledgment of deeds, mortgages and other documents (RCW 64.08.010):

1. A justice of the Supreme Court, or clerk thereof, or the deputy of such clerk;
2. A judge or clerk of the court of appeals;
3. A judge or qualified commissioner of the superior court, or a clerk thereof, or the deputy of such clerk;
4. A county auditor or deputy thereof;
5. A qualified U.S. commissioner appointed by any U.S. district court of the state.

Officers of Correctional Facilities

The superintendents, associate and assistant superintendents, business managers, records officers and camp superintendents of any correctional facility operated by the state may take acknowledgments and administer oaths for officers, employees and residents of such facilities, but without requiring a fee. "In certifying any oath or in signing any instrument officially, an individual empowered to do so under this section shall, in addition to his name, state in writing his place of residence, the date of his action, and affix the seal of the institution where he is employed" (RCW 64.08.090).

QUICK FACTS

Notary Jurisdiction
Statewide (RCW 42.44.060).

Notary Term Length
Four years (RCW 42.44.060), expiring at midnight on the appointment expiration date.

Notary Bond
$10,000, with a company qualified to write surety bonds in Washington (RCW 42.44.020[5]).

V–W

West Virginia

NOTARY SEAL

A West Virginia Notary Public must affix an official seal of office on every notarial certificate, and the seal's format must be as follows (WVC 29C-4-102):

Kind

Inked Rubber Stamp: "Under or near his official signature on every notarial certificate, a notary public shall rubber stamp clearly and legibly, so that it is capable of photographic reproduction ..." (WVC 29C-4-102). "The color of the ink is optional" (website, "Notary Seal").

An embossing seal may be used in addition to but not in lieu of the required rubber inking seal (WVC 29C-4-103). "If you use the embossing seal, you must carefully apply it so the indentations don't make the printing or writing on the document illegible" (NPH).

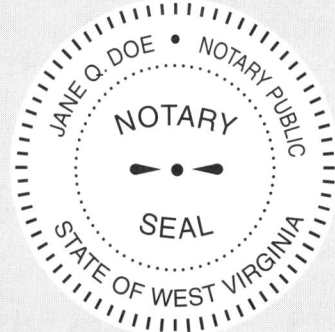

Examples

The above typical, actual-size examples of mandatory inking and optional embossing Notary seals are allowed by West Virginia law. Formats other than these may also be permitted.

NOTARY ADMINISTRATION

Office of Secretary of State
Business and Licensing Division
Notary Administrator   1-304-558-6000
State Capitol, Bldg. 1, Suite 157-K
1900 Kanawha Blvd., East
Charleston, WV 25305-0770

Website: www.wvsos.com/ business-licensing/notaries/Pages/default.aspx

NOTARY RULES

WVC — WEST VIRGINIA CODE
NPH — WEST VIRGINIA NOTARY HANDBOOK

Most Notary rules are in the West Virginia Code:

a. Chapter 29C ("Uniform Notary Act"), Articles 1 through 9;

b. Chapter 39, Article 1A, "Uniform Recognition of Acknowledgments Act."*

*This is the *Uniform Recognition of Acknowledgments Act* of 1968, adopted virtually verbatim.

Other guidelines for Notaries are in the "West Virginia Notary Handbook" published by the Secretary of State and available on the website.

Shape/Size

Rectangular: Not more than 1 inch high by $2^{1}/_{2}$ inches wide.

Customarily, the optional embossing seal is circular.

Border

The rectangular stamp must have a "serrated or milled edge" border surrounding the following components:

Components — Inked Rubber Stamp

1. "Official Seal";

2. "Notary Public";
3. "State of West Virginia";
4. Notary's name, exactly as in official signature, which must contain the surname and at least the initial of the first name (WVC 29C-2-207);
5. Business name, if a business address is used in seal;
6. Notary's business or residence address in the state;
7. "My commission expires _____(date)";
8. OPTIONAL: West Virginia State Seal: "Most notary stamp seals have the West Virginia State Seal on the left" (website, "Notary Seal").

Components — Optional Embosser
1. "Notary Seal";
2. Notary's name;
3. "Notary Public";
4. "State of West Virginia".

Illegibility of Notary Seal or Signature

The illegibility of the Notary's seal or signature does not affect the validity of a transaction (WVC 29C-4-104).

Obtaining a Seal

"When you order, send a photocopy of your commission letter which will include the exact information which is to be included on the seal, and the specifications. That way, if there is an error, the company should remake it at no extra charge. The name and address must be exactly as you were commissioned, and you must sign all notarizations with that name" (website, "Notary Seal").

Secretary of State Has Seal Imprint

Every applicant for a Notary commission must submit a specimen signature to the Secretary of State (WVC 29C-2-207) and, upon receiving a notification letter from the Secretary and having an official seal manufactured, a seal specimen (website, "Applying for a Notary Public Commission"). Then, after receiving a commission certificate, the Notary may begin notarizing.

A name or address change by the Notary requires a new seal, an imprint of which must be placed on the letter informing the Secretary of State of the change. The fee for recording this change is $2.

Security of Seal

"The security of the seal is liability protection for a notary public. Keep the seal in a safe place, where it can't be used or taken by anyone" (website, "Notary Seal").

Lost Seal

"Every notary public shall mail or deliver notice to the secretary of state within thirty days after he loses or misplaces his official seal" (WVC 29C-4-203). This notice should include the Notary's name, commission expiration date, address and date the seal was lost (NPH).

The fee for recording the loss of a seal is $2. An imprint of the replacement seal should be sent to the Secretary of State.

Disposing of Seal

The Notary must immediately destroy the official seal upon commission revocation or resignation, upon moving from the state or upon failure to be reappointed (WVC 29C-4-401 through 29C-4-404). In the case of the Notary's death, the seal should be destroyed as soon as possible by the heirs or personal representative.

"It is a good idea to destroy an old seal as soon as it is no longer legally useful. This happens when your 10-year term ends, or your name or address changes and you obtain a new seal with the new information. Destroying an old seal protects you against possible theft and fraudulent use" (website, "Notary Seal").

Wrongful Possession of Seal

"Any person who unlawfully possesses a notary's official seal or any papers or copies relating to notarial acts, is guilty of a misdemeanor, and, upon conviction, shall be fined not more than one thousand dollars" (WVC 29C-6-204).

Notary's Signature

"When you act as a notary, always sign your name exactly as you did on your application, and exactly as it appears on your seal" (NPH).

If the Notary has informed the Secretary of State of a name change but not yet obtained a new seal, the Notary may affix the old seal and sign the new official name, writing, "Commissioned as _____ (old official name)," underneath the signature (NPH).

Seal of Commissioner of Deeds

The seal of a West Virginia Commissioner

of Deeds must be an inking rubber stamp and contain: (a) the words "Official Seal"; (b) the words "Commissioner for West Virginia"; (c) the commissioner's name exactly as it is written as an official signature; (d) the city and state of residence of the commissioner; and (e) the words "My Commission Expires" followed by the date of expiration of the commission (WVC 29-4-15).

A stamped imprint of this seal, together with the official signature, must be filed in the office of the West Virginia Secretary of State. A person holding a commission prior to July 1, 2011, is not required to use a seal with the above specifications before expiration of the commission.

NOTARY POWERS

West Virginia Notaries are authorized to perform the following notarial acts (WVC 29C-3-101):
1. Take acknowledgments* and proofs** (WVC 39-1A-1);
2. Administer oaths*** and affirmations;
3. Certify copies****.

* Identifying Acknowledgers: "The person taking an acknowledgment shall certify that … (t)he person acknowledging was known to the person taking the acknowledgment or that the person taking the acknowledgment had satisfactory evidence that the person acknowledging was the person described in and who executed the instrument" (WVC 39-1A-3).

** Proof by Executing Witness: "Occasionally a person is unable to appear before a notary to acknowledge his or her signature. In this case, another person witnesses the first person sign the document, then appears before the notary as an executing witness to complete the notarization needed" (NPH).

An executing (subscribing) witness for a proof may not be related to the principal signer by blood or marriage, nor be named individually as a party to the transaction, nor receive any "advantage, right, title, interest, cash or property" as a direct result of the transaction (WVC 29C-5-103[b] and 29C-3-102).

*** Format for Spoken Oath: The wording for a spoken oath is substantially as follows: "You do solemnly swear or affirm, under the penalty of perjury, that the testimony you shall give in the matter in issue, pending between _____ and _____, shall be the truth, the whole truth, and nothing but the truth, so help you God?" (NPH and WVC 29C-5-102[b]).

**** Certified Copy Procedures: "A notary public may certify a facsimile of a document if he receives a signed written request stating that:

"(1) A certified copy or facsimile of the document cannot be obtained from the office of any recorder of public documents or custodian of documents in this state; and

"(2) The production of a facsimile, preparation of a copy or certification of a copy of the document does not violate any state or federal law ….

"Every notary public shall retain a facsimile of each document he has certified as a facsimile of another document, together with other papers or copies relating to his notarial acts" (WVC 29C-5-104).

Identifying Signers

"You don't need to ask for identification if you know the person signing the document, otherwise ask for a driver's license or some other identification" (NPH).

NOTARY DON'TS

A West Virginia Notary may (WVC 29C-7-101):
1. NOT represent or imply "from unauthorized use of his title of notary public that he has qualifications, powers, duties, rights or privileges that by law he does not possess";
2. NOT allow or permit "his name or his title of notary public to be used deceptively, fraudulently or in false or misleading advertising";
3. NOT notarize when "doubtful of the person's mental competence to understand the transaction" (NPH);
4. NOT engage in the unauthorized practice of law (WVC 30-2-4);
5. NOT "notarize the signature of someone you don't know without requiring proper identification" (website, "FAQs About Notary Practice").

Blank Documents Should Not Be Notarized

"Don't notarize a blank, unsigned document on the promise that a certain person is going to sign it later" (NPH).

"Never notarize a blank document" (website, "FAQs About Notary Practice").

Telephone Notarizations Not Allowed

"(T)he person must sign the document or acknowledge their signature in person — never on the phone" (website, "Practice FAQ").

Disqualifying Interests

A Notary may not notarize (a) if named individually as a party to the transaction requiring a notarial act, or (b) if receiving as a direct result any "advantage, right, title, interest, cash or property" exceeding in value the statutory fee for a notarization or the Notary's regular compensation as an employee (WVC 29C-3-102). "If you are a named party to the transaction or may receive direct benefit, such as cash, property or title from the transaction, you have a disqualifying interest and must refrain from notarizing any such documents" (website, "FAQs About Notary Practice").

Notarizing for Family: "Generally, be careful about notarizing papers for members of your immediate family if you could conceivably receive money or property interest from the transaction" (NPH).

Notarizing for Employer: "According to law, an employee is specifically allowed to notarize documents prepared by his or her employer as long as this is part of the regular duties of the job and no extra compensation is given as a result" (NPH).

"Employees may notarize for an employer, providing the transaction does not stand to benefit them in excess of their normal salary and benefits" (website, "FAQs About Notary Practice").

Attorneys Notarizing for Clients: "If you are an attorney and have prepared the documents for your client, the West Virginia State Bar advises that you have a third party perform the notarization" (NPH).

Government Employee Notaries Limited

"If you were commissioned in your capacity as a state or local government employee (with the application fee waived), you may act only as authorized by the government office or offices in which you are employed.

"If the office authorizes you to notarize private documents for walk-in clients, it is permissible, but you may not charge a fee. You should not perform notarial services outside the office except those specifically pertaining to office business" (NPH).

May Not Prepare Documents

"Any notary who is not an attorney should be aware that drafting legal documents is considered practicing law, and should reject any requests to help prepare any agreement, will, deed or any other legal document for signing and notarization. Also, notaries are not authorized to prepare vehicle title transfers" (website, "Compliance").

Criminal Misconduct by Notary

"Criminal misdemeanor charges may be brought against a notary public for official misconduct. The penalty for 'knowingly and willfully' committing official misconduct is a fine of up to $5,000 and a sentence of up to one year in jail."

"For 'recklessly and negligently' committing official misconduct, the penalty is up to a $1,000 fine" (website, "Compliance"). (See also WVC 29C-6-202[b].)

NOTARY SIGNING AGENTS

West Virginia is currently considered an "attorney-only" state in which only a licensed member of the state bar may conduct a real estate or loan closing. Thus, under West Virginia law as it is now officially interpreted, a non-attorney Notary Signing Agent may not notarize at closings unless under the supervision of an attorney.

West Virginia State Bar Opinion

An opinion issued by the West Virginia State Bar's Committee on the Unauthorized Practice of Law (Opinion No. 2003-01) explains why no non-attorney may preside at a real estate closing in West Virginia:

"Most importantly … it is inherent at the closing itself that buyers and sellers will have questions about the transaction and the document, which answers necessarily go to their respective legal rights and obligations. Such answers are advising on legal matters. Thus, in West Virginia, generally, real estate closings constitute the practice of law.

"In conclusion, it is clear that as a whole, real estate closings are the practice of law. The

Committee presumes that significant harm to the public occurs just by the practice of law by lay persons and holds such practices to be the unauthorized practice of law.

"The reference to lay persons in this section does not apply to a non-lawyer assistant employed, retained by or associated with a lawyer in accordance with Rule 5.3 of the Rules of Professional Conduct and consistent with all other Rules of Professional Conduct."

NOTARY FEES

The maximum fees that may be charged by a West Virginia Notary for a notarial act are (WVC 29C-4-301):

1. For each signature notarized: $2;
2. For certifying a facsimile, recording same in the Notary's journal, and retaining a copy: $2 for each $8^1/_2$ by 11 inch page kept;
3. For any other notarial act: $2.

Government Employees

"If you were commissioned in your capacity as a state or local government employee (with the application fee waived), you may act only as authorized by the government office or offices in which you are employed.

"If the office authorizes you to notarize private documents for walk-in clients, it is permissible, but you may not charge a fee. You should not perform notarial services outside the office except those specifically pertaining to office business" (NPH).

NOTARY CERTIFICATES

West Virginia has adopted the *Uniform Recognition of Acknowledgments Act*, including the short-form certificates (WVC 39-1A-6) for:

1. Acknowledgment by individual;
2. Acknowledgment by corporation;
3. Acknowledgment by partnership;
4. Acknowledgment by attorney in fact;
5. Acknowledgment by public officer, trustee, or personal representative.

The Notary's seal must be added to each certificate.

For the text of the above certificates, see "Uniform Recognition of Acknowledgments Act (1968)," Section 6, in Appendix 3.

In addition to the above forms, the following notarial certificates are recommended for Notaries by the West Virginia Secretary of State, who adapted them with minor modifications (i.e., adding "My commission expires _____,") from statute:

Short Form Acknowledgment by Individual (NPH and WVC 39-1A-6[1]):

STATE OF WEST VIRGINIA
COUNTY OF _____

The foregoing instrument was acknowledged before me this _____ (date) by _____ (name of person acknowledging). My commission expires _____.

_____   *(SEAL)*
Notary Public

Acknowledgment by Individual (Alternate Form) (NPH):

STATE OF WEST VIRGINIA
COUNTY OF _____

I, _____ (name of Notary), a Notary Public in and for said state, do hereby certify that _____ (name of person signing document), whose name is signed to the writing above, has this day acknowledged the same before me.

Given under my hand this ____ day of _____, 20__.

My commission expires _____.

_____   *(SEAL)*
Notary Public

Short Form Acknowledgment by Corporation (NPH and WVC 39-1A-6[2]):

STATE OF WEST VIRGINIA
COUNTY OF _____

West Virginia

The foregoing instrument was acknowledged before me this _____ (date) by _____ (name and title of person signing document) of _____ (name of corporation), a _____ (state or place of incorporation) corporation, on behalf of the corporation.

My commission expires _____.

_____   (SEAL)
Notary Public

Acknowledgment by Corporation (Alternate Form) (NPH):

STATE OF WEST VIRGINIA
COUNTY OF _____

I, _____ (name of Notary), a Notary Public in and for said state, do hereby certify that _____ (name of officer signing document), who signed the writing above, bearing the date of _____, for _____ (name of corporation), has this day acknowledged before me the said writing to be the act and deed of said corporation.

Given under my hand this _____ day of _____, 20___.

My commission expires _____.

_____   (SEAL)
Notary Public

Short Form Acknowledgment by Partnership (NPH and WVC 39-1A-6[3]):

STATE OF WEST VIRGINIA
COUNTY OF _____

The foregoing instrument was acknowledged before me this _____ (date) by _____ (name of partner or agent signing document), partner (or agent) on behalf of _____ (name of partnership), a partnership.

My commission expires _____.

_____   (SEAL)
Notary Public

Short Form Acknowledgment by Attorney in Fact (NPH and WVC 39-1A-6[4]):

STATE OF WEST VIRGINIA
COUNTY OF _____

The foregoing instrument was acknowledged before me this _____ (date) by _____ (name of attorney in fact) as attorney in fact on behalf of _____ (name of principal).

My commission expires _____.

_____   (SEAL)
Notary Public

Acknowledgment by Individual Who Cannot Sign Name (NPH and WVC 29C-5-101[b]):

STATE OF WEST VIRGINIA
COUNTY OF _____

On this _____ day of _____, in the year 20___, before me, _____ (name of Notary), a Notary Public in and for said state, personally appeared _____ (name of individual), known to me to be the person who, being unable to write his/her name, made his/her mark in my presence. I signed his/her name at his/her request and in his/her presence on the _____ (type of document) within and he/she acknowledged to me and the two witnesses who have signed and printed their names and addresses hereto, that he/she made his/her mark on the same for the purposes therein stated.

My commission expires _____.

_____   (SEAL)
Notary Public
_____
_____
(Signatures, addresses of the two witnesses)

Acknowledgment by U.S. Citizen Outside U.S. (WVC 29C-5-101[b]):

(Description or location of place where acknowledgment is taken)

On this _____ day of _____, in the year 20___, before me _____ (name and title of person acting as a Notary and refer to law or authority granting power to act as a Notary), personally appeared _____ (name of citizen), known to me to be the person who executed the within _____ (type of document), and acknowledged to me that he/she executed the same for the purposes therein stated.

_____   (SEAL)
(Official signature and official seal of person acting as a Notary and refer to law or authority granting power to act as a Notary)

Format for Acknowledgment Certificate

"The form of a certificate of acknowledgment shall be accepted in this state if: (1) The certificate is in a form prescribed by the laws or regulations of this state; (2) The certificate is in a form prescribed by the laws or regulations applicable in the place in which the acknowledgment is taken; or (3) The certificate contains the words 'acknowledged before me,' or their substantial equivalent" (WVC 39-1A-4).

Inappropriate Notarial Certificate

"Often, a notary will be presented with a document already prepared with an acknowledgment or oath form typed for the notary to simply fill out and sign. But if the proper form has not been provided on the document, it is the notary's duty to add text of the acknowledgment or oath" (website, "Notary Practices").

Proof by Subscribing (Executing) Witness (NPH and WVC 29C-5-103):

*STATE OF WEST VIRGINIA
COUNTY OF _____*

I, _____ (name of executing witness), do solemnly swear under the penalty of perjury, that _____ (name of person who does not appear before a Notary), personally known to me, has executed the within _____ (type of document) in my presence, and has acknowledged to me that he/she executed the same for the purposes therein stated and requested that I sign my name on the within document as an executing witness.

_____ *(signature of executing witness)*

Subscribed and sworn before me this _____ day of _____, 20___.

My commission expires _____.

_____   (SEAL)
Notary Public

Written Oath Format (NPH and WVC 29C-5-102):

*STATE OF WEST VIRGINIA
COUNTY OF _____*

*(TEXT OF OATH)
Subscribed and sworn before me this _____ day of _____, 20___.*

My commission expires _____.

_____   (SEAL)
Notary Public

Certification of Copy (NPH and WVC 29C-5-104):

*STATE OF WEST VIRGINIA
COUNTY OF _____*

I, _____ (name of Notary), a Notary Public in and for said state (or county), do certify that on _____ (date), I carefully compared the attached facsimile of _____ (type of document) and the facsimile I now hold in my possession. They are complete, full, true and exact facsimiles of the document they purport to reproduce.

My commission expires _____.

_____   (SEAL)
Notary Public

ELECTRONIC NOTARIZATIONS

The state of West Virginia has not yet adopted statutes or regulations expressly establishing rules, definitions and procedures for electronic notarization.

UETA Recognizes Notary's eSignature

West Virginia has adopted the Uniform Electronic Transactions Act (WVC 39A-1-1 through 39A-1-17), including the provision on notarization, thereby recognizing the legal validity of electronic signatures used by Notaries:

"If a law requires a signature or record to be notarized, acknowledged, verified or made under oath, the requirement is satisfied if the electronic signature of the person authorized to perform those acts, together with all other information required to be included by other applicable law, is attached to or logically associated with the signature or record" (WVC 39A-1-11).

NOTARY RECORDS

The notarial fee statute (WVC 29C-4-301) indicates that Notaries charge for the "notarization of each signature and the proper recordation thereof in the journal of notarial acts ...." This statute also states that, in certifying a facsimile, a Notary keeps an additional facsimile as an official record, in addition to recording the certification in the journal of notarial acts.

"In West Virginia, notaries are not required to keep a journal of their acts. However, if you are concerned about liability, keeping a notary journal listing the date, name and type of document notarized will help protect you" (NPH).

Disposition of Notary's Records

If a Notary commission is terminated by resignation, moving out of state, revocation or the death of the Notary, the Notary's official papers must immediately be sent by certified mail or delivered to the Secretary of State (WVC 29C-4-401 through 29C-4-403). In the case of the Notary's death, they should be mailed or delivered by "his heirs or personal representative, as soon as reasonably possible."

A Notary who is not reappointed to act as a Notary must send by certified mail or deliver the notarial records to the Secretary of State within 30 days after commission expiration (WVC 29C-4-404).

Wrongful Possession of Journal

"Any person who unlawfully possesses a notary's official seal or any papers or copies relating to notarial acts, is guilty of a misdemeanor, and, upon conviction, shall be fined not more than one thousand dollars" (WVC 29C-6-204).

AUTHENTICATION OF NOTARIAL ACTS

Secretary of State

Authenticating certificates for Notaries, including apostilles, are issued only by the office of West Virginia's Secretary of State (WVC 29C-8-101).

Fees: $10 for a certificate authenticating the act of a Notary or county clerk, or for an apostille. The cost for multiple certifications of various documents from the same Notary or public official is $10 for the first certification and $5 for each additional (Secretary's website, "Executive Records" at "Authentication of Documents for International Use").

Address:
Office of Secretary of State
Notary Administrator
State Capitol, Bldg. 1, Suite 157-K
1900 Kanawha Blvd., East
Charleston, WV 25305-0770

Telephone: 1-304-558-6000

Procedure: Mail or present in person the original notarized document(s), along with the appropriate fee and a completed "Authentication Service Request Form." Indicate the nation to which the document will be sent and the return address. A notarized document must include the Notary's original signature and rubber stamp seal impression, and a notarial form (acknowledgment, jurat, etc.). "Documents must be originals or certified copies — plain copies cannot be certified. If a certified copy cannot be obtained from an officer in West Virginia (such as a birth, marriage or death certificate, deed, will, or license), a notary is not authorized to certify a copy. A certified copy from a County Clerk, Circuit Clerk or Registrar must have an original signature of the clerk or a deputy and a raised impression seal...

"If you need express mail services, enclose a prepaid return Express Mail packet or a FedEx, UPS or other shipping service packet with your account number .... Complete requests with paper documents received by mail will generally be prepared and mailed back within 24-48 hours. Complete requests with proper documents received by express delivery will be prepared for the next pick-up, if possible, or within 24 hours.

Walk-in customers are served as soon as possible, usually within a few minutes" (Secretary's website, "Executive Records" at "Authentication of Documents for International Use").

Authenticating FBI Background Checks: As of August 1, 2009, the Secretary of State was no longer able to authenticate FBI background checks directly. These checks must now be notarized by a West Virginia Notary before they can be authenticated by the Secretary. "The background check can be photocopied by the person who owns it, and then an affidavit can be drafted, which would refer to the fingerprint/report, with general information stating where the fingerprint was obtained and the person it was obtained for. This affidavit must be signed in front of a notary by the person mentioned on the card and must be on a separate sheet of paper from the document. Once the notary has (notarized) this affidavit, send the affidavit, copy of the background check and criminal record (if applicable) to our office for authentication" (Secretary's website, "Executive Records" at "Authentication of Documents for International Use").

The website prescribes the following format:

I, _____ (name on fingerprint card), verify that the attached is an original background check that has been issued by the Federal Bureau of Investigation in _____ (town), West Virginia.

_____ (signature)
_____ (date)

STATE OF WEST VIRGINIA
COUNTY OF _____

I, _____, a Notary Public in and for said state (or county), do certify that on _____ (date), I carefully compared the attached original of _____ (name on fingerprint card) FBI background check and the copy I now hold in my possession. They are complete, full, true and exact copies of the document they purport to reproduce.

Notary Signature: _____ (SEAL)
My commission expires: _____.

COMMISSIONING AND ADMINISTRATION

Though West Virginia's Notaries have been appointed and commissioned by the Governor (WVC 29C-2-101[a]), it is the office of the Secretary of State that directly regulates and maintains records on them (WVC 29C-2-101[c]).

"Only the names, addresses, residence counties and commission dates of notaries public are public information. Other information in the application or the notary's record is not subject to release" (website, "Requesting Information"). See also WVC 29C-2-206.

Applying for Commission

Qualifications: An applicant for appointment as a West Virginia Notary must (WVC 29C-2-201): (a) be a citizen of the United States or of a country allowing U.S. citizens to become a Notary there, (b) be at least 18 years old, (c) not be disqualified from voter registration due to conviction for a felony, (d) be a resident of West Virginia or of another state who works at an office address within West Virginia, (e) be able to read and write English and (f) not have had a Notary commission revoked within the past 10 years.

No Course or Test: There is no requirement that applicants for a West Virginia Notary commission take a course of instruction or a test on their duties. "On the application you will be signing an oath that you have read and understand the requirements and will follow the law" (website, "Applying for a Notary Public Commission). The state's Notary laws are available on the website. Also downloadable on the website is a Notary handbook, and the Notary is directed to keep this guide handy whenever performing notarial acts.

Application: Every application for a Notary commission must be endorsed by three qualified electors of the state (WVC 29C-2-203). The accompanying oath must be witnessed by a Notary or other oath-administering official (WVC 29C-2-204). In addition, for state and local (but not federal) government employees who have their application fees waived, a letter from the pertinent government office head is required (WVC 29C-2-301); but federal employees may apply as regular Notaries and have their agencies pay the fees (website, "Application FAQ"). The commission application fee is $52 (WVC 29C-

2-202 and -207). It takes about three weeks for a commission to be issued after the completed application and payment are received (website, "Requesting Information").

For a renewal, the application process is the same. "If your current commission is due to expire, apply early so there will be no break between your old and new commissions…(If) you wish to keep the same month and day of expiration, please be sure to include that on the application form and apply at least two weeks prior to your expiration date" (website, "Applying for a Notary Public Commission").

Filing Seal Imprint Card: After receiving the application from the Notary commission applicant but before sending out a new commission to the applicant, the Secretary of State will mail the applicant a letter indicating the exact information that the new Notary seal must contain, along with a seal imprint card. The applicant must then obtain a new seal, affix an imprint of this seal on the card and mail the completed card back to the Secretary of State, whereupon the Secretary will send the Notary the official commission certificate. At that point, the Notary may begin notarizing.

Non-Residents: An out-of-state resident who works or has a business in West Virginia may apply to become a Notary in the state (WVC 29C-2-201).

Online Search: Information on Notaries that has been filed with the West Virginia Secretary of State may be accessed online by entering the Notary's first and last names. Information provided includes the Notary's name, address, city, zip code, county and commission starting and expiration dates. The Web location is http://apps.sos.wv.gov/business/notary/.

Changes of Status

If Notary Moves: "Every notary public shall mail or deliver notice to the Secretary of State within thirty days after he changes the address of his business or residence in this state" (WVC 29C-4-201). The fee to record this change is $2. A new seal with a new address must be obtained. "Write a letter requesting that your address be changed, and place an imprint of your new seal at the bottom of the letter" (website, "Making Changes"). This letter must also contain the Notary's old and new address and the commission expiration date (NPH). "You may wish to have the new seal made first, then file the change and the new seal imprint at the same time" (website, "Notary Seal").

If the Notary fails to maintain a business or residence address in the state, the Notary must immediately send in a letter of resignation, along with the official notarial records (WVC 29C-4-402).

"(T)he employer may not have the commission canceled. However, it is your duty to file a change of address and get a new seal immediately if your (former) employer's address is on your seal" (website, "Application FAQ").

If Notary Changes Name: "Every notary public shall mail or deliver notice to the secretary of state within thirty days after he changes his name, including with the notification a specimen of his handwritten official signature which contains his surname and at least the initial of his first name" (WVC 29C-4-202). The fee to record this change is $2. "Write a letter requesting that your name be changed, and place an imprint of your new seal at the bottom of the letter" (website, "Making Changes"). This letter must also contain the Notary's old and new name and the commission expiration date (NPH). "You may wish to have the new seal made first, then file the change and the new seal imprint at the same time" (website, "Notary Seal").

After notifying the Secretary of State of the name change, until a new seal is ordered, the Notary may use the old seal and sign the new official name on notarial certificates, writing, "Commissioned as _____ (old official name)," underneath (NPH). Destroy the old seal when the new one becomes available.

If Name and Address Change Together: "You may change both name and address with a single filing and a total fee of four dollars" (website, "Making Changes").

If Notary Resigns: A Notary who moves out of the state or otherwise acts to resign the commission must resign in writing and destroy the official seal (website, "Making Changes"). The law requires that the resigning Notary "send forthwith by certified mail or deliver to the secretary of state a letter of resignation and all papers and copies relating to his notarial acts" (WVC 29C-4-402).

COUNTY CLERKS

Effective July 1, 1984, West Virginia no longer commissions Notaries with just countywide powers. Thus, county clerks no longer keep records on local Notaries.

OTHER NOTARIAL OFFICERS

Commissioners of Deeds

The West Virginia Governor may appoint commissioners to take acknowledgments and oaths, in or out of the state, on deeds, leases and other documents pertaining to West Virginia property that will be recorded in the state (WVC 29-4-12 through 29-4-16). Such commissioners may also take affidavits and depositions. Commissioners need not be residents of West Virginia nor have a business address in the state. These commissioners will hold office for a term of 10 years and carry a $1,000 bond. The commissioning fee is $100. Specifications for commissioners' mandatory rubber stamp seals are listed above under "Notary Seal" / "Seal of Commissioner of Deeds".

This commission is used primarily by those representing businesses who conduct property or other legal transactions to be filed in West Virginia, and by court reporters who go outside the state to take depositions or affidavits to be filed in state courts.

QUICK FACTS

Notary Jurisdiction
Statewide (WVC 29C-2-102).

Notary Term Length
Ten years (WVC 29C-2-102).

Notary Bond
Not required by law.

<u>Employer Liability</u>: "The employer of a notary public is also liable to the persons involved for all damages, if: (a) The notary public was acting within the scope of his employment at the time he engaged in the official misconduct; and (b) The employer consented to the notary public's official misconduct" (WVC 29C-6-102).

V–W

Wisconsin

NOTARY ADMINISTRATION

Department of Financial Institutions
Notary Public & 1-608-266-8915
 Trademarks
345 W. Washington Ave., 3rd Floor
Madison, WI 53703

Mailing address:
P.O. Box 7847
Madison, WI 53707-7847

Website: www.wdfi.org

NOTARY RULES

WS — WISCONSIN STATUTES
NPI — NOTARY PUBLIC INFORMATION brochure
NPT — WISCONSIN NOTARY PUBLIC TUTORIAL

Most Notary rules are in the Wisconsin Statutes:

a. Chapter 137, Subchapter I, "Notaries and Commissioners of Deeds; Nonelectronic Notarization and Acknowledgment";

b. Chapter 706, including Section 706.07, "Uniform Law On Notarial Acts."*

 * This is the *Uniform Law on Notarial Acts* of 1982, adopted virtually intact.

Other guidelines for Notaries are in the "Notary Public Information" (Web Ed., July 2009) brochure published by the Department of Financial Institutions and available on the website.

In addition, the "Wisconsin Notary Public Tutorial," accessible on the website, contains helpful guidelines.

NOTARY SEAL

A Wisconsin Notary (including an attorney who is a Notary) must affix an official seal on all notarized documents (WS 137.01[4]), and the seal's format must be as follows (WS 137.01[3]):

Kind

Embosser or Inked Rubber Stamp: "Except as authorized in section 137.19 [regarding electronic notarization], every notary public shall provide an engraved official seal which makes a distinct and legible impression or official rubber stamp which makes a distinct and legible imprint on paper. The impression of the seal or the imprint of the rubber stamp shall state only the following: 'Notary Public,' 'State of Wisconsin' and the name of the notary. But any notarial seal in use on August 1, 1959, shall be considered in compliance" (WS 137.01[3][a]).

Examples

The above typical, actual-size examples of inking and embossing Notary seals are allowed by Wisconsin law. Formats other than these may also be permitted.

Attorneys who are Notaries are not exempted from the seal requirement ("Instructions for Wisconsin Attorneys' Permanent Notary Public Application").

A Notary may use both an embosser and a rubber stamp if samples of both are on file in the Wisconsin Department of Financial Institutions prior to use, and if the names are exactly the same on both (NPI).

Shape/Size

"The seal or stamp may be of any size or shape …" (NPI).

Components

Only the following components are authorized:
1. Name of Notary;
2. "Notary Public";
3. "State of Wisconsin".

IMPORTANT: According to the Notary commission application, no additional words, such as the expiration date or "My commission is permanent" may appear in the seal. Also, no title such as "Atty.," "Esq.," "Dr." or "CPA" should appear before or after the Notary's name.

Notary's Name

In the Notary seal, "[y]ou may use initials, or a shortened first name if you wish, but you must use your current last name in full … [and] you must always sign your name exactly as set forth on your notary seal or stamp" (NPI).

"Only the exact name you give and the seal or stamp you provide for filing with the Department of Financial Institutions may be used for notarization purposes. No other name, seal, or stamp may be used when performing notarial acts unless the Wisconsin Department of Financial Institutions is notified in writing prior to usage" (NPI).

Seal Change for Name Change: "If you change your name for any reason, it is strongly suggested that you purchase a new seal or rubber stamp stating your new name (and the words "State of Wisconsin" and "Notary Public") and obtain a Change of Name form from the Wisconsin Department of Financial Institutions. You are required to complete and submit the Change of Name form to the Wisconsin Department of Financial Institutions PRIOR to using your new name and seal for notary purposes (NPI).

Commission Expiration Date Must Appear

"[I]n addition thereto shall be written or stamped either the day, month and year when the commission of said notary public will expire, or that such commission is permanent [as in the case of attorneys]" (WS 137.01[4]). However, omission of this information may subsequently be corrected (WS 706.07[7]).

Seal May Not Be Preprinted

"[E]ach notarial act must be attested by an original impression of your notary seal/stamp. Do not preprint or photocopy your notary stamp/seal onto documents you will notarize" (NPT).

Lost or Stolen Seal

If a Notary's seal is lost or stolen, the Notary should notify the Wisconsin Department of Financial Institutions in writing immediately, then "order a new seal or stamp that has a different appearance than your previous one" (NPI). A sample of the new seal should be sent to the Department of Financial Institutions before it is used.

Seals of Other Officers

"All commissioned notaries public, including attorneys, must impress their notary seal on notarial certificates they issue. Other notarial officers specifically authorized by statute to perform notarial acts without a commission — such as judges, court commissioners, and county clerks — should state their title, and use their seals of office, if they are required to have one" (NPI).

Signature Must Be Handwritten

"Every official act of a notary public shall be attested by the notary public's written signature or electronic signature, as defined in Section 137.11(8)" (WS 137.01[4][a]).

"'Electronic signature' means an electronic sound, symbol, or process attached to or logically associated with a record and executed or adopted by a person with the intent to sign the record" (WS 137.11[8]).

"I will be notarizing a lot of documents. May I use a signature stamp instead of signing each one? — No! Every official act of a notary should be attested by his/her handwritten signature" (NPI).

"[Y]ou may not use a rubber signature stamp, photocopy, or preprint your notarial signature on documents you are notarizing" (NPT).

"[S]ign only and exactly the same name as the one on your notary seal/stamp…" (NPI).

NOTARY POWERS

Wisconsin Notaries are authorized to perform the following notarial acts (WSA 137.01[5] and 706.07[2]):
1. Take acknowledgments*;
2. Administer oaths and affirmations;
3. Take depositions;
4. Execute protests;
5. Take verifications** on oath*** or affirmation;
6. Witness or attest signatures****;
7. Certify or attest copies of documents or other items*****;
8. "[P]erform such other duties as by the law of nations, or according to commercial usage, may be exercised and performed by notaries public."

* Acknowledgments: "When a notary completes a certificate of acknowledgment, it will be assumed that the notary has done all of the following:
"1. Required that the acknowledging party be in the notary's presence, in person;
"2. Satisfactorily identified the party;
"3. Determined that the party knew what kind of document was being signed, and its intended purpose;
"4. Determined that the party signed the document voluntarily, of his or her own free will; and
"5. Witnessed the acknowledging party actually signing the document, or, if the document was signed previously, has shown the signature to the party, and asked the party to confirm having made the signature" (NPI).
"If the document [certificate] is an acknowledgment, the person need not sign in front of you, BUT MUST PERSONALLY APPEAR before you and acknowledge execution of the document" (NPI).

** Verification on Oath/Affirmation (Jurat): "When a notary takes a sworn statement, or a statement made under oath or affirmation, it will be assumed that the notary has done all of the following:
"1. Required that the party making the statement be in the notary's presence, in person;
"2. Satisfactorily identified the party;
"3. Required the party to specifically confirm that he or she swears, or affirms under penalty of perjury, that the statements in the document to be notarized are true; and
"4. Witnessed the party actually signing the document" (NPI).
"If the document is an affidavit or other document requiring an oath, the person MUST sign it in your presence....If the document is already signed, have the person sign again in your presence, above or below the other signature" (NPI).

*** Oath Wording and Ceremony: The "Notary Public Information" booklet issued by the Wisconsin Department of Financial Institutions suggests the following wording for the administration of an oath for a sworn statement: "Would you please raise your right hand. Now, do you solemnly swear that the statements in this document you have asked me to notarize are the truth, the whole truth, and nothing but the truth, so help you God?"

**** Witness or Attest Signatures: "When a notary notarizes an unsworn signature, it will be assumed that the notary has done all of the following:
"1. Required that the signing party be in the notary's presence, in person;
"2. Satisfactorily identified the party; and
"3. Witnessed the party actually signing the document" (NPI).

***** Certify Copies: "In certifying or attesting a copy of a document or other item, the notarial officer must determine that the proffered copy is a full, true, and accurate transcription or reproduction of that which was copied" (WS 706.07[2][d]).
"[Y]ou are strictly prohibited from making copies, certified or uncertified, of 'vital records,' which include certificates of birth, death, divorce, annulment, marriage, etc. Never notarize photocopies of vital records that a person may bring to you. Preparing or issuing anything that carries the appearance of an original or copy of a vital record could cause you to be fined not more than $10,000, imprisoned not more than 3 years, or both. Copies of vital records are appropriately obtained from their official custodian: a state or county office of vital records, or similar government records office" (NPI).
"'Vital records' means certificates of birth, death, divorce or annulment, marriage documents, fetal death reports and data related thereto" (WS 69.01[26]).

Identification Requirements

The following identification requirements apply to acknowledgments, verifications upon oath or affirmation and to witnessing or attesting signatures:

"A notarial officer has satisfactory evidence that a person is the person whose true signature is on a document if that person: 1. Is personally known to the notarial officer; 2. Is identified upon the oath or affirmation of a credible witness personally known to the notarial officer; or 3. Is identified on the basis of identification documents" (WS 706.07[2f]).

Types of ID: "Whenever you perform a notarial act, you must personally know the signer, or identify the signer upon oath or affirmation of a credible witness personally known to you, or ask the signer for satisfactory identification. It is your responsibility to determine what you consider to be 'satisfactory identification.' A current driver's license, photo identification card, picture credit card, student ID card, or employment ID may be enough proof for you to establish a customer's identity....If a customer cannot provide adequate identification, or makes excuses for having no ID, ask them to return later with proper identification, or to find a notary who knows them personally. Customers may know notaries through their insurance agents, financial institutions, schools or churches" (NPT).

Confidentiality Required of Notary

"(a) Except as provided in par. (b), a notary public shall keep confidential all documents and information contained in any documents reviewed by the notary public while performing his or her duties as a notary public and may release the documents or the information to a 3rd person only with the written consent of the person who requested the services of the notary public.

"(b) Deposition transcripts may be released to all parties of record in an action. A notary public may not release deposition transcripts that have not been made part of the public record to a 3rd party without the written consent of all parties to the action and the deponent. When a deposition transcript has been made part of the public record, a notary public who is also a court reporter may, subject to a protective order or agreement to the contrary, release the deposition transcript or sell the transcript to 3rd parties with the consent of the person who requested the services of the notary public.

"(c) Any notary public violating this subsection shall be subject to the provision of sub. (8) and may be required to forfeit not more than $500" (WS 137.01[5m]).

Foreign Documents and Signers

"There is no reference in the Wisconsin Statutes that prohibits you from notarizing a document written in a foreign language. However, if you do not understand the contents of the document, you are encouraged to find another notary who does understand it, or you may wish to refuse to notarize it. You might check with a university language department, or foreign students' office, or a consulate" (NPI).

Foreign Language Signer: "You may proceed with the notarial act if you are certain the signer understands the content of the document and realizes the consequences of signing it" (NPI).

NOTARY DON'TS

Incomplete Documents

"It is always advisable to check the document to be sure there are no blanks or incomplete statements" (NPI).

"Never notarize if...the customer withholds part of the document, showing you only the notarial portion. If the content of the document has lines that should be filled in and are left blank, has text that is blacked out or covered with 'white-out,' or refers to additional pages that are missing, do not jeopardize yourself by putting your name and seal on the document" (NPT).

Disqualifying Interests

According to the "Notary Public Information" booklet, issued by the Department of Financial Institutions:

1. Notaries should not notarize their own signatures ("Most filing officers [registers of deeds, county clerks, state offices, and courts, etc.] will not accept documents on which a notary has notarized his/her own signature.")

2. Notaries should not notarize documents from which they may derive a benefit since their right to receive that benefit may be jeopardized.

3. "A notary is not prohibited from witnessing the signatures of a spouse or relatives. However, if the document were to be questioned for any cause, the notarial act may be scrutinized more closely than if the notary were

not a spouse or relative."

Corporate or Bank Notaries: "It shall be lawful for any notary public who is a stockholder, director, officer, or employee of a bank or other corporation to take the acknowledgment of any party to any written instrument executed to or by such corporation, or to administer an oath to any other stockholder, director, officer, employee, or agent of such corporation, or to protest for nonacceptance or nonpayment bills of exchange, drafts, checks, notes, and other negotiable instruments which may be owned or held for collection by such corporation, if such notary is not a party to such instrument, either individually or as a representative of such corporation" (WS 220.18).

Do Not Dictate Notarization Type

"Performing a notarial act requires more than just affixing a notary seal and signature. In fact, simply signing and sealing a document is meaningless….However, you should not tell your customer what type of notarial act is required to 'notarize' their document, unless you are a notary public who is also an attorney" (NPI).

Unreasonable Claims

"[I]f the document contains blatant anti-government text, unreasonable claims, or if the notarial act is pre-printed and contains additional, non-standard language, you may choose to decline to notarize" (NPT).

Immigration Abuses by Notaries

According to Wisconsin law, a non-attorney Notary is forbidden to do the following (WS 137.01[1][i]):

"1. State or imply that he or she is an attorney licensed to practice law in this state.

"2. Solicit or accept compensation to prepare documents for or otherwise represent the interests of another person in a judicial or administrative proceeding, including a proceeding relating to immigration to the United States or U.S. citizenship.

"3. Solicit or accept compensation to obtain relief of any kind on behalf of another person from any officer, agent, or employee of this state, a political subdivision of this state, or the United States.

"4. Use the phrase "notario," "notarizaciones," "notarizamos," or "notario public," or otherwise advertise in a language other than English on signs, pamphlets, stationery, or other written communication, by radio or television, or on the Internet his or her services as a notary public if the advertisement fails to include, in English and the language of the advertisement, all of the following:

"a. The statement, if in a written advertisement, in all capital letters and the same type size: 'I AM NOT AN ATTORNEY LICENSED TO PRACTICE LAW IN WISCONSIN AND MAY NOT GIVE LEGAL ADVICE OR ACCEPT FEES FOR LEGAL ADVICE.' If the advertisement is given orally, the statement may be modified but must include substantially the same message and be understandable.

"b. The fees that a notary public may charge…"

The prohibitions under 2. and 3. above do not apply to a Notary who is an "accredited representative," as defined in 8 CFR 292.1(a)(4).

For a first-time violation of any of the above, a person may be fined not more than $10,000 or imprisoned for not more than nine months, or both.

NOTARY SIGNING AGENTS

Currently, there are no statutes, regulations or rules expressly governing, prohibiting or restricting the operation of Notary Signing Agents within the state of Wisconsin.

NOTARY FEES

The fees that may be charged by Wisconsin Notaries are (WS 137.01[9]):

1. "For taking the acknowledgment of deeds, and for other services authorized by law, the same fees as are allowed to other officers for similar services, but the fee per document shall not exceed 50 cents";

2. "For drawing any affidavit, or other paper or proceeding for which provision is not herein made": 50 cents per folio and 12 cents per folio copy;

3. Executing a protest: for drawing and copy of protest for nonpayment or nonacceptance, when protest required by law, $1; for drawing and copy of other protests, 50 cents; for drawing, copying, serving notice of nonpayment, 50 cents.

No Fee for Voting Oath

"No fee shall be charged by any officer for

administering or certifying any official oath, or any oath to any person relative to his right to be registered or to vote" (WS 887.02[2]).

NOTARY CERTIFICATES

Wisconsin has adopted the *Uniform Law on Notarial Acts*, including the short-form certificates (WS 706.07[8]) for:
1. Acknowledgment by individual;
2. Acknowledgment by representative;
3. Verification upon oath or affirmation;
4. Witnessing or attesting signature;
5. Attesting copy of document.

For the text of these certificates, see "Uniform Law on Notarial Acts (1982)," Section 8, in Appendix 2.

Form of Notarial Certificate

"(a) A notarial act must be evidenced by a certificate signed and dated by a notarial officer. The certificate must include identification of the jurisdiction in which the notarial act is performed and the title of the office of the notarial officer and may include the official stamp or seal of office. If the officer is a notary public, the certificate must also indicate the date of expiration, if any, of the commission of office, but omission of that information may subsequently be corrected. If the officer is a commissioned officer on active duty in the military service of the United States, it must also include the officer's rank.

"(b) A certificate of a notarial act is sufficient if it meets the requirements of par. (a) and it:
"1. Is in the short form set forth in sub. (8);
"2. Is in a form otherwise prescribed by the law of this state;
"3. Is in a form prescribed by the laws or regulations applicable in the place in which the notarial act was performed; or
"4. Sets forth the actions of the notarial officer and those are sufficient to meet the requirements of the designated notarial act ..." (WS 706.07[7]).

Representative Capacity Certificate

"When a document is signed in a representative capacity, language indicating that should be included in the notary certificate. Proper language to be added to a notary certificate to indicate a 'representative' signature may read, for example, as stated in the following [italic] text: a) For an acknowledgment: This instrument was acknowledged before me in Madison on June 1, 2001, by Sarah Smith, as the duly authorized executrix of the estate of John Smith. b) For an unsworn signature: This instrument was signed before me in Madison on June 1, 2001, by Robert Jones, as the duly authorized President of the ABC Corporation" (NPI).

"Loose" Certificate

"If there is not enough room at the end of a document to insert a jurat, you may place it on a separate sheet of paper and securely attach it to the sworn statement. When the jurat is not written on the document it applies to, a statement on the document should indicate that a jurat is attached. Also, the jurat should bear a statement identifying the document to which it is attached" (NPI).

ELECTRONIC NOTARIZATIONS

The state of Wisconsin has not yet adopted statutes or regulations expressly establishing rules, definitions and procedures for electronic notarization.

Webcam 'Notarizations' Not Authorized

The following notice appears on the website of the Wisconsin Secretary of State ("Authentications & Apostilles"):

"In Wisconsin, notaries must have the actual person or their agents before them at the time of the notarial act. Electronic signatures, signatures performed by webcam or over the telephone are not allowed, and will not be eligible for Apostille and Authentication."

Consumer Alert on Webcam Notarization: The following warning appeared in a "Consumer Alert" posted on the Department of Financial Institutions website in 2011:

"Online webcam notarization is invalid and illegal in the State of Wisconsin. A private company claims to have the first online notarization website; neither they nor any other company may provide online notarization in Wisconsin. The web-based platform purports to allow a person to submit copies of identification over the Internet and to use a webcam in lieu of a personal appearance in front of a Notary Public.

Appearance via webcam does not meet the requirement for notarization in Wisconsin....

Wisconsin law requires a person to appear personally before a Notary Public to obtain notarial acts. This means that party must be physically present before the Notary Public. A video image of other form of non-physical representation is not a personal appearance in front of a Notary Public under current state or federal laws."

UETA Recognizes Notary's eSignature

Wisconsin has adopted an amended version of the Uniform Electronic Transactions Act (WS 137.11 through 137.24, Chapter 137, Subchapter II, "Electronic Transactions and Records; Electronic Notarization and Acknowledgment"), including the provision, slightly modified, on electronic notarization and acknowledgment, thereby recognizing as legally valid electronic signatures used by Notaries:

"If a law requires a signature or record to be notarized, acknowledged, verified, or made under oath, the requirement is satisfied if the electronic signature of the person authorized to administer the oath or to make the notarization, acknowledgment, or verification, together with all other information required to be included by other applicable law, is attached to or logically associated with the signature or record" (WS 137.19).

No Seal for Electronic Notarization

"Except as authorized in section 137.19, every notary public shall provide an engraved official seal which makes a distinct and legible impression or official rubber stamp which makes a distinct and legible imprint on paper" (WS 137.01[3][a]).

Further, Wisconsin has enacted the Uniform Real Properly Electronic Recording Act (URPERA), which stipulates: "A requirement that a document or a signature associated with a document be notarized, acknowledged, verified, witnessed, or made under oath is satisfied if the electronic signature of the person authorized to perform that act, and all other information required to be included, is attached to or logically associated with the document or signature. A physical or electronic image of a stamp, impression, or seal need not accompany an electronic signature" (WS 706.25[2][c]).

Notary May Use Written or eSignature

"Every official act of a notary public shall be attested by the notary public's written signature or electronic signature, as defined in Section 137.11(8)" (WS 137.01[4][a]). "'Electronic signature' means an electronic sound, symbol, or process attached to or logically associated with a record and executed or adopted by a person with the intent to sign the record" (WS 137.11[8]).

NOTARY RECORDS

Wisconsin law does not specifically require a Notary to keep records, but it does specify the disposition of any such records in the event of the Notary's death or ceasing to hold office.

Records Are Encouraged

"Keeping a notarial log book, or journal, is not required in Wisconsin, although you are encouraged to do so. Depending on the amount and types of documents you are handling, recording your notarial acts in a journal may prove useful later if you need to recall specifics of a particular case.

"If you decide to keep a notarial log book, include items such as the date and type of notarial act, names and signatures of persons involved, and numbers from identification cards and driver's licenses presented" (NPI).

Records to Be Filed

"When any notary public ceases to hold office, the notary public, or in case of the notary public's death the notary public's personal representative, shall deposit the notary public's official records and papers with the department of financial institutions. If the notary or personal representative, after the records and papers come to his or her hands, neglects for 3 months to deposit them, he or she shall forfeit not less than $50 nor more than $500. If any person knowingly destroys, defaces, or conceals any records or papers of any notary public, the person shall forfeit not less than $50 nor more than $500, and shall be liable for all damages resulting to the party injured. The department of financial institutions shall receive and safely keep all such papers and records" (WS 137.01[7]).

Notarial Records Are Confidential

See "Confidentiality Required of Notary," above under "Notary Powers," regarding the Notary's statutory obligation to keep confidential all "documents and information reviewed by the notary public while performing his or her duties ..." The Notary is permitted to "release the documents or the information to a 3rd person only with the written consent of the person who requested the services of the notary public" (WS 137.01[5m]).

AUTHENTICATION OF NOTARIAL ACTS

Secretary of State

Authenticating certificates for Notaries, including apostilles, continue to be issued by the Wisconsin Secretary of State's office, rather than the Department of Financial Institutions (WS 137.01[6a]).

Fees: $10 per certificate for a regular authenticating certificate or an apostille. Payable to "Wisconsin Secretary of State." Personal and business checks, as well as money orders, are acceptable; no credit cards. For expedited service (1 to 5 business days), the fee is $35 per certificate.

Address for Mail:
Office of Secretary of State
Certification Desk
P.O. Box 7848
Madison, WI 53707-7848

Address for Couriers:
Office of Secretary of State
Certification Desk
30 West Mifflin St., 10th Floor
Madison, WI 53703

Telephone: 1-608-266-5503

Procedure: An "Apostille & Authentication Certificate Order Form" (available online) is submitted with the notarized document(s), along with the appropriate fee ($10 or $35 per certificate) and an addressed, stamped envelope (preferably with a tracking number) or a prepaid courier air bill. The documents may also be picked up in person. The information submitted must include the name of the foreign country involved, the Notary's exact name and commission expiration date, and contact information for the person submitting the request. Orders are typically processed within 10 business days after receipt. For expedited service, orders are processed within 1 to 5 business days after receipt; write "EXPEDITE" clearly on the outside of the envelope. Same-day service is not available. Improperly notarized documents will be rejected.

COMMISSIONING AND ADMINISTRATION

Though the Governor appoints Wisconsin's Notaries, the Secretary of Financial Institutions regulates and maintains records on them (WS 137.01).

All forms submitted to the Department of Financial Institutions regarding a Notary's commission are public records and subject to Wisconsin's Open Records Law (NPI). Thus, any person may inspect and copy a Notary's file for any reason.

Applying for Commission

Qualifications: An applicant for a commission as a Wisconsin Notary Public must (WS 137.01[1]): (a) be at least 18 years old, (b) have at least the equivalent of an eighth-grade education, (c) be a United States resident (i.e.., maintain a permanent dwelling place in the United States and be in fact living in this country [NPI]), (d) be familiar with the duties and responsibilities of a Notary, which can be shown by taking and passing the online tutorial described below, and (e) not have been convicted in state or federal court of a felony or a misdemeanor involving a violation of the public trust, unless a pardon has been issued. Notably, an applicant does not have to be a Wisconsin resident, nor a U.S. citizen.

Taking Online Tutorial Encouraged: No course of instruction or testing is required. However, the Department of Financial Institutions recommends that every Notary take a "free online notary public educational tutorial course," which includes a 50-question final assessment exam (NPI). The tutorial is available at www.wdfi.org. A passing score of 90% on the tutorial exam suffices as the required proof of familiarity with Notary duties; a "certificate of achievement" may then be printed out and submitted with the application in lieu of a separate signed and dated letter consisting of a written essay affirming that the applicant is familiar with the duties and responsibilities of a notary public and explaining how such knowledge was acquired.

Application: The application by a non-attorney for a four-year commission must include: a notarized oath of office; a completed $500 surety bond; an imprint of the Notary seal that will be used; a certificate verifying a passing score on the online tutorial or an a letter affirming familiarity with notarial duties, containing an explanation of how this familiarity was acquired; and a $20 fee payable to the "Wisconsin Department of Financial Institutions."

For renewals, the Department of Financial Institutions is required by statute to mail an expiration notice to each Notary's last known address; the reappointment procedure is otherwise the same as the initial appointment.

Attorneys do not have automatic notarial powers but must apply for a commission, either a regular four-year or a permanent commission (WS 137.01[2]). The application by an attorney licensed to practice law in Wisconsin for a permanent commission does not include an oath of office or a bond, but a seal imprint, a "Certificate of Good Standing" (no more than two months old) from the Wisconsin Supreme Court, and a $50 fee must be included. A permanent commission remains valid as long as the attorney is a U.S. resident licensed to practice law in Wisconsin (NPI).

Non-Residents: Any legal resident of the United States may obtain a Wisconsin Notary Commission, but the commission may only be used within the state.

Online Search: The roster of Wisconsin Notaries may be searched online by name, city, state, zip code and commission date of issuance at http://sos.nmtvault.com/notary.aspx. A Notary's address and commission expiration date will be provided.

Changes of Status

If Notary Moves: "The statutes require that a notary give written notice of any change of address to the Department of Financial Institutions within 10 days of the change" (NPI and WS 137.01[6m]). A form is available on the website. A Notary may move outside the state of Wisconsin and retain the commission.

If Notary Changes Name: A Notary with a new legal name must submit a change of name form (available on the website) to the Department of Financial Institutions prior to using the new name as a Notary. "If you change your name for any reason, it is strongly suggested that you purchase a new seal or rubber stamp stating your new name …" (NPI).

"For the remainder of your present commission … it is permissible to continue to perform notarial acts using a previous name if you sign your name exactly as stated on your seal or rubber stamp. A new or different name may not be signed in addition to the previous name, as in parenthesis or in a hyphenated manner. For notarization purposes, your signature must always exactly match the name indicated on your official notary seal or stamp" (NPI).

If Attorney-Notary Is Disciplined: "The supreme court shall file with the Department of Financial Institutions notice of the surrender, suspension or revocation of the license to practice law of any attorney who holds a permanent commission as a notary public. Such notice shall be deemed a revocation of said commission" (WS 137.01[2][c]).

A formal opinion of the Wisconsin Attorney General issued July 13, 2009, concluded that Wisconsin attorneys who have had their law licenses suspended or revoked for any reason, whether disciplinary or administrative, are not statutorily entitled to permanent Notary commissions. Upon restatement of their law licenses, however, the opinion stated that such attorneys are entitled to a fixed four-year commission that may be renewed.

COUNTY CLERKS

Due to statutory changes in 2001, Wisconsin Notaries no longer have the option to file signature and seal samples with local county circuit court clerks, nor to deposit their notarial records with such clerks; instead, their records must be filed with the Department of Financial Institutions. Thus, Wisconsin county circuit court clerks are no longer involved with the authentication of notarial acts or the archiving of notarial records.

OTHER NOTARIAL OFFICERS

Besides Notaries, the following officials have power to perform notarial acts in Wisconsin, their signatures and titles being "prima facie evidence that the signature is genuine and that the person holds the designated title" (WS 706.07[3]):

1. A judge, clerk or deputy clerk of a court of record;
2. A court commissioner;
3. A register of deeds or deputy register;
4. A municipal judge;
5. A county clerk or deputy county clerk.

Any Public Officer

"Any public officer entitled by virtue of his office to administer oaths, and any member in good standing of the state bar of Wisconsin, may authenticate one or more of the signatures on an instrument relating to lands in this state, by indorsing the instrument 'Acknowledged', 'Authenticated' or 'Signatures Guaranteed', or other words to similar effect, adding the date of authentication, his own signature, and his official or professional title. Such indorsement, unless expressly limited, shall operate as an authentication of all signatures on the instrument; and shall constitute a certification that each authenticated signature is the genuine signature of the person represented; and, as to signatures made in a representative capacity, that the signer purported, and was believed, to be such representative" (WS 706.06).

Seal and Title Required: "(N)otarial officers specifically authorized by statute to perform notarial acts without a notary public commission — such as judges, court commissioners, and county clerks — should state their title, and use their seals of office if they are required to have one" (NPI).

Commissioner of Deeds

"The governor shall have power to appoint one or more commissioners in any of the United States, or of the territories belonging to the United States and in foreign countries, who shall hold his office for the term of four years unless sooner removed. Every such commissioner shall take the official oath before a judge or clerk of one of the courts of record of the state or territory or country in which he shall reside, and file the same, with an impression of his seal of office and a statement of his post office address, in the office of the secretary of state ....

"A commissioner ... shall have authority to take the acknowledgment and proof of the execution of deeds, conveyances, and leases of any lands lying in his state, or written instruments relating thereto, or of any contract or any other writing, sealed or unsealed, to be used or recorded in this state; to administer oaths required to be used in this state; to take and certify depositions to be used in the courts of this state, either under a commission, by consent of parties or on notice to the opposite party; and all such acts done pursuant to the laws of this state and certified under his hand and seal of office shall be as valid as if done by a proper officer of this state" (WS 137.02).

QUICK FACTS

Notary Jurisdiction
Statewide (WS 137.01[5]). Out-of-state residents who qualify for a commission may notarize only within the state of Wisconsin.

Notary Term Length
Four years (WS 137.01[1]), expiring at midnight on the commission expiration date (WS 137.01[1]).

Lifetime Attorney Commission: Attorneys may apply either for four-year or for lifetime ("permanent") Notary commissions (WS 137.01[2]). "A permanent commission is valid as long as the attorney remains a United States resident licensed to practice law in Wisconsin" (NPI). Upon reinstatement of a revoked or suspended law license, a Wisconsin attorney may qualify only for a Notary commission term of four years (WS 137.01[2][am]).

Notary Bond
A surety bond of $500, provided by an insurance/surety company licensed in Wisconsin and approved by the Secretary of Financial Institutions (WS 137. 01[1][d]). No bond is required for permanent commissions held by attorneys.

Wyoming

NOTARY SEAL

A Wyoming Notary must authenticate all official acts with a seal of office, and the seal's format must be as follows (WS 32-1-106[a]).

Kind

Inked Stamp or Embosser: The Notary's seal must be "affixed by a seal press or stamp that will print or emboss a seal which legibly reproduces under the photographic methods" (WS 32-1-106[b]). According to the state's Notary Officer, embosser impressions should be "inked" to become photographable.

Shape/Size

Rectangular or Circular: If rectangular, not more than $3/4$ inch wide by $2^1/_2$ inches long. If circular, not over 2 inches in diameter (WS 32-1-106[b]).

Examples

The above typical, actual-size examples of inking and embossing Notary seals are allowed by Wyoming law. Formats other than these may also be permitted.

NOTARY ADMINISTRATION

Office of Secretary of State
Notary Division   1-307-777-5335
State Capitol Building
200 West 24th St.
Cheyenne, WY 82002-0020

Website: http://soswy.state.wy.us/Admin
    Services/NotariesOverview.aspx

NOTARY RULES

SOS-NOT — SECRETARY OF STATE'S NOTARY
    RULES IN WYOMING REGULATIONS
WNH — WYOMING NOTARY HANDBOOK
    (2010 WEB EDITION)
WS — WYOMING STATUTES

Most Notary rules are in the Wyoming Statutes:

a. Title 32, Chapter 1 ("Notaries Public");

b. Title 34, Chapter 26, Sections 101-109 ("Uniform Law on Notarial Acts"); 201-206 ("Powers of Notarial Officers"); and 301-304 ("Notarial Officer Fees").

Other "Notary Rules" are in the Wyoming Regulations promulgated by the Secretary of State.

Border

The seal must have a "serrated or milled edge border" surrounding the following components (WS 32-1-106[b]):

Components

1. Name of Notary;
2. "Notary Public";
3. Name of county* wherein Notary resides;
4. "Wyoming";
5. OPTIONAL: commission expiration date.

* If a Notary changes county of residence, a new commission and seal must be obtained (WS 32-1-101[d] and 32-1-106[a]).

Commission Expiration Date Must Appear

"If the officer is a commissioned notarial officer, the certificate shall also indicate the date of expiration, if any, of the commission office, but omission of that information may subsequently be corrected" (WS 34-26-107).

State officials allow the commission expiration date to be written in the seal by hand after "My Commission Expires _____."

Notary Seal Defined

"'Seal' means a device for affixing on a document an image containing a notarial officer's name, jurisdiction, commission expiration date and other information related to the notarial officer's commission and identity as required by WS 32-1-106" (WS 34-26-101[b][xix]).

Seal Cannot Be Sold

"(T)he seal of the notary public shall not be levied upon or sold" (WS 32-1-106[a]).

Report Lost or Stolen Seal

"What if my notary seal is lost or stolen?"

"Immediately notify the Secretary of State in writing. Then order a new seal or stamp. Safeguard the seal/stamp from improper use" (WNH).

Notary Signature Stamp Not Allowed

"I will be notarizing a lot of documents. May I use a signature stamp instead of signing each certificate?

"No. Every official act of a notary should be attested to by his/her handwritten signature in the same form that appears on his/her commission and stamp/seal" (WNH).

NOTARY POWERS

Wyoming Notaries and other Wyoming "notarial officers" are authorized to perform the following notarial acts (WS 34-26-101[b][iii]):

1. Take acknowledgments*;
2. Administer oaths and affirmations**;
3. Perform jurats***;
4. Witness or attest signatures****;
5. Certify or attest copies*****;
6. Note protests of negotiable instruments (WS 32-1-111)******;
7. Take verifications upon oath or affirmation*******;
8. Perform other acts authorized by Wyoming law********.

* <u>Acknowledgments</u>: "'Acknowledgment' means a declaration by a person that the person has freely and voluntarily executed an instrument for the purposes stated therein and, if the instrument is executed in a representative capacity, that the person signed the instrument with proper authority and executed it as the act of the person or entity represented and identified therein and that the person acknowledges that the instrument was executed and acknowledged freely and voluntarily" (WS 34-26-101[b]).

"A notarial officer commits a misdemeanor punishable by imprisonment for not more than six (6) months, a fine of not more than seven hundred fifty dollars ($750), or both, if he signs and affixes his seal to a certificate of acknowledgment when the party executing the instrument has not first acknowledged the execution of the instrument in the presence of, as defined in W.S. 34-26-101(b)(xxi), if by law the instrument is required to be recorded or filed and cannot be filed without a certificate of acknowledgment signed and sealed by a notarial officer" (WS 6-5-114).

** <u>Oaths and Affirmations</u>: "A person may be sworn by any form he deems binding on his conscience" (WS 1-2-101).

"Persons conscientiously opposed to swearing or to taking any oath may affirm, and are subject to the penalties of perjury as in the case of swearing an oath. Whenever any person is required to take an oath in any court, or before any person or officer authorized by law to administer oaths, it is lawful for the court, officer or person administering the same, to administer it in the following manner: the person taking the oath or swearing shall, with his or her right hand uplifted, swear or take the oath, concluding with the words 'so help me God'" (WS 1-2-103).

Wyoming law defines an oath as a notarial act, or part thereof, which is legally equivalent to an affirmation and in which an individual at a single time and place: (a) is personally known to the notarial officer or identified by the notarial officer through satisfactory evidence, and (b) makes a vow of truthfulness or fidelity on penalty of perjury while invoking a deity or using any form of the word "swear" (WS 34-26-101[b][xiv]). An acceptable oath would be: "Do you swear that the statements in this document are true?" (WNH).

Wyoming law defines an affirmation as a notarial act, or part thereof, which is legally equivalent to an oath and in which an individual at a single time and place: (a) is personally known to the notarial officer or identified by the notarial officer through satisfactory evidence, and (b) makes a vow of truthfulness or fidelity on penalty of perjury, based on personal honor and without invoking a deity or using any form of the word "swear" (WS 34-26-101[b][vii]). An acceptable affirmation would be: "Do you affirm that the statements in this document are true?" (WNH).

*** Jurats: Wyoming law defines a jurat as a notarial act in which an individual at a single time and place: (a) is personally known to the notarial officer or identified by the officer through satisfactory evidence, (b) signs the document in the presence of the notarial officer, "as provided in subparagraph (xxi)(A) of this subsection," and (c) takes an oath or affirmation from the officer vouching for the truthfulness or accuracy of the signed document (WS 34-26-101[b][xi]).

"A properly executed jurat satisfies any requirement for an acknowledgment" (WS 34-26-101[c]).

**** Witness or Attest Signatures: "In witnessing or attesting a signature the principal shall be personally known to the notarial officer or identified through satisfactory evidence, shall appear in person before the notarial officer and shall make the signature in the presence of the notarial officer" (WS 34-26-102[c]).

***** Certify or Attest Copies: "A notarial officer may certify or attest to a copy of a document or other item except that a notarial officer shall not certify or attest to a copy of a vital record, public record or publicly recordable document" (WS 34-26-102[d]). In addition, the certifying or attesting officer must (a) have the original document in his or her presence, (b) "copy or supervise the copying of the document or other item using a photographic or electronic copying process" and (c) "determine that the proffered copy is a full, true and accurate transcription or reproduction of that which was copied."

"(A) notary may be asked to acknowledge the signature of an official who is certifying a copy of a record maintained by that official. In such cases it is not proper for the notary to certify the record since the record is maintained and must be certified by the custodian of records for a government agency, school or other entity. The notary's function is only to verify the signing of the certified record by the custodial officer. In other words, the notarial action verifies the custodial official's signature and not the authenticity of the document" (WNH). Birth and death certificates, marriage licenses and school transcripts are cited as among the documents which may not be copy-certified by a Notary.

****** Protests: For guidelines on executing protests, Notaries may consult the "Uniform Commercial Code — Negotiable Instruments" (WS 34.1-3-101 through 34.1-3-905). Sections 34.1-3-104 and 34.1-3-505 will be of particular interest.

"A protest is a certificate of dishonor made by a United States consul or vice consul, or a notarial officer or other person authorized to administer oaths by the law of the place where dishonor occurs. It may be made upon information satisfactory to that person. The protest must identify the instrument and certify either that presentment has been made or, if not made, the reason why it was not made, and that the instrument has been dishonored by nonacceptance or nonpayment. The protest may also certify that notice of dishonor has been given to some or all parties" (WS 34.1-3-505[b]).

******* Verifications upon Oath or Affirmation: "In taking a verification upon oath or affirmation, the notarial officer shall determine, either from personal knowledge or from satisfactory evidence, that the person appearing before the officer and making the verification is the person whose true signature is on the statement verified" (WS 34-26-102[b]).

"'Verification upon oath or affirmation' means a declaration that a statement is true made by a person upon oath or affirmation" (WS 34-26-101[b][v]).

******** Other Acts Authorized by Law: The comprehensive revision of Wyoming's Notary law that took effect July 1, 2011, defined a notarial act called a "verification of fact," which was drawn from the National Notary Association's Model Notary Act—though it is unclear whether the Legislature was thereby authorizing Wyoming Notaries to perform this act, because it is otherwise not mentioned.

A verification of fact is defined as a notarial act in which a notarial officer reviews public or vital records to ascertain or confirm any of the following facts regarding a person: (a) date of birth or death, (b) name of parent, offspring or sibling, (c) date of marriage or divorce, or (d) name of marital partner (WS 34-26-101[b][xx]).

Identifying Document Signers

In taking an acknowledgment or a verification upon oath or affirmation, or in witnessing or attesting a signature, a notarial officer must identify the signer "from personal knowledge or from satisfactory evidence" (WS 34-26-102[a], [b] and [c]).

Personal knowledge of identity means "familiarity with an individual resulting from interactions with that individual over a period of time or any other reasonable corroboration sufficient to dispel any reasonable uncertainty that the individual has the identity claimed" (WS 34-26-101[b][xv]).

Satisfactory evidence of identity means: (a) the notarial officer's personal knowledge of the individual's identity; or (b) presentation of at least one current identification document issued by a federal, state or tribal government agency bearing the photographic image of the individual's face and signature and a physical description, "though a properly stamped passport without a physical description is acceptable"; or (c) the vouching under oath or affirmation of one credible witness unaffected by the notarized document or transaction who is personally known to the notarial officer and who personally knows the individual, or of two credible witnesses unaffected by the document or transaction who each personally knows the individual and shows to the notarial officer documentary identification as described in (b) above (WS 34-26-101[b][xviii]).

Credible witness means "an honest, reliable and impartial person who personally knows an individual appearing before a notarial officer and takes an oath or affirmation from the notarial officer to vouch for that individual's identity" (WS 34-26-101[b][x]).

Certain Representatives Must Be Sworn: In notarizing the signature of a person signing on behalf of a "business entity" (i.e., corporation, limited liability company, partnership or other entity, profit or non-profit) or of a trustee signing on behalf of a testamentary trust or an express trust created by a written trust instrument, the agent or trustee must be personally known by the Notary. In both cases, the agent or trustee must be put under oath by the Notary and swear that he or she is signing with due authority (WS 34-26-102[e] and [f]).

"A notary serves as an impartial witness to the signing of a document, establishes the identity of the person signing the document and attests that the signature on the document was made in his presence. If the person did not appear before the notary and sign the document in the notary's presence, the notary may acknowledge (sic) the person's signature when the person appears before the notary, presents the proper identification, acknowledges the signature is that of the person and the document was voluntarily executed by the person" (WS 32-1-105[b]).

Blank Spaces in Document

"The document signer should beware of any documents which have gaps or large blanks in the text…The document signer should beware of any document which has unsigned signature lines or signature blocks …

"Skim the document for blanks. Ask the signer to fill in all blanks or to write 'Not Applicable' before you notarize" (website, "Safeguards").

"It is always advisable to check the document to be sure there are no blanks or incomplete statements (this is not to review the document for legality, it is to make sure the document being signed remains the same as it was when signed)" (WNH).

Corrections

"Do not use 'white-out' or obliterate a name if a mistake is made on a (motor vehicle) title. The notarial officer may contact the County Clerk for instruction whether to strike-through the mistake and have the signer initial or remedy a mistake in some other manner" (WNH).

Signature by Mark

A notarial officer may certify the affixation of a signature by mark on a document presented for notarization if (WS 34-26-201[c]):

1. The mark is affixed in the presence of the officer and two witnesses unaffected by the document;

2. Both witnesses sign their own names beside the mark;

3. The notarial officer writes below the mark: "Mark affixed by (name of signer by mark) in presence of (names and addresses of witnesses) and undersigned notarial officer under WS 34-26-201(c)"; and

4. The notarial officer notarizes the signature

by mark through an acknowledgment, jurat or signature witnessing.

Signing for Person Unable to Sign

A notarial officer may sign the name of a person physically unable to sign or make a mark on a document presented for notarization if (WS 34-26-201[d]):

1. The person directs the notarial officer to do so in the presence of two witnesses unaffected by the document;

2. The notarial officer signs the person's name in the presence of the person and witnesses;

3. Both witnesses sign their own name beside the signature;

4. The notarial officer writes below the signature: "Signature affixed by notarial officer in the presence of (names and addresses of person and two witnesses) under WS 34-26-201(d)"; and

5. The notarial officer notarizes the signature through an acknowledgment, jurat or signature witnessing.

Foreign-Language Documents

"Wyoming's law does not prohibit notarization of documents written in a foreign language. What the document says has no bearing on the notary or the notarization…The notary's certificate should be written in English" (WNH).

Signing on Penalty of Perjury

"(a) A matter required or authorized to be supported, evidenced, established or proven by the sworn statement, declaration, verification, certificate, oath or affidavit in writing of the person making it, other than a deposition, an acknowledgment, an oath of office or an oath required to be taken before a specified official other than a notary public may be supported, evidenced, established or proven by the person certifying in writing 'under penalty of false swearing' that the matter is true. The certification shall state the date and place of execution and the following: "'I certify under penalty of false swearing that the foregoing is true'.

"(b) A person who knowingly makes a false certification under subsection (a) of this section is guilty of false swearing in violation of WS 6-5-303(c)" (WS 1-2-104).

"A person who knowingly makes a false certification under WS 1-2-104 is guilty of a felony punishable by imprisonment for not more than two years, a fine of not more than $2,000, or both" (WS 6-5-303[c]).

Availability of Notary

"There is no section of the Wyoming Statutes which makes it unlawful for a notarial officer to act on a Sunday or on a holiday. A notary commission does not however require a notary public to perform notarial acts at all hours or on every day of the week" (WNH).

NOTARY DON'TS

According to the Secretary of State's website, a Wyoming Notary should:

1. NOT postdate or antedate any certificate;
2. NOT notarize a document seen only partially ("The notary must see the signer's entire document and know what it is.");
3. NOT notarize a facsimile or a faxed copy of a signature;
4. NOT "take the acknowledgment of a person who does not speak the English language unless the nature and effect of the instrument to be notarized is translated into a language which the person does speak";
5. NOT date a notarial certificate before a document's date of signing ("The date of notarization must coincide with or follow the document's date of signing.");
6. NOT "invade the party's privacy" by reading the notarized document ("Merely identify the document to be notarized [deed, contract, etc.]. Record the type of document in your notary journal. Do not notarize a document you cannot identify.").

Notary's Disqualifying Interests

"Impartiality is having no conflict of interest. A notary must be an impartial witness. A notary is 'disqualified' from notarizing when the notary has a personal financial or beneficial interest in the transaction to which the document and notarized signature applies. Generally, this means you should not perform your notarial duties for yourself, your family or business associates where the notary could benefit. Courts hold (the) notary public to a high standard of independence and integrity because notaries are 'officers'" (website, "Principles").

"When in doubt about a conflict of interest in the transaction, the notary should refuse the notarial act and should seek to avoid even the slightest appearance of impropriety" (WNH).

Notarizing for Family Members: "The standard for notarization is impartiality and independence. A notary should not notarize if they have any financial or beneficial interest in the transaction. It is difficult to think of a notarial act where a spouse would not have a financial or beneficial interest in the transaction being notarized...(I)f the document was to be questioned for any cause, the notarial act will be scrutinized more closely than if the notary was not a spouse or relative" (WNH).

May Not Notarize Own Signature: "Since a notary must always be an objective and independent witness, notarizing your own signature defeats the very purpose of notarization. Don't do it" (WNH).

Bank or Corporation Notary: "It shall be lawful for any notarial officer who is a stockholder, director, officer or employee of a bank or other corporation to take the acknowledgment of any party to any written instrument executed to or by said corporation, or to administer an oath to any other stockholder, director, officer, employee or agent of such corporation, or to protest for nonacceptance, or nonpayment, bills of exchange, drafts, checks, notes and other negotiable instruments which may be owned or held for collection by any such bank or other corporation" (WS 34-26-201[e]).

Avoidance of Influence

When notarizing, a notarial officer who is not an attorney licensed to practice law in Wyoming under WS 33-5-101 through 33-5-117 shall not influence a person either to enter into or avoid a transaction involving a notarial act by the officer (WS 34-26-202[a]).

May Not Attest Lawfulness, Accuracy: In his or her capacity as a notarial officer, the notarial officer "has neither the duty nor the authority to investigate, ascertain or attest the lawfulness, propriety, accuracy or truthfulness of a document or transaction involving a notarial act" (WS 34-26-202[b]).

False Certificate

A Notary may not execute a certificate containing information known or believed by the Notary to be false (WS 34-26-203[a]).

Attachment outside Notary's Presence: A notarial officer may "not provide or send a signed or sealed notarial certificate to another person with the understanding that it will be completed or attached to a document outside of the notarial officer's place of business" (WS 34-26-203[b]).

Improper Documents

Under Wyoming law, the following documents may not be notarized, certified or authenticated: (a) a document without notarial certificate wording, and (b) a photograph (WS 34-26-204).

Intent to Deceive or Defraud

A Wyoming notarial officer "shall not perform any official action with the intent to deceive or defraud" (WS 34-26-205).

Testimonials

A notarial officer may not use the official title ("Notary Public" or "Notary") or seal "to endorse, promote, denounce or oppose any product, service, contest,candidate or other offering" (WS 34-26-206).

May Not Refuse Service

"Notaries may not refuse service to anyone who makes a reasonable and lawful request for a notarization and they must treat all persons equally" (website, "Principles").

Law Trumps Employer Instructions

"A notary's employer may not instruct the notary to perform a notarization which would violate state notary law. The notary must comply with all aspects of the notary law" (website, "Principles").

No Notarization without Physical Presence

"Being in the same building (with a signer), being in contact via the telephone, a notary's personal recognition of a person's signature, prior permission of the signer, or circumstances other than personal appearance before a notary are not permissible. Don't do it. The signer must appear in person before the notary" (WNH).

"A notarial officer, shall not perform a notarial act if the principal:

"(i) Is not in the notarial officer's presence at the time of notarization or is not personally known to the notarial officer;

"(ii) Is not personally known to the notarial officer or identified by the notarial officer through satisfactory evidence" (WS 34-26-201[b]).

Personal Appearance Defined: "'Personally appear,' 'in the presence of,' and 'appear before' mean for all purposes of this act except as used in paragraph (xi) of this subsection (Editor's Note: paragraph (xi) refers to performance of a jurat.) that:

"(A) The principal is in the notarial officer's presence at the time of notarization; or

"(B) The principal confirmed to the notarial officer that the principal signed the document…

"'This act' means WS 34-26-101 through 34-26-304" (WS 34-26-101[b][xxi] and [xxii]).

Penalty for Failure to Appear: "A notarial officer commits a misdemeanor punishable by imprisonment for not more than six (6) months, a fine of not more than seven hundred fifty dollars ($750.00), or both, if he signs and affixes his seal to a certificate of acknowledgment when the party executing the instrument has not first acknowledged the execution of the instrument in the presence of, as defined in WS 34-26-101(b)(xxi), the notarial officer, if by law the instrument is required to be recorded or filed and cannot be filed without a certificate of acknowledgment signed and sealed by a notarial officer" (WS 6-5-114).

NOTARY SIGNING AGENTS

Currently, there are no statutes, regulations or rules expressly governing, prohibiting or restricting the operation of Notary Signing Agents within the state of Wyoming.

NOTARY FEES

"For performing a notarial act, a notarial officer may charge the maximum fee specified in WS 34-26-302, charge less than the maximum fee or waive the fee" (WS 34-26-301).

Maximum Fees

The maximum fees that may be charged for a notarial act are (WS 34-26-302[a]):

1. For taking an acknowledgment, $2 per signature;
2. For administering an oath or affirmation without a signature, $2 per person;
3. For executing a jurat, $2 per signature;
4. For witnessing or attesting a signature, $2 per signature;
5. For certifying or attesting copies, $2 per page certified;
6. For taking a verification upon oath or affirmation, $2 per certificate;
7. For noting a protest of a negotiable instrument, $2 per protest.

Travel Fee

A notarial officer may charge a travel fee when traveling to perform a notarial act if: (a) the officer and the person requesting the notarial act agree on the travel fee in advance of the travel, and (b) the officer explains to the person requesting the act that the travel fee is both separate from the fee for the notarization, if any, and neither specified nor mandated by law (WS 34-26-302[b]).

Payment Prior to Act

A notarial officer may require payment of any fees specified in WS 34-26-302 prior to performance of a notarial act (WS 34-26-303[a]).

Any fees paid to a notarial officer prior to performance of a notarial act are nonrefundable if: (a) the act was completed, or (b) in the case of travel fees paid in compliance with WS 34-26-302(b), the act was not completed for reasons stated in WS 34-26-201(b) — i.e., the signer is not present or able to be identified through personal knowledge or satisfactory evidence — after the officer had traveled to meet the signer (WS 34-26-303[b]).

Fees of Employee Notary

An employer may prohibit an employee who is a notarial officer from charging for notarial acts performed as part of that employee's employment (WS 34-26-304[a]).

Governmental Employee Fees: "A governmental employer who has absorbed an employee's costs in becoming or operating as a notarial officer shall require any fees collected for notarial acts performed as part of the employee's employment either to be waived or surrendered to the employer to support public programs" (WS 34-26-304[b]).

NOTARY CERTIFICATES

Wyoming has adopted the *Uniform Law on Notarial Acts*, including the short-form certificates (WS 34-26-108) for:

1. Acknowledgment by individual;
2. Acknowledgment by representative;
3. Verification upon oath or affirmation;
4. Witnessing or attesting signature;
5. Attesting copy of signature.

For the text of these certificates, see "Uniform Law on Notarial Acts (1982)," Section 8, in Appendix 2.

In the sample notarial certificates provided on the Wyoming Secretary of State's website, the phrase "instrument/document entitled _____(title of document)" replaces the word "instrument" or "document" appearing in the forms for the Uniform Law on Notarial Acts (WS 34-26-108), thereby directing the Notary to insert the document's title on every short form certificate notarized.

Requirements for Any Notarial Certificate

"a. A notarial act shall be evidenced by a certificate signed and dated by a notarial officer. The certificate shall include identification of the jurisdiction in which the notarial act is performed and the title of the office of the notarial officer and may include the official stamp or seal of the office. If the officer is a commissioned notarial officer, the certificate shall also indicate the date of expiration, if any, of the commission of office, but omission of that information may subsequently be corrected. If the officer is a commissioned officer on active duty in the military service of the United States, it shall also include the officer's rank.

"b. A certificate of a notarial act is sufficient if it meets the requirements of subsection a. of this section and it:

"i. Is in the short form set forth in WS 34-26-108;

"ii. Is in a form otherwise prescribed by the law of this state;

"iii. Is in a form prescribed by the law or regulations applicable in the place in which the notarial act was performed; or

"iv. Sets forth the actions of the notarial officer and those are sufficient to meet the requirements of the designated notarial act" (WS 34-26-107).

Attaching a 'Loose' Certificate

"If there is insufficient space to affix a seal on a document, you may refuse to notarize or a separate page may be attached to the document for the notary certificate. The notary certificate need not share the same page as the signature being notarized since any notarial certificate is appended to the instrument and is not a 'part of the document text.' It is appropriate for the notarial certificate to make reference to the title of the document to which it is being attached" (WNH).

In regard to notarizing motor vehicle titles, "(i)f there is not room on the title for the notary stamp, a separate notarial certificate may be prepared and attached which includes the title number and the required signature and notary stamp" (WNH).

"When the jurat is not written on the document to which it applies, a statement on the document should indicate that a jurat is attached" (WNH).

Mere 'Stamping and Signing' Insufficient

"Every notarial act must be evidenced by a notarial certificate signed and dated by a notary public. It is not sufficient to just stamp a document and sign by your stamp. The notarial certificate must include the jurisdiction (state and county) in which the notarial act is performed. It must include words describing the type of notarial act performed such as the form of an acknowledgment or a jurat. The certificate must identify the title of the notarial officer (notary public). For notaries public, the certificate bears their seal or stamp and the notary's commission expiration date" (WNH).

Multiple Signers

"When two signers appear before a notary at the same time, the names may appear on the same certificate" (website, "Frequently Asked Questions").

Certificate Corrections

"Line through incorrect items in ink. Write corrections above lined-out material. Write initials and date adjacent to the correction. Never use 'white-out' products" (website, "Safeguards").

Fraud-Deterrent Tip

"It is a good idea to reference the name of the document on the notarial certificate to prevent its removal and placement on another document which the notary may not have witnessed" (website, "Sample Notarial Certificates").

ELECTRONIC NOTARIZATIONS

The state of Wyoming has not yet adopted statutes or regulations expressly establishing rules, definitions, and procedures for electronic notarization.

UETA Recognizes Notary's eSignature

Wyoming has adopted the Uniform Electronic Transactions Act, including the provision on notarization and acknowledgment (Title 40, Chapter 21, Sections 40-21-101 through 40-21-119), thereby recognizing the legal validity of electronic signatures used by Notaries:

"If a law requires a signature or record to be notarized, acknowledged, verified or made under oath, the requirement is satisfied if the electronic signature of the person authorized to perform those acts, together with all other information required to be included by other applicable law, is attached to or logically associated with the signature or record" (WS 40-21-111).

NOTARY RECORDS

"A notary journal is a permanent detailed written record of all notarizations performed by the notary. The notary journal protects the notary from accusations of wrong doing and it helps prevent the notary from engaging in wrong doing. Every journal entry is legally presumed to be truthful. Wyoming statutes do not require keeping a journal but it is wise and highly recommended by the Secretary of State" (website, "Journal"). "(R)ecording official notarial acts in a journal may prove useful later if you need to recall the specifics of a particular notarization. Such an instance might include testifying in a legal proceeding regarding your verification of a signer's identity..." (WNH).

Journal Permanent and Tamper-Proof

"The journal must be tamper-proof and permanent as a legal record of notarial activity. The journal must be permanently bound and have pre-numbered pages and entry spaces. The journal must never be shared and/or used by other notaries. A notary public should complete the journal entry immediately before notarization occurs and make an entry for every notary service provided" (website, "Journal").

Journal Entries

The website further states that every journal entry should include the following:

1. Document signer's signature;
2. Date and time of the notarization;
3. Date of the document;
4. Type of notarization performed and type of document notarized;
5. Document signer's address;
6. Statement on how the notary verified the signer's identity; and
7. Any special comments about the transaction.

AUTHENTICATION OF NOTARIAL ACTS

County Clerks

Authenticating certificates for a Wyoming Notary may be locally issued by the office of the county clerk where the Notary has filed an oath and bond. The fee for such a certification is $3 (WS 18-3-402[a]).

Secretary of State

Authenticating certificates for Notaries, including apostilles, are also issued by the Wyoming Secretary of State's office, as are authenticating certificates for county clerks.

Fees: $3 per document, covering authentication of a Notary or county clerk, or an apostille. Payable to "Wyoming Secretary of State."

Address:
Office of Secretary of State
State Capitol Building
200 West 24th St.
Cheyenne, WY 82002-0020

Telephone: 1-307-777-5335

Procedure: Mail or present in person the original notarized document(s), along with the

$3 fee(s). All signatures must be original. The country of destination must be specified. Indicate a return address and a daytime telephone number, in case there are questions. "All documents in a foreign language must be accompanied by a certified (notarized) English translation" (website, "Overview: Authentication Services"). Include an addressed, stamped return envelope, a prepaid air bill, or a pick-up date and time. A form is available at http://soswy.state.wy.us under "Authentication Services."

Authenticating School Transcripts: "The officer of the school must sign the transcript certification before a notary who is often an employee of the school (but does not need to be an employee). The notary may then attach a notarial certificate acknowledging the school official's signature. The notarized document may then be sent to the Secretary of State for the attachment of an apostille or certification stating the notary is a valid notary in Wyoming" (WNH).

COMMISSIONING AND ADMINISTRATION

The Wyoming Secretary of State commissions and maintains records on the state's Notaries (WS 32-1-101). "All applications and documents submitted to the Secretary of State or to the County Clerk regarding your Notary Public commission are public records and could be obtained under the Public Records Act. Any person may have the right to inspect and copy a notary application upon request" (WNH).

Applying for Commission

Qualifications: An applicant for a commission as a Wyoming Notary must: (a) be at least 18 years old, (b) be a resident of Wyoming and of the county from which applying and (c) be able to read and write the English language (WS 32-1-101[b]). A felon is not eligible to become a Notary (WS 6-10-106) unless the conviction has been reversed or annulled, the individual has been pardoned, or all rights have been restored under WS 7-13-105(a).

Self-Test Required: Applicants are asked to read the Notary statutes and the "Frequently Asked Questions" provided by the Secretary of State and to take the online "Notary Public Self-Help Test" which is a 20-question, true-false exam with correct answers provided. The test is not required and should not be sent to the Secretary of State with the application.

Application: "Instead of adopting the surname of the notary's spouse, a notary may…be commissioned as a notary by the name by which the notary is generally known" (WS 32-1-102[b]). The commission application fee is $30.

"The renewal procedure is the same as for a new commission. When renewing, do not submit your application more than six weeks prior to your current expiration date" (website, "Quick Info/How do I renew my notary?"). "A two or three week time frame is appreciated so the notary can be assured of no lapse in their commission" (WNH).

Non-Residents: Non-residents of Wyoming may not apply for a Wyoming Notary commission. However, a Notary of a contiguous state may notarize in Wyoming if that state grants Wyoming Notaries the same authority within that state (WS 32-1-105[d]). Montana currently is the only state extending such reciprocity.

Filing After Commissioning: After receiving notice from the Secretary of State and within 60 days of the commission's beginning date, the new Notary must file an oath of office and a $500 bond with the local county clerk (WS 32-1-104[a]). There will be a recording fee for the bond, which varies with the number of pages recorded and usually costs about $14 (WNH). The commission will be sent directly to the county clerk by the Secretary of State (WS 32-1-103). Upon the filing of the oath and bond, the county clerk will give the commission to the Notary and send a written notice of qualification to the Secretary of State. "Once you have filed your bond and received your Certificate of Commission from the county clerk, you can then begin performing the duties of a notary public" (website, "Frequently Asked Questions").

Changes of Status

If Notary Changes Name: The Secretary of State should be informed of any change of name by the Notary (website, "Name & Address Changes"). A Notary who changes a surname before expiration of a commission may either (WS 32-1-102):

1. Apply for a new commission in the new name at once or upon expiration of the current term (cost $30); or

2. Continue to use the old name (no cost); or

3. File a certified copy of the marriage certificate, divorce decree or court order of name change with the Secretary of State and the county clerk, allowing the Notary to add the new or restored name after the name appearing on the commission (cost $3 paid to state, plus county fee).

If Notary Moves: "You should notify the Secretary of State of (any) change of address so you can receive information about law changes or other courtesy mailings" (WNH).

A Notary's move to a new county automatically voids the commission. "A person holding a notarial commission who changes residence to a different county shall procure a new notary commission for the new county of residence" (WS 32-1-101[d]). A new Notary seal with the new county name must also be obtained (WS 32-1-106[a]).

Resignation: To resign a Notary commission, the Notary must submit a letter of resignation to the Wyoming Secretary of State (website, "Frequently Asked Questions"). A Notary who moves out of state during the term of office must resign the commission.

COUNTY CLERKS

To contact a Wyoming county clerk to obtain an authenticating certificate for a Notary, or for assistance in locating a given Notary, telephone long-distance information — 1-307-555-1212 — and ask for the phone number for the clerk of the appropriate county.

County	City/Town
Albany	Laramie
Big Horn	Basin
Campbell	Gillette
Carbon	Rawlins
Converse	Douglas
Crook	Sundance
Fremont	Lander
Goshen	Torrington
Hot Springs	Thermopolis
Johnson	Buffalo
Laramie	Cheyenne
Lincoln	Kemmerer
Natrona	Casper
Niobrara	Lusk
Park	Cody
Platte	Wheatland
Sheridan	Sheridan
Sublette	Pinedale
Sweetwater	Green River
Teton	Jackson
Uinta	Evanston
Washakie	Worland
Weston	Newcastle

OTHER NOTARIAL OFFICERS

Notarial acts may be performed in Wyoming by the following persons (WS 34-26-103):

1. A Wyoming Notary Public;
2. A judge of any court of the state;
3. A clerk or deputy clerk of any court of the state;
4. A clerk or deputy clerk of a county;
5. A district court commissioner;
6. A full-time magistrate as authorized by WS 5-9-208;
7. A part-time magistrate as authorized by WS 5-9-212;
8. Any other officer authorized under Wyoming law to take acknowledgments.

The above officers — and any others given notarial powers by Wyoming law — are designated as "notarial officers" (WS 34-26-101[b][iv]). The only officer on the above list that is required to be commissioned is the Notary Public; the rest have ex officio notarial powers.

Protests by Circuit Court Clerk

"When the holder of any instrument desires it to be protested, and no notary public can be found, it shall be lawful for any circuit court of the county wherein said instrument is required to be protested, to perform the services herein required to be performed by notaries public, and to be entitled to the same fees as are hereinafter provided for notaries public for similar services" (WS 32-1-111).

Notary of Contiguous State

"The administration of an oath or a proof of acknowledgment performed in Wyoming by a notary public of a contiguous state has the same effect under Wyoming law as if that act were performed by a Wyoming notary public, if that contiguous state grants Wyoming notaries public similar authority within that state" (WS 32-1-105[d]).

The following are defined as "authorized contiguous states": Colorado, Idaho, Montana, Nebraska, South Dakota and Utah, but only if they have "enacted a law or rule or regulation allowing a Wyoming Notary to perform acts within that state" (SOS-NOT-2 §1). When notarizing within Wyoming, such Notaries must use the seal of their own state (SOS-NOT-4 §1), but they may not charge more for their acts than Wyoming Notaries (SOS-NOT-5 §1).

Montana presently is the only state extending such reciprocity.

QUICK FACTS

Notary Jurisdiction
Statewide (WS 32-1-101[c]).

Reciprocity: "A Wyoming notary public may administer oaths or proofs of acknowledgment in a contiguous state if that state recognizes the Wyoming notary public's authority within that state to perform those acts. The administration of an oath or a proof of acknowledgment performed in Wyoming by a notary public of a contiguous state has the same effect under Wyoming law as if that act were performed by a Wyoming notary public, if that contiguous state grants Wyoming notaries public similar authority within that state" (WS 32-1-105[d]). Montana presently is the only state extending such reciprocity to Wyoming Notaries, who may thus notarize within Montana (website, "Duties & Principles").

Notary Term Length
Four years (WS 32-1-101[c]). For knowingly notarizing after commission expiration, the Notary may be fined no more than $500 and no less than $25 (WS 32-1-109).

Notary Bond
$500, executed by "two (2) sureties, to be approved by the county clerk, or by a surety company licensed in this state" (WS 32-1-104).

Appendix 1

TABLE OF ENACTMENT OF MODEL AND UNIFORM LAWS (2011)

Model acts of the National Notary Association and pertinent uniform acts of the National Conference of Commissioners on Uniform State Laws have been adopted as follows:

- ● Enacted virtually *in toto*
- † Substantial parts enacted or adopted
- * Only notarial forms enacted

	Model Notary Act (1984/ 2002/2010) (APPENDIX 1A)	Revised Uniform Law on Notarial Acts (2010) (APPENDIX 1B)	Uniform Law on Notarial Acts (1982) (APPENDIX 2)	Uniform Recog. of Acks. Act (1968) (APPENDIX 3)	Uniform Ack. Act (1939/1960) (APPENDIX 4)	Uniform Foreign Acks. Act (1914) (APPENDIX 5)	Uniform Acks. Act (1892) (APPENDIX 6)
Alabama							
Alaska				●			
American Samoa	†(2002)						
Arizona				●			
Arkansas					●		
California							
Colorado				●			
Connecticut				●	●		
Delaware			●				
District of Columbia			●				
Florida							
Georgia							
Guam	●(1984)						
Hawaii							
Idaho							
Illinois			*	●			
Indiana							
Iowa			*				
Kansas			●				
Kentucky				●			
Louisiana						●	●
Maine				●			
Maryland					●		
Massachusetts	†(2002)						●

Appendix 1

	Model Notary Act (1984/2002/2010) (APPENDIX 1A)	Revised Uniform Law on Notarial Acts (2010) (APPENDIX 1B)	Uniform Law on Notarial Acts (1982) (APPENDIX 2)	Uniform Recog. of Acks. Act (1968) (APPENDIX 3)	Uniform Ack. Act (1939/1960) (APPENDIX 4)	Uniform Foreign Acks. Act (1914) (APPENDIX 5)	Uniform Acks. Act (1892) (APPENDIX 6)
Michigan				●			
Minnesota			●				
Mississippi	†(2002)						
Missouri							
Montana			●				
Nebraska				●			
Nevada			●				
New Hampshire			●				
New Jersey							
New Mexico	†(2002)		●				
New York							
North Carolina	†(2002)						
North Dakota		●		●			
Northern Marianas	●(1984)						
Ohio				●			
Oklahoma			●				
Oregon			●				
Pennsylvania					●		
Puerto Rico							
Rhode Island	†(2002)						
South Carolina				●			
South Dakota					●		
Tennessee							
Texas							
Utah							
Vermont							
Virginia	†(2002)			●			
Virgin Islands				●			
Washington							
West Virginia				●			
Wisconsin			●				
Wyoming			●				

Appendix 1A

MODEL NOTARY ACT (2010)

Article I
Implementation and Definitions

Chapter 1 – Implementation

Comment

General: This chapter states the purposes and sets out the applicability of the Model Notary Act (hereinafter "the Act"). Section 1-2 is particularly noteworthy because its goals undergird most of the provisions found throughout the Act, and help justify a number of the positions taken. The balance of the chapter addresses standard legislative matters.

§ 1-1 Short Title.

This [Act] may be cited as the [Model Notary Act of 2010].

§ 1-2 Purposes.

This [Act] shall be construed and applied to advance its underlying purposes, which are:

(1) to promote, serve, and protect the public interest;

(2) to simplify, clarify, and modernize the law governing notaries;

(3) to foster ethical conduct among notaries;

(4) to enhance cross-border recognition of notarial acts;

(5) to integrate procedures for traditional and electronic notarial acts; and

(6) to unify state notarial laws.

Comment

Section 1-2 enunciates the overarching purposes of the Act. Although not necessarily listed in order of importance, the first two subparagraphs clearly constitute the driving spirit of the entire Act.

Subparagraph (1) places the public's interest above all else. The Act adopts the position that notaries are first and foremost public servants. Their powers are to be exercised only in the public's interest and not for personal gain. Other provisions elsewhere in the Act support and execute this operating precept. (See, e.g., Subparagraph 5-5(a)(1) (no notarization of one's own signature); Subparagraph 5-5(a)(3) (disqualification when signers are relatives); Section 5-11 (no testimonials); and Subsection 6-2(a) (no surcharges on fees).)

Subparagraph (2) stakes out equally important territory: bringing notarial laws into the 21st century. Some state notary laws are carry-overs from antiquated statutes (see, e.g., MASS. GEN. LAWS ANN. ch. 222, §§ 1 to 11), some are quite minimalist (see, e.g., VT. STAT. ANN. tit. 24 §§ 441 to 446), and others a patchwork product of numerous unrelated legislative amendments (see, e.g., CAL. GOV'T. CODE §§ 8200 to 8230 & CAL. CIV. CODE §§ 1181 to 1197). The Act offers a comprehensive statute that addresses all contemporary notarial issues, and introduces rules not only for paper-based documents but also for electronic transactions. It then integrates them into one workable piece of legislation. The Act makes the effort both to establish appropriate commissioning guidelines, and to detail proper procedures for performing notarial acts. The focus is clearly on ensuring that notaries understand their roles. This works toward satisfying the public interest objective set out in Subparagraph (1). The drafters addressed issues principally involving the commissioning of notaries and the performance of notarizations. Consequently, even if the Act is adopted, other legislation may still be needed to respond to related matters, such as ensuring that the statutory forms in other sections of the jurisdiction's law bear notarial certificate wording specified in Sections 9-4, 9-5, and 9-6.

Subparagraph (3) introduces a new concept: notary ethics. Although the Act does not establish any ethical standards, it recognizes that a notary owes special duties both to principals and the public, and consequently may be regarded as a professional. Professions impose ethical standards upon their members, and this should be the case as well for notaries. In 1998, the National Notary Association promulgated THE NOTARY PUBLIC CODE OF PROFESSIONAL RESPONSIBILITY. (Reprinted at 32 J. MARSHALL L. REV. 1123-1193 (1999) and available online at www.NationalNotary.org, clicking on "Best Practices.") It is a comprehensive ethics guide adaptable by state legislatures as a statute or by commissioning officials as an administrative rule. (See, e.g., AMER. SAMOA CODE ANN. § 31.0316, requiring notary commission applicants to take a course and pass a test that is based upon applicable law and THE NOTARY PUBLIC CODE OF PROFESSIONAL RESPONSIBILITY, which is provided by the Secretary of American Samoa as a study guide; and HAWAII ADMIN. RULES § 5-11-39 (12), listing as grounds for refusal to renew, reinstate, or restore a notary commission the notary's conduct or practice contrary to the CODE.) Absent taking this step, the Act provides rules and procedures that, when properly followed, encourage professionalism and foster ethical conduct.

Subparagraph (4) recognizes the modern reality of cross-border commerce. Principals who migrate from one jurisdiction to another or enterprises that conduct multi-state businesses need to have documents that are recognized wherever presented. A major objective of the Act, as stated in Subparagraph (6), is to unify notarial laws throughout the country. Problems relating to the recognition of out-of-state notarial acts can be eased or eliminated if the Act gains widespread acceptance.

Subparagraph (5) addresses the reality that electronic transactions are becoming more prevalent. One goal of the Act is to ensure that workable notarial procedures are in place to accommodate that fact. To this end, Article III of the Act is devoted to establishing rules for electronic notarizations.

[§ 1-3 Interpretation.

In this [Act], unless the context otherwise requires, words in the singular include the plural, and words in the plural include the singular.]

§ 1-[4] Prospective Effect.

The existing bond, seal, length of commission term, and liability of current notaries commissioned before the [Act's] effective date may not be invalidated, modified, or terminated by this [Act], but those notaries shall comply with this [Act] in performing notarizations and in applying for new commissions.

Comment

Section 1-4 protects valid notary commissions existing when the Act is adopted. The status of notaries holding such commissions continues according to the terms and conditions at the time of commissioning. However, recommissioning for these notaries will have to be done pursuant to the new rules of the Act. (See Section 3-5.) Significantly, although the status of a current commission is not affected, the new operating rules of notarization (see generally Chapters 5, 6, 7, 8, and 9) and concomitant obligations (see generally Chapter 12) must be followed by all notaries immediately, including those who were commissioned prior to the adoption of the Act.

§ 1-[5] Severability Clause.

If any provision of this [Act] or its application to any person or circumstance is held invalid, the invalidity does not affect other provisions or applications of this [Act] that can be given effect without the invalid provision or application, and to this end the provisions of this [Act] are severable.

[§ 1-[6] Repeals.

The following acts and parts of acts are hereby repealed: [_____].]

Comment

Section 1-6 recognizes that not all jurisdictions have a single act containing all of the rules regulating notaries and notarizations. Thus, legislators will have to identify existing statutes or portions thereof that are superseded by the Act and make the appropriate repeals. It is possible that some extant rules affecting notaries are not inconsistent with the Act, and ought not be repealed. This might include rules prohibiting notary fees for notarial acts related to elections or the securing of veterans' benefits. (See, e.g., CAL. ELEC. CODE § 8080, which prohibits a notary from charging a fee for verifying any nomination document or circulator's affidavit.)

§ 1-[7] Effective Date.

This [Act] shall take effect [_____].

Chapter 2 – Definitions Used in This [Act]

Comment

General: A number of recurring terms are used throughout the Act. Some have a technical meaning specific to notarial use, while others merely require elaborate explanation. Following the example of other statutes, these terms are defined in a separate section to simplify the text in the balance of the Act.

§ 2-1 Acknowledgment.

"Acknowledgment" means a notarial act in which an individual at a single time and place:

(1) appears in person before the notary and presents a document;

(2) is personally known to the notary or identified by the notary through satisfactory evidence; and

(3) indicates to the notary that the signature on the document was voluntarily affixed by the individual for the purposes stated within the document and, if applicable, that the individual had due authority to sign in a particular representative capacity.

Comment

In defining "acknowledgment," Section 2-1 makes clear that all three elements of the notarial act must occur at the same time and place. Subparagraph (3) explicitly requires that the principal voluntarily sign the document "for the purposes stated" therein. Although current statutes seldom directly address volition (but see GA. CODE ANN. § 45-17-8(b)(2) and (3)), it seems to be generally accepted by the courts as a requirement for an acknowledgment. The Act eliminates any doubt about the need for volition in a proper acknowledgment.

A second aspect of Subparagraph (3) raises other issues. The Act converts an acknowledgment from simply a formal statement that the signature on the document was freely made by the principal into one that also declares the intent to validate the document itself. Statutory acknowledgment forms often bear language stating that the acknowledger affixed a signature "for the purposes stated within the document." (See, e.g., ARK. CODE § 16-47-107, which states that the instrument was signed "for the consideration, uses and purposes therein mentioned and set forth.") Some drafters criticized this addition, fearing it could unwittingly impose unintended obligations upon the principal. The concern follows from the fact that a principal may read a document, not truly understand its effect, but nonetheless sign it. It was suggested than an acknowledgment ought not require the principal to speak to the purpose or intent of the document. In response, it was argued that apprehensions over this point can be put to rest by the intended reasonable interpretation of the provision. The definition does not make the acknowledgment in itself an admission that the principal understood the legal significance of the document. Indeed, it does not speak to the contents at all. The provision only means that signing serves to adopt the document as the principal's act. The legal ramifications of the document are subject to independent review. (See also Subparagraph 5-2(3), adopting the rule that a notary must not notarize a document if the principal does not appear to understand the significance of the transaction.)

In acknowledging a document, the principal does not make any statement regarding the truthfulness or accuracy of the contents of the document. (Compare Section 2-7 and Comment defining "jurat.") Moreover, there is no implication that the principal has even read the document. The acknowledgment speaks to the fact that the document was signed voluntarily for the purpose of validating the document.

Additionally, the principal asserts that he or she was authorized to sign the document if it was signed in a representative capacity. (See Section 9-4 for a model acknowledgment certificate form.)

§ 2-2 Affirmation.

"Affirmation" means a notarial act, or part thereof, which is legally equivalent to an oath and in which an individual at a single time and place:

(1) appears in person before the notary;

(2) is personally known to the notary or identified by the notary through satisfactory evidence; and

(3) makes a vow of truthfulness or fidelity on penalty of perjury, based on personal honor and without invoking a deity or using any form of the word "swear."

Comment

Section 2-2 offers a definition of "affirmation" that contains all of the standard components of an oath. An affirmation serves as the functional equivalent of an "oath" (see Section 2-11) for principals who prefer not to pledge to a supreme being. As required for most notarial acts, by definition, the principal must personally appear before and satisfactorily prove identity to the notary. In order to solemnify an affirmation, the Act compels the principal to understand that the statement is made under penalty of perjury.

The Act does not prescribe affirmation wording. It assumes that a simple statement including the language "I affirm" and "under penalty of perjury" will suffice. The notary may orally state the affirmation and have the principal positively assent to it, or the principal may speak the entire affirmation aloud. It is preferable for assent to be made by oral response, but any action (e.g., a hand gesture or nod) could constitute assent if clearly made for the purpose of adopting the affirmation, especially in the case of a principal who is physically incapable of communicating orally. While it is not necessary that the principal raise his or her right hand to make an affirmation, notaries are encouraged to require any ceremonial gesture that they feel will most compellingly appeal to the conscience of the principal. When associated with a notarial certificate, good practice would suggest that the notary read aloud any provided affirmation wording and obtain the principal's assent. The key point is that a proper affirmation requires a positive and unequivocal response by the principal.

An affirmation may be a notarial act in its own right, but most often it is administered as part of a jurat and the person making the affirmation will be required to sign an affidavit or other document. Note, nonetheless, even in those situations when a signed document is not associated with the affirmation, the notarial act should be memorialized in the notary's journal, with the entry including the principal's signature.

§ 2-3 Commission.

"Commission" means both to empower to perform notarial acts and the written evidence of authority to perform those acts.

§ 2-4 Copy Certification.

"Copy certification" means a notarial act in which a notary:

(1) locates or is presented with a paper or an electronic document that is neither a vital record, a public record, nor a recorded document;

(2) compares the document with a second paper or electronic document that either is:

(i) presented to the notary;

(ii) located by the notary; or

(iii) copied from the first document by the notary; and

(3) confirms through a visual or electronic comparison that the second document is an identical, exact, and complete copy of the image or text and, if applicable, metadata of the first document.

Comment

Section 2-4 defines and provides guidance on the notarial act of certifying copies. Subparagraph (1) prohibits a notary from making certified copies of certain documents. Generally, the Act assumes that only the duly appointed public custodians of official records and documents may certify copies of them. Thus, a notary may not certify a copy of a marriage license, birth certificate, or a recorded document such as a deed.

In Subparagraph (1), in a departure from the former Act, the drafters allow a copy of an electronic document to be certified, applying the same proscriptions against certifying a copy of a vital or recorded document. In another departure, the drafters recognize that a notary may be asked to locate the original paper or electronic document – possibly for a verification of fact (see Section 2-22) if vital or recorded documents are not involved – in contrast to the typical circumstance wherein the original document is presented to the notary. This expands the utility of copy certification.

Subparagraph (2) provides for three different scenarios, and the pertinent entry in the notary's journal of notarial acts should be clear on which applies for any particular copy certification. In the first, the notary would be presented with a second paper or electronic document to compare with the original described in Subparagraph (1). In the second scenario, the notary would personally locate this second document, perhaps in an office housing physical records or on the Internet. In the third scenario, the notary would personally make or supervise the making of a copy of the original document referenced in Subparagraph 1, whether that original were presented to or located by the notary. This copy would then be compared to the original. While the preferred situation from a fraud-deterrent perspective would always be for the notary to control production of the second document, this would limit the utility of copy certification. For instance, the notary might not have access to photocopying or electronic scanning equipment to duplicate an original paper document. Alternatively, the notary might be asked to certify the congruence of two electronic documents, one or both of which may already exist on the Internet. As long as the notary, through a careful visual or a reliable electronic comparison (see Subparagraph (3)), confirms that the two documents are identical, the certification will be meaningful.

Subparagraph (3) recognizes that electronic documents contain "hidden" coded information other than text or images. These "metadata," for instance, dictate the style, size, and spacing of the typeface in which the text appears. They might also include past editings that have been made to the electronic document. It may be very useful for a notary's client to know whether a certified copy of an electronic document does or does not include the same metadata prescriptions of its original. The copy certification certificate in Section 9-8 allows the notary to provide such information.

§ 2-5 Credible Witness.

"Credible witness" means an honest, reliable, and impartial person who personally knows an individual appearing before a notary and takes an oath or affirmation from the notary to vouch for that individual's identity.

Comment

Section 2-5 defines the term "credible witness." Consistent with the public interest goal of deterring fraud and creating reliable documents, the Act takes the step of removing any doubt as to who can qualify to act in this capacity. Particularly noteworthy is the impartiality requirement. This means that the witness neither has an interest in nor is affected by the transaction for which he or she is proving the identity of the principal in a notarization. Although not specifically required by the Act, witness impartiality may be measured by the same standards used to disqualify notaries from acting. (See Section 5-5 and Comment.)

The definition does not address whether a credible witness must be personally known to the notary or whether instead the witness may be identified through reliable identification documents. This matter, however, is resolved by the definition of "satisfactory evidence of identity" (see Section 2-20), which dictates that only in instances where two credible witnesses are vouching for the identity of a principal may the notary use identification documents to confirm the identity of a credible witness.

§ 2-6 Journal of Notarial Acts.

"Journal of notarial acts" and "journal" mean a book to create and preserve a chronological record of notarizations that is maintained by the notary public who performed the same notarizations.

Comment

This definition of "journal of notarial acts" differs from the definition in the former Act by its use of the word "book" rather than "device." The drafters' intention was to limit the application of the definition to a journal with paper or other tangible pages, and to let the definition of "electronic journal of notarial acts" in Section 15-4 address electronic devices for recording notarial acts. A notary or an electronic notary may elect to use either kind of journal. (See Sections 7-1 and 20-1.)

Another departure from the previous definition is the addition of the phrase "who performed the same notarizations." This clarifies that no person other than the notary who performed the notarial acts may make entries in the journal that records those acts.

§ 2-7 Jurat.

"Jurat" means a notarial act in which an individual at a single time and place:

(1) appears in person before the notary and presents a document;

(2) is personally known to the notary or identified by the notary through satisfactory evidence;

(3) signs the document in the presence of the notary; and

(4) takes an oath or affirmation from the notary vouching for the truthfulness or accuracy of the signed document.

Comment

Section 2-7 defines "jurat" as a particular type of notarial act, consistent with the current common usage in the notarial community. In so doing, it broadens the definition of the term commonly found in law dictionaries, e.g., "a certification added to an affidavit or deposition stating when and before what authority the affidavit or deposition was made" (see BLACK'S LAW DICTIONARY (7th ed. West 1999)). Mistakenly, some apply the term "jurat" to any notarial certificate form, including that for acknowledgments. It should be pointed out that the type of notarization designated as a "jurat" in this Act, is called a "verification upon oath or affirmation" in the Uniform Law on Notarial Acts (1982) of the National Conference of Commissioners on Uniform State Laws. This term is seldom used by notaries, who prefer the simpler "jurat."

The definition of "jurat" in Section 2-7 contains the commonly accepted components of this type of notarization. A central feature of the jurat is recognized in Subparagraph (4): the principal must take an oath (or make an affirmation) vouching for the truthfulness or accuracy of the contents of the document. This distinguishes the act from both an acknowledgment (see Section 2-1) and a signature witnessing (see Section 2-21). In the former, the principal merely indicates that a signature was voluntarily affixed to a document for the purposes of adopting the document. In the latter, the principal merely signs the document and nothing more is ascribed to the act. No commitment of conscience regarding the truthfulness or accuracy of the contents of the document may be inferred from either an acknowledgment or a signature witnessing, but that is the case with a jurat, which requires an oath or affirmation.

Notwithstanding that it is essential to a jurat, notaries often neglect formally to administer the oath or affirmation. When such omissions are challenged, courts have on occasion inferred that an oath was tacitly taken. The drafters believed that the significance attributed to a jurat as a statement under oath dictates positive action on the part of the notary to administer an oath or affirmation to the principal. Good practice demands that the oath or affirmation language be recited aloud and that the principal affirmatively respond before the notary completes the certificate. (With regard to the administration of oaths and affirmations, see Sections 2-11 and 2-2, along with their respective Comments.)

§ 2-8 Notarial Act and Notarization.

"Notarial act" and "notarization" mean any official act of certification, attestation, or administration that a notary public is empowered to perform under this [Act].

Comment

This definition of "notarial act" and "notarization" fleshes out the terser definition that appeared in the former Act, in order to distinguish ancillary acts that a notary is empowered or required to perform (e.g., reporting a change of address) from the central official function of a notary, which is to certify, attest, or administer.

§ 2-9 Notarial Certificate and Certificate.

"Notarial certificate" and "certificate" mean the part of, or attachment to, a notarized document that, in the performance of the notarization, is completed by the notary, bears the notary's official signature and seal, and states the date, venue, and facts attested by the notary in the particular notarial act.

Comment

This definition of "notarial certificate" differs from the definition in the former acts, in part, by addition of the phrase "in the performance of the notarization," in order to clarify that a notarial certificate must be completed at the time of the notarial act. The definition of "electronic notarial certificate" (see Section 15-6) is closely based on this section.

§ 2-10 Notary Public and Notary.

"Notary public" and "notary" mean any person commissioned to perform notarial acts under this [Act].

§ 2-11 Oath.

"Oath" means a notarial act, or part thereof, which is legally equivalent to an affirmation and in which an individual at a single time and place:

(1) appears in person before the notary;

(2) is personally known to the notary or identified by the notary through satisfactory evidence; and

(3) makes a vow of truthfulness or fidelity on penalty of perjury while invoking a deity or using any form of the word "swear."

Comment

Section 2-11 lists the elements of an "oath." An oath is the alternative to an affirmation. It serves the same purpose and has the same legal effect. The sole distinction between the two is that an oathtaker pledges to a supreme being or uses the word "swear" in any of its forms to indicate a solemn commitment of conscience. All of the procedural rules relating to affirmation apply equally to oaths. (See Section 2-2 Comment.) When making an oath, the principal need not swear on nor touch a Bible or other revered text. However, notaries have discretion to utilize gestures or ceremonies that they believe will most compellingly appeal to the conscience of the oath-taker.

§ 2-12 Official Misconduct.

"Official misconduct" means:

(1) a notary's performance of any act prohibited, or failure to perform any act or duty mandated, by this [Act] or by any other law in connection with a notarial act; or

(2) a notary's performance of an official act or duty in a manner that is negligent, contrary to established norms of sound notarial practice, or against the public interest.

Comment

Section 2-12 defines "official misconduct." In striving to promote the significance of notarial acts in general, the drafters felt it was important to emphasize proper notarial conduct. The Act broadly defines misconduct to include not only malfeasance (performing prohibited acts) but also nonfeasance (failing to perform required acts). (See Subparagraph (1).) Moreover, this type of misconduct is not limited to duties prescribed by the Act itself, but also extends to obligations imposed by other laws in connection with official acts by the notary. Additionally, misconduct includes misfeasance (negligent performance of acts), as well as actions that violate established standards of sound notarial practice. Recently a court held that the Model Notary Act of 2002 enunciated standards of sound practice and the failure to observe these standards can result in liability to the notary. (See Vancura v. Katris, 907 N.E.2d 814 (Ill. App. 2008).)

The drafters added the wording "or duty" to make notaries accountable not only for their official notarial acts, but also for any other related obligation imposed on them by this Act or any other law. (See, e.g., Chapter 12 for duties of a notary regarding the reporting of changes of status.)

Finally the Act recognizes a type of misconduct constituting a violation of public policy (i.e., "against the public interest"). For example, a notary who gouges a person needing at-home notarial services by overcharging for travel fees may be found in violation of public policy. (See Subsection 6-2(b) and Comment.) The commissioning official has discretion under Subparagraph (2) to determine whether a notary's action constitutes official misconduct.

§ 2-13 Official Seal.

"Official seal" means:

(1) a device authorized by the [commissioning official] for affixing on a paper notarial certificate an image containing a notary's name, title, jurisdiction, commission expiration date, and other information related to the notary's commission; or

(2) the affixed image itself.

Comment

The definition of "official seal" in Section 2-13 replaces the definition of "seal" that appeared in the former Act as Section 2-18. The replacement enables greater precision and economy of language in Section 8-2 and elsewhere in the Act. The two-part definition makes clear that the term "seal" may denote not only the inking, embossing, or other tangible device used by a notary to create an image containing certain information on a notarized document, but also may denote the image itself.

By contrast, the definition of "electronic notary seal" (see Section 15-8) refers only to certain information (i.e., the notary's name, title, jurisdiction, and commission expiration date) placed by the notary on an electronic notarial certificate. This definition does not refer to the device or process for creating this information in electronic form. Conceivably, the means registered by the notary for creating "registered electronic notary seals" (see Section 15-10) might include the notary's mere typing of the seal information on the electronic certificate.

§ 2-14 Official Signature.

"Official signature" means a handwritten signature made by a notary that uses the exact name appearing in the notary's commission and is signed with the intent to perform a notarial act.

Comment

Section 2-14 is new. It provides an important definition that enables greater precision and economy of language in Section 8-1 and elsewhere in the Act.

§ 2-15 Personal Appearance.

"Personal appearance before the notary" and "appears in person before the notary" mean that the notary is physically close enough to see, hear, communicate with, and receive identification documents from a principal and any required witness.

Comment

Section 2-15 defines "personal appearance before the notary" so as to mandate that the principal be in the physical presence of the notary at the time of notarization. This is necessary in order for the notary to perform the essential task of determining that the principal is exactly who he or she purports to be. Ascertaining identity is an integral part of most notarial acts. (See Sections 2-1, 2-2, 2-7, 2-11, and 2-21.) To properly perform this duty (see Section 2-20 for rules to determine "satisfactory evidence of identity") – and to make a necessary commonsense judgment that the principal appears to be acting without coercion and with adequate awareness – the notary must be able to question and closely observe the principal. A telephone call or an e-mail message to the notary will not serve this purpose.

In requiring each principal to appear in person before the notary, the drafters recognized that the Act bars electronic signatures from being notarized when the signer is at a location remote from the notary. One jurisdiction formerly recognized teleconferencing notarizations, with the signer at location A and the notary at location B (see former UTAH ADMIN. CODE R154-10-502), though this rule was repealed because its rigorous technical requirements were deemed impractical in the marketplace. The drafters believe that until teleconferencing equipment is refined to ensure ready and reliable determination of identity, mandating face-to-face personal appearance before a notary in the same room will remain necessary. The drafters are committed to re-evaluating this position as technological advances make reliable remote identification more feasible.

This definition was amended from that appearing in the former Act to clarify that the personal appearance rule also applies to "any required witness" needed to identify the principal. This would include credible witnesses (see Section 2-5) and witnesses to a signing by mark (see Section 5-3).

§ 2-16 Personal Knowledge of Identity.

"Personal knowledge of identity" and "personally knows" mean familiarity with an individual resulting from interactions with that individual over a period of time sufficient to dispel any reasonable uncertainty that the individual has the identity claimed.

Comment

Section 2-16 provides guidance on the critical concept of personal knowledge of identity. Although most notarizations will be based upon identification through evidentiary means (see Section 2-20), sometimes identity will be determined based on a notary's personal familiarity with another individual. Personal knowledge is a necessary element of the chain of proof when a sole credible witness is used. (See Subparagraph 2-20(2).) The Act provides a rule of reason for determining personal knowledge. (See Anderson v. Aronsohn, 63 CAL. APP. 737 (1923), which deals with the nature of personal knowledge of identity, stating that "the degree of acquaintance which would authorize a notary to certify that he had personal knowledge involves something more than mere casual meetings, and must be based upon a chain of circumstances surrounding the person tending to show that he is the party he purports to be.")

The definition does not quantify the number of interactions nor the period of time of acquaintance sufficient to convince a notary that an individual has a claimed identity. This is left to the notary's best judgment. However, the drafters firmly believed that any reasonable doubt on the part of the notary about whether a signer is "personally known" must result in reliance instead on acceptable identification documents or on at least one qualified credible witness.

A unique California law (see CAL. CIV. CODE § 1185) prohibits notaries from relying on personal knowledge to identify principals or credible witnesses in the performance of notarial acts. These provisions were recently enacted at the behest of the California law enforcement community, which has perceived an overly liberal interpretation of "personal knowledge" as the basis for too many identifications by notaries. The result, prosecutors complained, was a lack of recorded evidence in notary journals (e.g., identification document serial numbers) that might be useful in investigating criminal acts of forgery. The drafters of this Act decided not to take away from notaries the valuable option of using personal knowledge as the basis for an identification. Instead, they encourage notaries to supplement any journal notation that a signer was "personally known" with information from an identification document of the signer that might later be useful to law enforcement.

§ 2-17 Principal.

"Principal" means:

(1) a person whose signature is notarized; or

(2) a person, other than a credible witness, taking an oath or affirmation from the notary.

Comment

Section 2-17 defines a term used throughout the Act – principal. The drafters determined that it made sense to identify the person using the services of a notary as a principal. It makes for easier reading of the statute and ends ambiguities with respect to witnesses or other parties who may have dealings with a notary, but are not seeking the performance of a notarial act for themselves (e.g., a person asking a notary to serve a bedridden elderly parent).

§ 2-18 Regular Place of Work or Business.

"Regular place of work or business" means a stationary office or workspace where one spends all or some of one's working or business hours.

Comment

Section 2-18 establishes an important situs for purposes of the Act. A non-resident may qualify for a notary commission if he or she has a regular place of work or business in the jurisdiction. (See Subparagraph 3-1(b)(2).) The Act uses the word "regular" to ensure that a notary applicant has more than a passing relationship to the jurisdiction. The drafters intended "regular" to be reasonably construed. Clearly, having an office that is visited on a weekly basis qualifies, but visiting the office once every year would not. One significant limiting factor is that the workplace must be stationary, i.e., one may not claim a vehicle used for business in the state as a place of business.

§ 2-19 Requester of Fact.

"Requester of fact" means a person who asks the notary public to perform:

(1) a copy certification; or

(2) a verification of fact.

Comment

Section 2-19 introduces the new term "requester of fact" to designate a person who asks a notary to perform either a copy certification (see Section 2-4) or a verification of fact (see Section 2-22). In contrast to a "principal" (see Section 2-17), a requester of fact does not have a signature notarized nor personal identity confirmed by the notary. Indeed, the drafters determined that the personal identity of the individual requesting a copy certification or a verification of fact is not essential to the proper performance of these two notarizations. In performing either, the notary need not verify the requester's identity, volition, or awareness, as is necessary with a notarial act involving authentication of a principal's signature. Instead, the notary's focus is confirming or extracting a fact from public records, or confirming that two separate documents are congruent.

Thus, the drafters opened the door to the possibility that a copy certification or a verification of fact might be sought by the requester of fact from a remote location, perhaps over the Internet. This would enhance the public utility of the notary office and at times be of particular value in international child adoptions. The notary would still be required to record in the journal of notarial acts, at the least, the proffered name and address of each requester of fact (see Subparagraph 7-2(a)(5)), but not the requester's signature, evidence of identity, or thumbprint (see Subparagraphs 7-2(a)(4), (6), and (7)).

§ 2-20 Satisfactory Evidence of Identity.

"Satisfactory evidence of identity" means identification of an individual based on:

(1) at least 1 current document issued by a federal, state, or tribal government in a language understood by the notary and bearing the photographic image of the individual's face and signature and a physical description of the individual, or a properly stamped passport without a physical description; or

(2) the oath or affirmation of 1 credible witness disinterested in the document or transaction who is personally known to the notary and who personally knows the individual, or of 2 credible witnesses disinterested in the document or transaction who each personally knows the individual and shows to the notary documentary identification as described in Subparagraph (1) of this Section.

Comment

Section 2-20 manifests the tenet that positive proof of identity is integral to every proper notarization of a signature. A detailed definition of "satisfactory evidence of identity" was deemed essential to this Act. Many statutes refer to satisfactory evidence, but not all go on to define it precisely. The section allows a principal to prove identity in one of two ways. The first involves self-proof through the use of reliable identification documents. The second employs credible witnesses.

Subparagraph 2-20(1) describes the attributes of documents found in most self proving provisions. (See, e.g., CAL. CIV. CODE § 1185(b)(4). But see GA. CODE ANN. § 45-17-8(e); and IOWA CODE ANN. § 9E.9(6)(c), which allow the notary some discretion in determining what constitutes acceptable proof.) To eliminate any doubt, the Act specifically states that identification issued by a tribal government is acceptable. The Act also makes any valid current passport acceptable identification. This will ensure that visitors from foreign lands have the requisite proof of identity to access notarial services while they are in the United States. Of course, passports are excellent proofs of identity for United States citizens, as well. The Act requires the principal to produce only one identifying document. (Accord, FLA. STAT. ANN. § 117.05(5)(b)(2).) Nothing prohibits a notary from asking for additional proof of identity if any item presented by the principal raises questions as to its authenticity or is otherwise suspect. Indeed, notaries are obligated to satisfy themselves that the evidence presented positively proves the principal's identity.

Subparagraph (2) provides a second avenue for proving identity. It is designed for those principals who for one reason or another do not have identification documents. Primary beneficiaries of this rule are the elderly, especially those in nursing homes, who may no longer have valid driver's licenses or other current forms of government identification. Following the lead of California (see CAL. CIV. CODE § 1185(b)(1)(A)) and Florida (see FLA. STAT. ANN. § 117.05(5)(b)(1)), the Act allows credible witnesses of two types to prove the identity of the principal. (For a definition of "credible witness," see Section 2-5 and Comment.) Any credible witness must personally know the principal. (See Section 2-16 for a definition of "personal knowledge.") To prevent fraud and add to the integrity of the notarization, only persons disinterested in the document or related transaction may serve as credible witnesses. This is consistent with the requirement that credible witnesses be impartial. (See Section 2-5.)

Only one witness is needed if that witness is personally known to the notary. Otherwise two witnesses are required. The Act takes the view that the notary's personal knowledge of the identity of one credible witness is preferred to reliance on two witnesses, who must prove their own identities under the rules of Subparagraph (1). Note that a credible witness may not have his or her identity proven by another credible witness. The credible witness must either be known to the notary or this person must self-prove identity through acceptable identification documents.

Because proper identification lies at the heart of reliable notarizations, the drafters contemplated that the rules of this section will be narrowly construed and strictly enforced.

§ 2-21 Signature Witnessing.

"Signature witnessing" means a notarial act in which an individual at a single time and place:
(1) appears in person before the notary and presents a document;
(2) is personally known to the notary or identified by the notary through satisfactory evidence; and
(3) signs the document in the presence of the notary

Comment

Section 2-21 defines "signature witnessing," a notarial act recognized in a number of jurisdictions. (See, e.g., 5 ILCS 312 / 6-102(c); and states that have adopted the Uniform Law on Notarial Acts.) Technically, the act is neither an acknowledgment (see Section 2-1) nor a jurat (see Section 2-7). The drafters contemplate that the simple witnessing will be used in lieu of a jurat when an oath or affirmation is not needed, and as a substitute for an acknowledgment when a positive declaration that the principal accepts the terms of the document is not required. A signature witnessing has the same integrity as other notarial acts, and by definition must meet the same personal appearance and identification requirements in order to be valid. As with the jurat, affixation of the signature in this type of notarial act must be observed by the notary.

§ 2-22 Verification of Fact.

"Verification of fact" means a notarial act in which a notary reviews public or vital records, or other legally accessible data, to ascertain or confirm any of the following facts:
(1) date of birth, death, marriage, or divorce;
(2) name of parent, marital partner, offspring, or sibling;
(3) any matter authorized for verification by a notary by other law or rule of this [State].

Comment

Section 2-22 defines a notarial power that some may regard as being beyond the notary's traditional ministerial role. Locating, reading, and interpreting legal records is generally regarded as being in the bailiwick of attorneys. Yet, the extraction of certain basic information from public, vital, or other records – e.g., date of birth or death, date of marriage or divorce – is not a function requiring legal training. Such information, as certified by a notary, is often requested by foreign agencies in the context of adoption of a foreign child. Thus, in part to lessen the bureaucratic hardships imposed on couples attempting to adopt foreign children, this section gives lawmakers the option of allowing notaries to perform a verification of fact function. The statutory list of verifiable facts may be tailored to a particular jurisdiction.

The verification of fact certificate in Section 9-9 gives notaries the option of visiting a pertinent office that houses public, vital, or other records to ascertain the needed facts, or of accepting a record from an individual named in the certificate. Clearly, the former option is preferred, but notaries are given discretion in the latter case to assess the trustworthiness of any presented record. The notary is well-advised to positively identify the presenter, and to inspect the proffered document for evidence of tampering or counterfeiting, much like a notary inspects identification cards presented by principals.

In the former Act, this section was bracketed to indicate that the verification of fact was a notarization departing from the notary's traditional duties. After careful consideration, the drafters decided to remove the brackets in their effort to enhance the public utility of the notary office and in their belief that the new duties were not beyond the ken of notaries. This section also differs from that in the former Act in expanding the categories of verifiable facts beyond public and vital records to "other legally accessible data."

Article II
Notary Public

Chapter 3 – Commissioning of Notary Public

Comment

General: The Act codifies a comprehensive set of commissioning rules. Each adopting jurisdiction is thereby assured that only well-trained and knowledgeable notaries are serving the public. To meet this goal, the Act requires both the education and testing of applicants. (See Subparagraph 3-1(b)(5).) In an effort to protect the public from unscrupulous notaries, the Act also provides specific guidance to the commissioning authority regarding the types of behavior that justify denying an applicant a notary commission. (See Subsection 3-1(c).) As financial protection for the public against the notary's misconduct, the Act mandates that every notary be bonded. (See Section 3-3.)

§ 3-1 Qualifications.

(a) Except as provided in Subsection (c), the [commissioning official] shall issue a notary commission to any qualified person who submits an application in accordance with this Article.
(b) A person qualified for a notary commission shall:
(1) be at least 18 years of age;
(2) reside or have a regular place of work or business in this [State], as defined in Section 2-18;

(3) reside legally in the United States;
(4) read and write English;
(5) pass a course of instruction requiring a written examination under Section 4-3; and
(6) submit fingerprints to allow a criminal background check.

(c) The [commissioning official] may deny an application based on:

(1) submission of an official application containing material misstatement or omission of fact;
(2) the applicant's conviction or plea of admission or nolo contendere for a felony or any crime involving dishonesty or moral turpitude, but in no case may a commission be issued to the applicant within 5 years after such conviction or plea;
(3) a finding or admission of liability against the applicant in a civil lawsuit based on the applicant's deceit;
(4) revocation, suspension, restriction, or denial of a notarial commission or professional license by this or any other state or nation, but in no case may a commission be issued to the applicant within 5 years after such disciplinary action; or
(5) an official finding that the applicant had engaged in official misconduct as defined in Section 2-12, whether or not disciplinary action resulted.

(d) Denial of an application may be appealed by filing in proper form with the [administrative body hearing appeal] within [time limit] after denial, except that an applicant may not appeal when the [commissioning official] within 5 years prior to the application has:

(1) denied or revoked for disciplinary reasons any previous application, commission, or license of the applicant; or
(2) made a finding under Section 13-3(d) that grounds for revocation of the applicant's commission existed.

Comment

Section 3-1 addresses the personal qualifications needed for commissioning as a notary. Subsection (a) provides that, unless a statutory basis for denial exists, every otherwise qualifying applicant must be granted a commission. There is no limit imposed on the number of notaries that may hold a commission in the jurisdiction at any one time. Nor is the number to be linked to the jurisdiction's perceived need for notaries. (See contra HAW. REV. STAT. ANN. § 456-1(a).) The public is better served when there is an ample number of notaries available. The Act seeks to foster convenient access for all to notarial services, but it also promotes quality by imposing meaningful commissioning standards.

Subsection (b) spells out the personal requirements for commissioning. As is common throughout the country, Subparagraph (b)(1) sets the minimum qualifying age at 18 years. (See, e.g., ARK. CODE ANN. § 21-14-101(b)(1)(C); and N.M. STAT. ANN. § 14-12A-3(B).)

In addressing the residency requirement, Subparagraph (b)(2) adopts an increasingly common policy. The Act subscribes to the view that having a regular place of business (as defined in Section 2-18) within the jurisdiction creates a sufficient nexus for a non-resident to warrant notary commissioning. This position takes into account the "equal protection" argument available to persons doing business in a state, but who are denied notary status because they are not residents. (See Cook v. Miller, 914 F. Supp. 177 (W.D.Mich.1996), where the Court rejected the "equal protection" argument, but reconsidered its position for an out-of-state attorney licensed in Michigan seeking a notary commission to compete effectively with other lawyers. The legislative response supporting this position can be found at MICH. COMP. LAWS ANN. § 55.271(1)(e).) Although this problem can be handled through cross-border recognition of notary commissions (see, e.g., MONT. CODE ANN. § 1-5-605), the drafters believed the better response is to allow non-residents to become commissioned provided that they establish a sufficient nexus in the commissioning state. This will always give persons seeking legal redress against the notary a basis for jurisdiction and a place to serve court summonses or other official papers on the notary. Additionally, it will guarantee that there is an in-state location where the notary journal will be kept and be available for inspection. (For rules regarding access to notary journals, see Subsections 7-3(a) through (d).)

Subparagraph (b)(3) incorporates the current state of the law into the statute. Although some state statutes still nominally require the applicant to be a citizen of the United States (see, e.g., KAN. STAT. ANN. § 53-101), in Bernal v. Fainter (467 U.S. 216, 228 (1984)) the Supreme Court ruled that imposing a citizenship requirement for a notary was unconstitutional. Consequently, any legal resident may qualify for a notary commission, and the Act so holds.

Subparagraph (b)(5) imposes both an education and testing requirement on all notary applicants, including commission renewals. (See Section 3-5.) Some states mandate notary testing (see UTAH CODE ANN. § 46-1-3(5)) and a growing number additionally require a course of instruction for notary commission applicants (see N.C. GEN. STAT. § 10B-8(a)). Many states merely dictate that notary commission applicants attest to having read the local notary laws or have a familiarity with them. (See, e.g., R.I. GEN. LAWS § 42-30-5(b).) The Act takes the bold step of requiring notaries not only to understand relevant notary laws and practices, but also to satisfactorily demonstrate a command of that knowledge. The drafters believe this requirement serves the public interest by ensuring that all notaries are qualified to perform their duties. Additionally, the requirement helps to professionalize the office, a subsidiary goal of the Act. Finally, passing a written test helps prove that the applicant can satisfy Subparagraph (b)(4) – the ability to read and write English.

In regard to Subparagraph (b)(5), the drafters recognize that there is a financial cost associated with an education and testing requirement. The Act is silent as to when and by whom the cost is to be borne. This omission was intentional. The drafters believed it best to allow each state to determine the most appropriate method of funding the cost. Some states may have administrative budgets sufficiently ample to meet the added expense. Some will pass the cost along to notary commission applicants either by rolling it into a higher general application fee or by imposing a separate course or testing charge. Other states may allow private enterprise to play a role, letting notaries pay a non-governmental educational organization or institution for the requisite instruction and testing.

Arguably, passing the education and testing costs on to applicants heightens the entry barrier for the notary profession, which can translate into fewer independent notaries whose expenses are not underwritten by an employer. This, in turn, could mean there will be a smaller number of notaries available to serve the public, especially in economically disadvantaged areas. The drafters considered this possibility, but believed the benefits to the public outweighed any of the risks. Higher commissioning fees and strict testing requirements should limit applications only to highly motivated individuals who will take their duties seriously. Elevating standards in an effort to provide better trained and more devoted notaries can only redound to the public good. Should education and test costs restrict otherwise qualified and interested individuals from entering the field and serving areas in need, a commissioning authority is not precluded from instituting a "test fee waiver" program if it is deemed necessary or appropriate.

Subparagraph (b)(6) introduces a fingerprinting requirement as an added protection against dishonest persons becoming notaries. Fingerprints will allow commissioning officials to do computer-assisted background checks to determine whether the applicant has a criminal record. They also provide the opportunity to discover if aliases have been used, and, if so, whether criminal acts were committed under them. The federal Integrated Automated Fingerprint Identification System (IAFIS), linked to law enforcement data banks around the nation, simplifies the process of checking an applicant's prints. Additionally, requiring applicants to provide fingerprints should help ensure truthful responses to questions relating to prior criminal activity on the application. (See Subparagraph 4-2(7).) The fingerprint requirement should deter many unqualified applicants from trying to obtain a commission through deceitful means. Currently, one state requires fingerprints of notary applicants. (See CAL. GOV'T. CODE § 8201.1.)

Subsection (c) details specific grounds for denying a commission. Denials are within the discretion of the commissioning official. Although there was unanimous support for authorizing such discretion, some drafters felt the Act did not go far enough, and should have made certain past behavior automatic grounds for rejecting an application. In any event, because notaries hold positions of public trust, any matters within the purview of the subsection raised in the application are to be carefully scrutinized. In exercising discretion, the commissioning official should tip the balance in favor of the public's interest and not the applicant's desire to become a notary. The better approach is that, absent a clear showing of no risk to the public, the application should be denied. Although the Act contemplates that reviews will be made on a case-by-case basis, the appropriate body ought to consider maintaining accurate records to ensure that the rules are applied evenhandedly over the course of time.

Subparagraph (c)(1) provides a reasonable, minimum standard for denial. A person who is dishonest on an application cannot be trusted to faithfully execute notarial duties. The commissioning official will assess "materiality" of the misstatement or omission. The section allows the applicant to explain the error, and if it is excusable, to be granted a commission.

Subparagraph (c)(2) limits the commissioning official's discretion when the applicant has been held accountable for a felony or any crime involving dishonesty or moral turpitude. Examples could include crimes involving fraud, forgery, theft, securities law violations, and perjury. (The list is merely illustrative and not meant to be inclusive. It is contemplated that the commissioning authority will determine the appropriate crimes for these purposes.) The subsection mandates a five-year commissioning moratorium after a conviction, plea of admission, or nolo contendere plea. After that period has elapsed, it is expected that the commissioning official will scrutinize the circumstances to determine whether such an applicant is then fit or suited to be a notary.

The provision was purposefully written in broad terms. This allows the commissioning official the opportunity to determine those crimes which should provide a basis for applying the five-year rule. Also, it permits greater discretion after the five-year period has passed to determine which types of acts so challenge the applicant's integrity that commissioning would constitute too great a risk to the public. For the latter reason, some drafters believed that applicants with a history of fraud, forgery, or similar crimes of deceit ought never to be commissioned. Others felt that rather than provide a potentially incomplete list of acts warranting denial of a notary commission, it was best to let the commissioning authority exercise judgment on which acts warranted commission denial, taking into account what best suits the needs of the jurisdiction's citizenry.

Subparagraph (c)(3) reinforces the concept that honesty and reliability are cornerstones of the notarial office. Consequently, an applicant who has engaged in deceitful activity, even if not of a criminal nature, ought to be closely scrutinized. Absent a satisfactory belief that such actions will not be repeated, the application should be denied.

Subparagraph (c)(4) places sanctioned notarial and other professional license improprieties on the same footing as crimes involving dishonesty or moral turpitude. (See Subparagraph (c)(2).) Some drafters argued that revocation of a notary commission ought to serve as a permanent bar from future commissioning. The Act adopts the view that prior bad actors can be rehabilitated, but recognizes that certain acts require longer periods to prove rehabilitation. Hence, the five-year moratorium for professional misdeeds. After the moratorium expires, the commissioning official retains the discretion to deny the application if satisfactory evidence of rehabilitation has not been produced. Also, the commissioning official always has the discretion to examine the facts leading to the prior disciplinary action, and determine which acts are less likely to be repeated.

Subparagraph (c)(5) provides the commissioning official with general discretionary authority to reject applications of any notary found to have engaged in official misconduct as defined in Section 2-12 of the Act even if no disciplinary action had resulted. In essence, it serves as a backup to the other rules.

Subsection (d) permits the applicant to appeal a commission denial. The provision also requires the jurisdiction to establish an appeal board and an appropriate filing deadline. Presumably, the appellate body would establish its own procedures. The Act prohibits an appeal for any applicant who has had a notary commission denied or revoked by the commissioning authority within five years of the application; this time period is congruent with Subparagraph (c)(4)'s five-year ban on commission issuance after a disciplinary action. The Act contemplates that denials or revocations of non-notarial professional licenses are to be treated similarly, e.g., a real estate broker's license. Also, the applicant may not bring an appeal if a ground for revocation of a notary commission existed in a previous case, even though no official disciplinary action was taken on it. (See Subsection 13-3(d).)

§ 3-2 Jurisdiction and Term.

A person commissioned as a notary may perform notarial acts in any part of this [State] for a term of [4] years, unless the commission is earlier revoked under Section 13-3 or resigned under Section 12-3.

Comment

Section 3-2 addresses the scope of the commission. The Act adopts the modern view that a notary is authorized to act throughout the entire jurisdiction. (See, e.g., IND. CODE ANN. § 33-42-2-1.). Although the Act allows each jurisdiction to set the length of the notary commission term, a four-year term of office is recommended. Currently, some states set two or three-year periods (see DEL. CODE ANN. tit. 29 § 4307 (two years); and IOWA CODE ANN. § 9E.4 (three years)). The drafters felt this was too short, especially in light of the Act's rigorous education and testing components (see Subparagraph 3-1 (b)(5)). On the other hand, a five or six-year term, or longer, was considered too lengthy in that it does not provide sufficient contact between the notary and the commissioning official. (But see S.C. CODE ANN. § 26-1-10; and ARK. CODE ANN. § 21-14-101 (setting 10-year terms of office).) A few states offer lifetime appointments (see e.g., WIS. STAT. ANN. §137.01(2)(a), providing a lifetime appointment for attorneys in good standing). The drafters did not believe that the public's interest would be served by commission terms of such length that the commissioning official could not regularly reassess the qualifications of the notary nor apprise the notary of pertinent statutory changes or other developments affecting notarial duties.

§ 3-3 Bond.

(a) A notary commission shall not [become effective / be issued] until an oath of office and [25,000] dollar bond have been filed with the [designated office]. The bond shall be executed by a licensed surety, for a term of [4] years commencing on the commission's effective date and terminating on its expiration date, with payment of bond funds to any person conditioned upon the notary's misconduct as defined in Section 2-12.

(b) The surety for a notary bond shall report all claims against the bond to the [commissioning official].

(c) If a notary bond has been exhausted by claims paid out by the surety, the [commissioning official] shall suspend the notary's commission until:

(1) a new bond is obtained by the notary; and

(2) the notary's fitness to serve the remainder of the commission term is determined by the [commissioning official].

Comment

Section 3-3 addresses notary bonding requirements. Most jurisdictions now require notaries to obtain a surety bond covering their official acts (see, e.g., CAL. GOV'T. CODE § 8212; and 57 PA. STAT. ANN. § 154), but these are often for quite modest amounts (see, e.g., HAW. REV. STAT. ANN. § 456-5 ($1,000)); and WYO. STAT. ANN. § 32-1-104(a) ($500)). The Act favors a higher bond of $25,000, as opposed to the common $10,000 to $5,000 range (see, e.g., ALA. CODE § 36-20-3; KAN. STAT. ANN. § 53-102; and MISS. CODE ANN. § 25-33-1). It is important to note that the bond's function is to protect the public. The injured party can seek financial recovery against the bond, but is not limited to it. Excess damages may also be recovered against the notary. Even if the bond covers the damages, the notary is responsible to the surety company for any payments made on the bond.

The Act does not address notary errors and omissions insurance. This is a different issue. The drafters did not believe imposing an insurance requirement on notaries was warranted, as has occasionally been proposed. Other professions do not have it. It is hoped that the more stringent commissioning requirements, especially the education and testing components, will reduce if not eliminate notarial errors and concomitant claims.

Subsection (b) imposes a reporting requirement on the surety. This will help the commissioning official monitor notarial misconduct. It will also provide a record for future application reviews.

Subsection (c) puts teeth into the bond requirement. To protect the public, the notary commission is automatically suspended if the bond expires or is exhausted. Notably, once expired, the notary must not only obtain a new bond, but also undergo a fitness review. By its silence, the Act implicitly empowers the commissioning official to promulgate standards and procedures for this review.

§ 3-4 Commissioning Documents.

Upon issuing a notary commission, the [commissioning official] shall provide to the notary:

(1) a commission document stating the commission serial number and starting and ending dates; and

(2) a Certificate of Authorization to Purchase a Notary Seal stating the commission serial number.

Comment

Section 3-4 provides the means by which the notary can satisfy other sections of the Act. The Certificate of Authorization to Purchase a Notary Seal is needed to acquire a seal under Subsection 8-4(b).

§ 3-5 Recommissioning.

A current or former notary applying for a new notary commission shall submit a new completed application and comply anew with all of the provisions of Chapters 3 and 4.

Comment

Section 3-5 establishes an important rule that has far-reaching implications for protection of the public. The Act requires every notary commission applicant, specifically including those who are seeking "renewal" of a current commission, to comply anew with all of the provision of Chapters 3 and 4. Most importantly, this includes the education and testing requirements.

Although it is at odds with what some have termed a "rubber-stamp" renewal process in many jurisdictions (see, e.g., MD. CODE ANN., STATE GOV'T § 18-103(d); and N.D. CENT. CODE § 44-06-02), the drafters believed that the Act presents the better approach. By requiring that all components of the commissioning process be met anew, the Act ensures that every notary keeps abreast of changes and developments in notarial laws and procedures. It also compels individuals to re-examine their interest in remaining a notary, and filters out those who are not willing to go to the trouble of demonstrating proficiency. This serves the public's interest by ensuring that only those committed to the notary office are allowed to continue in it.

Chapter 4 – Application for Notary Public Commission

Comment

General: This chapter converts the commissioning requirements set out in Chapter 3 into an application form. The format provided is complete in itself, but there is allowance for modifications and additions. The Act is silent on a number of points that were considered to be best left to the discretion of the commissioning official.

§ 4-1 Application Materials.

Every application for a notary commission shall be made in a paper or electronic format established by the [commissioning official] and include:

(1) a statement of the applicant's personal qualifications, as described in Section 4-2;

(2) a certificate evidencing successful completion of a course of instruction, as described in Section 4-3;

(3) a notarized declaration of the applicant, as described in Section 4-4;

(4) a full set of fingerprints of the applicant;

(5) such other information as the [commissioning official] may deem appropriate; and

(6) an application fee, as specified in Section 4-5.

Comment

Section 4-1 establishes the components of an official application form. A notary commission may be granted only to applicants filing this official form. The section requires the commissioning official to provide the format for this application. It is implicit that the form will both be printed and made available by the commissioning official. Subparagraphs (1) - (5) set forth the elements of the application form as provided in the balance of the chapter. To the extent that any jurisdiction does not adopt a specific application requirement set out in the chapter, then the corresponding subparagraph of Section 4-1 should be deleted. For example, for those states that do not opt to impose an education requirement as prescribed in Section 4-3, Subparagraph

(2) will be deleted and the balance of the subparagraphs re-numbered.

§ 4-2 Statement of Personal Qualifications.

The application for a notary commission shall state or include, at least:

(1) the applicant's date of birth;

(2) the applicant's residence address and telephone number;

(3) the applicant's business address and telephone number, the business mailing address, if different, and the name of the applicant's employer, if any;

(4) a declaration that the applicant is a citizen of the United States or proof of the applicant's legal residency in the country;

(5) a declaration that the applicant can read and write English;

(6) all issuances, denials, revocations, suspensions, restrictions, and resignations of a notarial commission, professional license, or public office involving the applicant in this or any other jurisdiction;

(7) all criminal convictions of the applicant, including any pleas of admission or nolo contendere, in this or any other state or nation; [and]

(8) all claims pending or disposed against a notary bond held by the applicant, and all civil findings or admissions of fault or liability regarding the applicant's activities as a notary, in this or any other state or nation [; and

(9) if the notary elects to keep an electronic journal, the password or access instructions required by Section 7-6].

Comment

Section 4-2 incorporates into the application form the qualification requirements set out in Section 3-1. Subparagraph (3) is particularly important for non-resident notaries, whose nonresidency status is not a bar to commissioning if Subparagraph 3-1(b)(2) is satisfied. The business address requirement not only provides necessary information for the commissioning official, but also for parties seeking to serve legal papers (e.g., a summons or subpoena) on the non-resident notary or to access the non-resident notary's journal (see Section 7-3). Subparagraph (4) anticipates that the non-citizen applicant will attach a photocopy of the official paperwork that authorizes the applicant's legal residence in the country. Subparagraphs (6), (7), and (8) manifest the requirements of Subparagraphs 3-1(c)(2) through (5) and make clear that potential disqualifying acts are not limited only to those performed in the commissioning jurisdiction.

Subparagraph (9) requires those who elect to use an electronic journal in lieu of a bound paper record to include journal access information in their respective commission applications. By doing so, the applicant immediately complies with the journal-access requirements imposed by Section 7-6.

§ 4-3 Course and Examination.

(a) Every applicant for a notary commission shall take, within the 3 months preceding application, a course of instruction of at least 4 hours approved by the [commissioning official], and pass a written examination of this course.

(b) The content of the course and the basis for the written examination shall be notarial laws, procedures, and ethics.

Comment

Section 4-3 describes the education and testing requirement mandated by Subparagraph 3-1(b)(5). The applicant must both complete the course and pass the exam within three months before submission of the application. Notably, the Act does not waive the requirement for even highly experienced or credentialed applicants. This is contrary to practice in some jurisdictions. (See, e.g., N.C. GEN. STAT. § 10B-8(a) and (b).)

Both the course and test must be approved by the commissioning official. Nothing in the Act mandates that the commissioning official compose or teach the course, or develop or administer the test. These matters may be handled by an approved educational body. The degree of control over these matters is left to the discretion of the commissioning official. Some states may opt to have the course and test developed, administered, and graded by an approved independent provider. Others may want to administer both the course and test, or just develop and grade the test.

The educational program must be at least four hours in duration. The Act does not preclude requiring longer courses, and some jurisdictions may opt for that. Subsection (b) states that the course content shall include notarial laws, procedures, and ethics. Although the Act provides the rules for notary laws, it does not provide specific ethical standards for notaries. Nonetheless, the Act views notaries public as professionals, albeit with narrow powers, and as such implicitly suggests that they have ethical obligations to principals and the public.

THE NOTARY PUBLIC CODE OF PROFESSIONAL RESPONSIBILITY, promulgated by the National Notary Association (see www.NationalNotary.org), provides a comprehensive set of basic ethical standards. Commissioning authorities are encouraged to have education providers integrate the CODE into their courses.

As for the test itself, the Act requires only that it be written. (Currently at least one jurisdiction administers an oral notarial exam. See 17 D.C. MUN. REG § 2402.3. Other jurisdictions in which courts are the commissioning authority may base qualification on an oral interview with a judge. See, e.g., ALA. CODE § 36-20-1; GA. CODE ANN. § 45-17-1.1 and 2.1; and VT. STAT. ANN. tit. 24 § 441.) Written exams with only multiple-choice or "true-false" answers satisfy the provision. Online or other technologically generated exams are permitted. (See, e.g., http://notaries.dos.state.fl.us/ regarding Florida's online notary education and examination program.)

To facilitate implementing the examination requirement, the Act does not specify when the test is to be administered. The drafters intended that the test would be taken immediately after the course is completed when the material would be freshest in the mind of the student. Some jurisdictions, however, may want to allow the applicants time to reflect on the material. The Act does not mandate a formal classroom setting. Thus, aside from online teaching and testing, home study and mail-in tests are possible options, provided that the material and tests are from an approved education provider.

§ 4-4 Notarized Declaration.

Every applicant for a notary commission shall sign the following declaration in the presence of a notary of this [State]:

Declaration of Applicant

I, _____ (name of applicant), solemnly swear or affirm under penalty of perjury that the personal information in this application is true, complete, and correct; that I understand the official duties and responsibilities of a Notary Public in this [State], as explained in the course of instruction I have taken; and that I will perform, to the best of my ability, all notarial acts in accordance with the law.

_____ (signature of applicant)
(notarial certificate for a jurat as specified in Section 9-5)

Comment

Section 4-4 requires all applicants to swear or affirm on three points. The first is that the application is fully and accurately completed. This means not only that all statements are true, but also that there are not any pertinent omissions. The applicant then states that he or she understands the obligations of the notary office as taught in the mandatory four-hour course. Finally, the applicant takes what amounts to an "oath of office." Such a declaration is standard fare and required in all jurisdictions. (See, e.g., COLO. REV. STAT. ANN. § 12-55-105; IDAHO CODE § 51-105(1)(d); 5 ILCS 312 / 2-104; and VA. CODE ANN. § 47.1-9.) The oath impresses upon applicants that notaries public perform an important function in society, a role that must be faithfully fulfilled.

§ 4-5 Application Fee.

Every applicant for a notary commission shall pay to this [State] a nonrefundable application fee of [dollars].

Comment

Section 4-5 establishes the application fee. This will vary from jurisdiction to jurisdiction depending upon how the general operational costs of the office of the commissioning official are funded, how the specific expenses of processing applications are covered, and whether or not the cost of testing is to be borne by this fee or through a separate charge.

Jurisdictions that rely on third-party education providers for both the course and test may prefer to segregate the training/testing fee from the fee for application processing. Market forces should keep the educational costs reasonable and permit applicants to use factors other than cost (e.g., convenience) in satisfying their requirements.

Although the Act is silent on point, nothing prevents the commissioning official from waiving the fee in hardship situations. An overarching goal of the Act is to ensure that the public is properly served. The drafters recognize that providing notarial service in some economically depressed areas may be problematic. Thus, to encourage otherwise qualified members of those communities to meet notarial needs, fee waivers may be appropriate. (See Subparagraph 3-1(b)(5) Comment for similar issues with respect to testing fees.)

§ 4-6 Confidentiality.

Information required by Section 4-2(7) shall be used by the [commissioning official] and designated [State] employees only for the purpose of performing official duties under this [Act] and shall not be disclosed to any person other than:
(1) a government agent acting in an official capacity and duly authorized to obtain such information;
(2) a person authorized by court order; or
(3) the applicant or the applicant's duly authorized agent.

Comment

Section 4-6 mandates that the commissioning official keep all information regarding an applicant's criminal history confidential. Such information, however, may be used for all legitimate, official purposes by the office of the commissioning official. It must also be shared with other governmental officials operating within their authority, and is subject to lawful subpoena. The Act eliminates the need for the commissioning official to seek specific authority to release the information to the applicant's authorized agent. This should eliminate unnecessary paperwork and delay when legitimate requests for information are made.

The drafters considered whether all or more of the information in the application should be kept confidential. For example, some could not understand why the notary's home address and telephone number should be available to the public when a business address and number are listed. In certain situations, a state legislature could exempt certain notaries (e.g., law enforcement personnel) from the requirement to disclose a residence address and telephone number. The drafters decided that all matters related to prior professional licenses, public offices, and tort actions be available to the public. Notaries, as public servants, should be able to withstand the scrutiny of those who will use their services. Principals will depend on notaries to honestly and properly execute certificates and perform other notarial acts. These services will relate to important transactions for the principals and for innocent third parties relying on the notarized documents. Consequently, principals concerned about such matters ought to be able to screen a notary's qualifications to determine whether or not the notary satisfies the principal's expectations, and to find the notary for later legal action and redress in the event of misconduct. Realistically, the drafters expect that few requests would ever be made for such information.

Chapter 5 – Powers and Limitations of Notary Public

Comment

General: This chapter establishes the parameters for official notarial acts. It not only identifies authorized acts and related functions (see Sections 5-1, 5-3, and 5-4), but also specifically proscribes certain activities (see Section 5-2 and Sections 5-5 through 5-14). In some respects this chapter is the centerpiece of the Act. It introduces new procedural concepts, imposes rigorous execution standards, and provides sage guidance for notarial practice.

§ 5-1 Powers of Notary.

A notary is empowered to perform the following notarial acts:
(1) acknowledgments;
(2) oaths and affirmation;
(3) jurats;
(4) signature witnessings;
(5) copy certifications;
(6) verifications of fact; and
(7) any other acts so authorized by the law of this [State].

Comment

Section 5-1 identifies the permissible notarial acts. Subparagraphs (1), (2), and (3) list standard notarial acts recognized in all jurisdictions. (For the applicable description and general execution requirements of "acknowledgment," see Section 2-1 and Comment; of "oath" and "affirmation," see Sections 2-11 and 2-2 and Comments, respectively; and of "jurat," see Section 2-7 and Comment.) Subparagraphs (4) and (5) authorize two acts – "signature witnessing" and "copy certification" – not expressly recognized by statute in all jurisdictions. (See Section 2-21 and Comment for a definition and execution requirements of a "signature witnessing"; and Section 2-4 and Comment for a definition and execution requirements of a "copy certification.")

In the former Act, Subparagraph (6) was bracketed to indicate that a "verification of fact" is not a traditional duty for the American notary. In this revised section, the brackets have been removed by the drafters in their effort to expand the public utility of the notary office and in their belief that the duty of "verification of fact" is not beyond the ken of the notary. (See Section 2-22 and Comment.)

The former subparagraph authorizing a notary to perform electronic notarial acts has been removed and placed in its own section – Section 17-1. The drafters determined that performing electronic notarizations is so different from paper-based acts in certain regards that they merit separate consideration. Thus, only those notaries public who decide to enable themselves to perform electronic notarial acts pursuant to the rules provided in Article III are authorized to do so.

Subparagraph (7) expands a notary's authority to include acts permitted in the jurisdiction by other laws. This is not an uncommon practice. (See, e.g., ALA. CODE § 36-20-5; and R.I. GEN. LAWS § 42-30-7.)

The drafters realize that there are other notarial acts currently recognized in some jurisdictions but not listed in Section 5-1. These acts include protesting commercial paper (see, e.g., CAL. GOV'T. CODE § 8205(a)(1)) and solemnifying marriages (see FLA. STAT. ANN. § 117.045). In the case of protesting commercial paper, the drafters believed it better to mention this act and its requirements within a jurisdiction's Uniform Commercial Code, where it would be known to notaries with the requisite specialized knowledge, rather than in the general notary laws. Each jurisdiction is free to add as many notarial powers as it determines best meets the needs of its citizenry.

Conversely, a jurisdiction could delete an enumerated power. The drafters believe "acknowledgments," "oaths and affirmations," "jurats," "copy certifications," and "signature witnessings" are essential notarial acts that must be included in any comprehensive notary statute. Any of the other listed powers could be eliminated without substantially impacting the efficacy of the statute.

§ 5-2 Requirements for Notarial Acts.

A notary shall perform a notarial act only if the principal:
(1) is in the presence of the notary at the time of notarization;
(2) is personally known to the notary or identified by the notary through satisfactory evidence;
(3) appears to understand the nature of the transaction requiring a notarial act;
(4) appears to be acting of his or her own free will;
(5) signs using letters or characters of a language that is understood by the notary; and
(6) communicates directly with the notary in a language both understand.

Comment

Section 5-2 is derived from Subsection 5-1(b) in the former Act. It has been removed to its own section to emphasize its importance. The former subsection was rephrased to make clear that the requirements within it are positive obligations imposed upon the notary.

Section 5-2 prohibits a notary from performing a notarial act if any of the listed prerequisites are missing. These prescriptions guarantee the integrity and reliability of the transaction. Subparagraphs (1) and (2) specify requirements – the principal's physical presence and properly proved identity – that appear in the definition of all signature notarizations permitted by the Act. (See, e.g., Sections 2- 1, 2-7, and 2-21.) Although some jurisdictions do not specifically address these requirements, the drafters considered these two elements essential to all proper notarizations involving a principal, and deemed it worthwhile to iterate them.

Subparagraphs (3) and (4) address more controversial issues. The former follows the lead of two jurisdictions (see FLA. STAT. ANN. § 117.107(5); and GA. CODE ANN. § 45-17-8(b)(3)) requiring the notary to assess whether or not the principal is aware of the significance of the transaction involving the notarial act. The provision does not require the notary to inquire into the principal's knowledge or understanding of the document to be notarized. Nor does it mandate that the notary actively inquire into or investigate the transaction. Instead, it demands that the notary form a judgment from the circumstances as to whether or not the principal is generally aware of what is transpiring. Thus, if a principal presented a document entitled "power of attorney" and then asked the notary to notarize "this contract to purchase a burial plot," the notary might have a basis to determine that the principal was not aware of the transaction to which the notarization related. Usually, this provision will become critical only when the notary believes the principal suffers from mental infirmity. It also can come into play, however, for principals who are operating under the heavy influence of alcohol or drugs. It is expected that the notary will make a commonsense judgment about the principal's level of awareness, mainly through conversing with and observing the individual.

The obligation imposed upon the notary in Subparagraph (4) is similar to that set forth in Subparagraph (3) relating to the principal's awareness. In Subparagraph (4), the issue is volition. The subparagraph reinforces the view that a signing is the voluntary and intended act of the principal. If the principal is being unduly influenced by another or is acting under duress, the notary should not perform the notarization. As is the case with "awareness," notaries should pay close attention to principals who appear to have mental infirmities, as they are more susceptible to manipulation and exploitation by a third party. (For a more detailed discussion of volition, see Section 2-1 Comment.)

The final two subparagraphs, (5) and (6), are new. Subparagraph (5) recognizes that notaries may be asked to notarize a signature written in a foreign language or in characters they cannot understand. As a result, a notary may not be able to make a meaningful comparison of a signature affixed on a document with another signature or a printed name appearing on an identification document.

Subparagraph (6) takes a similar tack with respect to the notary's ability to communicate with the principal. If, for example, the notary cannot understand the spoken words of the principal, a meaningful judgment about this individual's awareness or volition cannot be made. (See the above discussions regarding Subparagraphs (3) and (4).) Moreover, a notary must not rely on an interpreter to communicate with the principal. Doing so would establish a dangerous policy. For any variety of reasons, an intermediary may not be capable or motivated to accurately represent the words of the principal or the notary. This subparagraph eliminates the risk of notarizing a document for someone the notary cannot understand.

§ 5-3 Signature by Mark.

A notary may certify the affixation of a signature by mark by a principal on a document presented for notarization if:
(1) the mark is affixed in the presence of the notary and 2 witnesses disinterested in the document;
(2) both witnesses sign their own names beside the mark;
(3) the notary writes below the mark: "Mark affixed by (name of signer by mark) in the presence of (names and addresses of 2 witnesses) and the undersigned notary

pursuant to Section 5-3 of [Act]"; and

(4) the notary notarizes the signature by mark through an acknowledgment, jurat, or signature witnessing.

Comment

Section 5-3 was Subsection 5-1(c) in the former Act, but was made into its own separate section to accord it more prominence. The section provides a simple procedure for certifying a principal's mark as his or her legal signature. The mark must be made in the presence of the notary and two disinterested witnesses. The witnesses must sign their names beside the mark. The notary must memorialize the ceremony in writing, and then execute the requested notarization.

§ 5-4 Signing for Principal Unable to Sign.

A notary may sign the name of a principal physically unable to sign or make a mark on a document presented for notarization if:

(1) the principal directs the notary to do so in the presence of 2 witnesses disinterested in the document;

(2) the notary signs the principal's name in the presence of the principal and the witnesses;

(3) both witnesses sign their own names beside the signature;

(4) the notary writes below the signature: "Signature affixed by the notary at the direction and in the presence of (name of principal unable to sign or make a mark) and also in the presence of (names and addresses of 2 witnesses) pursuant to Section 5-4 of [Act]"; and

(5) the notary notarizes the signature through an acknowledgment, jurat, or signature witnessing.

Comment

Section 5-4 was Subsection 5-1(d) in the former Act, but was made into its own separate section to accord it more prominence. The section provides a procedure to allow the notary to sign the name of a principal who is physically unable to do so. The same safeguards found in Section 5-3 for a mark made by a principal are present for a proxy signature made by the notary. There is one added protection: the notary may only affix the signature if specifically directed to do so by the principal. Moreover, this request must be made in the presence of the two disinterested witnesses. Once the proxy signature is affixed by the notary, the memorializing procedure is essentially congruent with the one spelled out in Section 5-3. The appropriate notarization may then be performed.

§ 5-5 Disqualifications.

(a) A notary is disqualified from performing a notarial act if the notary:

(1) is a party to or named in the document that is to be notarized;

(2) will receive as a direct or indirect result any commission, fee, advantage, right, title, interest, cash, property, or other consideration exceeding in value the fees specified in Section 6-2 of this [Act];

(3) is a spouse, domestic partner, ancestor, descendant, or sibling of the principal, including in-law, step, and half relatives; or

(4) is an attorney who has prepared, explained, or recommended to the principal the document that is to be notarized.

(b) Notwithstanding Subsection (a)(2), a notary may collect a nonnotarial fee for services as a signing agent if payment of that fee is not contingent upon the signing, initialing, or notarization of any document.

Comment

Section 5-5 describes situations in which a notary has a disqualifying interest and, therefore, must not proceed with a related notarization. Subparagraph (a)(1) states the basic rule that a notary may not notarize a document in which he or she is either a principal or otherwise named. This rule goes beyond the basic prohibition against notarizing one's own signature. It also prohibits the notary from acting if mentioned in the document. Being named in the document impugns the notary's disinterest in the transaction and casts in doubt whether he or she impartially can meet the obligations imposed by law.

Subparagraph (a)(2) addresses the "interest in the transaction" issue more squarely. It specifically prohibits a notary from performing an official act related to a transaction from which the notary could benefit. This rule is common to most jurisdictions. (See, e.g., 57 PA. STAT. ANN. § 165(e).) However, being an employee who performs a notarization for an employer does not create an interest governed by this subparagraph, unless the employee receives a benefit directly related to the completion of the act. Issues with respect to employee-notaries are specifically addressed in Sections 6-4 (fees), 7-4(b) (journal), 8-2(c)(4) (seal), and 13-1(c) and (d) (liability). Additionally, in recognizing that employees may notarize documents for their employers, it is contemplated that notarization in similar business relationships is permissible. A jurisdiction could specifically authorize corporate officers and directors to notarize documents for their business organizations. (See, e.g., ARK. CODE ANN. § 21-14-109.) The drafters did not feel this needed to be stated separately, concluding that it was implicitly permitted by language that did not specifically prohibit it. (But see Subparagraph (a)(4) which disqualifies attorneys from notarizing documents for clients.)

Subparagraph (a)(3) offers an expanded view of disqualifying relationships for a notary. Most jurisdictions that address the matter confine such disqualification to close family members, but the drafters felt that broader coverage best fostered the integrity of the notarial act. Particularly noteworthy is the position that for these purposes a domestic partner must be treated identically to a spouse. Also, the Act includes "in-laws," "half," and "step" relatives as family members who ought to have their documents notarized by completely independent and disinterested notaries.

Subparagraph (a)(4) raises a controversial issue. Attorneys often notarize their clients' documents. The drafters believed, however, that attorneys clearly have an interest in documents they draft or offer advice on for clients that should disqualify them from notarizing those documents. A separate nonnotarial fee probably is being earned for providing legal services in these cases.

Whereas it could be argued that an attorney's notarization of a client's document would run afoul of Subparagraph (a)(2), the drafters thought it best to state the disqualification separately. Another consideration was whether the attorney's role as advocate for a client is compatible with the notary's role as disinterested witness, especially if the notarized document becomes evidence in litigation and the attorney is asked to testify as the supposed impartial notary in a case in which he or she is representing the client.

Notably, nothing in Subparagraph (a)(4) would prevent a paralegal, legal secretary, or other notary associated with the attorney from notarizing the document. Even so, an attorney's employment of a notary does not relieve the notary from fulfilling all of the obligations imposed by the Act with respect to proper execution of a notarial act.

Subsection (b) addresses "notary signing agents," who perform a courier and clerical function in bringing loan documents to a borrower and, before notarizing these documents, ensure that they are signed in the proper places. The operation of notary signing agents has been challenged in a few states because their total fees exceed the maximums allowed by statute for notarial acts. (See, e.g., NOTARY PUBLIC GUIDEBOOK FOR NORTH CAROLINA (10th Ed., July 2006), which states: "Whether a notary may charge for mileage traveled in order to notarize an instrument is unclear, but a literal reading of GS 138-2 indicates that he or she may not.") The subsection allows signing agents to charge fees for their non-notarial functions, in addition to notarial fees, as long as payment of the nonnotarial fees does not depend on performance of a notarial act – for example, when a borrower signs a packet of loan documents. In other words, the notary signing agent who travels to deliver loan documents to a borrower must be paid for the assignment by the contractor even when the borrower decides not to sign, or when a discovered impropriety or discrepancy prevents the notary from completing the notarial act. This removes the signing agent's incentive to exert pressure on the borrower.

§ 5-6 Refusal to Notarize.

(a) A notary shall not refuse to perform a notarial act based on a person's race, advanced age, gender, sexual orientation, religion, national origin, disability, or status as a non-client or noncustomer of the notary's employer.

(b) A notary shall perform any notarial act described in Section 5-1 of this Chapter for any person requesting such an act who tenders the appropriate fee specified in Section 6-2(a), unless:

(1) the notary knows or has a reasonable belief that the notarial act or the associated transaction is unlawful;

(2) the act is prohibited under Section 5-2 or 5-5;

(3) the number or timing of the requested notarial act or acts practicably precludes completion at the time of the request, in which case the notary shall arrange for later completion of the requested act or acts without unreasonable delay; or

(4) in the case of a request to perform an electronic notarial act, the notary is not registered to notarize electronically in accordance with Chapter 16.

(c) A notary may but is not required to perform a notarial act outside of the notary's regular workplace or business hours.

Comment

Section 5-6 establishes important rules that help regulate a notary's conduct. The section gives guidance on the central issues of whether and when a notary may refuse to perform an official act. Most statutes are silent on these matters, yet this silence can prove to be troublesome for notaries in the field.

Subsection 5-6(a) reinforces the principle that the notary occupies a public office and therefore must treat all members of the public equally. The provision makes clear that a notary may not discriminate against any principal, and, absent some reasons justified by another section, must perform any requested notarization. The drafters' goal was to be as broad as possible in identifying protected classes. Listing specific groups was not intended to suggest that other persons are not entitled to the same protection, but merely to identify groups that often encounter discrimination. For example, people of advanced age were specifically identified because they are often the victims of discrimination on the presumption that they are not competent to handle their own affairs.

Subsection 5-6(a) also prohibits a notary from distinguishing between clients or customers and those who do not avail themselves of the notary's other professional or business services. The drafters were concerned that some employers might view an employee-notary as being available exclusively for the benefit of the employer. The language in this section is designed to emphasize two important points. First, there are no "notaries private," that is, officials commissioned for the sole purpose of handling a single employer's notarization needs. (Contra CA. GOV'T CODE § 8202.8.) Second, notaries are commissioned to serve all members of the public, including people who do not avail themselves of the notary's other business services. (Accord CONN. GEN. STAT. § 3-94(f).)

Subsection 5-6(b) begins by specifically requiring a notary to perform all authorized notarizations that are requested by anyone offering the statutory fee. The subsection then carves out four important exceptions to the rule. Subparagraph (b)(1) directs the notary to refrain from acting if he or she "knows or has a reasonable belief" that the notarization is associated with an unlawful act. The drafters did not contemplate that the notary would conduct an investigation of the underlying transaction. There is no duty for the notary to search beyond the readily apparent facts. Nonetheless, as a responsible public officer, the notary must always refuse to proceed with a notarial act when the illegality of the transaction is self-evident. The goal is to thwart illegal acts from being consummated – an entirely appropriate aim for any public official.

Subparagraph (b)(2) reinforces the position that notarizations should never be performed in certain circumstances in which exploitation of the principal or the parties relying on the notarization is possible or likely. The specific instances are set forth in Sections 5-2 and 5-5.

Subparagraph (b)(3) introduces a commonsense rule for notarial practice. The drafters recognize that at times there may be a tension between the notary's serving as a public officer and having other professional obligations. In reality, being a notary public is not full-time employment for most commission holders. A notary may not reasonably be expected to be at the instantaneous beck and call of the public. The notary may well have to attend to other duties. Consequently, there needs to be some flexibility in responding to the public's requests. This subparagraph makes clear that the notary is not constantly "on call" to perform notarizations, but may arrange to make reasonable accommodations to satisfy the public's need. When the number of documents presented makes notarizing all of them at one time unfeasible, the Act allows the notary to satisfy the request in a way that does not unreasonably interfere with the notary's other obligations.

Subparagraph (b)(3) is worded to address multiple notarizations, or any request made for notarial services during regular business hours when the notary is engaged in another task and it would be unreasonably disruptive for the notary to "drop everything" and immediately attend to the notarial services. In this situation, the notary would be encouraged to find a convenient juncture to attend to the notarization(s) within a reasonable time, or to arrange a mutually convenient alternate time to perform this function. A principal requesting a lawful notarial act should never be turned away without accommodation.

Subparagraph (b)(4) recognizes that notaries who have not taken the steps to educate, equip, and register themselves as electronic notaries (see generally Chapter 16) are not permitted to perform an electronic notarization.

Subsection (c) further reinforces the view that, notwithstanding status as a public servant, being a notary is not a round-the-clock job. Notaries may limit their availability to both a regular workplace and regular business hours. Whereas a notary has discretion to provide notarial services at any time or place within the jurisdiction, there is no obligation to do so outside of the notary's normal business hours or business place.

§ 5-7 Improper Influence.

(a) Unless Section 5-6(b)(1) applies, a notary shall not influence a person either to enter into or avoid a transaction involving a notarial act by the notary.

(b) A notary commission shall not authorize the notary to investigate, ascertain, or attest to the lawfulness, propriety, accuracy, or truthfulness of a document or transaction involving a notarial act.

Comment

Section 5-7 provides a rule to emphasize the notary's impartial role in performing official duties. Subsection (a) mandates that the notary play a neutral role and not attempt to influence any party from participating in or eschewing a transaction requiring a notarial act. The provision is written in broad terms and applies to a notary's dealings with all persons, including those who are not principals. Thus, for example, a notary is forbidden to influence a third party to act as a credible witness under Section 2-5 to prove a principal's identity. Notwithstanding the general rule, Subsection (a) does not apply to situations where the notary has reason to believe the underlying transaction is unlawful. (See Subsection 5-6(b)(1).)

Subsection (b) underscores the notary's limited role. The notary's duties are confined to the requirements established by the Act. A notary by virtue of holding a commission is neither authorized nor obligated to conduct an investigation into any aspect of a transaction. Indeed, the notarization promises no more than what the language in the certificate states. A notary never vouches for the legality, truthfulness, or accuracy of a document. The notary only verifies the principal's identity and participation in the notarial act. Nonetheless, a notary may "wear two hats" and by virtue of a professional credential, certification, or training (e.g., a real estate or insurance license) may be authorized and obligated to vouch for a document's legality, truthfulness, and accuracy.

§ 5-8 Improper Certificate.

(a) A notary shall not execute a notarial certificate containing information known or believed by the notary to be false.

(b) A notary shall not affix an official signature or seal on a notarial certificate that is incomplete.

(c) A notary shall not affix an official signature or seal on a notarial certificate other than at the time of notarization and in the presence of the principal.

(d) A notary shall not provide or send a signed or sealed notarial certificate to another person with the understanding that it will be completed or attached to a document outside of the notary's presence.

Comment

Appearing as Section 5-5 ("False Certificate") in the 2002 Act, Section 5-8 addresses improper handling of the notarial certificate, which is the essential manifestation of most notarial acts. (Simple oaths and affirmations as oral declarations may not require completion of a certificate.)

Subsection (a) prohibits execution of a certificate that the notary knows or believes contains incorrect information. "Known" information would be based on the notary's firsthand observation or experience, while "believed" information would be derived from other sources that the notary considers reliable. It is possible that notaries could be pressured by employers, clients, friends, and relatives to falsify a notarial certificate by inserting an incorrect date, or stating that an absent person was present, or a stranger was personally known. In these instances, notaries must keep in mind that the information in a notarial certificate may carry great weight in resolving disputes involving legal rights and interests. Much may depend on the truthfulness and accuracy of the statements in a notarial certificate.

Subsection (b) prohibits a notary from executing an incomplete certificate. The official signature and seal must not be affixed until all other portions of the certificate have been completed. If a notary signs and seals an incomplete certificate, an opportunity may be provided for an unscrupulous person to insert false information on the form.

Subsection (c), which did not appear in the 2002 Act, prohibits the not uncommon notarial practice of pre-signing and presealing stacks of certificates to save time. This is both an improper and a dangerous practice that could result in theft and subsequent fraudulent use of certificates without the notary's knowledge.

Subsection (d) reinforces the proposition stated in Subsection (c) that a proper notarization must be completed entirely at one time and place in the principal's presence. This subsection mandates that the notary not execute a certificate without also attaching it to the document to which it relates. The Act makes clear that an unattached certificate, whether complete or incomplete, may not be forwarded for attachment to the related document by a person other than the notary. The reason for this rule is quite simple. It would be too easy for an unscrupulous person to attach the signed and sealed certificate to a document for which it was not intended. Whereas it is true that, after a document with an attached certificate leaves the notary's possession, there is no way to prevent the certificate from being detached and then reattached to a different document (though there may be physical evidence of reattachment), Subsection (d) at least assures that the notary will not have abetted the illegal act.

§ 5-9 Improper Documents.

(a) A notary shall not notarize a signature:
   (1) on a blank or incomplete document; or
   (2) on a document without notarial certificate wording.

(b) A notary shall neither certify nor authenticate a photograph.

Comment

Section 5-9 identifies documents that may not properly be notarized due to significant omissions. Subparagraph (a)(1) bans notarizing a blank or incomplete document. A blank document is one that has no text. An incomplete document is one that has unfilled blanks in its text. Nothing in this section authorizes the notary to read the document itself. A principal's privacy rights are important. The notary should do no more than scan the pages for incomplete sections and to glean information about the document for entry in the journal. (For more information on this point, see THE NOTARY PUBLIC CODE OF PROFESSIONAL RESPONSIBILITY, Guiding Principal IX, Standards IX-A-1 and IX-A-2, and Commentary.)

Subparagraph (a)(2) extends the rule to prohibit a notary from notarizing a document that lacks notarial certificate wording, though subsequent authorized prescription of a proper certificate for the notary to use may remedy the situation. Subsection (b) specifies that a notary may not notarize a photograph. Although statutes do not specifically address this issue, it is important because of frequent requests that photographs be notarized, particularly for certain medical license applications. Making and certifying a subjective judgment about the accuracy, completeness, authenticity, or other attribute of a photograph, even if the notary had a hand in its production, is not an apt function of a notary. At best, a notary may notarize another person's signed statement of certain facts relating to the picture. Moreover, nothing precludes this statement and the notary's accompanying certificate from being executed on or across the photograph itself. But that notarization does not authenticate the photograph; it only verifies that a principal proved his or her identity, took an oath in the case of a jurat, and signed the statement.

§ 5-10 Intent to Deceive.

A notary shall not perform any official action with the intent to deceive or defraud.

Comment

Section 5-10 enunciates a basic rule that pervades the entire Act: a notary shall not engage in deceptive practices in the performance of official duties. This concept is self-evident, but is so essential to establishing integrity and reliability that the drafters believed it was well worth repeating through separate attention. Aside from being a positive obligation, it is also an ethical imperative. (See THE NOTARY PUBLIC CODE OF PROFESSIONAL RESPONSIBILITY, Guiding Principle IV, Standards IV-E-1 and IV-E-2, and Commentary.) A notary who violates this duty should incur both disciplinary and criminal sanctions. (See generally Sections 13-3 through 13-7.)

§ 5-11 Testimonials.

A notary shall not use the official notary title or seal to endorse, promote, denounce, or oppose any product, service, contest, candidate, or other offering.

Comment

Section 5-11 fosters maintenance of a neutral, independent, and respected notary office. To this end, the Act prohibits use of the office or any of its incidents for any commercial or political purpose. A similar rule has been promulgated in a number of jurisdictions. (See, e.g., UTAH CODE ANN. § 46- 1-10; and OR. REV. STAT. § 194.158(2).) The drafters adopted the rule because of a concern that uninformed members of the public could misunderstand the significance of a notary seal. It was feared that some might believe it carried with it a governmental imprimatur of approval. Of course, this is not the case. Indeed, a notary who uses his or her seal for such purposes with the intent to deceive someone into believing the seal imparted an official government endorsement would be in violation of Section 5-10, and subject to severe sanctions.

§ 5-12 Unauthorized Practice of Law.

(a) A non-attorney notary shall not assist another person in drafting, completing, selecting, or understanding a document or transaction requiring a notarial act.

(b) If notarial certificate wording is not provided or indicated for a document, a non-attorney notary shall not determine the type of notarial act or certificate to be used.

Comment

Section 5-12 has been reformulated from the former Section 5-9. The drafters determined that the section as it appeared in the former Act included provisions that, although related, deserved separate treatment. As a result the former Section 5-9 was parsed to create a series of sections that delivered their proscriptions and exceptions thereto in a succinct, direct manner. (See Sections 5-12, 5-13, and 5-14.)

Section 5-12 adopts the language of the former Subsections 5-9(a) and (b), but has reversed their order. The drafters determined that Subsection (a), as it appears here, provides the overarching proscription, and therefore should be placed first in the section.

This section draws a sharp line between notarial practice and legal advice. A significant underlying goal of the section is to protect the public, especially those who believe that notaries may lawfully perform some of the functions of attorneys. To this end, guideposts are provided to help ensure that the notary does not cross the line separating notarization from legal advice. Notaries who are not duly qualified attorneys are strictly forbidden from offering legal opinions to others. Those who do are engaged in the unauthorized practice of law. (See IDAHO CODE § 51-112(d); and TEX. GOV'T CODE ANN. § 406.016(d).) Aside from constituting official misconduct for notary purposes, it may also be actionable as a criminal offense.

Subsection (a) further clarifies the purely ministerial role played by a notary. It expands the proscription relating to notarial certificates to documents. A notary commission does not authorize the notary to provide any transaction-related assistance. Thus, the notary may neither complete an unfinished document nor draft a document for another person. Of course, this does not apply to completing the notarial certificate that is part of the document, including striking inapplicable language.

The notary should not recommend a document type to a principal, even if specifically asked. Notaries who have access to pre-printed legal forms must refrain from suggesting a form to another person even if the notary is confident about which form is needed. In addition, the notary must never interpret or explain either the purpose or contents of a document to another person. These acts constitute legal advice, and may only be performed by licensed attorneys, or by non-attorneys duly qualified, trained, licensed, or experienced within a particular professional field. (See Section 5-13.)

Subsection (a) underscores the fact that a notary is empowered solely to perform a requested notarization. It is inappropriate for a non-attorney notary even to suggest that a document needs to be notarized. The section is not limited in its application to principals (i.e., individuals for whom a notarization is performed), but applies to all persons, whether or not they ask to have a document notarized. Finally, notaries who are also attorneys are not covered by the subsection because an attorney is authorized to perform all of the otherwise proscribed activities in that capacity.

Subsection (b) establishes the rule that the notary's determination of the type of notarization needed or the type of certificate to be executed on a document is prohibited. An exception, of course, is made for notaries who are also attorneys. Some notaries may believe it is appropriate for them to assist principals in executing the notarization, and that recommending the act and certificate is consistent with this role. The drafters strongly disagree. Some documents may need an acknowledgment, others a jurat, and others only a signature witnessing. An improperly selected certificate could render the document ineffective. For example, a document with an acknowledgment or signature witnessing certificate would not be accepted as an affidavit, which speaks to the truth of the contents of the document. Neither of these types of notarization involves an oath or affirmation, an essential element of an affidavit. Such a mistake could prove costly if the transaction was voided because the truth of the document's contents was essential to its completion. A notary ought not to be involved in these matters; they belong in the attorney's realm. The drafters firmly believed that the notary public serves a ministerial role, one that does not entail giving advice or offering opinions. (Accord THE NOTARY PUBLIC CODE OF PROFESSIONAL RESPONSIBILITY, Guiding Principle VI.)

Nothing in this section prohibits a notary from putting or writing certificate wording on a document if the principal asks for a specific type of notarial act. Thus, if a notary is asked to take an acknowledgment of a principal's signature, but there is no certificate on the document, the notary may add the required wording for an acknowledgment certificate to the signature page. Prescribed certificate wording for different notarizations is provided in Chapter 9.

§ 5-13 Permissible Advice.

Section 5-12 does not preclude a notary who is duly qualified, trained, licensed, or experienced in a particular industry or professional field from selecting, drafting, completing, or advising on a document or certificate related to a matter within that industry or field.

Comment

Section 5-13 is the former Subsection 5-9(c) in the previous Act. The section recognizes that many notaries have other professional qualifications. So to speak, they may wear more than one hat. The Act provides that being a notary does not derogate from any authority or discretion the notary may derive from other professional licenses or certifications. A real estate agent, for example, may in that capacity give advice and assistance in executing a contract for the purchase of property. The Act permits this and similar activities of other professionals.

§ 5-14 Misrepresentation and Improper Advertising.

(a) A notary shall not claim to have powers, qualifications, rights, or privileges that the office of notary does not provide, including the power to counsel on immigration issues.

(b) A non-attorney notary who advertises notarial services in a language other than English shall include in the advertisement, notice, letterhead, or sign the following, prominently displayed in the same language:

(1) the statement: "I am not an attorney and have no authority to give advice on immigration or other legal matters"; and

(2) the fees for notarial acts specified in Section 6-2(a).

(c) A notary may not use the term "notario publico" or any equivalent non-English term in any business card, advertisement, notice, or sign.

Comment

Section 5-14 is a restatement of Subsections 5-9(d), (e), and (f) in the former Act. Subsection (a) forbids the notary from misrepresenting notarial authority. Immigration and other legal matters are of particular concern because in civil law jurisdictions the attorney-like notario publico may be authorized to deal with these issues. To prevent public confusion and thwart unscrupulous notaries from attracting business for unauthorized acts, the Act mandates that notaries not misrepresent the powers associated with the notary office. Nothing in the subsection prohibits an attorney-notary from claiming powers afforded by a license to practice law.

Subsection (b) is designed to supplement the rule against misrepresentation of authority spelled out in Subsection (a). The drafters recognize that there is a significant Spanish-speaking population in this country familiar with the powers of the notario publico. As an added precaution to avoid confusion and misunderstanding about the extent of the American notary's notarial powers, the Act requires any notary who advertises notarial services in a foreign language to stipulate clearly in the ad that the notary is not a lawyer and may not provide legal advice or counsel. Specific reference is made to immigration matters because it is often the subject of greatest interest to foreign-born residents who are less than fluent in English. To further deter exploitation of unknowledgeable aliens, the Act mandates that a notary who advertises in a foreign language state the statutory fees for notarial acts in the same language.

Subsection (c) takes the final step in attempting to clearly distinguish the United States notary from the notario publico of civil law Latin nations. The Act forbids a notary from using the term "notario publico" in any commercial communication to members of the public. Also prohibited is the use of equivalent non-English terms designating other attorney-like civil law notarial officers, including notaire (French) and notaio (Italian). Although the subsection speaks specifically to written material, the drafters intended the prohibition to extend to all types of solicitations, whether they be oral or electronic.

§ 5-15 Notarial Officers Other Than Notaries.

(a) Notarial officers, other than notaries public, who are given the power to perform notarial acts by other laws of this [State] shall comply with the following sections of this [Act], in the same manner as notaries public, in performing their authorized notarial acts:

(1) regarding prohibitions and restrictions, Sections 5-2 through 5-14;

(2) regarding maintenance of a journal of notarial acts, Sections 7-1 through 7-2; and

(3) regarding execution of notarial certificates, Sections 9-1 through 9-9.

(b) Notarial officers, other than notaries public, shall follow all pertinent laws of this [State], except those set down in this [Act] apart from this section, and the rules duly issued by their authorized employers in regard to:

(1) use or non-use of a seal of office;

(2) performance of electronic notarial acts;

(3) disposition of a seal of office and a journal of notarial acts after termination of status as a notarial officer; and

(4) all other matters, including discipline, related to their status as a notarial officer.

Comment

Section 5-15 did not appear in the Model Notary Act of 2002, but is included here to address the notarial responsibilities of officers who have been given the power to notarize by laws other than this Act. In most cases, such laws do not address basic notarial prohibitions and restrictions, maintenance of a journal of notarial acts, nor execution of notarial certificates, even though a notary's failure to attend to these matters can undermine the utility of a notarization. Subsection (a) identifies three parts of this Act that the drafters believed should not be ignored by ex officio notaries and others whose notarial authority derives from occupying an office or performing a function governed by statute or administrative rule.

Through Subsection (b), the drafters preferred to allow all other matters attendant to the duties of ex officio notaries – including, for example, seal use, performance of electronic notarial acts, disposition of seals and journals, and discipline for misconduct – to be addressed by dictates other than set down in this Act.

Chapter 6 – Fees of Notary Public

Comment

General: This chapter addresses a variety of issues concerning the setting and charging of notarial fees. The Act adopts the long recognized position that notaries are entitled to receive a fee for performing a notarization. The Act acknowledges that a notary may waive all or part of the fee, but must not use discriminatory bases in making that decision. As a convenience to consumers and to better serve the needs of the homebound, the Act introduces a "travel fee" concept. This permits notaries to recover their costs incident to bringing notarial services to those unable to leave a bed or residence and to those home refinancers and other borrowers who expect such conveniences in a competitive marketplace. Finally, the chapter also provides guidance on how the fees of employee-notaries are to be handled.

§ 6-1 Imposition and Waiver of Fees.

(a) For performing a notarial act, a notary may charge the maximum fee specified in Section 6-2, charge less than the maximum fee, or waive the fee.

(b) A notary shall not discriminatorily condition the fee for a notarial act on the attributes of the principal or requester of fact as set forth in Subsection 5-6(a), though a notary may waive or reduce fees for humanitarian or charitable reasons.

Comment

Section 6-1 states the basic rule that notaries themselves are to decide whether or not fees are charged. The drafters acknowledged that many notaries do not charge for their services, especially those who are employees. (See Section 6-4 for special rules applicable to an employee notary.) There are, however, some limitations on notaries' discretion in regard to fees. First, Subsection (a) makes clear that in no event may a notary charge more than the maximum allowable fee. (See Subsection 6-2(a) for the fee structure.) Second, Subsection (b) prohibits a notary from charging a fee predicated on an improper discriminatory basis. This antidiscrimination provision is new to notary statutes. The subsection specifically incorporates the Subsection 5-6(a) criteria for determining prejudicial acts, and applies to fees the same ban on unacceptable discrimination applicable to refusals to perform a notarial act.

Conceptually, as a public servant, the notary is precluded from engaging in any discriminatory practices. The Act reinforces the point. Subsection (b) carves out an exception for the notary who is motivated by philanthropic or charitable intentions. Thus, a notary who waives fees as a humanitarian act does not engage in discriminatory practice if he or she charges the maximum fee to others. Moreover, a notary may be selective in identifying those worthy charitable causes for which he or she chooses to waive the fee. The only limitation is that the notary may not use the characteristics specified in Subsection 5-6(a) as the basis for distinguishing those worthy causes.

§ 6-2 Fees for Notarial Acts.

(a) The maximum fees that may be charged by a notary for notarial acts are:

(1) for an acknowledgment, [dollars] per signature;

(2) for an oath or affirmation without a signature, [dollars] per person;

(3) for a jurat, [dollars] per signature;

(4) for a signature witnessing, [dollars] per signature;

(5) for a certified copy, [dollars] per page certified with a minimum total charge of [dollars];

(6) for a verification of fact, [dollars] per certificate; and

(7) for an electronic notarization, as specified in Section 21-2.

(b) A notary may charge a travel fee when traveling to perform a notarial act if:

(1) the notary and the person requesting the notarial act agree upon the travel fee in advance of the travel; and

(2) the notary explains to the person requesting the notarial act that the travel fee is both separate from the notarial fee prescribed in Subsection (a) and neither specified nor mandated by law.

Comment

Section 6-2 establishes the fee schedule. Subsection (a) identifies all of the different notarial acts, and provides a separate fee for each one. The drafters did not include fee amounts. It was determined that these decisions were best left to the respective jurisdictions. However, the drafters did express a preference for a fee of at least $10 for any notarial act, because this amount, authorized by law for most notarizations in a growing number of states (see, e.g., CAL. GOV'T CODE § 8211; FLA. STAT. ANN. § 117.05(2)(a); and S.D. CODIFIED LAWS § 18-1-9), was deemed to fairly compensate notaries for their time, effort, and potential liability. Enumeration of the various notarial acts was not intended to indicate that each should carry a different fee amount. More than one type of notarial act may command the same fee. (For example, the fee for an acknowledgment and a jurat may be the same.) The list provides the opportunity to set different fee amounts for the authorized notarial acts. Some jurisdictions stipulate a single fee for any and all notarial acts (see, e.g., 5 ILCS 312 / 3-104(a); and IND. CODE ANN, § 33- 42-8-1), while others prescribe a fee for each different type of notarial act (see, e.g., HAW. REV. STAT. § 456-17; and N.M.. STAT. ANN. § 14-12A-16(D)). By its specific reference, Subparagraph (7) applies only if the jurisdiction adopts Article III of the Act relating to electronic notarizations. If that article is not adopted, the subparagraph may be deleted. Should Article III be adopted without Section 21-2, then the fee schedule in this section shall also apply to electronic notarizations.

Subsection 6-2(b) addresses charging a travel fee incident to the performance of a notarial act. A few jurisdictions currently permit a notary to charge for these costs (see, e.g., ARIZ. REV. STAT. ANN. § 41- 316(B); N.M. STAT. ANN. § 14-12A-16(E); and UTAH CODE ANN. § 46-1-12(2)), and one jurisdiction, Nevada, sets a per-hour fee that varies according to the time of day the travel is performed (see NEV. REV. STAT § 240.100(3) and (4)). However, most state laws are silent on this point. There are many homebound disabled or elderly persons, as well as individuals in remote areas, who need notarial services. Given the relatively small fees that can be charged for notarial services, a notary may not reasonably be expected to personally bear the cost of traveling to accommodate these people. In response, the Act permits the notary to be reimbursed for necessary costs incurred to provide these special services. The Act does not impose rigid guidelines, but there is an expectation that the travel fee will be reasonable. Gouging or otherwise taking advantage of a person needing at-home services may violate public policy and constitute official misconduct. (See Section 2-12 and Comment.)

At a minimum, the travel fee covers costs such as public transportation fares, or, if a private vehicle is used, gas, parking, and tolls. The drafters contemplated that the travel fee could include additional expenses, as well. For example, if the situation necessitates that the notary spend a night away from home, reasonable accommodation and meal costs could be recoverable as part of the travel fee. Indeed, one state currently allows and sets per diem charges for notaries traveling to perform services within that geographically expansive state. (See ARIZ. REV. STAT. ANN. § 41-316(B).) Additionally, although the term "travel fee" is used, the section was written so as not to preclude a jurisdiction from allowing a notary to include a charge for time spent traveling. Each jurisdiction must balance the potential cost of a "time charge" against the benefit of special-needs principals having a notary come to them. Also, although perhaps not to be encouraged, nothing in the section would preclude a principal from paying a notary solely for the convenience of having the notary come to a home or office.

Subparagraphs (b)(1) and (b)(2) put two extremely important limits on the use of travel fees. First, and foremost, the notary and the principal or authorized principal's representative must agree upon the travel fee in advance. The drafters contemplated that this agreement will a) be made at the time the principal or representative asks the notary to travel and before the notary commits to the travel, and b) specify the actual dollar amount or an exact method for computing the amount of the fee. Second, the principal or representative must be informed that the travel fee is a) in addition to any notary fees to be charged for notarial acts, and b) not required by law but only payable by mutual agreement.

In regard to the new notarial act of verification of fact (see Subparagraph (a)(6)), it is anticipated that the notary's fee will be set at a level sufficient to cover the costs of obtaining any needed document copies from an office housing public or vital records. The costs of traveling to the office would be addressed by Subsection 6-2(b).

§ 6-3 Payment Prior to Act.

(a) A notary may require payment of any fees specified in Section 6-2 prior to performance of a notarial act.

(b) Any fees paid to a notary prior to performance of a notarial act are non-refundable if:

(1) the act was completed; or

(2) in the case of travel fees paid in compliance with Subsection 6-2(b), the act was not completed after the notary traveled to meet the principal because it was prohibited under Section 5-2, or because the notary knew or had a reasonable belief that the notarial act or the associated transaction was unlawful.

Comment

Section 6-3 addresses the problem notaries encounter when they expend considerable time and effort in traveling to perform a notarization, but are denied payment for travel when the notarial act could not be completed for due cause (see Section 5-2 and Subparagraphs 5-6(b)(1) and (2) or when the principal was dissatisfied with a properly performed act. Subsection (a) gives notaries discretion to require pre-payment of fees prior to performance of any notarial act. Some notaries may elect to invoke this provision only for acts necessitating travel, particularly verifications of fact (see Subparagraph 5-1(6)), wherein it is possible that the person requesting the verification may disagree with the notary's discovered facts and refuse to pay.

Subsection (b) stipulates that any fees paid to the notary prior to notarization are not returnable if a) the notarial act was completed, or b) the act was not completed for due cause when the notary had traveled to the site of the aborted notarization, in which case only the fee for the notarial act itself need be refunded. The travel fee would be retained by the notary.

§ 6-4 Fees of Employee Notary.

(a) An employer may prohibit an employee who is a notary from charging for notarial acts performed on the employer's time, but shall not condition imposition of a fee on attributes of the principal as described in Section 5-6(a).

(b) A private employer shall not require an employee who is a notary to surrender or share fees charged for any notarial acts.

(c) A governmental employer who has absorbed an employee's costs in becoming or operating as a notary shall require any fees for notarial acts performed on the employer's time either to be waived or surrendered to the employer to support public programs.

Comment

Section 6-4 addresses issues relating to the employee-notary who performs notarial services primarily for the employer or for customers of the employer. Employee notaries perform most, if not all, of their notarial duties at the employer's place of business, and they typically store their seals and journals at that site. (Subsections 7-4(a) and (b) require a notary to safeguard the journal when not in use. Subsection 8-2(c) imposes the same requirement for the official seal.) Oftentimes, an employer will pay for the cost of obtaining the employee notary's commission.

Subsection (a) recognizes that, since an employee is being paid during business hours, it is not unreasonable to allow the employer to dictate that notarial services in the employer's place of business be provided without a fee. However, the subsection provides that notary fees should not be discriminatorily imposed by an employer based on a given principal's status as a non-customer of the employer, or for any other prejudicial reason enumerated in Subsection 5-6(a). Note, the subsection is geared to the employment relationship and would apply to off-site notarizations performed in the scope of employment, as well. However, an employee-notary prohibited from charging during business hours could charge fees for notarizations performed off-site during nonbusiness hours, or for other notarizations not in the scope of employment. Nothing in this section should be used to imply that an employer may have an employee commissioned solely for the employer's business needs.

Subsection (b) reinforces the view that notarial fees may only be earned by and paid to the notary. The Act tries to balance the notary's independence as a public officer with the employer's right of control over an employee within the scope of employment. Whereas Subsection (a) tips the scale toward employer control over employees, Subsection (b) places greater weight on notarial independence. An employer may not collect the notary's fees, if for no other reason than that the employer is not a duly commissioned notary. The rule that only a commissioned notary may charge for notarial services cannot be questioned. (For penalties that may be imposed on an unauthorized person acting as a notary, see generally Chapter 14.) The effect of this proscription is to prevent the employer from offsetting the employee's salary cost by notary fees collected from third parties. Notwithstanding the above, nothing would prevent a notary from voluntarily giving the fee to, or sharing it with, an employer.

Subsection (c) provides a limited exception to Subsection (b). It permits certain government employers to take the employee notary's fees and use them for the benefit of the public, or to offer free notarial services as a public convenience. This applies in cases where the employing governmental agency absorbs the cost for maintaining the employee notary's commission. The Act intentionally uses the non-specific term "public programs" to allow discretion to the governmental unit availing itself of this opportunity. Presumably, using the fees to help defray the costs of commissioning the employee notary could fall within the definition of "public program."

§ 6-5 Notice of Fees.

Notaries who charge for their notarial services shall conspicuously display in their places of business, or present to each principal outside their places of business, an English-language schedule of fees for notarial acts, as specified in Section 6-2(a). No part of any notarial fee schedule shall be printed in smaller than 10-point type.

Comment

Section 6-5 provides a simple rule that notaries who charge for their services must prominently display a fee schedule. Notaries who travel to perform notarizations must carry a schedule with them and show it to any principal who inquires about fees. Fee posting provisions may be found in some existing statutes, though these laws do not require carrying and displaying such a schedule when traveling to perform a notarization. (See, e.g., NEV. REV. STAT. ANN. § 240.110; and OR. REV. STAT. § 194.164(3).) The drafters believed that the rule to post or display fees should help eliminate misunderstandings regarding charges for different services, as well as minimize opportunities for unscrupulous notaries to overcharge unsuspecting principals. The notice must be printed in English, but the drafters are equally concerned that non-English-speaking people, especially those from countries with notarios publicos, are not overcharged. Although not required, good practice suggests that notaries who usually deal with people not fluent in English also post or present a fee schedule printed in the language used by those persons. Any foreign-language advertisement for notarial services requires inclusion of a fee schedule in the particular foreign-language (see Subparagraph 5-14(b)(2)).

Chapter 7 – Journal of Notarial Acts

Comment

General: Notwithstanding their widely acknowledged critical value to the notarial act, notary journals have still proven to be a somewhat controversial subject. First, there is the threshold issue of whether or not a notary needs to maintain a journal. Many states require a notary journal (see ARIZ. REV. STAT. ANN. § 41-319; CAL. GOV'T CODE § 8206(a)(1); and 57 PA. STAT. ANN. § 161), but some do not. State law may mention notary journals without imposing a requirement to maintain one. (See UTAH CODE ANN. §§ 46-1-13 and 46-1-14.) No jurisdiction outlaws the practice. Second, if a journal is maintained, what entries are appropriate? Finally, who should have access to a journal? Most states do not address this issue, even though their notaries may be required or allowed to maintain a journal of notarial acts.

The drafters have adopted the view that journals are essential to good notarial practice and decidedly in the public interest. Entry requirements serve to help ensure that the notary records critical information about each notarial act. Such data can be extremely useful in answering any future questions that may arise concerning the document or its signer.

The Act nonetheless recognizes that there is a tension between principals' privacy rights and the right of the public to access information. Consequently, the drafters determined that while notary journals should not be considered public records per se, their public utility should be recognized and limited access granted in certain situations.

§ 7-1 Maintaining Journal of Notarial Acts.

(a) A notary shall keep, maintain, protect, and provide for lawful inspection a chronological journal of notarial acts that is either:

(1) a permanently bound book with numbered pages; or

(2) an electronic journal of notarial acts as described in Section 20-2 of this [Act].

(b) A notary shall keep a record of electronic and non-electronic notarial acts in the same journal.

(c) A notary shall maintain only 1 active journal at the same time, except that a backup of each active and inactive electronic journal shall be retained by the notary in accordance with Section 20-2(3) as long as each respective original journal is retained.

Comment

Section 7-1 mandates that every notary maintain and safeguard an official journal of all notarizations performed. The section also provides the specific authority for access rules (i.e., "provide for lawful inspection") that are spelled out in Section 7-3.

The notary is required to record notarial acts in chronological order. The Act permits the notary to choose a journal that is either in a bound paper or an electronic form, but Subsection (c) makes clear that only one active journal may be maintained. Thus, a notary may not have one book at home for recording notarial acts for friends and neighbors and another at the office for notarial acts completed at work, nor one to record paper-based notarizations and another to record electronic acts. To preserve the chronological integrity of the notary's record, there can be but one active journal. To facilitate adherence to the rule, good practice suggests that the notarial journal and seal be kept together at all times, thereby eliminating the opportunity to use the seal without having immediate access to the journal for recording the respective act. However, with the anticipated eventual advent of online electronic journals that may be accessed through any Internet connection, notaries will be given a new flexibility to enter notarial acts in the same journal from any location.

Due to the occasional malfunctioning of electronic systems, Subsection (c) mandates that a backup journal be retained for the active and for each inactive electronic journal. This will preserve a record of the notary's official acts in the event the original is lost or compromised. Ideally, such a backup electronic record would be maintained "off site" to prevent flood, fire, or other disaster from claiming both original and backup records.

Although the Act was intended to be a comprehensive unit of three articles, some jurisdictions may elect not to adopt the provisions regarding electronic notarization in Article III. At the same time, however, notaries in such jurisdictions may be allowed to maintain electronic journals for their paper-based notarial acts. This is an increasingly common practice, whether sanctioned by statute (see, e.g., TEX. GOV'T CODE § 406.014(e)) or permitted without express statutory authority. Subparagraph (a)(2) addresses this possibility. In jurisdictions not adopting Section 15-4 ("Electronic Journal of Notarial Acts") and Chapter 20 ("Record of Electronic Notarial Acts") from Article III but nonetheless permitting notaries to use an electronic journal, language defining and setting rules for such a journal should be added to Chapter 7. In those instances, the drafters recommend and encourage that the language from Section 15-4 and Chapter 20 be integrated into the chapter.

§ 7-2 Journal Entries.

(a) For every notarial act, the notary shall record in the journal at the time of notarization at least the following:

(1) the date and time of day of the notarial act;

(2) the type of notarial act;

(3) the type, title, or a description of the document or proceeding;

(4) the signature, printed name, and address of each principal;

(5) the printed name and address of each requester of fact;

(6) the evidence of identity of each principal in the form of either: a statement that the person is "personally known" to the notary; a notation of the type of identification document, its issuing agency, its serial or identification number, and its date of issuance or expiration; or the handwritten signature and the name and address of each credible witness swearing or affirming to the principal's identity, and for credible witnesses who

are not personally known to the notary, a description of the identification documents relied on by the notary;

[(7) the thumbprint of each principal and witness, or, in the case of an electronic journal, the thumbprint or other recognized biometric identifier, in accordance with Section 20-2(4) of this [Act];]

[(8)] the fee, if any, charged for the notarial act;

[(9)] the address where the notarization was performed, if not the notary's business address;

[(10)] the sequential number of any adhesive label bearing a notary seal image on the notarized document, in accordance with Section 8-2(d) of this [Act]; and

[(11)] in the case of an electronic notarization, the name of any authority issuing or registering the means used to create the electronic signature that was notarized; the source of this authority's license, if any; and the expiration date of the electronic process.

(b) A notary shall not record a Social Security or credit card number in the journal.

(c) A notary shall record in the journal the circumstances for not performing or completing any requested notarial act.

(d) A notary shall record in the journal the circumstances of any request to inspect or copy an entry in the journal, including the requester's name, address, handwritten signature, [thumbprint or other recognized biometric identifier,] and evidence of identity. The reasons for refusal to allow inspection or copying of a journal entry shall also be recorded.

(e) As required in Section 9-3(4), a notary shall append to the pertinent entry in the journal a notation of the nature and date of the notary's correction of a completed notarial certificate corresponding to the entry.

Comment

Subsection 7-2(a) both mandates that every notarization requires an entry in the notary's journal of notarial acts and specifies the proper components of such an entry. Most of the separate items enumerated in Subparagraphs (a)(1) through (a)(11) are currently required or allowed by jurisdictions legislating the use of notary journals. (See generally ARIZ. REV. STAT. ANN. § 41-319; CAL. GOV'T CODE § 8206(a)(2); and 57 PA. STAT. ANN. § 161.) There are, however, some innovations.

A new Subparagraph (a)(5) has been added to accommodate journal entries for verification of fact notarizations (see Section 2-19 and Comment), for which only the name and address of the requester of fact – and not the person's signature, thumbprint, and identifying information – need be recorded. Because the verification of certain other facts is the matter at issue (e.g., whether two separate documents are congruent), there is no need for this identity related information to be recorded in the journal. Indeed, it is not even necessary for the requester to be in the notary's physical presence. The drafters contemplated that verifications of fact might be requested by mail or electronic communication. If the requester of fact is present, the notary would not be prohibited from asking the person to sign the journal as evidence that the verification of fact certificate was delivered.

Subparagraph (a)(6) compels the notary to record how the identity of the principal was established, including a description of any identification documents or credible witnesses that were relied on. By requiring this entry, the Act reinforces both the essential role of the notary in authenticating signed documents – identity verification – and the proper methods of obtaining such verification. Additionally, the entry serves to memorialize proper performance of the act.

Offered as an option (i.e., bracketed) because it may be regarded as too intrusive or controversial by some lawmakers, Subparagraph (a)(7) requires capture of all principals' and witnesses' thumbprints, or, in the case of electronic records, other accepted biometric identifiers. This requirement sparked robust discussion among the drafters, a number of whom believed it demands too much of both the principal and notary. Proponents of the rule countered that modern technology has made fingerprinting clean, easy, and inexpensive. They argued that many impostors will thereby be deterred from forgery because they will not want to leave a thumbprint behind in the notary's journal as proof of their attempted crime. Also, it was asserted, prosecutors will be aided by the journal evidence in bringing forgers to justice.

For electronic journals, any other recognized biometric identifier (e.g., a retinal scan) may be captured in lieu of a thumbprint if the notary's journal technology so allows. No doubt, future technical advancements will make it easier for notaries who maintain an electronic journal to use biometric identifiers other than fingerprints, which a host of electronic products can now capture and store.

Subparagraph (a)(9) directs the notary to enter the location at which the notarization was performed, if not at the notary's normal business address. The purpose is to help protect the notary if the act is questioned in the future. Should the notary be called as a witness, this information can serve to refresh the notary's recollection regarding the transaction.

Subparagraph (a)(10) reflects that the Act recognizes official notary seals in forms other than the traditional metal embosser or inked stamp, as long as the seal satisfies the requirements of Chapter 8.

Subparagraph (a)(11) provides additional requirements for electronic notarial acts. It directs the principal to provide information about the origin and authenticity of any notarized electronic signature. If, for example, the signature were made using public key technology, the "authority issuing or registering the means used to create the electronic signature" would be the pertinent certification authority.

Subsection 7-2(a) mandates that the journal entry be made at the time of notarization. The Act does not specify whether the recording must be made before or after the notarial act is otherwise completed. Although completing the journal entry at the end might seem a logical choice, there is merit in completing the entry before the rest of the notarization is performed. The latter option prevents time-pressed principals from leaving with the notarized document before the journal entry is completed. Additionally, it allows the notary to refuse to act for those who will not provide a thumbprint or any other required entry component. Finally, the journal entries detail the essential elements of a proper notarization; by making the journal entry first, the notary reinforces the procedure that should be followed for each notarial act.

Subsection (b) responds to privacy concerns by precluding a notary from entering either a Social Security number or a credit card number in a journal. (See, e.g., TEX. ADMIN. CODE § 87.60, prohibiting notaries from recording identification document serial numbers in their journals.) Sophisticated criminals can exploit this information for illegal purposes. The drafters believe that this proscription is a prudent and necessary step toward protecting principals from identity theft and the concomitant hardships it can cause.

Subsection (c) is designed to provide a notary some protection against future claims regarding non-performance. The provision not only addresses instances in which a request for a notarial act was refused for due cause, but also those in which an act was begun and then discontinued due to discovery of an impropriety or other valid reason. The justification for nonperformance or discontinuation should be explained.

Subsection (d) requires a notary to record in the journal

the circumstances of any request to inspect or copy an entry in the journal, including the requester's name, address, signature, and evidence of identity. The reasons for refusal to allow inspection or copying of a journal entry must also be recorded. The notary is specifically cautioned to confine the entry to specific facts (e.g., inability to provide proof of identity), and not record purely subjective judgments. Again, the thumbprint requirement is bracketed to indicate a choice for lawmakers.

Subsection (e) is new and corresponds to the new Subparagraph 9-3(4), which requires a notation to be made in the journal in the event that a notarized document is returned to the notary for correction of an error in its notarial certificate.

§ 7-3 Inspection and Copying of Journal.

(a) In the notary's presence, any person may inspect and request a copy of an entry or entries in the notary's official journal during regular business hours, but only if:

(1) the person's identity is personally known to the notary or proven through satisfactory evidence;

(2) the person affixes a signature [and thumbprint or other recognized biometric identifier] in the journal in a separate, dated entry;

(3) the person specifies the month, year, type of document, and name of the principal or requester of fact for the notarial act or acts sought;

(4) the person is shown or given a requested copy of only the entry or entries specified; and

(5) the other entries on the same journal page are covered to prevent disclosure.

(b) If the notary has a reasonable and explainable belief that a person bears a criminal or harmful intent in requesting information from the notary's journal, the notary may deny access to any entry or entries.

(c) The journal may be examined and copied without restriction by a law enforcement officer in the course of an official investigation, subpoenaed by court order, or surrendered at the direction of the [commissioning official].

(d) Upon complying with a request for copies under Subsection (a), the notary shall charge not more than [dollars] per copy; and if a certified copy is requested, the fee is as specified in Section 6-2.

Comment

Section 7-3 addresses a controversial issue concerning the notary journal – whether or not it is a public record – and prescribes procedures for proper handling of the journal. Although a number of jurisdictions require notaries to maintain journals, not all consider the journal to be an accessible public record. The Act rejects the view that the journal is a true public record. Instead, it takes the position that the journal is quasi-public in nature. The Act controls and limits access to the journal by a) having it remain in the complete control of the notary, and b) restricting its inspection by the general public.

Subsection (a) establishes the principle that access to the journal is a privilege, not an absolute right. Thus, a person seeking to inspect the journal must be willing to give up some privacy in order to gain access. Specifically, the person must prove identity and both sign and impress a thumbprint in the journal, though, again, some jurisdictions may forego the thumbprint requirement. Additionally, the inspection must be made in the presence of the notary. In an effort to preserve the privacy rights of principals and eliminate "fishing expeditions," Subparagraph (a)(4) further promotes principals' privacy protection by limiting the inspection to only the specified entries. The Act requires the notary to exercise due care when making copies to ensure that other journal entries, or parts thereof, are neither revealed nor included as part of the copied material.

Except for an electronic journal (see Subsection 7-1(c)), a notary is not authorized to make a copy of the journal or any separate entry therein for personal use or as a "backup" record in the event the original journal is lost, destroyed, or stolen. Although having a copy of the journal might seem to be a sensible precaution, it invites other risks. A copy of a journal may not be adequately protected from unauthorized inspection. It is also possible that the notary by inadvertence or convenience might make an official entry in the copy, a violation of the dictate that the notary maintain only one journal.

In seeking to balance the public's rights against unwarranted invasions of privacy, the Act adopts the position that all specific inspection requests must be granted, unless the notary believes either a criminal or harmful purpose will be served by allowing the inspection. (See Subsection (b).) The notary must have a "reasonable and explainable belief" that the person requesting the inspection bears a wrongful motive. The drafters recognized that this standard is neither easily defined nor applied. Additionally, there was concern over how the notary would make such a determination. The drafters' intent was to allow a notary to deny or limit access in those situations where the notary has prior knowledge or is able to formulate a compelling opinion regarding the request. As to the former, the notary may have been informed by a principal that he or she is being stalked or is the target of identity theft. Regarding the latter, when asked by the notary why the journal information is needed, the person might not be able to give a plausible response. In these situations the notary is alerted to potential misuse of the information and should proceed with caution. To protect the personal safety and the private interests of persons named in the journal, Subsection (b) gives the notary discretion to deny access to the journal to any person the notary reasonably believes has a criminal or harmful intent. Notaries should be protected from becoming accessories to criminal or other wrongful acts. The subsection affords them this opportunity.

Subsection (c) makes it clear that, notwithstanding the protections provided by Subsection (b), notary journals are always subject to lawful inspection by appropriate authorities.

Subsection (d) authorizes the notary to provide a copy of a journal entry for any permitted inspection and to charge a statutory fee for the service.

§ 7-4 Security of Journal.

(a) A notary shall safeguard the journal and all other notarial records and surrender or destroy them only by rule of law, by court order, or at the direction of the [commissioning official].

(b) When not in use, the journal shall be kept in a secure area under the exclusive control of the notary, and shall not be used by any other notary, nor surrendered to an employer upon termination of employment.

(c) Within 10 days after the journal is discovered to be stolen, lost, destroyed, damaged, or otherwise rendered unusable or unreadable, the notary, after informing the appropriate law enforcement agency in the case of theft or vandalism, shall notify the [commissioning official] by any means providing a tangible receipt, including certified mail and electronic transmission, and also provide a copy or identification number of any pertinent police report.

Comment

Section 7-4 lays down rules for safeguarding the notary journal as a valuable and sensitive record of official acts.

Subsection (a) instructs the notary to protect not only the journal, but also any correlative notarial documents. This might include the notary's commission or copies of communications from the commissioning official. The notary's journal and records may only be surrendered pursuant to statute, court order, or a directive of the commissioning official. Note, although law enforcement officials are permitted to access journals, they are not entitled to take physical custody of the journal absent a court order.

Subsection (b) requires the notary to safeguard the journal at all times. The drafters recognize that journals often contain sensitive, confidential information that merits protection. The requirement that the journal be kept in a secure area lends itself to reasonable interpretation. The objective is to shield the information in the journal from unauthorized use. Clearly, keeping the journal locked in a desk under the notary's exclusive control meets the test. But other less secure measures might also be acceptable. Notaries who keep their journals at home must implement similar security measures.

This subsection reinforces the rule that the journal is the notary's property. No other notary has a greater right than any member of the general public to inspect the journal, nor may another notary use it. Consequently, a notary who performs a notarial act but does not have the journal available may not record that act in the journal of another notary. Also, in some instances a person may become a notary at the behest of an employer who may presume that the notary's services will be exclusively for the employer's benefit. The Act, however, does not recognize a "notary private" and considers every notary to owe obligations to the general public, notwithstanding the fact that an employer may have absorbed the notary's commissioning costs. Consistent with this view, the Act declares that the notary's journal belongs exclusively to the notary and not the employer. The employer has inspection and copying rights similar to those of other members of the public. Nothing prohibits the employer from exercising these rights to create a separate photocopied log of employer-related notarizations. (See, e.g., CAL. GOV'T CODE § 8206(d).) Consistent with this position, the journal goes with the notary when the employment relationship terminates.

Subsection (c) requires the notary to inform the commissioning official if, for any reason, the notary cannot continue to use the journal to record notarizations. Imposing this reporting requirement reinforces the view that the journal has official significance and must be handled with due care.

In the 2002 Act, Section 7-4 appeared as Subsections 7-4 (e), (f), and (g), but the drafters believed the topic of journal inspection and copying merited its own full section in this 2010 version.

§ 7-5 Disposal of Journal.

(a) Upon resignation, revocation, or expiration of a notary commission, or death of the notary, the journal and notarial records shall be delivered to the [office designated by the commissioning official] in accordance with Sections 12-4(a) or 12-5(3) by any means providing a tangible receipt, including certified mail and electronic transmission, allowing that an electronic journal may be delivered on disk, printed on paper, or transmitted electronically, in accordance with the requirements of the same office.

(b) In the case of an electronic journal and its backup copy whose disks or other physical storage media are not required to be surrendered, no further entries shall be made in the journal and its backup, both of which shall be safeguarded until both shall be erased or expunged after [5] years from the date of the last entry by the notary or the notary's personal representative.

Comment

Section 7-5 provides guidance on what to do with the journal and notarial records after the office is vacated or the commission terminated. This provision is consistent with the view that the journal contains sensitive, confidential information that must ultimately be turned over to an appropriate official for safekeeping. The journal should not be kept by another notary, or by the former notary's successors in interest. To do so would compromise the privacy rights of principals and others whose actions are recorded in the journal.

The drafters added new language in Subsection (b) to provide direction on how to dispose of electronic journals and backups after the notary vacates office or the commission terminates and the notary has complied with the journal disposition rules of Subsection (a). As with the paper journal, the objective is to safeguard the electronic journal entries from compromise or improper disclosure, while preserving them for a reasonable and justifiable period of time to allow proper public access.

In the Model Notary Act of 2002, Section 7-5 appeared as Subsection 7-4(h), but the drafters believed the topic of journal disposal merited expansion into its own section.

§ 7-6 Electronic Journal.

If a notary elects to keep an electronic journal pursuant to Section 7-1(a), the notary shall:

(1) provide to the [commissioning official] the access instructions that allow journal entries to be viewed, printed out, and copied; and

(2) notify the [commissioning official] of any subsequent change to the access instructions.

Comment

Section 7-6 contains provisions that ensure official access to the electronic journal of notarial acts in the event the notary is no longer alive or available to provide such access. Entries in the electronic journal may be made only by the custodial notary after a two factor access process is satisfied. (See Subparagraph 20-2(1) and Comment.) However, any person subsequently using the same access process may view, print out, or copy journal entries, but will not be able to alter any entry or its sequence. (See Subparagraph 20-2(2) and Comment.) Section 7-6 requires the notary to provide the access instructions to the commissioning official. (See Subparagraphs 4-2(9) and 16-4(3).)

As the official record of notarial acts, an electronic journal must be forwarded to an office designated by the commissioning official after the notary's death. (See Subparagraph 12-5(3).) In the event of death, this section anticipates that the notary's personal representative or other successor in interest will present proper proof of authority to the commissioning official to obtain access to the electronic journal for the sole purpose of forwarding it as required by law. In the event of the notary's disappearance or permanent incapacity, any other individual legally designated to attend to or settle the notary's affairs may also perform this function.

Chapter 8 – Signature and Seal of Notary

Comment

General: Notarizations involving a paper document typically require the notary to affix both an official signature and an official seal on the document itself. These two affixations together symbolize to the world that all of the statutory requirements for a proper notarization were satisfied. Because the signature and seal are the prime manifestations of the notarial act, guiding regulations for their proper use and protection are warranted. This is particularly true for the seal, which, if improperly appropriated, could lead to unchecked fraud. In many respects the seal is similar to the notary journal – both are incidents of the office and items for which the notary is the official custodian. (For notary journal rules paralleling those for the official seal, see Subsections 7- 4(a) through (c).) This chapter addresses basic "signature and seal" issues with an eye toward minimizing opportunities for fraud.

§ 8-1 Official Signature.

In notarizing a paper document, a notary public shall affix an official signature on the notarial certificate at the time the notarial act is performed.

Comment

Section 8-1 has been substantially revised from its appearance in the former Act and reduced to a short, succinct direction. The change was allowed by the introduction in this Act of a definition of "official signature." (See Section 2-14.)

Section 8-1 states the simple rule that a notary must place an official signature on the notarial certificate portion of any paper document that is being notarized. Section 2-14 dictates that this signature must be "handwritten." No other means of creating the notary's signature is authorized. Thus, the notary may not run a principal's document through a word processor and have a computer-generated signature validate the document's notarial certificate. The official signature that authenticates the notarial act must be handwritten by the notary.

In addition, Section 2-14, which defines "official signature," specifies that the notary's official signature must exactly match the spelling of the notary's name as it appears on the commission. Signatures that are shortened versions of the commission name are not valid.

Section 8-1 mandates that the notary's official signature be affixed only at the time of the notarization. The drafters believed that the practice of presigning multiple copies of standard notary certificates to save time is very dangerous, offering many opportunities for fraudulent abuse of the signed blank forms.

§ 8-2 Official Seal.

(a) In notarizing a paper document, a notary public shall affix an official seal on the notarial certificate at the time the notarial act is performed.

(b) The official seal of a notary public shall not be used for any purpose other than performing lawful notarizations.

(c) The official seal shall:

(1) be the exclusive property of the notary;

(2) not be affixed by any other person;

(3) be kept secure and accessible only to the notary; and

(4) not be surrendered to an employer upon termination of employment.

(d) An official seal affixed by an adhesive label shall bear a preprinted sequential number which shall be recorded in the journal of notarial acts for its respective notarization.

(e) Within 10 days after the official seal of a notary is discovered to be stolen, lost, damaged, or otherwise rendered incapable of affixing a legible image, the notary, after informing the appropriate law enforcement agency in the case of theft or vandalism, shall notify the [commissioning official] by any means providing a tangible receipt, including certified mail and electronic transmission, and also provide a copy or number of any pertinent police report. Upon receipt of such notice, the [commissioning official] shall issue to the notary a new Certificate of Authorization to Purchase a Notary Seal, which shall be presented to a seal vendor in accordance with Section 8-4.

(f) As soon as reasonably practicable after resignation, revocation, or expiration of a notary commission, or death of the notary, the seal shall be destroyed or defaced so that it may not be misused.

Comment

Section 8-2 provides detailed rules for the use, handling, and safekeeping of the notary seal. The drafters deemed them entirely appropriate for this most important of all the notary's tools of office. The seal is the internationally recognized symbol of the notary's authority and prima facie evidence of the facts attested in a notarial act.

Section 8-2 has been slightly revised and reorganized from its appearance in the former Act. In particular, Subsection (a) was changed to parallel Section 8-1 in order to indicate that the notary's seal and signature must be used in tandem to authenticate a notarial act.

Subsection (a) mandates that a seal impression be affixed by the notary for every notarization of a paper document. In contrast to the limitations on affixation of the notary's signature, however, the subsection does not preclude a seal image from being affixed by an electronic device or by an adhesive label, as long as the notary controls access to the sealing mechanism (see Subparagraph (c)(3)) and, in the case of an adhesive label, the labels bear preprinted sequential numbers, which must be noted in the journal for each notarial act (see Subsection (d)). Most often, however, the seal image will be affixed with an inked stamp.

Subsection (a) also mandates that the seal be affixed only at the time of notarization. This is the counterpart to Section 8-1, requiring notary signatures to be similarly affixed. Together, these two provisions work to reduce fraud, mistakes, and omissions because the notary will complete the entire notarization at one time, and that will be in the principal's presence. (See Subparagraph 5-2(1).) Otherwise, the notary might more readily forget to complete any open-ended act, leading to possible hardships for the principal. There would also be questions about where such an act should be entered in the sequential journal.

Subsection (b) dictates that an official notary seal may not be used for any purpose other than performance of lawful notarial acts. This subsection is supplemented by Section 5-11, which prohibits use of the "official notary title or seal to endorse, promote, denounce, or oppose any product, service, contest, candidate, or other offering." Subsection (b) offers a broader proscription, applying to use of the seal to lend authority or weight to any documentation, even that not amounting to a formal testimonial. For example, a seal's use by a notary on personal correspondence would be prohibited by this provision. The subsection is mirrored by Subsection 19-5(b), which applies to electronic notary seals.

Subsection (c) underscores that the seal belongs solely to the notary. It may not be used by anyone else, even if the other person is a notary. It is exclusively for the use of the notary to whom it was issued. Likewise, the seal of a notary whose commissioning fees and other notary-related costs were paid by an employer remains the property of the notary, not the employer. Consequently, if and when the employment relationship ends, the seal stays with the notary. This mirrors the rule with respect to notary journals. (See Subsection 7-4(b) and Comment.)

Subparagraph (c)(3) advances the view that the seal is an incident of the notary office and must be properly safeguarded. This provides the analog to Section 7-4, which contains the rules for proper care of the notary journal. As with the journal, a rule of reason is to be applied to determine what security measures satisfy the spirit of the requirement.

Again, good practice suggests that the seal and journal be kept together. Thus, steps to protect one may serve the same purpose for the other.

Subsection (d) reflects the position that an official notary seal may be in a form other than the traditional embosser or inked stamp. (For a corresponding provision regarding a notation in the notary's journal about the adhesive label seal, see Subparagraph 7-2(10).)

Subsection (e) imposes a basic notification rule in the event the seal becomes missing or in any way unusable for its intended purpose. It also imposes a duty on the notary to report any theft or vandalism of the seal to the appropriate law enforcement agency. This requirement underscores the importance of safeguarding the seal, which, in the hands of dishonest people, can enable production of forged documents and breed attendant problems. The subsection requires the commissioning official, upon receipt of a proper notice, to authorize the notary to obtain a new seal, as provided in Section 8-4.

Subsection (f) mandates that the seal be rendered unusable upon the notary's death or the resignation, revocation, or expiration of the commission. A new seal must then be issued for any subsequent new commission. This is consistent with the rule stated in Section 3-5 that the notary commission is not renewable automatically. Since every seal must contain the expiration date of the commission (see Subparagraph 8-3(a)(3)), every new commission requires a new seal.

§ 8-3 Image of Official Seal.

(a) Near the notary's official signature on each paper notarial certificate, the notary shall affix a sharp, legible, permanent, and photographically reproducible image of the official seal that shall include the following elements:

(1) the notary's name exactly as stated on the commission;

(2) the identification number of the notary's commission;

(3) the words "Notary Public" and "[State] of [name of jurisdiction]" and "My commission expires (commission expiration date)";

(4) the notary's business address; and

(5) a border in a [rectangular/circular] shape no larger than [dimensions], surrounding the required words.

(b) Illegible information within a seal impression may be typed or printed legibly by the notary adjacent to but not within the impression, or another impression may be legibly affixed nearby.

(c) An embossed seal impression that is not photographically reproducible may be used in addition to but not in place of the official seal described in Subsection (a).

(d) A seal as described in Subsection (a) shall not be affixed over printed or written matter.

Comment

Subsection 8-3(a) serves two purposes. First, its general language prescribes where the seal is to be affixed and how it shall appear. Second, the subparagraphs provide detailed specifications for an official seal. As to the former, the seal must be affixed near but not over the notary's signature. Since documents differ, the drafters realized that it would be impossible to identify one physical location for the seal that would serve all purposes. The document or certificate may indicate exactly where the seal should be placed, but both can be silent on this point, leaving the matter up to the notary. (See, e.g., certificate forms in Sections 9-4 through 9-9.) The Apostille is an example of a form that specifically designates where its signature and seal are to be affixed. (See Section 10-3.) Regardless of where affixed, the seal must be clearly readable and capable of being copied photographically. Accordingly, an inked rather than an embossing seal increasingly is the standard in modern jurisdictions, because an inked seal image is readily reproduced on microfilm or electronic media by county recorders.

Subparagraphs (a)(1) through (5) detail the components of the seal itself. The name on the seal must be exactly the same as that appearing on the commission. (See Subparagraph (a)(1).) Subparagraph (a)(2) requires that the notary's commission identification number be included. (See Section 3-4.) Although some jurisdictions require such numbers (see, e.g., CAL. GOV'T CODE § 8207; and FLA. STAT. ANN. § 117.05(3)(a)), others do not (see IND. CODE ANN. § 33-42- 2-4). The Social Security number should never be used as a substitute for an identification number because of its potential for co-option and misuse. The "business address" feature mandated by Subparagraph (a)(4) is required in one jurisdiction. (See W. VA. CODE ANN. § 29C-4-102(d).) The drafters felt it important to allow the public both to question the notary about a notarization and access the notary's journal in certain instances. By having the notary's address on the document, interested parties are given reasonable direction on where to find the notary and journal. Subparagraph (a)(5) gives each jurisdiction the opportunity to fashion the shape and design of the seal, and should result in uniform, easily recognizable seals.

Subsection (b) provides guidance for the notary when the seal does not create the legible image required by Section (a). Notaries are authorized to remedy unreadable portions of the seal by typing or printing the needed wording legibly, adjacent to the seal image. To avoid charges that the seal image was tampered with, notaries must not write over any portion of the seal nor make any marks within the area circumscribed by the seal border.

Subsection (c) addresses the use of nonphotographically reproducible embossing seals. Although they may not be used as the official seal and have no official status, they may be affixed to a document for both practical and ceremonial purposes. Adroitly affixed embossing seals can discourage fraudulent attachment of document pages and notary certificates, and facilitate acceptance of documents in foreign jurisdictions where embossments may be expected. Subsection (d) indicates that the notary's mandatory, photographically reproducible seal must not be placed over handwriting, printing or other images, lest wording within the seal image be obscured.

§ 8-4 Obtaining and Providing Official Seal.

(a) In order to sell or manufacture notary seals, a vendor or manufacturer shall apply for a permit from the [commissioning official], who shall charge a fee of [dollars] for issuance of this permit and maintain a controlled-access telephone number or Internet site to allow vendors and manufacturers to confirm the business mailing address and current standing of any notary in the [State].

(b) A vendor or manufacturer shall not provide a notary seal to a purchaser claiming to be a notary, unless the purchaser presents a Certificate of Authorization to Purchase a Notary Seal from the [commissioning official] and a photocopy of the respective notary commission, and unless:

(1) in the case of a purchaser appearing in person, the vendor or manufacturer identifies this individual as the person named in the commission and the Certificate of Authorization, through either personal knowledge or satisfactory evidence of identity; or

(2) in the case of a purchaser ordering a seal by mail or delivery service, the vendor or manufacturer confirms the business mailing address and current standing through the controlled-access telephone number or Internet site.

(c) A vendor or manufacturer shall mail or ship a notary seal only to a mailing address confirmed through the controlled-access telephone number or Internet site.

(d) For each Certificate of Authorization to Purchase a Notary Seal, a vendor or manufacturer shall make or sell one and only one seal, plus, if requested by the person presenting the Certificate, one and only one embossing seal.

(e) After manufacturing or providing a notary seal or seals, the vendor shall affix an image of all seals on the Certificate of Authorization to Purchase a Notary Seal and send the completed Certificate to the [commissioning official], retaining a copy of the Certificate and the Commission for [period of time].

(f) A notary obtaining a seal or seals as a result of a name or business address change shall present a copy of the Confirmation of Notary's Name or Address Change from the [commissioning official] in accordance with Sections 12-1 and 12-2.

(g) A vendor or manufacturer who fails to comply with this section shall be guilty of a [class of offense], punishable upon conviction by a fine not exceeding [dollars]. For multiple violations, a vendor's permission to sell or manufacture notary seals shall be withdrawn by the [commissioning official]. Such conviction shall not preclude the civil liability of the vendor to parties injured by the vendor's failure to comply with this section.

Comment

Section 8-4 establishes the procedure for producing and issuing notary seals. Most jurisdictions have little or no regulation regarding the production of seals. This can make it relatively simple for unscrupulous individuals to obtain a seal fraudulently. The drafters believed that imposing some measure of control over the issuance of seals was warranted. This is consistent with the position taken by some other jurisdictions. (See CAL. GOV'T CODE §§ 8207 to 8207.4; and OR. REV. STAT. § 194.031.)

Subsection (a) requires all seal vendors and manufacturers to be state-approved. The commissioning official must issue a permit to all seal vendors and manufacturers. To facilitate security with mail or Internet orders, the commissioning official must make available to vendors and manufacturers a controlled-access telephone number or Internet site. This allows any purchaser's good standing as a notary and the address to which the seal will be sent to be verified.

Subsection (b) prohibits a vendor or manufacturer from providing any type of notary seal unless a copy of the notary's commission and an original official purchase authorization certificate (see Section 3-4) is supplied by the notary. Additionally, before issuing the seal the vendor or manufacturer must verify that the person is the individual entitled to the seal. The notary must establish identity through satisfactory evidence, or, if the seal is mailed or shipped, the commissioning official's controlled-access roster of addresses must be used to guarantee that delivery is made only to an authorized person.

Subsection (c) reinforces the protection of Subsection (b) by expressly requiring that seals be mailed only to an address listed on the roster maintained by the commissioning official, as mandated by Subsection (a).

Subsection (d) provides that only one official seal may be issued upon presentation of a Certificate of Authorization to Purchase a Notary Seal. Notaries may not order duplicates to hold in the event the original seal is lost or destroyed. However, one embossing seal may be issued in addition to the official seal allowed for each Certificate of Authorization. (Regarding use of an embossing seal, see Subsection 8-3(c) and Comment.)

Subsection (e) provides a procedure for giving a sample of the notary's official seal to the commissioning official, allowing this official to survey issued seals for compliance with the law. The sample may also be useful as evidence in any investigations of the notary's conduct. Subsection (f) gives a procedure for obtaining a new seal in the event of a name or address change by the notary. The commissioning official also must put in place procedures for replacing a lost, stolen, or damaged seal. (See Subsection 8-2(e).)

Subsection (g) imposes criminal, administrative, and possible civil sanctions upon a manufacturer or vendor who violates any terms of the section. The drafters believed this was necessary to ensure that the rules would be properly followed. Imposing penalties is consistent with the view that reasonable efforts should be made to prevent fraud. Since an official seal can easily be used by anyone to generate false notarizations, taking appropriate steps to prevent that from happening is both prudent and justified.

Chapter 9 – Certificates for Notarial Acts

Comment

General: In the former Act, this chapter merely provided model certificates for use by notaries in performing the permitted notarial acts. In this Act, however, the drafters decided to address the common practical issues regarding both the completion and handling of notarial certificates. Three particular matters are addressed: identifying the essential components of a proper notarial certificate (see Section 9-1); properly attaching notarial certificates to notarized documents (see Section 9-2); and properly correcting an error in a notarial certificate (see Section 9-3).

§ 9-1 Notarial Certificate.

(a) For every notarial act involving a document, a notary public of this [State] shall properly complete a notarial certificate that contains or states:

(1) the official signature of the notary, in accordance with Section 8-1;

(2) an impression of the official seal of the notary, in accordance with Section 8-2;

(3) the venue of the notarial act, including the name of this [State] and of the pertinent [county] [parish] [district];

(4) the date of the notarial act; and

(5) the facts and particulars attested by the notary in performing the respective notarial act, as defined in Chapter 2.

(b) A notarial certificate shall be sufficient for a particular notarial act only if it meets the requirements of Subsection 9-1(a) and is in a form that:

(1) is set forth for that act in this Chapter;

(2) is otherwise prescribed for that act by the law of this [State];

(3) is prescribed for that act by a law, regulation, or custom of another jurisdiction, provided it does not require actions by the notary that are unauthorized by this [State]; or

(4) describes the actions of the notary in such a manner as to meet the requirements of the particular notarial act, as defined in Chapter 2.

(c) A notarial certificate shall be worded and completed using only letters, characters, and a language that are read, written, and understood by the notary public.

Comment

Section 9-1 is new and therefore has no counterpart in the former Act. Its focus is the notarial certificate, which provides proof of the performance of a notarization. Given its central importance, the drafters determined that the essential elements for a notarial certificate ought to be delineated beyond the basic definition in Section 2-9. Doing so allows a proper certificate to be recognized by the notary in the event a jurisdiction does not promulgate by statute or rule the certificate forms for permitted notarial acts. Should a document presented for notarization not contain a notarial certificate, or contain a questionable form, this section informs the notary of the minimum elements necessary for a proper certificate. The section does not authorize a notary to select or recommend a specific type of notarial certificate. That would violate the dictate of Subsection 5-12(b) proscribing the unauthorized practice of law. The section, however, does instruct the notary on how to prepare a notarial certificate that is requested or provided by the principal.

Subparagraphs (a)(1) and (2) require that every notarial certificate contain both the official signature and the official seal of the notary, as defined in Sections 2-14 and 2-13, respectively. The references to Sections 8-1 and 8-2 serve to reinforce the requirement that the certificate for notarization of a signed document be completed only in the presence of the principal at the time of the notarization. Notarial certificates for copy certifications and verifications of fact need not be executed in the presence of the requester of fact. (See Section 2-19 and Comment.)

Subparagraph (a)(3) requires every notarial certificate to identify the venue where the notarization was performed. The venue named on the certificate should be the site of the notarial act and not necessarily where the notary is commissioned. Subparagraph (a)(4) mandates that every notarial certificate bear the date of notarization. Subparagraph (a)(5) requires that the certificate state the elements of the particular notarial act performed (e.g., "…personally appeared before me and acknowledged…"). These elements are defined in Chapter 2 for each notarial act authorized in Section 5-1.

Subsection (b) states that a notarial certificate suffices if it is provided or authorized by statute or official rule. Subparagraph (b)(4) specifically recognizes the validity of a notarial certificate whose wording aptly characterizes a notarization but is not prescribed by law. Again, the subsection does not authorize the notary to draft or select the type of certificate to be used. That may constitute the unauthorized practice of law for any notary who is not licensed as an attorney (see Section 5-12) or duly qualified, trained, or licensed in a particular professional field (see Section 5-13).

Subsection (c) complies with the rules provided in Subparagraphs 5-2(5) and (6). The notary must be able to understand the notarial certificate on a document presented for notarization. If the notary cannot comprehend what the certificate says, the notary is prohibited from performing the notarial act.

§ 9-2 Attaching Notarial Certificate.

A paper notarial certificate that is attached to a document during the notarization of the signature of a principal shall:

(1) be attached by stapling or other method that leaves evidence of any subsequent detachment;

(2) be attached, signed, and sealed only by the notary and only at the time of notarization and in the presence of the principal;

(3) be attached immediately following the signature page if the certificate is the same size as that page, or to the front of the signature page if the certificate is smaller; and

(4) contain all of the elements described in Section 9-1 on the same sheet of paper.

Comment

Section 9-2 is also new and therefore has no counterpart in the former Act. The section sets forth the rules for attaching a so called "loose" notarial certificate to a paper document. The reference to "the notarization of the signature of a principal" indicates that the rules prescribed in Section 9-2 need not apply to requests for notarial acts (i.e., copy certifications and verifications of fact) by a requester of fact. (See Section 2-19 and Comment.) The notarial certificate for a copy certification and a verification of fact need not be attached in the presence of a requester of fact; and they typically will be attached as a cover sheet to the front of the certified copy or to copies of document(s) confirming a fact – although a verification of fact certificate may stand on its own. (See Section 9-9 and Comment).

In regard to notarization of the signature of a principal (see Section 2-17), Subparagraph (1) provides that any method of attaching a paper notarial certificate must leave evidence on the notarized document in the event that the certificate is detached (e.g., staple holes). Subparagraph (2) requires that the certificate attachment be made at the time of the notarization and in the principal's presence. This confirms to the principal that the notarial act is complete, and it lessens the possibility that the certificate will be attached to an unintended document. Subparagraph (3) identifies the proper location within the document for certificate attachment Subparagraph (4) provides the important rule that the certificate components be contained entirely on one page. This lessens the risk of fraudulent substitution of portions of the certificate after its execution.

§ 9-3 Correcting Notarial Certificate.

A notary public may correct an error or omission made by that notary in a notarial certificate if:

(1) the original certificate and document are returned to the notary;

(2) the notary verifies the error by reference to the pertinent journal entry, the document itself, or to other determinative written evidence;

(3) the notary legibly corrects the certificate and initials and dates the correction in ink, or replaces the original certificate with a correct certificate; and

(4) the notary appends to the pertinent journal entry a notation regarding the nature and date of the correction.

Comment

Section 9-3 also is new and therefore does not have a counterpart in the former Act. The section addresses how to correct a mistake in a notarial certificate. Subparagraph (1) makes clear that only the notary who completed the erroneous certificate may correct it. The notary may not authorize another person by telephone or e-mail to make a correction, nor may the notary mail or forward a corrected certificate. In order to make the correction, the notary must receive the original document and notarial certificate.

Subparagraph (2) mandates that any correction be corroborated by reviewing information either appearing on the document or entered in the notary's journal, or by reviewing other documentation (e.g., an identification card proving that a principal's name was misspelled on the notarial certificate).

Correctible errors and omissions include missing seals, signatures, and dates; misspellings of names; and incorrect insertions related to the gender or number of principals. Any request to change the nature of the notarial act (e.g., substituting a jurat for an acknowledgment) can be accomplished only by executing a new notarial act. If the principal's representative status was incorrectly stated on the certificate (e.g., attorney in fact rather than partner), it may be necessary for the principal to return to confirm this status. If, for example, the notary has to replace a statutory attorney in fact certificate with one for a signing by a partner – as addressed in Subparagraph (3) – a new notarization and new certificate date would then be needed if there is not any evidence, such as a journal notation, that the signer had declared the correct representative status at the time of the original notarization.

Whatever the corrective change, major or minor, Subparagraph (4) directs the notary to make note of the revision in the journal of notarial acts. (See Section 7-2(e).)

§ 9-4 General Acknowledgment Certificate.

A notary shall use a certificate in substantially the following form in notarizing the signature or mark of any person acknowledging on his or her own behalf or as a partner, corporate officer, attorney in fact, or in any other representative capacity:

[State] of _____
[County] of _____
On this _____ day of _____,20___, before me, the undersigned notary, personally appeared _____ (name of document signer),
  (personally known to me)
  (proved to me through identification documents, which were _____,)
  (proved to me on the oath or affirmation of _____, who is personally known to me and stated to me that (he)(she) personally knows the document signer and is unaffected by the document,)
  (proved to me on the oath or affirmation of _____ and _____, whose identities have been proven to me through identification documents and who have stated to me that they personally know the document signer and are unaffected by the document,)
to be the person whose name is signed on the preceding or attached document, and acknowledged to me that (he)(she) signed it voluntarily for its stated purpose(.)
  (as partner for _____, a partnership.)
  (as _____ for _____, a corporation.)
  (as attorney in fact for _____, the principal.)
  (as _____ for _____, (a)(the) _____.)

_____
(official signature and seal of notary)

Comment

Section 9-4 provides a general, "all-purpose" acknowledgment form adaptable to principals with different signing capacities. To comply with Section 2-20, the model form has language compelling credible witnesses to state specifically that they do not have any interest in the transaction related to the document being notarized. The form also includes language relating to the principal's volition in response to the rule for the notarial act of acknowledgment set out in Subparagraph 2-1(3). Both of these provisions are innovations not found in most notary acknowledgment certificates.

§ 9-5 Jurat Certificate.

A notary shall use a jurat certificate in substantially the following form in notarizing a signature or mark on an affidavit or other sworn or affirmed written declaration:

[State] of _____
[County] of _____
On this _____ day of _____, 20___, before me, the undersigned notary, personally appeared _____ (name of document signer),
  (personally known to me)
  (proved to me through identification documents, which were _____,)
  (proved to me on the oath or affirmation of _____, who is personally known to me and stated to me that (he)(she) personally knows the document signer and is unaffected by the document,)
  (proved to me on the oath or affirmation of _____ and _____, whose identities have been proven to me through identification documents and who have stated to me that they personally know the document signer and are unaffected by the document,)
to be the person who signed the preceding or attached document in my presence and who swore or affirmed to me that the contents of the document are truthful and accurate to the best of (his)(her) knowledge and belief.

_____
(official signature and seal of notary)

Comment

Section 9-5 provides a model form for a standard jurat certificate. As with the acknowledgment form (see Section 9-4), how the signer was identified must be specified. In many states, identification of the signer is not an express statutory requirement for a jurat, as it is with an acknowledgment. Attention should be paid to the form's language regarding the oath or affirmation, which the notary must not neglect to administer to the principal. (See Subparagraph 2-7(4) and Comment.).

§ 9-6 Signature Witnessing Certificate.

A notary shall use a certificate in substantially the following form in notarizing a signature or mark to confirm that it was affixed in the notary's presence without administration of an oath or affirmation:

[State] of _____
[County] of _____
On this _____ day of _____, 20___, before me, the undersigned notary, personally appeared _____ (name of document signer),
  (personally known to me)
  (proved to me through identification documents, which were _____,)
  (proved to me on the oath or affirmation of _____, who is personally known to me and stated to me that (he)(she) personally knows the document signer and is unaffected by the document,)
  (proved to me on the oath or affirmation of _____ and _____, whose identities have been proven to me through identification documents and who have stated to me that they personally know the document signer and are unaffected by the document,)
to be the person who signed the preceding or attached document in my presence.

_____
(official signature and seal of notary)

Comment

Section 9-6 provides a certificate for a signature witnessing. As defined in Section 2-21, this notarial act only requires the principal to appear, prove identity, and sign. Although silent on point, the certificate does not eliminate the need for the conscientious notary to take the standard precautions for ensuring the principal's awareness and willingness to sign. (See Subparagraphs 5-2(3) and (4).)

§ 9-7 Certificates for Signer by Mark and Person Unable to Sign.

On paper documents, certificates in Sections 9-4, 9-5, and 9-6 may be used for signers by mark or persons physically unable to sign or make a mark if:

(1) for a signer by mark, the notary and 2 witnesses disinterested in the document observe the affixation of the mark, both witnesses sign their own names beside the mark, and the notary writes below the mark: "Mark affixed by (name of signer by mark) in the presence of (names and addresses of 2 witnesses) and the undersigned notary pursuant to Section 5-3 of [Act]"; or

(2) for a person physically unable to sign or make a mark, the person directs the notary to sign on his or her behalf in the presence of 2 witnesses disinterested in the document, both witnesses sign their own names beside the signature, and the notary writes below the signature: "Signature affixed by the notary at the direction and in the presence of (name of principal unable to sign or make a mark) and also in the presence of (names and addresses of 2 witnesses) pursuant to Section 5-4 of [Act]".

Comment

Section 9-7 provides formats and procedures allowing use of the previous three certificates (see Sections 9-4, 9-5, and 9-6) when the principal's signature is made by mark or by the notary as a substitute signer (see Sections 5-3 and 5-4). In either case, it is possible that a credible witness who was used to identify the principal (see Subparagraph 2-20(2)) may additionally serve to witness the signing by mark or the proxy signing of the principal's signature by the notary.

§ 9-8 Certified Copy Certificate.

A notary shall use a certificate in substantially the following form in notarizing a certified copy:

[State] of _____
[County] of _____
On this _____ day of _____, 20___, I certify that the
  (attached or following paper document)
  (affixed, attached, or logically associated electronic document)
has been (visually) (electronically) confirmed by me to be a true, exact, and complete copy of the image (or text) (and metadata) of _____(description of original document),
  (presented/e-mailed to me by _____,)
  (found by me (online) at _____,)
  (held in my custody as a notarial record,)
and that, to the best of my knowledge, the copied document is neither a vital record, a public record, nor a publicly recordable document, certified copies of which may be available from an official source other than a notary public.

_____
(official signature and seal of notary)

Comment

Section 9-8 provides the form for a copy certification. It has been significantly revised from the former Act to allow for copy certification of electronic as well as paper documents. (See the corresponding new definition of "copy certification" in Section 2-4.) As more fully explained in the Comment for Section 2-4, the form accommodates a copy certification request by a person not in the physical presence of the notary; enables a notary to search and find online an electronic document that is to be copy-certified; and allows the notary to indicate whether hidden "metadata" are included in the copy. As did the former certificate for a certified copy of a paper document, the form accommodates certification of the notary's own records. The certificate makes clear that the notary is prohibited from certifying copies of certain records and that in making the copy the notary believes he or she is complying with that proscription.

§ 9-9 Verification of Fact Certificate.

A notary shall use a certificate in substantially the following form in verifying a fact or facts:

[State] of _____
[County] of _____
On this _____ day of _____, 20___, I certify that I have reviewed the following record(s) or data,
  (a) _____,
  (b) _____,
  (c) _____,
  (d) _____,
at the following office, Internet or electronic system locations, respectively,
  (a) _____,
  (b) _____,
  (c) _____,
  (d) _____ _____,
or upon the record(s) being presented to me by _____, and hereby verify the following respective fact(s) as stated in these records:
  (a) _____,
  (b) _____,
  (c) _____,
  (d) _____.

_____
(official signature and seal of notary)

Comment

Section 9-9 provides a certificate for the notary to complete in performing a verification of fact. (See Section 2-22 and Comment.) This type of notarial act can be used to confirm data on vital records such as birth certificates and marriage licenses, thereby certifying information often needed for the adoption of a foreign child.

While, in the interest of fraud deterrence, it is preferable that such records be reviewed by the notary in the offices of the records' duly designated public custodians (e.g., bureau of vital statistics or office of the county clerk), the form also allows the notary to review records presented by a private individual. It is left to the discretion of the relying third party as to whether such records are trustworthy.

Unlike other certificates in this chapter, this certificate need not be attached to another document. The certificate constitutes a complete notarial act in and of itself. It does not require the notarization of a signature and it need not be completed in the presence of the requester of fact. (See Section 2-19 and Comment.)

Chapter 10 – Evidence of Authenticity of Notarial Act

Comment

General: This chapter presents authentication forms that may be required by other jurisdictions of the United States or by foreign nations before recognizing notarial acts performed by a notary outside those jurisdictions. A principal goal of the Act is to establish uniform rules throughout the states of this nation. If achieved, state-to-state authentications might not be needed. Even if that overarching goal is realized, there would still be the need to authenticate notarial acts to enable their recognition by foreign nations. This chapter addresses that need, as well as offering the standard form for the internationally recognized Apostille.

§ 10-1 Forms of Evidence.

On a notarized document sent to another state or nation,

evidence of the authenticity of the official seal and signature of a notary of this [State], if required, shall be in the form of:

(1) a certificate of authority from the [commissioning official] and/ or [designated local official], authenticated as necessary by additional certificates from United States and/or foreign government agencies; or

(2) in the case of a notarized document to be used in a nation that has signed and ratified the Hague Convention Abolishing the Requirement of Legalization for Foreign Public Documents of October 5, 1961, an Apostille from the [federally designated official] in the form prescribed by the Convention and described in Section 10-3, with no additional authenticating certificates required.

Comment

Section 10-1 sets the rule that there are only two types of acceptable evidence of authentication. One is a Certificate of Authority provided in Section 10-2. The other is the Apostille found in Section 10-3.

§ 10-2 Certificate of Authority.

A certificate of authority evidencing the authenticity of the official seal and signature of a notary of this [State] shall be substantially in the following form:

Certificate of Authority for a Notarial Act

I, _____ (name, title, jurisdiction of authenticating official), certify that _____ (name of notary), the person named in the seal and signature on the attached document, was a Notary Public for the [State] of _____ [name of jurisdiction] and authorized to act as such at the time of the document's notarization.

To verify this Certificate of Authority for a Notarial Act, I have affixed below my signature and seal of office this _____ day of _____, 20___.

(Signature and seal of commissioning official)

Comment

Section 10-2 presents a Certificate of Authority evidencing the authenticity of a notary's signature and seal. Although this exact form need not be used, it provides all of the necessary information that must be included in such a certificate. Note, the certificate must be executed by the commissioning official or a designated local official, such as a county clerk, who has evidence of the notary's authority on file. In the case of official acts performed by electronic notaries, an adaptation of the form is provided in Section 22-2.

§ 10-3 Apostille.

An Apostille prescribed by the Hague Convention Abolishing the Requirement of Legalization for Foreign Public Documents of October 5, 1961, shall be in the form of a square with sides at least 9 centimeters long and contain exactly the following wording:

APOSTILLE
(Convention de La Haye du 5 octobre 1961)
1. Country: _____
   This public document
2. has been
   signed by _____
3. acting in
   the capacity of _____
4. bears the seal/stamp of _____
   CERTIFIED
5. at _____   6. the _____
7. by _____
8. No. _____
9. Seal/Stamp   10. Signature: _____

Comment

Section 10-3 sets out the Apostille form as prescribed in an annex to the Hague Convention Abolishing the Requirement of Legalization for Foreign Public Documents. This Convention was concluded on October 5, 1961, by the Hague Conference on Private International Law, and entered into force on January 24, 1965. The rules regarding the format of the Apostille, which may be used to authenticate the acts of a variety of state or territorial officials, must be observed exactly. An Apostille evidencing a notary's authority is to be completed by the office of a federally designated state or territorial official, normally the official who commissioned the notary. On line 3, the capacity "Notary Public" would be indicated, and on line 4 the name of the notary would be placed. The venue of the authentication, typically the state capital, would be written on line 5, and the date of the authentication on line 6.

§ 10-4 Fees.

The [commissioning/federally designated official] may charge:

(1) for issuing a certificate of authority, [dollars]; and

(2) for issuing an Apostille, [dollars].

Comment

Section 10-4 authorizes the authenticating official to charge a fee to cover the administrative costs of issuing a Certificate of Authority or an Apostille. The jurisdiction may wish to include in the fee schedule changes for special services such as "while-you-wait" or "overnight-return" authentications.

Chapter 11 – Recognition of Notarial Acts

Comment

General: This chapter has been added to the Act to remedy a deficiency of its predecessor. The drafters determined that a model act ought to have rules regulating the recognition of notarial acts from other jurisdictions. The rules provided here are congruent with the positions taken on point in the UNIFORM LAW ON NOTARIAL ACTS (14 U.L.A. 202 (2005)).

§ 11-1 Notarial Acts by Officers of This [State].

(a) A notarial act may be performed within this [State] by the following persons:

(1) a notary public of this [State];

(2) a judge, clerk, or deputy clerk of any court of this [State]; [or]

(3) [designation[s] of other officer[s]; or

(4)] any other officer authorized to perform a specific notarial act by the law of this [State].

(b) The official signature, seal, and title of a person authorized by Subsection (a) to perform a notarial act are prima facie evidence that the signature and seal are genuine and that the person holds the indicated title.

Comment

Section 11-1 provides general guidance on notarial acts performed within the jurisdiction. Subsection (a) identifies all of the officials authorized to perform notarial acts. Subsection (b) provides that the collective appearance on a notarial certificate of the signature, seal, and title of the person authorized to perform notarial acts self-proves the genuineness of those items and that the person actually holds the title indicated.

§ 11-2 Notarial Acts by Officers of Other United States Jurisdictions.

(a) A notarial act has the same effect under the law of this [State] as if performed by a notarial officer of this [State] if performed in another state, commonwealth, territory, district, or possession of the United States by any of the following persons:

(1) a notary public of that jurisdiction;

(2) a judge, clerk, or deputy clerk of a court of that jurisdiction; or

(3) any other person authorized by the law of that jurisdiction to perform notarial acts.

(b) The official signature, title, and, if required by law, seal of a person whose authority to perform notarial acts is recognized by Subsection (a) are prima facie evidence that the signature and seal are genuine and that the person holds the indicated title, and, except in the case of Subparagraph (a)(3), conclusively establishes the authority of a holder of that title to perform a notarial act.

Comment

Section 11-2 provides that notarial acts performed in other American states, districts, territories, and possessions are to be given the same effect as if they were performed by a duly authorized officer within the home jurisdiction, provided that the notarial act was executed by a person so authorized to do so in that other jurisdiction. As does Subsection 11-1(b), Subsection 11-2(b) allows a notarizing official's certificate to be self-proving if it bears the official's signature, title, and, if local law requires its use, the seal of office; however, unless the official is a notary or a judge, clerk, or deputy clerk of a court, further evidence may be needed to prove that a person holding the cited title has notarial powers.

While it might be argued that the "full faith and credit" clause of the United States Constitution renders this section redundant, notarial acts performed lawfully in one U.S. jurisdiction unfortunately may be rejected improperly in other U.S. jurisdictions, due to cosmetic inconsistencies or policy disagreements between governments. This section reinforces the obligation to honor lawfully performed notarial acts originating in other jurisdictions of the United States. (See, e.g., Apsey v. Memorial Hospital, 730 N.W. 2d 695 (Mich. 2007), in which the Supreme Court of Michigan ruled that an affidavit in a medical malpractice suit executed before a Pennsylvania notary must be accepted in a Michigan court without certification by the clerk within the notary's county.)

§ 11-3 Notarial Acts by Federal Officers of United States.

(a) A notarial act has the same effect under the law of this [State] as if performed by a notarial officer of this [State] if performed anywhere by any of the following persons under authority granted by the law of the United States:

(1) a judge, clerk, or deputy clerk of a court;

(2) a commissioned United States military officer on active duty;

(3) a foreign service or consular officer of the United States; or

(4) any other person authorized by federal law to perform notarial acts.

(b) The official signature, title, and, if required by law, seal of a person whose authority to perform notarial acts is recognized by Subsection (a) are prima facie evidence that the signature and seal are genuine, that the person holds the indicated title, and, except in the case of Subsection (a)(4), conclusively establishes the authority of a holder of that title to perform a notarial act.

Comment

Section 11-3 provides that notarial acts performed anywhere in the world by U.S. federal officers pursuant to lawful authority granted to them must be given full recognition and treated as if they were performed within the home jurisdiction by a duly authorized officer of the jurisdiction. Subsection (a) identifies federal officials who possess notarial powers. As do Subsections 11-1(b) and 11-2(b), Subsection 11-3(b) allows a notarizing official's certificate to be self-proving if it bears the official's signature, title, and, if federal law requires its use, the seal of office. If, however, the official is not a judge, clerk, or deputy clerk of a court, a commissioned U.S. military officer on active duty, or a U.S. foreign service or consular officer, further evidence may be needed to prove that a person holding the cited title has notarial powers.

§ 11-4 Notarial Acts by Foreign Officers.

(a) A notarial act has the same effect under the law of this [State] as if performed by a notarial officer of this [State] if performed within the jurisdiction and under authority of a foreign nation or its constituent units or a multi-national or international organization by any of the following persons:

(1) a notary public or other notarial officer;

(2) a judge, clerk, or deputy clerk of a court of record; or

(3) any other person authorized by the law of that jurisdiction to perform notarial acts.

(b) The official seal or stamp of a person whose authority to perform notarial acts is recognized by Subsection (a) are prima facie evidence that the signature is genuine, that the person holds the indicated title, and, except in the case of Subsection (a)(3), conclusively establishes the authority of a holder of that title to perform a notarial act.

(c) The authority of an officer to perform notarial acts is conclusively established if the title of the office and indication of authority to perform notarial acts appears either in a digest of foreign law or a list customarily used as a source for that information.

(d) An Apostille in the form prescribed by Section 10-3 conclusively establishes that the signature and seal of the notarial officer referenced in the Apostille are genuine and that the person holds the indicated office.

(e) A certificate of a foreign service or consular officer of the United States stationed in the nation under whose jurisdiction the notarial act was performed, or a certificate of a foreign service or consular officer of that nation stationed in the United States, conclusively establishes any matter relating to the authenticity or validity of the notarial act referenced in the certificate.

Comment

Section 11-4 puts notarial acts performed by duly authorized officials of foreign nations on the same legal footing as those performed by notaries in the home jurisdiction. Subsection (a) designates the types of foreign official whose notarial acts will be recognized. Subsection (b) allows a notarizing foreign official's certificate to be self-proving if it bears the official's seal or stamp. Again, if the official is not a notary or a judge, clerk, or deputy clerk of a court of record, further evidence may be needed to prove that a person with the cited title has notarial powers. Subsection (c) states that the authority to perform notarial acts of a foreign official is proven if the title and authority of such an officer is listed in a commonly accepted source. Subsection (d) mandates that an Apostille (see Section 10-3) authenticating a foreign notarial certificate must be accepted as genuine. Subsection (e) asserts that any matter related to the authenticity or validity of a foreign notarial certificate may be settled by the certificate of a U.S. foreign service or consular officer stationed in the respective nation, or by the certificate of a foreign service or consular official of that nation stationed in the United States. All of the subsections work together to ensure that notarial acts properly performed in foreign nations will be duly recognized in the jurisdiction adopting the section.

Chapter 12 – Changes of Status of Notary Public

Comment

General: This chapter addresses the administrative steps to be taken when a notary changes his or her name, address, or commission status. Easy-to-follow rules are established to ensure that proper notice is received by the commissioning official. Importantly, the Act does not merely impose a notification requirement, but goes on to mandate that the notifying party (the notary or the notary's representative) actually verify receipt of the notice. Any notice required by this chapter may be sent electronically.

§ 12-1 Change of Address.

(a) Within 10 days after the change of a notary's residence, business, or mailing address, the notary shall send to the [commissioning official] by any means providing a tangible receipt, including certified mail and electronic transmission, a signed notice of the change, giving both old and new addresses.

(b) If the business address is changed, the notary shall not notarize until:

(1) the notice described in Subsection (a) has been delivered or transmitted;

(2) a Confirmation of Notary's Name or Address Change has been received from the [commissioning official];

(3) a new seal bearing the new business address has been obtained; and

(4) the surety for the notary's bond has been informed in writing.

Comment

Section 12-1 imposes a notification requirement for any address change by the notary. The notification must be made within 10 calendar days after the change. Some address changes may impact commission status and necessitate resignation of the office. (See Subsection 12-3(b).) All notices must include both the old and new address. Since the notary's business address appears in the official seal, any change in business address requires that a new seal be obtained. (See Subparagraph (b)(3).) Further notarizations are prohibited until this is done.

§ 12-2 Change of Name.

(a) Within 10 days after the change of a notary's name by court order or marriage, the notary shall send to the [commissioning official] by any means providing a tangible receipt, including certified mail and electronic transmission, a signed notice of the change, giving both former and new names, with a copy of any official authorization for such change.

(b) A notary with a new name shall continue to use the former name in performing notarial acts until the following steps have been completed, at which point the notary shall use the new name:

(1) the notice described in Subsection (a) has been delivered or transmitted;

(2) a Confirmation of Notary's Name or Address Change has been received from the [commissioning official];

(3) a new seal bearing the new name exactly as in the Confirmation has been obtained; and

(4) the surety for the notary's bond has been informed in writing.

Comment

Section 12-2 provides guidance when a notary changes his or her name. The Act only contemplates official name changes, i.e., pursuant to court order or through marriage. Using a different name familiarly will not affect one's official name for notary public purposes. The notification process for a name change generally mirrors the procedure for an address change, including requirements to notify the commissioning authority within 10 calendar days and to obtain a new seal reflecting the change. (See Section 12-1) However, a notary may continue notarizing using a former name until a seal bearing the new name is obtained. (See Subsection (b).) In contrast, a notary having moved to a new business address may not notarize until a seal bearing that new address has been obtained. The drafters felt that knowing where to find a notary who has moved is more critical than keeping track of the current name of a notary at a known location in the event a questionable notarization has been performed.

§ 12-3 Resignation.

(a) A notary who resigns his or her commission shall send to the [commissioning official] by any means providing a tangible receipt, including certified mail and electronic transmission, a signed notice indicating the effective date of resignation.

(b) Notaries who cease to reside in or to maintain a regular place of work or business in this [State], or who become permanently unable to perform their notarial duties, shall resign their commissions.

Comment

Section 12-3 requires that proper notification be given to the commissioning official when a notary resigns a commission. Additionally, Subsection (b) establishes the rule that a notary who, because of a change of address, no longer has a qualifying nexus in the jurisdiction, must resign the notary commission. The rule applies equally to notaries residing outside of the commissioning jurisdiction who fail to maintain a regular place of business within the jurisdiction. The subsection also mandates that any notary who can no longer perform the duties of office resign. The Act thereby forces notaries to self evaluate their status, another step toward professionalizing the office.

§ 12-4 Disposition of Seal and Journal.

(a) Except as provided in Subsection (b), when a notary commission expires or is resigned or revoked, the notary shall:

(1) as soon as reasonably practicable, destroy or deface all notary seals so that they may not be misused; and

(2) within 30 days after the effective date of resignation, revocation, or expiration, dispose of the journal and notarial records in accordance with Section 7-5 of this [Act].

(b) A former notary who intends to apply for a new commission and whose previous commission or application was not revoked or denied by this [State], need not dispose of the journal and notarial records within 30 days after commission expiration, but must do so within 3 months after expiration unless recommissioned within that period.

Comment

Section 12-4 deals with the proper disposition of the incidents of office when a notary commission terminates for any reason. To prevent its unauthorized use, the notary must destroy or deface the official seal and any unofficial embossers. (See Subparagraph (a)(1).) How this is best accomplished is left to the judgment of the notary.

Subparagraph (a)(2) requires the former notary, within 30 calendar days after termination of the commission, to deliver the notary journal and any notarial records to the office designated by the commissioning official in Section 7-5. Subsection (b) carves out an exception to the 30- day-delivery rule. It allows a notary who intends to renew an expired commission up to three months to complete the process. If, however, within that time the commission has not been renewed, the journal and accompanying records must then be forwarded to the commissioning official.

§ 12-5 Death of Notary.

If a notary dies during the term of commission or before fulfilling the obligations stipulated in Section 12-4, the notary's personal representative shall:

(1) notify the [commissioning official] of the death in writing;

(2) as soon as reasonably practicable, destroy or deface all notary seals so that they may not be misused; and

(3) within 30 days after death, dispose of the journal and notarial records in accordance with Section 7-5 of this [Act].

Comment

Section 12-5 addresses disposal of a deceased notary's official seal and journal, and notification of the commissioning authority regarding the death. Destruction or defacement of the seal and proper delivery of the journal, to be performed by the notary pursuant to Section 12-4 after termination of a commission, are instead to be performed by the decedent's personal representative. Although in many cases this may be a surviving spouse, any proper successor in interest is authorized to perform this task. In regard to the disposition of an electronic journal upon the death of the notary, the notary's personal representative may first have to contact the commissioning official in order to learn journal access instructions (see Sections 7-6; 4- 2(9); and 16-4(3)) for the purpose of meeting the obligations imposed by this section.

In the event of the disappearance or permanent incapacity of the notary, any individual legally designated to attend to or settle the notary's affairs may perform the acts required in this section. (See Section 7-6 Comment.)

Chapter 13 – Liability, Sanctions, and Remedies for Improper Acts

Comment

General: This chapter provides rules for handling situations in which notaries have acted improperly incident to the performance of their official duties. The drafters believed notaries should be fully accountable for their official actions, and to this end imposed personal liability on them for any of their actions that result in damages to others. Additionally, since the Act mandates bonding (see Section 3-3), the drafters included rules to maximize an injured party's access to the bond. The Act also applies traditional liability rules to broaden the available resources from which damages caused by employee-notaries may be recovered. The balance of the chapter enumerates criminal and disciplinary sanctions that may be imposed on notaries who breach their obligations or violate rules of law in the performance of their official duties.

§ 13-1 Liability of Notary, Surety, and Employer.

(a) A notary is liable to any person for all damages proximately caused that person by the notary's negligence, intentional violation of law, or official misconduct in relation to a notarization.

(b) A surety for a notary's bond is liable to any person for damages proximately caused that person by the notary's negligence, intentional violation of law, or official misconduct in relation to a notarization during the bond term, but this liability may not exceed the dollar amount of the bond or of any remaining bond funds that have not been disbursed to other claimants. Regardless of the number of claimants against the bond or the number of notarial acts cited in the claims, a surety's aggregate liability shall not exceed the dollar amount of the bond.

(c) An employer of a notary is liable to any person for all damages proximately caused that person by the notary's negligence, intentional violation of law, or official misconduct in performing a notarization during the course of employment, if the employer directed, expected, encouraged, approved, or tolerated the notary's negligence, violation of law, or official misconduct either in the particular transaction or, impliedly, by the employer's previous action in at least one similar transaction involving any notary employed by the employer.

(d) An employer of a notary is liable to the notary for all damages recovered from the notary as a result of any violation of law by the notary that was coerced by threat of the employer, if the threat, such as of demotion or dismissal, was made in reference to the particular notarization or, impliedly, by the employer's previous action in at least one similar transaction involving any notary employed by the employer. In addition, the employer is liable to the notary for damages caused the notary by demotion, dismissal, or other action resulting from the notary's refusal to engage in a violation of law or official misconduct.

(e) Notwithstanding any other provision in this Act, for the purposes of this section "negligence" shall not include any good-faith determination made by the notary pursuant to the obligations imposed by Subparagraph 5-2 (3) or (4).

Comment

Subsection 13-1(a) establishes the basic rule that a notary is liable for damages directly resulting from the improper performance of a notarial act. The notary may be held responsible for either a negligent or an intentional act. Intentional acts that can create liability include acts that are either unlawful or constitute official misconduct. (See Section 2-12.) Consistent with the modern trend (see, e.g., IND. CODE ANN. § 33-42-4-2), the Act specifically rejects the antiquated view that a notary as a public official is entitled to sovereign immunity (see May v. Jones, 14 S.E. 552 (Ga. 1891)).

Subsection (b) obligates the surety for the notary's bond for damage recoveries permitted by Subsection (a). Recovery, however, is limited to the unused balance of the bond. A surety is not responsible for more than the dollar value of the bond. Multiple claims are to be prioritized pursuant to local law.

Subsection (c) limits the respondent superior doctrine for employee-notaries to a few, select situations. Although the doctrine may be applied in employee-notary situations without limitation (see, e.g., FLA. STAT. ANN. § 117.05(6)), the Act employs a more stringent application that requires additional action by the employer before imposing any liability for an employee notary's notarization. The drafters decided that the tension between the notary as an independent public servant and an employee warranted the approach adopted. To reinforce the independence of the office, the drafters wanted to iterate the fact that a notary is first and foremost a public servant, whose duty to the public overrides obligations to an employer. An employer cannot control a notary's performance of official duties. Consequently, it would be unfair always to hold the employer accountable for the employee-notary's behavior. Thus, the Act only imposes liability on the employer where the employer's own actions caused, facilitated, or permitted the improper behavior. (Accord VA. CODE ANN. § 47.1-27, which requires an employer to have actual knowledge of an improper practice, or reasonably be obliged to know, before liability is imposed.)

In order for an employer to be liable for a recovery permitted by Subsection (a), the employee must not only perform the notarization within the scope of employment, but the employer must also actively or impliedly "consent" to the notary's specific improper notarial act. Active "consent" includes directing, approving, or tolerating the notary's behavior. For these purposes, "tolerating" is the functional equivalent of tacit approval. It connotes an awareness of the behavior without taking any steps to correct or prevent it from recurring. Additionally, encouraging or expecting an employee notary to perform improper notarial acts will constitute active "consent." The facts of each particular case will have to be reviewed to ascertain when the employer encouraged the notary to perform an improper notarization. The same is true for those cases in which the injured party will try to demonstrate how the employer "expected" the behavior.

As to implied "consent," the Act simply provides that any past action or inaction by the employer concerning a particular improper notarization will carry forward to a later improper notarization. The theory is that the employee may reasonably rely on the employer's past action (or inaction, as the case may be) as a guide to a present act. If an objection was not raised earlier, there is no reason to believe it would be raised now. Thus, under the implied "consent" rule, an employer may be liable for a notarization despite being totally unaware it was performed by the employee-notary. The employer's failure to properly address a prior improper notarization can provide the basis for liability resulting from a future improper notarization.

The implied "consent" rule can be applied to an improper notarization by any of an employer's notaries. It is not limited to only the future improper notarizations of the notary who performed a prior improper notarization. The theory justifying the broad application of the rule is that employees are charged with knowledge of company policies and normally are aware of the acts of similar coworkers. It would be inappropriate to allow an employer to escape responsibility because a different employee-notary relying on past company practice performed the improper act. The Act effectively imposes an affirmative obligation on employers to promulgate and implement adequate internal controls to ensure that employee-notaries perform notarizations properly.

Subsection (d) serves to protect the notary financially from damages resulting from an improper notarization coerced by the employer. Generally, Subsection (a) makes the notary liable for damages resulting from all improper notarizations. The Act takes the position that if, under Subsection (c), the employer is found responsible for a specific improper notarial act, then the notary should be indemnified by the employer for any costs imposed upon the notary for following the employer's dictates. In adopting this position, the drafters recognize that a notary can be put in an untenable position: either perform the improper act or possibly suffer an employment penalty, including loss of job. Ideally, one would like to think the notary would demonstrate independence and refuse to perform the improper notarization. But reality suggests that usually this will not be the case, especially when the employee notary is young and inexperienced. Thus, although the notary remains primarily liable for his or her improper acts, the financial costs for those which are coerced by an employer should ultimately be borne by the employer who causes them. Nothing in this section exculpates the notary from responsibility for the improper act, and appropriate sanctions may be imposed by the commissioning official for it. (See Sections 13-3 and 13-4.)

This subsection also imposes financial obligations on an employer who penalizes a notary for failing to obey a request to perform an illegal notarization. The employer will be held responsible for recompensing the notary for any monetary loss incurred by any employment action taken by the employer that effectively constitutes retaliation for the refusal to follow the illegal request. The drafters believed that this rule was necessary to give teeth to the general proscription against coercing employees into performing illegal notarizations. Without it, an employer could too easily sidestep the ban.

Subsection (e) serves to insulate notaries who properly refuse to execute notarizations. The protection is specifically confined to those situations wherein the notary believes the principal lacks either the capacity to understand the underlying consequences of, or the independent volition to proceed with, the notarization. These are the mandates from Subparagraphs 5-2(3) and (4), respectively. The drafters strongly believe that notaries should refrain from acting in these situations, but feared they might be hesitant to do so. Whether a layperson could make the informed judgment required by the Act was a concern. The "good faith determination" defense was added to encourage notaries to adhere to the rule.

Notaries are not expected to make informed evaluations based upon either lengthy discussions with principals or reviews of medical documents. The Act simply calls for a commonsense assessment drawn from the circumstances attendant to the notarization request. Under these conditions, a notary who refuses to perform the notarization based on a good-faith determination that the principal failed to satisfy either the "capacity" or "volition" test is exculpated from any liability that might result from such refusal, Notaries are required to record refusals to notarize in their journals. (See Subsection 7-2(c).) The drafters, however, caution the notary to use care when making this entry. A simple recitation of the circumstances that led to the determination is sufficient.

§ 13-2 Proximate Cause.

Recovery of damages against a notary, surety, or employer does not require that the notary's negligence, violation of law, or official misconduct be either the sole or principal proximate cause of the damages.

Comment

Section 13-2 provides a special definition of "proximate cause" for purposes of the Act. It expands the traditional notion of "proximate cause" as applied in tort cases. Generally, "proximate cause" is the "primary," "dominant," or "moving" cause for an event. (See BLACK'S LAW DICTIONARY 234 (8th ed. West 2004).) The Act creates liability so long as the notary's wrongful official act contributes to the damages; it need not be the sole cause of the injury. (Accord 5 ILCS 312/7-103; and MO. REV. STAT. § 486.365.) For this purpose, "wrongful" refers to conduct identified in Subsection 13-1(a). Additionally, the provision imputes the same "contributing cause" rule to both the notary's surety and the employer who may be liable for the improper notarization pursuant to Subsection 13-1(c).

§ 13-3 Revocation.

(a) The [commissioning official] may revoke a notary commission for any ground on which an application for a commission may be denied under Section 3-1(c).

(b) The [commissioning official] shall revoke the commission of any notary who fails:

(1) to maintain a residence or a regular place of work or business in this [State]; and

(2) to maintain status as a legal resident of the United States.

(c) Prior to revocation of a notary commission, the [commissioning official] shall inform the notary of the basis for the revocation and that the revocation takes effect on a particular date unless a proper appeal is filed with the [administrative body hearing appeal] before that date.

(d) Resignation or expiration of a notary commission does not terminate or preclude an investigation into the notary's conduct by the [commissioning official], who may pursue the investigation to a conclusion, whereupon it shall be made a matter of public record whether or not the finding would have been grounds for revocation.

Comment

Section 13-3 both authorizes the commissioning official to revoke a notary commission, and prescribes procedural rules to effectuate the decision. Subsection (a) provides that a notary commission may be revoked for any of the reasons that may be used to deny a notary application. These are set out in Subsection 3-1(c). The drafters believed that an act sufficiently serious in nature to deny an application ought to provide the basis for a revocation if committed or discovered after the commission was granted. Thus, an act that could have provided the basis for an application denial, if properly disclosed upon the application, cannot become the basis for a subsequent commission revocation. If the act were not disclosed on the application, that may be a ground for revocation whenever discovered. To hold otherwise would encourage applicants to hide relevant information from the commissioning authority.

Subsection 13-3(b) implements the requirements of Subparagraph 3-1(b)(2) regarding having a sufficient nexus in the state to warrant receiving a notary commission. Section 2-18 defines "regular place of work or business" for this purpose. If the nexus is severed after the commission is granted, the commission must be revoked. (Accord NEB. REV. STAT. § 64-112.) The Act, by its silence, allows the commissioning jurisdiction to determine both local and United States residency.

Subsection (c) requires the commissioning official to give the notary proper notice of the revocation. The notice must inform the notary of a) the basis for revocation, b) the date when the revocation is to take place, and c) the notary's specific appeal rights. The Act holds that the notary may continue to perform notarizations until the effective revocation date on the notice. The commission, however, may be suspended during the pendency of any appeal.

Subsection (d) reinforces the view that a notary should be held accountable for any improper official act. Thus, resigning a commission or merely letting it expire will not end or preclude any investigatory process and possible subsequent disciplinary action. Moreover, the subsection provides that when the appropriate authority proceeds against a former notary, the action becomes a matter of public record.

§ 13-4 Other Remedial Actions for Misconduct.

(a) The [commissioning official] may deliver a written Official Warning to Cease Misconduct to any notary whose actions are judged to be official misconduct.

(b) The [commissioning official] may seek a court injunction to prevent a person from violating any provision of this [Act].

Comment

Section 13-4 permits the commissioning official to reprimand a notary for matters not warranting greater discipline. The Act establishes an Official Warning sanction. This disciplinary action allows the official to notify the notary that he or she is engaging in official misconduct and must cease such activity. Should the warning not prove effective, or the activities be sufficiently egregious, the commissioning official may seek injunctive relief from the courts. The subsection gives the commissioning official broad discretion to seek injunctive relief to prevent any provision of the Act from being violated. The drafters intended this authority to extend to nonnotaries as well. Thus, the commissioning official could seek to enjoin any person from violating the provisions of the Act. (For examples of non-notary infractions, see Chapter 14.)

§ 13-5 Publication of Sanctions and Remedial Actions.

The [commissioning official] shall regularly publish a list of persons whose notary commissions have been revoked by the [commissioning official] or whose actions as a notary were the subject of a court injunction or Official Warning to Cease Misconduct.

Comment

Section 13-5 requires a list of the names of notaries who have had their commissions revoked and of notaries who have received an Official Warning to Cease Misconduct to be published. The drafters thought that such a regular public posting would have a fraud ARTICLE deterrent utility in alerting the public about notaries who have been sanctioned. Also, it would impose a stigma that conscientious notaries would strive to avoid.

§ 13-6 Criminal Sanctions.

(a) In performing a notarial act, a notary is guilty of a [class of offense], punishable upon conviction by a fine not exceeding [dollars] or imprisonment for not more than [term of imprisonment], or both, for knowingly:

(1) failing to require the presence of a principal at the time of the notarial act;

(2) failing to identify a principal through personal knowledge or satisfactory evidence; or

(3) executing a false notarial certificate under Subsection 5-8(a).

(b) A notary who knowingly performs or fails to perform any other act prohibited or mandated respectively by this [Act] may be guilty of a [class of offense], punishable upon conviction by a fine not exceeding [dollars] or imprisonment for not more than [term of imprisonment], or both.

Comment

Section 13-6 sets out specific criminal penalties for notaries who violate critical provisions of the Act. Since criminal acts are involved, the Act requires that the notary knowingly violate the law. Mere negligence does not merit criminal sanction, and is addressed in Section 13-1. Nonetheless, repeated, knowing acts of negligence may result in suspension or revocation of the commission. If damage claims exceed the available bond, under Subsection 3-3(c) the commission will be suspended. When this happens, Subparagraph 3-3(c)(2) further requires the notary to prove fitness to serve out the remainder of the commission term. The request to continue may be denied. Further, the suspension could then serve as the basis for revoking the commission. (See Subsection 13-3(a) applying Subparagraph 3-1(c)(3).)

Subsection (a) targets three specific notarial functions – requiring a principal's physical presence, properly identifying the principal, and executing a true notarial certificate – for special treatment. These acts are the core features of notarizations that lend integrity and reliability to the notarial act, and therefore are given individual attention to reinforce their importance.

The drafters did not recommend specific criminal sanctions, preferring instead to have each jurisdiction determine whether violating these duties should constitute a felony, misdemeanor, or mere infraction. Appropriate fines and terms of incarceration would be determined by the status assigned to these offenses.

Subsection (b) makes any other knowing violation of the Act subject to criminal sanction. Again, the drafters deferred to the local jurisdictions to determine what penalties would best meet their needs. Examples of potential criminal violations could include charging a fee in excess of the statutory amount, creating a false journal record of a notarial act, or allowing another person to use the notary's official seal.

§ 13-7 Additional Remedies and Sanctions Not Precluded.

The remedies and sanctions of this chapter do not preclude other remedies and sanctions provided by law.

Comment

Section 13-7 makes clear that the criminal sanctions described in Section 13-6 are not exclusive. Certain Act violations may also trigger sanctions provided by the jurisdiction's penal code. For example, a non-attorney notary who dispenses legal advice might be in violation of the jurisdiction's unauthorized practice of law statute. Also, the criminal sanction will not serve as a substitute to block any civil remedies that may be available to injured parties.

Chapter 14 – Violations by Non-Notary

Comment

General: This chapter provides disciplinary sanctions to impose on non-notaries who wrongfully simulate or interfere with official notarial acts.

§ 14-1 Impersonation.

Any person not a notary who knowingly acts as or otherwise impersonates a notary is guilty of a [class of offense], punishable upon conviction by a fine not exceeding [dollars] or imprisonment for not more than [term of imprisonment], or both.

Comment

Section 14-1 addresses acting as a notary without authorization, and makes clear that such action is illegal and subject to criminal penalties. This position is common to many jurisdictions. (See, e.g., COL. REV. STAT. § 12-55-117; VA. CODE ANN. § 47.1-29; and W. VA. CODE ANN. § 29C-6-203.)

§ 14-2 Wrongful Possession.

Any person who knowingly obtains, conceals, defaces, or destroys the seal, journal, or official records of a notary is guilty of a [class of offense], punishable upon conviction by a fine not exceeding [dollars] or imprisonment for not more than [term of imprisonment], or both.

Comment

To protect against fraudulent notarizations and destruction of useful records, Section 14-2 makes the knowingly wrongful possession or corruption of the official notarial materials (seal, journal, and records) a criminal act. (Accord, see MO. REV. STAT. § 486.380; NEV. REV. STAT. ANN. 240.143; and W. VA. CODE ANN § 29C-6-204.)

§ 14-3 Improper Influence.

Any person who knowingly solicits, coerces, or in any way influences a notary to commit official misconduct is guilty of a [class of offense], punishable upon conviction by a fine not exceeding [dollars] or imprisonment for not more than [term of imprisonment], or both.

Comment

To preserve the integrity of the notarial act, Section 14-3 makes influencing or assisting a notary to commit an improper act a violation.

§ 14-4 Additional Sanctions Not Precluded.

The sanctions of this chapter do not preclude other sanctions and remedies provided by law.

Comment

Section 14-4 states that the penalties of Sections 14-1 through 14-3 are not necessarily exclusive, and allows imposition or pursuit of other sanctions as deemed appropriate. (Accord CAL. GOV'T CODE § 8207.4(b); and IDAHO CODE § 51-119(5).)

Article III
Electronic Notary

Comment

This article establishes the role of the electronic notary public. It constitutes a considerable advancement and refinement of the initial specifications for the role proposed in Article III of the 2002 Act. The changes reflect pertinent developments and demands of technology, business, and government over the intervening eight years. Like its 2002 predecessor, Article III in the Model Notary Act of 2010 acknowledges the significance of two legislative standards. The first is the widely enacted Uniform Electronic Transactions Act ("UETA"), adopted by the National Conference of Commissioners on Uniform State Laws on July 29, 1999. UETA recognizes the legal effect of electronic signatures, including those used by notaries. The second is the federal Electronic Signatures in Global and National Commerce Act ("E-Sign") (15 U.S.C.A. §§ 7001 et seq.), which is largely congruent with UETA and authorizes every state commissioned notary in the nation to use electronic signatures in performing official acts. Significantly, however, neither UETA nor E-Sign actually defines an electronic notarization, nor provides pertinent procedures, certificates, or qualifications for the officer performing such acts. This Act accomplishes those tasks.

Also like its 2002 predecessor, Article III in the 2010 Act is based on two cornerstone rules. The first is that the fundamental principles and processes of traditional notarization must apply regardless of the technology used to create a signature. No principle is more critical to notarization than that the signer must appear in person before a duly commissioned notary public to affix or acknowledge the signature and be screened for identity, volition, and basic awareness by the notary at the time of the notarial act. While technology may be improved, the basic nature of the human beings who use it, unfortunately, may not. Any process – paper-based or electronic – that is called notarization of a signature must involve the personal physical appearance of a principal before a duly empowered notary. Contrary to popular understanding, electronic notarization does not mean "remote" notarization, with the notary in front of a computer at location A and the principal before another computer at location B. In the Act, the definitions of the common notarizations apply, both to paper and electronic documents (see Sections 2-1, 2-2, 2-7, 2-11, and 2-21, respectively, for definitions of acknowledgment, affirmation, jurat, oath, and signature witnessing), and all embody the fundamental principle that the signer must appear in person before the notary at the time of notarization.

The second cornerstone rule of the article is technology neutrality. This Act neither embraces nor rejects any particular electronic signature technology. At the same time, it does not prevent or discourage a jurisdiction's prescription or proscription of a particular technology for electronic signatures or notary journals. Rather, the Act posits performance standards for electronic notarization which any qualifying technology must meet. (See, e.g., the performance standards for an electronic journal of notarial acts in Section 20-2.) The drafters preferred to let the forces of the marketplace winnow out less efficient technologies, and drive people toward those that combine maximum security with ease of operation.

The drafters considered it to be administratively problematic, if not in violation of E-Sign, to require special commissioning of electronic notaries. Instead, the Act merely requires interested paper-based notaries formally to register their intent to notarize electronically with the commissioning official, while submitting evidence of their electronic capabilities. (See Chapter 16, "Registration as Electronic Notary.") E-Sign authorizes every state-commissioned notary to act as an electronic notary – but only if the desire is there. Just as most notaries today elect to eschew any authority granted by statute to take depositions for lack of facility in shorthand reporting, so too, no doubt, many notaries will pass up the opportunity to notarize electronically for lack of facility in computers. A "regular notary" (i.e., one authorized to execute traditional paper based notarizations) is not obligated to become an electronic notary.

Developments and demands of industry and government have shaped the major changes to Article III that distinguish the 2010 Act from its 2002 predecessor. The new Act, for example, reflects a clear and growing consensus that electronic notarizations must both be "capable of independent verification" (see Section 15-1) and render any notarized electronic document as tamper-evident (see Section 15-12). According to the American Bar Association volume, FOUNDATIONS OF DIGITAL EVIDENCE (2008): "Concerning electronically notarized documents, an international and national edocument authenticity standard has emerged that reflects the evidentiary need for electronic documents to have the capability of authenticity testing. This standard requires that any relying party be able to verify the origin and integrity of the notarized electronic document. Establishing the authenticity of a notarized document thus requires the capability, in perpetuity, of independently authenticating the notary, and verifying whether the content of the electronic document is complete and unaltered."

Another marketplace demand reflected in the new Act is permission for the notary to register with the commissioning official more than one means for creating electronic signatures and electronic seals. Notaries may need to employ multiple technologies to accommodate the different electronic systems of their various clients. For example, one client might require the notary to use a portable plug-in token to notarize an electronic document, while another might require the notary to sign and seal electronically using an online server. Such electronic versatility benefits both the notary and the business world.

Chapter 15 – Definitions Used in This Article

Comment

General: Chapter 15 provides definitions of terms integral to the process of electronic notarization. Four are closely based on definitions in UETA (i.e., "electronic," "electronic document," "electronic signature," and "security procedure"). These UETA-inspired terms tie the Model Notary Act to fundamental understandings of electronic transactions that now permeate state and federal law, through enactments of both UETA and E-Sign.

One of the definitions is for a term ("capable of independent verification") often encountered without further explanation in state laws governing electronic signatures. Two others ("electronic notarial certificate" and "electronic notary seal") reflect definitions developed in guidelines for electronic notarization promulgated by the National Association of Secretaries of State. (See "National E-Notarization Standards," hereinafter "NASS Standards," adopted July 12, 2006.) Three of the terms ("electronic journal of notarial acts," "electronic notarial act and electronic notarization" and "electronic notary public and electronic notary") were defined in the 2002 Act but have been redefined by the drafters in this 2010 version. The remaining two original definitions are of unique terms ("registered electronic notary seal" and "registered electronic signature") that are key to the highly secure system for electronic notarization set forth in this Act.

§ 15-1 Capable of Independent Verification.

"Capable of independent verification" means that any interested person may confirm the validity of an electronic notarial act and an electronic notary public's identity and authority through a publicly accessible system.

Comment

Section 15-1 specifies what "capable of independent verification" means. This term or the term "capable of verification" is often found undefined in statutes to denote an attribute of a reliable electronic signature. (See, e.g., CAL. GOV. CODE § 16.5; FLA. STAT. § 117.021(2); N. MEX. ADMIN. CODE § 12.9.2.11(C); and CODE OF VA. § 47.1-16(D).) It is used in this Act to denote a desired and required attribute of an electronic signature used by a notary in performing an electronic notarial act. (See Section 19-2(2).)

An example of a system providing such verification may be accessed on the Internet at www.dos.state.pa.us/dos/site/default.asp, clicking on "Notaries" and "Electronic Notarization."

§ 15-2 Electronic.

"Electronic" means relating to technology having electrical, digital, magnetic, wireless, optical, electromagnetic, or similar capabilities.

Comment

Section 15-2 defines "electronic" consistent with the Uniform Electronic Transactions Act. (See UETA § 2(5).) The drafters employed terms that are compatible with UETA because that act has either been adopted by a number of jurisdictions (see, e.g., KAN. STAT. ANN. §§ 16-1601 to 16-1620; NEB. REV. STAT. §§ 86-612 to 86-643; UTAH CODE ANN. §§ 46-4-101 to 46-4-503; and ME. REV. STAT. ANN. tit. 10 chapt. 1051 §§ 9401 to 9419) or served as the starting point for other legislation enacted throughout the country (see, e.g., ARIZ. REV. STAT. ANN. §§ 44-7001 et seq.; MD. CODE ANN. (Commercial Law) §§ 21-101 et seq.; and OHIO REV. CODE ANN. §§ 1306.01 to 1306.23).

The term "electronic" is to be liberally construed to embrace not only computer generated signatures and documents, but also those created by other technologies that may currently be in use or developed in the future.

§ 15-3 Electronic Document.

"Electronic document" means information that is created, generated, sent, communicated, received, or stored by electronic means.

Comment

The definition remains unchanged from the prior version of the Act.

Section 15-3 defines "document" in a way that makes it the functional equivalent of the term "record" in UETA. (See UETA § 2(13).) The drafters preferred "document" to "record" because it strengthens the connection of electronic notarizations to paper-based official acts. The Act also seeks to eliminate any confusion about the term "record," which could be misunderstood to denote that the document has an official status or is considered an archive.

§ 15-4 Electronic Journal of Notarial Acts.

"Electronic journal of notarial acts" and "electronic journal" mean a chronological electronic record of notarizations that is maintained by the notary public who performed the same notarizations.

Comment

Section 15-4 has been changed from its 2002 version. The drafters decided to enumerate the specifications for an electronic notarial journal in a separate chapter (see Chapter 20), instead of following the approach in the former Act of including them in the definition itself.

For the purposes of this section, "record" is used in its ordinary, everyday meaning, and not as it is defined in UETA.

§ 15-5 Electronic Notarial Act and Electronic Notarization.

"Electronic notarial act" and "electronic notarization" mean an official act involving an electronic document that is performed in compliance with this Article by an electronic notary public as a security procedure [as defined in the Uniform Electronic Transactions Act].

Comment

Section 15-5 declares that every electronic notarization is itself a "security procedure," whose definition in Section 15-12 is closely based on the definition of the same term in UETA (see UETA § 2(14)). The UETA definition spells out that a security procedure is "employed for the purpose of verifying that an electronic signature, record, or performance is that of a specific person or for detecting changes or errors in the information in an electronic record." One of the clear standards that has arisen in the new field of electronic notarization is that an electronic notarial act must qualify as a "security procedure" with the important capabilities of establishing who signed and notarized an electronic document and rendering a notarized electronic document as tamper-evident. According to George L. Paul et al., FOUNDATIONS OF DIGITAL EVIDENCE, p. 212 (ABA, 2008): "Concerning electronically notarized documents, an international and national e-document authenticity standard has emerged that reflects the evidentiary need for electronic documents to have the capability of authenticity testing. This standard requires that any relying party be able to verify the origin and integrity of the notarized electronic document.

Establishing the authenticity of a notarized document thus requires the capability, in perpetuity, of independently authenticating the notary, and verifying whether the content of the electronic document is complete and unaltered." (See also NASS Standards 5-9; ABA SUBCOMMITTEE ON ETRUST: ENOTARY WORKGROUP WHITEPAPER ON ENOTARIZATION AT 3.3 (ABA, 2006), stating, "(T)he document being proffered must contain or be accompanied by evidence that it has not changed since it was first generated in its final form"; and Daniel J. Greenwood, ELECTRONIC NOTARIZATION: WHY IT'S NEEDED, HOW IT WORKS, AND HOW IT CAN BE IMPLEMENTED TO ENABLE GREATER TRANSACTIONAL SECURITY 10 (Nat'l Notary Ass'n, 2006).)

In this Act, at the core of each electronic notarization is the assurance that the notarized electronic document truly was signed by a particular real person and that the document will prominently display evidence of any subsequent alteration. In that way, all electronic notarizations are themselves security procedures.

The use of brackets in the definition allows jurisdictions that have not adopted rules inspired by the UETA definition to define "security procedure" in a manner more suitable to their own governing laws.

§ 15-6 Electronic Notarial Certificate.

"Electronic notarial certificate" means the part of, or attachment to, a notarized electronic document that, in the performance of an electronic notarization, is completed by the electronic notary public, bears the notary's registered electronic signature and seal, and states the date, venue, and facts attested to or certified by the notary in the particular electronic notarization.

Comment

Section 15-6 recognizes that every notarization, whether paper-based or electronic, requires a notarial certificate. The certificate may be either an integral or attached part of the paper or electronic document. This new section defines the electronic notarial certificate to parallel its paper counterpart. (See Section 2-9.)

The definition of "electronic notarial certificate" reflects the definition of the same term adopted by the National Association of Secretaries of State in 2006. (See NASS Standards, "Definitions" at 7.)

An "electronic notarial certificate" is not to be confused with a "public key certificate," which is a component of a technology widely used to create electronic signatures.

§ 15-7 Electronic Notary Public and Electronic Notary.

"Electronic notary public" and "electronic notary" mean a notary public who has registered with the [commissioning official] the capability to perform electronic notarial acts.

Comment

Section 15-7 defines "electronic notary public." The Act recognizes that any commissioned notary should have the opportunity to operate as an electronic notary, but ought not be compelled to do so if there is no interest.

Most authorities interpret E-Sign as giving electronic notarization powers to all current state-commissioned notaries. (E-Sign specifically states that it may be preempted by state law when certain requirements are met, but absent meeting those requirements, E-Sign controls (see § 7002).) Thus, the registration process itself does not empower registrants to notarize electronically. Instead, it enables the [commissioning official] to learn the specific electronic capabilities of a notary so that the notary's future electronic acts can be verified and authenticated by the [commissioning official] for such uses as become necessary.

§ 15-8 Electronic Notary Seal.

"Electronic notary seal" and "electronic seal" mean information within a notarized electronic document that includes the electronic notary's name, title, jurisdiction, and commission expiration date.

Comment

Section 15-8 defines "electronic notary seal" to be information both identifying an electronic notary and delineating in basic terms the notary's authority to act electronically.

E-Sign and UETA do not eliminate the need for the notary's addition to each electronically notarized document of authenticating information that is traditionally found in an official seal. This section defines that important information as an "electronic notary seal" in order to strengthen the connection between electronic and traditional paper-based notarial acts.

Unlike the definition of the "official seal" that is to be affixed on paper documents (see Section 2-13), this definition does not denote a device for imparting an image, nor the image itself. Inclusion of a digital image, however, would neither be required nor prohibited in an electronic seal, if the technology allowed it. (The required informational components of an electronic notary seal are prescribed in Subparagraph 18-2(3).)

§ 15-9 Electronic Signature.

"Electronic signature" means an electronic sound, symbol, or process attached to or logically associated with an electronic document and executed or adopted by a person with the intent to sign the document.

Comment

Section 15-9 essentially borrows the definition of "electronic signature" from UETA, substituting the term "document" for "record." (See Section 15-3; and UETA § 2(8).) The definition describes the different possible forms of an electronic signature, and is intended to be as inclusive as possible. No doubt, technologies not yet developed will create new ways to produce electronic signatures that would satisfy the definition.

It is important to note that this section only defines what an electronic signature is. It does not purport to authorize the use of a signature in a notarization. Only a registered electronic signature (as defined in Section 15-11) may be used by an electronic notary to perform an electronic notarization. Production of an electronic signature by a means not registered under Section 16-4 would render the attempted electronic notarization invalid.

§ 15-10 Registered Electronic Notary Seal.

"Registered electronic notary seal" means an electronic notary seal produced by a notary in the performance of an electronic notarial act by a means that was registered with the [commissioning official].

Comment

Section 15-10 introduces a new term to apply to electronic notarizations. Defining "registered electronic notary seal" enables more economy of language throughout the Article whenever reference is made to a notary completing an electronic notarization. ("Electronic notary seal" is defined in Section 15-8.) A "registered electronic notary seal" is an official seal of office for electronic notarial acts and an analog to a "registered electronic signature." (See Section 15-11.)

Only an electronic seal whose means of production has been registered with the commissioning official (see Section 16-4) may be used in an electronic notarization (see Section 19-1). The Act does not dictate how the seal must be produced. Instead, it specifies the required components of an electronic notary seal (see Subparagraph 18-2(3)), and gives the notary discretion to select the means of production. One such means of producing an electronic seal might be the simple process of typing in the required information comprising the seal – though such a process by itself would not result in a secure electronically notarized document. (For a discussion of the relative security of the different means for producing electronic notary seals and signatures, see generally Daniel J. Greenwood, ELECTRONIC NOTARIZATION: WHY IT'S NEEDED, HOW IT WORKS, AND HOW IT CAN BE IMPLEMENTED TO ENABLE GREATER TRANSACTIONAL SECURITY (Nat'l Notary Ass'n 2006).) By contrast, an electronic notary seal used in conjunction with an electronic notary signature with the attributes set forth in 19-2, including the attribute of rendering an electronically notarized document as tamper evident (see Subparagraph 19-2(3)) will produce a secure electronically notarized document.

Notably, more than one means for producing electronic notary seals may be registered by a notary. (See Section 16-5.)

§ 15-11 Registered Electronic Signature.

"Registered electronic signature" means an electronic signature produced by a notary in the performance of an electronic notarial act by a means that was registered with the [commissioning official].

Comment

Section 15-11 introduces a new term, "registered electronic signature," and distinguishes it from other electronic signatures that a notary may use for non-notarial purposes. ("Electronic signature" is defined in Section 15-9.) Only a "registered electronic signature" may be used by a notary in performing electronic notarizations. It is an official notary signature for electronic notarial acts and an analog to a "registered electronic notary seal." (See Section 15-10.)

Generally, in the paper world a person has only one signature and it is produced by the person's own hand. Thus, that same signature – with subtle variations in its image due to the fact that it is hand-drawn – is used for official notarial acts as well as for all other non-notarial signings. The same is not true in the electronic world, where an individual may use completely different personal electronic signatures produced by different processes. This Article dictates that despite the number of different ways a notary may make an electronic signature, only a signature whose specific means of production has been registered with the commissioning official (see Section 16-4) may be used in performing electronic notarizations (see Section 19-1).

Notably, more than one means for producing electronic signatures may be registered by a notary. (See Section 16-5.) Thus, an electronic notary may have and use multiple registered electronic signatures.

§ 15-12 Security Procedure.

"Security procedure" means a procedure employed for the purpose of verifying that an electronic signature, document, or performance is that of a specific person or for detecting changes or errors in the information in an electronic document. The term includes a procedure that requires the use of algorithms or other codes, identifying words or numbers, encryption, or callback, or other acknowledgment procedures.

Comment

Section 15-12 adopts the definition of "security procedure" provided in UETA (see UETA § 2(14)), with one change. To maintain consistency throughout the Act regarding adoption of language from UETA, "document" (see Section 15-3) has again been substituted for "record" (see UETA § 2(13)).

One of the prime innovations of this Act is applying the function of a security procedure as defined in UETA to electronic notarization. (See Section 15-5 and Comment.) There is congruence in the two processes. Indeed, the Comment for UETA § 2(14) states: "A security procedure may be applied to verify an electronic signature, verify the identity of the sender, or assure the informational integrity of an electronic record." This description demonstrates the overarching policy of the Act to have paper-based and electronic notarizations be as similar as possible.

Chapter 16 – Registration as Electronic Notary

Comment

General: Chapter 16 delineates the process for registering as an electronic notary. The drafters firmly believed that requiring a notary to obtain an additional commission in order to operate electronically would impose an impediment in violation of E-Sign's already existing permission, not to mention an administrative hardship on the commissioning body. The drafters, however, also believed it to be in the public interest and a reasonable accommodation to have some governmental oversight over electronic notaries. Such oversight would at the very least enable the commissioning body to authenticate a notary's electronic acts and to investigate an electronic notary's conduct in disciplinary matters.

Thus, this Act requires interested notaries to register with the commissioning official their capability of notarizing electronically before performing such acts. (See Section 16-1.) A notary who is not interested in performing electronic notarizations is not required to register as an electronic notary.

It was viewed as a reasonable public protection to require registrants first to prove their electronic competence by passing a course of instruction on electronic notarization. (See Section 16-2.) The registration would be valid as long as the notary's underlying commission remains in effect (see Section 16-3) or is not terminated for cause (see Section 24-2).

The electronic registration form requires the notary to inform the commissioning official about the specific means the notary will use to produce electronic signatures and notary seals in performing electronic notarial acts. (See Section 16-4.) Section 16-5 permits more than one means to be registered for each of these purposes or, alternatively, more than one "single element" combining the required features of both electronic signature and seal.

Sections 16-6, 16-7, and 16-8, respectively, address the administrative matters of material misstatement or omission of fact in the registration form, fees for registering, and confidentiality of information disclosed by registrants.

§ 16-1 Registration with [Commissioning Official].

(a) A notary public shall register the capability to perform electronic notarial acts with the [commissioning official] before notarizing electronically.

(b) Upon recommissioning, a notary public shall again register with the [commissioning official] before notarizing electronically.

(c) A person may apply or reapply for a notary commission and register or reregister to perform electronic notarial acts at the same time.

Comment

Section 16-1 requires the electronic notary to register with the commissioning official. In contrast to the former Act, this section has been reworded, lengthened, and transposed with the section titled "Course of Instruction and Examination," now designated as Section 16-2.

Registration serves a number of purposes. First, it demonstrates the electronic notary's proficiency in electronic communications and use of an electronic signature. Second, it provides the commissioning official with notice of the notary's intent to perform electronic notarizations. Third, it provides information (e.g., decrypting instructions) that may assist the commissioning official in any subsequent investigation of the electronic notary's conduct. Fourth, it allows the official to verify and authenticate the acts of the electronic notary.

Under Subsection (b), upon "renewing" a notary commission, an interested notary must in essence also renew the registration as an electronic notary. However, unlike the commission renewal process (see Section 3-5), reregistration as an electronic notary does not require renewed satisfaction of the education and testing requirements (see Section 16-2(a)).

Subsection (c) is new. It clarifies that a person may seek to be registered to perform electronic notarial acts at the same time the person submits an application for a commission – even an initial notary commission.

§ 16-2 Course of Instruction and Examination.

(a) Before initially registering the capability to perform electronic notarial acts, an electronic notary public shall complete a course of instruction of [4] hours approved by the [commissioning official], in addition to the course required for commissioning as a notary, and pass an examination based on the course.

(b) The content of the course shall be notarial laws, procedures, and ethics pertaining to electronic notarization.

Comment

Section 16-2 mandates that all notaries applying for registration to perform electronic acts (see Section 16-1) first satisfactorily complete an education and testing requirement. This is in addition to and not a substitute for the general education and testing requirement for basic notary commissioning. (See Section 4-3.) The Act adopts the position that, in order to protect the public, any notary who wants to perform electronic notarizations must prove the capability to do so. This section sets forth the mechanism for providing that protection.

The recommended education requirement has been raised to four hours, one hour more than was required in the former Act. The drafters believe that as the electronic world changes and becomes more complex, it makes sense for notaries to have additional "basic training" in order to start off abreast of the very latest developments affecting electronic notarization. The purpose is to ensure that the electronic notary is at a minimum proficient in performing certain electronic tasks. It is anticipated that the course and exam may be taken interactively online or in a more traditional classroom setting. Administrative matters may be handled in the same manner as are the basic notary education requirements. (See Section 4-3 and Comment.) Nothing in the Act precludes the electronic notary from taking additional courses to maintain or improve skills. Indeed, continuing education that keeps the electronic notary apprised of technological advances is encouraged. (See THE NOTARY PUBLIC CODE OF PROFESSIONAL RESPONSIBILITY, Principle X and Standard XA-4.)

§ 16-3 Term of Registration of Electronic Notary.

The term of registration of an electronic notary public

begins on the registration starting date set by the [commissioning official] and continues as long as the notary's commission remains in effect or until registration is terminated under Subsection 24-2(a).

Comment

Section 16-3 is new and fills a void in the former Act, viz., the starting and ending dates of the registration term. It provides that the commissioning official shall set the term. This section also provides that the term of the electronic registration runs concurrently with that of the notary's commission. When the commission expires or otherwise terminates, so does the electronic registration.

§ 16-4 Electronic Registration Form.

To register the capability to perform electronic notarial acts, a notary public shall electronically sign and submit to the [commissioning official] an electronic form prescribed by the [commission official] which includes:

(1) proof of successful completion of the course and examination required by Section 16-2;

(2) the following information:

(i) a description of each separate means that will be used to produce electronic signatures [and electronic notary seals];

(ii) any keys, codes, software, decrypting instructions, or graphics that will allow the electronic signatures [and seals] produced by the means described in Subparagraph (i) to be verified;

(iii) the names of any licensed authorities issuing the means for producing the electronic signatures [and seals], the source of each license, and the starting and expiration dates of each pertinent certificate, software, or process;

(iv) an explanation of any revocation, annulment, or other premature termination of any certificate, software, or process ever issued or registered to the applicant to produce an electronic signature or seal; [and]

[(v) a declaration that the notary public will use the means issued or authorized for issuance by the [commissioning official] for producing an electronic notary seal; and]

(3) if the notary will use an electronic journal of notarial acts as described in Chapter 20, the access instructions that will allow the journal to be viewed, printed out, and copied.

Comment

Section 16-4 provides the form for registering as an electronic notary. The form has been substantially revised from the version appearing in the former Act. The separate components of the form are drawn from requirements established in other sections of the Act that speak principally to the notary's ability to perform electronic notarizations in a secure and tamper-evident manner. The form itself must be signed and submitted electronically. Notwithstanding the fact that a notary may register more than one electronic signature (see Section 16-5), this section permits any electronic signature adopted by the notary, or required by the commissioning official, to be used to sign the registration form.

Subparagraph (2) requires the notary to submit to the commissioning official a description of the separate means that will be used to produce electronic signatures in future electronic notarial acts. This is done by providing both a verbal account of each means and certain items cited in Subparagraphs (2)(i) through (2)(iv), such as keys or codes, that will enable the resulting electronic signatures to be verified. These submissions also will allow the commissioning official to authenticate the notary's electronic signature.

The brackets in Subparagraph (2) accommodate two options for registering the means for producing the electronic notary seal. The first option is to register these means in the same manner as registering the means for producing the notary's electronic signature. The second is to give the commissioning official the duty either to issue the means for producing the notary's seal, or to authorize a trusted entity to issue such means.

Subparagraph (3) provides the mechanism for the electronic notary to comply with Subparagraph 20-4(1), which directs the notary to provide on the registration form access instructions for the notary's electronic journal.

§ 16-5 Registration of Multiple Means.

Under Section 16-4, a notary public may register at the same or different times 1 or more respective means for producing electronic signatures and electronic notary seals, or single elements combining the required features of both, consistent with the requirements cited elsewhere in this [Act].

Comment

Section 16-5 permits a notary to register multiple means for producing both electronic signatures and electronic notary seals. Notaries accustomed to the practices of the paper world might be uneasy that an electronic notary may use different methods for producing an official seal or signature on different electronic documents. However, it should be no more a matter of concern than the fact that a non-electronic notary might employ different pens to produce the same official signature on different paper documents, or might use both an inking and an embossing seal during a single notarization. The important thing is that, first, the differently produced signatures all refer to the notary as named on the commission (see Sections 19-1 and 19-2); second, that the differently produced seals all contain the same information about the notary's commission and jurisdiction (see Subparagraph 18-2(3); and, third, that their means of production are registered (see Section 16-4).

In today's electronic world, it is understandable why a business-savvy notary might want to register different means for producing an electronic signature or seal. Different clients or business situations, for example, might dictate use of different technologies by the notary. (For a fuller discussion of this point, see the introductory Comment to this Article.)

This section permits the combining of the electronic signature and the electronic notary seal into a single unit, which would be registered as such with the commissioning official under Section 16-4. The option to use such a combination has been specifically endorsed by the National Association of Secretaries of State. (See NASS Standards, Sections 3-4 and Comment.)

§ 16-6 Material Misstatement or Omission of Fact.

The [commissioning official] shall deny registration to any applicant submitting an electronic registration form that contains a material misstatement or omission of fact.

Comment

Section 16-6 is new. It reinforces the view that notaries hold a special position of trust. Material evidence indicating that a notary is not trustworthy will require the commissioning official to deny a registration request. This provision is consistent with the rule with respect to the application to become or be recommissioned as a notary. (See Subsection 3-1(c).)

§ 16-7 Fee for Registration.

The fee payable to the [commissioning official] for

registering or reregistering as an electronic notary public is [dollars].

Comment

Section 16-7 sets a registration fee that is distinct from the commissioning fee. The Act anticipates that the fee will be established at an amount to cover the commissioning official's administrative and related costs in overseeing electronic notarizations.

§ 16-8 Confidentiality.

Information in the registration form of an electronic notary public shall be used by the [commissioning official] and designated [State] employees only for the purpose of performing official duties, and shall not be disclosed to any person other than to:

(1) a government agent acting in an official capacity and duly authorized to obtain such information;

(2) a person authorized by court order; or

(3) the registrant or the registrant's duly authorized agent.

Comment

Section 16-8 serves as the counterpart to Section 4-6 regarding confidentiality of application information submitted for a notary commission. In this context, however, some of the information is even more sensitive because, if compromised, it could allow access to otherwise secure electronic documents and records. Moreover, these documents and records might belong to unsuspecting members of the public who had an expectation of privacy when they presented the instruments for notarization. Consequently, this section reinforces the need for strict confidentiality on decrypting instructions, codes, and related items. As with other confidential material, only duly authorized persons are entitled to obtain access to it. Additionally, the section seeks to preserve the security of the notary's keys or other means for producing electronic signatures. Doing so helps protect a notary's privacy.

Chapter 17 – Electronic Notarial Acts

Comment

General: Chapter 17 identifies those traditional paper-based notarial acts that may be performed electronically, and makes clear that certain fundamental requirements for nonelectronic notarial acts also apply in the electronic realm. While copy certification was not included as an authorized electronic notarization in the former Act, the drafters decided its inclusion now was essential. (See Subparagraph 17-1(4).) The pervasiveness of electronic documents, particularly in the arena of the Internet, gives increasing utility, if not necessity, to a process for electronic certification of such documents.

Section 17-2 specifies six basic requirements for electronic notarial acts, which are taken virtually verbatim from the mandates for non-electronic acts in Article II. Given primacy among these six is the need for the document signer to be in the physical presence of the notary for any notarization of an electronic signature. A new requirement that is particular to electronic notarial acts directs the notary to take reasonable steps to establish that a particular electronic signature is being used by the very person authorized to do so.

Section 17-3 provides a procedure allowing a person who is physically unable to make an electronic signature to direct an electronic notary to produce that signature on a particular document presented for notarization. Two other persons must be physically present to witness the process.

Section 17-4, complementing the six specific requirements of Section 17-2, requires notaries who perform electronic notarizations to adhere to all other applicable rules in this Act that govern the proper performance of non-electronic notarizations.

§ 17-1 Authorized Electronic Notarial Acts.

The following notarial acts may be performed electronically:

(1) acknowledgment;

(2) jurat;

(3) signature witnessing;

(4) copy certification; and

(5) verification of fact.

Comment

Section 17-1 identifies the five types of notarization that can be performed electronically.

Copy certification has been added to the list of authorized electronic acts. (See the corresponding new definition of "copy certification" in Section 2-4.) The drafters recognized that the pervasive presence of electronic and Internet documents upon which people rely in everyday personal and professional life has created situations where verifying the exact language or appearance of such documents is often necessary or useful. Since the content of electronic documents and Internet sites is readily changeable, electronic copy certifications will allow interested parties to possess an exact image, or an exact statement of language, used in a particular document or site on a particular date and at a particular time, as confirmed by a notary.

Oaths and affirmations are not mentioned because, being purely oral acts that require a face-to-face meeting of oathtaker and notary, they are not performed differently in an electronic context than in a paper environment. An electronic notary must still administer an oath or affirmation in person when executing an electronic jurat (see Section 2-7) or swearing in a credible witness (see Section 2-5) for an electronic acknowledgment, jurat, or signature witnessing.

Nothing in this or any other section of this Article derogates from the electronic notary's authority to perform any of the notarial acts authorized by Section 5-1 in a non-electronic setting.

§ 17-2 Requirements for Electronic Notarial Acts.

An electronic notary public shall perform an electronic notarization only if the principal:

(1) is in the presence of the notary at the time of notarization;

(2) is personally known to the notary or identified by the notary through satisfactory evidence;

(3) appears to understand the nature of the transaction;

(4) appears to be acting of his or her own free will;

(5) communicates directly with the notary in a language both understand; and

(6) reasonably establishes the electronic signature as his or her own.

Comment

Section 17-2 restates the basic requirements common to all notarizations, whether paper-based or electronic. The drafters thought it imperative to highlight the fact that electronic notarizations carry the same fundamental responsibilities as their non-electronic counterparts. Consequently, basic requirements for all notarizations, as set out in Section 5-2, mandating the principal's presence, proof of identity, awareness, and exercise of free will, also must be observed for electronic notarial acts. Subparagraph (1) clarifies that electronic notarization does not mean "remote" notarization. Not only must the principal be physically present before the notary, but the notary also must meet the same identity, volition, and awareness standards imposed for paper-based notarizations.

It should be pointed out, however, that the definition of "principal" (see Section 2-17) applies to "a person whose signature is notarized; or…a person, other than a credible witness, taking an oath or affirmation from the notary." Thus, the determinations about identity, awareness, and volition required of the notary by Subparagraphs (2), (3), and (4) do not apply to "requesters of fact" – i.e., persons asking the notary to perform either a copy certification or a verification of fact (see Section 2-19). Significantly, the drafters came to the conclusion that the personal appearance before the notary of a requester of fact is irrelevant in a notarial act in which the personal identity of the signer is not a central issue. In this Internet age, notaries must be allowed to certify needed electronic copies and to provide information available in local public records without imposing the inconvenience or hardship of requiring a client to present the request in person. Notaries serving such remote clients, of course, would be encouraged to use their best judgment and due caution by not engaging clients who are anonymous. Nothing in this section prevents a notary from asking for proof of identity from a requester of fact who does appear in person before the notary, but it is not required.

Two new requirements have been added to the section. First, the new Subparagraph (5) is drawn from the paper-based Subparagraph 5-2(6), which addresses increasingly common communication problems involving foreign-language documents and non-English-speaking signers. Second, the new Subparagraph (6) applies only to electronic transactions – added by the drafters as a fraud-deterrent measure. When paper-based notarizations are performed, normally the notary can easily read and recognize a handwritten signature as belonging to a person who has just been identified. Such ease of recognition may not be the case with electronic signatures, which can be produced at the mere touch of a computer key. To minimize the fraudulent use of another person's electronic signature, the Act now requires the notary to take affirmative action to ascertain that an electronic signature belongs to the individual using it. Some states already mandate such proactivity by the electronic notary – see, e.g., CODE OF VA. § 47.1-14(D), which directs the notary performing electronic acts to ensure that any registered devised used to create electronic signatures is current. Subparagraph (6) leaves to the notary's judgment the matter of what evidence reasonably identifies an individual as the rightful owner of an electronic signature made or acknowledged in the notary's presence.

The drafters chose not to incorporate the restriction of Section 5-2(5) (prohibiting the notary from notarizing a document written in a language the notary does not understand) because it would prevent many notarizations in the electronic world, where signatures may be processes or employ symbols not understood by the notary.

§ 17-3 Notary May Sign for Principal Unable to Sign Electronically.

An electronic notary public may electronically sign the name of a principal physically unable to make an electronic signature on an electronic document presented for notarization if:

(1) the principal directs the electronic notary to do so in the presence of 2 witnesses disinterested in the document;

(2) the electronic notary electronically signs the principal's name in the presence of the principal and the 2 witnesses;

(3) both witnesses sign their own names in the electronic notary's journal;

(4) the electronic notary writes on the electronic notarial certificate: "Signature made by the electronic notary at the direction and in the presence of (name of principal unable to sign electronically) and in the presence of (names and addresses of 2 witnesses) pursuant to Section 17-3 of [Act]"; and

(5) the electronic notary notarizes the signature through an acknowledgment, jurat, or signature witnessing.

Comment

Section 17-3 provides the procedure for an electronic notary to sign electronically the name of a principal who is unable to do so. This section mirrors Section 5-4 ("Signing for Principal Unable to Sign") but places the procedure in an electronic context. The same safeguards against fraud are in place (i.e., two disinterested witnesses) to protect both the principal and any third party who might rely on the electronic document.

Since some electronic signatures may be executed by the mere depression of a computer key, it is possible that the electronic procedure outlined in this section may not be used as often as its paper-based counterpart. Certainly, some individuals who are physically unable to sign or make a mark by pen might be able to negotiate the displacement of a button on a keyboard. It is noteworthy that there is no section in this chapter corresponding to the paper-based Section 5-3 ("Signature by Mark"), because a would-be electronic signer would either be able to perform the physical action required to produce an electronic signature (e.g., depress a key or type in a name) or not. At present there is not any electronic equivalent to a signature by mark.

Subparagraph (3) requires both witnesses to sign the notary's journal. Any electronic journal used for this purpose must be capable of capturing the witnesses' holographic or electronic signatures.

§ 17-4 All Notarial Rules Apply.

In performing electronic notarial acts, an electronic notary shall adhere to all applicable rules governing notarial acts provided in this [Act].

Comment

Section 17-4 makes clear that regardless of whether the document being notarized is electronic or non-electronic, the notary has to follow the fundamental rules that both prescribe and proscribe certain acts. Thus, for example, when notarizing an electronic document, the notary may not influence a person to act or refrain from acting (see Subsection 5-7(a)), execute a false certificate (see Subsection 5-8(a)), notarize a blank or incomplete document (see Section 5-9(a)), use the notary seal or title in testimonials (see Section 5-11), or engage in the unauthorized practice of law (see Section 5-12).

Chapter 18 – Electronic Notarial Certificate

Comment

General: Chapter 18 is the electronic counterpart of Chapter 9, which describes the components, form, and use of nonelectronic notarial certificates. Section 18-1 states that the notary must properly complete an electronic notarial certificate (see definition in Section 15-6) for every electronic notarization performed. Section 18-2 states that a proper electronic certificate is comprised of a registered electronic signature, a registered electronic notary seal, and attestation wording appropriate to the notarial act. Section 18-3 dictates that the form of this attestation wording must be the same as that described for non-electronic documents in Chapter 9 of the Act.

§ 18-1 Completion of Electronic Notarial Certificate.

In performing an electronic notarial act, the notary shall properly complete an electronic notarial certificate.

Comment

Section 18-1 requires that all notarized electronic documents bear an electronic notarial certificate. (See Section 15-6 for a definition of "electronic notarial certificate.") Notarial certificates likewise are required for notarization of all nonelectronic documents. (See Subsection 9-1(a).) A typical notarial certificate contains a venue, date of notarization, statement of the facts being attested (in the form of wording for an acknowledgment, jurat, or any other notarial act), testimonium clause (i.e., "Witness my hand and official seal..."), and the notary's signature and seal.

Whether electronic or non-electronic, the notarial certificate may be either an integral part of the document or an attachment to it. In this Article, the notary's electronic signature is the means for securing an electronic certificate to its intended document, and for enabling a certificate attachment to manifest subsequent tampering. (See Subparagraph 19-2(3).) The notary's electronic signature also provides evidence of alteration of the underlying document itself.

§ 18-2 Components of Electronic Notarial Certificate.

A proper electronic notarial certificate shall contain:

(1) completed wording appropriate to the particular electronic notarial act, as prescribed in Section 18-3;

(2) a registered electronic signature; and

(3) a registered electronic notary seal, which shall include:

(i) the name of the electronic notary fully and exactly as it is spelled on the notary's commissioning document;

(ii) the jurisdiction that commissioned and registered the electronic notary;

(iii) the title "Electronic Notary Public";

(iv) the commission or registration number of the electronic notary; and

(v) the commission expiration date of the electronic notary.

Comment

Section 18-2 sets forth the individual elements required for a proper electronic notarial certificate. They reflect the requirements for a non-electronic notarial certificate. (See Section 9-1.)

Only an electronic signature and an electronic notary seal whose means of production have been registered by the notary under the terms of Section 16-4 may be used with an electronic notarial certificate. The notary has the option of satisfying the requirements of Subparagraphs (2) and (3) by use of a single element that combines all the mandated features of a registered electronic signature and registered electronic notary seal. (See Section 16-5.)

Nothing in the section precludes the registered electronic notary seal from including a graphic image of a traditional seal.

§ 18-3 Form of Electronic Notarial Certificate.

(a) The wording of an electronic notarial certificate shall be in a form that:

(1) is set forth in Chapter 9 of this [Act];

(2) is otherwise prescribed by the law of this [State];

(3) is prescribed by a law, regulation, or custom of another jurisdiction, provided it does not require actions by the electronic notary that are unauthorized by this [State]; or

(4) describes the actions of the electronic notary in such a manner as to meet the requirements of the particular notarial act, as defined in Chapter 2 of this [Act].

(b) A notarial certificate shall be worded and completed using only letters, characters, and a language that are read, written, and understood by the electronic notary.

Comment

Section 18-3 prescribes the allowed forms for an electronic notarial certificate, and corresponds to its non-electronic counterpart. (See Subsection 9-1(b) and (c).) The essential congruity of the form and content of the electronic and non-electronic certificates reinforces a fundamental principle of this Act: the only true difference between electronic and non-electronic notarizations is the medium used.

Subsection (b) is consistent with Subsection (c) of Section 9-1, iterating that the notary must understand what the certificate states. Otherwise, the notary would not be able to execute the certificate with the knowledge that it is what it purports to be, i.e., an acknowledgment, jurat, or other notarial act.

Chapter 19 – Registered Electronic Signature and Seal

Comment

General: Chapter 19 sets forth rules for the secure use of registered electronic signatures and notary seals, starting with the fundamental requirement in Section 19-1 that any such signatures and seals be "attached to or logically associated with" (see UETA § 2(8)) a notarial certificate in such a way that both are attributed to the notary. The Act remains neutral about the type of technology or process to be used to achieve this end.

The security attributes of registered electronic signatures are detailed in Section 19-2. Registered electronic notary seals are not required to have all of the same security attributes. This difference speaks to the primacy of the notary's electronic signature in this Act, and to the drafters' economy in avoiding redundancy and needless cost. Even so, there is no prohibition in the Act against a registered electronic notary seal having all four of the same security attributes as a registered signature; indeed, if the signature and seal are combined into the same "single element" (see Section 16-5), they necessarily would share these attributes.

The fourth security attribute of Section 19-2 (i.e., keeping the means for producing a registered electronic seal "under the electronic notary's sole control") was considered so critical by the drafters that it was extended to registered electronic notary seals by Section 19-3. Further, Section 19-4 makes clear that even an employer who has paid for a notary's commissioning and electronic registration does not have a right to control or retain any means solely designed to produce an employee notary's electronic signatures and seals.

Section 19-5 provides that a registered electronic signature of a notary may be used for lawful purposes other than performing notarizations, as long as it does not label the user as a notary public. The same, however, does not hold true for registered electronic notary seals, which are restricted to official use only. This is consistent with the rules for use of traditional paper-based notary signatures and seals.

§ 19-1 Electronic Signature and Seal Attributed to Notary.

In notarizing an electronic document, the notary shall attach to, or logically associate with, the electronic notarial certificate a registered electronic signature and a registered electronic notary seal, or a registered single element in conformance with Section 16-5, in such a manner that the signature and the seal, or the single element, are attributed to the notary as named on the commission.

Comment

Section 19-1 applies the signature and seal requirements for non-electronic notarizations to their electronic counterparts. (See Sections 8-1 and 8-2.) The language "attach to, or logically associate with," adopted from UETA (see UETA § 2(8)), is a technology-neutral way to express how the signature and seal become part of the electronic notarial certificate.

The section recognizes that an electronic signature and seal may be combined into a single element. The Act permits the use of such a single element, provided that it meets all requirements pertaining to both a registered electronic signature and a registered electronic notary seal. (See Section 16-5.) These requirements are designed to deter fraud and help assure the security of the notarized document.

If a notary has registered more than one means for producing, respectively, electronic signatures and notary seals, any one of the resulting registered signatures may be used with any one of the resulting registered seals in notarizing an electronic document. Likewise, if the notary has registered more than one means of producing a combined signature and seal in a single element, then any one of the produced single elements may be used in notarizing electronically.

§ 19-2 Attributes of Registered Electronic Signature.

A registered electronic signature shall be:

(1) unique to the electronic notary public;

(2) capable of independent verification;

(3) attached to or logically associated with an electronic notarial certificate in such a manner that any subsequent alteration of the certificate or underlying electronic document prominently displays evidence of the alteration; and

(4) attached or logically associated by a means under the electronic notary's sole control.

Comment

Section 19-2 enumerates four attributes of electronic signatures commonly found in statutes. (See, e.g., CAL. GOV. CODE § 16.5; FLA. STAT. § 117.021(2); N. MEX. ADMIN. CODE § 12.9.2.11(C); CODE OF VA. § 47.1-16(D).)

Subparagraph (1) establishes that each notary must have his or her own distinctive means for performing electronic notarizations. Just as a notary could not simulate another notary's holographic signature to perform a notarization, an electronic notary may not use another's electronic signature. This rule drives the registration form requirements of Section 16-4.

Subparagraph (2) requires that the electronic signature be verifiable by independent means. (See definition of "capable of independent verification" in Section 15-1.) This permits third parties relying on electronically notarized documents to determine whether an electronic signature has been duly registered to a particular notary and is valid. The commissioning official could serve as the archivist of the means registered by notaries for producing electronic signatures, or that function could be performed by another trusted entity capable of maintaining a publicly accessible registration list. Although the Act is silent on point, it is conceivable that third parties seeking signature verifications might have to pay a fee to obtain the desired information.

Subparagraph (3) provides an extremely important attribute of the registered electronic signature, viz., that it render any change to the notarial certificate or document conspicuously evident. Electronic documents can be altered quite easily without any apparent trace. In order for third parties to rely on the authenticity of a notarized electronic document, there needs to be some assurance that the document reads exactly as it did when notarized. This third attribute of a registered electronic signature provides that assurance. Such resistance to tampering is promoted by the Uniform Real Property Electronic Recording Act (URPERA), which directs state panels adopting standards for electronic recording to consider "standards requiring adequate information security protection to ensure that electronic documents are accurate, authentic, adequately preserved, and resistant to tampering." (See, e.g., CODE OF S. CAR. §30-6-50(b)(5).)

Subparagraph (4) makes clear that the means for affixing a registered electronic signature must be under the exclusive control of the notary. This is consistent with the rules dictating that non-electronic notarial seals and journals be under the notary's sole control. (See Subsections 7-4(b) and 8-2(c).) An electronic signature may be applied with the touch of a computer key. Without proper safeguards, it can be easy for persons familiar with a notary's routine to co-opt the notary's registered electronic signature for fraudulent purposes. Mandating that the means for electronically signing be within the notary's exclusive control will deter fraud.

It should be understood that in the paper-based world, a person would need to take significant steps to forge or steal both a notary's signature and a notary's seal in order to perform a fraudulent notarial act. In the electronic world, however, the signature and seal can be combined and together employed with one strike of a computer key. (See Section 19-1.) Thus, a notary's failure to maintain exclusive control over the means of producing electronic signatures and seals offers easy opportunities for illegal acts. In one respect, the mandate of Subparagraph (4) may be met quite simply by designating a password known only to the notary to enable access to the means for producing a registered electronic signature. However, the conscientious electronic notary will be aware that passwords may be uncovered or subverted by technically sophisticated criminals, and therefore will be proactive in taking whatever measures are appropriate to prevent unauthorized use of a registered electronic signature.

§ 19-3 Security of Registered Electronic Notary Seal.

At all times the means for producing registered electronic notary seals, or registered single elements as described in Section 16-5, shall be kept under the sole control of the electronic notary.

Comment

Section 19-3 is essentially a continuation of Subparagraph 19-2(4). It extends the same mandate (i.e., exclusive control by the notary) from the means of producing an electronic signature to that for producing an electronic notary seal or a single element combining the required features of the signature and seal. (See Section 16-5.) Through use of the words "At all times," Subsection (a) heightens the notary's accountability for the security of these items. "At all times," of course, does not mean a constant physical presence by the notary, but it does mean employment of reliable systems to safeguard access when the notary is not present.

§ 19-4 Employer Shall Not Use or Control Means.

An employer of an electronic notary shall not use or control the means for producing registered electronic signatures and notary seals, or registered single elements combining the required features of both, nor upon termination of a notary's employment, retain any software, coding, disk, certificate, card, token, or program that is intended exclusively to produce a registered electronic signature, notary seal, or combined single element, whether or not the employer financially supported the employee's activities as a notary.

Comment

Section 19-4 is consistent with rules governing use and control of a notary seal for non-electronic notarizations. (See Subsection 8- 2(c).) The overarching principle here is that, regardless of who financed the notary's commissioning, the commission itself solely belongs to and is controlled by the notary, as are all the appurtenances of office – including the means for producing the notary's electronic signatures and seals. This does not mean that a notary leaving a company's employment is entitled to take every piece of "software, coding, disk, certificate, card, token, or program" used in producing a registered electronic signature or notary seal. Only those items "intended exclusively" to produce a registered signature or seal, or a combined single element, would be retained by the notary.

§ 19-5 Non-Notarial Use.

(a) A registered electronic signature may be used by the electronic notary for lawful purposes other than performing electronic notarizations, provided that neither the title "notary" nor any other indication of status as a notarial officer is part of the signature.

(b) Neither a registered electronic notary seal nor a combined single element containing the seal shall be used by the electronic notary for any purpose other than performing lawful electronic notarizations.

Comment

Section 19-5 applies certain principles of paper-based notary signatures and seals to their electronic counterparts.

Subsection (a) specifically allows the notary to use a registered electronic signature for non-notarial transactions, personal or professional, provided the signature does not contain any designations, such as the title "notary," indicating it belongs to an official with notarial powers. Otherwise, there could be confusion about whether a particular electronic document was or was not notarized. This corresponds to a notary's use of handwritten personal signatures on different paper documents in official and unofficial capacities, respectively.

In the future, the same electronic credential registered by a notary to produce electronic signatures for notarizations (see Section 16-4) might be used as well for the non-notarial purpose of systems access. For example, future notaries might be hired by organizations to perform electronic notarial acts but first will need to obtain access to a secure computer system using their electronic credentials in order to perform those official acts.

Subsection (b) lays down the simple and obvious rule that precludes a notary from using a registered electronic notary seal for any purpose other than performing an electronic notarization. This mirrors the rule with respect to improper use of an inking seal on paper documents. (See Subsection 8-2(b).) Because a single registered element combining the electronic signature and seal does indeed contain the seal (see Section 16-5), the same prohibition applies to the single element.

Chapter 20 – Record of Electronic Notarial Acts

Comment

General: In the former Act, no separate chapter existed to address record-keeping for electronic notarizations. Instead, the matter was largely dealt with in an expansive definition that the current drafters believed did not do full justice to the topic. Chapter 20 takes on this task.

Section 20-1 restates basic rules for maintaining a journal of notarial acts already set forth in Section 7-1 for paper-based notaries. Rather than insist that electronic notaries keep an electronic record of their official acts, the Act gives such notaries the option to maintain a traditional paper journal. Similarly, otherwise solely paper-based notaries may opt to keep electronic records. This flexibility was seen by the drafters as helpful at a time when many notaries are still transitioning to electronic processes.

Section 20-2 enumerates the required attributes of an electronic journal that, in the former Act, had been incorporated into the definition of "electronic journal of notarial acts." The attributes include a two-factor access procedure for the notary making entries or any person seeking to view or copy an entry (Subsection 1); a capability to prevent alteration of the content or sequence of a saved entry (Subsection 2); a backup system to compensate for loss of the original record (Subsection 3); and the capability of capturing, storing, and printing out the image of a handwritten signature, as well as data related to one other type of biometric identifier (Subsections 4 and 5). The "Comment" to Section 20-2 points out that an electronic notarial record is superior to a paper one in matters such as guarding the confidential data of signers.

Section 20-3 imposes on notaries who keep electronic journals the responsibility of obeying all applicable rules for traditional non-electronic journals.

Section 20-4 requires inclusion of electronic journal access instructions on the electronic notary registration form (see Subsection 16-4(3)), and notification of the commissioning official of any subsequent changes.

§ 20-1 Maintaining Journal of Electronic Notarial Acts.

(a) An electronic notary public shall keep, maintain, protect, and provide for lawful inspection a chronological journal of notarial acts that is either:

(1) a permanently bound book with numbered pages; or

(2) an electronic journal of notarial acts as described in Section 20-2.

(b) An electronic notary shall keep a record of electronic and nonelectronic notarial acts in the same journal.

(c) An electronic notary shall maintain only 1 active journal at the same time, except that a backup of each active and inactive electronic journal shall be retained by the notary in accordance with Subparagraph 20-2(3) as long as each respective original journal is retained.

Comment

Section 20-1 mandates that a notary who performs electronic notarial acts must maintain a journal. This is consistent with the rule established in Section 7-1 for nonelectronic notarial acts. The section does not require that electronic acts be recorded in an electronic journal. Subsection (a) permits notaries to record electronic transactions in a bound paper journal. Although a jurisdiction always may opt to require an electronic notary to maintain an electronic journal (see, e.g., 29 DEL. CODE § 4314(a); CODE OF VA. § 47.1-14(C)), the drafters decided that notaries should be given flexibility to perform this record-keeping function in the way that best suits them, especially in this era of continuing transition to electronic processes.

Conforming further with Section 7-1, Subsections (b) and (c) restate two important rules. First, a notary shall maintain only one active, official journal at a time and record all notarial acts (both electronic and non-electronic) in it. This averts possible later confusion about the completeness of any one journal. Second, if an electronic journal is used to record notarial acts, the notary must maintain a backup copy to accommodate the not inconceivable event of irreversible computer system failure or damage. (See Subparagraph 20-2(3).) Ideally, the backup journal would be retained in a separate, offsite system.

§ 20-2 Attributes of Electronic Journal.

An electronic journal of notarial acts shall:

(1) allow journal entries to be made, viewed, printed out, and copied only after access is obtained by a procedure that uses two factors of authentication;

(2) not allow a journal entry to be deleted or altered in content or sequence by the notary or any other person after a record of the notarization is entered and stored;

(3) have a backup system in place to provide a duplicate record of notarial acts as a precaution in the event of loss of the original record;

(4) be capable of capturing and storing the image of a handwritten signature and the data related to 1 other type of recognized biometric identifier; and

(5) be capable of printing out and providing electronic copies of any entry, including images of handwritten signatures and the data related to the 1 other selected type of recognized biometric identifier.

Comment

Section 20-2 enumerates the minimum attributes of an electronic journal. While in the former Act the attributes of the journal appeared in the definitions chapter (see the current much shorter definition of "electronic journal of notarial acts" in Section 15-4), the drafters decided that the more appropriate venue for these detailed specifications was this chapter.

Subparagraph (1) provides security to the journal by requiring a two-factor access process. There are three categories from which such authenticating factors may be drawn. These are based on 1) who you are (e.g., a user name or thumbprint), 2) what you have (e.g., a token or smart card), and 3) what you know (e.g., a password or knowledge-based question such as, "What is your mother's maiden name?"). Subparagraph (1) requires that access to the electronic journal be protected by at least two of these factors. Such protection is consistent with the rules in Section 7-4 for safeguarding a bound paper journal. It was the consensus of the drafters that while notary journals are not purely public records per se and should not be accessible at whim, their public utility should be recognized and limited access granted in certain situations.

Subparagraph (2) mandates that the electronic journal be tamper-resistant. It is critical that the system not allow changes by the notary or anyone else after a journal entry is electronically saved. Without such protection, the integrity of the electronic journal is compromised. In a paper journal, erasures or deletions are conspicuous and call attention to possible fraud, but electronic records often can be changed without detection. Thus, any reliable electronic journal must be tamper resistant.

Subparagraph (4) dictates that the electronic journal be able to capture a handwritten signature and one other type of recognized biometric identifier, such as a thumbprint. Nothing would prohibit the additional capability of capturing a photographic facial image of a principal. Indeed, a signature, thumbprint, and photograph would be convincing evidence that a particular individual appeared in person before the notary, and comprise a potent deterrent to forgers.

Subparagraph (5) requires that the electronic journal be capable of printing out any or all entries, including any or all associated images and supplemental information (e.g., signature dynamics data). This increases the public utility of the electronic journal and puts it on equal footing with its paper counterpart. (See Section 7-3.) Yet, in many respects the electronic journal is far superior to a paper one in the benefits it can provide to the public. For instance, the electronic journal much more easily enables the notary to protect the confidentiality of other entries from the unauthorized scrutiny of a principal, a witness, or a copy seeker who has been given proper access to view a particular entry.

§ 20-3 Rules for Electronic Journal.

In maintaining an electronic journal of notarial acts, a notary public shall comply with the applicable prescriptions and prohibitions regarding the contents, copying, security, surrender, and disposition of a journal as set forth in Chapters 7 and 12 of this [Act].

Comment

Section 20-3 simply imposes on the notary who maintains an electronic journal the same obligations in maintaining and disposing of this journal as exist for paper journals. (See, generally, Sections 7-2 through 7-5; and 12-4 through 12-5.) Notably, this rule applies as well to nonelectronic notaries who opt to record their paper-based official acts in an electronic journal.

§ 20-4 [Commissioning Official's] Access to Electronic Journal.

If an electronic notary public elects to keep an electronic journal of notarial acts pursuant to Subsection 20-1(a), the notary shall:

(1) provide to the [commissioning official] on the registration form described in Section 16-4 the access instructions that allow journal entries to be viewed, printed out, and copied; and

(2) notify the [commissioning official] of any subsequent change to the access instructions.

Comment

Section 20-4 requires that the commissioning official be given the means to access electronic journals kept by electronic notaries. Initially, this is done through the registration process. (See Subparagraph 16-4(3).) Subparagraph (2) directs the notary to inform the commissioning official of any later change in the procedure for gaining access to the journal. In the absence of the notary, such access instructions enable the official to glean information from any active or inactive journal should it ever be needed in authenticating an electronic or nonelectronic act, or in investigating the activities of the notary.

This section is similar to Section 7-6. The drafters believed that this same directive is needed in both the article guiding electronic notaries and that guiding non-electronic notaries, because notaries in either group may opt to maintain an electronic journal. Nonelectronic notaries, of course, do not use the electronic notary registration process to inform the commissioning official of their journal access procedure.

Chapter 21 – Fees of Electronic Notary

Comment

General: This chapter adapts the fee rules for paper-based notarial acts (see Chapter 6) to electronic notarizations. The drafters anticipated that jurisdictions will permit higher fees for electronic notarizations than for their paper-based counterparts because of the costs necessary to establish oneself and operate as an electronic notary. There also will be ongoing upgrade, maintenance, and security expenses. Electronic notary fees must bear a reasonable relationship to operating costs, yet be set at a level that does not make electronic notarial acts prohibitively expensive and thus discourage the use of electronic documents.

§ 21-1 Imposition and Waiver of Fees.

(a) For performing an electronic notarial act, an electronic notary public may charge the maximum fee specified in Section 21-2, charge less than the maximum fee, or waive the fee.

(b) An electronic notary shall not discriminatorily condition the fee for an electronic notarial act on the attributes of the principal or requester of fact as set forth in Subsection 5-6(a) of this [Act], though an electronic notary may waive or reduce fees for humanitarian or charitable reasons.

Comment

Section 21-1 essentially adopts the general rules regarding fees for paper-based notarizations (see Section 6-1) and applies them to electronic notarizations. As with nonelectronic acts, an electronic notary must neither charge a fee higher than permitted by statute, nor improperly discriminate in the setting of fees. (For a discussion of prohibited discriminatory fee practices, see, generally, Section 6-1 "Comment.")

§ 21-2 Maximum Fees.

(a) The maximum fees that may be charged by an electronic notary public for performing an electronic notarial act are:

(1) for an acknowledgment, [dollars] per signature;

(2) for a jurat, [dollars] per signature;

(3) for a signature witnessing, [dollars] per signature;

(4) for a copy certification, [dollars] per [500 characters] certified but in no event shall the fee be less than [dollars]; and

(5) for a verification of fact, [dollars] per certificate.

(b) An electronic notary may charge a travel fee when traveling to perform an electronic notarial act if:

(1) the notary and the person requesting the electronic notarial act agree upon the travel fee in advance of the travel; and

(2) the notary explains to the person requesting the notarial act that the travel fee is both separate from the notarial fee prescribed in Subsection (a) and neither specified nor mandated by law.

Comment

Section 21-2 sets the fee schedule for electronic notarizations, closely following the format of Section 6-2, which sets fees for nonelectronic acts. It is anticipated that these fees will be higher than those for paper-based notarizations. The exact fees should be determined by lawmakers who take into account the expenses associated with maintaining the capability to perform electronic notarizations. They must not be so high as to discourage citizens from availing themselves of electronic services. Since federal legislation (E-Sign) has paved the way for the widespread use of electronic documents and signatures, efforts should be made to foster that initiative. A reasonable, affordable fee structure will speed the absorption of electronic notarization into the stream of commerce.

In Subsection (a), the drafters were particularly challenged by the issue of how to charge properly for copy-certifying an electronic document, because charging per page, as is the rule with copy-certifying a paper original (see Subsection 6-2(a)), does not correspondingly accommodate lengthy "scroll down" electronic pages. Charging by character or word count seemed fairer, although this method is less useful when graphic images are involved. Some drafters proposed that "file size" be the determining factor in establishing the fee, but there often will not be direct proportionality between the size of an electronic file and the complexity of the copy-certification task. After considerable discussion, the drafters decided that it would be fairest in most cases for the electronic notary to charge based on the number of characters in the original electronic document, but with a "floor" or minimum fee in every case.

Subsection (b) restates the travel fee rules and restrictions for paper-based notarial acts (see Section 6-2(b)), and applies them to electronic notarizations. The provision reinforces the position that "remote notarizations" are not permitted. Principals must be in the physical presence of the notary for every notarization of a signature. There are not any exceptions made for electronic notarizations. Thus, if an electronic notary has a laptop computer or other portable means of notarizing a principal's electronic document, the notary may agree with the principal on an appropriate travel fee. (For further rules and discussion of travel fees, see Section 6-2(b) "Comment.")

§ 21-3 Payment Prior to Electronic Act.

(a) An electronic notary public may require payment of any fees specified in Section 21-2 prior to performance of an electronic notarial act.

(b) Any fees paid to an electronic notary prior to performance of an electronic notarial act are non-refundable if:

(1) the act was completed; or

(2) in the case of travel fees paid in compliance with Subsection 21-2(b), the act was not completed after the notary traveled to meet the principal because it was prohibited under Section 17-2, or because the notary knew or had a reasonable belief that the notarial act or the associated transaction was unlawful.

Comment

Section 21-3 adapts for electronic notaries the rules giving paper-based notaries discretion to require payment of fees prior to the performance of a notarial act. (See Section 6-3.) Under these rules, if a notarial act is not completed because of an action of the principal for whom the notarization is performed (see Section 17-2), then the notary may still retain the travel fee.

§ 21-4 Fees of Employee Electronic Notary.

The rules relating to fees for an employee notary public that are prescribed in Section 6-4 of this [Act] also apply to an electronic notary public in the performance of an electronic notarial act.

Comment

For electronic notaries who are employees, Section 21-4 adopts the same rules applicable to employees who perform non-electronic notarial acts. (See Section 6-4 and Comment.)

§ 21-5 Notice of Fees.

An electronic notary public who charges for performing electronic notarial acts shall conspicuously display in all of the notary's places of business and Internet sites, or present to each principal or requester of fact when outside such places of business, an English-language schedule of maximum fees for electronic notarial acts, as specified in Subsection 21-2(a). No part of any such notarial fee schedule shall appear or be printed in smaller than 10-point type.

Comment

Section 21-5 adopts for electronic notaries who charge fees a disclosure requirement similar to that for paper-based notaries. (See Section 6-5 and Comment.) In the case of a notary traveling to perform an electronic notarization, the Act would allow a fee schedule to be "presented" through an on-screen laptop display in lieu of a schedule printed on paper.

Chapter 22 – Evidence of Authenticity of Electronic Notarial Act

Comment

General: Chapter 22 provides for the authentication of electronically notarized documents so that they may be honored in foreign jurisdictions. Section 22-1 dictates that an electronic authenticating certificate be attached to or logically associated with the notarized document in a way that imparts the same level of tamper-evident security as did use of a registered electronic signature by the notary. Section 22-2 prescribes a form for the electronic certificate of authority, and Section 22-3 a maximum fee that may be charged by the commissioning official for issuance of the certificate.

§ 22-1 Form of Evidence of Authority of Electronic Notarial Act.

(a) On a notarized electronic document transmitted to another state or nation, electronic evidence of the authenticity of the registered electronic signature and seal of an electronic notary public of this [State], if required, shall be in the form of an electronic certificate of authority signed by the [commissioning official] in conformance with any current and pertinent international treaties, agreements, and conventions subscribed by the government of the United States.

(b) The electronic certificate of authority described in Subsection (a) shall be attached to or logically associated with the electronically notarized document in such a manner that any subsequent alteration of the notarized document, or removal or alteration of the electronic certificate of authority, produces evidence of the change.

Comment

Section 22-1 describes the electronic version of a certificate of authority, for use in authenticating a notarized electronic document. (See the rules for a nonelectronic certificate of authority in Section 10-1.)

Subsection (b) provides the same security protection for electronic certificates of authority as is given to notarized electronic documents themselves. Specifically, the section requires that the means for attaching or logically associating the certificate to the notarized document must produce evidence of any future tampering with either the certificate or document – thus, conforming with the NASS Standards. (See NASS Standards, Requirements for Issuance of Electronic Apostilles and Certificates of Authentication, 13 through 15 (2006) (www.nass.org). The drafters believed that a certificate from the commissioning authority that speaks to the authenticity of an electronic notary's act should maintain at the very least the same level of security as the underlying notarized document.

§ 22-2 Certificate of Authority for Electronic Notarial Act.

An electronic certificate of authority evidencing the authenticity of the registered electronic signature and seal of an electronic notary public of this [State] shall be in substantially the following form:

Certificate of Authority for Electronic Notarial Act

I, (name and title of commissioning official), certify that (name of electronic notary public), the person named as Electronic Notary Public in the attached, associated, or accompanying electronic document, was registered as an Electronic Notary Public for the [State] of [name of jurisdiction] and authorized to act as such at the time the document was electronically notarized. I also certify that the document bears no evidence of illegal or fraudulent alteration.

To verify this Certificate of Authority for an Electronic Notarial Act, I have included herewith my electronic seal and signature this ____day of _____, 20____.

(Electronic seal and signature of [commissioning official])

Comment

Section 22-2 prescribes a certificate for issuance by the commissioning official that in a straightforward manner provides the necessary assurances to third parties relying upon a particular notarized electronic document and confirms an electronic notary's authority to notarize that document. Implicit in this confirmation is the assurance that the document has the security features required by the Act. The certificate largely reflects the requirements of the authenticating certificate for non-electronic acts set forth in Section 10-2.

§ 22-3 Fee for Electronic Certificate of Authority.

For issuing an electronic certificate of authority for an electronic notarial act, including an electronic form of the Apostille set forth in Section 10-3 of this [Act], the [commissioning official] may charge a maximum of [dollars].

Comment

Section 22-3 authorizes the commissioning official to charge a fee for issuing a certificate of authority, including an electronic Apostille, for a notarized electronic document. This is consistent with the practice for non-electronic certificates of authority and Apostilles. (See Section 10-4.) The specific dollar amount is not set, but instead left to the discretion of the lawmakers of each jurisdiction.

Chapter 23 – Changes of Status of Electronic Notary

Comment

General: This chapter provides guidance for electronic notaries in reporting to the commissioning official pertinent changes in status. The provisions correspond to similar rules imposed on paper-based notaries (see Chapter 12), but the distinctive nature of the electronic notary's duties requires that some additional status changes be reported. However, nothing in this chapter relieves the notary from any obligations imposed by Chapter 12.

§ 23-1 Change of E-Mail Address.

Within [5] business days after the change of an electronic notary public's email address, the notary shall electronically transmit to the [commissioning official] a notice of the change secured by a registered electronic signature of the notary.

Comment

Section 23-1 imposes an obligation specific to the electronic notary to report any change of e-mail address. The reporting must be made electronically. This form of notification underscores the fact that the primary medium of communication between electronic notaries and the commissioning official is electronic. Whereas paper-based notaries are given 10 calendar days to report changes of physical address (see Subsection 12-1(a)), the drafters believed an e-mail address change can be reported more expeditiously without hardship to the notary.

§ 23-2 Change of Registration Data.

Any change or addition to the data on the electronic registration form described in Section 16-4, including any change to an electronic journal's access instructions, shall be reported within 10 days to the [commissioning official].

Comment

Section 23-2 mirrors the reporting requirements imposed on paper-based notaries. Because the commissioning official has discretion to ask for registration information from the notary in addition to that specified by Section 16-4, the drafters opted not to enumerate the information that might be changed, but instead just to address this data by reference to the registration form. Conceivably, such additional data might include the notary's name, telephone number, and business name. The drafters selected a reporting deadline of 10 calendar days to be congruent with the 10-day deadline for changes of name and address by paper-based notaries (see Sections 12-1 and 12-2) to enable the reporting obligations for both electronic and non-electronic status to be fulfilled by a single electronic communication.

§ 23-3 Change of Means of Production.

(a) Upon becoming aware that the status, functionality, or validity of the means for producing a registered electronic signature, notary seal, or single element combining the signature and seal, has changed, expired, terminated, or become compromised, the notary shall:

(1) immediately notify the [commissioning official];

(2) cease producing seals or signatures in electronic notarizations using that means;

(3) perform electronic notarizations only with a currently registered means or another means that has been registered within 30 days; and

(4) dispose of any software, coding, disk, certificate, card, token, or program that has been rendered defunct, in the manner described in Subsection 23-5(a).

(b) Pursuant to Subsection (a), the [commissioning official] shall immediately suspend the electronic status of a notary who has no other currently registered means for producing electronic signatures or notary seals, and if such means is not registered within 30 days, electronic status shall be terminated.

Comment

Section 23-3 recognizes the fact that a notary's registered electronic seal and signature are produced by specific electronic processes that are subject to change. For example, the electronic credential used by the notary to create electronic signatures may expire. Alternatively, heat or water may have damaged or destroyed the functionality of a pertinent disk or token; or theft or loss may have prevented any further use of the disk or token. Another eventuality that would qualify as a reportable change of status is the notary's voluntary discarding or destroying of the means for producing an electronic seal or signature. If the commissioning official determines that the notary's negligence or other misconduct compromised the means for producing an electronic signature or seal, the official has authority to terminate registration as an electronic notary. (See Subparagraph 24- 2(a)(3).)

Subparagraph (1) requires the electronic notary to notify the commissioning official of the change of status. This must be done even if the notary has registered other means for producing seals or signatures for electronic acts. For authentication and investigative purposes, the commissioning official must immediately be made aware of any changes of status in the capability to perform electronic acts.

Subparagraph (2) directs the notary to stop using any expired, invalid, or otherwise defunct means for producing an electronic seal or signature in notarial acts.

Subparagraph (3) dictates that the notary may continue to perform electronic notarizations only with a currently registered means for producing seals and/or signatures or with a means that will be registered within 30 calendar days. The drafters believed that electronic notaries should be given a "grace period" to update their expired electronic tools rather than have to suffer immediate termination of electronic notary status. Of course, if the notary possessed a still valid and registered second means for producing electronic seals and/or signatures, such termination would not be necessary.

Subparagraph (4) directs the notary to dispose of (i.e., "permanently erase or expunge") any defunct software, coding, disk, certificate, card, token, or program formerly used exclusively to produce electronic notary seals and signatures in notarial acts. The disposal must be accomplished as stipulated in Subsection 23-5(a).

Subsection (b) grants the electronic notary without another registered signature or seal a 30- day grace period to replace the defunct means for producing an electronic signature and/or notary seal and to register a new means. If this is not done within 30 calendar days, the notary's electronic status is terminated.

§ 23-4 Termination of Electronic Notary Registration.

(a) Any revocation, resignation, expiration, or other termination of the commission of a notary public immediately terminates any existing registration as an electronic notary.

(b) A notary's decision to terminate registration as an electronic notary shall not automatically terminate the underlying commission of the notary.

(c) A notary who terminates registration as an electronic notary shall notify the [commissioning official] in writing and dispose of any pertinent software, coding, disk, certificate, card, token, or program as described in Section 23-5(a).

Comment

Section 23-4 addresses matters related to termination of registration as an electronic notary. Subsection (a) states a basic rule: termination of the notary's commission, for any reason, concomitantly terminates the electronic notary registration. While the notary thereby would be prohibited from producing further electronic notary seals, there would be no such ban against future personal use of electronic signatures whose means of production was formerly registered, provided such signatures do not indicate status as a notary. (See Subsection 19-5(a).)

Subsection (b) makes clear that a notary may voluntarily terminate electronic notary registration without jeopardizing an otherwise valid notary commission. However, resignation of electronic notary status does not preclude an official investigation into an electronic notary's conduct. (See Subsection 24-2(c).) Official misconduct as an electronic notary is cause for the revocation of the underlying commission. (See Section 2-12 and Subsections 3-1(c) and 13-3(a).) The first two subsections make the point that while electronic registration is available only to duly commissioned notaries, not all such notaries may need or want to be registered.

Subsection (c) instructs the electronic notary on the steps to be taken for voluntary termination of registration.

§ 23-5 Disposition of Software and Hardware.

(a) Except as provided in Subsection (b), when the commission of an electronic notary public expires or is resigned or revoked, when registration as an electronic notary terminates, or when an electronic notary dies, the notary or the notary's duly authorized representative within [30] business days shall permanently erase or expunge the software, coding, disk, certificate, card, token, or program that is intended exclusively to produce registered electronic notary seals, registered single elements combining the required features of an electronic signature and notary seal, or registered electronic signatures that indicate status as a notary.

(b) A former electronic notary public whose previous commission expired need not comply with Subsection (a) if this person, within 3 months after expiration, is recommissioned and reregistered as an electronic notary using the same registered means for producing electronic notary seals and signatures.

Comment

Section 23-5 mandates that the software and other electronic devices used exclusively to create the notary's electronic seal and signature be properly disposed of to prevent their misuse by unauthorized parties. This corresponds to the rule for the proper disposal of the tools of office for the paper-based notary, i.e., seal and journal. (See Sections 12-4 and 12-5.)

Under Subsection (a), an electronic item need not be permanently erased or expunged if it were not used "exclusively" to produce a registered electronic notary seal or a registered single element combining the required features of an electronic signature and notary seal. Neither would the registered means for producing a notary's electronic signature have to be disposed of if the signatures produced did not indicate status as a notary. (See Subsection 19-5(a).) Such signatures could continue to be used on electronic documents in the notary's personal and other non-notarial affairs.

Subsection (b) allows a notary "renewing" a commission in accordance with Chapters 3 and 4 to avert the disposal procedure set forth in Subsection (a) if the notary intends to be recommissioned and reregistered within three months after the original commission expires. These two processes may be accomplished at the same time. (See Subsection 16-1(c).)

Chapter 24 – Liability, Sanctions, and Remedies for Improper Acts

Comment

General: Chapter 24 makes clear that the basic responsibilities and penalties belonging to the new functions of the electronic notary public are the same as those imposed by the traditional duties of the notarial office. (See Section 24-1.) Section 24-2 prescribes rules for the commissioning official to observe in terminating the registration of an electronic notary. These include the rule that voluntary resignation of status as an electronic notary not terminate an investigation into a notary's misconduct in the electronic arena.

§ 24-1 Penalties and Remedies for Improper Electronic Acts.

The liability, sanctions, and remedies for the improper performance of electronic notarial acts by an electronic notary public are the same as described and provided in Chapter 13 of this [Act] for the improper performance of non-electronic notarial acts.

Comment

Section 24-1 reinforces the position that electronic notaries are first and foremost duly commissioned notaries with traditional powers and responsibilities. As such, they hold positions of trust and confidence. Therefore, in the performance of electronic notarizations the public has the right to expect the same high level of integrity, honesty, impartiality, and trustworthiness that is demanded of notaries performing traditional paper-based notarizations. In recognition of that fact, the Act applies all of the liabilities, sanctions, and remedies set out in Chapter 13 for paper-based notarizations to electronic notarizations.

§ 24-2 Causes for Termination of Registration.

(a) The [commissioning official] shall terminate an electronic notary public's registration for any of the following reasons:

(1) submission of an electronic registration form containing material misstatement or omission of fact;

(2) failure to maintain the capability to perform electronic notarial acts, except as allowed in Subparagraph 23-3(a)(3); or

(3) the electronic notary's performance of official misconduct.

(b) Prior to terminating an electronic notary's registration, the [commissioning official] shall inform the notary of the basis for the termination and that the termination shall take place on a particular date unless a proper appeal is filed with the [administrative body hearing the appeal] before that date.

(c) Neither resignation nor expiration of a notary commission or of an electronic notary registration precludes or terminates an investigation by the [commissioning official] into the electronic notary's conduct. The investigation may be pursued to a conclusion, whereupon it shall be made a matter of public record whether or not the finding would have been grounds for termination of the commission or registration of the electronic notary.

Comment

Section 24-2 provides the bases and procedures for terminating registration as an electronic notary.

Subparagraph (a)(1) mirrors the commonsense rules applied to notary commission applications. (See Subsections 3-1(c); and 13-3(a).) There cannot be any reason to allow a notary who intentionally deceives the commissioning official to be given authority to perform notarial acts, either paper-based or electronic. Subparagraph (a)(2) mandates that registration terminate if the notary loses the technological capability to perform electronic acts. (This might result for any number of reasons, as outlined in the "Comment" to Section 23-3.) However, the subparagraph provides an exception if there is merely an interruption in the notary's capability to perform electronic notarizations. For example, if the electronic credential used by the notary to create electronic signatures expires, and the notary quickly (within 30 days, see Subparagraph 23-3(a)(3)) takes action to replace this credential and to register the new means of producing electronic signatures, then status as an electronic notary need not terminate. Subparagraph (a)(3) requires the commissioning official to terminate the registration of an electronic notary for official misconduct. (See definition of "official misconduct" in Section 2-12.) Such misconduct might include the notary's negligence in allowing the means for producing electronic notary seals and signatures to be compromised. (See Section 23-3 and "Comment.")

Subsection (b) provides the notice and appeal procedures to be used in a registration termination action. These ensure that the electronic notary is given a fair chance to respond to any allegations giving rise to termination. The procedures are similar to those used in cases of notary commission revocation. (See Subsection 13- 3(c).)

Subsection (c) specifically applies to endorse the rule enunciated in Subsection 13-3(d) regarding the need to continue to a conclusion any investigation into alleged misconduct of the electronic notary, even if the notary's registration or commission is resigned or expired prior to completion of the termination proceeding. Mere resignation or expiration of notarial powers is not a satisfactory response to egregious misconduct. It is important that any investigation go forward to ensure that misdeeds are exposed and appropriate measures taken and made public.

Chapter 25 – Violations by Person Not an Electronic Notary

Comment

General: This chapter addresses actions by third parties designed to bring about improper electronic notarizations. It also provides guidance with respect to criminal sanctions that may be imposed upon persons who improperly access, possess, or use the tools of office of an electronic notary.

§ 25-1 Impersonation and Improper Influence.

The criminal sanctions for impersonating an electronic notary public and for soliciting, coercing, or improperly influencing an electronic notary to commit official misconduct in performing notarial acts are the same sanctions described in Chapter 14 of this [Act] in regard to performing non-electronic notarial acts.

Comment

Section 25-1 establishes rules that parallel those set out in Sections 14-1 and 14-3 with respect to performing nonelectronic notarial acts without authority and influencing the execution of improper nonelectronic notarial acts. The section recognizes that an unscrupulous individual impersonating a notary could a) use an electronic signature and seal whose means of production have not been duly registered with the commissioning official to perform unauthorized electronic notarizations, or b) misappropriate and use a notary's registered means for producing an electronic signature and seal to do so. The section also imposes sanctions upon any person attempting to influence a notary to perform an improper electronic notarization.

§ 25-2 Wrongful Destruction or Possession of Software or Hardware.

Any person who knowingly obtains, conceals, damages, or destroys the coding, disk, certificate, card, token, program, software, or hardware that is intended exclusively to enable an electronic notary public to produce a registered electronic signature, notary seal, or single element combining the required features of an electronic signature and notary seal, is guilty of a [class of offense], punishable upon conviction by a fine not exceeding [dollars] or imprisonment for not more than [term of imprisonment], or both.

Comment

Section 25-2 is analogous to Section 14- 2, which relates to the wrongful possession or destruction of the seal or journal of a paper-based notary. This section imposes the same criminal liability for any person who engages in similar acts with respect to the tools needed to perform an electronic notarial act. The section does not specifically mention electronic journals because there is no distinction between a paper and an electronic journal for the purposes of Section 14-2. Thus, the electronic journal is protected under that section. In this Act, electronic and bound paper journals are interchangeable.

§ 25-3 Additional Sanctions Not Precluded.

The sanctions of this chapter do not preclude other sanctions and remedies provided by law.

Chapter 26 – Administration

Comment

General: Section 26-1 enables the commissioning official to administer the rules governing electronic notarization in the manner this official deems appropriate. The drafters anticipate that different officials will craft different methods to administer the Act most efficiently in their respective jurisdictions.

§ 26-1 Policies and Procedures.

The [commissioning official] may promulgate and enforce any policies and procedures necessary for the administration of this Article. ■

Appendix

Appendix 1B

REVISED UNIFORM LAW ON NOTARIAL ACTS (2010)

REVISED UNIFORM LAW ON NOTARIAL ACTS

Drafted by the

NATIONAL CONFERENCE OF COMMISSIONERS
ON UNIFORM STATE LAWS

and by it

Approved and Recommended for Enactment
in All the States

at its

Annual Conference
Meeting in Its One-Hundred-and-Nineteenth Year
in Chicago, Illinois
July 9–16, 2010

Without Prefatory Note or Comments

Copyright © 2010
By
National Conference of Commissioners
on Uniform State Laws

TABLE OF CONTENTS

Prefatory Note
SECTION 1. SHORT TITLE
SECTION 2. DEFINITIONS
SECTION 3. APPLICABILITY.
SECTION 4. AUTHORITY TO PERFORM NOTARIAL ACT.
SECTION 5. REQUIREMENTS FOR CERTAIN NOTARIAL ACTS.
SECTION 6. PERSONAL APPEARANCE REQUIRED.
SECTION 7. IDENTIFICATION OF INDIVIDUAL.
SECTION 8. AUTHORITY TO REFUSE TO PERFORM NOTARIAL ACT.
SECTION 9. SIGNATURE IF INDIVIDUAL UNABLE TO SIGN.
SECTION 10. NOTARIAL ACT IN THIS STATE.
SECTION 11. NOTARIAL ACT IN ANOTHER STATE.
SECTION 12. NOTARIAL ACT UNDER AUTHORITY OF FEDERALLY RECOGNIZED INDIAN TRIBE.
SECTION 13. NOTARIAL ACT UNDER FEDERAL AUTHORITY.
SECTION 14. FOREIGN NOTARIAL ACT.
SECTION 15. CERTIFICATE OF NOTARIAL ACT.
SECTION 16. SHORT FORM CERTIFICATES.
SECTION 17. OFFICIAL STAMP.
SECTION 18. STAMPING DEVICE.
[SECTION 19. JOURNAL.
SECTION 20. NOTIFICATION REGARDING PERFORMANCE OF NOTARIAL ACT ON ELECTRONIC RECORD; SELECTION OF TECHNOLOGY.
SECTION 21. COMMISSION AS NOTARY PUBLIC; QUALIFICATIONS; NO IMMUNITY OR BENEFIT.
[SECTION 22. EXAMINATION OF NOTARY PUBLIC.
SECTION 23. GROUNDS TO DENY, REFUSE TO RENEW, REVOKE, SUSPEND, OR CONDITION COMMISSION OF NOTARY PUBLIC.
SECTION 24. DATABASE OF NOTARIES PUBLIC.
SECTION 25. PROHIBITED ACTS.
SECTION 26. VALIDITY OF NOTARIAL ACTS.
SECTION 27. RULES
SECTION 28. NOTARY PUBLIC COMMISSION IN EFFECT.
SECTION 29. SAVINGS CLAUSE.
SECTION 30. UNIFORMITY OF APPLICATION AND CONSTRUCTION
SECTION 31. RELATION TO ELECTRONIC SIGNATURES IN GLOBAL AND NATIONAL COMMERCE ACT
SECTION 32. REPEALS
SECTION 33. EFFECTIVE DATE

Prefatory Note

This version of the Uniform Law on Notarial Acts ("ULONA") is a comprehensive revision of the Uniform Law on Notarial Acts as approved by the National Conference of Commissioners on Uniform State Laws ("NCCUSL") in 1982. Since that date, countless societal and technological as well as market and economic changes have occurred requiring notarial officers and the notarial acts that they perform to adapt. In addition, there has been a growing non-uniformity among the states in their laws regarding notarial acts. This version of ULONA adapts the notarial process to accommodate those changes, makes the Act more responsive to current transactions and practices, and seeks to promote uniformity among state laws regarding notarial acts.

Perhaps the most pervasive change since the adoption of the original version of ULONA has been the development and growing implementation of electronic records in commercial, governmental, and personal transactions. In 1999, NCCUSL approved the Uniform Electronic Transactions Act ("UETA"), thereby validating electronic records and putting them on a par with traditional records written on tangible media. The federal Electronic Signatures in Global and National Commerce Act, 15 U.S.C. Ch. 96 (2010) ("ESign") was adopted in 2000, and it also recognized and put electronic records on a par with traditional records on tangible media. In 2004, NCCUSL approved the Uniform Real Property Electronic Recording Act ("URPERA"), thereby permitting county recorders and registrars to accept and register electronic real estate records. Each of those acts also recognized the validity of electronic notarial acts (UETA §11; ESign §101(g); URPERA §3(c)).

This revision of ULONA further recognizes electronic notarial acts and puts them on a par with notarial acts performed on tangible media (Section 2(5)). It does this by unifying the requirements for and treatment of notarial acts, whenever possible, regardless of whether the acts are performed with respect to tangible or electronic media. While continuing the basic treatment of electronic notarial acts provided in UETA, ESign and URPERA, this Act implements structural and operational rules for those notarial acts that were absent in the prior laws. For example, Section 15 sets forth the requirements for certificates of notarial acts whether performed with respect to tangible and electronic records). In addition, Section 20 provides that before notaries public may perform notarial acts with respect to electronic records, they must first notify the commissioning officer or agency.

The Act seeks to provide integrity in the process of performing notarial acts. Regardless of whether the notarial act is completed on a tangible or an electronic record, it requires an individual to appear personally before a notarial officer whenever the officer performs a notarial act regarding a record signed or a statement made by the individual (Section 6), including an acknowledgment, verification, or witnessing of a signature (Section 5(a), (b), and (c)). A notarial officer who certifies a copy of a record must determine that the copy is a full, true, and accurate transcription or reproduction (Section 5(d)).

The Act commands a notarial officer to identify an individual before performing a notarial act for that individual. The Act provides two methods of performing that identification. Identification may be based on personal knowledge of the individual by the notarial officer (Section 7(a)). If an individual is not personally known to the notarial officer, the individual must provide satisfactory evidence of the individual's identity, which may be through the use of an identification credential or by means of an oath or affirmation of a credible witness (Section 7(b)). A notarial officer may require additional identification of an individual if the officer is not satisfied with the individual's identity (Section 7(c)). Furthermore, if an officer is not satisfied that an individual's signature is knowingly and voluntarily made or has concern as to the competency or capacity of the individual, the officer may refuse to perform the notarial act (Section 8(a)).

The Act strives to provide other assurances that also enhance the integrity of the notarial process. In addition to the familiar assurances when tangible records are used, the Act requires the use of tamper-evident technologies on electronic records (Section 20). It authorizes a commissioning officer or agency to adopt rules to implement this Act (Section 27(a)), including rules to insure that any change or tampering with a record bearing a certificate of the notarial act will be self-evident (Section 27(a)(2)). In order to encourage uniformity and interoperability, it provides that a commissioning officer or agency will consider national standards, the standards and customs of other enacting jurisdictions, and the views of interested persons (Section 27(b)).

Another means of assuring the integrity of the notarial process, strongly urged by commissioning officers and notarial associations, is to require that all notaries public maintain journals chronicling all notarial acts. This position is not without controversy, however, and other voices strongly argue that such requirements are unnecessarily burdensome. This Act includes optional provisions requiring a notary public to maintain a journal of all notarial acts that the notary public performs (Section 19), leaving the ultimate decision to the several states. A journal may be maintained on either a tangible or electronic medium, but not both at the same time. It further specifies the information that must be entered in the journal.

This Act replaces past references to a notarial seal with an official stamp. It defines an official stamp as a physical or electronic image and includes the traditional seal (Section 2(8)). Section 17 states the mandatory contents of the official stamp and requires that it be capable of being copied along with the record with which it is associated. Section 18 deals separately with the stamping device, which is defined as the means of affixing the official stamp to a tangible record or associating the official stamp with an electronic record (Section 2(13)). Section 18 also defines the responsibility of the notary public for controlling the stamping device and assuring that it not be used by others.

As with the prior version of the Act, this revision continues to recognize notarial acts performed by notarial officers in the adopting state (Section 10), another state of the United States (Section 11), or under federal authority (Section 13). It also recognizes notarial acts performed under the authority of a federally recognized Indian tribe (Section 12). The increasing frequency of international transactions requires the recognition of notarial acts performed in foreign states (Section 14). The Act continues to recognize an "apostille" complying with the Convention de La Haye du 5 octobre 1961 ("Hague Convention") as a means of providing conclusive authentication of notarial acts that are performed by a notarial officer of a foreign state (Section 14(e)). It also recognizes a consular authentication as an alternative means of providing that conclusive authentication of a foreign notarial act (Section 14(f)).

The prior version of this Act did not contain a licensing procedure for notaries public. As a result, the various states adopted their own provisions. Those provisions vary considerably. In order to promote unity, the Act establishes minimum requirements for the commissioning of notaries public (Section 21) as well as grounds to deny, suspend, or revoke those commissions (Section 23). The Act contains an optional section regarding educational and testing requirements for notaries public (Section 22).

The Act seeks to assure that a notarial officer does not act in a deceptive or fraudulent manner. It prohibits a notarial officer from performing a notarial act with regard to a record to which the officer or the officer's spouse is a party or in which either of them has a direct beneficial interest (Section 4(b)). The Act prohibits a notary public from drafting legal records, giving legal advice, or otherwise practicing law. It also prohibits a notary public from acting as a consultant or expert on immigration matters or representing persons in judicial or administrative proceedings in that regard (Section 25(a)). It further prohibits a notary public from engaging in false or deceptive advertising. In that regard, it expressly prohibits a notary public from representing or advertising that the notary may draft legal documents, give legal advice, or otherwise practice law; any representation or advertisement by a notary must contain a disclaimer to that effect in each language used in the advertisement (Section 25(b), (c), and (d)).

During the process of drafting this revision of ULONA, the Drafting Committee received invaluable assistance regarding current and developing notarial practices, regulatory matters, and available technology from numerous observers. The Drafting Committee wishes to express its appreciation to the National Notary Association, the United States Notary Association, the National Association of Secretaries of State, the Property Records Industry Association, the various vendors who demonstrated available technology, and all the other observers who assisted the Committee.

Revised Uniform Law on Notarial Acts

Section 1. Short Title

This [act] may be cited as the Revised Uniform Law on Notarial Acts.

Comment

This Act is a revision of the Uniform Law on Notarial Acts as approved by the National Conference of Commissioners on Uniform State Laws in 1982.

It provides for the recognition of notarial acts performed in this state, in other states, under the authority of a federally recognized Indian tribe, under federal authority, and in foreign jurisdictions. It applies to notarial acts whether performed with respect to tangible or electronic records.

Section 2. Definitions

In this [act]:

(1) "Acknowledgment" means a declaration by an individual before a notarial officer that the individual has signed a record for the purpose stated in the record and, if the record

is signed in a representative capacity, that the individual signed the record with proper authority and signed it as the act of the individual or entity identified in the record.

(2) "Electronic" means relating to technology having electrical, digital, magnetic, wireless, optical, electromagnetic, or similar capabilities.

(3) "Electronic signature" means an electronic symbol, sound, or process attached to or logically associated with a record and executed or adopted by an individual with the intent to sign the record.

(4) "In a representative capacity" means acting as:

(A) an authorized officer, agent, partner, trustee, or other representative for a person other than an individual;

(B) a public officer, personal representative, guardian, or other representative, in the capacity stated in a record;

(C) an agent or attorney-in-fact for a principal; or

(D) an authorized representative of another in any other capacity.

(5) "Notarial act" means an act, whether performed with respect to a tangible or electronic record, that a notarial officer may perform under the law of this state. The term includes taking an acknowledgment, administering an oath or affirmation, taking a verification on oath or affirmation, witnessing or attesting a signature, certifying or attesting a copy, and noting a protest of a negotiable instrument.

(6) "Notarial officer" means a notary public or other individual authorized to perform a notarial act.

(7) "Notary public" means an individual commissioned to perform a notarial act by the [commissioning officer or agency].

(8) "Official stamp" means a physical image affixed to or embossed on a tangible record or an electronic image attached to or logically associated with an electronic record.

(9) "Person" means an individual, corporation, business trust, statutory trust, estate, trust, partnership, limited liability company, association, joint venture, public corporation, government or governmental subdivision, agency, or instrumentality, or any other legal or commercial entity.

(10) "Record" means information that is inscribed on a tangible medium or that is stored in an electronic or other medium and is retrievable in perceivable form.

(11) "Sign" means, with present intent to authenticate or adopt a record:

(A) to execute or adopt a tangible symbol; or

(B) to attach to or logically associate with the record an electronic symbol, sound, or process.

(12) "Signature" means a tangible symbol or an electronic signature that evidences the signing of a record.

(13) "Stamping device" means:

(A) a physical device capable of affixing to or embossing on a tangible record an official stamp; or

(B) an electronic device or process capable of attaching to or logically associating with an electronic record an official stamp.

(14) "State" means a state of the United States, the District of Columbia, Puerto Rico, the United States Virgin Islands, or any territory or insular possession subject to the jurisdiction of the United States.

(15) "Verification on oath or affirmation" means a declaration, made by an individual on oath or affirmation before a notarial officer, that a statement in a record is true.

Comment

"Acknowledgment." An acknowledgment is a common form of notarial act in which an individual declares before a notarial officer that the individual has executed or signed the record for the purpose or purposes stated in the record. The declaration is made in the presence of the notarial officer. See Coast to Coast Demolition and Crushing, Inc. v. Real Equity Pursuit, LLC, 226 P.3d 605, 608 (Nev. 2010).

It is a common practice for the acknowledging individual to sign the record in the presence of the notarial officer. However, actually signing the record in the presence of the notarial officer is not necessary as long as the individual declares, while in the presence of the officer at that time the acknowledgment is made, that the signature already on the record is, in fact, the signature of the individual.

If the record is signed by an individual in a representative capacity, the individual also declares to the notarial officer that the individual has proper authority to execute the record on behalf of the principal (see Section 2(4)).

"Electronic." The adjective "electronic" is used to refer to electrical, digital, magnetic, wireless, optical, electromagnetic, and similar technologies. Electronic technologies are capable of generating, transmitting, or storing information in an intangible format that may subsequently be retrieved and viewed in a perceivable format.

As with the Uniform Electronic Transactions Act, the term "electronic" is descriptive and its reach is not intended to be limited to technologies that are technically or purely electronic in nature (see UETA §2, Comment 4). Rather, it is intended to be a collective term and applies to all "similar" technologies that involve the generation, transmittal, or storage of information in an intangible format.

Electromagnetic technologies that generate, transmit, and store information in intangible formats are electronic in nature. Thus, for example, the typical computer hard drive is a device that stores information electronically. Optical technologies that generate, transmit, or store information in intangible formats are also included within the meaning of the term. Although some aspects of optical technologies may not be truly electronic in nature, they are considered to be electronic because they create or manipulate information in an intangible format. Thus, for example, fiber optic cable is a means of transmitting information electronically.

The listing of specific technologies in this section is not intended to be static or limited to those created or in use at the time of the adoption of this Act. As electronic technologies continue to develop and evolve, even if they involve competencies other than those listed, they are also included in this definition if they perform the function of generating, transmitting, or storing information in an intangible format from which the information may subsequently be retrieved and viewed in a perceivable format.

The term "electronic" in this Act has the same meaning as it has in UETA §2(5), ESign §106(2), and URPERA §2(2).

"Electronic signature." An electronic signature is any electronic symbol, sound, or process that is attached to, or logically associated with, an electronic record by an individual with the intent to sign the record. An electronic signature on an electronic record is one that accomplishes the same purpose as a traditional "wet" or pen and ink signature on a tangible record; it associates an individual with an electronic record for the purpose of signing or executing the record. The technology that may be used for an electronic signature includes all the technologies that are encompassed within the definition of the term "electronic." Whether an individual in fact attaches an electronic signature to an electronic record with the intent to sign it is a question of fact to be determined in each case.

The term is similar to the definition used in UETA §2(8), ESign §106(5), and URPERA §2(4).

"In a representative capacity." The term "in a representative capacity" refers to the role in which an individual

signs a record or makes a statement with respect to which a notarial act is performed. Specifically, it indicates that the individual who signs a record or makes the statement is doing so as a representative of another person, a principal, and not on the individual's own behalf. A representative with proper authority binds the principal as if the principal signed the record. The authority to perform an act in a representative capacity may be derived from the position the individual holds (e.g. corporate officer) or from a specific grant of authority to the individual (e.g. attorney in fact). Whether a person is authorized to act in a representative capacity is a fact to be determined under the agency law of the state.

In this Act, the term is used Section 2(1) and in the short form acknowledgment provided in Section 16(2).

"Notarial act." The term "notarial act" encompasses a notarial act whether authorized in this Act or by other law of this state (see also Section 4(a)). This subsection lists those notarial acts specifically authorized by this Act. The listed notarial acts include taking an acknowledgment, administering an oath or affirmation, taking a verification upon an oath or affirmation, witnessing or attesting a signature, certifying or attesting a copy of a record, and noting a protest of a negotiable instrument.

This Act applies to a notarial act regardless of whether it is performed with respect to a tangible record, such as paper, or with respect to an electronic record. Other Uniform Laws, including UETA, ESign, and URPERA, specifically authorize the creation, transfer, storage, and recording of electronic records just as other law has traditionally authorized records on tangible media. This Act specifically authorizes notarial acts to be performed with respect to electronic records.

"Notarial officer." The term "notarial officer" includes a notary public as well as other individual having the authority to perform notarial acts under other state, tribal, or federal law or the law of a foreign state. Thus, for example, judges, clerks, and deputy clerks are notarial officers (see Sections 10(a)(2), 11(a)(2), 12(a)(2) and 13(a)(1)). Similarly, in some states, attorneys at law, by the fact that they are attorneys at law, are also notarial officers (see Section 10(a)(3)). Also, an individual designated as a notarizing officer by the United States Department of State for performing notarial acts overseas is also a notarial officer for that purpose (see Section 13(a)(3)). Other persons, whether by state law, federal law, tribal law, or the law of a foreign state, may also be notarial officers (see generally Sections 10 through 14.)

Many of the provisions of this Act apply broadly to all notarial officers regardless of the source of their authority. However, some provisions, such as those in Sections 17 through 25, apply only to notaries public.

"Notary public." A "notary public" is an individual who is issued a commission as a notary public by the commissioning officer or agency of a state pursuant to Sections 21 through 23. A notary public does not include those individuals, such as judges and clerks of court, who are authorized to perform notarial acts under other law or as a part of the official duties of an office or position they hold.

"Official stamp." The term "official stamp" refers to an image containing specified information that a notarial officer attaches to or associates with a certificate of notarial act, which is itself on, attached to, or associated with a record. The contents and characteristics of the "official stamp" are set forth in Section 17(a).

On a tangible record, the image is a physical one appropriately located on, or attached to, the certificate of notarial act. It may be applied to the surface of the certificate, as with a rubber stamp and ink, or it may be applied by compression or embossment, as with a seal. On an electronic record, the image is in an electronic format and attached to, or logically associated with, the electronic certificate of notarial act. Being an electronic image, the image must be viewed through a device such as a computer monitor or printed out in order to be humanly perceivable.

An "official stamp" is to be distinguished from the device by which the image is affixed on, attached to, or associated with a certificate of notarial act; that device is identified as a "stamping device" and is defined in Section 2(13).

"Person." The word "person" is broadly defined to include all persons, whether human individuals or corporate, associational, or governmental entities. When the definition of a "person" is intended to be limited to a human entity, the word "individual" is used in this Act rather than the word "person." The definition of "person" is the standard definition for that term as used in other acts promulgated by the National Conference of Commissioners on Uniform State Laws.

"Record." A "record" consists of information stored on a medium, whether the medium be a tangible one or an electronic one. The traditional tangible medium has been paper on which information is inscribed by writing, typing, printing, or other similar means. The information is humanly perceivable by reading it directly from the paper on which it is inscribed.

An electronic medium is one on which information is stored electronically. The information is humanly perceivable only by means of a device that interprets the electronic information in the record and makes it readable. For example, electronic information may be stored on a hard disk and it may be retrieved and read in a humanly perceivable form on a computer monitor or a paper printout.

Traditionally, especially if the tangible medium is paper, a record has been referred to as a "document." In this Act, the word "record" replaces the word "document" and includes information regardless of whether the medium is tangible or electronic. The definition of the word "record" in this Act is the same as the definition of that word in UETA §2(13) and ESign §106(9). It also is the same as the definition of the word "document" as used in URPERA §2(1).

"Sign" and "Signature." Subsections (11) and (12) of this Act define the related words "sign" and "signature." An individual may "sign" his or her name to a record either on a tangible medium or an electronic medium as long as the individual has the present intent to authenticate or adopt the record so signed. The verb "sign" includes other forms of the verb, such as "signing." Except as provided in Section 9, an individual must personally perform the act of signing a record.

A symbol located on, or associated with, a tangible or electronic record that is the result of the signing process is an individual's "signature." The usual symbol an individual uses as the individual's signature is the individual's given name. If, instead of using the individual's given name, however, an individual uses an alternative symbol as the individual's signature, such as an "X," the individual may affix that symbol to the record as the individual's signature.

Nothing in the definitions of the words "sign" or "signature" or of the word "record" (prior subsection) imposes a security process or standard in the definition of those words. When a means of security is imposed, it is done by a requirement in a separate section (see, for example, Section 20).

"Stamping device." A "stamping device" is the means by

which an official stamp is affixed to, embossed on, or associated with, the certificate of notarial act in a record. With a traditional paper medium, for example, the stamping device may be a rubber device that uses ink to impose a stamp on the paper. It may also be a device that compresses or embosses the paper and applies an impression seal.

In an electronic format, the stamping device is an electronic process or technology that associates unique information identifying the notarial officer with the certificate of notarial act that is affixed to, or associated with, an electronic record. The means of identifying the notarial officer may, for example, be a security card, password, encryption device, or other system that allows access to an electronic process that associates the officer's unique information with the certificate of notarial act on an electronic record. The electronic process may be located on, for example, a desktop or laptop computer; a flash drive or other peripheral device used in connection with a computer; a portable electronic device such as a Blackberry or iPhone; or a secure website on the Internet. The means of identifying the notarial officer and the electronic process are collectively the stamping device. The result, although attached to, or associated with, an electronic certificate of notarial act, will be perceivable only by means of a device such as a computer monitor that is capable of presenting it in a perceivable format.

"State." The word "state" includes any state of the United States, the District of Columbia, the United States Virgin Islands, and any territory or insular possession subject to the jurisdiction of the United States. This definition is the standard definition for that word as used in other acts adopted by the National Conference of Commissioners on Uniform State Laws.

"Verification upon oath or affirmation." A "verification upon oath or affirmation" is a common form of notarial act. It is a declaration by an individual before a notarial officer in which the individual states on oath or affirmation that the declaration is true. This declaration is sometimes referred to as an "affidavit" or "jurat." See Coast to Coast Demolition and Crushing, Inc. v. Real Equity Pursuit, LLC, 226 P.3d 605, 608 (Nev. 2010).

Section 3. Applicability

This [act] applies to a notarial act performed on or after [the effective date of this [act]].

Comment

This Act is not intended to be retroactive in effect. It applies to notarial acts performed on or after its effective date. The validity and effect of a notarial act performed prior to the effective date of this Act is determined by the law in effect at the time of its performance. (See also Section 28 regarding application of the Act to a notary public commission in effect on the effective date of the Act.)

Section 4. Authority to Perform Notarial Act

(a) A notarial officer may perform a notarial act authorized by this [act] or by law of this state other than this [act].

(b) A notarial officer may not perform a notarial act with respect to a record to which the officer or the officer's spouse [or civil partner] is a party, or in which either of them has a direct beneficial interest. A notarial act performed in violation of this subsection is voidable.

Comment

Subsection (a) is the enabling provision of this Act and grants a notarial officer the authority to perform notarial acts. It authorizes a notarial officer to perform notarial acts that are authorized by this Act as well as those authorized by other law of this State.

When taken in conjunction with the definition of a notarial act in Section 2(5), subsection (a) also authorizes a notarial officer to perform notarial acts regardless of the format of the record. Thus, a notarial officer may perform notarial acts on tangible records as well as electronic records. However, before a notary public may begin to perform notarial acts on electronic records, the notary must notify the commissioning officer or agency that the notary will be performing notarial acts with respect to electronic records (see Section 20(b)).

Subsection (b) prohibits a notarial officer from performing a notarial act in a circumstance in which performance of that act might create a conflict of interest. It provides that a notarial officer may not perform a notarial act with respect to any record in which the officer or the officer's spouse (or civil partner, as defined by state law) is a party. The prohibition is absolute and clear; there is no need to demonstrate a direct beneficial interest even though the interest may be obvious. For example, a notarial officer may not take an acknowledgment of a deed in which the officer or the officer's spouse is a grantor or grantee.

In addition, subsection (b) provides that a notarial officer may not perform a notarial act with respect to any record in which the officer or the officer's spouse (or civil partner) has a direct beneficial interest. This prohibition depends on whether there is a direct beneficial interest derived from the record (see, e.g. Galloway v. Cinello, 188 W. Va. 266, 423 S.E.2d 875 (1992)). For example, a deed by a third party (perhaps a grandparent) creating a trust in which a child of the notarial officer is a beneficiary might involve a direct beneficial interest to the notarial officer that is derived from the trust document (record), especially if the trust relieves support obligations of the officer. If it does provide a direct beneficial interest derived from the record, the officer would be prohibited from taking the acknowledgment of the deed of trust. While further information would be necessary to determine whether there is a direct beneficial interest derived from the record, a notarial officer should avoid performing a notarial act in any situation when doing so would raise the appearance of an impropriety.

This prohibition does not, however, extend to situations in which the beneficial interest is indirect and not the result of the operation of the record or transaction itself. For example, if the interest received is merely the payment of a notarial fee, the benefit is indirect and derived from the performance of notarial duties and not the result of the operation of the record or transaction itself (see, e.g. Hass v. Neth, 265 Neb. 321, 657 N.W.2d 11 (2003)). Similarly, a notary public who is hired by an employer to be available to perform notarial acts on multiple transactions does not derive a beneficial interest as a result of the operation of the records or transactions themselves. For example, a notary public may be an employee and the expenses of obtaining and maintaining the commission may be paid by the notary's employer. The obvious purpose of such an arrangement, at least in part, is that the notary public will perform notarial acts in appropriate situations as needed and requested by the employer. The fact that the notary public's salary and expenses are paid by the employer does not prevent the notary public from performing notarial acts when requested by the employer. Even though the notary receives a salary and the notary's salary may even depend on the fact that the notary performs notarial acts for the employer generally, the notary does not have a direct beneficial interest in the transactions or one that is derived from the operation of the records or transactions.

Likewise, if a notarial officer is an attorney, the attorney/notarial officer may perform notarial acts for a client as long as the attorney does not receive a direct beneficial interest as a result of operation of the record or transaction with regard to which the notarial act is performed. The fact that the attorney receives a fee for performing legal services, presently or in the future, is not a direct beneficial interest resulting from the operation of the record or transaction. Thus, receiving a fee for drafting a will or for subsequently representing the estate are fees for legal services and not a direct beneficial interest received as a result of the operation of the will (record) itself.

If a notarial officer should perform a notarial act in violation of subsection (b), the notarial act is not void per se. It may, however, be voidable in an action brought by a party who is adversely affected by the officer's misdeed. See Galloway v. Cinello, 188 W. Va. 266, 423 S.E.2d 875 (1992), where the court stated that the document was not void per se but was voidable; in making a determination the court should consider whether an improper benefit was obtained by the notary or any party to the instrument, as well as whether any harm flowed from the transaction. But see Estate of McKusick, 629 A.2d 41 (Me. 1993) in which the court questioned the validity of a will because the affidavit of a witness was made before a notary public who was the spouse of the witness.

Section 5. Requirements for Certain Notarial Acts

(a) A notarial officer who takes an acknowledgment of a record shall determine, from personal knowledge or satisfactory evidence of the identity of the individual, that the individual appearing before the officer and making the acknowledgment has the identity claimed and that the signature on the record is the signature of the individual.

(b) A notarial officer who takes a verification of a statement on oath or affirmation shall determine, from personal knowledge or satisfactory evidence of the identity of the individual, that the individual appearing before the officer and making the verification has the identity claimed and that the signature on the statement verified is the signature of the individual.

(c) A notarial officer who witnesses or attests to a signature shall determine, from personal knowledge or satisfactory evidence of the identity of the individual, that the individual appearing before the officer and signing the record has the identity claimed.

(d) A notarial officer who certifies or attests a copy of a record or an item that was copied shall determine that the copy is a full, true, and accurate transcription or reproduction of the record or item.

(e) A notarial officer who makes or notes a protest of a negotiable instrument shall determine the matters set forth in [Section 3-505(b) of the Uniform Commercial Code].

Comment

"Acknowledgment" – Subsection (a) provides that when taking an acknowledgment, a notarial officer certifies that: (1) the individual who is appearing before the officer and acknowledging the record has the identity claimed, and (2) the signature on the record is the signature of the individual appearing before the officer. The notarial officer must identify the individual either through personal knowledge of the individual or from satisfactory evidence of the identity of the individual (see Section 7). The acknowledging individual must also declare, as required in Section 2(1), that the individual in signing the record for the purpose stated in the record.

It is common practice for the individual to sign the record in the presence of the notarial officer. However, actually signing the record in the presence of the officer is not required as long as the individual acknowledges to the officer, when the individual appears before the officer, that the signature already on the record is that of the individual.

"Verification on oath or affirmation" – Subsection (b) provides that when taking a verification on oath or affirmation, a notarial officer certifies that: (1) the individual who is appearing before the officer and making the verification has the identity claimed, and (2) that the signature on the record is the signature of the individual appearing before the officer. The verifying individual must also declare, as required in Section 2(14), that the statements in the record are true. The notarial officer must identify the individual either through personal knowledge of the individual or from satisfactory evidence of the identity of the individual (see Section 7). A verification may be referred to as an affidavit or a jurat in some jurisdictions.

"Witnessing or attesting a signature" – Subsection (c) provides that when witnessing or attesting a signature, a notarial officer certifies that: (1) the individual who is appearing before the officer and signing the record has the identity claimed, and (2) that the signature on the record is the signature of the individual appearing before the officer. The notarial officer must identify the individual either through personal knowledge of the individual or from satisfactory evidence of the identity of the individual (see Section 7).

Witnessing or attesting a signature differs from taking an acknowledgment in that the record contains no declaration that it is signed for the purposes stated in the record and differs from a verification on oath or affirmation in that the individual is not verifying a statement in the record as being true. It is merely a witnessing of the signature of an identified individual.

"Certifies or attests a copy" – Subsection (d) provides that when certifying or attesting a copy of a record or item, a notarial officer certifies that: (1) the officer has compared the copy with the original record or item, and (2) has determined that the copy is a full, true, and accurate transcription or reproduction of the original record or item. This subsection directs the notarial officer to compare a record or item with a copy of the record or item. Therefore, the record or item must be presented to the notarial officer along with the copy so that the officer is able to make the comparison.

Certifying or attesting of a copy is usually done if it is necessary to produce a copy of a record when the original is in an archive or other collection of records and the archived record cannot be removed. In many cases, however, the custodian of the official archive or collection may also be empowered to issue an officially certified copy. When a copy officially certified by the custodian of the archive is available, it is official evidence of the state of the public archive or collection, and it may be better evidence of the original record than a copy certified by a notarial officer.

"Make or note a protest of a negotiable instrument" – Subsection (e) provides that a notarial officer may make or note a protest of a negotiable instrument under UCC §3-505(b). A protest is an official certificate of dishonor of a negotiable instrument. UCC §3-505(b) confers the authority to make or take a protest on "a United States consul or vice consul, or a notary public or other person authorized to administer oaths by the law of the place where dishonor occurs." In the United States a protest of a negotiable instrument may not be needed as evidence of dishonor (see UCC §3-505(a); see also UCC §3-503). A protest may be necessary, however, on international drafts governed by law of a foreign state (see UCC §3- 505, Official Comment). This subsection is designed to insure that there is no doubt as to the authority or a notary public to make or note a protest of a negotiable instrument when appropriate under the Uniform Commercial Code.

Section 6. Personal Appearance Required

If a notarial act relates to a statement made in or a signature executed on a record, the individual making the statement or executing the signature shall appear personally before the notarial officer.

Comment

This section expressly requires that when an individual is making a statement or executing a record with regard to which a notarial act will be performed by a notarial officer, the individual must appear before the officer to make the statement or execute the record. Thus, an individual who is acknowledging a record or verifying a statement on oath or affirmation before a notarial officer, or an individual whose signature is being witnessed or attested by a notarial officer, must appear before the officer to perform the specified function. See Vancura v. Katris, 907 N.E.2d 814, 391 Ill. App. 3d 350 (2009) which involved a notary public who performed notarial acts without the individual signing the instrument personally appearing before the notary.

To provide assurance to persons relying on the system of notarial acts authorized by this Act, notarial officers must take reasonable steps to assure the integrity of the system. It is by personal appearance before the notarial officer that the individual making a statement or executing a record may be properly identified by the notarial officer (see Section 7). It is also by personal appearance before the notarial officer that the officer may be satisfied that (1) the individual is competent and has the capacity to execute the record, and (2) the individual's signature is knowingly and voluntarily made (see Section 8(a)).

Personal appearance does not include an "appearance" by video technology, even if the video is "live" or synchronous. Nor does it include an "appearance" by audio technology, such as a telephone. At the time that this act is being drafted, those methods of "appearance" do not provide sufficient opportunity for the notarial officer to identify the individual fully and properly; nor do they allow the officer sufficient opportunity to evaluate whether the individual has the competency or capacity to execute the record or whether the record is knowingly and voluntarily made.

Section 7. Identification of Individual

(a) A notarial officer has personal knowledge of the identity of an individual appearing before the officer if the individual is personally known to the officer through dealings sufficient to provide reasonable certainty that the individual has the identity claimed.

(b) A notarial officer has satisfactory evidence of the identity of an individual appearing before the officer if the officer can identify the individual:

(1) by means of:

(A) a passport, driver's license, or government issued nondriver identification card, which is current or expired not more than [three years] before performance of the notarial act; or

(B) another form of government identification issued to an individual, which is current or expired not more than [three years] before performance of the notarial act, contains the signature or a photograph of the individual, and is satisfactory to the officer; or

(2) by a verification on oath or affirmation of a credible witness personally appearing before the officer and known to the officer or whom the officer can identify on the basis of a passport, driver's license, or government issued nondriver identification card, which is current or expired not more than [three years] before performance of the notarial act.

(c) A notarial officer may require an individual to provide additional information or identification credentials necessary to assure the officer of the identity of the individual.

Comment

Section 5, above, requires a notarial officer to determine, either from personal knowledge or satisfactory evidence, that the individual for whom the officer will perform a notarial act has the identity claimed. Section 7 specifies the means by which the notarial officer is to determine that identity. Subsection 7(a) describes when a notarial officer has personal knowledge of an individual's identity. Subsection 7(b) describes when a notarial officer has satisfactory evidence of an individual's identity.

Subsection (a) states that the notarial officer has personal knowledge of the identity of an individual only if the officer personally knows the individual through prior dealings. The prior dealings may be business dealings or personal dealings. Business dealings might simply be the performance of prior notarial acts for the individual. They may also arise because the notarial officer engaged in prior business transactions with the individual. Personal dealings may exist because the notarial officer is a friend or colleague of the individual. The dealings may also be mixed in nature such as where the notarial officer and individual work in the same office, school, or building. Regardless of whether the prior dealings are business or personal, they must be sufficient to provide the notarial officer with information that is adequate to identify the individual without the need to view any identification credentials or require any other means of identification.

Subsection (b) describes two methods by which a notarial officer may obtain satisfactory evidence of the identity of the individual even though the officer has no prior dealings with that individual. One method of identification is based on an identification credential issued to the individual (subsection (b)(1)). The other method of identification is based on an oath or affirmation of a credible witness as to the identity of the individual (subsection (b)(2)).

Subsection (b)(1)(A) allows a notarial officer to identify an individual by means of a passport, driver's license, or government issued nondriver identification card. The passport may the issued by the United States or by a foreign state. A United States passport includes the traditional passport book and the more recent passport card as well as any other form of passport the United States may issue. A driver's license may be issued by a state government, the federal government, a government of a foreign state as defined in Section 14(a), or a tribal, pueblo, or similar authority. A government issued nondriver identification card is a card issued by many states to an individual, which may be used as a means of identification instead of a driver's license. It may be issued to an individual who is not qualified to obtain a driver's license or it may be issued in lieu of a driver's license to an individual who is qualified to obtain a driver's license.

Although the notarial officer might usually expect the identification credential to be currently in force, this provision recognizes that even though an expired credential would not be effective for its primary purpose (e.g. as a license permitting the individual to drive an automobile), it may used for a period of up to [three years] after its expiration as a means for identifying an individual. As long as it provides the necessary information for identifying the individual, its identification function is satisfied. This subsection does, however, put a specific outside limit of [three years] beyond the expiration of the credential for its use for identification purposes.

Subsection (b)(1)(B) recognizes that some individuals may not have a passport, driver's license, or even a government issued nondriver identification card that is currently valid or not expired by more than [three years]. This subsection allows the notarial officer to base the officer's identification of the individual on another form of government issued identification as long as that form of identification contains the individual's signature or a photograph of the individual as a means by which the individual can be associated with the credential. This form of credential may include, for example, a military identification. However, this subsection also makes it clear that this alternative form of identification must be satisfactory to the notarial officer. If the officer is not satisfied with the identification that the credential provides, the officer may refuse to accept it as sufficient identification.

Subsection (b)(2) recognizes that an individual may require the performance of a notarial act even though that individual is not known to a notarial officer and does not have one of the identification credentials listed in subsection (b)(1), or at least the individual does not have the identification credential currently available. This provision allows a notarial officer to identify an individual through an oath or affirmation of a credible witness personally appearing before the officer. The credible witness must either be (1) personally known to the officer, or (2) identified to the officer by means of the witness' passport, driver's license, or government issued nondriver identification as long as the credential has not expired more than [three years] before the performance of the notarial act. If the identity of an individual is verified by a properly identified credible witness, it is established by satisfactory evidence.

The meaning of the term "personally known" in subsection (b)(2) is the same as in subsection (a); the meanings of the terms "passport," "driver's license," and "government issued nondriver identification" in subsection (b)(2) are the same as in subsection (b)(1)(A). Subsection (b)(2) does not allow for the identification of the credible witness by means of an alternative form of identification as is provided in subsection (b)(1)(B) for the identification of the individual for whom the notarial act is performed. Subsection (b)(2) also does not allow the identity of a witness to be based on an oath or affirmation of yet another witness; such a process could lead to a spiraling "witness to the witness."

Subsection (c) recognizes that, even if a specified identification credential is presented, a notarial officer may, in some cases, be uncertain as to the identity of the individual. For example, the identification credential may be defaced or have defects that make legibility difficult, or there may be changes in the physical appearance of the individual that may not be reflected in the image on the identification credential. If the notarial officer is uncertain as to the identity of the individual (whether the individual for whom the notarial act is performed or a credible witness for that individual), the officer may require the individual to provide additional information or identification in order to assure the officer as to the identity of the individual.

Identification of an individual based on an identification credential requires some flexibility. For example, it is not uncommon that an individual's name as used in a record may be a full name, including a full middle name; however, the name of the individual as provided on the identification credential may only use a middle initial or none at all. The inconsistency may be vice versa instead. The notarial officer should recognize these common inconsistencies when performing the identification of an individual. However, if a notarial officer is ultimately uncertain about the identity of the individual, the notarial officer should refuse to perform the notarial act (see Section 8.)

Section 8. Authority to Refuse to Perform Notarial Act

(a) A notarial officer may refuse to perform a notarial act if the officer is not satisfied that:

(1) the individual executing the record is competent or has the capacity to execute the record; or

(2) the individual's signature is knowingly and voluntarily made.

(b) A notarial officer may refuse to perform a notarial act unless refusal is prohibited by law other than this [act].

Comment

Subsection (a) allows the notarial officer to refuse to perform a requested notarial act in either of two circumstances. First, if the notarial officer is not satisfied as to the competency or capacity of the individual executing the record, the officer may refuse to perform the notarial act. Thus, for example, if the notarial officer is not satisfied that the individual has the mental status needed to execute the record, the officer may refuse to perform the notarial act. Second, if the notarial officer has concern about whether the individual's signature was knowingly and voluntarily made, the officer may refuse to perform the notarial act. Thus, for example, if the notarial officer is concerned that the individual's signature is coerced, the officer may refuse to perform the notarial act.

Satisfaction as to the competency or capacity of the individual making the record or with the fact that the signature is knowingly and voluntarily made are matters within the proper judgment of the notarial officer. No expertise on the part of the notarial officer as to those matters is required to refuse to perform the notarial act.

This subsection does not impose a duty upon the notarial officer to make a determination as to the competency or capacity of the individual nor as to whether the signature of the individual is knowingly and voluntarily made. It does not require the officer to perform a formal evaluation of the individual on those matters. It merely permits the notarial officer to refuse to perform the notarial act if the officer should not be satisfied as to those matters.

Subsection (b) gives the notarial officer the general authority to refuse to perform a notarial act for any other reason as long as the reason for the refusal is itself not a violation of other law of this state or the United States. Thus, for example, a notary public may be an employee whose employer has paid the expenses of obtaining and maintaining the notary public commission. Their understanding may be that the notary public will be available to perform notarial acts as needed by the employer but will not be available to perform them for general members of the public. A notary public under that arrangement may refuse to perform notarial acts for members of the public. In another context, a notary public may refuse to perform a notarial act with respect to an electronic record if the client demands that the notary use a technology for performing the notarial act that the notary has not selected (see Section 20(a)).

The subsection does prohibit, however, the officer from refusing to perform the notarial if the refusal is a violation of other law. For example, the notarial officer may not refuse to perform the notarial act due to discrimination that is prohibited by state or federal law. Indeed, such a refusal to perform the notarial act may also be punishable under the state or federal law.

Section 9. Signature if Individual Unable to Sign

If an individual is physically unable to sign a record, the individual may direct an individual other than the notarial officer to sign the individual's name on the record. The notarial officer shall insert "Signature affixed by (name of other individual) at the direction of (name of individual)" or words of similar import.

Comment

This section recognizes that some individuals may not be personally able to sign a record because of a physical disability. If an individual is physically unable to sign the record, this section allows an alternate process.

This section allows a disabled individual, who is executing

a record, to direct an individual other than the notarial officer to sign the executing individual's name to the record. It then requires the notarial officer to insert the quoted language in the record or to insert words of similar import. In effect, the executing individual is appointing another individual to act as the executing individual's agent for the purpose of signing the record.

Section 10. Notarial Act in This State

(a) A notarial act may be performed in this state by:

(1) a notary public of this state; [or]

(2) a judge, clerk, or [deputy clerk] of a court of this state[; or]

[(3) an individual licensed to practice law in this state][; or]

[(4) any other individual authorized to perform the specific act by the law of this state].

(b) The signature and title of an individual performing a notarial act in this state are prima facie evidence that the signature is genuine and that the individual holds the designated title.

(c) The signature and title of a notarial officer described in subsection [(a)(1) or (2)] [(a)(1), (2), or (3)] conclusively establish the authority of the officer to perform the notarial act.

Legislative Note: *Subsection (a)(4) recognizes, collectively and in general terms, the authority of other individuals holding notarial powers authorized under other law of this state. However, instead of the nonspecific collective recognition stated in this subsection, it would be preferable to list in this subsection other specific officers or individuals holding notarial powers and, if their powers are limited, the notarial powers granted to them. Such a listing would provide a practical reference for a person seeking to determine whether an individual or holder of an office is authorized to perform notarial acts in this state. This reference would be especially valuable if a notarial act performed in this state is to be recognized in another state under Section 11. Therefore, subsection (a)(4) is bracketed to show that a state may optionally insert a specific list of those officers authorized to perform notarial acts.*

Comment

Subsection (a) lists the individuals who are entitled to serve as notarial officers and perform notarial acts in this state. A notary public as well as a judge, clerk, or [deputy clerk] of any court of this state are specifically authorized to perform notarial acts.

This Act provides two optional groups of authorized individuals. Under subsection (a)(3), a state may authorize a duly licensed attorney at law to serve as a notarial officer by virtue of that individual's status as a licensed attorney. The attorney's authority to perform notarial acts does not depend on the issuance of a notary public commission by the commissioning officer or agency. This subsection would not be relevant, however, if an attorney must obtain a commission as a notary public from the commissioning officer or agency in order to perform notarial acts.

Subsection (a)(4) recognizes the authority of other individuals to perform notarial acts if the performance of notarial acts by that individual is otherwise authorized by state law. Usually, the individuals recognized in this subsection are incumbents in a particular office. For example, recorders or registrars of deeds, or commissioners of titles, may be authorized to perform notarial acts under separate legislation. See Legislative Note, above.

Subsections (b) and (c) deal with proof of the authority of a notarial officer to perform a notarial act. Establishing that proof usually involves three steps:

1. Proof that the signature in the certificate of notarial act is that of the individual identified as a notarial officer;

2. Proof that the individual named in the certificate of notarial act holds the designated office as a notarial officer; and

3. Proof that individuals holding the designated office may perform notarial acts.

Subsection (b) creates a prima facie presumption that a signature purported to be that of a notarial officer on the certificate of notarial act is, in fact, that of the named notarial officer. It also creates a prima facie presumption that the individual purporting to be a notarial officer in the certificate of notarial act does, in fact, hold the designated notarial office. These are the first two steps in the proof of a notarial act as listed above. However, being only prima facie evidence, these two elements may be disproved in a legal proceeding upon adequate proof.

Subsection (c) creates a conclusive presumption that notaries public, judges, clerks and [deputy clerks] of this state (and attorneys licensed to practice law in this state, if subsection (a)(3) is adopted) have the authority to perform notarial acts. Since this Act specifically authorizes individuals holding those offices to perform notarial acts, it is not possible to disprove that an individual holding one of those offices has the authority to perform notarial acts. This is the third step in the proof of a notarial act as listed above. However, this per se recognition does not extend beyond a notary public, judge, clerk or [deputy clerk] (or attorneys licensed to practice law in this state, if subsection (a)(3) is adopted) of this state. Authority of other individuals to perform notarial acts must be proven by reference to other law of this state.

Section 11. Notarial Act in Another State

(a) A notarial act performed in another state has the same effect under the law of this state as if performed by a notarial officer of this state, if the act performed in that state is performed by:

(1) a notary public of that state;

(2) a judge, clerk, or deputy clerk of a court of that state; or

(3) any other individual authorized by the law of that state to perform the notarial act.

(b) The signature and title of an individual performing a notarial act in another state are prima facie evidence that the signature is genuine and that the individual holds the designated title.

(c) The signature and title of a notarial officer described in subsection (a)(1) or (2) conclusively establish the authority of the officer to perform the notarial act.

Comment

Subsection (a) lists the notarial officers of other states whose notarial acts, when performed in those states, will be recognized in this state. The officers listed in subsections (a)(1) and (2) are identical to the officers listed in Subsections 10(a)(1) and (2), above. It provides parity of recognition for notarial acts performed by those officers. Subsection (a)(3) recognizes notarial acts performed by other notarial officers of other states, when performed in those states, if they are authorized by law of the other state. It is parallel to the recognition of other notarial officers of this state as provided in subsection 10(a)(4) (and subsection 10(a)(3) if attorneys at law are authorized to perform notarial acts in the other state by reason of their offices and not be reason of being issued commissions as notaries public). It clearly establishes that acknowledgements, verifications, affidavits, and other forms of notarial acts performed in another state by the listed notarial officers of that state meet the requirements of this section and are to be recognized in this state without the further need of a certifica-

tion or authentication of the notarial officer by an official of the foreign state (see Aspey v. Memorial Hospital, 477 Mich. 120, 730 N.W.2d 695 (2007)).

Subsection (b) creates a prima facie presumption that a signature purported to be that of a notarial officer of the other state on the certificate of notarial act is, in fact, the signature of the named notarial officer. It also creates a prima facie presumption that the individual purporting to be a notarial officer of the other state in the certificate of notarial act does, in fact, hold the designated notarial office. These are the first two steps in the proof of the authority of a notarial officer to perform a notarial act as listed in the Comment to Section 10. However, being only prima facie evidence, these two elements may be disproved in a legal proceeding upon adequate proof.

Subsection (c) creates a conclusive presumption that notaries public, judges, clerks and deputy clerks of the other state have the authority to perform notarial acts. Since this Act specifically recognizes the notarial acts of individuals holding those offices, it is not possible to disprove that an individual holding one of those offices has the authority to perform notarial acts. This abolishes the need for a "clerk's certificate," certification, or similar instrument to prove the authority of a notary public, judge, clerk or deputy clerk to perform a notarial act (see Aspey v. Memorial Hospital, 477 Mich. 120, 730 N.W.2d 695 (2007). This is the third step in the proof of the authority of a notarial officer to perform a notarial act as listed in the Comment to Section 10. However, this per se recognition does not extend beyond a notary public, judge, clerk or deputy clerk of the other state. Authority of other individuals to perform notarial acts may be proven by reference to law of the other state. In addition, other forms of proof of authority to perform notarial acts, such as a "clerk's certificate" or certification are acceptable.

Section 12. Notarial Act Under Authority of Federally Recognized Indian Tribe

(a) A notarial act performed under the authority and in the jurisdiction of a federally recognized Indian tribe has the same effect as if performed by a notarial officer of this state, if the act performed in the jurisdiction of the tribe is performed by:

(1) a notary public of the tribe;

(2) a judge, clerk, or deputy clerk of a court of the tribe; or

(3) any other individual authorized by the law of the tribe to perform the notarial act.

(b) The signature and title of an individual performing a notarial act under the authority of and in the jurisdiction of a federally recognized Indian tribe are prima facie evidence that the signature is genuine and that the individual holds the designated title.

(c) The signature and title of a notarial officer described in subsection (a)(1) or (2) conclusively establish the authority of the officer to perform the notarial act.

Comment

Subsection (a) lists the notarial officers acting under the authority and in the jurisdiction of a federally recognized Indian tribe (see 25 C.F.R. §83.1 et. seq.; see also 25 U.S.C. §9 (2010)) whose notarial acts will be recognized in this state. The officers listed in subsections (a)(1) and (2) are identical to the officers listed in Subsections 10(a)(1) and (2), above. It provides parity of recognition for notarial acts performed by those officers. Subsection (a)(3) recognizes notarial acts performed by other notarial officers acting under the authority and in the jurisdiction of a federally recognized Indian tribe, if they are authorized by the law of the Indian tribe. It is parallel to the recognition of other notarial officers of this state as provided in subsection 10(a)(4) (and subsection 10(a)(3) if attorneys at law are authorized to perform notarial acts under the authority of a federally recognized Indian tribe by reason of their offices and not be reason of being issued commissions as notaries public).

Subsection (b) creates a prima facie presumption that a signature purported to be that of a notarial officer acting under the authority of an Indian tribe on the certificate of notarial act is, in fact, that of the named notarial officer. It also creates a prima facie presumption that the individual purporting to be a notarial officer acting under the authority of a federally recognized Indian tribe in the certificate of notarial act does, in fact, hold the designated notarial office. These are the first two steps in the proof of the authority of a notarial officer to perform a notarial act as listed in the Comment to Section 10. However, being only prima facie evidence, these two elements may be disproved in a legal proceeding upon adequate proof.

Subsection (c) creates a conclusive presumption that notaries public, judges, clerks and deputy clerks acting under the authority of a federally recognized Indian tribe have the authority to perform notarial acts. Since this Act specifically recognizes the notarial acts of individuals holding those offices, it is not possible to disprove that an individual holding one of those offices has the authority to perform notarial acts. This abolishes the need for a "clerk's certificate," certification, or similar instrument to prove the authority of a notary public, judge, clerk or deputy clerk to perform a notarial act. This is the third step in the proof of the authority of a notarial officer to perform a notarial act as listed in the Comment to Section 10. However, this per se recognition does not extend beyond a notary public, judge, clerk or deputy clerk acting under the authority of a federally recognized Indian tribe. Authority of other individuals to perform notarial acts may be proven by reference to law of the federally recognized Indian tribe. In addition, other forms of proof of authority to perform notarial acts, such as a "clerk's certificate" or certification are acceptable.

Section 13. Notarial Act Under Federal Authority

(a) A notarial act performed under federal law has the same effect under the law of this state as if performed by a notarial officer of this state, if the act performed under federal law is performed by:

(1) a judge, clerk, or deputy clerk of a court;

(2) an individual in military service or performing duties under the authority of military service who is authorized to perform notarial acts under federal law;

(3) an individual designated a notarizing officer by the United States Department of State for performing notarial acts overseas; or

(4) any other individual authorized by federal law to perform the notarial act.

(b) The signature and title of an individual acting under federal authority and performing a notarial act are prima facie evidence that the signature is genuine and that the individual holds the designated title.

(c) The signature and title of an officer described in subsection (a)(1), (2), or (3) conclusively establish the authority of the officer to perform the notarial act.

Comment

Some notarial acts are performed by notarial officers acting under federal authority or holding office under federal authority. This section recognizes the notarial acts performed by those officers when performed in accordance with federal law. Subsection (a)(1) recognizes the notarial acts performed by judges, clerks, and deputy clerks under federal law. It is the federal law parallel to the notarial officers recognized in subsections 10(a)(2) and 11(a)(2).

Subsection (a)(2) recognizes the authority of certain individuals to perform notarial acts while in the military service or under the authority of a military service. These provisions are currently codified in 10 U.S.C §1044a (2010). At the time of the drafting of this Act, subsection (b) of the federal codification provides the following individuals with the authority to perform notarial acts for the purposes stated in subsection (a) of the enactment:

(b) Persons with the powers described in subsection (a) are the following:

(1) All judge advocates, including reserve judge advocates when not in a duty status.

(2) All civilian attorneys serving as legal assistance attorneys.

(3) All adjutants, assistant adjutants, and personnel adjutants, including reserve members when not in a duty status.

(4) All other members of the armed forces, including reserve members when not in a duty status, who are designated by regulations of the armed forces or by statute to have those powers.

(5) For the performance of notarial acts at locations outside the United States, all employees of a military department or the Coast Guard who are designated by regulations of the Secretary concerned or by statute to have those powers for exercise outside the United States.

Subsection (a)(3) recognizes the authority of an individual who is designated as a notarizing officer by the United States Department of State for performing notarial acts overseas. This has been a traditional function performed by a notarizing officer of the Department of State. In many parts of the world a notarial act performed by a notarizing officer of the Department of State may be the best means to perform a notarial act for records that must be recognized in the United States. See subsection 14(f) as to the effect of a consular authentication performed by an individual who is designated as a notarizing officer by the United States Department of State for performing notarial acts overseas .

Subsection (a)(4) provides recognition of the notarial acts performed by other notarial officers authorized under federal law who are not listed in the prior subsections. A variety of other federal officers may be authorized to perform notarial acts, such as wardens of federal prisons (see 18 U.S.C. §4004 (2010)).

Subsection (b) creates a prima facie presumption that the signature purported to be that of a notarial officer under federal law on the certificate of notarial act is, in fact, that of the named notarial officer. It also creates a prima facie presumption that the individual purporting to be a notarial officer in the certificate of notarial act does, in fact, hold the designated notarial office under federal law. These are the first two steps in the proof of the authority of a notarial officer to perform a notarial act as listed in the Comment to Section 10. However, being only prima facie evidence, these two elements may be disproved in a legal proceeding upon adequate proof.

Subsection (c) creates a conclusive presumption that a federal judge, clerk or deputy clerk, an individual in the military service or acting under the authority of a military service, and an individual designated as a notarizing officer by the Department of State has the authority to perform notarial acts. Since this Act specifically recognizes the notarial acts of individuals holding those offices, it is not possible to disprove that an individual holding one of those offices has the authority to perform notarial acts. This is the third step in the proof of the authority of a notarial officer to perform a notarial act as listed in the Comment to Section 10. However, this per se recognition does not extend beyond a federal judge, clerk or deputy clerk, an individual in the military service or acting under the authority of a military service, or an individual designated as a notarizing officer by the Department of State. Authority of other individuals to perform notarial acts under federal law may be proven by reference to federal law granting the authority.

Section 14. Foreign Notarial Act

(a) In this section, "foreign state" means a government other than the United States, a state, or a federally recognized Indian tribe.

(b) If a notarial act is performed under authority and in the jurisdiction of a foreign state or constituent unit of the foreign state or is performed under the authority of a multinational or international governmental organization, the act has the same effect under the law of this state as if performed by a notarial officer of this state.

(c) If the title of office and indication of authority to perform notarial acts in a foreign state appears in a digest of foreign law or in a list customarily used as a source for that information, the authority of an officer with that title to perform notarial acts is conclusively established.

(d) The signature and official stamp of an individual holding an office described in subsection (c) are prima facie evidence that the signature is genuine and the individual holds the designated title.

(e) An apostille in the form prescribed by the Hague Convention of October 5, 1961, and issued by a foreign state party to the Convention conclusively establishes that the signature of the notarial officer is genuine and that the officer holds the indicated office.

(f) A consular authentication issued by an individual designated by the United States Department of State as a notarizing officer for performing notarial acts overseas and attached to the record with respect to which the notarial act is performed conclusively establishes that the signature of the notarial officer is genuine and that the officer holds the indicated office.

Comment

Subsection (a) clarifies that, for purposes of this section, a "foreign state" means a foreign country and not the United States, a state in the United States federal system, or a federally recognized Indian tribe.

Subsection (b) provides for the recognition of notarial acts performed by notarial officers acting under the authority and in the jurisdiction of a foreign state or its constituent units. It also recognizes the notarial acts performed by notarial officers acting under the authority of a multinational or international governmental organization. An example of a multinational or international governmental organization is the United Nations.

Subsection (c) states that if the title of a notarial office and the authority of a person in that office to perform notarial acts appear in a digest of foreign laws or in a list customarily used as a source for that information, the authority of a notarial officer holding that office to perform the indicated notarial acts is conclusively established. This is the third step in the proof of the authority of a notarial officer to perform a notarial act as listed in the Comment to Section 10.

Subsections (d) states that the signature and official stamp of a notarial officer identified in subsection (c) provides prima facie evidence that (1) the officer's signature is genuine, and (2) the officer holds an office with the designated title. These are the first two steps in the proof of the authority of a notarial officer to perform a notarial act as listed in the Comment to Section 10.

Being only a prima facie evidence that the notarial officer's signature is valid and that the officer holds an office with the designated title, those elements may be disproved in a legal proceeding upon adequate proof. If the validity of a foreign notarial officer's signature or the fact that the officer holds an office with the designated title is challenged, ultimate proof in a judicial proceeding may be expensive and time consuming. Furthermore, the potential of post hoc challenges may be detrimental to the promotion of international commerce. Therefore, the Act recognizes two means by which the validity of the notarial officer's signature and the certainty that the individual holds a notarial office with the designated title can be conclusively established: (1) "apostille," and (2) consular authentication.

Subsection (e) recognizes an "apostille" as one means of conclusively establishing those facts. The United States is a party to an international treaty regarding the authentication of notarial acts performed on public documents. The treaty is known as the Hague Convention ("Convention de La Haye du 5 octobre 1961"). Under this treaty, an "apostille" may be prepared by a competent authority in a foreign state in accordance with the treaty and stamped on or attached to the record. A competent authority is one designated by the foreign state from which the public document emanates. The "apostille" may be in the language of the foreign state in which it is issued, but the words "APOSTILLE (Convention de La Haye, du 5 octobre 1961)" are always in French. The "apostille" should conform as closely as possible to the Model annexed to the Convention.

Subsection (e) carries out the provisions of Hague Convention and gives effect to an "apostille" complying with the treaty. It states that the "apostille" conclusively establishes that: (1) the signature of the notarial officer on the certificate is genuine, and (2) the officer holds an office with the indicated title. When combined with the conclusive presumption established under subsection (c) as to the authority of a notarial officer with a designated title to perform a notarial act, all three steps in the proof of the authority of a notarial officer to perform a notarial act, as listed in the Comment to Section 10, are met.

The "apostille" has the following form, which is set forth in the annotation to Federal Rules of Civil Procedure Rule 44:

The certificate will be in the form of a square with sides at least 9 centimetres long:

APOSTILLE
(Convention de La Haye du 5 octobre 1961)

1. Country: _____
This public document
2. has been signed by _____
3. acting in the capacity of _____
4. bears the seal/stamp of _____

Certified
5. at _____ 6. the _____
7. by _____
8. No _____
9. Seal/stamp: 10. Signature

Subsection (f) provides an alternative means by which (1) the fact that the signature of the notarial officer on the certificate is genuine, and (2) the fact that the officer held an office with the designated title may be assured. Under it, an individual designated by the United States Department of State as a notarizing officer for performing notarial acts overseas may provide that assurance by means of a consular authentication. A consular authentication conclusively establishes that (1) the signature of the foreign notarial officer is valid, and (2) the officer holds the indicated office. The consular authentication must be attached to the record with respect to which the notarial act is performed. When combined with the

conclusive presumption established under subsection (c) as to the authority of a notarial officer with a designated title to perform a notarial act, all three steps in the proof of the authority of a notarial officer to perform a notarial act, as listed in the Comment to Section 10, are met.

Section 15. Certificate of Notarial Act

(a) A notarial act must be evidenced by a certificate. The certificate must:

(1) be executed contemporaneously with the performance of the notarial act;

(2) be signed and dated by the notarial officer and, if the notarial officer is a notary public, be signed in the same manner as on file with the [commissioning officer or agency];

(3) identify the jurisdiction in which the notarial act is performed;

(4) contain the title of office of the notarial officer; and

(5) if the notarial officer is a notary public, indicate the date of expiration, if any, of the officer's commission.

(b) if a notarial act regarding a tangible record is performed by a notary public, an official stamp must be affixed to or embossed on the certificate. If a notarial act is performed regarding a tangible record by a notarial officer other than a notary public and the certificate contains the information specified in subsection (a)(2), (3), and (4), an official stamp may be affixed to or embossed on the certificate. If a notarial act regarding an electronic record is performed by a notarial officer and the certificate contains the information specified in subsection (a)(2), (3), and (4), an official stamp may be attached to or logically associated with the certificate.

(c) A certificate of a notarial act is sufficient if it meets the requirements of subsections (a) and (b) and:

(1) is in a short form set forth in Section 16;

(2) is in a form otherwise permitted by the law of this state;

(3) is in a form permitted by the law applicable in the jurisdiction in which the notarial act was performed; or

(4) sets forth the actions of the notarial officer and the actions are sufficient to meet the requirements of the notarial act as provided in Sections 5, 6, and 7 or law of this state other than this [act].

(d) By executing a certificate of a notarial act, a notarial officer certifies that the officer has complied with the requirements and made the determinations specified in Sections 4, 5, and 6.

(e) A notarial officer may not affix the officer's signature to, or logically associate it with, a certificate until the notarial act has been performed.

(f) If a notarial act is performed regarding a tangible record, a certificate must be part of, or securely attached to, the record. If a notarial act is performed regarding an electronic record, the certificate must be affixed to, or logically associated with, the electronic record. If the [commissioning officer or agency] has established standards pursuant to Section 27 for attaching, affixing, or logically associating the certificate, the process must conform to the standards.

Comment

Subsection (a) provides that a notarial act must be evidenced by a certificate of notarial act. It sets out the requirements of that certificate:

Subsection (a)(1) – The certificate must be executed contemporaneously with the performance of a notarial act. The performance of a notarial act may take some period of time to accomplish, especially in large transactions with long closings. The fact that the certificate is not executed by the notarial officer immediately after the individual signs and acknowledges a deed would not necessarily demonstrate a lack of contempo-

raneous execution. However, a certificate that is not executed until some days after an individual signs and acknowledges a deed and the transaction is closed would not be a contemporaneous execution.

Subsection (a)(2) – The certificate must be signed and dated by the notarial officer. If the notarial officer is a notary public, the signature must be signed in the same manner as the signature that is on file with the commissioning officer or agency. For example, if a signature on file with the commissioning officer or agency contains the notary public's middle initial, the signature on the certificate must also contain the initial.

Subsection (a)(3) – The certificate must identify the jurisdiction in which the notarial act is performed. This is normally done by identifying the state and county in which the notarial act is performed (see Section 16, Short Forms). (Some states allow, on a reciprocity basis, notaries public of this state to perform notarial acts in a neighboring state or in counties in a neighboring state. Nothing in this Act changes or limits that reciprocity).

Subsection (a)(4) – The certificate must identify the title of office of the notarial officer. For example, the office may be notary public or clerk of court. The notarial officer may also be an individual in a military service or performing duties under the authority of a military service, in which case the individual's rank or position should be identified.

Subsection (a)(5) – If the officer is a notary public, the certificate must contain the expiration date of the notary public's commission, if any. In some states, the expiration date will be part of a notary public's official stamp (see Section 17(1)) and the use of the official stamp will satisfy the requirements of this subsection. However, if a notary public's official stamp does not contain the expiration date because it is not required under Section 17(1) or if a notary public is not required use an official stamp under subsection (b), the expiration date of the notary public's commission must be separately inserted.

Subsection (b) identifies those circumstances in which the certificate of notarial act must contain the official stamp of the notarial officer.

If the notarial act is performed with respect to a tangible medium and is performed by a notary public, subsection (b) requires that the notary public's official stamp be affixed to or embossed on the certificate of notarial act.

If the notarial act is performed with respect to a tangible medium and is performed by a notarial officer other than a notary public, subsection (b) states that an official stamp may be attached to or embossed on the certificate of notarial act. However, although permitted, it is not required by this act. Whether a notarial officer other than a notary public is required to use an official stamp and what the contents of that stamp may be will depend on other law of this state. That law may not require the use of a stamp or it may require the use of a stamp but may specify other contents. Regardless of whether an official stamp is attached to or embossed on the certificate, the certificate nevertheless must, at a minimum, contain the information specified in subsections (a)(2), (3) and (4).

If the notarial act is performed with respect to an electronic record by a notarial officer, whether a notary public or otherwise, subsection (b) states that the officer's official stamp may be attached to, or associated with, the electronic certificate of notarial act. However, although permitted, this subsection does not require that a notarial officer's official stamp be attached to or logically associated with an electronic certificate. Regardless of whether an official stamp is attached to or logically associated with an electronic certificate, the electronic certificate nevertheless must, at a minimum, contain the information specified in subsections (a)(2), (3) and (4). These are the same provisions found in URPERA §3(c), UETA §11, and ESign §101(g) regarding the performance of notarial acts with respect to electronic records.

Subsection (c) provides that if the certificate of notarial act meets the requirements of subsections (a) and (b), it may be in (1) the appropriate short form set out in Section 16, (2) any other form permitted by the law of this state, (3) any other form permitted by the law of the place where the notarial act is performed if other than this state, or (4) any form that sets forth the actions of the notarial officer if those actions meet the requirements of Sections 5, 6, and 7 or law other than this act, whether state or federal. Thus, acknowledgments and other notarial acts may be in the short forms provided in Section 16 or may be in more prolix and elaborate traditional forms provided they contain the required information.

Subsection (d) emphasizes the obligation of the notarial officer to comply with the requirements of, and to make the determinations required by, Sections 5, 6, and 7. By executing the certificate, the notarial officer certifies that the officer has done so.

Subsection (e) provides that the notarial officer may not sign the certificate until the notarial act has been fully performed (compare N.C. Gen. Stat. §10B-35 (2009)).

Subsection (f) seeks to assure the unified integrity of the record and the related certificate of notarial act. With respect to a notarial act evidenced on a tangible record, this subsection requires that the certificate must be a part of, or securely attached to, the record. If the certificate is not a part of the record itself, the means of attaching the certificate to the record are not specified. However, stapling is a common means.

Affixing an electronic certificate to, or associating it with, an electronic record requires sophisticated technology. There are multiple technologies by which the affixing or associating may be accomplished and those technologies will undoubtedly change over time as technologies improve and change. Accordingly, subsection (f) does not adopt any particular technology or limit the affixing or associating to technologies that are currently available. Rather, it provides that the certificate must be affixed to, or logically associated with, the electronic record in accordance with standards as may be approved by the commissioning officer or agency. The standards are left to the determination of the commissioning officer or agency under Section 27 and will depend on the available technology and the degree of security provided by available technology. In the absence of standards adopted by the commissioning officer or agency, the notary public may proceed with performing notarial acts with respect to electronic records as long as the notary public employs tamper evident technologies as required by Section 20.

Section 16. Short Form Certificates

The following short form certificates of notarial acts are sufficient for the purposes indicated, if completed with the information required by Section 15(a) and (b):

(1) For an acknowledgment in an individual capacity:

State of _____
[County] of _____

This record was acknowledged before me on _____ by _____
Date   Name(s) of individual(s)

_____
Signature of notarial officer

Stamp
[_____]
Title of office
[My commission expires: _____]

(2) For an acknowledgment in a representative capacity:

State of _____
[County] of _____

This record was acknowledged before me on
_____ by _____
Date   Name(s) of individual(s)
as (type of authority, such as officer or trustee) of (name of party on behalf of whom record was executed).

_____
Signature of notarial officer

Stamp
[_____]
Title of office
[My commission expires: _____]

(3) For a verification on oath or affirmation:

State of _____
[County] of _____

Signed and sworn to (or affirmed) before me on
_____ by _____
Date   Name(s) of individual(s)
           making statement
_____
Signature of notarial officer

Stamp
[_____]
Title of office
[My commission expires: _____]

(4) For witnessing or attesting a signature:

State of _____
[County] of _____

Signed [or attested] before me on _____ by
_____   Date
Name(s) of individual(s)
_____
Signature of notarial officer

Stamp
[_____]
Title of office
[My commission expires: _____]

(5) For certifying a copy of a record:

State of _____
[County] of _____

I certify that this is a true and correct copy of a record in the possession of _____.
Dated _____

_____
Signature of notarial officer

Stamp

[_____]
Title of office
[My commission expires: _____]

Comment

This section provides statutory short form certificates of various notarial acts. These forms are sufficient to document a notarial act in this state. See Section 15(c)(1). Other forms may also qualify as stated in Section 15(c)(2), (3), and (4).

These certificates may be used for notarial acts performed on tangible records as well as those performed with respect to electronic records. They are available for notarial acts performed by notaries public as well as notarial officers who are not notaries public. Under Section 15(b), an official stamp is required on the certificate if the notarial act is performed on a tangible record by a notary public. Under Section 15(b), if the notarial act is performed on a tangible record by a notarial officer other that a notary public or is performed by any notarial officer on an electronic record, an official stamp is optional, but the information or acts specified in Section 15(a)(2), (3) and (4) must be supplied. The short forms provided in this section call for the insertion of that information or the performance of those acts.

The calls in each of the forms for state and county information refer to the state and county where the notarial act is performed.

Section 17. Official Stamp

The official stamp of a notary public must:

(1) include the notary public's name, jurisdiction, [commission expiration date,] and other information required by the [commissioning officer or agency]; and

(2) be capable of being copied together with the record to which it is affixed or attached or with which it is logically associated.

Legislative Note: Among the elements of a notary public's official stamp, paragraph (1) includes the expiration date of the notary public's commission. Under the current law of some states, notary public commissions do not have an expiration date. A legislature may wish to continue the practice of issuing notary public commissions without expiration dates (see Section 21(e)). In addition, the current practice in some states is not to require that the expiration date be included as one of the elements of the official stamp, but rather to allow it to be inserted by means of another stamp or by hand. A legislature may wish to continue that practice. Therefore, the provision in paragraph (1) requiring the official stamp to include the expiration date of the commission is optional.

Comment

This section sets forth two requirements for a notary public's official stamp, whether the stamp is a physical image attached to, or embossed on, a tangible certificate of notarial act or an electronic image attached to, or logically associated with, an electronic certificate of notarial act.

Subsection (1) provides that the official stamp must state the notary public's name. Since Subsection 15(a)(2) requires that a notary public sign the notary's name as it appears on file with the commissioning officer or agency, the name of the notary on the official stamp should also conform with the name on file with the commissioning officer of agency. The official stamp must state the jurisdiction in which the notary public is commissioned. An optional provision states that the official stamp must set forth the date on which the notary public's commission expires. Finally, the official stamp must include any other information that is required by the commis-

sioning officer or agency.

Subsection (2) requires that the official stamp be capable of being copied together with the record to or with which it is attached or logically associated. Thus, for example, an official stamp that is affixed with a rubber stamping device and ink must provide a clear image in an ink that is capable of being copied. An official stamp that is affixed by embossing must do so in such a way that the information in the embossment is capable of being copied. An official stamp that is attached to, or logically associated with, an electronic record must be capable of being copied by the same technology by which the electronic record is copied.

Section 18. Stamping Device

(a) A notary public is responsible for the security of the notary public's stamping device and may not allow another individual to use the device to perform a notarial act. [On resignation from, or the revocation or expiration of, the notary public's commission, or on the expiration of the date set forth in the stamping device, if any, the notary public shall disable the stamping device by destroying, defacing, damaging, erasing, or securing it against use in a manner that renders it unusable. On the death or adjudication of incompetency of a notary public, the notary public's personal representative or guardian or any other person knowingly in possession of the stamping device shall render it unusable by destroying, defacing, damaging, erasing, or securing it against use in a manner that renders it unusable.]

(b) If a notary public's stamping device is lost or stolen, the notary public or the notary public's personal representative or guardian shall notify promptly the commissioning officer or agency on discovering that the device is lost or stolen.

Legislative Note: *The second sentence of subsection (a) require a notary public to render the notary's stamping device unusable upon the resignation, revocation, or resignation of the notary's commission. Similarly, the third sentence requires that upon the death or adjudication of incompetency of a notary public, the notary's personal representative or guardian, if knowingly in possession of the stamping device, must render it unusable.*

These two sentences are provided for states that consider that it is important to render a former notary public's stamping device unusable. However, the enactment of these two sentences is not essential for the uniformity of the act. They are bracketed to show that they are optional.

Comment

In order to protect and maintain the integrity of notarial acts, it is important that a notary public's stamping device be kept secure and out of the hands of other individuals who might use it fraudulently or erroneously. Accordingly, subsection (a) provides that a notary public is responsible for maintaining the security of notary's stamping device. Similarly, it provides that a notary public may not allow another individual to use the device.

In order to assure the integrity of the notarial system, the optional (bracketed) sentences of subsection (a) provide that the notary public may not continue to possess the official stamp once the notary is no longer serving as a notary public. The first optional sentence provides that upon the resignation of the notary public's commission, the revocation or expiration of the notary's commission, or the expiration of the date set forth in the stamping device, the notary must disable the device by destroying, defacing, damaging, erasing or securing it in a manner that renders it unusable. Similarly, the second optional sentence provides that upon the death or incompetency of a notary public, if the notary public's personal

representative is knowingly in possession of the stamping device, the representative must render the stamping device unusable by destroying, defacing, damaging, erasing or securing it. (Compare N.C. Gen. Stat. §10B-36(a) (2009).)

Subsection (b) recognizes that if the official stamp is lost or stolen, the possibility of fraudulent activity or misuse is also raised. Thus, a notary public is required to notify the commissioning officer or agency as soon as the notary discovers that the stamp is lost or stolen. The commissioning officer or agency may be able to take other steps to provide notification that will further protect the public (compare Ariz. Rev. Stat. §41-323 (2010); N.C. Gen. Stat. §10B-36(c) (2009).)

[Section 19. Journal

(a) A notary public [other than an individual licensed to practice law in this state] shall maintain a journal in which the notary public chronicles all notarial acts that the notary public performs. The notary public shall retain the journal for 10 years after the performance of the last notarial act chronicled in the journal.

(b) A journal may be created on a tangible medium or in an electronic format. A notary public shall maintain only one journal at a time to chronicle all notarial acts, whether those notarial acts are performed regarding tangible or electronic records. If the journal is maintained on a tangible medium, it must be a permanent, bound register with numbered pages. If the journal is maintained in an electronic format, it must be in a permanent, tamper-evident electronic format complying with the rules of the [commissioning officer or agency].

(c) An entry in a journal must be made contemporaneously with performance of the notarial act and contain the following information:

(1) the date and time of the notarial act;

(2) a description of the record, if any, and type of notarial act;

(3) the full name and address of each individual for whom the notarial act is performed;

(4) if identity of the individual is based on personal knowledge, a statement to that effect;

(5) if identity of the individual is based on satisfactory evidence, a brief description of the method of identification and the identification credential presented, if any, including the date of issuance and expiration of any identification credential; and

(6) the fee, if any, charged by the notary public.

(d) If a notary public's journal is lost or stolen, the notary public promptly shall notify the [commissioning officer or agency] on discovering that the journal is lost or stolen.

(e) On resignation from, or the revocation or suspension of, a notary public's commission, the notary public shall retain the notary public's journal in accordance with subsection (a) and inform the [commissioning officer or agency] where the journal is located.

(f) Instead of retaining a journal as provided in subsections (a) and (e), a current or former notary public may transmit the journal to the [commissioning officer or agency] [the official archivist of this state] or a repository approved by the [commissioning officer or agency].

(g) On the death or adjudication of incompetency of a current or former notary public, the notary public's personal representative or guardian or any other person knowingly in possession of the journal shall transmit it to the [commissioning officer or agency] [the official archivist of this state] or a repository approved by the [commissioning officer or agency].]

Legislative Note: *This section is provided for states that consider it to be good policy for notaries public to maintain* *journals of the notarial acts that they perform. However, the enactment of this section is not essential for the uniformity of the act. It is bracketed to show that it is optional.*

Subsection (a) contains further optional provision. The optional provision requires attorneys who obtain commissions as notaries public to maintain journals. However, by custom and professional practice, attorneys often retain copies of documents upon which they perform notarial acts for their clients. The retention of those copies generally provides the same assurances for the integrity of the notarial system that this provision is designed to accomplish. This subsection is provided for states that consider it to be good policy for notaries to maintain journals. However, the enactment of this provision is not essential for the uniformity of the act. It is bracketed to show that it is optional.

There are two additional considerations that were not adopted as part of this uniform act but which a state legislature might wish to consider with regard to the journal requirement. Subsection (b) requires that a notary public maintain only one journal at a time. Subsection (c) requires that a notary public make the entries into the journal at the time that a notarial act is performed. This may create a difficulty for a notary public who performs notarial acts with respect to electronic records and also performs notarial acts on tangible records. If a notary maintains an electronic journal (especially if the technology the notary uses automatically performs electronic journaling), the notary will have difficulty journaling a notarial act performed on a tangible record if the notary is away from the computer containing the electronic journal. For example, if a notary's electronic journal were installed on a desktop computer maintained in the notary's office and the notary were asked to perform a notarial act on a tangible record at an individual's bedside in a hospital, the notary might not be able to enter the notarial act into the electronic journal at the time the notary performs the notarial act. Under this section, as written, a notary would either have to maintain a journal on a tangible record or would have to install the journaling software on a portable computer. As another alternative, an adopting legislature may wish to allow a notary public to maintain a portable journal on a tangible record in addition to the regular electronic journal (see Or. Rev. Stat. §194.152(1) (2010)).

Another alternative that a legislature might wish to consider is adding a provision to subsection (c) requiring an individual for whom a notary public performs a notarial act to sign the journal. This would assure that the entry in the journal is made at the time of the performance of a notarial act and that the individual has reviewed the entry made by the notary public (see Cal. Govt. Code §8206(a)(2)(C) (2010)).

Comment

Creating and maintaining a journal of the notarial acts that a notary public performs provides a number of assurances that will protect the integrity of the notarial system. Among other benefits, it helps to assure, or at least determine whether, a notarial act that is performed in the name of a particular notary public was indeed performed by that notary. As an ordinary business record the journal may provide evidence that the act was performed by the notary or, by the absence of an entry in the journal, it may provide evidence that the act was not performed by the notary. In that regard, it provides protection to both the notary and to the public whom the notary serves (cf. Vancura v. Kartis, 907 N.E.2d 814, 391 Ill. App. 3d 350 (2008)).

Subsection (a) requires a notary public to maintain a journal of all the notarial acts that the notary performs. A notary must maintain the journal for at least ten years after the performance of the last notarial act chronicled in that journal. For example, if a particular journal volume chronicles a notary public's notarial acts for the period from January 1, 2005 to December 31, 2009, the entire journal volume must be maintained until December 31, 2019 despite the fact that some entries may be nearly fifteen years old by that date.

The optional exception provided in this subsection for attorneys licensed to practice law in this state applies regardless of whether the attorney is authorized to perform notarial acts by the fact that the attorney is licensed to practice law (see Subsection 10(a)(3)) or the attorney must obtain a commission as a notary public from the commissioning officer or agency.

Subsection (b) allows a notary public to decide whether to use a traditional journal on a tangible medium or an electronic journal. However, the notary may maintain only one active journal at a time. If the notary maintains the journal on a tangible medium (e.g., paper), the journal must be maintained in a permanent, bound register with numbered pages. It may not be in a loose-leaf or similar volume with pages that can be removed or torn out without evidence of their removal. If the notary decides to use an electronic journal, the electronic journal must be maintained in a permanent, tamper evident electronic format as prescribed by the rules of the commissioning officer or agency (see Section 27).

Subsection (c) provides that a notary public must make the entries in the journal contemporaneously with the performance of the notarial act. The performance of a notarial act may take some period of time to accomplish, especially if is part of a large transaction with numerous notarial acts. Thus, the fact that the entry in the journal not made immediately after an individual signs and acknowledges a document such as a deed does not necessarily demonstrate a lack of contemporaneous entry. Nevertheless, the entry must be made reasonably promptly and by the end of the transaction.

Subsection (c) also lists certain information that must be included in the journal entry for each notarial act performed. These include: (1) the date and time of the notarial act; (2) a brief description of the record, if any, and the type of notarial act performed (e.g., deed with acknowledgment); (3) the full name and address of each individual for whom the notarial act is performed; (4) if identity of the individual was based on personal knowledge (see Section 7(a)), a statement to that effect; (5) if identity of the individual was based on satisfactory evidence (see Section 7(b)), a brief description of the method of identification (i.e. identification credential or credible witness), and, if an identification credential was used, the date the credential was issued and its expiration date; and (6) the fee, if any, charged by the notarial officer (compare Cal. Govt. Code §8206 (2010)).

Because of the importance of journals and their continued maintenance by notaries public, subsection (d) requires a notary public to notify the commissioning officer or agency, upon discovery, if the journal is lost or stolen. Similarly, if pages in a notary's permanent, bound register, as required in subsection (b), are lost or stolen, the notary public must notify the commissioning officer or agency upon discovery. The reporting of this information to the commissioning officer or agency not only protects the members of the public whom the notary has served but also the notary him or herself.

The retention and maintenance of a notary's journals continue to be important after the termination of the notary's commission. Thus, subsection (e) provides that upon the resignation of a notary public from the notary's commission, or the revocation or suspension of the notary's commission, the notary must continue to retain the notary's journals for the ten year period provided in subsection (a) and provide the commissioning officer or agency with information about where the journals are located.

Subsection (f) allows a current or former notary public, instead of retaining journals for the ten year period provided in subsection (a), to elect to transmit them to the [commissioning officer or agency] or [official state archivist] or a repository approved by the commissioning officer or agency.

Subsection (g) directs that upon the death of a notary public, the notary's personal representative, guardian, or any person knowingly in possession of the journals must transmit the journals to the [commissioning officer or agency] or [official state archivist] or a repository approved by the commissioning officer or agency.

Section 20. Notification Regarding Performance of Notarial Act on Electronic Record; Selection of Technology

(a) A notary public may select one or more tamper-evident technologies to perform notarial acts with respect to electronic records. A person may not require a notary public to perform a notarial act with respect to an electronic record with a technology that the notary public has not selected.

(b) Before a notary public performs the notary public's initial notarial act with respect to an electronic record, a notary public shall notify the [commissioning officer or agency] that the notary public will be performing notarial acts with respect to electronic records and identify the technology the notary public intends to use. If the [commissioning officer or agency] has established standards for approval of technology pursuant to Section 27, the technology must conform to the standards. If the technology conforms to the standards, the [commissioning officer or agency] shall approve the use of the technology.

Comment

Subsection (a) provides that a notary public may elect to perform notarial acts with respect to electronic records and, for the purpose of performing those notarial acts, may select one or more technologies. This allows a notary to use more than one technology in order to accommodate clients using different technologies to perform their electronic transactions. However, a notary public may determine whether to use a technology requested by a client and may refuse to do so.

Any technology that the notary selects must be a tamper evident technology. A tamper evident technology is one that is designed to allow a person inspecting an electronic record to determine whether there has been any tampering with the integrity of a certificate of notarial act logically associated with a record or with the attachment or association of the notarial act with that electronic record.

Subsection (b) requires that, before performing the notary public's initial notarial act with respect to an electronic record, a notary public must notify the commissioning officer or agency that the notary will be performing notarial acts with respect to electronic records. When a notary provides a notification to the commissioning officer or agency, the notary must also identify the technology or technologies that the notary intends to use to perform the notarial acts.

If, at the time that a notary public provides the notification to the commissioning officer or agency, the commissioning officer or agency has established standards for the approval of technology to be used to perform notarial acts with respect to electronic records, any technology selected by the notary must conform to those standards. If the technology conforms to those standards, the commissioning officer or agency must approve it for use by the notary. In the absence of standards adopted by the commissioning officer or agency, the notary public may proceed with performing notarial acts with respect to electronic records as long as the notary public employs tamper evident technologies as required by this section.

Section 21. Commission as Notary Public; Qualifications; No Immunity or Benefit

(a) An individual qualified under subsection (b) may apply to the [commissioning officer or agency] for a commission as a notary public. The applicant shall comply with and provide the information required by rules established by the [commissioning officer or agency] and pay any application fee.

(b) An applicant for a commission as a notary public must:
 (1) be at least 18 years of age;
 (2) be a citizen or permanent legal resident of the United States;
 (3) be a resident of or have a place of employment or practice in this state;
 (4) be able to read and write [English]; [and]
 (5) not be disqualified to receive a commission under Section 23[; and
 (6) have passed the examination required under Section 22(a)].

(c) Before issuance of a commission as a notary public, an applicant for the commission shall execute an oath of office and submit it to the [commissioning officer or agency].

(d) [[Not more than [30] days after] [Before] issuance of a commission as a notary public, the [notary public][applicant for a commission] shall submit to the [commissioning officer or agency] an assurance in the form of a surety bond or its functional equivalent in the amount of $[____]. The assurance must be issued by a surety or other entity licensed or authorized to do business in this state. The assurance must cover acts performed during the term of the notary public's commission and must be in the form prescribed by the [commissioning officer or agency]. If a notary public violates law with respect to notaries public in this state, the surety or issuing entity is liable under the assurance. The surety or issuing entity shall give [30]-days notice to the [commissioning officer or agency] before canceling the assurance. The surety or issuing entity shall notify the [commissioning officer or agency] not later than [30] days after making a payment to a claimant under the assurance. A notary public may perform notarial acts in this state only during the period that a valid assurance is on file with the [commissioning officer or agency].]

[(e)] On compliance with this section, the [commissioning officer or agency] shall issue a commission as a notary public to an applicant [for a term of [ ] years].

[(f)] A commission to act as a notary public authorizes the notary public to perform notarial acts. The commission does not provide the notary public any immunity or benefit conferred by law of this state on public officials or employees.

Legislative Note: *Subsection (d) requires that a notary public provide a surety bond or its functional equivalent. It is provided for states that consider it to be good policy for a notary public to post an assurance in the form of surety bond or its functional equivalent. However, the enactment of this subsection is not essential for the uniformity of the act. It is bracketed to show that it is optional.*

The qualifications that an individual must meet for the issuance of a commission as a notary public under various state statutes are quite varied. The requirements listed in subsection (b) are common although not uniform among the states. They should be considered to be the minimal requirements for an individual to be entitled to the issuance of a commission as a notary public. Adopting states may add other provisions.

Comment

Subsection (a) provides that an individual qualified under subsection (b) may apply to the commissioning officer or agency to obtain a commission as a notary public. The subsection *applies to an individual seeking an initial or renewal commission. It leaves the form of application, the process for applying, and the timing of the process, as well as other administrative matters to be determined by the commissioning officer or agency pursuant to authority provided in Section 27. It also allows the commissioning officer or agency to establish the fee to be charged for issuance of the commission, if otherwise permitted by law of the state. Although the statutes of some states specify the process and timing for issuance of a commission in varying detail (compare Ariz. Rev. Stat. §41-312 (2010); Cal. Govt. Code §8206 (2010); Del. Code Ann. tit. 29, 4301 (2010)), this Act leaves the determination and implementation of those provisions to rules adopted by the commissioning officer or agency.*

Subsection (b) sets out qualifications that an applicant must meet in order to be entitled to the issuance of a commission as a notary public. The qualifications under various existing state statutes are quite varied. The requirements listed in this subsection are common although not uniform among the states (compare Ariz. Rev. Stat. §41-312(E) (2010)). They are the minimal requirements for an individual to be entitled to the issuance of a commission as a notary public.

The requirement in subsection (b)(1) which provides that an applicant must be at least 18 years of age is a minimum age requirement. A state may wish to increase the age if another age better comports with other law of the state. The word "English" in subsection (b)(4) is bracketed because, in some jurisdictions such as Puerto Rico, the legislature may wish to use another language either as a substitute or as an alternative.

Subsection (c) provides that before an applicant will be issued a commission as a notary public the applicant must execute and submit an oath of office to the commissioning officer or agency (compare 5 Me. Rev. Stat. Ann. §82(3-A) (2010)).

Subsection (d)is an optional provision. Depending on the version selected by the legislature, it provides that a notary public must either submit an assurance in the form of a surety bond or its functional equivalent to the commissioning officer or agency not more than 30 days after the notary has been issued a commission, or that an applicant must submit the assurance to the commissioning officer or agency before the issuance of the commission (compare Fla. Stat §117.01(7)(a) (2010); Tex. Govt. Code §406.010(a) (2010)). If the legislature enacts the alternative requiring a notary public to submit the assurance within thirty days after the notary has been issued a commission, the last sentence of this subsection prohibits the notary from performing a notarial act until the assurance is on file with the commissioning officer or agency. An example of an assurance that is the functional equivalent of a surety bond would be an irrevocable letter of credit issued by a bank as long as that letter of credit meets the requirements established by the commissioning officer or agency under Section 27(a)(6).

The monetary amount of the assurance is not specified and is left to the state legislature to determine. It is recognized that an assurance that would cover the full amount of many transactions for which notaries perform notarial acts would be very large and might be prohibitively expensive. Nevertheless, limited but reasonable assurance amounts would cover the amount of some ordinary transactions and would provide some, although limited, recovery in other transactions. Requiring a surety bond or its functional equivalent should also emphasize to a notary that the notary's function is a significant one and that it is not a meager or trivial one.

An assurance must be issued by a surety or other entity that is authorized to do business in this state. It must be in the form prescribed by the commissioning officer or agency under Section 27(a)(6). It must cover acts performed by a notary during the term of the notary's commission. A surety or issuing entity will be liable under an assurance if the notary violates the law of this state with regard to the performance of notarial acts during the term of the assurance. A surety or issuing entity must give the commissioning officer or agency 30 days notice prior to cancelling a bond or other form of assurance and must notify the commissioning officer or agency within 30 days after making a payment to a claimant under a bond or other form of assurance. A notary public may perform notarial acts only while an assurance is on file with the commissioning officer or agency.

Subsection (e) provides that upon compliance with the requirements of subsection (a) through (c), or (a) through (d) if subsection (d) is adopted, the commissioning officer or agency will issue the applicant a commission as a notary public. The term of the commission is to be determined by the state legislature; the legislature may also determine that the commission is to be without term.

Subsection (f) recognizes that a notary public is an individual licensed by the commissioning officer or agency and not a public official or employee of the state. Accordingly, it provides that a notary does not have any of the immunities or benefits conferred by the law of this state on public officials or employees.

[Section 22. Examination of Notary Public

(a) An applicant for a commission as a notary public who does not hold a commission in this state must pass an examination administered by the [commissioning officer or agency] or an entity approved by the [commissioning officer or agency]. The examination must be based on the course of study described in subsection (b).

(b) The [commissioning officer or agency] or an entity approved by the [commissioning officer or agency] shall offer regularly a course of study to applicants who do not hold commissions as notaries public in this state. The course must cover the laws, rules, procedures, and ethics relevant to notarial acts.]

Legislative Note: *This section requires an applicant for a commission as a notary public to pass an examination based on a course of study regarding the laws, rules, procedures, and ethics relevant to notarial acts. It is provided for states that consider it a good policy that an applicant for a commission as notary public be required to pass an examination based on such a course of study. However, the enactment of this provision is not essential for the uniformity of the act. It is bracketed to show that it is optional.*

Comment

An increasingly common requirement for the issuance of a commission as notary public is the applicant's passage of an examination based on a course of study relevant to the law of notarial acts (compare Neb. Rev. Stat. §64-1-1 (2010)). Professional education enhances the effectiveness and integrity of the notarial system. The course of study envisioned in this section is designed to educate a prospective notary public about the laws, rules, procedures, and ethics relevant to notarial acts.

Subsection (a) provides that an applicant for a commission as a notary public who does not currently hold a commission as a notary public must pass an examination administered by the commissioning officer or agency or an entity approved by the commissioning officer or agency. An applicant who does not currently hold a commission as a notary public includes an applicant who never held a commission as a notary public as well as an applicant who previously held a commission as a notary public but whose commission has since expired. The examination is to be based on the course of instruction provided in subsection (b). The subsection leaves administration of the examination to the commissioning officer or agency through rules adopted pursuant to Section 27(a)(7)(A).

Subsection (b) provides that the commissioning officer or agency or an entity approved by the commissioning officer or agency must regularly offer a course of study to applicants (compare Cal. Govt. Code §8201(a)(3) (2010)). To achieve the objective of enhancing the effectiveness and integrity of the notarial system, the course of study is designed to educate a prospective notary public in the laws, rules, procedures, and ethics relevant to notarial acts. The subsection leaves administration of the course to the commissioning officer or agency through rules adopted pursuant to Section 27(a)(7)(B).

Section 23. Grounds to Deny, Refuse to Renew, Revoke, Suspend, or Condition Commission of Notary Public

(a) The [commissioning officer or agency] may deny, refuse to renew, revoke, suspend, or impose a condition on a commission as notary public for any act or omission that demonstrates the individual lacks the honesty, integrity, competence, or reliability to act as a notary public, including:

(1) failure to comply with this [act];

(2) a fraudulent, dishonest, or deceitful misstatement or omission in the application for a commission as a notary public submitted to the [commissioning officer or agency];

(3) a conviction of the applicant or notary public of any felony or a crime involving fraud, dishonesty, or deceit;

(4) a finding against, or admission of liability by, the applicant or notary public in any legal proceeding or disciplinary action based on the applicant's or notary public's fraud, dishonesty, or deceit;

(5) failure by the notary public to discharge any duty required of a notary public, whether by this [act], rules of the [commissioning officer or agency], or any federal or state law;

(6) use of false or misleading advertising or representation by the notary public representing that the notary has a duty, right, or privilege that the notary does not have;

(7) violation by the notary public of a rule of the [commissioning officer or agency] regarding a notary public; [or]

(8) denial, refusal to renew, revocation, suspension, or conditioning of a notary public commission in another state[; or]

[(9) failure of the notary public to maintain an assurance as provided in Section 21(d)[; or]

[(10) insert other state specific provisions or reference to other state statutes].

(b) If the [commissioning officer or agency] denies, refuses to renew, revokes, suspends, or imposes conditions on a commission as a notary public, the applicant or notary public is entitled to timely notice and hearing in accordance with [this state's administrative procedure act].

(c) The authority of the [commissioning officer or agency] to deny, refuse to renew, suspend, revoke, or impose conditions on a commission as a notary public does not prevent a person from seeking and obtaining other criminal or civil remedies provided by law.

Legislative Note: *Subsection (a)(10) is an optional provision and allows the state either to insert other specific grounds for the denial, refusal to renew, revocation, suspension, or imposition of a condition on a commission as a notary public or to insert references to specific statutes elsewhere in the law of this state providing those grounds. It is bracketed to show that it is optional.*

Comment

Subsection (a) lists the grounds upon which the commissioning officer or agency may deny, refuse to renew, revoke, suspend, or impose a condition a commission. The general grounds listed include a lack of honesty, integrity, competency, or reliability on the part of the applicant or current notary public. The grounds are similar to those provided in many states (compare Ariz. Rev. Stat. §41-330(A) (2010); N.C. Gen. Stat. §10B-5(d) (2010)).

Subsections (a)(1) to (6) and (8) enumerate specific grounds upon which the commissioning officer or agency may deny, refuse to renew, suspend, revoke or impose a condition a commission. Subsection (a)(7) allows the commissioning officer or agency to refuse to renew, suspend, revoke, or impose a condition a commission because the notary public has violated rules adopted by the commissioning officer or agency regarding notaries public.

Although the grounds for disciplinary action stated in this subsection provide the commissioning officer or agency with substantial authority to invoke discipline on the applicant or notary public in order to protect the public, paragraph 10 allows legislatures to add other specific grounds.

Because notaries public deal with financial, personal, and confidential matters for their clients, trustworthiness and honesty are essential qualities of a person holding a commission. Many of the disciplinary grounds provided in this subsection deal with breaches of those qualities (compare Cal. Govt. Code §8201.1(a) (2010)). Subsections (a)(2), (3) and (4) specify several situations in which lack of those qualities, i.e. fraud, dishonesty and deceitfulness, may arise and upon which the commissioning officer or agency may deny, refuse to renew, revoke, suspend, or impose a condition on a commission. Subsection (a)(6) allows disciplinary action if dishonesty or deceitfulness is displayed by the use of false or misleading advertising. If optional Section 21(d) is adopted, subsection (a)(8) allows disciplinary action if a notary public refuses to obtain, has been unable to obtain, or has been denied, an assurance in the form of a surety bond or its functional equivalent.

In determining whether to deny, refuse to renew, suspend, revoke, or impose a condition on a notary public's commission based on an applicant's or commission holder's prior felony under subsection (c), the commissioning officer or agency should take into consideration the relevance of the felony to the performance of the notary public's duties as well as the length of time that has transpired since the performance of the felonious act. The commissioning officer or agency has discretion when making the determination and should weigh all the facts and circumstances before making a decision.

Subsection (b) states that an applicant or notary public whose commission has been denied, revoked, or suspended, or upon whose commission a condition has been imposed, or who has been refused a renewal of a commission is entitled to a timely notice and a hearing. Such a notice and hearing are likely required by the state's administrative procedure act but are restated here for clarity.

Subsection (c) provides that the fact that a commissioning officer or agency has the authority to deny, refuse to renew, suspend, revoke or impose a condition on a commission does not prevent additional relief provided by law. Either the commissioning officer or agency or a person aggrieved by the action of a notary public may seek appropriate relief, whether the relief is civil or criminal.

Section 24. Database of Notaries Public

The [commissioning officer or agency] shall maintain an electronic database of notaries public:

(1) through which a person may verify the authority of a notary public to perform notarial acts; and

(2) which indicates whether a notary public has notified the [commissioning officer or agency] that the notary public will be performing notarial acts on electronic records.

Comment

This section requires the commissioning officer or agency to maintain an electronic database of notaries public. The objectives sought by this provision are twofold. First, it is a disclosure of information and a means by which a member of the public may verify whether an individual who claims to be a notary public in fact has a commission as a notary public. Second, by also requiring that the database indicate whether a notary public has informed the commissioning officer or agency that the notary will be performing notarial acts with respect to electronic records, it provides information to members of the public who are seeking to find a notary public capable of performing notarial acts with respect to electronic records.

Section 25. Prohibited Acts

(a) A commission as a notary public does not authorize an individual to:

(1) assist persons in drafting legal records, give legal advice, or otherwise practice law;

(2) act as an immigration consultant or an expert on immigration matters;

(3) represent a person in a judicial or administrative proceeding relating to immigration to the United States, United States citizenship, or related matters; or

(4) receive compensation for performing any of the activities listed in this subsection.

(b) A notary public may not engage in false or deceptive advertising.

(c) A notary public, other than an attorney licensed to practice law in this state, may not use the term "notario" or "notario publico".

(d) A notary public, other than an attorney licensed to practice law in this state, may not advertise or represent that the notary public may assist persons in drafting legal records, give legal advice, or otherwise practice law. If a notary public who is not an attorney licensed to practice law in this state in any manner advertises or represents that the notary public offers notarial services, whether orally or in a record, including broadcast media, print media, and the Internet, the notary public shall include the following statement, or an alternate statement authorized or required by the [commissioning officer or agency], in the advertisement or representation, prominently and in each language used in the advertisement or representation: "I am not an attorney licensed to practice law in this state. I am not allowed to draft legal records, give advice on legal matters, including immigration, or charge a fee for those activities". If the form of advertisement or representation is not broadcast media, print media, or the Internet and does not permit inclusion of the statement required by this subsection because of size, it must be displayed prominently or provided at the place of performance of the notarial act before the notarial act is performed.

(e) Except as otherwise allowed by law, a notary public may not withhold access to or possession of an original record provided by a person that seeks performance of a notarial act by the notary public.

Comment

In general, subsection (a) provides that a notary public does not have the authority to render legal services merely by the fact that the individual has a commission as a notary public. It does recognize, however, that a notary public who is also an attorney at law licensed to practice law in this state may, by the fact that he or she is a licensed attorney, provide those legal services.

Subsection (a) lists four specific activities prohibited to notaries public:

(1) A notary public may not assist persons by drafting legal records or giving legal advice; more generally a notary public may not practice law (compare Colo. Rev. Stat §12-55-110.3(3)(b)(I) (2010)).

(2) A notary public may not act as an immigration consultant or an expert on immigration matters (compare Colo. Rev. Stat §12-55-110.3(3)(a) (2010)).

(3) A notary public may not represent a person in any legal or administrative proceedings relating to immigration, United States citizenship or related matters (compare Colo. Rev. Stat §12-55-110.3(3)(b)(III) (2010)).

(4) Since a notary public may not perform the above listed activities, a notary public may not receive or collect compensation for performing or attempting to perform those activities (compare Colo. Rev. Stat §12-55-110.3(3)(b)(II)-(III) (2010)).

Subsections (a)(2) and (3) specifically reference immigration matters because many immigrants, especially those from civil law countries, are familiar with the civil law office of "notario publico" or "notario." A holder of that civil law office may have the authority to provide immigration advice or assistance in the foreign country. Because of the similarity in the names of the offices, an immigrant from a civil law country may believe that a notary public is authorized to provide the same assistance in this country. Confusion on the part of the client, however, should not be a reason for a notary public to attempt to provide that assistance. Those subsections clearly prohibit a notary public from providing the assistance. See also subsection (c) for further requirements in this regard.

Subsections (b), (c), and (d) attempt to reduce or eliminate misleading or deceptive advertising by notaries public.

Subsection (b) directly and simply prohibits a notary public from engaging in false or misleading advertising. This prohibition includes the false or misleading advertising specifically described in this section as well as other forms of false or misleading advertising prohibited by other law.

Subsection (c) prohibits a notary public, other than one who is also an attorney licensed to practice law in this state, from using the term "notario publico" or "notario" in the notary's advertising, title, or informational material. As described above, many immigrants from civil law countries are familiar with the civil law office of "notario publico" or "notario," a holder of which may have the authority to draft legal records or provide legal advice, including advice on immigration. To prevent notaries public from taking advantage of the similarity of title by using the term "notario publico" or "notario," this subsection prohibits any advertising using either of those titles (compare Colo. Rev. Stat §12-55-110.3(3)(b)(V) (2010)). Since licensed attorneys have, by reason of their attorneys' licenses the authority to draft documents and provide legal advice, this subsection does not apply to licensed attorneys.

Subsection (d) prohibits a notary public, who is not also an attorney licensed to practice law in this state, from advertising that the notary may draft legal records, provide legal advice, or otherwise practice law. In addition to that prohibition, it makes two specific requirements in any advertising or representation that the notary uses:

(1) Any advertising or representation by the notary must include a specific disclaimer as to the notary's authority to practice law, to provide legal services, or to collect a fee for those activities. The disclaimer must be provided regardless of whether the advertising is written or oral, or a combination of the two. Included among the situations in which that disclaimer must be provided are advertising or representations made on broadcast media (e.g. television and radio), print media (e.g. newspapers, newsletters, and magazines), and the Internet (e.g. web pages and banner ads). If the advertising or representation is not made on broadcast media, print media, or the Internet, and if the inclusion of the disclaimer is not

possible due to the small size of the advertisement or representation (e.g. business card), the disclaimer must be displayed prominently or provided at the place of performance of the notarial act, including any off-premises locale at which the notary performs a notarial act.

(2) The disclaimer must be provided in each language used in the advertisement or representation. To make sure that any advertising aimed at individuals who are not fluent in English or for whom English is a second language, this subsection requires that the disclaimer must be in each language used in the advertisement or representation.

Subsection (e) prohibits a notary public from retaining an original record presented by a person to a notary. A notary's duties as a notary public are to perform the notarial act and, when completed, return the record to the presenting party or as directed by the presenting party. However, a notary public who is also an attorney licensed to practice law in the state may retain a record for purposes consistent with the performance of legal services. In such a case the attorney is not retaining the record in a notarial capacity.

Section 26. Validity of Notarial Acts

Except as otherwise provided in subsection 4(b), the failure of a notarial officer to perform a duty or meet a requirement specified in this [act] does not invalidate a notarial act performed by the notarial officer. The validity of a notarial act under this [act] does not prevent an aggrieved person from seeking to invalidate the record or transaction that is the subject of the notarial act or from seeking other remedies based on law of this state other than this [act] or law of the United States. This section does not validate a purported notarial act performed by an individual who does not have the authority to perform notarial acts.

Comment

This section makes it clear that, except as otherwise provided in subsection 4(b), the failure of a notarial officer to perform the duties or to meet the requirements of this act does not invalidate the notarial act performed by the notarial officer. For example, a notarial act performed by a notary public whose assurance or surety bond may have expired or been cancelled is not invalidated. However, this provision only applies to a person who is a notarial officer. The section does not legitimate a notarial act attempted to be performed by a person who does not have the authority to perform the act. For example, an individual who does not have a valid commission as a notary public cannot perform notarial acts and any attempted notarial act would be invalid.

Despite the fact that a notarial act may be valid, the underlying record or transaction may be invalid and may be set aside in appropriate legal proceedings. For example, the underlying record may be the product of fraud, whether performed by the notarial officer or by a third person. In accordance with other law of this state, an action may be brought to invalidate or set aside the record and obtain restitution and other relief.

Section 27. Rules

(a) The [commissioning officer or agency] may adopt rules to implement this [act]. Rules adopted regarding the performance of notarial acts with respect to electronic records may not require, or accord greater legal status or effect to, the implementation or application of a specific technology or technical specification. The rules may:

(1) prescribe the manner of performing notarial acts regarding tangible and electronic records;

(2) include provisions to ensure that any change to or tampering with a record bearing a certificate of a notarial act is self-evident;

(3) include provisions to ensure integrity in the creation, transmittal, storage, or authentication of electronic records or signatures;

(4) prescribe the process of granting, renewing, conditioning, denying, suspending, or revoking a notary public commission and assuring the trustworthiness of an individual holding a commission as notary public; [and]

(5) include provisions to prevent fraud or mistake in the performance of notarial acts; [and]

[(6) establish the process for approving and accepting surety bonds and other forms of assurance under Section 21(d)][; and]

[(7) provide for the administration of the examination under Section 22(a) and the course of study under Section 22(b)].

(b) In adopting, amending, or repealing rules about notarial acts with respect to electronic records, the [commissioning officer or agency] shall consider, so far as is consistent with this [act]:

(1) the most recent standards regarding electronic records promulgated by national bodies, such as the National Association of Secretaries of State;

(2) standards, practices, and customs of other jurisdictions that substantially enact this [act]; and

(3) the views of governmental officials and entities and other interested persons.

Comment

Subsection (a) is comprehensive authority for the commissioning officer or agency to adopt rules to implement this Act. Any rules adopted with respect to the performance of notarial acts on electronic records must be technology neutral; they may not require or favor one technology or technical specification over another. This is the same requirement provided in ESign, 15 U.S.C. Ch. 96, §102(a)(2)(ii) (2010).

Subsection (a)(1) authorizes rules that prescribe the manner of performing notarial acts, whether with respect to tangible or electronic records. The provisions of this Act itself were not intended to specify all the possible requirements or procedures that now or in the future may be appropriate for performing notarial acts. Thus, it allows the commissioning officer or agency to adopt rules to further implement the Act

Subsection (a)(2) authorizes rules that will ensure that any change to, or tampering with, a record bearing a notarial act will be self-evident, i.e. tamper evident. Such a procedure will allow an individual inspecting the record to determine whether there has been any tampering with the integrity of a notarial act performed on, or with respect to, a record or with the attachment or association of a certificate of notarial act with the record. This provision applies both to notarial acts performed on tangible records and notarial acts performed with respect to electronic records. Regarding tangible records, this would allow a rule, for example, that requires a certain method of attaching the certificate to the record so that the removal or addition of a page would be readily discernable. With regard to electronic records, this would allow a rule, for example, that requires the technology or process used provide a means of testing to determine whether there has been any change to the electronic certificate or record. Note, however, that such a requirement must be technology neutral and may not require or favor one particular technology or technical specification. See subsection (a).

Subsection (a)(3) authorizes rules that will ensure integrity in the creation, transmittal, storage, or authentication of electronic records or signatures. This would allow a rule, for example, that requires that a certain level or degree of security be achieved in attaching an electronic certificate of notarial act to, or associating it with, an electronic record, and in its transmission or storage. Once again, the requirement must be technology neutral. See subsection (a).

Subsection (a)(4) authorizes rules for granting and revoking commissions and assuring the trustworthiness of individuals holding a commission. As stated in the Comment to Section 21, that section leaves the form of application, the process for applying, the timing of the process, and other administrative matters to be determined by the commissioning officer or agency. This section authorizes the commissioning officer or agency to adopt a rule, for example, that implements a method by which the prior history of an applicant for a commission could be reviewed with regard to the applicant's trustworthiness.

Subsection (a)(5) authorizes the adoption of rules that will prevent fraud or mistake in the performance of notarial acts. It would authorize the adoption of a rule, for example, that specifies what additional information should be provided in order to guide notaries public under Section 7(c) regarding additional information to identify an individual for whom a notarial act will be performed.

Subsection (a)(6) allows the commissioning officer or agency to adopt rules regarding the approval and acceptance of surety bonds and other forms of assurance if Section 21(d) is adopted by the legislature.

Subsection (a)(7) authorizes the commissioning officer or agency to adopt rules to implement and administer the examination of applicants for notary public commissions if Section 22 is adopted by the legislature. The rules may also administer the provision of a course of study for applicants for a commission as well as the process of selecting and approving of an entity to offer the course.

Subsection (b) directs the commissioning officer or agency, when adopting, amending, or repealing rules regarding notarial acts performed with respect to electronic records, to consider, so far as is consistent with this Act, the most recent standards promulgated by national bodies such as the National Association of Secretaries of State and also to consider the standards, practices, and customs of other jurisdictions that substantially adopt this Act. The purposes of this provision are to bring to the commissioning officer or agency the best practices and information concerning notarial acts performed with respect to electronic records and to encourage uniformity of those provisions among the various states.

Section 28. Notary Public Commission in Effect

A commission as a notary public in effect on [the effective date of this [act]] continues until its date of expiration. A notary public who applies to renew a commission as a notary public on or after [the effective date of this [act]] is subject to and shall comply with this [act]. A notary public, in performing notarial acts after [the effective date of this [act]], shall comply with this [act].

Comment

This section states that an individual who has a commission as a notary public that is in effect on the date of the adoption of this Act may retain that notary commission until the scheduled date of expiration, if any. Other than as may apply to the length of an existing commission, however, the provisions of the law previously in effect do not carry over after the adoption of this Act. Thus, after the effective date of this Act, a notary is subject to the provisions of this Act with respect to a refusal to renew the commission or a revocation or suspension of the commission. This Act is also applicable to all notarial acts performed after its effective date regardless of whether the commission predated or postdated the effective date of this Act.

Section 29. Savings Clause

This [act] does not affect the validity or effect of a notarial act performed before [the effective date of this [act]].

Comment

This section expressly provides that the enactment of this Act does not affect either the validity or effect of any notarial act performed prior to the effective date of the Act under a law that was repealed by this Act. The validity and effect of that notarial act will continue to be determined under the repealed law.

Section 30. Uniformity of Application and Construction

In applying and construing this uniform act, consideration must be given to the need to promote uniformity of the law with respect to its subject matter among states that enact it.

Comment

This provision seeks to encourage construction that will maintain uniformity among the various states adopting the Act.

Section 31. Relation to Electronic Signatures in Global and National Commerce Act

This [act] modifies, limits, and supersedes the Electronic Signatures in Global and National Commerce Act, 15 U.S.C. Section 7001 et seq., but does not modify, limit, or supersede Section 101(c) of that act, 15 U.S.C. Section 7001(c), or authorize electronic delivery of any of the notices described in Section 103(b) of that act, 15 U.S.C. Section 7003(b).

Comment

This section responds to the specific language of the Electronic Signatures in Global and National Commerce Act and is designed to avoid preemption of state law under that federal legislation.

Section 32. Repeals

The following are repealed:
 (1) [The Uniform Acknowledgment Act (As Amended)].
 (2) [The Uniform Recognition of Acknowledgments Act].
 (3) [The Uniform Law on Notarial Acts].

Comment

This section lists laws that this act supervenes.

Section 33. Effective Date

This [act] takes effect ….

Comment

This is the standard effective date provision for uniform laws. ■

Appendix 2

UNIFORM LAW ON NOTARIAL ACTS (1982)

UNIFORM LAW ON NOTARIAL ACTS

Drafted by the

NATIONAL CONFERENCE OF COMMISSIONERS
ON UNIFORM STATE LAWS

and by it

Approved and Recommended for Enactment
in All the States

at its

Annual Conference
Meeting in Its Ninety-First Year
in Monterey, California
July 30–August 6, 1982

With Prefatory Note and Comments

Approved by the American Bar Association
New Orleans, Louisiana, February 9, 1983

Commissioners' Prefatory Note: *This Uniform Act is designed to define the content and form of common notarial acts and to provide for the recognition of such acts performed in other jurisdictions. It thus replaces two Uniform Laws, the Uniform Acknowledgment Act (As Amended), and the later Uniform Recognition of Acknowledgments Act. The original Acknowledgment Act served to define the content and form of acknowledgments. The Recognition Act later provided for more specific rules for recognition of acknowledgments and "other notarial acts" from outside of the state, although its title was more narrowly stated.*

This statute is thus a consolidation, extension, and modernization of the two previous acts. It consolidates the provisions of the two acts relating to acknowledgments of instruments. It extends the coverage of the earlier act to include other notarial acts, such as taking of verifications and attestation of documents.

In addition, the act seeks to simplify and clarify proof of the authority of notarial officers.

Uniform Law on Notarial Acts

Sec.
1. Definitions.
2. Notarial Acts.
3. Notarial Acts in This State.
4. Notarial Acts in Other Jurisdictions of the United States.
5. Notarial Acts Under Federal Authority.
6. Foreign Notarial Acts.
7. Certificate of Notarial Acts.
8. Short Forms.
9. Notarial Acts Affected by This Act.
10. Uniformity of Application and Construction.
11. Short Title.
12. Repeals.
13. Time of Taking Effect.

Section 1. Definitions

As used in this [Act]:

1. "Notarial act" means any act that a notary public of this State is authorized to perform, and includes taking an acknowledgment, administering an oath or affirmation, taking a verification upon oath or affirmation, witnessing or attesting a signature, certifying or attesting a copy, and noting a protest of a negotiable instrument.

2. "Acknowledgment" means a declaration by a person that the person has executed an instrument for the purposes stated therein and, if the instrument is executed in a representative capacity, that the person signed the instrument with proper authority and executed it as the act of the person or entity represented and identified therein.

3. "Verification upon oath or affirmation" means a declaration that a statement is true made by a person upon oath or affirmation.

4. "In a representative capacity" means:

   i. for and on behalf of a corporation, partnership, trust, or other entity, as an authorized officer, agent, partner, trustee, or other representative;

   ii. as a public officer, personal representative, guardian, or other representative, in the capacity recited in the instrument;

   iii. as an attorney in fact for a principal; or

   iv. in any other capacity as an authorized

representative of another.

5. "Notarial officer" means a notary public or other officer authorized to perform notarial acts.

Commissioners' Comment: *This Uniform Law defines common notarial acts and provides for the recognition of notarial acts performed in other states and in foreign jurisdictions. It does not prescribe the qualifications of notaries public or other officers empowered to perform notarial functions, nor does it establish the procedure for their selection or term of office.*

The Act uses the term "notarial officer" to describe notaries public and other persons having the power to perform "notarial acts." These notarial acts are described in Section 2. Section 3 then describes who, in addition to notaries public, is a notarial officer in this state; Sections 4, 5, and 6 provide for the recognition of acts of notarial officers appointed by other jurisdictions.

Section 2. Notarial Acts

a. In taking an acknowledgment, the notarial officer must determine, either from personal knowledge or from satisfactory evidence, that the person appearing before the officer and making the acknowledgment is the person whose true signature is on the instrument.

b. In taking a verification upon oath or affirmation, the notarial officer must determine, either from personal knowledge or from satisfactory evidence, that the person appearing before the officer and making the verification is the person whose true signature is on the statement verified.

c. In witnessing or attesting a signature the notarial officer must determine, either from personal knowledge or from satisfactory evidence, that the signature is that of the person appearing before the officer and named therein.

d. In certifying or attesting a copy of a document or other item, the notarial officer must determine that the proffered copy is a full, true, and accurate transcription or reproduction of that which was copied.

e. In making or noting a protest of a negotiable instrument the notarial officer must determine the matters set forth in [Section 3-509, Uniform Commercial Code].

f. A notarial officer has satisfactory evidence that a person is the person whose true signature is on a document if that person (i) is personally known to the notarial officer, (ii) is identified upon the oath or affirmation of a credible witness personally known to the notarial officer or (iii) is identified on the basis of identification documents.

Commissioners' Comment: *This section authorizes common notarial acts. It does not limit other acts which notaries may perform, if authorized by other laws.*

Subsection (a) specifies what a notarial officer certifies by taking an acknowledgment. The notarial officer certifies to two facts: (1) the identity of the person who made the acknowledgment and (2) the fact that this person signed the document as a deed (or other specific instrument), and not as some other form of writing. The personal physical appearance of the acknowledging party before the notarial officer is required. An acknowledgment, as defined in Section 1(2) is a statement that the person has signed and executed an instrument; it is not the act of signature itself. Hence a person may appear before the notarial officer to acknowledge an instrument which that person had previously signed.

Similarly subsection (b) specifies the requisites of taking of a verification on oath or affirmation. There are again two elements: (1) the identity of the affiant and (2) the fact that the statement was made under oath or affirmation. Here again, the personal physical presence of the affiant is required.

Subsection (c) defines the requirements for witnessing (or attesting) a signature. Here only the fact of the signature, not the intent to execute the instrument, is certified by the notarial officer.

Subsection (d) defines the standards for attestation or certification of a copy of a document by a notarial officer. This is commonly done if it is necessary to produce a true copy of a document, when the original cannot be removed from archives or other records. In many cases, the custodian of official records may also be empowered to issue official certified copies. Where such official certified copies are available, they constitute official evidence of the state of public records, and may be better evidence thereof than a notarially certified copy.

Subsection (e) refers to a provision of the Uniform Commercial Code which confers authority to note a protest of a negotiable instrument on notaries and certain other officers.

Subsection (f) describes the duty of care which the notarial officer must exercise in identifying the person who makes the acknowledgment, verification or other underlying act. California law, for example, provides an exclusive list of identification documents on which the notarial officer may rely. These are documents containing pictorial identification and signature, such as local driver's licenses, and U.S. passports and military identification papers, issued by authorities known to exercise care in identification of persons requesting such documentation.

Section 3. Notarial Acts in This State

a. A notarial act may be performed within this state by the following persons:

   1. a notary public of this State,

   2. a judge, clerk or deputy clerk of any court of this State,

   [3. a person licensed to practice law in this State,] [or]

   [4. a person authorized by law of this State to administer oaths,] [or]

   [5. any other person authorized to perform the specific act by the law of this State.]

b. Notarial acts performed within this State under federal authority as provided in section 5 have the same effect as if performed by a notarial officer of this State.

c. The signature and title of a person performing a notarial act are prima facie evidence that the signature is genuine and that the person holds the designated title.

Commissioners' Comment: *Subsection (a) lists the persons who are entitled to serve as notarial officers in the state. In addition to notaries public, all judges, clerks and deputy clerks of courts of the state may automatically perform notarial acts. The language follows the more modern form of the Uniform Recognition of Acknowledgments Act. It is more abbreviated than the Uniform Acknowledgment Act, in that it consolidates the several judicial offices into one listing.*

Several optional additional notarial officers are listed. A state may authorize all duly licensed attorneys at law to serve as notaries public by virtue of their attorneys' licenses. It may also authorize other individuals who have authority to administer oaths to do so. If other particular officers, such as recorders or registrars of deeds or commissioners of titles, may perform notarial acts in the state it would be advisable to list them here, because this list will be a ready reference point for those who seek to determine the validity of their acts, when they are used in another state.

Proof of authority of a notarial officer usually involves three steps:

   1. Proof that the notarial signature is that of the named person,

   2. Proof that that person holds the designated office, and

   3. Proof that holders of that office may perform notarial acts.

Subsection (c) sets forth the presumption of genuineness of signature and the presumption of truth of assertion of authority by the notarial officer, the first two elements of authentication. Since the officers listed in subsection (a) are authorized to act by this statute, no further proof of the third element, the authority of such an officer, is required.

Section 4. Notarial Acts in Other Jurisdictions of the United States

a. A notarial act has the same effect under the law of this State as if performed by a notarial officer of this State, if performed in another state, commonwealth, territory, district, or possession of the United States by any of the following persons:

   1. a notary public of that jurisdiction;

   2. a judge, clerk, or deputy clerk of a court of that jurisdiction; or

   3. any other person authorized by the law of that jurisdiction to perform notarial acts.

b. Notarial acts performed in other jurisdictions of the United States under federal authority as provided in section 5 have the same effect as if performed by a notarial officer of this State.

c. The signature and title of a person performing a notarial act are prima facie evidence that the signature is genuine and that the person holds the designated title.

d. The signature and indicated title of an officer listed in subsection (a)(1) or (a)(2) conclusively establish the authority of a holder of that title to perform a notarial act.

Commissioners' Comment: *Sections 4, 5, and 6 of this act are adapted from Sections 1 and 2 of the Uniform Recognition of Acknowledgments Act. That Act set forth the individuals outside of the state who could take acknowledgments or perform other notarial acts, and separately set forth the authentication of those acts which was necessary. Different standards applied in the cases of persons acting under the authority of another state, of the federal government, or of a foreign country. This statute distinguishes between the three kinds of authority from outside the state, and provides the authentication separately for each type.*

Subsection (a) is adapted from Section 1 of the Uniform Recognition of Acknowledgments Act. Subsection (b) gives prima facie validity to the signature and assertion of title of the person who acts as notarial officer. It follows Section 2(d) of the Uniform Recognition of Acknowledgments

Act. It thus provides the first two elements of proof of authority of the notarial officer set forth in the comments to Section 3.

Subsection (c) provides the third element of that proof of authority. It recognizes conclusively the authority of a notary public or of a judge or clerk or deputy clerk of court to perform notarial acts, without the necessity of further proof that such an officer has notarial authority. It is copied from Section 2(a) of the Uniform Recognition of Acknowledgments Act. These two subsections abolish the need for a "clerk's certificate" to authenticate the act of the notary, judge, or clerk. The authority of a person other than a notary, judge, or clerk to perform notarial acts can most readily be proven by reference to the law of that state. Any other form of proof of such authority acceptable in the receiving jurisdiction, such as a clerk's certificate, as is currently provided by Section 2(c) of the Uniform Recognition of Acknowledgments Act, would also suffice.

Section 5. Notarial Acts Under Federal Authority

a. A notarial act has the same effect under the law of this State as if performed by a notarial officer of this State if performed anywhere by any of the following persons under authority granted by the law of the United States:

1. a judge, clerk, or deputy clerk of a court;

2. a commissioned officer on active duty in the military service of the United States;

3. an officer of the foreign service or consular officer of the United States; or

4. any other person authorized by federal law to perform notarial acts.

b. The signature and title of a person performing a notarial act are prima facie evidence that the signature is genuine and that the person holds the designated title.

c. The signature and indicated title of an officer listed in subsection (a)(1), (a)(2), or (a)(3) conclusively establish the authority of a holder of that title to perform a notarial act.

Commissioners' Comment: *Some acknowledgments are performed by persons acting under federal authority, or holding office under federal authority. This section provides for the automatic recognition of those notarial acts within the enacting state. The list of persons whose acts are immediately recognized by this section is drawn from Section 1 of the Uniform Recognition of Acknowledgments Act, but has been simplified. This law no longer limits recognition of the notarial acts performed by military officers to acts performed for persons in the military service "or any other persons serving with or accompanying the armed forces of the United States." Such a limitation in recognition merely places another cloud on the validity of the notarial act. The Act does not purport to extend the authority of military officers to perform these acts, but merely immunizes the private party relying on them from any consequences of the officer's excess of authority. Both in the case of commissioned military officers and foreign service officers, the language has been modified to reflect modern descriptions of the offices in question. In both instances, the further reference to "any other person authorized by regulation" has also been omitted as duplicative of paragraph 4 of this subsection.*

Subsection (b), like its counterpart in Section 4, is drawn from Section 2(d) of the Uniform Recognition of Acknowledgments Act. It confers prima facie validity upon the signature and assertion of rank or title by the notarial officer, thus providing the first two elements of proof described in the comments to Section 3.

Subsection (c) is drawn from Section 2(a) of the same law. It provides the third element of proof of the notarial officer's authority. It immediately recognizes the authority of a judge or clerk, or military officer or foreign service or consular officer to perform notarial acts, without the necessity of further reference to the federal statutes or regulations to prove that the officer has notarial authority. There is no need for further authentication of these persons' authority to perform notarial acts. A variety of other federal officers may be authorized to perform notarial acts, such as wardens of federal prisons, but their authority must be demonstrated by other means. The authority of such an officer to perform the notarial act can most readily be demonstrated by reference to the federal law or published regulation granting such authority. Any other form of authentication, such as a clerk's certificate, could also be used.

A military officer who performs notarial services should insert the appropriate title (e.g., commanding officer) in the place designated for "title (and rank)" to conform to 10 U.S.C. Sec. 936(d). The officer's rank and branch of service should also be inserted there.

Section 6. Foreign Notarial Acts

a. A notarial act has the same effect under the law of this State as if performed by a notarial officer of this State if performed within the jurisdiction of and under authority of a foreign nation or its constituent units or a multi-national or international organization by any of the following persons:

    1. a notary public or notary;

    2. a judge, clerk, or deputy clerk of a court of record; or

    3. any other person authorized by the law of that jurisdiction to perform notarial acts.

    b. An "Apostille" in the form prescribed by the Hague Convention of October 5, 1961, conclusively establishes that the signature of the notarial officer is genuine and that the officer holds the indicated office.

    c. A certificate by a foreign service or consular officer of the United States stationed in the nation under the jurisdiction of which the notarial act was performed, or a certificate by a foreign service or consular officer of that nation stationed in the United States, conclusively establishes any matter relating to the authenticity or validity of the notarial act set forth in the certificate.

    d. An official stamp or seal of the person performing the notarial act is prima facie evidence that the signature is genuine and that the person holds the indicated title.

    e. An official stamp or seal of an officer listed in subsection (a)(1) or (a)(2) is prima facie evidence that a person with the indicated title has authority to perform notarial acts.

    f. If the title of office and indication of authority to perform notarial acts appears either in a digest of foreign law or in a list customarily used as a source for that information, the authority of an officer with that title to perform notarial acts is conclusively established.

Commissioners' Comment: *This section deals with the authority of notarial officers empowered to act under foreign law. Note that the act of any notary is recognized, as well as that of judges or clerk of courts of record. The notarial acts of other persons will be recognized if they are authorized by the law of the place in which they are performed.*

Proof of validity of foreign notarial acts is a more difficult problem than recognition of such acts from other states of the United States, because the relative authority of public and quasi-public officers may vary. See the special rules previously provided under the Uniform Recognition of Acknowledgments Act, Section 2(b).

The United States is now a party to an international convention regarding the authentication of notarial and other public acts. The first method of recognition of foreign notarial acts is that set forth in the treaty. The Apostille may be stamped on the document or an attached page by a specified officer in the foreign country. It has the following form.

APOSTILLE
(Convention de La Haye du 5 octobre 1961)

1. Country: _____
This public document
2. has been signed by _____
3. acting in the capacity of _____
4. bears the seal/stamp of _____.

CERTIFIED

5. at _____ 6. the _____
7. by _____
8. No. _____
9. Seal/Stamp 10. Signature: _____

It may be in the language of the issuing country, but the words "Apostille (Convention de La Haye, du 5 octobre 1961)" are always in French. Under the terms of the treaty, to which the United States is a party, the Apostille must be recognized if issued by a competent authority in another nation which has also ratified it. The text of the convention is reproduced in the volume of 28 U.S.C.A. containing the annotations to Rule 44 of the Federal Rules of Civil Procedure, and in Martindale-Hubbell.

Although federal law provides for mandatory recognition of an Apostille only if issued by another ratifying nation, this statute provides for recognition of all apostilles issued by any foreign nation in that form. They are, in effect, no more than a standard form for authentication. Use of the form eases problems of translation.

Recognition may also be accorded in a number of other ways, which are taken from Section 2(b) of the Uniform Recognition of Acknowledgments Act.

Section 7. Certificate of Notarial Acts

    a. A notarial act must be evidenced by a certificate signed and dated by a notarial officer. The certificate must include identification of the jurisdiction in which the notarial act is performed and the title of the office of the notarial officer and may include the official stamp or seal of office. If the officer is a notary public, the certificate must also indicate the date of expiration, if any, of the commission of office, but omission of that information may subsequently be corrected. If the officer is a commissioned officer on active duty in the military service of the United States, it must also include the officer's rank.

    b. A certificate of a notarial act is sufficient if it meets the requirements of subsection (a) and it:

    1. is in the short form set forth in Section 8;

    2. is in a form otherwise prescribed by the law of this State;

    3. is in a form prescribed by the laws or regulations applicable in the place in which the notarial act was performed; or

    4. sets forth the actions of the notarial officer and those are sufficient to meet the requirements of the designated notarial act.

    c. By executing a certificate of a notarial act, the notarial officer certifies that the officer has made the determinations required by Section 2.

Commissioners' Comment: *This section requires a written certification by the notarial officer of the notarial act. That certification may be simple. It need only record the notarial act and its place and date, together with the signature and office of the notarial officer. Subsection (b) provides that the certificate may be in any one of the short forms set forth in this act, or in any other form provided by local law, or in any other form provided by the law of the place where it is performed, or in any form that sets forth the requisite elements of the appropriate notarial act. Thus acknowledgments or other notarial acts executed in the more elaborate forms of the former Uniform Acknowledgment Act or the Uniform Recognition of Acknowledgments Act would continue to qualify under subsection (b)(4). Subsection (c) reemphasizes the obligation of the notarial officer to make the determinations required by Section 2 and to certify that the officer has done so.*

Section 8. Short Forms

The following short form certificates of notarial acts are sufficient for the purposes indicated, if completed with the information required by Section 7(a):

1. For an acknowledgment in an individual capacity:

State of _____
(County) of _____

This instrument was acknowledged before me on _____ (date) by _____ (name(s) of person(s)).

(Seal, if any)
_____ (Signature of notarial officer)

_____ Title (and Rank)
[My commission expires: _____]

2. For an acknowledgment in a representative capacity:

State of _____
(County) of _____

This instrument was acknowledged before me on _____ (date) by _____ (name(s) of person(s)) as _____ (type of authority, e.g., officer, trustee, etc.) of _____ (name of party on behalf of whom instrument was executed).

(Seal, if any)
_____ (Signature of notarial officer)

_____ Title (and Rank)
[My commission expires: _____]

3. For a verification upon oath or affirmation:

State of _____
(County) of _____

Signed and sworn to (or affirmed) before me on _____ (date) by _____ (name(s) of person(s) making statement).

(Seal, if any)
_____ (Signature of notarial officer)
_____ Title (and Rank)
[My commission expires: _____]

4. For witnessing or attesting a signature:

State of _____
(County) of _____

Signed or attested before me on _____ (date) by _____ (name(s) of person(s)).

(Seal, if any)
_____ (Signature of notarial officer)

_____ Title (and Rank)
[My commission expires: _____]

5. For attestation of a copy of a document:

State of _____
(County) of _____

I certify that this is a true and correct copy of a document in the possession of _____.
Dated _____

(Seal, if any)
_____ (Signature of notarial officer)

_____ Title (and Rank)
[My commission expires: _____]

Commissioners' Comment: *This section provides statutory short forms for notarial acts. These forms are sufficient to certify a notarial act. See Section 7(b)(1). Other forms may also qualify, as provided in Section 7.*

A notarial seal is optional under this Act. See Section 7(a). A military officer who is acting as a notarial officer will normally enter both title (e.g., commanding officer, Company A, etc.) and rank (Captain, U.S. Army) as identification.

Section 9. Notarial Acts Affected by This Act

This [Act] applies to notarial acts performed on or after its effective date.

Section 10. Uniformity of Application and Construction

This [Act] shall be applied and construed to effectuate its general purpose to make uniform the law with respect to the subject of this (Act) among states enacting it.

Section 11. Short Title

This [Act] may be cited as the Uniform Law on Notarial Acts.

Section 12. Repeals

The following acts and parts of acts are repealed:
1. [The Uniform Acknowledgment Act (As Amended)]
2. [The Uniform Recognition of Acknowledgments Act]
3. _____.

Commissioners' Comment: *This statute is intended to replace the Uniform Acknowledgment Act and the Uniform Recognition of Acknowledgments Act, and may also replace other state legislation on this topic.*

Section 13. Time of Taking Effect

This [Act] takes effect _____. ■

Appendix

UNIFORM RECOGNITION OF ACKNOWLEDGMENTS ACT (1968)

UNIFORM RECOGNITION OF ACKNOWLEDGMENTS ACT

Drafted by the

NATIONAL CONFERENCE OF COMMISSIONERS ON UNIFORM STATE LAWS

and by it

Approved and Recommended for Enactment in All the States

at its

Annual Conference
Meeting in its Seventy-Seventh Year
Philadelphia, Pennsylvania
July 22 — August 1, 1968

With Prefatory Note and Comments

Approved by the American Bar Association
at its
Meeting at Philadelphia, Pennsylvania
August 7, 1968

Prefatory Note

Reasons for Proposed Uniform Act. Since its first Uniform Acknowledgment Act in 1892, the National Conference has promulgated, amended and revised acts in 1914, 1939, 1942, 1949 and in 1960. Each of these acts had a multiple purpose: to establish a simplified and certain form for taking acknowledgments both within and without the state; and to specify how acknowledgments and other notarial acts taken out of the state could be taken so as to be recognized in the enacting state. Each amendment or revision has been made necessary and desirable by technological changes (e.g., use of facsimile signatures); by the mobility of the American population (e.g., acknowledgment without the United States) and by changes in titles of officers, other than notaries public, who are authorized to take acknowledgments in various parts of the United States and the world.

Impetus for the present consideration of acknowledgments by the National Conference has come from the Secretary of State of the United States. He has advised the Conference that the existing acts, both of the Conference and of the individual states which do not have the Uniform Act, are out of date in listing the titles of officers of the foreign service who may take acknowledgments. Thus, the act refers to taking an acknowledgment before a "secretary of a legation" but not before a "secretary of an embassy" and currently the United States has only two legations in the world and in every other country the United States has an embassy. In the course of examining both state laws and federal law on the subject, other instances of federal personnel operating in other states and throughout the world who have acknowledgment powers came to our attention. Thus, the Coast and Geodetic Survey and Weather Service have vessels stationed outside the jurisdiction of the United States and the personnel of this service have need for notarial services while on active duty. Wardens of federal prisons have been authorized to take acknowledgments for inmates of these institutions, but many of these titles are not found in the acknowledgment acts of the various states and, therefore, may not be recognized in the state where it is desired that the notarial act be used.

Rather than preparing another "minor amendment" which wastes time of state legislatures, it is proposed in this draft that there be a major independent act concerning recognition in the enacting state of acknowledgments and other notarial acts performed elsewhere for use in the enacting state. The present draft proposes to describe, in sufficiently general terminology, the persons whose notarial act will be recognized in the enacting state that new designations of officers will not require additional amendments. Thus, instead of listing a series of special titles such as "ambassadors, ministers, charges d'affairs, consul general, etc." which may take acknowledgments and which titles may change as tables of organization of the Secretary of State change, this draft refers only to an "officer of the foreign service" and other persons designated by regulation of the foreign service to perform notarial acts.

This act does not require amendment of existing acknowledgment law in the state unless that state chooses to make an amendment. This act deals only with "recognition of notarial acts" and it is a recognition statute "in addition to any other recognition statute now in effect in the state." While as a matter of tidying-up the statute books, it may be desirable to repeal some of the existing recognition statutes such as the earlier Uniform Acknowledgment Acts, this is not necessary. This act may stand alone.

The act proposed lists the officers whose performance of notarial acts will be recognized in this state (Section 1); it prescribes where authentication of the power of the officer is necessary for recognition of the acknowledgment (Section 2); it states what the officer performing the notarial act shall certify (Section 3); and it states what certificates used by the officer taking the acknowledgment will be recognized (Section 4). The act also prescribes a short form of acknowledgment which will be recognized if used. The short form does not prohibit the use of any other form.

Need for Uniformity. The major need for uniformity is the need of notaries and persons outside the enacting state who have been asked to notarize a document for use in the enacting state. Currently, the personnel regulations for the foreign service of the United States have more than 10 pages of instructions to consuls and others admonishing them that if the acknowledgment is to be used in state X only a vice-consul may take the acknowledgment, but if it is to be used in state Y either a consul or a consul general may take an acknowledgment. The other major use outside the enacting state is by personnel of the Armed Forces of the United States who are asked by persons connected with the Armed Forces installation to perform a notarial act for use elsewhere.

A uniform act on the subject of recognition of acknowledgments is becoming increasingly more imperative as more and more citizens of the United States are employed by the federal government and American industry away from their state of origin or property management. The federal government has designated various officials to serve their employees and others by authorizing them to take acknowledgments. This service can be performed efficiently and certainly only if the federal official has a simple method of taking an acknowledgment which is uniformly effective in any state. For a state to enact this Uniform Recognition Act it would substantially help its citizens and residents conduct affairs having significance in the enacting state at places wherever they happen to be at the time the notarial act is performed.

In this Act there is no attempt to say what instruments shall be acknowledged or when proof of execution of an instrument is required. All that this Act does is to provide that whenever the laws of the enacting state require an act of acknowledgment to be performed and whenever they authorize a notary public of the enacting state to perform the act, then the officers designated in the proposed Act may perform the act and it is to be recognized in the enacting state.

Uniform Recognition of Acknowledgments Act

Section 1. (Recognition of Notarial Acts Performed Outside This State.)

For the purposes of this Act, "notarial acts" means acts which the laws and regulations of this State authorize notaries public of this State to perform, including the administering of oaths and affirmations, taking proof of execution and acknowledgments of instruments, and attesting documents. Notarial acts may be performed outside this State for use in this State with the same effect as if performed by a notary public of this State by the following persons authorized pursuant to the laws and regulations of other governments in addition to any other person authorized by the laws and regulations of this State:

1. a notary public authorized to perform notarial acts in the place in which the act is performed;

2. a judge, clerk, or deputy clerk of any court of record in the place in which the notarial act is performed;

3. an officer of the foreign service of the United States, a consular agent, or any other person authorized by regulation of the United States Department of State to perform notarial acts in the place in which the act is performed;

4. a commissioned officer in active service with the Armed Forces of the United States and any other person authorized by regulation of the Armed Forces to perform notarial acts if the notarial act is performed for one of the following or his dependents: a merchant seaman of the United States, a member of the Armed Forces of the United States, or any other person serving with or accompanying the Armed Forces of the United States; or

5. any other person authorized to perform notarial acts in the place in which the act is performed.

Comment: *This section refers to persons whose title is created by the laws of another place whose notarial act is directed to be recognized in this state. Under federal laws there are several classes of persons who now fall within subsections (3), (4) and (5). As an example, the following are* *authorized to take acknowledgments: 1. Wardens, clerks and parole officers of federal penal and correctional institutions for employees and inmates, 18 U.S.C. § 4004. 2. Commissioned and warrant officers of the Coast Guard, 14 U.S.C. § 636. 3. United States commissioners, 5 U.S.C. § 92, 28 U.S.C. § 637. 4. Commanding officers of coast and geodetic survey vessels not in the jurisdiction of the United States, 33 U.S.C., § 875. 5. Foreign service officers of the United States, 22 U.S.C. § 1203 and C.F.R. Tit. 22, § 92.2.*

Section 2. (Authentication of Authority of Officer.)

a. If the notarial act is performed by any of the persons described in paragraphs 1 to 4, inclusive of section 1, other than a person authorized to perform notarial acts by the laws or regulations of a foreign country, the signature, rank, or title and serial number, if any, of the person are sufficient proof of the authority of a holder of that rank or title to perform the act. Further proof of his authority is not required.

b. If the notarial act is performed by a person authorized by the laws or regulations of a foreign country to perform the act, there is sufficient proof of the authority of that person to act if:

1. either a foreign service officer of the United States resident in the country in which the act is performed or a diplomatic or consular officer of the foreign country resident in the United States certifies that a person holding that office is authorized to perform the act;

2. the official seal of the person performing the notarial act is affixed to the document; or

3. the title and indication of authority to perform notarial acts of the person appears either in a digest of foreign laws or in a list customarily used as a source of such information.

c. If the notarial act is performed by a person other than one described in subsections (a) and (b), there is sufficient proof of the authority of that person to act if the clerk of a court of record in the place in which the notarial act is performed certifies to the official character of that person and to his authority to perform the notarial act.

d. The signature and title of the person performing the act are prima facie evidence that he is a person with the designated title and that the signature is genuine.

Comment: *Subsection (a) is a change from existing law in some states. Practically all states provide that if the notarial act is performed by an officer of the United States, the signature of the officer and a statement of his rank is sufficient proof of the authority of the holder of the office to perform the notarial act. Subsection (a) also provides that no authentication is necessary of the power of an officer designated by the laws of a state in the United States. Thus, a notary of another state may, by signing his name and his title and his number, if any, establish his proof authority of a notary to perform the notarial act.*

Subsection (b) requires authentication if the notarial act is performed by a person authorized by the laws of a foreign country to perform the act. Two methods of authentication are made. Authentication may be made by a certificate by a foreign service officer of the United States resident in the foreign country or a certificate by a diplomatic officer of the foreign country resident in the United States that a person holding the office is authorized to perform the notarial act or authentication may be made by affixing an official seal of the officer.

In some states, title companies, banks and law digests maintain lists of officials authorized to perform notarial acts. Subdivision (3) of subsection (b) gives official recognition to this practice as an alternative method of proof of authority.

Subsection (c) is a "catch-all" to cover authentication where the person taking the acknowledgment does not fall within the categories covered by subsections (a) and (b).

Subsection (d) distinguishes proof of the authority of the holder of the office from proof of the genuineness of the signature and the genuineness of the claim that the person is an officer.

Section 3. (Certificate of Person Taking Acknowledgment.)

The person taking an acknowledgment shall certify that:

1. the person acknowledging appeared before him and acknowledged he executed the instrument; and

2. the person acknowledging was known to the person taking the acknowledgment or that the person taking the acknowledgment had satisfactory evidence that the person acknowledging was the person described in and who executed the instrument.

Section 4. (Recognition of Certificate of Acknowledgment.)

The form of a certificate of acknowledgment used by a person whose authority is recognized under section 1 shall be accepted in this state if:

1. the certificate is in a form prescribed by the laws or regulations of this state;

2. the certificate is in a form prescribed by the laws or regulations applicable in the place in which the acknowledgment is taken; or

3. the certificate contains the words "acknowledged before me," or their substantial equivalent.

Section 5. (Certificate of Acknowledgment.)

The words "acknowledged before me" means

1. that the person acknowledging appeared before the person taking the acknowledgment,

2. that he acknowledged he executed the instrument,

3. that, in the case of:

i. a natural person, he executed the instrument for the purposes therein stated;

ii. a corporation, the officer or agent acknowledged he held the position or title set forth in the instrument and certificate, he signed the instrument on behalf of the corporation by proper authority, and the instrument was the act of the corporation for the purposes therein stated;

iii. a partnership, the partner or agent acknowledged he signed the instrument on behalf of the partnership by proper authority and he executed the instrument as the act of the partnership for the purposes therein stated;

iv. a person acknowledging as principal by an attorney in fact, he executed the instrument by proper authority as the act of the principal for the purposes therein stated;

v. a person acknowledging as a public officer, trustee, administrator, guardian, or other representative, he signed the instrument by proper authority and he executed the instrument in the capacity and for the purposes therein stated; and

4. that the person taking the acknowledgment either knew or had satisfactory evidence that the person acknowledging was the person named in the instrument or certificate.

Section 6. (Short Forms of Acknowledgment.)

The forms of acknowledgment set forth in this section may be used and are sufficient for their respective purposes under any law of this State. The forms shall be known as "Statutory Short Forms of Acknowledgment" and may be referred to by that name. The authorization of the forms in this section does not preclude the use of other forms.

1. For an individual acting in his own right:

State of _____
County of _____

The foregoing instrument was acknowledged before me this _____ (date) by _____ (name of person acknowledged).

_____ (Signature of Person Taking Acknowledgment)
_____ (Title or Rank)
_____ (Serial Number, if any)

2. For a corporation:

State of _____
County of _____

The foregoing instrument was acknowledged before me this _____ (date) by _____ (name of officer or agent, title of officer or agent) of _____ (name of corporation acknowledging), a _____ (state or place of incorporation) corporation, on behalf of the corporation.

_____ (Signature of Person Taking Acknowledgment)
_____ (Title or Rank)
_____ (Serial Number, if any)

3. For a partnership:

State of _____
County of _____

The foregoing instrument was acknowledged before me this _____ (date) by _____ (name of acknowledging partner or agent), partner (or agent) on behalf of _____ (name of partnership), a partnership.

_____ (Signature of Person Taking Acknowledgment)
_____ (Title or Rank)
_____ (Serial Number, if any)

4. For an individual acting as principal by an attorney in fact:

State of _____
County of _____

The foregoing instrument was acknowledged before me this _____ *(date) by* _____ *(name of attorney in fact) as attorney in fact on behalf of* _____ *(name of principal).*

_____ *(Signature of Person Taking Acknowledgment)*
_____ *(Title or Rank)*
_____ *(Serial Number, if any)*

5. By any Public Officer, trustee, or personal representative:

State of _____
County of _____

The foregoing instrument was acknowledged before me this _____ *(date) by* _____ *(name and title of position).*

_____ *(Signature of Person Taking Acknowledgment)*
_____ *(Title or Rank)*
_____ *(Serial Number, if any)*

Section 7. (Acknowledgments Not Affected by This Act.)

A notarial act performed prior to the effective date of this Act is not affected by this Act. This Act provides an additional method of proving notarial acts. Nothing in this Act diminishes or invalidates the recognition accorded to notarial acts by other laws or regulations of this State.

Section 8. (Uniformity of Interpretation.)

This Act shall be so interpreted as to make uniform the laws of those states which enact it.

Section 9. (Short Title.)

This Act may be cited as the Uniform Recognition of Acknowledgments Act.

Section 10. (Time of Taking Effect.)

This Act shall take effect _____. ■

Appendix

Appendix 4

UNIFORM ACKNOWLEDGMENT ACT
(1939, AMENDED 1960)

UNIFORM ACKNOWLEDGMENT ACT

Drafted by the

NATIONAL CONFERENCE OF COMMISSIONERS
ON UNIFORM STATE LAWS

and by it

Approved and Recommended for Enactment
in All the States

at its

Forty-ninth Annual Conference
at San Francisco, California

July 3 — 8, 1939

with Prefatory Note

Approved by the American Bar Association
at its Meeting at
San Francisco, California, July 14, 1939

Prefatory Note

In 1892 the Conference of Commissioners on Uniform State Laws adopted an Act for the acknowledgment and execution of written instruments. In 1914 the Conference adopted an Act for the acknowledgment of written instruments taken outside the United States.

These two Acts differed in many essential respects and at later sessions of the Conference it was concluded to rewrite the Acts so as to eliminate the confusion of inharmonious and contradictory provisions. The matter was accordingly referred to the appropriate section of the conference, which made an exhaustive study of the subject, as a result of which a Uniform Act was adopted at the 1939 Conference of the Commissioners on Uniform State Laws held at San Francisco, California, and which is now being presented to the Legislatures of the various states for adoption.

In the Act adopted there is no attempt to say what instruments shall be acknowledged – the Act merely provides that where by the laws of the State the acknowledgment of an instrument is required to be made, it may be made in the manner and form now provided by the law of the State or in the manner and form as prescribed by the Act. It should be explained to the Legislatures that there is no attempt to repeal the existing laws on the subject but the Act proposed is merely permissive in that an acknowledgment may be made either in the manner and form now provided by the law of the state or in the manner and form fixed by this Act. Thus a modern, uniform Act is being proposed for adoption in those states which desire it, without any attempt to alter or change the existing form and method in the event that form or method should be preferred over that proposed.

The Act likewise provides for the recognition within the State of acknowledgments made in other states, provided they be authenticated in the manner prescribed by Section 9 Sub-section 2 of the Act.

In addition to the adoption of the Act by the Conference of Commissioners on Uniform State Laws, this Act has likewise had approval of the American Bar Association, and it is accordingly recommended to the States for adoption in the strong belief that it represents a decided improvement in legislation on the subject.

There is not only a demand for a more modern enactment on acknowledgments in many of the States, but more uniformity on the subject in all the states. This act will provide both without disturbing the existing law for those who want to use it.

Uniform Acknowledgment Act

An Act Relating to Acknowledgments of
Written Instruments and to Make Uniform the
Law with Relation Thereto.

Be it enacted by the _____.

Section 1. (Acknowledgment of Instruments.)

Any instrument may be acknowledged in the manner and form now provided by the laws of this State, or as provided by this Act.

Section 2. (Acknowledgment Within the State.)

The acknowledgment of any instrument may be made in this State before:

1. A Judge of a court of record;
2. A Clerk or Deputy Clerk of a court having a seal;
3. A Commissioner or Register (or Recorder) of Deeds;
4. A Notary Public;
5. A Justice of the Peace; or
6. A Master in Chancery or Register in Chancery;
7. A duly licensed attorney at law.

Section 3. (Acknowledgment Within the United States.)

The acknowledgment of any instrument may be made without the State but within the United States or a territory or insular possession of the United States or the District of Columbia or the Philippine Islands and within the jurisdiction of the officer, before:

1. A Clerk or Deputy Clerk of any federal court;
2. A Clerk or Deputy Clerk of any court of record of any State or other jurisdiction;
3. A Notary Public;
4. A Commissioner of Deeds;
5. Any person authorized by the laws of such other jurisdiction to take acknowledgments.

Section 4. (Acknowledgment Without the United States.)

The acknowledgment of any instrument may be made without the United States before:

1. An Ambassador, Minister, Charge' d'Affaires, Counselor to or Secretary of a Legation, Consul General, Consul, Vice-Consul, Commercial Attache', or Consular Agent of the United States accredited to the country where the acknowledgment is made.
2. A Notary Public of the country where the acknowledgment is made.
3. A Judge or Clerk of a court of record of the country where the acknowledgment is made.

Section 5. (Requisites of Acknowledgment.)

The officer taking the acknowledgment shall know or have satisfactory evidence that the person making the acknowledgment is the person described in and who executed the instrument.

Section 6. (Acknowledgment by a Married Woman.)

An acknowledgment of a married woman may be made in the same form as though she were unmarried.

Section 7. (Forms of Certificates.)

An officer taking the acknowledgment shall endorse thereon or attach thereto a certificate substantially in one of the following forms:

1. By Individuals:

State of _____
County of _____

On this the _____ day of _____, 19__, before me, _____, the undersigned officer, personally appeared _____, known to me (or satisfactorily proven) to be the person whose name _____ subscribed to the within instrument and acknowledged that _____ executed the same for the purposes therein contained.

In witness whereof I hereunto set my hand and official seal.

_____
_____ Title of Officer

2. By a Corporation:

State of _____
County of _____

On this the _____ day of _____, 19__, before me, _____, the undersigned officer, personally appeared _____, who acknowledged himself to be the _____ of _____, a corporation, and that he, as such _____, being authorized so to do, executed the foregoing instrument for the purposes therein contained, by signing the name of the corporation by himself as _____.

In witness whereof I hereunto set my hand and official seal.

_____
_____ Title of Officer

3. By an Attorney In Fact:

State of _____
County of _____

On this the _____ day of _____, 19__, before me, _____, the undersigned officer, personally appeared _____, known to me (or satisfactorily proven) to be the person whose name is subscribed as attorney in fact for _____, and acknowledged that he executed the same as the act of his principal for the purposes therein contained.

In witness whereof I hereunto set my hand and official seal.

_____
_____ *Title of Officer*

4. By any Public Officer or Deputy thereof, or by any Trustee, Administrator, Guardian, or Executor:

*State of _____
County of _____*

On this the _____ day of _____, 19__, before me, _____, the undersigned officer, personally appeared _____, of the State (County or City as the case may be) of _____, known to me (or satisfactorily proven) to be the person described in the foregoing instrument, and acknowledged that he executed the same in the capacity therein stated and for the purposes therein contained.

In witness whereof I hereunto set my hand and official seal.

_____
_____ *Title of Officer*

Section 8. (Execution of Certificate.)

The certificate of the acknowledging officer shall be completed by his signature, his official seal if he has one, the title of his office, and if he is a Notary Public, the date his commission expires.

Section 9. (Authentication of Acknowledgments.)

1. If the acknowledgment is taken within this State or is made without the United States by an officer of the United States no authentication shall be necessary.

2. If the acknowledgment is taken without this State, but in the United States, or a territory or insular possession of the United States, the certificate shall be authenticated by a certificate as to the official character of such officer, executed, if the acknowledgment is taken by a Clerk or Deputy Clerk of a court, by the presiding judge of the court or, if the acknowledgment is taken by a Notary Public, or any other person authorized to take acknowledgments, by a Clerk of a Court of Record of the County, Parish or District in which the acknowledgment is taken. The signature to such authenticating certificate may be a facsimile printed, stamped, photographed or engraved thereon when the certificate bears the seal of the authenticating officer. A Judge or Clerk authenticating an acknowledgment shall endorse thereon or attach thereto a certificate in substantially the following form:

*State of _____
County of _____*

I, _____, (judge or clerk) of the _____ in and for said county, which court is a court of record, having a seal, do hereby certify that _____, by and before whom the foregoing (or annexed) acknowledgment was taken, was at the time of taking the same a notary public (or other officer) residing (or authorized to act) in said county, and was authorized by the laws of the said state to take and certify acknowledgments in said state, and, further, that I am acquainted with his handwriting and that I believe that the signature to the certificate of acknowledgment is genuine.

In testimony whereof I have hereunto set my hand and affixed the seal of the court this _____ day of _____, 19__.

3. If the acknowledgment is taken without the United States and by a Notary Public or a Judge or Clerk of a Court of Record of the country where the acknowledgment is made, the certificate shall be authenticated by a certificate under the Great Seal of State of the country, affixed by the custodian of such Seal, or by a certificate of a diplomatic, consular or commercial officer of the United States accredited to that country, certifying as to the official character of such officer.

Section 10. (Acknowledgments Under Laws of Other States.)

Notwithstanding any provision in this Act

contained the acknowledgment of any instrument without this State in compliance with the manner and form prescribed by the laws of the place of its execution, if in a State, a Territory or insular possession of the United States, or in the District of Columbia, verified by the official seal of the officer before whom it is acknowledged, and authenticated in the manner provided by section 9 subsection 2 hereof, shall have the same effect as an acknowledgment in the manner and form prescribed by the laws of this State for instruments executed within the State (except where the instrument is a deed by which a resident of this State purports to convey his homestead in this State and the deed is not additionally acknowledged in the form prescribed by the law of this State for the validity of a conveyance of a homestead).

Section 11. (Acknowledgments Not Affected by This Act.)

No acknowledgment heretofore taken shall be affected by anything contained herein.

Section 12. (Uniformity of Interpretation.)

This Act shall be so interpreted as to make uniform the laws of those States which enact it.

Section 13. (Name of Act.)

This Act may be cited as the Uniform Acknowledgment Act.

Section 14. (Time of Taking Effect.)

This Act shall take effect _____. ∎

UNIFORM FOREIGN ACKNOWLEDGMENTS ACT (1914)

Uniform Foreign Acknowledgments Act

AN ACT

To Make Uniform the Law of Acknowledgments to Deeds or Other Instruments Taken Outside the United States

Be it enacted, etc.

Section 1

All deeds or other instruments requiring acknowledgment, if acknowledged without the United States, shall be acknowledged before an ambassador, minister, envoy or charge' d'affaires of the United States, in the country to which he is accredited, or before one of the following officers commissioned or accredited to act at the place where the acknowledgment is taken, and having an official seal, viz.: any consular officer of the United States; a notary public; or a commissioner or other agent of this state having power to take acknowledgments to deeds.

Section 2

Every certificate of acknowledgment, made without the United States, shall contain the name or names of the person or persons making the acknowledgment, the date when and place where made, a statement of the fact that the person or persons making the acknowledgment knew the contents of the instrument, and acknowledged the same to be his, her or their act; the certificate shall also contain the name of the person before whom made, his official title, and be sealed with his official seal and may be substantially in the following form:

_____ (name of country).
_____ (name of city, province or other political subdivision).

Before the undersigned _____ (naming the officer and designating his official title) duly commissioned (or appointed) and qualified, this day personally appeared at the place above named _____ (naming the person or persons acknowledging) who declared that he (she or they) knew the contents of the foregoing instrument, and acknowledged the same to be his (her or their) act.

Witness my hand and official seal this ____ day of _____, 19__.

(SEAL)   _____ (name of officer)
          _____ (official title).

When the seal affixed shall contain the name or the official style of the officer, any error in stating, or failure to state otherwise the name or the official style of the officer, shall not render the certificate defective.

Section 3

A certificate of acknowledgment of a deed or other instrument acknowledged without the United States before any officer mentioned in Section 1 shall also be valid if in the same form as now is or hereafter may be required by law, for an acknowledgment within this state. ■

Appendix

UNIFORM ACKNOWLEDGMENTS ACT (1892)

Uniform Acknowledgments Act
An Act Relating To Acknowledgments On Written Instruments

Section 1

Either the forms of acknowledgment now in use in this State or the following may be used in the case of conveyances or other written instruments, whenever such acknowledgment is required or authorized by law for any purpose:

(Begin in all cases by a caption specifying the State and place where the acknowledgment is taken.)

1. In the case of natural persons acting in their own right:

(Caption)

On this _____ day of _____, 19__, before me personally appeared ___(AB)____ (or ___[AB and CD]___), to me known to be the person (or persons) described in and who executed the foregoing instrument, and acknowledged that he (or they) executed the same as his (or their) free act and deed.

2. In the case of natural persons acting by attorney:

(Caption)

On this _____ day of _____, 19__, before me personally appeared ___(AB)___, to me known to be the person who executed the foregoing instrument in behalf of ___(CD)___, and acknowledged that he executed the same as the free act and deed of said ___(CD)___.

3. In the case of corporations or joint stock associations:

(Caption)

On this _____ day of _____, 19__, before me personally appeared ___(AB)___, to me personally known, who, by me duly sworn (or affirmed) did say that he is the president (or other officer or agent of the corporation or association) of _____ (describing the corporation or association), and that the seal affixed to said instrument is the corporate seal of said corporation (or association) and that instrument was signed and sealed in behalf of said corporation (or association) by authority of its board of directors (or trustees) and said ___(AB)___ acknowledged said instrument to be the free act and deed of such corporation (or association).

(In case the corporation or association has no corporate seal, omit the words "the seal affixed to said instrument is the corporate seal of said corporation (or association), and that" and add, at the end of the affidavit clause, the words "and that said corporation (or association) has no corporate seal.")

Section 2

The acknowledgment of a married woman when required by law may be taken in the same form as if she were sole and without any examination separate and apart from her husband.

Section 3

The proof or acknowledgment of any deed or other written instrument required to be proved or acknowledged in order to enable the same to be recorded or read in evidence, when made by any person without this state and within any other state, territory or district of the United States, may be made before any officer of such state, territory or district, authorized by the laws thereof to take the proof and acknowledgment of deeds, and when so taken and certified as herein provided, shall be entitled to be recorded in this state, and may be read in evidence in the same manner and with like effect as proofs and acknowledgments taken before any of the officers now authorized by law to take such proofs and acknowledgments, and whose authority to do so is not intended to be hereby affected.

Section 4

To entitle any conveyance or written instrument, acknowledged or proved under the preceding section, to be read in evidence or recorded in this state, there shall be subjoined or attached to the certificate of proof or acknowledgment, signed by such officer, a certificate of the Secretary of State of the state or territory in which such officer resides, under the seal of such state, territory, or a certificate of the clerk of a court of record of such state, territory or district in the county in which said officer resides or in which he took such proof or acknowledgment under the seal of such court, stating that such officer was, at the time of taking such proof or acknowledgment, duly authorized to take acknowledgments and proof of deeds of lands in said state, territory or district, and that said Secretary of State, or clerk of court is well acquainted with the handwriting of such officer, and that he verily believes that the signature affixed to such certificate of proof or acknowledgment is genuine.

Section 5

The following form of authentication of the proof or acknowledgment of a deed or other written instrument when taken without this state and within any other state, territory or district of the United States, or any form substantially in compliance with the foregoing provisions of this act, may be used.

Begin with a caption specifying the state, territory or district and county or place where the authentication is made.

> *I, _____, clerk of the _____ in and for said county, which court is a court of record, having a seal (or, I _____, the Secretary of State of such state, or territory) do hereby certify that _____ by and before whom the foregoing acknowledgment (or proof) was taken, was, at the time of taking the same, a notary public (or other officer) residing (or authorized to act) in said county, and was duly authorized by the laws of said state (territory or district) to take and certify acknowledgments or proofs of deeds of land in said state (territory or district), and further that I am well acquainted with the handwriting of said _____ and that I verily believe that the signature to said certificate of acknowledgment (or proof) is genuine.*
>
> *In testimony whereof, I have hereunto set my hand and affixed the seal of the said court (or state) this ____ day of _____, 19__.*

Section 6

The proof or acknowledgment of any deed or other instrument required to be proved or acknowledged in order to entitle the same to be recorded or read in evidence, when made by any person without the United States, may be made before any officer now authorized thereto by the laws of this state, or before any minister, consul, vice-consul, charge d'affaires, or consular agent of the United States resident in any foreign country or port, and when certified by him under his seal of office it shall be entitled to be recorded in any county of this state, and may be read in evidence in any court in this state, in the same manner and with like effect as if duly proved or acknowledged within this state. ∎

Appendix 7

HAGUE CONVENTION ON AUTHENTICATION (1961)

Hague Convention Abolishing the Requirement of Legalization for Foreign Public Documents

Concluded October 5, 1961

Entered into Force by the United States of America on October 15, 1981

"The Hague Conference on Private International Law, established upon the initiative of the Netherlands Government, has been active in the field of the unification of private international law since 1893....

"The Convention (Abolishing the Requirement of Legalization for Foreign Public Documents) is one of the most widely adopted of the Hague Conventions prepared by the Conference....

"The purpose of the Convention is to abolish the requirement of diplomatic and consular legalization for foreign public documents. Such legalization or authentication is frequently the last step in a time-consuming and burdensome process known as the chain-certificate method of document certification. Under this method when a document is to be used in a foreign legal proceeding a chain of certifications is ordinarily required beginning with the issuer of the document and leading ultimately to a consul of the recipient country sitting in the country of origin.

"The first certification is of the authenticity of the signature or seal of the issuer and each certifier thereafter merely certifies the signature, seal or stamp of the certification immediately preceding his. As an example, the signature chain for a power of attorney executed in Iowa for use in the Netherlands might run as follows: (1) grantor; (2) public notary; (3) county clerk; (4) Secretary of State of the State of Iowa; (5) Secretary of State of the United States; (6) Consul of the Netherlands sitting in Chicago. Sometimes a recipient country additionally requires that the signature of its consul be certified in the recipient country by its own department of foreign relations.

"The purpose of the chain of certificates is to provide a foreign recipient of a document evidence of authenticity upon which he may rely without undertaking the difficult task of personally certifying the document directly with the original issuer.

"The Convention establishes a simplified system for attaining the same objective. The key elements are (a) substitution of a standard certificate bearing one signature for the chain-certificate and (b) abolition of diplomatic or consular authentication of that certificate. The result is elimination of the costs, delays and frustrations of the present system and reduction of the administrative burden on judges, clerks of court, diplomatic and consular officers, and other officials of certifying each other's signatures...

"The Convention consists of nine substantive articles, six formal articles, and one annex, the model of the certificate established by the Convention...."

Joseph J. Sisco
Acting Secretary of State
United States of America
April 8, 1976

Convention Abolishing the Requirement of Legalization for Foreign Public Documents

The States signatory to the present Convention,

Desiring to abolish the requirement of diplomatic or consular legalization for foreign public documents,

Have resolved to conclude a Convention to this effect and have agreed upon the following provisions:

Article 1

The present Convention shall apply to public documents which have been executed in the territory of one contracting State and which have to be produced in the territory of another contracting State.

For the purposes of the present Convention, the following are deemed to be public documents:

a. Documents emanating from an authority or an official connected with the courts or tribunals of the State, including those emanating from a public prosecutor, a clerk of a court or a process server ("huissier de justice");

b. Administrative documents;

c. Notarial acts;

d. Official certificates which are placed on documents signed by persons in their private capacity, such as official certificates recording the registration of a document or the fact that it was in existence on a certain date and official and notarial authentication of signatures.

However, the present Convention shall not apply:

a. To documents executed by diplomatic or consular agents;

b. To administrative documents dealing directly with commercial or customs operations.

Article 2

Each contracting State shall exempt from legalization documents to which the present Convention applies and which have to be produced in its territory. For the purposes of the present Convention, legalization means only the formality by which the diplomatic or consular agents of the country in which the document has to be produced certify the authenticity of the signature, the capacity in which the person signing the document has acted and, where appropriate, the identity of the seal or stamp which it bears.

Article 3

The only formality that may be required in order to certify the authenticity of the signature, the capacity in which the person signing the document has acted and, where appropriate, the identity of the seal or stamp which it bears, is the addition of the certificate described in Article 4, issued by the competent authority of the State from which the document emanates.

However, the formality mentioned in the preceding paragraph cannot be required when either the laws, regulations, or practice in force in the State where the document is produced or an agreement between two or more contracting States have abolished or simplified it, or exempt the document itself from legalization.

Article 4

The certificate referred to in the first paragraph of Article 3 shall be placed on the document itself or an on "allonge"; it shall be in the form of the model annexed to the present Convention.

It may, however, be drawn up in the official language of the authority which issues it. The standard terms appearing therein may be in a second language also. The title "Apostille (Convention de La Haye du 5 octobre 1961)" shall be in the French language.

Article 5

The certificate shall be issued at the request of the person who has signed the document or of any bearer.

When properly filled in, it will certify the authenticity of the signature, the capacity in which the person signing the document has acted and, where appropriate, the identity of the seal or stamp which the document bears.

The signature, seal and stamp on the certificate are exempt from all certification.

Article 6

Each contracting State shall designate by reference to their official function, the authorities who are competent to issue the certificate referred to in the first paragraph of Article 3.

It shall give notice of such designation to the Ministry of Foreign Affairs of the Netherlands at the time it deposits its instrument of ratification or of accession or its declaration of extension. It shall also give notice of any change in the designated authorities.

Article 7

Each of the authorities designated in accordance with Article 6 shall keep a register or card index in which it shall record the certificates issued, specifying:

a. The number and date of the certificate,

b. The name of the person signing the public document and the capacity in which he has acted, or in the case of unsigned documents, the name of the authority which has affixed the seal or stamp.

At the request of any interested person, the authority which has issued the certificate shall verify whether the particulars in the certificate correspond with those in the register or card index.

Article 8

When a treaty, convention or agreement between two or more contracting States contains provisions which subject the certification of a signature, seal or stamp to certain formalities, the present Convention will only override such provisions if those formalities are more rigorous than the formality referred to in Articles 3 and 4.

Article 9

Each contracting State shall take the necessary steps to prevent the performance of legalizations by its diplomatic or consular agents in cases where the present Convention provides for exemption.

(Articles 10 through 15 deal with formalities and technicalities related to a nation's ratifying and implementing the Convention. – *The Editor*)

Annex to the Convention

Model of certificate. The certificate will be in the form of a square with sides at least 9 centimetres long.

APOSTILLE
(Convention de La Haye du 5 octobre 1961)

1. Country: *United States of America*
   This public document
2. has been signed by _____
3. acting in the capacity of _____
4. bears the seal/stamp of _____

CERTIFIED

5. at _____ 6. the _____
7. by _____
8. No. _____
9. Seal/Stamp 10. Signature _____

Nations Adhering to Convention

The following 102 nations are adherents to the Hague Convention Abolishing the Requirement of Legalization (Authentication) for Foreign Public Documents, according to the Hague Conference on Private International Law, as of November 14, 2011 — see *www.hcch.net/*:

Countries

Albania
Andorra
Antigua and Barbuda
Argentina
Armenia
Australia
Austria
Azerbaijan
Bahamas
Barbados
Belarus
Belgium
Belize
Bosnia and Herzegovina
Botswana
Brunei Darussalam
Bulgaria
Cape Verde
China, People's Republic of *
Colombia
Cook Islands
Costa Rica
Croatia
Cyprus
Czech Republic
Denmark
Dominica
Dominican Republic
Ecuador
El Salvador
Estonia
Fiji
Finland
France
Georgia
Germany
Greece
Grenada
Honduras
Hungary
Iceland
India
Ireland
Israel
Italy
Japan
Kazakhstan
Korea, Republic of
Kyrgyzstan
Latvia
Lesotho
Liberia
Liechtenstein
Lithuania
Luxembourg
Macedonia
Malawi
Malta
Marshall Islands
Mauritius
Mexico
Moldava, Republic of
Monaco

Mongolia
Montenegro
Namibia
Netherlands
New Zealand
Niue
Norway
Oman
Panama
Peru
Poland
Portugal
Romania
Russian Federation
Saint Kitts and Nevis
Saint Lucia
Saint Vincent and the Grenadines
Samoa
San Marino
Sao Tome and Principe
Serbia
Seychelles
Slovakia
Slovenia
South Africa
Spain
Suriname
Swaziland
Sweden
Switzerland
Tonga
Trinidad and Tobago
Turkey
Ukraine
United Kingdom of Great Britain and Northern Ireland
United States of America
Uzbekistan
Vanuatu
Venezuela

* The convention applies only to the Special Administrative Regions of Hong Kong and Macao, as a result of extensions made by the United Kingdom and by Portugal, respectively. When Hong Kong and Macao were restored to the People's Republic of China on July 1, 1997, and December 20, 1999, respectively, China declared that the Convention will continue to apply for both Hong Kong and Macao.

Questions

Persons having questions about the operation and implementation of this Convention may address their inquiries to:

U.S. Department of State
Authentications Office
518 23rd St., N.W. SA-1
Columbia Plaza
Washington, DC 20520

Telephone: 1-202-647-5002

Website: www.state.gov/m/a/auth/ ∎

About the NNA

NATIONAL NOTARY ASSOCIATION

Since 1957, the National Notary Association has served the nation's Notaries Public — today numbering nearly five million — with a wide variety of instructional programs and supporting services. The Association's *Notary Public Code of Professional Responsibility* is widely regarded as the American Notary's code of ethics.

As an organization dedicated to professionalizing Notaries in the United States, the NNA offers five "Core Values of Membership":

I. Compliance

Notary laws, regulations, official directives and legal rulings require that the Notary understand practical procedures and their implementation. This information is often not available through state agencies or other organizations and Notaries may be left on their own to seek training, guidance and clarity to avoid serious administrative or legal consequences. *NNA membership* ensures that Notaries receive timely notice of new laws, rules and other information necessary to provide sound notarial services.

II. Liability Protection

The Notary is liable for both intentional and unintentional acts. Notaries must perform notarizations in a manner that reduces or removes the possibility of liability exposure for themselves and their employers. Courts regularly hold employers liable for the errors of their employee Notaries. *NNA membership* provides Notaries with the knowledge and skills that can reduce this liability exposure and protect both themselves — and their employers — from charges of misconduct, negligence and other adverse and costly consequences.

III. Risk Management

Important documentary transactions are notarized to minimize the possibility of contractual disputes or lawsuits among the parties to a transaction. The role of the Notary is to follow legal, customary and ethical practices and procedures that will limit risks to the signer, the person or agency relying on the document, and the Notary's employer. *NNA membership* provides Notaries with programs and specialized guidance enabling them to prevent fraudulent transactions, reduce instances of identity crimes, and avoid civil and criminal lawsuits.

IV. Professionalism

Notaries may hold their notarial office in addition to full-time occupational employment, but must develop, possess and maintain distinctive qualifications and skills in order to perform their official duties. The legal and business communities rely on Notaries to act with reliability, competence and integrity. *NNA membership* demonstrates to the public that the Notary has been trained in all applicable laws and standards of professional practice and will perform with superior dependability, trustworthiness, and the highest standard of ethics.

V. Opportunities

Notaries can enhance the value of holding a state-issued commission and increase their potential to earn additional income by pursuing professional development to master and maintain standards of practice beyond statutory laws. *NNA membership* offers access to exclusive and proprietary certification programs, such as the Trusted Notary, Notary Signing Agent and the Trusted Enrollment Agent credentials, which are recognized and specifically sought by businesses and governmental agencies that require high levels of training and qualification to carry out their secure documentary transactions.

As the country's clearinghouse for information on notarial laws, customs and practices, the NNA educates Notaries through publications, seminars, instructional videos, webinars, annual conferences, and a Notary Hotline that offers immediate answers to specific questions about notarization.

The Association is the nation's preeminent publisher of information for and about Notaries and is also the nation's standard setter for best practices. Its *Model Notary Act* — conceived in 1973 and updated and expanded in 1984, 2002 and 2010 — has been adopted as law governing Notaries by more than 40 U.S. states and jurisdictions. ∎

Appendix

To Order More Copies

Across the nation every year, notarial procedures, certificates and seals are directly affected by hundreds of changes in statute, regulation, case law and attorney general opinions.

Thus, the *U.S. Notary Reference Manual* is an invaluable updating resource for government officials, document investigators, attorneys, consular officers, seal manufacturers, Notaries, and many others. It is published by the National Notary Association every two years.

To order additional copies of the 2012–2013 *U.S. Notary Reference Manual*, please use the form below.

Bulk Order Quantities

The *U.S. Notary Reference Manual* is available at special discounts when ordered in bulk quantities. For information, contact:

Customer Service
Telephone: 1-800-US NOTARY
        (1-800-876-6827)

Fax: 1-800-833-1211

Email: services@nationalnotary.org

Detach and return with your remittance to the NNA

Yes...I would like to receive _____ copy(ies) of the 2012–2013 *U.S. Notary Reference Manual* (No. 15339) at $79.95 per copy for NNA members ($95.95 for non-members), plus $11.95 ($13.95 for non-members) shipping per copy.

Name _____

Organization _____

❏ Business
Address ❏ Home _____

City _____ *State* _____ *Zip* _____

Daytime Telephone _____

NNA Member No. (required for member price) _____

❏ *Check Enclosed* (Payable to National Notary Association)

❏ *American Express*   ❏ *Discover*   ❏ *Visa*   ❏ *MasterCard*

Card Expires _____

Card No. _____

Signature _____

Total Order $ _____

Add sales tax for shipments to: CA & WA* $ _____

Add Shipping Charge $ _____
($11.95 ea. for NNA members; $13.95 ea. for non-members)

TOTAL ENCLOSED $ _____

*For WA, include tax on shipping charge.

NATIONAL NOTARY ASSOCIATION
P.O. Box 541032, Los Angeles, CA 90054-1032
1-800-US NOTARY (1-800-876-6827) • Fax: 1-800-833-1211
www.nationalnotary.org

Source Code: A45786